THE
ORIGINS OF THE
INQUISITION

THE
ORIGINS OF THE
INQUISITION

in Fifteenth Century Spain

B. NETANYAHU

RANDOM HOUSE

NEW YORK

Library of Congress Cataloging-in-Publication Data
Netanyahu, B. (Benzion)
The origins of the Inquisition in fifteenth century Spain / B.
Netanyahu.
p.   cm.
Includes bibliographical references and index.
ISBN 0-679-41065-1
1. Inquisition—Spain. 2. Converts from Judaism—History.
3. Jews—Spain—History. 4. Antisemitism—Spain—History.
I. Title.
BX1735.N48 1992
272'.2'0946—dc20   92-53643

Manufactured in the United States of America
2 4 6 8 9 7 5 3
First Edition

This book is dedicated
with unrelieved grief
to the memory of my beloved son
J O N A T H A N
who fell while leading
the rescue force at Entebbe
on July 4, 1976

Unless otherwise indicated, the terms Conversos, Marranos and New Christians are used in this work synonymously. Each of them has long served to designate the same group in Jewish, Spanish and European scholarship.

Spanish names of persons and places are given in this book in their Spanish forms, except in cases where the English usage is long established—e.g., Seville, Cordova, Ferdinand and Isabella.

Italicization in quotations from works written before the end of the 16th century is in all cases the author's.

Biblical translations follow standard English versions, except when occasionally modified by the author to fit his understanding of the original.

Contents

BOOK THREE

ENRIQUE IV AND THE CATHOLIC KINGS

BOOK FOUR
THE ORIGINS OF THE INQUISITION

APPENDICES

Introduction

The vast literature on the Spanish Inquisition created in the course of half a millennium includes a large number of superb studies on almost every aspect of the Inquisition's activity and every phase of its evolution. Conspicuously absent from these master works is a thorough investigation of the first phase, exploring the origins and causes of the Inquisition and the circumstances from which it emerged. Although the subject has been repeatedly discussed, primarily in histories of the Inquisition, it has more often than not been treated perfunctorily, sometimes partially or one-sidedly, and never in a manner befitting the importance of the questions involved.

This lacuna in so ramified a history is certainly an oddity that calls for explanation. One would naturally assume that the renown of the Inquisition, its centuries-long duration and far-flung sway and, above all, the great influence it wielded on the history of Spain, Europe and the world should have excited the curiosity of many a scholar to dig deep until its roots were exposed. That this did not happen was due, in our judgment, to the firm belief entertained by most scholars that they were in possession of all the necessary facts to determine the primary cause of the Inquisition. That cause, they were sure, was the presence of a heresy, steadily spreading and highly contagious, which threatened the future of Christianity in Spain. The Inquisition was created to crush that heresy and, if possible, to destroy it root and branch.

There were several reasons for the deep inculcation of this belief in literature and in the public mind. The heresy referred to was a *Judaizing* tendency claimed to be rampant among the Marranos (known also as conversos or New Christians), almost all of whom descended from Jews converted to Christianity during the persecutions of 1391 and 1412. That such a tendency actually existed seemed credible, first, from the cardinal fact that most of the above-mentioned converts were *forced*—a circumstance inclining one to assume that, though outwardly Christian, these converts remained Jewish, secretly upholding their old tenets and rites and also transmitting them to their children. Apart from this, there was the *structure* of the Inquisition, which was likewise conducive to that presumption. Its guidelines, its laws, its modes of operation were all a replica of the earlier inquisitions which, without exception, were designed to fight heresies. It stood to reason that, like all its predecessors, the Spanish Inquisition was created for the same purpose—that is, to arrest some deviation from the faith. And this presumption was further supported by testimonies of the highest authority and reliability. We refer to the bull of Pope Sixtus IV (1478), which sanctioned the establishment of the Inquisition in Castile, and the royal proclamation made public in Seville upon the commencement of the Inquisition's activity (Jan. 1481). In both these documents it was stated explicitly that the sole purpose of the new tribunal was to put an end to the *Judaic heresy* that had infected the camp of the conversos. Finally, that purpose was reaffirmed by the Inquisition in both the judgments it pronounced and many other statements by which it sought to justify its punitive acts—those acts which indeed appeared more telling than all the above indications put together. For the Spanish Inquisition attacked the Marranos with a savage ferocity that by then was outmoded; it burned them by the thousands, confiscated their possessions, incarcerated them in its dungeons, branded them as outcasts, robbed their sons of their rightful inheritance while denying them the right to public office, and subjected them all to a reign of terror, which "turned their lives into something worse than death," as Mariana, the Spanish historian, put it. Is it possible that all this could be done if there had not been that reason— that *sole* reason—so repeatedly given by the kings and the Inquisition for its establishment and operations? Common sense rebelled against such an assumption.

Thus we can see how that belief was founded. It was based on the testimonies of the authors of the Inquisition, i.e., the Spanish kings and the inquisitors themselves—that is, on their verdicts and assertions. These testimonies appeared sufficient for most scholars not only to determine the causes of the Inquisition, but also to serve as a standard of judgment for all other evidence that came their way. As a result, no diverse and free-ranging inquiry into the origins of the Spanish Inquisition was attempted, or at least evolved to a significant degree. And what further hindered or blocked such evolution was the overwhelming influence of a special development which is often overlooked.

Writing in the middle of the 16th century, Samuel Usque, a Portuguese

Jewish author, called the Inquisition a "wild monster of such terrible mien that all of Europe trembles at the mere mention of its name." When Usque wrote these words, the Spanish Inquisition had just passed the peak of the persecution that characterized the first period of its activity—namely, its persecution of the conversos—and was moving ahead, through its attacks on the Moriscos and other Spanish groups whom it charged with dissidence, to its battle against the Reformation. There was not of course any historical connection between the original reasons for the founding of the Inquisition and its subsequent fight against the "heretical" Reformers. But its perform-ance in that period, which was indeed devoted to the struggle against a variety of heresies, tended to substantiate its claims about the motives for its creation and earlier activity. In fact, that second period covered with oblivion the original purpose of the first; and thus, by the turn of the 18th century, it was universally believed that the Spanish Inquisition was created to fight heresies, among which the Jewish heresy was merely the first it encountered on its historic route.

I mentioned the turn of the 18th century because later, with the rise of modern historiography, that reigning concept about the origins of the Inqui-sition was totally discarded and replaced by another view. Scholars in Spain, Germany and France, including the leading historians of the age, noticed certain features in the Spanish Inquisition which contradicted the old hy-pothesis. They observed that, unlike all earlier inquisitions, the Spanish Inquisition was ruled, from its inception, much more by the king than by the pope; they saw how the king sought to appropriate to himself more and more papal powers in governing the Inquisition; how he spurned the pope's cen-sures of its excessive persecutions, and how he used the incomes of the Inquisition for his own needs and none for the needs of the Catholic Church. Thus they concluded that the Spanish Inquisition was a royal rather than a papal institution, that its real aims were secular rather than religious, and that it was actually erected to finance the king's ventures and promote his abso-lute power.

One can well understand why the authors of such a theory felt no necessity to undertake a major inquiry into the origins of the Inquisition. For in their view its origins were right in its beginnings, in the mind of King Ferdinand, whom they judged to be its founder. Their theory appeared self-sufficient, and plausible enough to attract adherents. Nevertheless, it was ultimately abandoned—and not without good reason. It failed, to begin with, to explain what made Ferdinand embark on a plan so bizarre and complex in order to promote his monarchic interests. Nor did it explain how the conversos came to play such a tragic part in that unprecedented scheme. It was hardly credible that so fierce a persecution, reflecting the dominant sentiment of a *nation*—and this not for one but for *many* generations—could be the product of the cupidity or ambition of one man, however powerful and influential. Consequently, in the controversy about the causes of the Inquisition that ensued in the second half of the 19th century, the pendulum of scholarly opinion swung back to where it was at the turn of the 18th.

It is strange that throughout this battle of opinions no importance was attached to a peculiar phenomenon that, no less than the other peculiarities mentioned, rendered the Spanish Inquisition distinct from all preceding inquisitions. This was its adoption of the principle of *race* to discriminate against all conversos. Why should an institution constitutionally dedicated to the defense of Christian cult and doctrine adopt a policy so alien to Christianity and so opposed to its laws, teachings and traditions? Some scholars already noted this anomaly more than a century ago, but insofar as the origins of the Inquisition were concerned, they treated it as of no consequence. In 1905, Henry Charles Lea portrayed for the first time the full extent of that anomaly and its far-reaching influence on Spanish life, but explained it by the oversensitivity of the Inquisition to anything that might give grounds to suspect the presence of a Judaic heresy. Since he adhered so firmly to the old view regarding the primary cause of the Inquisition, he could naturally offer no other explanation for that enigmatic phenomenon. And so it happened that the great historian of the Inquisition—indeed, the greatest of all time— failed to inquire into the origins of the Inquisition in a manner that could expose the true reason for its racism and thereby also the motives for its establishment. Indeed, when he composed the chapter in his history that dealt with the beginnings of the Spanish Inquisition, he left many blank pages to be written in due course by some of his later students and admirers. This brings me to the genesis of the present work.

When many years ago I first approached the study of the history of the conversos and the Spanish Inquisition, there was no doubt in my mind that almost all the Marranos were crypto-Jews who followed the laws of Judaism, thereby arousing the ire of the Church, which could not tolerate such conduct within its ranks. Naturally I viewed the Marranos as moral heroes who courageously withstood the terrors of the Inquisition and adhered to their faith under grueling tortures, frequently even unto death. Once again, I thought, the Jewish people, which produced the first religious martyrs in history and gave so many martyrs to the faith in the Middle Ages, demonstrated its capacity for suffering and self-sacrifice for its moral principles and religious convictions.

In 1944 I began my inquiries into the life and times of Don Isaac Abravanel, the outstanding leader of the Jewish exile from Spain (1492), and soon I was startled to come across documents that threatened to shatter my aforementioned view. To be sure, I found evidence that some of the Marranos were indeed secret adherents of Judaism. But the idealistic conception and heroic image I had of the Spanish Marranos as a group was greatly undermined by the above documents. For what they revealed was that, about the year 1460, most of the conversos were conscious assimilationists who wished to merge with the Christian society, educate their children as fully fledged Christians, and remove themselves from anything regarded as Jewish, especially in the field of religion. What is more, I discovered that this situation resulted from a long-lasting, ongoing process, so that the number of the Christianized Marranos was rising from generation to generation, while the number of clandestine Jews among them was rapidly dwindling to the vanishing point. In 1481, when the Inquisition was established, the Judaizers formed a small minority in both relative and absolute numbers. Inevitably, I came to doubt the common view concerning the reasons for the establishment of the Inquisition. If only a fraction of the Marranos were still Jewish and more and more of them kept becoming Christian, what sense was there in establishing the Inquisition? Surely there was no need to eliminate by *force* a phenomenon that was disappearing by itself.

These were the conclusions I reached in that inquiry and indicated, in part, in my work on Abravanel, which first appeared in 1953 (4th edition, 1982). So great was the discrepancy between these conclusions and the prevailing view of the causes of the Inquisition that I naturally had to give thought to the question of what brought about the adoption of that view, and especially of the factors that made it prevail. It occurred to me that perhaps the most significant of these factors was the reliance of most scholars on the documents of the Inquisition. To be sure, I was baffled by the great credence given by historians to those documents and to the claims made by the Inquisition on their basis. Little value, I thought, could be attached to evidence originating in witnesses who remained anonymous and could not be cross-examined by the accused; little weight should be imputed to statements exacted under torture or fear of torture, and little store should be set in documents subjected to the Inquisition's censorship. I could not understand why scholars of all persuasions, well aware of these crucial facts, somehow belittled their momentous meaning. Just the same, I could well understand why the picture they had commonly painted of the Marranos coincided with the portrait drawn by the Inquisition.

It became obvious to me that, in order to determine what the Marranos were religiously, evidence about them must be obtained from sources that were absolutely free of the Inquisition's influence. Clearly, such evidence could, in the main, be found in documents that antedated the Inquisition and whose authors were not subject to its threats and punishments. These sources I set out to investigate according to the group from which they stemmed (that is, Jewish, Marrano and Old Christian). I was hoping that such a manifold inquiry would yield conclusions about the Marranos' religion—that is, their religious views and practices—on which we could safely rely. I also believed that having reached such conclusions—and, indeed, only after having reached them—would we be in a position to identify the factors responsible for the establishment of the Inquisition.

The Marranos of Spain, which appeared in 1966 (enlarged edition, 1973), formed the first part of this investigation. It included a summary of my studies of the Marranos according to contemporary Hebrew sources from the late 14th to the early 16th century. In studying these sources I also examined certain documents that originated after 1481, when the first Inquisitional tribunal was erected; but in doing so, I did not depart from my guideline— i.e., the criterion of free expression. As Jews, the Hebrew authors concerned were not subject to the Inquisition's jurisdiction and, moreover, they wrote after the Expulsion or lived outside Spain before 1492. What was common to these sources was the judgment they pronounced on the Marranos' religious beliefs and conduct. It was a progressive judgment, tending in one direction—parallel to the Marranos' own changing attitudes toward Judaism and the Jewish people; and these changes fully confirmed the results of my earlier partial investigation. What I gathered from them was that Marrano Christianization had been steadily advancing for three generations (from 1391 on), so that at the beginning of the 1480s, when the Spanish Inquisition was established, virtually all Jewish authorities in Spain and elsewhere regarded the mass of the Marranos as renegades—that is, as apostates or gentiles. By any of these definitions they were Christians, and in no way Judaizers or crypto-Jews.

The value of this evidence appeared to me incalculable, as it ran contrary to the wishes, tendencies and interests of the Spanish Jews. What is more, the traditional attitudes and policies of Spain's Jews called for a friendly consideration of forced converts who retained their Judaism in a clandestine manner; it called for treating them patiently and benevolently in order to strengthen their attachment to the faith. Had the Marranos been secret Jews, the Jewish scholars and leaders who authored our sources would have been the first to confirm this fact, as indeed they did whenever they noticed any of the conversos behaving as Jews. But the evolution of Marranism dashed all their hopes that the conversos would ultimately "return" to Judaism, and although they first tried to offer "excuses" for the Marranos' non-Jewish behavior, they finally had to face stark reality with its incontrovertible message. For just as their tradition obliged them to respect and encourage secret Jews among the converts, it also commanded them to denounce real converts as traitors to their religion and their people. Hence, if they came to the point of so describing the conversos, it was because they could not describe them otherwise, or, more clearly, because the Marranos' religious attitudes toward Judaism precluded any other description.

The evidence of the Jewish sources, therefore, flatly contradicted the Inquisitional charges. Its lesson was that the New Christians were generally what their name suggested—that is, *Christian* in spirit and intent—and thus the aim of the Inquisition in persecuting them was not, and could not possibly have been, to excise a Jewish heresy from the Marranos' ranks. Its aim must have been quite different.

When I reached this conclusion as the major deduction from my researches into the Jewish sources, I confess I did not see how it could be refuted, especially since the knowledge I had gained of the Marranos from a variety of *non*-Hebrew sources contained nothing to offset that conclusion. I realized, however, that a more comprehensive and more penetrating inquiry into the *non*-Hebrew sources was necessary before I could be assured of their import. For only the results of such an inquiry would enable me to test, in the light of their lessons, the inferences I had drawn from the Hebrew writings. Hence, the second stage of my investigation concerned itself with the Spanish and Latin sources that originated in pre-Inquisitional times and related to the religious views and conduct of the Spanish conversos.

I began the second stage of my inquiry with a study of the documents of converso origin—and this for an obvious reason. What was the conversos' *own* view of their attitudes toward Judaism and Christianity? This question, it would seem, should have been high on the agenda of all scholars who dealt with the subject. But, surprisingly enough, it was not. Hundreds of articles and books have been written about the Spanish Inquisition, but not one of their authors took the trouble to examine the testimony of the conversos about themselves. This in itself was highly irregular, indicating that something was basically wrong with the studies related to the history of the Inquisition. In the present work we have tried to correct this irregularity. We have investigated and analyzed the Marrano sources to the extent we have found them pertinent to our question; and we hope that we have come up with an answer which is as definitive as it is substantive. This answer fully confirms the results of our inquiry into the Hebrew sources; for what we gather from it is that Judaism in the Marrano camp was a marginal phenomenon already in the middle of the fifteenth century; that by the turn of the seventies it had almost passed from sight, while Christianity had almost engulfed it all; and that the conversos, who valiantly defended their Christianity, were indeed overwhelmingly Christian and bent upon a course of complete assimilation.

To be sure, some critics may hasten to remark that the testimony of the

Marrano sources on the conversos reflects only a one-sided and hence a partial view. The Marranos, they may argue, were an interested party, and they naturally sought to clear themselves of the charges that had been leveled against them. But, we may ask: Are there opinions of any concerned party that are *not* one-sided? Is not the *Old* Christians' negative opinion of the conversos, in which so much stock has been put by the historians, one-sided too? Were the Old Christians a *neutral* party, or were they not as deeply involved in the quarrel as the Marranos themselves? When one wishes to establish the facts of a case, discern the actual causes of events, and determine what is true and what is not in any controversy, the correct thing to do is to hear *all* sides, to compare testimonies, and judge their value from every pertinent standpoint. Especially must one hear the *accused* party, which in this case was that of the conversos. This is indeed what we have done. We have examined every piece of Marrano evidence touching the conversos' religious position and carefully weighed its merits. We considered the possibility that our Marrano witnesses would tend toward self-justification. But in studying their testimonies, we also bore in mind that the claim of innocence is no evidence of crime and that passionate self-defense may represent truth no less than fiery accusation. In brief, we believe we have judged duly and correctly, and that the conclusions we drew from the Marrano literature will stand the test of scrutiny by competent inquirers.

Next came the study of the documents about the Marranos that were written by Old Christians. The special importance of these documents for our inquiry was evident to us from the outset. For apart from the testimonies of the Inquisition, most scholars relied primarily on these sources for their judgments and conclusions. Our review of these sources has, first, revealed to us that not all of them are of the same hue. More clearly, we found that what they tell us of the conversos, or rather of their stand toward Judaism and Christianity, consisted of different or conflicting accounts. Some of them agreed with the lessons we have drawn from the converso and Jewish sources—that is, they viewed the Marranos as good Christians, except for a small, indefinite minority that could not affect the character of the group. Others appeared to be of two minds, sometimes strongly defending the Marranos and at other times supporting their foes. A third group, however, unreservedly labeled all or most Marranos as "heretics" and "false Christians" who believed in Judaism and were addicted to its rites. It was obvious that only this latter group of sources might offer full justification for the thesis that a large secret Jewish or semi-Jewish underground existed in the Marrano camp. Consequently, we examined each of the charges leveled against the Marranos in these documents—a task which was complicated by the necessity to determine not only the reliability of each source, but also the grounds of, or reasons for each claim. The reader will find the fruits of our labor duly presented in the pages of this work, and he will also find that the sum total of this effort—that is, of our inquiries into the Old Christian writings—in no way affected the conclusions we arrived at in our study of the Jewish and Marrano sources. Indeed, it was this set of writings—i.e., the anti-Marrano Old Christian documents—that more than any other group of sources convinced us of the falsehood of most of the charges leveled at the conversos. For what they showed, beyond any doubt, was that the standard accusation that the Marranos were "Jews" was a weapon of a vilifying propaganda; that the evidence offered in support of that charge bears all the symptoms of a popular invention; and that consequently the religious condition of the Marranos could offer no justification, and therefore no real reason for the establishment of the Inquisition.

This radical conclusion of ours, drawn from *all* our sources on the Marranos, stood in such contrast to the prevalent views on the factors that caused the establishment of the Inquisition that we came to see our inquiry into the subject, rather than terminated, almost back at its starting point. Since the basis of the common view of the Inquisition had been shattered or, more truly, removed, the theoretical structure that rested upon it collapsed into a heap of ruins. Obviously, the two major questions that now loomed before us were: Why did the Inquisition attack so fiercely a community that was essentially *Christian,* and why did it seek, in so many ways, to stamp it as *non*-Christian and heretical? It was evident that only when we answered *these* questions would we know why the Inquisition was established.

Thus the focus of our attention shifted from the religious to the social and political fields. Since the Spanish Inquisition represented the wishes of a large part of the Spanish people, its treatment of the Marranos had inevitably to do with the relations that developed between that part and the conversos. Consequently, we had to study the evolution of these relations from the beginning of Marranism in 1391 to the establishment of the Inquisition in 1481. This required a review of Marrano history in that period against the background of Spain's general history. Such a review is found in this volume, and it helps, we believe, provide definite answers to the crucial questions we have posed above.

As we see it, these answers throw new light on the nature of the Inquisition, its policies and activities. They present the historical movements and forces that played a major role in precipitating the Inquisition; they reveal the difficulties encountered by the promoters of the Inquisition and the struggles they waged to remove the obstacles in their way; and finally, they show how a variety of social drives converged to achieve that goal—i.e., to translate the idea of the Inquisition into a social and political reality. Thus were unraveled the origins of an institution that was born at the opening of the new age, spread its tentacles across half the world, and set—through its theories, policies and actions—precedents and examples to systems of government that still hold in their power a large part of mankind.

I do not delude myself that the conclusions of this book will be speedily accepted by all the scholars in the field. Views which have been rooted in the public mind for five centuries cannot be easily or speedily uprooted. This is especially so with the Spanish Inquisition. Any critical study of its history is sure to be greeted with a chorus of objections produced by myth, bias, preconceptions and vested interests, national and religious. But I am encouraged by the reactions of scholars in many countries to my former work on the Marranos. Although the controversy raised by that work is still unsettled, more and more scholars have come to support my views, either under the direct impact of my study or as a result of their own researches. I was especially gratified that eminent scholars lauded my work in unqualified terms, and that a celebrated historian like Cecil Roth, who had stood for the thesis of Marrano Judaism, retreated from his own much-publicized position and embraced more or less the same view of the Marranos that I had presented in my studies on the subject. These and many similar symptoms— and above all the labor of some outstanding scholars, whose recent contributions have greatly enriched our knowledge of the Marranos' literature and history—inspire me to believe that we are approaching the point at which the real picture of Marrano life will at last be unfolded in its true setting. And who knows? Perhaps the new developments in the historiography of the Inquisition will help revolutionize research also in other fields of history which had long been half obscured by subterfuge and distortion, and, above all, by the blight of prejudice, which is only another name for man's stubborn refusal squarely to face some disturbing truths.

BOOK ONE

HISTORICAL BACKGROUND

CHAPTER I

The Jewish Question

I

On September 27, 1480, the Spanish sovereigns Ferdinand and Isabella issued an order to establish in their kingdoms tribunals to judge cases of "heretical depravity,"[1] and shortly thereafter, probably in November, they set up in Seville the first of these tribunals, to become known collectively as the Spanish Inquisition.[2] The royal decree explicitly stated that the Inquisition was instituted to search out and punish converts from Judaism who transgressed against Christianity by secretly adhering to Jewish beliefs and performing rites and ceremonies of the Jews.[3] No other group was mentioned, no other purpose indicated—a fact that in itself suggests a close relationship between the creation of the Inquisition and Jewish life in Spain. Other facts, too, attest that relationship. The converts referred to in the royal decree were, for the most part, offspring of Jews converted to Christianity during those fatal fifty years (1367–1417) in which furious persecutions forced multitudes of Jews—actually, the majority of Spanish Jewry—to abandon their religion and become Christians.[4] Obviously, the establishment of the Spanish Inquisition was linked in some way to those persecutions, and an inquiry into their causes must inevitably lead us to consider their social and political background. This, in turn, impels us to look into the factors that made up the Jewish question in Spain.

The Jewish question in Spain, however, was not a pure outgrowth of Spanish soil. It was part and parcel of the Jewish situation in the Europe of the Middle Ages; and that situation, like most medieval phenomena, had its roots in Roman and pre-Roman times. A detailed description of the evolution of the Jewish problem from antiquity to the birth of the Spanish Inquisition would clearly be outside the purview of this work. But a brief account of that evolution, and above all of its patterns and key elements, seems essential to our discussion. Without it we can hardly explain the emergence of the Inquisition, its nature, its objectives and its historic course.

II

"Jew hatred and incitement against the Jews," said Mommsen, "are as old as the Diaspora itself."[5] When Mommsen made this cardinal statement, his attention was focused on the aversion to Jews that prevailed in large parts of the Hellenistic world. But that unique hostility which he designated "Jew hatred" and the specific "incitement" which accompanied that hostility were by no means "as old as the Diaspora." It took special political and social circumstances, and a long development of certain public attitudes, to produce the particular genre of hatred that Mommsen had in mind.

The condition of alien minorities in general was no happier in antiquity than in later times. Toleration was rare and usually limited to brief visits of traders, who brought desired goods. When their stay was prolonged with the rulers' consent, the negative reaction to their presence was lessened. But even then their intentions were questioned by the people, their movements were watched by both people and rulers, and their freedom of action was usually confined to the specific limits approved by the authorities. Some sociologists believe that at the bottom of this attitude lay the instinctive fear of strangers as potential enemies—a fear linked to the resistance of many living species to outsiders' encroachments upon their domains. This feeling, which the Greeks called *xenophobia*, dictated their policy toward aliens. But the policy, like the feeling, was not unique to them. It was virtually universal.

Out of this experience there inevitably emerged the custom for any group, tribe, or nationality that wished to settle in a foreign land to accompany that settlement by military force. The Greek colonies in Asia Minor and Sicily, like the Phoenician colonies in North Africa and Spain, were not only economic but also military outposts. The Jews in the period of the First and Second Temple lacked the will or the capacity for such military ventures. They would not therefore settle in any foreign land without the express consent of its rulers, which implied, and often explicitly assured, government protection. Obviously, no ruler would grant such assurances unless he considered it advantageous to his interests and, furthermore, believed himself powerful enough to cope with his people's likely opposition. There was no telling of course under what constraints the authorities' protection might be withdrawn and the life of the minority cut short as a result. But to sustain it, it was clear, two conditions were essential: the minority had to be permanently useful; the rulers, permanently strong.

The first Jewish settlements in the Diaspora, however, did not proceed from voluntary arrangement but from compulsory imposition of conquerors. We have no indication of any special burdens imposed on the Israelites transferred to Assyria (in 724 and 721 B.C.E.) or on the Judeans exiled to Babylonia (in 597 and 586 B.C.E.)—that is, burdens heavier than those endured by the exiles of other conquered nations. Nor do we have any evidence of "Jew hatred" or of any "incitement against the *Jews*" in these circumstances. In contrast, what we know rather indicates the absence of such special persecution. For it appears that within fifty years after the beginning of their second exile, the Judeans in Babylonia were able to extricate themselves from their earlier hardships and limitations and enter the mainstream of Babylonia's economy as free and effective participants.[6] They were even in a position to extend impressive aid to many thousands of Judeans who returned to their homeland in 536 B.C.E.[7] As for the Jews who remained in the dispersion, their condition under Persia took an upward swing both socially and politically in the empire's first century.[8] From the second century, however, we have several indications of troubled relations between the Jews and the authorities, as well as certain segments of the empire's population. To be sure, our information on these occurrences is too scarce to permit any definite conclusions; but it would not be too far-fetched to assume that the troubles resulted from the growth of intolerance toward the prosperous Jewish community. For it is an iron-clad rule in the history of group relations: *the majority's toleration of every minority lessens with the worsening of the majority's condition, especially when paralleled with a steady improvement of the minority's status.* Any serious decline in the power of the rulers is then seen by the people as a suitable opportunity to strike at the minority with its entire force; and this is what probably happened in Persia in the period of the disorders that tore the empire apart.[9] But whatever the cause and nature of these developments, they did not occur at the *start* of the Diaspora but centuries after it began.

These brief remarks were a necessary preliminary to the following observations on our main scene of interest. That scene is Egypt of the twenty-sixth dynasty at about the opening of the sixth century B.C.E. Egypt's pharaoh, Psametich II, then potential ally of Judea against Babylonia, enlisted from among Judean immigrants to his country a group of farmer-soldiers to guard Elephantine (Jeb), his southernmost fort facing the Ethiopians, with whom Egypt was engaged in a long-running war.[10] Other positions on the northeastern frontier were probably likewise manned by Judeans who fled to Egypt in 586 B.C.E., after Judea fell prey to Babylonia. If we interpret correctly some biblical allusions, many of these migrants joined existent settlements established by Judeans who sought safety in Egypt during earlier invasions of their country[11]—a development that could not possibly have occurred without Egypt's friendly disposition. It stands to reason that this friendliness persisted as long as Egypt faced danger from the east and its political condition vis-à-vis its neighbors did not drastically change.

Such a change, however, occurred in 525 B.C.E., when the Persians, who had crushed Babylonia, invaded Egypt and annexed it to their empire. In the course of their invasion they no doubt came in touch with the Jewish garrison at Jeb; and rather than disband it, they preferred it to continue as guardian of the southern frontier.[12] We may easily discern the motive for this preference. Surrounded by a huge Egyptian population seething with hostility toward their army and administration, the Persians looked eagerly for points of reliance on which they could lean in times of trouble. Jeb offered them such a point, since all Jews were then known as friends of Persia because of its assistance to their national rebirth. The Jewish troops in Jeb must have readily joined Persia's military forces in Egypt, probably without feeling any compunction in making their new commitments. They had been, after all, mercenaries of a sovereign that had ceased to exist and could no longer employ them; therefore, they could view themselves fully entitled to offer their services to another lord. The Egyptians, however, may have seen their behavior in a different and rather unfavorable light. The eagerness of those Jewish troops to serve Persia could not, it stands to reason, be concealed; and their readiness to bolster Persia's rule over Egypt at the very moment of Egypt's defeat could be seen by the Egyptians as a gross impropriety and a repellent switch of allegiance.

The altered position of a small Jewish garrison in one of the farthest reaches of Egypt may appear insignificant in the broad scheme of things. Actually, if our analysis is correct, it was of exceptional significance, for it started a chain reaction that was destined to affect the history of the Jewish people ever after and, with it, the history of mankind. The paucity of our records from those remote times obscures from our vision many pertinent events. But certain developments may be taken for granted in any plausible reconstruction. Thus we may assume that the Jewish troops in Jeb (and possibly in other Persian outposts in Egypt) opposed the Egyptians and defended Persian interests during the Egyptian rebellions against Persia in 485 and 464 B.C.E.; and we may further assume that both their loyalty to Persia and opposition to the rebels increased the Egyptians' odium for the Jews. Thus links were forged in a chain of circumstances that extended to the year 411 B.C.E., when Jeb was attacked by its Egyptian neighbors and the Jewish temple there was razed to the ground.[13] That this attack was led by Egyptian priests need not necessarily lead us to the conclusion that it was merely an act of religious hostility. The Egyptian priests were a guiding force in Egypt's national insurrections against Persia, and their assault upon Jeb may have spearheaded the revolt that broke out a few years later (in 405) and freed

Egypt from Persia's yoke for almost six decades. In all probability, the attack on Jeb's garrison was stimulated by both national and religious motives. It may have marked, in fact, an attempt by the majority people—perhaps the first attempt of its kind in history—to wipe out, by violence, the Jewish minority in its midst.

This event might have closed that sorry chapter in the annals of Egyptian-Jewish relations, had not history created new, complex situations which brought the two peoples together again and intertwined them almost inextricably. For Egypt did not regain its independence with the abolition of Persian rule; that rule was merely replaced with Greek conquest during the southward thrust of Alexander the Great (in 322 B.C.E.). Following that epochal event, Jewish life in Egypt again began to quicken. The favorable view the Greeks had formed of the Jews from their first encounters with them in the 4th century[14] facilitated the development of friendly relations between the Greek conquerors of Persia and the Jewish people; and this development had far-reaching consequences. Like the Persians, the Greeks needed outside help to control the vast territories they had seized; and they viewed the Jews as trustworthy and fit to fulfill both military and civil functions. Accordingly, they repeatedly invited Jews to settle in the empires they had established in the East. The Ptolemies welcomed them to Egypt and Libya (notably, to Alexandria and Cyrene)[15]; the Seleucids, to the northern regions (notably, to Antioch, Lydia and Phrygia).[16] Alexandria, especially, offered the Jews a variety of great attractions. It was not without their industry and creativity that this city became, in due time, after Rome, the greatest metropolis of the ancient world.

To understand the ensuing events, however, we must turn our attention again to the Egyptians. They hated the Greeks who governed their country, and they aspired to overthrow Greek rule; but even more than the Greeks they hated the Jews, whom they viewed as their rulers' servants. To be sure, the Jews had nothing to do with Egypt's takeover by the Greeks, just as they had played no part in its capitulation to the Persians. Just the same, from the Egyptians' standpoint, the Jews were now seen for the second time aligned with subjugators of their country—an occurrence that inclined them to view the Jews as their historic foe. In addition, the fact that the Jews, by Greek arrangement, belonged to Egypt's higher social classes while the Egyptians were graded as the lowest[17] made them see themselves subject to the Jews; and their rage over this humiliating condition increased with the growth of the Jews' numbers in the country and the steady rise of their influence. The movement to free Egypt from its "servitude" to the Jews matched the movement to free it from the Greeks; but neither movement made much headway. Sporadic revolts broke out in certain areas; but Greek control of Egypt remained firm and unshakable; and the leaders of the opposition, who were again mostly priests, could not bring about a real revolution. Their burning hate and aggressive urges, therefore, had to find other outlets.

In 270 B.C.E. the Egyptian priest Manetho published in Greek a *History of Egypt* in which he described the Jews' ancestors as a band of foreign conquerors who, mixed with a crowd of Egyptian lepers, were known for their cruelty and misanthropy; isolated by the Egyptians in the city of Avaris, they were finally banished altogether from the country, but not before they had lorded it for thirteen years with exceptional savagery and inhumanity.[18] This account of the origin of the Jewish people, which does not have much truth to commend it, represents the first written antisemitic piece to come down to us from antiquity. When the work was composed, the Jews had been enjoying a generally positive reputation, which contributed, as we have noted, to the trust the Greeks put in their loyalty and ability. Manetho wished to ruin that reputation and thereby undermine the Greeks' faith in the Jews; and, judged by the repercussions of his work, his success exceeded his expectations. From him sprang the anti-Jewish agitation which was to assume unsurpassed ferocity and make an unprecedented impact. Its main transmitters were native Egyptians who had mastered the Greek language and learned how to address Greek audiences. It is they who, as Josephus observed, poisoned the Greeks' mind against the Jews,[19] though the poison, we should note, could not take effect before the body politic of Hellenistic Egypt was conditioned to absorb it.

The change was brought about by a series of developments in the century that followed Manetho's campaign—developments on which, in the present context, we can touch only cursorily. On the one hand, the Ptolemaic kings of that century drew nearer to the Egyptian cults and customs (and consequently to the Egyptian priesthood), while on the other, there was a growing Hellenization of Egypt's elite and upper middle class. Both trends helped bring together certain segments of the Egyptian and Greek higher classes; and as the prospect of Egyptian opposition diminished, the Jews' value as aides of the Greeks was reduced. Another factor contributing to this effect was the massive Greek immigration to Egypt—an immigration that included many middle class elements and masters of all professions.[20] These were now struggling to improve their lot; and since the Jews were engaged in virtually all trades, many Greeks tended to see them as standing in the way of their own advancement. Intolerance, born of economic competition, was inevitably growing.

But Greek intolerance toward the Jews of Egypt was nursed not only by economic rivalry; it was also nurtured by the Jews' social progress, by their rise to the highest political spheres, and by the influence they gained in the royal house. Their inevitable involvement in political conflicts earned them not only the enmity of their adversaries—that is, of their partisan political opponents—but also the ire of the Greek populace, which hated to see a foreign minority decide the destinies of their country. The volatile nature of these involvements and the dangers they held for the Jews of Egypt may be aptly illustrated in the following.

In the middle of the 2nd century B.C.E., two Egyptian Jews, Onias and Dositheos, attained leading positions in Egypt's military organization. According to Josephus, Ptolemy VII Philometor and his consort Cleopatra placed their whole army under their command[21]; and judging by the conditions in which the kings found themselves, this information appears credible. Philometor was engaged in a bitter struggle with his brother Euergetes, who aspired to replace him and was strongly supported by the residents of Alexandria, both the Greek and the Egyptian. Philometor could suspect treason in every quarter, save that of his Jewish subjects. Following Philometor's death (146 B.C.E.), we are told, Cleopatra II, the Queen, was faced with the same menace; but entering Alexandria at the head of his troops, Onias stilled the opposition in the city and made it acquiesce in the Queen's rule.[22] Euergetes, however, did not forget the obstacles the Jews had placed in his way and, in 145, when he became king, planned to avenge himself on Egyptian Jewry. It was only by a miraculous turn of events that the Jews managed to avert disaster[23]; yet this did not deter them from further striving to attain high levels of power. Thus, in the days of Cleopatra III (116–102 B.C.E.), Helkias and Ananias, sons of Onias, were the chief generals of the Egyptian army, and when Cleopatra's son (Ptolemy X Lathyros) rebelled against his mother, they fought him in both Cyprus and Syria.[24]

Such high attainments in the country's army could not be isolated incidents, disconnected from the general state of affairs. Onias' sons, like their father, may first have been in charge of the Jewish forces in Leontopolis (guarding the southern approaches to the Delta); but it is hardly believable that they became Egypt's top generals without Jewish support in the royal administration. Indeed, Josephus tells us that Philometor and Cleopatra "entrusted the whole of their realm to Jews,"[25] and while this assertion may be judged an exaggeration, it doubtless reflects a Jewish occupation of leading positions in Egypt's central government.

III

It is evident that certain elements of the Jewish minority were anxious to be part of Hellenistic society in its most elevated spheres. The tendency manifested itself not only in economy, politics and the military, but also in the realms of spiritual endeavor; and the results of rivalry in these fields, too, were of far-reaching significance.

Long before they encountered the Jews, the Greeks had developed the

notion of themselves as the choice nation on earth. Their evident superiority
in the arts and sciences and their great capacity for analytical thinking made
them view other nations with disdain, or at least as culturally inferior. Their
military victories over the Persian empire appeared to them only a natural
confirmation of their view of themselves as the master race of mankind. So
did their cultural conquest of the East, which long outlived their political
dominion. Indeed, the imprint they left upon the East lasted for more than
a millennium.

   This amazing cultural superiority, to which the Roman empire also
bowed, was challenged by only one people. Like the rest of the peoples in
the eastern regions, many Jews looked with bewilderment and admiration at
Greek achievements in so many fields; but most Jews remained unimpressed.
Their own traditions, concepts and ideals retained a far greater hold on their
minds; and careful comparison with the Greek way of life reinforced their
basic feelings. In the eyes of these Jews, Jewish culture and beliefs remained
what they were in the eyes of their forefathers prior to their encounter with
the culture of Hellas—that is, the beliefs, laws and customs that raised them
above all the nations of the world. The conviction of these Jews about the
superiority of their own laws, moral concepts and way of life was met with
a like conviction of the Greeks about their own civilization. That a violent
clash between the bearers of these postulates was bound to occur sooner or
later was obvious to insightful observers.[26]

   The astounding Hasmonean victories in Palestine marked not only the
beginning of the end for Greek political hegemony in the East; they also
signified the beginning of a drive to establish Jewish moral and religious
superiority. From their political center in Palestine, and all over the Hellenistic world, Jews were now spreading the message of their Prophets as
aggressively as the Greeks were disseminating the teachings of their great
poets and philosophers; Jewish missionaries in Hellenistic countries endeavored to convert the gentiles to their faith, and while agitating for Judaism
they inevitably criticized Greek religious views and customs. It would be
unrealistic to assume that these criticisms were usually inoffensive and only
rarely provocative. However courteous the Jewish propagandists were (and,
obviously, they were often not courteous at all), they could not conceal or
suppress their scorn for the pagan beliefs, cults and customs—that scorn
which Emperor Claudius counseled and cautioned them to avoid.[27] The sight
of a minority mocking the majority—which meant, in Egypt, both Greeks
and Egyptians—and the success of the Jews in converting gentiles could not
but contribute to the hatred of the Jews. Evidently, the fear that the Jewish
campaign might end in a Jewish religious triumph was bound to throw some
Greeks and Egyptians into occasional spells of panic. No wonder that Apion's
attack upon the Jews centered not on their moral character (as had that of his

forerunner, Manetho) but on their religious worship, which he took pains to portray as the most barbarous cult of mankind.[28]

As has been suggested, the religious struggle emerged from a broader cultural encounter; but other aspects of this crucial conflict must be noted even in this brief review. We refer above all to the intellectual contest between Greek and Jewish authors, most notable of whom was Philo of Alexandria (died c. 40), whose works were essentially a series of attempts to subject Greek thinking to Jewish ideals.[29] The Hellenistic world, or at least most of it (before it took a sharp turn to Christianity), could not help rejecting these attempts with chagrin. And thus two proud peoples, or rather two proud cultures, each convinced that it had the exclusive right to serve as the ultimate model for mankind, clashed in a field that was politically explosive and controlled by a third, foreign power: Rome.

The causes of the conflict between Jews and Greeks, therefore, covered the whole gamut of human interests; they were political, social, economic, religious, and intellectual—and we list them here in order of importance. In no other country in the ancient world did such a large array of factors combine to form the background of a lasting conflict between Jews and non-Jews as it did in Egypt and its dependencies (Cyprus and Cyrenaica). And as if all this were not enough to inflame the social atmosphere, there was the insistence of the Jews of Alexandria to be recognized as full-fledged citizens—and this in addition to the privileges they were granted in consideration of their religious needs.

Like the other characteristics we have noted above, this struggle of the Jews for civil equality was peculiar to the Greek-Jewish confrontation. For what was involved were not claims for rights such as trading facilities or freedom of movement, but for full participation in the country's life, to be shared on a par with all other citizens. The Greeks, however, balked at the Jews' demands; and the vigorous fight that the Jews of Alexandria (and in their wake, of other Greek cities) put up for their full rights as citizens bespoke an irrepressible desire for equality surpassing any similar claim put up by any other minority. The demand appeared strange, impudent and unjust to all majorities among whom the Jews lived; but it did not appear strange to the Jews. Perhaps it was no coincidence that the ancient Jewish code was the only one in the world which called repeatedly for equal treatment of the "alien who resides in your midst."[30]

All these antagonisms came to a head when Rome, following the conquest of Syria, became the real arbiter of Egyptian affairs. In the struggles between the Ptolemies backed by Roman power and those favored by numerous Egyptians, claiming to represent Egypt's national interests, the Jews of Egypt could not remain indifferent. Consequently, they found themselves in critical situations that often put them to severe test. Such was the situation they encountered in 53 B.C.E. under Ptolemy XIII Auletes. This king, fearing the populace and the army, fled Egypt to Rome in 58, thus enabling the opposition peacefully to enthrone his daughter Berenike in his stead. But three years later he reappeared before Pelusium, together with an army led by Gabinius, the powerful Roman proconsul of Syria, and Judean troops under Antipater, and asked the Jewish forces who guarded that fortress to give him free passage to Alexandria. The Jews of Pelusium, who then held the fort for a government bitterly opposed to Auletes, had of course to overcome a serious dilemma when they gave that request a positive response.[31] It is hard to believe that such a crucial decision was taken by them without the counsel and consent of the Jewish leadership in Alexandria. Undoubtedly, the latter justified their action by their allegiance to the "legitimate" king of Egypt who was returning home after a forced exile; but one can imagine the Greeks' feelings toward the Jews when Gabinius, after entering Alexandria, restored Auletes' royal authority and stationed three Roman legions in the country to secure the rule of the hated King.

Eight years later, in 47 B.C.E., the Jews of Egypt faced a similar test when Julius Caesar was besieged in Alexandria and the force that came to his rescue from the east—headed by Mithridates, king of Pergamon, and assisted by Judeans led by Antipater—had to pass through an area (the "Land of Onias") held by a strong Jewish military corps. Once again the Jewish force could block or hinder the advance of the foreign invaders, but instead it received them as friends and allies and enabled them to reach Alexandria in time to save Caesar from his predicament.[32] As a result Cleopatra, the rejected queen, became mistress of Egypt under Roman protection. Once again the Jews' conduct must have appeared to many Greeks, especially to those who opposed Cleopatra, if not actually treacherous, at least most improper—a meddling in Egypt's internal affairs through the intervention of a hostile power. The Jews no doubt argued that this intervention was desired by the Queen of Egypt, and therefore what they did was done in obedience to the country's legitimate authority.

It would be wrong to regard such explanations as excuses, since legitimacy was the main principle of policy—in fact, the only policy—the Jews of Egypt could pursue. However risky and shaky a foundation it provided for their future existence, it was the only policy that could offer them security amid a majority which begrudged their successes and gave clear signs of deepening enmity. Thus, the only justification of their political conduct, which the Jews of Egypt could possibly give, though essentially truthful, would not be the whole truth. It was loyalty to the Crown *and* their communal interests that combined to determine their stand.

Rome knew how to appreciate the help it received at that juncture from the Jews in the East. It realized that the Greek population in Egypt, with its old traditions of mastery and independence, would always oppose Roman supervision, and that the native Egyptians, whether Hellenized or not, would invariably share the Greeks' attitude. Rome therefore looked for factors in the region to counterbalance those two national entities. But where could such factors be found? Across the border lay Judea, which was a friendly Roman base (in the days of Herod), while in Egypt proper and its former dependencies the Jews constituted a great force. Accordingly, Rome expanded the boundaries of Judea and confirmed the Jews of the Diaspora countries in all the privileges they had gained in the past.[33] In Egypt itself, this policy was promulgated as soon as the country was annexed to the Empire (in 30 B.C.E.).[34]

The great cross-currents of Rome's internal struggles and, above all, its rooted colonial system, based as it was on "divide and rule" and a frequent reassessment of local resistance to its ever-changing imperial plans, were bound, however, to affect Rome's initial attitude toward Egyptian Jewry. Once its rule in Egypt was firmly established, Rome reappraised the force and utility of the various contending groups in the country, and consequently revised its original policies toward both Jews and Greeks. While upholding the Jews' economic positions as masters or controllers of the river's ports, it reduced their civic and political status, but not to a degree that would satisfy the Greeks. On the other hand, the Jews did not take the curtailment of their "traditional" rights lying down.[35] They persistently fought for their full restitution, thereby clashing with the Greeks, who kept urging Rome to reduce the Jews' status still further. Rome, however, rejected these counsels, retaining the position it had allotted to the Jews, while refusing the Greeks, who enjoyed full civil rights, a higher political status.[36] Though evidently seeking to attain equilibrium, for the Jews this policy bore seeds of disaster which began to germinate before long. In their growing but impotent rage against Rome, the Greeks intensified their campaign against the Jews who, they feared, might finally regain their former superior position. The Emperors, they knew, more often than not showed the Jews of Egypt a friendly face.

The rise of Greek hatred for the Jews, however, can be better understood if attention is paid to two additional factors. Rome's initial policy toward the Jews of Egypt, as well as the latter's responses to it, evoked among the Greeks the same reaction that their own earlier policy toward the Jews had aroused among the Egyptians. Like the Egyptians, the Greeks came to believe that the Jews had now joined Egypt's foes for the third time against the clear will of its people and spokesmen. At the same time, the numbers of Greeks in Alexandria were "swelled by a host of Egyptians" (as Josephus put it),[37] and these Egyptians, of whom many were Hellenized, fanned the hatred of the Greeks for the Jews. In consequence, the old Jew hatred of the Egyptians merged with the recent Jew hatred of the Greeks, attaining thereby unprecedented heights of malevolent aggressiveness. No longer could that hatred be satisfied with mere insults, with vehement censure, maligning and abuse. It sought expression in violence. It was finally given opportunity for such expression in the pogrom of Alexandria in 38 C.E.

The pogrom of 38 was the first manifestation of antisemitism in its fullest form. It originated in circumstances peculiar to Egypt in both the Greek and early Roman periods. These were (a) the reliance of the Jews for their protection and security on the country's rulers, who were mostly foreign; (b) the occasional assistance the Jews offered the rulers against the wishes of large sections of the non-Jewish population; (c) the stubborn insistence of the Jewish minority on equality of rights with the country's upper classes; (d) the rise of many Jews to high social levels; and (e) the projection by the Jews of a religious victory over the pagan cults and beliefs. These were the factors that joined to set ablaze the Greek world with the fire of Jew hatred.

They provided, moreover, the fertile soil in which the tree of antisemitism grew. But what watered that soil, and made the plant produce the variety of poisonous fruit it bore, was the *particular campaign that had developed in Egypt since the days of Manetho.* It was a campaign that relied on nothing but lies, the most atrocious lies and the most absurd libels, but it attained its purpose of reviling the Jews, besmirching their name, and rendering them an object of intense hatred. This was, in one word, defamation—the most extreme and unscrupulous vilification of a people, without which the appearance of antisemitism, its growth and achievements would have been utterly impossible. It emerged from the particular environment of Egyptian-Greek society and culture and the particular complications in the course of Egypt's history, and prior to that emergence we see nothing of the kind anywhere in the ancient world. This is why we agree with that clear-sighted scholar who said, unreservedly, in plain language: "Antisemitism was born in Egypt."[38]

IV

In their search for the origins of antisemitism in the Middle Ages, which they regard as the forerunner of modern antisemitism, many leading scholars arrived at the conclusion that the roots of antisemitism must be sought in Christianity, its teachings and the campaign it conducted against the Jews. One of the most eloquent spokesmen of this view is the well-known Christian scholar James Parkes, whose numerous works on the Jewish question are all distinguished by vast learning, sound judgment and lucid exposition. Parkes is also more consistent and convincing than most of the scholars who share his approach. We shall therefore examine some of his statements as representative of this line of thought.

Parkes does not overlook the fact that Jews were disliked and molested by their neighbors a considerable time before Christianity arose, but he claims that this dislike originated in reasons "similar to those which have animated dislikes of other peoples" in many times and places. Parkes considered such dislikes "normal," stemming from the natural collective antagonisms that underlie conflicts between neighboring groups. Accordingly, he says, "the dislike of the Egyptians for the Jews of Alexandria was a normal dislike. The jealousy of the Greek cities in the time of Pompey was a normal jealousy." In contrast, he regards the massacres of 1096, during the first Crusade, as "abnormal," for they indicate a "disparity between cause and effect." "This is the abnormality whose ultimate explanation lies in the history of the Christian Church."[39]

Elsewhere, too, Parkes tries to convince us that the "anomalous" hatred known as antisemitism was not to be found in the pre-Christian world. For in that world, he claims, many instances could show "how completely Jewish-Gentile relations followed the *normal pattern of relations between neighbors,* now good, now bad, now roused to active enmity by some special irritation, now moved to approval and imitation by something which was admirable. But it would bring us no nearer the understanding of antisemitism. For antisemitism is a unique expression of group prejudice, and arises out of a unique cause."[40]

Parkes, then, makes a sharp distinction between antisemitism in the Middle Ages and Jew hatred in the Greek world. In his opinion, the two developments belong to two different categories of phenomena and two separate historic courses. The later course—i.e., the medieval—had its own starting point and stemmed from a different cause. That cause, he insists, was Christianity, or rather the "action of the Christian Church," which "changed the normal pattern of Jewish-Gentile relations."[41]

With this view of Parkes we sharply disagree. To our way of thinking, his whole view of the relations between Jews and gentiles in antiquity misses the core of the historical reality that produced ancient antisemitism and sustained it. Because of this he sees no similarity and no real link between Jewish-gentile relations in the ancient world, which he regards as "neighborly," and the medieval hostility toward the Jews, which alone he designates as antisemitism. Our own view, in contrast, is that the Jewish question in antiquity was produced by essentially the same factors that fashioned it in later times; that antisemitism in the Christian period was, fundamentally, a continuation of the anti-Jewishness that preceded it; and that the origins and manifestations of both phenomena were fundamentally the same.

To prove this, it is sufficient, we believe, to compare some expressions of Jew hatred in the Hellenistic world with those we know from medieval Europe. Philo, who left us a vivid description of the pogrom in Alexandria in 38, provides ample information for such a comparison. As he put it:

So excessive were the sufferings of our people that anyone who spoke of them [i.e., of the Jews] as undergoing wanton violence and outrage would be using words not properly applicable. [Such a man would lack] adequate terms to express the *magnitude of cruelty so unprecedented* that actions of conquerors in war, who are also merciless to the conquered, would seem kindness itself in comparison.[42]

Philo supports this general evaluation with numerous data of a horrid nature. "Multitudes" of Jews were destroyed in Alexandria with "manifold forms of maltreatment," he recounts; for "any Jews who showed themselves anywhere" in the city "were stoned and knocked about with clubs," the blows being first aimed at "the less vital parts," so that a speedier death might not give the victims "speedier relief from the consciousness of their anguish."[43] But "more pitiable," he adds, "was the fate of those who were burnt to death in the middle of the city." For sometimes "through lack of proper wood," the pogromists collected brushwood, and "after setting it on fire, threw it upon the victims who perished half burnt more through the smoke than by the fire."[44] Even this, however, did not mark the peak of the atrocities. For "many," Philo tells us,

> while still alive, they [i.e., the pogromists] tied with thongs and nooses and, binding their ankles, dragged them through the middle of the market, leaping on them and not even sparing their dead bodies. For, more brutal and savage than fierce wild beasts, they severed them limb from limb and piece from piece and trampling on them destroyed every lineament, so that not even the least remnant was left which could receive burial.[45]

I do not know wherein this outburst of savage hatred differed essentially from the anti-Jewish outbursts that Parkes relates to the era of antisemitism. During the Crusades, when the Jews of the Rhineland were butchered and robbed in orgies of violence, or when the Jews of Alsace in 1338 were hacked to pieces by the murderous gangs of Zimberlin (the Armleders), the methods of killing may have differed from those commonly used by the Greeks in Alexandria, but the cruelty and inhumanity of the killers were the same. Nor do we see greater disparity between cause and effect in the medieval atrocities than in the ancient excesses. Rather the reverse seems often the case. For when the Jews of Colmar—men, women and children—were pushed into one cave to be burned there together, or when the Jews of Strasbourg, two thousand strong, were all driven into a lighted pyre, there was ostensibly a justifiable reason for these outrages: The Jews were charged with having caused the Black Death. But what similar libel could have motivated the Greeks to burn the Jews of Alexandria? Above all, the wild outburst in Egypt we have just mentioned was not by any means an isolated occurrence, suggesting a one-time irregular deviation from an otherwise "normal" course of behavior. As we have indicated above, and shall further show below, it reflected a trend of rising hatred which was aimed at one goal: the Jews' annihilation. Nor was the pogrom in Alexandria its peak.

E. H. Flannery, another Christian scholar who, like Parkes, surveyed the history of Jew hatred, said that "after Apion Greek antisemitism withered."[46] This conclusion, too, is based, in our judgment, on a misconception of the actual development. The opinion of the Jews preserved from such authors as Nicarchus and Damocritus, Aristides and Philostratus, Clearchus and Ptolemaeus and many others indicates that the antisemitic current in Greek literature was flowing strongly after Apion's time; and we ought to bear in mind that the documents that have reached us represent only a fraction of the literature produced. Indubitably, many pamphlets and propaganda sheets composed by second-rate writers were not preserved, and there is also no doubt that, more than by writings, the agitation against the Jews was carried on by public speeches, abusive talk and offensive deeds. Had this not been the case, Josephus would not have been impelled to write his great apology for the Jewish people, and his passionate counterattack against the pagan antisemites, more than sixty years after Apion had committed his anti-Jewish railings to writing. For Josephus' book was no mere exercise in theoretical wrangling, aimed at proving the antiquity of the Jews or confuting false arguments against them which he found in old books. When we read his work, we have a live feeling that he was fighting current libels and calumnies widely circulated in *his* time, and indeed he often speaks of the foes of the Jewish people in the present, not in the past tense ("The Egyptians *are* notoriously our bitterest enemies").[47] In any case, the great fire of hatred for the Jews, which burst out in the pogrom of 38, was by no means suppressed after Apion; it continued to burn and spread; and if additional disasters like that of 38 did not occur shortly thereafter, it was because Rome was on guard to prevent them and because the Jews' ability to defend themselves was still a real deterrent. But as soon as conditions seemed opportune, the Greeks returned to the use of force. This happened in the year 66, following the outbreak of the great Jewish revolt against Roman rule in Palestine.[48]

Believing that the Romans would now refrain from disturbing them, the Greeks resumed their assault upon the Jews in many cities, including Alexandria. Though the data we possess about these events are far from adequate to reconstruct them in full, they are sufficient to show that the pogroms of that year proved another stage in the escalation of antisemitism in the countries around the eastern Mediterranean.[49] Indeed, when Josephus wrote his work against Apion, he must have felt a thickening atmosphere of danger; and perhaps he thought that he might help to clear it by means of his counteroffensive. If so, he was mistaken. For not many years later the treatment of the Jews in Egypt became so abusive and humiliating—indeed so provocative and intolerable—that the Jews of Egypt, Cyrenaica and Cyprus (that is, of the whole former Ptolemaic empire) decided to rise against their tormentors and try to inflict on them so heavy a punishment as to deter them from further acts of aggression. That is how the so-called Jewish War of 115–117 broke out.[50]

The Greek authors who wrote about this war went out of their way to describe the brutalities committed by Jews against Greeks.[51] That in addition to true facts they reported false rumors circulated by avowed enemies of the Jews is evident from the contents of their narratives.[52] But bearing in mind the barbarous atrocities perpetrated against the Jews during the first pogrom in Alexandria, we may readily agree that many of the Jews, moved by an ungovernable urge for vengeance, treated many Greeks who fell into their hands in just as ruthless a manner. In all likelihood, however, their main aim in the war was, as we have indicated, not vengeance but preemption, or rather suppression of the Greeks' desire to repeat their assaults upon them. It was of course an unrealistic hope, yet it does not appear too fantastic when we note that the Jews had the upper hand in many theaters of war, until the Romans, who sought to restore order, interfered. Even then, the war did not end soon; it went on for almost three years, and in some places perhaps for a decade. In any case, it involved not only clashes like those of the year 66 which, however terrible, had gravely affected a rather limited number of cities. What we have before us is a conflict far more violent and of incomparably greater magnitude. It embraced vast regions in three countries; the casualties on both sides amounted to many myriads[53]; whole provinces were laid waste in its wake[54]; and countless communities were wiped out. How can one talk, in view of these developments, of the "withering of Greek antisemitism after Apion" or define the relations between the Jews and the Greeks as "normal relations between neighbors"?

V

If the pogroms of 38 and 66 provided the background of popular strife against which the war of 115 broke out, the war itself must have further deepened the antagonism between Greeks and Jews. If until that war many Greeks were still inclined toward Judaism and the Jewish people, the suffering of many innocent Greeks, struck down inadvertently by the Jews' retaliation, must have made Greek hatred of the Jewish name far more widespread and intense. One would assume that this drastic deterioration in Greek-Jewish relations adversely affected the chances of the Christians to draw support from those Greeks, whose sympathy for Christianity was based, in large measure, on their sympathy for Judaism. One might conclude that conversions to Christianity were greatly reduced in the wake of the war; and this indeed seems to have been the case in the first decades following the upheaval. Shortly thereafter, however, Christianity resumed its forward march on a front much broader and at a pace much swifter than those that marked its earlier progress. To understand this seemingly irregular development, we have to note the following.

The spread of Christianity from the middle of the 2nd century until it became, in 325, the dominant religion of the Roman empire has usually been ascribed to its ideological evolution and the irresistible influence exercised by its message on the pagan population of the Empire. Since the impact of the Greek-Jewish conflict has generally been excluded from the causes of that evolution, the expansion of Christianity was commonly portrayed as an abstract outgrowth of religious theories, with little regard to the sociological factor that lay at the bottom of that development. That factor was the Greek-Jewish relationship, which after the war of 115–117 must have become more tense and troubled, since the war left the Greeks more hostile toward the Jews than they had ever been. As this hostility has generally been underrated, and more often than not completely ignored, what should have been the crucial question for historians has rarely even been considered. And thus we remained with the puzzling query which applies especially to the time referred to: How could the masses of the Hellenistic world, imbued as they were with burning hatred for the Jews, accept a basically Jewish doctrine, originating in Jewish thought and literature and advocated by Jewish apostles? Or, to put it more succinctly: How can we explain the swelling current of converts to Christianity from about the year 150 onward—a current that engulfed the eastern half of the Empire and overflowed into its western regions?

The answer to this question lies in the crucial change effected in the posture of Christianity toward Judaism and in its relationship toward the Jewish people. The change implied not merely greater emphasis upon the distinction between the two faiths, but also a total separation of Christianity from Judaism as a religion, a cult, and a way of life.

It may of course be argued that the trend toward separation was already begun by Paul, when he freed the gentiles from the burden of the Commandments and thereby made it easier for them to accept his version of Christianized Judaism. There is no doubt much truth in this contention, as there is in the claim that many pagans in the Empire had long been craving a message of salvation of the kind offered by Jewish messianism. Yet while these factors paved the way for Christianity, they could not draw to it the enormous gentile following that it was to gain in the course of time.

In fact, as we see it, "Jewish" Christianity had from the outset no chance of becoming a mass movement among the Hellenists, whose masses became increasingly permeated with hatred of the Jews. Paul, with his praise of his Jewish "brethren," and his limitless admiration for their achievements, could not perform the feat. Nor could the writers of the first three Gospels, as they too were steeped in Jewish thinking, Jewish religious and legal concepts, and Jewish hopes of redemption. It was only a Christianity that broke with Judaism in all that truly mattered to its essence—a Christianity that developed a new view of God, new dogmas, and a new historic outlook, quite different and indeed remote from those of Judaism—that could become an attraction to the gentile world.

This radical departure from Judaism can first be noted in the Gospel according to John which, judging by available information, was composed about 125.[55] It was this Gospel that first replaced the Jewish idea of God with the conceptual basis of the Trinity,[56] the Jewish view of the Messiah (as the son of David) with the notion of the incarnated *logos,* and the Pauline view of His universal mission with a revised conception that does not grant the Jews any preference in any respect. Nowhere can we find here, of course, an indication that Israel was the sole object of Jesus' mission, such as occurs in other Gospels—e.g., that Jesus came to redeem only the "lost sheep of Israel," that the "bread" of salvation assigned for the "sons" (i.e., the Jews) cannot be thrown to the "dogs" (i.e., the gentiles), or that His disciples were forbidden by Him to preach among the Samaritans.[57] On all these matters the Gospel of John takes quite a different position.[58] Nor does it present Jesus as an advocate of strict adherence to the Law—indeed to its last jot or tittle (Matt. 5.17–18)—but rather as its direct and open antagonist. For when addressing the Jews, who opposed His views, He calls the Law "*your* Law" (i.e., not *His*), thus making it apparent that He differed from them not on interpretative but on substantive issues.[59] What is more, while the other three Gospels make it clear that Jesus' foes among the Jews were specific groups (the Pharisees and the Sadducees, the "chief priests" and the elders), the Gospel of John points out—indeed stresses—that His conflict was not only with those groups but with *the Jews in general,* and accordingly, that *the Jews* sought to kill Him, even *with their own hands.*[60] It is in conformity with all these assertions that we find there Jesus' sharp reproach to the *Jews* as the sons of the Devil, the arch-murderer, as an explanation of their desire to take His life.[61]

Such a presentation of Jesus' divinity, of His relations with the *Jews,* and of His view of the Jewish people could of course appeal to the Greek pagans, who were filled with hatred of the Jews. It could help to convince them that the Christians were not just a "Jewish sect" and Christianity not a mere version of Judaism, as so many had believed and asserted, but a religion quite independent of Judaism, which differed from it on all major issues and was in such bitter conflict with Judaism as to admit no compromise and no reconciliation. The Greek pagans' growing inclination to embrace Christian-

ity from the middle of the 2nd century—indeed, the fact that, from about that
time, the narrow flow of pagan converts to Christianity became an ever
broader stream—must be related to the evolution of the new ideas whose
beginning we note in the Gospel of John. This, however, represents only part
of the explanation of that unique phenomenon. The other part must be
related to a parallel development which was of no lesser importance.

For with all the radical changes that took place in the basic religious
concepts of Christianity, there remained the problem of the reliance on the
Bible and the admiration for the Prophets and Israel's heroes as reflected in
the words of both Jesus and Paul—a reliance that stood in direct contradiction to the anti-Jewish sentiment of the Greek masses. The question which
arises from that contradiction may perhaps be best framed as follows: How
could the Hellenistic masses come to view the Bible, which was produced by
Jews, as the supreme spiritual expression of mankind, and how could they
accept the ancestors of the Jewish people with such unqualified veneration,
when they so hated their descendants and disciples? The answer lies in the
work done by a throng of Christian apologists, teachers and exegetes, who
interpreted the Bible in such a way that it appeared not as a pro- but an
anti-Jewish book—a book in which the Fathers of Israel assumed the role of
the Fathers of Christendom, now perceived as the True Israel, while Israel
the people was presented as the false Israel, which was identified with the
Jews. Naturally, the attainment of such a result called for an indefatigable
effort and a relentless process of casuistic thinking; every sentence and word
of the Bible had to be interpreted so as to agree with all the other parts as
newly construed; and consequently, allegoric and symbolic understanding
had often to replace the plain, unvarnished meaning. But the "final sentence"
could at last be pronounced: "The Old Testament, from cover to cover, has
nothing whatever to do with the Jews."[62] To be sure, it was argued, the Jewish
teachers "illegally and insolently had seized upon it, confiscated it, and tried
to claim it as their own property; they had falsified it by their expositions, and
even by corrections and omissions." "But every Christian must . . . deny them
the possession of the Old Testament. It would be a sin for Christians to say,
'this book belongs to us *and* to the Jews,' seeing that the book belonged from
the outset, as it belongs now and evermore, *to none but Christians,* whilst the
Jews are the worst people, the most godless and God-forsaken, of all the
nations upon earth, the devil's own people, . . . a fellowship of hypocrites
. . . stamped by their crucifixion of the Lord."[63] As Harnack said in summarizing the whole process:

> Such an injustice as that inflicted by the Gentile church on Judaism
> is almost unprecedented in the annals of history. The Gentile church
> stripped it of everything, she took away its sacred book; herself but a

transformation of Judaism, she cut off all connection with the parent religion. The daughter first robbed her mother, and then repudiated her![64]

This disengagement of Christianity from Judaism represented its battle for a new identity—a battle that indicated its deep dissatisfaction with itself as a Jewish or semi-Jewish sect. We ought to bear in mind that by 125, and certainly by 150, the overwhelming majority of Christians were gentiles, or rather of gentile origin—a fact which should be taken into consideration in any attempt to explain that discontent. It should also help us realize that what Christianity was then yearning for was not some formal change, but a new inward life and outward appearance that would make it *clearly* distinct from Judaism, and bring it much closer to Greek habits of behavior and Greek forms of speculation. The force of this peculiar desire may be gauged by the strength of the aversion for the Jewish people that animated Christian ranks at the time, and it was indeed the rising anti-Jewish feeling that moved many Greek Christians to "rethink" their Christianity and try to adjust it to their frame of mind. Then came the theologians, and performed the task of theoretical accommodation. Christian theology did not create or initiate the hatred of the Jews that saturates its teachings—it was, on the contrary, created and shaped by it. The instinct of hatred was simply hardened into a doctrine that constituted the foundation of the new religious edifice.

VI

If no ordinary evolution of theological thought can explain the transformation of the Christian faith from its Pauline form to that of the Nicene Creed; if indeed that transformation cannot be explained without bearing in mind the background of emotions which forced Greek thought to employ its ingenuity in that extraordinary and anomalous manner, it must also be conceded that the leading Christian thinkers, representing the mainstream of Christian theology, could not have formed their final positions without making a careful, pragmatic calculation of the needs that Christianity had to meet at the time. Only by considering these needs and that approach can we explain their tenacious adherence to the Old Testament as the fountainhead of the Christian faith.

For one thing must be taken for certain: the intellectual ferment that evolved in Greek Christianity in the wake of the war of 115–117 produced conflicting pressures upon the Christian theologians from both poles of Christian opinion. On the one hand, there were the extreme antagonists of Judaism, chief among whom were Marcion and his followers, who urged complete desertion of the Old Testament as the very antithesis of true

Christianity, while, on the other hand, there were Greeks who remained faithful to the Judaic heritage in Christianity and sought to preserve it at all costs. These were the Monarchians (of the "dynamic" brand) who, in reaction to the Marcionites, again raised the banner of pure monotheism and viewed Jesus as essentially a prophet, entrusted by God with the mission of salvation and therefore endowed, more than the other prophets, with supernatural powers. The mainstream theologians, however, rejected both these approaches. In no way could they approve the fundamentally "Judaic" view, which they considered suicidal for Christianity, but they were equally opposed to the idea that Christianity ought to abandon the Old Testament. They conceded that to make the "Jewish" Bible conform to the dominant view of Christianity about the Jews, it had to be differently comprehended and interpreted—a Herculean task no doubt, whose feasibility could be questioned. But they also realized that Christianity would be groundless, shorn of authenticity, and denied far-reaching influence, if it could not rely on the Old Testament's antiquity, sanctity, authority and fame. Consequently, they preferred to divorce Judaism from the Bible rather than divorce the Bible from Christianity.

But the task on which these Christian authors embarked aimed not only at the reinterpretation of the Bible; it aimed also at the expurgation from Christianity of any Jewish trait, notion or custom affecting any part of its religious life—i.e., its dogmas, its forms of worship and, above all, its conception of God. It is indeed by the effort of so many Christian thinkers to shake off from Christianity anything "Jewish" that one may best gauge the depth of their antipathy toward Judaism and the Jewish people. In the two centuries of Christianity's transformation from the Pauline mold to the Nicene Creed (c. 125–325), it is difficult to find a single Christian writer who did not disparage Judaism and its followers. But it is not in the invectives, or criticisms, or denunciations hurled at Judaism by such Christian authors as Justin Martyr or Tertullian or Athanasius that the true attitude toward the Jews was revealed. In the altered political climate of Rome—which since 150 appeared favorable to the Jews, but hostile and frequently stormy for the Christians—the Christian author would often moderate his style, so as not to give offense that might provoke persecution. In his comments on the Bible, however, and his discussions of its teachings—all seemingly of a purely academic nature—he could freely express his opposition to Judaism, and thereby give vent to his anti-Jewish feelings. This is why we believe that in that particular age, Christian hatred for Judaism and the Jewish people should be assessed less by the sharpness of the shafts then flung by Christian authors against the Jews than by the intensity of the labor those authors invested in building the new Christian doctrine.

The greatest effort was undoubtedly put into the formation of the new concept of God, where obstacles were met at almost every step. Here again the struggle centered on the measure of Jewishness that the opponents of the theory upheld by the mainstream sought to retain in the idea of the Godhead. So bitter was the struggle on this issue that nothing less than excommunication was the punishment considered fit for the opponents. This was indeed what the Council of Nicaea decreed for Arius and his followers. The Arians denied the full divinity of Jesus, thereby approaching the Jewish view of the Savior, and consequently demoted the concept of the Trinity, which had been made the cornerstone of the new Christian faith.

The Nicaean blast at Arianism, however, did not crush it as many had expected, and the battle against it continued unabated until the Council of Constantinople (381), whose decision, supported by Theodosius I, proved fatal to Arianism in the Roman empire. Triumphant over its great enemy within, Christendom developed a multiple attack upon the enemy without—the Jewish people. We say "multiple" because the *literary* assault upon the Jews and Judaism had never ceased, and, in the decades preceding the Council of Constantinople, had become more violent than ever before. Having frequently enjoyed since 325 the outspoken favor of the Roman empire, most Christian authors abandoned all restraint in their attacks upon the Jewish people. The works of such writers as Ephraem Syrus, Gregory of Nazianzus and Gregory of Nyssa are notorious for their venomous vituperations against the Jews. But none surpassed in vehemence and ferocity the anti-Jewish diatribes of John Chrysostom of Antioch and none contributed as much as he did to the transition from literary attacks upon the Jews to physical forms of aggression against them.

Chrysostom began his campaign against the Jews in 387, and shortly thereafter, in the following year, some Christians in Syria came to believe that, like their Greek forefathers in the first and second centuries, they could accompany their insults with violence. Accordingly, they destroyed the Jewish synagogue at Callinicum, an event which signaled the opening of a new era in the history of anti-Jewish persecution—an era characterized by popular violence carried on under the banner of the cross.

The reaction of the emperor, Theodosius I, to the Christian-Greek insult at Callinicum (he would not let the culprits go scot-free) showed that Rome was still holding fast to its traditional legal and religious policies. What bolstered these policies in preceding decades had been the opposition to civil discrimination on the part of the pagan forces in the Empire (who were still strong, especially in its western part) and the leaning of some emperors toward Arianism, which moved them to uphold the principle of toleration. But by the end of the fourth century paganism was enfeebled, while Arianism in the Empire proper was crushed. This changed the situation materially. When the anti-Jewish forces in northern Syria decided to take the law into their own hands, they were driven to do so not only by their Jew hatred (which had long sought an outlet in violence), but also by their newborn feeling of strength, generated by the great expansion of Christianity and the unification of its ranks. What gave that feeling its peculiar vigor was the widespread opinion, raised to axiomatic levels, that to hurt the Jews was a holy duty; and this reigning view was of crucial value. For when hatred and jealousy drive the masses to a point at which they are eager to break the law, an ideology justifying their wishes is needed to give them the necessary moral support. The anti-Jewish ideology of Christianity now performed the task which in earlier centuries had been fulfilled by the Hellenistic theories of Jew hatred. It proved its effectiveness not only in the agitation that preceded the attack at Callinicum, but also in the defense it offered the crime after it had been committed. Such was the intellectual climate of the time that St. Ambrose, then bishop of Milan, was able to move the all-powerful emperor to withdraw his order to punish the lawbreakers. It was a minor retreat involving a single case, but it foreshadowed the breakdown of the imperial system, once it was subjected to greater strain.

In 395, such a strain developed when a radical change took place in the structure of the Roman government. The Empire was divided into two parts; the influence of the West was greatly diminished both by the division and by the reduction of its power under the impact of the barbarian invasions, while the eastern half could be considered Greek and virtually dominated by the Christian population. Under Theodosius II, the emperor of the East, the authorities increasingly displayed their inability to resist the pressures of the antisemitic masses. The license and impudence of the latter grew, and at the beginning of the fifth century, pogroms against the Jews broke out in Illyria and other parts of the Empire. Most serious was the attack upon the Jews of Alexandria, followed by their expulsion at the order of the bishop, Cyril of Alexandria, their sworn enemy (415). The emperor later confirmed the order, which foreshadowed his own decree to banish the Jews from Constantinople.[65]

Yet the most sinister development touching the Jews of the Empire took place in the field of law. We have seen that the first goal of the Greeks in the East was to reduce the Jews, socially and politically, to a *legal* level inferior to their own. And there can be no doubt that the spokesmen of the Christians—direct heirs of the Greek antisemites—began to press for anti-Jewish legislation from the moment they felt that Rome's internal policies were veering in their direction. The emperors, however, were generally not anxious to renounce the equal treatment granted by their laws to all the citizens of the Empire (and all licit religions) and adopt a policy of discrimination against the Jews; and Constantine the Great set the example in this respect. Although he imposed some restrictions on the Jews, all formally related to religious matters, these restrictions were presented as defensive of Christianity rather than as offensive to Judaism, and, with one exception, none of them affected the Jews' economic and social interests. This exception, which consisted of a ban on the purchase of Christian slaves by Jews, had of course nothing to do with religion or with humanitarian considerations. Its sole purpose was to give the Christian Greeks a competitive economic advantage over the Jews. The Roman authorities soon recognized this fact, and the law was simply not enforced. Then it was reenacted by Constantius, only to fall again into disuse. But the restraining attitude displayed by the government toward this and other anti-Jewish edicts virtually disappeared within two decades after the division of the Empire.

Thus, in 417 the law forbidding Jews to employ Christian slaves was reissued for the third time, with the supplement prohibiting the Jews from owning pagan slaves as well.[66] In 418 the Jews were debarred from the offices of imperial inspection, as well as from those of the Court and the army.[67] In 429 they were hit politically when the Patriarchate in Palestine was abolished.[68] Then, after 429, they were denied the right to practice law, and in 438 they were forbidden to serve in any administrative or public office.[69] Yet even this did not constitute the end of the repression. More legal restrictions were enacted under Justinian; and under Phocas (602–610) bloody outbreaks occurred in Antioch, notorious as the scene of such outrages. In the course of a quarrel between the city's Jews and Greeks (in 608), the emperor subjected the Jews of Antioch, and probably also of large neighboring regions, to a decree of forced conversion.[70] The decree moved the Jews of Antioch to rebel, which was in accord with their known martial vigor. But the rebellion was quelled after fierce resistance, following which the surviving Jews of Antioch were banished from the city.[71]

What emerges from the above observations may be summarized as follows. The genesis of antisemitism, its growth, and its development to full maturity and prime capacity took place in the Hellenistic world—that is, geographically, in the belt of lands encircling the southeastern Mediterranean. Here was the birthplace of that particular hatred which far surpassed the animus that any majority may ordinarily feel for a minority. For here first appeared that particular *campaign* (termed in our own time *propaganda*) which was aimed at mobilizing public opinion against the Jews as a prelude to violent attacks upon them; here also developed the method of besmirching them, of sullying their reputation and of rendering them odious by means of *libels, calumnies and lies* of the most vicious kind—in brief, of their *defamation;* here also was the birthplace of the *popular outbreaks* (known in modern times as *pogroms*), whose purpose was to cause the Jews such heavy losses as to annihilate them or frighten them away; here, too, was inaugurated the *anti-Jewish legislation,* specifically designed to degrade the Jews socially, and subject them perpetually to a variety of restrictions—civil, economic and political; here evolved that particular form of an intensely anti-Jewish Christianity, which was to serve as a dominant *ideology* justifying the repression and harassment of the Jews; and here, finally, arose that *state persecution* of the Jews which culminated in *expulsions and forced conversions.* Thus all the forms of warfare against the Jews in the Diaspora had their origin in regions dominated demographically by Greek masses, inspired culturally by Greek civilization, and organized politically as the Eastern Roman Empire. When, at the beginning of the 7th century, antisemitism was about to strike in the West, it had before it the heritage and model of the eastern movement.

CHAPTER II

The Spanish Scene

I. Earlier Stages

I

If the eastern part of the Roman empire became, after the division of 395, more and more a national state, united in language, culture and religion and surging toward ethnic homogeneity, the western part of the Empire evolved in the opposite direction. From the beginning of the fifth century until the middle of the sixth, it was subject to invasions by great Germanic tribes, who cut it up into different dominions and disrupted the influence of Latin civilization, which was molding their peoples into a uniform whole by its language, jurisdiction, and way of life. In consequence, these invasions left behind them a heritage of political and cultural diversity, considerably strengthened by the changes they wrought in the ethnic structures of the peoples involved. In due course, however, these medleys of influences gradually blended into new unions—the entities that served as the cores or foundations of the modern Western nations.

It is questionable of course whether Romanization, if left undisturbed for a much longer period, would have produced in the West the kind of unified society that Hellenization had produced in the East. But whatever its final result might have been in different historical circumstances, it is clear that already by the turn of the third century its amalgamating process had produced several large unions from the different segments of the western populations. It need scarcely be said that Rome's administrative structures, established in natural geographic confines, were of great aid to this development. They united neighboring, often kindred tribes into extensive "provincial" entities, whose members were aware of their common "belonging" as well as of the ties that bound them together. In the course of the fifth century, and for decades thereafter, this awareness on the part of the indigenous populations increased in the face of the invading hordes and gave rise to a stronger sense of identity, akin to a feeling of national consciousness. It was a feeling that united all the inhabitants of each province, with the notable exception of one group: the Jews.

By that time the Jews in the western Empire had a considerable history behind them and stood out everywhere as a group apart, of peculiar character and special status. Though Roman citizens from 212 and favored by Rome as opponents of Christianity, they gradually fell into disfavor in the provinces, whose peoples, steadily drawing together, came to view them as a foreign element, wedded to its customs, religion, and nationality, with obvious pretensions to superiority. The spread of Christianity in the fourth century, especially in Gaul and Spain, further contributed to the unification of their peoples, hitherto separated by their different cults, and to the growing opposition of these peoples to the Jews, Christianity's resolute antagonists. We see the first evidence of this attitude in Spain, whose self-consciousness was more acute than Gaul's and whose antagonism to the Jews was possibly bolstered by a special Hellenistic-Egyptian influence.[1] The Council of Elvira, convened about 306,[2] gave the first clear evidence of Spanish antisemitism cloaked in contemporary Christian garb. It preached total dissociation from Jews and Judaism and total separation from Jews as from the plague.[3] Then came the anti-Jewish laws, promulgated by the Empire in the 4th and 5th centuries (from 325 to 438), which denied the Jews many basic rights and rendered them second-rate citizens. It was obvious that had this process continued, the Jews would have ultimately been reduced to the level of semi-pariahs.

The process, however, was checked by the invasions, which created new social and political confrontations of far greater significance to the western populations than their quarrel with the Jews. What divided the invaders from the peoples of the West was the natural opposition between conquerors and conquered, between natives and aliens, between Teutons and Celts (or other races), between Arians and Catholics, between speakers of Latin and various German dialects, between bearers of different customs and traditions, and between adherents of different laws. Inevitably, these divisions produced distrust and discord, which were to persist for a long time. And it was because of this manifold conflict that the general condition of the Jews in the West radically changed for the better.

To be sure, most differences mentioned above divided the Germans from the Jews, too, but here there were factors that overrode the differences and laid a basis for trust and cooperation. Indubitably, both the Jews and the invaders were quick to discern the similarities in their condition and their common ground in the situation that confronted them. Both were minorities amidst a hostile population, and each could benefit from the other's aid. The Germans needed the Jews' loyal services; the Jews needed the Germans' protection. From these basic interests, an understanding was born which led to a favorable treatment of the Jews by the invading Germans. In consequence, Jewish life in the West came to rest on the same political foundations that had repeatedly sustained it in the East: an alignment of the Jewish minority with the conquerors for mutual support against the majority population.

Contrary to their behavior with the Greeks and Romans, the Jews did not attempt to get from the Germans written assurances with respect to their rights. Nor, in all likelihood, would they have received any if they had asked the Germans to grant them. Such commitments on the part of the invaders would be out of line with their general policy, which was aimed at establishing a clear-cut division between themselves and the subject populations. To emphasize that division, and to minimize friction, they applied their own laws only to themselves and left the conquered peoples subject to the laws that had governed their lives before the invasions. Roman law (the Theodosian Code) thus remained in force for all non-Germans, including the Jews, who, as Roman citizens, were under that jurisdiction. To be sure, the Jews' rights as citizens were curtailed by Roman law as codified by Theodosius II; but the Germans treated these restrictions in a manner that could hardly cause the Jews real harm: while they issued no new laws in the Jews' favor, they ignored the old laws in their disfavor, and thus virtually restored the Jews to the position of equal Roman citizens.[4] This was certainly not the usual way for governments to execute national policy, but it was not actually a novel one either—and it gave the Jews relief from harassment and discrimination for periods ranging from a century to two.

Many historians have repeatedly asserted that the favorable condition of the Jews under the Germans lasted as long as the latter were Arians, but was radically altered—if not totally reversed—when the Germans adopted the Catholic faith. This seems to imply that religious intolerance was the sole cause of the drastic change. But the evidence does not confirm this view. Rather does it indicate that, besides religion, there were other factors working inexorably toward worsening the Jewish condition.

The matter becomes strikingly apparent from a comparison of the policies pursued toward the Jews by the Franks in Gaul and the Visigoths in Spain. The Franks converted to Catholicism in 496, and from 507 to 534 seized the whole of Gaul, save Septimania, which remained under Visigothic rule. Shortly after the completion of that conquest, the Third Council of Orléans met in 538, and became one of the first Gallic Councils to decree against the Jews. In its thirteenth canon, the Council urged all Christians to protect

Christian slaves who fled their Jewish masters and sought asylum in Christian homes or churches. In such cases, the Jew was forced to free the slave for a fixed, but suitable, payment. Otherwise, however, Jews could hold Christian slaves as long as they did not attempt to convert them.[5] This makes it evident that the Jews owned Christian slaves with the authorities' full permission, although this privilege was explicitly denied them by the Roman imperial (i.e., Christian) codes. It further shows that the Council did not go to the full length of restoring Roman law, undoubtedly because it wished to show the king that its own position did not differ from his. Three years later, in 541, the Fourth Council of Orléans reissued this decree,[6] which indicates that even the few concessions that the preceding Council had sought to attain were disregarded by both the Jews and the authorities. But this decision fared no better than the former. The situation apparently remained unchanged, as it took another forty years before the Council of Mâcon (581) made another step in the direction of revision. It decreed that Christian slaves could be freed from Jewish bondage if Christians ransomed them for a fixed price.[7] But this injunction, too, was far from the old law, which prohibited the possession of Christian slaves by Jews. The Council of Rheims (c. 627) moved closer to that goal. It forbade the sale of Christian slaves to Jews,[8] but as yet did not prohibit the Jews from using Christian slaves they owned or had acquired by inheritance or gift. Only years later, when the Frankish kings adopted a drastically anti-Jewish policy, was the full execution of the Roman law on this issue urged by the Council of Châlons-sur-Sâone.[9]

The Catholic Franks took the same position also with regard to other limitations imposed by Roman law upon the Jews. As indicated above, the Theodosian Code prohibited the occupation by Jews of public offices, both military and administrative. But in 535 the Third Council of Clermont decreed only against the appointment of Jewish judges.[10] From this we should not gather that, of all public offices, only those of judges had been occupied by Jews. What later conciliar resolutions indicate is that Jews served, under Frankish rule, in various state and public offices, and hence that the Third Council of Clermont simply thought it more prudent to request a change in only one profession. That this demand, however, remained unheeded we can see from the decree of the Council of Mâcon (581), which again forbade the appointment of Jewish judges, while adding to this prohibition the demand that Jews be forbidden to serve as tax collectors.[11] This decree, too, it seems, remained long unenforced, although further broadening of the demands in that direction is noticeable in later conciliar decisions. Thus, in 614 the Fifth Council of Paris adopted the full imperial law that forbade Jews to serve in *any* military or administrative office[12]; and a parallel decree to the same effect was issued in the same year by Chlothar II.[13] This was the first time that a Frankish king had sanctioned a council's decision against the Jews. But this was more than one hundred years after the Franks' conversion to Catholicism!

Hence, the common notion that the German invaders' adoption of Christianity in its Catholic form automatically altered their policy toward the Jews stands in need of correction. The factors that led these invaders of all tribes originally to view the Jews with toleration were the same factors that placed them apart—and aloof—from the populations they had conquered. We have noticed at least seven such factors insofar as the Arian Goths were concerned.[14] By adopting Catholicism as their religion, the Franks, to be sure, removed one of the divisions that separated them from the majority population, but the other six still remained standing. In fact, with respect to culture and language, they stood far more apart from the native peoples than the Goths, who had been influenced by Roman civilization and sought to accommodate themselves to its ways. It took the Franks—or rather their kings—several generations of sojourn in Gaul and of getting to know their Gallo-Roman subjects before they could see the latter as *their* people on whom they could rely for the materialization of their plans. This does not mean that the kings had noticed an ethnic coalescence between Franks and Gallo-Romans or even a far-reaching assimilation. Many more years would have to pass before such merging occurred.[15] But by the turn of the sixth century, the Frankish kings could see their Gallo-Roman subjects bound to them by bonds of loyalty and obedience. These bonds, to be sure, were not forged by the kings but by the Gallo-Roman leaders, the bishops; but the kings were naturally inclined to strengthen them by responding in some measure to the bishops' wishes. Of these wishes, they knew, the most ardent and constant was embodied in their demands (expressed partly in their councils) to reduce the Jews' status and narrow their rights. The readiness of the kings to accede to these demands developed nevertheless rather slowly, and it grew with their respect for the Gallo-Roman bishops and the mass of the people for whom they spoke. It was therefore no coincidence that Chlothar II, seeking popular support for his rule over Gaul (united under him after internecine conflict), took a strong position against the Jews. And it was again no mere chance that his son Dagobert, who made strenuous efforts to secure Gaul's unity (and likewise counted heavily on the Gallo-Romans' aid), who went to the extreme with his anti-Jewish policy by ordering the Jews to convert or leave the country (629).[16]

Something similar, though in some respects more complex, took place in Visigothic Spain. More than a century and a half had passed since their settlement in the Iberian peninsula before some of the leading Visigothic nobles came to think of a united Spanish people. It was not an idea that they all shared, and certainly not in the same measure or form, but it was given great impetus when adopted by Leovigild (567–586), perhaps the most important occupant of the Spanish throne throughout the whole period of Visigothic rule. Leovigild dreamed of uniting the whole peninsula, territorially and nationally, into one entity. Three Iberian regions were beyond his control—one in the northwest, held by the Sueves, and two in the south, ruled by the Byzantines. Leovigild attacked the Sueves, annexed their country to his kingdom, and forced them to readopt Arianism (which they had changed for Catholicism only decades before).[17] He evidently considered it too risky for him to assail the Byzantines at that stage. In the meantime, he thought, the most important task for him and his administration to accomplish was to unite the two main peoples of his kingdom—the Hispano-Romans and the Visigoths—into a single nation.

When he came to power, the Romanization of the Visigoths had advanced to a point where few cultural differences could be noticed between them and the Hispano-Romans. The barriers that still kept them apart were, in the main, ethnic and religious. Leovigild was determined to remove those barriers. He attacked the ethnic issue by abolishing the law prohibiting intermarriage between Visigoths and Romans. But little headway was made toward ethnic fusion following that enactment; nor could real progress be made in that direction as long as intermarriage between Catholics and Arians was prohibited by religious law.[18] Leovigild was of course aware of this obstacle, and it increased his determination to unite both peoples under one religious aegis. He would certainly have preferred the Spanish Catholics to convert to Arianism rather than vice versa, and he made various attempts to facilitate such conversions. Thus, he first induced a synod of Arian bishops, convened in Toledo in 580, to decree that Roman converts to the Arian faith need not be rebaptized and, in addition, would be financially advantaged.[19] We are told that this decision moved "many" Catholics to exchange their religion for Arianism, but obviously no mass movement ensued. Leovigild then proposed a compromise between the faiths; he admitted the identity of Christ's substance with the Father's but denied this identity to the Holy Spirit.[20] This compromise, too, drew some Catholics to Arianism—that is, in its mutilated form; but again, no significant change occurred in the general condition of the opposed camps. Leovigild came gradually to the conclusion that Spain's common, unifying religion would have to be Catholic Christianity, and his ambassadors showed a tendency to yield to the whole set of Catholic dogmas.[21]

Leovigild himself, however, did not make the final move, but his attempts at compromise between the two religions show that his faith in Arianism was tepid and his attempts on its behalf were probably made not so much to satisfy his conscience as to reduce the expected opposition of some Arians (especially their bishops and the zealots in their ranks). Insofar as his own beliefs were concerned, he would not, in all likelihood, have minded very much which theological formula was accepted, if it served the cause which was paramount in his mind—that of national unification.

Leovigild died without realizing his vision, but left his son Reccared the triple conviction that Spain, to rise higher, must be ethnically united, that religious unity must precede ethnic merger, and that the only religion which could serve the purpose was that of the majority—Catholic Christianity. Reccared, who inherited his father's aspirations, also adopted his father's tactics. He went through the motions of social accommodation, showing great respect for the Arian bishops while displaying what seemed to be an honest curiosity and an impartial search for truth. He called three episcopal meetings to consider the differences between the two Christian creeds—first, a meeting of Arian, then of Arian and Catholic, and finally of Catholic bishops. At the last meeting he informed the assembled bishops that he had decided to become a Catholic[22]—a decision he had probably reached before he called any of the above gatherings. We need not be impressed by the praises of his faithfulness sung by Catholic leaders. Bearing in mind the background of his conversion, we are entitled to doubt his religious convictions. What Reccared truly believed in, it seems, was the value of the asset he gained from his conversion—the prerequisite for having the main peoples of his kingdom united into one nation.

The above may help us understand what moved Reccared to reverse the Gothic policy toward the Jews when he sanctioned the anti-Jewish laws of the Third Toledan Council (589).[23] What motivated him was the consideration that led him to adopt Catholicism in the first place: he wanted to come nearer to the Hispano-Romans so as to ease their merger with the Goths. Thus in Spain, as in Gaul, the anti-Jewish policy adopted by the German kings did not stem essentially from a change of religion, but from a *change in the royal position toward the peoples subject to their rule.* It stemmed from their goal of national unification and their feeling that the principal peoples of their countries were prepared to move toward that goal. It was clearly meant to serve a political purpose, and hence was rooted primarily in political, not in religious motives.

Reccared knew that his conversion to Catholicism was opposed by a large body of Visigoths, who differed from him on the religious issue or took no part in his political idea. Fearing assassination, he was converted in secret, but the act became known, and assassination was attempted. In addition, he had to crush several conspiracies before he could see himself safe on the throne.[24] Scholars summarize these occurrences, which took place in the first years of his reign, under the heading "the Arian Reaction," but the Arian reaction was not limited to those events, nor did it end with the King's death in 601. Though their formal proselytization progressed rather rapidly, many

Arians resented their change of religion—and with this, inevitably, their change of status. The nobles, especially, were split in their attitude toward the policy of unification. The elevation of the Ibero-Roman bishops to the level of legislators and royal councillors inevitably reduced the authority of the nobles; and the opinions of the kings who reigned after Reccared ranged from unreserved support of his policy through a lukewarm neutrality to complete opposition.

Ten years after Reccared's death, when Sisebut ascended the throne (612), he noticed that the anti-Jewish laws of Reccared had fallen into abeyance. Sisebut blamed the nobility for the neglect,[25] but there is no doubt that his predecessors on the throne shared the nobility's responsibility. They may have belonged to the anti-union party or questioned the wisdom of Reccared's moves—including his policy toward the Jews—and this is why they failed to enforce it. Sisebut, who sought to remedy the situation, first issued several harsh laws against the Jews,[26] by which he hoped to prevent recurrence of the abuse and perhaps induce many Jews to convert; but seeing the Jews' reactions to his rulings and their unremitting efforts to scuttle his decrees, he came at length to radical conclusions concerning the solution of the Jewish question in Spain. In 616 he issued an order for the Jews to convert or leave the Spanish kingdom on pain of capital punishment.[27] As most Jews were simply unable to emigrate, the order amounted to a decree of forced conversion—and as such it indeed became known.

Sisebut was the first Visigothic king to launch a severe persecution of the Jews, and his example was followed by other Gothic kings, who surpassed him in their anti-Jewish drives. Apart from Sisebut, all these kings tried to work in close cooperation with the Councils, which enacted the laws that governed the kingdom and also laid down the policy toward the Jews. As the kings saw it, most scholars believed, the difficulties presented by the Jews to the state stemmed from their stubborn refusal to convert, and this view is presumed to have been fully shared by the Spanish Councils, too. Hence, both the monarchy and the clergy are generally believed to have favored every conceivable measure that could lead the Jews to conversion. Yet a careful analysis of the various positions taken by the Councils and the kings toward the Jews reveals that the monarchy and the Church did not see eye to eye on the Jewish problem.

Ordinarily, one would be inclined to assume that the Councils, representing both the Church and the people, should have been more adamant and extreme in their demands to suppress Judaism in Spain. But already more than a century ago the great Jewish historian Heinrich Graetz observed that the "initiative to tyrannize, by legislative means, the Jews of Spain [under the Visigoths] emerged not from the clergy, but from the Kings," and that while the kings issued a series of harsh laws aimed at forcing the Jews to convert, the Church openly opposed forced conversion and adopted, on the whole, milder measures. "Were the Catholic kings of Visigothic Spain, from Reccared to Egica," Graetz asked, "more orthodox than the clergy, more Catholic than Gregory I," who repeatedly expressed, in no uncertain terms, his objection to the forced conversion of the Jews? Graetz, however, while discerning the problem, did not offer an acceptable solution and, furthermore, diminished the force of his query by concluding—erroneously, as we shall show below—that most of the kings' laws referring to "Jews" were actually aimed at Jewish converts to Christianity.[28] Nor did other scholars who noticed inconsistencies in the monarchic or conciliar attitudes toward the Jews offer a satisfactory explanation. Consequently, in trying to comprehend these developments, we ought to consider the following two questions: What moved the Gothic kings—or rather some of them—to depart from the tradition of religious toleration that had characterized Gothic rule for two centuries? And why did the Church councils, which were imbued with Jew hatred, oppose the alternative of "conversion or expulsion" that the kings offered the Jews of Spain? Only if we answer these questions satisfactorily can we understand Spain's policies toward the Jews in the century following Sisebut's succession.

While scholars have failed to identify the reasons for the policies pursued by the Gothic kings toward the Jews—or even to notice any *patterns* in their conduct—attention has been focused on Sisebut's activity and the considerations that motivated it. Juster believed that his conversion decree was simply inspired by a "neophyte's zeal,"[29] and this view was followed by other scholars, who apparently, like Juster, saw no connection between that decree and some political objective. Yet while Sisebut may have been a devout Catholic, as some of the relevant sources suggest, he was, as we see it, no less a devotee of the principle of Spain's unity. For the sake of this principle, he fought a bloody war against the Catholic Byzantines in the south, which cleared the way for his successor, Swinthila, finally to drive them out of the peninsula. His alleged "Christian piety," which did not deter him from causing the death of thousands of Catholics (on both his own and the Byzantine side) when a political-national cause was involved, was not, in our judgment, the prime mover of his order against the Jews either.

Juster's explanation would have appeared more plausible if Sisebut had been a convert from Judaism and emotionally involved in a conflict with the Jews (as were other Jewish converts who became their people's scourge). But Sisebut was a convert from Arianism, not Judaism, and as a neophyte Catholic, however zealous, he was likely to act, in the case of the Jews, strictly in accordance with the guidance of the Church and the relevant instructions of its authoritative leaders—that is, *if purely Christian interests had motivated his conduct.* But no Christian religious authority advised Sisebut to take that step against the Jews. Isidore of Seville, whose views must have been known to him, roundly disapproved of his proposed decree, and he may have also informed Sisebut that the famed Pope Gregory (d. 604) had been opposed to coercion in matters of faith.[30] Nor did Sisebut call a Church Council to consider his proposal and pronounce judgment, which, as a faithful member of the Church, he was in duty bound to obey. He must have suspected that with Isidore's objection, he would not draw the Council to his side, and he therefore decided to act on his own, potentially against the Council's position and against the position of the Roman pope. Why? The only answer we can suggest to this question is that Sisebut's conduct in this case was determined, as it was in his war with Byzantium, not by a religious but by a political consideration. Yet what could that consideration be if not one that was intimately connected with the idea of Spain's national unification? If so, this idea *loomed larger in his eyes than Church policy that might obstruct its realization.*

It is hard to comprehend his radical move, however, unless the union he aspired to was broader than the one that Reccared or Leovigild had had in mind. While these kings had sought to amalgamate *two* peoples—the two main components of Spain's population—Sisebut's conception of the national union embraced *all* segments of Spain's population and required religious uniformity of them all as a prerequisite for joining the union. Consequently, he would tolerate no separate people and no dissident religious group in Spain, whether pagan, Arian, or Jewish. Hence, laws enacted against any of these sects made sense to him only if they led to conversion as a prelude to their assimilation. Since he concluded that no discriminatory law would achieve this objective in the case of the Jews, he decided to break their resistance by force or get rid of them by expulsion. Thus, the Church had nothing to do with Sisebut's far-reaching decision; nor did any outside influence move him to take that extreme measure. The forced conversion of the Jews in Antioch decreed a few years earlier by Phocas may have served as an encouraging example.[31] But this could have only a marginal effect. Both the intention and resolution were Sisebut's, and they sprang from the reasons indicated above.

No extant record gives us any clue to the number of Jews converted under Sisebut; but judging by the imprint they left on Spain's history, their number must have been large indeed, perhaps embracing no less than half of Spain's Jewish population. That the policy of coercion was actually enforced is attested, among other things, by the hurried migration of many Spanish Jews to Gaul.[32] But the persecution lasted only five years. Sisebut died in 621, and his successor, Swinthila, relaxed the severity that had marked Sisebut's policy toward the Jews. Not only was forced conversion discontinued, but those who had gone abroad could return and openly resume their practice of Judaism.[33] What is more, the special laws restricting Jewish rights enacted by

Sisebut at the beginning of his reign were now disregarded, as were those of Reccared in the reign preceding Sisebut's accession. One can see here the beginnings of that zigzag course of royal policy toward the Jews of Spain which continued until the end of Gothic rule in that country and, possibly more than any other factor, accounted for the survival of Spanish Jewry.

It must be understood, however, that the changes in this course were not produced merely by incidental views held by the occupants of the throne. As we have indicated, the great Gothic nobles were divided on Reccared's and Sisebut's aims, and the constant support that many of them lent the Jews in their struggle against discrimination and oppression reflected, in the main, the opposition of those nobles to the "unionist" idea in either of its forms— i.e., the moderate and extreme. Consequently, when any of those nobles became king, the policy he pursued on the question of the "union" expressed not only his *personal* views but also those of his *nobiliar faction*. And thus one may say that, from Reccared onward, the Gothic kings reflected in their treatment of the Jews *two conflicting policies on the issue of the union*, although occasionally the definite attitude was replaced by considerable vacillation or indecision. This is why the Councils, over whom all kings, however shaky their position, exerted influence, had frequently to include in their legislation on the Jews retractions from or changes or reaffirmations of their earlier positions.

Swinthila's successor was Sisenand, who gained his royal power through rebellion and held it less than six years (631–636). He was undoubtedly a unionist king, and as such sought to have both the Jews and converts surren- der their faith under repressive legislation. The two harsh laws which the Fourth Toledan Council (633) issued against Jews and Jewish converts to Christianity were enacted, as the Council stated, "at this order."[34] He was however so insecure on the throne and so much in need of popular support that he had to give the bishops a great deal of leverage in formulating these laws as they saw fit. Nor could he oppose the Council when it criticized and, as we shall see, to a large extent deviated from the unionist extreme line.

A much firmer stand on the Jewish question than Sisenand's was taken by his successor, Chintila, who ruled for four years (636–640). His declaration in the Sixth Toledan Council (638) that he would not permit non-Catholics to live in Spain leaves no doubt as to his political alignment. He was one of the extreme "unionist" kings whose prototype was Sisebut and whose attitude toward the Jews was determined by the view that Spain's religious unity must be absolute and that no exceptions to this rule could be allowed. Chintila's declaration was incorporated by the Council in its third canon as a statement presenting the ultimate goal of the king's policy on the Jewish question. It was not, as Graetz and Hefele thought, an order of expulsion from Spain of all Jews who might refuse to convert to Christianity.[35] As it did not speak clearly of the need to depart, or of the time limit set for departure, or of any punishment involved in violation, the law was no more than a statement of policy whose way of execution was still to be defined. There were doubtless more teeth in the special measures that Chintila applied to the "baptized Jews," and their harassment by this king, we have reason to believe, assumed some of the grimmest forms.[36] But his reign was short, and Chindaswinth's decade (642–652) gave the Jews of Spain another respite from oppression before another drive, fiercer than ever, was launched against them after his death.

King Receswinth (653–672), the author of that drive, was clearly a follower of Sisebut and Chintila in his desire to see all religious groups in Spain and all the elements of the Spanish population fused into a single nation. He exhibited this aspiration in two legislative acts whose meaning cannot be disputed. He issued a law that specifically permitted intermarriage between Goths and Romans,[37] and he published a unified code for the kingdom, replacing the Roman and Gothic codes of law.[38] If we are to believe his own assertion at the opening session of the Eighth Toledan Council, as well as in his own code, "all the heresies [that had existed in Spain] have been extirpated root and branch," save Judaism, which still "defiles the soil of the Kingdom."[39] Receswinth was determined to correct this defect, and there was hardly a harsh law that he refrained from using in his effort to enforce his decision. As compulsory conversion was prohibited by the Church, he did not reinstate Sisebut's decree, but included in his code a series of laws that denied the Jews the right to practice their religion, undoubtedly hoping that by means of these restrictions he would bring Judaism to the verge of disappearance. Thus, he forbade the Jews to celebrate their Passover, to observe the Sabbath, to circumcise their children, to keep their dietary laws, to marry by Jewish rites (or by any other rites save Christian).[40] Since violation of these and similar laws amounted to a capital crime, his decrees bordered on compulsory conversion and matched the worst religious persecution the Jews had suffered since the days of Hadrian.

Graetz believed that Receswinth's laws against "the Jews" were actually intended for baptized Jews only, whereas unconverted Jews were treated by him basically in accordance with Roman law—that is, as citizens restricted in certain matters (such as slavery and public offices), but free to perform their religious duties.[41] Graetz' arguments in defense of his thesis, however, were decisively refuted by Juster,[42] and one may only add, in support of Juster, that Receswinth's pronouncements on the Jewish question bespeak his determination to fight the overt Jews no less, if not more, than the covert ones—i.e., the false converts. Thus, addressing the Eighth Toledan Council, he first denounced the life and customs of the overt *Jews*—"because of whom alone" the land, as he put it, was still "contaminated with the pest of heresy," and only then touched upon the *converts* who still clung to the "laws of perfidy."[43] Similarly, in summarizing his anti-Jewish decrees, he warned all Christians of whatever authority not to offer in any manner, openly or surreptitiously, encouragement or protection to any [unbaptized] Jew who "remains in the practice of his detestable faith," as well as to any "baptized Jew who returned to the observance of his perfidious ceremonies."[44] Certainly, if Receswinth's laws against the *Iudei* did not aim at the professing Jews, the latter needed no "encouragement" and "protection" in practicing their religion.

Receswinth's treatment of the converted Jews was no less severe than his treatment of the overt ones. To make sure that the converts were to suffer the same punishments assigned to overt Jews for performing Jewish rites, he included in his code Chindaswinth's decree that if a convert, or a convert's son, "has practiced circumcision, or *any other Jewish rite,*" he "shall be put to ignominious death . . . under the most ingenious and excruciating torture."[45] Furthermore, he exacted from the converts an unqualified commitment that they carefully watch their fellow converts, and if any convert was found to have relapsed into any of his former errors, or transgressed Christian rulings, however slightly, the converts themselves should "punish him by stoning or by burning him to death."[46] Thompson, who wrote the best work we possess on the history of the Spanish Visigoths, made in this connection the summary observation: "This was the first systematic attempt to use the whole power of the State to eliminate Judaism in Spain.[47]

II

We have pointed out the basic reason for this policy of Receswinth and some of his predecessors on the throne. We still have to deal with other Gothic kings who tenaciously followed the same policy. But before doing so, we must again turn to the Councils convened during that time and see whether their stand on the Jewish question matched that of the kings, and if not, wherein it differed and why. More precisely, we would like to know what role the Councils played in the struggle against the Jews as it evolved in the 7th century and what motivated their course of action, assuming that this course had one direction and was heading toward a preconceived goal.

The German scholar Dahn, who was among the first to produce detailed studies of the Goths in Spain, believed that the Councils' role was decisive. "It was the Church," he said, "not the State, that took the initiative in the persecution" of the Jews, and the "secular arm"—i.e., the kings—"served the Councils in this matter merely as a tool."[48] Subsequent scholars, with few exceptions, shared on the whole Dahn's opinion. Our own analysis of the available sources leads us, however, to a different conclusion.

We do not suggest, of course, that Dahn and his followers did not notice that, from Sisebut to Egica, the harshest laws against the Jews originated with the kings and not with the Councils. They probably assumed that the kings enacted those laws on the advice of the Catholic bishops—an assumption which could arise from their failure to discern the true factors that impelled some Gothic kings to pursue severe policies against the Jews of Spain. Actually, however, there was no real harmony between the plans of the Councils and those of the kings with respect to the ultimate fate of the Jews; and a mere comparison between the laws of the kings (incorporated in the Visigothic code) and those of the Councils concerning Jews and converts is sufficient, we believe, to make this apparent. But in order to perceive the main considerations that moved the Councils to take their own positions, we ought to retrace some of our steps and touch on some pertinent points.

We have noticed that already at the start of the invasions (that is, at the beginning of the fifth century) there existed a deep rift between the Ibero-Romans and the Jewish community of Spain.[49] In the following two centuries that rift broadened until it assumed the form of a gulf. What caused this development was, to begin with, (a) the numerical growth of Spanish Jewry by a steady migration from the Hellenistic East, and (b) the growing involvement of the Jews in Spanish life under the favorable rule of the Goths. Viewing the Jews as a foreign minority that competed with them both economically and socially, the Spaniards resented this double competition and the influence the Jews gained as a result. Soon this resentment turned into a hatred, which was nursed by the Jews' friendship with the Goths, who were viewed by all Ibero-Romans as subjugators, and by the Catholic Spaniards also as heretics and enemies of their religion.

Against this background we can readily understand why the Third Toledan Council (589), convened by King Reccared, subjected Spanish Jewry to some of the restrictions imposed on the Jews by Roman law. The Council, however, did not go in its enactments to the full length of the Roman restrictions and limited itself to several demands, which were essentially in agreement with the decrees concerning Jews issued by the Gallic councils. Thus they concentrated on three prohibitions—to marry Christian women, to buy Christian slaves, and to assume public offices that entitled them de jure to inflict penalties on Christians.[50] The only innovation these laws contain touches children born to Jewish-Christian parents. Such children, the law stipulates, must be baptized to Christianity—a condition that might have deterred some Jews from having conjugal relations with Christians.[51] The law concerning Christian slaves owned by Jews was moderate compared to the final position taken on this issue by the Roman codes. If such slaves are circumcised, the law states, they are to be returned to Christianity and be freed without compensating their Jewish masters.[52] The reason for this self-restraint must have been the Council's fear that the king, at this point, might not agree to effect a drastic change in Gothic policy toward the Jews and that if they asked too much, they might get too little.

Sisebut's harsh decrees against the Jews[53] encouraged Spain's Church to go considerably further in its anti-Jewish legislation, and the Fourth Council of Toledo (633) gave expression to this attitude in a new set of laws. Regarding mixed marriages, it not only resolved that the children of such unions must be reared as Christians, but also that Jews who married Christian women must convert to Christianity or part with their wives.[54] Regarding slavery, it forbade Jews to own Christian slaves or buy Christian bondmaids or receive them as gifts.[55] But in addition, it went to the extreme in denying Jews the right to assume *any* public office (and not only such as entitled them to punish), on the ground that, through the occupation of such offices, they might "cause some injury to Christians."[56]

No less hostile, but much more complex, was the Council's attitude toward *converts* from Judaism. To begin with, the Council lashed out against King Sisebut, who effected a conversion of Jews under duress. It declared such conversions to be in violation of what it called the "full form of justice" and ordered that "no Jew would from then on" be moved "to believe by force or necessity,"[57] referring most likely by "necessity" to *exile*, which was offered by Sisebut as the alternative to death. The Council, however, decided to recognize the validity of Sisebut's forced conversions, because denial of that validity, it argued, would amount to a "debasement and depreciation" of the faith. Since these converts, the Council explained, have "received the divine sacraments, the grace of baptism, were anointed by the chrism, and partook in the body and blood of the Lord, it is proper that they keep the faith," although they admitted to its truth under compulsion.[58]

For all its acute theological sophistry, the Council's argument appears incoherent and, in fact, self-contradictory. It would have made some sense if, while decrying forced conversion, it had recognized the forcibly converted as real converts on the ground that it discerned in their religious conduct—despite their basic attachment to Judaism—the beginnings of a tendency to become true Christians. No such recognition, however, was acknowledged. The Council did not say that it noticed an improvement in the basic attitude of the converts toward Christianity. All it said was that it is *proper* for them to keep the faith they had received through the process of conversion, however coercive that process was. Accordingly, the forced converts were to remain in Christendom not of their own free will, as required by the "full form of justice," but by the legal coercion of the Council, which thereby committed the same injustice it had denounced in Sisebut.

That the Council's attitude toward forced conversion was in principle not as negative as suggested by its criticism of Sisebut's action appears also from the following. We have seen that the Council regarded conversion as coerced not only when effected by *force* (which presumably meant the threat of death) but also under the pressure of "necessity." The Council, however, ordered separation of Jewish husbands from their Christian wives unless the former converted to Christianity,[59] as well as separation of small children from their parents (Jewish converts to Christianity who had relapsed into Judaism), so that the children might not get accustomed to Jewish usages and beliefs.[60] Yet what greater "necessity" could there be imagined than total detachment of husbands from their wives or of small children from their parents? Nevertheless, conversions resulting from such pressures, which were "forced" by the Council's own definition, were accepted by it without any reservation. What other conclusion can we draw from this except that the Council was not opposed to forced conversion *in principle,* or at least under *all* circumstances? This leads us to the conclusion that its aforesaid decree concerning Sisebut's forced conversion did not represent its real or full stand on the question at issue; and hence, that it was motivated by more compelling reasons than the theological subtleties by which it justified that decree. Yet what were those reasons? Or, more plainly, what were the aims the Council sought to attain in its laws against the Jews and the converts?

Of the various factors that determined the Council's stand on the Jewish question, the large size of the Jewish community in Spain—large in both absolute and relative terms—constituted no doubt the core of the problem.[61] The masses of Jews who were brought into Christendom by Sisebut's forcible conversion were released from the restrictions imposed on them as Jews and soon confronted the Ibero-Romans as a strong competitive force. This threatened the Ibero-Romans with the loss of all the gains they had made through the restrictions imposed on the Jews by Reccared, and consequently they looked for every possible way to forestall such an outcome. Ultimately, their leaders—i.e., the bishops—came to believe that they had found a way out. Well aware that Jewish rites and customs were still observed by many neophytes, they thought they could declare all converts "suspect"—that is, possible infidels and false Christians—and place them on the legal level of the Jews.

We ought to look carefully into this charge, which was made so much of by the Fourth Toledan Council and led most scholars to believe that by 633 all converts from Judaism (or almost all of them) were Jews in deed as well as at heart. Indeed, no author dealing with the subject ever questioned the validity of that belief. But what do we really know about this matter? Let us first note the Council's own words:

> Very many of the Jews who, some time ago, were promoted to the
> Christian faith, are now not only known to blaspheme Christ and

perform Jewish rites; they are also presumed to practice the abominable circumcisions.[62]

From this formulation one cannot determine whether *all* those who had converted and comprised "many of the Jews" relapsed into Judaism after their conversion, or whether only "very many" of the converts did so, while the rest of them behaved as Christians. However, if the authors of that formulation had referred to *all* Jews who had converted, they would, it seems, have stated this explicitly, for by such a statement they could justify the laws they intended to issue for *all* converts. Since they did not use such clear language, we must conclude that they *could not* use it—apparently because besides the many converts who were "known" to have followed the ways of the Jews, there were others, who behaved, at least outwardly, as Christians and who may also have been numerous. Obviously, the bishops found it impossible to denounce this body of converts as renegades, and thus they opened the afore-cited decision with a phrase which *could* mean that only *many of the converts,* but by no means all of them, had transgressed against Christianity. It is also possible that the bishops lacked proof of the guilt of many of the converted Jews who were allegedly "known to have performed Jewish rites"; and thus they may have had little to go on even with respect to this group. If so, we have here the real reason why they recognized Sisebut's forced conversions. The reason was not what they had stated in their decree (because the converts "were anointed by the chrism" etc.), but because, practically and legally, they could not see their way clear to nullify the conversions.

Yet, while they could not *de-Christianize* the converts, they could *downgrade* their Christianity by raising doubts about its worth. They attained this aim by the mere ambiguity of their statement on the converts' religious attitudes—an ambiguity which planted in the minds of many Christians the idea that *all* converts may have been Judaizers, thus permitting the Council to treat them all as "suspects" and as such deny them all basic rights. It was a novel experiment in the history of persecution that the Councils had embarked on in their conduct toward the converts. They would not permit them to live as Jews, but they would not allow them to live as Christians either. They would simply treat them as a caste apart, outside both the Jewish fold and the Christian society. And what was perhaps worst of all: it denied them the avenue of rehabilitation or the right to prove their innocence.

That many converts may indeed have been innocent—that is, did not observe Jewish law and carefully fulfilled all Christian rulings—is evident from the Council's own decree on the issue of the offices. Had the Council wished to deny the offices only to converts who "prevaricated" against the faith, it could have stated this clearly in its decree. But no such stipulation was included in the law, evidently because the Council feared that many converts could *prove* the faultlessness of their conduct. Therefore, to achieve its own purpose, it decreed that "Jews and *those who are of the Jews*" are debarred from public office.[63] "Those who are of the Jews" is an ambiguous term that may mean *adherents of Jewish law*, and thus it would not involve the Council in departure from Christian doctrine and practice. But it may also mean *those who stem from Jewish stock*, and thus the law would apply to *all* converts, in complete disregard of their religious record as well as their claims and intentions. That is indeed how the law was understood, and that is how it was carried out. The prohibition was commonly justified on the ground that *all* converts were not only "suspect" but actually considered "guilty" ("those *who are of the Jews*," according to the first interpretation)—so "guilty," indeed, that if any of them happened to have been appointed to office, he was declared to have gained that appointment "surreptitiously" (presumably, by misleading the appointing judge to believe that he was a true Christian); consequently, *without any inquiry into his case,* the convert was punished by public flogging, and the judge involved by excommunication. And thus, apart from being judged guilty, the convert was given no chance to prove his innocence—not only at the time of the judgment but also in the future, under changed circumstances. Nothing, as we see it, shows more clearly and decisively that it was not true conversion or religious probity that the bishops were after.

What they were after may be clearly deduced from both the laws they accepted and those they rejected. What they wanted was to have the Jews degraded and repressed, segregated from the Christians and, if possible, banished—if there was a country ready to accept them. But they did not want to have all of Spain's Jews converted and fused with the Spaniards. As Christian theologians they could not object, of course, to Jewish conversion to Christianity; nor would they object to having small numbers of Jews absorbed by the Christian society[64]; but a massive assimilation of the Jews among the Spaniards appeared to them most undesirable, and this was precisely the kind of development threatened by a general forced conversion. Sisebut's action, though completed only partly, presented them with an almost insoluble problem. On the one hand, they could not utterly reject it, for the reasons indicated above, but on the other, they could not approve of it either as they did not wish to have so many Jews join the ranks of the Spanish people. To escape both horns of the dilemma, they formally recognized the forced converts as Christians, but in practice treated them all as Jews on the grounds that their conversion was forced.

That the bishops did not seek a mass conversion of Jews is apparent also from the stand they took on all that pertained to the Jews' passage to Christianity. None of the references to the converts in the laws enacted by any of the Toledan Councils contains a single kind word about the converts, or a single phrase showing a friendly attitude or any consideration of their difficulties. In contrast, we have seen that the Councils' canons imposed severe anti-convert restrictions that both Jews and converts must have viewed as wrong, if not actually wicked. It cannot be imagined that these harsh laws could attract any of the forced converts to Christianity; nor can it be assumed that this treatment of the converts could serve as an inducement to any overt Jew to exchange his Judaism for Christianity. Rather could one foresee that such treatment of the converts would strengthen their resolve to adhere to Judaism or push them back into its fold if they had ever left it. Is it conceivable that the shrewd bishops of the Councils who wrote the anti-convert laws did not envisage these results? As this is unbelievable, we are led to the conclusion that most of the bishops, who were Hispano-Romans, were not happy at the prospect of having Spain's Jews brought into the Christian orbit. While ready to accept, or rather absorb, a limited number of Jewish converts, they did nothing to promote the mass conversion of the Jews, but did much to upset and block it.

That this was indeed the position of Spain's bishops is attested also by their reaction to the appeal that King Receswinth addressed to the Eighth Toledan Council. When the King asked them to do their utmost in order to effect the conversion of all "infidels" (i.e., Jews),[65] they did not follow the course the King outlined in his code, but limited their response to a confirmation of the resolutions that had been adopted in the Fourth Toledan Council.[66] They so acted, it appears, because most of them feared that if they adopted more extreme measures, such as were embodied in Receswinth's laws, the Jews would have no choice but to convert and the converts no alternative but to stay Christian. Since such an outcome was not to their liking, for reasons we have explained above, they had to conduct a balanced policy which set limits to their persecution of the Jews and, consequently, to the Jews' conversion.

The letter of Pope Honorius I, chastising Spain's bishops for their stand on the conversion issue (calling them "dumb dogs that cannot bark"),[67] shows that information had reached Rome that the bishops were refraining from doing their utmost to blot out Judaism in Spain. Indubitably, the information suggested that the bishops were sabotaging the conversionary efforts of the kings, for otherwise the Pope, in addressing the bishops, would not have insulted them so sharply. In its answer to the Pope's letter, drafted by Braulio, bishop of Saragossa, the Council admitted its measured pace, but claimed that it "proceeded slowly on purpose." This was true, of course, as was the bishops' claim that their conduct did not stem from "negligence or fear"[68] but from reasons related to their policy. But they evaded the truth and hid their real motives when they attributed the slowness of their action to their attempts to convert the Jews by preaching.[69] No one knew better than the

Spanish bishops that they could not count on mere preaching and persuasion to convert Spain's Jews to Christianity. Hence, their policy on the issue of conversion was rooted in different considerations.

III

This policy, as we have indicated, was not that of the kings who favored unification. But at this point we must take another look at that policy and reexamine the motives of the kings who pursued it. There can be no doubt that they all adhered to the principle of "total union" and worked toward the goal set by Sisebut in his decree of "conversion or exile." Chintila made this clear by his declaration that no non-Catholics (not only Jews!) would be permitted to live in Spain, and Receswinth by his announcement that the Jewish heresy must share the fate of all other heresies which had been extirpated from Spanish life. Nevertheless, the extremely harsh measures that some of the kings applied against the Jews, so untypical of traditional Gothic tolerance, are puzzling for several reasons.

Ziegler, who closed his book on Gothic Spain with an important chapter on the Jews under the Visigoths, asked: "Why did the kings wax so fanatically zealous?"[70] Prima facie, Ziegler thought, the Church was the only force that might have moved the monarchs to take this attitude. "Catholic kings less dependent on the Church," he said, "could scarcely have persecuted subjects so assiduously and cruelly for their religion"[71]; but actually the Church often curbed the kings' zeal, and the bishops, "at least to some extent, championed freedom of conscience."[72] Ziegler noticed a dichotomy in the bishops' attitude, but failed to identify its reasons.

Ziegler concluded that avarice was probably the motive of the kings' policy toward the Jews.[73] Yet this could hardly have been the case. When Receswinth or the kings who followed in his footsteps included confiscation among their harsh penalties, they meant to put enough pressure on the Jews that would ultimately force them to convert. But if conversion was the goal which, as they believed, could be achieved by drastic measures, there could be little hope of gain by confiscation.

Ziegler's answer reflects his conviction that religious zeal could not possibly have motivated the Visigothic kings' decrees against the Jews. And the record of these kings justifies that conviction. Neither in character nor in deed was any of them known for piety. In fact, they were accused by their contemporaries of debauchery, guile, fraud and other crimes. Had zeal inspired their laws against the Jews, their fanaticism would have extended to the Arians and pagans, who were still present in Spain in substantial numbers when Receswinth boasted of their disappearance. In fact, they persisted to the end of Gothic rule[74] without ever being subject to the same kind of harassment that tormented the Jews of Spain. But if neither avarice nor zeal inspired that harassment, whence that ferocity toward the Jews?

To answer this question, we ought to bear in mind that besides the goal of union, which the anti-Jewish kings were presumed to pursue for *national* reasons, they had another objective of *direct interest to them* both as persons and as rulers. That objective was related to their safety and the protection of their heirs and inheritance. As we shall see, this pressing issue impelled the kings to embark on their anti-Jewish policy and pursue it stubbornly and unremittingly.

It has long been noted that the Visigothic monarchy was a feeble and unstable institution. Of the six kings enthroned before Leovigild, four were murdered by enemy rivals; and of the eighteen who reigned after Leovigild, seven were deposed, if not assassinated. In addition, all of them were frequently harassed by treacheries, conspiracies, and threats of rebellion. That is why they often appealed to the Councils for special laws to increase their prestige and make it difficult for rebels to assail them personally or rob their heirs of their possessions. It was in this atmosphere of lurking danger and unrelieved fear of sudden insurrection that the theory was fashioned that the Jews must be suppressed—indeed, if possible, eliminated altogether—if that danger was to be substantially reduced.

The potential enemies of the Visigothic kings belonged to the higher nobility, which is how the Jews became involved. The connection had already been sensed by Sisebut when he enacted his first laws against the Jews. The Jews, he observed, could ignore the restrictions that the laws of Reccared had imposed upon them because "they had *corrupted the minds of the princes.*"[75] By "corruption" he evidently meant *the funds that the Jews supplied to the great nobles of the kingdom* in return for their promises of protection. In subsequent years, we repeatedly hear of the "bribes" the Jews gave both "laymen and clerics," by means of which they allegedly succeeded in preventing the enforcement of the anti-Jewish laws, or managed to escape punishment for their violation. Most scholars have assumed that by this large-scale bribery the Jews defeated the kings' rulings against them and retained their religious and economic way of life. But such an assumption is untenable. No minority can bribe a whole officialdom to violate the laws of church and state; nor can most officials be moved to do so merely by private inducements. What happened, we believe, was different.

The Jews provided large sums of money to some of the nobles who governed large provinces, and once the pro-Jewish attitude of these nobles became common knowledge, their subordinates—the judges and other officials—behaved in accordance with their wishes. Occasionally, the Jews no doubt gave minor gifts to some members of the nobiliar administration, but these individual gestures of appreciation could hardly determine the common behavior of the great majority of the officials. In any case, it was not these gifts or recompenses that troubled the unionist kings. What no doubt troubled them was the Jews' pouring large sums of money into the nobles' coffers. These funds helped the nobles acquire more weapons, keep more retainers, and hire more spies and secret agents, all of which increased their capacity to conspire and emboldened them to start an insurrection. The kings knew that the Jews had no share in these seditious activities and therefore did not accuse them as rebels.[76] All the same, as steady financial supporters of the nobles, they were viewed politically as a menace, quite apart from the question of religion.[77]

There were only two ways of putting a stop to Jewish funding of the nobles—the "corruption" referred to by Sisebut. The first was to force all Jews to convert and, once converted, to behave like real Christians. In that case they would have no *need* to pay the nobles. The other way was to impoverish the Jews, so that they would be *unable* to pay them. Recceswinth hoped to achieve both these ends by imposing death and confiscation on Jews and converts for almost every infraction of his laws. The kings who followed him, as we shall see, alternated between the two methods.

We cannot make even the most general assessment of the extent to which any of these methods proved effective. But whatever the extent, the question must be raised: If the kings were so anxious to end the flow of Jewish money to the conspiratorial nobles, why did they not rescind their measures against the Jews and thus free them from the *necessity* of making those expenditures? The answer is that they could not. To begin with, there was the unionist ideology, which prompted them to seek the extirpation of Judaism, and ideologies have a way of retaining their influence despite the forces of reality that gather against them. But even if the kings were prepared to give up their drive for the Jews' conversion, they must have realized that this would not solve the problem that beset them.

For the funding of the nobles began, as we have noticed, shortly after Reccared issued his laws that curtailed the Jews' rights to own slaves and hold offices—laws "proposed" to him by the Third Toledan Council and made public in its 14th canon.[78] The prohibitions touching slavery were much intensified by Sisebut, while those touching offices were expanded and made harsher by the Fourth Toledan Council. The quarrel therefore was not only about conversion, but also about economic and social restrictions which impaired the Jews' welfare and undermined their existence. Had the kings now abolished these restrictions, they would have lost the support of the Ibero-Roman masses—a support whose acquisition was their main incentive in launching their unionist policy in the first place and on which they pinned their hopes—despite all disappointments—in their struggle against the no-bility. Such a loss they could not afford.

The conversion of the Arians in Spain to Catholicism thus entrapped the kings in a vicious circle. They gave concessions to the Catholics at the expense of the Jews, but they thereby roused the Jews to aid the nobility without getting from the Catholics the needed cooperation to compel the Jews' total surrender. The only course of action that seemed open to the kings was somehow to break out of that circle. They had to unfurl the unionist banner and make every effort to persuade the Councils to adopt the extreme measures they urged against the Jews. This was indeed the goal which later kings repeatedly sought to attain.

IV

Receswinth's immediate successor was Wamba who, like Chindaswinth, was neither a unionist nor a follower of the Church Councils. Striving to attain monarchic independence based on a strong and faithful army, he saw no reason to persecute the Jews and left the laws against them unenforced. Wamba had the making of a great king, but underestimated the strength of the restive opposition. After ruling successfully for eight years (672–680), he was removed by a cabal of dissatisfied bishops and unionist nobles headed by Erwig.

Resolved to achieve his partisan aims, Erwig, who replaced Wamba as king, began immediately after his accession to draw up a series of anti-Jewish measures which he sought to induce the Council to adopt. He knew of course that Receswinth had failed in his efforts to convert the Jews by his drastic laws, but believed that the bishops were responsible for that failure. The bishops, who repudiated Receswinth's legislation (as is indicated by their refusal to adopt it at their Councils), criticized it especially on the grounds of its severity—citing the capital punishment it imposed in every instance of performance of almost every Jewish rite. Fearing that such punishments might produce a mass conversion, they denounced them as amounting to religious coercion, which was prohibited by the Fourth Toledan Council. Erwig, who sought the bishops' support, ostensibly agreed with this criticism. From now on, he promised, punishment would no longer be as uniform as it was, but would be graded in accordance with the crime. As we shall see, he failed to keep this promise; but he abolished the death penalty, which he replaced with deportation, accompanied by other harsh chastisements. Deportation, he knew, the bishops would welcome, as it diminished the threat of mass conversion and might reduce—at least to some extent—the number of Jews living in Spain. He thus proclaimed (in the first law of his code) his intention to use this measure, and stressed its stringency by adding the assurance that even if the culprit "should, at any time, renounce the errors of his perverse sect, he shall under no circumstances be permitted to return from exile."[79]

Erwig's stress on deportation as the prime penalty was made, however, for a larger purpose. The threat of deportation, like the death penalty, he knew, could deter many Jews from observing their laws, but it would not necessarily lead to conversion or even to emigration. Thus he concluded that there was only *one* measure that would bring the Jews to religious submission, or to their departure from Spanish soil. This was the measure so strongly desired and sternly urged by Chintila and Receswinth, but repeatedly turned down by the Councils—namely, a decree that offered Spain's Jews only one alternative to exile: conversion. The problem, then, was how to overcome the bishops' opposition.

He decided to appeal to the bishops in a manner never attempted by any King before him. "With tears in my eyes, I implore your venerable assembly"—he said to the Twelfth Toledan Council—"to devote all your zeal to purge the country of the plague of *corruption*. Stand up, and disrupt the *plots* of the criminals, chastise the evil ways of the renegades . . . and, above all, eradicate the Jewish pest, root and branch."[80] No other Gothic King, addressing a council, had so prostrated himself before it. Erwig thus acted because he wanted the bishops to endorse a move that went against their grain, against their convictions and their established policy. He wanted them to decree forced conversion.

To bolster his plea and facilitate its acceptance, he entrusted the bishops with the main responsibility for the execution of the laws he recommended. Perhaps this is what really made the difference. As executors of the laws, the bishops may have felt, they could determine the rigor of their implementation; they could manipulate the activity of the Spanish judges so as to prevent a large-scale conversion, or channel the movement of the frightened Jews into the avenue of emigration.[81] Other influences may have been at work, too. But whatever they were, the end result was that the Council accepted all of Erwig's laws, including the decree that all the Jews of Spain must accept baptism within one year, or else be subject to expulsion.[82]

Erwig did not count only on this law in his plan to bring the Jews to their knees. But it was the key law in a set of regulations that were aimed to break down Jewish resistance. Besides the prohibitions enacted by Receswinth especially against overt Jews, his own laws included severe restrictions, some of them new, against Jewish converts. Thus no baptized Jew could "leave the Christian faith, or assail Christianity in word or deed, or take flight so as to escape from it, or hide any one who did so."[83] Punishments for violation were usually draconic, and this applied equally in cases of overt Jews. Thus, among other things, the latter were forbidden to read books "rejected by the Christian faith" on pain of receiving a hundred lashes, forfeiture of property and perpetual exile.[84] Other punishments were of the same order, but one was especially gruesome. Circumcision of either Jews or Christians was punished by both the confiscation of property and amputation of the genitals of both offenders—the circumciser and the circumcised.[85]

There is no doubt that Erwig's savage laws caused many Jews to flee Spain for North Africa, the only country in that part of the world that was open to Jewish immigration. The majority of Jews, however, remained in Spain, struggling to survive under Erwig's tyranny. Egica, his successor, was not slow to realize that Erwig had not got much farther with his laws than Receswinth with his own enactments. This led him again to change the legislation touching on both Jews and converts. He relaxed the persecution of the converts on condition that they pledged to be faithful to Christianity—a pledge to be accompanied by a "number of sureties"—and also abolished the decree of forced conversion, which was issued by Erwig. But he enacted a series of economic measures that were bound to reduce the Jews to bankruptcy—if they persisted in their Jewishness. Thus he ordered them to sell to the Treasury, at a price to be fixed by the latter alone, all the slaves, lands, buildings and other property they had acquired from Christians.[86] In addition, he forbade all Jews to trade with Christians either in Spain or abroad,[87] thereby preventing them from earning by commerce what they could no longer earn from agriculture (owing to the restrictive regulations concerning slavery) or from work as officials in the public service (owing to the prohibitions on their holding office). But at length, when he realized that none of his maneuvers yielded the desired results, he decided to settle the annoying Jewish problem by the use of a libelous charge. Addressing the Seventeenth Council of Toledo (on Nov. 9, 694), the King made public some shocking news: The Spanish converts and their brethren overseas conspired to overthrow the King's rule in Spain, "exterminate the Christian people and [destroy] their homeland."[88] What is more, this plan was part of a larger scheme that the same evil men contrived against Christendom, and indeed in some countries the kings had caught the rebels and put them to death. This plan which, according to Egica, was discovered through "confessions" of some of the conspirators, showed how vicious the Jews were, and that they were indeed beyond correction. He begged the Council to approve the measures he considered necessary to deal with the Jews: their properties should be confiscated; they should all be enslaved and dispersed across the land among Christian masters; and their small children, from seven years up, should be removed from them to be reared as Christians.[89] The Council approved the King's recommendation and put it, in its eighth canon, into law.[90] Confiscation, enslavement, and partial assimilation were measures the Council could subscribe to.

We do not know what part, if any, of Egica's plan was enforced. It was obviously based on a total invention, void of any sense or reality, and the fact that eminent scholars gave it credence[91] cannot make it more believable. It was no doubt met with much resistance by the nobles, and in the days of Egica's heir, Witiza (702–710), it may have been completely abandoned.[92] In any case, shortly after Witiza's reign, Christian rule in the peninsula was terminated. In 711, the Moors invaded Spain, and the nightmare of Jewish existence in that country—a nightmare which had lasted a whole century— came at last to an end.

II. The Second Cycle

I

The Moorish-Arab conquest of the Iberian peninsula in 711–714 ended the first cycle of Jewish life in Christian Spain. In the isolated spots of northern Spain that remained under Christian control, no Jews lived after 714; nor did Jews live in any of the territories "reconquered" by the Spaniards in the course of the eighth and the early ninth centuries.[1] Those who did not flee southward to the Moslems were killed by Christian raiders or conquerors. Consequently, a hiatus of at least one hundred years separated the end of the first cycle of Jewish life from the beginning of the second. The second cycle was twice as long, but territorially Christian Spain was for most of the period less than half its former size. Although in retrospect it seems to have steadily been growing, in fact it often contracted and expanded, as if seized by frequent convulsions. What occasioned these changes was the ebb and flow of war which kept affecting its borders.

The curtain rises slowly upon the stage of Jewish life as it evolved in Christian Spain over more than two centuries following the hiatus we have referred to. Out of the fog that covers the events (owing to the scarcity of relevant sources), certain isolated facts stick up like solid rocks, suggesting a broader and more intense development than may be gathered from the extant records. The facts we have in mind indicate the presence of three Jewish communities which, viewed geographically, form points on a line stretching from the Mediterranean (Barcelona) to the Atlantic (Coimbra), through a midpoint in the center of the Christian-held area (Castrojeriz).[2] No evidence is available of any direct links, social or historical, between these communities, but common sense suggests that such links existed and that the three places mentioned were not the only ones where Jews then lived in the Christian-held regions. Nevertheless, it is only from the beginning of the 11th century, when the heavy mist obscuring Jewish life in Christian Spain begins to lift in some areas, that certain parts of the Spanish landscape appear dotted with Jewish communities. From that time onward, the flow of information concerning Jewish life in northern Iberia becomes ever wider and fuller, so that we may take the year 1000 as marking the beginning of a new great thrust by the Jewish people into Christian Spain. It is in this period that the Jews inhabit the Christian lands in growing numbers, first in Catalonia, Asturias and León, then in Castile, Navarre and Aragon. First they come in small groups as migrants (mostly from the north, along the routes of trade); then they prefer to remain under the

Christians when the latter recapture their towns from the Moslems, and finally they flock to Christian Spain as refugees, fleeing Moslem lands in times of persecution. Their number soon increases by leaps and bounds, and their network of communities gradually spreads across the land as a whole. Thus Christian Spain became for the Jews, in the second cycle of their life there, not only a land of immigration and a haven, but also the foremost stage of their influence, political and economic, the center of Jewish prestige and power to an extent attained nowhere else in the Middle Ages.

In attempting to explain this remarkable phenomenon we must of course consider it in its entirety—that is, we ought to include in our purview the eighth and ninth centuries, during which only few Jews lived in Christian Spain, but in which this puzzling development began. Indeed, the beginning of this evolution poses the question that inevitably lies at the heart of our discussion: What was it that moved the Jew to return to Christian Spain, a land torn by war, virtually a battleground of two fierce and uncompromising rivals—a land of traditional, fanatical Jew haters—which brought to his mind recollections of sad, even bitter experiences from the not too distant past? And related to this question—in fact, inseparable from it—is another query which is no less perplexing: What was it that moved the Christian rulers of the north to change so radically their policy toward the Jews so that, rather than excluding them from their domains, they accepted them in ever growing numbers? And the question becomes even more bewildering when we recall that these rulers offered help to the Jews, and granted them privileges and special rights, at a time when all the norms of the Christian Middle Ages were radically opposed to such treatment, and when unmitigated pressure from Rome called for the cancellation of all Jewish privileges and indeed for the Jews' outright degradation. For this was the time of the Fourth Lateran Council, of Pope Innocent III and the popes who succeeded him, when ecclesiastic power was at its height and Church anti-Jewish legislation at its peak. What is more, this was the time of the Crusades, when Europe, from one end to the other, was swept by anti-Jewish agitation, when its cities were the scenes of frequent massacres of Jews, and when the Jews were expelled from England and France. It is this disparity of attitudes toward the Jews—of Europe on the one hand and Christian Spain on the other—that poses the key problem of Jewish history in Spain in that particular period. However we look at it, the problem is not easy, and it appears even more difficult when we bear in mind the following important facts.

For Christian Spain's friendly policy toward the Jews was pursued at the very time when that country was involved in the great struggle of the Reconquest, a struggle waged in the name of religion. In fact, Christian

Spain found itself in the throes of a *constant crusade*—that is, in conditions in which any Christian country was likely to develop a persecution of the Jews, as happened in Germany, France, and England. Why did such a movement not develop in Spain? Why, on the contrary, do we find the Jews advancing, in the very midst of the Reconquest, from one position to another? And why do we find opposition to them stiffen, and persecution flare up, *after* the main drive of the Reconquest was over, or rather after that drive had achieved its principal objectives?

In attempting to explain this remarkable phenomenon, one cannot ignore the relations that evolved between the Jews of Spain and the Moslem conquerors of the peninsula in the first three centuries following the invasion. We have noted that after the Moslem conquest, no Jew could live in Christian Spain, and we may attribute this fact to the traditional hostility that imbued the Christian Spaniards' attitude toward the Jews. That hostility reached its peak on the eve of the invasion, and was further heightened by a new set of legends about the schemes the Jews had allegedly contrived against Spain and the Spanish Christians. The gist of these legends was that the Jews had incited the Moors and the Arabs to invade Iberia, and were thus responsible for Christian Spain's ruin. The accusation evolved of course from the violent charges hurled at the Jews by the Gothic king Egica in the Seventeenth Toledan Council (694)—charges whose falsehood and crude inventiveness are clear from their very contents. One can realize how much the accusation was believed by the Christian Spaniards of that age when one recalls that even in modern times great scholars did not consider it unlikely, and accordingly did not reject it as such.[3] Hate, coupled with the shame of defeat, produced also other, less fantastic myths, such as that the Jews opened to the Moors the gates of many beleaguered cities and even betrayed Toledo, the capital, to the Moors at the cost of hundreds of Christian lives.[4] In the turmoil and anarchy that then dominated the country, it was often hard to tell facts from falsehoods, and it was especially hard for those who preferred to have the falsehoods regarded as facts. That was precisely the attitude of the Christians toward the rumors spread about the Jews, and thus the stories portraying the Jews as traitors were impressed upon the minds of the Christian Spaniards and formed part of their collective memory. Yet it is also clear that, in this instance, truth came to the aid of fiction.

The Jews of Spain greeted the Moslems as their saviors from intolerable oppression, and their jubilant reception of the victorious Moorish forces was undoubtedly well noted by the Spaniards. What is more, the Jews performed various tasks in support of the Moslems' military campaign. For there can be no doubt that the Jews helped the Moors guard and administer many of the towns they had seized in their march of conquest.[5] The invading forces, whose number was small, were of course depleted by losses in battle, and if they had to garrison the captured towns, they would have been unable to sweep rapidly through the vast peninsula. Thus, the aid the Jews gave them at that juncture constituted in effect a material contribution to the Moslem conquest of Spain. We may also assume that, besides that aid, the Jews provided the invaders with various supplies and other facilities which expedited their advance. That this demonstration of manifold cooperation with the enemies of the Spanish people and Christianity intensified the Spaniards' animus toward the Jews may be taken as a matter of course.

It would not be surprising therefore if, at that stage of their history, the Jews saw themselves as allies of the Moslems and that they were seen as such by all concerned.[6] As a minority whose very existence had been jeopardized by the majority of the Spanish population, they sought to be tied to the conquering power, from which they expected special consideration in return for the services they were prepared to render. This, as we have seen, was the political arrangement on which they had repeatedly relied in their dispersion, and now it appeared that, for several reasons, it had even better chances to endure. There were no cultural or religious affinities between the Moslems and the Spaniards, such as had existed between the Romans and the Greeks or even between the Visigoths and the Ibero-Romans. What is more, Islam was at war with Christendom and there was no sign that the Islamic expansion was about to falter. In these circumstances, the prospect that the Moslems would respond in kind to the friendly Jewish overtures appeared reasonably realistic.

Reality fell short of expectation. But some Jewish hopes were nevertheless fulfilled. Scholars are divided in assessing the conditions of the Jews in Moslem Spain in the 8th and 9th centuries; and in view of the paucity, ambiguity, and one-sidedness of the available sources, the question may never be finally answered. Both Moslem theory and common practice, which assigned to all non-Moslems an inferior status, militated against granting the Jews full equality, and the spirit of domination that imbued all Moslem factions helped strengthen the same tendency. Nevertheless, it seems that, unlike the Christians, the Jews knew how to gain the rulers' confidence, and while accommodating themselves to the restrictions imposed on them, they gradually attained, by patience and obedience, what they could not obtain by their original assistance. "They tied their destiny to Moslem dominion," writes Ashtor about their position at the time, "and stood by it loyally in all areas of life."[7] Then he adds: "It stands to reason that their loyalty earned them a large measure of appreciation at the royal court."[8] This latter assertion is no mere assumption, since (as many think) it is strongly supported by the general course of Jewish history in Moslem Spain. The facts that for more than two hundred years we hear no Jewish complaints of Moslem mistreatment; that Jewish migration to Moslem Spain from the East continued throughout that period[9]; and that in the 10th century the Jews in Moslem Spain reached the top of the administrative pyramid show that something of the Jewish-Moslem friendship that had arisen during the invasion persisted and was expressed in a more benevolent attitude toward the Jews than the one exhibited toward the Christians. In any case, in the first century and a half following the Moslem conquest, Spain's Christians viewed all Spanish Jews as confirmed friends of the Moslem rulers, and hence as their own implacable foes, and this view was another factor that intensified their enmity for the Jews and their determination to keep them out of their borders.

This, of course, adds to the complexity of the question we posed in the foregoing: What led Christian Spain to change its attitude toward the Jews from utter rejection to partial acceptance in circumstances that argued against such a change? For the facts of the case cannot be doubted: Sometime in the course of the ninth century, at the very time when the kings of Asturias were locked in deadly battle with the Moors, Christian Spain began to reverse its Jewish policy. We shall now attempt to identify the factors that brought about that reversal.

II

In 798, the forces of Charles the Great invaded northern Catalonia, put an end to Moslem rule there, and annexed the province to Charles' domains. This was not the first time that the Gauls had fought the Moslems in an effort to keep them beyond the Pyrenees; nor was it the last.[10] During most of the 8th century, when the kingdom of Asturias was waging war to push the Moslems southward, the rulers of Gaul were endeavoring to achieve the same aim in their own realm. In their battles with the Moslems—which, though sporadic, took a whole century to complete—they managed to force the Moslems out of Gaul, first by capturing Septimania and its capital (Narbonne) and finally by establishing the Spanish March—a protective Frankish zone south of the Pyrenees that extended to the Mediterranean coast. Here the March was anchored in Barcelona, the southernmost point of their penetration, which they captured in 803.

Forming the two poles of a semicircle that bulged into the northwestern Mediterranean, Narbonne and Barcelona were the prime achievements of the Carolingian kings in their southern domains. The importance of both places for Charlemagne's empire far exceeded their military value. Narbonne came to play a key role in broadening the empire's economic horizons and thereby wielded a far-reaching influence on the history of European civilization; and Barcelona helped it to fill that role while simultaneously promoting the interests of Christian Spain. Both cities could perform these tasks largely thanks to their Jewish communities—a remarkable feat which has to be noted if we wish to understand the developments under review.

In our present rapid survey of Hispano-Jewish history we can touch on this development only very briefly. Even so, we must call the reader's attention to some crucial conditions then obtaining in Europe—conditions that inevitably lead us to the theories so forcefully espoused by Henri Pirenne.[11] Despite the criticisms leveled at these theories,[12] it is hard to find fault with their main postulates. The facts are that, as Pirenne has pointed out, during the 8th and 9th centuries, the western Mediterranean basin was dominated by the Moslems owing to their control of North Africa and Spain and later of Sicily and the Tyrrhenian Sea. In consequence, it was closed to free Christian shipping, so that the northern Christian ports of the Mediterranean were soon virtually paralyzed.[13] Commerce between East and West almost ceased, and Europe soon felt the disastrous consequences. Its stagnated economy left its marks, among other things, in decayed cities, half-ruined roads and a declining standard of living. There was only one way to remedy the situation: to open the clogged arteries of communication and allow the lifeblood of trade to flow once again into Europe's abandoned markets. But this meant breaking the Moslem blockade, with no naval force available to do it. It was in this apparently hopeless impasse that the Jews of Narbonne and its neighboring communities stepped in and changed the situation.

Narbonne, which belonged to the Spanish state throughout the period of Visigothic rule, had a strong Jewish community whose importance was so great that even at the height of Visigothic Jew-baiting it was repeatedly freed from the extreme persecutions to which the rest of Spain's Jews were exposed.[14] In 719 Narbonne was captured by the Arabs and thus was again part of Spain, now Moslem. In the following four decades, before it was seized by the Carolingians, Narbonne lay at the end of the route by which goods coming from the East through Moslem Spain could reach the border of the Christian West. The city no doubt profited from this condition, but Gaul benefited relatively less. Lacking a professional merchant class, it could neither absorb a vast supply of goods nor mobilize a large equivalent for exchange.

This state of affairs began to change, however, when Narbonne was taken by Pepin I (759) and later included in the empire of Charles the Great. Its Jewish merchants could then acquire wares and products from Charles' vast dominions and move them to market from remote places, including the faraway eastern regions. They could also increase imports by establishing contact with suppliers in the Orient, thanks to the ties they retained with Moslem Spain from their former association with that country. Indeed, Moslem Spain was used by them primarily as a bridge to North Africa and the East, while their connections with Spain's Jews served them as links to the Jewish merchants in North Africa and the East. Thus they could form an international organization whose commercial net spread across immense areas, ultimately extending far beyond the limits of both Christendom and Islam. Their agents traversed routes that embraced eastern Europe as well as enormous stretches of Asia, reaching India long before Vasco da Gama and China long before Marco Polo. With the goods they brought to Europe, they established new trading stations, revived deserted towns, and formed many nuclei of new urban centers. Thus, in the empire of Charles and his heirs, including the kings of the Holy Roman Empire, they became known as builders of cities as well as masters of wholesale trade.

The story of these international Jewish merchants, known by their common designation as the Radhanites, has been told many times by scholars in the field.[15] What has not been duly emphasized, however, is the primary part that the city of Narbonne played in giving birth to their organization, and the secondary, but by no means insignificant, part played by Barcelona in its development. The special importance of Barcelona to their empire was indubitably recognized by the Franks all along, and it was for good reason that in order to capture it they were ready to besiege it for two whole years. Barcelona served the Carolingian rulers not only as the tip of a military wedge driven into eastern Moslem Spain, but also as a harbor in whose neighborhood their merchants could board Moslem ships to cross the Mediterranean or proceed to North Africa along the Spanish coast.[16] Needless to say, it was no easy voyage, free from legal and financial complications; and to carry it out required ingenuity, an enterprising spirit and, above all, courage. The Jewish merchants of Narbonne and its neighboring communities (especially Arles, Béziers and Marseilles) evidently possessed these qualities, for many of them returned from their distant travels laden with goods that brought them much wealth, high social standing and further opportunities. Pirenne, who noted their unique functions, summarized part of their achievement by saying that it was through the Jews that the Occidental world was then kept in touch with the Orient.[17] Even more far-reaching was his cardinal statement: "The Jew was the professional merchant of the Carolingian age."[18]

This development had far-reaching consequences, on which we can touch here only very briefly. Because of the function fulfilled by its Jews in the evolution of Europe's economy, Narbonne could play an unprecedented role in the history of European Jewry. Recognizing the services rendered by the Jews in relieving the economic distress of his empire, Charles took little notice of the decrees enacted against the Jews by the Christian legislators and, with minor concessions to Church laws and principles, granted the Jews of Narbonne basic freedoms and the full protection of his government.[19] The same rights and privileges were soon extended by him, as well as by his heir Louis I, to all other Jews who wished to trade in their realms; and thus Narbonne's Jews became instrumental in reopening the West to renewed Jewish life. What is more, the West in which the Jews now resettled included not only the realms of Gaul but also those of the Holy Roman Empire. Here, indeed, even more than in France, the Jews enjoyed prosperity and peace for three centuries and more.

III

It did not take long before Charles' novel—indeed revolutionary—policy toward the Jews produced a notable effect on Christian Spain. The capture of Barcelona by the Frankish forces must have drawn to the city a number of Jews from Narbonne and other Septimanian towns who came there intending to start or advance new mercantile projects. It is possible that they found there at least part of the community that had lived in Barcelona under the Moslems, for the Franks, it is certain, did not order the Jews to leave the city after they had conquered it. In any case, judging by at least two sources, a Jewish community existed in Barcelona probably as early as 825. It was apparently the first Jewish community in any part of Spain under Christian control, and the way it was treated by the empire's authorities must have astounded the Spanish Christians. If Alfonso II, king of the Asturias (798–842), looked with admiration at Charles the Great as the future deliverer of Spain from Moslem bondage, he inevitably contemplated with no little wonder the internal regime of the Frankish empire. It must have occurred to him that if the Jews could be so helpful to and so highly regarded by the great Christian king as to make him forgo almost all the old laws that had been enacted against them, they might also be of assistance to him and his hard-pressed kingdom, then fighting for its life. In brief, we believe it safe to assume that the favorable treatment of the Jews of Barcelona by the authorities of the northern empire served as a model for the treatment of the Jews of Spain by the Christian Spanish sovereigns.

We do not know whether Jewish settlement in Asturias began as early as the days of Alfonso II, but there is no doubt that it started not long thereafter, perhaps already in the days of Ordoño I (850–866), but certainly in those of Alfonso III (866–909).[20] In any case, if it expanded as it did, it was due not only to the influence of the "model", but also, and primarily, to the services the Jews rendered to the Spanish rulers and their newborn kingdoms. Indeed, these services were more varied and manifold, and certainly no less vital to their countries, than those they offered to the kings of Gaul.

In discussing the functions fulfilled by Spain's Jews during the period of the Reconquest, the Spanish historian Sánchez-Albornoz refers to their share in repopulating the places captured by the Christian warriors from the Moors. "The urgencies of the Reconquest and the repopulation," he says, "determined the Jewish policies of the Christian Kings"; for "when it was necessary to populate a city that had been gained from the enemy, the devil in person would have been well received in it as repopulator."[21] When Alfonso VII, the same author reminds us, captured Oreja in 1139, he invited as settlers "every class of delinquents, homicides and abductors and even those who incurred royal ire . . . save traitors. With how much greater pleasure would he accept the industrious Jews!"[22] We may be forgiven if we suspect Sánchez-Albornoz, who is well-known for his anti-Jewish bias, to have made his remark about the "devil in person" as a sideline justification of the noble king's decision to invite Jewish settlers to his kingdom; but the stress he laid on the scarcity of repopulators is in full accord with historical reality—except that we should add that the scarcity of settlers, and the pressing need to find them, was felt not only in the days of Alfonso VII but also in those of Alfonso III, as well as a considerable time before that. This is another reason why we believe that Jewish settlement in the "reconquered" localities had already begun in the middle of the ninth century and that the document from Coimbra (900) indicates not only what occurred then and there, but also earlier in other captured towns. Indeed, just as the need for "repopulators" was pressing long before Alfonso III's reign, it was felt, in various degrees, also after it—in fact, to the end of the main period of the Reconquest (that is, until 1252).[23] This is largely true of Spain's other needs, many of which were met by the Jews to a greater or lesser extent. Accordingly, what we shall say later on about the Jewish contribution to Christian Spain applies to the entire period.

In assessing that contribution, we ought to bear in mind that when the kings sought "repopulators," they were looking first of all for men who could bear arms and were capable of defending the newly conquered places. We should also note that Christian Spain was at war with an enemy which, for long periods, was far superior in both manpower and resources, and this superiority encouraged the Moslems to harass the Spaniards and provoke new conflicts. Especially exposed to Moslem raids and incursions were the Christian frontier outposts, which were often poorly manned and inadequately fortified, and the Jews, who came to live in these places, realized that they would have to take part in their defense. Indeed, they committed themselves to the task, and in some places formed the sole or main force that bore the brunt of the attacks. This was especially the case in fortresses which were placed by the kings in their exclusive custody and which they undertook to settle and guard.[24] Later on, when their numbers increased, the Jews also took part in the campaigns of the Reconquest, either in separate military units or through individual enlistments. Evidence of this comes from various quarters—Moslem, Christian and Jewish—covering the long period of Castile's Reconquest from Alfonso VI to Fernando III.[25]

By this we do not mean to suggest that the Jews constituted a major factor in the Christian-Moslem military struggle that unfolded in Spain in those centuries; but we do mean to emphasize that they took part in that struggle more than we have generally been led to believe and that they shared with the Christian Spaniards the burden of Spain's war of liberation. What cannot be gauged even roughly, however, is the total effect of their military contribution, since the sources offer no solid ground for any such assessment. Nevertheless, one ought to bear in mind that in all life-and-death military clashes, when the adversaries involved strain their efforts to the limit, any addition or detraction of strength may determine the outcome. In the long history of the Reconquest, many such crucial clashes occurred, and therefore it is not at all excluded that, in certain critical situations, the Jews' contribution to the Spanish war effort, however small compared to the Christians', may have made the difference. In any case, Christian Spain was for the Jews not just a trading post and a land to settle in, from which they could derive only peacetime benefits. It was also a land that confronted them with dangers akin to those faced by the Christian Spaniards.

Yet the Jews' chief contribution to Spain and its rulers was not in the military but in the economic field. At a time when most able-bodied Christians in the north were engaged in fighting the battles of the Reconquest, there were not enough Christians to garrison the forts taken, often half destroyed, from the Moors; and even smaller was the number of Christians who were willing to perform that difficult task at their expense. Such people, however, were precisely the kind with whom the kings wished to populate those places. Unable to support a paid regular army, they sought soldiers who could draw their living from the soil by working the fields adjacent to their fortresses or from some manual art in which they were trained. Like their Christian neighbors, therefore, the Jewish settlers in those places cultivated the arable land around them—that is, outside their fortifications—and tried to derive from it whatever food they could. But no less was the effort they devoted to the practice of various manual arts. Craftsmen, in fact, were eagerly sought, not only because they were able to sustain themselves, but also because they could meet vital needs of the defensive forces. Above all, they could keep the clothes, weapons, and other equipment of the troops in good shape so that the latter would be ready for battle. Here indeed the Jews were especially useful. For the Christians, having long been devoted to the war, were woefully short of trained craftsmen, while the Jews, who came from civil surroundings, had them in impressive numbers.[26]

Agriculture and manual trades thus formed the main occupations of these Jewish settlers, but there was also a third sphere of activity that inevitably attracted their attention. For neither the farmers nor the artisans could perform any of their tasks without supplies; and the Christian settlers could not meet this need, which was obviously a requisite for their continued stay. It was, however, met by another group of Jews, who arranged for a steady flow of commodities to the reconquered areas and military bases. And thus, the Jewish settlers offered Christian Spain, both its authorities and its frontier population, not only soldiers, farmers, and craftsmen but also merchants and suppliers of goods. Directly or indirectly, the latter formed part of the great commercial net the Jews had spread over a large part of the world.[27]

Américo Castro, who noted the paucity of Christian activity in craftsmanship and commerce for long periods of the medieval era, said that the "diligent Jews occupied the place vacated by the Christians in the life of the nation" and that they thus "constituted the economic base of the peninsular medieval society."[28] This statement may apply to the earlier rather than the later periods and to those Christian artisans who abandoned their trades while dedicating themselves to the art of war. But insofar as commerce was concerned, the place of the Christians was not "vacated" in this field, since the great majority of the Christian repopulators had not occupied it to begin with. The free Christian peasants and small proprietors who distinguished themselves in fighting the Moors, and thus earned the king's decision to make them *ciudadanos* (i.e., burghers) and grant them tracts of land, buildings, and rights, had never been engaged in commercial activity. What occurred in their case with respect to commerce illustrates the rule observed by Wilhelm Roscher, according to which many societies, in certain early stages of their history, "permitted a foreign people of superior cultural standing to provide for their commercial needs. Then the native people, as they matured, sought to free themselves from the tutelage." Their efforts to shake off the foreign controls, adds Roscher, "were often accompanied by fierce struggle."[29] This is indeed what happened in Christian Spain in the earlier centuries of the Reconquest.[30]

It would be wrong, however, to assume that the Jews' work in the above professions constituted the limit of their participation in Spanish life. To be sure, in the earlier stages of the Reconquest the Jews labored primarily in basic economic fields. But later their efforts rapidly expanded to embrace a large variety of spheres. What Bofarull pointed out with respect to their activities in Barcelona in the 11th, 12th and 13th centuries[31] may apply to most of Spain's cities and regions, and to some of them even later, too. Thus we see the Jews offer Christian Spain, besides the military aid referred to, not only farmers, artisans and merchants, but also physicians, land surveyors, engineers, mathematicians, salt miners, tax collectors, tax farmers, administrators, translators, diplomatic emissaries, and functionaries in a variety of other professions, in which they excelled and kept perfecting themselves from generation to generation. Most of these professions were of tremendous value to the development of Spain's economy, to its fiscal administration, to its diplomatic efforts and to its military accomplishments. Is it any wonder that the kings invited these newcomers to the newly occupied towns, "offering them houses and even whole boroughs, granting them judicial guarantees and conceding them administrative and judicial autonomy?"[32] Similarly, one can readily understand why, far from persecuting the Jewish communities they had found in the conquered Moorish towns, they did their utmost to induce them to stay in these towns along with the new Christian settlers."[33]

Thus it was not the mere "industriousness" of the Jews but their know-how in many fields that was vital for the state—as well as the other qualities they possessed, such as their loyalty, reliability and devotion to their task—that moved the Christian kings to court the Jews and accept them in unlimited numbers. That the kings knew how to appreciate the unique and multifold contribution of the Jews to their administration—and, more broadly, to the country as a whole—is evident not only from the protection they gave them, and the special rights and privileges they granted them, but also from the variety of high offices they offered them in almost all the departments of their government. In adopting this practice, Christian Spain may have followed a pattern suggested by Moslem rulers in the peninsula, who had appointed some outstanding Jewish individuals to the highest positions of government. But what happened in Moslem Spain only occasionally, and for a relatively short period, occurred in Christian Spain rather regularly—and for a very long time. Thus, we can note that for three hundred years (from approximately 1075), there was not a reign in Castile in which Jews did not occupy high offices in the royal administration—above all, in diplomacy and finance. The names Ferrizuel (in the days of Alfonso VI), Yehuda Ibn Ezra (in the time of Alfonso VII), Avenxuxen (in the period of Alfonso VIII), Don Çulema (in the reign of Fernando III), and other names from those and later times, clearly attest this pattern.[34] Indeed, in no other country in the medieval era did the Jews play such a major part in the management of the royal finances—and, directly and indirectly, also in other departments of the royal administration—as they did in medieval Christian Spain. Nor did they gain anywhere else so many signs of recognition and appreciation of their services, expressed in special rights, grants of property, and other gifts of perpetual income, as they did in Spain between 1000 and 1252. Thus, for Spanish Jewry this was a period of establishment, rapid growth, and steady rise in status and influence, with the support of the kings and the grandees—a period which may be characterized as the happiest in their long history in the Iberian peninsula.

IV

And yet it would be wrong to assume that even in that period the Jews of Christian Spain could steadily, or even frequently, enjoy the sensations of freedom and security characteristic of societies in which mutual toleration and basically friendly attitudes prevail. However strong their belief in the solidity and durability of the social and political structure that sheltered them, they could not help being terrified from time to time by occurrences threatening their very existence. For despite the seemingly serene surface of their social and economic life, the earth beneath them was constantly trembling, and from time to time the tremors were followed by eruptions that claimed many victims. Such were the massacre in Castrojeriz in 1035; the pogroms in Toledo, Escalona and other towns in 1109; and again the pogrom in León in 1230. To understand this unrest and the disturbances it produced, we ought to consider several additional factors, and especially those that governed the relations between the Jews and the Spanish people.

What we must first bear in mind is that the Christian Spain with which the Jews negotiated the terms of their resettlement was not the Spain of the common people. It was the Spain of kings, princes and grandees who, the Jews believed, owned the land and all its assets to dispose of in any way they wished. Actually, the situation was far more complex and, in addition, was constantly affected by the growing pressure of the rulers' subjects. To be sure, the kings' orders went a long way to shape popular behavior toward the Jews; and the multifarious aid the Jews extended to the Christians in the early phases of their life as neighbors did much to assuage the people's animus for the Jews and lessen the distrust they had commonly felt for them. Yet this period of peaceful symbiosis was bound to be affected by the changing circumstances. Its duration was not uniform in all places and depended on the local state of affairs. But generally, it tended to be rather short, with its approaching end usually signaled by mounting tensions between Jews and Spaniards. Eventually toleration, however obligatory, turned into open intolerance.

The causes of this transmutation of attitudes were inherent in the nature of things—that is, in the condition of the Jews as a minority group within the great majority of the native Spaniards. This condition of course was not peculiar to Spain but common to the whole of medieval Europe, and in large measure, though in lesser intensity, to many countries beyond Europe as well. Pointing to the root cause of the antagonism that evolved toward the Jews in the medieval West, Baron defined it as the "alienage of the Jews," which was generally viewed as irreversible. "In the mental picture of most medieval men," he wrote, "the Jew appeared as a *permanent* stranger."[35] This is undoubtedly a correct observation which touches the key issue of Jewish

life in the Middle Ages. But it has to be amplified: The Jew was seen as a
"permanent stranger" not only by non-Jews but by the Jews themselves.[36] It
was the coincidence of both views—the Jewish and non-Jewish—that was
largely responsible for the resultant condition, equally well noted and defined by Baron, that the "Jewish community was a corporate body . . .
consisting of a group of permanent 'aliens,' " who were *essentially living
apart" from the Christian society.*[37]

The concluding part of this definition requires, we believe, some elucidation—at least insofar as it touches the second cycle of Jewish life in Christian
Spain. That the Jews lived apart from the Christian society in all that related
to their *religious* conduct may be taken as a matter of course. But they also
lived apart from that society *politically*—that is, if we view the "city" as the
main habitat of the Jews and recall that the Jews took no part in its administration, nor demanded to have any share in it. Furthermore, since the Jewish
community in Spain was not subject to the city's jurisdiction, it lived apart
from the Christians *judicially* as well; and accordingly, while conflicts among
its own members were settled by its own courts, conflicts between Jews and
Christian commoners were settled by special judges chosen by the king.[38] In
addition, they lived apart from the Christians insofar as their *fiscal obligations*
were concerned; for the Jews paid most of their taxes to the king and little
to the cities in which they dwelt. Finally, they lived apart from the Christians
also in the narrow *territorial* sense, since they usually sojourned in well-
defined neighborhoods especially assigned for their habitation. It was only in
the economic field that the Jews did not live—or wish to live—apart from
the Christians; for in this sphere, separation would put an end to their
economic activity and abolish the conditions that enabled them to exist.

In time, as we shall see, the Christian Spaniards manifested a tendency to
restrict, if not totally cut off also their economic ties to the Jews. The origin
of the tendency must be ascribed to the same cause—the alienage of the
Jews—that led to their exclusion from other major spheres of the nation's life.
Like all strangers, the Jews were tolerated in some measure as long as their
special skills and functions were considered helpful to the majority. But when
the tasks performed by the Jews could be accomplished also by certain
Christian Spaniards, the activity of the Jews appeared not only superfluous
but also disturbing and hurtful. In consequence, the Jews' success would
produce only jealousy; their competition, increased antagonism; and their
success and competition, taken together, outbreaks of hatred that proved
hard to suppress. What contributed to this development, apart from economic rivalry, was a periodic shortage of funding, which hampered the
Christians' activity. As latecomers to their fields, the Christian craftsmen and
small merchants, lacking superior training and experience, could not for
some time earn enough to save up for times of stress. This was one reason

they incurred debts, which they often could not pay and only worsened their situation; but they fell into debt for other reasons, too, as we shall see below. It was the part of the people that was faced with these hardships—mostly of the lower and some of the middle class—that raised the most violent battle cries against the Jews; it was they who carried the war against the Jews with fire and sword into the Jewish neighborhoods; and it was they who finally moved the authorities to settle the Jewish question along the lines they recommended, or rather demanded by their spokesmen.

If this effort to oust the Jews from Spain's economy, and thereby from the life of the Spanish people, took almost four centuries to accomplish—in fact, until the Jews' expulsion from Spain—it was due to the strength of the Spanish monarchy, which shielded the Jews with exceptional steadfastness. To be sure, from 1250 on the kings frequently withdrew, under pressure of the masses, from some of their traditional positions, but these withdrawals were in most cases tactical and usually corrected after a short time. On the whole, the people had their way only when the royal power disappeared (through death) or became ineffective (through an interregnum). Thus, the pogrom that erupted in Castrojeriz in 1035 occurred shortly after the death of King Sancho the Great; the pogroms that broke out in Toledo, Escalona and other cities in 1109 occurred after the death of Alfonso VI; and the one that took place in León in 1230 followed the death of Alfonso IX, king of León. Shortly thereafter, once the monarchy was reestablished, the pro-Jewish policy was reinstated and the vigorous defense of the Jews was resumed.

V

At this point a few brief remarks are called for on a well-known theory that has influenced many works touching the evolution of Jewish economy in the Middle Ages. According to this theory, the leading occupations in which the Jews engaged in the medieval era were taken up not by their own choice but under pressures applied by hostile princes or regimes. Accordingly, the Jews embarked on international trade because they were forced out of agriculture, and then embarked on moneylending and banking when they were forced out of international trade. The theory, however, is only partly valid; it is true for some periods in certain regions, but not for all periods and all parts of Europe; and certainly it cannot be substantiated for the *beginnings* of most of the indicated courses. On the whole, the process was not that passive; it was also a result of calculated choices, of the seizure by the Jews of economic opportunities suddenly provided by changing circumstances. Thus, the Jews shifted from profession to profession not only when the one they held appeared precarious, or became forbidden by the country's law, but because the one they adopted was more in demand, and hence more lucrative, and hence more likely to serve their ends. This is what happened especially in Spain with respect to moneylending and tax collection—the two occupations that became in the 12th century the most salient features of the economic and social life of Spanish Jewry.

Manuel Colmeiro and other Spanish scholars who recognized the indispensability of credit for the economic development of all societies found it possible to denounce, without reservation, the evils of the "Jewish usury," which they attributed to the natural tendencies of the Jews.[39] We see in such assertions no explanations but merely reflections of traditional prejudices, which bring us no nearer to, but rather remove us, from the heart of the problem. In pursuing this subject, we must note, to begin with, that moneylending in Spain at no time embraced such a large section of the Jewish community as it did in France or in England, and that most Spanish Jews who engaged in it (at least, to the end of the 14th century) belonged to the lower classes. While the hunger for credit was universal, in Spain it was felt most acutely in the cities among the Christian artisans and small merchants, whose number increased with the urban expansion and who needed, to withstand the growing competition, new instruments, more goods and better facilities, for whose acquisition they required capital. As Church law forbade Christians to lend money at interest and no Christian would lend them money gratis, such artisans or merchants would often turn to the nearest and only available source they knew—their Jewish neighbors, who were often engaged in the same profession at a higher economic level. These usually preceded the Christians in practicing certain trades and professions and managed to save, by their thrift and hard labor, considerable sums of money. To risk these savings by lending them to poor Christians without receiving adequate securities was certainly not an attractive proposition. Such securities were indeed obtained by pawns or contracts authorized by government, but their realization was not always free of trouble. The real attraction was the chance of high profits—and this is how the process began.

The first point to realize, then, is that in Spain—i.e., in both Castile and Aragon—most borrowers were "small people," while most lenders belonged to the lower middle class. In the pogroms perpetrated in Segovia and Avila in 1368 (during the Civil War), the pogromists took care to destroy the documents recording their indebtedness to Jews, or to recover whatever they had given as security to their moneylenders.[40] Similarly, during the pogrom in Barcelona in August 1391, the "small people" forced the bailiff of the city to give them the documents he kept at his disposal, which indicated the sums they owed to Jews.[41] The pogromists, "small people," were usually artisans and other members of the lower classes. The loans they would receive would inevitably be small, and the rich would have no interest in granting them. Only small Jewish merchants and artisans, who needed extra money to supplement their income, would be the natural lenders to such clients.[42]

This does not mean that some Jews who belonged to the higher classes did not engage in moneylending or that exorbitant rates of interest were not exacted, especially in the early period. As with all commodities, the cost of money fluctuated in accordance with the law of supply and demand, and the main fault lay, as was pointed out by Vives, in the "incapacity of the Castilian burgher class to create banks and bank deposits" that would supply credit at much lower rates of interest.[43] Later on, when the government intervened (during the reign of Alfonso X) and reduced the rate of interest to 25 percent, the situation was somewhat relieved, but not settled. Bankruptcies continued, and so did the criticisms that compelled the government to intervene again with moratoria on loans and other measures. Finally, in the Cortes of Alcalá (1348), Alfonso XI completely prohibited lending money at interest; but this proved to be no solution either. A few years later, the procurators requested the restoration of Jewish moneylending to Christians on the terms that prevailed before the prohibition.[44] Evidently, Jewish credit was helpful to many and not as ruinous as it had been described.

It is questionable to what extent all this concerned the Jewish upper class, the financial elite, who lent money to the nobles and great Christian merchants. Baer believed that if the ban on moneylending had become effective, it would have "prevented Jews from acting as tax-farmers."[45] This contention, however, is wrong. If either of these occupations—tax farming and moneylending—depended on the other, it was not the former that depended on the latter. The major source of wealth for the Jewish financiers was tax farming, not moneylending, and it was the large profits they made from tax farming that enabled them to grant large loans to the nobles, and occasionally to the kings too. Had Alfonso XI or Enrique III believed that their laws forbidding moneylending at interest might endanger Jewish farming of their revenues, they would never have issued those laws. No financial arrangement was guarded by them more jealously than the collection of their revenues by Jewish tax farmers.

If moneylending affected the economic conditions of many individual Jews but changed only marginally the Jewish communal situation, the gathering of revenues, and especially tax farming, involved a much smaller number of Jews, but had a great impact on the general condition of the Jewish community as a whole. This was due, first of all, to the direct linkage of the tax-farming system with the royal administration. The gathering of the king's revenues was carried out under the guidance and supervision of the Chief Treasurer of the realm (or of the *Contador Mayor*) who, until the end of the

14th century (when his office was taken over by conversos), was almost invariably a Jew. The influence of this official was often far-reaching, exceeding by far his financial responsibilities, and therefore deserving special attention. The medieval Spanish chronicles, however, referred to the Jewish courtiers cursorily and only with the briefest possible remarks, while modern scholarship, as Ballesteros observed, has scarcely investigated their lives and performance.[46] Nevertheless, even at this stage of our knowledge, we can state with full assurance that the Jewish treasurer at Court was the main pillar of the Jewish economic structure and the central force in what may be defined as the political power of Spanish Jewry.

Indubitably, most of this power derived from the tasks the Jews fulfilled in acquiring and managing the finances of the royal estate. The tax-collection system, controlled by the treasurer, was mostly, if not entirely, in Jewish hands. Heading its various sections and divisions, which covered all regions and all types of imposts, were tax farmers, who were in most cases Jewish, and whose assistants, their assessors and collectors, were usually Jewish as well. As a result, the Christian commoners of each city found themselves subjected to Jewish tax gatherers who, armed with royal powers, could force them to pay taxes in accordance with their own assessments. What occurred as a result could of course be expected. The cities raised their voice in violent protest against their alleged subjugation to the Jews and demanded a revision of the whole tax-gathering system and the removal of all Jewish officials from it. As these demands produced no positive response, the protests became louder and fiercer; yet their effect remained the same: nil. This was one issue on which the kings would not yield; and tax collection remained largely in Jewish hands until the end of Jewish sojourn in Spain.

It was primarily because of the functions of the Jews as the king's revenue gatherers in the urban areas that the cities saw the Jews as the monarch's agents, who treated them as objects of massive exploitation. By serving as they did the interests of the kings, the Jews seemed to be working against the interests of the cities; and thus we touch again on the phenomenon we have referred to: the fundamental conflict between the kings and their people—a conflict not limited to financial matters, but one that embraced all spheres of government that had a bearing on the people's life. It was in part thanks to this conflict of interests that the Jews could survive the harsh climate of the Middle Ages, and it is hard to believe that they did not discern it when they came to resettle in Christian Europe. Indeed, their requests, since the days of the Carolingians, for assurances of protection before they settled in a place show (a) that they realized that the kings' positions on many issues differed from those of the common people and (b) that the kings were prepared, for the sake of *their* interests, to make common cause with the "alien" Jews against the clear wishes of their Christian subjects. In a sense, therefore, the Jews' agreements with the kings in the Middle Ages resembled the understandings they had reached with foreign conquerors in the ancient world.

This situation, as we may gather from the above, was not by any means unique to Spain; it was common to many countries in Europe. But in two respects Spain differed from the latter. In Spain, the kings were almost constantly engaged in a war of national liberation, and therefore it was their people's war no less than their own. The Reconquest was indeed the common ground on which the wishes of kings and people met, and as long as that war continued, no real rupture could occur between the king and his Christian subjects. In addition, as leaders of all military campaigns against the people's most dangerous enemy (the Moslems), the authority of the kings became so dominant that few dared to act against their decisions.

But on the other hand, Spain was the scene of a development that limited the ability of the Spanish kings' to conduct their pro-Jewish policy freely—that is, in any way they wanted. The needs of the war, which lasted for centuries, compelled the kings of Spain to grant the people rights, which became ever more impressive both quantitatively and qualitatively, in order to arouse their enthusiasm for the war and their readiness for self-sacrifice. Thus Spain became the first country in Europe where the seeds of democracy sprouted and, in consequence, the people gathered enough courage to criticize their leaders and demand reforms. As long as the war of the Reconquest continued, these criticisms could be quelled by the kings with little effort. But when the war was halted for a long time, the voice of the people became ever louder and steadily more audacious and effective.

The radical change came in the middle of the 13th century, when the Reconquest had attained its major goals with the capture by the Christians of Seville (1248) and Jaén (1252), and when the third estate in Spain—the democratic force, which was centered in the cities—at last gained representation in the Cortes of Castile (almost nine decades after it had gained it in Aragon). From then on, Castile's cities incessantly conducted a vigorous campaign against the Jews, marked by frequent forceful assaults, which the kings, in need of the Jews' services, repeatedly tried to ward off. The following two hundred and fifty years (1250–1492), representing the second half of Jewish life in Christian Spain (insofar as the bulk of the second cycle was concerned), was a period of incessant struggle between the Jews and the Spanish cities. During the first century of that period the Jews still appear to be holding their own, repeatedly succeeding in repelling attempts to abolish or restrict their rights. In this one hundred years (1250–1348) we still see the Jews in charge of Spain's finances, in the councils of government, in the leading embassies, in the supply of armies, and in many of the other tasks and professions in which they had engaged in the preceding era. Moreover, in this very century we see them rise in the echelons of power, producing some of their most eminent courtiers, such as Çag de la Maleha (under Alfonso X), Abraham el Barchilon (under Sancho IV), Don Samuel (under Fernando IV), and Don Joseph de Écija (under Alfonso XI). One may conclude, therefore, that even in this period the Jews of Spain were advancing in almost all fields; but it was an uphill advance, against many impediments; and as they reached the top of the pyramid, the specter of annihilation faced them for the first time.[47]

Then came a period of great crisis and transition, which lasted four decades (1350–1390), followed by a century which began with catastrophe, continued with stabilization on a much lower level, and ended with the precipitate fall of the Expulsion (1492). Throughout this period of transition, as well as for most of the subsequent century (1390–1492), we see the kings making determined efforts to defend the Jews against a rising opposition that steadily became more intense and widespread until it assumed menacing proportions. Thus, in this period the Spanish kings pursued their distinctly pro-Jewish policy not only against world opinion—i.e., the Christian world, of which their kingdoms were part—but also against the dominant opinion of their own people. This shows that some, if not most, of the services the Jews rendered their administrations were considered by the kings vital for their regimes and that therefore they were anxious to retain them. The kings continued to defend the Jews' traditional positions even against constantly increasing odds. But they ultimately lost.

The winners were the cities. More precisely, they were the lower classes, the great majority of the cities' population, who represented the will of the common man. They got only occasional support from Rome and infrequent help from isolated elements of the Church leadership in Spain. But they were strongly aided by the lower ranks of the hierarchy of the Spanish Church, and they spoke in the name of religion. To gain a better comprehension of what occurred in Spain, and especially of what motivated the urban drive against the Jews, we have to take a closer look at the Castilian cities.

III. The Castilian Cities

I

The cities were semi-independent republics that owed whatever rights they possessed to the kings. It was from the kings that they received their charters *(fueros)*, or what we may call their constitutional laws, and it was from them that they obtained from time to time special *privileges*—that is, revisions, annulments or amplifications of the original rulings. These privileges were usually granted to the cities in response to requests they addressed to the kings when their inhabitants came to regard some old laws as no longer applicable or tolerable. Especially would the kings respond to such requests when they sought the cities' aid (financial or political) and when the cities had grown rich and strong enough to make large-scale contributions to the Crown. To get what he asked of them, the king often felt that he had to give the cities something in return; for in negotiating with the king the issues in question, the cities were moved by two desires. While willing to render vital services to the kings in all matters related to national security, they wished to get greater consideration for their views concerning the management of the kingdom's affairs. Especially did they seek to curb, if not free themselves from royal interference in their internal life.

There is no evidence that the cities of Spain had ever aspired to an independent status such as was attained by some cities in Italy or by the Hanseatic League. The war of the Reconquest, which clearly required the unification of all national forces, precluded the development of such schemes; and so did the smallness of the Spanish cities, which, excepting Seville, Barcelona and Valencia, could not compare in population and resources with their European counterparts. But what the Spanish cities could not gain individually they tried to gain together, as a collective force, and what they sought to attain was a leading position among the factors determining the national life of Spain.

These factors, as indicated, were primarily three: the king, the nobility and the urban oligarchies, each of which aspired to wealth and power—more wealth to gain greater power, or more power to gain greater wealth. No other aspiration can be seen as decisive in the intermittent conflicts among these forces, and no other can be viewed as truly significant in shaping their attitude toward the Jews. For that attitude was established primarily by the view that each of them took of the Jewish role—i.e., whether it was judged to be helpful or harmful to their economic and political aspirations.

The reader who is used to defining the Jewish problem in primarily religious or spiritual terms may wonder at our exclusion from the list of the factors that shaped the fortunes of the Jews in Spain (a) the Spanish clergy, which was one of the estates and (b) the Catholic Church, with its seat in Rome, which established policies for the Jews in Christendom. That the local and Roman churches had a share in shaping the destinies of the Jews in Spain as elsewhere, it is not our purpose to deny. But it is our wish to draw a dividing line between *determining* and *supportive* factors; and as far as we can judge, the role of the Church, both Spanish and universal, was secondary in the gathering storm against the Hispano-Jewish community. Viewed in due perspective, the cardinal facts, attested by evidence we consider conclusive, indicate this quite clearly. We shall note this evidence and probe it.

Yet before doing so, we ought to take another look at the specific issues that served as *casus belli* between the Jews and the cities—their relentless and, in fact, most dangerous foes.

II

It has long been noted that the first public attack upon the Jews as gatherers of the royal revenues in Castile took place during Sancho IV's reign in the Cortes of Haro, 1288, where the cities demanded that the Jews be removed from the offices of farmers and collectors of taxes.[1] What has not been noted, however, is that this demand was not conceived as an exclusively anti-Jewish move—that is, as a move against the Jews qua Jews. The facts of the case controvert such an assumption totally and conclusively.

For in that very Cortes the burghers asked the king to refrain from farming out the taxes (*servicios,* or other tributes) to *any* person and, in order to obtain the revenues due him, to appoint only *collectors.* These collectors, the cities further argued, should be *omes buenos* (i.e., "good people") who "know how to serve God and the king and guard their souls and the communities *(los pueblos)*."[2] *Omes buenos* was the common designation of a special segment of the urban aristocracy, which constituted the town's moral elite and supplied a good part of the council's membership. Hence, what the cities asked the king in that Cortes was to stop the farming of taxes altogether, to limit the procedure of tax gathering to collections, and, finally, to transfer the responsibilities of tax collection to their own chosen and "trustworthy" members, who, by virtue of their integrity and reliability, would serve both the king and the people. This much is clear from the response the king gave to the petition addressed to him on that issue. What is not clear, however, is whether the ban on tax farming was meant to be absolute, inviolable in all circumstances, or whether the prohibition on "any person" (besides the Jews as a group specifically mentioned) was directed against certain non-Jewish tax gatherers who were opposed by the cities as performers of this task for some undisclosed reason.

In the Cortes of Valladolid, 1293, the cities took steps to clarify their intent and put teeth into their previous petition. Instead of asking the king to forbid tax farming "to any person"—which made the request appear too general and hence might permit undesirable exceptions—they now asked specifically that the farming be prohibited to *ricos omes* (the high nobility), *caballeros* (nobles of lower rank), *alcaldes* (royal city judges), *merinos* (royal provincial judges) and, finally, to Jews.[3] Thus, the term "any person" in the petition of 1288 served merely to avoid open confrontation with certain highly placed Christians, whom the townsmen indubitably objected to as tax farmers no less, and perhaps more, than they opposed the Jews. If we compare their two petitions on tax farming in the Cortes of Haro and that of Valladolid, we may conclude that apart from the groups they disqualified from tax farming, there were no other tax farmers, actual or prospective. That was why they could safely extend their proposed prohibition to "any person." They could do so also for the obvious reason that they themselves were not prepared to become tax farmers (for reasons to be discussed). But the cities went further in their antagonism to having any of the above groups—i.e., the nobles (of all ranks), the high officials, and the Jews—involved in the gathering of the revenues. Thus, in the same Cortes of Valladolid they asked the king to remove the latter not only from tax farming but from tax collection as well.[4] But insofar as tax collection was concerned, the burghers would not extend the prohibition they requested to "any person," for they themselves had a strong, abiding interest in assuming the role of tax collectors. In fact, just as they wanted to have none of the tax farming, they wanted to have all of the tax collection.

III

That this opposition to appoint Christians of authority to any of the above-mentioned tasks and offices was not determined by a passing mood but by deep-rooted attitudes and convictions is evident from the petitions presented to the king only a few years later, in 1301, in the Cortes of Burgos and that of Zamora. Judging by the king's response in Burgos, the petition of the cities on that occasion was concerned primarily with the collection of the *servicios;* and regarding this they expressed their radical opposition to having *caballeros, clerics* and *Jews* participate in that function in any capacity—whether as farmers, collectors, or inquirers. Their demands in Zamora were essentially the same with respect to the groups they wanted excluded, but extended to cover, beyond the *servicios,* all forms of royal taxation. Specifically, what the cities asked in this Cortes was that "neither *ricos homes,* nor *infanzones,* nor caballeros, nor clerics, nor Jews" be allowed to act as farmers or collectors of either the *servicios,* or the *monedas,* or the *diezmos de puertos* (duties imposed on transported goods), or any of the tributes that might be required by the king in some future time. Similarly, they demanded that all these taxes be collected "in fidelity" for the king by *"caballeros* and *omes buenos* of the towns" and by "residents of the other royal places" and that these collectors be "remunerated" for their efforts in the form of fixed salaries."[5]

This stipulation again makes it clear that the cities refused to have the taxes of the king farmed and collected not only by Jews but by any noble of whatever rank, and that they likewise opposed having members of the *clergy* engaged in these undertakings. Their position with regard to tax collection was identical with the one they maintained on tax farming, except that they agreed to have the towns' *caballeros* join with the local *omes buenos* in assuming the offices of tax gathering. The inclusion by the cities of these *caballeros* among the tax gatherers resulted no doubt from the difficulty they felt in denying the *caballeros* this right. As citizens involved in the governance of the cities, the city *caballeros* formed a bridge between the first and third estates— or rather, between the grandees and the city. Formally members of the nobility, the *caballeros* were actually closer to the burghers, and they often represented them in Cortes as *procuradores* of the town councils (*concejos*). Thus, in a sense, they were in the same category as the *omes buenos,* and as such they no doubt demanded—and received—the right to serve as tax gatherers in the cities. On the other hand, no such consideration was shown to any member of the clergy. Clerical participation in tax collection was categorically opposed.

It seems that the difficulties the nobles of all ranks began to encounter in obtaining royal contracts for both the farming and collection of taxes (as a result of the decisions of Cortes on these matters in 1288 and 1293) provided an opportunity for members of the clergy to assume positions refused to others. Since in the decision of 1293 they were not mentioned among the prohibited groups (even though the Cortes of 1288 prohibited tax farming to "anyone"), the formulation seemed to offer a loophole in the law, which the clergy could use to their advantage. It is also possible that, since the clergy was not mentioned among the groups forbidden to farm or collect taxes, some clerics were engaged by members of the other classes to act formally as their contractors of tax farming or tax collection—most probably, for some assured profit or on the basis of partnership. Yet whatever the cause of the clergy's sudden entry into the field of royal tax gathering, the cities were quick to close this loophole in the law and made it clear that their objection to the clergy's action in this field was as strong as that to the nobility's. In fact, it may have been stronger. For the burghers could suspect that the moral authority and judicial privileges enjoyed by tax-farming clergymen would make it even harder for the cities to resist them (in case of abuses) than many members of the noble class. In any case, their objection to the gathering of taxes by churchmen indicates most emphatically that other motives than religion were determining the cities' position on this issue.

That the cities disapproved of both clerics' and nobles' involvement in the gathering of the revenues no less than they opposed that of the Jews seems again to be indicated in the petitions they submitted in the Cortes of Medina del Campo (1305). These petitions again reiterated the demand that Jews be forbidden to serve as collectors, supervisors of collectors *(sobre cogedores),* and farmers of taxes, and further stipulated that "neither *ricos omes* nor *caballeros* nor any other person" be allowed to farm the revenues.[6] It is at this point, we should note, that the king states the reason given by the petitioners for this particular objection—i.e., that this method of gathering the revenues would "lay waste the land."[7] To be sure, these effects were ascribed to tax farming regardless of who performed the task, yet the fact that the magnates and other *caballeros* were singled out for mention in this connection seems to indicate that they were notorious as harsh and injurious tax farmers. Perhaps this remark was prompted by the ruthlessness displayed by *some* members of the nobility in collecting the taxes they had farmed; in any case, it is clear that what the cities demanded in this Cortes, as in the preceding ones, was that tax farming be totally prohibited to both Jews and Christians and that the collection of taxes be entrusted to people who were "citizens and residents" of the towns *(vecinos et moradores)* and, apart from this, that the collectors be appointed by the cities.[8] They evidently saw in these measures a guarantee against frequent violations of their proprietary rights and illegal expropriations of the fruits of their labor, or of their inherited possessions.

In light of the above, it is not difficult to understand what is implied in the king's reply to a petition submitted to him on this matter in the Cortes of Valladolid, 1307:

> With respect to the request they made concerning the taxes [*pechos*] which they would have to give me—[namely,] that I refuse to have them gathered [from now on] by those who habitually collect them, nor by other people from outside the places [in which the taxes are to be levied], for [in this way] many wrongs are done to the land; and [furthermore] that I see to it that the taxes be collected by the towns' *caballeros and omes buenos* who should be men of substance, so that they may serve me *and guard the land from harm,* I say that I hold it for good that I appoint the collectors, and that these be rich and trustworthy *omes buenos* of the towns, and that no Jew be [from now on] collector or farmer of the revenues.[9]

Even though only the Jews are here mentioned among those to whom the prohibition applied, there is no doubt that some of the above terms (those "from outside the towns," and those who "habitually collect the taxes" and consequently cause, in the cities' opinion, "wrongs" and "harms" to the land) referred to the same groups which were described by the *procuradores* in previous petitions. And these included of course the aristocrats and the clerics, whose participation in the tax-gathering process the cities, as we have seen, had violently opposed. That the king now refrained from mentioning these groups and preferred to speak in general terms must be attributed to his political concerns—i.e., to his desire to minimize offense to both the high nobility and the clergy, then actively cooperating with him in preparations for a war against Granada. Yet both the positive and negative parts of his decision—the assignment of the tax collection to townspeople only and the exclusion of all those who are "outside the towns"—made it quite clear that not only Jews, but also the higher classes of the Christian society fell within his prohibition.

All anonymity was dropped in the Cortes of Palencia (1313), in which the cities vigorously resumed the attack on various matters that concerned them, including taxes. Now, as on previous occasions, they were assured not only that taxes would not be farmed out but that no *caballero*, or clergyman, or Jew, or any "other mischievous persons" *(omes reboltosos)* would be engaged in collection of taxes.[10] The stipulation also indicates a definite hardening of the cities' position toward their "own" caballeros. Like all other members of the aristocracy, they too were now forbidden to engage in tax collection, which was hereafter left exclusively, as the king's reply specifies, in the hands of *omes buenos*. Two years later, in the Cortes of Burgos, this exclusion of the caballeros from the tax collection, even in their own places of residence, was allowed to suffer one exception: in Extremadura the caballeros of the towns were permitted by the cities, for an undisclosed reason, to collect taxes in their places of residence, as were the *omes buenos*.[11] But this provision, which was clearly presented as the sole exception to the proposed rule, only shows how stern and determined was the cities' opposition to the nobles' engagement in this field. In fact, their objections to caballeros, clerics and Jews either as farmers or collectors of taxes are repeated in this Cortes with special force.[12] With similar emphasis, though less comprehensively, the cities restated their position on the subject in the Cortes of Carrion, 1317. "No caballero, no cleric, and no Jew will farm any part of the revenues or the tributes which rightfully belong to the king."[13]

So great indeed was the cities' opposition to the nobles' participation in the gathering of the taxes that in the Cortes of Valladolid, 1322, they not only repeated this demand but also forbade the admission to the profession of any townsman who "lives or was friendly with any *rico ome* or caballero or lady of high rank," or with noblemen or ladies of lesser rights,[14] obviously because such townsmen might serve as media for the nobles' penetration into the tax-gathering system. No doubt many nobles used trustworthy townsmen as undercover agents to act as collectors—nominally on their own, but actually on the nobles' behalf—to circumvent the laws that prohibited the latter from acting as tax gatherers of any sort. The new stipulation regarding such townspeople was intended to stop that practice.

Similarly, the cities restated their objection to having clerics share in the collection of the revenues, just as they again reaffirmed their opposition to having Jews participate in that function. "Clerics and Jews" are again linked together as undesired persons in the field, and classed with them here are also the Moors, who seem to have entered the royal fiscal system, perhaps because they had not been specifically mentioned among the prohibited groups. Thus, the burghers' demand was now extended to read that "neither clerics, nor Jews, nor Moors be involved in the tax collection, and [furthermore] that the taxes not be farmed."[15] The request that tax farming be prohibited was of course meant to be general in scope, but the fact that it is mentioned alongside the interdict intended for the above three groups (i.e., clerics, Jews and Moors), and not mentioned in conjunction with the nobles, indicates, it seems, that by that time the nobility had withdrawn from the tax-farming business (no doubt because of the previous enactments)[16] and merely tried to retain, by various subterfuges, its reduced position in the field of tax collection.

In the Cortes of Madrid of 1329, neither the great lords (and the nobility in general) nor the clerics serve anymore as targets of attack in the burghers' petition on the issue of the taxes. From this we may conclude that under pressure of the cities, both the nobility and the clergy had abandoned tax collection and tax farming altogether. This left the field open to Jews and Moors, who hastened to increase their holdings in it. No wonder that Jewish and Moorish tax gatherers now attracted the fire of the burghers' criticism, and it is evident why the Jews, who were by far the main tax lords, both by tradition and experience, as well as by their greater financial power, were now singled out as especially ominous.[17] Faced for the first time with only the Jews as their main competitors in this field, the burghers soon concluded that unless they came up with some new solution to the problem of the revenues, they had no chance of winning the contest. They realized that the secret of the Jews' hold on the system lay in their excellent services as tax farmers, and that unless a suitable substitute was offered, the kings would continue to engage them. In consequence, the burghers made a major shift of policy and suggested, for the first time, that they, together with the towns' caballeros, be appointed as tax farmers and tax collectors.[18] It is significant that in responding to this petition, Alfonso XI gave a qualified consent to their anti-Jewish demands,[19] but failed to indicate any support for their proposal that the taxes be farmed and collected by the burghers. Evidently, he considered that proposal so impractical—or so inimical to his interests—that he refused to indicate any support for it, let alone commit himself to it to any extent.

That the burghers lost the contest with the Jews in this field, and that the latter became in the succeeding decades the only dominant factor in tax farming (and no doubt, as a result, also in tax collection), is evident from the petition the cities submitted to the king in the Cortes of Burgos of 1367. Complaining this time merely that the king (Enrique II) farmed out to Jews the debts that the cities owed for past taxes, without making clear what the farmers and collectors still owed the treasury, the cities asked the king that an order be given to collect the latter debts first, and that this collection be farmed out to "Christians who may enjoy the king's favor."[20] Significantly, this time there is no indication of the class or kind of Christian tax farmers that the cities would approve of, and certainly there is no insistence that they be "trusted sons" of the cities concerned. It is obvious that the cities had failed to build a tax-farming system of their own, and that after ousting the nobles and the clergy from the field, they could not put forward members of their own groups as potential tax farmers. Their suggestion that unspecified Christians ("whoever might be acceptable to the king") assume the responsibilities involved indicates only that they themselves could not propose anyone for the task, and merely hoped that some Christians, of one class or another, might be willing to accept the position. But that such a hope was unrealistic is evident from the following response of the king:

> The truth is that we have ordered the said revenues to be farmed out
> to Jews because we have not found any others who would take it
> ... but if some Christians would *like* to take it, we would order to have
> it given to them for a much smaller amount than the one for which it
> was farmed to the Jews.[21]

Like the petition itself, the response indicates the collapse of the burghers' campaign on this issue and the total exposure of their abortive plans to offer substitutes for Jewish tax farming. Indeed, there were no substitutes. In the Cortes of Toro of 1371, in which the cities' attack upon the Jews reached a new peak of ferocity, the burghers again demanded that Jews be denied the right to farm taxes,[22] but made no counterproposals to compensate the king for his expected losses. It is clear that what the cities wanted was not only to remove the Jews from tax farming but—as they had stated time and again—to have the whole institution abolished and deny this activity to non-Jews no less than to Jews. What they wanted was to have the tax gathering performed

only by *tax collectors chosen from their own fold*. Indicated in this was no doubt
distrust for anyone outside their own communities—whether Jew or non-
Jew—and self-defense against abusive exploitation of their own members by
outside elements. Yet there is no doubt that apart from this, the cities sought
to secure for themselves—or rather for their rich and leading citizens—the
profits to be derived from managing the tax collections. Eager as they were
to lay their hands on any source of income that the state could provide, they
were especially anxious to control those sources to which they saw themselves entitled by right. Regardless of the arguments they presented to the
king—which emphasized their care for the interests of the Crown, no less
than for the "land," which they sought to protect—it is obvious that the
economic advantage referred to was very much on their minds. Those who
paid the taxes, the cities felt, were entitled to the benefits derivable from that
payment.

This feeling, we should add, was steadily intensified by their general
jealousy for their independence, by their intense desire to run their own
affairs, and by their fierce objection to foreign interference—that is, to have
outsiders command or police them, determine their right to their possessions
and thereby dictate their economic fortunes and indeed control their lives.
By "foreigners" and "outsiders," it must be understood, the cities meant
anyone outside their corporation—that is, who did not belong to their
commune—whether or not he lived inside their walls. Consequently, this
"alienship" applied to anyone who was not legally bound by the city's
decisions. In the case of taxes, the burghers' struggled against "alien" controls
of their material assets and "alien" impositions upon their economic life.
Thus, their opposition to the Jews in this area was rooted in the same
interests and considerations that motivated their opposition to the nobility
and the clergy, except that the alien status of the Jews was felt by the
burghers more keenly, and therefore aroused stronger antagonism, for reasons to be discussed below. Even so, the cities' opposition to the Jews was
inseparable from their general objectives. Hence it remained essentially, in
all circumstances, a secular rather than a religious opposition. It was part of
the far larger, centuries-old struggle that the cities had been waging, in Spain
as elsewhere, for economic and political self-determination.

IV

In view of the above, one might consider it superfluous to demonstrate that
the cities' appeals to the kings to bar all public offices to Jews stemmed
likewise from social, economic and political rather than religious interests.
Yet so much stress has been laid by most historians on religion as the prime
cause of those appeals that one feels duty-bound to examine this claim from

every possible standpoint. One is further impelled to make such an examination in light of the fact that the cities' demand that the Jews be denied the right to public office was the primary and best-known postulate of their anti-Jewish policy.

Forming part of the imperial legislation since the days of Theodosius II (418–438), and reinforced by the decisions of the Third Toledan and Fourth Lateran Councils (589; 1215), the proposed measure to bar the Jews from public office was in full consonance with established Church law. It was obviously meant to be applied more stringently against holders of high public office than against low-grade officials. Yet the kings of Castile disregarded this intent and, as we have seen, kept appointing Jews to the highest positions in their court and administration. King Alfonso VI initiated this tradition,[23] and when Pope Gregory VII found it necessary to remind him that Jews should have no authority over Christians,[24] the king simply ignored the papal reproof. In fact, the engagement of Jews as courtiers and high officials became such common practice in Castile that future popes would not even issue "reminders" on this matter, evidently because they realized that their protests would be slighted and their complaints remain, to the discredit of the Church, a mere exercise in futility.

The first time the cities of Castile demanded that Jews be excluded from *all* offices at Court, and not only from the gathering of the king's revenues, occurred during the minority of Fernando IV in the Cortes of Valladolid, 1295.[25] To be sure, the Jews were the only group explicitly mentioned as unacceptable for these positions; yet two other demands the cities made on that occasion show that their requested change in the officialdom touched also others besides the Jews. What they wanted was no less than the removal from the Court of all the favorites and officials of Sancho IV (the previous monarch), most of whom belonged to the higher estates, with the possible exception of some of them, whom the Regents and the cities would consider suitable.[26] Never had such an audacious demand been presented by the cities of Castille, and its far-reaching implications can be properly assessed only in conjunction with the reported fact that the cities had appointed certain *omes buenos* to choose, with the Regents, the new candidates for office.[27] There can be no doubt that what the cities wanted was that most officials of the Court be not only approved by their *omes buenos*, but be in fact members of the urban upper class. Thus, their objection to Jews serving at Court was not a specifically anti-Jewish position, but, like the stand they took on tax farming, part of a much larger issue, involving, besides Jews, the nobility and the clergy. In fact, what it reflected was the cities' aspiration to take over the entire central administration from its royal governors and rulers, Jews and non-Jews alike. It was a struggle for control, for power, and for the perquisites of office, not for religious values.

In the Cortes of Valladolid, 1312, King Fernando IV, in his reply to the cities' petitions on this question, avoided criticism of his officials—clearly, not to show consideration for any plan to discriminate against them in the governance of the kingdom.[28] But during the minority of Alfonso XI, when the government was run by a divided regency, the cities returned to press the same demands with renewed and even greater vigor. Again we hear them urge (in the Cortes of Palencia, 1313) that no Jew be allowed to assume any office at the Court of the king and repeat, in this connection, the old Church argument that Jews, as officials, do much harm to Christians by their deceitful claims and impositions.[29] This sharp denunciation of the Jews (as Jews) does not, however, alter the fact that, in the same Cortes, the cities again urged the removal of the nobility from almost all the positions at Court. Moreover, they insisted that the Council of Regency, which was planned to comprise twenty members, should include sixteen representatives of the cities and four nobles, none of whom were to be favorites or courtiers of the former King (Fernando IV) and only such as would be acceptable to the cities.[30] This audacious demand, which obviously meant to eliminate the nobility as a political force, was matched by another, no less audacious, which was aimed at achieving the same objective. Essentially, it was the same demand that the cities made in 1295, but this time spelled out more clearly, so as to leave no doubt that what they sought was a permanent arrangement and not a stop-gap to cope with a temporary emergency. Thus, the cities demanded that the offices of the Court, which were traditionally occupied by the high nobility, such as the offices of *camarero, coperero* and *portero mayor,* as well as all the other offices of the Court, be placed in the hands of townspeople (*caballeros* and *omes buenos*),[31] and, on top of this, they demanded that the judges and *escribanos* serving at Court on behalf of the various "kingdoms" be all *omes buenos,* and that such be the *merinos,* who must be also natives of the regions or provinces for which they were appointed.[32] In brief, what they demanded amounted in effect to a revolutionary change in the whole system of government: a total takeover by the cities of the royal administration—central, regional and municipal alike.

That this was indeed what they wanted to achieve, and that their attempts to oust the Jews from their royal offices formed part of their effort to deny these offices to all nonburgher elements, was further confirmed in the Cortes of Valladolid, 1322. In this Cortes the cities were asked to support the Queen's new plan—i.e., to have the Infante Don Felipe serve as "tutor" to the young king, and thus as the de facto head of government. The cities seized the opportunity then offered them by the divided and weakened regency, and approved the Queen's proposal on condition that the new tutor extend their administrative controls and strengthen their grip on the national government. They now stipulated that the Supreme Council of State should be enlarged to comprise twenty-four members, *all* of whom should be representatives of the cities (*caballeros* and *omes buenos*) and that these should examine and determine all matters that came before the king.[33] This means that the cities now saw an opportunity to clear the highest echelons of government of all baronial and clerical elements by refusing admission to the Supreme Council even to the small minority of *ricos omes* to which they had consented in 1313. The cities of course repeated their demands that the notaries at the King's Court and all the judges and *escribanos* in the country be chosen from their own people[34]; but to make their hold on the government more secure, they now also demanded that all alcazars and castles in the royal cities be governed by members of the local communities (i.e., *caballeros* and *omes buenos*), and not by members of the landed aristocracy, as was the common practice until that time.[35] All this attests the aggressive policy that the cities followed in their quest for control.

It would be surprising if in this Cortes the cities had not launched an attack upon the Jews—or rather upon the Jewish officials in the administration. And indeed, after stipulating that the holders of the king's seals must be chosen only from his subjects in the cities,[36] they presented the demand that "neither clerics nor Jews nor any one who represents them" be allowed to hold a post in the chancellery, in the notaries, in the Office of the Seal and all other offices that pertain to the chancellery."[37] All these posts must be manned by city people; the clerics and Jews who now serve in them must be dismissed; and should Don Felipe refuse to act accordingly, the cities would cease to recognize him as tutor and withhold their support from him.[38] This extraordinarily strong formulation made it clear that the cities were not prepared to temporize or compromise on this issue; but, again, it should be noted that the cities' demand extended not only to Jews but to representatives of the Church, including prelates[39]; and hence it was not zeal for Christianity that dictated this stipulation but major secular-earthly concerns—namely, the desire to attain full control of all key positions in the state.

In the next few decades the cities made no demands to eliminate the Jews, the clergy and the nobility from the offices of government. But this does not mean that they had changed their attitudes toward the Jews and the other estates or their political and economic aspirations. In the days of Alfonso XI's majority and those of his successor, Pedro I, it was simply inconceivable for the cities to dictate the structure of government to these strong monarchs. In this period, indeed, the influence of the cities declined, and that of the Jews and the other estates rose, in the royal administration. It was only in 1367, under Enrique II, before the conclusion of the Civil War, that the cities resumed, at the Cortes of Burgos, their attack upon the Jews in positions of power, and accompanied this attack by a renewed effort to penetrate the highest echelons of government. We must, however, note the new tactics that the cities employed on this occasion. Having abandoned the extravagant demand that the nobles and clerics be banished from the administration, they now merely asked for twelve *omes buenos* to be included in the royal Council, not as replacements but as an addition.[40] On the other hand, they now abandoned all restraint in their complaints against the Jews. They plainly demanded that all Jews be ousted from the royal court and the courts of all members of the king's family, justifying this demand by the many evils, injustices, deaths and evictions that "the cities suffered in the previous reigns at the counsel of Jews who served as favorites or officials of the kings."[41] It is significant that while the king responded positively to the first request (namely, the addition of *omes buenos* to his Council), he totally rejected the second. "Never, he said, "was such a petition presented to any of the other kings of Castile."[42]

Such requests, as we have seen, had been presented in the past, not once but several times, even though they were actually addressed not to kings but to regents. The king must have known this, and his response indicated a search for excuses in support of his reply. But the burghers were not deterred by his rejection. Several years later, in the Cortes of Toro, 1371, they renewed their attempt to penetrate the king's Council, though in a more cautious way. This time they did not demand the inclusion in the Council of any fixed number of their members, but only some of their citizens that the king would find fit.[43] But they intensified their attack upon the Jews and demanded their ouster from all the offices—that is, not only from those of the royal adminis- tration but also from the administrations of the nobles.[44] What we see here was no doubt a change of tactics, not of general goals. There are enough signs to indicate that the cities were slowly redeveloping their attack upon the nobility and their drive to replace it in the administration. It was precisely because they had to exercise caution and restraint with respect to the nobles that they strengthened their assault upon the Jews. It meant hitting the system at its weakest point and trying to establish their position in govern- ment by first replacing the Jews. But Enrique II would not yield. In the Cortes of Burgos, 1377, however, he formally acceded to one request of the cities: the Jews would not occupy any more positions in the administrations of the nobles.[45] By this concession, the cities not only came closer to their goal with respect to the Jews; they also struck a blow at the nobles, whom they always regarded as their major adversaries and whom they wished to strip of their great economic and political power.

V

What has been said about the attitude of the cities toward Jewish occu- pancy of high offices in general, and the offices of revenue gathering in particular, can be said about their attitude toward other rights and privileges that the Jews had received from the kings of Spain. The special status the Jews had been enjoying in the country's judicial system was perhaps as characteristic of the Jewish condition in Spain as the functions they fulfilled in the royal administration. Certain that the society in which they lived would be reluctant to treat them fairly and equally—and, in fact, would be inclined to discriminate against them—in legal clashes between them and its Christian members, the Jews of Spain asked for and received the right to have their legal disputes with Christians heard by special judges appointed by the king. These judges would take into consideration Jewish as well as non-Jewish law; and no case could be decided against any party on the basis of Christian or Jewish witnesses alone. Inevitably, these arrangements complicated procedures and often blocked the execution of justice, but they helped protect the Jews against legal action originating in prejudice, or in the natural desire of the Christian communities to guard the interests of their members.

From the standpoint of the cities, however, such privileges constituted a violation of their basic rights. As permanent residents of their territories, they reasoned, the Jews should be subject to *their* laws; they should appear before the ordinary judges, who handle the cases of all residents; and a Christian plaintiff should not need Jewish witnesses to have his case against a Jew validated in the courts. Consequently, the cities incessantly endeavored to abolish these judicial rights of the Jews, while the Jews steadily resisted these endeavors and generally succeeded in heading them off. No doubt they managed to convince the kings that if this legal shield were removed, the Jews would be frequently denied justice and their life in the city would become precarious, if not altogether impossible. Nevertheless, there were several exceptions, notably in Toledo, Seville and Murcia, where the cities succeeded in breaking this rule, which had been firmly upheld in the rest of Castile, and the king had to stipulate in their *fueros* that, save in disputes related to tax farming, Jews who had litigation with Christians should have their cases tried by the city judge.[46]

These concessions, which isolated cities wrested now and then from the Castilian kings, paved the way for the general demand that the cities finally presented in Cortes for a similar nationwide arrangement. In 1286 they gained at least a partial and temporary victory when Sancho IV agreed to end the appointment of special judges for the Jews and instead to assign one of the local judges to deal "separately" with Christian-Jewish litigation. The new setup lacked the prestigious status of the special court that dealt with such litigation and also reduced the chances for the judge to be neutral, since like all local judges, he was an *ome bueno*, aspiring to gain or retain the friendship of his fellow Christian citizens. However, since he was appointed by the King, and therefore responsible to the Crown for his decisions, he could be

expected to treat fairly both sides. Even so, Sancho IV ordered the judge to
take into consideration both Christian and Jewish law, so that in "mixed"
cases "the Christians would have their law *(derecho)* and the Jews theirs."[47]
Actually, however, the balance of the compromise tilted heavily in favor of
the cities, even though the requirement of mixed testimony apparently
continued to be enforced.

It seems, however, that the law was interpreted to mean that the Jews had
the right to *choose* from the local judges the one who would decide their
conflicts with Christians—a right which gave them considerable leverage—
and it was this right that the cities now tried to rescind in order to abolish
the "separate" court. They failed in their attempts at the Cortes of Valladolid
in 1351[48] and again at the Cortes of 1385, which met in the same city.[49] That
the kings repeatedly rejected their petitions indicates how vital this remnant
of the old privilege was considered for the Jewish community in Castile. It
was only in 1412, with the total collapse of the Jewish social and legal position,
that the cities finally attained their goal in this particular area, too.[50]

Now, ostensibly this struggle of the cities to abolish the judicial privileges
of the Jews in their litigation with Christians seems to be related to the Jews
qua Jews; and indeed if we consider the letter of their petitions, this seems
to have been the case. Actually, however, all this was merely part of a broader
struggle, waged by the cities for their judicial independence and a reflection
of their determination to subject to their laws *all persons outside their communities* who had any dealing with their citizens or residents. Thus, the cities
demanded relentlessly not only that all their judges should be sons and
residents of the places where they exercise their duties,[51] but also that the
judges at the King's Court should be *omes buenos* from the King's towns, who
would safeguard the rights of every litigant and the *fueros* of every group and
place.[52] Above all, they demanded that if any "grandee, caballero or hidalgo,"
or any nobleman of whatever rank, have a claim against plebeians of a royal
domain, that he present it "according to the fueros of the defendants and
before the judges of their locality." Only if dissatisfied with the decisions of
these judges could the nobles appeal to the King's Court for a retrial[53]; but
this Court, too, was packed with *omes buenos,* in whose fairness the nobles put
little faith when it came to conflicts between members of their own class and
members of the third estate. This is why they demanded to be judged by
nobles only, in accordance with the old law and custom; and in the Cortes
of Burgos in 1271, Alfonso X yielded to this demand.[54] Nevertheless, Sancho
IV was compelled to rescind this decision of his father when he responded
affirmatively to the cities' petition in the Cortes of Valladolid, 1293.

And no less symptomatic of the cities' jealousy for their judicial independence, and their stern opposition to any interference with or encroachment
upon their legal system, were their repeated rebukes of the *ecclesiastical courts*

whenever they tackled secular cases. It was the wish of the *procuradores* that all prelates and vicars and commanders of religious orders be forbidden to adjudicate in cases that did not fall, clearly and directly, under their jurisdiction, and that no layman should dare to summon another layman before any ecclesiastical judge.[55] Moreover, the cities demanded, and were assured by the king, that "no cleric or man of a [religious] order should be allowed to summon [before an ecclesiastical court] any layman from the king's domain, according to orders received from Rome, in disputes over landed estates or [other] temporal matters."[56] If they have a claim against any layman with respect to a temporal matter, they should present it to the King's Court, according to the fuero of the person involved, but if they themselves sentence any layman, or attach any part of his property, their sentence and action cannot be recognized as valid and should be opposed by the local judges.[57]

It is clear that the cities wanted their own judicial system and their own laws to serve as the only legal means by which their citizens could be judged when claims against them were made by outsiders who were not subject to the local laws (such as the nobles and the clerics), and it is clear that they wished to extend this procedure also to cases that involved claims of their citizens against outsiders. Hence, the cities' opposition to the Jews' special rights in the field of judicial procedure was in line with their opposition to any judicial privilege that would give the barons and the clergy an advantage over their own citizens.

Tied up with their struggle against separate courts for Jewish-Christian litigation was their opposition to the Jews having their separate *escribanías*. The cities wanted the Jews' legal documents to be prepared by the public notaries *(escribanos)* that each city council had at its service. This meant that all legal instruments that were to serve the Jews in their business transactions would be subject to the discretion of officials of the councils, in whom the Jews had little confidence. The king had rejected this demand of the cities, first voiced in the Cortes of Burgos (1301) and again in that year in the Cortes of Zamora[58]; and it had never been raised at Cortes since then. Perhaps the cities believed that this goal could be achieved only with the abolition of the separate courts. In any case, the desire to abolish the separate *escribanías* was not a passing phenomenon. As with respect to other institutions, the city's attitude toward the "Jewish" *escribanías* reflected their firm, abiding determination fully to control this important vehicle of legal and economic activity. Thus they repeatedly demanded from the king that he appoint as *escribanos* in each place only townspeople (later: *omes buenos*), that he *remove from them any cleric* occupying the post of *escribano* and, finally, that he forbid clerical *escribanías* to serve the needs of laymen.[59] Indeed, the struggle to place the work of the *escribanías* entirely in the hands of *omes buenos* left numerous and very clear traces in the proceedings of the Castilian Cortes. But here again, even more than in other issues, it was directed not only against the Jews but also—and far more—against other elements, notably the clergy. There is no reason, therefore, to assume that in this as in similar matters, the cities' position was determined by anything but economic and political interests.

VI

Only a few more remarks are needed to conclude this discussion. The prohibition against the acquisition by Jews (and Moors) of landed property in the urban territories, first petitioned by the cities of Castile in 1293,[60] seems to be of religious origin. Yet despite the religious overtones heard in these petitions, the prohibition involved did not stem from religious interests. What motivated the cities' stand on this matter was primarily their objection to having city property fall into the hands of outsiders. Their repeated requests to prohibit the acquisition of landed estates in the city by noblemen, clerics and members of religious orders, all of whom were subject to outside jurisdiction,[61] offer sufficient support of our thesis that the cities' objection to the acquisition of similar property by Jews reflected the same position.

That the struggle against the Jews was essentially motivated by social and economic, rather than religious considerations is further evident from the cities' position on other controversial matters. In a petition submitted at the Cortes of Valladolid, 1312, the cities claimed that more than five thousand rich Jews were freed from any payment of taxes; they demanded that these "exceptions" be abolished and that from then on *all* Jews share the burden of taxation.[62] Exemption from payment was one of the special privileges of the nobility, and the aforesaid demand, like many others, was aimed at eliminating the wealthy Jews from the position of a privileged, special class, similar to that of the Spanish aristocracy. But it also aimed to open new sources of income for the royal administration and thus reduce the fiscal pressure on the cities. Fernando IV, to whom the petition was addressed, responded in a noncommittal manner, but shortly thereafter, following his death, the demand was renewed in the Cortes of Palencia (June 5, 1313) and approved by the Infante Juan, guardian of Alfonso XI.[63]

That the cities were anxious to have the nobility share a greater burden of the state's fiscal obligations goes without saying; but it was only in the days of Enrique II (1373) that the monarchy first responded to this wish and began to impose on the aristocracy payments from which it had hitherto been exempt.[64] In the Cortes of Zamora, 1432, the cities complained that the prelates, clerics, abbots, and other ecclesiastical persons were shielding communities and individuals from the obligation to pay taxes on the grounds that they were exempt from such payments by virtue of privileges or customs[65]; and in the same Cortes they demanded action against the numerous newly declared caballeros, originally *omes de poca manera* who had acquired noble rank for the sole purpose of avoiding the payment of tributes.[66] The matter is again taken up in the Cortes that met in Valladolid in 1442, in 1447, and in 1451.[67] It is clear, then, that the cities sought to broaden the tax base and that their attacks upon the exemptions of rich Jews signified a general tendency in this regard, which received partial royal support in the late 14th century and, as we have noted, came to full expression in the century that followed.

Thus, we see a fundamental equality between the cities' position toward the Jews on issues relating to law, tax farming, offices, property acquisition and exemption from taxes, and their position on all these issues toward the nobility and the clergy. Even their demands for a low rate of interest were not based on a specific attitude toward the Jews and were not directed solely against them.[68]

Moreover, the same attitude prevailed not only in the cities but in other social entities, and in times preceding the establishment of Cortes in the Castilian kingdom. The very fact that for two full centuries—from 1050 to 1252—the Jewish question was hardly discussed in the Spanish legislative assemblies (in which the cities were not represented) is in itself a clear indication that the policy toward the Jews was not, in the main, determined by religious considerations. For the Spaniards in those centuries were certainly no less Christian and the Jews no less Jewish than they were in later times. Furthermore, the same attitude was reflected not only in the secular legislative bodies but also in the ecclesiastical ones. From 1137, religious matters were dealt with separately by Church councils, presided over by dignitaries of the Church and not, as in earlier times, when the governmental councils, which dealt with both ecclesiastical and secular matters, were presided over by the kings. Thus, Jewish affairs were now to be dealt with by two independent legislative bodies; and what is symptomatic and revealing in this respect is that the Jewish question came up for discussion, for the first time after a long period of silence, not in the religious but in the secular assemblies—that is, in the Cortes of 1252. In fact, the Church councils were mute on the Jewish question for almost the entire preceding two centuries, including the period of more than a century in which they assembled without secular overlordship. They continued to keep silent for the next two generations (from 1252 to 1313).

That the Spanish Church took such an attitude at the time when the cities' *procuradores* at Cortes were launching repeated attacks against the Jews and trying to dislodge them from their positions offers further proof that it was not ecclesiastical but secular forces—and, more precisely, the cities of Spain—that impelled the anti-Jewish drive and sustained it throughout this period. Therefore, when we see the Church Council of Zamora, 1313, taking

an anti-Jewish stand for the first time, we must conclude that it was under
the influence of the cities—and the inflammatory agitation they had conducted for decades and reached a special height in that very year—that the
Church finally decided to move in the same anti-Jewish direction. In other
words, the Catholic hierarchy in Spain was for hundreds of years aligned
with the kings and the nobility, and not with the people. This does not mean,
of course, that the sentiment of the population was not shared by many of the
clergy, especially those of the lower ranks. It was. But it took a radical change
in the social circumstances for the Church to join the general attack upon the
Jews.

IV. Debacle and Transition

I

The views voiced in Cortes by the *procuradores* embodied the cities' formal demands. But the cities' population was not of one mind. Its upper strata sought to achieve by agitation and by petitions to the king (both in and outside Cortes) the enactment of new laws that would limit the Jews' rights and narrow their spheres of activity. In other words, they sought to reduce the Jews' position—social, economic and political—by legal means. The lower strata wanted the Jews out of the cities, and were ready to use the most brutal methods, especially when the rulers of the cities—their spokesmen—failed to get substantial concessions from the king in response to their anti-Jewish demands. Nevertheless, they would not dare attack the Jews unless the city leaders joined them in the assault, while the latter, even when inclined to aid the masses, would not take the course of naked aggression without the support of some great nobiliar force. Such support, however, they rarely received; and in consequence, all classes of the Christian urban population felt paralyzed in a way when they wished to fight the Jews. What held them in this state of impotence, they knew, was their fear of the king and the great nobles, who all seemed committed to the Jews' defense. Their chance of attacking the Jews, they realized, lay only in a serious disruption of relations between the monarchy and the nobles who stood behind it.

Such a chance arose unexpectedly out of a chain of unforeseeable developments. Alfonso XI, king of Castile, had died in the great plague (1350) and the throne was occupied by his son Pedro. Relations among the heirs of the departed king were poisoned, and they infected the great nobles associated with them. Inevitably, these relations led before long to rifts among various nobiliar factions, and these rifts, in which the king became involved, eroded his prestige and the popular affection on which royalty in Spain usually relied. This was the background of the ensuing troubles and the ultimate collapse of the king's power.

The king himself was another source of growing unrest in the kingdom. Perhaps never before was Spain in greater need of a self-controlled, wise and patient ruler who might allay the apprehensions, distrust and ill will that dominated the conflicting parties. But Pedro I was not such a ruler. He was impetuous, headstrong and exceedingly sensitive about his royal rights and honor. Above all, he was moved by the same factionalism that imbued the main nobiliar contenders. He belonged, from the outset, to one of the parties, and so did his leading guides and counselors.[1]

When Pedro ascended the throne he was fifteen years old and under the influence of his chief minister, Don Juan Alfonso de Albuquerque, who had been his tutor, and of his mother, María de Portugal, the estranged wife of Alfonso XI. Albuquerque was an able statesman, highly educated and devoted to the King, but was prone to see in political opponents personal enemies who ought to be removed. María, a hard and vindictive woman, shared his jealousy and intolerance. Shortly after Pedro's enthronement, she ordered, no doubt with her son's consent, the arrest and execution of her rival, Leonor.[2] But the foul act backfired. It aroused deep resentment among the great nobles who had been close associates of Alfonso XI and friends of his assassinated mistress. Judging by the evidence, only Leonor's sons, especially Enrique, Count of Trastámara, displayed tendencies of rebellion,[3] while some of the nobles expressed their opposition merely by criticisms of the regime. The main target of these criticisms was Albuquerque, the mastermind of the government's policies, who assumed virtually dictatorial powers. Under his influence, young Pedro soon treated all critics as rebels who must be destroyed. In the purge that followed, many nobles were seized and brutally dispatched without trial.[4] This stamped Pedro in the eyes of many, from the outset, as a ruthless, lawless and tyrannic king.

The reign thus began with vengeance and bloodshed, the twin evils that marked its whole course; and it was unfortunate for the Jews that the initiator of this course was Albuquerque, their staunch defender. Albuquerque brought into the royal administration his own financial steward, Samuel ha-Levi, and made him *Tesorero Mayor* of the realm.[5] Don Samuel became a great favorite of the King,[6] so much so that he dared take a stand against his patron, when Albuquerque clashed with the King on an issue that caused a break in their relations. Don Samuel actually replaced Albuquerque as the King's chief favorite and minister. He also became a member of the Royal Council[7]—an appointment dictated by his manifold responsibilities and his close friendship with the king.

Don Samuel was one of the foremost courtiers the Jews of Christian Spain had ever had. Only Joseph de Écija and Abraham el Barchilon possibly matched him in influence.[8] Both his rapid rise to honor and power and his tragic fate after ten years of service cast their shadow on the period of transition which ended with the catastrophe of 1391.

Don Samuel assumed his high royal office when Spain was still smarting from the afflictions of the plague, and popular hostility to the Jews was rising in both Castile and Aragon.[9] To be sure, in 1350 Spain did not permit such atrocities against the Jews as those perpetrated in Savoy, Switzerland and Germany during the Black Death. Of all regions of Spain, only Catalonia witnessed assaults upon the Jews during the plague[10]; Castile saw no evidence of them. But this does not mean that hostility to the Jews was milder in Castile than elsewhere in the peninsula. The petitions addressed to Pedro I in Cortes (Valladolid, 1351) gave clear evidence of this attitude.[11] The cities demanded that the Jews be segregated, live in separate boroughs, and be marked off as inferior both in appearance and in civil rights. Thus, they asked the King that Jews be forbidden to use Christian names, wear precious clothes, and engage Christian nurses for their infants.[12] It is amazing that such matters occupied their minds at a time when the kingdom was beset with urgent problems touching the health, security and livelihood of the great majority of the people.

Indeed, from the proceedings of the same Cortes we learn that the country was filled with bands of brigands who, "fearing neither God, nor the king, nor his punishment," caused "many deaths, destructions of Churches, highway robberies, thefts, rapes, abductions and imprisonments," so that one could no longer feel safe in his domicile.[13] As for the economic condition of the people, we can assess it from the fact that the procurators petitioned to repeal the law enacted in the Cortes of Alcalá (1348) forbidding the Jews to lend money at interest.[14] So barely three years after they had won the hard-fought battle of "Jewish usury," the cities abandoned the fruit of their victory and requested the restoration of the *status quo ante*. What could prove more decisively the hollowness of their claim, repeated by them for over a century, that the Jews' lending money at interest had ruined them (and should therefore be prohibited) or demonstrate more clearly the flimsiness of their pretext (the Church law by which they "justified" that demand)? Now as before, what they sought to attain was relief from their material woes and hardships, which stemmed from a half-feudal economy that could not adapt itself to the nascent mercantilism, but which they blamed, out of hatred, on the Jews, whose offers of credit could only alleviate—though by no means remove—the evils of the system. One cannot fail to be astonished at the insolence, as well as the absence of any sense of shame, manifested in their efforts to degrade the Jews while seeking to get vital help from them through renewal of the moneylending they had so reviled. No wonder they asked the King to withdraw the permit the Jews had received to buy land (near the Duero) as a substitute source of income when their right to lend money was abolished.[15] Not only did they want the Jews to be allowed to engage in the "sinful" profession; they apparently sought to have them placed in a condition that might compel them to engage in it extensively.

The royal response to the aforesaid petitions was virtually negative. The King, his answer said, would look into the matter and act in accordance with what would serve his interests and the interests of the land.[16] The royal response represented, in effect, the decision of the chief minister, Albuquerque, "through whom were made and passed [at the time] all the decrees of the Kingdom,"[17] while the latter's moves with respect to the Jews were made, in all likelihood, after having been approved by his friend and counselor Samuel ha-Levi, now treasurer of Castile. Many Jews must have come to the conclusion that moneylending under the new conditions was a most uncertain business. In view of the cancellation of a quarter of all debts owed by Christians to Jews under contractual agreements,[18] and the repeated moratoria decreed on these debts by Alfonso XI since 1345,[19] moneylending came closer to loss than to profit, and there was no clear reason for the Jews to engage in it and give up their right to buy land. Indubitably, the cities saw a Jewish influence in the King's unsatisfactory response to their petition, as well as in his refusal to grant the moratorium they requested on debts "owed by Christians to Jews."[20] That Don Samuel was believed to have inspired these answers may be taken for granted.

It was perhaps already at that time that Count Enrique saw in the King's pro-Jewish policy and the growing influence of Don Samuel at Court an excuse to stir up public hatred for Don Pedro and a way to mobilize support for himself—if, in contrast to the King, he appeared as the Jews' enemy and the champion of the people's cause. It was not easy for him to take such a stance as long as the government was run by Albuquerque. But when a rift developed between the minister and Don Pedro, and Don Samuel took the King's side, Enrique thought that the opportunity he was waiting for had at last arrived.

The cause of the rift was Albuquerque's choice of bride for the young King of Castile. Both he and Pedro's mother, the strong-willed Queen, wanted him to marry Blanche of Bourbon, niece of the king of France. Pedro, however, was then enamored of the daughter of one of his second-rank nobles—María de Padilla—whom he may even have secretly married. Forced by Albuquerque and his domineering mother, Pedro went through a marriage ceremony with Blanche, but left his wife two days after the wedding in favor of his paramour, María de Padilla.[21] His mother was furious. She would not allow her son to repeat the same evil that his father, Alfonso, had committed against her. Albuquerque supported her for political reasons; and drawing to their side many nobles and cities, they thought they might compel the young prince to mend his ways and smother a burgeoning scandal. Actually, they managed to split the kingdom and bring it to the verge of civil war.

To be sure, Albuquerque and the widowed Queen did not intend to topple Pedro's rule. But some of the nobles gathered around them may have fostered conspiratorial schemes. Such schemes, in any case, were doubtless on the mind of Count Enrique de Trastámara who, rather incredibly, joined the party of Queen María, the presumed murderess of his mother. Enrique would permit no moral principle, no consideration of decency and honor, to hinder his political ambitions. His goal was to destroy Don Pedro and replace him as king of Castile.

Carefully concealing his real aims, he appeared in the guise of defender of Queen Blanche, whose wounded honor he was out to restore. He intended to transform the widespread disapproval of Pedro's mistreatment of his wife, the Queen, into a national anti-Pedro mood, which might soon assume a rebellious character. Before long he confided his plans to some friends, who must have approved them and promised support. For he finally decided to make a bold move which, he hoped, would lead to insurrection.

His plan was to capture Toledo, in whose alcazar Queen Blanche was held prisoner, and turn it into the headquarters of the rebels and a rallying point in defense of the Queen. He enlisted the aid of his brother Fadrique who, as Master of Santiago, could place at his disposal some troops of his great military order. The decision to act was probably taken before May 1355, when Enrique met his brother at Talavera, accompanied by a small army.[22] It may have been prompted by the King's arrival in Torrijos (only five leagues from Toledo), which aroused their suspicion that he was going to Toledo to transfer the Queen from the alcazar of that city to a better-guarded fortress. As this would have wrecked their entire plan, they resolved to act without delay.

Approaching Toledo at the head of eight hundred cavalry, they were met outside the city by the local nobility, who inquired about the purpose of their coming. They had come, they answered, in fulfillment of their pledge to aid the people of Toledo to defend Queen Blanche. It seemed to them that the Toledans might need such aid now, since the King, who was in the neighborhood of Toledo, might come to the city and cause harm to the Queen. The caballeros replied that, at that very moment, their emissaries were trying to influence the King to take a more conciliatory attitude toward the Queen, and if at this point they were to receive his brothers, along with their military force, into the city, they might undermine the delicate negotiations.[23]

This exchange took place near the Gate of San Martín, the principal entrance to Toledo, and ended in a stalemate. The Count and the Master could not persuade the caballeros to open the gate to their troops. But other Toledans, who were no doubt anxious to have Count Enrique among them at the time, guided him to the Gate of Alcántara, which apparently was under their control. There the brothers entered the city, and immediately saw to it that all the gates of Toledo should be placed at their command.[24]

Pero López de Ayala, the historian of the reign, who wrote his *Crónica de Don Pedro* after having joined Enrique, offers us no coherent account of the Count's first moves in the city. His narrative, however, contains some intimations which, combined with other extant data, are sufficient to convince us that what then happened in Toledo was part of a well-prepared plan.

According to Ayala, the nobles of Toledo were unevenly divided in their attitude to Enrique, but only a few were prepared to help him. While most nobles turned to the alcazar, where they sought to defend themselves and the Queen, some of them went to the Jewish fortress to aid its Jewish defenders.[25] This suggests that Enrique, upon entering the city, revealed to the nobles his plan to turn it into an anti-Pedro stronghold. That he failed to obtain their approval of his plan is apparent from Ayala's account of their reaction, as well as from the fact that when the King regained the city, he did not punish a single nobleman. In contrast, he imposed draconian sentences on many commoners for having collaborated with the Count. Yet it is unlikely that this collaboration, which amounted to an actual rebellion against the King, was agreed on by distinguished men of the community within a few hours after the Count's arrival. Enrique must have been in touch with their spokesmen well before he came to the city, and it was no doubt they who opened to him the Gate of Alcántara.[26]

The night following his arrival in Toledo determined the fate of his adventure, for during that night Enrique attempted to capture the *judería* of the city. Undoubtedly, the attempt was part of his plan to seize Castile's capital city, as it was impossible to hold Toledo without controlling its walled Jewish borough. Enrique was anxious to accomplish this task as quickly as possible, since he was aware that the King and his army were only five leagues away from the city. The *judería*, he reasoned, must be captured before Pedro learned of what was happening in Toledo and could come with his army to its rescue. Obviously, every hour counted. Nevertheless, before assailing the fort, he ordered his soldiers to attack the smaller *judería*, known as Alcana, which was situated beyond the main Jewish quarter and was not protected by any fortification. The soldiers, Ayala adds, "robbed and killed the Jews they found there, men and women, adults and small children, to the number of 1,200 souls."[27]

What was the purpose of this terrible massacre, which cost precious time, delayed the attack on the main *judería*, and thereby endangered the entire undertaking? Ayala's *crónica* says nothing to explain this. Enrique's reasons, however, can be clearly gathered from the sequence of his activities in Toledo and his published motives on similar occasions. The massacre of the Jews was meant to secure for him the support of Toledo's Christian populace, which was bursting with anti-Jewish feelings, and this is why he gave it first priority on his Toledan agenda. But this was not all he expected to gain from it. In fact, by that action he sought to demonstrate to all Spaniards where he stood on the Jewish question and thereby enlist the support of all Jew haters in all the towns and cities of Castile. From what we know of this Toledan affair, we must conclude that the plan of the Alcana massacre had likewise been known to his collaborators in the city and approved, if not advised, by them before he came to Toledo.

When the fortified *judería* was attacked, the Jews and some of the loyalist nobles defended the borough with fierce determination. No sign of surrender was shown by the besieged even when the assailants began to penetrate the fortress through several breaches they made in the walls.[28] The outcome of the struggle now depended solely on the defenders' capacity to hold back Enrique's troops. But matters did not come to that crucial test. King Pedro, informed of what was happening in the city, rushed to the aid of his faithful subjects. When he came to Toledo, he found all its gates firmly held by Enrique's men, and he had to storm the bridge of San Martín and set the wooden gate on fire. But at the same time he did something else. Fearing that the resistance of the *judería* might be crumbling, he ordered three hundred of his troops to attempt an entry into it from the side where the Tagus was its natural barrier. The river was exceptionally shallow that year, and the King's men were therefore able to cross it with the aid of cords the Jews had thrown them from their ramparts. That is, says Ayala, how Pedro's soldiers joined "those of his party in the castle of the *judería.*"[29]

Enrique, who failed to prevent the King's entry, was soon forced into headlong retreat. He left the city as he had entered it—that is, through the gate of Alcántara—and made his way in the direction of Toro, where many discontented nobles had assembled. Pedro was in no hurry to follow him. He first saw to it that Queen Blanche should be removed from the alcazar of Toledo, where she was imprisoned, to the castle of Sigüenza, which he now placed under more trustworthy command.[30] Then he looked for Enrique's supporters and imposed harsh penalties upon the culprits. He executed some of Enrique's men who had been left behind during his hasty escape and sentenced twenty-four leading citizens *(omes buenos)* to death. According to Ayala, these men were thus punished for "having conspired with Enrique to rouse the city in revolt."[31] Nevertheless, it seems that they were punished for their share in the Alcana massacre too, both because it was a major crime that Pedro, as king, could in no way tolerate, and because the destruction of the Jews was regarded by the rebels as a means and an end of their insurrection. In the Letter of Forgiveness that he sent to the city on October 12, 1355 (almost five months after the uprising), from his army camp besieging Toro, Pedro excluded from forgiveness the Toledan Moors and ten Christian individuals, all commoners, for having committed outrages against "my Jews."[32] The above exceptions, together with the death sentences he issued against the *omes buenos,* as well as the fact that no death sentence was pronounced against any of Toledo's nobles, show that Enrique's base of popularity was among the common people. There could be no reason for that popularity at the time except for Enrique's presumed intention to destroy Toledan Jewry. Undoubtedly many of Toledo's Christians favored that intention. They viewed the elimination of the Jews from the city as their reward for supporting Enrique's party.

This fierce anti-Jewish mood was not limited to Toledo. Enrique used it to build a following for himself in other cities as well. In consequence, he soon became known as the standard-bearer of the anti-Jewish movement, and support for his political position became identified with opposition to the Jews. The most violent Jew haters among the cities' lower classes were inclined to flock to his banner, and where the city's nobility was aligned with Enrique, the masses—in accordance with their habitual reaction—were emboldened to plan bloody assaults upon the Jews. This is what happened in Cuenca.

Alvar García Albornoz was a leading nobleman who, in the days of Alfonso XI, was closely associated with the king and his mistress Leonor de Guzmán. He raised their young son Don Sancho (b. 1340) and now kept him under his protection in Cuenca, which was the base of his political power. He and the clique of nobles about him were considered Enrique's natural allies, and Cuencans of all classes became vociferous critics of King Pedro and his regime. We do not know whether the urban elite intended to take part in Enrique's plan; but they probably tolerated, if they did not encourage, the popular outbreak against the Jews in Cuenca. In any case, that outbreak reflected Enrique's wishes, was in full accord with his schemes and aims, and of course betrayed a rebellious stand against King Pedro.

Unlike the atrocities committed in Toledo, those perpetrated against the Jews of Cuenca occurred without Enrique's presence and without the aid of outside soldiers. They were the work of the citizens of Cuenca themselves, who could not possibly have achieved their ends without the knowledge and consent of the local nobility. Both the invasion of the *judería* and the capture of its towers, where many of the Jews had fled for shelter, could not be accomplished without causing Jewish casualties along with massive plunder; but, in addition, some Jews were imprisoned and others, men and women, banished from the city on the ground that they supported the position of the King.[33]

Pedro left Toledo for Cuenca, intending to stifle the agitation there against him and punish the assailants of the Jews. But fearing his punishment, both nobles and commoners shut the city gates against him. Cuenca was a strongly fortified place, and Pedro knew he could not take it by assault. To reduce it under siege would take a long time, and Pedro was anxious to go to Toro, where his chief adversaries, headed by Enrique, had assembled under his mother's aegis. He therefore concluded an agreement with Albornoz, by which he undertook to withdraw from the city and pardon its citizens for their misdeeds in return for Albornoz' and the city's commitment to stay loyal to the Crown. The King kept his promise regarding the pardon,[34] and the blood of the Jews shed in Cuenca was to remain unrequited.

Pedro was not admitted to Toro, but took the city after a long siege. He allowed the Queen Mother to leave for Portugal after he had killed several nobles in her presence.[35] He also granted Enrique, who had escaped to Galicia, a safe-conduct to France.[36] When Albornoz, the lord of Cuenca, learned of the fate of the Toro conspirators, he feared that the King would now return to his city and punish him for his alliance with the rebels. He made haste to take young Sancho, his protégé, and leave with him for Aragon.[37]

II

Pedro was now at the height of his power. His four-year conflict with the nobles of the opposition had ended in his complete victory. His financial condition appeared promising as his treasurer, Don Samuel, had developed new methods for the collection of the revenues.[38] Pedro, it seemed, could now enjoy peace; but this was not to be his fate, or the fate of Castile during his reign. Less than a year after his victory at Toro he was embroiled in a war against Aragon—a bloody and costly war which lasted ten years and ultimately led to his ruin.

P. E. Russell, whose study of Don Pedro is rich in illuminating data, tried to place responsibility for the war on Aragon's king, Pedro IV, called by his people the *Ceremonious*.[39] The truth, however, is that the king of Castile was the main instigator of that war. It was legitimate for Don Pedro to seek satisfaction from Aragon for an offense against his honor and Castilian interests committed by one of Aragon's ship captains, but he placed before the Ceremonious such "terms of satisfaction" as no self-respecting monarch could accept.[40] Furthermore, it was the Castilian king who had started the war by invading Aragon, and thus he was clearly the aggressor. Had he not attacked Aragon as he did, there would probably have been no war.

These are plain facts that cannot be ignored; and yet they do not explain everything. The remaining question is: What was behind the facts? National interests or personal impulses? Some modern historians believe that the truth should be looked for in the first direction,[41] while earlier scholars, including the old chroniclers, opted for the second.

Thus, according to Ayala, Pedro rushed into the war because he was an addict of combats, "because he had always loved wars,"[42] whereas Balaguer, in his *Historia de Cataluña* (1860), says that it was the "impudence of a Catalonian mariner and the haughtiness of D. Pedro *the Cruel* of Castile that ignited the war" between Castile and Aragon.[43] This does not mean, however, that Pedro's assumed faults were not shared in large measure by his antagonist. In fact, Balaguer, in his final assessment, seems to apportion blame equally to both kings; both, as he put it, were known to have "demonstrated tendencies of domination, rage, and arrogance," and both were "at bottom desirous of the war."[44] This view approaches that of Zurita, who attributed to both kings "ferocious spirits bent on vengeance rather than on clemency."[45]

Pedro attacked Aragon by both land and sea and carried the war into the enemy's domain. He emerged victorious from most battles and took from Aragon many towns and much land; but the war dragged on for five years, and finally, in May 1361, Pedro concluded a peace treaty in Terrer by whose terms he was to return to Aragon all the towns and territories he had captured.

What moved Pedro to make a treaty by which he lost all that he had gained in five years of hard and bitter conflict? Several theories have been advanced,[46] but none of them seems satisfactory. The answer may be found in the impact of three factors (financial, political and military), and three personalities (Samuel ha-Levi, Count Enrique and Juan Fernández de Henestrosa) whose misfortunes, failures, or achievements at the time influenced Pedro's decision.

Juan Fernández de Henestrosa was uncle of María de Padilla, Pedro's beloved since his youth and later his legally recognized wife. Undoubtedly the King's most trusted counselor, he was Major Chancellor of the Secret Seal *(Sello de Poridad)* and one of Castile's chief military captains. Zurita says that the "King of Aragon hated him intensely, as he was blamed more than others for inducing Pedro to persevere in his stand [against Aragon] and continue in the prosecution of the war."[47] In September 1359, however, Henestrosa died in the battle of Araviana, and the war party of Castile had thereby lost one of its most passionate advocates. It is possible that without Henestrosa's influence, the protagonists of peace managed to sway Pedro to listen more attentively to their counsels.

Enrique de Trastámara was certainly the chief villain in the drama of Pedro's life. From the moment he reached France in 1355, he kept denigrating Pedro as "King of the Jews," who had delivered Castile into their hands, as was evidenced, so he claimed, from the activities of Don Samuel, whom Pedro appointed Chief Treasurer of the kingdom and virtually chief ruler of the country. Moreover, Enrique spread the story that Pedro was actually the son of a Jewess who was exchanged for the King's newborn daughter with her own mother's consent.[48] From the time of his arrival in Aragon, as ally of its king (August 1356), he continued to disseminate these calumnies against Pedro, which were carried into Castile and avidly repeated there. At the same time, he kept portraying himself as champion of the rights of his Christian countrymen and as enemy of their Jewish oppressors.

He also demonstrated this enmity in practice. While fighting on Aragon's side, he invaded Castile in March or April 1360, at the head of a thousand horse and three thousand infantry, and occupied some towns on the right bank of the Ebro which were the home of old Jewish communities. On reaching Nájera, he urged its Christian citizens to join his soldiers in massacring the Jews. "The killing of the Jews of Nájera," says Ayala, "was ordered by Count Enrique because the people [of the town] did it willingly and because the very deed made them fearful of the King and consequently led them to take the Count's side."[49] He employed the same method of gaining adherents also in other places he seized, among them the town of Miranda de Ebro, whose Jewish community, like that of Nájera, dated from the 11th century. Don Pedro, who moved eastward from Burgos, forced Enrique to retreat toward the border, but while pursuing his enemy he stopped at Miranda because the Christian residents of the town, as Ayala tells us, "had robbed the Jews there and joined the party of the Count."[50] The word "robbed" in the statement just cited does not indicate merely a sack; it stands for a pogrom that included a massacre, as may be gathered clearly from the broader account in the *Crónica Abreviada*. According to this *crónica*, the Christians of the town "robbed and *killed*" their Jewish neighbors and "joined Enrique's party."[51]

Thus, as in Toledo five years before, Enrique now believed that he could gain the people's aid by showing himself as the nemesis of the Jews. King Pedro, on the other hand, considered it his duty to see to it that justice be done and that those who killed and robbed Castilian Jews be treated as rebels. Convinced as he was that only great fear might arrest tendencies to break the law, he inflicted frightful punishments on the culprits. Thus, he executed in Miranda de Ebro at least five of the town's citizens, probably the organizers of the pogrom, one of whom he ordered to be boiled and another to be roasted in his presence.[52] These gruesome punishments curbed the pogromist movement, but they increased the people's hatred of Pedro and augmented Enrique's following.

This is precisely what Enrique expected. Both his invitation to assail the Jews and Pedro's harsh treatment of their assailants served his purpose; for both increased his popularity in the cities, especially among the lower classes. All this was made possible because hatred of the Jews had reached such extremes that killing them was no longer considered a crime by the majority of the populace; in fact, it was regarded as commendable—an act which "the people did willingly," as the historian Ayala affirms. Enrique recognized these facts and concluded that they could be of great use to his campaign.

Only a few historians who dealt with Pedro's reign paid due attention to the major part played by antisemitism in Enrique's rise to power and, consequently, in the radical change that took place in Castile's dynasty and the condition of its noble class.[53] What ought to be especially emphasized in this connection is the fact that Enrique was the *first nobleman in Spain to use antisemitism as an instrument of propaganda and a means of attaining political control.* In later times other Castilian nobles would follow in his footsteps.

Pedro no doubt realized that Enrique's campaign against the Jews was a maneuver conducted against him, but he knew of no strategy by which he could defeat it. It may indeed have occurred to him that because he was losing the war at home, he could not win it abroad.

III

Pedro's inability to cope with the Jewish question eventually left its mark on his administration, which was run, virtually from the start of the war, by Don Samuel ha-Levi. Toward the end of 1360, his relations with Don Samuel must have taken a sharp turn for the worse, and soon deteriorated to a point where Don Samuel was imprisoned, charged with embezzlement, and tortured to exact from him detailed information about the hiding places of his treasures. He died under the hands of the King's torturers, probably around the middle of 1361.[54]

What was it that so radically changed the king's attitude toward the man who was his "very great favorite," who stood by him during all his tribulations and followed him in the thick of his struggles? The old chroniclers do not offer much to go by, and modern historians have dealt little with the question, as if the issue involved was of minor importance and had no bearing on the fortunes of the reign. Most likely, however, it had a great bearing, for it must have affected Pedro's state of mind and the crucial decisions he took at the time.

Amador de los Ríos evidently attempted to solve the mystery of Don Samuel's death. He did not offer a hypothetical explanation which, in view of the limits imposed by the sources, would be the most that could be expected; but his inquisitive mind led him to pose several important questions. Why did King Pedro destroy his Jewish favorite? "Did he propose," asked Amador, "to remove all pretexts for the libelous rumors by which he was defamed in both Castile and abroad? Did he aspire to satisfy the complaints of the clergy? Did he pretend at last to change his policy toward the cities which were oppressed by Don Samuel's severe administration?" Or perhaps could "such a disruption of relations and such a death be explained, as some have claimed, only by the King's avarice?"[55] To these pertinent queries of Amador a few more may be added. Was Don Samuel's sudden downfall connected with the state of Castile's finances? Was it related to Castile's military condition? Did it have anything to do with the peace treaty with Aragon that Pedro was about to conclude? These queries go beyond the Jewish question, as well as the specific tasks of treasurer which Don Samuel performed in the administration. Since the case of Don Samuel touches the fate of the last great Hispano-Jewish courtier, we shall digress for a moment to consider the activities and, what is more important, the general situation of the Jewish courtiers in Spain.

IV

The common view of this situation is based on the assumption that the functions of the Jewish Chief Treasurers in Spain were limited to the provision of funds. But this prevalent assumption is wrong; and perhaps no other misconception related to the subject has done more to obscure historical reality. It must be conceded that almost any Jew who reached the high position of the King's Chief Treasurer was endowed not only with financial skills, but with a broad understanding of various problems affected by the realm's economic condition. Some of these problems touched foreign relations, including decisions on war and peace, and the Chief Treasurer was impelled by the duties of his office, if by nothing else, to make his views on all critical developments known in due time to the King. This was the source of the close contacts that evolved between the monarchs and their Jewish financiers. But it was also a source of bitter resentment that some Christian courtiers, whose authority was affected, felt toward the Jews' frequent interference in the spheres of their own responsibility.

Yet the close association of the Jewish treasurer with the King, and the advice he gave him on a great many matters, also involved him in the internal conflicts of the realm. It was natural for the King to trust and consult one group of nobles more than the others, and since the Jewish courtier had no choice but to side with the party of the King's favorites, he inevitably made their opponents his enemies. Thus he became involved in fierce power struggles, which he was often believed to have affected by his influence on the King or on some of the grandees. Despite the scanty remarks on this subject in the medieval Spanish chronicles, it is apparent that the Jews' participation in Spain's politics was constant, and sometimes far-reaching.

We have touched on one of the important factors that made the condition of the Jewish courtiers in Spain at once strong and precarious. Don Samuel ha-Levi was not the first Jewish courtier to be executed by a Castilian king. He was preceded by two others who were sentenced to death by Alfonso X (one of whom was the famous Çag de la Maleha), and by Samuel ibn Wakar, who died under torture while imprisoned by Alfonso XI. It is hard to conjecture, and impossible to determine, how the deadly intrigue against any of them started and who was instrumental in promoting it. Since the Jewish courtier faced the constant enmity not only of his rivals (usually nobles) but also of the burghers who sought to replace him, as well as of the Church, which denied his right to office, plans for his removal from the royal Court could be contrived in many quarters. Yet we do not know of a single Jewish treasurer or any other Jewish high official at Court who resigned his position of his own volition. They realized that they were on dangerous ground, and yet they refused to abandon it. Why?

Material gains alone cannot possibly explain this stubborn adherence to such hazardous positions. Other factors were involved which must be taken into account. The striving for equality and a dignified status—which was latent in the thinking of all Jewish minorities—was given in the particular circumstances of Spain an opportunity to be realized more than elsewhere. The Jewish courtier symbolized that opportunity and, in a way, fulfilled that striving. Then there was the political urge, which had been awakened early in the life of Spain's Jews and became intensified in the course of generations—an urge which is stronger than any possible menace to life, health, and fortune. In addition, most of these courtiers felt that the opportunity afforded them by their position to wield influence upon the King was the one strong shield protecting their community against the designs of its enemies. It was a call of duty they could not ignore.

V

Don Samuel must have encountered the same difficulties that were met by other Jewish officials and experienced the same hostile reaction from various Christian sources. It may even be assumed that the hostility for him was especially intense and widespread, since the tasks he performed in the governance of the kingdom were more numerous, and touched the interests of more people, than those performed by his Jewish predecessors. The Spanish sources do not say a word about his activity in foreign affairs, but two non-Spanish documents (one Hebrew and one Portuguese) attest his efforts in this field.[56]

Even more far-reaching must have been his involvement in the internal conflicts of the realm. Early in his association with the royal Court, he had to take a stand against Albuquerque, the king's half-brother Count Enrique, and their various powerful allies. Other crucial issues raised in later years must also have forced him to take similar positions, and inevitably he became the target of denunciations by nobles and commoners alike.[57] Even if he had not served a king like Pedro, who was, to say the least, controversial, the mere occupation of his high office was sufficient to make him, as Jew, a target. But he did serve a king whose ruthless behavior made the task of his minister all the more difficult, and this in the midst of a civil war, when feelings of hatred ran high on all sides and when a Jewish official could easily be accused of many of his king's misdeeds. That he was not responsible for Pedro's atrocities need hardly be pointed out; but that he was often believed to have had a share in them cannot be doubted either. What produced that belief was the rising antisemitism that then pervaded Castilian society, as well as the fact that Don Samuel's influence was in many spheres truly decisive. Not only the Jew haters but also the Jews considered him the leading minister of Castile. In their view, he held the highest place ever attained by a Jew in Spain.[58]

It was virtually inevitable that so great an influence confronted with such a fierce hatred would lead to tragic consequences. But besides the above factors which worked for that end, Don Samuel was beset by a further difficulty of a particularly disturbing nature. This was the ruthless competition he encountered from other Jewish courtiers.

Here, too, we touch a phenomenon that was not peculiar to Don Samuel, but common to many royal courtiers who arose among the Jews of Spain. Politics breeds jealousies, hatreds and fierce struggles in all peoples and at all times, and the Jewish magnates of Spain, like all seekers of power, did not always achieve their goals by fair means. Nevertheless, in Spanish Jewry these contests had long been controlled—that is, limited to forms that did not endanger the lives of the contenders. Gradually, however, they became more ferocious, and in the generation of Don Samuel, if not decades earlier, they assumed a murderous character. Perhaps it was the enormous wealth gathered by Jewish courtiers from tax farming that raised the passion for power of some of them to levels heretofore unknown in Spanish Jewry; or it may have been the influence of the Spanish nobility, which seldom shrank from the use of foul means in order to attain selfish ends. Be that as it may, Don Samuel ha-Levi, like Don Joseph de Écija and others before him, was confronted with insidious plots fomented by his Jewish rivals.[59]

According to the *Sumario de los Reyes de España*, "several Toledan Jews, jealous of the favor the King had shown Don Samuel," told the King that Don Samuel was the "richest man in the world," because he has "robbed your Kingdoms for more than twenty years." They suggested that the King should ask him for the money he had stolen from his revenues, and if he refused to comply, put him to the torture. As the story goes, the King asked Don Samuel for a loan of two thousand gold marks, which he badly needed as dowry for his children. The King also suggested that the loan be paid from the taxes the Treasurer was about to gather. Don Samuel's response, however, was inflexibly negative: he could not lend the King even a single mark. Infuriated, Don Pedro ordered his arrest.[60]

The legendary character of this story, as well as its antisemitic theme, scarcely needs demonstration. Its purpose was to depict the Jewish Treasurer not only as an embezzler who had robbed the Spanish people, but also as an ingrate, a person so mean as to refuse even a modest loan to the King, his benefactor, when the latter found himself in financial straits. The charge of embezzlement has never been proven, and no doubt merely rested on the immense fortunes discovered in Don Samuel's possession.[61] But this discovery in itself cannot explain his arrest any more than the clearly fictitious assertion that he had rudely refused the King's request for a loan. Don Samuel no doubt acquired his great wealth from the profits he amassed during his long service as Treasurer (of both Albuquerque and the King) and from the investments he made with those profits. He had no need to resort to illegal means to become a millionaire, or even a multimillionare, and he would not have been so rude and foolish as to refuse the King a personal favor, which he could easily do. But if so, the puzzling question remains: What caused the breach between the King and his favorite and the quarrel that must have preceded it?

Ayala, who devotes a chapter in his *Crónica* to Don Samuel's imprisonment and financial assets, does not say that his incarceration was based on a charge or suspicion of fraud. In fact, he does not tell us what the charge was. But the arrest of Don Samuel, along with all his relatives, and the immediate confiscation of their possessions, was in accordance with the King's treatment of culprits whom he had sentenced, before their imprisonment, to death.[62] We must therefore assume that Don Pedro's harsh sentence against his Chief Treasurer sprang from some fault he ascribed to him, and that this alleged fault was viewed by the King as highly injurious to the realm.

If our analysis of the sources has led us to reject the oft-repeated notion that Don Samuel's fall was due to his misappropriation of the King's revenues (a notion dismissed, among others, by Amador[63]), our attempt to present a more plausible reason is based on a hypothetical explanation. Our hypothesis relates the downfall of Don Samuel to a major event that occurred at the time—namely, the cessation of the war with Aragon and Pedro's consent to the Peace of Terrer. We have asked: What moved Pedro to sign that humiliating peace? And the answer, we believe, should be looked for in Castile's economic condition.

VI

Don Pedro, in all likelihood, suddenly discovered that his treasury was exhausted and that he was financially in no position to continue the war, or even keep all the places he had won from Aragon.[64] While immersed in his battles against the enemy, Pedro relied on his able Treasurer to supply him with the funds necessary for the war; and Don Samuel undoubtedly did his utmost to meet the King's financial needs. But following the failure of Pedro's naval effort (June 1359), which was preceded by the costly provision of his fleet, and the losses his generals suffered in Castile (Sept. 1359), Don Samuel must have found that the kingdom's resources were in an extremely precarious state. We may assume that the King presented to him one day, following his extensive counter-attacks, which carried him back to the far north (Nájera, April 1360), a plan for a new land campaign based on the mobilization of additional forces. This of course required a large outlay of money, and the King may have proposed the imposition of new taxes. Don Samuel, however, who knew the people's mood and how weary they were of the endless war, was also well aware of their economic hardships and the shortages under which they labored. He may have realized that it would be next to impossible to exact heavy taxes from them at the time. Consequently, he may have opposed the King's proposal and sought to lead him gradually to the conclusion that the best solution for Castile under the circumstances was to find a way out of the war. Don Pedro, enraged, may have accused his Treasurer of failure to apprise him in due time of the kingdom's true financial situation, thereby endangering—or even annulling—his triumphs and the sacrifices of the army. We may imagine other arguments tossed in both directions, but the result was that the King became disenchanted with Don Samuel, and accused him of criminal negligence and a desire to end the war against his wishes.

This, we believe, may have been the main cause of the rupture between the two men, and this may have provided the historic kernel of the account we have cited from the *Sumario de los Reyes*—namely, that the conflict between Don Samuel and the King evolved from a quarrel over money.[65] There may have been, however, also another cause which served to deepen the breach, and that cause, too, may have been reflected in the *Sumario*'s story.

VII

Pedro no doubt felt that he must do something radical to counteract the charge that he was "king of the Jews," fighting a Jewish war, and bleeding the people to attain Jewish ends. Perhaps it was under the impact of that feeling that he resolved to remove Don Samuel from his post. He began to look for a suitable excuse to dismiss his most able and devoted servant, and this inclined him to listen to the hostile hints that Don Samuel's rivals, Jewish tax farmers and courtiers, directed against him from time to time. Encouraged by the King's altered attitude toward his favorite and his willingness to hear accusations against him, one of these courtiers may have suggested that Don

Samuel could not have acquired his huge fortune legally and hence that he must have stolen large sums from the King's revenues. Don Pedro was certainly too shrewd to attribute any substance to such charges, but in his agitated state of mind at the time, he could have been induced to permit an inquiry into the assets of his Chief Treasurer. Understandably, Don Samuel was so offended by the suspicion and, above all, by the way he was treated by Don Pedro—the king whom he had served so devotedly and unflinchingly—that he refused to answer his investigators' questions. He was transferred to Seville, where he was put to the torture, but he retained his pride—and his silence—to the end.[66]

Perhaps Don Pedro expected the investigation to end differently.[67] In any case, he was now freed from the embarrassment that the powerful Jewish minister had caused him by his very position in the government. Baer says that Don Samuel's place was filled by other Jewish tax experts.[68] But this is not true. Pedro did not appoint as Chief Treasurer any of the Jewish courtiers or financiers who had intrigued against Don Samuel and hoped to replace him. Nor did he appoint any other Jew to that office. His new *Tesorero Mayor* was a Christian, Martín Yáñez de Sevilla, and "all the revenues and the tax-collections of the Kingdom were now under his control."[69] This was the conclusive proof Pedro gave his countrymen that he was neither a "lover" of the Jews nor their "instrument," and of course not a Jew himself. Both moves may have weakened the impact of the personal campaign conducted against him, although his enemies could still claim that his general policy remained pro-Jewish, without any noticeable change.

J. B. Sitges, who devoted many years to the study of Don Pedro's reign, and who carefully scrutinized almost every incident in the King's career, completely ignores his clash with Don Samuel, whom he nonetheless mentions on other occasions.[70] Sitges sought to rehabilitate the King and, above all, clear his stained reputation, and managed to produce a much fairer portrait of Don Pedro than that drawn of him in the *crónicas*. He presents Pedro as "right" in almost all the disputes where others considered him "wrong" and as "just" where he was generally viewed as "guilty," although here and there he does not pass in silence over acts of the King which he thought to have been foul. But regarding Pedro's punishment of Don Samuel, Sitges offers neither explanation nor criticism. He obviously did not accept the embezzlement theory and therefore could not justify the King's punishment of Don Samuel. Nor could he denounce that punishment, as he did not detect its real cause. Evidently, he misunderstood it. And his misunderstanding, as we see it, stemmed from his failure to discern the great part the Jewish question played in Spain's history during Pedro's reign.

VIII

Following the execution of Don Samuel, Yáñez, his successor, must have imposed new taxes and begun slowly, if not aggressively, to collect them, and Pedro delayed the withdrawal of his garrisons from most, if not all, of his captured towns. Perhaps the stalemate might ultimately have ended for Don Pedro in a less humiliating peace, leaving some of his Aragonese conquests in his possession. But if there was any prospect of such a peace, it was to prove chimerical in the end. What wrecked it was the interference of Enrique, Pedro's implacable foe.

Shortly after the Peace of Terrer, the Count left for France with a new set of arguments with which he believed he could persuade Charles V to lend him support in a drive to smash Pedro and take over the kingdom of Castile. This time the war, he was to point out, would be led by himself and not by the Ceremonious, who was too hesitant in his military moves and too dependent on the allocations of his Cortes. No doubt he also intended to point out Pedro's total financial exhaustion, indicated by his peace terms with Aragon and by his quarrel with Don Samuel, his treasurer. In addition, he could stress the disgust the people felt for Pedro's rule and his war, and assure Charles that one strong blow could now suffice to bring down the hated monarch and establish himself as master of Castile. All he needed from France was to allow him the use of the "White Companies"—that group of mercenaries committed to France's service, who were famed for their great fighting skills no less than for the atrocities they habitually perpetrated against the civil populations they happened to encounter. Enrique intended to assure their leader, Bertrand du Guesclin, one of Europe's great warriors, of rich rewards for his assistance.[71]

His negotiations with Charles and Guesclin ended well. France, embroiled in her endless war with England, wanted to remove from her southern border a Castile allied to England since 1362. But one major difficulty had to be overcome. To reach Castile, the notorious White Companies would have to pass through Aragon, and the Ceremonious would certainly be reluctant to permit this wild horde to descend upon his country. Enrique went to Aragon and persuaded the Ceremonious to open a narrow corridor for the passage of the mercenaries, in exchange for an enormous prize: he promised him that, once he became king, he would surrender to Aragon about a sixth of Castile.[72]

Pedro learned of the new negotiations between the Count and the Ceremonious, and of the latter's intent to accept Enrique's plan. Almost a year had passed since the death of Don Samuel, and in this period he managed to collect new funds and recruit troops for another army. He now had two courses open to him, and he chose the one that was more in accord with his pride, his ambitions and his bellicose nature. Instead of withdrawing his soldiers from Aragon, as he was obliged to do under the treaty of Terrer,[73] and combining them with his new recruits into a force that could meet the newly planned invasion, he decided to launch a lightning attack on Aragon directed at its capital, Saragossa, and aimed at controlling the country's north, where he might block the entry of the French. It was a wrong decision from every standpoint. Had he adopted the alternative solution, he would have denied the Ceremonious the support of his own people, who, like the Castilians, were tired of the war and were all hankering for peace. Pedro's sudden attack, however, gave the Ceremonious an indisputable reason to remobilize his people behind him.

Pedro opened his campaign with an attack on Calatayud, which surrendered to him after a long siege,[74] and thus cleared his way to Saragossa from the south. He chose, however, first to capture Tarazona, and thus threaten Saragossa from the northwest too.[75] The way to the capital seemed open to him, and yet he refrained from besieging it. Instead, he removed his main army to the south, capturing many towns on the way to Valencia, and finally reached that metropolis and besieged it.[76]

Several theories have been offered to explain why Pedro retreated from Saragossa and chose Valencia as his theater of war. The true reason was probably indicated by Balaguer, who pointed out that, at the crucial moment, the Catalonians were seized by a patriotic ardor and sent to Saragossa a large force of volunteers.[77] Pedro must have realized that under these circumstances, he might be bogged down in a long siege, which would deny him any concrete achievement; and he needed a decisive victory quickly to sustain the war effort of his countrymen. He therefore removed his army southward, where he thought he could gain such a victory. But here too he was unpleasantly surprised. The Catalonians sent Valencia a strong naval force, which bolstered its defenses and spirit of resistance.[78] Pedro eventually saw no sense in continuing the difficult siege of Valencia and withdrew from that city as well. Before long he found himself again exhausted, not only financially but also militarily, with no decisive victory to his credit and no concentrated force behind him.

The Ceremonious, however, was exhausted too, and this time he was ready to sign a peace which left Pedro with many of his conquests. This was a peace that Pedro could live with and that might actually save him from his predicament. But nothing came of it. Considering the peace terms too humiliating for Aragon, the procurators of Catalonia rejected them, and in consequence the treaty became null and void. Pedro remained stuck with a war he could not finish and could not continue either.

IX

It was at that moment that Enrique de Trastámara, with his White Companies, burst into Castile from its northern region. Since they were met with no opposition, the timing of the invasion could not have been better. Enrique must have correctly assessed the exhaustion and helplessness of his adversary. Upon reaching Calahorra, close to the border, he declared himself King of Castile, and shortly thereafter, on March 29, ordered his coronation in Burgos. On their way to this city, Enrique's mercenaries attacked the Jewish community of Briviesca, massacring its two hundred families to a man. As nobody bothered to give the dead burial, "their corpses," a contemporary author wrote, "served as food to the birds of the sky and the beasts of the field."[79] It can hardly be doubted that this massacre, too (like those of Alcana, Nájera and Miranda), was carried out at Enrique's order (or at least with his consent), as antisemitic slogans were still the watchwords of his anti-Pedro campaign. They appear even in the formal invitation he issued to his coronation, in which he accused Pedro of having "enslaved" "the whole land" by "raising as lords the Moors and the Jews" and "casting down the Catholic faith."[80] In further accord with his anti-Jewish policy, he imposed on the Jewish community of Burgos a fine of one million maravedis—well beyond the community's means[81]; and shortly thereafter he declared that all Christians were released from their duty to pay their debts to Jews.[82] No better encouragement was needed by the Christians in cities such as Avila and Segovia to attack the *juderías* and rob their residents of the documents attesting their indebtedness to Jews.[83]

Pedro hastened to Toledo with the hope of obtaining military aid there; but Enrique followed fast in his footsteps and forced him to retreat further to Seville. Upon reaching Toledo, Enrique, styled king, repeated the act of communal robbery he had perpetrated against the Jews of Burgos. Toledo's Jews, too, were compelled to pay him, within two weeks, 1 million maravedis—a payment which, as in the case of Burgos, exceeded their financial resources. Consequently, it left many of them destitute, while it doomed many others to enslavement.[84]

By the time Enrique came to Seville, Pedro had already left the city. He went to Gascony, then in English hands, in order to enlist the aid of England. He took with him a portion of the royal treasure, and sent its main part to Portugal in a riverboat commanded by his treasurer, Yáñez. But Enrique's agents in Seville, who followed Yáñez, caught up with him and took the treasure. Yáñez was brought to Enrique, who hastened to enlist him in his financial service. Was Yáñez in collusion with Enrique's robbers? The conjecture seems extremely far-fetched. But Pedro, who later sentenced him to death, may have suspected Yáñez of betrayal.[85] In any case, this entire episode, which helped, as we shall see, seal Pedro's fate, would most likely not have occurred if the treasure had been guarded by Don Samuel.

X

Enrique was now ruler of the whole country save Galicia, which remained faithful to Pedro. Believing that the war was virtually over, Enrique now concentrated on building his administration, and with the shameless cynicism and cold pragmatism that typified all his actions, he now reversed his policy toward the Jews. His antisemitic campaign, which had helped him achieve power, was no longer of any use to him, and he saw no reason to continue it. Consequently, he now looked for able Jewish financiers who could set up for him a tax-gathering system of the kind that had served the needs of his predecessors. Thus, during his visit to Seville he got in touch with two Jewish financiers who had *not* been associated with Pedro's administration and now expressed their willingness to work for him. They were the wealthy and well-known Sevillian Jews Joseph Pichon and Samuel Abravanel.

That Enrique entrusted the collection of his revenues to these men, and not to any of the Jews who held such offices under Pedro, was probably due to the latter's refusal to help Enrique in managing his affairs. As they must have been aware that Pedro was negotiating with the English in Bayonne to secure their assistance, they did not give up hope for his return; and, as long as such hope persisted, they could not enter the service of his enemy.

Like most Castile's Jews, they must have viewed with disapproval, if not severe criticism, the consent of Pichon and Abravanel to aid Enrique—the butcher of Alcana and Nájera and the robber of Jewish fortunes. From the outset, therefore, Pichon and Abravanel must have been opposed by the major Jewish tax farmers—a fact that no doubt hindered their efforts to enlist experienced tax gatherers to their service. Nevertheless, it did not take long before the various posts in Enrique's treasury began to be filled by Jews.

If Castile's leading Jews were dismayed by this development, the antisemites in the country were amazed and enraged. Consequently, "all the cities, towns and places" represented in the Cortes of Burgos (Feb. 1367) reminded Enrique of his former assertions—namely, that "all the evils, damages, deaths and banishments that took place in past times occurred because of the counsels of the Jews who were the favorites and officials of the past Kings" (a broad hint at Samuel ha-Levi). Accordingly, they petitioned Enrique that no Jew should be appointed to *any* office (including that of physician) in the Courts of the King, the Queen and the Infantes. Enrique answered that never had such a petition been addressed to any other Castilian king and that, although some Jews "move about in our Court *(casa)*, we do not include them in our Council" (in contrast to Pedro and Alfonso XI, who did place Jews— Samuel ha-Levi and Joseph Nasi—in their councils) nor "do we grant them such power by means of which they could cause some harm to our land."[86]

This, however, was not the only demand the procurators then raised with respect to the Jews. They also wanted the King to appoint Christians as commanders of the fortresses the Jews had been guarding in Castile and asked that the walls encircling the Jewish boroughs (such as those in Toledo) be demolished. They obviously sought to denude the Jews of their defenses and have their neighborhoods open to assault. Enrique, however, rejected their arguments that the Jewish command of forts was "harmful" to the Christians; nor was he moved by their mention of Toledo, which was meant to remind him of the troubles he encountered when he besieged that fortress in 1355. He flatly refused the petition on this score by indicating that he saw through the petitioners' intention. Fulfillment of their request, he said, would bring about the destruction of the Jews, and this would be to his disservice.[87] He was not, however, oblivious of his need to cater to the cities in *some* matters. In response to their requests that he cut by half the Christians' debts to Jews (since the other half allegedly represented concealed interest) and that a moratorium of three years be given for settling them (since many of their citizens had been made destitute by the war and the "exactions of the tyrant who called himself King"—i.e., Pedro), he reduced the debts by a third and granted a moratorium of two years.[88] These were important concessions of course, but far different from his call that the Christians not pay their debts to Jews at all—the call he had issued only a few months earlier, before he became king.

XI

When Enrique called the Cortes of Burgos he thought that his conflict with Pedro was over. But already at the closing sessions of that Cortes he learned that Pedro had swayed England to assist him and that an English invasion of Castile was imminent. And indeed, in March 1367, Pedro crossed the border accompanied by a strong force of Gascon and English troops, headed by the Black Prince, King Edward III's son, a renowned military leader. The Prince soon justified his great military reputation, when he roundly defeated Enrique's army in Nájera on April 13, 1367. Apart from many left dead on the battlefield, the enemy lost seven thousand prisoners. Enrique, however, managed to escape to Aragon, whence he proceeded to the French court.

The victory gained by Pedro and his allies removed Enrique from the Castilian scene but did not reestablish Pedro's national authority. Actually, control of Castile was now divided between Pedro and the Prince of Wales—

two strong men who did not see eye to eye on a number of major issues. In all probability, Pedro's inability to meet his financial commitments to the Prince lay at the bottom of their disagreements. Thus, the Prince refused to deliver to Pedro the seven thousand prisoners he took in Nájera, because many of them were men of great wealth who could pay him much ransom for their release; and the Prince was in great need of money to cover the cost of the expedition. It was perhaps partly for this reason that his troops were allowed to rob the Jews—robberies which were usually accompanied with bloodshed. Thus, in the course of these attacks many communities, such as Villa Diego, were annihilated, while others, such as Aguilar de Campo, were subjected to massive carnage.[89] So great was the terror which these soldiers struck in the hearts of Spain's Jews that many of the latter, to escape rape and murder, were converted to Christianity.[90] Apparently, Pedro could not prevent these outrages, as he had no power over the Prince's troops; and because of his strained relations with the Prince he may not even have tried to do so. His restoration to the throne, therefore, had in no way diminished the sufferings of Spain's Jews; rather it increased them and complicated their tragedy by the appearance of many converts. In the coming years, some of these converts may have played a special part in embittering the lives of their former brethren.[91]

Pedro made desperate efforts to extricate himself from his financial straits and pay his debt to his English allies; but all his attempts ended in failure.[92] The Prince of Wales, unpaid, returned to Gascony, full of contempt for Pedro and Castile, which appeared to him ready to be taken over. In fact he contrived, behind Pedro's back, to form an alliance with Aragon and Portugal, to partition Castile among themselves.[93] Rumors of his plans, which must have reached the French Court, may have prompted it to provide Enrique once again with a new army for the conquest of Castile. In May 1368, Enrique's forces, including many of the ransomed prisoners of Nájera, descended unexpectedly upon the prostrated country to subject it to further travails. To Pedro, this new invasion must have looked like a natural disaster. He knew he could not resist it.

Enrique now again advanced westward on the road leading to Burgos, but this time his advance was not marked by the sack or massacre of Jewish communities. Neither his own soldiers nor his French mercenaries, nor the townsmen of the cities through whose territories he passed, attacked the Jews, robbed or molested them, evidently because he had sternly forbidden them to cause the Jews any harm. When he now punished Jews, as he did in some places, it was only where they denied his authority and opposed him as rebels to their king. Thus, he imposed on the community of Burgos another enormous fine of one million maravedis—because they closed their fortress to his troops and compelled them to enter it by force.[94] He inflicted equal punishment on the Jews of Toledo (in May 1369), because they too shut the gates of their borough and fought him to the bitter end[95]; and a rebellious attitude toward his sovereignty must also have caused him to impose a heavy fine on the community of Palencia. The anti-Jewish outbreaks that occurred in Valladolid, Paredes and Jaén, when these towns declared for Enrique as king,[96] were doubtless not of Enrique's doing, but an expression of the sentiments of the local mobs, who believed that, by striking at the Jews of their cities, they were acting in accord with Enrique's wishes—the Enrique they knew from his premonarchic anti-Jewish campaign.

Enrique moved quickly on his southbound route without encountering serious resistance. It was only upon reaching Toledo that he met the first determined opposition, of which the city's Jewish community formed the hard core. Heavily reduced by starvation and disease, the defenders of Toledo were still holding out after eleven months of relentless siege, still waiting for their king, Don Pedro, to deliver them from their ordeal. While working in Seville on the recruitment of new soldiers and the building of a new army, Pedro decided to go to their aid before his work was completed. His force was considerable, some three thousand cavalry, but half of them were Moslems, who had no intention of risking their lives in battles between Christians. A surprise attack by Enrique and du Guesclin, who had been constantly watching his moves, forced Pedro to seek shelter in the castle of Montiel, which was soon surrounded by the enemy. Negotiating his escape with du Guesclin, he relied on the latter's false promises and allowed himself to be brought to his tent. There he met Enrique, who killed him in a struggle, but not without du Guesclin's aid.

XII

Pedro's reign left Spanish Jewry deeply wounded, impoverished, half destroyed. Except for Toledo, most of the punishment was taken by the northern communities. It was they who suffered most of the casualties, and it was they who experienced the agony of conversion out of despair and deadly fear. In the days of wrath to come, it was northern Spanish Jewry that was to show the least resistance.

Once Enrique was established as king, the situation of the Jews immediately improved. General security was soon restored and the Jews resumed their former position. Joseph Pichon, who in 1367 was still defined in the documents as a "Jew of the King's house,"[97] was raised to the high office of *Contador Mayor,* despite the promise Enrique gave the cities (in the Cortes of Burgos, Feb. 1367) not to appoint a Jew to any office that allowed him dominion over Christians. Indubitably, Samuel Abravanel too was given extraordinary powers, as were other Jewish tax experts who were charged with the administration of the royal revenues.

It is hard to believe, however, that the deep resentment that the leaders of Castilian Jewry felt for Pichon and Abravanel was dissipated during Enrique's reign. Both Pichon and Abravanel served Enrique throughout the long Toledan siege; and their support of Enrique in those frightful days increased the antipathy for them among the Jews. And yet, following Pedro's death, many Jews in Castile must have come to the conclusion that Pichon's and Abravanel's association with Enrique turned out to be of help to Spanish Jewry. Open criticism of them was no longer voiced among either the rank and file or the leadership. But the majority's evaluation of their characters, it seems, did not basically change; it was merely suppressed.

Not unrelated to that silenced criticism was the altered attitude that the great Jewish tax farmers must have taken toward Enrique's administration. They, who had occupied high posts in Pedro's treasury, had to swallow their pride and do work for Enrique under the command of the newcomers, Pichon and Abravanel. Along with these tax farmers there came into the Court many Jewish officials who served in related fields, and the royal treasury assumed its old form of a "Jewish" organization. The new rise of the Jews to authoritative positions sparked a violent reaction from the antisemitic elements, who saw themselves betrayed by King Enrique—the man they had so ardently supported because he promised to end Jewish influence in Castile. In the Cortes of Toro (Sept. 1371), they expressed their protest against the King's pro-Jewish policy in a fiery language perhaps never heard before in any Castilian Cortes:

> Because of the great license and power given to the enemies of the faith, especially to the Jews, in all our kingdoms, in the court of the King and the courts of the nobles . . . and because of the great offices and honors they have, which impel all Christians to obey and fear them and show them the greatest possible reverence, matters have reached the point that all the councils of the cities, towns and places of our kingdoms, and each of their individual persons, are in the captivity of the Jews—that is, subjected and terrified by them—both because they see the high ranks they hold and the honors they enjoy in the Courts of the Kingdom, and because of the gathering of the revenues which they control and the offices they occupy [in the administration]. For this reason, the aforesaid Jews, brazen and evil people as they are, enemies of God and of all Christians, perpetrate with great daring many wrongs and briberies, so that all our kingdoms, or their greater parts, are being destroyed and driven by the Jews to a state of desperation.

Then, after having presented the evils which the Jews, in their opinion, have brought upon the kingdom, the petitioners indicate the corrective measures they would like the King to take:

> Since it has been the kings' wish that this bad company live in these kingdoms, let them agree in their mercy that they [i.e., the Jews] be marked and separated from the Christians as God has commanded and as the laws have ordered—[namely,] that they wear signs as they do in other kingdoms, so that they might be recognized among the Christians and be less inclined to cause so much evil and do so much harm as they are presently doing. Apart from this, let the kings see to it that they have no office either in their own courts or in the court of any lord ... nor serve as farmers of the royal taxes—offices by means of which they commit, through their falsehoods, many violations of rights. . . . Since they have to live as bearers of testimony to the death of our Lord Jesus Christ, let them live and work only in the offices [that suit them and] to which they have been habituated, as they live and work in other kingdoms which some of them inhabit.[98]

No other petition addressed to Enrique exhibits so clearly the antisemitism of the time, the causes that imbued it with special ferocity, and the arguments employed in its support. The Jews are "brazen and evil people," who "perpetrate with great daring" many "falsehoods," "briberies," and "evils"; they "destroy the kingdom" and "drive its people to despair." They subjugate the Christians and control their lives through the taxes they impose on them and the offices they run. Indeed, they manage not only the revenues of the King, but also the estates of all the nobles of the land. Their style of life, which is like that of the nobility, helps them perform their harmful deeds; for, dressed in fine clothes and riding mules, called by Christian names and residing among Christians, and, on top of this, not wearing the badge, they often conceal their real identity. Thus, we see how social and economic reasons—the old roots of hatred for the Jews—are clearly reflected in the above complaints; and we likewise see them accompanied by old arguments—the justifications supplied by Christian theory and opinion. Thus, the Jews are "enemies of God and of all Christendom"; they are allowed to live only because they attest the death of Christ—namely, the Crucifixion, for which, as all know, they were responsible; but they are allowed to live not as Christians do, let alone as Christian noblemen, but in a humble and repressed manner, limited to a few low professions, as they are in other Christian countries.

By accepting only two of the requests—concerning the "names" and the wearing of the "badge," which was never meant to be enforced, Enrique showed how little value he ascribed to these claims and arguments. He continued to engage Jews in his Court wherever they could be of use to him, and ignored the growing clamor of the critics, who kept reminding him of his Christian duties. In 1377, in the Cortes of Burgos, the *procuradores* returned to the charge. But realizing that they could not have their way in anything that concerned the royal administration, they concentrated their petitions on matters touching loans, or rather their unpaid debts to the Jews, and were allowed several concessions.[99] In addition, they asked that no Jew be permitted to hold high office in the estate of any *noble*. The King found it easy to grant this request which, he knew well, was unenforceable and he likewise endorsed the cities' petition to free them from collective punishment for Jews occasionally killed in their territories.[100]

Enrique thus gave in on non-substantial issues, while stubbornly adhering to the main objectives of the pro-Jewish policy of his predecessors. His financial administration remained in Jewish hands, and if anything was to disturb its structure, the disturbance came from Jewish, not Christian sources.

XIII

We have already referred to the prevalent opposition to Pichon and Abravanel among Castile's Jews, and especially among their aristocracy. Stemming originally from communal motives, it was later nursed by the personal ambitions of certain major figures in Pedro's administration. Having had no choice but to join the system led by Pichon and Abravanel, they were forced to show a friendly face to these arbiters of Enrique's finances. But they never acquiesced in their leadership and constantly looked for ways to thwart it. Above all, they looked for suitable occasions on which they might point out to the King any flaw or failure in their financial management, and thereby bring about their dismissal.

The main target of their efforts was of course Pichon, whose powerful position as *Contador Mayor* was the prize they sought to win by their ceaseless machinations. It is not at all unlikely that the same Jewish courtiers who were instrumental in the downfall of Don Samuel were now involved in a similar attempt against Joseph Pichon.

Whoever they were, or whoever were their aides, they must have been extremely clever and efficient to be able to weave such a web of intrigue to undermine Pichon's authority. We may also assume that their keyman or ringleader had gained the full confidence of Pichon, who no doubt enabled him to approach Enrique freely, and thereby wield direct influence upon him. The intrigue must have taken a long time, but finally an opportunity presented itself to strike at the *Contador Mayor*.

The tactics appear similar to those that had apparently been employed against Samuel ha-Levi. Pichon was accused of submitting false accounts of his tax collections and earnings, and the King, who may have given some credence to these charges, ordered his arrest and a full investigation.

Pichon, however, did not react as had Don Samuel. Offended as he was, he did not remain silent; he fought back vigorously and made a strenuous effort to prove the groundlessness of the charges leveled against him. Ultimately, both the investigators and the King must have become convinced of his innocence, for otherwise he would not have been restored to his position, with none of his honors and powers diminished.[101] Enrique, however, yielding to his avarice, could not miss the chance to extract from Pichon a huge fine for the defects that the royal investigators allegedly noticed in his conduct. They probably found some minor flaws in Pichon's handling of one or more accounts, and Enrique ordered them to exaggerate these sins, so that they could impose a heavy fine. Pichon paid, and put an end to the affair.[102]

He knew, of course, who had maligned him, who was the chief intriguer, and who were his collaborators. He had many ways of striking at them; he could deny them large contracts, or raise their tax rates. But he realized that he had to be careful. By heavily fining Pichon as he did, the King, in a way, became a party to his accusers and, to some extent, their validator too. Action against his enemies might, with their connivance, appear to be an action against the King. Pichon preferred to let bygones be bygones and left the crime against him unavenged.

His foes, however, could not believe that he had either forgotten or forgiven, and were apparently in constant suspense and fear of the schemes he might contrive against them. When Enrique died in May 1379, their fear turned into panic. What Pichon did not dare do in Enrique's lifetime he might readily do under his heir, Juan I. They decided to forestall such dangerous action before Pichon could manage to cement close relations with the new king.

As leading tax farmers and extremely wealthy men, they wielded great influence in the Jewish community; and now they decided to exploit that influence. The plan of action they adopted seemed simple, but it took great daring to implement.

The Jews of Castile, like those of Aragon, had the right to sentence to death individuals who had falsely accused their fellow Jews, or their community, of violating certain laws or avoiding tax payments—crimes that might involve them in conflicts with the kings or the Christian citizenry. Their death sentences, however, required the King's sanction, and execution was entrusted to royal officials. Pichon's enemies now went to the chief rabbis, described to them the crimes he had allegedly committed—as well as the designs he was harboring against them, which might endanger the whole of Castilian Jewry—and demanded that Pichon be condemned to death as a delator and enemy of his people.[103] Perhaps unaware of the accusers' motives, the rabbis sentenced Pichon to death. No doubt what moved them to issue that sentence was not only the testimony of Pichon's rivals, but also their own prejudiced opinion of Enrique's *Contador Mayor*. It was essentially his lingering bad reputation since the days of the Civil War that led to his condemnation.

The crucial part of the conspiracy, however, was still to be fulfilled; but the conspirators had their scheme worked out and followed it tenaciously to the end. The new king, Juan I, was still celebrating his coronation, which had taken place a few days before, and while engrossed in the joyous affair, was approached by several Jewish leaders with a request to confirm a death sentence of the Jewish court against an especially vicious informer. Informers were usually known to belong to the vilest class of men, and the King, not suspecting that the sentenced person was one of the highest officials of the realm, gave his confirmation without asking for the name of the criminal involved. With this confirmation the conspirators rushed to the office of the royal executioner and induced him, despite his aroused suspicions, to carry out the verdict promptly. Then they proceeded to Pichon's house, where the King's executioner beheaded him.[104]

Pichon's execution and the circumstances surrounding it shocked the whole kingdom. Overcome with wrath, the King announced that he had been duped, and ordered the Jewish leaders who deceived him to be hanged and quartered. Even the executioner was severely punished—his arm was cut off—for having callously killed the famous man. Rabid antisemites used Pichon's murder as an excuse to mount a new campaign against the Jews. They claimed that the Jews of Castile killed Pichon because of his friendly attitude toward Christians. They, who for years had been urging the King to dismiss every Jew in his administration who wielded any power or authority over Christians, could not find words enough to praise the dead man, who was the chief of those officials and the strongest of them all. That their new charge contradicted their earlier claims could not of course be concealed. But inconsistency never stood in the way of hateful incitement. In the Cortes of Soria (Sept. 1380), the Jews of Castile were denied their old right to judge criminal cases[105] and forbidden to occupy any office in the royal and nobiliar courts.[106] This time the laws were enforced. From then on, no Jew was appointed *Contador Mayor* in the royal administration of Castile.

XIV

It is hard to assess the damage caused by this double blow to Jewish interests and prestige. It is still harder to believe that it was all the making of the Jewish grandees and courtiers. Baer says that, judging by the sources,

Pichon's "character was not above suspicion," that his "hands were apparently not clean," and hence that it was not without reason that he was killed as an informer.[107] A careful study of the sources used by Baer yields nothing to justify these assertions. The underhanded manner and the great haste in which Pichon's execution was carried out do not suggest consideration for justice, but rather a plot to remove a person presumed to have posed a danger to the plotters.

Writing thirty-five years after the event, but probably as a contemporary,[108] the great Jewish moralist Solomon Alami accused the Hispano-Jewish courtiers of major responsibility for the misfortunes of Spain's Jews. Lashing out against their scandalous behavior, he points out among the crimes they had perpetrated their "speaking evil of each other before the Kings and the grandees [purely] out of envy of each other's attainments." Their sole aspiration, he adds, "is to increase their wealth and expand their estates in the lands of their enemies" (i.e., the Spaniards), and "in all their conspiracies their interests are focused on the *shedding of innocent blood*."[109]

Alami speaks here of the jealousies and ambitions that led to the killing of Jewish courtiers from the time of Alfonso XI on. But as a contemporary of Pichon, he must have referred primarily to him. Indubitably, Alami considered Pichon "innocent" of the wrongdoings ascribed to him.

Alami attributed to the Jewish courtiers, who contrived their schemes in "surreptitious consultations," the "expulsion" of the high Jewish officials from the courts of both the kings and the great lords (another indication that it was the Pichon affair that was on his mind while writing the above), and he also pointed out the historic consequences of that crucial development. By losing control of the royal finances and their positions of power at Court, the Jews lost their most influential defenders against the attacks planned by their foes.[110] This no doubt facilitated the latter's task and contributed materially to their ultimate triumph.

Viewed in proper historical perspective, the moral deterioration of the Jewish courtiers appears to have stemmed from that of Spain's nobility, of which the Jewish magnates strove to be a part. The principle that "all is fair in war," viewed as valid also in internal strife—the principle by which most nobles lived and which permitted the excesses of a man like Enrique—determined the behavior of the Jewish magnates, too—or rather of many of their leaders. Alami would probably have agreed with this. It was in the Jewish courtiers' disregard for their own people's "sacred Law and morality" that he saw the main root of the woes and tribulations that befell the Jews of Spain.

XV

Before closing our review of the period of transition that generated the great crisis in the life of Spanish Jewry, we ought to make a few additional remarks on both the primary and secondary causes of the catastrophe that followed. By the primary causes we mean the conditions that prepared and made possible the disaster, by the secondary, the factors that aggravated the malady that lay at the root of the troubles. The breakdown of Jewish power in Spain, on which we have touched in the preceding chapter, was doubtless one of the secondary causes. Such were also the rule of King Pedro and the challenge to that rule by Count Enrique.

King Pedro of Castile was certainly maligned and his true image seriously distorted by the authors of his own and later times. But even if we discount half of their censures, enough will remain to force us to draw a grim portrait of his personality. Sitges tried to absolve him of the evils of which he was often accused by the people, and replace the title "Cruel" affixed to his name with that of "Strictly Just" *(el Justiciero)*.[111] It was a vain attempt. A man who would kill any person in the realm whom he merely suspected of rebellious designs, or who happened to have been a companion of his enemies, cannot be considered just by any standard. Nor could a man who executed opponents in the presence of his mother, their political ally, be an ordinarily just judge, free of a sadistic streak. Nor could such a judge be a king who wished men he had sentenced to cruel death to be boiled and roasted in his presence; or one who commanded his officials to send him the heads of adversaries (actual or potential) whom he had ordered killed. He was cruel, all right, whatever kind of "justice" may be attributed to his acts.

Nor can we agree with Russell and Hillgarth, who view his brutal deeds in the light of his age and consider them no worse than the excesses committed by some of his contemporaries. It is true that his father, Alfonso XI, Pedro IV of Aragon, and other sovereigns of his time likewise assassinated rivals and antagonists and paid little attention to the requirements of the laws when they considered their rule threatened. But while Pedro followed their principle of conduct, he applied it more readily and far more often. His biography reveals on almost every other page a public execution or a clandestine assassination carried out on his orders.

One thing, however, may be said in his defense. He would not execute ordinary opponents but only those who were actually or presumably involved in rebellion or conspiracy. It was his royal prerogative, he was certain, to determine their involvement (and their guilt) on the basis of his impressions, his feelings, and the information he acquired, without resorting to any due process of law. In his own mind he was certain that the sentences he issued were "right" and "just"; and his distorted view of kingship by divine right, along with his poor sense of what was legal and illegal, led him to believe that the people had no right to question his motives, and that his judgment would ultimately be accepted as correct. The people, however, thought differently. They often considered his judgments wrong, malicious, or vengeful, and many came to think of him as a killer-king.

Inevitably, such a ruler was constantly feared not only by his enemies but also by his friends, and consequently was bound to lose the support of ever larger sections of the people. That his rule caused irreparable damage to the Jews may be taken for granted. The hatred which he aroused against himself unavoidably engulfed the Jews, too, since his evil deeds were often attributed to the evil designs of his Jewish counselors. His protection of the Jews thus ultimately served to mobilize the antisemitic forces against them. This would have been the effect of his reign even if it had not been beset by other troubles, internal and external.

Enrique's share in aggravating the Jewish situation exceeded by far that of Pedro. Inferior to Pedro from every moral standpoint, since considerations of justice had no place at all in his quest for power and struggle to gain it, he was nevertheless careful not to leave behind him a long array of victims calling for vengeance. His tactics were aimed at attracting supporters and minimizing the number of his antagonists—that is, among the Christians of all classes. Insofar as the Jews were concerned, he treated them as game in open season. While his initial persecution of the Jews was intended to draw the Spanish people to his side, the final consequences of that persecution went far beyond his original aims. It was he who showed the Spaniards for the first time how Jews may be butchered by the hundreds in the cities, leaving their killers unpunished by the rulers (save in isolated cases). It was he again who showed them how the Jews may be pillaged, robbed of their possessions, and sold into slavery if they fail to meet the obligations imposed on them. To him, again, must be ascribed the destruction of many Jewish communities by his French mercenaries, who imitated the deeds of his own soldiers, as well as by the English mercenaries, who imitated the French; and consequently we must also attribute to him the large-scale conversion movement that ensued. Above all, it was his ferocious agitation, and the massive violence that accompanied it, that made hatred of the Jews, intense as it was, still more intense and soar to new heights. Though, once he became king, he reversed his attitude toward the Jews, he could not undo what he had done.

Yet great as was the impact of these factors upon the condition of Spanish Jewry, it could not compare, in effectiveness and scope, with the internal developments in Castile's cities, which were then making a strenuous effort to maintain their precarious position of influence, and this when the living standards of their citizens were undergoing a sharp decline. We have already dealt with the cities' interests and motives that led their Christian populations to act against the Jews. In the following chapter we shall touch on the impact that national adversity had on those populations and, consequently, on the condition of the Jewish communities in the Spanish kingdoms.

CHAPTER III

The Age of Conversions

1391–1417

No popular outbreaks against the Jews in the Middle Ages çaused the Jewish people such staggering losses as the Spanish riots of 1391. To be sure, Jewish casualties in the Rhineland during the first Crusade (1096) or in Germany during the Black Death (1348) were heavier, in proportion to the Jewish population, than those of the Jews of Spain in 1391. But if we take into account the Jews who left Judaism under the impact of the pogromist threats, the losses of Spain's Jews in 1391 far surpassed those the Jews had borne elsewhere in the wake of popular assaults. Within two or three years from 1391, Spain's Jewish community, the largest in the world, was reduced by nearly one third—in both geographic and numerical terms, the greatest catastrophe that had hitherto befallen European Jewry.

Like all earlier popular attacks upon the Jews, the outbreaks of 1391 resulted from a long and progressive aggravation of the Jewish question. Yet like all such outbreaks, they would not have occurred without the rise of popular intolerance to high levels due to social and economic distress caused by some national misfortune. In fact, the outbreaks of 1391 came in the wake of a series of misfortunes which struck Spain from 1348 on. Both Castile and Aragon, as we now well know, were severely hit by the Black Death; both were soon thereafter plunged into a war, in which they bled each other for about ten years; and both became involved in that terrible conflict which became known as Castile's Civil War (1366–1369). Before long Castile increased the load of its troubles by invading Portugal, which it sought to annex. But the abortive attempt ended in disaster (the defeat of Aljubarrota, 1385), to be accompanied by another fearful epidemic that killed about a third of Andalusia's population. Finally, following the death of Juan I (1390), the kingdom was administered by a split regency, which soon lost all effective control. It was then that the riots of 1391 broke out.

These developments, however, merely facilitated the outbreaks, but were not their real, underlying cause. In the West, as in the East, the primary cause was the rise of an alien defenseless minority, with royal support, above the masses of the majority, whose constant aversion for that minority was thereby turned into a fiery hostility. In civilized societies such a hostility, to be translated into action, requires an *ideology*—or, more plainly, moral "justification," and this need was supplied by the defamation of the Jews, which was fostered for five centuries in the East and reached its apogee in the doctrine of the deicide. The deicide implied that the Jew was condemned—an implication the masses understood and embraced as fitting their innermost desires. They failed to comprehend, however, despite the Church's explanations, why Christianity forbade them to kill Jews, rob them and, generally, violate their "natural rights." Consequently, when fear of punishment did not curb them, they threw all these prohibitions to the winds. It was thus against the Jews as killers of Christ that the war against Spanish Jewry was launched.

Like all great events in the history of mankind, the disasters that befell the Jews in the Middle Ages resulted from the interaction of social conditions and the deeds of certain persons at a given time. As a rule, Jewish historiography concentrated on unraveling the social background of the calamities, but paid relatively little attention to the part played by individuals in their occurrence. Paucity of data was one reason for this lacuna; but scant appreciation of men of great influence was frequently another reason. Whatever the cause, the results were disappointing. The accounts produced resembled a drama whose actors remained behind the scenes, and the picture they offer of Jewish life in the Middle Ages is much less colorful, vivid and comprehensible than it might have been had the leading personalities involved been given greater attention.

We shall try to depart from this tradition. Accordingly, we shall describe in some detail the man who, more than any other person in his time, was responsible for the war declared on Spanish Jewry—the war which, after a century of clashes, ended in the establishment of the Spanish Inquisition and the removal of the Jews from the land of Spain.

I. Ferrán Martínez

I

He was Ferrán Martínez, a Castilian priest, who never rose in the hierarchy of the Church above the median positions of archdeacon of Ecija and provisor of the church of Seville.[1] Judging by our sources, he was a man of poor learning,[2] and he may also have been of humble origin, which could perhaps explain why he failed to attain a more elevated position in the Church. This might also partly explain the great rapport he apparently had with the lower classes, his ability to move, guide and control them, and also his fiery hatred of the Jews, perhaps a heritage from peasant ancestors that passed to their sons in the cities.

Be that as it may, the archdeacon of Écija was an outgrowth of the conditions that prevailed in Castile and determined the attitude toward the Jews in that kingdom in the period following the Black Death. Ardently anti-Semitic like so many of his generation, he must have seen in King Enrique II the deliverer of Castile from the Jewish blight. The fierce and protracted anti-Jewish campaign conducted by Enrique during the Civil War, and the wholesale massacres of Jews by his troops which were reportedly carried out at his order, must have excited Martínez' hopes that Enrique was embarked on a policy of extermination which alone, he thought, could rid Spain of its Jews. We can take it for granted that Ferrán Martínez was one of Enrique's most enthusiastic partisans throughout the period of the Civil War, and we can also imagine his disappointment and resentment when he saw that Enrique, once victorious and in power, reversed his declared attitude toward the Jews and proceeded along the same pro-Jewish path followed so tenaciously by his royal predecessors.[3] Martínez knew that his bitter disappointment was shared by the majority of the common people; that they considered Enrique a betrayer of the trust, which they, the people, had faithfully placed in him; and that they responded with affection, enthusiasm and admiration to Martínez' exhortations that Castile should readopt the policy against the Jews which Enrique once pursued and then abandoned.

Martínez could experience these reactions while exercising his function as Church preacher; and, backed by public favor, he went to the extreme in heaping abuse and contumely upon the Jews as he urged their elimination from Spanish life. He did not have to invent denunciations or look for Christian authorities to support him. Church literature was full of them. But Martínez chose from the anti-Jewish writings the epithets most likely to rouse hatred for the Jews and stimulate the actions he proposed and implemented. Thus, his harangues against the Jews were followed by instructions he addressed to several small towns in the archbishopric of Seville, ordering their councils, under pain of excommunication, to expel all Jews from their confines and refrain from any converse with them.[4]

By the time Martínez began his campaign (apparently, in 1378), expulsion of Jews was no novelty in Europe. Jews had been ousted from cities and provinces (in Italy and Germany) as well as from the kingdoms of England and France. Spain, however, differed from these countries; it had not yet reached the state of anti-Jewishness that would move its kings to take such measures. But Martínez thought differently. He evidently paid little heed to Church teachings, which permitted, even advocated, the presence of Jews in all Christian dominions. Rather than the theory and law of the Church, Martínez preferred to follow the lay rulers, who had banished the Jews from their domains. The *concejos* of Andalusia, however, refused to act on so important an issue at the behest of a second-rate Church official. Yet this did not deter Martínez from trying to hurt the Jews in ways which, though conforming to Church orders, were certain to conflict with the civil law.

Apart from his ordinary tasks as archdeacon, Martínez, as we have indicated, performed another function. He was diocesan judge *(provisor)*, nominated by the archbishop of Seville, and in this capacity he claimed the right to adjudge cases in which Jews were involved. The popes favored such adjudication and sought to introduce it wherever they could; but the kings of Spain had constantly opposed it, and the will of the kings prevailed. Martínez could not be ignorant of this fact. He knew that by taking the action he did, he was violating the laws of Castile, which provided that in disputes between Jews and Christians, special judges appointed by the king would hear the litigants and render judgment. Martínez decided to test the King's resolve to abide by that policy against rising criticism; and he carefully prepared his moves.

It seems that, for certain specific situations, he had received special permission from the King to act as arbiter and final judge in disputes between Christians and Jews,[5] and he used this permission to extend his authority over other cases as well. On the same grounds, it appears, he also attempted to persuade the lay authorities to enforce his decisions; but the authorities involved found enforcement difficult. Armed with old royal privileges that forbade Church interference in their lawsuits with Christians, the Jews protested Martínez' actions, stating, in addition, that the sentences he pronounced were unfair and inimical to their interests. Martínez of course realized that sooner or later the Jews would carry their grievances to the Court; but he evidently intended to stand his ground. He knew that by sentencing Jews the way he did, he enhanced his popularity among the Christian populace; and he may have looked for an open conflict with the Crown by which he might effectively defend his position and thereby elevate his public standing.

If this was indeed what he expected to attain, the subsequent events proved him right. His illegal interference in Christian-Jewish litigation and the partial support he received from the *concejos* compelled the Jews to take their case to Court, and the king had no choice but to decide which law prevailed—the law decreed by his royal predecessors or the one enunciated by Martínez. Apparently, the Jews had at no time any doubt as to what the King's reaction would be, and they seemed to have had no difficulty in eliciting that reaction promptly. Prominent in the Court of Enrique II were then the Sevillian Jews Pichon and Abravanel, and these could actually have prepared for the King the order they wished him to sign. Enrique II was obviously convinced that Martínez' impudent acts must be halted. He sent him an unqualified order: "Do not dare to interfere in judging any dispute which involves any Jew in any manner."[6]

This clash between Martínez and the King occurred in April or May 1378. In July, the King was expected in Seville, and Martínez decided to suspend his activity until after the royal visit. As soon as the King left the city, however, he resumed his interference in Jewish-Christian litigation, while continuing from the pulpit his unbridled incitement of the Christian populace against the Jews. What is more, to these tactics of stirring up trouble, he now added an even more disturbing move. Over his signature, and that of other Church officials, whom he had persuaded to join him, letters were issued to many towns of the diocese, demanding, under pain of excommunication, that they deny the Jews the right of residence in their midst and accordingly eject them from their territories. The town councils that received these letters, however, were slow to act on his command. After all, they knew that no Church law had ever endorsed so extreme a measure, and no royal decree had ever sanctioned it. But Martínez would not give up. He knew that even if one town in Andalusia followed his instructions and evicted its Jews, the action would be imitated by other towns, and the whole diocese would be in an uproar. He therefore went to Alcalá de Guadaira in hopes of inducing the authorities there to execute his expulsion order. The results he attained fell short of the mark, but the danger his activities posed for the Jews was not by any means over. The latter now had, however, a stronger case against him and again carried their complaint to the Court.

Enrique's reaction was again swift, and now it was directed not only at Martínez but also at the judges and police chief of Seville and at "all the officials of all the towns and places of Seville's archbishopric." After expressing his amazement that Martínez continued, despite royal prohibition, to adjudge cases involving Jews, the King again ordered him in no uncertain terms, to desist from passing judgment "in any dispute that relates to any Jew or Jewess, in any manner whatever." Furthermore, "we command all Jews and Jewesses you have summoned," the King wrote to Ferrán Martínez, "not to appear before you as judge, or respect any sentence you may issue against them." Similarly, he ordered all the officials of the cities to "refuse to enforce any sentence" that Martínez might hand down to the Jews in their localities, and not to "seize the Jews' persons or possessions" on the basis of his verdict or order.[7]

No less forceful was the King's reaction to Martínez' letter to the councils of his diocese urging the rupture of all relations with the Jews and preventing their living among Christians. Not only was the archdeacon strictly forbidden to issue such instructions against the Jews; he was also prohibited from making "any move" against them or causing "their degradation in any thing in any manner." Also, the authorities of all the towns were enjoined "not to place any restriction upon the Jews with respect to their dwelling places, their shops, or their offices; and if something was done to this effect, that they undo it"—that is, restore the situation to what it had been before they changed it on Martínez' instructions. Both Martínez and the urban authorities were warned that disregard of these orders from then on would result in punishment in body and possessions, according to the King's pleasure.[8]

The stern warning had an immediate effect upon all the councils of the archbishopric and forced Martínez to retreat. It was clear that without the support of the *concejos,* he could not carry out any part of his program, and the councils were obviously unwilling to act against the King's explicit orders. In consequence, Martínez had to abandon his actions against the Jews in the judicial sphere, as well as his attempts to induce the councils to banish the Jews from their territories. It may be safely assumed, however, that his inflammatory preaching was not interrupted on this account and that, on the contrary, it became more rancorous and aggressive under the impact of the frustration he experienced. Before long, however, his feeling of frustration gave way to jubilation. Luck came to Martínez' aid.

II

On May 30, 1379, Enrique II died unexpectedly at the age of forty-six, leaving the throne to his son, Juan I. Then followed the assassination of Don Joseph Pichon, the Jewish *Contador Mayor,* by his Jewish rivals, which provided ammunition for the campaign against the Jews[9]; and soon afterward the Cortes of Soria, meeting on September 18, 1380, denied the Jews of Spain their age-old privilege to judge their own criminal cases.[10] This was a far-reaching decree that hit hard at Jewish judicial independence and constituted the first move toward the abolition of other judicial privileges still enjoyed by the Jews of Castile. What is more, the same Cortes took another step aimed at curtailing Jewish rights: it reaffirmed Enrique II's decree forbidding Jews to serve in the nobiliar administrations and underscored it with the King's assurance that "from now on the law would be guarded."[11] This law suggested that Juan I had embarked on an anti-Jewish course, though such a far-reaching conclusion was wrong. In any case, Martínez' prestige grew. It was easier for him now to persuade the citizens who were favorably disposed toward his plans that further pressure in the directions he indicated would ultimately lead to the desired end.

Encouraged by the change in the royal policy toward the Jews, he resumed his activity as judge in legal disputes between Christians and Jews; and he must now have received active support from some of the towns' officials. Again the Jews turned for help to the Crown. They referred to the orders of the deceased King, showed papal bulls they had procured in their defense,[12] and requested the King to take severe measures against Martínez' agitation and persecution.[13] Once again the royal reaction was positive. On March 3, 1382, the King sent Martínez a stern missive reminding him of the late king's commands and stressing that they were in full force. He also informed him of his own wish to have the Jews "guarded, defended and kept as something that is ours and our chamber's"; he therefore forbade him to use in his "preaching or other [public] utterances any words that may harm or prejudice the Jews or raise a tumult against them." He also let him know that he must not judge cases involving Jews and Jewesses and that "any dispute relating to the Church which may be against a Jew or a Jewess shall be handled from now on by the Archbishop, or by anyone the latter may assign for the task, and not by you." Finally, the King commanded all the judges, the police chief, and the council members of the city of Seville that they "do not allow" Martínez to act against the Jews in "whatever is against what is stated in this order, and that neither you nor they do anything in this matter under pain of punishment according to our wish."[14]

The King's letter cleared up misunderstandings and put to rest some false assumptions. It offered no ground for the current belief that Juan I's position toward the Jews differed fundamentally from that of his predecessor, and accordingly there was no reason to expect that he would act in an antisemitic spirit. The *concejos* had evidently to comply with his wishes and deny Martínez the arm of enforcement; and in consequence Martínez was compelled to cease all his anti-Jewish *judicial* activities. Soon, however, he found other ways to molest and injure the Jews.

He began a campaign of conversion to Christianity among the Moorish slaves owned by Jews in Seville. Since Jews were forbidden to own Christian slaves, their Moslem slaves, once converted to Christianity, would have to be set free; and such a conversion movement, if it spread, could harm Jewish economic interests. Martínez also continued his incitement against the Jews without respecting the prohibitions and warnings of Juan I any more than he had heeded those of Enrique. In fact, his tirades against the Jews became more inflammatory and provocative, going as far as assuring his audiences that he personally knew that if any Christian killed or injured a Jew, the King and Queen would be pleased with his deed and, on issuing judgment, would pardon him. In fact, Martínez guaranteed that such a man would suffer no harm at all. Such assurances, which amounted to calls for bloodshed, alarmed the Jews of Seville. Again they petitioned aid from the King, who, on August 15, 1383, issued another *alvalá* (directive) against Martínez' actions.

The new royal order forbade Martínez to Christianize Moorish slaves held by Jews, since this is against "the privileges granted the Jews in this matter by the kings from which we hail." Above all, he was ordered peremptorily to cease inciting the populace against the Jews. The King expressed his astonishment at Martínez for his audacity in involving the royal pair in his harangues. "Since when," the King asked, "have you been on such intimate terms with us that you may know our intention and that of the Queen?" It was clear to the King that unless the incitement of the archdeacon was stopped, "the *aljama* of this city would be destroyed and the Jews would lose what they have." He therefore gave Martínez a grim warning that "if you do not abstain from this behavior, we shall punish you so that you regret what you have done and no other person will dare to do likewise."[15]

The threatening language of the royal directive must have had a temporary effect; in any case, more than four years passed before the *aljama* of Seville found it necessary to lodge a new complaint against him. This does not mean of course that Martínez was inactive throughout that long period, or that he ever ceased his campaign against the Jews. We may fairly assume, however, that at least for some time—perhaps until the end of 1385—he refrained from conducting his illegal intrusions into affairs that concerned Jews, and he may have also stopped claiming or insinuating that the killing of Jews would incur no penalty. We assume so because the authority of Juan I was high in Castile until the war with Portugal—or rather until the disaster of Aljubarrota (1385)—and the Jews then acquired a strong protector in the court through the person of Don Gedalya Negro. But Don Gedalya died in 1385, and the great defeat in Portugal led the King to seek the goodwill and support of the Castilian cities. He dreamed of renewing the war with Portugal and of winning a victory so great and decisive that it would wipe out the shame of his defeat. For this he sought new financial allocations from the councils, which granted his request, but apparently only after they had seen to it that the King would yield to some of their demands. Thus, meeting in Valladolid in December 1385, Cortes further struck at the old privileges of the

Jews. Cohabitation of Jews with Christians was prohibited,[16] and occupation by Jews of offices in the Court was once more strictly forbidden (now under the pain of property confiscation).[17] For the second time since 1383, the Jews had to forgo a third of the debts owed them by Christians and, in addition, to grant a fifteen-month moratorium on the payment of debts that were due to them.[18] Above all, the royal Council, reconstructed by the King, now consisted of four bishops, four nobles, and four *procuradores* (i.e., representatives of the cities). It was obvious that the Jews had lost most of their standing and much of their protection at Court, and in these circumstances, Martínez gathered courage to resume his judicial harassment of the Jews, urge their complete separation from the Christians, and demand, in addition, the destruction of all synagogues built in the archbishopric since the Reconquest.[19]

So charged became Seville's social atmosphere as a result of this ferocious agitation that, at the beginning of 1388, the Jews of the city felt that something must be done to stop Martínez' campaign. Their only recourse, it would seem, was to turn to the King, but they were evidently cautioned by their friends at Court that the time was not propitious for a Jewish petition. The mood of the monarch was clearly anti-Jewish; and rather than risk a lukewarm reply that might encourage Martínez further, they decided to take their case against Martínez to the highest court in Seville. And so on February 11, 1388, the representative of the community, Don Judah ben Abraham, presented to the chief judge of Seville a formal complaint against Martínez' campaign which was aimed at the destruction of their synagogues. Don Judah cautioned Martínez, and indirectly the judges, that should this complaint remain unanswered, the Jews would turn to the King. "They will show how he, Martínez, violated what the King had ordered him to do," and how he acted against the royal command which clearly forbade him to do certain things.[20] This argument was of course a tactical maneuver: traditional royal support of the Jews was invoked as a *threat* when it could no longer be relied on in *fact*.

Martínez, however, must have sensed their weakness. A week after the Jews had submitted their complaint, he gave his response. Using the occasion to launch a new attack, he described the Jews as incorrigible criminals who attempted to cheat even God Himself, and nobody should therefore be surprised that they were cheating the kings and the princes. Had not Jesus said to his disciples when he sent them to preach the Gospel that anyone who would refuse Jesus' reign should be viewed as His enemy and as son of the devil? Whom does this definition fit more than the Jews, who have consistently rejected His reign from the days of the apostles on? What he, Martínez, says of the Jews is identical with what Jesus had said of them; hence, he cannot speak otherwise. Nor did he do anything wrong, either morally or legally. He urged the separation of Christians from Jews because this is *what the law commands* and what the archbishop of Seville has ordered, and also because the archbishop told him to attend to this matter.[21] He demanded the dismantling of the Jewish synagogues because this is what the law requires, and, had he been truly faithful to the law, he said, the "twenty-three synagogues the Jews built in Seville . . . would all have been razed to the ground."[22] As for his judicial actions, it is true that the King gave him certain instructions, but these instructions were based on false information supplied to the King by the Jews. "They said that I pronounced wrong sentences in the disputes which were entrusted to me by the King, our lord. To this, Señor, I answer: Let them show me which sentences I have pronounced against Jews and Jewesses, and if they were wrong and given against the law, I wish to pay for them all." He of course will not desist from preaching despite the King's instructions, since such instructions make no sense; for what he preaches is the word of God, by which not only God is served but also the King.[23]

The Jews obviously got no satisfaction from their appeal to the local authorities. They did not turn to the King as they had threatened, doubtless for the reasons pointed out above. But they developed a plan to check Martínez' drive through another medium. They turned to the deacon of the church of Seville, who presented the case to the chapter.

III

There is no doubt that even before they made this move, the Jews of Seville had received intimations that the leadership of the church of Seville was displeased with Ferrán Martínez' conduct and therefore was prepared to hear their complaints against his behavior. These intimations may have surprised the Jews, but they clearly indicate that not all Seville's Christians were heart and soul with Martínez. Here we can see that a part of the citizenry, an organized segment of Christian society—in all likelihood, at its upper levels—opposed Martínez' agitation and actions, which, they felt, went far beyond the limits permitted by the country's laws. And thus, after discussing the Jews' complaints and appeal, the chapter decided to send a delegation to the King, with a petition to curb Martínez' activity. The answer the King gave them was hardly encouraging: he would order his Council to consider the petition, but he felt it necessary to add that "although the zeal of the Archdeacon is holy and good, it must be watched that he does not arouse the people against the Jews with his talks and sermons; for although the Jews are bad and perverted, they are under my shelter and royal power, and they should not be wronged except through just punishments in cases where they offended against the law."[24]

In all this there was more double-talk than a straightforward answer. The

King called for the protection of the Jews, but failed to recommend any action against Martínez. He completely ignored the stern warnings that he and Enrique had given Martínez and, instead of reprimanding him, praised his "holy zeal" and threw a sharp reproach at the Jews. As for the petition, he limited his reaction to the expression of his view that Martínez should be "watched," but avoided a concrete and straightforward reply by turning the matter over to the Council, thus shirking direct responsibility. Undoubtedly the king was obliged to cater to the feelings of the antisemitic party, which was strongly represented in the royal Council. Three years after Aljubarrota, Juan I was not the same king he had been before that debacle. No action against Martínez came from the King's Court; indeed, no such action could have come from it at the time.

The attempt to enlist the local Church against Martínez thus ended in disappointment. Not only did it fail to stop him; it rather increased his audacity. His sermons against the Jews became more frenzied than ever, for now he believed that his goals were within reach. His overconfidence, however, unbalanced him, and in consequence he stumbled. He presented himself as the ultimate authority on anything that concerned the Jewish question. He even claimed that the pope had no right to issue bulls allowing Jews to establish new synagogues. He spoke in the name of the church of Seville as if he were its chief representative, and his audacity assumed a form of impudence that undermined the prestige of the Sevillian archbishop. There is no doubt that a strong body of opinion now opposed him in the cathedral chapter. The archbishop decided to take action.

Pedro Gómez Barroso, the archbishop of Seville, was, according to Amador de los Ríos, one of the most distinguished leaders of the Spanish Church, both for the "purity and integrity of his doctrine and the mild gravity of his manners."[25] He realized that in attempting to stop Martínez he would have a tough fight on his hands, and he did not want to make this fight personal. He therefore appointed a committee of experts, both lay and ecclesiastic, to examine the charges leveled at the archdeacon, and bring him before the committee to answer them, if he could. Martínez appeared. He was first questioned whether it was true that he denied the pope's right to give the Jews license to build new synagogues. Martínez confirmed the claim. He was then asked to give his reasons for that view, as it was commonly held that the opposite was true. The archbishop and the other members of the committee gave reasons in support of the contrary opinion; they mentioned the position of Juan Sánchez in the *Novela* and the fact that Popes Alexander (III) and Clement (VI) and other Holy Fathers issued bulls permitting the building of many synagogues. To diminish the pope's power against all this testimony is an "error," they stressed, which, unless duly justified, must be retracted. Martínez, however, refused to retract or justify his statement. He was prepared to give his reasons, he said, in the presence of the "officials and others of the *people*,"[26] thereby indicating his inability to provide legal arguments that might satisfy the learned, and his need to rely on the "common people," whose ears were ever open to his claims. The archbishop responded that such matters can be examined only by scholars, and not by laymen unduly informed of Church law and regulations. Martínez was asked to show obedience to the Church by refraining from making such questionable assertions until his statements are examined by a committee of experts, who should determine whether or not they constituted a deviation from the teachings of the Church.[27] Martínez refused to agree to this, too. He continued his preaching in the same vein.

The archbishop then issued a formal sentence in which he forbade Martínez to deliver any sermon until his case was decided by competent judges. Furthermore, in view of his open disregard of the order given him by the archbishop and the examiners, as evinced by his latest pronouncements, he made himself "contumacious, rebellious, and suspect of heresy." And, what is worse, since with every passing day he affirms that what he had said represented the truth, he appears to be "hardened in error." In addition, the archbishop called his attention to the fact that, besides the above statement concerning the pope, he had also said that the "pope cannot grant dispensation for a priest to marry, nor can he dispense with vows made, or absolve any person from his sins, and other matters which for those who understand might be considered a good opinion, but for the simpletons and even for those not very learned could be a cause of great scandal, as well as of contempt of the pope."[28] Martínez was denied, on pain of excommunication, not only the right to preach, but also to act as judge or official of the archbishop until judgment on his statements was pronounced. This severe sentence of the archbishop, we should note, was issued on August 2, 1389.[29]

Martínez was now in real trouble. He had antagonized the chapter, incurred the enmity of the archbishop, and was divested of all his rights, facing an investigation involving heresy. But luck again was on his side. On July 7, 1390, Archbishop Barroso died, and Martínez' supporters were soon on the stump. Their immediate goals were to persuade the chapter to disregard the pending investigation against Martínez, reinstate him in his position as archdeacon of Ecija and elect him as one of the provisors. A game of political intrigue ensued, probably guided by Martínez himself, through which all the above aims were achieved. No doubt opposition to him in the chapter was so weakened by the archbishop's death that many of its members believed they had no choice but to join the bandwagon of the victor. Martínez was now in the saddle again, and in a much more formidable position.

IV

Three months after the archbishop's death, Juan I also passed away, leaving as heir his minor son and debatable instructions concerning the Regency. Formed after troubled negotiations, the Regency was soon so divided as often to become almost paralyzed, while the representatives of the cities now formed a major part of the royal government. Thus, the Regency could hardly be expected to take strong measures in defense of the Jews. Martínez was now sure that his moment had come. On December 8, 1390, he issued orders to the clergy of various towns in the diocese that they destroy, within three hours of the receipt of his instructions, the synagogues in their localities. Écija and Alcalá de Guadaira, where support of Martínez was overwhelming, were the first towns to carry out these instructions; Coria and Cantillana came next; and then the same orders were issued by Martínez to all other places in the diocese. If there was resistance anywhere, he warned, the town would be put under interdict until the order was obeyed and carried out.[30]

It need scarcely be said that the Jews of Seville realized the gravity of the peril overhanging them. There was nobody now in Seville to appeal to. Martínez behaved like master of the city, and nobody seemed willing or able to resist him. Only one course still appeared open: to turn to the Regency and try to get its aid. The Jews of Seville used this avenue. They sent an urgent plea to the leaders of Spain's Jewry, then assembled in Madrid, where Cortes met. They described their plight and warned that, if no remedy was provided, the Jews of the archbishopric would have to leave the region.[31] It was not hard to foresee the disastrous consequences of such an eventuality for all of Spain's Jews.

Faced with the remonstrances of the Jewish leaders, the Regency was moved to action. It realized that no time could be lost; and on December 20, 1390, it sent the dean and chapter of the church of Seville a vigorous missive, reaffirming the position of King Enrique II in that protracted conflict. Bearing the name of the young King, and countersigned by all the leading members of the Council, the letter, besides attacking Martínez, sharply criticized the cathedral chapter. To understand the developments that followed, we should note in some detail what it said.

The Regency expressed its amazement that the chapter, having known Martínez and his ways, and aware that he was under suspicion of heresy and prohibited from exercising his former functions, including even the right to preach, chose to elect him as one of the provisors and, furthermore, tacitly consented to his plans by failing to interfere with their implementation, or even reprimand him in any form. The Regency subscribed to the view of the Jews that the chapter, by both its action and inaction, shared responsibility for Martínez' activities and for the harm and injury he caused the Jews. It therefore charged the chapter to restore at its own cost the synagogues razed at Martínez' orders and make amends to all Jews and others who suffered damage as a result. But besides this, the Regents ordered the chapter to take specific actions against Martínez himself. He was to be denied the provisorship, by whose powers he had committed his latest offenses; he was also to be prevented from preaching against the Jews or their worship in Seville's synagogues; he was to be placed under ecclesiastic censure (as the law required); and finally, he was to "redo, restore and repair" all the synagogues whose destruction he had ordered.

The letter ends with a stern warning that severe fiscal punishment will be imposed if the chapter does not follow the King's instructions and does not remove Martínez from the provisorship. "Be certain . . . that we shall order you to pay for all damages from your own private possessions, and if these will not suffice, from the possessions of your *mesa capitular* [resources of the chapter], plus a fine of a thousand doblas for each violation, besides other penalties at the royal pleasure, so that this may be due punishment to you and an example for those who will notice this."[32]

The strong and uncompromising letter of the Regency was calculated to frighten the chapter into action in accord with the wishes of the Jews, and this indeed was its effect. It was the predisposition of the chapter's leaders, however, that made this result possible. Had the members of that leadership shared Martínez' views and sought as he did to destroy Seville's Jewry, they would have contested the Regency before obeying it. They could have looked for reasons to exempt themselves from guilt—i.e., from responsibility for Martínez' actions; they might even have protested against interference with their right to elect to their offices whomever they wished; and they might have sent a delegation to Madrid, where they had many friends who could support their case. But this is not what they did. Five days after they had taken formal notice of the Regency's letter, the chapter met again (on January 15, 1391) and declared its willingness to honor the King's orders. This shows that the great majority of the chapter resented the arbitrary actions of Martínez; that many disliked or even hated him personally as an obnoxious and dangerous individual; and, again, that the patrician elements in the cities, and the upper strata of the Church's hierarchy, did not favor violent action against the Jews, even though they wanted to reduce their legal status, force them into positions of subservience to the city, and remove them from the mainstream of Sevillian life by legal means—that is, in conformity with the king's law and, of course, the laws of the Church.

The meeting of January 15 was attended not only by the leaders of Seville's church. Present were also several Church notables from other cities of the archbishopric (such as the archdeacons of Jerez, Reyna, and Castro), as well as twelve canons and beneficiaries of the church of Seville. In the presence of all these, the deacon of Seville's church declared in his own name, and the name of all present, except for one canon who demurred, that they considered the letter of the King as a command, which they were duty-bound to obey, and that accordingly they deprived Martínez then and there of the office of provisor to which they had appointed him; they further ordered Martínez to refrain from preaching in a manner that might cause disturbance and scandal, or any evil or harm to the Jews and their synagogues. Furthermore, they ordered him to rebuild or repair, within the space of a year, all the synagogues he had destroyed in the archbishopric; and he was warned that failure to comply with these demands would result in his excommunication.[33]

From this action of the chapter it is clear that its officials had never been in collusion with Martínez in his plan to demolish the synagogues; nor had they ever cooperated with him in issuing or enforcing the orders of demolition. Had this not been the case, they could not so easily have shirked responsibility for these occurrences; nor could they have told Martínez to his face that he (and he alone) had to repair the synagogues which *he* (and he only) had ordered destroyed. Martínez, as we shall see, was trying to ascribe responsibility for his actions to the deceased archbishop, and he would certainly have been quick to point out in his reply (which we shall presently consider) that the chapter had agreed, if not collaborated, with him in the proceedings taken for the razing of the synagogues, if he had any basis for such a claim. Evidently, he had no such basis. And thus we must limit the responsibility of the chapter, insofar as the destruction of the synagogues was concerned, only to its passivity—that is, its failure to stop or interfere with the execution of Martínez' instructions. Yet that passivity did not stem from consent or indifference but rather from fear of Martínez and his cohorts—the same fear that may account for his election as provisor after the death of the archbishop. Probably one of Martínez' supporters, perhaps the one who now opposed the chapter's decision, proposed his election to that position, while the others, suspecting personal injury if they openly opposed the dangerous man, failed to indicate their objections to the proposal and thus brought about Martínez' election. If they now mustered courage to come out against him, it was because they counted on the backing of the Regency and, in addition, were threatened by its punishments if they failed to fulfill its instructions.

The leaders of the chapter no doubt realized that Martínez would be hard to defeat. Indeed, he remained dauntless and unyielding. In his reply to the chapter, which he gave then and there, he made it clear that he had no intention of obeying either the order of the Regents or the instructions of the chapter. Jesus Christ, he said, gave His followers two swords, with which they were to punish the evil and defend the good; one of them He placed in the hands of the kings, the other in those of the Church, "which is the Pope, the Cardinals, the Prelates, and the whole clergy." These, then, are two different jurisdictions, and hence neither the Church nor any of its clergy can be sentenced by royal judges; therefore, neither the King nor those who signed the letters which were issued against him had the right to do so, for he, Martínez, is under the jurisdiction of the Church—and the Church only. Nor could he consider of any value the decision taken against him by the chapter, for these people are *not* his judges *episcopi jure;* therefore, he does not have even to appeal such a sentence or order, because it is per se null and void. Furthermore, in the judgments issued against him, the law was flagrantly ignored even in the elementary requirement that he be heard in his own defense, and thus he was condemned solely on the basis of the accusations leveled at him by the Jews, the "traitors, the enemies of the faith." Finally, he was ready to prove that the late archbishop ordered the destruction of the synagogues inasmuch as they were built against the Church and against God and without permission from any person. He further mentioned that he destroyed two synagogues during the lifetime of the archbishop, and he does not regret what he did.[34]

In view of this defiant answer, it was obvious that Martínez was far from suppressed. What was now to follow was a contest of wills between the Regency and the chapter on the one hand and Ferrán Martínez on the other. We do not know whether Martínez could, in fact, continue with his functions as provisor; in any case, he was still the archdeacon of Écija and an official of the church of Seville, and in these capacities he continued to preach and urge the people to support him. There can be little doubt that in the sermons he delivered he portrayed his struggle with the Jews' "friends" at Court and in the Sevillian chapter, and how, despite all their impending threats, he was not ready to budge an inch. Nor can we doubt that the tale of his fortitude, aggrandized by Martínez and his aides, increased the popular admiration for him and served as further inducement to his followers to stand firmly behind him. Martínez was now at the peak of his influence among Seville's lower classes, who formed of course the great majority of the city's population. How was he going to employ this force? He knew that he could not move the Crown, or the Regency, or the city council, or the chapter to take any action in his support. His strength lay with the masses of his followers. These had long been clamoring for action and were awaiting his signal.

V

Feeling the storm fast gathering about him, Martínez could not have failed to realize that the hour of decision had come. The political situation, he knew, was propitious; the Regency was divided; it was most unlikely that it would dare move against him in the event of a general outbreak. The *concejo* and the chapter were hiding behind the Regency and would not initiate action on their own. The avalanche he could now unleash, Martínez felt, was too strong for any of these bodies to withstand, and he concluded that the time was ripe for a major attack upon the Jews. This is indeed what he and his aides now decided on, keeping secret all the time the scope, objectives, and date of the assault. Only the rising ferocity of Martínez' agitation indicated its imminence.

Seville's *judería* was now surrounded with an ugly pogromist atmosphere. Its residents were daily insulted and molested by members of Martínez' party, no doubt with the aim of provoking disturbances and raising the fever of the aggressive mobs. Violent reactions to these insults became more and more unavoidable; and whether on their own initiative or in response to the Jews' requests, the chief royal officials in Seville decided to suppress the pogromist movement. They believed that if they showed a strong hand, they might deter the populace from bloodshed. Two nobles of the great family of Guzmán were the King's chief officers in Seville; one of them, Juan Alonso Guzmán, Count of Niebla, was the governor *(adelantado)* of the whole province; another, Alvar Pérez de Guzmán, was the *alguazil mayor* (chief of the royal police) of Seville. They seized two of the rabble who hurled insults at the Jews and ordered them flogged and imprisoned. But the action backfired.

The *Cuarta Crónica General* tells us that the "small people" (the *pueblo menudo*)—i.e., those who formed Martínez' main following—were infuriated by the way their fellow rioters had been treated. Resorting to force, they freed the two prisoners and captured in the process the *alguazil mayor*. Then they carried the freed men to the great church, where only two months before the chapter had issued its harsh judgment against Martínez. There wild harangues were delivered against the Jews and against their Christian protectors. The "small people" shouted that the *alguazil* must be stoned, and that the Count of Niebla, too, should be slain. Nevertheless, the mob was soon compelled to free Alvar Pérez. It was obvious that otherwise a major clash would ensue between the nobiliar forces and the crowds of Martínez—a clash that he evidently wanted to avoid. He did not wish to turn the conflict with the Jews into a conflict with the nobility. He ordered the release of the *alguazil*.[35]

A strange calm now descended on Seville which, rather than reassuring the Jews, frightened them. The release of the flogged culprits in defiance of the public sentence pronounced by authorized royal judges showed that the hand of the law was broken and that the real masters in Seville were Ferrán Martínez and the aggressive mobs that followed him. Nevertheless, it appears that although the *alguazil* could not take any of the rioters to court, he did not entirely abandon his duties as head of the city's police. He must have prepared his men to meet new outbreaks, since rumors abounded that assaults upon the Jews were being planned in Seville and the neighboring towns. The menaced Jews, for their part, sent signals of alarm to their leading notables, then meeting in Madrid; and the leaders, realizing the gravity of the crisis, rushed to the regency and demanded action. The Regency again hastened to respond as well as it could with its limited resources. It realized of course that, in the circumstances it faced, the only effective way to prevent disorders was to send to Andalusia detachments of troops to protect the *juderías*. But this the Regency could not afford to do. Divided more than ever, and increasingly menaced by the forces of its antagonist, Don Pedro Tenorio, archbishop of Toledo, it was itself in need of military aid. And so instead of troops, it sent special messengers to Andalusia's most agitated towns, ordering their *concejos* to keep the peace. It also made a diplomatic move which, it hoped, would alleviate the situation: it removed Alvar Pérez from the office of *alguazil* and replaced him with the highly prestigious noble Pero Ponce de León, lord of Marchena.[36]

The action, taken on April 29, was meant to appease the extremists in Seville, who demanded the removal of Alvar Pérez from his post. Yet rather than improving the city's security, it accelerated its deterioration. For soon thereafter a sharp quarrel broke out between the new *alguazil* and the governor of the province, Juan Alfonso Guzmán, thereby splitting the forces of Seville's nobles, who now no doubt differed on the policy to be pursued toward Martínez and his aides. In any case, Ponce de León must have shown a rather friendly face to the latter, either in the hope of reducing their aggressiveness, or because of his need to enlist their support against the powerful Count of Niebla. Meanwhile, the fierce agitation continued. "The people were so aroused," says Ayala, "that they now had no fear of any one, and the desire to rob the Jews was increasing from day to day."[37]

With the populace thus stirred and readied for action, with a divided Regency in Madrid and a divided nobility in Seville, and with the urban aristocracy afraid to intervene, the conditions for an anti-Jewish outbreak seemed more favorable than ever before. Events moved inexorably toward a climax. It took only one month and five days from the replacement of Alvar Pérez by Ponce de León for the attack on the Jews of Seville to take place.

VI

We have presented Martínez' struggle against the Jews from the start of his agitation to the outbreak of the riots insofar as we could reconstruct it from the sources. What conclusions can we draw from this account that may help us understand the sequel?

To begin with, there is Martínez' character as reflected in the documents touching his conduct, and what we gather from them contradicts most epithets applied to him by the chroniclers and historians. According to these epithets, which no doubt agreed with his reputation among the masses, Martínez was a religious zealot, distinguished by "unusual devoutness" to the faith; but actually he lacked the main qualities—moral integrity and ideological consistency (together with a degree of naivete)—required for the possession of true religious zeal. The record shows this unmistakably. He claimed that the King, or any other lay authority, had no jurisdiction over him and his actions since, by virtue of his clerical status, he was under the exclusive jurisdiction of the Church; but when Archbishop Barroso appointed a committee of jurists and theologians to consider his conduct, he refused to state his arguments before them, declaring that he would present his case only before the *people's* "officials," who of course were all laymen. How he evaluated Church jurisdiction, to which he resorted again and again, is similarly attested by his arbitrary, cynical and, indeed, contemptuous treatment of the archbishop's judgment, which suspended him from all his positions and put him under suspicion of heresy; for as soon as the archbishop died, he did not hesitate to disregard that verdict as if it had never been issued. He was restored to his position by an action of the chapter, which also made him provisor of the Church; and he readily accepted these decisions of the chapter, although they were made not *jure episcopi* but clearly and openly against it. Yet when the same chapter removed him from the provisorship, he claimed that his removal was illegal, as such action against him could be taken only *jure episcopi*. He displayed the same attitude in his repeated claim to have acted only in accordance with Church law; but he did not hesitate to disregard that law when it conflicted with his actions against the Jews. Thus, while Church law repeatedly forbade slaying Jews merely because of their Jewishness, Martínez urged the masses to do precisely that, and even assured them exemption from punishment by the authorities. Another fateful instruction of his—the one that related to forced conversion—was likewise based on a violation of the canons and disregard for the teachings of the Church.[38] We shall deal with this point further below.

A man who could treat Church laws and precedents with such inconsistency for his own convenience could hardly be filled with the "holy zeal" that some of the sources attribute to him; nor could he exemplify exceptional "devoutness," while adroitly manipulating his contradictory arguments to win his battles against his opponents. What appeared as religious zeal in Martínez was actually his burning hatred of Jews. The other misconceptions about his "virtuous" behavior must likewise be interpreted in the light of that hatred.

He was rightfully noted for his iron will and unwavering determination to achieve his objectives. And his strength of character, his ruthlessness and cunning, as well as his unscrupulousness and daring, made him virtually irresistible. Thanks to this combination of qualities he overcame the pressure of two kings, a Regency, the archbishop of Seville, the *concejos* of the cities, Seville's cathedral chapter, and the powerful Sevillian nobility. And what further increased his fame and popularity was his oratory, which must have been stirring and especially suited to move masses. It was indeed primarily by this oratory that he captured the imagination of the Christian lower classes, who saw in him the champion of their cause—a hero who withstood the determined attacks of his and their own foes.

But here we touch a point related to his leadership, and more broadly to his tactics and influence, which deserves special consideration.

The outbreak in Seville was the first massive strike of the tidal wave of hatred for the Jews that soon swept over the whole of Castile as well as most of Aragon. Martínez' responsibility for the outburst of that fury, unprecedented in the annals of Spain, is stressed by all historians of the period, but the main part he played in shaping these events has not yet been fully defined.

When Martínez began his campaign against the Jews, hatred for them was widespread in Spain, and in the lower classes it was intense. His chief contribution to the great riots, therefore, was not the creation of public opinion against the Jews, even though he raised the anti-Jewish fever by more than several degrees. For this in itself would not have made the mobs replace their nonaggressive behavior toward the Jews with the pillage and butchery that followed. To move the people of Seville, Andalusia and Castile to do violence to the Jews on such an enormous scale, certain prerequisites had to be met. And it was in the provision of these prerequisites that Martínez fulfilled his crucial function.

Except for the grim but sporadic attacks on the Jews of Castile during the Civil War, Castile had not seen bloody riots against the Jews for almost three hundred years—that is, since the outbreaks in Toledo and its environs in 1109. To solve the Jewish question by means of massive bloodshed, or other forms of popular assault of the kind perpetrated in Germany and other countries, was clearly not in the tradition of Castile. Maintaining relentless pressure upon the King that he follow their demands with respect to the Jews, the oligarchies of the cities pursued a legal course to which they tenaciously adhered. It was primarily through Cortes, and occasionally through privileges the kings gave them outside Cortes, that they sought to carry out their plan for the Jews—but not through acts of violence. Such acts would constitute rebellion against the King, which was the last thing the *concejos* would support. They knew that whatever autonomy they enjoyed they had obtained from the kings, who, from the middle of the 1380s, had encouraged them to believe that ultimately they would raise them above the other estates. Hence the *concejos* in both Castile and Aragon adhered, at least formally, to their legal duties with respect to both the King and the Jews— before, during and after the riots—in practically all the cities involved.

The masses, however, were straining at the leash. They were bursting with desire to fall upon the Jews with all the violence they could muster; and what held them back was fear alone—their dread of the cruel and terrible punishments they knew the Crown could inflict upon them. Martínez taught the masses to overcome that fear. Not only did he *preach* violation of the laws insofar as the treatment of Jews was concerned, but he *perpetrated* such violations himself. He sought to prove to the masses that by doing certain things—for instance, destroying the synagogues—they did not risk any harm to themselves; and to induce them to take such actions, he argued that by taking them they would not break the law but guard it, for this was what the laws—both canon and civil—required them to do. By his illegal actions, for which he was not punished, and which he sought to disguise as legal, he served the Spanish masses as a model of behavior which moved them to believe that, if they hurt the Jews, they would not be punished or incur guilt. Thus, he encouraged them to brave the authorities and take the law into their own hands. A crafty demagogue and clever mentor, he calculated his moves with great sagacity, accustoming the masses to rely on his judgments and, finally, to obey his orders.

That his Jew hatred and that of the masses who followed him were products of a long social evolution is of course unquestionable; and this evolution we have tried to explain. But Martínez was not just riding the waves. He had to steer a ship—the ship of his party—through many dangerous straits and whirlpools, and he piloted it to its appointed destination. Martínez's share in the developments that ensued was therefore immense.

In his own way, Ayala indicated that share when he said: "And the beginning of all this [namely, the pogroms] and the harm done the Jews was. the *preaching and incitement* that the Archdeacon of Écija did in Seville."[39] As a reference to the initial cause of the events, the statement is undoubtedly correct; but as explanation of how those events evolved, it is incomplete and may be misleading. For the "beginning" to which Ayala referred may be taken to mean a mere starting point, the first link in a chain of developments and an indication of a rather brief time. But Martínez' activity, as we have seen, spanned no less than fourteen years, and involved not only persuasive preaching but numerous clashes, struggles and maneuvers, without which the ultimate results he had striven for would not have been attained. Indeed, judging by his entire course of action and, above all, by its conclusive stages, it is clear that from the outset, Martínez' goals were not limited to the Jews of Seville or Andalusia, but encompassed the whole of Spanish Jewry. Except for him and his closest aides, perhaps only the Jews of Seville fully realized that the destruction of their community as planned by Martínez would be the beginning of the end for all the Jews of Spain.

THE ASSAULT

Castile

I

The storm erupted on June 4, 1391, more than two and a half months after the disorders of March 15.[40] According to Amador, "no suspicion or symptom of the tumult" was noticeable in the interval between the two dates. But this is hardly possible. The assault upon the Jewish borough, as we shall see, resulted in a bloodbath of massive proportions that all but annihilated the Sevillian *judería*. Such an attack could not be carried out without large-scale preparations and mobilization of forces, and such activities could not remain hidden from the authorities and the Jewish community. Surely "symptoms" and "suspicions" of the forthcoming events must have abounded in Seville and its neighborhood; and Amador was probably wrong to assert that on the day of the pogrom, the Sevillian population "saw itself suddenly agitated *en masse*."[41] There was nothing "sudden" or "surprising" about that agitation. Nor was there surprise in the ensuing events. Undoubtedly, the Jews expected the onset, and the pogromists awaited the order to attack them. The only item they may have been in doubt of was the precise date of the onslaught.

For weeks, if not months, the Sevillian *judería* must have been on the alert, with its walls guarded and its gates shut. No doubt the planners of the attack realized that penetrating the *judería* by scaling its walls would be a costly operation. They decided therefore to invade it through its wooden gates, which could be set on fire from the outside—perhaps by torches thrown from a distance. This method of capturing the *juderías* was practiced also in other places.

On the day the riots broke out in Seville, the royal forces charged with keeping the peace failed to intervene on behalf of the Jews—a failure so conspicuous as to suggest that no such forces then existed in the city. There can be no doubt that the Regency expected the royal forces in Seville to resist any assault. But the prestige of the Regents of Castile was low; their orders were slighted; and Ponce de León, their representative in Seville, followed a policy of his own. He evidently did not wish to be embroiled in a conflict with the riotous Sevillian populace, and the pogromists must have known from the start that the Jews would receive no military aid. Any opposition they might encounter, they realized, could come only from the Jewish defense units, and these were reputed to be small in numbers and inadequately trained and equipped.

The attack began at dawn, with the forces of Martínez striking simultaneously at several positions of the Jewish borough. Poorly defended, these positions crumbled, and the hordes of attackers burst through. What followed was an orgy of bloodshed and rapine on a scale that Spain's Jews had never seen before. Thousands of Jews, mostly men, were butchered, while many more thousands of women and children were taken captive to be sold into slavery. Exempt from this fate were only those Jews who hastened to announce their consent to be baptized, and these must have constituted the great majority (probably no less than 20,000).[42] They must have been aware that only conversion could save them from immediate death; and leaving behind them their homes and possessions, they rushed in droves to the baptismal fonts. When they returned from the churches, they found little left of their former abodes. Most of the buildings, after being sacked, were burned. Following the riots, Zúñiga tells us, the *judería* looked like a wasteland.[43]

The riots in Seville fulfilled Martínez' hopes; and they must also have suited his further plans. Amador de los Ríos and other historians described the effect of those riots as "contagious,"[44] as an "example" that inflamed the fanaticism of the masses throughout the archbishopric of Seville. But these assertions are only partly true. The basic attitudes of the Jew haters of the archbishopric who lived outside the capital city were not formed by the Sevillian fury. Long exposed to Martínez' campaign, which embraced all the towns and townlets of the diocese, they were all imbued with a fierce hatred of the Jews which sought an outlet in violence. But the success of the pogromists in Seville, we may assume, prompted them to follow in their footsteps; thus the outrages committed in the capital were soon repeated in the provincial towns. Alcalá de Guadaira, Carmona and Écija (the headquarters of Ferrán Martínez) were among the places hit hard, and so were the communities of Santa Olalla, Cazalla and Fregenal, which were virtually wiped out. But the fury soon spread beyond the limits of the archbishopric and ravaged Cordova and its neighboring towns. No doubt the pogroms were planned by the same men who organized the attack on the Jewish quarter in Seville. They must have been prepared simultaneously.

We gather this from letters written five months before the riots by Cordovan and Sevillian Jews, in which Cordova is mentioned as a major target of

Martínez' incitement.[45] Also, the size of the Cordovan community, the walls of its borough and its strong castle, as well as the forces of the Crown and nobility, which it could possibly enlist for its protection, were factors the aggressors had to consider if they wanted their attack to succeed. The planning and organization of such a complex operation required therefore more than a few days. Yet the riots in Cordova must have occurred within about a week of those of Seville. Hence, the disturbances in both cities were prepared more or less at the same time.

The *Cuarta Crónica General* combines its account of what happened in Cordova with certain events that took place in Jerez. "In both these cities," says the *crónica*, "the *menudos* [i.e., the "small people"] rose against the grandees, threw them out of the city, and appointed other officials in their stead."[46] This is an important piece of information which is offered by no other source and which historians have bypassed inadvertently. No doubt these occurrences were intimately connected with the development of the pogromist movement. The grandees in Cordova and Jerez, we may assume, tried to block the attack upon the Jews in these cities as they had attempted to do in Seville, but the *menudos* overcame them as they had done in Seville. The urban administrations were consequently reorganized in accordance with the wishes of the mobs. If this is what happened in Cordova and Jerez, the conduct of the *alguazil mayor* in Cordova is easily explicable. He followed in the path of Ponce de León, and for the identical reasons.

On the basis of the above, we may safely conclude that the burden of resisting the attackers in Cordova fell wholly on the Jewish community and that, as in Seville, its defensive units were unequal to the task. From the limited records that have reached us, we can gather that once the Jewish borough was invaded, a large-scale massacre proceeded undisturbed, accompanied by plunder and devastation. Many fled to the nearby castle, hoping to find there a safe refuge, but the castle too was invaded by the rioters, and the brutal crimes committed in the borough were soon repeated in the fortress. Here, too, the survivors realized that conversion was their sole alternative to death, and this alternative was finally chosen by the great majority of the Cordovan community.

"Recovered from his initial surprise," José Amador de los Ríos writes, "the *alguazil* of the city appeared [in the *judería*] with a substantial force of caballeros and soldiers to put an end to the barbarous slaughter. His astonishment and indignation had no measure when he saw that more than two thousand corpses were piled up in the streets, houses and synagogues."[47] The implied assumptions of this statement, however, cannot be accepted for obvious reasons. The *alguazil* could not have been "surprised" at the attack, because a pogrom of such magnitude must have been, as we have indicated, in preparation for some time, and the head of police must undoubtedly have received more than a few hints of its preparation. He allowed the outrage to go on unopposed as long as the pogromists had work to do, and appeared on the scene when it was practically over and when only a few Jews were left alive. Was his absence a result of collusion with the pogromists? Or was it due to his reluctance to confront an opposition he had reason to believe he could not cope with? One way or the other, the *alguazil* shirked his duties.

According to the extant evidence from Cordova, it appears that although the force of the attackers consisted mainly of the *populo menudo*, it also included some urban patricians who lived with the caballeros (as their favorites and agents), as well as some priests (of the lower clergy). But the sources also indicate that behind the rioters there was somebody of authority who guided the attackers—a man against whom, when it was all over, the King's investigators did not dare to move.[48]

In Cordova, therefore, Martínez' followers included not only the *menudos,* but at least a fraction of the upper classes, who shared in the execution of their plans. This again suggests that the pogrom in Cordova, no less than in Seville, was not a spontaneous outbreak, but a carefully planned and organized attack led by Martínez and his allies.

II

Following their bloody triumph in Cordova, and in full accord with their behavior in Seville, the ruthless attackers issued calls for action to their friends in other places in the bishopric—to towns like Montoro and Andújar, where Martínez had campaigned for many years and his agents had secretly prepared the ground for a brutal assault upon the Jews. Soon the storm passed to the province of Jaén, engulfing, besides the capital city, the important towns of Úbeda and Baeza, which were "inundated with Jewish blood."[49]

No sooner was Andalusia aflame than the scourge advanced northward to Villa Real, and then further north, invading the center of Castile and its eastern part (including Cuenca). The great Toledan community, which was attacked on June 20, could not resist the aggressors any more than had the communities of Seville and Cordova. Many of its members were put to the sword, thrown into the river, or burned alive, while their wives and children were sold into slavery. There were no doubt many martyrs in Toledo, but there, too, many more, it seems, were saved from death by conversion.[50]

From Toledo the pogromist movement continued its northward course to Madrid, thence to Segovia, and from there, through Soria and Logroño, to Burgos, which it reached about August 12.[51] In contrast to the sources for the southern areas, those for the north betray no sign of martyrdom, or losses of life in the course of self-defense, while they clearly refer to large-scale conversions, which virtually wiped out whole communities.[52] The Jews of

Burgos, we know, bore arms[53] and had a strong fortress at their disposal. Nevertheless, when the riots broke out, most of them rushed to the churches to be baptized, while a minority, apparently significant, preferred the shelter of patricians' homes to that of their citadel, which could have been defended. The conduct of Burgos' Jews was no doubt affected by the massacres and conversions in the south. The virtual destruction of the southern communities seemed to indicate that Spanish Jewry was doomed and that neither resistance nor martyrdom could reverse or substantially alter its fate. This may have been why the Jews of the north left no record of either self-defense or Sanctification of the Name. The situation must have appeared to them so hopeless as to lead them to surrender rather than fight.

The precise dates of the riots in the north are not indicated in the extant sources, but judging by the available data, the northern communities were hit in the same order that marked the outbreaks in the south. Thus they formed part of a common trajectory that indicated a northward thrust. It is hard to assume that this direction, which marked the general expansion of the riots, was merely the result of geographic proximity, or that the intervals between one pogrom and another merely signified the time which the local "contagion" required to take effect. Only ten days were needed for the pogrom in Seville to become known throughout the country; and if the strong desire to strike at the Jews had been the sole cause of the outbreaks, there was no apparent reason for Seville's example to recur in geographic order. Ideas do not necessarily spread along the pattern followed by pestilent diseases, and Burgos did not have to take its cue for action from a second-rate town to its south.

What appears more likely is that, besides the social atmosphere, which was everywhere charged with anti-Jewish feeling, there was a hard nucleus of agitators and organizers to whom we must ascribe the course of the outbreaks. This nucleus, in all likelihood, was formed by Martínez and consisted of his agents, who spread his gospel and executed his plan to destroy the Jews of Spain. Moving from place to place along preagreed routes, their task was to exploit local hatreds for the Jews and organize popular attacks. In the circumstances the task may not have been difficult, but the desired results would not have been attained if it had not been performed. This is, we believe, how the direction of the outbreaks, their timing, the methods of assault (which were everywhere the same), the treatment of the vanquished (which was likewise identical), and the uniformity of the assailants' peculiar message (to which we shall refer in the following) may be duly explained.

The scanty data we possess about the pogroms in Castile will not sustain further speculation. But our conjectures concerning Castile are supported by the parallel events in Aragon, which left behind them a long trail of evidence.

It is on this elaborate and reliable evidence that we shall now focus our attention.

Aragon

I

In 1391 Aragon differed from Castile in having a mature and functioning king, Juan I, who was on good terms with both the nobles and the ruling elites of the cities. He also had special respect for the law and took responsibility for the safety of his Jewish no less than his Christian subjects. But his authority among his countrymen was not high. He was known for shunning the hard work of government and devoting himself to a life of hunting, music, and poetry. Thus, he earned for himself the double title of *el Cazador* (the Hunter) and *el Indolente* (the Idle One). When the pogroms against the Jews broke out, however, he became unexpectedly active. He showered letters and instructions on the governors and the *concejos*, in which he denounced the outrages in sharp terms and demanded severe punishment of the culprits. ("For in such an enormous crime every haste is tardiness and every severity is leniency and softening of justice."[54]) Perhaps in dealing with this particular problem the Indolente was at his best, but his notoriety as an irresolute king undermined his resolute orders. Nevertheless, the *concejos*, though skeptical of his steadfastness, could not disregard his instructions. Nor were they really anxious to ignore them. Generally speaking, the members of the city councils hated the rioters and abhorred the riots, but did not dare go too far in curbing them. They feared the mobs more than the King.

Though we lack full answers to many pertinent questions, the available information on the riots in Aragon allows us to form a much clearer idea of the causes of the outbreaks, their movers and operators, as well as the reaction of the various authorities (monarchic, nobiliar and urban) to the pogroms at the start of the disturbances and in their later stages. The most detailed accounts for Aragon are those left by the councils of Valencia and Barcelona; and they are also most instructive for another reason. In many respects, what occurred in these cities was repeated throughout their surrounding regions. The accounts of these urban occurrences, therefore, deserve special attention.

II

Valencia had been in a state of social turmoil almost since 1367, when it was besieged by Pedro I of Castile in the second phase of his war with Aragon.

The ravages inflicted on Valencia's province by the invading army of Pedro I, which captured, in its march to that coastal city, the fortresses of Teruel, Murviedro and Sogorbe, were hardly remedied with the retreat of the invaders. For shortly thereafter Valencia was the scene of a long, bloody war between its chief nobiliar families, who recruited many of the city's inhabitants, especially from the lower classes.

Thus disorder increased in the city as did the poverty of the workers and peasants, who were mercilessly squeezed by the warring factions, seeking money for their wasteful lives as well as their military ventures. Valencia, says an authoritative scholar, was in those days (i.e., 1391) "like a meeting point for all the vagabonds, roughnecks, gamblers, and adventurers of the kingdom, enemies of all work, who expected to find in it a field and opportunity to dedicate themselves to their perverse inclinations." Prostitution was likewise rampant in the city, and "saloons and gambling dens were established without shame in the streets, in the market places and even in the square of the Bishop's palace." From these areas "emerged all the broils and quarrels that stained the city's streets with blood. The chief of the vigilants and his agents could not guarantee personal security or the inviolability of the domicile."[55]

Given this situation and the misery of the lower classes, who were indebted to the Jews and sought to get rid of them, it is not astonishing that they received with enthusiasm the news of the pogroms in Andalusia and Castile and that their minds were open to every proposal that they too rob and kill the Jews. Such prospects were in fact discussed in Valencia, and all that was needed for their implementation was a competent leadership whom the masses could trust. Before long, as we shall see, such a leadership appeared, presenting its own plan of action, which the Valencians hastened to accept.

Faced with a rising pogromist movement, the Jews of Valencia turned for help to the bailiff and the *concejo*. The latter was also urged by the King to forestall a repetition of the Castilian disorders. In consequence, the judicial authorities of Valencia, as well as other notables of the city, decided to take some precautions. They convened, to begin with, all the city officials and forbade them to support any action against the Jews, "since this is prohibited by the laws of Church and State and subject to grave punishments."[56] To convince the people that this punishment would be forthcoming, they placed gallows with pitchforks in the squares and streets adjacent to the *judería*. They also saw to it that the city's chief judge, accompanied by many guards, move around the *judería*, especially at night. These measures may have calmed the threatened Jews and the well-meaning officials. They did not, however, diminish the preparations for the assault.

The *judería* thus remained subject to attack, depending for its survival solely on its own forces, stationed behind its strong wall, whose construction had been completed only recently. Under the impact of the Castilian riots and the pogromist preparations in their own city, the Jews of Valencia had mobilized a force to meet the expected attack upon their borough, but in view of the brief time at their disposal, they could not give that force adequate training. Apart from this, as Danvila pointed out, they "lacked order and a plan of defense."[57] It would seem that most of them also lacked a fighting spirit and confidence in their success. What was true of the Jews of Castile appears to have been true of the Jews of Valencia, and indeed of Aragon as a whole.

On July 9, at noon, forty to fifty men, no doubt Castilians, approached the Gate of Figuera, which was the *judería*'s chief entrance. The gate was open at that time of day, and some of the attackers entered the *judería*, only to find the gate closed behind them and their friends unable to enter. Perhaps a brawl developed inside the walls, in which some of the intruders were wounded, while those outside the gate hastened to shout that their friends were being murdered. Soon a large throng gathered in the square. It consisted, we are told, of "alien vagabonds," licensed seamen and other "men of low condition" *(hombres de poca y pobre condición)*.[58] Probably, these men were waiting in the neighborhood for a sign that the gate of the *judería* had been seized so that they could rush in.

Fearful of the consequences, the royal officials hastened to impart the news of these developments to Don Martín, the King's brother, Duke of Montblanch and lieutenant of the kingdom, who happened to be in Valencia at the time. Followed by a few horsemen (probably his bodyguard), Don Martín rushed to the Gate of Figuera, which by then was besieged by an excited crowd. Upon reaching it, he asked the Jews behind the gate to release the few Christians they held as captives. But the Jews declined to do so, assuring the Duke that the Christians in their hands were safe. Don Martín now argued that once the people saw that the captives were unharmed, they would quiet down and withdraw from the place. Furthermore, he claimed, if the gate is opened, it will be possible to place guards inside the *judería* and prevent further violence. The Jews, however, refused to give in; and this accelerated the pace of the developments. The infuriated mob approached the gate to break it down. Don Martín and the royal officials who were with him could hardly stop them from making the attempt.

This is the account which the representatives of the city later gave King Juan I. They obviously sought to blame the pogrom on the Jews, who refused to listen to the Infante. Would the riots have been averted if the gate had been opened and the Jews had released the captured Christians? The answer must be in the negative. Evidently, the Jews, who had little faith in the ability of the Infante to quiet the mobs, did not dare take his advice. Don Martín's promise to place guards near the gates must have been regarded by them as hollow, since he came accompanied by only few men, and the isolated guards he might possibly place there would add little to the Jews' own force. Had Don Martín first moved the crowds away from the walls, so that the Jews would feel safe in opening the gate for the short time needed to release the prisoners, there would have been room to criticize their judgment. As matters stood, however, they must have thought that an open gate would serve as an invitation for the pogromists to burst in; that the slightest urging or excuse could stir them to take such action; and that the presence of the Infante would not deter them from the execution of their plan.

While these events took place near the Gate of Figuera, another group of pogromists tried to enter the *judería* through the entrance of Valladar Viejo. The wooden gate was attacked, the Jews placed themselves in the breach, and a "terrible battle ensued, body against body." One Christian was killed and another wounded. Finally the besieged "repelled the attack and remained the masters of the passage."[59] But the defensive force, as events soon showed, was too small to withstand the pressure.

The organizers of the riots now carried the body of the killed Christian among the assembled mob and urged vengeance on the killers. The assault was soon resumed with greater fury, and the assailants found a way to penetrate the *judería*. The Jewish defense units were ultimately dissipated, though some of their members still defended their homes with bolts shot from crossbows. Twelve pogromists were killed and many more wounded, but this did not change the course of events. The robbery and killing of the residents of the *judería* proceeded virtually unchecked. All forms of violence had their heyday; many sacked houses were set on fire, and strewn among the ruins were the corpses of approximately 250 Jews. Some Valencian Jews fled to ships in the port, others to the mountains, while seven thousand souls—the overwhelming majority—were saved from death by carrying crosses and expressing their wish to be baptized. Their conversion marked the total extinction of the Jewish community in Valencia.[60]

III

The results of the pogrom in Valencia, the first city in Aragon to be attacked, strengthened the determination of the organizers of the riots to expand their activity in that kingdom. The next few weeks appeared uneventful, but they were doubtless filled with feverish preparations to put in operation a plan of attack that the King would be unable to disrupt. Speed and ferocity in the execution of the plan were considered vital for its success, and so were secrecy and the element of surprise. In one measure or another, all these factors were present in the Aragonese outbreaks. And thus, after a period of illusory peace, when the riots had almost subsided in Castile, there began in Aragon a series of outbreaks which followed one another in rapid succession: on August 2 in Palma, the capital of Majorca; on August 5 in Barcelona; on August 10 in Gerona; on August 13 in Lérida, and on August 17 in Perpignan. As in Castile, so in Aragon, the rioters moved generally from south to north, storming the great urban centers in the east, especially those located near the coast, where the Jews had long been the most favored targets of the lower classes' hostility and violence.

If the dates of these outbreaks suggest the speed of the pogromist advance, the fierce determination that inspired the assailants may be indicated by the following events. In both Palma and Lérida, the mobs turned furiously against the city officials and forcibly removed them from the way. In Majorca, the governor was almost killed in his futile attempt to defend the Jews, while the governor of Lérida lost his life, having permitted the Jews to take shelter in the alcazar, and then defended the place as well as he could. The fortress, however, was invested by the pogromists, who set fire to its gates and adjacent buildings, and the governor perished in the flames. The attack upon the officials of the crown was general, and we are told that many of them were stoned and wounded while attempting to protect the Jews. In Perpignan, the Jews escaped to the castle after many of them had been killed or converted following the invasion of the *judería*. Here, however, the defenders of the castle succeeded in holding it against the aggressors. In Majorca, the *aljama* was "taken by storm," and in Gerona it was "forced," which clearly indicates that in these places, too, there was some measure of self-defense.[61]

Much more is known about the riots in Barcelona, where the pogrom broke out on August 5, with some fifty Sevillians, who came through Valencia, forming part of the aggressors' vanguard. The attackers took the Jewish quarter by storm, killing about a hundred Jews. The remainder of the residents, deserting their possessions, withdrew to the new castle of the city. Once the aggressors invaded the *aljama*, they hastened to set fire to the *escribanías*, which contained many documents attesting to debts owed by Christians to Catalonian Jews. During the rest of the day and the following night, they sacked the Jewish quarter, paying no heed to the many reproofs of the royal and city authorities.

"On the following day, Sunday," says one of our sources, "the royal officials, the councillors and many notables strengthened the guard of the New Castle," to prevent its capture by the "small people." They also arrested the Castilian rioters and recovered much of what had been stolen. The imprisoned men were put in the carcel of the Court of the vicar of Barcelona. But besides these data, we are informed of a development that throws much light on the events in Barcelona and especially on the attitude of its upper classes toward the pogromists and the Jews:

On Monday, August 7, a full meeting of the Council was held in its accustomed place. Apart from the Councillors, it was attended by many nobles, *caballeros, escuderos,* doctors, honored citizens, merchants and office holders. All of them unanimously maintained that the satisfaction of justice and the damages done to the Republic of Barcelona required that the Castilians, and especially ten of them who took part in the assaults upon the *juderías* of Seville and Valencia, should be executed on the gallows. But while the vicar of Barcelona, Guillermo de San Clemente, wished to carry out the sentence of the Council, arranging for the criminals to make their confessions before they ascended the scaffold, the plebeians broke out in a riot. Equipped with crossbows and other arms, raising banners and shouting: "Long live the people and the King!" they hurled themselves at the royal officials, knocked down the vicar, the councillors and the notables; and so ferocious was the attack that the honorable Jaime Soler, citizen of Barcelona, and a righteous and God-fearing man, succumbed to it, pierced by an arrow of a crossbow, while many others fell wounded. Then the plebs forced their way into the carcel and freed the bandits, both Castilian and Catalan, after overcoming the governor and the other royal officers who were charged with the custody of the prisoners. Only one prisoner, Pedro Vilardell, accused of homicide, did not avail himself of the opportunity [to escape] and refused to leave the prison without an order to do so by the legitimate authorities. He was a citizen of Barcelona.[62]

Having done this, some of the "small people" used sickles to break down the gates of the city walls, and some of them climbed to the bells of the churches and called the peasants to arms, shouting that the "fat" ones (i.e., the rich) were destroying the "small" ones (i.e., the poor). Brandishing torches, the rioters seemed anxious to burn the houses of the burghers. They would have carried out their intent, we are told, had they not been restrained by the "grace and pity of God."[63]

The reference to the "grace and pity of God" at this crucial point of the account raises the question of how the danger then threatening the burghers was averted. Our curiosity, however, is satisfied by another source (the account of Mascaró), according to which "one of the menaced citizens," Mosen Pons de la Sala, understood how to "turn around to the rioters" and persuade them to spend their fury on the Jews rather than upon the Christians.[64] Judging by our original document, this happened on August 8. "In the afternoon of that day," it tells us, "the rebellious people closed in upon the New Castle and attacked it with arrows, stones and other throwable arms. The royal standard that waved over the castle was of no aid to its defenders. The combat lasted until the late hours of the night. In the darkness, about the middle of the night, most of the Jews left the castle and found shelter in various houses of Christians."[65]

"Most of the Jews," to whom this document refers, comprised the majority of those who *remained* Jews after the rest had been converted. From Mascaró's account, we note that the besieged, "combatted with arrows and even more so by hunger and thirst," expressed on that day of August 8 their wish to be baptized to Christianity, while some of them (especially the women) preferred death to conversion. The majority, however, realized their wish. For this purpose a procession of men moved from the Cathedral Church to the Castle, where the cross [of the baptizers] was upheld all that afternoon."[66]

It follows that the Jews who were converted on August 8 comprised the majority of the community, while most of the remainder found shelter in the homes of Christian patricians. A number of Jews, however, refused or were unable to avail themselves of such a refuge. They remained in the castle only to discover that they would have to leave it the following day. Faced with the threats of the besieging mobs and fearing that he would be unable to resist them, the governor ordered the Jews out. Thus they were back in the *judería*, but this time homeless and defenseless. "Those of them who refused to accept baptism were immediately slain, and their corpses, stretched in the streets and the squares, offered a horrendous spectacle."[67] The number of those slaughtered on that day and the next, August 10, amounted to more than three hundred. August 10 was the last of the six days in which the gruesome rape of the Jewish community of Barcelona, the greatest in Aragon, was perpetrated.

There is a significant denouement to this story. On the night following the Jews' conversion, the "peasants invaded the Court of the bailiff, and reduced to ashes all the papers of the archives and the property registers that they could get hold of." And on the following day some rustics forced the vicar to supply them with documents officially "testifying to the abolition of their debts."[68] Together with the burning of the *escribanías*, these events provide a glimpse into the social background and the economic catalyst of the riots. As in all previous outbreaks against the Jews in the Middle Ages, their fiercest enemies in 1391 were the downtrodden elements, the poor, the have-nots, who had borrowed from the Jews to meet their needs and then were unable or unwilling to repay them. It is they who became soldiers of the agitators against the Jews, especially of those who urged that they be looted, degraded and, above all, expelled. The upper classes, the Jews' real competitors, who sought to restrict their rights in the cities, were generally, as we have seen, opposed to violence as a means of settling the Jewish question. And though some of them rejoiced over the mobs' deeds as a heaven-sent answer to their secret prayers, they were careful to conceal their joy under the cover of alleged regret or discontent. There were, however, burghers who felt genuine sorrow for the terrible fate that befell the Jews, and others who offered them shelter and protection, sometimes at considerable risk. Had there not been such burghers in Spain, few Jews of those who had failed to convert would have survived the attacks of 1391.

These reports of the pogrom in Barcelona, originating in authoritative Christian sources, constitute the fullest account we possess of the riots in any Spanish city. From them, it is evident that the vanguard of the rioters included a band of some fifty Castilians, who had participated in the pogrom in Seville and came to Barcelona via Valencia, where they partook in the pogrom in that city. Here in Barcelona, as elsewhere, they followed the same procedures of attack—assaulting, killing, and robbing all Jews who refused to be converted—and here as elsewhere they clashed with the authorities when the latter tried to interfere. The destruction of the city's archives, as well as the insistence of the "small people" on renouncing their debts to the Jews, indicate, apart from the robberies themselves, the economic inducement for the attack, while the actions of the city patricians show that most of them were anxious to punish the culprits, but did not dare to challenge the rioting mobs. Thus they sentenced to death only ten of the fifty Castilians who had led or collaborated with the local rioters, but were soon convinced that the populace would not tolerate any action against their fellow pogromists from Castile. The outbreak against the Jews was on the point of becoming an outburst against the burghers, and the pillage of the Jews could easily extend to the Christian elite as well. Deficient in moral courage, and possibly also in military resources, the burghers lacked, above all, strong leadership to whom duty and honor were values worth fighting for. The vicar was certainly no such leader. When he ousted the Jews from the castle into the streets, he bought peace and security for himself, and possibly for his family and comrades, at the cost of hundreds of Jewish lives. It was far from being an honorable act, and Crescas, the head of the Jews of Aragon, seems to have judged him too leniently.[69]

IV

However scanty our data for the riots in Castile and however incomplete for those in Aragon, the combined information suggests certain conclusions regarding the nature, causes and objectives of the outbreaks.

It has been commonly believed that the pogroms in Spain in the summer of 1391 broke out spontaneously following the riots in Seville, which merely spurred the Jew haters across the country to inflict deadly blows upon the Jews. There is truth in this opinion, but not the whole truth.

To be sure, the pogrom in Seville served to stimulate Jew-baiters in many places in Castile to strike at the Jews; but this stimulus alone would not have produced so many assaults; nor can it account for their extreme and large-scale violence, as well as their unprecedented results. Already while discussing the riots in Castile, we expressed our opinion that the *order* of the outbreaks there, their direction and timing, imply a guiding and controlling force. This view gains strength from the parallel course observable in the riots of Aragon. There, too, they spread from south to north and were separated from each other by brief intervals. In light of this order, it is hard to assume that the riots were a merely spontaneous response of the Aragonese people to the pogroms in Castile. Had these riots stemmed from sheer impulse, they would have broken out in scattered sites and not extended as they did from south to north. Actually, there was little in this phenomenon that was merely of an imitative nature. Rather do we have here a premeditated extension of an activity whose origin was in the south. That origin could be none other than the archdeacon Ferrán Martínez.

Our view that the riots in Castile resulted from a planned action of an organizing force was based on certain suggestive symptoms. Regarding Aragon, the same view may be upheld not only on the grounds of such symptoms, but also on the basis of clear-cut evidence offered by contemporary sources. Thus these sources, as we have noted, reveal that the attacks in both Valencia and Barcelona were led by a group of some fifty Castilians, who included the vanguard of the rioters in Seville. These facts in themselves strongly suggest that these men did not just happen to be in Valencia and Barcelona during the pogroms, and thus merely *chanced* to partake in them, but came to those cities on a special mission to organize the assaults on their Jewish communities. But in addition to the above evidence, which leads us to this plausible conclusion, we possess another important testimony that turns the plausibility into a certainty.

In April 1392, the authorities of Aragon seized a certain priest who was Martínez' nephew, and put him in the prison of the archbishop of Saragossa. They had evidently been looking for him for a long time and regarded his activity as extremely harmful, since his capture was considered so important that three public bodies—the high court of Aragon, the police of Saragossa and the council of that city—hastened to inform the King of his arrest. The nature of the harm done by the prisoner is not specified in these notifications; it is indicated, however, in the King's responses to his aforementioned informants.

In these responses the imprisoned man was called by the King *"the cause of the riots and of the destruction of our aljama of Jews."*[70] Undoubtedly the King made this momentous statement on the basis of many reports he had received; and it is also certain that the same view was shared by the recipients of the King's responses. Martínez' nephew was thus seen by the authorities as not merely a participant in the riots but as their "cause"—namely, as their instigator and organizer and, more precisely, as the man *without whose activity the riots would not have occurred, or at least would not have had such calamitous results*. Accordingly, the authorities attributed to him not only the destruction of *one or two* Jewish communities, but of *all* the communities in the Aragonese kingdom that were ruined by the pogroms (or, as the king put it, he was the "cause of the destruction of *our aljama* of Jews." Hence, we must conclude that Martínez' nephew led the pogromist drive in all the towns of Aragon that took part in the bloody persecution.

In light of this, one can hardly doubt that he acted as Martínez' agent. Nor can we assume that he was the *only* Castilian who carried out that complex and large-scale mission. The fifty Castilian pogromists in Valencia and Barcelona were surely part of that force which was sent to Aragon by Martínez and took its orders from the arrested priest. No wonder that the King warned his officials to guard the prisoner well, lest he escape and avoid the severe punishment he deserved ("For such people should not be allowed to live").[71] It seems that the King also considered the possibility that, with his man in prison, Martínez himself might come to Aragon to lead the pogromist movement, as he probably did not consider such a movement possible without a highly efficient organizer and inciter. Thus he added in his letter to the authorities of Saragossa that if this indeed happens—i.e., "if Martínez comes to your city" [and you manage to seize him], "send him to me or throw him into the river."[72]

As far as is known, Martínez did not come to Aragon; nor are there records of additional riots in that country after the arrest of his nephew. Perhaps the imprisonment of Martínez' chief agent and leading organizer of the riots led to the abrupt demise of the pogromist movement. In any case, it is evident that the outbreaks in Aragon were not, as had commonly been assumed, merely a product of popular impulses, stimulated by the pogroms in Castile, but also the result of a guiding hand and mind—the hand and mind of Martínez.

V

This conclusion, which conforms to the inference we drew about the "prime mover" of the riots from their common traits in both Castile and Aragon, is further supported by another feature that characterized these riots in all places. This was the *uniformity of their results*, which cannot be explained without the guidance and control of a strong and effective leadership.

The most significant of these results was undoubtedly the exceptionally large number of converts compared with the relatively small number of martyrs. This fact does not square with the common behavior of other Jewish communities in Europe who underwent similar experiences. Especially does it stand in stark contrast to the conduct of German Jewry during the first crusade (1096) who, in the great majority of cases, chose death rather than conversion. What was the cause of this striking difference? Could it have been merely, as has often been argued, the different degrees of dedication to Judaism that characterized the communities involved? Or were there possibly other reasons?

There can be nò doubt that the Jews of Germany had far surpassed the Jews of Spain in religious devotion and readiness for martyrdom. Judging by the principles that inspired them, their self-immolation in defense of their faith set an example of moral grandeur that had never been excelled in the annals of mankind.[73] And yet Spanish Jewry cannot be downgraded to a low level of religious devotion. The thousands of martyrs it produced during the onslaughts of 1367 and 1391 offer clear evidence of this. But to understand more fully the results of those onslaughts, certain relevant facts should be noted.

Some of these facts are clearly related to the past history of Spanish Jewry. Their forced conversion under the Almohades (1147), which they managed to overcome as secret Jews, led many of them to believe that forced conversion was not the end of the world; and in addition there were the teachings of Maimonides who, while hailing martyrdom, did not denounce forced conversion, and thus gave a kind of moral sanction to conversion under duress.[74] Neither such experiences nor such teachings affected the Jews of Germany in 1096. But there was also another factor, peculiar to Spain, which no doubt helped incline the Spanish Jews toward this form of conversion.

That factor stemmed from the behavior of the pogromists, which was not the same in Germany as in Spain. To be sure, as in the Rhineland, the pogromists in Spain were moved above all by a pent up hatred which sought an outlet in bloodshed and pillage; in both countries the assaults were "justified" by the need "to avenge the blood of Christ;" and in both the Jews could escape destruction by declaring, through baptism, their abandonment of Judaism and adoption of the Christian faith. Yet the process of their "escape" in 1391 was characterized by a special innovation.

It is doubtful whether during the Spanish Civil War (in Briviesca and Miranda de Ebro) the attacked Jewish communities, which were wiped out to a man, were even offered the opportunity of conversion. The assailants simply wanted to kill the Jews and rob them, and were hardly interested in anything else. This was no doubt the main aim also of the crusading bands in Germany who fell upon the Jews like packs of hungry wolves, and were to give up their desired prey only when warned by lay or Church authorities against killing Christians (which the converts would become).[75] This was not what happened in Spain in 1391. In the pogroms of that year, as evidence suggests, the assailants announced, prior to their attacks, that what they wanted was to have the Jews converted, and only if met with no positive response would they resort to violence. Thus, whereas in the Rhineland type of pogroms conversion was the alternative to death, in the pogroms of 1391 death was the alternative to conversion. Granted that in Germany this change of order would have made no difference. In Spain, as we see it, it made a big difference, psychologically and materially.

To begin with, it is obvious that when murder, rapine, robbery and arson were the sole or main objectives of the attackers, it was extremely hard to divert them from their aims by the victims' expressed consent to convert. There is no doubt that in the fury of such attacks, many appeals for conversion were ignored. The case was different, however, when conversion was offered not by the assailed but by their assailants, and the threatened Jews had from the outset a choice between conversion and death. The emphasis put on this choice by the attackers *necessarily inclined some Spanish Jews to consider the alternative*; it increased hesitation, especially of the faint-hearted, and weakened their resolve to fight to the end.

These characteristics of the riots of 1391 may help explain the great multitude of conversions in each of the attacked communities, and the fact that many of these conversions took place before the attacks started. Let us recall that royal decrees offering conversion as the alternative to death produced even in most faithful communities almost total conversion of all their members. The riots of 1391 combined in a way the procedures followed by coercive governments and those in great pogroms by incited masses, whose aim was primarily robbery and murder. Hence the mixed results: a large number of converts and an incomparably smaller, though by no means insignificant, number of martyrs for the faith.

We shall get a better sense of this development when we consider Martínez' strategy. It is clear that Martínez' hatred of the Jews was such that it moved him to seek their annihilation; and we have seen that he had occasionally conducted an openly murderous agitation. Yet when it came to the final test, he saw himself restrained, as archdeacon of the Church, from explicitly expressing his desire. Church instructions forbade the killing of Jews for whatever reason and under any circumstances, unless ordered by the courts as expiation for crimes deserving capital punishment. Martínez was of course aware of these instructions. It would have been too dangerous for him to order his hordes plainly, "Go and kill all Jews!", and thereby assume personal responsibility for hundreds of thousands of deaths. Instead, he commanded them to let the Jews know that they ought to convert if they wished to live, and only if they failed to respond in the affirmative, to treat them as stubborn enemies of Christ who deserved all the punishments the people might inflict on them. On the basis of this approach Martínez could claim that he aimed not to destroy the Jews but to save them—that is, save their souls through conversion to Christianity—and that the threat of punishment accompanying his appeal was a necessary stimulant to the obstinate infidels who would otherwise not convert.

That the riots of 1391 followed this pattern consistently was due to Martínez' strong hold on his followers and the faithfulness of his deputies to his orders. There is no doubt that in his harangues against the Jews, Martínez inflamed hatred for them to the point of moving the populace to destroy them. But it is also clear that as a Church official, he wanted to remain within the limits of Church law, and therefore he attached to each of his campaigns some concrete anti-Jewish order, based in one measure or another on Church law—an order which the Christians urged the Jews to fulfill and which the Jews would find it impossible to follow.

Such, for example, were his demands to oust the Jews from their quarters, or destroy their synagogues, or force them to accept ecclesiastical adjudication. Since the Jews resisted all his proposed measures, Martínez urged his followers to *enforce* them on the ground that they were decrees of the Church. His campaign of 1391 followed the same method. This time his concrete demand was the most difficult for the Jews to accept and for the Christians to carry out: the Jews were required to convert, and if they refused, they were to be killed; if, however, in the course of the attack they changed their mind and chose to convert, the violence ought to be terminated at once and their request to be baptized should be granted.

Conversion effected under *such* a threat of death could be considered none other than forced, and the Church had legally opposed forced conversion, even though (since the days of Isidore of Seville) it recognized its validity after the fact. But Martínez was no stickler for legal niceties, especially when these did not suit his purpose; and he did not have to do much hairsplitting to prove that in this case logic was on his side. If conversion effected under threat of death was ultimately accepted by the Church as valid, why should any Christian avoid effecting it and refrain from saving more souls for Christ? Only sophisticated theologians could reconcile the *acceptance* of such a conversion with the *prohibition* to perform it. Martínez rejected such subtleties. He adopted St. Isidore's final conclusion that *forced* converts should be viewed as *ordinary* converts, and disregarded the prolegomena that led to it. Perhaps this is why theologians like Paul of Burgos considered him a man of poor learning. But Martínez was not so ignorant. In any case, he misinterpreted some teachings of the Church not out of ignorance but by design. It was his method to use *some* decrees of the Church, or *some* sayings of Christian authorities, in disregard of contradictory sayings and decrees if the former would suit his purpose. We have already seen that this habit of his had brought him to a frontal conflict with the Church and the brink of being sentenced as a heretic.

That the "small people" who attacked the Jews came to believe, due to Martínez' agitation, that forced conversion was permitted by the Church, or even that it was commanded by it, is evident from the repeated attempts of Juan I of Aragon to challenge that belief. The King chastised the rioters by letting them know that, though the Church welcomed the conversion of the Jews, it prohibited their conversion under duress. The masses, however, paid little attention to the King's "theological instructions" and preferred to take Martínez' word as to what the Church's teaching was. And not only the *populo menudo* believed him. Martínez' views on forced conversion spread also among the middle class, as well as among the cities' patricians. Matters reached such a pass that the King had to issue instructions to the citizens of Valencia who offered the Jews shelter in their houses *not to use coercion in the conversion of the fugitives.*[76] In the course of the riots, it is quite clear, Martínez and his agents managed to persuade vast sections of the people that conversion (voluntary, if possible; forced, if impossible) was the only way to solve the Jewish problem. In Perpignan the city councilors urged the King to see to it that all the Jews convert, and thereby put an end to the disorders.[77]

It is a testimony to the hold Martínez had on his movement and to his far-reaching influence on the Spanish masses that his instructions were carried out almost fully, or at least to a great extent. It was easy to incite mobs to rob the Jews and kill them; it was not easy to suppress the aroused passions of the mobs by the mere consent of the Jews to convert. The suppression was nonetheless made possible in most cases because the masses were prepared for it by Martínez' agitation and well disciplined by his lieutenants to use violence against the Jews only on condition that they refused conversion. Since legitimation of violence depended on that refusal, the offer of conversion *had* to be made, and the opportunity to effect it *had* to be given. Martínez saw to it that this lesson was inculcated as thoroughly as his instructions on what to do with the Jews if they rejected that offer. His followers knew that they could begin their killing and pillage immediately after the first refusal, and generally treat the Jews brutally as befits the enemies of Christ.

The authors of the extant accounts of those events were so impressed by the bloodshed and destruction that they tended to see in the threat of death alone the cause of the massive conversion. Rarely do they touch on Martínez' campaign beyond stating that it was fiercely anti-Jewish. But that he stressed in his campaign the alternative of conversion is evident from a variety of contemporary sources. It is apparent from the demands which the peasants of Majorca had addressed to the Jews of Palma before they started their attack; the peasants told the Jews that they must convert if they did not wish to die.[78] Of the Jews of Barcelona, who were forced to leave the castle near the *judería*, we are informed that *when they refused to convert*, they were immediately cut down[79]; this suggests that before they were killed, they had been given the opportunity to convert. Similarly, the "small people" who besieged the castle of Geronelia (on the outskirts of Gerona) demanded that the Jews convert to Christianity or leave the city.[80] Similar evidence is offered by other sources. Rafael Ramírez de Arellano, who studied the documents related to Cordova, noticed the double thrust of Martínez' agitation when he summarized the events in the city as follows:

"The Cordovese, *under the pretext of obliging the Jews to convert to Catholicism,* entered the *judería* and the castle [which was within it], robbing what they found and killing all Jews who stood in their way."[81] The same "pretext" was reflected also in the taunts, which the ruffians who attacked the Jews in Valencia hurled at the besieged community. "The archpriest of Seville," they said, "came with his cross to baptize the Jews, and *those who will not baptize themselves will die.*"[82] Referring to Martínez' agitation preceding the great outbreak in Seville, Zúñiga says that it reflected a "new intemperance," indicating that Martínez "wanted to convert the Jews almost by force."[83]

Indeed, Martínez' campaign of 1391 represented the only pogromist movement in Jewish history that inscribed on its banner the conversion of the Jews. Ostensibly, Martínez did not mean to hurt the Jews but to do them enormous good. Thus he could mobilize many of the neutral and less antisemitic elements of the populace by claiming that he conducted a campaign of conversion—a positive, legitimate, acceptable campaign—and that only if the Jews insisted on their perfidy would they be punished as deserved. We must bear all this in mind to understand the rapid spread of the campaign (which indicates support from different quarters) and, above all, its major consequence.

This consequence was the appearance of a large New Christian population. Indeed, the conversion of the Jews in 1391 might not have assumed such large proportions if the pogromist campaign of that year had been conducted in the spirit, and with the approach, of the pogromist movements of 1096, or 1190, or 1348, or 1649—that is, if its obvious primary aim had been the extermination of the Jews. Matters turned out the way they did because the conversion, and not the destruction, of the Jews was the declared purpose of the attacks. This facilitated the transfer of many Jews to Christianity; and thus was born the converso problem.

II. Paul of Burgos

None of Spain's converts had made such great efforts to bring about the Christianization of all of Spain's Jews and none had attained such success in his endeavors as Solomon ha-Levi, chief rabbi of Burgos, who went over to Christianity during the riots of 1391. He was known thereafter by his various Christian names—Pablo de Santa María, or Pablo de Cartagena, or the Bishop of Burgos (*Episcopus Burgensis*, in Latin theological literature), but he is also referred to in the Spanish sources as Pablo de Burgos—the designation we shall use here in English form.[1]

He was born in Burgos about 1352 to a rich and well-connected family, apparently of Aragonese descent.[2] His education followed the pattern then common among the wealthy Jewish families of the peninsula, comprising all branches of traditional Jewish learning, the philosophies of the Middle Ages, and some of the sciences.[3] From the Jewish philosophers, primarily Maimonides and his disciples in the 13th and 14th centuries, a short road led to the Christian scholastics, who were notable for their rationalistic bent. As followers of Aristotle in one measure or another and as bearers of "philosophical truth," their views, though saturated with Christian ideas, could be partly accepted by Jewish students of philosophy, just as the works of Averroes could be admired by them all despite their Moslem veneer. Tradition has it that Paul became infatuated with the works of Thomas Aquinas.[4] There is no need to doubt this tradition.

His vast acquaintance with Jewish literature and his mastery of the Jewish sources of law were at least partly responsible for his appointment as chief rabbi of Burgos. But his mastery of Latin brought him also in touch with the anti-Jewish Christian authors (from the Church Fathers on), and aware of their arguments against the Jews and Judaism, he could devise counterarguments to refute them. In the second half of the 14th century, theological disputations between Jews and Christians abounded in Spain, especially in Castile. Paul used his wide learning, keen mind and debating skill to defend the Jewish faith against its critics. He became known among both Jews and Christians as a formidable advocate of the Jewish case.[5]

In the 14th century the Jewish community of Burgos was one of the three leading communities of Castile, not only because of its size and wealth but also because of its political influence, Burgos then being a major base of power of the Castilian kingdom.[6] His position as chief rabbi of the great community, however, did not satisfy Solomon ha-Levi's ambitions. He aspired also to the position of courtier, such as many Jews still enjoyed in Castile until the beginning of the 80s. As head of the Burgos Jewish community and member of one of its wealthy families, he could easily gain access to the leaders of the administration and try to make his way into the diplomatic service. He may have actually been approaching this objective, for we know that in 1388 he was chosen by the king, Juan I, to serve, with other courtiers and notables, as one of Castile's hostages in England.[7] The hostages were given as security for the dowry Juan I was to give the Duke of Lancaster, in accordance with the terms of the contracted marriage of Catalina, the Duke's daughter, to Enrique, Juan's son. In a show of special devotion to the King, Solomon may have offered his candidacy for the task, which was by no means pleasant or free from risk. This is the only case we know in which a Jew played such a part in a medieval kingdom; and we may assume that Paul's candidacy was accepted not because of, but despite his being a Jew and a rabbi. It was accepted because he was a wealthy individual and highly regarded in the royal Court.

Solomon ha-Levi must have fallen in love with the style of life of the Christian aristocracy,[8] just as he must have become an admirer of scholastic and philosophical Christian literature. Perhaps the debates he had with Christian scholars, which compelled him to study Christian writings against the Jews, led him to the conclusion, not admitted by him openly, that on some points at issue the Christian views were sound, grounded in authority, and hardly refutable. This does not mean, however, that he came to view himself as closer to Christianity than to Judaism. It is more likely that the questions, doubts and uncertainties he encountered in the course of his inquiries and debates turned him gradually into a skeptic. He could see that by the same scholastic tactics, and the same reliance on Holy Writ, one could prove the veracity of any religion, Christianity included, or conversely, the dubiousness of any faith, Judaism not excepted. In any case, his original belief in Judaism as the sole bearer of religious truth was seriously undermined, or at least debilitated to a considerable extent.

He must have been in this frame of mind, with his social ambitions unfulfilled and his religious views in turmoil, when the riots in the south broke out. He was certainly not ready to make great sacrifices either for his way of life as a Jew or for his adherence to Judaism as a religion. As long as the Jews of Spain retained their status as a privileged and protected minority, a man like Paul might see no vital need to abandon his flock for a higher position or a more attractive society. But when Judaism posed a danger to his existence, Paul would not risk his life for its sake.

He was no doubt informed of the massacres in Andalusia shortly after their occurrence, and it did not take him long to make up his mind about the course he was to take. He decided to convert. We have seen that already on

June 16, only twelve days after the outbreak in Seville, the Regency warned
the authorities of Burgos against the pogromist movement in their city. Paul,
as chief rabbi, must have dealt with these authorities about the measures of
protection sought by his community, and he must have soon been convinced
that no real protection could be expected and, hence, that in case of an attack
conversion was the only avenue of escape. Paul drew from the information
he possessed what seemed to him the only logical conclusion: Why await the
attack, suffer many casualties, and then convert in the course of a sack like
the Jews of Seville, Cordova and Toledo, when they could convert before the
attack, save themselves and their possessions from destruction and avoid
intolerable suffering?

If this was indeed his train of thought when he arrived at this decision, his
ensuing conversion might still be regarded, in a sense, as "forced." But what
we know from subsequent sources is that Paul presented his conversion as a
voluntary act that stemmed solely from his religious convictions. How he
made that reversal in the brief time between the outbreak of the riots and his
adoption of Christianity is obscured by the sources. But a casual remark of
his in a letter he wrote shortly after his conversion gives us a clue to some
of the events related to his transition. From that remark it appears that he
made the drastic move not alone, but together with other Burgensian Jews,[9]
and this fact may serve as basis for a plausible reconstruction of what
happened. As head of his community, he no doubt communicated to its
notables the data he gathered and the opinions he formed about the situation
that confronted them; and another source gives us reason to suppose that
they agreed with his assessments and conclusions.[10] As a result, Paul could
be encouraged to believe that he would be converted with a large group—
perhaps that he might even persuade his whole community to follow him to
the baptismal font.

From this point we may perhaps be permitted to proceed with our reconstruction somewhat further. It would not, as we see it, be excessive to assume
that Paul then called a general meeting of his community and presented to
its members his thoughts on the grave crisis with which they were faced. One
can imagine the tenor of his address. He must have painted a gloomy picture
of the condition of the Jews in Spain, stressing the hopelessness of their
situation. He may also have described the condition of the Jews in other
countries of the West, mentioning the persecutions in England, France and
Germany and drawing the conclusion that the end was approaching for
Jewish life in the Iberian peninsula, too. In any case, he must have stressed
the futility of the attempt to adhere to the Jewish faith under the current
circumstances in Spain, and the terrible consequence that such an adherence
would entail for every individual Jew. It does not stand to reason that on that
occasion he tried to prove to his perturbed audience that Christianity was

superior to Judaism as a religion. He may have pointed out, however, its relentless conquest of one region of the earth after another, and that even the Moslems had to retreat before the invincible might of the cross. In line with this he may have added that the Jews had resisted the pressure of Christianity more than any other people; it is a pity, of course, that all their efforts, their suffering and sacrifices were in vain. But it is time to face reality and cease shedding more blood for what experience has proven unattainable.

Whatever arguments Paul used in that address which, as we conjecture, he most probably delivered, it was not received with general acclaim. In fact, it must have caused shock and consternation among many of those who attended that meeting, and arguments refuting his contentions and conclusions must have been voiced by some of them.[11] Indubitably the latter did not fail to accuse Paul, hitherto seen as their leader and teacher, of both appalling treachery and shameless cowardice; and the grave insults hurled at him on that occasion may have been so offensive and so hard to take that he could never forget or forgive them. Perhaps the seeds of his future hatred of the Jews—that is, of the Jews who had stuck to their religion—that hatred which seethed in his later writings, had its origin in that bitter experience and his subsequent encounters with the faithful Jews of Burgos in those crucial days.

II

Nevertheless, judging by our sources, most notables of the Burgos community accepted Paul's analysis of the situation and found no solution in their extremity except the one suggested by Paul. They knew of course that intensive preparations were in progress for an attack upon the *judería*, and they decided to preempt the planned assault by their public baptism in the Major Church. They fixed the date of their conversion for July 21, and invited all the Jews of the community to join them. Only a minority, however, agreed. The remainder consisted of determined opponents and others who could not make up their minds—that is, who decided to cross the bridge when they reached it, hoping for a miraculous turn of events. No miracle, however, occurred. Paul and his family (with the exception of his wife)—his three brothers, his children and his mother—together with a group of followers, were converted on July 21, 1391,[12] only a few weeks before the outbreak of the pogrom in Burgos.[13] Many members of the community converted after the *judería* had been invaded and its residents were forced to abandon their homes. But many others found refuge in the homes of patricians, who offered them shelter for handsome rewards.[14] Thus Paul's presumed prognostications did not prove entirely true. Rich Jews *could* have saved themselves without being converted.

In the following months the regency was stabilized and the pogromist movement in Castile was checked, while in Aragon it may have been arrested with the incarceration of its chief organizer. Paul felt he had nothing to do in the ruined and divided community, where he was exposed to the violent denunciations of the Jews who had stuck to their religion. He was then thirty-eight years old, full of vigor and yearning for new achievements. He decided to go to Paris and study theology in its famous university, making use of his mastery of Latin and considerable knowledge of Christian litera-ture. He was a scholar, a lover of learning and inquiry, but he was also a man of strong social ambitions, which he was not prepared to give up. It is hard to believe that he went to Paris without having a Church career in mind.

In Paris he devoted three years to his studies and graduated as Master of Theology.[15] But this was not his only accomplishment. In the course of his stay there, he became acquainted with Pedro de Luna, Cardinal of Aragon, who then resided in the French capital as Clement VII's *legatus a latere* for France, England, Scotland and the Low Countries. The cardinal must have been deeply impressed with Paul's personality, breadth of knowledge and original ideas. In fact, Paul formed a strong friendship with the legate, who became such an admirer of his that in October 1394, when he was elected Pope under the name of Benedict XIII, he hastened to invite Paul to Avignon and entrusted him with highly responsible tasks.[16] It stands to reason that already in Paris, the former rabbi disclosed to the cardinal his plans for the conversion of all the Jews of Spain, possibly of Europe. And now, in Avignon, Paul began immediately to use his position in the papal court to put some of his ideas into effect.

1394 was another disastrous year for the Jews of western Europe. In Sep-tember of that year, Charles VI, King of France, expelled all the Jews from his domains. Paul was in Paris when the decree was issued and could witness the plight of the uprooted community, one of the last in western Europe to survive the medieval persecutions. Only a few places in France agreed to receive the exiles, the papal territory of Perpignan among them. Paul thought the time opportune to address the deportees, who crammed the small Jewish quarter of Perpignan, and point out to them the terrible fate awaiting all Jews who kept denying Christ. He is said to have made many converts among the exiles,[17] and one tends to assume that there is truth in this report, bearing in mind his ability as disputant, the influence of his past position as chief rabbi, the prestige he gained from his office in the curia and, above all, the state of misery and desperation in which the newcomers to Perpignan must have found themselves at the time.

Paul was not satisfied, however, with mere preaching. He also worked out an anti-Jewish plan comprising a series of oppressive measures, but was prevented from implementing it by the Cardinal of Pamplona, Martín Salva, a confidant of Benedict XIII.[18] We do not know what that plan was and against which Jewish group (or groups) it was directed. But in view of the above, it is reasonable to assume that he urged Benedict XIII to decree the expulsion of the French exiles, or of all Jews who lived in his domains, unless they agreed to convert to Christianity. The adoption of such a measure would be contrary to the policies followed by all popes; and if this was indeed the gist of Paul's plan, we should not be surprised that the Cardinal of Pamplona could persuade Benedict to reject it.

But Paul worked against the Jews in other ways, too. Through the contacts he developed with Juan I of Aragon, he managed to have some "annoying" decrees issued against the Jews of that country. Under different circumstances, the Jews of Aragon would probably have asked for the repeal of those decrees. But Crescas, the leader of Aragonese Jewry, who knew that their petition would be brought to Paul's attention, considered the latter's intervention so dangerous that he preferred to suffer the annoyances involved rather than give Paul another opportunity to interfere in the affairs of the Jews of Aragon.[19] Obviously, by then Paul had become known as a fierce enemy of the Jewish people.

These developments occurred shortly after Paul's appointment to his office in the curia—in any case, not later than 1395.[20] It is doubtful whether in the following four years (the period of Paul's stay in Avignon) he had time to concern himself with the Jewish question. He was busy managing the curia's affairs, which were in a sorry state, and, above all, upholding his pope's cause. Antagonism to Benedict continued to increase in the wake of the growing opposition to the Schism. In July 1398, France withdrew its obedience from him, and in December of that year Castile followed France. Apart from the political issues involved, Benedict was beset with financial problems. Paul was in the thick of these developments, and proved to be in those difficult years a pillar of strength to Benedict and his cause. Esteem for him in the curia grew, and its members viewed him as a leading figure, destined to occupy the highest Church positions, including that of cardinal.[21] But the tasks he fulfilled and the contacts he established also gained him an international reputation—above all, in the Spanish peninsula.

In 1398 Benedict decided, in view of his waning influence in Castile, to send Paul back to his country of origin, hoping that Paul might manage to restore there his authority with the King and the Spanish Church. He appointed him archdeacon of Treviño, a large province in the diocese of Burgos, and made him his official representative in Castile. Paul's reputation undoubtedly helped him to establish himself in his new positions. The King accorded Paul a most friendly welcome and appointed him royal chaplain. Thus began Paul's association with Enrique III, and the second phase of his great career in Christendom, this time in the sphere of monarchic authority.

III

Paul's rapid advance in Castile, following his great success in the Church, leads us to conclude that he was endowed with some outstanding personal qualities. This conclusion is also supported by the records. "There was no doubt a great reason for the fact that he was loved by every discreet King or Prince," says the contemporary Spanish poet and historian Pérez de Guzmán of Paul.[22] Guzmán believed that the intimate friendship Paul formed with some of the potentates of his time was based on the trust one could place in his discretion. "These are virtues and graces," Guzmán adds, "that make a man worthy of gaining the favor of any discreet King." But this is hardly a sufficient explanation. Paul must also have been a great diplomat, ingenious deviser of solutions to hard problems; and besides, he must have had the appearance and deportment of a great personage.[23] It was presumably in part thanks to these qualities that Paul succeeded, after years of patient labor, in moving Enrique III to submit once more to Benedict's authority. This happened toward the end of 1402.[24]

In recognition of this outstanding achievement, Benedict appointed Paul, on July 30, 1403, bishop of Cartagena, the diocese of which Murcia was the capital; and at the same time he was formally appointed the Pope's ambassador to the Castilian Court.[25] In the following years, Paul cemented his relations with Enrique III and became one of the King's closest friends, if indeed not the closest of them all. In 1406 Enrique appointed him one of the three executors of his will, Major Chancellor and the tutor of his son, Juan II.[26]

Following Enrique's death (in 1406), the papacy came under increasing attack by the European powers, which were now more determined than ever to put an end to the Schism. It was in no small measure due to the relations that Paul had established with Castile's Regency that Castile did not withdraw its obedience from Benedict XIII. Of the two Castilian Regents at the time—Queen Catalina, the late king's widow, and the Infante Fernando, the late king's brother—the latter became the main power in the kingdom and the leading influence in Castile's nobility. Paul, while on amicable terms with the Queen, forged special ties of friendship with Fernando. As we shall see, this friendship was to form the basis of Paul's future activity and career.

In March 1403, Benedict XIII, his palace besieged by French troops, fled Avignon for Castroreinaldo, in the domain of the Duke of Orléans. Some two months later, however, France, following the Castilian example, resumed its submission to Benedict; but the latter never returned to Avignon. He established his residence in Marseilles, where he stayed several years. But the rising pressure for his abdication inclined him to go to northwestern Italy, where he sought to persuade Gregory XII, his rival in the papacy, to give up his position. Nothing came of these attempts; and, faced with mounting criticism and growing hostility, he finally decided to move to Perpignan, then in Aragon's dominion. He arrived there by boat—"almost as a fugitive," as one historian of the Schism put it[27]—on the eve of Saint James Day, 1408.

IV

What was Paul's position toward the Jewish question throughout his stay in Castile from 1399 on? We can deduce it, we believe, from the attitude toward the Jews displayed by Castile's Enrique III, who became, as indicated, Paul's intimate. In the years following the King's assumption of power (in the second half of 1393)—that is, prior to Paul's return to Castile—we can detect no anti-Jewish attitude on Enrique's part. The King persisted in pressing the cities to pay the fines for the losses caused to the Crown by the pogroms; and although it was obvious that this effort represented a fiscal interest of the King, it also carried with it the concept of collective guilt and a warning that no attack upon the Jews was to remain unpunished. More indicative of the King's pro-Jewish policy was the uninterrupted occupation by Jews of high positions in the King's administration, such as tax farmers, revenue collectors and provincial treasurers.[28] But toward the end of his reign we see the King enact, in the Cortes of Madrid (December 1405), a number of laws that were offensive to the Jews, reduced their social status and hurt them economically. What brought about these enactments at a time when the Jews were still smarting from the wounds of the pogroms and when their economic recovery from the blows they had suffered was supposed to be in the interest of the Crown? In our judgment, this new legislation should be attributed in the main to the influence of Paul.

Most of these laws deal with the interest the Jews took on loans they had given to Christians. *Prima facie,* they repeat similar decrees issued by preceding kings since 1348 (by Alfonso XI).[29] Yet a careful study of this legislation shows that the new laws differed from the old ones in several important respects. Most notably, they reflect a return to the position taken by the Church prior to the decree of 1348.

As is known, the struggle of the third estate in Castile against Jewish moneylending at interest was encouraged by the Church's campaign against usury. In 1306, the Toledan Church, relying on orders of Pope Clement V, instituted trials against local Jews who lent Christians money at interest. Not only did its judges cancel all interest owed Jews by Christian borrowers, but they sentenced Jewish lenders to return the interest they had already taken on loans. Moreover, they excommunicated some Christians who collaborated with Jews in such transactions. Sternly forbidding the Toledan Church to follow the Pope's instructions in this matter, King Fernando IV annulled the sentences issued by the ecclesiastical court,[30] and thereafter nobody was excommunicated for similar alleged offenses. In contrast, King Enrique III, in his decree, "orders and requests" the prelates of his dominion to impose a sentence of excommunication on any judge or official who respects notes or contracts obliging Christians to pay interest on loans.[31]

The other difference touches the penalties to be imposed upon both Jews and non-Jews for usury. To begin with, these penalties reduce the debts which Christians owe Jews (according to contracts, sentences, or witnesses). Since it is not credible that, "in view of their faith (por razón de la seta), Jews would lend Christians anything without usury, all such debts as those mentioned above are presumed to be usurious"—namely, to contain not only the principal but also the interest agreed on between the parties, even though this is not mentioned in the contracts. Accordingly, the King decided to decree a large reduction of all the sums that Christians owed Jews.

In themselves such reductions were no innovation. They had repeatedly been made in response to complaints over the high rates of interest the Jews had charged and the economic distress in which the Christians found themselves. Thus, in 1348 Alfonso XI reduced the Christian debts to the Jews by a quarter[32]; in 1367 and again in 1377, Enrique II reduced them by a third[33]; and in 1385, Juan I again reduced them by a quarter.[34] Enrique III, however, went a step further: he reduced the Christians' debts to Jews by *half*.[35]

In line with earlier enactments, however, Enrique III agreed to make exceptions for loans contracted *before* the issuance of his law. He agreed that if trustworthy Christians testify that the payment demanded by the Jewish lender contains no interest at all, or if the debtor himself confirms this claim through unimpeachable Christian witnesses, the Christian must pay the entire loan, as demanded by the Jew.[36] But such exceptions are no longer to be made in future borrowings. Since the Jews, in their efforts to defraud the law, also manage to induce Christian borrowers to confess that they have received what they actually have not—namely, pure principal without any interest—Enrique now decrees that such confessions are totally invalid. Judges and other officials are forbidden to issue a sentence on that basis, and if they do, the sentence will not be honored; "from now on I regard as null and void any sentence that may be issued in deception and defraudation of the laws."[37]

What is more, since fraudulent claims concerning such loans could also come before ecclesiastical judges, Enrique decreed that if a Christian confesses before any judge—ecclesiastical or lay—that he owes a Jew gold, or silver, or money, or any other thing, and the Christian makes that confession under oath in a lawsuit or in testimony—the Christian who makes that confession in any of the above forms shall pay a penalty equal to the debt concerning which he had confessed, and the Jew who would demand of the Christian such an admission would likewise be penalized by the same quantity.[38]

Thus, Enrique's law introduced new elements into the prohibition on taking interest: (1) the permission for ecclesiastic judges to intervene in such cases; (2) the reduction of debts by half of their contracted value; (3) the disqualification of any admission made by the borrower that he received no loan on interest; (4) the punishment of any debtor who might "confess" to the Jewish claim with a sum equaling the one he confessed about; and (5) the punishment of the Jewish lender with the same sum if he demanded such a confession from the Christian. These provisions include not only harsh punishments for the violation of the prohibition on lending money at interest; they also eliminate any possibility of circumventing the law or finding loopholes in it—and thus enable a judge to compel a Christian not to pay his debt to a Jew. Whence stemmed this extreme severity, and this determination to close any avenue for Christians to borrow money from Jews?

As we see it, the purpose of this law was more to hurt the Jews than to benefit the Christians. Moneylending at interest was an important source of income not only for the great Jewish financiers, but also for many of the Jewish lower classes. Our assumption that Paul had much to do with pushing the prohibition to new extremes, so as to close this source of income to Jews, is based on our examination of *all* anti-Jewish laws enacted from that date through 1412. What distinguishes them is not only their studious employment of all previous laws on the subject, but also their going beyond those laws, both in the extent of their regulations and in the severity of the penalties they impose for violations. Above all, they display exceptional cleverness in foiling any attempt to circumvent them. Since these qualities characterize the laws of 1412, which, as we shall show, were composed by Paul (or framed under his guidance), we may assume that the preceding laws resembling those of 1412 were likewise inspired by him at least in part, as stages in a legal drive he contemplated to bring the Jews of Spain to religious capitulation.

V

It seems logical to suppose that till the end of 1402 Paul could not divert much of his energy to his plans for solving the Jewish question in Spain. His task of defending Benedict's cause and moving Castile back to his obedience no doubt took most of his time and energy. But things must have changed radically in this respect after he had gained Castile's support for the Pope and cemented his own relations with the King. In the following three years Paul no doubt had many opportunities to present to the King his views on the Jews and how they should be treated, and it seems that he gradually moved the

King to take an anti-Jewish stand on a number of issues. Thus, he may have influenced the King's decision to enforce the decree regarding the wearing of the badge, which had been on the books since 1348[39] but remained virtually a dead letter. Not only does the law of 1405 contain precise instructions concerning the badge (such as touch its form and size), but also a specific order that Jews who serve at Court must wear the badge, like all other Jews.[40] Just as the law concerning interest was meant to harm the Jews *materially*, the law about the badge meant to hurt them *morally*—especially their upper class, whose pride and status would be greatly reduced by wearing the badge at Court.

The death of Enrique III caused no decline in Paul's influence upon the royal administration—at least with respect to its policy toward the Jews. On the contrary, as chief arbiter of Church affairs in Castile and the leading convert in the kingdom, the bishop of Cartagena must have been generally regarded as the foremost expert on Jewish affairs. We do not know which of the two regents was more moved by Paul to take a stand against the Jews; but it seems pretty certain that he influenced them both. In any case, on October 25, 1408, barely two years after Enrique's death, a new anti-Jewish law was enacted of the most far-reaching import and consequences. This law, which was issued by both regents, forbade the Jews to act in any capacity as farmers and collectors of the revenues.[41]

Why should the regents decree such a law when they were under no pressure to do so? No petition to this effect was presented at Cortes, and the law was issued at a time when Castile was in a state of truce with the Moslems and after the cities had made—and fulfilled—their financial pledges for the prosecution of the war. To be sure, the regents may have needed more funds for the resumption of the war at the conclusion of the truce (in February 1409), and to move the cities to supply those funds, they presumably sought to buy their goodwill with an anti-Jewish law. But the war was resumed only in 1410, and the sums the cities paid in 1409 were far smaller than what the tax farming by the Jews was supposed to bring in within a year or two. Nor is there any hint in the law that it was issued in response to a public demand. What we gather from its reading is that the regents enacted it without having consulted even their own Council. And yet enactments against tax farming by Jews, as we know, had always been opposed by the kings and their treasurers. Even Enrique III, when in 1405 he forbade all Jews to receive from Christians any document indicating their indebtedness to Jews, exempted from this prohibition letters showing such indebtedness to collectors of the revenues. What was it, then, that led the regents to ignore the acknowledged interest of the Crown in Jewish tax farming, and part with a traditional policy which the kings had invariably upheld against critics and opponents?

We have no full answer to this question. Perhaps there was a special need that has not been divulged by the sources. But even so, we feel certain that beyond the need there operated the persuasiveness of Paul of Burgos. As a churchman, Paul must have mentioned to the Regents that the Church had frequently prohibited Jews from gaining power over Christians and that, in addition, Spain's civil law had repeatedly sanctioned that prohibition. But he no doubt realized that this reasoning, which was ignored by Spain's kings for many generations, would not move the Regents to do what he proposed. Paul must therefore have centered his argument on the political aspect of the issue—that is, on the people's persistent demands that the Jews be removed from the gathering of revenues and on their deepening disappointment and frustration over the fact that the kings kept rejecting their petitions in this matter. Along these lines, he could of course argue that, if the Regents fulfilled the people's requests and issued a clear-cut law to that effect, they would unite the country behind them to an extent that no other measure possibly could, and that such mobilization was indeed vital for victory in the war with Granada—and thus for attaining the great goal of the Reconquest.

Like the law on interest, this decree, too, sought to embrace all possibilities and deny any excuse for violation. It forbids every Jew "of whatever condition" to farm the king's revenues; it enumerates all the taxes and tributes that fall under this prohibition; it is binding on all the lords of the country beyond the specific royal dominions, be they secular or ecclesiastic princes; it prohibits the Jews from acting in this matter not only publicly but also secretly— that is, it forbids them to act in behalf of Christians as it forbids Christians to act in behalf of Jews. If a Jew tries to defraud the law and is discovered, he will pay *double* the sum he undertook to pay through farming; if his property will not suffice to meet his penalty, he will lose all his possessions and will be publicly flogged. If any Christian is involved in any manner or degree in granting the Jews such farming, he too will be penalized by a sum twice as large as the one committed to by the farmer; if his possessions won't suffice to cover the fine, he will lose them all and, in addition, will serve a year in one of the castles on the frontier.[42] Clearly, the same spirit that influenced the composition of the law concerning interest also shaped the law on the gathering of revenues.

To Paul of Burgos, such a decree would be his second major blow at Jewish existence in Spain, for tax farming and moneylending provided the foundations of the Jewish economy in Castile, and far more than moneylending, tax farming formed the basis of Jewish political and social influence. Without these two professions the Jewish community was bound to be impoverished, and its value as a source of income for the Crown would be reduced in the same degree. In consequence, the Crown would have little interest in protecting the Jews against the populace; the latter would soon sense its opportunity to attack them; and once the days of wrath return, what choice will remain for the Jews of Spain except to convert to Christianity?

VI

Shortly after the promulgation of the law of October 1408, Paul left for Perpignan to take part in the Council convened by Benedict XIII as a counterweight to the preparations then in progress for the meeting of the Council of Pisa. As Benedict's leading aide and chief spokesman for Castile, Paul was included in the Council's commission, whose assignment was to work out a plan for the dissolution of the Schism. Nothing came of their efforts and proposals, and meanwhile Benedict's condition worsened. His council adjourned in February 1409, but already on January 12, he was informed by the French Court that, if by the opening of the Council of Pisa (scheduled for March 25, 1409) no progress had been made toward the unification of the Church, France would once again deny him obedience.[43] By the end of May the threat materialized, and several weeks later Benedict was hit again when the Council of Pisa deposed both him and his rival, Gregory XII, as heretics and schismatics who were tearing apart the One Holy, Catholic and Apostolic Church. However, by electing, in June 1409, a new pope, named Alexander V, the Council of Pisa did not abolish the Schism. It rather made it less resoluble, for now the Church had three popes instead of two.

Paul was by then back in Castile, where he had to labor hard to secure the continued adherence of the Regents to Benedict. But in December of that year, he was again in Barcelona at the Pope's side when the latter issued his blast against the Council of Pisa in a special bull countersigned by Paul.[44] The following developments brought Benedict no relief. In May 1410, Alexander V died, but his cardinals proceeded to elect a new pope, John XXII, leaving the Church's problem unresolved and as complicated as ever. The demands in Europe to end the Schism grew steadily louder and more urgent. Benedict understood that he must do his utmost to tighten his hold on the Spanish dominions if he wished to retain his papacy. But what could he do?

It was probably at this juncture that Paul proposed to him that he launch a nationwide campaign in Spain with the aim of converting all the Jews of that country to the Catholic faith.

Taken as a whole, the Christians in the cities (especially the lower middle class, the artisans and the laborers), not to speak of the peasants and the people of the countryside, were seething with hatred for the Jews; and the laws of 1405 and 1408 did not mollify their hostility. That the Jews were no longer permitted to lend Christians money at any rate of interest did not make them more loved by the hard-pressed Christian craftsmen, who desper--

ately needed funds to finance their trades and now had nowhere to turn for help. On the contrary, they now may have disliked the Jews more intensely for allegedly having the means to help them but refusing to come to their rescue. As for the Jewish gatherers of the taxes, they certainly did not disappear from the field upon the publication of the law of 1408. As stated in the decree, it did not apply to royal tax farmers whose contracts were still in force[45]; and such contracts, we should note, were usually made for a number of years. In consequence, the pressure of Jewish tax farming on Christians continued to be felt after 1408. On the other hand, the large-scale commitments by the cities in support of the war with Granada almost drained their financial resources and constituted a heavy burden on their citizens. Thus, little happened to relieve, while much occurred to exacerbate the old tensions between Christians and Jews. Any friction between the groups could prove intolerable and explode in violent conflict.

It was this social atmosphere, thick with Jew hatred, that gave birth in Castile to a terrible persecution, which claimed many Jewish victims. The pretext was one of those preposterous accusations that had embittered Jewish life in Germany and France but had only rarely been raised against the Jews of Spain. It was probably in 1410 that the Jews of Segovia were charged with the "torture" of a consecrated Host according to their "alleged custom." Many Jews were implicated in the charge, including their chief leader, Meir Alguades, formerly physician to Enrique III. Under torture, Don Meir "confessed" not only to his share in the crime against the Host, but also to having poisoned King Enrique and thereby causing his death. He was sentenced to be hanged, drawn and quartered, while other Jews, charged with desecration of the Host, suffered similar punishments.[46] But this did not mark the end of the ordeal to which the Jews of Segovia were subjected. The bishop of Segovia, Don Juan de Tordesillas, who was judge of the aforesaid case, found a way to prolong the persecution. He claimed that the Jews bribed his cook to kill him by poisoning his food, and a number of additional Jews were arrested, tortured, confessed and executed in the same cruel manner.[47]

Meir Alguades and Paul of Burgos had probably been friends before Paul's conversion,[48] and later the friendship was replaced by that enmity which usually separated Jews from converts. In their case the enmity must have been especially acute. For besides having been Enrique's physician, Meir Alguades acted at Court as chief spokesman of the Jews and guardian of their interests, and thus may have clashed head-on with Paul, who sought to implement his anti-Jewish schemes. The two men, the physician and the bishop, no doubt competed for the King's favor, and the contest was finally won by Paul, as shown by the King's law on usury. When Don Meir was prosecuted by the Segovian bishop, no one knew better than Paul of Burgos the groundlessness of the charges for which he was tried. We may take it for granted, however, that he did not lift a finger to establish the truth and save his former friend, the Jewish leader, from ignominy, torture and death. Instead, he must have chosen to stay aloof and completely detached from the case. To expose the libel of Host desecration would stamp him, he knew, as a protector of the Jews and cloud the sincerity of his conversion. He may also have been pleased that the Jewish community in Spain, whose destruction he so ardently desired, lost its valiant advocate at Court.

The news of these shocking events had of course a great, though different, impact upon the Christians and the Jews. Since many more Christians now regarded the Jews as guilty of the crime imputed to them, Christian hostility toward the Jews grew, while many Jews, appalled by the terrible persecution, were driven to desperation. Paul may now have thought the situation propitious to launch a new campaign against the Jews, with a view to attaining a new mass conversion. With their upper classes hit economically and their influence at Court at its lowest ebb, the Jews, frightened by the growing hostility, might be induced to seek refuge in Christianity, especially if the agitation against them were accompanied by further restrictions. Paul knew of course that the campaign he was thinking of would be far more effective if led by the Pope. But what reason could he give Benedict, then engrossed in the battle for his papacy, to divert his energies to such an effort? Ostensibly, no such reason was available. But Paul was a crafty schemer, and he soon devised arguments to convince the Pope that, by sponsoring his plan with respect to the Jews, he would not only advance the cause of Christianity, but also offer invaluable support to his position as the sole true leader of the Church.

VII

Judging by prevalent scholarly opinion, the campaign for the conversion of the Jews of Spain was undertaken by Pope Benedict XIII to draw the Christian world to his side. Accordingly, the Pope and his aides believed that if that campaign ended in success, all Catholic countries would applaud his achievement and recognize him as the only true pope. It is unlikely, however, that Benedict and his counselors were so naive as to believe in such a forecast. They knew the ambitions, the interests and the theories stubbornly upheld by the powerful men who propelled the movement for his deposition, and they realized that the conversion of Spain's Jews to Christianity would not make the slightest difference to them. Nevertheless, since Benedict agreed to launch the conversion campaign at a time which was so critical for his fortunes, he must have regarded it as highly valuable to his struggle for the papacy.

It is not hard to see in what way he thought it could be of assistance to his cause. By the end of 1409 and in 1410, following the withdrawal of France from his obedience, Benedict could see himself banished from Europe and shorn of any influence there. Aragon was now his only safe base, and except for Aragon, his dominion embraced only the neighboring kingdoms of Castile and Navarre, and small, isolated Scotland. His position in Christendom rested, in fact, on these three countries of the peninsula, and to secure his hold on them, he evidently intended to become more involved in Spanish life and politics. By heading a campaign to convert the Jews, he thought, he could make a big step in that direction, not so much due to its declared aim as to the methods used for its achievement. Such a campaign, he knew, would necessarily abound in sharp censures of Judaism and its bearers, and nothing would appeal more to Spain's Christian masses than a steady flow of anti-Jewish invective from the headquarters of the Pope. In fact, the Pope's very declaration that he was out to put an end, once and for all, to the existence of Judaism in Spain would endear him to the great majority of the people, so that they would view him as a spiritual leader who must be protected at all cost. Indeed, if this attitude became dominant, who in Spain would dare join the effort to depose him?

Such was the reasoning that could move Benedict to launch the campaign for the conversion of the Jews, which was proposed, as we believe, by Paul. We ought, however, to touch on another consideration that could induce him to support the plan. As we see it, the Pope could consider it useful also as a diversionary tactic. In the popular excitement against the Jews and Judaism that the campaign was expected to generate, public attention would turn away from the Schism and the arguments for his deposition. All that was necessary was to see to it that the campaign would indeed be effective. Fortunately for the Pope, there was among his aides one who could be counted on to attain that end.

VIII

He was Vicente Ferrer.[49] A Dominican friar who saw his life's mission in the propagation of Christianity among the infidels, as well as among deviators from the faith, Ferrer had carried his message across Spain, France, Italy and other countries with singular success. He was known as a great apostle of Christianity and one of the truly saintly men that Spain gave the world in his generation. To bring the Jews into the Christian fold was one of Ferrer's primary goals—a goal for which his Dominican schooling had especially prepared him[50]; and when asked by the Pope to lead a nationwide campaign aimed at the conversion of Spanish Jewry, his response must have been enthusiastic. He had by then passed his sixtieth year, an old man by medieval standards. No greater idea could be conceived, he no doubt felt, to crown his life's missionary efforts.

Ferrer now faced his greatest opportunity, but also his most difficult task. Would he justify the hopes placed in him? Encouraged by his past experience, Ferrer believed that he could convert almost any sinner, if given the proper opportunity; but now he was assigned a special task. The Jews were known to be particularly stubborn and exceptionally hard to draw to the faith, and all attempts to do so by mere persuasion had so far failed, except in few cases. Now he was expected to achieve by eloquence what others had achieved only by violence—namely, the conversion of masses. Could it be done?

Ferrer opposed forced conversion,[51] and so did Benedict, who would not officially depart in this matter from the traditions of the Church. Consequently, the Pope would not sanction or agree to a repetition of the riots of 1391, and he must have realized that the lay authorities would not tolerate them either. Yet if the threat of death as the alternative to conversion was to be excluded from the campaign, what were the prospects of success? Neither he nor Paul could have possibly believed that Ferrer would achieve their common goal with his oratorical skills alone. Therefore, they thought that although the threat of death must be excluded as a spur to conversion, the adoption of some oppressive measures, based on either Church law or precedent, could be urged by Ferrer in arguing his case. The impact of his agitation would thus be increased, as it would depend not only on theoretical arguments, but also on some practical considerations that the Jews would be unable to ignore.

They must have conveyed to Ferrer their misgivings and the general line of the solution they proposed, though Ferrer, as they could have anticipated, was unlikely to greet their proposal with enthusiasm. All his life he believed that in religious conversion the "word" alone, and not the "sword," must be employed; and by "sword" he meant all intolerable measures that virtually amounted to compulsion. Certainly, he would not like his campaign against the Jews, which was to be the pinnacle of his career, to be marred by charges that its results were achieved not by the inspiration of his preaching but by threats of harsh impositions. Nevertheless, he finally agreed to advocate the adoption of one repressive measure: the transfer of the Jews who lived with Christians in mixed neighborhoods to separate boroughs of their own. The justification of this measure was related to Ferrer's mission: it would be unreasonable to allow the new converts, who were brought to the faith after so much persuasion, to be exposed to the dangerous influence of the Jews. The proposed move would thus be presented as necessary to protect the gains of Ferrer's efforts, thereby weakening the sting of the claim that it was a means of coercion. But coercive it was, and one can see in the very structure of the argument—the stress on the needs of the *newly converted*—the stamp of Paul's sharp thinking.

The idea that the Jews should live in boroughs of their own, totally apart from the Christian population, was not born in 1410. Usually, when settling in a Christian city in the Middle Ages, the Jews themselves insisted that a special zone be assigned for their residence. They required this not only for communal and religious needs, but also for their security, and that is why the area allotted to them was habitually surrounded by a protective wall. This was part of their way of life in all the countries of western Europe. In Spain, however, after long periods of peace, the Jews often settled outside their boroughs, and not always with Christian consent. Thus, in the privilege which Alfonso X granted the city of Murcia in 1272, he stipulated, no doubt at the request of the Christian citizens, that "no Jew would reside among the Christians" of the town and that the Jews would have their "separate *judería*" in a place assigned to them by the King.[52] The concession may be viewed as an extension of the *fuero* that Murcia had received only six years before[53] and need not serve as indication of the King's intent to establish the same order throughout the kingdom. But the negative attitude of the Murcian Christians toward living next door to Jews was not limited to them alone. Testifying to this is the royal confirmation, in the Cortes of Valladolid in 1351, of the agreements made between several Jewish communities and the lay and ecclesiastic authorities of their towns regarding the Jews' residence in separate quarters—a confirmation made to satisfy the burghers, who sought to prevent the expansion of the Jews beyond the confines originally fixed for them.[54] But no Spanish king had ever enjoined such a restriction for the entire country, nor did any ecumenical council adopt it, nor had any pope ever confirmed it. In 1215, when the Fourth Lateran Council sought to separate the Jews more effectively from the Christians, it ordered the Jews to wear a special sign, and considered this measure sufficient for the purpose. This was also the position of Castile's civil law, as indicated in the *Partidas* and later affirmed by Enrique II and Enrique III. Neither the former nor the latter legislation confined the Jews to separate boroughs. Only one ecclesiastic enactment could serve as precedent for Ferrer's demand, and that was the decision of the Council of Palencia in 1388.

Indeed, in that year the above Council decreed that the Jews and Moors should live in separate quarters.[55] What led that assembly to make that regulation? Undoubtedly, it was made under the impact of the agitation then conducted by Ferrán Martínez. The Council, however, was more considerate than Martínez, who simply urged the towns to eject the Jews. While it forbade the Jews to live among Christians, it called upon the cities to designate special sites in which the Jews could build houses for themselves.

It also permitted them to have, in addition to their dwelling places, houses and habitations in the cities' squares and markets, where their merchants, craftsmen and officeholders could conduct their business with the Christians.[56] There is no indication that Ferrer was opposed to any of these arrangements. In any case, when he, Benedict and Paul advocated residential separation of the Jews, they could lean on the decision of that Council of Palencia. But they were linked to that decision also in another way. Presiding over the Council of Palencia was none other than Cardinal Pedro de Luna, later to become Benedict XIII.[57]

IX

Ferrer began his campaign in Castile in the southwestern part of the kingdom bordering Valencia, his native country. He first visited the city of Murcia, in the diocese of Cartagena, whose bishop was then Paul of Burgos, and proceeded through the provinces of Albacete and Ciudad Real (then Villa Real) toward Toledo, which he entered on May 30, 1411. We cannot really assess the yield of his campaign in any of the Castilian cities he visited, although we are informed that he gained many converts, especially among the social and economic elites. Some scholars have assumed that Ferrer made these conquests not so much by means of his arguments as by means of the social atmosphere he created. His blistering tirades against Judaism, it has been claimed, unleashed a new storm against the Jews, and the flagellants who accompanied him helped inflame the passions of the cities' mobs against them. Under these circumstances, it is not surprising that many Jews thought that what they were seeing was a prelude to new riots like those of 1391. For though Ferrer was determined not to permit violence to interfere with his campaign, the Jews could not be sure of his determination, or his ability to control the agitated crowds. We may therefore conclude that in the heated atmosphere created by Ferrer's inflammatory sermons, it was the dread of assaults more than anything else that drove many Jews to the baptismal font. In addition, Ferrer pressed the *concejos* to remove the Jews from the Christian neighborhoods, and this too may have strengthened, in some places, the tendency of some Jews to convert. Nevertheless, we cannot really tell to what extent that demand of Ferrer was heeded and how it affected the conversion movement. After all, there was no state law ordering the *concejos* to oust the Jews from their homes in predominantly Christian areas, and the Jews could be assisted by the courts and royal officers in defending their private and collective rights. In addition, such actions required much time and left room for negotiation.

As a result Ferrer must have found his campaign often hampered or hard going, and far from yielding the harvest he expected; and when the results he hoped for did not materialize, he would sometimes lose his patience and go beyond the limits that he himself had set to the use of force. This, we are told, happened in Toledo, where he expelled the Jews from their synagogue, which he thereupon consecrated as church.[58] On the whole, however, he stuck to his principles and curbed any tendency to violence among his followers. Yet this in itself did not calm the Jews, who became more nervous with every passing day. In fact, the more the campaign expanded, the more ominous Ferrer's calls sounded, and the more convinced the Jews became that Christendom had declared on them a war to the finish.

Judging by the trend of Christian opinion, Ferrer's campaign justified Benedict's expectations. It centered public attention on the Jewish problem and moved the Spanish masses to urge the implementation of the proposed anti-Jewish measures. But from the standpoint of its religious achievements, it was hardly a success. To be sure, Ferrer's followers might applaud the impact of his powerful sermons; and indeed for one man to draw to Christianity thousands of Jews in so short a time was a remarkable feat. But to Paul of Burgos, who wanted the campaign to trigger a conversion of mass proportions, the results appeared meager, indeed disappointing. What difference could a few thousand converts make to Spain's Jewry, which still numbered hundreds of thousands? And how long could Ferrer, a weak old man, continue that hard labor? It was obvious to Paul, now more than ever, that Ferrer's agitation must be reinforced by extraordinary oppressive legislation, if the hopes placed in his ability to stir the masses, and move the Jews to convert, were ever to materialize.

He evidently did not change his mind about the potential effect of the residential segregation which Ferrer urged the cities to enact, but he realized that unless it was backed by the Crown, the measure could hardly be enforced. In any case, it affected primarily the Jews who lived in mixed neighborhoods; it hurt less the Jews who lived in their own boroughs, and the number of these was still large. Paul's plan of anti-Jewish strictures would strike hard at *all* the Jews of Spain, regardless of their dwelling place, class, or occupation. However they resist, he was sure, that plan would force them to religious surrender. Yet it all depended on the full cooperation of the authorities of the state.

Astute and determined to achieve his goal, Paul now devoted his great persuasive powers to influence the two regents of Castile, Queen Catalina and the Infante Fernando, to accept his proposed legislation for the Jews. No doubt he pointed out to them that, since the Jews had been debarred from tax farming and moneylending, their financial usefulness to the Crown would drop sharply. On the other hand, their continued converse with the populace would produce tension and friction. Thus, they were a cause of irritation and unrest, and a source of religious demoralization. It now remained for Spain to take the final step to bend the Jews to religious submission and create, at last, the religious unity that would finally pacify the country. Once the Jews were converted and assimilated, Spain could have the benefit of their abilities without the damage caused by the division and ill feeling that would always prevail between them and the Christians. He undoubtedly lauded Ferrer's campaign and wanted it to continue and expand, but explained that for the campaign to succeed, it must be supported by a series of laws that would make the Jews decide in favor of conversion. The people would of course welcome such laws and hail the rulers who would issue them.

Such arguments could be viewed as valid. But however appealing or convincing they might be, it is hard to believe that they alone could move the regents to reverse so completely the policy which Spain's kings had pursued for centuries on the Jewish question. Yet it was precisely such a reversal that was implied in the laws proposed by Paul. If, nevertheless, the regents finally decided to respond positively to his proposal, we must attribute that response not only to the reasons offered by Paul in support of his plan, but also to a special political consideration which was at that moment uppermost in their minds and which, we may be certain, Paul must have alluded to on every suitable occasion.

X

Martín I (the Humane), king of Aragon, died on May 31, 1410, without leaving direct heirs to the throne. He had been known for some time to be in failing health, and the question of his succession became a burning issue when his only surviving son, Martín the Young, King of Sicily, died in July 1409. There were several contenders for the throne in Aragon, each with his supporters and opponents. Prelates and magnates took sides in the quarrel, which threatened to throw the country into civil war. But a contender appeared also outside Aragon. He was the Infante Fernando, Castile's Regent, who was nephew of the departed king. By virtue of this kinship he saw himself entitled to the Aragonese succession.

He had been, in fact, possessed by the idea for some time, and persistently moved toward its realization. Already in August 1409, when he sent his condolences to Martín the Humane over the sudden demise of his son, he pointed out that the latter's death made him the rightful lord of Sicily. In the following year, when he left Granada after having seized Antequera (in June 1410), he asked his legal experts to examine the rights of the various claimants to the Aragonese throne and inform him of their findings. They emerged with the opinion he expected: he was the only person legally entitled to inherit the position of the late king.

On October 31, he communicated his claim to the Cortes of Aragon, then

meeting in Barcelona, and he also informed Queen Catalina of the conclusion reached by his jurists on the matter and of his intention to act accordingly. The Queen, however, did not take the decision of Fernando's jurists
as the last word on the subject. She had no doubt been informed that had her
late husband, Enrique III, been alive, he would have succeeded Martín the
Humane; and she believed that since their son Juan II inherited his father's
rights, he owned the right to the Aragonese throne. She saw indeed no reason
that Juan II should not add Aragon to his kingdom, and she submitted the
matter to the examination of her own experts. These, however, came up with
the strange opinion that the succession belonged both to King Juan II and to
the Infante Don Fernando.[59] They evidently could not make up their minds
which of the two had priority in the matter, but the fact that they mentioned
Juan II before Fernando was enough for her to conclude that her son was first
in the line of succession, and certainly had no less a claim than his uncle.

She intended to campaign for her position in Aragon and was on the point
of sending a delegation there when she was dissuaded from doing so by the
shrewd Fernando, who suggested that before they speak to the Aragonese,
the question of his own or Juan's priority should be settled among the
Castilians themselves. Catalina had no choice but to agree. The question was
again submitted to experts, and these, as the chronicler of Juan II tells us,
unanimously decided in favor of Fernando.[60] Whether this was a free or
biased jury, manipulated by the clever Infante, we have no way of knowing.
But it would not be far-fetched to assume that Catalina had doubts about the
propriety of its decision. She seems to have stopped her activity in this
direction, ostensibly leaving the field to Fernando; but what designs she
harbored, or what hopes she entertained, it is impossible to determine. She
realized of course that the final decision rested, after all, with the Aragonese;
and she may have expected that Aragon's leaders, once they examined the
rights of all claimants, would arrive at the conclusion that it was her son, Juan
II, and not the Infante who was the rightful heir.

When Vicente Ferrer was traversing Castile, both regents knew that the
question of the succession was approaching the critical stage. It was also
believed that Vicente Ferrer, who commanded great influence in Aragon,
would play a leading part in deciding the issue. Thus far, however, he had
given no hint as to where he stood in the raging controversy. In July and
August, both he and the Pope may still have been groping their way among
the disputants, seeking to determine, among other things, which of the
claimants would be more likely to uphold Benedict XIII's cause. What is
certain, however, is that the Pope's other aide, Paul of Burgos, had made up
his mind which candidate to support; and, as we shall see, his opinion went
a long way in influencing the Pope's and Ferrer's position.

It can hardly be doubted that Paul of Burgos saw in the contest for the

Aragonese Crown not only an opportunity to promote his own as well as
Benedict's papal interests, but also an occasion to advance his cherished
plan—the conversion of the Jews of Spain. He was well aware of course that
both Fernando and Catalina aspired to win the monarchic prize of Aragon;
he must have repeatedly pointed out to them that both the Pope and Ferrer
would have a decisive voice in the selection of the King; and he must also
have stressed that the attitude of Castile's rulers toward the conversion of the
Jews would go far in determining the Pope's and Ferrer's choice. He did not
have to demonstrate to either of the regents the truth of his contentions—
Ferrer's strenuous and relentless agitation confirmed it fully—but he had to
explain why Ferrer's great effort had thus far not brought the expected
results. Ferrer, he no doubt argued, did not succeed in his campaign because
he lacked the necessary state support, which could be provided only by
suitable legislation. Let the regents approve the laws which he, Paul, had
prepared for the purpose, and the Jews would convert in large masses. If the
regents issued such laws at this point, the Pope and Ferrer could not fail to
be impressed by their enormous contribution to Christianity.

It need hardly be added that both Fernando and Catalina were aware of
Paul's influence on the Pope and Ferrer, and each of them wished to win his
favor. Both fell for his arguments and no doubt assured him that the laws he
proposed would be drafted by their jurists, who would of course seek his
counsel and approval, and made public without delay. They also agreed to
invite Ferrer to the Court in order to deliver a sermon there as a prelude to
their publication.

In December Ferrer came to Ayllón, the residence of the Court at the
time, saw the regents, and, apparently unaware of what they had promised
Paul, asked for one thing only: their formal approval of his proposal regarding the segregation of the Jews.[61] Before long he was informed of their
intention to issue not only the law he requested but also additional important
laws, which might contribute to the Jews' conversion. Ferrer could hardly
object.

The laws they had promised Paul to enact had to be issued by each of them
independently in their respective areas of government. Fernando asked for
some delay in the publication of the new laws in his own domain until he
removed certain difficulties he faced there, but Catalina insisted on the
immediate fulfillment of their promise in her part of the kingdom. In all
likelihood, she wanted to show Ferrer that here was a queen who really
meant business and was capable of solving the Jewish question in Spain
precisely as he and the Pope would have it. She did not have to indicate the
implied conclusion: should her son be elected King of Aragon, the same
policy would be inexorably pursued in that country, too.

This is what accounts for the unusual speed with which the action was taken—again, not under the pressure of Cortes, but under the political exigency of the Aragonese succession. Perhaps Paul asked Ferrer not to depart from the Court before the new laws were issued. But there seemed to have been no reason for concern. The laws referred to, known as the laws of Catalina, were published in Valladolid on January 2, 1412.

THE LAWS OF CATALINA, 1412

Save for the decrees of "conversion or expulsion" issued against the Jews in various countries, the laws of Catalina were the harshest ever published against the Jews in Christendom before 1412. Many historians have analyzed these laws and commented on their contents, but, as we see it, their uniqueness and purpose still require elucidation.

Amador de los Ríos, who was the first to present a detailed summary of the laws of 1412, described them as directed against the Jews, although as formulated they applied to Moors too. He pointed out their aim as follows:

> The capital idea which stood out in this edict, in all and each of its stipulations, had as its object to put the unfortunate proscribed people outside the old laws of Spain, narrowing more and more the iron ring within which it was to be annihilated. Except for its preamble and first disposition, which deals with the separation of living places, the entire ordinance had as its target the legal annulment of the Jewish people as such; all of it was designed to reduce that people to a state of the greatest misery and impotence and put forever an end to the influence which it had gained in the Republic.[62]

It is hard to find fault with Amador's description if one considers separately the edict's stipulations. But the "capital idea" that binds them together, or more clearly—i.e., the edict's main goal—is not indicated in Amador's statement. As we shall show below, Amador touched on some of the means provided by the edict for the attainment of its end; the end itself, however, he failed to point out.

Sharing some of Amador's assessments, Graetz said that the aim of the edict was to "impoverish and humiliate the Jews, and reduce them to the lowest grade in the social scale."[63] And in the wake of both Amador and Graetz, though unlike them he referred also to the Moors, Henry Charles Lea concluded that the edict was "designed to humiliate [both Jew and Moor] to the utmost, to render their lives a burden, to deprive them of the means of livelihood and diminish their usefulness to the state."[64] This conception of the aims of the edict as presented by Lea and Graetz suffers from the same omission that we noted in the case of Amador. As we shall see, however, in a subsequent discussion Lea revised his opinion of the laws of 1412.

Coming to later leading historians, we shall first touch on the view of Baer. The laws of Catalina, he asserted, "reflect the tendencies of the Church militant and the Estates," whose "combined object was to undermine the Jewish economy, abolish the political freedom of the Jewish communities, and reduce the Jews to the status of pariahs."[65] Like Lea, however, Baer was evidently uncertain of the accuracy or completeness of this assertion, for in his final observations on the subject, he modified his view of the "combined objective" of the laws of 1412. "Generally speaking," he said, "there is hardly a uniform purpose or a definite program in the various provisions of the laws of Valladolid."[66] As the reader will see, however, these laws do represent a uniform purpose and, to no lesser extent, a definite program.

In line with Baer's original description, Parkes and Serrano believed that the laws of 1412 comprise most of the enactments ever made against the Jews, except that Parkes thought they were of ecclesiastic and Serrano of secular origin. Thus, Parkes said that the laws of 1412 were "almost entirely based on canonic regulation,"[67] whereas Serrano claimed that Catalina's ordinance "was no doubt the work of the Royal Council" and "there is nothing in it which had not been clearly legislated at Cortes."[68] Both these opinions are wrong, as we shall presently show.

As we see it, the laws of 1412 were unique in more than one respect, and to note their innovations and uniqueness, we shall have to examine their various stipulations in the light of earlier legislation. Of these stipulations we shall first touch on the one that was closely related to Ferrer's campaign—the law that confined the dwelling places of the Jews and the Moors to special areas assigned by the authorities, in complete separation from the Christians. Once these areas were designated, the Jews were to move, according to that law, to their special locations within eight days, and those who failed to do so were to be subjected to the *loss of all their possessions and to corporal punishment.*[69]

We have already indicated that no such limitations concerning the Jews' dwelling places had ever been enacted by any Church authority before the Council of Palencia in 1388. But the law of 1412 goes far beyond that conciliar decision. Not only does it fix too short a time for its execution and too harsh punishments for its violation, quite unlike the Palencian decree, but it is also marked by the extreme extent to which it carried the principle of separation. For the Council of Palencia stipulated, as we have noted, that although the dwellings of the Jews should be confined to certain areas, the Jews might have their place of business in the common public squares and markets. In contrast, Catalina's edict does not offer such a concession; in fact, it explicitly denies it. Thus, the second law of this edict states that no Jew or Moor should "keep publicly or secretly warehouses, shops or tables for selling"; and that "any Jew or Moor who acts contrary hereto, shall incur the penalty of ten thousand maravedis for each violation, besides the corporal punishment he may be subject to according to the King's pleasure."[70]

What is more, to avoid any misunderstanding of the above prohibition, the sixth law makes it clear that even in their own boroughs or dwelling places, Jews and Moors should not have *squares or markets* to buy from, or sell food or drinks to Christians, under pain of five hundred maravedis for each violation, though they may have victuals and drinks in their enclosures to trade among themselves.[71]

Thus, we see that some major stipulations of the laws of 1412 regarding the dwelling places and markets of the Jews are not to be found in any earlier enactment; on several vital matters they are new. The same is true with respect to other laws, as we shall presently see.

We have noted that the decrees of both Church and state prohibited Spain's Jews from occupying high office in the administrations of the kings, the Church and the nobility, and that the law of 1408 specifically forbade them to serve as farmers and collectors of revenues in both royal and seniorial estates. This provision was repeated, with special emphasis, in the edict of 1412.[72] But never before had Jews been forbidden, as they were under the edict of 1412, to serve Christians as "smiths, carpenters, doublet-makers, tailors, clothworkers, shoemakers, butchers, carriers, or clothiers."[73] Nor had they ever before been forbidden to sell Christians any edible thing, such as bread, flour, and butter, or any article of clothing, such as shoes, doublets, or breeches.[74]

The difference between the edict of 1412 and previous enactments is conspicuous and far-reaching in other areas as well. Thus, earlier Church decrees prohibited Jewish physicians, surgeons and apothecaries from treating Christian patients and preparing medicine for them; but the laws of Catalina forbid them to serve altogether in the medical professions.[75] Needless to say, the purpose of this prohibition was not to protect Christians from the lethal designs that Jewish doctors allegedly harbored against them (as the prevalent libels and myths suggested), but to deny the Jews an important source of income and prevent the development of friendly relations between Christians and the Jewish physicians who cured them (and thereby with Jews generally). The same intent dictated the laws that forbade Jews to "visit Christians in their illness, or give them medicines, or talk idly to them, or send them presents of dried herbs, or spices, or any article of food."[76] And we may add to this category also the laws forbidding Jews to attend Christian weddings and funerals or take part in any ceremony in which Christians were honored.[77] It is true that the tendency embodied in these laws goes back to the earliest Christian laws against the Jews[78]; in the edict of 1412, however, it went further than ever before.

For its ultimate aim was not merely to prevent the development of friendships; actually, it was part of a broader policy, whose aim was to effect a complete separation—and permanent isolation—of the Jews from the Christians. Perhaps nothing is so suggestive of this aim as the law forbidding Jews to shave their beards or trim their hair, and ordering them to "wear them long as they grow naturally."[79] The purpose of this law—whose violation entailed the harsh punishment of a hundred lashes, besides a fine of one hundred maravedis—was obviously to increase the Christians' desire to separate themselves from the company of Jews (for the very appearance of the Jew should be such as to repel Christians from associating with him). The same purpose imbues the enactment prohibiting Christian women, whether married or single, from entering Jewish neighborhoods even by day, while previous laws limited that prohibition only to specific times and occasions.[80] Likewise, the older laws forbidding Jews to engage Christian domestics were extended by the laws of 1412, so as to forbid them also to employ Christians as plowmen, shepherds and herdsmen.[81] This law, however, had an additional purpose, on which we shall touch in the following.

It has sometimes been wondered why the laws of 1412 do not include a specific prohibition against Jews lending Christians money at interest. Obviously, this lacuna does not suggest that such activity was permitted. The prohibition was omitted because the authors of the edict did not wish to conflict with the law on this subject issued by Enrique III (at the Cortes of Valladolid, 1405). While forbidding the Jews to lend money at interest, Enrique's law permitted them to buy tracts of land on both sides of the Duero, in order to supplement their income by agriculture.[82] The authors of the laws of 1412 were evidently opposed to this concession, but considered it impolitic to suppress or ignore it by issuing a new law against usury. They chose therefore to rely on Enrique's law, which forbade Jews to lend Christians money at interest, while seeking to forestall the Jews' settlement on land by other restrictive regulations. Such a regulation was the aforementioned law forbidding Jews to employ Christian workers in their fields, as well as the law prohibiting the Jews from imposing any tax on their own members without the authorities' specific permission.[83] Obviously, the majority of Spain's Jews lacked the funds needed to settle on the land. It could be expected that special taxes might be imposed by the Jewish communities on their richer members to supply at least in part the needs of the poor. The law prohibiting internal taxation, however, eliminated this possible source of help. With these and all the other obstacles before them, the transfer of hundreds of thousands of Jews from urban conditions to rural life became a virtual impossibility.

As no minority can survive economically totally cut off from the majority of the population, the laws of Valladolid should not be viewed merely as economic and social constraints. Their purpose was not economic oppression, but complete economic strangulation; and socially, their aim was not merely degradation, separation and segregation, as some of the authors we have cited suggested, but total exclusion from Spanish life. For their aim was not merely to restrict all intercourse between Jews and Christians to the minimum, but to cut it off altogether. The preamble to the edict openly stated that the laws were designed to terminate all converse between the Christians and the infidels; and the reason given for this termination was the need to prevent the faithful from falling into the errors that converse with the infidels might occasion.[84] This shabby excuse was of course a cover for an entirely different purpose.

To discern that purpose we merely have to consider the inevitable results of the laws of 1412, were they to be enforced for a considerable time. The spectacle of Jews living under those laws in their special enclosures (we may call them reservations) would resemble that of a herd of penned animals confined to a certain limited area and cut off from almost all their sources of sustenance. Of what use could such a group be to the country or the government that placed them in that condition? Obviously, of no use at all. Since their earning capacities were gone, or reduced to almost nothing, they were unable to contribute anything of value to the royal revenues, and thus one might assume that the edict of 1412 was issued to force the Jews to emigrate. But several laws included in that edict invalidate this assumption. Thus, the sixteenth and twenty-third laws forbid the Jews to remove themselves from their neighborhoods, prohibit the nobles from offering them shelter and, above all, impose the most severe penalties on any Jew trying to leave the country. Accordingly, law 23 reads:

> All Jews and Moors departing from my Kingdom and dominions, and taken in the road or any other place, shall lose whatever they have with them, and be my slaves forever.[85]

Since the road of emigration was cut off, the question must be asked: What was the purpose of all the above restrictions? The only answer that can come to mind is: conversion to Christianity.

For the laws of 1412 constituted a plan which prevented the Jews from taking any path that could possibly lead them to safety. Free emigration could of course provide an escape route for many or most of them. But the laws on emigration blocked that route. It was the door that closed the trap. Thus, conversion was left to the Jews of Spain as the only open way for their survival.

If we see the edict as aimed at this objective, we can understand also its other clauses, which, like some of those we have cited, have no precedent in the laws of Church or state. Such was the law that prohibited the Jews from using their own judges in their internal disputes, not only in criminal but also in civil cases, and forcing them to use the *alcaldes* of the cities, towns and villages where they reside.[86] These *alcaldes* were of course Christian; they would not judge according to Jewish law, and their verdicts would inevitably compel the Jews to infringe on their own laws. This was at least the expectation of the legislator, who may well have assumed that the new legal circumstances would narrow the gap between the life of a Jew and that of a convert to Christianity.

Similarly, the twelfth law forbidding any Jew to be designated Don was not meant so much to deny the Jews the dignity as to dash any hope they might entertain that their notables would abolish the bad decrees. The law made it clear that there would be no more Jewish courtiers who might influence the rulers: even the comparatively low title Don was prohibited to any of their members. Evidently, the main intent of the law was to have a practical effect on their thinking regarding their chances of extricating themselves from the death trap into which they were driven.

So, contrary to the views of Baer and other scholars, the laws of 1412 did have a "uniform purpose and definite program." Their sole objective was conversion, and each of them was calculated to attain this end. It was obvious that if the laws were implemented, the rich Jews would be impoverished and the poor would starve. The Jewish community would collapse economically and morally. The difficult and virtually insoluble questions posed by these laws regarding the Jews' housing, professions, income, and even the practice of their own law, combined to place the Jews under terrible strain, to expose them to excruciating suffering, and make them realize that conversion to Christianity was their only avenue to survival.[87]

And indeed from the moment the law was enacted, a steady stream of Castilian Jews flowed to the baptismal fonts. We have evidence of this from various sources, as we shall see below. The pressure continued for at least seven years, in the course of which many Jewish communities were swallowed up by the tide of conversion. There may be disagreement on the number of converts that the new wave of conversion brought in, but there can be no doubt that it was huge. According to Zacuto, the fifteenth-century Jewish chronicler, it was the "largest forced conversion that had ever taken place in Jewish history."[88] And this was written by a man who was well aware of the scope of the disaster of 1391.

Who Was Responsible?

From our preceding account of the events and developments leading to the promulgation of the laws of 1412, the reader could sense clearly that we imputed their genesis to the convert Paul of Burgos, then bishop of Cartagena. This imputation was based, to begin with, on our view of Paul's ambition to convert the Jews, of his evaluation of the Jews' resistance to conversion, and of the evolution of his thoughts on the subject from the beginning of his Church career. There were, however, additional reasons that led us to the above conclusion, and we consider it necessary to present them here in order to shed as much light as we can on the causes and aims of the laws of 1412.

Amador de los Ríos was the first modern historian to suggest that this entire legislation—apart from its preamble and first stipulation—originated with Paul of Burgos.[89] Graetz shared Amador's opinion, and so did other historians, notably Lea.[90] But Cantera and Serrano, Paul's modern biographers, considered the idea prejudiced. Serrano claimed that it lacked any foundation,[91] and Cantera asserted that the available evidence (the testimony of the historian Alvar García, Paul's brother) attributed the laws to the "initiative" of Ferrer.[92]

Let us first consider the evidence of García, on which Cantera so heavily relies. According to the account of this historian, the friar met the Queen at Valladolid in December 1411, and then and there urged her to separate the Jews and Moors from the Christians. "And the noble queen, moved by the Friar, issued her order in her entire province to designate special dwelling-places for the Jews and Moors. She also ordered that the Moslems wear yellow hoods with bright moons and the Jews turbans with long beards." This, we should note, is García's account according to the manuscript of his *crónica* in the Academia de la Historia, Madrid.[93]

This account differs in some details from that of the *Crónica de Juan II*, which was edited by Pérez de Guzmán within a few years after the king's death. According to this source, the friar met both the Queen and the Infante in Ayllón (and not in Valladolid) and delivered there a sermon, in which he asked both the Queen and the Infante that they

> order in all the cities and towns of the Kingdoms the separation of the Jews and the Moors from the Christians, because from their continued converse with the latter stem great dangers, especially to those who were newly converted to our Holy Faith. And thus it was regulated, ordered and put in effect in most cities and towns of these Kingdoms. And then it was also ordered that the Jews wear turbans with red signs and the Moslems hoods with a bright moon.[94]

This account of Ferrer's meeting with the regents is clearly more accurate than that of García. Ferrer, it seems, met the Queen more than once—first, together with the Infante in Ayllón, and then in Valladolid, her main residence. In Ayllón he presented his demand for "segregation" not in a private talk (as suggested by García), but in a sermon delivered before the two regents, and it was there that he asked them to issue a decree ordering all the towns and cities in the kingdom to effect that separation. This is indeed what actually occurred.[95]

It is hardly conceivable that Alvar García was unaware of all these facts. What moved him then to suppress Fernando's share in that important occurrence—important especially to García's own group, the conversos, and opposed to the position of his brother Don Pablo, who was known to be partial to Don Fernando? As we see no reason for Alvar García to present Ferrer's visit in so distorted a manner, we must conclude that some editor tampered with his manuscript and made several alterations in the text. The meeting place was changed from Ayllón to Valladolid, which was the headquarters of the Queen (and thus Fernando could be eliminated from the picture); and while describing the Jewish apparel, he passed over the requirement to wear the "sign" and instead mentioned the stipulation about the "beards," which he got from the law itself.[96] Yet whatever the correctness of any of the above versions, none of them indicates that the ordinance of Valladolid was inspired by Ferrer. Both limit the friar's influence only to one point: the residential segregation of the Jews. The instruction concerning the "sign" seems to have originated in some other influence, although the friar probably gave it his consent. What we can say with certainty, therefore, is that he pleaded only for a royal order supporting his demand for separate boroughs (for reasons that have been explained) and possibly sanctioned the imposition of the "sign"; but in this we see no grounds to conclude that he inspired the whole edict of 1412.

In fact, as we have noted, the imposition of the "sign" had long before been stipulated by Castile's civil law (1348), and separate living quarters for the Jews had been urged by the Council of Palencia (1388) and approved by the kings for certain cities since 1272. Yet these regulations did not call for the total elimination of the Jews from the economy or the suppression of their civil jurisdiction, or the prohibition on their leaving the country, or throwing them out of their houses in eight days, or threatening them with personal enslavement; nor did they call for most other measures included in the edict of 1412. Had these measures been in Ferrer's mind, they would somehow have been indicated by him in his campaign. But they were not demanded by him at any time. They appeared only in the laws of 1412, which were enacted at the conclusion of his campaign in Castile. Hence, they stemmed from a different mind—the mind of a man who did not believe that Ferrer's agitation, unsupported by repression, could induce the Jews to convert to Christianity—a man who thought that, while a decree for segregation might move *some* Jews to abandon their religion, it would be far from sufficient to bring all or most Jews to religious surrender. It had to be a man who was intimately familiar with the Jews' readiness and capacity to suffer for their religion, and at the same time commanded great influence at Court. And who could that man be if not Paul of Burgos?

But Paul had not only the motive and the inclination to influence the regents in that direction; he had also the opportunity to do so. He was not detached from the Court as Ferrer was, but permanently attached to it. As the Major Chancellor of the kingdom, as tutor of the young king, and as intimate friend of both Fernando and Catalina, he could speak to them on the issues related to the above laws as often as he wished. And he had to discuss those issues with them *many* times if he wanted his advice to be accepted. For what was involved was a complete departure from Spain's centuries-old policy on the Jewish question, and the adoption of laws more severe and repressive than either Church or state had ever proposed. There is also no doubt that Paul had to counteract strong influences which the Jews could still mobilize in their defense, and he obviously needed considerable time to develop all the arguments, political and economic, that could move the regents to accept his plan. Ferrer, on the other hand, could not possibly have managed, during his short visit at Court, to work out the numerous laws of the edict, touching on so large a variety of issues, some of which were specifically Castilian and closely related to Castile's life and law. We must assume therefore that when he came to Ayllón (in December 1411) the edict of January 2, 1412 had already been drafted; that Paul and the regents delayed its publication until they could "rely" on Ferrer's appeal; and finally, that their edict included the order about the Jews' residential segregation, and hence that even the initiative for publishing *this* law did not come from Ferrer (as Amador thought). It was all carefully planned and prepared, and finally also coordinated with Ferrer, by Paul of Burgos—the man who could, in his shrewdness and perspicacity, combine both the religious and political elements, the internal factor of the Jewish question with the external issue of the Aragonese succession, and bring them all to bear in a ruthless legislation (the one he had striven and worked for so long) during that brief period of Ferrer's visit to the Court.

Was Paul of Burgos morally capable of subjecting the Jews to such hardships and suffering, which were sure to doom many of them to death? His *Scrutinium Scripturarum*, the large work he composed to prove the truth of Christianity from the Scriptures,[97] offers a clear answer to this question. In this book he defines the Jews as greater criminals than the people of Sodom, worse than the rebels Dathan and Aviram, who were justly destroyed in a single moment when they were devoured by the earth. The punishment given to those criminals, therefore, was, in his opinion, insufficient for the Jews. They deserved a prolonged chastisement and agony to make their punishment heavier, and hence their long exile and the tortures it entails.[98] Nowhere does he indicate that the sufferings of the Jews, the bloody persecutions to which they were subjected, were disproportionate to their alleged sins. On the contrary, all the troubles and tribulations they have endured since Christ's time are viewed by him as a just penalty for their horrible crime against the Son of God; and in the massacres and atrocities of 1391 he saw not only a part of that penalty, but also a divine answer to the Jews' foolish (and criminal) desire to become rulers of Spain.[99] The answer was given them by Ferrán Martínez, whose murderous actions against them were motivated, according to Paul, solely by the desire to "avenge the blood of Christ" *(Deo ultionem sanguinis Christi excitante)*[100]—a desire he could not consider illegitimate. And when he comes to the reign of Juan II, he says that "many things were instituted" by the Regents against the "Judaic wickedness" which were "mostly observed in their courts and kingdoms, and under which, with divine help, the Judaic, as well as the Saracen infidelity is being suppressed."[101] Here too, then, not a word of criticism is uttered against the laws of 1412, but rather the highest praise. Moreover, he sees them as the source of a double goodness. "At the very time that the Jewish experts believed to be the age of the coming of their redemption, there began the destruction of the perfidious infidels, and salvation, life and resurrection of the faithful converted to Christ."[102] Paul of Burgos, then, not only justified these laws; he also regarded them as necessary measures to rid the world of the great infidelity and bring about the great conversion movement which had developed in Spain.

And let us note the following point, too. While he clearly indicates that Ferrán Martínez was responsible for the riots and conversions of 1391,[103] he does not refer at all, even by allusion, to Vicente Ferrer, who was commonly regarded as the sole author of the legal innovations which took place in the period of Juan II and which he, Paul, hailed as an act of God. Indeed, when Paul wrote about the laws of 1412 (probably c. 1430), he did not relate them in any way to Ferrer, though the name of the saint, of whose missionary activity legend had woven miracle stories and who was known as the great Apostle of the Faith, could have helped Paul to justify those harsh measures as having been urged by a holy man. Why, then, refer to Martínez, the murderer of the Jews—who, he knew, was a man of little learning, though he described him as one of "laudable life," and ignore the learned man whose life was not only laudable but generally considered saintly? Why not mention Ferrer, who not by acts of violence, but by pure persuasion, as it was believed, moved so many Jews to convert to Christianity and influenced the Kings to enact those laws in which he, Paul, saw an act of God? The answer is that Paul of Burgos knew that what was attributed to Ferrer in this connection was not true; because he knew that the major responsibility for the laws of 1412 was not Ferrer's but his; and himself he would not praise. By the time he discussed this subject in his work, he could no longer correct what was written in the history books and what was generally accepted as fact. Yet he could not bring himself to support a notion which he knew full well to be wrong, or at least highly exaggerated, and which in effect denied him the credit of his own achievement. Paul of Burgos, therefore, chose silence as the only alternative open to him. It was left to the Augustinian friar Sanctotis, who wrote Paul's biography about 1590, to point out his real share in the edict of 1412 and stress that he worked with all his might for the acceptance of those laws, which were "organized, instigated and made public by his influence, in order to bring about the devastation of Judaism and the augmentation of the Christian Religion."[104] Like Paul, Sanctotis does not mention Ferrer's name either.

XI

Shortly after the laws of Valladolid became public, Ferrer received the Pope's urgent call to return to Aragon. He was needed there in connection with the evolving conflict over the election of the King. Ferrer knew that he would have to cut short his campaign in Castile, but he wished, before returning to Aragon, to visit the country's northwestern cities. He must have done this in the following two months (January–February), heading toward León through Palencia and Paredes, and then turning southward toward Zamora through Astorga and Benavente. On his return to Aragon, which he started in March, he visited such important cities as Segovia, Avila and Salamanca,[105] and a number of smaller communities, devoting to each only a very brief time. But the results of his campaign were astounding. Barely fifteen days after the laws had been issued, and before starting his northern drive, he could announce the incredibly "good news" that "the Jews and Moors of Valladolid are all converting themselves."[106] Soon he could see the same phenomenon in all the places he visited on his tour. Thousands of Jews hastened to be baptized and whole communities were almost wiped out.[107]

What accounted for Ferrer's success was of course the edict of 1412. One can understand the rush for conversion evidenced shortly after its publication among the Jews of Northern Castile, which was under Catalina's jurisdiction. The law gave them only eight days to leave their places, and they were seized with panic that any day they might be thrown out of their homes. Paul of Burgos was thus proven right when he claimed, as we assumed, that Ferrer's agitation would be highly effective only if accompanied by legal pressure. And the pressure was indeed strong and incessant, since the authorities were everywhere strict and uncompromising in executing the new laws.[108] In fact, the conversion movement started by Ferrer could now continue on its own momentum, or rather under the impetus constantly provided by the laws of 1412.

When he returned to Aragon (probably by the end of March), Ferrer plunged into the wrangle over the issue of succession, which by then had stirred the entire country. On March 14, 1412, he was chosen as one of the nine arbiters representing the three great provinces of the kingdom—Valencia, Catalonia and Aragon—to select their new king. When they met the following month in the castle of Caspe, Ferrer (who arrived there on April 12) was the first to express his opinion; and he spoke unreservedly in favor of Fernando. His view won over the majority of the voters, and Fernando was elected king.[109] In June of that year Fernando left Castile, but—contrary to Catalina's expectations—did not resign the regency. Instead, he elected four men to represent him, one of whom was the bishop of Cartagena. Fernando was not ungrateful. He knew how to value what Paul had done for him when he influenced Ferrer in his favor. Indeed, thanks to this particular influence, Paul of Burgos became one of the men who shaped the destinies of the Spanish kingdoms.

On June 24, 1412—that is, shortly after his election as king—Fernando published in Cifuentes, in the province of Guadalajara, a modified version of the laws of Catalina for the part of Castile controlled by his regency, and nine months later, on March 20, 1413, he published in Barcelona the same version for Aragon.[110] His own laws were not as extreme and brutally anti-Jewish as those of Catalina, but essentially they contained all that was needed to force the Jews to conversion. Fernando thus fulfilled his own part of the bargain he had made informally with Paul.

Even before the new laws were issued in Aragon, Ferrer returned to the stump; and he resumed—and intensified—his conversionist activity shortly after their publication. Covering in his campaign the whole of Lower Aragon, he proceeded from there, through Valencia, to Majorca, and then through Catalonia to Rosellón.[111] Of course, the majority of his converts were now coming to Christianity under the impact of the laws of Barcelona, rather than under the influence of his preaching. But his preaching helped, and it served the papacy by supporting its contention that the conversionist achievements resulted from its efforts.

But the Pope was also thinking of other ways to justify his claims about those achievements. He must have received advance notice from Fernando about the issuance of the laws of Cifuentes in Aragon, and he may also have coordinated with him the time of their publication. Toward the end of 1412 he developed the idea that he should identify himself more personally with the conversion movement by opening its forthcoming drive in Aragon with an outstanding dramatic act: a public disputation between Jews and Christians on a scale larger than ever before.

It would not be surprising if this idea, too, was proposed to him by the bishop of Cartagena, since it was Paul's disciple, Joshua ha-Lorki (known since his conversion as Jerónimo de Santa Fe), who was appointed by the Pope, no doubt on Paul's advice, to lead the Christian disputants against the Jews. According to the plan adopted by Benedict, he himself would invite the Jewish communities of Aragon to send their representatives to the disputation.

Joshua ha-Lorki, a physician from Alcaniz, must have excelled in the medical profession, for otherwise he would not have been chosen by Benedict as his personal physician.[112] Commanding a broad general education and mastering some of the medieval sciences, Lorki was also at home in Hebrew learning, and undoubtedly was believed to be capable of meeting the arguments of the Jewish scholars. He seemed especially fitted for the task because, following his conversion, he had written a work sharply censuring the Jewish faith *(Contra Perfidiam Judaeorum)*, to which he appended a special tract on the errors of the Jews according to the Talmud. Lorki planned to pick up the line of argument followed by the Christians in an earlier disputation—the one held in Aragon in 1263 between the convert Paulus Christiani and Moses Nahmanides, one of the foremost scholars Spanish Jewry had produced. On that occasion Christiani tried to prove from post-Biblical Jewish literature— i.e., the Midrashim and the Talmud—that the Messiah had already come and that he was none other than Jesus, whereas Nahmanides sought to demonstrate that the evidence and arguments presented by Christiani were nonsensical and utterly unfounded.[113] Jews and Christians were divided in their opinion about the outcome of that celebrated debate. Now Lorki undertook to complete the task begun by Paulus Christiani, and to prove the case of Christianity so convincingly that the Jews would be compelled to admit their error and abandon their religion.

Lorki was not naive; nor was he a mystic who truly believed in the Christian import of the Sages' sayings he intended to cite in support of his thesis. He was aware, of course, of Nahmanides' refutations of the assertions made by Christiani to that effect, and could not fail to see that they were unanswerable. If he now undertook to perform a task which he knew was theoretically impossible, it was because he believed that the Jews of the time were in no position to defend themselves effectively. Faced with Ferrer's conversionist campaign and the repressive laws of 1412, and aware that both the Pope and the Kings were resolved to eliminate Judaism from Spain, the Spanish Jews saw their horizon covered with clouds presaging a heavy storm. Lorki was sure that in this state of mind, governed by desperation and fear, the Jews would be reluctant, or extremely hesitant, to take a clear-cut stand against his arguments. His opening remarks show that he counted on their mood, more than on anything else, to win his case. By now, he thought, the Jews must realize that conversion was their only way to survive; and he wanted of course to strengthen that realization from the very start of the debate. He began by citing Isaiah's verses: "Come and argue, said the Lord. If you be willing and hear me, you shall eat the good of the land, but if you refuse and provoke my irascibility, you will be devoured by the sword."[114]

The disputation opened in Tortosa, after much preparation, on February 7, 1413. It was given a most ostentatious form, to make it appear as a major event in the history of the Church. Honored by the presence of Benedict XIII, his cardinals, and most of his archbishops and bishops, the opening session was also attended by some one thousand invited guests, including courtiers, nobles and notables from various parts of the kingdom. Twenty-two Jewish savants, representing the best that Jewish scholarship could then muster, came to serve as spokesmen of the Jews. Turning to them at the opening of the discussion, the pope made it clear that they were invited to Tortosa not to determine the truth of either Judaism or Christianity, "for I know that my own faith is true whereas yours *was* true and has been abolished. You were asked to come here to present your views on Jerónimo's claim that the authors of the Talmud, who knew more than you do, admitted that the Messiah had come."[115] The Pope wanted to limit the argument to that point, but the Jews, who sought to avoid as much as possible the issue of Jesus' messiahship, expanded the discussion to embrace the basic differences between the two faiths.[116] But by broadening the discussion, they prolonged it, so that it lasted much longer than expected. After nine sessions of oral debates, ending on February 20, 1414, the parties began to argue in writing, presenting their views in detailed memoranda read in common meetings, and then rebutted.[117]

From the standpoint of a modern layman, judging the arguments of both sides by rationalistic-historical criteria, there can be no doubt that the Jewish disputants refuted most claims made by the convert. But the debate at the time was hardly judged by purely rationalistic-historical standards. What is more, it was Jerónimo de Santa Fe who summarized the results of the various discussions, and these summaries were always tendentious and often plainly distortive. Finally, on April 19, 1414, in the sixtieth session, Jerónimo presented his final "conclusions," according to which the Jews lost the debate. This was the official verdict.[118]

The Tortosa Disputation was the longest and most crucial of all the medieval debates of its kind. It was crucial because it served as an effective instrument of the conversion campaign as it developed at the time. It gave thousands of Jews, who had decided to convert for purely social and economic reasons, a convenient excuse to carry out their wish: they could argue that the debate at Tortosa had proven Christianity right.[119] Most Jews who looked for such an excuse belonged to the upper classes, but their claims and pretenses demoralized many others and added impetus to the conversion movement, which thus assumed massive proportions.

In the following year, in his bull of May 11, the Pope summed up the achievements of Tortosa and also sanctioned the laws of 1412 and 1413, which were issued, after all, by lay rulers.[120] It was now clear to him that without those laws, no large-scale conversion could have materialized, and in consequence, both Ferrer's agitation and the Tortosa Disputation would have lost their significance, as their whole importance lay, from his standpoint, in giving the mass movement, which the laws had created, the image of a voluntary conversion. He knew that, more than to anyone else, he owed this achievement to Paul. He appointed his son, Gonzalo de Santa María, then archdeacon of Briviesca, as the executor of his bull,[121] and on December 18 rewarded Paul with the bishopric of Burgos.[122]

XII

By making this appointment Benedict not only expressed his appreciation of Paul's past services; he also indicated his expectation that Paul would continue to serve him effectively in the days ahead. The month of September was especially crucial for Benedict's fortunes. Following the abdication of the two other popes (John XXII and Gregory XII), the German emperor Sigismund, who made great efforts to terminate the Schism, and whose influence on the Council of Constance was far-reaching, sought to move King Fernando, Benedict's chief ally, to impress on the Pope the unavoidable necessity for him to follow the path of his rivals. Fernando understood that no other course was left; but tied to Benedict by personal commitments, he looked for an honorable way out. He first appointed a committee of four bishops, two from Castile and two from Aragon, to examine the abdication papers of the rival popes and report to him on their propriety. Paul was one of the two Castilian appointees and, like the other three members of the commission, found no fault in the documents of abdication and the procedures by which they were obtained. Although all four examiners were supporters of Benedict, they unanimously decided that "since it is clear that both John and Gregory have renounced the papal dignity, Benedict, too, ought to do the same, if he sincerely wished to restore peace and concord to the Christian world."[123]

It is obvious that Paul was now completely on the side of King Fernando and was determined to implement the latter's plans. But it is also obvious that he was astute enough to let Benedict believe that, come what may, he would not forsake him. Accordingly, he accompanied Benedict to the island of Peñiscola, where he moved on November 9; and it was in Peñiscola that he was appointed by the Pope as bishop of Burgos.[124]

Before they left for Peñiscola, on November 9, a secret meeting was held by the representatives of Castile and Aragon in which it was decided to approach

Benedict three more times with requests for abdication; if he still refused, both Castile and Aragon would withdraw their obedience from him. Paul participated in the delegation that presented to Benedict the third request to abdicate. But there can be no doubt that he managed to convince Benedict that, regardless of his own view of the issue of abdication, he would continue to influence both Castile and Aragon against withdrawing their obedience from him. Had Benedict been given the slightest intimation that Paul would act differently, Benedict would certainly not have increased his authority by granting him the important Burgensian position. Paul thus acted toward Benedict in bad faith. He dissimulated unalterable friendship for the Pope as long as he hoped to obtain the prize position that was available at the time—namely, the bishopric of Burgos. But once he got the desired appointment, he discarded Benedict like an old glove and left him to his miserable fate.

Following the Pope's rejection of the third request, Paul left Peñiscola never to return; nor did he ever, from that day on, renew his contacts with the Pope. On February 4 he swore to the agreement reached earlier (on December 13, 1415) in Narbonne between representatives of Castile, Aragon and Navarre to participate in the Council of Constance with the intent of abolishing the Schism in the only way left—that is, by deposing Benedict from the papacy.[125] In all this Paul displayed his capacity for double-dealing and political maneuvering, as well as his lack of moral fiber. His conduct in those days was determined first and foremost by his desire to promote his own interests—i.e., his power and aggrandizement—the same motive that had played a major part in his conversion to Christianity.

His attainment of the bishopric of Burgos, however, was the last achievement in his political career. On April 2, 1416, only a few weeks after Paul had committed himself to the Narbonne agreement, King Fernando died, and this completely altered Paul's position in Castile. Queen Catalina, who now realized that Paul had never been her true friend, and that he persistently supported Fernando, excluded him from the council of regents, which she reorganized following Fernando's death. Soon the direction of political affairs in Castile passed into the hands of Paul's old enemy and rival, the Burgensian Sancho de Rojas, whom Benedict XIII had appointed archbishop of Toledo on June 10, 1415, well before Castile withdrew its obedience from him on January 15, 1416. From then on, Paul exercised no direct influence upon the affairs of Castile or the universal Church. His activities were limited to the management of his bishopric and to literary production, especially to the writing of his two major works: the *Additiones* to Nicholas de Lyra's biblical commentary which he completed in 1429,[126] and *Scrutinium Scripturarum*, his magnum opus—a large-scale polemical discourse on Judaism and Christianity, which he finished in 1434,[127] one year before his death at the age of eighty-three.

III. The Conversos Enter Spanish Society

The mass conversions of Spanish Jews in 1391 and 1412 created in Spain a new social entity which formed a large part of the urban population and posed unprecedented problems to the cities. Legally freed from the various restrictions that limited the Jews' economic activities, the converts sought to enter economic fields hitherto exclusively occupied by Christians. As a result, the Old Christian population in the cities was put under constant pressure by the newcomers, whose competitive force was felt before long in the crafts, free professions and officialdom. How did the cities react to this influx? And how did this reaction affect the absorption of the new element by the Old Christian population? The sources offer sporadic and only partial data. In a later chapter we shall see to what extent they may provide answers to the above questions.

But the entry of the converts into Spain's Christian society raises a number of other questions, too. How did this large body of Jews who adopted Christianity under *duress* conduct itself in the new environment? Obviously, not all members of this group shared the same attachment to Judaism. Yet whatever their inward religious attitudes, it is certain that most of them were extremely reluctant to stop performing *all* the Commandments, and even more so to take part in Christian rites and ceremonies. Nevertheless, such behavior was dictated to them not only by the laws of Church and state, but also by economic necessity; in fact, their survival depended on their readiness to behave publicly as Christians.

To appreciate the gravity of this necessity, several facts ought to be noted. Following the riots, the majority of the converts, like the majority of the Jews in the stricken areas, were in dire economic straits. When they returned to their homes from the baptismal font, they found their houses sacked and half ruined.[1] Craftsmen had lost the tools of their trade, which, if not stolen, were usually smashed; businessmen lost their Jewish partners, who, if not killed, were scattered to every corner; and moneylenders were often deprived of the documents or the collateral they had received for their loans. Both the conditions that obtained during the pogroms and the contemporary evidence from various quarters lead us to conclude that most converts were destitute when they entered Christendom.[2]

In these circumstances, it is obvious, the majority of the converts urgently needed remunerative work. But this urgent need could hardly be met by their own convert communities. The number of Jews who had converted *before* the riots, and thereby saved at least part of their possessions, was too small to sustain the majority, who were now in danger of starvation. Nor could needy converts find work among Jews in the places stricken by the pogroms; for most of these Jews faced similar hardships, and their despoiled communities could hardly take care of their own emergency cases.[3] The only chance for the converts to get work, therefore, was to turn to the Christian burghers; but the Christians, who would generally not engage Jews unless moved by some special reason to do so, maintained the same attitude toward the converts. Inevitably, to induce a Christian to employ them, the converts would reduce the cost of their labor; and this would require them to work longer hours and often do their work in Christian neighborhoods. This meant that during much of the day, as well as in the early hours of the evening, they had to avoid the performance of the Commandments, ignore the Jewish dietary laws, and behave in all other respects like Christians. This also meant that they had to work on the Sabbath and Jewish holidays, and avoid working on Sundays and Christian festivals. On such days they also had to go to church, hear mass, and participate in other Christian ceremonies. They obviously also had to perform Christian rites related to births, deaths and marriages.

It is evident that in such circumstances little time and opportunity were left to the converts to observe Jewish law. No doubt at first many among them, determined to perform the Commandments secretly, would rise early to recite the Jewish prayers before they went to work for their Christian employers and would fulfill other religious duties when they returned to their homes in the evening. Others would organize in small groups that met on certain holidays for religious worship. But the strain involved in leading a double life and the tension caused by fear of discovery would inevitably take their toll. Attendance at the secret gatherings declined, as did the number of followers of Jewish law in their homes, as well as the number of laws they would follow. Thus, Judaism among the converts receded, while attachment to Christianity was on the rise.[4]

For a time, we should add, this development was aided by the general reaction of both Jews and Christians to the converts' religious behavior. Since most Jews sympathized with the forced convert's plight, they would usually give him the benefit of the doubt when they saw him violate Jewish law[5]; they tended to assume that on such occasions, he considered it perilous to expose his Jewishness. It was of course natural that many a convert took advantage of this prevailing Jewish attitude and permitted himself to be rather lax in the fulfillment of the Commandments. He knew that his failure to act like a Jew would be excused not only by his fellow converts, but also by most Jews, who "understood" his predicament and trusted his judgment as to what he could or could not do as a forced convert. On the other hand, he could not expect such "understanding" from Christians should they find him violating Christian law or custom. Social convention and public opinion, which from the start was distrustful of forced converts, would invariably condemn such behavior. Here, therefore, he had to be especially careful if he wished to avoid punishment by the authorities and not undermine his relations with the Christian society, upon which his livelihood depended. Thus, while keeping Jewish law was optional for the forced convert, obeying Christian law was obligatory. Consequently, he was habituated more and more to live like a Christian and less and less to behave like a Jew. His conduct could not remain long unnoticed. In 1393, only two years after the riots, the philosopher Profiat Duran, himself a forced convert, observed that a "part" of the converts is so remiss or failing in the practice of Judaism that it is generally believed to have left the fold, while others among them so "enjoyed" their freedom from the burden of the Jewish precepts as to put in question even the possibility that they might ever return to the right path.[6]

Three years later, in 1396, that same author informs us of a new development of a far more serious nature. The camp of forced converts is now teeming with "rebels," who brazenly denounce the Jewish faith and actively campaign for full Christianization.[7] Their message was evidently gaining acceptance, but not without arousing strong opposition. Sharp debates broke out between the Christian protagonists and the converts who remained Jews at heart; and these debates spread so rapidly among the converts and engulfed such large sections of their camp that it appeared, as Duran put it, that the "entire people was at strife."[8] In the turmoil and confusion that accompanied these disputes, it could nevertheless be seen that Christianity was the winner, so much so that the philosopher Hasdai Crescas, then leader of the Jews of Aragon, looked for ways and means to stop the steady progress Christianity was making among the forced converts. It occurred to him that the pro-Christian agitation should be combatted with anti-Christian arguments, and he thought that such arguments should be made available to the "Jewish" converts, who could not apparently stand their ground when confronted with the Christian agitators. Thus Duran wrote, at Crescas' request, a detailed confutation of Christianity, which was followed up by a critique of Christian dogma written by Crescas himself.[9] Both works are powerful attacks on Christianity, the best that Jewish polemics had produced. Perhaps they had some vitalizing effect upon the hard-pressed defenders of Judaism among the converts. But the trend toward Christianity was not halted.

Who were those who in the middle of the nineties began that agitation among the forced converts? They belonged, we presume, to the group of *voluntary* converts who campaigned for Christianity among the Jews of Castile shortly before the riots of 1391.[10] They were the latest of a long succession of such converts who had been active in Spain since the 12th century and who managed to produce, despite their small number, a large and diversified anti-Jewish literature. Their oral propaganda, too, was varied and marked by its different approaches to Spain's Jews, including that of public disputations. But despite their manifold efforts at persuasion, their conversionist achievements were limited. They constantly looked, however, for opportunities to increase them, and now they thought that the camp of the forced converts, depressed, perplexed and fearful as it was, offered them such an opportunity. In this instance the results proved them right. They must soon have acquired among the forced converts not merely followers but able disputants, whom they taught how to argue against Judaism. This would explain the indication of the sources that the agitators for Christianity among the converts were "numerous,"[11] so numerous indeed that they could split the converts' camp as suggested by the "strife" we have referred to.[12] Thus, the campaign to Christianize the forced converts had made, even in its early stages, deep inroads into their ranks and started the process which, within a few decades, drew most of their camp to the Christian side.

The altered position of the forced converts was not expressed in a formal conversion (for formally the converts had *been* Christian), but by an inward change of attitudes. Actually, it meant withdrawal from *all* Jewish practices and voluntary identification with Christianity—essentially an extension of the double process which began, as we have noted, among the forced converts shortly after their conversion. It is hard to assume that the later stages of this process did not evolve from the earlier ones and were products of entirely different causes, such as the conversionist campaign. It is more likely that what radicalized the movement that abandoned Judaism and veered to Christianity were the hardships inherent in the converts' situation—hardships that increased with the passage of time and eventually became unbearable. In this condition, it would seem, the missionaries offered many converts an honorable way out, a cover for their flight from Judaism out of weakness or out of what appeared as ulterior motives. But it must also be recognized that many other converts were led by the missionary campaigners to believe that Christianity was indeed the ultimate creed, and sincerely embraced it as the only true faith. Had this not been so, the foremost Jewish authors of the 15th century would not have kept writing polemical works in defense of Judaism and refutation of its critics. Moreover, in the middle of the 15th century, one of these authors, Hayyim ibn Musa, admits the great influence which the conversionist literature—that is, literature produced by Jewish converts—had on many Jews, and furthermore notes that the arguments made by converts (and Christians by birth) in religious disputations had a similar effect.[13] To be sure, when Ibn Musa refers to Jews, he may have had in mind *overt Jews* and not *Jews at heart* among the forced converts; but what he said about the influence of the Christian arguments could obviously apply to the latter, too. In fact, it could apply especially to them, since forced converts, who sought relief from their troubles, were especially vulnerable to the conversionist agitation.

Besides the conversionist campaign, however, there was another "spiritual" factor that contributed to the Christianization of the forced converts. In 1861 Renan observed that owing to the influence that the philosophy of Averroes wielded on Jewish thinking, "the Jewish people became one of the principal representatives of rationalism in the second half of the medieval era."[14] If by the term "the Jewish people" Renan meant small sections of the Jewish communities in southern France, Italy, and Spain, his observation was a true statement of fact. But for a long time nobody related this fact to the general state of religion in Spanish Jewry, or to the rapid retreat from Judaism of the forced converts of 1391 and 1412. Such a relationship, however, existed, though it was indirect and not always apparent.

There is no doubt that, in the last analysis, Averroism was a denial of religion. Its lessons, however veiled, implied negation of such concepts as the immortality of the soul, the afterlife and a world governed by reward and punishment. Thus, it conflicted with the fundamental beliefs not only of Islam (Averroes' own religion), but of Christianity and Judaism as well. Jewish students of Averroes tried for a long time to coordinate his views with the tenets of religion, but finally the development of Jewish philosophy brought to the fore bolder spirits, who spelled out the implications of Averroes' teachings in clear and definite terms. It did not take long before their conclusions spread from the intellectual elite, which upheld them, to the social elite of the Jews of Spain; and no special insights are needed to envisage how ties were formed between these groups. It was primarily the rich who could afford to give their young not only Jewish but secular education, including philosophy, the supreme science of the time; and thus some of the rich, more than members of other groups, came to be affected by religious skepticism. But this development in their thinking, we should note, did not incline them to convert to Christianity. Of all religions, mystical Christianity was the least acceptable to the Jewish skeptics, while Judaism (especially in its ancient state) appeared the least objectionable. Their position, however, would be instantly reversed if adherence to Judaism involved mortal danger. As no religion, including Judaism, appeared to them worth risking their lives or fortunes for, conversion to Christianity in times of peril was to them an acceptable solution.

Perhaps the first evidence of this was offered during the pogroms that broke out in Catalonia during the Black Death. A document of the Jewish communities meeting in Barcelona on December 16, 1354, refers to those converts, who were "born to great wealth," as "children of crime" and says that "those who had risen to the highest spheres were those who converted."[15] In 1348 most of the Jewish communities in Spain were not in danger, and the majority of the elite even in the attacked communities was probably not yet infected with faithlessness. In 1391 conditions changed. Faithlessness must have been more pervasive among the elite groups, as suggested by the behavior of the Jewish leaders in Burgos.[16] By 1412–1414 disregard for Judaism on the part of leading Jews became far more widespread and also more pronounced. Speaking of the Jewish notables of Aragon who came to attend the Tortosa Disputation (1413–1414), the poet Bonafed, who saw and heard them, says that many of them *wished* to be converted even before the disputation ended. Bonafed also explains why: Their faith in Judaism was so enfeebled as to make them utterly unable to resist the temptation to convert to Christianity.[17]

Bonafed thereby denies the common presumption that the propensity to convert, which was noticed among the elite, stemmed from their unwillingness to part with their wealth and the life of comfort they were used to. Whatever truth there is in this presumption, it does not touch the core of the problem. During the frightful persecutions in Germany from the 11th to the 14th century, the wealthy Jews, who belonged to the elite, were a model of religious devotion and self-sacrifice. So also were the wealthy Jews in England in 1190 and those of the Ukraine during the massacres of 1648. What sustained them all was their great faith, which remained unshaken—and indeed unaffected—in the face of overwhelming tragedy. In these Jewries, one should add at this point, philosophy was never studied.

This does not mean that the study of philosophy was the sole factor that made the difference in the attitude toward religion between the Jews of Spain and those of northern or eastern Europe. But it was undoubtedly one of the factors, and probably not the least of them. Throughout the 15th century, leading Jewish authors repeatedly attributed the mass conversions of Spain's Jews to the philosophers, who taught skepticism and denial and thus weakened the faith of the Spanish Jews. But these testimonies have generally been ignored by modern scholars. Only Baer noted the close relationship between the influence of Averroism on Spanish Jewry and the skepticism and denial that prevailed in certain circles of the Jewish aristocracy, especially among the courtiers.[18] This would explain why many of the wealthy were inclined to convert, but it would not explain the rapid tendency toward Christianization that appeared among the masses—i.e., among the converts of 1391 and later among those of 1412. The impact of philosophy upon the faith of the masses could be established only if a link could be found between the religious attitudes of the skeptical elite and those of the common people who did not study philosophy. Such a link, as we have shown elsewhere, existed.[19] It was formed by the collapse of the people's belief in the reality of reward and punishment—a major foundation of the Jewish faith—whose absence, many thought, had been tangibly demonstrated by the great catastrophe that befell the Jews of Spain. Amid that catastrophe, the philosophers' summations reverberated in the minds of the persecuted masses, and supplied the approval of the "great" and the "learned" to what they saw around them.[20] Thus, faithlessness became widespread, engulfing large sections of Spanish Jewry. "Look hard," said Alami, "and you will find that *faith no longer exists in the majority of the people.*"[21]

Alami wrote this in 1415, but much of it must have been true in 1391 and the years that followed. Otherwise, it would be hard to explain the rapid Christianization of the converts of 1391—as well as those of 1412—of which we have abundant evidence. Thus, the impact of philosophy on Spain's Jews must be added to the factors that moved forced converts to abandon Judaism and embrace Christianity—in most cases, to be sure, not as an act of faith but of faithlessness, of taking the one open avenue to survival when all other avenues were closed.

But all this applied to the first generation of converts. Their children, educated in Christian schools and attuned to Christian teachings, were prone to abandon the opinions of their parents, whether learned or unlearned. Intellectually, they were part of the Christian world, and saw no reason why they should not be part of the Christian society about them. The current discrimination against Jews, they no doubt realized, affected them, as offspring of Jews, adversely. But by the end of the second decade of the 15th century, things were beginning to change. All the leading men of the preceding generation who were involved in the anti-Jewish campaign had either died or lost their influence. In January 1419, Pope Martin V issued a bull virtually freeing the Jews from most of the limitations of the laws of 1412. The civil authorities in Spain were in no hurry to obey it. But there was some relaxation of the anti-Jewish persecution, which seemed to augur well for the conversos, too. It was a slight change, to be sure—hardly noticeable, but sufficient to encourage the sons of converts to believe that they were on the threshold of better times.

BOOK TWO

THE REIGN OF JUAN II
1419–1454

CHAPTER I

The Struggle for
Monarchic Superiority

I. The King and His Minister

I

Thus opened the period of Juan II, which might more aptly be called the age of Alvaro de Luna, the king's chief minister and ruler of the kingdom for almost the whole of that long reign (1419–1454). For more than any of his contemporaries, Alvaro affected the course of Castile's history and exerted a deep and lasting influence on most of the major developments of his time. As for the history of the conversos in that period, it was so closely linked to Alvaro's deeds and policies that not even a single phase of it can be described, or any of its great events understood, without considering Alvaro's involvement. Alvaro's biographies and most related histories (such as those of Spain and the Spanish Inquisition) pay scant attention to this fact. We shall try to fill this odd lacuna.

It may be reasonably assumed that the expansion of the conversos, or rather their penetration into the Old Christian society, could also have occurred under a different regime from that established by Alvaro. But the scope of that expansion would have been much narrower, its pace much slower, and its various achievements much more limited. Under Alvaro's regime, however, the attainments of the conversos were nothing short of phenomenal. Within one generation the New Christians in Castile, who had been (till 1420) a rather humble group, rose to the highest positions of leadership in almost every field of the nation's life. And directly related to this development was the mid-century political crisis that precipitated Alvaro's downfall. As the reader will see, Alvaro's fortunes were inextricably bound up with those of the conversos, just as the fortunes of the conversos were tied to Alvaro's rise and fall.

Similar to the conversos' social advancement, though by no means equal in national importance, was the rapid progress made by Spain's Jews under Alvaro's rule. In barely one decade they were transformed from a deprived, degraded and impoverished community into one that regained its former social status and much of its lost wealth. As in the case of the conversos, so in that of the Jews, it was Alvaro de Luna who was largely responsible for this radical change. In fact, the ups and downs in the condition of the Jews reflected the condition of their protector. Alvaro firmly supported both groups (the Jews and the conversos), which, though sharing certain social characteristics, differed in most vital respects. What moved Alvaro to adopt this policy which clearly ran counter to the trend of his times? Later on, in discussing his goals, we hope to offer an answer to this query.

Alvaro's life (1389–1453) falls into two periods of almost equal length, but so disparate and dissimilar that they seem to belong to two different men. Ending after his thirtieth year, the first of these periods was completely devoid of public activity of any kind; the second, which continued almost to his death, was marked by his ceaseless, intense involvement in the political and social life of Castile. And while in the first period Alvaro appears as a blithe and carefree *caballero,* in the second he impresses us, right from the outset, as a statesman of stature and far-reaching goals, for whose achievement he worked without letup. Could such a transformation take place overnight? Was there nothing in Alvaro's first three decades that prepared him for his second stage of life—or rather, for the great and crucial part he played in the history of Spain? So meager is our knowledge of his life in those three decades that any definite answer is precluded.[1] Nevertheless, certain links between the periods may be vaguely discerned.

II

Alvaro de Luna was the illegitimate son of an Aragonese nobleman of the same name who settled in Castile, had a few estates there and served as cupbearer to Enrique II. We are told that his father, who raised him, did not like him and left him, when he died, a small pension. The orphaned child, then seven years old, went to live with Juan Martínez de Luna, an uncle who served as *alférez* (subaltern) of the co-regent Fernando de Antequera. This association seems to have lasted to the end of Alvaro's boyhood. Then he had to change his home again. He went to live with Pedro de Luna, his other uncle, who became archbishop of Toledo. Already Juan Martínez, the *alférez,* had noticed in Alvaro a flair for knighthood, and started to train him in that direction. The archbishop must have approved of that judgment, for when Alvaro was eighteen years old, he arranged for Queen Catalina, then regent, to accept him as *doncel* at her Court. Alvaro remained there for the following twelve years, and thus, one may say, his social milieu was throughout his first period nobiliar. He adopted all the manners, most of the values, and some of the views of Castile's nobility. Among other things, he retained the religious tolerance that typified the attitude of most grandees toward the Jews—and this despite the anti-Jewish bias of Queen Catalina and her circle.

Although Alvaro's education and social setting were nobiliar, he was only half noble by birth, for his mother was by all accounts a plebeian. Perhaps this explains his inclination to associate with members of the third estate, form close friendships with some of them and later appoint them to high office. This may also explain his rather skeptical view or low evaluation of nobility by birth and his keen appreciation of nobility by achievement,[2] and why so many commoners were raised in his time to the rank of nobles. His half-plebeian origin may also have influenced his positive attitude toward the conversos, who, with only few exceptions, were all commoners in the early 1420s.

Denied a mother's care and a father's love, and lacking a permanent home in his youth, Alvaro developed a sense of insecurity and a strong tendency to caution and suspicion. His dependence on the goodwill of those who gave him shelter often compelled him to use dissimulation, and often it must also have induced him to be courteous, pleasing, helpful and obedient. With these qualities he made his way in the Court, which he wanted to turn into his safe haven. Indubitably he was quick to notice the fascination he exercised on Juan, the lonesome child-prince, and came to think that it offered him an opportunity to render a service that the Queen would welcome. Alvaro fostered his friendship with the Prince to a point where the latter became addicted to his company, and within less than two years he was formally appointed as the future king's page. There was undoubtedly an anomalous element in the relationship between the lad of twenty-one and the child of four or five, which did not become much less anomalous in the course of the following decade. It must have put a tremendous strain on Alvaro which, in different circumstances, he might have shunned. His ability to take it, however, can be explained by his determination to hold on to his position as the King's companion. It was the only anchorage he had ever found that could offer him some security.

The above casts some light on Alvaro de Luna's social attitudes and habits, but none on the development of his interest in politics. Nor does it explain his attachment to conceptions that were to determine his political activities. From the records of his contemporaries we learn nothing of his stand on any of the political issues of that time. But this does not mean that he was unaware of what was going on in the political arena. The court was, in fact, the best school for studying Spain's politics in the making, and Alvaro could get there firsthand information about the tactics, stratagems, and maneuvers employed by the various forces involved. He certainly did not lack authoritative sources. One of his close friends was Inés de Torres, who for years was the favorite of Queen Catalina. This lady most likely revealed to him what she knew and thought of the political situation. Like Leonor de López, the Queen's former favorite, Inés de Torres hated and distrusted the co-regent, Fernando de Antequera. Fernando, as is known, enjoyed the reputation of a man who was the mirror of fairness, as well as of a regent whose main concern was to secure the Prince's welfare. Agreeing with this view of Fernando de Antequera, Spanish historiography, both old and new, has heaped abuse on the Queen and her two favorites for their negative opinion of Fernando. It is questionable, however, whether the abuse is justified. Catalina and her favorites could not have failed to notice that the co-regent kept depleting the Crown's assets by transferring many of them to his children. Alvaro no doubt watched Fernando's moves with the same distrust as did Ínes de Torres, and like her, he extended this negative attitude to the regent's sons, Juan and Enrique. But while he observed, judged, and drew conclusions, he kept his thoughts to himself. Fernando and his sons had their agents at Court, and they could easily remove him from his post if they found any fault in his behavior. Alvaro continued to feign indifference to everything, save his duties to the heir apparent.

His interest in politics must have grown immensely with the approach of Juan's maturity. Following Fernando's death in 1416, the Queen entrusted the government of the realm to Don Sancho de Rojas, Archbishop of Toledo, although he was known as Fernando's staunch friend. Rojas, however, retained his old attitudes, and whoever opposed Fernando's sons, and especially the Infante Juan, was to him persona non grata. He expelled Inés de Torres from the court, and would doubtless have ousted Alvaro, too, if the latter had given him ground to believe that he was hostile to the Infantes. Matters did not change in this respect at all after Catalina's death (in 1418). Sancho de Rojas retained his position and even increased his domination of the Court. But the nobles became impatient with his dictatorship; and to weaken his hold on the royal administration, they decided to enthrone the heir apparent as soon as he reached maturity.

Alvaro could see how the forces of the nobility had now split into three groups, one headed by the Infante Juan, another by his brother, the Infante Enrique, and a third, which was opposed to both. The latter group was the weakest of the three; the most dangerous was that of Enrique. This prince was not satisfied with his prime position—the mastership of the great Order of Santiago, gained for him by his father. He sought to obtain also the marquisate of Villena, the large rich tract in the heart of the country, as dowry of Catalina, King Juan II's sister, whom he desired to marry. But he was not the only grandee in Castile who aspired to additional estates. Alvaro saw the great nobles of the country gathering around the Crown to get close to the boy-king in order to satisfy their political ambitions and, above all, their craving for wealth. No other image could he form of them than of a pack of rapacious wolves, circling the young king before they attacked him and tore his patrimony to pieces. What could save the defenseless young monarch was a balance of power among the competing bands, each of which wanted the whole kingdom for itself. But how could such a balance be created? And how, if created, could it be maintained? Alvaro began to form his plans.

III

On March 7, 1419, Cortes met in Madrid for the purpose of transferring the government of Castile into the hands of the young prince. As primate of Spain and head of the administration, Don Sancho de Rojas opened the proceedings with a speech in which he was expected to indicate the tasks facing the nation and the King. Rojas, however, confined his speech to a discussion of one task only—the future distribution of royal grants—and he even thought the occasion proper to make specific recommendations. After devoting half of his address to eulogizing Fernando, the late regent, who by then had been dead for three years, he went straight to his main point: the king was under a heavy obligation to "do favors and grant benefits" to Fernando's sons in recompense for their father's achievements. Among these achievements, remarkably enough, Rojas included also the "great services" Fernando had rendered the kingdom on the seas "by sending your [i.e., the King's] uncle, the admiral Alonso Enríquez, who is present here, to do battle with the fleets of the kings of Belamarin, Tunisia and Granada." The admiral, he said, gained a signal victory in that battle, and it was hardly necessary to point out that the King should remunerate his services.[3]

Having thus concluded his remarks on the reasons that moved him to recommend the above as grantees, Rojas proceeded to propose to the King a general policy and line of conduct with respect to the concession of royal favors. "It is proper, Señor," he said, "that from now on . . . you look hard at those who have served you well and loyally, and who will [so] serve you from now on, and to those individuals you do favors . . . For liberality and magnanimity are most suitable to kings, as they gain for them the love and affection of their subjects, while cupidity makes them abhorred." Rojas finished his exhortation with a warning: "Kings who are hated are served poorly and begrudgingly."[4] He evidently thought it superfluous to spell out the anarchy that would follow such service.

This was essentially all the guidance the first minister had to give the young prince upon his assumption of power. Rojas clearly wanted his address to buy him the goodwill and support of the Infantes of Aragon and their influential uncle, the Admiral of Castile. The King was told bluntly that he should be particularly "liberal" toward the sons of Fernando of Antequera, as if the late regent had not sufficiently provided them with royal and ecclesiastical assets. But his address was designed to gain for him the support of the other grandees as well, for whom he recommended royal grants not only "according to the quality of their services," but also *according to who they were"* (namely, their rank, reputation, etc.).[5] The grandees no doubt liked this approach, and Admiral Enríquez, while addressing Cortes, urged the King to *"commit to memory* the things said to him by the Archbishop of Toledo."[6] To Alvaro, all this must have sounded like a plan for systematic spoliation of the royal estate.

Rojas seemed to have obtained what he wanted. The nobles decided to let the Royal Council remain unchanged in membership and structure, and consequently Rojas retained his position as first councillor of the king. But the Infante Enrique was dissatisfied. Rojas was a follower of his brother, Juan, who opposed Enrique's ambitions in Castile; and despite the archbishop's high-sounding statements about the King's "great duty" to reward Fernando's "sons" (in the plural), Enrique was not at all sure that Rojas would go far enough in rewarding him, Enrique. Especially did he doubt Rojas' readiness to support his claim to the marquisate of Villena, which he was most anxious to have. In fact, it all depended on Rojas, for he alone in the royal administration had the right to propose such large royal grants. Enrique now sought to wrest that right from Rojas and vest it in one of his partisans.

A surprise stroke he prepared with some of his friends enabled him to gain this objective. When the members of the Council met with the King for his formal confirmation of what they had agreed on, one of them moved that all important grants be processed by Don Gutierre de Toledo, the highly respected archdeacon of Guadalajara, who would by no means act on this matter by himself. He would first present his suggestion to a committee, composed of five leading members of the Council, the consent of whose majority would be needed for Gutierre to submit his proposal to the king.[7] The councillors proposed as members of that committee were holders of the highest offices of the nation, and the name of Rojas headed the list. There seemed to be no reason to oppose an arrangement that assured less bias, and more balanced judgment, in the choice of grantees. Consequently, the move was approved by the King before Rojas could muster arguments to defeat it.

The Council thus underwent a major change in Don Enrique's favor. Rojas was no longer the all-powerful lord from whose hand, in a sense, all the nobles had to eat. Enrique could now count on the clever Don Gutierre, a devoted follower of his, to gain for him the prize he was so eager to obtain.

It did not occur to him that a small-time *caballero,* a virtual nobody like Alvaro de Luna, could foil his entire plan.

IV

It was inevitable that the King's coronation would affect Alvaro's position at Court. So long as Juan was heir apparent and Alvaro merely his page and companion, Alvaro could stay at Court with the approval of the Queen or her successors. As a minor Juan had no power, and his requests to retain Alvaro in his post would mean little or nothing if the heads of the administration made up their minds to dismiss him. Once Juan became king, however, he was legally endowed with the highest authority, and Alvaro could now rely on that authority for a large measure of protection and support. From the standpoint of his tenure of office, therefore, his condition greatly improved. Nevertheless, Alvaro still thought it premature to expose his political intentions. He knew that the administration and the kingdom as a whole were virtually in the hands of the grandees, who could find ways to remove him from their path if they found his activities disturbing. He therefore deemed it necessary to go on pretending to be a man who shunned politics, and consequently avoided wielding influence in any political quarter. Moreover, now that he intended to put stumbling blocks in the path of the great nobles, simulation appeared to him more vital than ever. Whatever political moves he was planning, therefore, he decided to make undercover, or to make look innocent as long as he could.

In light of the developments that were soon to follow, it is not hard to reconstruct his plan. He concluded that to save the King's independence, two measures had to be urgently adopted: One would strengthen the royal finances, which were fast approaching a state of bankruptcy; the other would prevent the royal patrimony from constant diminution to the vanishing point. A thorough overhaul of the tax-collection system was obviously called for to restore the treasury, and the King must hold fast to the marquisate of Villena, which would demonstrate a new policy with respect to grants. Obviously, both lines of action could be followed only if supported by some major force. But where could such a force be found in Castile if not in the circles of government and Court? Inevitably Alvaro began his search for allies among the leaders of the administration.

It was fortunate for him that Sancho de Rojas was no longer controller of the royal grants. Offended by his deposition from that office, he withdrew from both the committee on grants and the administration as a whole. Sancho de Rojas was incapable of sharing the responsibilities of leadership with anyone else, and thus he had assumed during his service at Court a number of positions, which now fell vacant. There were no doubt nobles who offered their candidacies for some or all of Rojas' former posts, but we may assume that Alvaro influenced the King to withhold acceptance of these offers. Rojas' withdrawal offered Alvaro an opportunity which he did not intend to miss.

He set his sights on Hurtado de Mendoza, the Major Majordomo, who was married to his cousin María de Luna. The family relationship no doubt helped Alvaro to establish closer contacts with Mendoza, acquaint him with his views on a variety of issues, and see whether he could be a party to his schemes. Finally, he decided to unfold before Mendoza his entire plan for economic recovery as the only means of rescuing the Crown from rapid decline to insignificance. Alvaro no doubt assured Mendoza that if, as Major-domo, he subscribed to his plan, he, Alvaro, would do his utmost to have the King appoint him to Rojas' former posts.

To step into the shoes of the powerful Rojas and assume the position of head of the administration was a bait very hard for Mendoza to resist. He had served for many years as Major Majordomo without making further progress at Court, but he must have dreamed, like his peers, of greater grandeur and much higher achievement. Now Alvaro opened to him a door of opportunity which he could not ignore. But lacking the mettle of true leadership, he did not dare pass through it either. At that point, it seems, he needed the assurance of a man on whose wisdom and strength he could rely; and it was probably then that he put Alvaro in touch with Fernán Alfonso de Robles.

Robles, a plebeian career official, who rose from the post of a common *escribano* to the highest financial office of the realm (he became the kingdom's *Contador Mayor*),[8] was endowed not only with professional skills, but also with a sharp intelligence and a daring that reflected his strong personality. His critics considered him a "bellicose man" who would offer "dangerous counsels,"[9] but there can be no doubt that he was highly influential, and also hard to oppose. As former secretary of Leonor López, Queen Catalina's first favorite and guide, he no doubt shared his mistress' dislike of the late co-regent Fernando de Antequera, and we also know that he had strenuously opposed the transfer of the marquisate of Villena to Enrique. Thus, he was partly attuned by background to Alvaro's point of view. But he must also have grasped and appreciated the importance of Alvaro's novel and far-reaching plans. Before long the two developed such strong links of amity, confidence, and common purpose that Alvaro came to depend in large measure on Robles' counsel and consent. No doubt Robles helped convince Mendoza that Alvaro's ideas were sound and workable, and the Major Major-domo soon began to act along the lines of Alvaro's proposals.

Backed by the King, who was guided by Alvaro, Mendoza became the chief power in the administration, and with Mendoza's support, Alvaro and

Robles proceeded to put their plan into practice. They agreed that their first task was radically to change the system of tax collection established in 1412 that forbade the gathering of royal revenues by Jews. Alvaro and Robles were well aware that the system suffered from both corruption and inefficiency and could not be remedied by its own resources. Many of the officials, appointed by the nobles and enjoying their unreserved support, did not care much about the size of their collections or about the honesty of their agents. The income kept dwindling through sluggish gathering, and was further diminished by theft and waste. Inevitably, Alvaro and Robles concluded that the only way to increase the royal revenues was to bring the Jews back into the system and restore tax farming in all the king's domains.

Hurtado de Mendoza agreed with this assessment and sanctioned the implementation of the plan. Moreover, he proposed to entrust the revenue collections to the man he considered best fitted for the task. This was Don Abraham Bienveniste, the Jewish tax farmer and financial expert who managed Mendoza's own estate.[10] Mendoza, it appears, had to share his financier with the central royal treasury, or transfer him completely to the King's service, if he wanted the plan he adopted for the Crown to get under way and succeed. In doing so, however, he followed an old path. For this was usually how Jews became courtiers or other high officials of the King. Thus Don Joseph de Écija became financial minister of Alfonso XI at the recommendation of the Infante Felipe, whom Don Joseph was serving at the time, and Don Samuel ha-Levi became treasurer of Pedro I at the advice and urging of Juan Alfonso Albuquerque, whose finances were then managed by Don Samuel. And, as in the case of these Jewish courtiers, Bienveniste's aid and counsel were soon extended from the field of tax collection to other areas touching the governance of the realm.

Judging by the sources at our disposal, all this happened within the first year after the King's accession, and we do not know the extent to which the new proposals worked out by Robles and Bienveniste were actually implemented at the time. In any case, Castile's restless grandees soon threatened to obstruct their work. What disturbed them now especially was Mendoza's rising influence, just as in the past they had been upset by the growing authority of Rojas. They therefore sought to reduce Mendoza's power before he became entrenched in his position and replace him with a government whose very structure might prevent a similar menace. It was difficult of course to achieve both ends, but finally they agreed on a plan: the administration would be ruled by three quintets of nobles, each to reside in the Court for four months. None of the Infantes was included in the quintets, although their supporters were present in them all. It was a balanced arrangement, or at least it so appeared, but for that very reason it was spurned and opposed by the most ambitious nobles.

The main opposition no doubt stemmed from the Infantes. It was not hard for them to see that their exclusion from the Court would only serve to reduce their influence and thereby block their ambitions. Each of them, therefore, urged his followers to claim that the "common good" of the kingdom called for their leader to be "near the King" as long as possible. But the non-aligned nobles objected. They feared, as the *Crónica de Juan II* tells us, that "if any of the Infantes be close to the monarch, he would [ultimately] govern [the kingdom] with his followers" (namely, take over the administration), and the "other grandees would be badly served."[11] Once again the nobility split into three groups: the followers of Juan, the devotees of Enrique, and those who remained independent of both. Seeking to get the King's approval of their views, each of these groups now tried to enlist Alvaro de Luna's aid. They knew, the same *crónica* explains, that "more than any other person he could sway the King's will" and influence his thinking.[12]

From all this we can see what kind of figure Alvaro now cut in the nobles' eyes. The former entertainer of the heir apparent was now regarded as the monarch's trusted friend, who could influence or even determine his stand on administrative and political issues. To be sure, Alvaro's persistent simulation of a person who had no real interest in politics continued to form their basic judgment. In fact, it misled them. They considered him indifferent to their disputes and quarrels, and consequently neutral toward all their parties. That is why all three groups of nobles felt free to seek his intervention with the King. They knew, of course, that he had helped Mendoza obtain the King's approval of his proposals, but this assistance they saw merely as a favor done by one relative to another. Consequently, they did not consider Alvaro the initiator of Mendoza's actions. Only later did they realize that although "it *appeared* that all the affairs of the kingdom were managed by Juan Hurtado, *in reality they were governed only by the will of Alvaro de Luna.*"[13]

Feigning neutrality and political indifference, Alvaro found it easy to head off the appeals that the various groups of grandees addressed to him, and also refuse Enrique's requests that he help him obtain the marquisate of Villena. Evidently, Enrique too was convinced that Alvaro agreed to help Hurtado de Mendoza only because of their family relationship, and as we shall see, this belief was crucial to Alvaro's future activity. To understand this, however, we must go back a few steps and see what happened in Enrique's case.

We have noted that Don Gutierre de Toledo, archdeacon of Guadalajara and partisan of Enrique, was entrusted with the task of proposing royal grants, and there can be no doubt that Gutierre was not slow in submitting his proposal concerning the marquisate of Villena to the Grants Committee appointed by the Royal Council. The chances of approval seemed to be good, since the committee, following Rojas' resignation, consisted of only four members, two of whom were Enrique's men. But Mendoza, who was one of the remaining two, managed to prevent a majority decision. It stands to reason that he influenced the admiral, the committee's non-aligned member, to refrain from voting until he heard the opinion of the foremost expert on the royal patrimony—namely, the *Contador Mayor*. This, we assume, is how Alfonso de Robles came into the picture.

It was probably under Robles' influence that the admiral voted against the proposal and, as a result, the committee was deadlocked. In vain did the Infante urge Robles to change his mind, and just as useless was his attempt to gain the support of Mendoza. It was then that he must have turned to Alvaro, asking him to move the King to intervene. Alvaro, needless to say, declined. And he could readily excuse himself by pointing out that Enrique's case had become highly controversial and that he, Alvaro, had always refrained from siding with any of the nobles against the others; he could not depart from this principle.

Enrique concluded that his cherished dream of getting the marquisate of Villena was doomed as long as the government of Mendoza was in power. He refused, however, to give it up; and driven as he was by his passion for power, he finally decided on a course of action that had no precedent in the annals of Castile.

V

The coup d'état was fixed for July 12, 1420, when Enrique's brother, the Infante Juan, was scheduled to be out of the country, celebrating in Pamplona his marriage to Doña Blanca, heiress to the crown of Navarre. And thus in the predawn hours of that day Enrique's troops surrounded Tordesillas, where the King and the heads of the administration were staying, occupied the palace, and arrested the Majordomo and his nephew, who was the king's bodyguard. Then Enrique and his chief associates proceeded to the royal chamber, awakened the King from his morning slumber, and informed him of the arrests they had just made and of the "reasons" for their action. They came, they said, to free the King from his "subjection" to men who caused him "great harms and disservices" by perpetrating "many ugly and indecent things in his house and his kingdoms."[14] Alvaro was also present when they said this, for he had slept that night in the King's room, and both he and the King were reluctant to accept the Infante's explanations. They evidently put hard questions to him, because two of his companions had to come to his aid and got involved in the discussion. *"Each of them gave as many reasons as he could to prove that what they did was done for the King's service and the general good of his kingdoms."* The culmination of their arguments in support of their move was their claim that Mendoza was "acting under the guidance of a Jew called Abraham Bienveniste."[15]

This argument could not have been invented on the spur of the moment, and like all other moves related to the coup, it was decided upon in advance. The conspirators felt the need to justify their action by some readily acceptable excuse, and looking for such an excuse, they hit upon Mendoza's relationship with "his Jew." That they disliked this relationship, and strongly opposed it, may be taken for granted. It symbolized the new fiscal policies of the administration, which were calculated to strengthen the power of the king and thereby weaken the nobility's grip on the monarchy and the country as a whole. But *this* reason they would not reveal, of course. Instead, they chose to strike at Mendoza by exploiting the widespread anti-Jewish sentiment and demonstrating their adherence to the laws of 1412, which prohibited the appointment of Jews to high office. They pretended to have been shocked and alarmed by Mendoza's blatant violation of those laws, and to strengthen this pretense they drew to their side the bishop of Segovia, Don Juan de Tordesillas.

Their choice of this bishop as participant in the coup, and also as performer of the tasks they assigned him, had of course its special reasons. Don Juan de Tordesillas was known throughout Castile as one of the fiercest Jew haters of the day. He was the man who, a decade before, had sentenced eight Jews to death for "desecrating a Host" and who, by means of torture, forced Don Meir Alguades, Enrique III's Jewish physician, to "confess" that he had poisoned the King. To such a man, the fact that a Jew like Don Abraham occupied a position of great influence in the Court was more than a mere excuse for the coup. To him it might be a compelling reason to seek the overthrow of the government. Naturally, he could be counted upon as propagator of his views across the kingdom. But, above all, he was needed for another purpose, which was both urgent and vital. Enrique and his aides had reason to assume that the prelate of Segovia could mollify the King if he showed stubborn resistance. Thus, he could tell him that it was he, the bishop, who revealed to the world that a Jew had killed his father, and therefore his warnings should not be slighted when they touched that other Jew, Bienveniste. Alvaro, needless to say, slighted them; he knew precisely *why* the coup was engineered and what Bienveniste's real functions were. Nevertheless, he nodded consent, and the King no doubt followed his example.

The Infante, we have good grounds to believe, was satisfied with Alvaro's performance. Hence, before leaving the King, he assured him that he meant no harm whatever to Alvaro, that he wanted the latter to stay with the King and continue to offer him his good advice, and that he even considered Alvaro fit to become a member of the Royal Council.[16] Thereupon, he proceeded to take a few measures necessary to secure his hold on the government. He dismissed Mendoza's officials in the court, including Robles, who left for Valladolid, and replaced them with men of his own. He put a heavy guard on both the King and his companion, allegedly to protect them against abduction. Then he moved the Court to Avila, where he intended to convene Cortes.

VI

In his history of Juan II's reign, Suárez Fernández noted that Enrique committed a "very grave error" in allowing Alvaro de Luna to stay at the King's side after the coup.[17] Though subsequent events justify this assessment, the cause of that error still needs to be explained. As we see it, Enrique's mistake did not stem from his underassessment of Alvaro's ingenuity (and hence of his capacity to liberate the King); it stemmed, in our judgment, from his gross misconception of Alvaro's personal motives and intents. Enrique still labored under the wrong impression implanted in his mind by Alvaro's simulation, and thus continued to believe that he was devoid of any political interest or conviction. Under trying circumstances such a man, he thought, could easily turn into a political opportunist who would readily serve anyone in power. Alvaro, Enrique reasoned, was now in such circumstances; he was firmly held in the clutches of his captor; and the councillor's post that Enrique then offered him clearly shows what he thought of Alvaro, his political incentives and his moral fiber. Enrique kept Alvaro at the King's side because he believed he could turn him into a pliable instrument that would facilitate his control of the King.

Alvaro read Enrique's mind. Realizing that his dissimulation had saved him from the fate of Mendoza and Robles, he concluded that further simulation now constituted his only salvation. He therefore did his utmost to foster and deepen Enrique's misconception of his person. He advised the King to fulfill without demur all of Enrique's requests and demands, so as to lead the Infante to believe that the King acquiesced in a puppet's role; and the King, relying on Alvaro's judgment, agreed to play his part to the full. Thus, in response to Enrique's appeals, he proclaimed his consent to Enrique's actions; he helped persuade his sister Catalina, who, fearing Enrique, had fled to Tordesillas, to accompany him and the Infante to Avila; and while in Avila, he agreed to call Cortes in order to get what Enrique desired—i.e., the nation's approval of the coup.

Cortes met in Avila in September of that year. Almost all the nobles and prelates who attended were known as Enrique's supporters; the others were conspicuously absent; but all the cities, save Burgos, were represented, and this was the most that Enrique could expect. Opening the proceedings with a single sentence, the King told the assembly that he had summoned them for reasons to be explained on his behalf by the archdeacon of Guadalajara.

Thereupon, the latter went up to the pulpit to recount the events that led to the coup.

Gutierre de Toledo, learned and respected, was destined for higher positions in the Church than that of the archdeaconry he occupied at the time. He was to become successively bishop of Palencia, archbishop of Seville, and finally archbishop of Toledo. But the picture drawn of him by Pérez de Guzmán is not altogether favorable. In his talk and manners, Guzmán said, he "resembled caballeros more than prelates" (i.e., laymen more than men of God); he was "neither magnanimous nor generous," and he was too "harsh and rigorous" in his judgments, though his zeal and intentions, Guzmán believed, were basically well directed.[18] In pronouncing this belief, however, Guzmán may well have been too generous. Gutierre's speech at Cortes certainly suggests this.

Gutierre claimed that the agreement reached shortly after the King's coronation concerning the governance of the kingdom had been violated by those who took over the administration; yet this was not the worst thing that had happened. The worst thing was that Hurtado de Mendoza, who had gained the King's trust and become his favorite, "behaved and governed in accordance with the counsels he received from [the Jew] Don Abraham Bienveniste." Furthermore, he stressed, he consulted this Jew not on financial matters alone but on *"all the affairs of the Kingdom,"* and thus, following the latter's advice, "many things were done which were wrongful and outrageous and contrary to the service of God and the King."[19] He concluded by saying that the Infante and his associates, seeing the kingdom driven to "perdition," felt they had to make the "move of Tordesillas" in order to "repair the damages done and prevent those expected" in the future. This is why the King had approved their deed, and also ordered all the grandees and members of his Council, as well as the procurators of the towns and cities, to express approval of that action.[20]

It need scarcely be said that Gutierre's account of the reasons for the coup and the King's position was full of half truths, distortions and inventions. Gutierre, as Enrique's close friend, could not possibly have been unaware of this. Yet in expounding the antisemitic argument, he may have expressed his own thinking. In any case, he employed this argument as a means of influencing public opinion. By this we do not mean that Gutierre used it to gain the support of the nobles and prelates. They, who knew well why the coup was undertaken, would anyhow sanction it for partisan considerations. But he did intend to win the favor of the cities, whose approval of the coup was a prerequisite for advancing Enrique's designs. To the cities, of course, any action that prevented the growth of Jewish influence at Court was likely to appear praiseworthy. Obviously, Don Gutierre wanted to impress them that insofar as the Jewish question was concerned, Enrique had been true to the laws of 1412 and the traditional position of the Church. Not in vain did Enrique choose Gutierre, a churchman, to present his case in Cortes.

Enrique's tactics paid off. Not only the prelates and nobles who attended, but also the *procuradores* of the cities solemnly declared their approval of his action on behalf of King and country. And his victory at Cortes was followed by another triumph, which was the main goal of his maneuvers. He decided to move southward toward Andalusia, where his main military strength lay, and on the way there he persuaded Doña Catalina to give him her hand in marriage. The King immediately granted her as dowry the marquisate of Villena, which he now declared a duchy, while conferring on Enrique the title of duke. Thus, only four months after the coup, Enrique had gained more than he had bargained for in his negotiations with the previous administration. Above all, he had won the greatest prize of all: full control of the King.

The King, he noted, gave him no trouble, and he rightly credited his behavior to Alvaro. Thus, he concluded that his evaluation of Alvaro, and the hopes he placed in him, had been confirmed by experience. His confidence in Alvaro grew from day to day, and Enrique decided to show it. Whereas immediately after the coup, the King and Alvaro were accompanied by a guard of 200 armed men, later that guard was reduced to 150, then to 100, then to 50 men, and finally abolished altogether. The King could now hunt twice a day with whomever he chose as his companion. He virtually regained his freedom of movement, though still in restricted areas and for limited times.[21] Alvaro could now contemplate escape—that is, the realization of the single idea that had possessed his mind since their imprisonment. And thus, pretending to go hunting, the King and Alvaro left Enrique's camp in the predawn hours of November 29 on what they hoped would be their road to freedom.

VII

Judging by all extant accounts of this flight, it was not properly prepared. Consequently, the chances of success were poor and left largely to luck. Only a few of the King's most devoted aides were let in on the secret. One of them was Diego López de Ayala, lord of the neighboring castle of Villalva, four leagues from Talavera, where Enrique was stationed with his troops. At this castle they planned to make their stand against any attempt to recapture them; but when they reached the castle, they found it indefensible, which compelled them to move on to Montalbán, another castle four leagues away, on the other side of the Tagus. It was only at Villalva that they heard of this place as the nearest fortress that might suit their purpose, and their going there was a shot in the dark, as they relied on the advice of only one man who was supposed to know the region.[22] Caught off guard, the defenders of the fortress, which belonged to the Queen of Aragon, surrendered, and the place was occupied by the fugitives. The fortress appeared to be in good shape, and this was the first piece of luck to come their way since their escape from Talavera.

They realized of course that they would soon be followed, and prepared themselves for a siege. But how could they withstand Enrique's army with their own small force? Before leaving Talavera, they received assurance of support from only one source: Don Fadrique, Count of Trastámara. The latter and the Count of Benavente, Don Rodrigo Alfonso Pimentel, were dissatisfied with Enrique because his chief aides, the Constable and the Adelantado of Castile, had excluded them from his circle of advisers and consquently wished to align themselves with the King. Alvaro had many talks with them; and once he became convinced of their intentions, he revealed to them his plan of escape. Don Fadrique provided fifty armed men, who were awaiting them hidden in a forest near Villalva. This was the only military force on which they could count.

The fortress of Montalbán lacked supplies, however, and the first thing they did was to issue a call to the neighboring *hermandades,* the special police forces of the cities, to offer the King provisions and defenders.[23] They also informed the Infante Don Juan and the Archbishop of Toledo of their whereabouts and condition, and asked for their immediate aid. Upon leaving Villalva, the King also dispatched a notice to Enrique that he was going to Montalbán, and ordered the Infante to stay in Talavera and there await his instructions. This was the first move of defiance and independence that the King made toward his captors.[24]

Five hundred of Enrique's troops, led by the constable and the adelantado, soon encircled the castle of Montalbán and prevented supplies from reaching it. Nevertheless, some twenty men, who had responded to the King's call for aid, managed to join the defenders. The King ordered the besiegers to retreat, but they answered that they came to "save" him from his "captors." We shall hear this cynical argument repeated a thousand times during Alvaro's career, and its recurrence shows that the gross lie involved never served as an obstacle to its propagation.

Enrique, too, planned to go to Montalbán; but before doing so he asked the bishop of Segovia to demonstrate once again the persuasive skills which, he thought, he had displayed during the coup. The present task of Don Juan de Tordesillas was to convince the King that, for his own good, he should return immediately to Enrique's camp. The bishop, however, could hardly tell the King that he had been taken to Montalbán "forcibly" by his "captors." He therefore built his argument on a truthful basis: the King came to Montalbán of his own free will, except that his decision to do so was wrong; it was based on an error of judgment.

No approach could be more deceitful than the one now used by the prelate of Segovia; but the lies involved were too transparent. When the bishop entered the fortress, he could see that its defenders were reduced to living on the corpses of their horses. Yet he had the audacity to tell Juan II that everything Enrique and his men did in Montalbán was done strictly "in the King's service" and without the slightest "intent to annoy him." All they asked of the King was that he change his location, one could gather from the bishop's argument; for if the King would agree to settle in Toledo or in any other place of his choice, he could keep with him anyone he wished, and no one would contradict his will. Why then stay in Montalbán and cause infamy to himself and the grandees of the kingdom (namely, Enrique and his associates)? It was all, after all, a matter of honor.

To this tissue of lies and false arguments the King gave a straightforward answer. He would not leave the castle while Enrique's troops encircled it. Nor did he desire to return to these people. His stay among them had pained him greatly and they had gravely offended him. Let the bishop tell them that it would comply with his service if they abandoned the siege without a moment's delay. Once they were gone, he would leave Montalbán and go to a town or city "of his choice."[25]

The argument and the response throw clear light on the nature of the quarrel that was to disturb the tranquility of Castile in the following three decades. And equally enlightening is Enrique's reaction to the bishop's account of his talk with the King. "He [Enrique] would not," he said, "depart from that place [i.e., Montalbán] for anything in the world until the King had left the castle. For he did not believe that *it was the King's own will that dictated his answer, but the will of those who carried him there.*"[26] And the same reply he gave to Pero Carrillo de Huete, the King's Major Falconer, who formally presented him with the King's demands and later wrote the story of his reign.

On the fourth day of the siege a new stratagem was tried. Enrique's three leading associates asked Alvaro to meet them outside the castle. Alvaro agreed, and came to the meeting accompanied by two men. Enrique's delegates threw at him the charge: it was he who had brought the King to "that castle," thus doing great damage to the Infante and his followers; and they expressed their astonishment that he had so acted, as he had never received from them anything but favors. Alvaro answered that the King came to Montalbán because he could not tolerate his condition any longer. He assured them that all the King sought was his freedom; that he did not want to hurt the Infante or his associates; and once they left the place, he would go to some city where he could deal with the "pacification of these kingdoms." Until matters are duly settled, he promised them, the King would not permit the infante Don Juan or any of his partisans to stay in the Court. Ultimately, the King would invite them all, and then, being free, would issue an order that would be for the good of his kingdoms.[27]

Enrique and his party, then, were now certain that it was Alvaro who had engineered the King's escape and that he was after something quite different from the favors he could expect from Enrique for his services. Enrique, nevertheless, would not give up. He now tried to influence the King through the procurators who had remained in Talavera. When they came to Montalbán, they were allowed entry into the castle and soon met the King. Now they heard from the King's own lips all the grave evils done to him by Enrique and his men since the coup at Tordesillas, and the plain fact that they had put him in a servitude from which he was compelled to escape. Once again he asked them to communicate his order that the besiegers leave the place at once.

When the procurators returned with the King's answer, Enrique realized that he had committed a grave error. The procurators had been exposed to the truth, and they now understood what he had done since the attack in Tordesillas. They might be opposed to Juan Hurtado's policies, but they would never agree to keep their King in bondage. Enrique was forced to back down. The *Crónica de Juan II* summarizes the three reasons that compelled him to lift the siege of Montalbán: "Since the will of the King had become known, and a great part of the Kingdom was responding to his call, and the Infante Don Juan was approaching with a great force, including many grandees who were in the King's service, it would not suit [Enrique's men] to stay there any further, but rather act in accordance with the King's order."[28]

On the tenth of December, which was the eighth day of the King's stay in the castle, Enrique allowed passage of all victuals into the fortress, and on that day he also asked the King's permission to visit him prior to his departure in order to "do him reverence and kiss his hands." The request was denied, as "the King did not wish to see him at the time." The Infante was ordered to go to Ocaña and there await further instructions.[29]

VIII

Thus ended the King's captivity and the hazardous venture of his liberation. Within eight days a veritable revolution took place in his entire condition. His rebuff of Enrique's request to see him, coupled with the order he gave him, signified not only his restored freedom, but also his return to a state of kingship that Castile had not known since Enrique III. A barrier was placed between the sovereign and the barons which emphasized the King's elevated status and which the magnates, especially those suspected of disloyalty, found it thenceforward often hard to pass. Even such a leading noble as the Infante Don Juan was soon to experience this difficulty. A few days later, near Talavera, where he came to "do his reverence" to the King—and of course to congratulate him on his liberation—he was dismissed, after a brief meeting with the King, with all the others who came there for that purpose; and like the others, he too was ordered to return to his place and there await the King's instructions. Then, when Don Juan asked Alvaro for permission to stay several more days at Court, so as to enable him to discuss with the King certain matters that concerned both him and other grandees, his request was forthwith denied. "And the Infante Don Juan," the King's *crónica* tells us, "having seen the will of Alvaro de Luna, understood that it would not suit him to insist on staying there" as he had intended; and he left for his camp in Fuensalida.[30]

In this remark the *crónica* unwittingly touched upon a change of historical importance. For at that moment a major new factor appeared on the scene of Castile's politics: "the will of Alvaro de Luna." The mask had fallen from Alvaro's face and everyone could see the real man: a statesman of stature with a firm grasp on the helm of Castile's ship of state. That ship, which, as Mariana saw it, had been floundering without a captain in a stormy sea, was navigated hereafter with great courage and astuteness by its new master, Alvaro. It took only a few weeks for his abilities to be recognized and his authority to be established throughout the country.

IX

We have dealt in detail with some basic data touching the first period of Alvaro's life, including his earliest approaches to politics, because they reflect some of his characteristics and motives, whose recognition, we believe, is necessary to understand both his methods and policies. It need scarcely be said that our judgment of Alvaro should not be founded solely on these data. To form a fuller view of his character, of his personal incentives and political aspirations, we must of course consider his entire conduct throughout his long public career. But beginnings have an importance of their own. They often play a decisive part in determining the direction of our drives; and Alvaro's beginnings still require, as we see it, considerable elucidation. Despite all that has been written about him, Alvaro remains a historical enigma.

A careful analysis of what is known about his life just before his assumption of power may help us, we believe, to decipher his code. Two important aspects in particular throw light on most of his activities. It is hard to say that they have not been sensed; yet they have not received the emphasis they deserve.

The first of these aspects, and by far the more decisive, was Alvaro's dedication to a special cause which he judged to be both social and political. That *cause* was the supremacy of kingship as the determining factor in all human affairs within the sphere of the King's authority. What we mean by that cause is not merely a policy based on a principle of royal government. Such a policy might render *service* to the cause; but the cause must be viewed as separate from the policy, just as a target is separate from the arrow that flies at it. Hence, while the policy may occasionally fluctuate under the pressures of changing needs and circumstances, the cause remains a fixed, unaltered ideal which is not subject to change. It is this kind of cause that Alvaro served; and in this respect he was an idealist. He was probably the only idealistic statesman that Spain produced in those Machiavellian times.

We cannot even guess how it came about that Alvaro dedicated himself to that cause (so little do we know of his thinking!). He may have been moved by his reflections on Castile's political situation; or by some mystical adoration of kingship which may sometime in his youth have been planted in his mind; or by a chivalric instinct which drove him to defend the threatened and defenseless young prince. Whatever the root of that dedication, its presence cannot be questioned. And it was only because he was possessed by that ideal that he was ready to risk his life to free the King and end his humiliation. It is senseless to see that desperate attempt, made against all apparent odds, as a reckless gamble for gain and honors which would be characteristic of some daring adventurer. If gain and honors had been Alvaro's goal, he could have secured them more safely by serving Enrique rather than the powerless King. Nor would he have undertaken the burden of simulation, and lived a feigned life for such a long time, had he not been lured and inspired by the vision of raising Castile's kingship from its degraded condition to a state of supreme power and grandeur.

In our forthcoming discussion we shall have to draw a line between Alvaro's idealistic view of royalty and his rather realistic, conservative attitude toward other social and governmental problems. But his view of kingship, we may say with certainty, colored the whole of his political career. It was that view, more than anything else, that made him a guardian of the King's rights and involved him in bitter conflicts with the nobles; and it was his elevated concept of kingship, to which he remained faithful throughout his life, that led him to move Cortes to recognize royal rule as absolute, boundless and decisive—and this in a nation that was the first in Europe to fight for the restriction of royal powers and the increase of popular rights and liberties.

Related to Alvaro's attitude toward kingship was another characteristic, which can likewise be discerned in his earlier period. This was his readiness to take any measure, however opposed by the majority of the people, and follow any policy, however unpopular, if he considered such a measure or policy *necessary* for the advancement of the royal cause. We see this tendency manifest in his plan to reengage Jews in the royal treasury, and especially in the gathering of the king's taxes, which was certain to rouse widespread opposition. It was of course not hard for Alvaro to envision—and, in any case, he could learn from experience—that his positive attitude toward the Jews would result in strong antagonism to his administration, as well as bitter hostility to himself; and yet he stubbornly persisted in that course, riding roughshod over all obstacles, because he believed that the Jews were essential to restoring the King's financial power. Thus he reversed almost singlehand-edly Castile's policy on the Jewish question, and gave Spanish Jewry, which was almost in its death throes, a new lease on life for three generations, until the last years of the century.[31]

Here again, the policy he pursued toward the Jews during his clandestine political activity helps explain the policy he embraced toward the conversos upon his formal assumption of office. Both policies—toward the Jews and the conversos—were interrelated; in both he encountered many of the same problems, and in both he displayed the same obstinacy and determination in adhering to them against all odds. It would be correct to say that in following both policies Alvaro was going against strong historic currents, and in both he displayed a blatant disregard for the force of public opinion. Here, we may observe, lay his main strength, as well as his main weakness. The story of his moves in the political arena, of his triumphs and defeats, his achievements and his failures, including his ultimate fate, evolved from these two diverse tendencies, which together directed and determined his activities often at one and the same time.

X

The speed with which Alvaro de Luna took over the reins of government after the King's liberation offers a striking demonstration of his innate capaci-ties for both governance and leadership. Had he not been endowed with these abilities, he, who had never before been involved in any diplomatic wrangling with the grandees, would not have succeeded in overcoming so quickly all attempts at interference by these crafty diplomats, including the shrewdest of them all, the Infante Don Juan. Nor would he, who had never held office, have managed to build in such a short time a Royal Council in which the neutralized nobles could not disturb him in the execution of his plans. But these talents alone, it must be added, would not have produced lasting results had they not been supported by his view of the particular government he wanted to create.

Quintana and Rizzo, Alvaro's biographers, said that his main political innovation consisted in his creation of the "party of the King" amidst the various parties that split Spain's society.³² But one must question the validity of this assertion. It is difficult to see in the shifting alliances that marked Alvaro's political career a truly pro-royal entity. Both nobles and cities kept changing their positions according to their own, not the king's interests, and a pro-royal constancy can be discerned only among isolated elements of the higher estates. Perhaps these elements formed the nucleus of the movement that later supported Enrique IV and finally became a partisan force in the days of the Catholic kings. Yet if the creation of a royalist party cannot, in our judgment, be ascribed to Alvaro, we can without doubt attribute to him the creation of a royalist bureaucracy; and here, as we see it, lay his contribution to Castile's practical politics.

Alvaro's decision to create such a bureaucracy grew out of his long observation of the manner in which the royal administration operated in Castile. He came to the conclusion that not only its upper crust—i.e., the bodies which formed its policies—but also its various executive branches were marked by a dual if not multiple allegiance, and hence by a basic faithlessness to the King. He saw how the great nobles of Castile, who occupied the chief positions in the government, discharged their official duties and responsibilities, how much time they devoted to their own promotion and how little to the tasks they were entrusted to fulfill. Even worse, he saw how their self-indulgence, their partisan interests, and their lack of deep concern for the Crown's authority and the nation's needs seeped down from their elevated ranks and positions to the lowest levels of the royal administration; and thus he perceived how the lower officials, if they were loyal to anyone at all, were not loyal to the King, whom they swore to serve, but to the grandee or prelate who had put them in office and could also dismiss them whenever he wished. What kingdom could prosper or even endure, Alvaro de Luna must have asked himself, with such a malfunctioning administration?

This evaluation of most of the officials who served in the various departments of government was no doubt crystallized in Alvaro's thinking to the point of becoming an unshakable conviction after the coup of the Infante Enrique. Enrique, as we have indicated, discharged all the officials who had worked in Mendoza's administration, and Alvaro knew that he would have to remove all the officials appointed by Enrique, if only because he had reason to suspect that they would function as Enrique's agents. In fact, Alvaro then concluded that the King's administration could not truly rely on any of the nobles, their aides and servants. There was too much treachery and connivance in their ranks to consider them and their assistants trustworthy. But aware of the ambitions of the urban oligarchies, he could not rely on them either. Whence, then, could he take the manpower needed to build a trustworthy administration? This is where the conversos came in.

Heirs to a tradition of faithfulness to the Kings which characterized the

Jews in Spain and elsewhere, the conversos offered the royal bureaucracy candidates of unquestionable loyalty to the King and great eagerness to serve in his administration. But they also had other invaluable qualities which their Jewish forebears lacked. Well adjusted to the Christian way of life, they could approach all Christians freely and naturally; and trained in Christian schools, especially in law, they were professionally equipped to fill a great variety of administrative posts. Above all, as Christians, they could not be denied the right to assume authority over Christians. And thus they had all the assets of the Jews without any of their liabilities. With these able and spirited men, Alvaro proceeded to build a bureaucracy that was to serve as an effective instrument of government and a bulwark against all subversive attempts to subjugate the Crown to the estates.

Before long, the nobles could see what he had done and tried to find faults in his creation. They hated the new bureaucracy he had established and the obedience and faithfulness it constantly showed him. They resented this body of learned commoners and professional public servants who performed their duties efficiently and objectively, without showing much concern for the claims of the nobility to preferential treatment. They saw in these officials usurpers of their rights, almost as much as they did in Alvaro; and they naturally were anxious to find flaws in their performance where others ordinarily would see merit. Thus, certain steps these officials would take, in accordance with the laws and in keeping with their tasks, were often presented by the nobles as breaches of both the laws and the officials' duties. Above all, the claim often made by these officials that they were, in the main, servants of the king was presented as merely a substitute for the reality of their being Alvaro's agents.

We see this resentment and criticism of these officials expressed in a letter criticizing Alvaro which Alfonso V, King of Aragon and brother of the Infantes Juan and Enrique, sent to Pedro Núñez de Herrera, lord of Pedraza, in 1425. Among the accusations he leveled at Alvaro, the one which dealt with the royal officialdom formed his major and central charge. According to Alfonso, Alvaro put near the King men of "low standing and condition" who, while appearing as the servants of the King, actually followed Alvaro's instructions. What is worse: this behavior resulted not only from the lack of moral backbone common to such men, but also—and mainly—because Alvaro's officials "favored him and his tyranny."[33] The meaning of this statement cannot be questioned. It meant that the officials appointed by Alvaro were not only his most obedient servants, but also his "partisans," who genuinely supported his policies, his methods, and his leadership.

Fifteen years later, in 1440, the nobles uttered the same complaints and hurled the same virulent accusations at Alvaro and his officialdom; but to fortify their censures they added a few charges which are necessary for us to consider. Thus, in a letter they sent the King that year, the nobles repeated their claim that the officials appointed by Alvaro for the royal administration were all chosen from among his partisans and that these men would abide by his instructions and consider nothing else. Moreover, they stressed that all these appointments were made without the King's slightest knowledge, implying thereby that, had the King been informed, or rather involved in the process of selection, he would have chosen as officials men faithful to *him* rather than to Alvaro de Luna. But the criticism indubitably fell short of the mark. Obviously, the king could not see a contradiction between devotion to Alvaro and devotion to himself, and he would have considered it foolish for Alvaro to choose for any position of authority neutral men, or men who might oppose him, object to his instructions or system of government. Certainly, he should have made it clear in advance that the candidates for office supported his policy—namely, the absolute royalist policy which the king himself would defend to the hilt; and as for the rest—i.e., all that related to the examination, selection and appointment of officials—the King was no doubt grateful to his minister for freeing him from these onerous tasks, to which he, the monarch, had never been attracted; he may also have judged most of these tasks to be beneath his royal dignity.

We should, however, note also another point made by the nobles in that document. Trying to separate Alvaro from the King by undermining the King's faith in his officials, the nobles presented them as conniving *against* the King, and slyly inducing him to approve measures which ordinarily, if he knew all the facts, he would never have sanctioned. Thus, they told the King that the high officials, before they meet with the King in Council, "go to Alvaro's place [of lodging] and get a feeling of what he wants," so as to know what positions to take on the issues to be discussed. "Thus behave," the nobles stress, "all or most members of your Council; and those who do *not* act in this manner are subjected by him [i.e., Alvaro de Luna], with the support of your lordship, to all the evil he can inflict upon them."[34]

Alvaro's conduct was thus presented to the King as a criminal conspiracy engineered behind his back, which the nobles, in their letter, now revealed to his Majesty for the first time. But if we examine the contents of this charge, we can see that it, too, held no water. What it pointed out was the ordinary relationship that exists in most governments between the chief minister and the highest officials of the various departments. Such officials are commonly briefed on the policies supported by the head of the administration, and are often subjected to loss of favor, or reduction of influence, or dismissal from office, when their views differ from those of the chief minister on all or some of the major issues. The facts which were denounced by the nobles, therefore, were common to all monarchies governed with efficiency—especially where the King showed no real desire to go into the problems facing the government and the chief minister was actually responsible for the conduct of the affairs of state.

One is tempted to remark that this is how state affairs are often managed in democratic governments, where cohesion between the prime minister and members of the cabinet is considered an asset rather than a liability. In the centralist government maintained by Alvaro no other form of management was possible. But it is precisely here that the interest of the grandees clashed with Alvaro's administrative system. Concerted action, directed from above, was something that went against their grain. Each of them wanted to pull the administration, and the country as a whole, in the direction he desired, and real leadership whose will and views permeated the leading organs of the state, as well as the entire bureaucratic apparatus, appeared to them as tyranny.

How to overcome this tyranny was of course the nobles' main problem, and they knew of no way to resolve it except by drawing the King to their side. Inevitably this meant that they had to exonerate the King of direct responsibility for the tyranny they opposed, and to ascribe his support of the regime and its actions to the duplicity of Alvaro and his officials. To "explain" to the King that these officials opposed him no less than they did the nobles, his servants, seemed to them the most effective attack upon Alvaro and his administration. Thus a case was built against these officials; they were Alvaro's "creatures," "tools" and stooges, and they constantly kept the King misinformed, so that he would make wrong decisions in favor of Alvaro, their master.

How much truth, if any, was there in these charges? Alvar García de Santa María, the official chronicler of Juan II from 1426 to 1435, supplies us with important testimony on this subject. He writes:

> Since the King entrusted his affairs to the Constable [i.e., to Alvaro de Luna], he [Alvaro] did not entrust them to himself, for everything that was done in the administration of justice, as well as in the financial estate of the King, was decided by those of the King's Council. That Council consisted of two parts: one dealing with the granting of royal favors and the issuance of expedient orders, and another which dealt with judicial matters. And since the Constable wanted that all matters related to favors and expediencies be dispatched more properly and without raising suspicion [that they involved some impropriety], the Constable advised the King that these matters be entrusted to the doctors Periáñez and Diego Rodríguez de Valladolid (of whom this history made mention many times); for these were very skillful jurists, well informed of the affairs of the King and the realm, and they took a long time to discuss and decide whatever related to each matter. *They were also very loyal to the King, and they were not persons who would advise*

or inform the King or the Constable any thing which would be against justice
or reason, neither for gifts nor for requests, nor for love, or ill will; and
thus the Constable would not do, or say, or counsel the King, or
determine anything in the royal affairs except with the counsel of these
doctors.[35]

These reforms which Alvaro introduced in the royal administration, continues our chronicler, were of "much help and advantage for the dispatch and
arrangement of matters in just the right way, as befits the service of the King,
the Administration of Justice and the government of the kingdoms." But to
have things "well deliberated, ordered and counseled," he adds, "would not
suffice for the purpose of good government, had not the right decisions been
supported by a good and free execution." And to have this condition fulfilled,
"the King was served by another person, of a kind no other king, as far as is
known, has ever had before. This was Doctor Fernán Díaz de Toledo. He was
the *oidor,* the *Relator,* the *Referendario* and Secretary of the King."[36]

Thus, Alvar García was convinced that Alvaro's reforms in the structure
of the administration, and the new officialdom that he created, constituted his
outstanding contribution to the welfare of the realm. With such people
around him for "ordering and consulting, and such a man as Fernán Díaz to
carry out decisions, the Constable could justify the great confidence that the
King had placed in him,"[37] while the King could be certain that the affairs
of the kingdom were properly conducted.

This chronicler's inside view of the inner workings of Alvaro's government
flatly contradicts the evaluations of that government by the rebellious nobles.
Indeed, as we see it, those evaluations represent, at most, only one of the
aspects of Castile's political reality—an aspect that most likely was seen, or
shown, by them in a decidedly wrong light. Of course, as the official chronicler of the realm, Alvar García may be suspected of exaggeration in his praise
of the administration of which he was part; and as a converso, he may have
been prejudiced in favor of the King's officials at the time, many of whom
were New Christians. Yet even this must be said with great hesitancy, as we
really have no evidence that the facts of the case differed from his description.
Alvar García tends in his writing to be circumspect, balanced and cautious,
and his truthfulness was praised by such a critical observer, and antagonist
of Alvaro, as Pérez de Guzmán. On the other hand, we have every reason to
doubt the veracity of the nobles' assertions. They certainly had an ax to grind.
To overcome Alvaro and oust him from his office was their constant and most
ardent wish. At stake, they believed, were their fortunes and positions, their
influence in the country and their chances to assume power; and to head off
a danger which threatened these assets, or which they believed was threatening them, they were ready to use more extreme measures than to slander
Alvaro's officials.

Yet with all this, we should note, the nobles of the opposition placed some restraints upon their censures. However critical they were of the new bureaucrats, and much as they assessed them as men of low quality, lacking the powers, the dignity and the courage to stand up for their convictions and defend their rights, they never attacked them on religious grounds or on the grounds of their ethnic origin. The reasons for this may be readily discerned.

To begin with, Alvaro's officials of all grades included Old Christians of plebeian stock; and second, the estates and finances of the great nobles themselves were managed by Jews and New Christians. Usually these managers were distinguished by their integrity, and the nobles would not think of offending or annoying them by attacking their religion or their stock. Their campaign against the royal administration, therefore, even when aimed at the leading officials, was directed primarily against Alvaro, their master, who chose as his servants men fitted for his purposes—bad men, of course, men of low quality, but such as may be found in all groups, including the Old and New Christians of Spain.

This was indubitably the prevalent view among most of Castile's great nobles and prelates, and this was no doubt their formal stand as well. Nevertheless, it is hard to assume that their fierce agitation against "Alvaro's officials" did not stir anti-Marrano feelings among vast sections of the Old Christian population or that the nobles who conducted it did not aim at this result. They knew that the people would be quick to identify "Alvaro's officials" with the conversos who formed a considerable part of the administration, and they realized that this identification in itself would lend credibility to their accusations, which were otherwise hardly credible. It was part of their tactics to enlist the people—i.e., the third estate—in their campaign against Alvaro, and they had grounds to believe that the results of these tactics would be favorable to their cause.

XI

For the appointment of conversos to the Royal Council and other high offices of the central administration roused the opposition of another social entity, whose members aspired to the same positions. This was the urban upper aristocracy, which had long been fighting a losing battle with the monarchy for its right to share the governance of the nation.

We have noted their repeated demands to exclude all Jews from high royal office, especially that of *Contador Mayor*, and we have also seen that they achieved that objective at the beginning of the 1380s. But that achievement hardly fulfilled all or most of their wishes. For not only did they want all *Jewish* officials ousted from their high posts in the Court; they also wanted *the other high positions vacated by their clerical and nobiliar holders*. What they really aspired to was ultimately to become the real and sole governors of the realm—of course, under a king who would be guided by their counsels and in fact do their bidding.

They began their pressure in this direction by requesting the King that a number of "citizens" *(ciudadanos)* be included in the Royal Council, but they did not mean just *any* citizen that the King might appoint to that position. In the petition they presented in the Cortes of Toro, 1371, they indicated their wish that the King choose these councillors from among their patricians (the *omes buenos*)—i.e., from among the urban aristocracy—and that these men participate in *all* the King's councils, for the good of the kingdom and the King's dominion. In his answer, Enrique II stated that the judges of his Court and the High Tribunal already included men "from the provinces" (i.e., the towns) and that he would agree to have them join his Council.[38]

This was obviously a negative reply. What the cities sought was higher status not for some commoners distinguished as jurists, but for their *recognized civic leaders;* and this was of course quite a different matter. Nevertheless, they used the King's reply as a partial admission of the rightness of their claim, and kept pressing for its full satisfaction. Finally their endless prodding, on the one hand, and the King's frequent need of their support, on the other, forced the King to retreat. In 1385, Juan I, then much weakened by his defeat at Aljubarrota, enabled the cities to come nearer to their goal: he allowed them entrance to the Royal Council and granted them four of its twelve seats. Five years later, after the King's death, the cities achieved a greater breakthrough. In the Cortes of Madrid, November 1390, they formed the majority of the Council's members (thirteen *procuradores* against eleven representatives of the nobility and the clergy). But this gain proved to be short-lived. In the Cortes of Madrid, 1391, the grandees reduced that majority to a parity.

The cities would probably have gone ahead still further had not the storm of 1391 thrown the country into semi-anarchy. Under the circumstances the higher estates managed to stop the cities' progress in the Council, without preventing them, however, from overstepping the limits stipulated in Juan I's testament. The late king, it appears, was inwardly opposed to the grant he gave the cities in 1385, for in the regency he appointed in his testament, he did not include even one of their spokesmen, conceding them only the right to counsel but not the right of decision. To be sure, in the Cortes of Burgos, 1392, the cities replaced the right to counsel with a veto power, but they never restored their former influence in the Council, where, numerically, they balanced the other estates. Their presence there no doubt helped Enrique III (Juan I's heir) to humble the insubordinate nobles; but having done this, he dismissed the representatives of the cities from his Council, denying them a privilege that the kings of Castile never wanted to give them to begin with.

This happened in 1406, fifteen years after the great conversion and shortly before Enrique III's death. In the period of Juan II's minority, the cities were given no representation in the Councils of regencies of Catalina and Fernando. But their urge to be represented in those Councils remained undiminished, and they looked forward to the accession of Juan II to renew their pressure in that direction. In the Cortes of Madrid at which Juan was enthroned, 1419, they presented a well-argued petition for their renewed participation in the Council. They reminded the King of supportive precedents (some of his ancestors, "both when minors and of full age" [*hedad complida*] recognized their right to representation, they said), but refrained, out of caution, from going too far. They did not ask that *all* cities be represented, or specify how many seats they wished to get; instead, they petitioned the King to permit "*several persons* acting in behalf of *some* of the cities" to enter the Council and have a voice in its proceedings. Avoiding a commitment, the King replied that he would look into the matter and then act in accordance with what in his opinion would be useful to his service.[39]

Six years later, in the Cortes of Palenzuela, 1425, the *procuradores* reminded the King of his promise, and expressed their hope that he would indeed recognize that the incorporation of the cities' representatives in his Council would be of great benefit to his service. They also thought it useful to point out again that the same thing was done by his grandfather, Juan I, and his great-grandfather, Enrique II (now omitting any reference to Enrique III!). The King, however, answered that his Council was "well provided for" by members of all three estates. It included "dukes and counts, prelates and *ricos hombres,* jurists and *caballeros* and persons who are *my natural subjects of the cities and towns of my Kingdom.*"[40] Essentially, this was the same reply given to the cities by Enrique II. It avoided the real issue that had triggered the petition and was based on the obviously feigned assumption that all the cities wanted was to have a few townsmen included in the Royal Council.

The cities of course realized that the Crown was dead set against urban representation in the Council, and abandoning their hope that the King might change his policy, they withdrew many of their demands. In the Cortes of Zamora, 1432, they asked only for two of their *procuradores,* chosen by all their representatives in Cortes, to stay in the Court between the meetings of Cortes and advise the King concerning matters affecting the public welfare of the cities. The King responded to this petition, too, with a "peremptory veto."[41]

XII

It was no secret to the cities that these responses of the King were all dictated by Alvaro de Luna, and they also knew why he acted as he did.

Ostensibly, he was merely following a policy pursued by Castile's kings for centuries, but actually he was more determined and extreme in upholding it than any of those monarchs. It was clear to the cities that Alvaro refused to return to the position taken by Juan I (in 1385) or his successor Enrique III, in the earlier stages of his reign. Alvaro sought to lessen the pressure on the monarchy by reducing the power of the higher estates, and he saw no sense in increasing that pressure by raising the status and influence of the cities. Nor could the cities hide from Alvaro their ambition to become the dominant force in the governing bodies of the kingdom. He therefore decided to keep them out of these bodies and, above all, of the Royal Council.

Yet however apparent these considerations were to the cities' patricians and ruling circles, and however convinced they were that it was Alvaro who blocked their entry into the government, they could not help laying part of the blame at the door of the conversos. For these were known, as we have indicated above, not only as Alvaro's "partisans"—that is, as followers of his political philosophy—but also as his genuine friends and supporters for both psychological and practical reasons. The New Christians in the administration were well aware that they owed their positions to Alvaro and his policy and, moreover, that he often placed them in those positions against the will of powerful opponents. This awareness attached them to him by special ties of gratitude and fidelity; and that relationship, the city leaders reasoned, could not be ruptured in foreseeable circumstances. The converso officials at Court, they believed, would support *automatically* all of Alvaro's policies, including his policy on urban representation. Consequently, they appeared to the cities' oligarchies as their outright political opponents.

Correctly sensing the conversos' attitude toward their inclusion in the Council, the cities also realized that the aforesaid reasons, however important, were merely secondary. The main reason, as they knew, lay elsewhere: The conversos opposed the cities' presence in the Council because the cities opposed the conversos' presence there. In fact, there was no group whose presence in the administration, in both its lower and upper levels, was so resented by the cities as the conversos.

To appreciate the depth of that resentment, we must relate it to the cities' conflict with the Jews. After many years of struggle for a place in the government and a share in determining the nation's affairs, the cities found the doors of the royal administration shut in the face of their spokesmen; and this final result of their arduous efforts naturally disappointed and angered them. But the anger turned into wrath, and the disappointment into exasperation, when they saw who occupied the seats of authority to which, they believed, they themselves were entitled. They thought they had got rid of the Jews in high office after a long and bitter struggle, but now they witnessed the conversos—the Jews' progeny—in the very offices from which the Jews had been ousted, and in many others which they had never held. To the patricians of the cities it appeared as if history had played a cruel joke upon them.

It is possible that in different circumstances the cities would have acquiesced in their lack of representation in the government (they did so under the Catholic Kings!). But frustration and rage often spur people to resume their fight for causes considered almost lost. Something of the kind now happened to the patricians. The King's statement that the townsmen in his Council (many of whom were conversos—that is, men who were viewed by the cities as their enemies) ought to be regarded as *their representatives* was taken by them as an insult to their intelligence, added to the injury which, they thought, it foreshadowed; and this statement in itself, apart from other reasons, prodded them to new resistance. The cities now realized that, besides Alvaro de Luna, they would have to overcome the opposition of the conversos, who now constituted a formidable force. For they occupied not only many seats in the Council but also high positions in the Royal Treasury, the Chancellery, the High Tribunal and the King's secretaryship. That they would not give up these positions willingly was of course taken for granted; but something else became likewise apparent. Aware of the cities' desire to replace them, the highly placed conversos would use their influence to prevent the cities from gaining even a foothold in the central administration. It became obvious to the cities that the first task in their struggle for the national offices was to oust the conversos from their positions. Their battle against Alvaro thus turned more and more into a battle against the New Christians.

XIII

If the cities' yearnings for national offices placed them in confrontation with the converso officials at Court, that confrontation was far from representing their entire anti-converso front. For however anxious they were to unseat the conversos in the national administration, they had to devote much effort to the home front—that is, to curb the converso expansion within the cities themselves.

Here the developments were almost uniform in all cities. Economic progress and social elevation pushed the conversos ever closer to the sensitive centers of political control, and the local Old Christians, who held the reins of power, soon saw themselves forced to defend their positions against the invading newcomers. By "positions" we mean here the offices of city government; and to comprehend the nature of the struggle that developed between the Old and New Christians over these offices, it is necessary for us to consider the difference between what the city administrations meant to their oligarchies and what the national administration meant to the nobles.

We have seen that the grandees could hardly check their fury when they spoke of Alvaro's officials in the Court, and this because the latter had replaced them in some offices in which they had performed ministerial functions and exercised a measure of national authority. Nevertheless, the great nobles did not view these officials as competitors for their positions in the nation. For the nobles' social status and political strength rested much less on their administrative offices than on their nobiliar condition—that is, on their titles, their estates, their castles, their vassals, and their fortunes—in brief, the bases of their power. From these bases, the nobles were sure, the new bureaucrats did not seek to dislodge them. It was Alvaro alone who attempted to do so, because he wished, they believed, to rob them of their power together with their possessions. It was he alone, therefore, who was their real rival, both social and political. Consequently, it was he, and not his officials, who became the main target of their violent attacks.

Quite different was the competition that evolved between the Old and New Christians in the cities. Like all established aristocracies, the Old Christian patricians disliked the upstarts joining their ranks even when these were *Old* Christian; when they were *New* Christians, they would like them much less. Consequently, when many New Christians became rich and thereby formed part of the urban upper class, the Old Christians of that class were unhappy about it; and yet they had reason to restrain their emotions. For although some conversos now matched them in wealth, they could still regard themselves as the urban elite since it was *they* who served as governors of their cities and the highest officials of their administrations. Thus they were still the superior element and, in a sense, the true upper class. Yet when the conversos crossed this line of demarcation and some of them became high urban officials, the comparative status of the groups began to change to the Old Christians' disadvantage. It seemed to them that if the share of the conversos in the government of the city continued to increase and more of them assumed leading positions, they might become the actual rulers of the cities. In consequence, their upper class might attain superiority over the Old Christian elite and the city's social order might be turned upside down.

This is what made the resistance of the burghers to the appointment of conversos in their urban administrations so different from the opposition of the nobles to the converso officials at Court. To the burghers, the conflict with the conversos was a *struggle for both social and political superiority*, which was not the case with the nobility, and it was also a struggle for their *security*, wherein they also differed from the nobles. For when the latter lost their offices at Court, they still had their fortresses and their armies to rely on, but when the Old Christians lost their offices in the cities, they had nothing to fall back on. The defense of their properties, their rights and privileges would be in the hands of the city's rulers; and the rulers would now be conversos. This was a situation they could not accept.

XIV

If this in itself was sufficient for the oligarchies to oppose converso presence in their administrations, the policy adopted by Alvaro toward the cities could only bolster that opposition. That policy had one objective: to establish the Crown's absolute dominion over the cities' residents and resources—and this meant to disregard the cities' privileges, their councils, and their oligarchies. In pursuit of this policy Alvaro did not launch a frontal assault upon the cities' rights; nor did he ever admit his purpose. His tactics for winning this battle of supremacy were similar to those he had employed against the nobles. He sought to appoint to the urban administrations men who would never oppose the King's orders, and block the appointment of candidates who were likely to give priority to their councils' instructions. Since the choice of candidates for high urban offices was in most cases up to the King, Alvaro filled many of these offices with devoted servants of the Crown. Thus, he expected to have the city administrations transformed from pro-urban to pro-royal, and thereby transfer control over the cities from their councils to the royal administration.

Alvaro was not, it must be pointed out, entirely an innovator in this field. Already under Enrique III the *concejos* had noticed the tendency of the Crown to increase the royal power in the cities at the expense of popular liberties. In 1396 Enrique established the new office of *corregidores*, who were sent to cities where complaints were raised about mismanagement or malfunctioning of their administrations. Ostensibly co-rulers with the city's own officers, the *corregidores* were actually armed with authority that placed them high above the *regidores*, as well as all other urban officials. Their formal task was to see to it that the King's laws were observed and that the magistrates carried out their duties, but actually they broadened their powers to include the dismissal of *regidores* and *chief judges*, as well as the appointment of others in their stead. Under Alvaro, this tendency became more pronounced, and the cities' oligarchies correspondingly became more disturbed and restless. Irritated by the growing monarchic interference in their civic life and governmental order, they were infuriated when they saw their highest offices, including those of *regidores* and *corregidores*, given by the King to conversos.

Obviously, Alvaro, who had implicit faith in the New Christians' loyalty to the King, did not doubt their readiness to carry out his orders even when these were clearly opposed to the councils' policies and instructions. The conversos of course would not act otherwise, and many of them were naturally eager to assume the honorable and lucrative city posts which the crown made available to them. It is questionable, however, whether they foresaw the rage that these appointments would arouse, or whether such foresight would have led them to refrain from accepting those positions. In any case, they soon felt the incendiary hatred of the urban oligarchies and their constituencies. For more than the King's Old Christian appointees, his converso appointees were viewed by the cities as usurpers of offices that belonged to the oligarchies and as agents of the King who sought their subjection.

The records of the Castilian Cortes of that period reveal the great struggle between the cities and the monarch over the King's persistent imposition of officials upon the urban administration. Time and again the cities asked the King to send them *corregidores* only in cases when *all* their council members, or at least their majority, explicitly asked him to do so. But the King continued to ignore this request, and appointed *corregidores* for minor reasons or at the request of a few citizens. Similarly, the cities implored the King to limit the number of *regidores*, judges *(alcaldes)*, police officers *(alguaciles)* and notaries *(escribanos)* according to the accepted rules of each place; the King, however, kept raising the number of these officials, whose salaries were paid by the city. The cities likewise asked the king that the offices whose occupants were nominated by him for life (such as those of *alcaldes, merinos* and *regidores*) be given only to natives of the cities who were also permanent residents.[42] The King, however, hardly heeded this appeal and often appointed to those offices outsiders who had never resided in the city. The King also created conciliar offices without waiting for the *regidores* to petition him to do so, which was a time-honored procedure in the cities; he thus multiplied the number of city councillors far beyond the city's needs, solely to secure his control of the *concejos*. Above all, they requested that the King stop interfering in the election of their representatives to Cortes, and also stop paying the expenses of their procurators, which made them, in a way, subservient to the Crown.[43] But these requests, too, were formally denied or practically circumvented.

Under Alvaro's relentless attack, the cities were forced into steady retreat, but they fought this retreat every step of the way. Repeatedly they pointed out in Cortes how almost all the King's appointees in the cities infringed upon their rights, violated their privileges, breached custom, and flagrantly disregarded the King's assurances. They also watched carefully the conduct and performance of each of the officials appointed by the Crown, noted their faults and publicly exposed them, though without mentioning names, at every meeting of Cortes. They compelled the King to admit his errors and repeat his promises to end the abuses. But as one historian correctly pointed out when referring to the promises of Juan II:

"Rarely did he refuse a petition of the *procuradores,* but rarely did he also fulfill what he granted."[44]

The cities knew what the Crown was aiming at, but refrained from stating that aim openly. Without the support of the nobles, they knew, they were no match for the King's forces, and thus they chose to take the King at his word and appear *as if* they believed his claim that all he had done with respect to his appointments was done for the cities' own good. But in 1440 the nobles changed their posture; they decided to rebel; and anxious to draw the cities to their side, they brought into the open the King's acts against the cities, which the latter had habitually chosen to conceal. In the brief they addressed that year to the King, the nobles said that Alvaro de Luna had appointed his servants to urban posts, so that he "might gain a stronger hold on the King's towns and cities," and that, in addition, he planted his men in various key areas of the cities so that no proposal could be passed or discussed there without their knowledge or counsel.[45] To be sure, in keeping with the line of their campaign, the nobles attributed these alleged actions not to Alvaro's royalist policy, which aimed at securing the king's dominion in the cities, but solely to his selfish despotic designs. And although these motives could not be ascertained, nobody could doubt the veracity of the facts to which the alleged motives were related. Thus, it became the prevalent opinion that Alvaro de Luna, whatever his motives (personal or monarchic), pursued an anti-urban policy of subjugation, whose most evident manifestations were the numerous appointments he made arbitrarily against the cities' will.

That the councils did not care to refute these conclusions must be taken for granted. And we must further assume that, as a result, the populace came to view the "King's officials" (i.e., those whom he appointed to the urban administrations) not as officers of the cities (which paid their salaries), but as servants of the King (or his tyrannical minister) whose aim was to repress the cities and exploit them. It is difficult to believe that the criticized officials took all these accusations lying down. In the public debates which inevitably followed, at least some of them must have tried to clear their names, while most of the conversos among those officials no doubt took Alvaro's side. To them Alvaro was the King's chief minister, whose instructions were in fact the King's supreme orders which, they believed, ought to be obeyed, regardless of whether one liked them or not. Yet their defense of Alvaro must have served their enemies as proof that they were in the tyrant's service; and the debate, rather than subsiding, persisted, like a festering wound in a sick body politic.

We can hear the echoes of this debate in the campaign of the Toledan rebels in 1449, when control of public offices again became the central issue in the struggle between the Old and New Christians.[46] In the meantime, however, the political scene changed. Alvaro fell and rose again, and after his victory at Olmedo over the party of the Infantes, he thought he could resume his old policy against the cities. In fact, his disregard of the cities' privileges must have progressively increased, and hence his occasional appointment of officials who were not equal to their tasks. Evidence of this may be adduced from the petitions the cities addressed to the King in the Cortes of Valladolid, 1447, in one of which they demanded public investigation of "all the *alcaldes, merinos, alguaciles, regidores,* and the other officials appointed by the Crown."[47] All this reflected the fierce campaign which the councils conducted against Alvaro de Luna to undermine his prestige and the authority of his officials. As a result, the latter found themselves confronted with a hostile public that disregarded their instructions, or even obstructed their implementation. Disobedience increased; clashes followed; and the oligarchies placed the responsibility for the disorders squarely at the door of the officials themselves. Since the evidence at our disposal is one-sided, we may consider it far from objective. The truth may have been that the harassed officials tried to restore order by using force, whereupon the populace accused them of brutality, which was another point in their disfavor. Thus Alvaro de Luna's policy collapsed, having been vanquished by the councils' agitation. He sought to establish the King's control over the oligarchies; but what he achieved was a state of semi-anarchy and a ferment of revolution.

The revolution came, like so many others, in a series of spasmodic, short-lived waves, the first of which was the outbreak in Toledo in 1449; and its causes, again like those of other such outbreaks, were a complex of old and new factors. Of the latter, the most important was no doubt the fact that the conversos had become unwittingly involved in the battle for supremacy waged by the King against the forces that encroached on his authority. In the two-pronged attack launched against these forces—i.e., the nobility and the cities—the conversos were placed in both cases in the front line; thus they attracted the heaviest fire and suffered most of the casualties.

It is clear that the conversos were anxious to avoid, rather than provoke, these confrontations; but they were on a collision course that led them to clashes they could not possibly prevent. Hence if Alvaro, the author of the King's strategy, was responsible for the rise of converso power in Castile, he was also responsible for the growth of the forces that sought to destroy that power. In consequence, there arose a fierce hatred of the conversos such as they had never experienced before.

Yet it would be wrong to assume that this alone shaped the outlines of converso history at the time. For besides the hostility toward the conversos that grew out of their involvement in the political conflict, there was the old, deep-rooted hatred for Jewish converts which had always been felt by the

Christians of Spain. That hatred formed the substratum of the hostility, and, in addition, its breeding ground. In a sense, therefore, the *old* hatred was the *root* of the new one, and to assess it correctly we have to note its manifestations in the relations between Christians and Jewish converts as they evolved in the history of Christian Spain.

II. Precursors of Toledo, 1449

I. OMINOUS PORTENTS

I

If we are to believe some modern Spanish scholars, the Toledan outbreak of 1449 signaled the beginning of the anti-Marrano movement in the kingdoms of both Castile and Aragon.[1] Accordingly, the period following that outbreak was marked by increasing hatred for the conversos, while the preceding one, starting with the mass conversion (1391–1449), was characterized by a show of goodwill and amity on the part of the Old Christians toward the New. No period of transition from the friendly to the hostile attitude is noted by these scholars; consequently, we may conclude that in their opinion, the change was as swift as it was radical—that it assumed, in fact, the form of a break. The break came with the Toledan riots of January 1449.

This conception of the development under review is plainly unhistoric. It does not explain the antecedent events related to the occurrences of 1449, and by the same token, it leaves unexplained the *causes* of these occurrences. Inevitably, it also fails to suggest the true impact of the development in question and, hence, its historical significance.

Thus, according to Menéndez Pelayo, the outbreak in Toledo was "the first spark" of the persecutory hatred that was to engulf the conversos.[2] Yet this notion is obviously wrong; for the Toledan outbreak was not a spark but a conflagration, and one of great magnitude and force. It was a popular eruption, and like all such eruptions, it was long in the making. Therefore, if it played any part at all in starting new lines of development, in itself it was the *climax* of a long evolution. That evolution must be carefully traced if we wish to understand how the outbreak came about and what it ultimately led to.

Essentially, as we see it, "Toledo '49" was no "turning-point" in Marrano and Spanish history. At a turning point, history changes its course; here it did not. Yet seen in perspective, Toledo '49 opened a new phase in the protracted conflict between the Old and New Christians in Spain. Other phases, with still higher climaxes, were to follow in succeeding decades, but all formed part of the same social drive, moving relentlessly toward the same ends.

It is possible, of course, that to many conversos, as well as to many Old Christians at the time, the ferocious attack upon the Marranos in Toledo came as a total surprise. The first large-scale earthquake in any area often does come as a surprise; but this is so only where its preceding tremors, rumblings and warning signs go unheeded—or, if heeded, are misread. It is clear that in the case of the social explosion known as the Toledan outbreak, the tensions that preceded it could not have built up entirely in the dark. They repeatedly signaled both what was happening and what was bound to occur. But as far as the conversos were concerned, most of these signs were ignored or misconstrued. We need not be astonished by this misconstruction. The annals of all peoples testify to the fact that impending disasters are rarely perceived.

If the failure of peoples to discern the future should not ordinarily amaze us, the failure of historians to discern the past calls, in this instance, for an explanation. Trained researchers, it would seem, should have been able to detect in the sources, which they repeatedly investigated, the trend leading to Toledo '49. But no such trend is depicted or suggested in any of the studies dealing with the subject. Contrariwise, they tend to portray the period preceding '49 as one of peaceful coexistence between the Old and New Christians. To cite Menéndez Pelayo again, "Spanish Society received the neophytes [i.e., the converts of 1391 and 1412] with open arms,"[3] and according to him, this friendly "reception" seems to have lasted a very long time. To be sure, he states that this attitude reflected a one-sided love that remained unrequited, or was not repaid by the conversos in kind. Yet in spite of this, he believes that the break in relations, or the turning of that "love" into virulent hate, did not take place before 1449.

There were several reasons for the acceptance of this view, and we shall discuss them later on,[4] but one of them must be mentioned here: the absence, in all the chronicles of the period, of any sign of conflict between the Old Christians and the New. This absence was interpreted as a sign of peace, as proof of harmonious coexistence. In fact, it resulted from something quite different: from the censorship that interested parties imposed on the chronicles of the period preceding 1449. So thorough and so subtle was this censorship that its very existence has hardly been noticed, and thus one cannot be truly surprised that many a researcher was misled. Nevertheless, it was impossible that the documents should not preserve some vestiges of the suppressed truth. And these vestiges, once subjected to analysis and related to known, pertinent facts, reveal to us the hidden side of the developments that led to Toledo '49.

II

To trace these developments back to their beginnings, we must review all large-scale conversions of Spanish Jews to Christianity during the period of the Reconquest, and also the reactions to those conversions on the part of the Spanish people.[5] We shall try to observe these twin phenomena as they appeared in that period, beginning with the first link in the chain—i.e., the conversions of 1109.

Like the conversions of Jews to Christianity in the Rhineland during the first Crusade (1096), and like those in Spain in 1391, the Spanish conversions of 1109 came in the wake of a series of massacres which, like a tidal wave, hit and devastated many communities at almost the same time. The communities affected were those of Toledo (and its neighborhood), those of northern Castile (around Burgos), and those in León (around the capital city). We have direct, though insufficient, information about the massacres and the ensuing conversions[6]; we have no direct information at all about how the converts were received.

Nevertheless, from several laws included in the *fuero* granted to Toledo by Alfonso VII in 1118,[7] we can arrive at relatively safe conclusions about the "reception" accorded the converts at the time. These laws came to meet the demands that the burghers had addressed to the King's counselors on matters pertaining to the Jewish question, and the first of these laws refers not only to Jews but also to Jewish converts to Christianity. It reads as follows:

> Wishing to obey and fulfill the instructions of the Holy Fathers [of the Catholic Church], the king has decreed that neither Jew nor recent convert may assume authority over any Christian in Toledo and its territory.[8]

That Jews should assume no post or position in which they might exercise authority over Christians had been part and parcel of Christian law since the days of Theodosius II.[9] But Alfonso VI, conqueror of Toledo, placed the interests of the state above the law of the Church, and appointed Jews to a number of posts that commanded high authority and prestige.[10] In 1081 Pope Gregory VII rebuked Alfonso for these appointments,[11] but the King ignored the Pope's rebuke just as he ignored the Church's old prohibition. In doing so, however, Alfonso VI flouted not only the wishes of the Pope, but also the sentiments of his Christian subjects, many of whom bitterly resented the appointment of Jews to high office. When the former realized that no authority in Christendom could move Alfonso to alter his policy, their pent-up rage turned to violence or, more precisely, to political murder. They ambushed and assassinated Solomon ben Ferruziel, Alfonso's courtier and ambassador-at-large, upon his return to Toledo, his hometown, from a royal mission to Aragon.[12] In retrospect, this assassination appears as a lightning flash in a charged atmosphere. Occurring about a year before the massacres, it could or should have given clear warning of the gathering storm. We have no indication that it did.

The storm broke on August 15, 1109,[13] a month and a half after Alfonso VI's death, before a new government could be firmly established and when the country was divided on the question of the succession. As we have indicated above,[14] periods of interregnum were often times of trouble for Jewish communities in the West, especially when, coupled with political unrest, the country was suffering from a military debacle or a grave economic setback. These were precisely the circumstances in Castile at that particular time.

Only about a year before Alfonso's death, his armies had suffered a crushing defeat at the hands of the Almoravides in Uclés, leaving, by all available accounts, many thousands dead on the battlefield. That the blame for the defeat was ascribed to the Jews who formed part of Alfonso's army at Uclés is possible or even likely, although the conduct of the Jews in that crucial battle, and the related details as set forth by Amador, remain unsubstantiated to this day.[15] Of course, such charges, if leveled at the Jews, could help fan the flames of hatred against them, but the ensuing fury could have occurred even if these charges were never made. As we see it, under the conditions then obtaining, the military debacle itself was sufficient to try the people's patience to the breaking point. It removed their own self-control at a time when external controls were missing or deficient, owing to the interregnum.

Never before in her long history had Spain seen such a large-scale attack upon the Jews as that of August 1109, and, in a sense, never had Europe seen anything like it either. For the perpetrators of the offenses against the Jews in Spain differed, in one important respect, from those who had struck the Jewish communities in Germany about a decade earlier. The frenzied rabble who made the latter assaults were, in their overwhelming majority, outsiders to the cities in which the Jews lived, while in Spain the assailants were ordinary city dwellers who rose, sword in hand, against their Jewish neighbors and exposed them to all forms of outrage.[16] There can be no doubt that by these bloody acts a message was sent to the rulers of Spain: The Christian populace of the Spanish cities wants no Jews in its midst.[17]

The kings of Castile and León, however, were not inclined to heed this message, nor were the burghers probably explicit in some of their formal claims on the Crown. They did, however, insist on at least one demand, which they no doubt had repeatedly presented—namely, that Jews be denied all public office, royal or municipal, by royal decree. But as before, the Crown rejected this demand, and likewise declined the citizens' request that it overlook the crimes committed against Jews during the riots of 1109. Both propositions were against the Crown's interests, and the dispute over them dragged on for years, until the turn of events forced Alfonso VII to grant the stubborn Toledans their wishes. He did this in the form of specific legislation included in the *fuero* he granted Toledo on December 16, 1118—the day on which he entered the city as the newly appointed ruler of the realm.[18]

To be sure, we have no direct information about the controversy that must have preceded this decree, but the decree itself is at our disposal, and it offers some clues as to what had occurred. As we have noted, the law did not forbid *all* converts to hold public office in the city; it applied only to *recent* converts. But what did the term "recent converts" mean? The expression used in the text of the privilege, which was written in Latin (and is extant in that language), is *nuper renati*,[19] and this may mean one of two things—either "recent converts" or "*the* recent converts." In the first instance it refers to *all recent converts, of whatever faith and in whatever period,* in the second, to *the* recent converts who were known to one and all in Toledo and other cities—i.e., those who went over from Judaism to Christianity under the impact of the massacre of 1109. Moreover, as we have seen, the law relied for its enactment on the "Holy Fathers" of the Catholic Church. But the Fathers of the Church were never opposed to appointing "recent converts" to public office[20]; nor did they recommend anywhere in their works that *Jewish* converts be barred from such appointments.

Whatever the author of the *fuero* had in mind when he used the expression *nuper renati*, there can be no doubt that he referred primarily to the Jews converted in 1109. This formulation could satisfy the Old Christians—at least, at the time when the law was enacted. Nine years after the conversion, the converts of 1109 could still be classed as "recent," and any Toledan could readily assume that *nuper renati* alluded to them. But what was the attitude of the Old Christians toward the converts in the decades succeeding the enactment of that law? What, especially, was their attitude in Toledo, then living under its new constitution?

No documents from the century following the *fuero* are extant to clarify this matter, but evidence from the 15th century indicates that such documents were then available.[21] According to this evidence, there is reason to believe that, about 1145, Alfonso VII granted the Toledans another privilege, according to which no Jewish convert, or any offspring of such convert, might at any time have the right to public office in Toledo and its territory. If such a privilege was indeed granted—as this evidence suggests—it must have been in response to appeals by Toledans who were probably hard-pressed by the converts on that matter. The latter could then claim the right to public office in accordance with the *fuero* of 1118.[22] They might have argued that the *fuero* denied this right to *recent* converts, but their own association with Christianity and Christendom, by then already several decades old, could no longer be defined as "recent."[23] The burghers, however, opposed this claim and asked Alfonso VII to issue a new order which would vindicate their opposition. It is possible, of course, that they asked him to confirm that by *nuper renati* he meant *the* recent converts (i.e., the neophytes of 1109), so that those who were barred from public office in the city would be subject to that law because of their *origin*—i.e., their Jewish stock or background—and not because of their "recency."

We need not elaborate the point further, except to say that the second privilege of Alfonso, to which the later documents refer, soon fell into disuse.[24] No doubt the Church opposed its basic concepts, which went against its views and traditions. It is also possible that most converts and their descendants migrated from Toledo after the issuance of that privilege, so that, de facto, convert equalization was no longer a concrete issue in the city.[25] Whatever the case, the alleged second privilege was never confirmed by subsequent kings. And while the confirmation of the Toledan *fuero* by Alfonso VIII in 1178 retained the stipulation about *nuper renati*,[26] the expression must have come to mean, at least formally, *recent converts* to Christianity from *all* religions, and not necessarily *Jewish* converts, and certainly not the Jews who went over to Christianity in the course of the riots of 1109. This is also what we gather from the equivalents of *nuper renati* in other Spanish documents.[27]

But something else should be said in this connection that is highly relevant to our discussion. Between the formal rendering of the expression in Spanish and the meaning it assumed in the public mind, there was a marked and important difference. The constant appearance of the expression "recent converts" in conjunction with the term *Jews* ("neither Jews nor recent converts will have any right to public office") led many to assume that the converts referred to were converts only (or primarily) from Judaism[28]; and since the accent of the prohibition was on *Jewish* converts, the issue of their recency assumed secondary importance. Thus, *all* converts from Judaism of whatever date came to be considered recent, their recency now measured not by months or years but by decades, or even generations.[29] In due course, the term "recent converts" was changed into New Christians, and their "newness" (like their earlier recency) would remain outside the bounds of time.

The significance of this development lay in the fact that it was not limited to Toledo or to the towns in which Jews were converted during the riots of 1109. The problem spread to other places, to which some of the converts or their offspring must have moved. If that migration represented an attempt to escape the discrimination they felt in their hometowns, it more often than not must have proven futile. For like the sentiment against the Jews, the feeling against the converts invariably followed them in their migrations, and consequently, its scope, rather than narrowing, constantly broadened in the process. What is more, there is evidence to the effect that this anti-convert feeling was lasting. When, several generations after 1118, the Toledan *fuero* was extended to other cities—that is, to Cordova (1241), Carmona (1247) and Alicante (1251)—the stipulation regarding the converts was retained,[30] while its various alterations indicated the persistence of the old attitudes.[31] It is also significant that in the *fuero* of Carmona the prohibition was broadened to embrace *all* converts (rather than only recent converts), while the designation used for converts in that privilege is the abusive term *tornadizo* (turncoat), suggesting both hatred and contempt.[32] All this shows that the law concerning converts in the Toledan *fuero* was not transferred automatically to the new *fueros* with the remainder of the old Toledan laws, but was carefully weighed, rephrased and altered to suit the burghers' particular views, or accommodate their views to those of the King.

III

That this antagonism to converts from Judaism was not at all of a local nature—that is, peculiar to the towns thus far mentioned—but rather of a national, all-Spanish character, we can clearly gather from other documents of approximately the same period. Of these documents we should mention first Alfonso X's code, the *Fuero Real*, which was completed in 1255.

Unlike the *fueros* granted by Castile's kings to particular cities, such as those we have mentioned, this code was meant to apply to many towns which still lacked their own constitutions; and it was also hoped that it would ultimately replace the law in the cities which had *fueros* of their own. The *Fuero Real* therefore was designed in a way to suit the interests of the nation as a whole. Hence it is significant that it forbids reference to a convert by the vilifying term *tornadizo*.[33] From the penalty imposed upon the violators of this order (twenty maravedis for each instance), we can see that the law aimed at checking the abuse; but the habit of insulting converts was so general, and the feeling to which it gave vent so strong, that the law had little if any effect. This is evident from Alfonso's second code, the famous *Las Siete Partidas,* whose compilation was completed ten years later (1265).[34] It contains two important laws on the subject of conversion—or rather on the treatment of converts to Christianity. Of these one is general and the other specific, the former relating to *all* converts to Christianity, the latter solely to converts from Judaism. The general law opens with the following preamble:

> Many people live and die in foreign faiths who would prefer to become Christians, had they not seen the humiliations and abuses, in word and in deed, to which the others, who did turn Christians, were subject, having been called turncoats (*tornadizos*) and reproached in many other evil and insulting manners. We hold that all [people] are in duty bound to honor such persons [i.e., the converts] *for many reasons,* rather than disgrace them.[35]

Several important conclusions can be drawn from this introductory passage. To begin with, it is obvious that the law does not refer to hypothetical cases; it rather touches upon a concrete situation in which converts to Christianity have been scorned and abused. That this treatment was not exceptional is evident from the fact that the lawmaker regards it as a *well-known custom,* so well known, indeed, that in his opinion, it deters "many" of other faiths from going over to Christianity. Obviously, the lawmaker finds no justification for this systematic attack upon the converts, expressed in "many evil and insulting manners." He certainly does not believe that the converts could be blamed for the treatment they received—that they were, for instance, unfaithful to Christianity or insincere in their Christian beliefs (as could be gathered from the term "turncoat"),[36] for in this case he would not have stated so emphatically that all people are in *duty bound to honor them.* Apart from treating the converts honorably, therefore, the law insists that all Christians *do them good,* and do so *"in every manner they can,"*[37] precisely as they would or should have treated converts who had come from their own stock.[38] Indeed, the law maintains that converts from alien stocks have to overcome difficulties that converts from the same stock do not encounter or experience—such as the "parting from parents and relatives, from the way of life to which the converts were accustomed and from all the other things that caused them pleasure."[39] Since the sacrifice involved in the conversion of such people is greater than that offered by converts of the same stock, plain fairness would require that all other Church members show them special consideration. If the lawmaker did not spell this out clearly, his argument at least implies that *equal* treatment for such converts is the *minimum* they should get from their fellow Christians. This is of course the very *opposite* of the treatment prescribed for converts by the Toledan *fuero.* Thus, the policy of discrimination proposed by that *fuero* was not only abandoned—it was reversed.

Accordingly, the lawmaker viewed with special severity the abuse of converts from foreign races and demanded a "more cruel" punishment for such abuses than would be imposed for similar offenses committed against persons of native extraction.[40] It is obvious from this law that the foreign origin of the converts loomed large in the eyes of the Old Christian populace in determining its negative attitude toward converts, while, contrarily, that origin is considered by the law as a factor in the convert's favor—not only when it points to the way he *should* be treated, but also when it fixes penalties for those who abused his elementary rights.

The other law on converts contained in the *Partidas,* which deals specifically with "Jewish" converts, also bears witness to the same effect. It says:

> Since some Jews may be converted to Christianity, all the subjects of our dominions are ordered to honor them, and no one dare refer to them or their lineage by way of an insult. They should retain all their goods and their rights of inheritance as if they were Jews, and they can have all the offices and honors which other Christians have.[41]

It is clear that the insults hurled at converts from Judaism included reminders of their "origin," or their stock, and that these "reproaches" were readily aimed not only at Jews who themselves had been converted, but also at their descendants who were born in Christendom.[42] This law, like the other, does not indicate that any of these converts were to blame *religiously* for any of the abuses they may have suffered; the fault which could supposedly be imputed to them was related not to their *present* but *past* faith, extending to the faith of their ancestors, which was of course not necessarily theirs.[43] This is clear evidence from *that* time of the prevalent refusal to treat converts as equals, purely on the grounds of their "lineage," or their stock. A strong racial feeling is revealed here, although still veiled with a religious excuse (their ancestors' belief in the Jewish religion).

But something else becomes apparent at this point which has to do with the position of the king. As we have noted, Alfonso VII of Castile prohibited the appointment of converts to public office (in 1118)—a prohibition that must have been upheld in many places until the middle of the 13th century; and thus, in this respect, the status of the converts was no better than that of the Jews. Now, however, the *Partidas* introduced a change in this matter. While the law repeats the old prohibition against *Jews* occupying public office,[44] it states that *converts* from Judaism to Christianity "may have *all* the offices and honors" held by Christians. The victory that the burghers had won on this issue, and whose fruits they held firmly for a century and a half, now appeared lost. The old Castilian policy toward converts from Judaism was not only discarded; it was reversed. And the question to be asked now is, quite obviously: What was the cause of this reversal?

IV

In searching for an answer to this question, we cannot, to our regret, be assisted in any measure by previous investigation. The fact is that the entire burgher-convert quarrel from the beginning of the 12th to the end of the 14th century was outside the purview of the historians of the period. Since they failed to notice this whole line of evolution, they naturally failed to see any break in it, such as was made by Alfonso's legislation. Consequently, they saw at this point no problem that called for a special solution. The following is merely a cautious attempt to throw some light on this obscure area.

As we see it, there were several reasons for the King's change of policy toward the converts, the most important of which were the following: (a) the rise of Dominican influence in Spain and (b) the Crown's desire to cater to the Church for a reason to be touched upon below.

These were the years in which the Dominicans conducted a vigorous conversionist campaign in Aragon, and we may safely assume that their plans for conversion included Castile as well. In any case, their leader, Raymond de Peñafort, former General of the Dominican Order, used his great influence to push that campaign in all possible directions.[45] While he and his associates devised new methods to persuade Jews to abandon their faith—methods relating to the theological side of the Jewish-Christian controversy—they were not so naive as to ignore the social and economic problems involved. They centered their conversionist activity in Aragon, where they found these problems less disturbing, although the popular attitude toward converts in that country was likewise anything but friendly. Indeed, there too converts from Judaism were often reviled in such offensive terms as "renegades," "turncoats" and the like; and as long as this habit persisted, conversion to Christianity could hardly be attractive.

The Dominicans, therefore, saw to it that Jaime I, king of Aragon, issued, on March 9, 1242, a decree prohibiting the abuse of all converts and also removing some other obstacles from the path of their conversionist campaign.[46] From then on, the Dominicans believed, the conversion of Jews and Moslems in Aragon would depend, at least largely, on their own performance—that is, their ability to convince Jews and Saracens of the veracity of Christianity, or its superiority to all other faiths. But conditions in Castile were quite different. There the Dominicans could hardly expect to induce many Jews to go over to Christianity so long as the common attitude toward converts was marked not only by social aversion but also by sharp legal discrimination, as was evident from the laws on their right to hold office included in many of the country's *fueros*. For the Spanish Dominicans the situation in Castile must have been intolerable; they realized that their first task in that country was to remove the legal disabilities against converts and establish their equality with all other Christians.

They saw an opportunity to achieve this aim through the work of codification then in progress in Castile, and they doubtless thought it both fitting and feasible to influence the lawmaker in accordance with their goals. Since Alfonso X wished his law books to conform as closely as possible to the laws of the Church, and since Raymond de Peñafort was known throughout Christendom as the foremost expert in canon law, he was no doubt consulted by the king's lawmakers on all major issues related to Church law—including of course the issue of conversion. Thus, it was probably not without his influence that the *Fuero Real* of 1255 included—for the first time in Castile—a clear prohibition against abusing converts. Above all, one may assume that the laws in the *Partidas*, which speak so strongly in defense of the converts, were drafted under his or his colleagues' inspiration.[47] This is also evident from the preambles to the laws which deal with conversion to Christianity generally, as well as specifically with conversion of Jews. Both laws were clearly designed to meet the needs of conversion to Christianity[48]—that is, the needs of the Church militant and the current Dominican campaign.

But apart from the general influence of the Dominicans on the *legal* positions taken by the Crown, another factor must have moved Alfonso to pay special attention to their demands. The Dominicans were regarded as emissaries of the papacy and executors of the pope's will, and Alfonso X had a special reason to be on good terms with the pope. Since the beginning of his reign (in 1252) Alfonso had striven to be crowned Emperor of Germany. He had some hereditary claims to this title, and the support of the papacy was vital to their acceptance and thereby to the fulfillment of his dream.[49] In 1257 Pope Alexander IV seemed to favor Alfonso's election as emperor, but demanded that Alfonso and his rival at the time submit their claims to the Roman curia and yield to the Pope's final verdict. Since Alfonso refused to fulfill this condition, the papal attitude toward him changed, becoming indecisive or even antagonistic (at least until 1265). Alfonso, however, did not cease scheming to attract the papacy to his side, and while he cherished his political independence, he was ready to pay homage, on suitable occasions, to the pope's authority in matters of faith. The Dominican proposals on the convert issue fell within the sphere of that authority, and here Alfonso could demonstrate cooperation with the papacy's plans.

But in addition to the Dominican activity at the time and the King's interest in pleasing the popes, another factor must have played a part in producing the new legislation. This was the influence of the converts themselves, which had been on the rise in Spain for some time. As a rule, one may assume that no decree or law designed to protect a minority in the Middle Ages was issued without a determined effort on the part of the minority involved. So it was with all the privileges that the kings of Europe granted the Jews, and this was doubtless also the case with Alfonso's laws in favor of the converts. By the middle of the 13th century, it appears, converts had occupied some important positions in the royal administration of the Castilian cities,[50] and it is also well known that at that very time they exerted real influence in monastic circles.[51] It was probably through their Dominican friends that the converts worked their will on the royal legislators, but even so, it took them years of effort before they saw their wishes fulfilled. The law against the abuse of converts that is included in the *Fuero Real* must have been their first breakthrough in Castile, but the laws of the *Partidas* on the issue of conversion marked their ultimate triumph. Morally and religiously, as well as socially, they could not hope for better laws; nor could their interests be better protected vis-à-vis the Jews as well as the Christians.[52] The laws evince attention to all the converts' needs, and this in itself testifies to the role which their spokesmen played in this legislation.

The triumph of the converts, however, was premature, for like the other laws of the *Partidas*, the laws on conversion remained ineffective for the next eighty-five years—that is, until 1348, when Alfonso XI declared the *Partidas* to be the law of the country. From then on, indeed, their laws on conversion became guiding principles for the kings' policies and the final authority to which the converts turned for the protection of their rights.

V

There was special significance in the fact that these laws became operative in 1348, for shortly thereafter the problem of the converts rose again to the fore in Castile's social life. The Castilian Civil War of the 1360s was accompanied by bloody attacks upon the Jews, which were in turn followed by a new wave of converts seeking entry into Christian society.[53] Since the law of the country now assured them equality with all other Christians, the converts may have expected a tolerable reception on the part of the Old Christians. But the new influx of converts into Castile's society was greeted with a fresh outbreak of hostility, which the laws of the kingdom were powerless to stem. Symptomatic of this was the frequency of abuse, now directed against converts everywhere, and the rapid spread of the new insult—*Marrano*, meaning "pig" or "swine."[54] So ugly and disturbing had the public mood become that in 1380, Juan I found it necessary to enact a new law against the use of such terms, and imposed a fine of three hundred maravedis for every violation.[55] This was a penalty many times larger than the one imposed by the *Fuero Real*,[56] yet the King went beyond even this. If the offender, the law added, could not pay the fine, he was to be imprisoned for fifteen days.[57]

These harsh measures were meant to match the severity of the situation. By means of them the King hoped to stop or restrain a habit that could lead to an irreparable social rift. We do not know what effect, if any, his law had in the coming few years. In any case, about a decade later, the riots of 1391 broke out, and these produced new masses of converts—far more than Spain had ever known before. All the legal dams erected till then to check the abuse of converts from Judaism were swept away by the tide of hostility which was moving relentlessly against the newcomers to Christianity. The term *Marrano* as an offensive designation was soon to be on everybody's lips.

Thus, when the dust settled after the great riots, Spain appeared affected by her old malady, for which no cure had been found in the preceding centuries. The country had been seething with discontent, and the tension resulting from convert penetration was testing hard the tolerance of the people. The conditions obtaining after 1391 could only aggravate that tension. If Juan I still earnestly believed that he could check the verbal attacks on the conversos, the next administration, that of Enrique III, realized the futility of this attempt. It could see how the old "war of words" not only continued unabated, but was paralleled by a "war of deeds," which was a far more serious matter. It turned its attention to the latter.

II. THE RISING TIDE (1391–1449)

I

From the evidence presented above, we believe, we may draw a most significant conclusion, without which we cannot duly understand the development of relations between the Old and New Christians. Much has been said in historical literature about the tradition of Jew hating that was discernible in Spain even in the benign periods of the Reconquest; but *parallel to the Spanish tradition of Jew hatred there ran a tradition of hatred for Jewish converts;* and of this phenomenon hardly anything has been said. Like the former tradition, the latter too had its quieter and stormier periods, depending on social and political conditions, on the number of converts in the country, and the like. Yet under the surface it never disappeared, and it was as restive, as virulent and growing in intensity as was the animosity for the Jews.

This is what characterized the relationships in the period of 1118–1391. What happened after 1391 only lends support to this conclusion.

Barely fourteen months after the mass conversion—i.e., in October 1392— Enrique III addressed the council of Burgos with a letter touching on a new kind of problem. It is the first extant document of a number available, all bearing witness to the same trend. The letter refers to a complaint the king received from the residents of Santa María la Blanca, a borough of Burgos, near the citadel, which was inhabited by New Christians. Prior to the riots of 1391 the borough was a Jewish neighborhood, and now, since it was settled by Christians, it was entirely under the city's jurisdiction. What the New Christians complained of in their brief was that some people in the city in positions of authority—apparently officials of the city council—purely out of malice toward the conversos *(por los querer mal)* had molested and injured them in various ways, such as incarcerating conversos charged with any offense, whether criminal or civil, in private jails *(carceles privadas)*.[58]

What is of especial interest in this document is the stress on the *ill will* shown the New Christians which was expressed in a systematic persecution. It seems that, in the eyes of the New Christians, the most disturbing element of that persecution was the imprisonment in private jails, where apparently they were not protected by the laws that governed the public prisons. In consequence they could be exposed there more easily to maltreatment, privation and abuse of all sorts.

It is evident that the New Christians of the Burgensian borough were subjected to a reign of terror, the arrests having aimed, as far as we can judge, at frightening the community into leaving the area. Moreover, these actions, the same document suggests, violated a privilege which Burgos had received in the wake of an inquiry into the converso problem apparently conducted by the king's agents.[59] The document is not sufficiently elaborate to indicate the exact circumstances of that inquiry and the full content of the ensuing privilege. It is evident, however, that the relations between the Old and New Christians in Burgos had already been troubled before October 1392; that a special investigation had been instituted about the conversos in which they were fully exonerated; that as a result they were recognized as equal citizens in the privilege the city received shortly thereafter; and finally, that this privilege did little to improve the conversos' social conditions. Despite its stipulation in the conversos' favor, the city officials ignored Marrano rights and the laws that vouchsafed the conversos' equality, forcing the latter to appeal to the king for redress of these wrongs.

These developments were related to the riots that broke out in Burgos against the Jews on August 12, 1391. In the course of the upheavals, or shortly thereafter, most of the community was converted to Christianity.[60] But this did not save the remaining Jews from threats of renewed aggression. On July 30, 1392, the king found it necessary to write to the city urging its leaders to guard those Jews against further attacks by the lower classes (*omes rafezes de pequeño estado*).[61] In consequence of the riots, the king pointed out, the Jews had become virtually destitute; and unable to pay their taxes and their debts, they were often subject to arrests and confiscations. But they were also subjected to harassment of other kinds, as we shall presently see.

For the eleven months that passed since the great riots had sufficed to produce deep antagonism between the Jews and the new converts. Jews who had fled the *judería* during the riots refrained from returning to it, partly because they feared some of the new converts, who "persecuted" them, caused them many harms, and urged them to attend their conversionist sermons.[62] And yet despite the Christian zeal and anti-Jewish feeling manifested by at least some of the neophytes, the populace, including the city's officials, harbored, as we have seen, ill will toward them all. If the people of Santa María la Blanca (i.e., the conversos) turned to the king with their complaint, it was *because they could not find attentive ears in the city's administration*. It was customary for Jews to resort to the king—their traditional protector, legally and in fact—with complaints about persecutions they had suffered and requests to provide for their security. Now the Marranos learned that in this respect their situation remained fundamentally unchanged. The king had to write to the municipality of Burgos demanding fair treatment for the conversos, just as a few months earlier he had had to write to it demanding humane treatment for the Jews.

"And you well know," says the King's letter of October 14, 1392, "that the said residents *(vezinos)* of the said neighborhood are Christian and newcomers to the Catholic faith and that you ought to treat them as brothers. They are to enjoy all the privileges, liberties, good uses and customs that the said city enjoys . . . either by virtue of the abovementioned inquiry as well as for other [obvious] reasons, and that you should not consent that anyone, unless he is a *merino* in the said city acting under the orders of my judges, dare seize the person or the property of any of the said residents, and that, furthermore, if any of them be arrested as indicated [that is, by a *merino* and at a royal judge's order] that he be put in the customary place of imprisonment, and in no other place." Violation of this order, the letter concludes, would involve a penalty of one thousand maravedis payable to the king's chamber.[63]

From all this it is apparent that the imprisonments of conversos were acts of brigandry committed by Old Christians, without any regard to due process of law and with the connivance or consent, active or passive, of the city's administration; that the victims therefore could find no relief from the harassment through appeals to the city's authorities; and that they were regarded by the same authorities as excluded from the privileges granted to the city. Phrased in strong language, the king's letter was obviously a reprimand to the city. It placed the New Christians on equal footing with the Old Christians—a condition which, according to the letter, the fathers of the city ought to have known, but which they chose to ignore.

Burgos was not the only city in Castile in which tension developed between the New and Old Christians; for Enrique III issued similar orders to other cities as well. The Marranos were compelled to submit to him complaints about "injuries, disgraces and damages" which they suffered in Toledo and other cities of the kingdom,[64] after their appeals to the local authorities had evidently proved futile. Thus, Toledo had been a focus of dissension between the Old Christians and the New even in the days of Enrique III—that is, *more than five decades before the outbreak of 1449!*

Judging by the king's letter to Toledo, the like of which must have been sent to other cities too, the abuses perpetrated against the conversos were aggravated by a special issue on which the Old and New Christians differed. For the king ordered all judicial authorities, officials and nobles of the city of Toledo, as well as all his subjects in the realm, to "*honor and receive the said good people and faithful Christians* who were recently converted in Toledo, and in all the cities, towns and localities in his kingdoms and dominions, in which they now stay or will stay and in which they are or will be residents *(vicini), to both offices and honors of all kinds by which the other Old Christians are honored.*"[65] In addition, while decreeing that "no injury be done to the [converts'] possessions or persons," he stressed again that they equally *"enjoy all privileges, honors, customs, advantages and employments which are or may be enjoyed by the Old Christians in the said city."*[66]

It is clear, then, from this statement, which urged so strongly the equalization of the New Christians, that the Old Christian communities in Castile's cities, led by the new and old capitals of Castile (Toledo and Burgos), had been adamantly opposed to converso penetration into positions of authority and prestige, and that they refused to share with the New Christians the cherished privileges which their forefathers had won from kings and nobles after long and bitter struggles. The conversos, as is evident from all the above, insisted on the fulfillment of the laws of Church and state that entitled them to *full* equality, thereby stirring up an Old Christian resistance that was equally stubborn and unremitting. So the conflict kept producing assaults upon the conversos, who saw themselves, as a result, in danger. That is why the king had to order the authorities that they be "protected and defended."

All this occurred before 1406, the year of Enrique III's death, and probably before the turn of the century. For there is good reason to believe that the above decree was the letter of privilege *(carta de privilegio)* which, a reliable source tells us, was granted the conversos by Enrique III in the days of Don Pedro Tenorio, Archbishop of Toledo.[67] Tenorio, who assumed his position in Toledo in 1376, died in 1399, and that means that the privilege was given only a few years after the mass conversion of 1391. Countersigned by the archbishop and by Dr. Periáñez, both leading members of the Royal Council, the privilege was obviously approved by the Council, and as such it indicated, when the King was still a minor, that this was the official policy of the realm.[68] All this makes it clear that stern opposition to placing the New Christians on equal footing with the Old was manifested in many Castilian cities at a very early date in the history of their relationship after the riots of 1391.

II

The anti-converso actions of the populace in Burgos, Toledo and other Castilian cities, and the cooperation of the city administrations in those actions, show that the mass conversion of Jews to Christianity in 1391 presented the Old Christians with unusual irritants stemming from the new realities.

We have seen that the general aversion to converts intensified in Castile following the Civil War, when the number and influence of converts in the country rose to new, much higher levels. Nevertheless, the converts still constituted at that time a small minority in the general population, and though their presence disturbed many Old Christians, their limited interference in Spanish life was still endurable to many others. But what had been a small minority in 1380 swelled to large proportions in 1391. Now the cities had to cope with a whole set of problems they had hardly ever known—at least, on such a scale. Thus, there was the question of living in separate boroughs; there was the question of how to incorporate the conversos into the stratified society of the cities; and, above all, there was the question of the rights and privileges to which the conversos claimed to be entitled, but which the cities were reluctant to grant.

The most important part of this last question related to the right to hold public office, on which we have touched repeatedly in the foregoing. No other issue created so much friction in the relations between the Old Christians and the New, and no other issue generated so much heat in the controversies that evolved between the two groups. We have noticed the determined opposition of the Old Christians to converso equality in this domain, and we have noted that they lost much ground in this struggle after the *Partidas* became the country's law, in 1348. But now, after the conversions of 1391, they seemed on the verge of losing the whole battle. In addition to the presence of converso masses, which constituted a strong pressure in itself, there was the influence wielded by some outstanding conversos at the Royal Court of Castile. Only about a decade before 1391, the cities registered an important triumph when they compelled the kings, after centuries of resistance, to prohibit Jews from serving in the royal administration.[69] But this victory would become meaningless if the conversos, who had already penetrated the high places, now also invaded the Crown's municipal positions that were usually filled with the king's appointees.[70]

Garibay, the 16th century Spanish historian, tells us that the noted converso leader Don Pablo de Santa María, bishop of Burgos, advised Enrique III, king of Castile, to accept neither Jew nor converso in the service of his house, or in the king's Council, or in the administration of the royal patrimony, or in any other royal office.[71] Such advice, if indeed it was given, would have indicated great wisdom on the part of Don Pablo, for nothing generated so much hate for the conversos as the role they were to play in the royal administration. But it is extremely doubtful that such counsel was offered at any time by the converso leader. To put the conversos in a position of inferiority with respect to the rest of the Christian population would be, from all we know, contrary to everything Paul of Burgos believed and wanted. In fact, after his return to Castile in 1399, he received three court appointments from Enrique III, culminating in that of chief chancellor of the kingdom (1406), contrary to the solicitous advice that Garibay ascribed to him.[72]

The order issued by Enrique III gave the conversos, in their fight against discrimination, the governmental backing that they vitally needed. But the

Old Christians' struggle against their equalization did not end with this enactment; on the contrary, it intensified. Facing a new wave of converts (following the persecutions of 1412) and a new stream of converso complaints about their mistreatment by the Old Christians, Juan II, Enrique III's successor (or rather the regents who acted in his name) found it necessary to issue a new privilege, in which he incorporated the decree of Enrique III and insisted that it was the law of the country. This is how part of that privilege reads:

> Considering the good and sacred intention which the king, our lord, my father, and my own lord had in granting and expediting the said letter for the service of God, i.e., the exaltation of the Catholic faith;
> And considering also what the laws of the *Partidas,* as well as what the cities of our kingdoms and dominions ordered in such cases, and especially what is contained in Law VI under the title of "Jews," in Book VII, which says thus:
> "Likewise, we order that, if any of the Jews be converted to the Christian faith, all people of our dominions treat them respectfully, and that none dare detract them or their lineage by mentioning, in an insulting manner, the fact that they had been Jews. [We further order that] they [i.e., the converts] may have all the offices and honors which the other Christians have."
> Therefore, out of our own volition, and with definite knowledge and royal power, we approve and confirm through this letter—which we order and wish to have the force of law, as if it were issued in Cortes— the said letter and privilege of the King, our father, which is above incorporated in this letter . . . and I wish and order that it be observed and implemented now and in perpetuity, in all its points and every respect, and under the penalty specified therein.
> I also approve and confirm the said law of the *Partidas* which is cited above, ordering that it be observed in all its points and in every respect, and for all times.[73]

The reference to the *Partidas,* the revered code of law which bears the stamp of Alfonso X, obviously meant to give the policy toward the conversos, enunciated by Enrique III, the sanction of *old* laws and traditions. Since Enrique was the first Spanish king to confront mass conversion of Jews and the ensuing difficulties in the Spanish cities, his policy might be seen as the result of inexperience or bad counsel. Unless it was based on the *old* laws, therefore, it could be viewed by some as likely to be overruled, sooner or later, by the king's successors. By referring to the *Partidas,* the privilege sought to show that the governmental policy had deep roots in Castile, that it was no invention of Enrique III, and that it was to remain in perpetuity ("for all times"). Thus, the privilege expressed the government's resolve to establish the equality of the conversos—not only in law, but also in life—and oppose any attempt to undermine that equality or reduce it in any measure. Indeed, it aimed at settling, once and for all, the question of the rights of the New Christians in Spain.

III

The decrees issued by the Castilian kings could not, of course, fail to affect the relations between the Old and New Christians. Under the protective shield of the law, the Marranos could now defend themselves against assaults and advance along a broad social front. All the fields of public endeavor that had been firmly closed to Jews appeared to be open to the conversos. Their opponents were now legally disarmed and politically outmaneuvered. But the hatred of the converts was not quenched, and the opposition, although largely suppressed, was far from dead or impotent. Furthermore, it was manifested in a sphere that traditionally had been the converts' stronghold.

This was the sphere of the Spanish Church, whose leaders, while fulminating against the Jews, habitually catered to converts from Judaism and usually defended their rights and interests. Now, however, there appeared Church dignitaries in Spain whose stand on the converso issue was diametrically opposed to the traditional views and practices of the Church. And it was from their circles that the principle of *limpieza*—the discrimination against the converts on purely racial grounds—surfaced in Spain for the first time.

The new attitude seems to have been demonstrated in the course of the establishment of a college for religious studies, later known as the Colegio Viejo de San Bartolomé, in Salamanca. The architect and founder of this institution was Don Diego de Anaya, then bishop of Cuenca,[74] and among the statutes of the constitution he laid down for the college was the provision that no descendants of Jews be admitted as collegians. The language in which that provision is cast indicates quite clearly the extreme position taken by this high dignitary of the Church:

> Since it has always been our will and intention that no person of Jewish origin should be allowed entrance to this college, and since we cannot permit this wish of ours to be forgotten in the course of time, we have stipulated and we order that no one who originates in the said stock [of the Jews], whether from both sides or from one, be admitted to the collegiate and chaplaincy of the said College, and that in this matter no difference be made, whether the grade of origin is remote or near.[75]

According to this regulation, then, anyone even *partly* of Jewish stock, *however remote the degree of kinship,* would be barred from admission to the

school. The regulation was no doubt too extreme to have been adopted c.
1410—that is, at the time when the college was founded, or in 1414–1416, when
its first constitutions were composed.[76] This raises the question of the statute's date, especially since the document in which it is included (the *Statuta
Rectoris et Collegialium*) came down to us undated.[77]

Luis Sala Balust believed that it originates from the middle of the 15th
century,[78] probably because this was the time when Castile was first swept
by a strong anti-Jewish racial agitation. If this were so, the ruling referred to
could not have been proposed by the founder of the college, since Don Diego
died in September 1437.[79] But such a conclusion would not only conflict with
the formal inscription related to this statute, which clearly ascribes it to Don
Diego,[80] but also to other testimonies we possess, which likewise attribute to
the founder of the college the advocacy and institution of its racial policy.
Thus, constitutions and statutes established for the college by the rector and
collegians in 1507 contain the following regulation:

> In conformity with the will of the *archbishop our lord*, of which we are
> certain and which is also known to us from *the collegians who saw his
> letter*, we confirm the statute forbidding any descendant "of the race of
> Jews or Saracens" to be a collegian. And if it is necessary, we issue this
> regulation again by virtue of the authorization we have received from
> Pope Julius II [to establish constitutions and statutes for the College of
> San Bartolomé].[81]

This statute, then, again refers to the archbishop (who could be no other
than Don Diego de Anaya) as the originator of the racial policy in the college,
and it relies on the evidence of certain collegians who saw a letter of the same
archbishop, urging the pursuit of such a policy. But the statute they cite as
containing the words *of the race of Jews and Saracens* was obviously not the
one ascribed to Anaya in the above-mentioned *Statuta Rectoris*, etc.,[82] since
the latter document did not include those words; nor did it deal with descendants of Saracens, but with descendants of Jews only. The statute referring to both Jews and Saracens must have been, therefore, of a later date; it
may have been proposed by Anaya himself in one of his letters to the
authorities of the college, or formulated and introduced by these authorities
following Anaya's proposal.[83]

Coming back to the testimony regarding the "letter," which allegedly
included that proposal, it is strongly supported by other evidence, which
seems unimpeachable. I refer to certain statements included in the biography
of Don Diego de Anaya, written by Ruiz de Vergara y Alava, a member of
Spain's Supreme Council of Justice, and published in Madrid in 1661. In this
work, speaking of Anaya's wish that no person of "impure blood" be admitted
to the college, the author states that the Archbishop Don Diego exhorted the

collegians to fulfill his wish *"in different letters signed by his own hand which we have seen and are kept in the Archives, box 9, numbers 18 and 24."*[84] We may take it for certain, then, that letters urging discrimination against converts *were* written by Don Diego, the founder of the college, since they were *seen* by the author of his biography and their *place in the archives* was clearly pointed out. Moreover, the same biographer attests that Don Diego also formed certain regulations aimed at "guarding and executing" his *limpieza* policy. These "constitutions of the Archbishop our Lord," he says, *"signed by his seal and title,* are found in a sealed sheet of paper in the same box 9, number 9."[85]

The "constitutions" Ruiz de Vergara referred to were most probably the *Statuta Rectoris et Collegialium* that include his ruling about the race of the collegians[86]; and in the light of the afore-cited evidence it is clear that this ruling, too, was made by Don Diego, and not by someone else (as surmised by Sala Balust). Evidently, the archbishop pressed the authorities to adopt that policy for a very long time (probably, from the very foundation of the college), as is suggested in the opening of the undated race statute: "Since it has *always* been our will and intention that no person of Jewish origin shall be allowed entrance to this college . . ."[87]

The letters, which may have been written in Seville (where Anaya served as archbishop since 1418), indicate that the rector and the other college leaders found it difficult to comply with the founder's wishes, even though they may have been in full accord with his thinking and intentions. Moreover, Don Diego de Anaya himself must have found it difficult to implement his policy, for otherwise, it seems, he would not have postponed the formulation of the racial clause from 1414–1416 (the time when he composed the first statutes of the college) to some two decades later, as we shall see below. He was evidently apprehensive of making such a ruling without explicit papal approval, especially since his relations with the papacy were strained and fragile for many years. We should recall that following his appointment as archbishop by Pope Martin V in 1418, he began to agitate against the Pope, so that the latter deprived him of his office (perhaps as early as 1420).[88] And although Anaya was restored to his position on January 13, 1423, he must have known that he had lost the Pope's trust and that he had to be careful not to slip again. In 1431 Martin V died, but Anaya was involved then in a quarrel with his chapter that led to his second dismissal from office in that very year (1431) by Pope Eugene IV. It was only in 1435 that Anaya regained his Sevillian see,[89] and it was, we believe, only then that he felt safe to propose the *Statuta Rectoris et Collegialium*, which contain the racial clause.

One more remark is necessary to complete the story of this document. Anaya left it undated because, in view of its controversial nature, he probably regarded it as a draft proposal which he sent to his friends in Salamanca for consideration, and it *remained* undated because his associates in the college could not see their way clear to accept it. No doubt they believed that, lacking papal sanction, Don Diego's racial policy would cause a scandal in the Church and lead to a conflict between the college and the papacy. They must have communicated their reasons to the archbishop, but shelved the *Statuta Rectoris* for future reference, or until it might be possible to enact them. Understandably, they filed them with the other statutes which Anaya then composed and which they accepted.

This is how we see the sequence of events related to the racial statute of Anaya. Perhaps another more plausible explanation could be offered for the various problems involved.[90] But whether events unfolded thus or otherwise, what occurred in Castile in connection with the founding of one of the major colleges of Salamanca was highly symptomatic of what was brewing in Spain with respect to the converso problem. It shows that opposition to converso integration was not limited to secular society, but had penetrated ecclesiastical circles as well. Anaya may have been then the only Spanish prelate who took such a hard anti-converso line; but there is no doubt that he represented other churchmen, both within and outside his college, who did not have the courage of their convictions. Indeed, to come out in so extreme a manner against the conversos in 1416–1437 meant to court defeat and ignominy. For formally and factually, the Church as a whole stood for the conversion of the Jews in Spain, as well as for the full equality of converts and Old Christians. Similarly, the governments of both Castile and Aragon stood firmly behind this double policy, believing that it represented the only—or best—solution of the Jewish question.

IV

Under the impact of the new realities created by the mass conversion, however, that solution was sorely tested. The resentment stirred by converso penetration into Old Spanish Christian society was bound to be galvanized into formal opposition. And even though anti-converso opinion was in the beginning more subdued than expressed, it was there, and it gathered momentum. New waves of converts were now hitting the shores of Spain's Christian society, and the inroads they made into that society only increased its resentment and stiffened its opposition to their continued penetration.

We have no clear picture of the social processes that developed in this connection at the time. It is manifest, however, that many Old Christians sought legal ways to block converso thrusts into the social spheres they considered vital, while the New Christians resisted these attempts with all the countermeasures they could muster. A legal and political battle ensued, the traces of which can be clearly seen in contemporary documents.

One such document represents the decision of the Council of Basle concerning Jews and converts, which was passed in its nineteenth session, on September 15, 1434. While the Council was radical in its wish to abolish most privileges still enjoyed by Jews in Christian countries, and while insisting on the implementation of the laws enacted in Spain in 1412—including the prohibitions on Jews assuming offices and living in common boroughs with Christians[91]—it came out again in favor of conversion and also in support of converts. It assured any would-be convert that his possessions, whether mobile or immobile, would remain inviolable, and that only property acquired by usury would be restored to the Christian (or Christians) from whom the usury was taken. If that person (or persons) cannot be found, the Church permits the convert to keep his profit on the understanding that he use it for pious ends.[92] As far as poor converts are concerned, "the diocesans should not only encourage the Christian laity to offer these converts aid, but they should also use, as much as they can, Church income to support them. They should also defend them with fatherly affection against insult and contumely, whatever their source."[93]

Following this, the decree makes clear the position of the Church on the issue of equality. "And since they [i.e., the converts] became, by the grace of baptism, fellow citizens with the saints and members of the House of God, and since the regeneration of the spirit is by far more important than the birth in the flesh, we decree it as law through this edict that they enjoy the privileges, liberties and immunities of those cities and localities in which they were regenerated by the sacred baptism in the same measure as the natives and other Christians enjoy therein."[94]

In addition, the decree orders the bishops to see to it that the baptized, both before baptism and after, are instructed in the articles and laws of the new faith, as well as the rites of the Catholic Church. They should further see to it that converts do not converse, at least for a long time, with Jews or other infidels. What is more, they should urge the newcomers to the faith to contract marriages with original Christians.

Passing from the duties of the Old Christians toward the converts to the duties of the converts themselves, the decree lays stress on the following points: "It is forbidden to these neophytes, under grave penalties, to bury the dead according to Jewish custom or to observe the Sabbath, holidays and other rites of their former sect in whatever manner. Just like other Catholics, they should frequently attend our Churches and sermons, and conform to all usages of the Christian faith. Those who violate these rules will be subject to inquiry by their bishop or inquisitors of heresies, and, if found guilty, will be delivered to the secular arm and be punished, so that they may serve as examples to others."[95]

Although the decree was directed to all Christians as a universal law of the

Church, and does not mention Castile or any other Spanish realm, it is clear that the authors were especially concerned with conditions obtaining in Spain. Responding to pressures and counterpressures that were brought to bear upon the papacy and the Council, the decree represents the Church's answer to questions raised by those concerned.

From the anti-Marrano party, we may assume, the Church received complaints against converts from Judaism on both economic and religious grounds. Some of the complaints of the first category (i.e., those that related to economics) may be reconstructed as follows. Many Jews were converted to Christianity merely or primarily to save their fortunes, but these fortunes were accumulated illicitly—that is, through usury, which is forbidden by the Church, and excessive extractions from Christians.[96] As long as these usurers were Jews, there was hope that someday they would be brought to account; but conversion, it seems, gave them the opportunity to escape unpunished with their booty; it legitimized the robbery. Later these converts make use of their wealth to buy positions of power in Christendom, by which they assume control over the Old Christians whom they had first despoiled.

Against this, no doubt, the pro-Marranos claimed that only a few Jews had joined Christendom with some wealth, and still fewer had accumulated that wealth through usury, whereas the great majority of those who came to Christ were in a dismal material position. For the converts forfeit their inheritance rights when they abandon the Jewish fold,[97] lose their economic connections and positions, and actually enter the Church without means. Then, instead of being aided by Old Christians, who now became their coreligionists, they are ignored by them or treated with ill will. It is against these claims and counterclaims that the first point of the decree is directed. It clearly takes both sides into account by trying to accede to the views of those who directed their criticisms against the *rich* conversos, and the counterposition of those who criticized the attitude of the Old Christians toward the *poor* neophytes. But what emerges from all this is that both rich and poor converts were confronted with hatred and abuse, and that all of them faced a general desire to deny them the share in the common welfare which they believed was rightfully theirs.

In attacking the conversos on religious grounds, their opponents must have sought to justify the refusal to grant them equal status by claiming that, in reality, the conversos were not Christians, but Jews who covertly followed Jewish law. In response, the converso advocates no doubt claimed that if some conversos were not yet fully committed to the Catholic faith and way of life, or even practicing some Jewish rites, it was only because they had never received proper religious instruction. The Church accepted this explanation and ordered the bishops to instruct the neophytes both before and *after* baptism. On the other hand, it issued a stern warning to the converts to avoid following customs of their "ancient sect" (such as those regarding burial and observation of the Sabbath), while it also enjoined them to be scrupulous in observing Catholic dogma, law and ritual.

Thus, the decree of Basle reflected the tense conflict that was developing in Spain between the Old and New Christians. While it assured the conversos equality of rights, it also threatened them with an inquiry; and this was probably the first time that the idea of applying an inquisition for the conversos appeared in the literature of the period. It was a compromise that aimed at satisfying both parties and, in all likelihood, fully satisfied neither. Yet on balance the decree favored the conversos. They had sought the council's confirmation of their status as Christian citizens who were rightfully on a par with all other such citizens; and this they obtained. The decree equalizes the converts with the Old Christians; it reaffirms their right to public office; it forbids denunciations to be uttered against them on grounds of their former religion; it recommends the extension of help to their poor, not only morally but also materially; and it urges intermarriage between converts and Old Christians as the best means of bringing the groups together and ultimately eliminating the conflict. Doubtless the statement was made in reaction to the tendency toward racial segregation which, by then, already had many advocates; and the assimilationist leaders of the conversos, such as Alonso de Cartagena, chief delegate from Castile, welcomed—or demanded—its inclusion in the decree.[98]

As for the paragraph concerning the inquisition, it seems that it too represented a compromise. While the conversos insisted that all religious inquiries concerning the New Christians be conducted by the ordinary ecclesiastical authorities (i.e., the bishops), the anti-Marranos no doubt demanded that these inquiries be made by special inquisitors appointed to the task of investigating heresies.[99] The formulation of the Basle decree on this point reads "bishops *or* inquisitors," thus legitimizing each party's view and actually leaving the question unresolved. To the representatives of the Marranos, however, it was clear that the Basle formulation on this point, though it thwarted the plan to establish an inquisition for the conversos *in the near future*, did not remove the threat of its establishment at some later time. In any case, it is unlikely that they opposed to the end the proposed stipulation as ultimately accepted. It is more likely that, sooner or later, they felt obliged to nod their consent. For ostensibly, there was nothing in that formulation to which a true Catholic could object.

V

It is difficult to say what practical effect the Basle decree had on the conversos' condition. In Castile, it was probably used by the Crown to justify its policy with respect to the New Christians; and the foremost converso leaders in that country, who occupied high positions in the Church, must have publicized it far and wide. Perhaps the conversos in Castile could note concrete gains as a result of the Basle decree. But insofar as Aragon was concerned, no such gains were visible, it seems. We gather this from a formal petition submitted by the Aragonese conversos to Pope Eugene IV on January 31, 1437.

The submission of this petition to the Pope indicates that the conversos could expect no relief from either the municipal authorities in Aragon or from the royal administration. Alfonso V, king of Aragon, was engrossed at the time in his Italian affairs; and while he lived in Naples, Aragon was run by his wife, Doña María, and his brother, Juan of Navarre, father of the future Ferdinand the Catholic and himself the future king of Aragon. All this strengthened the position of Cortes, the representatives of popular opinion, which in any case was more influential in Aragon than it was in Castile.

Referring to the origins of the conversion in Aragon—namely, the outbreaks of 1391—the conversos' petition begins by pointing out that the new converts entered the Church deprived of all their earthly possessions. This is a straight reply to the charges about the conversos' ill-acquired wealth, which were echoed, as we have seen, in the Basle decree of 1434. "Christ, however, in His pity," the petitioners continued, "saw to it that those who were so baptized would prosper," and thus "by their legitimate labors and talents they gained many possessions" and have their crafts. Almost all who were baptized on the occasion of that riot are dead by now, while "all of the survivors were, for the larger part, born in the Catholic faith, educated in it, and live according to its rites."[100] There are, however, others who, "under the influence of Pedro de Luna, once known in these countries as Benedict XIII, and the preaching of some notable men, recognized the truth and, illumined by the true light . . . , have voluntarily and eagerly obtained, together with their wives and children, regeneration through the sacred waters [of baptism], shedding the old man and acquiring the new. And thus there were baptized, thanks to Christ's help, more than three thousand persons who have ever since lived as good and true Catholics.[101] They retain no memory of their infidelity and glory to be protected in the fold of the true and eternal Shepherd."[102]

Two things are emphasized here. First, that the original generation of converts who went over to Christianity during the riots of 1391 has almost disappeared, while the new generation, which constitutes the overwhelming majority of the conversos, was born and reared in the Catholic faith and lived according to Catholic law. Second, that the camp of New Christians contained many converts who came to Christianity not coercively but of their own volition (such as those who joined Christendom after the Tortosa

Disputation). This description of the background or origins and way of life of the conversos of Aragon meant, of course, to show that there was no reason to assume that a large number of conversos lived secretly as Jews or lacked devotion to the Catholic faith.

"Certain sons of iniquity," however, "who are Christians only in name"—the document continues—"strive to separate these recent converts to Christianity, and not only them, but also their descendants, who were begotten in the bosom of Holy Mother Church, from the other Christians by refusing them admission to the public offices or to the councils and government of the cities.[103] To this end, they have enacted certain statutes and ordinances in which they treat these conversos and their descendants as infidels. They "refuse to enter into matrimony with them" and, on top of this, "subject them to such vituperation that they [i.e., the conversos] now find themselves in a condition worse than they would be in if they still were Jews. Indeed, the Jews and other infidels ridicule them by saying that they gained no improvement by their baptism and that they would have fared better if they had remained in the Judaic blindness." Because of this, many Jews are changing their minds with respect to conversion, "giving up their original intent to go over to Christianity."[104]

These citations point very clearly to the religious and social conditions of the conversos in Aragon in the middle of the thirties. Religiously, they saw themselves as Christians; they had "abandoned" Judaism, were "educated" in Christianity, and "behaved" as true Christians do. Yet socially, they were discriminated against and, in fact, regarded as outcasts. A wall had been raised between them and the Old Christians by denying them admission to the public offices; by refusing to contract marriages with them; and by the nationwide campaign of denunciation and vilification which was incessantly waged against them. The Council of Basle, as we have seen, forbade all these abuses, but its decree was evidently of little effect. In their petition, the conversos do not hesitate to state that their condition is worse than that of the Jews, that socially they might have fared better in the Jewish fold, and that their degradation has deterred many Jews, who otherwise would have converted to Christianity, from taking that radical step.

Whether factual or conjectural, the argument was calculated to influence the Pope, who appreciated the great role that the oppression of the Jews played in their conversion. But no doubt it also reflected the views of many conversos concerning their own problem and the Jewish question in general; for they came to believe that it was in their interests, as well as those of their former brethren, that the latter follow in their footsteps and join the Catholic Church. But if the status of the converts was unenviable—if, like the Jews, they were subject to abuses, recriminations and disabilities of various kinds—the movement toward conversion would naturally end.

The extent to which the conditions referred to were intolerable to the conversos is indicated by the following statement: "When the said converts, their children and progeny see themselves thus oppressed and separated from the Church and the sheepfold of Jesus Christ, who adopted His precious flesh out of their own people—the people whom he first sought to redeem . . . and with whose converts He established the . . . foundations of the Church—they turn with tears and heartache, and with great concern, to the Pope who is the vicar of Christ on earth and whose duty it is to lead the sheep to one fold and guard the unity of the Christian Church."[105]

Even though couched in religious terms, the complaint clearly transcends the religious issue and has distinct social and racial overtones. The emphasis of the Marranos upon the principle of Church unity and their protest against the attempt to "cut them off from that union" and "separate them from the bosom of the faithful" is, of course, another way of indicating their struggle against social and racial segregation. Similarly, their reference to the out-standing facts (a) that Jesus emerged from their people and (b) that Jewry was the cradle of Christianity was made not merely to underscore the injustice done them, or to move the Pope to show them special consideration, but also—and above all—to indicate the falsehood of the criticisms made of their racial origin. Echoing their response to these criticisms by which they were accused of racial baseness and thus declared unfit for intermarriage, the argument advanced here is essentially the same as the one presented in 1449, when the issue of Marranism as a question of race exploded in the midst of a political storm. Another remark in this document, as we shall see, further supports our interpretation that the mention of their kinship with Jesus, which seemingly implies claims of racial superiority, was essentially a re-sponse to the charges leveled at them concerning their alleged racial inferior-ity. Deeply offended by these charges and the atmosphere of contempt that surrounded them, the conversos, understandably, *liked* to point out their ethnic relationship to Jesus Christ. It bolstered their dignity, which they cherished, and it served simultaneously as an effective answer to the claims of their critics and vilifiers. The situation was both agonizing and complex, and the Marranos turned to the Pope, as they say, "with tears and with heartache and with great concern." We may take this statement as actually denoting their state of mind at the time.

They beseech the Pope to "encourage" the conversos, whom they describe as "oppressed and distressed," by "annulling all the statutes and ordinances against them that serve to the degradation of the orthodox faith." They also ask him to instruct the diocesan authorities that, under pain of ecclesiastical censure and other measures, they "restrain and prevent the secular officials of whatever rank, the communities and other persons, public and private, from doing the above-mentioned things, and thus insure that the newly converted and their descendants be treated in all matters and in every respect in the same manner as all other Christians, and that no difference be made between them and others under the pretext of their descent from the Jewish people."[106]

The last sentence clearly relates to what we said about the racial aspect of the anti-Marrano agitation. As we gather from our document, it was in the bureaucracies and administrations of the towns that most of the opposition to the Marranos was centered, indicating that the Marranos' persistent attempts to penetrate the royal and municipal officialdom had encountered strong resistance. It was therefore primarily from these circles that the racial agitation against the Marranos emerged. In any case, discrimination against them was practiced in these areas not only by means of administrative procedures, but also through formal and legal measures. We know that *statutes and ordinances were enacted against them*—or rather against their admission to the councils, as well as all other public offices—for they asked the Pope to have them annulled; and these statutes were evidently based not on a religious but on a racial principle or, in the language of our documents, on the "pretext" that the conversos "descended from the Jews." Thus, the discriminatory racial ruling proposed by Anaya for the college of Salamanca did not remain an isolated incident. *There was a direct line of development leading from Salamanca through the enactments in Aragon to the* Sentencia-Estatuto *of 1449.*

It is apparent that no action on behalf of the conversos was taken at the time by the kings of Aragon, and that no special decrees or privileges were then issued in their defense. Otherwise, the petitioners would have mentioned this fact, or might not have turned to the Pope in the first place. This is where the situation of the conversos in Aragon differed radically from that in Castile. For in Castile the kings did take stern measures in defense of the conversos' rights, and their consistent policy on this issue enabled the conversos to move steadily ahead. The result was that in Castile, unlike Aragon, the Old Christians were faced with real opposition, and though they were the larger faction, they saw themselves on the losing side. Consequently, the situation could not be decided in favor of one party or the other. For the losers refused to accept defeat, while the winners refused to give up their gains; and both parties kept building their strength—the Marranos by acquiring new positions, the anti-Marranos by acquiring new followers. To those who could read the signs of the times, it must have been evident that both sides were headed irreversibly toward a violent collision.

VI

At about the time that the Council of Basle was grappling with the converso problem, certain events occurred in Castile that clearly revealed the social background against which the Basle decree was enacted. They indicate, above all, that the hatred of the conversos, and the opposition to their social integration, had not diminished in Spanish society, but, on the contrary, had increased and assumed a potentially explosive nature.

The events referred to were related to the revolt which Don Fadrique, Count of Luna, sought to organize in Seville in 1434. Seville, as we know, was an old center of virulent and ingrained anti-Jewish feeling. In its precincts there broke out, in 1391, that tidal wave of pogroms which swept across the peninsula and almost put an end to Spanish Jewry. In that very year, in the midst of a massacre, most of Seville's Jews went over to Christianity, and the presence of a large converso community was thenceforth a part of Seville's social scene. We may assume that here—as elsewhere in Spain—the industrious and ambitious Jews turned Christian, now freed from the shackles of their past disabilities, advanced toward the attainment of economic affluence and social influence and prestige. What reaction this engendered among their Christian neighbors, what feelings they harbored toward the New Christians, what the communal climate in the city was, and how the Old and New Christians got along together, can be guessed from what we know about Castile as a whole. The events related below, however, allow us to exchange our guesses and conjectures for more definite knowledge.

The Count of Luna—son of Martín the Young, king of Sicily, who died in 1409—settled in Castile in 1430. Politically, the Count was a frustrated politician, for he had aspired to the throne of Aragon, which he thought was his by right of inheritance, but was turned over to Fernando de Antequera, who bequeathed it to his son Alfonso V. While originally his relations with Alfonso were friendly, later they seemed to have been strained or ruptured; and from information that reached Castile about the Count, it appeared that he was in a rebellious mood and, furthermore, intended to leave his country and put himself at the service of the Castilian king. Since Castile was at odds with Aragon, it was probably believed by Alvaro de Luna that the Count, an enemy of the adversary, could be useful to the Castilian Crown. Thus, no doubt on the advice of Alvaro, Juan II granted Don Fadrique an estate that enabled him to live honorably in Castile.

The Count, however, soon became dissatisfied with both the passive role and the limited income assigned to him by King Juan's administration. Settling in Seville, at the home of his sister, who was married to the powerful Count of Niebla, he befriended several Sevillian nobles, such as Fernán Alvarez Osorio and Lope Alfonso de Montemolín, and made himself popular in their circles. Then, feeling the rising tide of unrest in a city that was leaning toward the Infante Enrique, he persuaded himself that he could play a major part in Spain's political life. He knew that his chances of gaining real influence in the Castilian Court were actually nil. He had nothing to offer the Crown of Castile; but he could make a contribution to the Crown of Aragon, and reestablish himself in its good graces, if he joined the Aragonese party in Castile and delivered to it such an asset as Seville—the most important commercial center of the country and the richest of all Castilian towns. The capture of Seville could pave the way to a complete overthrow of Alvaro's government and to the establishment of one of the Infantes of Aragon in the seat of power in Castile. The Count could then present an account for services that were actually beyond remuneration.

The social conditions he found in Seville appeared to suit his ambitions. Much of the city's wealth and commerce seemed to be concentrated in the hands of two groups, which the Sevillians regarded as alien and hence as unwanted competitors. These were the conversos and the Genoese. It seems that the resentment toward these groups was so strong that the Count and his associates seriously believed that if their plans for the rebellion would secure the elimination of these two groups from the city, the citizens of Seville would join them in the uprising. It was, after all, the government of Alvaro that backed these hated intruders.

This, then, in our opinion, is how the rebels' considerations ought to be reconstructed. There is no direct intimation of this in any of the sources related to that affair. It can be inferred, however, from the annals of the time—though only after much search and speculation, for the annals conceal rather than reveal all that relates to the Marranos in this case. And as we shall see, this concealment was not limited to this case alone.

VII

The most detailed account of Don Fadrique's plot is found in the *Crónica de Juan II* which was written by Alvar García de Santa María. García, the brother of Paul of Burgos and himself a notable converso, served at the time as the official chronicler of the kingdoms of Juan II. There is no doubt that he was well informed of the facts relating to the case under consideration, and particularly those concerning the Marranos. Yet what he tells us about it, in his own words, is limited to the following statement:

> We have already mentioned in some of the earlier years[107] how Don Fadrique, Count of Luna, came to the kingdom, and of the grants of towns, villages and incomes that the king gave him every year, both such as included the right of inheritance and others that were only for

life, as well as the many honors that the king Juan II bestowed upon his person. Nor should one pass in silence over the patience the king showed in consenting to the many bad deals that the count made with the grants he had received; for he sold the towns and villages the king gave him, except for the town of Cuellar. He also sold some of the incomes he had gotten, both those with inheritance rights and those given for life.

The moneys he received from these sales, he did not invest in necessary matters; nor did liberality motivate the manner in which he spent these funds. He was lavish, wasteful and devoid of moderation, and he squandered the money with men of low station and little value. He also became involved in many rows and brawls with other persons of the same manners and other dishonest pursuits.

So great was the speed with which he spent the money acquired from what he had sold, that it would last only a few days after he had received it. Considering these and other misdeeds of his, the king could justifiably refuse to consent to so many bad arrangements. The matter concerned the king, for when the Count was short of money, the king had to sustain him, although from what he had originally obtained from the king he could well maintain a larger estate than the one he had in Aragon. But the king, being well disposed toward him and not wishing to displease him, tolerated his actions and agreed to the aforesaid bad arrangements and many others that he had made.

The Count of Luna, however, did not esteem all these favors, honors and aid that he had received from the king; and having forgotten all about them, he plotted, while in Seville and this land, with some people of Seville and *Andalusia,* that they rob and kill, in the city *and outside it,* those whom they wished to, and *that they rise with Andalusia* in favor of the kings of Aragon and Navarre and the Infantes, their brothers, *with whom, prior to this, he had dealings and discussions* through letters and messengers. The plotters were certain that they would not receive, from the administration of justice, the punishment they deserved, for (so they thought) very soon they would be joined by the above-mentioned [i.e., the rulers of Aragon], with whom the Count had his talks, and they would defend them.

It did not please God that this evil plan of his and those allied with him should materialize; for, since in the negotiations that were conducted many persons of good intention were involved, these revealed the matter to the king or to others who revealed it to him. The king, before taking any action in this matter, ordered a secret inquiry to be made, through which what we have said above, or most of it, was discovered; for a document was found with the signatures of those who negotiated the conspiracy.

Therefore, when the Count of Luna came to the court at Medina and stayed there for fifteen or twenty days, the king ordered his arrest, and instructed García Fernández Manrique, the Count of Castañeda, that he put Don Fadrique in his place of lodging. There he was imprisoned for a few days, before he was transferred to the Castle of Urueña.[108]

So much for the Count himself. Alvar García's account, however, also offers some data about his partners in crime:

> From what was established through the inquiry, and from what appeared in the [related] documents, the king ordered the arrest in Seville and in the Court of certain persons whose names, as we have indicated, appeared on the document which bore upon those negotiations. They were Lope Alfonso de Montemolín, Fernand Alvarez Osorio, Pero González, public notary of Seville, and González Martín of Medina.
>
> Others, who were also arrested with these, were released after having been found guiltless. As for the four mentioned above, they were brought to the Court, interrogated in due manner, and after they had confessed to their evil actions, the King ordered their public execution, namely, that two of them, Lope Alfonso and Fernand Alvarez, be quartered, and the other two beheaded. He also ordered the perpetual imprisonment of a certain Franciscan friar, a native of Portugal, who was involved in these negotiations. Prior to his imprisonment he was to suffer the shame of being placed by the bishop on a rostrum in the public square [as a treacherous conspirator].[109]

Alvar García was both a circumspect historian and an accomplished writer; but he was also a court chronicler and a diplomat. Giving much thought to what he said and left unsaid, he carefully weighed the contents, structure and order of his statements. As chronicler, García's task, as he saw it, was both to *portray* the events and *explain* them—that is, to point out their causes; and his accounts are usually distinguished by their clarity, accuracy and incisiveness. His tale of the Count of Fadrique, however, is a notable exception. It contains ambiguities and unexplained data, and it raises more questions than it answers.

Above all, we are not clear about the motives (particularly the *main* motive) of the rebels—that is, the Count and his chief associates, Lope Alfonso de Montemolín and Fernand Alvarez Osorio. Both of the latter were, as we have indicated, Sevillian nobles of no mean repute, and one of them, Alfonso de Montemolín, was actually in charge of Sevillian affairs. It was not the first time that Castilian nobles, who felt they had scores to settle with Alvaro, or were deeply dissatisfied with his regime, had turned to the party of the Infantes; and so we may assume that the abovementioned nobles developed their highly ambitious scheme. But then we do not know what is behind the statement that they planned "to rob and kill those whom they wished to." Were these intended victims personal foes or political rivals of the conspirators? Or were they such staunch supporters of Alvaro, or such faithful officials of the king, that the conspirators deemed their liquidation essential for the success of the uprising? If the latter answer is correct, we are still puzzled about the plan to *rob* them—or perhaps others as well. Robbery during revolutions or riots was often carried out by mobs, but was not the common practice of rebellious nobles who intended to gain wealth by power. And why should the rebels have concentrated on "robbing" when they set out to capture the richest territory in Castile and, ultimately, the whole country? Yet Alvar García mentions the robbing *as if it were the first item on their agenda.*

One may gather from this that the Count, the reckless squanderer, and his chief associates, who may have been as greedy, wanted to become rich overnight at the expense of their intended victims. If so, it is clear that this plan of theirs to satisfy their private craving for wealth could be of no interest to the numerous Andalusians whose active support they must have sought. In fact, we wonder what kind of promises were held out to the latter. What were the motives, we ask, that could induce—or be regarded by the rebels as capable of inducing—many citizens of Seville and Andalusia to rise against their king? Was it concern for the nation's welfare, or a desire to solve some vexing *local* problems? Or perhaps was gain by robbery also offered *them* as a means of attracting them to the conspiracy? Perhaps, indeed. But in this case, the people who were designated to be robbed must have constituted a large group to satisfy the numerous would-be attackers, and consequently, our curiosity again turns to the question: Who were they "whom they wished to rob and kill"?

Since García does not offer answers to these questions, we turn to another contemporary *crónica*—that of Pedro Carrillo de Huete, who was known as the King's Falconer *(el Halconero)*. He, too, was an official chronicler of Juan II, and his work is a major source for the period, especially from 1435, when the services of García as Court Chronicler were terminated for reasons still unclear. Carrillo, however, did not start his chronicle with a narrative of the occurrences of 1435. He wrote a history of the reign from its very beginnings, and thus his work includes an account of the Fadrique affair in 1434. What came down to us of Carrillo's chronicle, however, is not the original, but revised versions, mostly abridged. One of these, which was recently published as the *Refundición de la Crónica del Halconero,* served as source and basis for the well-known *Crónica de Juan II,* commonly ascribed to Pérez de Guzmán. Guzmán, however, follows this source not from 1435, as has often been suggested,[110] but from 1433, and thus, his account of the conspiracy of

Don Fadrique is based not on García, but on Carrillo—or rather on Carrillo's abridged account, as found in the version that Guzmán used. Let us see, then, what Guzmán's *Crónica* holds for us on the Fadrique affair.

After recounting the Count's arrest, the confiscation of his property and the unsuccessful intercession on his behalf by his sister, the Countess of Niebla, the *Crónica de Juan II* comes to the point which interests us most. It says:

> The reason for the imprisonment of the Count of Luna, was that it was found, by inquiry, that he negotiated with certain caballeros and other persons of the city of Seville for the purpose of appointing him as leader and delivering into his hands the arsenals and the Castle of Triana and that they rob the richest citizens [*ciudadanos*] and the Genoese of the city.[111]

Now, if we examine the version of the Halconero that Guzmán's *Crónica de Juan II* followed—i.e., the *Refundición*—we find that it offers an identical account of the rebels' aims, except that the *Refundición* omits the reference to the Genoese. It merely says that they wanted to "rob the richest citizens" of Seville.[112] So either the *original* text of the Halconero which was used by Guzmán contained the words "and the Genoese," or Guzmán may have taken this information from a different source. More significant, however, than the addition of the words "and the Genoese" in the *Crónica de Juan II* is the omission (in both this *Crónica* and the *Refundición*) of any mention of the political association of the rebels with the Infantes of Aragon. By suppressing this important fact, which is attested by Alvar García, the rebellion is made to appear as if it had a local purpose only. If we had not known from Alvar García that the rebels allied themselves with the Aragonese on whom they pinned their hopes for help; had we relied for our information only on the *Crónica* of Guzmán and its source, the *Refundición*, we would not understand how the rebels could expect to get away with their crimes. Yet it is evident that this was precisely what Guzmán's *Crónica* and the *Refundición* wanted to convey—namely, that the conspirators had no other motive except the desire to satisfy local interests or, more clearly, to become masters of Seville and "rob the rich" of the city. Moreover, the proclamation of the town crier of Medina del Campo concerning the execution of the chief rebels, which the editor of the *Refundición* appended to his account, seems to agree with this interpretation, or at least does not indicate any other motive. The text runs as follows:

> This is the judgment which the King our lord ordered to do to these people who made alliances and a conspiracy in the King's disservice, and took for themselves a leader in order to get control of the arsenals

of Seville and of its Castle of Triana and to rob and kill the rich and honored citizens of that city.[113]

The reader who knows what Alvar García tells us may suspect of course that by the "alliances and conspiracy" which were made by the rebels "in the King's disservice" the alliance with Aragon is alluded to; but we have no way of knowing this from the *Crónica de Juan II*, which was edited by Guzmán, or from the version of the Halconero which that *Crónica* followed. The Aragonese aspect of the story was clearly suppressed, and thus we may assume that an attempt was made here to present the entire abortive revolt as the mere brainchild of some Sevillian adventurers who envied the "rich, and the honored" in the city and aspired to get their positions and fortunes.

Nevertheless, the item concerning the "Genoese" in Seville, who were singled out for attack by the rebels—an item found only in Guzmán's *Crónica de Juan II*—falls in with the broader plan of the rebels, which is indicated by García. Genoa was then embroiled in bitter conflict with Alfonso V of Aragon, and an attack upon the Genoese colony in Seville would certainly have pleased the Aragonese. As we have indicated, the Sevillians, too, looked with much disfavor on the prosperous Genoese colony in their midst. That this colony could exist in Seville at all was due to the special charters and privileges the Genoese received from the Castilian kings[114]; and therefore an attack upon the Genoese in Seville would also be construed as an act of rebellion against the king of Castile. Thus, by piecing together the relevant elements in the three sources cited—Alvar García, the *Refundición*, and the *Crónica de Juan II* edited by Guzmán—we can see that besides the desire to bring to power the party of the Infantes of Aragon, there was also a local irritant—the Genoese—which could serve as a desirable target for attack. Still, we cannot clearly see the motive that could have been considered likely to cement a popular force behind the rebels' union. To be sure, we may assume that many Sevillians had grudges against the Genoese in the city; but if so, how could this be expected to induce many citizens in *other* Andalusian towns, which did *not* have Genoese colonies in their midst,[115] to join the rebels' ranks? Nevertheless, it is obvious that the plotters relied on some genuine rancor, or interest, or desire shared by *many* in the Andalusian *cities* and not only by the people of Seville, if they expected to draw a substantial part of their populations to their side. Yet what that factor was, or could possibly be, is not apparent in the accounts we have examined.

We would not even have begun to suspect that the Marrano issue played a major role in the plans of the conspirators to gain popular support had there not survived another version of the *Halconero*, which likewise remained unpublished until our own time. That version, too, is not the original *Hal-*

conero, but only a revised abbreviation of it; yet at least at one point it is closer to the original than the version used by Pérez de Guzmán. Its tale of the conspiracy is even more abridged, and the aims it ascribes to the leading rebels seem even vaguer in its summarized narrative; but in presenting the text of the town crier's proclamation, the *Halconero* supplies a startling item of information which is missing in the other accounts. The text, in this version, reads as follows:

> This is the judgment which the king our Lord ordered to do to these people who made alliances and a conspiracy in his disservice, and took for themselves a leader in order to get control of the arsenals of Seville and its Castle of Triana *and kill the conversos,* and rob those whom they might be able to in the city of Seville, and deliver the arsenals and the Castle of Triana to the enemies of the King.[116]

It is clear, therefore, that the editor of this version, who saw himself free to abbreviate and alter the original account of the *Halconero,* so as to suggest that the conspiracy was nothing but a plan of a robber band to sack the rich or "some" of the rich people of Seville, found himself stymied when he was confronted with the text of the town crier's proclamation. He obviously felt that to change such a text, and to let the changed text appear as the original— as did the editor of the other version of the *Halconero*—would amount to outright falsification, and therefore he left the proclamation untouched. Thus, its text reveals what the other versions or accounts based on the *Halconero* conceal—namely, that there was a secret alliance between the conspirators and the "King's enemies" (i.e., the Infantes of Aragon), to whom they wanted to deliver the arsenals of Seville and the Castle of Triana (which is in full agreement with what is related in the *crónica* of Alvar García de Santa María).[117] But it also tells us what was suppressed by all the other chronicles we have cited, including that of Alvar García—namely, that the first planned action of the rebels after capturing the city was to carry out a *massacre of the conversos*—and this, of course, explains how and why they could attract "many" to their plan, not only in Seville but also in other Andalusian cities, in almost all of which the conversos formed a considerable element of the population.

Thus, the political alliance with the Aragonese party was bolstered by the strong resentment that many Andalusians felt for the conversos. Killing and robbing the conversos, together with the other rich "aliens"—the Genoese— may have served as a sufficient inducement for many to join the conspiracy and side with the party of the Infantes, whose invasion and conquest of Andalusia could be seen as the only means by which the local Old Christian population could rid itself of all the hated "aliens," and especially of the conversos, and establish themselves as the real masters of Andalusia's administration and economy.[118] This also explains the special role that a Portuguese friar could play in a plot which, according to all available accounts, related to Castilians and Aragonese (but not to Portugal) and which had economic and political motives but no religious connotations at all. A planned attack upon the conversos, however, did have a religious aspect. In such a plan any churchman of whatever country could play an effective part, depending on his views and powers of persuasion. The Portuguese friar seems to have offered the rebels the religious approval which they needed and which they had evidently failed to obtain from the Church leaders of Andalusia or Seville.

There can be no doubt that the Halconero, who was fully familiar with all the elements of the case (as all the courtiers of Juan II must have been), recorded the main facts indicated in the town crier's proclamation, which he incorporated in his original account. There can also be no doubt that the editors deliberately changed his narrative so as to weaken its national significance, and that their desire to omit all mention of the conversos overrode all considerations of truth. In one instance, as we have seen, they went so far as to mutilate the very text of the town crier—an official document which indicated clearly both the findings of the judges (in the case of the accused) and the official reasons given for the public executions. Who could be interested in suppressing the converso aspect of the Sevillian conspiracy? As we shall show elsewhere in this work, it was only converso historians or editors, or someone closely allied with the conversos, who had substantial reasons to do so.[119]

Alvar García was a converso. He did not want to present the revolt of Don Fadrique as an attempt based on the provocative assumption that the populace of Seville and other cities of Andalusia could be persuaded to take up arms against the king only if they were allowed, in the first stage of the uprising, to rob and massacre the conversos. Evidently, he refused to inform his readers that hatred for the Marranos had reached such extremes that it served as an inducement to rebellion against the King. Obviously, some people might gather from this that the Marranos endangered the existence of the state. Consequently, he chose to eliminate from his account *any* mention of the conversos; and since he refrained from touching upon *them,* he obviously had to avoid mentioning the Genoese. Thus, he covered *both* groups with the obscure and non-committal assertion that the rebels planned "to rob and kill whom they wished to," and presented the whole affair as the brainchild of a corrupt and callous adventurer opposed by all "citizens of good intentions" and shorn of any social significance.[120] The facts of the case, however, were quite different. Whatever the aims and ambitions of the conspirators, it is clear that they believed that the hatred of the conversos— and, in fact, the ardent desire to destroy them—was so widespread in Seville and other cities that it could serve as a vehicle for their plans. And since some of them were Sevillian leaders, few could know better than they the public moods and social conditions in Andalusia. It can hardly be doubted, therefore, that the Marrano situation there offered fertile soil for the conspiracy. What the rebels did was merely to prompt its growth by promising assistance from an outside party.

The discovery of the plot in due time and the exemplary punishment of the rebel leaders nipped the conspiracy in the bud. But what had actually been in the making was the rebellion of a great Castilian city against the King, nurtured by the desire to destroy the conversos, and encouraged by the hope of obtaining support from the King's foes in Aragon. What was incipient in Seville in 1434 came to life fifteen years later, in the Toledan rebellion of 1449.

VIII

On July 13, 1444, Juan II issued a cedula to the councils of the principal cities in the kingdom, demanding that their administrations of justice avoid any discrimination against the conversos, that the latter be treated "as if they were born Christians," and that they fully enjoy the right to be admitted to "all honorable offices of the Republic."[121]

The date of the cedula is significant. Less than a month earlier, on June 16, the King had escaped from the virtual captivity in which he was held by Juan of Navarre, the head of the Aragonese party, and now he was making a strenuous bid to recapture the power he had lost. In the north he was engaged in a military campaign aimed at conquering all the strongholds on the Duero controlled by the Infantes; and on July 18, five days after he had signed the cedula referred to, he launched his assault on the castle of Peñafiel, which was to last until August 16. In addition, the King was faced with the task of overcoming the forces of the Infante Enrique, who held in his grip a good part of Andalusia and was moving northward toward Toledo.[122] What led Juan II at such a time, in the midst of hasty preparations for battle, and while taxed with so many pressing problems, to issue that cedula on behalf of the conversos?

What is more, as Amador de los Ríos tells us, the cedula was addressed not to one or two cities, but to all the principal towns and cities of the kingdom.[123] Thus, it amounted to a royal declaration of national policy on the converso issue and, consequently, assumed extraordinary significance. So the question we have raised may now be posed as follows: What made Juan II declare that policy at the very beginning of his reborn reign?

Since there are only a few data to go on, any reconstruction can be only hypothetical. Nevertheless, from the available facts several conclusions may be drawn with certitude.

To begin with, it is obvious that the Marrano problem—the struggle of the Old Christians to reduce the status of the New—had become so widespread and assumed such proportions that no longer was it considered a "local" issue—that is, limited to a few places—but one that assumed *national* proportions and required treatment on a national scale. This is why the King's order was directed to all major towns and cities of the kingdom.

Second, it is obvious that the problem had become *acute*—namely, that the struggle against the Marranos had intensified, that it was expressed in many abuses of their rights, and that the Marranos felt themselves so hard-pressed as to solicit the King's help. We draw these conclusions from the following assumptions, which we regard as hardly controvertible: first, that no such intervention on behalf of the Marranos would have been made by the King, especially at that time, unless preceded by strong Marrano pleas; and second, that the Marranos had been waiting *impatiently* for the change that now took place in the regime, and lost no time in making their requests once Juan II resumed his independence. This leads us inevitably to the additional conclusion that something untoward had happened to the Marranos during the reign of the Infantes of Aragon—something that caused a deterioration of their situation—and that the calls for help they had addressed to the Infantes had evoked no favorable response.

The main causes of this deterioration are not too difficult to guess. In the three years during which the royal administration was virtually in the hands of Juan of Navarre, the grip of the Infantes on the country was loose and decidedly insecure. Confronted by a nobility with divided allegiances and constantly shifting political positions, the Infantes could hope only for the support of the cities. But the cities, traditionally opposed to the great barons and especially distrustful of the rapacious Infantes, were more interested in exploiting their weakness than contributing to its elimination. In the meantime, secure in their strategic strength and the rulers' great need of their assistance, the cities felt free to disregard some or all of the laws that protected the conversos. Cautious and pragmatic, Juan of Navarre, who was heading the party of the Infantes, refused to turn the converso issue into a *casus belli* with the cities.

But on June 16, 1444, when Juan II escaped from his captivity, the political scene changed overnight. Juan of Navarre hastily withdrew eastward to the borders of Aragon, and power was again seized by the King and Alvaro de Luna. The war, however, was far from over; the opposing armies were hardly reduced, and there was every likelihood that Juan of Navarre, supported by substantial forces from Aragon, would soon return to the field. Surely it was in the King's vital interest to mobilize the nation behind him at that hour; the cities were a major part of the nation; and he ought, it seems, to have looked to them for both financial and military aid. A cedula rebuking them on their policy toward the conversos of the kind he sent them on July 13 was certainly not the best way to win their friendship at the opening of his restored rule.

And yet the cedula was issued. This, we believe, supports the assumption that, besides making their own appeals, the Marranos used some of their Old Christian friends to bend the Crown to their position. Men like Bishop Lope de Barrientos, whose influence was great at that stage, could have been responsible for the issuance of the cedula.[124] It is also likely that Marranos contributed large sums to the war chest of the King. This could counter-balance, at least to some extent, the delayed or all too limited assistance the cities were ready to offer at that point.

But whatever influences the Marranos brought to bear, whether political or material or both, the issuance of the cedula at that time must have been seen as a bold stroke of policy by the government of Juan II. Indeed, the case of the Marranos could well be one in which Alvaro's political strength was tested. For nothing so symbolized the reinstatement of Alvaro and the re-sumption by the King of his royal duties as the declaration of the policy of full equality for the Old and New Christians.

Alvaro, however, was fighting at the time not only for his favored, tradi-tional policies, but also, and first of all, for his political survival; and as a pragmatist and shrewd calculator, he avoided risks when these were not essential. No doubt the issuance of the pro-Marrano cedula involved a certain risk for his administration; he must have weighed the pros and cons and probably decided that the gamble was minor and, in any case, worth taking. Thus we touch on the most important reason for the issuance of the cedula.

Indubitably, Alvaro assessed the country's mood and the alternatives avail-able for at least the largest cities. And what he concluded must have been encouraging. *Politically*, most cities, like the country as a whole, were aching to shake off the rule of the Infantes, who came to be seen as exploitative foreigners using Castile for their private ends[125]; and *militarily*, the latter were viewed as no match for the forces allied with the king. The coalition of Alvaro and Prince Enrique, the heir apparent, together with the nobles in league with them, was considered sufficient to defeat the Infantes, whatever support they might hope to enlist; and Juan of Navarre's headlong retreat seemed only to demonstrate this fact. Thus both politically and militarily, most cities had no alternative but to join the king's camp.

If this was in fact Alvaro's assessment, the issuance of the cedula at that time presented no real problem. The cities' lack of choice paralyzed their resistance, and this paralysis was also apparent when they met in Cortes the following May and yielded to the extreme political demands presented to them by the Constable.[126]

That meeting took place just a few days before the crucial battle of Olmedo. And if this was the cities' stand at the time, it is not hard to imagine what it was after the battle was over. For Alvaro, who emerged as the decisive victor, was strengthened even further. The party of the Infantes was virtually smashed, and the country lay prostrate before the powerful chief minister, who was the conversos' friend. In the next few years, the pro-Marrano policy was vigorously enforced. But it was enforced in the teeth of opposition.

For now came the turn of the Old Christians—or rather the anti-Marranos among them—to see themselves as oppressed. Of course, legally they were not worse off than the conversos, but socially and economically they believed they had been hurt. For Marrano equality was viewed by them not only as harmful to their present well-being, but also as a springboard for Marrano advancement—or, more precisely, as a means for the Marranos to attain superiority over them, the Old Christians. Thus, they came to identify their failures with the successes of the conversos, and vice versa. Yet, what could they do about it? De Luna's iron hand was felt everywhere, and the Marranos—entrenched in the royal Council, the chancellery, the treasury and other high offices—jealously guarded their rights from violation and saw to it that the declared policy of the kingdom was actually carried out. There appeared to be no way to circumvent the government's policy, and no change could be expected in that policy as long as that government remained in power. The results were inevitable. When all hope is lost that the authorities will use the law to correct a hateful situation, the radical elements are usually tempted to take the law into their own hands.

Thus was set the stage for Toledo 1449.

III. The Outbreak of the Rebellion

I

Judged by the attitudes of its Christian population, the history of Toledo from its reconquest onward was largely a history of pride and prejudice. The pride was heightened by the city's past glory, when Toledo was the capital of Spain. The prejudice was deepened by the period of ignominy, when Toledo was subject to Moorish rule. In the main, these attitudes stemmed from old hatreds toward both Moors and Jews—the infidel "sects" whom the Christians despised and with whom they believed they had accounts to settle. When Moslem Toledo was forced to surrender, the Christians assumed that their hour had come—that now they could give vent to their feelings toward the two subjugated groups. But the conqueror of Toledo, King Alfonso VI, had other plans in mind for his non-Christian subjects.

Faithful to the policies pursued in the Reconquest by himself and his predecessors in Castile, Alfonso wanted both Jews and Moors in Toledo to go on living in peace. To this end he established a legal framework which was supposed to offer them protection.[1] But the ill will and hostility of the Toledan Christians were pressing hard against his legal defenses. Flagrant violations of the laws he laid down soon spelled danger to the entire structure.[2] But Alfonso refused to give in. He insisted on maintaining the established order.

The Toledan Moors had no illusions about their future in the city. Faced with the raging, ongoing war between the Almoravides and the Christian armies, they knew they would be regarded by the Christians as the "enemy within." Their solution, they realized, lay in emigration; and south of Toledo, in Spain and beyond it, there lay vast Moslem lands to migrate to. Bearing all these matters in mind, and no doubt prodded by Christian harassment, they began their gradual departure from the city shortly after its conquest. By the mid-12th century only a remnant, consisting of the poorer part of the community, survived of Moorish Toledo.[3]

Different was the reaction of the Jews. They did not see themselves as enemies of the Christians, and even less as friends of the Almoravides. Nor did they see in the offing any land that might provide them a more secure haven. They felt they could rely on the pledges of the king, which were reciprocated by their faithful services; and more than such pledges, they knew, they could not get in any other country. Rather than migrate from Toledo, therefore, they chose to move to it in growing numbers. Soon

Toledo gave signs of becoming the most important center of Spanish Jewry.[4]

The Toledan Christians were increasingly irritated—in fact, they were outraged—by this development. Some two and a half decades after Toledo's liberation, they struck hard at the Jewish population, hoping to frighten it away from the city.[5] But the attempt failed. Like the rest of the Jews in Spain's Christian dominions, the Jews of Toledo were defended by the kings, and their community grew and prospered almost steadily until the war of the mid-1350s.

This was the war between King Pedro of Castile and his half-brother Enrique de Trastámara. The Jews of Toledo, as we have noted, remained to the end faithful to the king and paid an exorbitant price for their faithfulness. So heavy were their losses, both in lives and fortunes, that they came to the brink of extinction.[6] They had hardly recovered from that catastrophe when the riots of 1391 broke out and almost destroyed the entire community.[7] Many of its members who survived the massacre sought refuge in conversion to Christianity, and many of the remainder followed the same course during the persecutions of 1412–1418.[8] From then onward, the Jews of Toledo were no longer a major annoyance to the burghers. The latter's attention was now centered on the problems posed by the New Christians.

The patterns of history may repeat themselves endlessly, but they never repeat themselves fully—not even in their outlines. Toledo provides an example of this rule in the policies it pursued toward the converts from Judaism. Following the conversions of 1109, the Toledans opposed convert equalization[9]; and following the conversions of 1391, they displayed the same opposition.[10] Yet while on both occasions their reactions were the same, the social and legal effects were different. On the earlier occasion the Toledans had their way: The kings, as we have seen, acquiesced in their demands.[11] On the latter occasion, their wishes were thwarted: the kings took a firm pro-converso stand,[12] and Toledo was compelled to abide by the rules that applied to the rest of the kingdom. The result was that formally, and to a large extent factually, converso rights were established in Toledo in all public domains.

The Toledan objection to converso equality was thus suppressed or silenced, but did not disappear or diminish. On the contrary, it festered and swelled—until it finally erupted. In the course of this eruption the Toledans attempted to crush the conversos by sword and by law—and the impact of this attempt was immense. Indeed, its repercussions were felt throughout Spain for ten generations.

Of all Spanish cities, Toledo was the leader in the drive against the conversos. It was so not only by virtue of its traditions (dating at least from

1109) and the tensions they produced time and again. It was so also by virtue of its prestige and the model it provided to the nation as a whole. Seville and Cordova could doubtless match Toledo in their hatred of Jews and Marranos. But Toledo, a major political center and historically Spain's ecclesiastic capital, was more susceptible than any other Spanish city to the issues of control and authority. Hence, the converso community in Toledo, particularly strong in numbers and wealth,[13] presented a problem to its Old Christian neighbors. If equal opportunity became the rule of life, their hold on Toledo—some of them feared—might be lost to the conversos. To the Toledan Christians who harbored such fears, the thought was hardly bearable.

Whether it was all imaginary or not, many Old Christians kept an anxious eye on every forward move of the conversos. They saw a steady converso advance in all fields of public authority—fields the Old Christians considered their own; and the more this converso expansion continued, the more restless and resentful the Old Christians became. Their resentment, however, was held at bay. Not only was it checked by the royal administration, as well as by the highest authorities of the Church; it was also restrained by the high nobility, which in Toledo, as in other urban centers, controlled much of the city's life.[14] Together these three public forces—the monarchy, the Church, and the local great nobles—kept the lid upon Toledo's social kettle. But in the beginning of 1449, as we shall see, this condition changed: the highest Church authority was away from Toledo[15]; the old nobiliary control had been removed[16]; and the royal authority was undermined to a point where it lost its hold on the city population. In the absence of all these controlling forces, the lid flew off. An anti-converso outbreak took place which was the first of its kind in Spain.

II

The family of nobles that held sway in Toledo was that of the famous Pero López de Ayala, a statesman of renown and chancellor of the kingdom under the first three kings of the house of Trastámara. Old Ayala's interests were national in scope, but his son, of the same name, made Toledo his power base and became immersed in its politics and problems. In 1398 the younger Ayala was appointed by the King as Toledo's chief magistrate *(alcalde mayor),* and sometime later he was given, in addition, command of the alcazar and the other city strongholds. He may have been entrusted with these military posts—which made him, in fact, governor of the city—by Fernando de Antequera, the famous regent, and perhaps it was his allegiance to Fernando that Ayala later transferred to his sons. He was especially attracted to the third, Enrique, the boldest and most daring of them all, and—at least as Ayala perceived him—the most promising politically, too. In any case, he must have had little faith that Juan II, aged fourteen when crowned king, would retain his hold on the kingdom. In the struggle for power that developed in Castile following the death of Queen Catalina in 1418, Ayala cast his lot with Don Enrique.[17] Yet when the struggle seemed to end in the king's favor, he hastened to make peace with Juan II—or rather with his favorite, Alvaro de Luna. He did not gain Alvaro's confidence, but he evidently was too strong and influential (and Alvaro too new in the seat of power, and therefore too eager to make friends) for his overtures to be rejected. Thus, the second Pero López de Ayala kept his grip on Toledo.

He remained formally faithful to the regime when, in 1429, new trouble flared up between the reckless Enrique and Juan II. Ayala proved right to hold his peace, for Enrique again withdrew defeated. But a decade later, when the political tide seemed to turn in Enrique's favor (1440), Ayala joined him again. Not only did he align himself with the restive nobles who demanded Alvaro's withdrawal from the Court; he also defied the King's explicit order to keep Enrique out of Toledo.[18] Openly intransigent, Ayala was now risking the outraged monarch's retaliation. Yet this time he was on the winner's side: Alvaro was removed from the Court, and the Infantes took over the royal administration; but as it turned out, not for long.

In June 1444, Juan II managed to extricate himself from the grip of the Infantes, attacked them and forced them to retreat.[19] Once more Ayala was ready to change sides, and the King was again prepared to accept him. Accordingly, on September 4, the King granted Ayala a full pardon for his actions against the Crown and invited him to enter the league of nobles which, headed by his son and heir apparent, Prince Enrique, was aimed against the Infantes of Aragon.[20] Formally, Ayala's response was positive; he joined the league, but evaded his duties, or at least his expected assistance as ally. When the conflict between the King and the Infantes intensified, approaching the moment of a military clash, Ayala remained neutral. His forces were not present at Olmedo.[21]

His absence from that crucial encounter, however, may have been Ayala's major blunder. His shiftiness, faithlessness and evident duplicity had at last caught up with him. He lost his chance to be counted among the grandees who had a say in the running of the state, or even to remain in the King's good books.

III

Pero López de Ayala ruled Toledo with an iron hand. But at no time did he act so harshly as during his rebellious stand against the king in 1440 and 1441. In that period he expelled from Toledo many nobles (of both low and middle rank) who disagreed with his antiroyal acts, robbed many of his opponents of their possessions, and even put some of them to the torture. As the *Crónica de Juan II* put it: Ayala had "committed great outrages."[22] Entrenched as he was in his high office, he managed to silence his critics; and it was only after the battle of Olmedo that the *regidores* of the city summoned the courage to appear before the King and give him an account of Ayala's lawlessness and violence. They urged that Ayala be removed from his posts in both the alcazar and the administration of justice, adding that, unless their plea was heeded, they would leave the city for fear of his vengeance.[23]

The grave accusations of the *regidores* played directly into the King's hands. For some time now, both he and Alvaro had desired to strip Ayala of his powers and oust him from his royal positions in Toledo, which he used so frequently to the Crown's disadvantage. They needed only an opportune moment. And such a moment came after the victory of Olmedo, when no nobleman or city in the whole country would dare oppose the King or the Constable. So in December 1445, the King deprived Ayala of the command of the alcazar and all other fortified places in the city,[24] and shortly thereafter removed him from the office of Chief Judge of Appeals.[25] Thus ended Ayala's rule in Toledo, which had lasted for almost three decades.

But Ayala was not a man to give up. Trying to recover his lost positions, he enlisted the support of Prince Enrique, the heir apparent, to whose party he still formally belonged and to whose protection he thus seemed entitled.[26] Once again at odds with the royal administration, though not to the point of total break, the Prince wished Toledo to be held by Ayala, his allegedly newly won ally. He therefore interceded on Ayala's behalf, but with no apparent success. The King was not moved by his son's appeals and remained unusually firm. Nevertheless, the Prince continued his entreaties, and the king at last partially yielded. He agreed to let Ayala resume his position as Chief Judge of Appeals in Toledo, but categorically denied him the command of the alcazar or any other military post.[27]

Yet the king's concession was not implemented. It was objected to by the new governor of the city, a nobleman by the name of Pero Sarmiento, whose loyalty to the Crown and obedience to the King had hitherto been unquestioned. Now he completely changed his stand and his behavior as royal official. In the following we shall deal with the causes of this change, which ultimately made him leader of a rebellion, but whatever they were, Sarmiento's altered attitude must be seen in the light of Ayala's past behavior. It was Ayala's repeated manifestations of defiance of his royal overlord, Juan II, that encouraged Sarmiento—and the Toledans who followed him—to resist the King; and it was Ayala's lawless and ruthless dictatorship, displayed especially during the last rebellion, that served as model for Sarmiento's conduct when *his* turn came to rule the city. Thus both as rebellious official and governor, Ayala contributed in a variety of ways to the developments that followed.

IV

Our story will go back now to the first stage of the conflict between Pero López de Ayala and the royal administration. When Alvaro de Luna and Juan II decided to remove Ayala from his posts, they had their eyes on Pero Sarmiento as a suitable successor. Sarmiento was one of the better-known courtiers; he was the King's Chief Butler *(Repostero Mayor)*, member of the Royal Council and of the King's inner circle. Furthermore, he was scion of a noble family, which had given distinguished service to the Crown,[28] and he himself was always on Juan II's side when the King did battle with his enemies.[29] In fact, because they knew of his faithfulness to the King and his stern opposition to their own aspirations, the Infantes of Aragon had raided and destroyed his estates near the border of Navarre.[30] No other person in Juan II's Court seemed more reliable and dedicated to the King than his *Repostero Mayor*. He seemed therefore to offer the best possible choice for the future governor of Toledo.

Sarmiento, however, must have been for some time deeply dissatisfied. No doubt he believed that, compared to other nobles, he had been poorly repaid for his exertions. In 1448, after eighteen years of service, he was still, in effect, a second-rate nobleman, with mediocre estates and moderate income.[31] But then came the appointment in Toledo, and Sarmiento believed that his day had come. To be the King's *asistente* in Toledo, the governor of its alcazar and its chief judicial officer, meant to occupy lucrative and prestigious posts. At last, he must have thought, the King and Alvaro had realized that his reward was overdue.[32]

Therefore when, on May 15, 1446, the King informed Sarmiento that "for the present" he was revoking his Chief Judgeship of Appeals, which was to be restored to its former incumbent,[33] he was bitterly disappointed. In fact, he was so shocked that he lost his self-control and began to act like a rebel. He prohibited the publication of the King's order in Toledo and prevented Ayala from performing the duties assigned to him by the King. On June 28, Juan II sent Sarmiento a stern reminder of his order,[34] reiterating his command to stop all interference in the matter of the judgeship.[35] But Sarmiento continued to defy the King's instructions.[36] He may have believed that his record of service, or perhaps his place in the King's affections, would protect him against punishment or disfavor.

If so, he miscalculated. His audacious and unexpected disobedience provoked misgivings in the minds of Alvaro and the King. Perhaps Sarmiento later tried to assure them that his failure to follow the King's instructions concerning Ayala was intended to prevent a *fait accompli* that both the King and the Constable would regret; or that he was sure that they would hear him out before they proceeded with the matter any further. Apparently, he had exacted a promise from Juan II that the case would be reconsidered. But he failed to restore the confidence he had lost by his precipitate action.

His arguments, to be sure, may have led Alvaro and the King to reexamine their latest decision—that is, to restore the Chief Judgeship of Toledo to Pero López de Ayala, the proven traitor; but by now they must also have questioned the wisdom of placing all the military positions of Toledo in the hands of Pero Sarmiento. Having noticed his capacity for flagrant disobedience, the King and Alvaro came to believe that Sarmiento had revealed his true colors. They now saw him in a new light, in which he appeared far less reliable than they had originally thought.

Negotiations on the judgeship lasted more than two years. Finally, it was decided to withdraw from Ayala the post of Chief Judge of Appeals and appoint him one of the two "major judges," a considerably lesser post.[37] It was also decided to deny Sarmiento the control of the city gates and other forts, so that of all the posts he had been promised, he was now left only with the command of the alcazar.[38] The latter decision was obviously taken to prevent Sarmiento from using Toledo against the King, and showed how little faith the King and Alvaro now placed in Sarmiento. The vacant judicial and military positions were filled by Alvaro de Luna himself, who appointed his deputies to run them.

Sarmiento was informed of these decisions about the middle of December 1448. Six weeks later, the city of Toledo was up in arms against Alvaro and the King, with Sarmiento at the head of the rebellion.

V

This reconstruction of the Toledan events may help us comprehend the urges and motives that drove Sarmiento into a rebellious mood. It cannot, however, explain his final resolution to take the fateful step and actually rebel. To understand that resolution, we must consider other factors that came into play in that particular situation.

Some chronicles explain Sarmiento's decision by his desire to regain what he had lost, or what the King was presumably obliged to give him.[39] We take it that these chronicles refer to the posts that had been promised Sarmiento and then denied him. Sarmiento's distress over these losses, his resentment at the way he had been treated, and especially his grievances against Alvaro de Luna were doubtless common knowledge at the court of Juan II and in the political circles of Toledo. Many therefore thought it reasonable to assume that his rebellious actions stemmed from that resentment, and from his refusal to acquiesce in the "injustice" done him by the King and the Constable. This is also why the chronicles ascribe his uprising to his determination "to get back what was his." Yet this seems too easy an explanation for such a decisive move.

No doubt his removal from the post of chief judge inspired Sarmiento's reveries of insurrection. His initial reaction to the King's notification that his appointment to that post had been revoked offers support to this supposition. But it is a far cry from rebellious musings, or even an insubordinate attitude, to planning an uprising and actually leading it politically and militarily. No one would go to such great lengths merely to recover the office of a judgeship or the command of some gates and bridges. No one would assume the terrible risks involved in a rebellion against the King of Castile simply for the limited benefits entailed in the control of such positions. Shrewd, practical and extremely cautious, Sarmiento would certainly not endanger his estates, his rank and revenue, and even his life, for an office inferior to the one he held. A much stronger motive must have impelled him to push aside all other considerations and take the rebel's path. That motive, as we see it, was his great apprehension—or rather his fear—of an impending disaster.

But what was the cause of that fear? To understand this, we must take a closer look at some of the elements of the precarious situation in which Sarmiento believed he was involved.

VI

If his refusal to surrender the chief judgeship cost him much of the King's goodwill, he must have lost still more royal favor in his subsequent struggle for the office.[40] No doubt his dismissal from the command of the city gates added to Sarmiento's hurt feelings and further strained the already tense relations between him and the administration. But essentially, it must have confirmed his belief that Alvaro had read his mind correctly. He was known to hold a grudge against Alvaro, and Alvaro regarded him therefore as an enemy. Sooner or later, Sarmiento was sure, Alvaro would oust him from the bureaucracy.

From his long association with the Court of Juan II, Sarmiento knew how Alvaro got rid of his enemies. The blow would come suddenly, without warning, and at the least expected moment. The victim would courteously be invited to the King for a presumably friendly discussion, and then and there would be arrested and sent away to some fortress prison. Sarmiento saw with his own eyes how this method was applied to López de Ayala when the latter was divested of his offices in Toledo,[41] except that Ayala was not imprisoned, probably out of consideration for the Prince. Sarmiento, however, could not expect such consideration. He was not allied with any potentate and did not belong to any party. Politically, he was completely isolated, and whatever action was contemplated against him could be taken with impunity.

The concern for his safety, which most likely began troubling him in June 1446, turned into real and growing anxiety after the arrest of a group of great nobles in Zafraga on May 11, 1448.[42] Though most of these nobles had once belonged to the opposition party, they had since made peace with the King and gave no cause for such harsh treatment. No reason was given for the sudden arrests and the ensuing large-scale confiscations, and no one was sure of the real reason. It was generally agreed, however, that the action was taken with complete disregard for both law and custom, and the nobility were alarmed. As the *Crónica de Juan II* put it, "the great nobles and the median ones, as well as the minor *caballeros* of these kingdoms, were very concerned, scandalized and discontented, since they believed that *the same harm could come to all of them.* In their opinion, all this was done because the Master of Santiago Don Alvaro de Luna felt no restraint whatever in carrying out his will."[43]

Ranking as he did below the leading nobles, Sarmiento may have thought he had reason to be *especially* concerned. If Alvaro could thus mistreat the great nobles simply because he doubted their loyalty, why should he not treat him, too, in precisely the same manner?

If we interpret his thinking correctly, Sarmiento believed that his skirmish with the administration, as well as the crucial position he held, placed him high on the list of the unwanted. Then came the reduction of his military authority—i.e., his removal from the command of the gates—and Sarmiento could not fail to understand what this meant. It meant open mistrust of his loyalty to the King, to Alvaro de Luna and the royal cause, and it further confirmed his gravest suspicions about what the near future held in store for him. Above all, it was a warning compelling him to realize that he had but one course: to preempt the coming blow with a counterstrike against his dangerous enemy.

VII

The Toledan insurrection is generally perceived as a popular outbreak that nobody planned and of which Sarmiento assumed the leadership only after the rebels had captured the city. This perception is fallacious. As the reader will see, hard evidence is available that Sarmiento led the rebellion from the start.[44]

The proximity of the date on which King Juan II announced his decision on the government of Toledo and the date on which the rebellion broke out do not refute this conclusion. On the contrary, they confirm it. It is unlikely that such a rebellion could have been organized within so brief a span. Therefore, we must conclude that the plan of insurrection, which materialized in January 1449, was conceived *before* the preceding December, along with the preparatory moves it called for. We have seen how such moves may have been on Sarmiento's mind for almost two years, and how the main motive that helped push him to the brink became more compelling toward the end of '48. Yet motive alone cannot explain what happened in the following month. The rebellion of Toledo, as is common in such cases, was a cross between motive and opportunity.

That Pero Sarmiento had been looking for an opportunity to carry out his rebellious scheme may be taken for granted. And we may also assume that such an opportunity could be offered, to his thinking, by the state of the kingdom. Watching the political scene as he did, he must have been searching for signs of developments that might give him hope for cracks in the regime. Sparks of such a hope were, we may suppose, kindled in his mind not infrequently. For the kingdom was plagued with growing unrest and some of its border regions were in turmoil.

To begin with, the northeastern frontier became a theater of war in June 1446, when the important fortresses of Atienza and Torija fell to Juan I of Navarre.[45] Stuck deep like thorns in Castile's flesh, these fortresses served the Aragonese as staging grounds for raids against the neighboring countryside.[46] And while this part of the border was ablaze, another frontier, further to the south, burst into flames in February 1448. There the troublesome Rodrigo Manrique, who claimed the title of Master of Santiago (the very title borne by Alvaro), established himself as lord of Murcia and, using it as a base for his operations, attacked the areas of Molina and Seville.[47] He was assisted in these raids by the Moslems of Granada, thus aggravating the problem then posed for Castile by its southern Moslem neighbor.

It soon turned out that the problem was not limited to raids causing losses in men and livestock. The Moslem assaults in 1447 resulted in the capture of several strong places, such as Arenas, Huéscar, and the two forts of Vélez (*blanco* and *rubio*) that guarded the approaches to Lorca and Murcia.[48] With no ready army available to stop it, the Moslem penetration seemed likely to go on. According to the *Crónica del Halconero,* the Moslems were encouraged to launch their assaults by the tumults and divisions they had noticed in Castile which rendered it almost defenseless.[49] This judgment of the chronicler echoed Alvaro's opinion. To him and the king, it was apparent that these troubles resulted from the agitation, incitement and unrest fomented by Juan I of Navarre.

It was perhaps as part of his general plan to start a war against Aragon, or prevent an all-out Aragonese invasion, that Alvaro arrested the leading nobles of the opposition. He may have seen this action as a precautionary measure that would deny Navarre support from Castile's restive barons. But the action succeeded only in part, and in the end recoiled against the Crown. For while Alvaro managed to weaken the opposition by arresting some of its troublesome members, he strengthened it by drawing to its ranks many others who came to fear his moves and intentions. In addition, two members of the old Infantes' group, Admiral Fadrique and the Count of Castro, did not fall into the trap of Zagara. They fled to Saragossa and there urged Juan, King of Navarre and Viceroy of Aragon, to declare total war on Juan II and Alvaro. No doubt they claimed that should Aragon and Navarre invade Castile quickly, they would rally to their standard most of Castile's nobles, who were yearning for Alvaro's downfall. Inclined to believe this, Juan of Navarre sent the admiral to his brother, King Alfonso in Naples, in order to get his approval of the plan.[50] The chances of an all-out Aragonese invasion, rather than diminishing as a result of the arrests, now seemed to have considerably increased, while Aragonese raiders kept harassing the countryside, spreading destruction wherever they went, and carrying away booty and captives.

Toward the end of 1448, all these troubles came to a head. The Count of Benavente, Alfonso Pimentel, one of the nobles arrested in May, escaped in December from his prison in Portillo, and reaching safety in his castle of Benavente (near the Portuguese border), raised there the standard of revolt against the King.[51] In the same month the Moors launched an attack upon Hellín (south of Albacete), with deadly results to its defenders.[52] And on January 10, 1449, a raid by the Aragonese on Requena and Utiel ended in heavy losses to these towns.[53] Thus, the turn of the year 1448 saw gathering clouds in the skies of Castile.

To Sarmiento, however, these clouds may have indicated that light was not far behind. At the very time when his fortunes were declining and the personal danger to him was rising, the royal administration appeared almost paralyzed and the kingdom defenseless in the face of its foes. The regime was now simultaneously attacked from the east, the west and the south. Sarmiento, most likely, could not help thinking that if it were attacked in the center too—that is, if Toledo now rose against the King—the pressure on the monarchy might prove unbearable, and Juan II, to pacify the realm, might be compelled to discharge his favorite. Alvaro would again be removed from the court—and this time probably forever.

Such were the considerations that must have influenced Sarmiento's assessment of the chances of an uprising. The political situation appeared propitious, almost an invitation to take action. The only thing he was still not sure about was his own political and military potential.

VIII

This brings us to consider the popular force that constituted the source of Sarmiento's potential—the lower classes of the city of Toledo, which might possibly serve as the vehicle for his plan. We have noted the motives that inclined Sarmiento to take the rebel's path. But what could move the Toledan population to join him in such a hazardous venture? Evidently, none of Sarmiento's aims concerned them. And yet it was the populace of Toledo that rebelled and delivered the city into his hands. No doubt a link was somehow established between Sarmiento and the people of Toledo—that is, between his goals and their desires, which could not possibly be similar. It all resembled a feat accomplished; the question is how it was done.

At the outset, it seems, he could not draw much encouragement from the Toledan conditions as he knew them. His only military asset, he realized, was his command of Toledo's alcazar; but the alcazar alone, without the city, was not a position he could hold for long. And the leaders of the city, as he well knew, were not at all in a rebellious mood. The patricians were traditionally on the side of law and order; they comprised the *regidores,* the city council, the upper middle class and the lower nobility. They had generally been opposed to antiroyal moves during the period of Ayala's rule; and nothing that happened after that period had made them change their minds. As for the great nobles—i.e., the Ayalas—they would never follow Sarmiento's lead. To them, he was just a second-rate nobleman with no resources of his own to speak of. In addition, they obviously disliked—and distrusted—him as one who was after their former positions. Judging by all this, he had little to count on. The control of Toledo seemed far from his grip, a dream that could scarcely come true.

This is how matters appeared to Sarmiento before he met one Marcos García, who happened to have returned to Toledo after a long absence. Marcos García de Mora (or Mazarambroz), more commonly known as Marquillos (a nickname of diminution and probably of contempt, given him perhaps by the conversos, his opponents), was a man of no mean abilities and also of no minor shortcomings. We have only isolated data about his background prior to his involvement in the Toledan rebellion, but the little we know may suffice to provide a general biographical outline. He described himself as both a native of Toledo and "the son of an honored man," an "hidalgo."[54] Actually, however, he was the son of a peasant who lived in the territory of Toledo.[55] By some stroke of fortune, and aided by his talents, he rose from the low station of his birth to the respectable position of bachelor-of-law. But his social ascent had been a struggle and involved him, most likely, in some brushes with the law. Thus we find him also described as a vile man, reputed to be of evil life, and accused of many crimes and transgressions.[56] His hatred for the conversos, which was fierce and implacable, may have been a heritage from his peasant background, or a product of conflicts with converso litigants or perhaps competitors in the legal field. In any case, in Toledo García found many who shared his animus toward the conversos and were ready to take some action against them. These were primarily laborers and artisans, whose interests García claimed to represent. But he also acquired friends among the clergy and some of the young Old Christian professionals. Above all, he gained the confidence of Sarmiento, who probably appointed him his legal counselor before the rebellion broke out.

A shrewd observer, García must have sensed Sarmiento's problems and concerns, and soon came to know his cherished dream—to rise with Toledo against the royal administration and thus become the focus of the national opposition to the rule of Alvaro de Luna. It was no doubt García who showed Sarmiento how to get hold of the city. He, too, must have realized, like Sarmiento, that Toledo's aristocracy would not rebel, but believed that Toledo could be stirred to revolt by someone who knew how to arouse the *común*. The *común* (namely, the laborers, the artisans, and also some parts of the lower middle class), he was sure, could be mobilized in only one way— that is, by fanning their hatred of the conversos and assuring them satisfaction of that hatred. Accordingly, he assumed, the *común* would join a rebellion against Alvaro if the Constable were described as the conversos' friend and identified as their "protector."

If we may judge by later developments, Sarmiento accepted García's idea, or at least agreed to test it in some form—that is, to check the feelings it might generate among some members of the *común*. Again, it must have been Marcos García who undertook to do the required test without involving Sarmiento or Sarmiento's name in his cautious probes and inquiries. He must have recruited to what he called their "cause" several of his trusted friends and associates who, together with him, began to do the necessary agitational groundwork in the city. They were careful not to advocate rebellion, for such advocacy, they knew, would have stopped them in their tracks. Yet they could freely denounce the conversos and bitterly complain about Alvaro, their supporter, especially among the artisans and laborers. Thus they could create a revolutionary ferment among the *común*, which might follow them when the need arose.

This is, we believe, how the populace of Toledo, or rather a segment of that populace, was won over to Sarmiento's side. His narrow, strictly personal interests were now sustained by a popular movement and supported by what its members considered their common or even "holy" cause. Never was a stranger, unholier marriage effected between a leader and those he was to lead; but it bore fruit—bitter, to be sure, but endowed with a vitality that was to endure beyond what anyone could then foresee.

IX

On January 25, on his way to Ocaña, Alvaro paid a brief visit to Toledo to ask the city leaders for a loan to the Crown of 1 million maravedis. In fact, he did not *ask* for that loan; he peremptorily demanded it. The money was urgently needed, he said, to organize defenses against the country's enemies, who were attacking it from both the east and the south; and under the strain of these needs, he added, the city could not be exempted. But the leaders of the city remained unconvinced. Seemingly astounded by Alvaro's demand, they reminded him that Toledo, by ancient privilege, was exempt from granting such loans. Alvaro countered by pointing once again to the emergency in which the country found itself, and he left Toledo apparently confident that the leaders he had spoken to would provide the loan.[57]

His confidence, however, was misplaced. Meeting shortly after his departure, the city council decided to resist his demand and sent a delegation to the Constable in Ocaña to inform him of their decision. But Alvaro remained firm and unyielding, and the delegates returned to Toledo downhearted.[58] The council now realized that they had no choice but to grant Alvaro the requested loan; and they instructed their treasurer, Alonso Cota, who happened to be a converso tax farmer, to proceed with the necessary collection.[59]

Sarmiento who, as the king's *asistente*, must have attended the council's meeting, knew that many of the citizens were outraged.[60] They simply dismissed Alvaro's claims, ignored his political arguments and considerations, and merely insisted that his demand for the loan constituted a gross violation of their rights. If they finally consented to the loan as they did, that consent was given for one reason only: they believed that continued objection on their part would result in open conflict with Alvaro, and nobody wished to appear responsible for promoting such a conflict. But an ugly mood of disappointment and frustration spread from the council to the community, and while Cota proceeded to collect the loan, the preparations for a popular insurrection had begun.

There is no doubt that Alvaro's visit to Toledo, and his gloomy account of the state of the nation, thrust Sarmiento into a jubilant mood and strengthened his intention to rebel. While the majority of the council thought that Alvaro's assessments were deliberately exaggerated, so as to strengthen his case for the loan, Sarmiento in all likelihood believed that those assessments were essentially true. He must have felt certain that Juan of Navarre, in concert with leading Castilian nobles, was indeed planning an invasion of Castile, just as Alvaro had stated. This led him to conclude that, nationally, the time was propitious for a rebellion. However, he had to be also assured that the time was ripe locally, too.

This assurance he probably received from García and his friends. In the hasty consultations he must now have held with them, he undoubtedly asked for their opinion. What they told him can be gauged by the results. They judged the mood of the *común* to be right for the start of a general uprising. They thought that *any* provocation could ignite the powder keg of the Toledan rabble, and believed they could use the "loan" as the tinder that would touch off the explosion. Sarmiento gave the go-ahead sign, and they proceeded to put their plan into effect.

According to the chronicles reporting these events, certain people were inciting the lower classes to refrain from taking part in the collection of the loan. Hostile rumors were spread about Alvaro and Cota, according to which they had devised the loan for their own personal gain; Cota was to reap his profit as tax farmer, and Alvaro was to get his bribe from Cota.[61] When one of the artisans who refused to pay his share cried out raucously while being dragged to prison, the whole town broke into an uproar.[62] Soon the bells of the cathedral were ringing, calling the people to a meeting. There, fiery speeches were delivered, and the crowd was exhorted to go to Cota and inflict due punishment on that converso as the architect of the criminal scheme. Cota escaped, but his houses were sacked and then set on fire.[63] These were the opening moves of the rebellion and the war against the conversos. They occurred on Monday, January 27.[64]

In line with what we have indicated above, most *crónicas* describe these events as a spontaneous reaction of the *común*, or the poor, to the exaction of a tribute which was beyond their means.[65] It is possible of course that some of the *común* were unable to meet the demands of the collectors, but such incidents were by no means rare. They appeared in Spain in *all* tax gatherings conducted on any considerable scale, and they could not in themselves inspire a city to rebel, if it was not prepared for mutiny. The outbreak in Toledo betrays too many signs of planning and preparation, as well as the presence of a guiding hand, to attribute it all to spontaneity.

In the history of the Jewish people in the Diaspora, Jewish communities were all too often subject to riotous attacks (later known as pogroms) which to many appeared incidental. Rarely, however, did a pogrom occur "suddenly" without preceding incitement, intense rabble-rousing, and determined organization of a hard core of pogromists who were to lead the attack. The Toledan rebellion of January 1449 was clearly an outbreak of this kind. Those who called the meeting in the cathedral knew full well what they sought to achieve. They included, in all likelihood, the two canons of the cathedral, Pero Lope de Galvez and Juan Alonso, who are later to be found among García's comrades and chief allies in the rebels' leadership.[66] They may also have spoken at the meeting in the cathedral and urged the people to attack Cota's houses, without intending, of course, to have the disturbance end with that attack. Obviously, the crowds who rushed to the cathedral, from which they proceeded to take violent action, did not hear there for the first time the harangues and accusations that were uttered from the rostrum. They came there seething with hatred for the conversos, as well as for Alvaro de Luna, their "protector." The image of Alvaro as the oppressor of the people, as well as the ally of their enemies, the conversos, was no doubt by then well established in their minds.

Such extreme and provocative views could certainly breed hostility. But mobs do not act in a concerted manner when they translate their emotions into violence. To do so, they must be led by individuals whom they trust and regard as mentors and guides. It is such people who can move them to do battle and bring them to the field of action in the first place.

We have presented our conclusions as to the identity of the instigators of the Toledan populace; and in this judgment we are not alone. Zurita identified the source of the agitation that swept Toledo prior to the outbreak when he explicitly said that it was Pero Sarmiento who "incited the people" to rebellion.[67] But it was of course Sarmiento acting *indirectly* through his aides, who were prodded by García. Zurita speaks of García, too, in this connection as one of the two prime movers of the events. He describes him as "a great counselor and leader,"[68] and there is no doubt that it was García who had actually "incited the people" of Toledo and openly *led* the insurrection from the start.

It must have been relatively easy for García to move the *común* to sack Cota's houses, and it could be expected that afterward they would proceed to attack the converso neighborhood.[69] Yet somebody had a far broader design than satisfying the *común's* rage. The crucial task now was to capture the strongholds under Alvaro de Luna's control—i.e., the gates that were guarded by his men—and thus prevent him from bringing in reinforcements that could nip the rebellion in the bud. The insurgents were ordered therefore to attack the gates; and their rapid compliance with this order shows again that they included a hard core of partisans who loyally followed their leadership.

That Sarmiento was the actual head of this leadership is, in our judgment, not open to doubt. Essentially, this was also the opinion of Zurita, who mentioned him first among the "instigators" of the rebellion. But Sarmiento was not only the chief instigator. From the outset he was the chief leader, although in the beginning both his leadership and incitement were conducted surreptitiously.

What made Sarmiento remain behind the scenes even at this late hour, when the crowds of the *común* were surging forward in full compliance with his will and design? The answer is obvious. It was his fear of Alvaro, as well as the doubts he must still have had about the rebels' capacity to carry out his plan. He was told that he could rely on the *común* for the capture of

Alvaro's strongholds in the city, but—like most noblemen—he had little faith in the military ability of the lower classes, and may have wished to test the intensity of their feelings and their readiness to do battle for their cause before openly committing himself to the rebellion.

Nevertheless, while remaining behind the scenes, he directed the rebels' activities, or at least their major moves. In fact, months later, in an official document, which he addressed to the Pope and King Juan II, Marcos García stated explicitly that the *gates of the city of Toledo were captured by Sarmiento's authority and command*.[70] What better evidence is needed to convince us that the rebellion was not a spontaneous outbreak but a planned affair, engineered by Sarmiento? This also explains the mob's daring assault upon the fortified gates and bridges of the city, when all the military positions in Toledo were ostensibly in Alvaro's hands. Doubtless the assailants were assured by their commanders that they need not fear the forces in the alcazar, since the governor, Sarmiento, was on their side.[71] Such an assurance could give wings to their movements, while a rumor to that effect, deliberately spread, would dampen the spirit of the defenders of the gates. In any case, the insurgents quickly captured three of the four gates of the city, encountering resistance only at one point, the Tower of San Martín. But the commander of this fort, too, was soon forced to surrender.[72] Thus, all of Alvaro's strongholds in the city fell to the rebels.

The insurgents then put the gates and bridges under the command of their own men. Could these appointments have been made by a rabble that lacked leadership and planning? One would not expect such actions of a mob that had burst into a spontaneous outbreak. Such a mob, having spent its fury, tends to disperse and disappear. In Toledo the attackers behaved differently. The captains entrusted with guarding the gates, the bridges and other strategic outposts were no doubt chosen before the outbreak, with a view to securing these positions once they were captured by the rebels. The plan was to prevent Alvaro de Luna from entering the city with his troops.

Toledo was now closed to Alvaro's men, and the first goal of the conspirators was attained. Sarmiento at last came into the open, but continued with his disguise. He formally "negotiated" with their acknowledged leaders (i.e., those he had directed during the uprising), and got from them an assurance under oath that they would yield to his authority. He then outlined the policy to be pursued by the city. He spoke only of the need to remove Alvaro from the Court and his other positions, of the privileges of the city which the Constable had violated, and of the need to secure the city of Toledo against further such encroachments on its rights.[73] In his first open act of intervention he uttered no complaint against the conversos, either in Toledo or elsewhere in Spain. Perhaps he still hoped to win over the upper middle class, which included influential conversos, and some members of the council who were angry with Alvaro solely for his imposition of the loan. But if this was his strategy, it did not gain him much. None of the city notables, including the *regidores,* supported the insurrection. Sarmiento now learned his first great lesson: to sustain the revolution, he could rely only on those who propelled it—namely, the lower classes.

He received from the rebels the keys of the gates and declared himself formally, with their consent, head of the city's administration and chief commander of its military forces.[74] He clothed himself again with the honorable title of which he had been divested by the King—i.e., that of Chief Judge of Appeals—removing from this post Alvaro's deputy, who agreed to become his aide.[75] All this was accomplished effectively, swiftly, and seemingly without a hitch.

Sarmiento now had the situation well in hand. From mere commander of the Toledan alcazar he became master of Toledo.

IV. Toledo Under the Rebels

I

Like most events of historic significance, the Toledan rebellion of 1449 resulted from the meeting of several drives moving from different directions. We do not really know all the currents, social and personal, that converged at that point; but three of them stand out clearly. They may be identified with Pero Sarmiento, Marcos García, and the Toledan *común*. If Sarmiento represented a private factor and the Toledan *común* a social one, García served as the tie between them. The forces that impelled him were both personal and collective, as we shall presently see.

To understand the partnership between Sarmiento and García, we should take another look at these two men as they are reflected in the sources. The sources, to be sure, do not offer us a finished, well-rounded portrait of either of them, but they do indicate their main characteristics and these should be sufficient for our reconstruction. Sarmiento's character seems far less complex, and therefore his image appears more clearly. Both Palencia and Pulgar stressed his "depravity,"[1] though, unlike Palencia, Pulgar ascribed it to the influence of "evil" men (and hence not to his innate tendencies).[2] We cannot go along with Pulgar. Sarmiento impresses us as a hard, cruel man, narrow-minded and brutal, a cold-blooded egotist. The sources describe him as excessively greedy and, furthermore, as a man who, to satisfy his greed, was capable of any and every crime. In this, however, he was not exceptional. His "inordinate" avarice was in fact typical of many in his baronial class; yet what distinguished him from most of his peers was his complete lack of social motivation. To be sure, in the course of the Toledan revolution he claimed to have fought for the rights of the city, or even to have championed the cause of the nation; but coming from him, these claims were hollow. His main concerns, as betrayed by his actions, were self-preservation and material gain. His Toledan record, bleak as his person, remained to the end unrelieved by any deed of higher or nobler aspiration.

Unlike Sarmiento, García's main passion was not for wealth, but for fame and glory. He sought prestige in a society that scorned him, and he tried to change the attitude of that society by becoming a "tribune" of the common people. He believed that he was charged with a mission, and also with the talents required to fulfill it; and these beliefs spurred his natural boldness to the verge of fatal recklessness. What is more, his courage and spirit of adventure were fueled by his violent hatreds (particularly those he felt for the conversos), and these feelings, more often than not, helped unbalance his judgment.

Although he related his hatreds to his morals, to his sense of duty and religious principles, in reality his moral attitudes were formed by his grudges more than by anything else. So were his views of what was legal, "according to both canon and civil law." As a jurist, who knew the relativity of the law, and how it could be changed, bent and misconstrued, he wielded the law as a pliant instrument of what he called his "just and holy purpose."[3] All these beliefs, qualities and propensities affected his political activities in Toledo and thus, in large measure, determined his own fate and the course of the Toledan revolution.

Judging by the characters of these two men, as well as by their different backgrounds, it is obvious that they had little in common except for their cynical attitude to morality (at least in its strictly legal sense). What united them was their ardent desire to see the rebellion they led succeed; but here, too, they differed in their goals as they did in their major motives. Sarmiento's goal was to destroy Alvaro; García's was to destroy the conversos. But to achieve what they sought, they had to join forces. García was Sarmiento's link with the *común,* without which the rebellion could not materialize. Sarmiento was García's link with the nobility, without which the rebellion could not end in success. And just as they had to join forces, they also had to combine their aims. Sarmiento accepted García's plans for the conversos, while diverting them, in part, to his private ends; García accepted Sarmiento's plan against Alvaro, adapting it to his anti-converso drive. Obviously, such a union called for mutual accommodation—and mutual concessions.

II

Sarmiento's assumption of a dictator's role may well have resulted from such a concession. García, who hated to be a subordinate and knew how self-centered Sarmiento was, would doubtless have preferred that all major decisions be adopted by a majority of the rebellion's leaders. Yet realizing that Sarmiento would never agree to put himself in the hands of commoners, he had no choice but entrust his own and his friends' fate to Sarmiento. The latter, for his part, must have assured García that he would use his power in the service of the revolution and direct it only against its enemies.

On the basis of this clear understanding, Sarmiento established his rule in Toledo, which soon assumed the form of a tyranny. Political opponents, actual and potential, were banished from the city or put behind bars, while some of his supporters, who hailed his activities, were given positions of authority and trust. He justified his actions on the pretext that the city was in a state of war; that it must prepare for an onslaught by Alvaro; and that everyone who spoke in Alvaro's favor was in effect a traitor. Under these circumstances all opposition ceased; the council was suppressed, the *regidores* silenced. As the *Crónica* of the *Halconero* put it,

> Whether out of love or out of fear, there was not a man in the city who dared utter a single word against the will of Pero Sarmiento.[4]

As far as the people of Toledo were concerned, "love" for Sarmiento could then be felt only in the ranks of the *común*, which was his power base and many of whose members undoubtedly expected to be rewarded for their support. But except for the *común*, which must have then enjoyed Sarmiento's preferential treatment, political persecution affected all sections of the city's population, including the clergy and the nobility. From the outset, however, the conversos were the rebels' first and primary target. The policy pursued against them was atrocious even by the standards of that harsh regime. It was doubtless framed by García and his friends, and carefully calculated to achieve their goals. Perhaps they did not reveal their aims fully at the very outset of the new regime, although it was obvious that what they wanted most was to wreak their vengeance upon the hated group. Yet in urging the government to adopt their policy, they could employ pragmatic arguments. Thus, they could stress that the people of Toledo rebelled primarily to put down the conversos, and that the people expected the government they installed to act in accordance with their wishes. This was also what the people had been promised; and if the rebels wished to have their support, they must keep faith with them in this matter. Such arguments could not fail to impress Sarmiento; but his decision to take an anti-converso line stemmed also from other—personal—considerations in which García (and his friends) probably had no share.

For Sarmiento saw in the persecution of the conversos an opportunity to fulfill his lifelong dream, which was to amass a great fortune. He must have worked out a plan of action, and, as we have indicated, could be encouraged in his planning by Ayala's behavior eight years before. But besides this example, there were two more factors that made his task much easier: the *común*'s attitude toward the conversos and the conversos' attitude toward the rebellion. Indeed, the latter's stand provided him with an excuse for whatever action he might take against them.

If the measures he took against certain Old Christians were strongly resented by Toledo's upper classes, the measures he took against the conversos could not generate such opposition. And if members of the higher classes did react negatively to his anti-converso acts, their reaction must have been in most cases subdued, while that of the *común* was enthusiastic, loudly supporting Sarmiento's policy and his hostile treatment of the New Christians. Deep-rooted group feelings were no doubt responsible, mainly or largely, for these varied reactions; but objective factors also played a part.

While the Old Christians of *all* classes were divided in their attitude toward Alvaro de Luna, the conversos were definitely not. They had no reason to come out against Alvaro, whose attitude toward them had always been friendly, and every reason to oppose the rebels, who had always shown them deep aversion and disdain. Politically, then, the conversos were viewed not merely as opponents of the rebellion, but also as enemies of the new regime and, of course, of the *común,* which installed it. All that Sarmiento had to do in their case was to prove that their apparently passive hostility was in effect covertly active, that they were in collusion with the dangerous Constable and planned to overthrow his government.

He had no difficulty in obtaining such proof. As chief of the military forces in the city and as head of the city's administration of justice, he ordered the arrest of leading conversos and had them tortured until they "confessed"— that is, admitted their complicity with Alvaro against the city's new government.[5] The proud, rich converso upper class was especially hated by the lower classes, and its open subjection to torment and humiliation elated the *común.* Sarmiento realized that by allowing the mobs to vent their feelings against the conversos, he was strengthening their loyalty to the regime and feeding the fires of his rebellion. But more important was the second purpose which he sought to attain through that persecution. For once he had extorted "confessions" from the accused of their complicity with Alvaro, he could formally judge them guilty of treason and "legally" confiscate their possessions. His government was badly in need of funds and he himself a living mass of greed. We do not know how he divided the spoils, but a lot of them went into his own coffers. Then he put the "guilty" to cruel death (or "cut them to pieces,"[6] as Higuera tells us), thereby giving even greater satisfaction to the mobs howling for converso blood.

A night of terror descended upon Toledo, most appallingly upon its conversos. What could the latter do to save themselves? By all accounts, it seems, very little. Yet we know that some measures were taken. They turned for help to certain nobles in the city, and at least some limited assistance came forth[7]; they closed their boroughs to Sarmiento's men and vowed to resist further arrests; but clashes occurred between their armed groups and some of Sarmiento's followers in the city, and in one of these clashes some conversos were killed, among them their commander, Juan de la Cibdad. He was shot to death and then hanged, feet up, in the central square of Zocodover.[8] This seems to have dampened the conversos' spirit and impelled them to change their tactics.

What precisely happened is not clear. Possibly, the conversos were now faced with a choice (offered by Sarmiento himself) between resistance to an all-out assault upon their boroughs (an assault that could well end in a massacre) and reliance on Sarmiento's pledge that he would prevent such an attack if they laid down their arms. They seem to have chosen the latter course as the lesser of two evils, or possibly because Sarmiento promised to tone down the persecution. However, what happened after their surrender must have exceeded their worst expectations. Arrests, banishments, and expropriations followed in rapid succession, and no converso knew when his turn would come to be jailed, tortured, killed or expelled. A general pogrom, however, was avoided. Sarmiento did not want to let the mob loose to burn and destroy what he could take for himself, or confiscate for his government. Apparently, the Chief Judge of Appeals wished to give his crimes some semblance of legality; and this desire was no doubt sustained also by another nagging thought. For however reckless Sarmiento was, he must still have considered the possibility that he might someday have to account for his crimes; and he pondered the impact of his behavior in Toledo on his potential future judges and public opinion.

III

It nevertheless may be taken for granted that both García and Sarmiento intended to punish the whole converso community. But they faced a dilemma. It was one thing to "prove" by means of torture the "connection" between the conversos and Alvaro and another to make it generally credible for all, except for the lower classes who needed no convincing. How could a conspiracy between Alvaro and the conversos actually have been planned and implemented in Toledo when all the entrances to the city had been shut since the very beginning of the rebellion and tightly guarded by the rebel government? No doubt Sarmiento's interrogators could show general attitudes, sympathies and desires; but it was difficult to condemn a whole community on the basis of political leanings alone. Such a plan was probably considered, but ultimately rejected as impolitic. In any case, they realized that new excuses, other than political, had to be employed.

It is a fact that has escaped scholarly attention, but ought to be noticed and duly assessed: no religious charge was leveled at the conversos in the first stage of the Toledan persecution. Only later did the charges shift from politics to religion. In all probability, the reasons for the shift lay partly in the difficulties noted above, and it is reasonable to assume that the new line of attack was urged by García and his clerical friends. One of the latter, Pero Lope Galvez, was vicar of the cathedral church of Toledo and, with the archbishop absent from the city,[9] head of the church's judicial system. As such he was viewed as the highest authority in all cases involving religious crimes.

That the religious accusation was more suitable than the political for the purposes the rebels then had in mind could be argued on a number of grounds. To begin with, charges of a religious nature did not require for their substantiation a link between the accused and an outside force (such as Alvaro). Second, such charges could publicly be hurled at the whole converso community of Toledo, while a political conspiracy could obviously be pinned only on a limited number of persons. Third, the religious accusation was not new; it had roots in Old Christian opinion and therefore would be more readily believed. All that was necessary was now to repeat it and drive it forcefully into the public mind.

Such or similar considerations must have moved the rebels to launch the new campaign. Soon they began to describe the conversos as secret Jews, heretics and traitors—not only to the city of Toledo and to Spain, but of course to Christianity and the Christian world. The epithets spread, the charges caught on; for the enemies of the conversos, especially in the *común*, were quick to see in these vilifying slogans effective weapons against the hated breed. But there can be no doubt that many Old Christians then greeted the new accusation with amazement, unconcealed skepticism or plain disbelief, and occasionally, when not stifled by fear, with open criticism and sharp reproach.

To answer these criticisms, and justify the steps it was planning to take in the new direction, the government decided on a special action. In the midst of its clamorous and persistent agitation against the conversos as Judaizers and heretics, it announced the appointment of a commission of inquiry to investigate all the charges, claims and complaints made against the conversos with respect to their religion.[10]

It is easy to imagine how this announcement was greeted by the conversos. They knew who the members of the commission were, what their attitude toward the conversos was; and they could have no doubts about the nature of the guidelines the "inquirers" had received from their superiors. Naturally, they were certain that the "findings" were predetermined and designed to serve a sinister plan. They may not have known what that plan was, but even if they did, they could do nothing about it. They were helpless prisoners in the hands of deadly foes who would stop at nothing to hurt them.

The commission soon produced its conclusions: the ranks of the New Christians were filled with secret Jews who followed Jewish rites and beliefs. It also presented an account of its proceedings and a detailed summary, under twenty-two headings, of the non-Christian practices it had discovered.[11] On the basis of these "findings," which nobody dared question, the government felt safe that public opinion was prepared for its next move. It established a tribunal to judge the Judaizers, and invited good Christians who knew of their heresies to come forward and bear witness against them. The first inquisitional tribunal was thus established in Castile.

Many decent and learned Old Christians must have been shocked at what they now saw. The proceedings were authorized by neither pope nor arch-bishop, only by the vicar of the cathedral church, Galvez, who was notori-ously an enemy of the conversos and one of the leaders of the rebel group.[12] But the *común* rejoiced. The sight of conversos being dragged to court, subjected to the most ignominious accusations, sentenced to death and then burned in the squares[13] must not only have excited their passion for ven-geance but also fired their hopes that soon, at last, they would be rid of the hated group. Then came the confiscation of all the goods of the conversos judged guilty by the religious courts; and while we do not know how these properties were divided, it seems likely that Sarmiento gave a share to the Church and those involved in the proceedings (judges, executioners, clerks and the like). The popular jubilation over the punishment of conversos, now generally designated as crypto-Jews, was thus fortified by the immediate profits that many Old Christians had derived from their destruction. To the enemies of Christ in Toledo, it seemed, the Day of Judgment had come ahead of time.

It is impossible to say how long this frenzy would have continued, or how it would all have ended, if, shortly after the proceedings had begun, the attention of the rebels had not been diverted from the orgy of persecution to other matters. They had to get ready to fight for their lives.

IV

On May 1, 1449, the King and his army, on their way to Toledo, reached the small town of Fuensalida, only five leagues from the rebellious city. When the outbreak occurred the king was far away, besieging the village of Benavente, several miles from the Portuguese border, and it was there that he received Alvaro's appeal to abandon the siege and hasten to Toledo.[14] But the King deferred action on that appeal, and spent three full months in a futile attempt to reduce the stronghold of the rebel count. Perhaps he had thought that victory in Benavente might facilitate his effort to pacify Toledo, but as things turned out, his failure on that front must only have stiffened the Toledans' resistance. In any case, by delaying his departure for Toledo, he gave the rebels time to establish their regime, strengthen their hold on the great city, and prepare it for a long siege.

Above all, the delay gave Sarmiento time to build his case against the administration and develop a campaign in the city and the country that lent him a posture of a national leader. The arguments of that campaign centered on the conversos and connected the converso issue with Alvaro in a way that had never been done before. It is safe to assume that most of these arguments were provided by Marcos García de Mora, who in all probability had used at least some of them in his prerebellion agitation. Now, however, they combined into a cogent theory that could serve as the rebels' official view. What the rebels wanted was to have that view accepted—first, in Toledo, then in other towns, and finally throughout the realm. And there is no doubt that, in the period referred to, they attained no mean part of that goal. When at the beginning of May 1449 they presented to the King their memorandum (or "Petition"), including a summary of their position, there is reason to believe that it was backed, at least partly, not only by the *común*, but by a much broader section of the Toledan public.[15]

Before submitting that Petition, however, Sarmiento informed the King in Fuensalida that "if he wished" to enter Toledo, he "should please come only with a limited force, and without Alvaro de Luna or his men."[16] In addition, he made the King's entry subject to the following two stipulations: (a) that Sarmiento be assured of his command of the alcazar, and (b) that he would never be called to account for any action he had taken since the outbreak of the rebellion.[17]

As could be expected, the King rejected these demands and proceeded to Toledo to lay siege to the city. It was in his army camp outside Toledo that he received Sarmiento's Petition, in which the rebels set forth their grievances and demands.[18] These demands included the calling of Cortes in order to "remedy" the condition of the realm, but essentially they focused on the ousting of the conversos and of Alvaro, their promoter, from the royal administration. The two demands were presented as inseparable—in fact, as a single bipartite demand[19]; and the King was informed that, if he failed to comply with it, the city would stop treating him as King and would transfer its allegiance to his son, Prince Enrique.[20]

"The King," says the *Crónica de Juan II,* "was very much annoyed" by the Petition.[21] He did not dignify it with a reply, and continued with his siege of Toledo. But soon he could assess the difficulty of the task. The spirit of resistance and defiance he encountered attested Sarmiento's strong hold on the city, or rather the fact that many Toledans agreed wholeheartedly with his actions and demands. The city could doubtless withstand a long siege. But Sarmiento's patience was giving way. He realized that, if he continued to depend solely on the support of the *común,* he could not hold out in this quarrel for long. To overcome his isolation and the deficiencies it entailed, he knew he had to join a body of nobility that would protect him as one of its own.

Now, as before, he was certain that his interests could best be served by the Aragonese—that is, the party of Juan I of Navarre; and indeed, shortly after having seized Toledo, he wrote to that troublemaker and political meddler, who so often disturbed the peace of Castile, offering him alliance and requesting his aid. Juan of Navarre answered on March 17, praising the Toledans to heaven for their rising and solemnly assuring them that he would do his utmost to assist them as speedily and effectively as possible.[22] Nothing, of course, could be gathered from that answer as to how and when that aid would arrive, and yet Juan's reply may well have breathed new life into Sarmiento's waning hopes. He knew that Navarre was awaiting the response of the King of Aragon, Alfonso V, then in Naples, to the appeal of Don Fadrique (the escaped Castilian nobleman) that he authorize an Aragonese invasion of Castile[23]; and Sarmiento may have had good reasons to believe that the response would be favorable, as it actually was. In any case, the tenor of the Petition, which the rebels then addressed to the king of Castile, suggested (or perhaps was just meant to suggest) that, politically and militarily, they felt secure. They may have overrated the low state of the kingdom and underrated the resourcefulness of Alvaro de Luna, as well as the endurance of Juan II. But the King's flat rejection of their proposals, and his blunt refusal even to discuss them, may have acted as a powerful jolt, forcing them back to reality. At least, it compelled them to change their strategy.

Since no concrete aid could come soon from Aragon, and none was even promised so far, Sarmiento fell back, with much reluctance no doubt, on the only alternative that was open to him: an alliance with another nobiliar force—that of Prince Enrique.[24]

The Prince and heir apparent Don Enrique constituted one of the foci of opposition to the rule of Alvaro de Luna. Shortly after the victory at Olmedo, he abandoned his father's camp once more, evidently dissatisfied with his share of the spoils that had fallen to the victors. Again, he felt, Alvaro stood in his way, and again he sought to reduce, if not ruin, the Constable's influence at Court.

Commanding large estates and allied with great nobles who were joined with him in a powerful league, the Prince was a force not to be ignored by any nobleman or city in Castile. In his current posture toward the King and Alvaro, he appeared to Sarmiento as a possible ally, and yet a most questionable one. For the Prince was known for his political instability, and, in addition, was subject to the influence of his favorite, the wily and notoriously unscrupulous Pacheco. An agreement with the Prince, Sarmiento realized, was unsafe, whatever its terms; yet he had nowhere else to turn.

He must have sent feelers in the direction of the Prince even prior to the King's arrival in Fuensalida, without seeking, however, to strike a deal at that particular moment. But the King's flat rejection of his Petition, and especially his investment of the city, made the alliance with the Prince urgent and quickened the process of negotiations. Sarmiento offered the Prince and Pacheco a bait he was sure they would take. The leadership of Toledo and its partial rule, he thought, was a trump card that no one would reject— that is, no one engaged as passionately as they were in Castile's game of politics. Agreement was soon reached on some major points, but its conclusion had to be delayed until both sides were sure that it could be carried out. It was obvious that, unless the Prince could secure both his entry into Toledo and the lifting of the siege, there was no basis for the contemplated agreement, as these were prerequisites for the realization of both Sarmiento's and Enrique's desires. Accordingly, the Prince requested the King, his father, to allow him entry into Toledo with a military force, arguing that this was the only way to return the city to the King's authority; but the King and Alvaro remained unimpressed and rejected the Prince's appeals. They had no more faith in the Prince's declarations than they had in Ayala's or, in fact, in Sarmiento's. The Prince, however, had taken the bait. He proceeded toward Toledo with a military force considerably larger than that of the King; and the latter, to avoid a clash with his son, or fearing a war in both his front and rear, hastened to raise the siege of Toledo. On May 24, he began his retreat toward Valladolid.[25]

V

The lifting of the siege and the withdrawal of the king's army were undoubtedly hailed as a great victory for Sarmiento—and not among his supporters alone. The event seemed to justify his political tactics and vindicate his stamina and foresight. Inevitably his prestige rose, and many of those who had been undecided were now drawn to his camp. The general view was that Sarmiento was now the uncontested master of Toledo.

But he and his associates knew better. Soon, they realized, they would have to give up much of their authority. To begin with, their understanding with the Prince would forbid them to negotiate with any political party. From the moment the Prince became the city's patron, Toledo's "foreign relations" were to be in his hands, and any action of the rebels in this field—against his will, or behind his back—would be regarded as betrayal. Obviously, Sarmiento could not help realizing that the Prince had freed him from the King's siege only to place him in his own cage.

He tried to weaken the grip of this constraint on his political and military freedom by holding on, as far as he could, to the internal gains of the Toledan revolution. The retreat of his enemies from the city's walls gave him some relief and a breathing spell, and upon resuming his negotiations with the Prince, he tried to strike a hard bargain. To begin with, he secured continued control of his main military and judicial positions (i.e., command of the alcazar and the chief judgeship of appeals).[26] He allowed the Prince the right of entry and exit through only two of the city's gates, which the Prince would control, but kept in his own hands the two other gates, including the Tower of St. Martín. He also prohibited the King's visits to Toledo except as companion to the Prince—a humiliating provision which in effect nullified the prospect of the King's visit to the city—at least in the immediate future.[27]

All these terms seemed to have secured Sarmiento's *internal* control of Toledo; and yet he realized that even internally his freedom was sharply curtailed. Indubitably, the Prince informed his agents that he would refuse to patronize the city of Toledo if it continued to be the scene of lawless actions as it had been in the preceding months; and, among other things, he must have insisted that the savage persecution of the conversos cease. The only concession Sarmiento got from him insofar as his former conduct was concerned was an assurance that he could keep the goods he had taken, justly or unjustly, from any citizen of Toledo, and that he would never be called to account for any deaths, banishments and other sufferings caused to any citizen at his order. He also obtained specific promises concerning the conversos—namely, that those of them he had ousted from the city would never be allowed to return; that conversos he had removed from their offices and honors would not be permitted to resume these posts; and that those he had appointed in their stead would be allowed to keep their positions.[28]

It would seem that these far-reaching concessions should have satisfied Sarmiento's requirements. And yet he was troubled and uneasy, as no doubt were also his principal aides. They knew that the die had been cast against them. They had lost their main asset—their full mastery of Toledo—and in this, they realized, they had to acquiesce. But what caused their disquiet was a special problem that urgently called, they felt, for a solution. Finally, they hit upon a plan of action designed to allay their concerns. The outcome of that plan was soon to throw Spain into a furious controversy. It was known as the *Sentencia-Estatuto*.

VI

On June 5, 1449, a meeting was held at Toledo's town hall *(Sala de los Ayuntamientos)* to proclaim a law which was meant to govern the city's relations with the conversos. The law was enunciated with great pomp, in the presence of the governor, Pero Sarmiento, the judges, the chiefs of police *(alguaziles)*, and members of all classes of the city's population, with the exception of the high nobility. To be sure, many of Toledo's former leaders, including the *regidores*, the city's formal "rulers," were likewise absent from that gathering. Nevertheless, the meeting in the town hall represented a cross-section of the city's population and perhaps the majority of its citizens.

The law, as formulated, comprised two parts: (1) a preamble, which set forth an "opinion" (or "judgment") of the conversos' social and religious conduct; and (2) the legal limitations to be imposed on the conversos on the basis of that "opinion." Hence the double name of the law in its entirety:

Sentencia-Estatuto (Judgment and Statute). As for the Judgment, its major innovation lay in its view of the Jewish people as constituting a problem that cannot be solved by conversion to Christianity. As for the Statute, it proclaimed certain measures to be taken in accordance with that view. Stripped to its essentials, it denied all conversos the right to any office (either public or private), the right to any ecclesiastical benefice (again, both public and private), and also the right to give testimony in court, both in Toledo and its territory. Furthermore, the Statute declared these denials binding also upon the conversos' offspring—that is, both their immediate descendants and their progeny in later times.[29]

The Statute was obviously intended not only to humiliate the conversos and degrade them. Its immediate aim was to create a deep cleavage between the conversos and all other Christians, while its ultimate aim was to push the conversos outside the pale of Christian society. As such, the Statute was meant to attain for the anti-conversos their most desired goal. But, as we shall see, it also represented a new treatment of the conversos and the converso problem—a treatment that differed fundamentally from the one which the rebels had applied in the preceding months. Hence we must ask: Why the change? And why did it occur when it actually did—just before the end of the rebels' rule, or rather *independent* control of Toledo?

VII

It would certainly not be far-fetched to assume that what worried Sarmiento most at this juncture was his future safety in Toledo. To be sure, he had been solemnly promised by the Prince that at no time would he be brought to judgment for any of his actions during the rebellion. But the validity of that promise was obviously limited to the Prince's tenure as Toledo's lord. After that, he realized, he could rely on it no more than on a broken reed.

He must have been especially haunted by the prospect of a possible rapprochement between the Prince and the King, in which the assurances the Prince had given him would be sacrificed in exchange for the King's concessions to the prince. If this happened, he knew, the King and Alvaro would be free to act against him as they wished; and he also knew that in such circumstances the conversos would resume their influence. If so, they would not be slow, he was sure, to take legal action against him; and he could easily foresee the inevitable outcome of these judicial procedures. Indeed, he must have dreaded the day when conversos—both lawyers and witnesses—would reveal in the courts his horrid deeds and, what was worse, when converso magistrates would sit in judgment over his crimes. Such a prospect must have alarmed him no less than the fear of Alvaro's vengeance.

Sarmiento, obviously, could do nothing at the moment to secure Alvaro's downfall. Anything that related to the future of the realm was now to be handled by the Prince alone. But it occurred to him and the other rebel leaders, who must have shared his concerns and anxieties, that they still might be in a position to minimize potential converso reprisals. They seem to have concluded that this could be achieved if their judicial prosecution by conversos were forbidden. More clearly, they believed that if a law to this effect were adopted by the city while they were in power and enforced thereafter for a considerable time, the chances were that it would be honored also later by whomever might rule Toledo in the future.

The *Sentencia-Estatuto* was meant to be that law. Under its ruling, the New Christians were denied the right to assume public office, which meant, among other things, that they could not serve as judges, lawyers and public notaries. Moreover, they were denied the right to bear witness in any legal proceedings, and thus their capacity to sue the rebels was reduced almost to nothing.

These were, as we see it, the *personal* considerations that moved the rebels to enact the *Sentencia*. But no less compelling were the *political* considerations that prompted them to take this action. As we have indicated, the Prince promised the rebels to pardon them all their *past* misdeeds; but this also implied—and he no doubt made it clear—that such actions would not be tolerated in the future. This meant that there would be no more arrests, expulsions, and executions of New Christians in Toledo, which in turn seemed to spell the end of the rebels' anti-converso drive.

Inevitably, the matter was closely related to their ability to hold the city. They knew that it was the *común* alone from which they could expect support and sympathy, but they also knew that the *común*'s loyalty had to be constantly fed and fostered. What nourished that loyalty, they had no doubt, was the persecution of the conversos. But if this persecution were to stop and be replaced by what might look like toleration, the *común* might turn its back on the rebels. Its enthusiasm for the rebellion would give way to disappointment, indifference, or even contempt. It would judge the rebel leaders as failures, if not as traitors to their own cause.

The *Sentencia-Estatuto* was meant to indicate that the rebels were faithful to their word. By declaring the conversos unfit to be equal, in rights and function, to all other Christians, and by denying them, both legally and factually, all participation in the city's government, they showed to the *común*, and the rest of the people, that their struggle against the conversos went on. The social degradation of the conversos, which the city administration was to enforce, would certainly be hailed by the lower classes, which chafed at what they viewed as converso "oppression," but it would also be welcomed by the middle classes, which resented the conversos' great public influence and eagerly sought to curb it. Thus, there was good reason to hope that, as a result, most of the citizens would come to support Sarmiento's government—and not on the converso issue alone.

Thus, it appears that the change in the regime and the apparent uncertainty of Toledo's future raised in the rebels' minds the question of their security, as well as of their future hold on Toledo. The *Sentencia-Estatuto* came to offer at least a partial solution to both these problems. From the rebels' standpoint it was an emergency measure, but it indicated their adaptability to new situations and their ability to keep to their chosen course in the face of obstacles and hardships. Just as in the first stage of the rebellion the persecution of the conversos had assumed a new form when it passed from political to religious lines, it now changed its form again when it passed from religious to social lines. A new phase began in the struggle against the conversos; and soon we shall see where it led to.

The rebels had little time at their disposal to carry out their new plan. The date of the Prince's arrival in Toledo, no doubt fixed by agreement, was fast approaching, and the rebels were determined to beat the deadline. They wanted to pass the law they had in mind while they still were sole masters of Toledo, and in this, as we have stated, they succeeded. Thus, a new anti-converso campaign, or rather an old one, reshaped and re-formed, was launched upon an agitated people in the throes of an ongoing civil strife.

V. The Rebels Under the Prince

I

Shortly after the issuance of the *Sentencia-Estatuto*, Toledo was the scene of another event that had been eagerly awaited by its citizens. This was the arrival of Prince Enrique in Toledo, which gave rise to a medley of hopes and apprehensions; for in view of the unsettled political situation, the most fervent optimism could easily dwell alongside the most pessimistic forecasts. This, as we see it, was the Toledans' state of mind on the eve of the Prince's visit.

According to the *Crónica del Halconero*, he entered Toledo "in the beginning of June."[1] But in all probability, the author of this *crónica* was ignorant of the precise date. He may have been informed: "early in the month" and understood this to mean "in the beginning, etc." In our judgment, the prince's arrival in Toledo *followed* the issuance of the *Sentencia-Estatuto*.[2] It is unlikely, therefore, that he entered the city before June 8.

Both his entry and reception were intended to befit the royal heir to the throne. Flanked by his favorite, Juan Pacheco, and Juan's brother, Pedro Girón, the Prince rode into the city at the head of a procession that included many nobles and 1500 horsemen.[3] He was received with great pomp by Pero Sarmiento, who acknowledged the Prince as the city's lord, and with jubilant festivities by the citizens, who viewed him as both friend and patron. For despite all uncertainties surrounding the future, one thing was clear for the present: the Prince had freed them from the royal siege, the agonies of war, and the danger of occupation; he also freed them from the fear of punishment by a vengeful minister and an outraged king.

During the Prince's visit to Toledo (which, according to the sources, lasted fifteen days),[4] two changes were made in the city's governance: one military, the other civil. The military change consisted of the transfer of the Gates of Alcántara and Visagra to the Prince[5]; the civil change was expressed in the new policy that had just been adopted toward the conversos. The people of Toledo could now clearly see that the city's military control was divided. And they doubtless also noticed the different treatment that was now accorded the New Christians.

For gone were the trials, executions and expulsions which had raised the spirits of so many Toledans. Gone was the violence that had characterized the actions taken against so many New Christians. To be sure, the conversos were still persecuted, but it was persecution of a different kind. It was marked by contempt, acid hostility, subtle affronts and, above all, discrimination—

sharp, blatant and painful discrimination, in full accord with the rules and spirit of the *Sentencia-Estatuto*.[6]

What was the Prince's reaction to the Statute, of which he must have heard upon his entry to Toledo, if he had not been informed of it before? We have no indication that he reacted at all, and there is good reason to believe that he did not. He or his advisers must have realized, of course, that the Statute was a clever legal subterfuge aimed at sanctioning criminal acts—the kind of acts he must have forbidden when he negotiated with Sarmiento the terms of his entry. Yet he also knew that the rebels could claim that they had done nothing beyond the terms agreed to; that the measures they adopted were strictly preventive, aimed at protecting their rights and interests; and that their new rulings were actually not new, but anchored in old laws and privileges. Hence, if the Prince wished to repeal them, he would have to enter into a legal dispute, which could not be settled quickly to his liking, unless he was prepared to use force. But nothing was further from his mind at the time than legal wrangling or the use of force. He therefore ignored the publication of the Statute as if it were the city's internal affair, and as if it did not concern him directly as Toledo's patron and master.

Sarmiento and his aides, one may assume, awaited the Prince's reaction with anxiety. They knew they had tricked the Prince into a corner from which he would find it hard to assail them; yet there was no telling what a prince might do once he realized that he had been cheated. The rebels may have counted on Pacheco's pragmatism and his customary preference of the useful to the honorable, and they knew that to him Toledo was a power base that he would not like to jeopardize by a quarrel with its people. Just the same, they must have been relieved by the Prince's failure to criticize the Statute. It was the first test of their relations with the Prince in their common future control of the city, and the test passed smoothly to their satisfaction. Sarmiento could now govern Toledo on the basis of the newly enacted law.

Far different must have been the reaction of the conversos to the Prince's silence on their terrible degradation. Indubitably, they were both amazed and disappointed. They had hoped that the Prince's coming to Toledo would restore their former condition in the city, or at least mark the start of that restoration. But what actually happened gave them little hope that this would indeed be the case. To be sure, they could now breathe more freely. The assaults upon their persons and property had ceased, or at least been greatly diminished. But at the same time, the discrimination against them continued and was vigorously enforced. From this they could gather that all the Prince had done was to stop the most ghastly forms of persecution, but that actually he approved of, or at least acquiesced in, the Statute and all it involved. Such a conclusion could make the conversos, both in Toledo and elsewhere in Castile, shiver with fear and apprehension.

For however grim was their view of the sufferings they had endured under the rule of Sarmiento, they viewed with much greater concern and misgiving the enactment and enforcement of the *Sentencia-Estatuto*. For this was no longer an unruly action by antiroyal rebels who had captured a city. This was the formal policy of a city, now run primarily by a national leader. The Statute was therefore persecution institutionalized. The fact that such a law, and such a regime, could be tolerated by Prince Enrique, the heir apparent, the future king of Castile and León, seemed to spell disaster for all New Christians. Sooner or later, the example of Toledo would spread to other cities in the country, and finally embrace the whole of Castile and the rest of the peninsula.

That this was not just a nightmarish vision, born of panic and shorn of reality, soon became apparent from the attacks upon conversos that occurred in various places in the country.[7] Especially terrible were the disturbances in Ciudad Real that broke out on July 7, 1449, precisely one month after the issuance of the Statute. Of all the places in which the conversos were assailed, Ciudad Real gave the most brutal evidence that the spirit of Toledo was catching. A pogrom was organized by the Old Christians of the city against their New Christian neighbors, and crimes and atrocities were committed of a kind not seen in Spain since 1391. Since the attack on the conversos in Ciudad Real was neither connected with a political objective (such as freeing the city from Alvaro's rule) nor led by rebels who could rouse the mobs to support their plans and ambitions (as was the case in Toledo), the fury of the Old Christians in Ciudad Real seemed a natural response to the popular calls that then swept the city, such as *Kill the conversos!* and *Sack their homes!* The results were disastrous. Most of the borough of the richer conversos, the fashionable neighborhood of Barrionuevo, was destroyed in an orgy of pillage and bloodshed that lasted no less than two weeks (from July 7 to 20). Twenty-two conversos were killed; many others were maimed and wounded. Most of those killed were dragged through the streets, and then, following the Toledan example, hanged, feet upward, in the central square.[8]

Two great cities in the heart of the country had now tangibly demonstrated the feelings of their citizens toward the New Christians. That a widespread dislike for conversos existed in many parts of Castile and Aragon was common knowledge in both realms; what was not known, however, was that this dislike could reach such extremes of violence and hate. Toledo and Ciudad Real sounded a warning; but it was still too early to determine what it meant. Did the outbreaks there indicate a deep-seated attitude of the average Old Christian in the urban centers, or did they reflect the ability of some agitators to drive the cities' masses to acts of madness? Toledo, which appeared to be captured by such men, seemed to support the second proposition; Ciudad Real gave more credence to the first.[9]

Be that as it may, the conversos refused to yield to counsels of despair. They agreed, to be sure, that many Old Christians could be moved, under incitement, to behave like brutes, but most of them, they believed, were reasonable men, who could be swayed to act lawfully by an honest appeal; hence, together with these Old Christians, they, the conversos, could cure the country, now seized with fever, by putting an end to the Toledan regime, the source of the spreading disease.[10] Especially dangerous in their eyes was the Statute—the ultimate expression of that regime—which legitimized the feelings, intentions and actions of the conversos' enemies everywhere. Thus, the destruction of the Toledan regime, together with the annulment of the *Sentencia-Estatuto,* became the conversos' most urgent aim.

To achieve this aim, they mobilized their best forces, all their connections in the government and the Church and all their influence at home and abroad. Alfonso de Cartagena wrote several letters concerning the Toledan events to King Juan II.[11] One of their ecclesiastic notables in Toledo went to Rome to move Pope Nicholas V to pronounce the rebels and their Statute anathema.[12] Letters and memoranda were sent to the Curia, and Cardinal Torquemada was urgently requested to take up the cudgels on behalf of the conversos.[13] The cardinal threw himself into the battle and, as we shall see, his contribution and achievement were of signal importance.

We have no indication that all this activity was coordinated with the King, Juan II, but it was no doubt aided by the steps he had taken in that very direction. For the King, too, appealed to the Pope for his immediate intervention.[14] The King's appeal, we have reason to believe, focused on the rebels' antiroyal moves, while that of the conversos centered on their crimes against faithful Christians and against Christianity. Both complaints led to the same conclusion and ended in the same request—namely, that the Pope denounce the rebels and anathemize them and their abettors.

The Pope was thus under double pressure (that is, from both the King and the conversos) to take immediate action. His denunciation of the rebels could be made within days, at most within weeks. But the Pope took his time; he procrastinated. Other pressures, and other considerations, were obviously at work.

II

One of the sources of that pressure must have been the rebels' delegation to Rome. It probably arrived there early in July, close on the heels of the conversos' delegate, and its task was to convince Nicholas V of the legality and propriety of the Toledan outbreak and, above all, to prevent him from heeding the appeals of both the King and the conversos. Its members must have come to Rome well prepared, backed by the "evidence" they had assembled in their Inquiry and the documents that served as basis for their Statute. And it all meant to show, we may take it for granted, that the rebellion was both inevitable and justifiable because the people could not take any longer what they faced: the terrible crimes of the false Christians and the shocking conduct of their royal patrons. Their argument, they hoped, would impress the Pope, especially when presented by the head of their mission, the highly respected García de Villalpando, whose record seemed to indicate not only ability but also integrity and civil courage.[15] But all these hopes soon came to nothing. The delegates were not given a chance even to present their case to the Pope.

Influenced by Cardinal Juan de Torquemada, Nicholas V refused to accept them,[16] fearing no doubt that an audience might lend them an aura of legitimacy. The delegation, however, did not give in. Unable to speak to Nicholas V, it found receptive ears among members of the curia and these no doubt communicated its arguments to the Pope, or some of his aides and advisers. Thus, it is likely that these arguments inspired certain statements in the Pope's bull on the conversos.[17] In all the rest, the delegation was a failure. The Pope was probably already disposed to come out against the rebels by the middle of July. Nevertheless, two more months passed before he finally decided to do so. Why?

The reason, as we see it, was the Pope's doubts about the viability of Juan II's rule and his favorite's ability to avoid the collapse that threatened his administration. No doubt early in July the Pope was informed that Alfonso V, king of Naples, his neighbor, had instructed Aragon, his other kingdom, to mount an all-out invasion of Castile; and he knew that in Castile a dozen smaller armies, led by the foremost nobles of the country, were ready to take the field against their king once such an invasion began. What sense would there be in censuring Toledo, one rebellious spot in the kingdom, if the fires of rebellion were about to spread across the whole length and breadth of Castile? What is more, in the circumstances, a bull against the rebels might be seen as an attack upon their allies, too—and Nicholas V did not wish to be involved in a quarrel with Naples and Aragon. Cautious and hesitant, the Pope bided his time, waiting to see what would happen.

A good many days, however, were to pass before the trend of events finally emerged from the mist of confusion that engulfed it. At the beginning of July, when the admiral of Castile returned to Saragossa with King Alfonso's response, things looked bleak for the kingdom of Castile. Alfonso V had ordered the Aragonese to place at the disposal of his brother and the admiral both cavalry and infantry for an attack upon Castile. He also ordered them to pay the salaries of the troops that his brother might bring from Navarre for that purpose. And apart from this, he gave the admiral's delegation "much money" from his own treasury in Naples, no doubt to show the seriousness of his intentions and his own readiness to support the war effort.[18] There seemed to be good reason to believe that the King's express wishes would be honored by Cortes and that an Aragonese-Navarrene invasion of Castile would soon be under way. Even the prudent Juan of Navarre seemed sure that this was the case.

He hastened to convene the Cortes of Aragon in order to ratify the King's instructions and discuss with them the manner in which these instructions should be carried out.[19] Cortes, however, did not come up to expectations. It strongly objected to the King's instructions, claiming that according to the terms of peace, which Aragon had recently concluded with Castile, they could not go to war against it.[20] Juan of Navarre and the admiral of Castile tried hard to move Cortes to change its position, but what they achieved fell short of the mark. Cortes adhered to its adamant refusal to involve Aragon in war with Castile. It agreed, however, to "serve the King of Navarre with a large sum of money"—even larger than that which their King, Alfonso, "ordered them to give him."[21]

An Aragonese invasion of Castile at this time might have imperiled Juan II's rule, and the dismissal of the plan by the Cortes of Aragon must have brought relief to Alvaro and the King. But not for long. For as soon as that major danger was removed, another conspiracy began to take shape. Old threats gave way to new.

III

The King and Alvaro were of course right in opposing the Prince's entrance into Toledo and in mistrusting the vows and assurances he had given them before making that move. They realized that his purpose in entering the city was not, as he claimed, to wrest it from the rebels in order to return it to his father. His aim was to use it as a means of advancing his own military and political plans. To be sure, when he entered the city of Toledo, these plans were not yet completed. His next moves, he realized, would greatly depend on the outcome of Don Fadrique's mission to Naples. But one of two options appeared possible. Should Aragon and Navarre invade Castile, the Prince would assist them on the clear condition that control of Castile remain solely his. Otherwise, he would negotiate with his father for an alliance that would yield him further gains.

But Aragon's refusal to join the battle of Castile forced the Prince to adopt new plans, just as it compelled Juan of Navarre to revise and readjust his own. Stubborn and resourceful, Juan was unwilling to abandon his old designs on Castile, but he knew that whatever schemes he now contrived, he could count on only two assets. These were (a) the pledge of the Aragonese Cortes to offer him financial aid, and (b) the ardent desire of most Castilian nobles to overthrow Alvaro's regime. These assets would have to do, he thought; and he hoped that Castile's leading nobles of the opposition would agree with him on this. Accordingly, he appealed to Prince Enrique and "all the other Caballeros of the Kingdom" to join him in "defense of their rights."[22]

Seeking to allay the patriotic misgivings of at least some of the nobles concerned, while trying to excite their fear of Alvaro, Juan of Navarre stressed in his appeal to them that the effort he suggested would in no way be aimed at the kingdom of Castile or at its king, Juan II, but solely against the terrible Alvaro, who threatened them all with ruination.[23] His appeal, as he could see, was well received, but he also noted that the nobles he turned to preferred to follow a Castilian chief rather than the king of Navarre. In consequence, the leadership of the struggle against Alvaro passed almost automatically to the Prince; for now it was he, the Prince, and no one else, who could rally the mutinous nobility.

On July 26, he convened in Coruña a meeting of nobles who were in his league and others of Alvaro's major opponents. It was attended by representatives of the Prince (Pacheco), the king of Navarre (Admiral Fadrique) and the powerful houses of Haro and Mendoza (Count Pero de Velasco and the Marquis of Santillana), as well as by the fiery Rodrigo Manrique. The assembled nobles pledged to mobilize their forces and meet near Peñafiel within one month. It was further agreed that the King of Navarre and the friendly nobles then outside Castile would join with them at the same place and time, provided that before entering Castile they subscribed to the terms of Coruña.[24]

These terms must have related to matters of leadership in the planned struggle, as well as to postwar arrangements in Castile once the alliance gained the upper hand. In any case, it appears that those assembled in Coruña thought that Navarre might object to their terms, in which case they agreed not to be deterred from taking on Alvaro by themselves. Evidently, they believed that their combined forces could emerge victorious from an encounter with the King, or compel the King to open negotiations that would spell the end of Alvaro's rule.

The agreement of Coruña must have moved Alvaro to take some precautionary measures; but this was not his only worry. In the middle of the year, the Moors of Granada had renewed their raids into Castile in great force, reaching at times the environs of Baena, Jaén, and even Seville. Leaving behind much devastation, they brought back to Granada many captives and much livestock. "In all this," says the *Halconero*, "they met no resistance in the whole of Andalusia."[25]

It seemed certain that if in such a precarious situation Juan II were attacked by Prince Enrique, aided by his league of nobles and Navarre, the

Moors would join the latter in great force and help topple the regime. As a matter of fact, the King of Granada wrote in July to Juan of Navarre, advising him to invade Castile at once, and assuring him that if the invasion took place, the Granadans would besiege and capture Cordova and then put it at the disposal of Navarre. Expressing thanks for this intended help, Juan of Navarre answered Granada that he was indeed planning to invade Castile, and when the time came, he and his nobles would consult the Granadans on the course they should follow.[26]

But beyond these threats Juan II of Castile had still other things to worry about. In April, when the King departed from Benavente, he left the castle besieged by his forces and the village in the hands of his lieutenants. However, when the Count of Benavente, then in Portugal, heard of the King's withdrawal from Toledo, he returned to Benavente with troops he had assembled and compelled the King's soldiers to abandon the siege and retreat from the occupied village. Months of effort by the King and his army thus went up in smoke. Again Benavente became a center of rebellion and a base for war against the King's men; but faced with the "great necessities" of his kingdom, the King could do nothing about it.[27]

The news of these setbacks for Juan II was no doubt dispatched with utmost speed by the rebels of Toledo to their delegates in Rome, and quickly reported by the latter to the curia, with the aim of communicating them to the Pope. Obviously, they wanted the Pope to believe that the days of Alvaro's rule were numbered, and, under the circumstances, the Pope could assume that there was a good basis for that forecast.

Throughout that period, we may take it for granted that Alvaro's agents in Rome were attempting to minimize the impact of the rebels' agitation.[28] Unlike the rebels, they had access to the Pope, and thus could present to him directly the arguments they judged helpful to their case. The Pope, however, remained unconvinced. He kept withholding action on behalf of the King— or, for that matter, against the rebels. He also refused to issue a bull in defense of the conversos.

It was only in mid-September, it seems, that he finally made up his mind. He was no doubt informed that the forces of the alliance were scheduled to meet in August; but August passed and nothing happened. Alvaro's agents must have played up the fact that none of the parties to the Coruña agreement, except Prince Enrique, came to Peñafiel,[29] and they probably explained this by what they must have known of the factors that pulled the coalition apart. Accordingly, they could declare with confidence that Castile faced no danger from within or without and that the "nobles' rebellion" was to prove as chimerical as the "Aragonese invasion." The facts they cited in support of their claims could not fail, it seems, to have impressed the Pope.

In any case, he was led to believe that the Castilian regime was there to stay, and on September 24 he finally signed the long-awaited bulls against the rebels.

IV

The bulls constituted powerful blasts against the rebels and the anti-Marrano movement, and, from the standpoint of Marrano history, they probably represent the strongest position taken by the Church on behalf of the conversos. That does not mean that the New Christians were satisfied with everything contained in these bulls. But they were on the whole pro-converso statements; and this was the most the conversos could achieve.

Of the three bulls issued on September 24, one was devoted to the rebellion per se, another to the converso problem in Christendom; the third dealt with a personal matter: it abolished a judgment issued by the rebels against the archdeacon of the Toledan church.[30]

The bull on the rebellion is directed entirely against Sarmiento and his aides.[31] To them the bull attributes three kinds of crimes: against the King, against Toledo and against the city's inhabitants. The actions against the King are classed by the bull as a crime of *laesa majestas*[32]; the actions against Toledo are summarized as an attempt to "overthrow" the city's laws and lordship[33]; the actions against the inhabitants consist of various crimes, which are described by the bull as follows:

> Many of the inhabitants, especially among the conversos, he [Sarmiento] robbed and arrested under manipulated charges of heresy; he laid violent hands on clerics; he expelled members of the religious orders [*regulares*] from the city; and he committed other criminal offenses, which not only work to the detriment of the faith, but also pose a danger to the state of the kingdom and bring about the destruction of its subjects.[34]

Thus, the rebels' actions against the conversos are placed on a par with their crimes against the clergy, the "regulars," and the faith as a whole, which fact in itself shows clearly and conclusively that the Pope viewed the charges of "heretical depravity," leveled by the rebels against the conversos, as fabricated excuses lacking any substance. This is why he called them *exquisitae assertiones* and classed them with the rebels' other crimes, which he called "manifest and notorious."[35] Nevertheless, in enumerating those notorious crimes, the Pope failed to mention the most notorious of them all—i.e., the *burning* of conversos as "heretics," even though, as indicated, he had generally denounced what was done to them on such a pretext. Surely these crimes were more heinous than robberies or unjust expulsions and incarcerations, which the Pope *did* mention in his bull. But if so, why the evasive language in *this* instance and the failure to reveal the whole truth? We shall have to return to this matter later on.

In punishment for all the aforementioned crimes, the Pope imposed on Sarmiento and his "familiars," as well as his "companions, supporters, followers and adherents," the sentence of excommunication, denying them the right to give testimony (or make a will) and "depriving them of all the seigniories, properties, lands, honors, dignities and offices, both ecclesiastic and civil," which they may possess. Similarly, he made them "perpetually subject to all the other sentences, censures and penalties established by the law and by the common custom against the perpetrators of such offenses."[36]

Moreover, these harsh penalties were not all the punishments that the rebels could expect. For the Pope also issued a call to the princes, dukes, barons, and all other temporal lords—as well as to all the city councils, territories, towns, castles and places, and to all (military) captains and anyone who had in his pay armed men, on both horse and foot—in the dominions of Juan II that if, "within a month after the bull is published, they be required to do so by the King, they will proceed by force against Sarmiento and his aides, seize them and keep them imprisoned until such time as due satisfaction be made to the King and all those who suffered at their hands."[37]

Furthermore, the Pope made it clear that his orders were to be obeyed under pain of grave punishment. He warned all the cities, territories, towns, castles and places that, should they fail to carry out the instructions of the bull, they would be put under an *interdict,* while the princes, dukes, counts, nobles and captains, as well as the officials of the various public bodies, who disobeyed the above instructions, would be subject to excommunication.[38] Finally, the Pope instructed all the officers of the Church "solemnly to publish," in all the churches and other places where the faithful are wont to assemble, both the crimes of Pero Sarmiento and his aides and the punishments imposed upon them by the Pope.[39] Obviously, the Pope wished the execution of the punishments to be as swift and effective as possible. He wanted it to match the severity of the crimes.

Yet if in his bull against the rebels of Toledo the Pope did his utmost to defend the King, the royal rights and the king's subjects, in his bull against the conversos' foes the Pope did not take such a clear-cut position. For this bull contains several phrases and allusions that leave room for various interpretations, and it also lacks certain overt indications that seem to have been called for in such a document. Nevertheless, the bull, as a whole, was a *pro-converso* statement. The tenor of its argument, and some of its pronouncements, offered in their totality a defense of the conversos, as we shall presently see.[40]

To begin with, the Pope placed the attack on the conversos in a historic perspective which was favorable to them when he linked it with the attack of the gentile converts on the Jewish Christians in the days of St. Paul. The Apostle compared those who differentiated between Christians on the grounds of their origin or former religion to sowers of weeds in the field of the faith, in order to prevent the growth of the wheat which that field was expected to yield. Such sowers of weeds, the Pope declared, were now trying to undermine the foundations of Christianity—i.e., the unity and peace of the Church—"especially" in the kingdoms of Castile and León.[41] "Audaciously they assert that those who came to Christ from gentilehood, or Judaism, or any other error, should be denied admission to the honors, dignities, offices and notaryships because of their recent acceptance of the faith." What is worse, they want these limitations to apply also to the children of these converts, and, in addition, they vilify and injure them in a variety of ways by word and deed. Such claims and conduct, the Pope declares, are totally alien to the teachings of Christianity, and as such they contradict the divine authorities, the "sacred canons" of the Church, and the secular laws, for they clearly contravene the various decrees that the princes of Castile have issued against such falsehoods. The Pope took this occasion to confirm the laws enacted in this matter by Castile's Alfonso VIII, Enrique III and Juan II, including the penalties laid down therein. And in order to strengthen this royal position, he added the following declaration:

> Under pain of excommunication we order each and every Christian of whatever station, rank or condition, both ecclesiastic and civil, to admit each and all of those who were converted, and those who will be converted in the future, either from gentilehood or from Judaism, or from any other sect, as well as the descendants of these converts, both lay and clerical, who live as Catholics and good Christians, to all the dignities, honors, offices, notaryships, the bearing of witness and all the other things to which are usually admitted all other Christians who are older in the faith.[42]

Further, the Pope ordered, under the threat of the same punishment, all the above-mentioned groups of all classes that "no difference be made between recent converts and other Christians"; that the latter refrain from dishonoring the former either by word or by deed; that no permission be given for such things to be done, but rather should they be opposed unreservedly. Finally, the converts should be treated with charity, and every honor should be given them as to all other Christians without regard of persons.[43]

However straightforward the statement may appear, it raises certain questions about its objectives. The bull threatens with punishment all who *will* discriminate against the converts in the future; but it does not impose any punishment on those who injured the conversos in the recent past. Why? Perhaps, one may assume, because such punishments are indicated in the Pope's bull against the rebels. But the rebels it referred to acted mostly in Toledo, while many crimes and outrages against conversos were perpetrated outside Toledo as well. In fact, the bull itself clearly indicates that the troubles were not limited to the city of Toledo, or to one or two more isolated spots. It speaks of a *movement* that embraced whole countries, touching most probably Aragon too, but one that infected in a special manner *the kingdoms of Juan II*.[44] Why then leave unpunished all the crimes and transgressions perpetrated against conversos in these kingdoms and treat them as if they had not been committed? There seems to be only one plausible answer: the Pope wished to mitigate the intensity of his conflict with the strong anti-Marrano movement in Spain.

Second, the bull states that the object of that movement was to discriminate against converts of *all* origins—"from gentilehood, Judaism and any other error." But the Pope knew well that this movement was directed against converts from Judaism *only;* that there was no other body of converts in Castile (or, for that matter, in the "kingdoms of Juan II") that seemed to pose a "problem" to the Christians; and that the *Sentencia-Estatuto* enacted in Toledo did not refer to any converts to Christianity other than converts from Judaism. Why then did he blur the real issue by mixing it with other phenomena that were either imaginary or insignificant?

That tactical considerations were involved in the formulation of "converts from gentilehood, Judaism and other sects" cannot be doubted, in our opinion. But this does not mean that the Pope invented the issue, or that it had no basis in fact at all. We may readily assume that in some Spanish towns to which the wave of discrimination had spread, the campaign against converso equalization was aimed against converts from Islam as well. But even in these cases the converts from Judaism undoubtedly were the main object of attack, and if the agitators against them denounced, in their slogans, converts from Islam as well, they must have mentioned the latter not as the primary but as the secondary target. The Pope, however, reversed this order. In his list, the converts censured and hurt are, first of all, "gentile," then "Jewish," and then those who came from "other sects." The reason for this strange presentation of the problem is, in our judgment, not hard to detect. The Pope did not wish to appear as a defender of the New Christians only. He wanted to be seen as the protector of *all* converts, and above all as the advocate of a Christian principle hallowed in the Church since the days of St. Paul.

In this, as in his failure to stipulate punishment for whomever had molested conversos anywhere, we note again his desire to avoid confrontation with the popular anti-Marrano force. This is also why he failed to refer to such crimes as the burning of Marranos as "heretics." To have mentioned them alone would have exacerbated the conflict and forced him to punish the culprits.[45] Instead, the Pope wished to show the opposition due consideration for its arguments and claims, and this he did through several provisions which he included in his bull.

One such provision consisted of the words *catolice et quod Christianum decet viventes* ("who live catholically and in a manner befitting a Christian"), which specified the converts who deserved equal treatment.[46] The provision seemed of course right and self-evident, and yet it cast a stigma of suspicion upon the converts as more likely than any other Christian group to depart from the Catholic way of life. For obviously, any Christian group whose members would violate Christian law and customs, or show disbelief in Christian doctrines, would be considered unfit to occupy offices, dignities, notaryships and the like. So if the "self-evident provision" was needed, it should have applied to all Christians. On the other hand, if it was superfluous, as it seemed to be, it ought not to have been made in this case either (i.e., with reference to the converts). Why, then, was that provision introduced? This becomes clear from the following clause, which is likewise included in the bull:

> But if it is found that some of these people, after having been baptized [to Christianity] do not savor the Christian religion, or fall for the errors of the Jews or the gentiles, or do not guard the precepts of the Christian faith, either because of malice or of ignorance, in this case there should enter into force what was established by the Toledan Councils in the chapter *Constituit*, as well as in another place, wherein it is stated that apostates of this kind should not be admitted to such honors [as indicated] on a par with other Christians.[47]

Needless to say, the very suggestion that heretical phenomena may appear in the converso camp had the effect of distancing that camp to some extent from the ordinary faithful. For heretics could be found in *any* Christian group, whether it consisted of Old or New Christians; and there seemed to be no reason to single out the converts as more likely to harbor heretics in their midst. Especially disturbing was the papal instruction to apply the chapter "Constituit" of the Fourth Toledan Council if "some" of the converts were found to have slipped,[48] when the well-known prohibitions imposed by that decree (on appointment to office, etc.) referred not only to the renegades themselves but to all who were related to them ethnically—i.e., to all converts of Jewish origin.[49] No doubt the conversos opposed the inclusion of this dangerous clause in the Pope's bull. But it is also clear that they could not prevent it. Strong and far-reaching as their influence was, it obviously had its limits. But what they failed to achieve in Rome, they later tried to correct in Castile, as we shall presently see.

V

If in signing these bulls the Pope had relied on a positive assessment of Castile's situation, or rather on the strength of its administration, that assessment was soon confirmed by the course of events. At the beginning of October, when the two major partners of the Prince's coalition (the Count of Haro and the Marquis of Santillana) finally met the Prince at Los Gumieles, it could be clearly seen that Castile was not faced with a large-scale nobiliary uprising. It was apparent that these two great nobles had undergone a change of heart and were looking for excuses to extricate themselves from their joint commitment at Coruña.

According to our sources, the nobles and the Prince could not reach an accord (a) because the parties did not trust each other, and (b) because all of them now raised new demands, aimed at satisfying private interests at the expense of the general plan.[50] In all probability, the second obstacle was merely a face-saving device; but the first was undoubtedly real. The Count and the Marquis were fully aware of the value of promises made by Pacheco; they could not be sure that he would not betray them even at the last moment (perhaps for some reward that Alvaro might offer him). With all this, it seems that another reason (one which the sources chose not to mention) was uppermost in their calculations.

They weighed their chances of beating Alvaro de Luna against the terrible punishments they were certain to take in the event of defeat in battle—and their courage forsook them. Alvaro, they knew, could muster a strong force; he was also cunning and unpredictable; he was expert in avoiding snares and pitfalls and worming his way out of tight spots. The Count and the Marquis had too much at stake; and they judged their alliance with the Prince too shaky—and, without Aragon, also too weak—to challenge such a formidable foe. The Prince, too, must have had second thoughts about the feasibility of beating Alvaro, especially in view of the lack of determination he noticed in his prospective partners. And so they all arrived at the conclusion that, while remaining united in their league, they would forsake their military plan against Alvaro, including an invasion by Juan of Navarre and the Castilian nobles who stood by him. Instead, they would seek accommodation with the King, reducing the terms of accommodation to one: the Prince would return Toledo to the King, while the King would return the castle of Burgos to their ally, the Count of Plasencia. Thus, the balance of power in the country would

not change in Alvaro's favor. The Prince undertook to carry out this understanding within a year from the date of their meeting.[51]

VI

The news of this agreement, so disastrous for the rebels, must already have
reached them in October, but it was only during the Prince's visit to Toledo,
where he arrived at the beginning of November,[52] that they fully realized its
grim meaning. Coming in the wake of those condemnatory bulls and Aragon's decision *not* to fight Castile, the agreement of the nobles was the third
hard blow to strike the rebels in rapid succession. In a sense, it was the worst
of them all, for it dashed their last hope for a change in the regime.

The Prince lost no time in starting negotiations with his father and Alvaro
on the delivery of Toledo, but before long the negotiations bogged down in
a quagmire of disagreements.[53] The Prince, however, believed that in the end
his father would be forced to accept his demands. In the meantime, he
decided to go to Toledo to wrest the alcazar from the hands of Sarmiento and
remove him from the city's judiciary; but he also intended to talk to some
notables whom he wished to take over the Toledan administration. He
wanted to inform them of his plans for the city and secure their support and
allegiance.

He came to Toledo with an impressive retinue, including the leading
members of his court, "many caballeros and *gentil hombres*" and, in all probability, a strong military force.[54] As usual, he was accompanied by Pacheco
and Girón, and this time also by Don Lope de Barrientos, the bishop of
Cuenca, who had joined his council. The bishop was known as the King's
man, and his function at the time as the Prince's adviser led some to assume
that he had changed sides.[55] But such a move would be out of keeping with
Barrientos' political record.[56] No doubt the Prince, foreseeing great difficulties in his forthcoming negotiations in Toledo, asked Barrientos to help him
sway the Toledans to accept his proposed settlement. He must have told the
bishop that he wanted the Toledans to agree to terms acceptable to the King,
and Barrientos could not see in such an assignment anything opposed to his
loyalties.

Toledo gave the Prince a joyous welcome, followed by more than a week
of celebrations, which doubtless expressed the city's desire to strengthen its
ties with its royal patron. Evidently, the Prince was now viewed by most
Toledans as their future deliverer from the rebels' rule, as well as their
protector against the King, his father, who still threatened them with punishment. To impress Sarmiento with the people's attitude, the Prince allowed
the celebrations to last; but as soon as the festivities were over, he broke the

news of his plans for the city both to the rebel chiefs and to some of the notables who were outside the rebels' party.

The annals of the time retain no record of these talks of the Prince with the Toledans. It is possible, however, to reconstruct their trend on the basis of other contemporary sources. Indubitably, the Prince explained to the Toledans that, in the circumstances, they had no choice but to make peace with the King. They might of course seek and obtain some concessions on several matters of no mean importance, but they had to realize the basic conditions which an agreement with the King entailed. These conditions include their acceptance of Alvaro as actual ruler in the country, and they also include the abolition of the *Sentencia* and the restoration of converso equality. Then he pointed out the ultimate conclusion at which he was driving from the very start: it would be inconceivable for the present administration to stay in office under the new arrangements, and the city would have to choose and establish a new municipal government.

The rebels' reaction to these proposals was of course negative—full of reproach and bitter criticism. They reminded the Prince of the terms he had agreed to before they allowed him to enter the city. They made him patron of Toledo, they said, to protect them against Alvaro's oppression, and now he proposes, and seeks their consent, to have them thrown to the tyrant's wolves. They further stressed that they accepted him as lord because he promised to safeguard their rights and privileges; and now he wants them to abolish the *Sentencia*, which is based on their oldest and most cherished privilege. Finally, they reminded the Prince of the assurances he gave Sarmiento regarding his positions—namely, that they were his to keep indefinitely —and now he disregards these assurances, too, and wants Sarmiento to yield all his posts.[57] What answer could the Prince expect them to give him except a categorical no?

No less determined and no more encouraging was the reaction of the notables. To be sure, they wished to get rid of Sarmiento and the hated rebels who swarmed about him, and of course they wished to resume their authority as leaders and governors of the city. But they did not at all relish the prospect of Alvaro's renewed control of Toledo, and they feared his vindictiveness and increased exactions once the city was again in his hands. In addition, they seemed sternly opposed to the restoration of converso equality, and they sought to hold on to the *Sentencia-Estatuto*, which appeared to conform to their views and interests. In fact, on this, as on other issues, there was no great gap between the notables and the rebels; and so the Prince realized that he faced in Toledo a rather united antiroyal front. He no doubt tried hard to allay the fears that all sections of the city population then shared—that is, with regard to the punishments they expected and regarding their special immunities and exemptions. He would do his utmost, he no doubt assured them, to obtain the King's pardon to the city and its citizens, and he would also see to it that the King reconfirm all or most of their royal grants. None of this, however, calmed their spirits; and seeing the stubborn resistance he encountered, Enrique, at some point, must have told the Toledans that he would take their objections into consideration and possibly revise his entire plan. Marcos García, who was then still working on the draft of his reply to the Pope's bulls, must have been impressed with this seeming indecision, and still assumed that the Prince could be swayed to support the rebels' old program. He appealed to the Toledans to stand firm on their rights and not to be attracted by the lure of positions.[58] And he included in his draft a call on the Prince, which is at once a reproach, an entreaty, and a warning:

> O, illustrious Prince and powerful Señor Don Enrique! How did the bad friar[59] deceive you and made you forget the oaths and promises you had given to the holy city of Toledo? You have known the intention of the city and its residents and you have found that intention to be holy and good, and you have approved its actions and motions as just . . . and you have signed with your name and sealed with your seal a letters patent [to this effect], and you have sworn and promised to defend the city and secure full justice and peace and concord between her and the King your father. . . . Why, then, Señor, to the detriment of your soul, and in great disservice to God and the King, and in such great damage and destruction to the said Kingdoms and the city [of Toledo], you wish to approve what you have reproved—namely, the said tyrant and the said heretics. [Why do you wish to] bring about a rise in the tyranny of that tyrant [i.e., Alvaro de Luna] and enable the heretics to increase the mendacity [which they practice] against the Catholic faith and take crude vengeance on the Christian people and on the said city. I beg your Lordship to stand by what you have sworn and promised to this city, and [accordingly] to guard it. For what you have promised is just and licit, and the oath you gave was given of your own will, without any pressure or coercion. Neither the false bishop of the stock of the Jews,[60] nor any other prelate will be able to absolve you from it. Otherwise [namely, if you go back on your promises], the said city will protest as it has been said and as it has [actually] protested.[61]

Enrique, however, did not abandon his attempts to draw the Toledans to his point of view. Before long it became clear to the rebels that the Prince had but one goal in mind: to reach an accord with Alvaro de Luna and deliver Toledo to the King.

The rebels were both confounded and alarmed. What course could they possibly take *now* to avert the imminent hazards they faced? They had little doubt that if their own security, including their promised exemption from punishment, stood in the way of the planned accord, the Prince would forsake them without much ado, promises notwithstanding. After all, they were seen as rebels not only by Alvaro de Luna and the King; they were rebels in the Prince's eyes, too, and he had little sympathy with their aims. Nor did they have any doubt about the fate—or rather the horrors—they were all to suffer once they were delivered to Alvaro's hands. There remained, it seemed, only one avenue of escape: to try for their own accommodation with the king before he received Toledo.

Favoring this attempt were all the leading rebels, with the exception of one—Sarmiento. But Sarmiento was their chief; he had the final say; and he possessed also the only real asset—i.e., military control of the city—that the rebels could offer in their negotiations with the King. But Sarmiento remained opposed to their proposal, and, of course, he had his reasons. No doubt he thought that the rebels had no chance of coming to terms with the King to begin with, while a break with the Prince—which their action would amount to—would cost them the only support they could count on. Sarmiento's answer, then, was no.[62]

His arguments, however, did not convince his friends or alleviate their anxieties. They saw only one course open to them: to act without Sarmiento's knowledge. Perhaps they believed that if they actually managed to reach an agreement with Alvaro and the King, and present Sarmiento with suitable terms, he would welcome it and join in their efforts. As matters stood, however, they faced the hard task of convincing Alvaro that they were in a position (without Sarmiento's support or consent) to deliver the city to his hands. The Gate of Calatrava was under the command of Fernando de Avila, who was one of their group,[63] and they must have had friends and associates among the guards of the Tower of San Martín, too. Their sole military task was to take over the gates which were held by the Prince's men, and for this, it appeared, they formed a plan.[64] Then they had to work out a line of negotiations and come up with some ready, appealing arguments, as well as suggestions for future arrangements; and finally, they had to establish communication with the Constable or the King. All this was done and negotiations started, or were about to start. But fortune was not on their side. By accident or treachery, their venture was divulged.[65] Early in December, while hunting in Requena, the Prince got wind of this development. He interrupted his hunt and made haste to Toledo.[66]

Judging by the swiftness of the Prince's action, he probably believed that a deal was in the making. Perhaps it was. Despite all their rumblings against Alvaro de Luna, it is possible that the rebels now proposed to him something that he was inclined to consider. After all, he was extremely reluctant to give up the castle of Burgos, and he knew how tough Pacheco could be when he was in a position to squeeze a rival. If the rebels could open the city gates to his troops, he would be freed of the Prince's pressure, while Toledo would again be in his hands. Such a prospect may have prompted Alvaro to view the rebels' proposals with favor. In any case, the negotiations, if already begun, had hardly passed their first stage when the Prince decided to forestall their development and prevent a positive outcome.

Back in Toledo, he lost no time in establishing the true facts. He ordered a quiet inquiry to determine the identity of the rebels involved in the affair; and he may not have been surprised to find that these were none other than the rebel chiefs: García and his friend Fernando de Avila, a bachelor of law, and the two canons Galvez and Alonso. He also established that Pero Sarmiento was not a party to their attempt, and that whatever arrangements they had planned or made were contemplated without his knowledge.[67]

The hour of decision was now at hand, the Prince felt, and he did not intend to miss it. Probably about the tenth of December, he called an urgent meeting in the town hall, to which he invited Toledo's *regidores, omes buenos* and other notables—that is, the city's legitimate "rulers" and representatives of the patrician class.[68] This is significant. Neither the *regidores* nor the *omes buenos* participated in the issuance of the *Sentencia-Estatuto*. They were, in all likelihood, opposed to the rebellion and therefore excluded from Sarmiento's government; thus, they played no part in shaping its policies and managing the city's affairs. Now the Prince invited these men to support him—and the actions he was planning to take. Obviously, this was an anti-rebel meeting, and by calling it, the Prince gave public notice that he viewed those invited as Toledo's true leaders, legitimate authorities and spokesmen. He thus signaled to Pero Sarmiento that his rule was about to end.

To the Prince, we may assume, it was a matter of course that the delivery of the city to the King must be preceded by total suppression of the rebellion—which meant the removal of all the rebel chiefs from the political scene. The Prince had no doubt that the real leader of the rebels, their moving spirit and most dangerous troublemaker, was Marcos García de Mora. That is why he must have decided to do away with him as soon as possible. By making the mistake of negotiating with the King, García gave the Prince a valid excuse to proceed against him by law. The Prince, however, did not wish to seem arbitrary; that is why he called the meeting in the town hall, expecting it to give him unqualified support.

Into this gathering he threw his bombshell: the news of negotiations between the rebels and the King with a view to delivering Toledo into his hands. He presented this attempt as an act of treason—not only against himself, but also against the city, whose patron he was and with which he was allied. We may take it for granted that none in that audience dared dispute his conclusions.

García and his friends were invited to the meeting but were wise enough not to attend.[69] They could expect nothing positive from that assembly and had a clear notion as to why it was convened. They had no doubt that the gathering would condemn their action and call for their arrest and punishment. There was no sense in entering the trap that had been laid for them by the Prince. Yet soon they discovered that the whole of Toledo had become for them a trap with no apparent exit. They were now desperately seeking refuge, but none was available. They could not find it in the alcazar, since Sarmiento had evidently washed his hands of them—either because they had acted behind his back or because he feared to attract the Prince's ire. Having no place to hide or escape to, they fortified themselves, with the aid of some friends, in the tower of the cathedral church[70]—the same tower whose bell had served barely ten months before to call the people to the meeting that started the revolution. There they awaited the impending attack of Prince Enrique's forces.

But the Prince did not want his men to undertake this attack on their own. He ordered the town crier to call the *común* to join him in the assault on the cathedral tower.[71] It was a clever move. No doubt his forces were sufficient to overcome the small band of defenders. But he wanted the *común* to be involved in the action—perhaps to let them know that he considered them his allies, or to preclude their later criticism. In any case, he had good reason to believe that the *común* would now respond.

They did; and this shows that the rebels had lost much of the support they had enjoyed among the plebs. Probably by then many of the latter were deeply disappointed with the rebel government, perhaps because they felt it had not rewarded them for their exertions in its behalf. Some of them may have judged the moment opportune publicly to join the party of the Prince, and thereby evade prosecution and punishment for their misdeeds in the preceding months. And so, as the *Crónica de Juan II* tells us, "those of the *común* and the people of the Prince who were at that time in the city, went all armed to the Church."[72]

A large crowd now besieged the tower and began to fight its few defenders. Soon these were forced to surrender and the archrebels were dragged down. The canons of the cathedral, Galvez and Alonso, were incarcerated to await ecclesiastical trial. García and Fernando tried to escape, but were caught as they fled and met a cruel death.[73] Both were drawn and quartered by order of the Prince, or at least with his tacit consent.[74] Thus ended the life of this prophet of hate, who learned from experience the fickleness of the "people" on whose behalf he had spoken with such fiery eloquence and in whom he had placed so much faith.

VII

The execution of García and Fernando de Avila and the imprisonment of Galvez and Juan Alonso dealt a crushing blow to the rebel government. Their removal from the scene deprived Sarmiento not only of his most effective assistants but also of the moral authority that these men imparted to his regime. In addition, he could not have failed to understand that the hostility manifested toward his aides and associates was aimed at *him* no less than at *them*. And what was doubtless no less important: The circumstances of their capture made it quite apparent that there was no longer any group in Toledo that was ready to fight for the rebels' cause; all segments of the city's population seemed anxious to place themselves at the disposal of the Prince.

Obviously, these lessons could not pass unnoticed by the Prince and his shrewd councillors either. And thus they concluded that conditions were ripe to put an end to the rebels' rule. They decided to strike.

The chroniclers of the reign of Enrique IV have generally portrayed the Prince as phlegmatic, as a feeble, unstable and indecisive politician. But this is not the figure he cut in his handling of the Toledan crisis. Perhaps it was Pacheco who worked out his plans, or masterminded his major moves, but no doubt the Prince had a considerable share in both the resolution and the execution. In any case, in Toledo, at crucial moments, we often see him in the forefront of the action, sure of himself, never slipping, always in command of the situation. These were the qualities he displayed also now, when he came to put an end, once and for all, to Sarmiento's grip on Toledo.

Accordingly, the Prince now sent word to Sarmiento, "requesting" him politely, but firmly, to surrender the alcazar and the chief judgeship.[75] In view of his earlier talks with the Prince concerning the "need" for his resignation, Sarmiento must now have expected such a move; and yet when it came, he felt "bitter" about it,[76] perhaps because he realized that it left him no choice. Nothing that he might say or do, he understood, would deter the Prince from his decision. Of course, he could try to hold on to his strongholds and put up a fight for his positions, but he did not see much sense in doing so. The two city gates he controlled would soon fall into the Prince's hands, he was sure; and then the alcazar would be besieged by the Prince and the city's entire population. That such a siege would end in his death was a foregone conclusion.

He answered Don Enrique that he would be "pleased" to comply with the Prince's double "request," but reminded his patron that it was customary in Castile to receive compensation for positions thus surrendered.[77] He also raised the question of his personal security, to which the Prince responded by assuring him protection and the grant of a safe-conduct. He also promised to compensate Sarmiento for the income he would lose with the loss of his positions[78]; and ostensibly on the basis of these assurances, Sarmiento resigned from all his posts. Thereupon, without much ado, the command of the alcazar was transferred to Girón, the Master of Calatrava.[79]

The Prince, however, was not satisfied with this, and within a few days made another move against the fallen rebel. Through his emissary Bishop Lope de Barrientos, the Prince got in touch with Sarmiento again. This time the Prince did not come with a "request," but plainly expressed his definite "will" that Sarmiento settle his affairs in Toledo and quit the city for good.[80]

What made the Prince at that point so eager to oust Sarmiento from the city? After all, shorn of the authority which his former positions had lent him, Sarmiento seemed unable to block or impede any of the Prince's contemplated moves. The Prince, however, evidently did not think so. Cunning and devious as Sarmiento was, he could still do much harm, he no doubt thought. Sarmiento must still have had friends in Toledo and important connections in influential circles, and the Prince was then faced with the difficult task of moving the Toledans to support his plans. Once he had left the city, he feared, Sarmiento might incite them to take a hard line and stiffen their resistance to his proposed arrangements. Obviously, the prince would feel more secure if Sarmiento were out of Toledo.

Sarmiento was surprised by the new order, for which, he thought, he had given no cause. According to the sources, he was "exasperated,"[81] and apparently with good reason. Leaving Toledo at that moment seemed to him tantamount to a sentence of death. He had no safe haven in Castile, and the country was teeming with the King's agents, authorized to arrest or kill him on sight. He tried to object, but the bishop explained to him that he had no choice in the matter. Toledo was, in fact, less secure for him now than any other place in the country, and he was living there solely by the Prince's grace. Sarmiento again made a rapid decision. He expressed his consent to leave Toledo, provided he could take with him all his possessions and settle in the Prince's citadel, Segovia. For this, however, he needed the Prince's consent. He went to see Don Enrique.[82]

The Prince granted him all his requests, including the right to stay in Toledo for a few more weeks to settle his affairs. Sarmiento even managed to get from the Prince a definite commitment of a landed estate to indemnify him for the lucrative posts he gave up at the Prince's request.[83] Finally, he got Don Enrique to agree that they go to Segovia together, so that he be protected on the road from attacks by the King's men.[84]

The latter arrangement, however, did not come to pass. On February 6, 1450, Don Fernando de Luxán, bishop of Sigüenza, made public his sentence on the execution of the bull which the Pope had issued against the rebels (Si ad reprimandas). The sentence, which was addressed to Don Enrique,

ordered all Christians to stay away from Sarmiento, who was to be anathema.[85] Under the circumstances, the Prince did not wish to appear in Sarmiento's company. He did not retract the permission he had given him to go
to Segovia if he still wished to do so, but ordered him to leave Toledo at
once, unprotected by the Prince's force. Sarmiento of course had to comply.
Sometime in the middle of the month of February, only a few days before
the Prince's own departure, he left the city in the dead of night with his
family and possessions.[86]

Thus ended Sarmiento's rule and his violent interference in Toledo's life,
and thus vanished the sinister thrall in which he had held the city for more
than ten months. What the Prince did to rid Toledo of his presence was
indubitably hailed by all segments of the citizenry, except for one group—
the conversos. Happy as they were over the downfall of the man from whom
they had taken the most terrible punishments, their happiness was mixed
with bitter disappointment and helpless indignation. For this was not how
they envisaged the end of Pero Sarmiento's career. His departure from the
city as a protected man, holding a safe-conduct from Prince Enrique, and
taking with him all the wealth he had stolen, was to the conversos not only
offensive but shocking and intolerable. They protested and remonstrated in
the name of justice, only to find the Prince unmoved.[87] They could not
understand how such a thing could happen—how the laws could be so
flouted and plain justice so ignored by the man who was to be their future
king. But what they witnessed was the usual triumph of political expediency
over morality—as common in Castile in the 15th century as in other countries and other times. Once again, the conversos learned from experience the
"practical" value of the principles of law on which they had relied for their
protection.

CHAPTER II

The Great Debate

I. First Attack on the Conversos

I. THE PETITION

I

Of the sources related to the conflict that erupted between the Old and New Christians in Toledo, three documents dating from the year of the rebellion, 1449, present with great clarity the views on the Marranos as upheld and propagated by their opponents. These are (a) the Petition, which the city of Toledo addressed to Juan II on May 2, 1449; (b) the *Sentencia-Estatuto*, the statutory decree against the conversos issued by the city of Toledo on June 5, 1449; and (c) the *Memorial*, written by Marcos García de Mora against the conversos and their "defenders," most probably in November 1449.[1] Each of these documents bears witness to the motives, attitudes, doctrines, and convictions that shaped the views of the anti-Marrano party.

The first of these documents—the Petition—was written, as we have seen, at the height of the struggle between the king and the rebellious city.[2] It was a critical moment for the rebels and one that required great tenacity on their part to persist in the course they had chosen. The king's forces were drawing near the city; if there was to be a siege of Toledo, the rebels knew they lacked the strength to break it; and although they had some prospects of outside help, they could not be *assured* of assistance from any quarter. Nevertheless, the Petition betrays no conciliatory tone, or any softening of their position. They were clearly not ready to compromise with Juan II at the expense of what they regarded as their rights, and they made it palpably clear that their demands must be met if the monarch wished to keep their allegiance. More than a formal request to a king, the Petition sounded like an ultimatum; and this is indeed what it was.

This unbending, bellicose stand taken by the rebels toward the king can hardly be viewed as clever tactics. In the prevailing circumstances any shrewd politician could perceive that the rebels' inflexible stance would yield no positive results and, in fact, merely aggravate matters. Rather than the outcome of cold calculation, therefore, the extremism of the Toledans must be seen as precipitate, determined by a revolutionary fervor that had seized their minds and emboldened their spirits.

Also, the fiery style of the Petition and the passionate argument running through it suggest that the Toledan discontent and tenacity were nurtured by some revolutionary vein. Thus, a local grievance over an abuse of rights assumed the character of an explosive force, and turned the case of Toledo, in the rebels' minds, into a national cause. Indeed, the rebels claimed that they spoke not only in the name of Toledo, their own city, but also "in the name of the republic" of all the kingdoms and "in the name of *all* other cities" in the realms of Juan II.[3] It was a bold claim to a mandate never given. But revolutionaries do not await authorization to speak in the name of "the people."

Whether the petitioners had reason to believe that they represented the sentiments of the Spanish people, or at least of its majority, is a moot point. We shall return to this question later[4] and try to determine to what extent such a belief could be justified at the time. In any case, as self-proclaimed spokesmen of the nation, the petitioners made it clear that they demanded much more than satisfaction of local grievances. What they sought were solutions to major problems, national in scope and monarchic in character. More plainly, they asked for the elimination of evils which stemmed from the central—i.e., royal—government and which, in direct, unavoidable consequence, afflicted *all* the subjects of the king.[5]

Advocating large-scale, radical reform and proposing steps for its implementation, the Petition therefore may be viewed as presenting the political program of a vigorous opposition. Yet it was more than that: it was a propaganda piece, aimed at the public no less than at the king. In fact, it was a *manifesto* addressed to the whole people and, as such, intended to communicate to the people the rebels' political *credo*.

What one declares and what one believes in are often two different things, however. Were the authors of the Petition standard-bearers of a "faith," moved by real conviction, or were they cunning, unscrupulous demagogues, as several historians of Toledo have maintained? This is one of the questions posed by this document that we shall have to tackle.[6]

II

According to the authors of the Toledan Petition, the evils afflicting the Castilian people insofar as they were related to the government flowed primarily from two sources: Alvaro de Luna and the converso officialdom. The criticisms leveled by the Toledans at the conversos touch directly on the present inquiry; they will therefore form the prime object of our attention. Yet to judge them correctly, we must also dwell upon the charges made by the Toledans against Alvaro. In fact, both sets of charges—against Alvaro and the conversos—were presented by the petitioners as inseparable. Here, for the purposes of our analysis, however, we shall examine them separately.

Generally, the petitioners' charges against Alvaro followed closely the accusations leveled at him by the nobles who followed the Infantes of Aragon. This becomes apparent from a comparison of the Petition with the various "complaints" lodged against Alvaro by his rivals and enemies in the Castilian nobility—such as the letter addressed by Alfonso V of Aragon to Pedro Núñes de Herrera in 1425,[7] or the brief submitted by the nobles of the opposition to Juan II in February 1440.[8] As in these documents, so in the Petition, Alvaro is termed virtually a dictator, a "tyrant" and "usurper" of the powers of the Crown[9]; and here, as there, he is described as possessed of an insatiable passion for wealth.[10] Again in both complaints, he is accused of having plotted against the nobles who wished to serve the Crown and also of having intrigued among them for the purpose of separating them from the king.[11] Like the nobles' briefs, the Petition accuses Alvaro of having ignored or violated the rights of the cities,[12] as well as of having imposed upon the country "unjust and illegal" tributes.[13] Finally, the Toledans, like the nobles before them, hurl at Alvaro the charge of theft—that is, of having appropriated for himself a good part of the revenues.[14] The list of similarities, as we see, is long. Let us look at the differences.

While the brief of the nobles claimed that Alvaro de Luna "blocked many elections" to Church prelacies and dignities since he wanted the posts filled by people of his choice, so that he might get, by simony, "a part . . . of the incomes of those dignitaries,"[15] the Petition of Toledo imputes to the same motive—i.e., Alvaro's insatiable greed—a much greater variety of appointments to public office. In fact, it says, addressing itself to the king, "this constable of yours, by reason of his *greed,* has caused the offices of the government, of the administration of justice, and also the temporal and spiritual offices, and *all other offices* [of the kingdom] to be sold and bought for money."[16] Similarly, while the nobles' brief claims that Alvaro de Luna, in order to attain control over the finances of the kingdom, appointed to all the offices of the treasury and tax collection people who would be "obedient" to him *only* (which may or may not hint at his financial corruption),[17] the Toledan Petition states explicitly that the Constable "farms out your revenues, taxes and duties *(derechos)* in a wholesale manner *(por via de masa)* . . . so that he may become a partner of the tax farmers in sharing the spoils of their collections *(seyendo el participe con ellos).*"[18] With respect to the cities, while the nobles' brief says that Alvaro has imposed tributes on *some* cities in violation of all precedent and custom,[19] the Petition goes clearly beyond that when it says (after dealing with the tribute imposed on Toledo) that he also "robbed the lands and vassals" of "*the other cities*" in the realm (thereby implying *all* of the cities, without any reservation).[20] In like manner, with reference to his struggle with the nobility, while the brief says that Alvaro secured the death of *several* nobles, imprisoned some, and exiled others (of those whom he could not neutralize or befriend),[21] the Petition says plainly that his purpose had been to "liquidate" *all* the nobles (without exception).[22] Finally, while the brief accuses Alvaro of striving to become the real ruler in the country—and, accordingly, to gain such influence over the king that the latter would not "understand, wish, or say" anything except what conformed to Alvaro's will[23]—the Petition charges that Alvaro's aim was not only to become the virtual master of the land but also to "become master *in name as well as in fact*,"[24] a charge which seems to indicate that Alvaro de Luna aspired to the throne.[25] Thus, the charges presented in the Petition of the Toledans are not only more sweeping than the accusations of the nobles, but also much graver. Both quantitatively and qualitatively they go to extremes.

Nevertheless, it is not these differences alone that make the charges of the Petition appear markedly different from those in the nobles' brief. What makes them even more distinct is their basic content. For the Petition contains a new argument against the government which is not to be found in the nobles' memorandum and goes beyond the problems raised in the earlier censures. The new complaint relates to the place occupied by the conversos in Alvaro's administration and, through the administration, in the country as a whole. So strongly emphasized and so elaborately presented is this complaint in the Petition that it looms as the most crucial problem that Spain had ever faced. By so presenting the converso question, the Petition not only brought it into the open, but also placed it in the forefront of Spain's internal politics. In that position it was to remain for decades—and in some respects for centuries—to come; and it is this fact, and this fact alone, that lends this manifesto of the Toledan rebels historical significance.

III

Thus, according to the Petition, Alvaro's tyranny and greed were by no means the sole source of the troubles that befell the land. Nor did the evils of his regime stem mainly from the fact that the offices of government, including the chancellery and treasury, were in the hands of his henchmen. Something more sinister was involved. For Alvaro had followed the prohibited practice of "granting the offices [of the government of Castile] to *infidels and heretics,* enemies of our sacred faith, our king, our persons and our estates."[26] Thus, the ruthless implementation by these officials of Alvaro's policy did not result merely from obedience to a tyrant, but also from something far worse and more dangerous—namely, the great enmity that these immoral characters felt for the king's subjects. Thus, the exploitation of these subjects proceeded not only with thoroughness and determination, but also with zeal and vengeance. In fact, besides being despoiled, many of them were wantonly killed. And so it happened, concludes the Petition, that officials "who were authorized to defend and protect and govern your subjects . . . have, under the guise of doing so, and with the power of the offices entrusted to them, robbed and destroyed the whole land."[27]

The Petition leaves no doubt as to the identity of these "heretics and infidels," these robbers and killers, who have committed their crimes in the name of the government and the law. They are, it says bluntly, "the conversos from the lineage of the Jews of your dominions . . . who, *in their majority,* have been found to be *infidels and heretics*"; who "have Judaized and are Judaizing"; who "have guarded the rites and ceremonies of the Jews, apostatizing the chrism and baptism which they received"; and who have demonstrated by deed as well as by word that the water of baptism "touched [only] their skins, but neither their hearts nor their wills."[28] As secret Jews, "many of whom bitterly blaspheme Christ and His mother," while others among them "worship idols,"[29] they are, of course, hostile to Christianity; and because of their hostility to this religion, they are obviously enemies of its believers, the Christians—i.e., the real or *Old* Christians, so called to distinguish them from the conversos. Thus, says the Petition, "these people" [i.e., the converso officials], because of their hatred for the king's subjects,[30] "have usurped, with the power of the offices [given them], the lordship which belongs to the great of our kingdom, and have applied their powers to the possession of the Old Christians and all their estates."[31] The "King's subjects," of course, are the "Old Christians," who alone deserve this designation, for only they are the true and faithful subjects of the King; and it is they who are brutally maltreated and tyrannized by the treacherous despots and exploiters—i.e., the conversos—who fill the ranks of Alvaro's administration.

In granting the crucial offices of the kingdom to members of this inimical group, Alvaro, in the petitioners' view, committed not an error but a crime—and one for which he must be made to suffer the harshest possible punishment. For it was not a result of shortsightedness on his part, but of a calculated policy which he stubbornly pursued, even though its disastrous consequences had become known to all. This is evident from his whole attitude toward that converso group. "For it is notorious that the said Alvaro de Luna, your Constable, has publicly defended and accepted the conversos from the lineage of the Jews of your kingdom."[32] The formal support he lent the conversos, and the favorable opinion he endeavored to create for them, were part and parcel of his criminal design to entrust the government to their hands. It was through the services offered by these infidels that he could dislodge the nobles from their positions of power, and it was by means of such officials that he could tyrannize the Castilian people. Thus, the conversos were Alvaro's tool in establishing and maintaining his oppressive rule, just as he was their natural ally in attaining their own particular ends. In fact, both parties had a common goal (the subjugation and exploitation of the Spanish people) and both agreed on how to achieve it (by removing the nobles from their governing positions and abolishing their influence in the state). These objectives were fully attained. For while Alvaro usurped the powers of the King, the conversos usurped those of the nobility.[33]

The conversos are thus portrayed as opponents of the great nobles, whom they virtually displaced, and as enemies of *all* classes of the Spanish people. From mere "instruments" and obedient servants, as Alvaro's officials are described in the nobles' brief (which did not identify them as conversos), these officials became, in the Toledan Petition, partners in crime of the king's chief minister. As for the origins of the converso penetration into the highest echelons of government, they should not be looked for, according to the Petition, in Alvaro's plans alone. There was more to it than that.

For it was not by mere chance, in the petitioners' opinion, that the conversos were available for Alvaro's service; nor was their presence in Spain's Christian society fortuitous. It was planned by the conversos themselves long before. To be sure, there is no denying the fact that they were formally converted to Christianity, but they did this to achieve, "under the guise of Christians," a purpose quite incompatible with conversion. Their real and secret aim, the petitioners said, was to "squeeze the souls and bodies and possessions of the Christians who are old in the Catholic faith"[34]— namely, the Old Christians. And this is indeed "what [the converts] have been doing and are doing today."[35] Thus, the conversos did not just "fall in" with the tyrannical plans of Alvaro de Luna. While serving him they actually followed their own scheme, executing all the time their devilish design against Christianity and the Spanish people.

We have thus touched the main point of difference between the Petition of 1449 and the Memorandum of 1440, and indeed between the Petition and the other baronial documents that had previously been composed against Alvaro and his administration. The nobles, who wrote the documents of 1425 and 1440, saw the government of Castile as a group of functionaries who did Alvaro's bidding. To the petitioners, however, it appeared as something different—as an arm of an enemy that invaded the kingdom, entrenched itself within it in positions of power, and from these positions, under cover of the law, moved into all the fields of life and carried out its plan of conquest and subjugation of the Spanish people. What was necessary, therefore, according to the Petition, to save the Spanish people was not only to oust Alvaro, the tyrant, from his position of supreme authority, but also to eliminate the whole bureaucracy—and restore the government to the people.

IV

The question we now have to ask of course is what, if anything, is true in these charges which so heavily tax our credulity. Anyone familiar with the history of antisemitism, and the history of persecution in general, might tend to dismiss most or all of them as typical products of intense group hatred— that is, as charges that have little to do with the facts and much to do with ill will. Yet such a dismissal would not serve our purpose, which is to establish, on the basis of clear evidence, the precise borderline between the false and the true in all that was ascribed to the Marranos and their life. We shall therefore examine the above allegations not only in the light of kindred precedents, but also in the light of the social conditions in which they were made, spread and promoted. Thus, we shall now touch on the Toledans' first charge—Alvaro's "deal" with the conversos.

We have seen that the portrayal of Alvaro in the Petition is basically the same as that drawn by the nobles in their various "complaints" against the Constable. So similar, indeed, are the two descriptions that one must conclude that the authors of the Petition had read the related baronial statements, and especially the memorandum which the nobles addressed to Juan II in February 1440. This document served them as both source and model for their attack upon Alvaro, although the changes they made were significant.

We have shown that the crimes which the nobles of the opposition imputed to Alvaro were grossly exaggerated.[36] Hence, the authors of the Petition, by broadening these imputations, exaggerated even further. But this fact did not trouble them. They knew they were following a safe campaign track, beaten by the nobles for twenty-five years, and that the harsh opinions they voiced about the Constable were merely an extension of familiar charges. As such they involved no real shock and were ready for "public acceptance." But the petitioners must also have discovered what became common knowledge five centuries later—namely, that a "big lie" is more effective than a "small lie" if it is expressed boldly and unequivocally and repeated often enough. Accordingly, in their attack on Alvaro de Luna they minced no words and spared no offense. They dropped the reservations that accompanied the accusations of the nobles and carried these accusations to new extremes. The result was more or less what they expected. Alvaro now became an object of mass hatred, with his name more besmirched and his prestige more under-

mined. His image, already much distorted, now appeared as a twisted caricature, hardly resembling the real person, with his faults and virtues combined.

All this relates to the charges against Alvaro which are found in both the
nobles' briefs and the Petition. As for the charge found *only* in the Petition—
the one that ascribes to Alvaro the promotion of the conversos for his
criminal ends—it must be examined separately. Of course, the fact that all
the charges against Alvaro turned out to be so wildly exaggerated must in
itself cast strong doubts upon the truthfulness of that particularly strange
claim concerning the conversos. In fact, we are tempted by mere analogy to
discard it as so much fodder for public agitation. But analogy, which can
suggest leads for inquiry, cannot serve as a substitute for proof. We shall
therefore probe the question of Alvaro's attitude toward the conversos without relating it to the validity of the other charges leveled at the constable.

So according to the Petition, Alvaro appointed to his administration conversos *who were all secret Jews* and who, by virtue of this fact, hated the Old
Christians and strove to destroy them. To assume that Alvaro made these
appointments unaware of the nature of his appointees—and of their "hostility" to the Old Christians—is, to put it mildly, untenable. For Alvaro must
have known what, according to the Petition, every man in the street knew;
and he was in a better position to know it, having at his disposal many agents
and informers who could acquaint him with the true facts. Yet if he *knew* what
the conversos were, what they were planning, and what they were *doing,* then
he must have chosen to deliver the administration into the hands of secret
Jews and, in effect, permitted them to persecute, subjugate and torment the
Old Christians.

But now another question arises which obviously must be asked: Why
should Alvaro have done so? The answer offered by the petitioners is implied
in their general argument. Alvaro, according to this argument, was a tyrant
and, like most tyrants, sought power and riches; to achieve these aims, he
had to subjugate the people, and for this purpose he employed the conversos—the best possible instruments for accomplishing that task—since they,
too, sought to oppress the Spanish people, even though primarily for other
reasons.

Ostensibly logical, the explanation, in truth, was not logical at all. For only
a mad tyrant, consumed with hatred for his people, or a vicious foreign
conqueror bent on destroying a prostrate nation, would pursue such a course
as this. Alvaro, however, did not fit any of these categories; therefore he could
not have chosen as officials—and certainly would not have retained long in
office—individuals whose purpose was not only to satisfy their own insatiable greed (apart from his), but also, and above all, to implement their own
scheme of ruining the people and bleeding them to death. However dull he
may have been (and who would say that Alvaro was dull?), he would cer-

tainly have realized that the extermination of the people over whom he ruled would eliminate not only his source of wealth, but also his base of power. And why should he allow his officials to act so patently against his interest?

All this may seem too obvious to elaborate. But the Toledan claims about the conversos' "real" attitudes and the designs they had on the Spanish people received such great currency at the time, and were echoed so strongly in the past two centuries in so many works of scholarship, including famous histories,[37] that we felt we should examine them from every angle. Accordingly, we shall consider one more argument which may be briefly summarized as follows.

Since bureaucrats sometimes extend their authority beyond their formal guidelines, the converso officials, once in the saddle, may have executed their own plans, regardless of the chief minister's wishes. But can such an argument apply in this case? It is true that officials sometimes deviate in their actions from the lines prescribed for them by their superiors, but they generally do this within certain limits, and to a far lesser extent in a dictatorship. In Castile of Juan II, however, the alleged deviation was supposed to be *extreme*, and the government in power was allegedly a dictatorship of the most resolute and effective kind. Thus, if Alvaro was, as his opponents claimed, a tyrant who carefully chose his servants, and if one of his major conditions for choosing them was their complete obedience to him, he would certainly not have tolerated actions on their part that went far beyond any measure he dictated, merely to satisfy their own desires—and sadistic desires at that. Hence, we cannot escape the following conclusion: either Alvaro was a ruthless dictator as the Toledans described him, in which case his officials could not have executed their plans against his wishes and interests, or the officials were the real rulers of the country and impudently and boldly implemented their *own* plan in total disregard of Alvaro's wishes; but then Alvaro was no dictator at all, but a puppet or captive in the hands of his officials, which nobody assumes he was. It follows that the theory of the Toledans in both its parts—(a) that Alvaro granted the conversos power to do with the Castilian people what they wished and (b) that the conversos used this power for the destruction of that people—was nothing but a figment of a wild imagination, created to serve a political end.

V

But something else should be considered at this point. While the accusations against Alvaro de Luna, which the petitioners borrowed from the rebellious nobles, were exaggerated and untenable, the accusations they made against Alvaro's officials had no basis in fact at all. It scarcely needs proof that the converso officials, especially in the Court and central administration, could not guard Jewish law and custom,[38] and that the plans they allegedly contrived against the Old Christians—the plans imputed to them by the Toledans—could never have been implemented. If these officials were even half as astute as the Toledans described them, they must have realized this all along and never embarked on such a course.

There remains, however, one element of these charges—the element that served, in a way, as their foundation—which thus far has not been examined. It is that the Marranos or their Jewish forebears adopted Christianity to bring ruin upon the Spaniards. Here is an allegation clearly related not only to a few of the conversos (the officials), but to the group as a whole; and it refers not only to aims and motives, presumably hidden or half hidden, but to historical facts occurring in broad daylight and thus more readily observed.

To be sure, the conclusions we have reached about the charges brought by the Toledans against the converso officials are sufficient to undermine the accusations leveled against the converso group as a whole. Obviously, if this group harbored a conspiracy of the kind suggested by the Toledans, the converso officials would have served as its spearhead, especially in view of the petitioners' own claims regarding the conspirators' strategy and tactics; but since the Marrano officials, as we have indicated, could not have fulfilled the function ascribed to them, the basis of the whole charge is shattered. Nevertheless, it may be argued, the accusation as a whole ought not to be so quickly disposed of. For the motives attributed by the Toledans to the Jews—the ancestors of the Marranos—for their conversion to Christianity could still apply to most of the conversos, while the conspiracy against the Christians could still linger on—if not among the converso high-office holders, then in some other part of the group. Let us, then, consider the matter a little further.

Since the Toledan rebels conducted an Inquiry into the Marranos' beliefs and actions, we naturally wonder whether it produced any evidence to substantiate that charge. In this Inquiry the Toledans used torture; and one may assume that with such drastic methods, the truth about the treacherous "Marrano plot" might have been brought into the open. Yet neither the Petition nor Alonso de Espina, who presents a detailed summary of the "findings" of that Inquiry,[39] offers any evidence that any segment of the Marranos was involved in an attempt to destroy the Spanish people, or that any number of Jews were converted for that purpose. Had they been provided by the Inquiry with such evidence, the Toledan rebels would no doubt have hastened to present it to the public, since it would have helped them to arouse the Spanish people and enlist its support for their aims. Indeed, such evidence would have been mentioned repeatedly in the succeeding decades, when the same allegations were publicly restated by the Marranos' foes and critics. Yet no testimony to that effect has ever come from the Toledan inquiries. Even the Inquisition could not rely, for this purpose, on the investigations conducted in Toledo. To sustain the myth that Marranos and Jews had clandestine plans to destroy the Christians, the Inquisition had to produce new "evidence" in an "inquiry" solicited, planned, engineered, and conducted by its own officials.[40]

If evidence in support of the conspiracy theory could not be drawn from Marrano life, could the theory possibly be supported by certain trends in the history of the Jews? But, the answer to this query too must be negative. There was no such intention, scheme or development in any of the movements of Jewish conversion, either in Spain or anywhere else. When large masses of Jews went over to Christianity in 1391, or when many of them did so during the Civil War (1366–1369), they changed their religion not, as the Petition claimed, for the purpose of "squeezing the souls and bodies of the Christians," but rather to prevent the Christian Spaniards from "squeezing" their own bodies and souls. Nor did the conversion of 1412 result from "connivance" or a chosen plan of action on the part of the converted Jews, but from circumstances that left them hardly any choice if they wanted to survive.[41] And if some Jews, clearly a small minority, adopted Christianity of their own free will, they did so to improve their own lot, not to worsen that of the Christians. There is, in fact, no evidence either in Hebrew or in non-Hebrew documentation for any sizeable conversion with such an aim in mind. It is questionable whether there was even a single Jewish lunatic who embraced such a cause or followed such a course.

Yet this lunacy was now attributed to a group numbering hundreds of thousands. It was presented in a document addressed to the King by the representatives of the foremost city in the country. It was stated as a "fact" which claimed the attention of the whole Spanish people; and it was seriously used as a major argument for justifying the revision of an old, established policy. Evidently, such a claim would not have been advanced unless it was expected to be believed, at least by some. If so, what was it that made it credible, though clearly so contrary to the facts?

In vain shall we try to answer this question on the basis of Spanish precedents alone. To understand the origins and nature of the attack on the conversos in Toledo in 1449, and get a clear insight into the arguments of the attackers, of whom the petitioners formed a part, we must refer the reader to our earlier discussion of the development of Jew-hatred in antiquity and the Middle Ages.[42] All the major factors that produced the great enmity for the Jews in the medieval era, and all the main excuses used to justify a large-scale, bloody campaign against them, were now present in segments of the Spanish society for whom the conversos were no longer bearable. Just as German antisemitism in the fourteenth century produced the myth of poisoned wells to justify the mass murder of Jews; just as Russian antisemitism in the nineteenth century produced the myth of the Elders of Zion to justify Russia's persecution of the Jews, so did Spanish antisemitism in the fifteenth century produce the myth of the "officials' plot" to justify the removal of the Marranos from their posts and their elimination from Spanish society. In all these instances, a conspiracy was alleged to have been organized by cunning and devilish schemers who were ready to go to any imaginable length to satisfy their thirst for Christian blood. In all these cases, as in many others, there was not the slightest substance to the allegations, but all were nevertheless believed.

We may, therefore, conclude our analysis as follows: No evidence was presented to prove the existence of the "Marrano plot" because no such evidence had been discovered; and no such evidence was ever discovered because no such plot had ever been conceived. Obviously, the Toledans made their allegations on the sole grounds that they considered them "acceptable." And they *were* acceptable because they stemmed from old traditions, widespread accusations, deep-rooted hatreds and notions about the Jews that the people of Spain shared with other Christian nations throughout the second half of the medieval era.

VI

To complete our examination of the Toledans' Petition, we shall now turn to the last set of charges presented in the opening of this chapter—that is, those which refer to the Marranos' Judaism. The Petition, as we have seen, contains three accusations concerning the conversos' religious views. These were (a) that they had been "for the most part" Judaizing—i.e., following the rites and ceremonies of the Jews; (b) that "many of them" were blaspheming Christ and His mother; and (c) that "others among them" were worshiping idols.

It is obvious that the last of these accusations was meant to illustrate the baseness of the conversos' religion. Yet the claim that the Marranos were worshipers of idols is hardly consonant with Jewish beliefs. Indeed, so bizarre and unusual is it that we must ask on what grounds could the petitioners have made it.

Fortunately, a contemporary source is available which gives us a precise indication of these grounds. It is the *Fortalitium Fidei* of Fray Alonso de Espina, who was an ardent follower of the Toledan party. Espina had access to the findings of the Inquiry *(pesquisa)* conducted against the conversos in Toledo, and he summarized these findings in 22 paragraphs in one of the chapters of his book.[43] The twentieth paragraph deals with the assertion that "conversos were worshipers of idols"—an assertion regarded by Espina as a fact that cannot be doubted. To prove this, he supplies the evidence unearthed by the Toledan inquiry.

According to this evidence, a certain converso couple prayed daily in Arabic at noontime and in the evening before four human images or statues made of wood, which they kept hidden in their attic. Their Christian servant, the witness, would bring these statues from the attic toward prayer time and return them thereafter. The witness performed the task assigned to him as long as he lived with those conversos.[44]

This, then, was the foundation of the claim concerning idol worship among the Marranos. On the basis of one reported case involving a single converso couple, the Toledans asserted that, in addition to the Judaizers and the blasphemers among the conversos, "others among them" were worshiping idols[45]—"others" meaning a group or a trend, but by no means isolated cases. Furthermore, they made this grave charge on the basis of the testimony of a *single* witness, whose moral worth and intelligence were so low as to allow him to cooperate regularly in idol worship. Was not the testimony of such a witness invalid? Can it really be believed that he had seen what he reported, or understood what he had seen? Whatever the value of that testimony, and assuming it was given in good faith, it indicates how reckless the Toledans were in making their religious charges.

The second of these accusations—blaspheming Christ and the Virgin Mary—was taken by Christians to have been a Jewish custom since the beginnings of Christianity. Of course, from a Christian point of view, whatever the Jews said—or could say—about Jesus, even the mere negation of His divinity was gross blasphemy. From a Jewish standpoint, however, such statements were anything but "blasphemy," since the Jews never regarded Jesus as God and Mary as the Mother of God. Whatever may be said concerning this matter, therefore, relates to the first charge—namely, that of Judaization—to which we shall presently pass.

There are several things in the Toledans' statements on this issue which appear, to say the least, discordant. To begin with, in discussing the Marrano officials, the petitioners designate them *all* as "heretics," "infidels," etc.; when they speak of the Judaism of the Marranos generally, they say that a *majority* of them were found to have been "infidels." Not "*all* of them" or "*almost* all of them," not even "an overwhelming majority," but just "for the greater part."[46] Does not this imply a tacit admission that a considerable minority of the Marranos could be Christian—that is, *sincerely* Christian—after all? Evidently, the petitioners did not dare go beyond this indefinite generalization. They even refrained from qualifying their "majority" so as to render their statement more inclusive. Moreover, when they referred to the converso "blasphemers," they did not even say that they formed a majority within the converso group, but only that "many" of the conversos belonged to this category[47]; yet "many" could mean a minority, too. Why this restrained language? If the "majority" of them were indeed *secret* Jews, as the Toledan authors alleged, why did they not say that a "majority" of them were also covert blasphemers of Christ? Do we not have here a retreat from an assertion that would not be easily believed?

Second, we must examine the statement: "It has been *found* that the *majority* of the Conversos were infidels and heretics."[48] We must ask: By *whom* and *when* and *how* was it "found"? If the reference is to the investigations about the Marranos conducted by the rebel government of the city, we cannot help doubting the validity of the conclusions reached in these investigations. To begin with, those conclusions related, we are told, to the conversos in all the realms of Juan II. How could a determination on a subject like this be made in such a short time with regard to so great a multitude of people, living in all parts of the country? And could such an investigation be to any extent impartial when conducted by such extreme partisans as the Toledan petitioners? What value, one must ask, may be ascribed to conclusions reached by such inquiries and such investigators?

Very little indeed, or virtually none, to go by this document.

For since all the other charges of the Petition were found to be wild distortions of the truth, and creations of minds possessed by hatred and a desire to destroy the objects of that hatred, should we not treat in the same way the charge that the conversos were secret Jews? Above all, can we rely on the generalizations of such accusers? If they could make generalizations such as that the Jews who went over to Christianity did so for the purpose of "squeezing the souls and bodies of Christians," that the conversos engineered a "plot" to capture the government of Castile, and that a section of the conversos were idol worshipers—charges that were based on *no truth at all*—could they not also make untruthful generalizations with regard to the Marranos' secret Judaism on the basis of *some* factual data? Suppose a few Marranos were discovered to have been Judaizers or performers of some Jewish rites and customs; would not the Toledans have rushed to conclude that *the* Marranos—or *most* of them—were secret Jews and practicers of Jewish rites? This tendency of the petitioners to exaggerate, invent charges and produce theories to suit their fancy, or rather their political and social ends, must render unreliable and untrustworthy their charge of "widespread Judaism" among the Marranos—simply because it was *they* who made it.

And let us remember one more thing: the very thesis that the Marranos embraced Christianity for the purpose of killing or ruining the Old Christians *necessitated* the assumption that they were Jews at heart. For without this assumption, there could be no explanation for the hatred the conversos allegedly felt for the Old Christians and for their alleged plan to destroy

Christendom. Indeed, once this assumption is discarded, the whole theory of the Marrano conspiracy must be discarded with it. Thus we see that besides the tendency to exaggerate the faults of a hated party—the tendency that characterized all the charges in the Petition—the Toledans had an ulterior motive in making their claim of Marrano Judaization. For there can be no question at all that their sharpest blow against Alvaro's rule and their most impressive appeal to the masses, and also their most effective means of sowing fear and suspicion of the royal administration, and moving the people to support the rebellion, lay in their claim that the government of Castile was in Jewish hands.

Afterthoughts

We have analyzed in detail the contents of the Petition submitted by the Toledans in May 1449 because the arguments it contains served as basis for later pronouncements of the Toledan rebels, and because it harbored the kernel of far greater developments than those that concerned its authors.

As far as we know, the Toledan Petition was the first public expression of the anti-Marrano sentiment which, as we have indicated, was rife in Spain but hitherto had been formally suppressed. It was, moreover, the first formal position taken by an organized section of the Spanish people toward the Marranos and the Marrano question. In addition, it was the first expression of a philosophy that was to penetrate every walk of Spanish life. It was also the beginning of a violent campaign that was to engulf the whole of Spain and continue unabated for several centuries. Above all, it marked the opening of a drive that was to culminate in the founding of the Spanish Inquisition and emerge, through its agency, as a force that affected the course of world history.

Who at the time would have attributed to this document such far-reaching consequences? No one, may be the common answer. Once the crisis passed and the city seemed pacified, the Toledan rebellion came to be seen as a development of local and temporary significance. This evaluation, however, was wrong. The Toledan rebellion indicated the surfacing of a subterranean current, which was to swell into a river and later into a flood.

The new development is also suggested in the Petition's terminology. We have seen that "the King's subjects," in the language of the Petition, is another designation for the Castilian people; but actually it represents, in embryonic form, a much more developed and modern concept. At a time when internal strife was ceaseless and class divisions sharp and pronounced, the Petition glosses over the old conflicts between the various sectors of Castile's society and groups them all under "the King's subjects." It speaks on behalf of the nobles, the burghers and the laborers *(labradores)* as a common target for the enemy, the Marranos, and therefore united in a common cause. In fact, the petitioners sought to create the impression that they represented a broad front, combining all classes of the Spanish people. It was a fictitious pretense, no doubt. But it served as a "factor" in the common drive toward national unification and self-determination.

For the forces working toward nationalism in Spain coalesced in the face of a "common enemy." First it was the Moors, then the Jews and the Moors, and finally the conversos (in addition to the Jews and Moors). In the struggle against the "enemies" of the people, the Spaniards found their identity. Alvaro disappeared from the political scene a few years after the Toledan rebellion; the external enemy—the Moor—was crushed four decades later (in 1492); and in the same year the Jews were banished; but the struggle against the "hidden enemy," the crypto-Jews—and later the crypto-Moslems—continued. The Moriscos—the Moorish converts to Christianity—were finally expelled c. 1610; but the war against the "Jewish" conversos dragged on for another two centuries. We have here in a sense the start of a crusade, which was as far reaching as it was determined, and whose standard-bearers upheld ideas of the Petition as dogmas of an old religion.

II. THE SENTENCIA-ESTATUTO

If the Petition was the opening shot of the rebels' public campaign against the Marranos, the *Sentencia-Estatuto* they enacted in Toledo on June 5, 1449 served them as a major instrument of warfare. But like the Petition, its impact was not limited to that time only. Indeed, few documents originating in the 15th century could match the *Sentencia* in lasting influence on the conflict between the Old and New Christians. We have indicated the short-range purposes of the *Sentencia* and its political motivation.[1] We shall now turn to its long-range goals and the legal, religious, and social reasons adduced in its justification.

1. *The Legal Reasons*

According to the Toledans, all their doings and proceedings were characterized by adherence to the law: it was by law, and in order to preserve the law, that their so-called "rebellious" acts were performed, whereas their foes, Alvaro and the conversos, were perpetual lawbreakers.[2] Thus they argued that the anti-converso Statute they had enacted was perfectly "legal," since it agreed with the laws, decrees and regulations that governed the kingdom of Castile. Moreover, they claimed that this statute was no *new* enactment, but a combination of several old laws, drawn from various sources.

Was this true?

According to the Toledans, their *Sentencia-Estatuto* was in full accord with (a) canon law; (b) civil law; and (c) a special privilege that was given to Toledo by a Castilian king. Both canon and civil law, they argued, decreed that "converts of Jewish descent, because they are suspect in the faith of Christ, in which they often vomit while they readily Judaize,[3] should not be allowed to hold offices or benefices, either public or private, by means of which they may injure, offend and mistreat the Old Christians; nor can their testimony against these Christians be of any validity."[4]

There is no doubt that in referring to canon law, the Toledans had in mind the sixty-fifth decision of the Fourth Toledan Council,[5] which was incorporated in Gratian's Decretum.[6] That decision consisted of the famous prohibition that "Jews, or those who are of Jews" should in no wise seek public office, because in such circumstances they may cause harm to Christians; and by "those who are of Jews" *(hi qui ex Iudeis sunt)* they understood, as others did before and after them, all converts to Christianity of Jewish extraction.

It is not clear, however, to which civil law they referred. In fact, even the

Forum Judicum, the ancient Spanish Visigothic code—which of all Spain's codes takes the harshest stand against both Jews and converts from Judaism—does not contain a law that prohibits *all* such converts from assuming public office. On the contrary, it contains a special law which frees sincere converts from certain disabilities that apply to Jews.[7] In indicating the burdens to be removed from these converts, the law mentions the special taxation to which Jews were subject at the time, and the prohibition on Jews' trading with Christians; but it does not refer to matters such as testimony and the holding of public office. From this, one may gather that these latter disabilities (then in force with respect to the Jews) were valid also for the "sincere" converts, let alone for the "insincere" ones. Yet such a conclusion would doubtless be wrong, since the law, read correctly, assures sincere converts freedom from *all* "Jewish" disabilities,[8] and the references to "taxation" and "trade" in this law were made either for the sake of offering illustrations or because the lawmaker wished to provide concrete answers to some "burning" questions that had to be resolved.[9] In any case, the law did not *except* the rights in question (i.e., to public office and to testimony) from the general freedom it granted sincere converts; nor was there another civil law on the books that explicitly prohibited converts from Judaism from filling public offices, even though such a prohibitive law is found with respect to testimony in court.

This is the law in the *Forum Judicum* which states that "Jews, whether baptized or not," are forbidden to testify against Christians.[10] Perhaps by "baptized" Jews the codifier understood *insincere* converts who remained Jews at heart even after their formal conversion,[11] and thus he would not see in this law a contradiction to the one that relates to *sincere* converts who were freed from the limitations that applied to Jews. This is indeed how the law was understood by later experts on civil law[12]; but this is not how the Toledans read it. As far as they were concerned, the law applied to all converts from Judaism, or rather to *all* Jews who were baptized into Christianity, whatever their post-baptismal behavior. Since the law referred to was issued in a period when laws equating Jews with converts from Judaism were repeatedly promulgated by the Church councils, the Toledans' interpretation may indeed have fitted the original intent of the law.[13] In any case, it was *this* and no other law to which they could refer with some justification when they spoke of their reliance on "civil" law. Even so, it was not true that each of the two laws, canon and civil, supported both prohibitions indicated by the Toledans, as may be gathered from their assertions. At most, they could lean on canon law for one restriction (i.e., with respect to offices and benefices) and on civil law for the other restriction (i.e., with respect to testimonies).

Yet even with this important limitation, the Toledans' assertion that their Statute agreed with both canon and civil law was a gross exaggeration. For if, besides the laws cited above, one considers all other related pronouncements in canon and Spanish civil law,[14] one can see that the Statute not only failed to represent them, but violated their instructions in both letter and spirit.

It was no doubt because they realized the weakness of their legal position insofar as reliance on the codes was concerned[15] that the Toledans pointed out, with special emphasis, another legal basis for their enactment. This was the privilege which, in their words, was granted them by Alfonso, king of Castile and Leon, and which prohibited every convert from Judaism to Christianity not only from assuming any office in Toledo, but also from receiving ecclesiastic benefices.[16] Because no such privilege has been found in the archives and because the identity of the king was not specified (there were a number of Alfonsos in Castile), some scholars believed that no such privilege had been granted and that the whole argument was pure invention.[17] It is likely, however, that the Toledans possessed such a privilege (given them by Alfonso VII), and therefore, as far as this point is concerned, they were probably reporting a fact.[18] Nevertheless, in this matter, too, they were clearly at odds with the truth, not so much for what they said as for what they left unsaid. For they failed to mention that the old Alfonsine privilege had fallen into desuetude,[19] that the prevailing law and custom had disqualified it, and that it was superseded by subsequent royal orders that established quite different laws for the converts both in Toledo and the country as a whole.[20] The Toledans chose to ignore these facts, which had affected the validity of the privilege they referred to, just as they ignored the canon and civil laws that disqualified the laws upon which they relied.

2. The Religious Reasons

In justifying the laws enacted in the past against equalizing *Jewish* converts to Christianity with other Christians, the Statute presents as the *main* reason the claim that these converts were "being suspect in the faith."[21] Similarly, in indicating their own reasons for issuing the new *Sentencia-Estatuto*, the authors of this document list, in the first place, the attitude of the conversos toward Christianity. As they put it, "it has been proven" and it "has appeared ... evident" that "a very large part of the conversos of this city, descendants of the lineage of the Jews who lived in it, are persons who are *very* suspect [as disbelievers] in the Holy Catholic Faith."[22]

According to the same authors, this "suspicion" rests on a variety of presumptions about these converts. If we examine these presumptions, which are presented by the Toledans as both definite and factual, we find that they include two general and three specific accusations. The *general* charges are that the conversos (a) "adhere to and believe in very great errors" (i.e., heretical opinions) "against the articles" of Christianity; and (b) that they "guard the rites and ceremonies of the Old Law."[23] The *specific* charges are that they [the conversos] say that (a) "our Savior . . . Jesus Christ, was a man of their stock who was hanged and whom the Christians worship as God"; (b) that they claim that "there are a God and Goddess in heaven"; and (c) that "on Maundy Thursday *(en el Jueves Santo),* when the holy oil of the Chrism is being consecrated in the Holy Church of Toledo . . . they, following the custom of the Jews, slaughter lambs and eat them, and make other sorts of burnt offerings and sacrifices."[24] All this, adds the Statute, "is described in greater detail in the Inquiry *(pesquisa)* which was made in this matter by the vicars of the said Holy Church of Toledo, by virtue of which the royal administration of justice, following the prescriptions of the law, proceeded against some of them [i.e., the conversos] by way of fire."[25]

If the conversos were truly Judaizers, there would be nothing to say against the two general accusations—namely, that they held erroneous beliefs from the standpoint of Catholic dogma and that they kept Jewish rituals and ceremonies. Nor could anyone say anything against the first of the three specific accusations—namely, that they considered Jesus not a man *and* God (as all true Christians hold Him to be), but a mere man of Jewish extraction who underwent capital punishment for some crime. This was certainly the view of Jesus which was prevalent among the Jews everywhere, and if the conversos were Jews at heart, there is no reason to assume that they did not share it. Also, this agrees with the Petition's statement that they "blaspheme" Jesus and the Virgin Mary. From a Christian standpoint, such talk about Jesus is clearly outright blasphemy.

No special inquiry, of course, was needed to establish these facts with respect to Jews. Every Christian knew that the Jews hold different beliefs, have their own ceremonial laws, and completely deny the divinity of Jesus. The authors of the Statute, however, claimed that a special Inquiry discovered that these beliefs and practices were shared, as they put it, by "a very large part" of the Toledan conversos.[26] Yet one might be more inclined to accept these claims had the Toledans not added to this "discovery" the two other charges which are included in their accusation.

The first of these evidently came to illustrate the *beliefs* allegedly adhered to by the Judaizing or "heretical" conversos; and these, to begin with, included the belief in the existence of "a God and a Goddess in heaven." The imputation of such a belief to conversos—let alone to "a very large part" of the conversos—undermines the reliability of the Toledan Inquiry no less than the charge mentioned in the Petition that "others among them worship *idols.*"[27] We have seen upon what kind of dubious evidence that charge of "idolatry" was based; what kind of proof was offered to substantiate it; and how the single testimony offered in its behalf was used as the basis for a generalization.[28] The absurdity of the claim that the so-called Judaizing Marranos believed in the existence of "a God and Goddess" is no less apparent than the fabricated charge that some of them worshiped idols.

As the text of the proceedings of the Toledan Inquiry is not extant and we have no other source for the Judaizers' belief in a "God and a Goddess" (such as provided by Espina for the conversos' idol worship), we can only conjecture its origin. Perhaps an echo is heard here of the Cabbalistic concept of the *Shekhina,* communicated and misinterpreted in a vulgar fashion either by some Judaizing converso or by some Jew with whom the Toledans came in touch. Literally mistranslated and fundamentally misconceived, the term[29] could suggest that, besides God, there is a Goddess in heaven. Even so, it is difficult to assume that such a misconception developed, or could develop, in the minds of Jews, whether clandestine or not. For the Jews were known for their emphasis upon the absolute unity of God; and facing, as they did in the medieval era, the tremendous propagandistic onslaught of Christianity, their view of God's unity served them in good stead against the Christian doctrine of the Trinity, which, despite all explanations to the contrary, appeared to them as endorsing or implying the existence of three divine beings. The Cabbalists also, it should be pointed out—even though they believed in the theory of the *Sephirot* (which may be viewed as emanations from the divine essence), or in the doctrine of the meeting within the essence of God of the two opposite elements of the cosmos (the masculine and feminine)[30]—never presented these doctrines with a view to indicate a plurality of divine persons but, on the contrary, to stress again and again the definite and absolute unity of God,[31] in whom all opposites so inhere as to constitute a single indivisible being. It is likely, therefore, that the view of the "God and Goddess" was a hostile interpretation of the idea of the *Shekhina* or of the dualistic Cabbalistic doctrine just mentioned—hostile because, in all probability, it was presented before the Toledan inquirers by a Christian "witness" who claimed that he had "heard" the notion propagated by some converso, just as another such Christian witness claimed that he had "seen" a converso couple worship idols. Also, if the idea was expressed by a converso who was investigated by the Toledan inquisition, it could be forced out of him under torture, or threat of torture, against his true convictions or beliefs; and in this instance, we may assume that the inquisitor who questioned him was bent upon confirming his own interpretation of some of the notions he had gleaned from Jews. But whatever the truth about the origin of the charge, it is obvious that at no time was there among the Marranos a *large number*— let alone "a very large" body—of believers in the existence of "a God and Goddess." Hence, what we have here is a wild generalization grounded in a single instance or isolated cases of false or forced or misinterpreted testimonies regarding the issue in question. This gives us once more an idea about the nature of the *pesquisa* and the quality of the findings on which the Toledans based their judgments concerning the Marranos' religion.

Equally preposterous was the third specific charge leveled at the conversos in the *Sentencia*—namely, that on Maundy Thursday (i.e., on *every* Maundy Thursday), the conversos were "slaughtering lambs and eating them and also making other-sorts of burnt offerings and sacrifices."[32] This procedure is described in the *Sentencia* as being in accordance with the "manner of the Jews"[33]—presumably on Passover eve. But *was* this the manner of the Jews? Granted that prior to the destruction of the Temple the Jews would offer, on the *eve* of that holiday, the Passover Sacrifice and the Sacrifice of the Festivity.[34] In addition they would make, on the first day of the holiday, the Pilgrim's Burnt Offering and the Felicity Peace Offerings.[35] And apart from this, they would bring on each day of the holiday the Sacrifice of the Congregation offered on new moons.[36] But all these sacrifices, as is known, were abolished—in fact, were *prohibited*—after the destruction of the Temple.[37] Certainly, the Marranos, if they were Judaizers—and that means followers of Jewish law and ritual—were not trying to preserve laws and customs that no longer existed among the Jews, or to revive customs that were clearly forbidden by established Jewish law. How, then, did the Toledan inquisitor arrive at such a strange conclusion? Did he derive it simply from the book of Exodus (XII 3:7, 8) or from other sources about ancient Jewish custom? Perhaps he was able to "confirm" this conclusion through a frightened witness who responded affirmatively to some of his questions that implied those assumptions—and this sufficed for him to claim that it was the custom of the Marranos not only to slaughter lambs on Passover eve, but also to make all kinds of "sacrifices and holocausts" according to the "manner of the Jews."

But this is not the only strange part we find in these assertions. For they include also the claim that the conversos were offering their "sacrifices" on Maundy Thursday. But why should they have done this on that day? If the reference was, as it appears to have been, to the Jewish celebration of the Passover, the date marking the eve of this festival is not Maundy Thursday but the 14th of Nisan, which never falls on a Thursday.[38] If, on the other hand, the authors of the *Sentencia* meant to indicate that the conversos, in their hatred for Christianity, turned the day of solemn sorrow for the Christians into a day of festivity for themselves, they could not say that the "sacrifices and burnt offerings" brought on that occasion constituted Judaization. For Judaizing meant, as the Toledans defined it, the following of the laws and ceremonies of the Jews; yet there has never been a law, rite, or custom that prescribed for the Jews such conduct on that day. Inevitably, we revert to our original understanding that by the Maundy Thursday celebration mentioned in the *Sentencia* the reference was to the celebration of the

Passover, and so we must conclude that the inquisitor made here another blunder: he assumed that just as Maundy Thursday (the day of the Last Supper) was in Jesus' time the day of the Passover feast, so it was for the Jews ever since; and he may also have had a responsive witness who, out of ignorance or fear (or perhaps both), nodded agreement to his allusions. Above all, we can see how several related data, taken from the Old and New Testaments alike, combined to form the strange accusation, which had no basis in fact.

It was, then, for such crimes of faith and worship—the offering of "sacrifices" on Maundy Thursday, the belief in the existence of "a God and a Goddess," and the "worship of idols"—"crimes," which no doubt were never committed, that some of the conversos were sentenced to be burned. However, according to the authors of the Statute, the faithlessness of the conversos was also indicated by their negative reaction to these harsh sentences, or as the Statute puts it: "The majority of the Marranos *do not feel good* about the faith" because the holy decrees consider it right that heretics should be punished by burning.[39] It was presumably supposed that had they been real Christians, they would have welcomed these harsh sentences. Even so, such an argument could be made only if the conversos were convinced of the truth of the accusations leveled against some of their members. But the conversos, we know, were not convinced of this at all. On the contrary, they denied the right of the rebel judges to sentence people to death and send them to the stake on the basis of the kind of evidence they possessed.[40] It should also be noted that according to Christian law, the finding of some deviation from the faith in itself constitutes no proof of heresy[41]; and furthermore, if heresy *is* established, the culprit must be given an opportunity to repent before he is declared a stubborn heretic who must be purged by the ultimate punishment.[42] There is evidence that the Toledan tribunal disregarded all these legal requirements,[43] and we should not be surprised that many Marranos sharply criticized its actions. They no doubt repudiated the right of such a court to sentence people to death even if it found them to be holding false beliefs[44]; and it stands to reason that some conversos expressed doubts or criticisms about the very assumption that culprits of faith should be so punished. This, of course, could be interpreted by the Toledans as sure evidence of their "bad feelings" about the Catholic faith as a whole.

But these reactions of the conversos to the trials place in further doubt the Toledans' claims concerning Marrano Judaization. For if the Marranos were secret Jews, they would have shared with other Jews their criticism of Christianity for its *major* beliefs, for *all* its dogmas, and for the *oppression* to which it had subjected them. In other words, they would have "felt badly" about Christianity for reasons quite apart from its treatment of "heretics," and long before they experienced such treatment. If it was, however, *this* experience which caused the conversos' "bad feelings" about Christianity, it suggests that they had not been secret Jews but rather followers of the Christian faith, who were shocked by what happened in Toledo—in fact, by what happened to them as Christians. Indeed, it suggests that the Toledan occurrences moved some of them to examine their attitude toward Christianity and question the very propriety and worthwhileness of their association with it. Such people may have asked themselves: What kind of religion is this if such atrocities can be committed in its name, and allegedly on the strength of its laws? That such critical thoughts stirred the minds of *some* Marranos and changed their attitude toward Christianity from positive to negative may be gathered also from other sources.[45] But this development, which was a *result* of the persecution, could not serve as the *reason* for it. To present it as the reason would virtually amount to reversing the order of cause and effect.

It is difficult to assume that the authors of the Statute did not sense the fallacy of their thinking. Yet the fact that they resorted to such an argument, and presented the Marranos' reaction to their "trials" as proof of the latter's dislike of Christianity, suggests that their Inquiry offered them little—indeed, very little—to go on. For it shows that in their efforts to justify their enactment—i.e., the *Sentencia-Estatuto*—they seized every argument, however questionable, in order to buttress their case.

Finally, we must consider the following two points, which appear especially important. In the Petition, as we have noted, the Toledans branded *most* of the conversos as Judaizers.[46] The authors of the *Sentencia*, however, retreated from this charge; instead they said merely that "a very large part" of the "conversos of this city" were found to be religiously unfaithful.[47] It is obvious that if they could have ascribed this condition to an *overwhelming majority* of the conversos, or even to *any sort of majority*, they would not have refrained from doing so. Their *failure* to do this can only be attributed to their *inability* to do so, or rather to the realization of at least some of the Toledans that in a legal document such as the *Sentencia* they must avoid patently exaggerated expressions and easily refutable statements. Evidently, their Inquiry did not supply grounds for a broader, more definite statement. The indefinite term "a very large part" was, in the circumstances, the best they could use.

Second, the *Sentencia* does not say that this part, whatever its size, was actually "heretical" (as is claimed in the Petition). What it says is that this part was found to be "very suspect" of religious impropriety—suspect of adhering to beliefs and practices that were Judaic or repugnant to Christianity. But "suspect," and even "very suspect," does not mean "guilty," or otherwise incriminated religiously in a manner that would justify penal measures. Obviously, the Inquiry could not establish anything definite even concerning *that* "part"; and since we have concluded that the term it used (i.e., "a very large part") stood at most for a substantial minority, it follows that the Inquiry established nothing certain even with respect to that minority. What it did establish, according to its own claim, was that *some people*—or, rather, several people—were found by the inquirers to be guilty of heresy, so that the secular authorities had to proceed against them "by means of fire." These results of the Inquiry could not, understandably, satisfy the authors of the Statute. Therefore, while attempting to find justification for an enactment that would apply to *all* conversos, they found it necessary to add that "the *majority* of the conversos feel badly about Christianity on account of its position on the burning of heretics,"[48] and furthermore, that "beyond what has been said, *it is notorious in the city*, and as such we hold and declare it as notorious, that the said conversos live and behave [*tratan*] without fear of God, and also have shown and show themselves to be *enemies of the said city* and its Old Christian residents."[49]

The authors of the Statute thus finally reached the point they needed for their religious accusation. They effected the transition from "a very large part" (allegedly based on the findings of the Inquiry) to a "majority" (of the conversos who reacted negatively to their Sentence), and then to the conversos generally, without exception; and they further moved, in their choice of terms suggestive of the conversos' guilt, from the vague "suspect" through the "feeling badly about the Christian religion," which is a clear allusion to a negative attitude, to the concrete and all-embracing accusation that they "lived without fear of God," which was supposed to stand for outright violation of all the laws of Christian morality and faith.

3. The Social Reasons

This brings us to the third set of reasons that the authors of the *Sentencia* give for their enactment. It relates to the social attitudes of the conversos toward the Old Christians of Toledo and the country as a whole, and especially to the way they exercised their functions as holders of public office.

Already in the preamble to the *Sentencia-Estatuto*, the conversos are exposed to biting criticism for the way they acquired the *escribanías* (i.e., the public notaries) in Toledo, most of which, according to the *Sentencia*, were at the time in their possession. They acquired them, the *Sentencia* claims, in a "tyrannical" manner—that is, against the will of the citizens—by "purchasing" them with money, or by assuring certain "favors" to those who could grant these offices, or "by other subtle and deceitful means," which the authors do not care to specify.[50] Later on, in the body of the *Sentencia*, this attack upon the converso office holders is both broadened and sharpened. And it turns from the question of how the offices were *acquired*—which may be viewed as rather incidental—to the fundamental question of how they were *managed*.

Pointing to the converso management of the King's fiscal administration, the *Sentencia* accuses the converso officials of "having stolen large and innumerable quantities of maravedis and silver from the King our Lord and from his revenues, taxes and tributes." Also, they "have brought devastation upon the estates of many noble ladies, caballeros and *hijos dalgo*" and, altogether, "have oppressed, destroyed, robbed and depraved most of the old houses and estates of the Old Christians of this city, its territory and jurisdiction."[51] Indicated in all this is a system of spoliation aimed at the Old Christians of the city—especially of the lower nobility and the middle class—which had already wrought havoc upon "most of the old houses and estates". And, of course, since the management of the King's fiscal administration was not limited to Toledo and its environs, what was said with respect to Toledo applied equally to "all the kingdoms of Castile."[52] In consequence, the whole country became a sorrowful scene of the same common and widespread evils—robbery, oppression, and economic ruin—which were of the making of that officialdom. In brief, it was a national, not a local, calamity, for which the conversos were responsible.

Having thus described the illegal manner in which the conversos acquired their offices (as in the case of the *escribanías*) and the criminal manner in which they ran them (as in the case of the financial administration), together with its catastrophic consequences, the authors turn again to Toledo and speak of the conversos' doings in that city in more specific terms. To be sure, here, too, the discussion is limited to the conversos' occupancy of public offices, but it no longer deals with their possession of such offices in this or that field of the administration, but with the manner, purpose, and result of their control of *all* the public offices they hold. Furthermore, it describes the impact of that control not only upon the individual property owners (the nobles and their dependents, as indicated before), but also upon the public property of Toledo. Accordingly, it charges that "during the time in which the conversos have held the public offices of this city, as well as its regimen and government, not only has a great—or the greater—part of the [private] places of the city become depopulated and destroyed, but also the land and places of its public property have been lost and alienated."[53] As for the remainder of the public resources, "all the incomes of the rents and of the public possessions are being spent on [the promotion of] the private interests and estates [of the conversos], so that all the goods and honors of the fatherland [*patria*] are being wasted and destroyed, while they [i.e., the conversos] become lords [of the land] in order to destroy the Holy Catholic Faith and the Old Christians who believe in it."[54]

Thus, according to this document, the conversos held not only most of the notarial posts, but also many other public offices of the city, and were actually in control of the city administration (they "held its regimen and government"). They also controlled the King's fiscal administration, by means of which they acquired a stronger hold on the King's subjects in the city, and in fact in all the kingdoms of Castile. Consequently, both city and country felt the disastrous effects of their rule; but these effects, the Statute makes clear, must not be related to such flaws of management as negligence, blunder, or inefficiency. On the contrary, the converso occupants of these offices demonstrated in their actions great care and deliberation; they made thorough and efficient use of the positions they had assumed—though not for the purposes for which those positions were established, but for the conversos' own goals. In the process of pursuing these goals, they committed every crime in the book: bribery, corruption, oppression, robbery, and theft, and generally subverted the public offices into varied and all-purpose instruments of crime. This, then, is *how* those officials operated; these were their methods and their means! And their ends? Their ends were, of course, to enrich themselves at the expense of the subjects over whom they ruled (to serve their "interests" and "increase their estates"); but beyond this was the overriding, ultimate aim: to destroy Catholicism and those who believed in it.[55]

Thus, we have here again a clear allusion to the alleged conspiracy of the conversos: to seize control of key positions in the government—for the purpose of oppressing and destroying, first the best and noblest of Christian Spain, and ultimately all the Old Christians in it. No proof is offered to substantiate any of these grave charges. No proof seems to be needed; "for this is notorious and we hold it to be so."[56]

Nevertheless, while the authors of the Statute do not find it necessary to present tangible evidence—or any evidence at all—with respect to the behavior of the converso officials, they evidently seek to bolster their charge by pointing to incidents in Toledan life that might illustrate the attitude of both the Jews and the conversos (the Jews' progeny) toward the Old Christians, and thus "explain" the conduct of the converso officials as an expression of the will and attitude of the community to which they belong.

The first of these incidents relates to the alleged activities of the Jews; and to find an instance of Jewish behavior that would illustrate their assertions, the authors of the Statute had to go back more than seven centuries in the history of Toledo. At this point, they thought, they encountered an occurrence which offered support to their claim—namely, that the Jews so hated the Christians that they engineered the deadliest conspiracies against them. Here, in the city of Toledo, they say, the "Jews lived in ancient times"; and, as the old chronicles relate, "when the city was encircled by the Moors, our enemies, under [the leadership of] Tarife (Tarik) . . . the Jews made a deal with the [besieging] enemy, sold him the city and its Christian population, and enabled the Moors to enter it. As the result of this treaty and agreement, 306 Christians of this city were massacred, and more than 106, both men and women, children and old persons, were dragged from the Iglesia Mayor and the Church of Santa Leocadia and carried away as captives."[57]

The story is first told by Lucas of Túy and repeated by the *Primera Crónica General*.[58] However, it is confirmed by no authentic source, and for this, as well as other reasons, it is considered questionable, if not fictitious.[59] We cannot, however, blame the authors of the *Sentencia* for having relied on Lucas's story. Whatever was written in any reputable work, and especially in one assumed to be a "history," was taken to be true in those days; and there is no reason to doubt that the authors of the *Sentencia* believed in the verity of that account.[60] But had they had any sense of fairness or any respect for the *whole* truth, they would also have considered some related developments of which they were certainly aware—namely, that the alleged Jewish alliance with the Moors followed a century of anti-Jewish persecution, and that if the Jews did conspire against the rulers, they were not alone in that adventure but joined by a large segment of the Christian population, headed by Count Julian, the sons (or brothers) of Witiza (the deposed king), and Oppas, the Metropolitan of Seville.[61] Surely the Christians who supported the Moslems were not enemies of Christians, but of their country's rulers, just as the Jews could have been too. Yet such conjectures, which could throw a favorable light upon the Jews of Toledo and the Jews generally, would not enter the minds of the writers of the *Sentencia*. And what emerges from their account is that the Jews, unprovoked, betrayed the Christians of Toledo, with whom they seemingly lived in amity, and brought misfortune upon them and the city, for no other reason than their old hatred for the Christians since the Passion of Christ.

Having presented what they viewed as evidence proving the perfidy of the Jews, the authors of the Statute add that similar conspiracies with the same intent—to betray the city and destroy its Christian population—were organized by the Toledan conversos. Indeed, only "a short while ago," they assert, "the conversos of this city organized an insurrection, joined together and armed themselves, and put into deed and effect, as is notorious, a plan aimed at destroying and putting an end to all Old Christians" in Toledo, "including one Pero Sarmiento, their chief."[62] Among the goals they sought to achieve, the Statute lists: (1) "to obtain control of the city; (2) to throw the Old Christians out of Toledo; and (3) to deliver the city to its enemies"—namely, to Alvaro de Luna and his associates, "according to what has been reported, and is public knowledge and notorious."[63]

Obviously, the reference here is to actions taken by the conversos during the Toledan rebellion; and the cited account is another example of how biased and deceptive these authors could be—not only with respect to facts from remote periods, but also from the most recent times. For the truth was the opposite of what the Statute said. The conversos organized and armed themselves not out of *their* hatred for the Old Christians but in reaction to the latter's hatred for *them*, made manifest in many aggressive acts. Furthermore, the conversos armed themselves not to destroy the Old Christians of Toledo or oust them from the city, as the *Sentencia* claimed, but to defend themselves against the destruction and expulsion planned for *them* by many Old Christians. It is highly improbable that they planned to capture the city—first, because they were considerably weaker, numerically and militarily, than the Old Christians, and second, because the alcazar and all other strongholds were tightly held by the Old Christian rebels. But even if they entertained such far-reaching plans, it is clear that these plans were in no way directed against *all* the Old Christians of Toledo but only against the rebel party; and if indeed they schemed to reduce that party and oust its leaders from the city, it was not because it was made up of Old Christians, but because it was in rebellion against the King—and, above all, because it was bent upon the oppression, persecution, and destruction of their own group. Thus, we see how facts, causes, motives, and aims are so falsely presented in the *Sentencia* that obvious truths are replaced by their opposites: the rebels and conspirators accuse their opponents of rebellion and conspiracy; the desperate self-defense of the conversos is portrayed as cold-blooded, premeditated aggression; the persecution initiated against them by the Old Christians is neatly exchanged for a persecution *of* the Old Christians planned and organized by the conversos. And thus the paramilitary steps taken by the persecuted solely to defend themselves appear to have been prompted by a different motive: the Marranos' traditional, undying hatred for Christianity and its followers, the Christians.

The Statute further claims that the conversos were responsible for the recent siege of Toledo by the royal army. According to the authors of the *Sentencia*, this action which the King took against the city resulted from the converso conspiracy—or, as they put it:

> It is notorious that it was at their [i.e., the conversos'] *request, instigation and solicitation* that a besieging army was placed round the city by the Constable Alvaro de Luna and his followers, urging cruel war upon us with an armed hand, with blood and fire, accompanied with destructions, damages and robberies, as if we were Moors.[64]

Thus, while the Petition indicates that conversos were in the King's entourage when he was approaching the city with his army, and that they were there under Alvaro's protection (an allusion to their connivance with Alvaro), the Statute states unequivocally that the whole military campaign against the city was undertaken at the conversos' instigation. But was this true? Indubitably, the conversos *wanted* the King to capture the city and put an end to the regime that threatened their existence in Toledo. It is also very likely that some of the conversos who were members of the King's Council and accompanied the King were among those who advised Juan II to take stern action against the city. This advice they could certainly render as faithful servants and counselors of the King both out of their conviction that the action they suggested was in the King's vital interest and out of their sincere belief that the conversos, loyal subjects of the King and citizens of the republic, had the right to be fully protected by the Crown. But whether such advice was given or not, it could hardly have been the major factor in determining the king's moves against Toledo.

The determining factor undoubtedly lay first in Alvaro's position in the matter and then in the offensive, unacceptable terms that the rebels presented to the king in their Petition. We have, in fact, the evidence of Carrillo, the King's chronicler, that it was Alvaro de Luna (and hence not the conversos) who urged the King, shortly after the outbreak of the rebellion, to come to Toledo in order to pacify the city "either by negotiations or by force."[65] Since the rebels' demands were clearly not negotiable from the King's and Alvaro's point of view, the King had no choice but to use force—the alternative envisaged by the Constable. It was precisely to avail himself of this alternative that the King brought his main army with him; and it was doubtless in connection with the military steps that he expected the King to take against Toledo that the Constable sought, at about the same time, the aid of the Master of Alcántara.[66]

It is difficult to assume that Sarmiento and his partisans were unaware of these steps of the Constable, or that they failed to realize that their own presentations—the terms of peace, or rather of agreement, which they submitted to the King as conditions for their obedience—left Juan II no choice but to take military action against them and the city which they held in their grip. Obviously, for tactical reasons they preferred to attribute the failure of their Petition, and of their mission to the King, to their sworn enemies, the conversos, by claiming that it was the latter who "persuaded" the King to disregard their pleas and beleaguer the city. By this claim, we assume, they could divest themselves of the blame for all the hardships, sufferings and troubles that befell the city as a result of the siege, and lay it on the shoulders of the hated conversos, the "enemies of all Christians."

4. The Racial Reasons

Now, what the Jews allegedly did to the Toledan Christians during the Arab conquest of Spain, "the said conversos, the descendants of the Jews, have been doing and are doing every day."[67] In other words, they are bringing upon the Old Christians the "same harms, evils, and wars which the Jews, the enemies of our Holy Catholic faith, have always brought, and are still bringing about, since the passion of our Savior Jesus Christ."[68]

To the authors of the Statute, the sameness of the means allegedly employed by the conversos and the Jews indicated the sameness of the hatred which both groups felt toward the Christians. Nevertheless, the identification of these enmities—i.e., of the conversos and the Jews—was not meant here merely to indicate the identity of the *religious* position of the two groups. Determining the sameness of their hostility to Christianity was, apart from their common Jewish religion, another, more powerful and more crucial factor: their common *racial* origin.

This view of the authors of the Statute is already implied in their identification of the conversos—those bearers of a deadly hatred for the Christians—as "the descendants of the Jews." For by saying "the conversos, the *descendants* of the Jews," they meant to signify not an extraneous, but an inherent, unalterable relationship. For "descent" is conceived by them not merely as a factor that establishes contact between generations through certain attitudes, beliefs and customs transmitted from one generation to another, but as the very *root* of the common attitudes, etc., and their related forms of behavior. The identical conduct toward the Christians by both the conversos and the Jews is thus explained by the identical cause of that conduct: the common "descent," or race.

That this is indeed what the Toledans had in mind is evident from the first statement of the *Sentencia*, which identifies the conversos—i.e., the whole group—as the offspring of the "perverse lineage of the Jews."[69] It is "perversity," or the inherent deficiency of their race, that is responsible for their social and religious crimes; and since *all* of them share the same deficiency, *all* of them, without need of any proof or inquiry, must be treated as outcasts from Christian society, and consequently denied the right to public office, or even the right to testify in court. Moreover, because it is not an accidental, but an *organic* condition that causes their moral depravity and sinfulness, they are not only "unsuitable" to the aforesaid social functions, but also inherently "incapable" of fulfilling them—in all circumstances and at all times.[70] Indeed, since racial qualities are immutable, the above limitations apply to *future* conversos, as well as to those of the *present* and the *past;* and hence, "this Sentence . . . must be viewed as valid for the converts of the past, the present and the future."[71]

The Statute was thus based on a principle which superseded all moral and religious considerations, and it was not on the basis of such considerations that it judged the conversos as individuals and as a group. To be sure, it repeatedly pointed to and stressed the alleged deviations of the conversos from morality—i.e., the proper social and religious norms; but this was done to illustrate or prove the assertion about their "perverse race." The latter term is doubtless the key title among the Statute's various designations for the Marranos, but by no means the only one that reflects the same view. In fact, a whole theory of race and race relations is inherent in the Statute's terminology.

Three times does the term *lindos* (pure) appear in the *Sentencia* as a title of *christianos viejos,*[72] emphasizing, no doubt, that in its authors' view, the "purity" which characterizes the Old Christians emanates from their "pure" origin, just as the corruption of the New Christians emanates from their impure, "perverted" source—i.e., the "stock and breed of the Jews."[73] This, of course, is a much more serious flaw than the transfer of religious customs and traditions from one generation to another. Such a transfer could presumably be halted by Christian environment and education. But can one escape a heritage of immorality which flows neither from custom nor from ancestral authority but from one's own constitution? The policy promulgated by the Toledan *Sentencia* was predicated upon the denial of this possibility.

This, then, was the main innovation implied in the terminology used by the Toledans in their statements on the converso question; and this was the first time in Spain that any social or political organization—let alone one that represented a great city—formally adopted a racial principle and made it the cornerstone of its policy.[74] A new ideological current was born that was to be carried along, with occasional checks, not only by the winds of social hatred, but also by the force of governmental power. Before long, and for centuries to come, Spain's attitudes toward the Marranos were to be influenced—or even determined—by the letter and spirit of the Toledan Statute.

This completes our presentation of the reasons offered in the *Sentencia* for the various decrees it promulgated against the conversos. As we have noted, these reasons rest on four foundations, or rather four categories of arguments. So well coordinated are these arguments, and so passionate the pleas made in their behalf, that one can easily be swayed into the belief that they make in their totality a strong case. When closely examined, however, they yield a different impression. In fact, the whole structure of the Toledans' accusations collapses, upon analysis, like a house of cards.

For legally, as we have seen, the Statute was based on very weak and inadequate grounds, and stood in direct and open opposition to the govern-ing law, both canon and secular. Socially, it was based on a morbid imagina-tion, the product of hate, fear, and jealousy, and presented a decidedly distorted account of the Marranos' aims and functions in the Christian society. Religiously, it was based on fantastic claims that stemmed from ignorance and wild rumor. And racially, it was grounded on arbitrary as-sumptions which could not be supported by either history or theology or any pattern of phenomena in social life. That this is so will be shown in greater detail in some of the fothcoming chapters. At this point, however, we should note some differences between this document and the Petition, which pre-ceded it.

It is clear that the Statute echoes, in large measure, the views and senti-ments expressed in the Petition. But it is less extreme and less sweeping in its anti-converso charges. Thus while it claims, as the Petition does, that a converso conspiracy is afoot in the country to take over the government and destroy the Old Christians, it drops the accusation, found in the Petition, that the Jews had been converted to attain this end. Similarly, while the Petition states definitely that the *"majority"* of the Marranos are *"heretical"* and *"apostatic,"* the Statute merely says that *"a large part"* of them—which obvi-ously meant less than a majority—is only *"suspect"* in the faith. Evidently the authors of the Toledan Statute eliminated or weakened some major accusa-tions—no doubt because they did not wish to be criticized for taking posi-tions that were clearly indefensible.[75]

But while the *Sentencia* is more "moderate" than the Petition in its refer-ences to the scope of the Judaic "heresy," it is more extreme in marking the expanse of the Marranos' enmity toward the Old Christians. For it extends that enmity from the "heretics" per se to the Marranos generally; and thus, instead of *erejes enemigos,* which is the term used by the Petition,[76] the Statute speaks of *vecinos enemigos*[77] meaning thereby the whole Marrano group. Likewise, the measures proposed by the *Sentencia* to combat the "enemy" as described above are more sweeping than those indicated in the Petition. For while the Petition seeks to oust the Marranos, together with Alvaro, from the *royal* administration, the *Sentencia* prohibits them from holding *any* office (public or private) and receiving *any* benefice (again, public *or* private) and even from testifying in the public courts. What is more, it extended these prohibitions to the descendants of the Marranos for generations to come—an extension made not merely on the grounds of "religion" or rather of the Marranos' religious suspectability, or of their alleged hatred for the Chris-tians—but also, and primarily. on the grounds of racial origin—that is, because, as the Statute puts it, they belong to the "perverse race" of the Jews.

These are the differences between the Petition and the Statute; and we have to consider whether these differences—what the Statute omitted and what it added—are not somehow related. In fact, major practical and ideological considerations were responsible for both the omissions and the additions. And these, as we shall see, touch upon the question: Why was the race theory created? But to answer this question we must first examine all other pronouncements on the same issue that were made in the course of the campaign under review.

II. Converso Counter-Attack

I

Of the extant Marrano documents on the *Sentencia-Estatuto* and the anti-Marrano views that inspired it, the Instruction directed to the bishop of Cuenca by Fernán Díaz de Toledo in October 1449[1] was the first to be completed and made public.[2] This chronological fact may have contributed to the influence the work exerted on the evolving controversy between the Old and New Christians. In the main, however, its effect must be attributed to its brilliant style and striking arguments, to its author's fame as the Relator, and to some of the qualities of his colorful personality, which are reflected in his writing. The Relator was witty, subtle, clever, occasionally sarcastic, more often diplomatic, and always reliable in his assertions. For his statements of fact were based on solid knowledge and his judgments on sound reasoning. His views, moreover, formed an integral part of a harmonious world outlook, resting on the foundations of Christian law, religion, morality, and history, with a number of amplifications, additions, and emphases derived from his Marrano background.

In describing Fernán Díaz, Amador de los Ríos defined him as "one of the principal conversos who attained great esteem in the Castilian Court."[3] The description, though correct, is incomplete. For as we shall see, Fernán Díaz de Toledo was the object not only of esteem and admiration, but also of hate and abuse. Yet whether praised or censured, he was one of the most powerful officials at the Court of Juan II, and in the closing years of Juan II's reign probably the most influential of them all.

Even though his name is often mentioned in the numerous documents that have come down from that period, the data we possess about his life and activity can barely suffice for the briefest sketch. Born to a Jewish family of Alcalá de Henares,[4] he was probably converted in early childhood, during the pogroms of 1391. His father must have been one of those converts who followed the assimilationist line and, consequently, sought to give his son a thorough Christian education. Fernán, in any case, received such an education and, as a result, was equipped with skills that secured for him a place in Spain's higher society. As expert in law, both canon and civil, he was well fitted to serve in the legal profession, but Fernán's interests exceeded the limits of this calling and inclined him toward the field of government. Thus we find him, in October 1420, serving as secretary of Juan II—a position to which he may have been appointed when the administration was headed by

Juan Hurtado de Mendoza, Alvaro de Luna's friend and relative.[5] If so, the change in the royal administration resulting from Infante Enrique's coup d'état did not seem to affect adversely Díaz' standing. In any case, when the coup was subverted and Alvaro de Luna became Constable of the kingdom, he appointed Fernán Díaz to one of the highest posts in the royal bureaucracy. It was the newly created office of Relator,[6] which Díaz made famous by the way he managed it and which was to be identified with his person.

It is difficult to establish the precise date on which Fernán Díaz was appointed to this office. In any case, his rise in the bureaucratic hierarchy was exceptionally rapid. In 1423—only two and a half years after Alvaro took over the reins of government—we find Díaz occupying, besides the position of secretary, also that of the king's auditor (*oidor*) and referendary (*referendario*) and shortly thereafter also that of Relator.[7] Four years later, in 1427, we see him simultaneously holding all these offices, as well as that of notary of the royal chamber (*Escribano de la Camara*). He was also chief notary of the Rounded Privileges; and at the same time, and possibly even earlier, a member of the King's Council.[8] Thus within a brief period, Fernán Díaz succeeded in concentrating in his hands more bureaucratic powers than any other man in Alvaro's administration, except Alvaro himself.

"To be sure," says the historian Alvar García de Santa María when writing the annals of the realm in 1429, "anyone who will hear that all these offices were entrusted to one person . . . will maintain that they were ill provided for."[9] But this, he adds, could be assumed only by one who does not know Fernán Díaz. For he who knew the man and saw with his own eyes how he worked and what he had produced, who noticed his "astuteness," "great loyalty," and the "purity" of his dealings, who observed, in addition, the great "diligence" with which he handled the affairs of the king, as well as the "liberality" with which he dispatched them, will realize that "all these tasks were well taken care of."[10]

This gives us an idea of the personal qualities which, according to García, enabled Fernán Díaz to perform responsibly all the administrative tasks that were imposed upon him. Even so, these traits alone, unaided by great talent, cannot explain Fernán Díaz' achievement. For the work that emanated from his office, says the chronicler, was "nothing short of prodigious." Through his hands passed practically all the royal business, for only "very few documents were processed by any other secretary of the king."[11] It is he who prepared and discharged all the letters issued in the king's name: diplomatic correspondence with foreign powers, papers related to internal negotiations, and instructions to towns, nobles and officials, as well as announcements and stipulations of royal grants given to localities and individuals. This included the allocations of rights, offices, incomes, and lands, and royal decisions in cases of dispute.[12] Even when judged by its mere amount, Fernán Díaz' industry was a cause of amazement. But even more astounding than the quantity of his work was its remarkable quality.

We can get a fair notion of that quality from the numerous documents that have come down to us bearing the Relator's signature. They display a clarity and smoothness of style that are distinctly his and are marked by his ability to formulate convincingly whatever position he undertook to present. So strongly, indeed, do these documents reflect his brilliance as jurist and his shrewdness as diplomat that one does not wonder why he was entrusted with such numerous and complex responsibilities.

But apart from all these manifold distinctions that made Fernán Díaz' services so desired, he was known for still another characteristic which made him particularly respected and sought after. He could not be bribed—or even hired. Magnanimous in offering his valuable services for the settlement of many difficult disputes (some no doubt outside the scope of his duties), he consistently refused to be remunerated financially beyond what he received ordinarily from the king. Says concerning this the historian García: "For all those letters [that Fernán Díaz dispatched], from which, without imposing any burden upon his conscience, and without any violation of custom . . . he could have earned as much money as could have made ten *Escribanos de Cámara* rich and opulent, he is not known to have taken a single penny; nor did he get anything for his reports on litigations, nor for any of the other matters for which people customarily earn large sums of money, even though on many occasions he was entrusted with their settlement."[13] In an age when the rapacity of courtiers was proverbial and the hunt for gain the pursuit of most officials, it was difficult to find a man in high office so immune to the contagious disease of avarice.[14]

It was no doubt because he was so deeply impressed by the particular combination of administrative abilities and moral qualities that Fernán Díaz displayed—and not simply because he was the first to occupy the newly established office of the Relator—that Alvar García said, when referring to him, that he was an official the like of which "neither this king [i.e., Juan II], nor any other king before him was known to have had."[15]

II

According to Alvaro's initial design, the Relator was to be the main dynamic force in the efficient bureaucracy he sought to create—a bureaucracy which was to put into effect his plan to centralize the monarchic government. By assuming so many major responsibilities, and by displaying that enormous capacity to fulfill them, the Relator actually represented in his person the concentration of powers which Alvaro espoused. He became the nexus of the royal administration and, in some respects, the symbol of the Alvarian regime.

As such, however, he was bound to become, regardless of the excellence of his performance, a target of sharp criticism and rebuke on the part of the ever-restive opposition. This could not be otherwise, even if Fernán Díaz tried to exercise—as actually may have been the case—the utmost fairness and impartiality in the execution of his duties. In the relentless struggle that developed in Castile between Alvaro de Luna and the Infantes of Aragon, hardly anyone in the political arena could remain truly neutral, or be considered as such. As a central figure in Alvaro's administration, and as one who was put in office by Alvaro, the Relator was inevitably seen by the opposition as Alvaro's "creature."

This alone was reason enough for him to be regarded as persona non grata by the party of the opposition. Yet in addition, this party assumed that Fernán Díaz played a special role in cementing Alvaro's relations with the King; and that meant that the functions he fulfilled were vital for Alvaro's retention of power. This assumption was based on the fact that the Relator was the only royal counselor who was virtually always at the King's side, and therefore could, more that anyone else, influence Juan II in favor of the Constable—or for that matter, against him.

The tactics of the opposition were aimed for a long time at driving a wedge between the King and his favorite. Naturally, they saw Fernán Díaz de Toledo as a major obstacle to the attainment of that aim. To shatter the King's faith in Alvaro, they reasoned, they had first to undermine his faith in the Relator, the guardian of Alvaro's alliance with the King. No wonder, therefore, that in the brief of complaint which they sent Juan II in February 1440, the rebellious nobles described Fernán Díaz as Alvaro de Luna's secret henchman at court. As such, they claimed, the Relator was following the King's orders only ostensibly, while actually he was taking his instructions from the Constable.[16] To be sure, in that brief we find the same charge directed at other officials as well. In fact, it is claimed there that all of Alvaro's appointees, whether inside or outside the Court, were committed to Alvaro's bidding and gave him their "first loyalty." Nevertheless, the Relator was the only one of these officials whom they designated as exemplar of this rule and singled out as Alvaro's arch-agent in the King's most intimate entourage. All this indicates that the Relator was not just an ordinary supporter of Alvaro— merely one of the many whom the barons disliked—but a prime target of a special attack in that bitter political contest.

That the party opposed to Alvaro de Luna took such a harsh view of the Relator precisely because they believed him to have been a staunch and effective friend of the Constable is evident also from an incident that occurred in March 1441. At that time, Fernán Díaz and two other courtiers were sent by Juan II to the Infante Don Enrique with the aim of persuading the latter to leave Toledo, which he had entered against the King's prohibition. In response, Don Enrique arrested the ambassadors and kept them imprisoned, in defiance of the King's order that he set them free at once.[17] Finally, yielding to the arguments of his ally the duke Don Fadrique, the Admiral of Castile, he agreed to release two of the ambassadors on their assurance that instead of returning to the Court, they would retire to their estates.[18] The Relator, however, was not one of the two. We do not know whether he was approached with a similar offer by the Infante, and if so, what his answer was. What we do know is that Don Enrique insisted that freedom be denied to Fernán Díaz and that he remain under guard in the admiral's care, in the fortress of Casarrubios del Monte.[19] Obviously, Don Enrique attached great importance to keeping the Relator detached from the King, believing that his counsel to Juan II could only harm the Infantes' cause.

Nevertheless, shortly thereafter the Admiral of Castile must have freed the Relator, for only several months later, in August of that year, we find Fernán Díaz again in the Court, signing royal documents as the Relator. Some of these documents embodied the decision taken by the four arbiters who were appointed by the King, after negotiations with the disgruntled nobles, to determine the political fate of the Constable.[20] As is known, the arbiters' decision was that the Constable be separated from the Court for six years.[21] The Constable complied with that decision and left; all his friends in the royal administration were likewise removed from their posts[22]; but Fernán Díaz was an exception. He continued to serve as the King's Relator even when the administration was actually taken over by the party of the opposition.[23]

The secret of the Relator's political survival at that crucial phase of Castile's internal turmoil lay, as we see it, in the staunch support offered him by Juan II. Perhaps now more than ever the King needed by his side a man of great wisdom, efficiency and loyalty, in whom he could have implicit faith; and Fernán Díaz was such a man. In vain did the opposition try to persuade the King that the Relator was Alvaro's henchman. Juan II knew better. Fernán Díaz may have owed a debt of gratitude to Alvaro for having installed him in office; he may also have personally liked to see Alvaro continue as Constable of the kingdom; but if a conflict arose between Alvaro and the King and the Relator had to choose sides, the King could have no doubt whatever where Díaz' first loyalty would be.

Therefore, in 1440, when Juan II saw that he had no choice but to make a deal with the Infantes and sacrifice Alvaro's position in the Court, he nevertheless adamantly refused to sacrifice the services of Fernán Díaz. No doubt before transferring the administration to the Infantes, he insisted on obtaining their unreserved commitment that Díaz would continue as Relator, and also retain all his other posts.[24] If this was the actual development, as we assume, the Infantes must have yielded to the King's wishes, believing that with Alvaro out of office, Fernán Díaz presented no danger to their rule.

III

We have no indication as to what influence he wielded during the administration of Juan of Navarre. But it stands to reason that he was not included in the inner circle of the Navarrian's confidants. Apart from the purely political fact that he was regarded as "Alvaro's man," and so, no doubt, watched with suspicion, he must have been the subject of hostile gossip by the infantes' followers. His work, we may assume, was now limited strictly to administrative functions, and we may further assume that he himself controlled his actions so as not to overstep these limits. In the atmosphere of ill will that now surrounded him, any move of his that might appear questionable could provoke his enemies to pounce upon him. He could not be too careful.

It is further clear that his enemies included opponents who were not strictly "political." More often than not, political antagonisms evolve into personal hatreds; and Castile in the '30s and '40s of the 15th century was no exception to this rule. Obviously, the hatreds generated for the Relator in the period of Alvaro's stay in power were carried over to the period that followed. But apart from his political alignment, there were two other causes of enmity for the Relator, which stemmed from his very position.

The first of these was probably connected with the almost mad rush for possessions and income that characterized the nobility of Castile. As arbiter in many financial disputes, which in one way or another touched the administration, the Relator had the ears of both the King and the Constable and was regarded as their confidential adviser. At least some who emerged as losers through his judgments, or whose hopes for royal favors were dashed, may have come to consider *him* responsible for their failures. Thus, grudges were born against the Relator; and such grudges, once rooted and nurtured, could grow into fierce animosities.[25]

But in addition to these reasons (political and financial), there was a third source of hatred for the Relator, which was perhaps the deepest of all. This one related to his origin and background—that is, to his being a converso. His very presence in a position of power at the Court of Juan II bitterly irked the anti-Marrano elements, both in the administration and in the country as a whole. To the latter, the Relator symbolized the extent of "Jewish" penetration into the government of Castile and the skill of the "Jews" in occupying positions that rightly belonged to Old Christians. No wonder that he was among the first conversos to be sentenced in absentia by the Toledan rebels as a heretic and a Judaizer.[26]

That he was no Judaizer and no heretic goes, in our opinion, without saying. All the indications about his life and activity clearly substantiate this fact. We have already pointed out what is generally ignored, but what must be regarded as self-evident: a converso of Jewish origin who wished to live as Judaizer—that is, to lead a secret Jewish life—would not have sought high office in the royal administration, and that if he did seek and achieve such an office, he would not have been able to keep it.[27] Such an attempt would have failed especially in the case of a man who served as the Relator, as the king's secretary, and in all the other posts that were filled by Fernán Díaz. For the numerous tasks of such a man exposed him so frequently to the public eye that he lived as if in a glass house. Yet nothing was ever noticed about him that could justify a suspicion that he was a Judaizer. Had such a suspicion been aroused and had it been found of any substance, he would not have been able to retain his post for any considerable time.

Several more arguments may be adduced in support of this conclusion. Alvar García de Santa María, the official chronicler of Juan II, praised Fernán Díaz unstintingly. This in itself might ordinarily not have any bearing on the point of this discussion. But Alvar García was a converso and one who belonged to and, in a way, represented the family of Paul of Burgos. Total detachment from their Judaic past and complete integration into Christian life marked the behavior of this family, and we have no reason to assume that Alvar García was in this respect a dissenting member. Had he not been utterly convinced of the Relator's dedication to the new converso creed, which advocated full assimilation into Christendom; had he suspected Fernán Díaz of secret Jewish leanings, he would certainly not have praised him so unreservedly. Fearing a future scandal that might compromise all involved, he would in all likelihood have refrained from lauding such a questionable man.

Nor would the writer of the "Note of Celebrated Converts" (who was doubtless a converso of the same brand—i.e., of the type of the Santa María family, or perhaps an Old Christian who was friendly to the Marranos) have included Fernán Díaz among the converso great—among those who were famous for their "devoutness and religiosity" and, more particularly, were preeminent in the fields of canon law, Christian theology, and Church leadership—had he harbored any doubt of the Relator's Catholic loyalty and devotion.[28] Furthermore, the author of the *Chronicle of Alvaro de Luna* was clearly hostile to the conversos. He did not hesitate to disparage Juan de la Cibdad, the Toledan converso leader who was killed in 1449, because some of his relatives had left Spain and "returned" to Judaism[29]; he was certainly hostile to Fernán Díaz as well, because he knew the great part the latter had played in the destruction of his hero.[30] Yet he could not point to even one flaw in the religious conduct of the Relator, because he evidently could not find one.[31] Finally, the nobles of the Aragonese party opposed him because of his faithfulness to Alvaro; had they been able to accuse him of "heresy," they would certainly not have refrained from doing so. But they did not—obviously, because they could not.

No, nothing could be said against the true Christianity of Fernán Díaz or his offspring.[32] Consequently, the accusations of the Toledans against him, and their sentencing him in absentia as a secret Judaizer, were not taken seriously by anyone who knew him. In fact, they backfired against the accusers, for they made them appear as irresponsible vilifiers. The attempt of the Toledan rebels to force him out of office failed, as had the previous attempts of the rebellious barons. The Relator continued to function as such. He held this position uninterruptedly for thirty-four years, through all the changes of governmental power, through all the political storms that swept the kingdom and all the attacks of so many ruthless enemies to which he was exposed.[33] The stress was enormous, but so was the challenge, and the Relator proved equal to it. He was a great man.

IV

Whether it was under the impact of the attacks that were directed at him as a converso that the Relator was moved to take up the cudgels on behalf of his vilified group, or whether it was a long-standing interest in the fate and fortunes of the Marranos generally that impelled him to join the battle in their behalf, one thing stands out clearly: in the struggle that ensued over the conversos' rights following the rebellion of 1449, the Relator emerges as a major figure among the defenders of the Marranos' cause. In fact, he appears as a crafty strategist who carefully calculated his every move, so much so that one is tempted to believe that it was he, Fernán Díaz, who concentrated in his hands the defense of the conversos; that it was he who devised and set in motion the various actions taken on their behalf; and finally, that it was he who marshalled all the forces engaged in repelling the furious attack which threatened the Marranos' very existence in Spain.

All this is borne out not only by the charges of Marcos García,[34] but also by the evidence the Relator himself left us about his part in the struggle. This evidence consists of a single document, but one in which the Relator appears as the spokesman of his "nation" (i.e., the New Christians), as the advocate of its rights, and also as the one who supplied its defenders with effective arguments against its foes. Moreover, that document contains many insights into the converso problem at the time, and especially a variety of the

Relator's reflections on the question of Old-New Christian symbiosis. It is a summary of thought which for Fernán Díaz constituted established, self-evident truths and which, he believed, must serve as the basis for any treatment of the Toledan outbreak. Carefully chosen, phrased and argued, his advice as to how to cope with the problem, which clearly threatened to get out of hand, is known as the *Instruction of the Relator to the Bishop of Cuenca, Don Lope de Barrientos.*[35]

As the document itself clearly indicates, the *Instruction* was written shortly after the arrival of the papal bulls against Sarmiento in Castile and the papal briefs to the King and Prince Enrique (all of which were sent to the royal chancellery).[36] Since the bulls (and also the briefs, we may presume) were issued on September 24, they must have reached their destination a few weeks later, probably in the middle of October. By virtue of his position, Fernán Díaz was doubtless among the first in Castile to have seen and studied these documents, and he was anxious to have them forwarded to the Prince as soon as possible. Yet two considerations occasioned some delay in the dispatch of the papal papers. The first was that they were written in Latin—and the Relator wanted them rendered into the vernacular, so that the Prince and his closest advisers, Juan Pacheco and Pedro Girón (none of whom had, apparently, mastered Latin), would be able to understand them.[37] But in addition, he wanted the documents to be accompanied by a memorandum of his own, containing facts and arguments of which, he believed, the Prince and his counselors should be apprised.

Prepared in haste, and laden with emotion, though well controlled and kept within bounds, the memorandum preserved the natural flow of his ideas expressed under the stress of the critical situation. Under such pressures spokesmen for causes, if truly gifted and equal to their tasks, often rise to their highest stature. So it was now with the Relator. His memorandum is a masterpiece of apologetics, brilliant in thought and eloquent in style. No wonder it soon came to be viewed not only as a clever defense of the conversos, but also as a first-rate instrument of propaganda on behalf of the converso cause. Yet when Fernán Díaz wrote it, we should note, it was not at all meant to be such an instrument. Its aim was to influence not the general public but four individuals—and them alone. These were Prince Enrique, the heir to the Castilian throne; his favorite and guide Juan Pacheco; Pedro Girón, the latter's brother; and the bishop of Cuenca, Don Lope de Barrientos.

Forming the Prince's closest entourage and his inner council on political matters, these three men were clearly in a position to influence the Prince's policies and stand on any pressing question. Of the three, however, only Don Lope was regarded as faithful to Juan II and as one who had the Crown's interests at heart. He was also known to have been friendly to the conversos and helpful in defending them in the past.[38] It was to him, therefore, that the Relator dispatched his memorandum, the Pope's bulls and letters to the King and the Prince, and some other related documents.[39] It was only the bishop, the Relator thought, who could set in motion the kind of action that he, the Relator, considered absolutely vital if the attack on the conversos was to be repelled.

V

What made the writing of the memorandum so urgent was the awareness of the Relator that the Prince intended to resume negotiations with Sarmiento and the Toledans regarding the settlement of the conflict between the city and the King. He was no doubt informed of the crucial decision reached by the Prince and some of the great nobles to return Toledo to the King, but he must also have realized the difficulties involved in the implementation of that decision. He knew of course that the rebels' hold on Toledo had weakened as a result of their political reverses and the economic hardships to which the city had been subject since the beginning of the rebellion, but he could not overestimate this fact. For he was well aware that the rebels still commanded both military strength and much popular support. In any case, he realized that many in Toledo were still adamantly opposed to have the city placed—or rather re-placed—in the dictatorial grip of Alvaro de Luna, and even more so in the hands of his "converso agents." The latter, he further knew, were now not only hated, but feared as prospective avengers of wrongs; and for this reason, too, the converso question in Toledo was so emotionally charged and built up to such proportions that it threatened to serve as an impassable obstacle to any reconciliation with the King.

Faced with these hard realities, and lacking the restraining force of principle, the Prince and his advisers, the Relator suspected, could easily conclude that there was no other way to achieve their aim—that is, of restoring the city to the King—than to give Toledo firm assurances that, first, its old privileges would be respected and, second, that its anti-converso regime would be retained under the King's rule. There is no doubt that the Relator considered the possibility of an agreement on such a basis; and perhaps he got wind of the Prince's readiness to come to terms with the Toledans at the conversos' expense. In any case, he realized that should the Prince *commit* himself to the perpetuation of the *Sentencia-Estatuto,* and should the King resume his mastery of Toledo on the basis of such an understanding, the *Sentencia* would become established in Toledo as a permanent fixture. The ultimate effect was not hard to predict. Not only would Toledo become unlivable for the conversos and soon be cleared of its converso population; it would also become a model to emulate for other cities throughout the kingdom. Once recognized and accepted by the king of Castile as the law of the country's chief city, the discriminatory Statute could not fail to affect the status of the conversos everywhere.

Thus, it was obvious to the Relator that the *Sentencia-Estatuto* would have to be abolished if converso life in Spain was to continue to flow with any reasonable measure of normality. The problem was how to effect that abolition at that particularly crucial moment. Things would have looked better for the conversos if they could have counted on the determined support of the King and Alvaro de Luna. But the King and the Constable were now interested, above all, in the recovery of Toledo and its inclusion in their domain, and the restitution of the Marranos' status in the city did not seem to them a matter of immediate concern. They may even have considered it tactically wrong to tackle that problem at that particular time, and therefore left it in the hands of the Prince and his advisers to deal with as they saw fit. Yet whatever the considerations of the King and the Constable, they were clearly not identical with those of the conversos. For the latter could not view with tacit equanimity the making of an agreement between the Prince and the city in which their rights would be jeopardized, or even sacrificed, for the sake of political expediency.

It was at this juncture that the papal bulls, and the accompanying briefs of September 24, arrived at the Castilian court. As far as the conversos were concerned, the bulls could not have come at a more opportune moment; nor could they have asked for more from Nicholas V. The bulls were clearly a great victory for the conversos, for the cause they stood for and the principles they espoused. Not only were Sarmiento and his followers excommunicated as rebels against the king; they were also denounced as heretics to Christianity and enemies of the Church—and this for their anti-converso stand. What is more, Toledo was threatened with an interdict if it continued to support Sarmiento and his band, offer them shelter, and obey their instructions.[40] All this could facilitate the task of the Prince in wooing Toledo away from the rebels. It could also enable him to take a vigorous stand on behalf of converso rights.

That he would use the bulls for the first purpose could hardly be questioned. But would he use it for the second? The Relator, evidently, was by no means sure. After all, the Prince had already once acceded to Sarmiento's demands with respect to the conversos (that is, prior to his entry to the city),[41] and he might well accede to them again, despite the prohibitive order of the Pope. This would not be the first time that papal directives had been evaded in Castile for the sake of political considerations. The question therefore was what arguments could be used, apart from those employed by the Pope, to induce the Prince to side with the conversos.

Nothing illustrated more clearly and emphatically the fatal weakness of the Marranos in Spain than the fact that the fate of the entire group could now depend on the attitude of a young prince who, though his influence was not inconsiderable, was not actually in power. Yet however dismal the situation might appear, there was nothing, Díaz realized, to be done at that moment except to try to develop effective arguments and find the right approach to the Prince. Yet this was a most difficult task. Besides being unstable and unpredictable—and anxious to aggrandize, by almost any means, his own position as against his father's—he was very much under the influence of Juan Pacheco and the latter's brother, Pedro Girón. It would be futile to try to win the Prince's favor for the converso point of view without first securing a good measure of support from Pacheco and Girón; yet these counselors of the Prince, like the Prince himself, were known to have been shifting their ground with the ebb and flow of the political tides. Cold, unscrupulous, and pragmatic as they were, they had little regard for moral arguments—for considerations of fairness, justice, and legality—unless these suited their personal interests. Pacheco in particular saw Toledo and its rebel group, as well as its converso situation, as nothing but pawns in a political game to be played to his own advantage.

There was only one person in the entourage of the Prince who could be counted upon to take a firm stand on behalf of any cause he embraced. This was the bishop of Cuenca, Don Lope de Barrientos, a man of principle and moral fervor, who was then acting as the Prince's third counselor. The Relator did not question his basic attitude, but he doubted his awareness of all the main issues that might be raised in the forthcoming debate. To counteract the excuses that had been given in justification of the conversos' degradation, the bishop, he felt, had to be equipped with solid arguments to overcome the opposition. Above all, Prince Enrique and his two favorites had to be convinced that it was worthwhile and necessary for *them* to quash the Toledan *Sentencia*. In brief, a set of arguments had to be worked out which was calculated to appeal to the bishop as a Christian leader, to the Prince as a ruler, and to the interests of the brothers Pacheco and Girón as members of the new noble class in Spain. Thus, he wrote the paper that was to become known as *La Instrucción del Relator al Fray Lope de Barrientos*.

VI

Don Lope de Barrientos was a "man for all seasons," combining in his person a multitude of talents and many of the qualities that make men great. Scholar and theologian, orator and historian, a Dominican friar and man of the world, Don Lope was also an accomplished diplomat and a statesman of no mean stature. Endowed with great sagacity, dauntless courage, and unquestioned patriotic zeal, the bishop was destined to play more than once a crucial role in the history of Castile. Time and again, when the Court or the country was faced with a major political crisis, Don Lope appeared on the troubled scene and offered a strong helping hand. So it was now, too. As the Toledan scandal reached its crucial stage, Don Lope, while known as the King's confidant, managed to make himself counselor of the Prince. To the Crown, this involvement was a boon; to the conversos, it was a lucky break.

For as is obvious from the opening of the *Instruction,* the bishop was known for his support of the conversos and his amicable relations with the Relator. Furthermore, he had some converso relatives with whom he was clearly on intimate terms.[42] Rumor even had it that he himself was of converso or partly converso origin. This was not true, as he himself pointed out[43]; but so involved did he become in the defense of the conversos, and so identified with their cause, that the rumor seemed credible and therefore spread. His own, as well as the conversos' enemies contributed of course to its dissemination.[44] In any case, it persisted a long time. Even two centuries later, when the *Tizón de España* listed famous Spaniards of Jewish origin, his name was included in the list.[45]

Appealing to the Old Christian prelate, the Relator found it necessary to offer an explanation why it was to *him* that he turned with his plea. He appealed to the bishop of Cuenca of all people because he believed that the matter *pertained* to him, Don Lope, more than to any other devout Christian—first, because he was not only a bishop, but also an expert in the "Sacred Theology," and the issue at question, as the Relator was to show, had many Christian theological implications; and second, because of his attitude toward the conversos, because "he had always helped, sheltered and protected us."[46] The word "always" indicates repeated intervention of Don Lope de Barrientos on behalf of the conversos, while the word "us" suggests that he and the Relator belonged, by their origin, to different groups. In closing the Instruction, the Relator refers to him as "our principal advocate and our Father,"[47] and virtually the same appellations are found in the opening of the Instruction as well.[48] We should not be induced by the term "our father" to assume that the bishop was a converso (a view held by scholars for some time). He is called here "our father" in a symbolic sense—in the sense of a kind and reliable protector. Adds the Relator: "As such [i.e., as "father"] we all regard him, and singularly I, for never have I found anyone who did me so much good as your grace, without having offered him any service on my part, and without having merited it."[49] The Relator clearly asks here a *special* favor, not one based on the natural claim of kinship; and this is also evident in the opening of the *Instruction,* where he "commends himself" to the bishop, not only for himself, "but also for all this poor and harassed Nation of the lineage of our Lord Jesus Christ according to the flesh."[50] It is an appeal to

a person who was most friendly to the Relator, and to the conversos generally, but it is an appeal to an *outsider*.

There are three sets of arguments in the *Instruction* that may be designated
religious, legal, and social. All are interrelated, and all rest, in greater or lesser
degree, upon Christian ideological foundations. Nevertheless, each of them
was aimed in the main, if not exclusively, at a different component of the
Prince's group. Thus, the religious arguments were directed primarily to the
bishop of Cuenca, Don Lope. The part of the legal argument relating to
canon law was of course also intended for him, while its other part, dealing
with *secular* law, was intended mainly for the Prince. The *social* argument also
had the Prince in mind, but, as we shall see, was aimed especially at the
Prince's favorites, Pacheco and Girón.

The Relator opened his presentation with an assertion that was calculated
to impress a leader of the Church. What he first seeks to prove is that the
Toledan persecution does not only hurt the conversos attacked, but also, and
much more, the Church as a whole. *For it endangers the advancement of the
Church militant, and even threatens to stop it in its tracks.* In fact, he points out,
it has already produced two clearly negative results to that effect: first, it
halted the conversion of the Jews *and of others outside the faith* (Moslems); and
second, it scandalized the conversos themselves to the point that "it aroused
among some of them the desire to go to the lands of the Moors and other
kingdoms in order to become Jews once again."[51] Nobody should be surprised at noticing the first occurrence (i.e., the stoppage of conversion to
Christianity). "For seeing how badly were treated [by the Old Christians]
those who came to the [Christian] faith," as well as "their descendants" who
were born in it, the candidates for conversion among the Jews and others
came to believe that if they would be converted, they too would be subject
to the same fate. The result is that they remain in their state of disbelief;
"they keep blaspheming against the faith every day;" and "they will continue
to blaspheme against it" in the future if the present persecution persists.[52]

That some of the conversos now have second thoughts about the worthwhileness of being Christian, and even think of "returning" to Judaism, must
be viewed as danger signals for the future, even though at the moment the
number of such conversos is very limited indeed. According to the Relator,
these cases of "rethinking," or of reconsideration of their religious position,
appear especially among the uneducated—among those who survived of the
original converts and do not understand much in matters of faith.[53] The very
fact, however, that such thoughts could arise among people who lived—and
wished to live—as Christians indicates that something very wrong and sinister is at work in the ranks of Christian society—something which has given
these people a *reason* for that radical change of heart. In fact, one can
understand what led them to such thoughts, for they say that the "faith does

not protect them against the evils" that befell them as a result of their conversion and that they are actually "more persecuted than the Jews."[54] Consequently, they are looking for aid and succor in different directions.

All this, of course, is "a disservice to God and an opprobrium and offense to our Holy Catholic faith."[55] It is a reverse for Christendom and a blow to its hope of bringing the Jews—and, in fact, all infidels—to the bosom of the Church, to the fold of Christ. A Christian bishop, committed to the Chruch militant no less than to the aims of the Church triumphant, cannot look with equanimity upon a situation in which the Church loses, rather than gains, souls; in which the faithful decrease in number and the "blasphemers" increase. Yet this is precisely what is happening and will happen; this is what *must* happen if the scoundrels of Toledo are allowed to continue their nefarious campaign.

Such was the opening shot of the Relator's Instruction. It was fundamentally a moral argument calculated to arouse the bishop's sense of duty to all the members of the Church without distinction, and his special paternal responsibility for those who were maltreated and appealed to him for help. But it was also a pragmatic political argument that could appeal to an aggressive churchman like Barrientos who, faithful to the idea of the Church militant, would oppose anything and anyone who presented an obstacle to the Church's expansion. As such, it could also be aimed at achieving a certain psychological-tactical goal; for it conditioned the bishop to review and assess the conflict between Christian policy, on the one hand, and the anti-converso drive of the Toledans as reflected in the Statute, on the other.

THE LEGAL CONSIDERATIONS

Of the various specific arguments of the rebels, those that touched upon the Statute's legality seemed to loom largest to the Relator. The rebels claimed that their Statute relied on old and established Church laws, and if this were so, how could one argue that they had committed a religious outrage? In addition, they insisted that the action they had taken was consonant with the secular law; and if this were so, no one could argue that they were in breach of the laws of the state. The first claim was of major interest to the bishop; the second was of special importance to the Prince. To prove therefore to the bishop and the Prince alike that these claims were groundless from any standpoint was the Relator's first task.

Pointing to the alleged legal basis of the Statute, the Relator makes clear that there are only two laws which, *prima facie*, may limit the right of *all* converts from Judaism, regardless of their inward religious attitude. One of these is canonic and the other secular (which Marquillos has also canonized, he adds mockingly).[56] The first is represented in the sixty-fifth decision of the

Fourth Toledan Council (633), which prohibits the granting of public offices "to Jews or to those who are of the Jews."[57] The second is included in the old *Fuero* compiled by King Egica c. 693, which forbids "Jews, whether baptized or unbaptized," to testify against Christians.[58] While the second decree was never included in any collection of Church law—despite the statement to the contrary by Marcos García—it must be understood, just as the first decree should be, as referring not to *all* converted Jews but to those Jews who, after having been converted, apostatized and returned to their old religion. This is indeed how the sixty-fifth decree was interpreted by the archdeacon Guido de Baysio,[59] one of the most authoritative glossators of Gratian; and this is also how the law in the *Fuero* must be interpreted if properly understood.[60] To clothe these laws with the meaning that García attributes to them in so definite a manner would signify not only poor understanding of their content ("poor even for a bachelor like Marquillos"), but also "a great blasphemy against God, and against His Holy Faith, and against all reason, and against all law."[61] Moreover, it would be a "notorious heresy," which would necessarily be rejected by the "sacred theology" and the teachings of its doctors, the "holy authorities of the written law, as well as the Law of Grace, apostolic and canonic alike."[62] There is a chapter in the canon, the Relator points out, which specifically says that no one should be abused, discriminated against, or denied any honor, dignity, or position, merely for having been a Jew prior to becoming a Christian.[63] And the doctors who comment on this legislation find it necessary to make the significant observation that not only should these converts in no way be abused; they should rather be favored[64]; and this agrees with the words of the Apostle: "Jew, first, and [then] Greek."[65]

We must pause and say a word about this understanding of the two laws on which the rebels relied in shaping their Statute, for it may help clarify the trend of Díaz' thinking and his basic approach to problems of law—more precisely, of "Christian" law—which determined his position in this case. It was proper for him to claim that the law in the *Fuero Juzgo* (which denied baptized Jews the right to testify against Christians) ought to be interpreted in the same vein as the decree of the Fourth Toledan Council (which denied them the right to public office). Both laws emanated, as the Relator pointed out, from the same period (the seventh century) and from the same place (Toledo); both sprang from the same social, religious, and political conditions (those of Visigothic Spain at the time); and both were trying to cope with the same problem—that of the "Jews, whether baptized or not." But he was wrong of course in trying to read into these laws a meaning which they clearly sought to avoid. Surely these laws did not refer, as he suggested, to a certain "kind" or "segment" of the converts, but to all of them without exception; and the phrase "those who are of the Jews" had unquestionable racial connotations. Indeed, the whole purpose of these laws, as we see it, was to make clear that, in the matters they referred to, there was no distinction between Jew and convert and between one class of convert and another. Hence, if Christian policy had to be determined by the original intent of these laws, García's interpretation was correct and that of Díaz mistaken.

Christian policy, however, was not determined by these laws alone; for taken as a whole, the Church consistently opposed any discrimination against converts in general and converts from Judaism in particular. Faced with these contradictory positions, what could the Relator do? He did what commentators of the law before him (such as Guido de Baysio, whom he cited, and others) had done in such cases. In an age that gave little or no concession to a critical, historical approach to Church documents, when all the ecclesiastic enactments of all times had to be grasped as one solid whole, as part and parcel of a cohesive system, no contradiction in terms and attitudes could be admitted to be found in any part; hence, any law that apparently conflicted with other parts of canonic legislation had to be "coordinated" with those parts—which meant to be "explained" accordingly. The Relator did, therefore, what a skilled Church lawyer had to do in such circumstances: he "interpreted" the one or two exceptions so as to make them agree with the rest, or rather with the bulk of the Church's teachings. Also, García fundamentally presented a part of the law as reflecting the *whole* of it, but he refused to see that on the issue he tackled, the law as a whole contained inconsistencies. Essentially, the difference between García and Díaz was that the latter wanted to fit the exception to the rule, while the former wanted to make a rule of the exception. There can be little doubt as to which of them was "heretical"—that is, deviated from the prevalent and legally accepted position of the Church.

Having demonstrated, as he thought, that the theory of García was radically opposed to canon law, the Relator proceeded to show that it conflicted also with the laws of the country—the secular law—and the privileges granted by the kings. We have seen how he tackled the law on Jewish converts which is included in the *Fuero Juzgo* (i.e., the one that forbids them to testify against Christians), and we have seen that he interpreted this law as referring not to *all* Jewish converts but only to some of them—specifically, to those who reverted to Judaism. What, however, was the attitude of the secular law toward sincere and steadfast converts from Judaism—that is, toward those who are recognized by the Church as Christians to all intents and purposes? To this question, the Relator points out, the country's codes provide a clear answer. For the laws of the *Partidas*, compiled by Alfonso the Learned, prohibit any discrimination against converts from Judaism and proclaim their full and complete equality with all other Christians. In vain, he says, did Marquillos refer to the law of the *Fuero Juzgo*. Even if he understood the law correctly, which he did not, this was not a law that could serve as a guideline for the people's behavior in our time; "for it is the laws of the *Partidas* by which the country must be governed, and not by any other laws,"[66] including those of the *Fuero Juzgo*. The reason: the latter were replaced by the laws of the *Partidas*, which became the governing laws of the kingdom—that is, the laws which, in fact and in theory, are the only ones that are binding in Castile. What is more, the same laws about converts from Judaism (i.e., those which are included in the *Partidas*) were reaffirmed by Alfonso XI in the *Ordenamiento of Alcalá* (1348) and, on top of this, received added force in the laws issued by the present King, Juan II.[67] All this demonstrates beyond any doubt the position taken by the secular law on the question of converso rights. Yet apart from all this, there is the law on this matter that was issued by one of the kings of Castile, who was confronted with a problem not unlike the one plaguing the country today.

"For sixty years ago," says the Relator, "this very question came for consideration before King Enrique III. This was at the time when Don Pedro Tenorio served as archbishop of Toledo, when many among the Toledans had been converted to Christianity, while others among them, like Marquillos [today], expressed about these converts the same opinions"—namely, that the converts should not be granted equality of rights [with the other Christians]. But the King, in concert with his council, thought otherwise. He "declared the opposite," and "the letter of privilege which he gave to this effect was countersigned by the Archbishop and Dr. Periáñez [representing the Royal Council]."[68]

At least twice in the course of his reign, and only five years before, in 1444, Juan II decreed, as we have indicated, equal treatment for New and Old Christians.[69] Yet the Relator merely mentioned Juan II amongst others who confirmed the old laws; and instead of pointing to the most recent royal action, he preferred to refer to a decree of another king, which was issued more than half a century before. A tactical consideration, psychological and political, was no doubt involved in this preference.

To begin with, Juan II was not held in great esteem by his son, Prince Enrique, the heir apparent, whom the Relator now sought to influence. The Prince, who often flouted his father's orders, might assume that the Toledans, with good reason, could likewise flout his decrees on the conversos. In fact, these decrees were declared by the rebels null and void for reasons the Prince might have considered valid—first, because they were, in effect, Alvaro's and not the King's own voluntary edicts; and second, because the barons were not consulted on their enactment, as they should have been, according to law.[70] Avoiding, therefore, a detailed exposition of the legislation of Juan II, the Relator concentrated on presenting the position of Enrique III. For here was a king revered by all, whose enactment in this matter was endorsed by his Council—not one that the rebels could say was "packed" by the wily Alvaro de Luna, but a "real" council comprising the great of the kingdom, including Pedro Tenorio, archbishop of Toledo, who was one of the most respected churchmen of Castile. Both state and Church were thus duly represented in the issuance of this particular decree, which would indicate that both took the same stand on the converso problem. Accordingly, the Relator says:

> I truly believe that our Lord the Prince is so Catholic [a ruler] and of such good conscience that he will neither permit, nor offer an opportunity for anything to be done against what such an august King as Don Enrique [III] did, ordered and declared in accord with the said Lord Archbishop, and other magnates of his kingdoms and his Council.[71]

It was clear to the Relator that in any future discussion between the Prince and the Toledans on the conversos' social status, the Toledans would claim that the laws of the country entitled them to pursue the *Sentencia*'s policy. What, therefore, could be more useful for the Prince and his counselors, in their negotiations with the Toledans, than to have before them this pertinent document which, apart from representing the legal position of both Church and State on the issue involved, was related to practically the same situation (a hostile reaction to the equalization of the conversos) in the same city of Toledo. Accordingly, the Relator sent Barrientos a copy of the privilege of Enrique III, together with the recent bull of the Pope in both the original and Romance translation, and he likewise provided him with a transcript of the decretal *Eam te* from *De Rescriptis*, the relevant decrees of the Council of Basle and of "what the Laws of the *Partidas* wish and order that in this matter be observed and practiced, and be established as custom for all time in these kingdoms and in the whole Church of God."[72]

All these documents were clearly intended to serve as an armory of legal weapons to be used against the Toledan leaders, if and when they insisted, as was expected, on their legal right to do what they had done. Doubtless, from a purely judicial standpoint, this material appeared quite adequate to overcome the Toledans' objections on legal grounds. But the Relator realized that apart from the legal aspect, other aspects of the Statute must equally be dealt with. Their implications and possible repercussions in Christendom far transcended, he knew, what might be gathered from a mere exposure of the Statute's illegality. Thus, he moved to examine the Statute also from other related standpoints—and first of all from that of Christian policy and practice throughout the Church's existence.

THE CHURCH AND THE CONVERSOS

That the policies of the Church and its traditions of behavior were opposed to discrimination against converts from Judaism can be made clear, according to the Relator, even from the most cursory survey. In fact, the Church's guidelines in this matter allow no other conclusion. "Holy Scripture says in several places that all should *honor* those who come to the Faith and treat them like brothers, and give them a share in the inheritance of the land and in all other matters, such as receive those who are already of the faith. And, if this was done—as it should have been done—by the Law of Scripture, which is a shadow of the truth, how much more should it be observed by the Law of Grace *which is the same truth,* prophesied and promised."[73] Indeed, says the Relator, if there were room in Christianity for the view propagated by Marquillos, "I would be unable to understand how it could be compatible with the fact that the holy canon and the civil law on the one hand, and the Holy Fathers and the Doctors of the Church on the other, tell us that those who are outside the faith—and especially the Jews—should be invited to it, and [even] attracted to it, by cajolery, and requests, and benefits, and other ways of good and gracious instruction . . . and that the Christians ought to help, and succor and honor them, and treat them fraternally and charitably and even with love, without making any separation and distinction between the Old [Christians] and the New."[74] Moreover, the Old Christians should in certain matters discriminate *in favor* of the converts; they should offer them more advantages than to other Christians, until they become planted and rooted in the faith, as is done to the novices of the religious orders. This is indeed what the Council of Basle decreed—"a Council in which ambassadors of Castile participated"—and this is what the Church actually did when it raised converts from Judaism to all the offices in its hierarchy, including the highest—i.e., that of Pope. For was not Linus, the first Roman pope (after St. Peter), the son of a Jew, Judah of Beth-Lehem? And was not St. Julian of the 7th century a converso and son of a Jew? Was he not, moreover, archbishop of Toledo, of this very city where the heretics claim, and declare so impudently, that converts from Judaism cannot be appointed to any Church office? As for the present time, not only in Spain, but also in other countries, there are prelates who came from this Nation.[75] There can therefore be no question as to the practice of the Church and its policies in this matter from its earliest days on.

Boring beneath the surface of the law enacted against the conversos in Toledo, the Relator points out that what was involved was much more than an ordinary, or even gross, violation of sanctified Church policies, norms, and attitudes. What was involved was a specific theory that *justified* that violation and in this way sustained it. This, says the Relator, was the *theory of race,* which takes the issue out of the area of law breaking and brings it into direct confrontation with central Christian tenets. Hence, it must be seen as fundamentally opposed to the very spirit and essence of Christianity.

It was this theory, more than anything else, that the Relator sought to refute in his paper, and it was in fact to this special task that he dedicated most of the Instruction. To assume, he says, that, on the grounds of mere origin, Christianity authorized discrimination against converts is nothing but a "great" and "notorious" "heresy."[76] It is directly opposed to Christian doctrine, as expressed in both Laws, the Old and New; it goes counter to the teachings of the Church Fathers, and all other sources of Christian theology; and it undermines, if it does not openly deny, what is implied in some articles of faith.[77] Among other things, it emasculates the Dogma of Baptism, which is central to the Christian religion. For the notion that the convert always carries within him, and transfers into his Christian existence, all the immoral qualities and propensities that he possessed in his pre-Christian life nullifies the belief in the efficacy of baptism, which is supposed to make of the baptized a "new man." Indeed, as all true Christians believe, "it washes him and frees him from any blame, so that he is in no need of doing penance, and it clears him of any transgression so thoroughly that it leaves on him no trace of defect."[78] Obviously, there cannot be a "new man" if the "old man" has never changed—and all the more so if he *can* never change, as the race theorists claim.

If their theory must be viewed as anti-Christian on the general grounds of Christian doctrine, it must be seen as doubly so because of its position—or rather concentration—on the race of the Jews. For the theory which heaps abuse and contumely upon the race of the Jews, and upon converts from Judaism *because* of their race, stands in such flagrant contradiction to Church thought—as well as to Church history, cult, and worship—that if accepted, it must perforce lead one away from Christianity. It is impossible to see how one can adhere to this theory and at the same time consider oneself Christian and "apply himself to guard whatever relates to that faith." For "how can he honor the holidays of our Lord, our head, who came from that lineage [of the Jews] in flesh; or how can he celebrate those of the Virgin, our glorious lady Mary, His mother, or those of the Apostles, Saints and Martyrs who [likewise] were of the same lineage" and "whom Holy Scripture defines as the *basis of the Election*" (i.e., of the whole Christian world).[79] "For it is [mostly] on *their* vigils that we fast, and very few [on those] of others; for it is *they* who were the foundation of the Church of God, and it is with *them*, and their words, that we are baptized; it is to *them* that we confess every day; and it is with *their* authority, based on God's will, that the Popes and Prelates absolve us. It follows that it is with the power that *they* had delegated to the priests, the confessors, who act as *their* agents, that the latter absolve us from our sins."[80] In brief—when we are born, while we live, and when we die, when we pray and say mass, "we are always with them, and never do we separate ourselves from them if it is Christians that we wish to be."[81]

If a Christian comes to abhor the Jewish race, he must logically also abhor Christianity, and even abhor himself as Christian. For a Christian qua Christian is what he is thanks to the Jewish contribution to Christianity—thanks to the fact that Jews, and Jews alone, have created that faith and established the Church and served as its main inspiration to this day. It is impossible to ignore this contribution or avoid recognizing its ceaseless impact upon the life of every Christian. Yet despite all these decisive facts, including the fact that the Savior Himself, the Lord, the Son of God according to the flesh, came from no other race than that of the Jews, "we kill those of his race, rob and defame them"—and this "while the Church prays every day to God that He bring them to His faith."[82]

No one had exposed more forcefully and poignantly the contradiction between what Christendom owes the Jews and how it pays its debt to them in practice. For it is not only García and his fanatic followers—and not only the conversos, their chosen targets—that were now on the Relator's mind. What he was thinking of was the behavior of *all* Christians—or, more correctly, of the Christians taken generally—toward *all* those who belonged to the Jewish race, whether converted to Christianity or not. Note how subtly he passed from the limited to the broader accusation: "We kill those of his race, etc." "We," all Christians, and not only the heretical anti-Marranos, and "those of his race," not only the converts.[83] Almost uncontrollably, the sentence bursts from the Relator's pen, concealing under the subtle and biting irony the painful truth which he sought to hide. If asked for an explanation, he could of course have said that what he actually meant was the general image that "we," the Christians, assumed in the eyes of the persecuted Jewish converts—"we" who persecute and "we" who tolerate the persecution by allowing the outrages to go on unpunished as if they were no crime at all. To be sure, all this can be read into that statement—and the Relator no doubt referred to this, too. Yet out of all this subtlety, and above it, there rises a ringing voice of protest—the protest of a Jew against the entire Christian world for its shocking ingratitude to the Jewish people, its cynical and cruel treatment of the people that was its greatest benefactor.

The true Christian who was a convert from Judaism could not have felt differently. For nothing revealed that cynicism so blatantly as the other contradiction, which pained him even more and was part and parcel of the same attitude—that between the manner in which converts from Judaism *should* be treated according to what true Christianity dictates and the manner in which they are *actually* treated by large segments of Christian society. In essence, it is the conflict between theory and practice that is exposed here before those who held on to both, and hence the implication of cynical hypocrisy that recurringly emerges from these bitter charges. Yet in the Relator's language all this is presented—or at least calculated to appear—as a conflict between Christianity on the one hand and its followers (the "people") on the other; between the "Church of God" and this worldly society, which, strangely, considers itself Christian. Indeed, the Church is conceived by him, in a way, as an abstract, unchangeable, monolithic entity, reflecting in both its leadership and teachings the pure spirit of Christianity, its theory and its principles. This view, of course, did not conform to reality—or to many of the Church's features in real life—and the Relator appears to have been a shrewd observer. Nevertheless, this sublimation of the Church ought not to be seen as an arbitrary move taken for tactical consideration. It was a major component of converso ideology, and it constituted the backbone of converso psychology, which kept the conversos from losing all hope and being submerged in the darkness of despair. And it was, in addition, an attitude backed by no small amount of historical experience. For it was the *Church of Rome* that was the last refuge to which the conversos turned in hours of trial; it was indeed the popes to whom they repeatedly appealed for help and succor in their tribulations; and it was in fact the Church that *offered* them help, repeatedly and consistently, for three generations. Now, too, the voice of the Pope rang out forcefully in their defense.

Yes, the Church *does* represent the heart and soul and ultimate truth of Christianity—of this the Relator was certain, as were most of the leading conversos at his time. Nor could he doubt that its position toward converts (and converts from Judaism in particular) would always remain as it had been and should have been, as indicated above. If the conversos encountered such hostility and so much abuse of their basic rights, it was not the Church as such that was at fault but those who, though formally counted as its members, disregard its policies and flout its orders, which they seek to replace with rulings of their own. What is worse, while they deny the Church's doctrines, and substitute for them theories of their own—theories which are the very opposite of these doctrines—they brazenly claim to represent the Church's teachings as if they were its true adherents. This is where the special danger lies in the campaign of such men as Marquillos. It is a "great heresy" that they propagate, of course—"great" in the sense that it is far out of tune with anything that is truly Christian—and one wonders "what pious Christian ears can hear it or what faithful Christian can tolerate it."[84] Yet, the Relator knew only too well, many Catholics not only heard and tolerated, but also endorsed and ardently supported it. Evidently, like other heretics, the spokesmen of the "race" heresy succeeded in confusing many of the faithful, and thus misled them into paths of evil.

And from this position the Relator goes over in one bold step to the defense of the conversos. If the heresy referred to, he asks, has confounded so many *Old* Christians as it has, should it be surprising that its very appearance, and its capture of such a following in Christendom, has confounded and misled some of the *New* Christians, though in a different manner? One need not be surprised if, under such circumstances, some backsliders appear among the conversos. Rather should one view with astonishment and admiration the steadfast devotion that the group *as a whole* displays toward Christianity, its teachings and institutions.

For the newly converted, when he considers all this—i.e., all that he sees and all that he endures—"what patience must he have that may suffice for him to stick to the Catholic faith [which he had adopted], and what willpower should he have to persevere in what every good Christian must do?" How can he understand why *he*, who was converted and joined the faithful, "should be judged *ipso facto* as one who had erred and suffer so great a punishment and injury, without having committed any sin?" How can the converts be expected to react "when they see that they are thrown out of every honor, office, dignity and benefice as are the heretics and infidels, and when such a discredited person as Marquillos heretically affirms it?"[85] The answer appears self-evident.

HERETICS AND JUDAIZERS

Nevertheless, one should not see in this any attempt to defend the backsliders among the Marranos. What the Relator sought to explain was how and why a breakdown might occur in the religious thinking of some New Christians; but it is one thing to understand why, in certain circumstances, a person may stumble or be tempted to commit a crime, and another to condone the crime if committed and forgive the criminal. Understanding is by no means tantamount to forgiveness. But understanding is necessary for the leaders of the Church to know how to cope with the heresy of Marquillos and how to forestall its evil consequences. The stumblers must of course be properly punished if they fail to repent after receiving due warning; but the solution is not in punishing the stumblers, but in uprooting the cause of the stumbling—the heretical persecution of Marquillos.

The Relator had no doubt about the necessary measures to stop the advance of the dangerous movement. He indicates quite clearly that should Marquillos persist in propagating his ideas among the faithful, he ought to suffer the punishment decreed for all heretics by Christian law and practice. That punishment was death by fire, of which the Relator fully approves as a treatment of heresies that cannot be cured. He left no doubt as to the nature of the culprits who were to be subject to the gruesome punishment: stubborn heretics, who had been duly admonished but blatantly refused to mend their

ways. And to make it unmistakably clear that he favors the application of the
laws concerning heresy as a matter of *general principle*, and not merely in the
cases of García and his followers, he states that he would not hesitate to
recommend it for any heretical convert, whether he comes from Judaism or
any other faith. If there is, he says,

> any New Christian who keeps behaving in an evil manner after he has
> been duly admonished, it is right and just that such a person be pun-
> ished and chastised in a cruel fashion. And I shall be the first to bring
> firewood to burn him and the first to ignite the fire.
>
> Furthermore, if this New Christian happens to be a descendant from
> the Israelitic stock, he ought to be punished more severely and cruelly;
> [for it may well be assumed that such a culprit sinned not out of
> ignorance but] out of knowledge, [having] more information about the
> law and the Prophets [than any other kind of New Christian may have].
> This very thing had been indicated by the Apostle when he said: *Jew
> and Greek*; the Jew first—in punishment no less than in honor.[86]

That the Jewish convert who deviated from the Faith should be subject to
a singularly harsh punishment is a theory which the Relator borrowed from
the arsenal of the rabidly anti-Jewish Church fathers.[87] But what is of interest
for us at this point is not the theoretical source itself, but the application
made of it by the Relator. While he indicates by his very treatment of the
subject—i.e., of the way heretics should be punished—his conviction that his
own group, taken as a whole, was virtually free of the scourge of heresy, he
also indicates—even more clearly—his anxiety about the spreading heresy
of Marquillos. His statement that he would be the first to put the torch to
heretics if such were found among the New Christians is merely a dramatic
way of showing his impartiality and of strengthening his demand to apply
that form of punishment to Marquillos. Obviously, he came to believe that
only the most severe measures, including death by fire, could stop the
campaign of the racists. He could perhaps have looked for, and found,
excuses for showing greater consideration to the backsliders to Judaism than
to heretics whose religious past and background were never other than
Christian. But the Relator does not look for such excuses. On the contrary,
he imposes a heavier onus of crime on the New Christian than on the Old.
Surely there is more to this than a mere display of objectivity; and, in fact,
he is not objective here at all, but rather discriminatory against the New
Christians. Yet this discrimination may have been merely formal. Indeed, as
we see it, he dared say what he said because he did not believe that there
were heretics (i.e., Judaizers) among the conversos in any appreciable number, and furthermore, that if there were some, their intransigence was not of
such a nature as to be incurable by effective instruction. Thus, for both

reasons, the Relator believed, the conversos were actually far removed from the stage of heretical burning.

One need not, however, merely infer this. For the question: Did the Marranos include many Judaizers? is given by Fernán Díaz a straight answer—and it is categorically negative.

Thus, while speaking of those through whose mind may pass the notion of fleeing Spain, in order to go to the lands of the Moors and there to return to Judaism, he says that *the number of such people is very small today*—"for I doubt whether in the whole of Toledo there would be [even] ten of these."[88] It should be noted that he adds, in qualifying this statement, that such thoughts could occur only to those who both have little understanding *(que no tanto entienden)* and passed some time of their lives as Jews,[89] and these must have comprised, by 1449, a comparatively small number. Evidently, he speaks here of the remnants of those who were *themselves* converted in 1391 or 1412. It is primarily among these that some might have developed—and perhaps *did* develop, under the stress of the circumstances—an inclination to "return" to Judaism. But what does it mean in general terms? If in a large city like Toledo there could be no more than ten candidates for "return" or for migration to Moslem countries, their total, as he saw it, in the whole of Spain must have been extremely small.

But this is not all he has to say on the subject. While attacking the basic conceptions of Marquillos with regard to the treatment of Jewish converts generally, he avers that these conceptions are especially preposterous when related to the conversos of Spain. For who are these Spanish New Christians? In the overwhelming majority of cases, they are the offspring of persons who were converted to Christianity some forty or sixty years ago; and since this is the case, "I do not see how one can designate as 'converts' those who are children and grandchildren of Christians; *those who were born in Christianity and do not know anything about Judaism or its rites.*"[90] Since in the middle of the 15th century, the descendants of the Jewish converts to Christianity constituted the overwhelming majority of the New Christians, we can conclude from the above, if we rely on the Relator, that the overwhelming majority of the Marranos were Christian and considered themselves *as such* only. Nor did they regard themselves as "converts"—or wish to be regarded as such. "Born" as Christians, they knew from infancy only their native religion—Christianity—and thus had no notion whatever of Judaism, either in theory or in practice. And since they were *unaware* of it, they obviously could not follow it. Thus, we have here a categorical denial, based on both fact and logic, of the charges made by the anti-Marrano party concerning the "Judaism" of the conversos.

From the same time, and from quite a different direction, there comes down to us a similar testimony on this subject in almost identical language.

In a responsum dated c. 1450, the great Algerian rabbi Solomon Duran tells us that the descendants of the converts from Judaism should not be blamed for believing in Christianity or for taking the anti-Jewish attitudes they display, since, having been reared from childhood as Christians and believing in what their fathers had taught them, they are totally ignorant of Judaism and its commandments and, consequently, of what it stands for.[91] This is a direct confirmation of the statement just cited from the Instruction about the conversos (almost all of whom were in 1449 "descendants" of conversos); and indirectly, it strengthens Díaz' other statements about the Christian propriety of the conversos generally and the paucity of Judaizers among them.

Was it possible that the enemies of the conversos had wrong notions about the latter's religious attitudes, and thus their attacks upon the conversos were simply the result of an honest mistake? The Relator discarded this possibility. As he saw it, the symptoms of converso Christianity were too clear and evident to be ignored, and the contrast between them and the anti-Marrano charges too sharp and blatant to be misjudged.[92] He concluded therefore that the anti-Marranos, in their campaign, had *knowingly* employed false accusations; and consequently, their attacks upon the conversos stemmed from reasons other than those claimed. But, then, what *were* those reasons? The Relator seemed to have no doubt in the matter. The way he saw it, the reasons in question stemmed not from moral and spiritual, but from immoral and material considerations. It was the "inordinate greed" and irrepressible desire of the persecutors of the Marranos "to rob them of their possessions"— that desire which is at "the root of all evils."[93]

Thus, the Relator gives the same explanation for the anti-Marrano outbreaks in Toledo that we repeatedly find in the chronicles of the period,[94] as well as in the testimonies of other Marrano leaders.[95] It was greed and desire for earthly goods that were at the root of all the troubles, not zeal to punish religious offenders. And there could be no room for such zeal, simply because there were no such offenders. Thus, insofar as religion was concerned, the Marranos were innocent victims.

VII

This is a direct testimony about the state of Judaism among the Marranos and the number of possible Judaizers among them by one of the most responsible representatives of the converso society at the time. Briefly, it tells us that in the middle of the 15th century—that is, prior to the Toledan persecution—Judaism among the Marranos was practically nonexistent. It is not an isolated testimony, we should stress, but one that fits with other testimonies, highly reliable and highly authoritative, which have come down to us from those times. What the Relator says on the religious position of the conversos of the second and third generation is confirmed, as we have seen, by Jewish sources, and is presented as a matter of common knowledge that no one could honestly deny. Further, what he says of the Toledan trials, and the actual results of their inquiries, is, as we shall show, fully corroborated by other contemporary sources. And finally, what he says of the possible number of the Judaizers in his time must be judged in the light of his broader assertions about the descendants of the original converts. Since these descendants formed at the time the overwhelming majority of the Marranos, the paucity of the Judaizers, as described by the Relator, falls in with the general picture.

It is no more than an estimate, of course, and he may have estimated the number of the Judaizers in Toledo as considerably lower than it actually was. Possibly, he would have been closer to the truth if he had judged the number to be fifty or a hundred rather than ten. But this would not have changed the general impression which he wished to convey. It would still mean that their number was insignificant, even though it might lead to the conclusion that small groups (or nuclei) of Judaizers existed in Spain, especially in the large cities, and were possibly dispersed across the country. The Relator must have considered such a conclusion wrong, however; and it is perhaps precisely for the purpose of denying it—or rather of palpably showing its absurdity—that he quoted the low figure he did.

To be sure, today this statement sounds extreme, and every extreme statement seems to border on exaggeration. Nevertheless, it is the very extremism of this—and perhaps also of his other statements on the subject— that argues, in this instance, against making such a judgment. For we must always bear in mind that the author of these statements was one of the greatest Spanish jurists of his time, and one who was trained and habituated by his profession to weigh his words carefully. Moreover, his position as the Relator—who would regularly report to the King on all matters of interest or concern to the royal administration—would compel him to see to it that his statements were factual, or at least did not flagrantly contradict the facts. Therefore, had there been in Castile or Toledo a large number of conversos dedicated to Judaism, the Relator would not have been able to say that there were "perhaps ten" such individuals in Toledo, or declare the innocence of the group as a whole in such strong and definitive terms; nor would he have denounced the accusations of the Toledans (concerning the Marranos' alleged infidelity) as fraudulent, groundless and stemming from their greed, and from no other motive. Moreover, by the time he was making these assertions, the conclusions of the Inquiry conducted in Toledo were already a matter of public knowledge, and doubtless many people in the city knew their contents and their worth from the standpoint of truth. Had he believed that the Inquiry had brought up something substantial against the conversos, it would have been foolish on his part to deny it—and especially in such an unqualified manner. After all, he was addressing himself to men like Lope de Barrientos and Juan Pacheco, shrewd men who were soon to visit Toledo (or were there already) and who would receive, he realized, much information from reliable Toledan sources. It is inconceivable that in his "defense" of the Marranos, he would have offered them arguments that could be easily discounted as contrary to fact.

We must therefore conclude that the Relator denied in all earnestness the existence of Judaizers among the Marranos in any appreciable number. Since the question of the number of Judaizers in Castile is of paramount importance in any attempt to reveal the origins of the Inquisition and discern its true motives, the Relator's testimony on this matter must be given the most careful attention and studied from every possible standpoint. What matters, in examining this testimony, is that it constitutes both a diagnosis and prognosis of the Judaizing situation. The Relator did not ignore the fact that isolated individuals appeared here and there who began to consider or preach "return." This was essentially his diagnosis. But in these isolated cases he saw a *symptom* of what was coming, or was bound to come—the beginning of splits in the solid Christian front that the Marranos presented at that time. In fact, it appears that he did not seek to minimize, but rather to play up the danger of Judaization posed by the racial persecution—a danger that, in his opinion, could become real if the persecution did not stop. Still, he viewed it as a mere *possibility*, as something that might happen under the impact of the atrocities, and he may have felt free to discuss this possibility precisely because he knew that the *reality* was so positive. In any case, he could not see anything contradictory between his insistence on the religious innocence of the Marranos (and the extreme paucity of Judaizers among them), on the one hand, and the danger of increasing, perhaps large-scale Judaization, which he presented as a likely development, on the other.

With all this we must recall that he was a diplomat and a tactician engaged in repelling a hostile attack, and he may also have had a covert reason for taking that particular stand. He evidently considered the potentiality of "return," though limited, realistic under the circumstances; and should cases of "return" actually materialize, the party of Marcos García, he knew, would make the most of them in its campaign. By pointing out the *cause* of such possible occurrences, he transferred the blame from the conversos to their detractors and removed the sting of the sharp accusations that could be leveled at the former on this account. More clearly, he sought to forestall the attack by cautioning the Prince, his favorites, and the bishop against being unduly impressed by the stories they might hear, whether true or false, about Judaizers in Toledo. Above all, he used the occasion to guard them against falling into the trap of the wild generalizations which the anti-Marranos were making all the time, and were certain to make even more emphatically if actual cases of "return" were discovered.

VIII

The method of generalization employed by the Toledans was indeed the problem that concerned Fernán Díaz perhaps more than any other aspect of this controversy. After all, any characterization of a group depends on its relevance to most of its members—and, more properly, to its great majority; and such characterization, to be honestly made, must be based on manifold and reliable data, cautious and prolonged observation and, above all, a meticulous search for truth. To miss the truth and present a false picture is common even among investigators who inquire into collective phenomena without any bias or preconceived notions. If they fail, their failure must be related—assuming their powers of judgment are adequate—to the absence of one or more of the prerequisites for reaching correct conclusions. In the case of the Toledan campaigners, Díaz knew, none of the necessary prerequisites existed, and their strong anti-converso prejudice made any argument with them pointless. Yet the general public—even its neutral elements, and even those who may have tended to be friendly to the conversos—might easily be taken in by the claims that their generalizations were, in fact, based on thorough inquiries and careful evaluation of all available data. This brings us back to the incidents of Judaization that might have occurred, or could occur shortly. To demonstrate these claims, the Toledans might employ such incidents as "examples" of what they called the rule, of an allegedly *common* phenomenon, while actually these examples proved the opposite of that rule by being mere exceptions to it. The Relator felt he had to rebut such "proof" by the following argument.

To attach a stigma of heresy to a *group* because some of its members deviated from the faith is as unreasonable as it is unjust, the Relator sternly points out. Backsliders to Judaism, if there be such cases, must be seen in the perspective of other heresies that sprang up in Spain and other Christian regions. Thus, in the North of Spain, among the Basques, there arose the heresy of Durango; in the South, in Andalusia, Islam receives converts from Christianity daily; but this does not mean that all the Basques, or all the Christians living in Andalusia, should be declared or regarded as heretics. Similarly, "if some heresy will arise in Castile, one should not deduce from this that all the Castilians were its partisans."[96] The burden of responsibility must be laid, solely and strictly, upon the individuals involved, and not upon the community or the group to which they happen to belong. As the prophet Ezekiel said in the name of God: *"The soul that sinned, it shall die."*[97]

"If some heresy *will* arise in Castile . . . " It is clear that the Relator discussed here a future possibility, and not a current reality—even though it is evident that he was concerned with the possibility of a *Judaic* heresy. Deliberately, he chose to speak of such groups as Basques, Andalusians, Castilians, because in this way he could suggest that heresies among the Spaniards—or, more precisely, among the Christian Spaniards—should be indicated only by their regional, and not by any other affiliation. Reflected here once more is the assimilationist view that sought to ignore all differences of origin and emphasize the commonality of all Christians living within given geographic limits. To be sure, in imputing the sins of individuals to a group (in this instance, the Marrano collectivity), the Toledans were using not geographic, but purely ethnic criteria; but this only highlights their fallacy. It shows that they generalized on the basis of a principle that is wholly unacceptable to true Christians, as well as to subjects of the Spanish realms. "For if the law of God and the laws [of the country] do not wish a father to be punished for his son (and vice versa) nor a woman for her husband (and vice versa), how much less should we punish other persons *who have nothing to do with the crime in question,* even though, as they say, they all descend from the same *people.*"[98] Certainly, "descent from the same people" represents less of a social relationship than that of wife and husband, and therefore should involve no responsibility for crimes committed by any member of that people.

"The soul that sinned, it shall die." In this insistence upon the individual's responsibility for all his religious sins and transgressions, the Relator stood of course on firm ground, both legal and moral. Evidently, his purpose in emphasizing the old maxim was to free the great majority of the Marranos— or, more precisely, the group as a whole—from any involvement in any form of misconduct on the part of some of its members. What we have here is a resort to Christian ethics, and also to the basic principles of jurisprudence upon which the secular state must rest. From the standpoint of the Relator, both as Christian and as jurist, the argument appeared flawless.

Nevertheless, however flawless his reasoning, he was still far from satisfied, for he knew that there was still a stumbling block to pass. The Prince's chief counselors were Pacheco and Girón, hard-boiled politicians who looked only for their interests and could hardly be impressed by considerations of the kind he had presented thus far. Yet he knew that without gaining their support, or at least their friendly neutrality, he would not accomplish much, if anything. For the Prince would not adopt a policy which they opposed; nor would the bishop manage to move him to take a proper stand on the issue. Thus, the Relator looked for an argument that would touch directly upon the selfish interests of these self-seeking politicians—an argument which would show that the doctrine of Marquillos, and the laws and policies that stemmed from it, threatened their own well-being.

IX

Juan Pacheco and Pedro Girón were known to be descendants of Moors on their father's side and of Jewish converts on their mother's side. By the middle of the fifteenth century, their Moorish blood was much diluted through intermarriage with Old Christians, but their Jewish ancestry was of more recent origin, even though it too, according to the *Tizón,* was from five generations before their own.[99] In any case, it was no secret that their great-great-grandmother was Jewish.

The Pachecos, of course, considered themselves Christian—or rather Old Christian—through and through. That they had no interest or emotional involvement in Judaism need scarcely be pointed out. Yet the rebels claimed that they considered "Jewish" any descendants of Jewish converts at least up to the fifth generation,[100] and the Pachecos had thus barely made it. Should they be concerned with the racial campaign that was being conducted against the conversos when their own relationship to the Jews is so remote, and antiquated at most? They must have answered with an emphatic no, it seems, to nobody's surprise.

The Relator thought differently, however, and he set out to prove the point.

To show the range of aristocratic families that might be affected by the race theory, he presented a list of many nobles in the kingdoms of both Castile and Aragon who had a partly converso ancestry, or who were intermarried with conversos.[101] The range appeared enormous. Embracing many or most of the houses of the Spanish barons and magnates, including some of the foremost among them, the list shows that, if the racial principle were adopted, more than half of the rulers of Spain would and should be excluded from office. The results of such a policy, were it enforced, would obviously be disastrous. Many noble houses would be divided and weakened, many relationships would be impaired, and the right to many estates would be questioned. Not only would this result in chaos, both social and economic, but also the efficacy of the nobility as a ruling class would be greatly jeopardized, if not ruined. The social distinction which is associated with its membership and evokes the natural respect of the masses would be so undermined, and so diminished, by the charges made by the race protagonists that its prestige would be drastically reduced and gradually replaced by disrespect and scorn. Could the race theory go that far? Could such a thing really happen? *It has already begun to happen,* the Relator pointed out. It has already caused no little damage to the nobility as a whole, for it "casts a stain" upon the honor of all those who are related, in any measure or form, to the conversos of Jewish origin.[102] All these "great lords, counts and countesses, and the very notable Prelates who are today in the Church of God, the

Knights, and the Masters of the military Orders, and also the Members of the monastic orders, the hidalgos and Doctors (of theology and law), as well as the auditors and officials of the king and members of his Council, and many other notable persons *who have a part in this lineage*" are now subject to "ignominy, vilification and contumely."[103]

Was this already the actual state of things, or was the Relator merely pointing to the future consequences of the race theory for the people involved? There is no doubt that the racists of Toledo were inquiring into the background of every member of the ruling classes, especially those who were opposed to them, and looking for racial flaws in their origins, as well as their family relationships. Hatred, gossip, and the usual delight which the common people take in running down the famous, in finding flaws and faults in the lives of the great, were naturally pushing in this direction, even though formally, the leadership of the rebel movement was still avoiding an overt attack upon the "mixed" elements of the nobility. In any case, the Relator was quite sure that such an attack was in the making, that the *potential* was bound to become *actual*—unless the race doctrine, and those who spread its germs, were outlawed and suppressed in time.

Several times does the Relator stress that the main danger posed by the practices of the Toledans lies in their espousal of a new principle and their reliance on a new philosophy. "Above all, what is more evil [morally] and worse [also otherwise]," he says, "is the dogmatization of the error."[104] Had the outrages of Toledo been merely a product of social maladjustments, jealousies, and friction, one might assume that the harm would be limited to the New Christians of Toledo—or perhaps also to those of some other cities in which similar conditions prevail. More precisely, the troubles could be regarded as confined to some limited areas and special circumstances, and therefore also more likely to pass in a relatively short time. But this is not the case with the Toledan persecution. It is carried not only by the emotions aroused by the common antagonisms between groups and classes but also by a new philosophy, a *dogma*, which transcends all local or temporary considerations. Such a theory cannot be limited to Toledo; in fact, it will not remain limited to Castile. "Not only does it already hurt the nobles of Castile, but also of those of all the *Españas* [the Iberian kingdoms], and even of the whole world."[105]

The "world" of which the Relator spoke was of course the Christian world; and that is what he really wished to emphasize. As he saw it, the "error" (or "heresy") of Marquillos, although it is clearly anti-Christian, claims to represent "true" Christianity, and as such it will inevitably seek to attain dominance in the whole Christian world. For a theory operates by the force of its principle and moves forward, unless stopped, by its own momentum. There is no question that the Relator realized all this, and there is likewise no doubt that he correctly assessed the strength of the driving force of the race theory. It was enormous, or "diabolical," as he put it.[106]

The main purpose of the Relator's lengthy listing of the nobles who could be affected by this drive (that is, who could be classed as "part-Jewish" and, hence, racially "impure") was therefore not to bring the theory *ad absurdum,* as may perhaps appear at first glance. His main purpose was undoubtedly to emphasize the threat posed by that theory to the Spanish aristocracy and, consequently, to the whole social order of Castile and other countries as well. In simpler terms, what he wished to indicate was that intermarriage between conversos and the Spanish nobility had advanced to a point where the two groups were inseparably intertwined, and the downfall of the one would inevitably cause the downfall of the other. In vain will some nobles who are racially "polluted," according to the theorists of Toledo, try to remain indifferent to the sufferings of the conversos, who now carry the brunt of the battle. However distant they are from the scene of troubles, or however remote their racial connection with the Jews, the "theory" is ultimately bound to overtake them, if it is allowed to run its course. Nor will it stop before any eminence—of rank, or dignity, or achievement; it will even reach to royalty itself; and the Relator goes on to show that also the royal houses of Navarre, Aragon, Castile, and Portugal are "tainted" with Jewish blood.[107]

Such an argument, the Relator thought, must have some effect upon the Prince (whose own house, incidentally, was intermarried with the royal houses of Navarre and Aragon), and especially upon the brothers Pacheco and Girón, whose partly Jewish origins were no secret and who harbored plans of marriage with great nobles, some of whom were mentioned by the Relator. In any case, the Relator made doubly sure that his point would not be missed. He expressed his belief that "the Señores who are near his Grace [namely, the favorites Pacheco and Girón], out of respect for their virtue, *and for their persons, and dignities, and origins,* will not like to be involved in matters of such bad example, which are against God and against his Holy Faith, and so dangerous to the souls, and so *defamatory* toward God and toward the *World.*"[108] Note especially the words: *out of respect for their origins,* in which the Relator wanted to say that they *must* consider themselves involved, even though their partly Jewish ancestry dates back five generations; these matters which are of *"such bad example"*—namely, which are not going to be confined to Toledo, or to the rules laid down by the Toledans— are of course "dangerous to the soul" (because they are so anti-Christian and so heretical). But the religious garb in which the threat is cloaked is too thin to veil its main intent. *The "example" will spread,* and anyone whose descent can be traced to Jewish ancestry, however remote and however partial, will be faced with the danger of defamation. It is *"defamatory toward the world."* The defamation will affect one's religious as well as secular position (for it is directed "toward God and toward the world"). What is more, the word *world* here had more than one connotation and hinted at another negative result: Those who will be hit by the race calumny will have no place to hide or escape from it; it will follow them wherever they go. For the nature of such calumnies is that they besmirch a person before the whole world.

The observation was incisive and the prognosis far-sighted. In due time, the nobility was to feel the brunt of the race theory that spread from Toledo and to take severe punishment as a result. Nor was the span of four or five generations sufficient to "clear" one of racial "pollution." The day was to come in Spain when any taint of Jewish blood was sufficient to affect the "purity" of any person, however elevated his rank or notable his achievement.

X

This concludes the Relator's argument against the Marranos' enemies. It is a clear, well-aimed, hard-hitting argument, and its objectives can be easily discerned. Nevertheless, to understand it fully, one must bore somewhat deeper. One must unravel the major idea that connects its parts and underlies its thoughts—at once the source of the Relator's reasoning and the principle of his speculative drive.

How can one distinguish in Christendom, he asks, between one people and another—or, more clearly, between any two Christians by dint of their descent? To be sure, "the Church of God consists of a combination of *two* peoples *(pueblos)*—the Israelite and the Gentile. Since its foundation, there were always converted to it, from time to time, now from these and now from the others, and similarly they will go on being converted to it from these and the others to the end of days."[109] But from all these converts who come from these two peoples "our Lord has made—and is making—one people *(un pueblo)* by his Holy Passion, and it is for *all* of them that he suffered."[110] Thus for more than fourteen centuries, Christendom has been fashioned by a perpetual intermixture of Jews and gentiles, and this was especially the case in Spain, where all the Jews at one time, seven hundred years ago, were converted to Christianity. In consequence, "no longer is it known who descended from whom," and there is not one Christian who can safely say that he stems from a purely gentile stock.[111] The upshot of all this is that differentiation between groups according to their origin—that is, whether it is Jewish or gentile—is impossible in the Christian world, just as it is abhorrent, morally and religiously, to the spirit of Christianity and the teachings of the Church. Indeed, it is no accident that this is so; for Christ suffered and died for this very purpose of abolishing the distinction between Jew and gentile and for making of both one people.

"One unified people!"—this is what Christ began to accomplish; this is what the Church has been creating from its beginning; and this is the ultimate goal of history and the final destiny of mankind. "One people"—the whole assimilationist view of the conversos is embodied in these remarks. There can be no doubt that for Fernán Díaz de Toledo, as well as for the majority of the conversos in Castile, intermarriage with Old Christians represented the solution—the ultimate solution—of the converso problem. Assimilation was their wish, their aspiration, and their "end," and intermarriage the best "means" to attain it. Yet so great is the complexity of the human mind that it produces baffling contradictions of attitudes, and so it did in the case of the conversos when they came face to face with their identity.

For preaching assimilation and favoring intermarriage did not deaden the consciousness of their group affinity, nor did it stifle their pride in their origin. And thus, while adhering in principle to the theory that the Church was built by both Jewish and gentile converts, and that it effaced all the signs by which they were distinguished in their pre-Christian condition, the conversos continued to see a major difference between the converts from Judaism and those from gentilehood. Moreover, that difference appeared to be so crucial that the former-Jews and former-gentiles in the Church came to be viewed by them not as interchangeable (i.e., as equal converts to Christianity), but as two distinct categories with quite different characteristics. As a matter of fact, the Relator tells us, the designation "convert" does not even *fit* those "who came to Christianity" from Judaism. This is why the author of the *Ecclesiastical History* pointed out that in the ancient Church only gentiles, but not Jews, who came to the faith were called "converts."[112] "For the latter [i.e., the Jews] were in their home and their Law, and all they needed [to become Christians] was to baptize themselves and believe that Jesus was the Messiah whose coming had been promised by the Law and the Prophets."[113] This was a comparatively easy task, as *Jerome* had pointed out. All it required of the Jews was to see in a clearer light the meaning of *the same Law* which they were following and upholding and which "our Lord Jesus Christ did not come to abolish, but to fulfill." In contrast, the gentiles, to become Christians, had to go through a basic and far-reaching transformation; "they had to pass from evil to good, from infidelity to Faith"; they had to be converted.[114] And therefore it is to them—and to them alone—that in truth the name "converts" should apply.

This, then, is the view of the Relator, and, as we shall see, it was shared by—and animated—other leading conversos at the time. It is the view of one who had been brought up from childhood not only on the traditional teachings of Christianity, but also on the teachings of Paul of Burgos and other Jewish converts of the same brand who appeared in the Spanish domains.[115] Later on, we shall touch on the various considerations that moved the conversos to adopt that view.[116]

II. JUAN DE TORQUEMADA

I. GENERAL BACKGROUND

I

Several months after the Relator had written his Instruction to Don Lope de Barrientos, another rebuttal of the *Sentencia* was completed by another outstanding apologist of the Marranos. The author was Cardinal Juan de Torquemada (uncle of the famous Inquisitor General)[1]; the place was Rome and the language was Latin. The date of this document[2] and its language, among other reasons,[3] accounted for the fact that it lagged behind the Instruction in its impact on Spanish public opinion. But this in no way diminishes its importance as a source for the developments we now seek to unravel. In fact, it surpasses the work of the Relator in revealing certain parts of these developments. In particular it throws light on the anti-Marrano campaign, the methods employed in it, its aims and slogans, and the theoretical premises on which it rested. At the same time it offers us a better understanding of the Marranos' own view of themselves—of their lives as Christians in the Spanish society and their historical function in the Christian world.

Invaluable in itself, Torquemada's testimony gains added importance from its author's great prominence—from the fact that he was a "star of the first magnitude" in Church life of the 15th century.[4] Oddly enough, this outstanding testimony failed for many years to engage the interest of scholars, and the work containing it was published only recently.[5] But no thorough analysis has yet been made of it, and its real meaning has been lost for most readers— no doubt because of the orthodox approach that prevailed in scholarship toward the issues involved.

II

He was born in Valladolid,[6] probably in 1388,[7] to an Old Christian father by the name of Alvar Fernández de Torquemada and, most probably, a New Christian mother, whose name remains unknown.[8] The father belonged to a family of hidalgos hailing from Torquemada, a small town in the province of Palencia, in which Alvar had once served as *regidor*. Some of the members of Torquemada's family were knights in the entourage of Castile's kings Alfonso XI and Pedro I,[9] and one of them, Rodrigo Rodríguez de Torquemada, was, in the days of the latter monarch, *adelantado mayor* of Castile.[10] He was the only one of Torquemada's ancestors who attained national distinction.

At the age of sixteen he joined the Dominican Order and entered the Convent of St. Paul in Valladolid,[11] "and from that time on he dedicated himself to a life of piety and studies."[12] It is not clear that he ever studied in Salamanca, as some of his biographers have asserted.[13] But wherever he studied, he must have distinguished himself as both student and friar. In 1416, when Fray Luis de Valladolid, prior of Torquemada's Convent of St. Paul, was appointed by King Juan II of Castile as his legate to the Council of Constance, he chose Torquemada to accompany him as *socius*, most probably in the capacity of secretary and aide.[14]

They left for Constance in April 1417, when the council was already in its fourth year, and arrived in time to attend the thirty-fifth session.[15] It was only ten months before the council's dissolution, but much crucial work still lay ahead. In July of that year they could see the deposition of Benedict XIII as "heretic and schismatic," and in November they could attend the election of a new pope (Martin V), this time of a reunited Church. They could also witness the violent discussions about the proposed supremacy of the Council over the pope—discussions that left major issues unresolved and the way open for future conflict. The role Fray Luis played in the Council was so pleasing and helpful to Martin V that the pope expressed his appreciation of that role with special recompenses.[16] Since in matters of faith Martin V opposed appeals to the council against papal decisions,[17] we may assume that Fray Luis' position on this issue leaned toward that of the pope. Perhaps the seed of the view of papal primacy, which so distinguished Torquemada in later years, was planted in his mind during those discussions. He may have been influenced by the views of Fray Luis; or the latter may have been strengthened in his stand by the aid and advice of his young *socius*.

Whatever the case, Torquemada's assistance was highly appreciated by Fray Luis de Valladolid, for he rewarded his *socius* with the best prize that a friar in his position could hope for. He sent Torquemada to Paris to specialize in theology, no doubt with a view to appoint him teacher in the new theological school that Fray Luis was then planning to establish in Valladolid.[18] Juan went to Paris directly from Constance and entered the Gymnasium of Saint-Jacques. He became a student of the University of Paris, from which he received, in March 1424, his licentiate in theology, and about a year later his degree of master.[19] Shortly thereafter he returned to Valladolid, but his plan of teaching there may have been abandoned, for Fray Luis died and Torquemada was appointed prior of the Convent of St. Paul in his stead. Before long, however, he exchanged this position for the priorship of the Convent of Pedro Mártir in Toledo.[20]

In the following years (until 1432) we see him occupy the same position, growing in stature until he became known as Spain's leading Dominican. Although we lack direct evidence for this assertion, we can infer it from two important facts. He was chosen by Juan II of Castile as his legate to the Council of Basle (which opened in 1431), and was appointed by the General of the Dominican Order as his procurator in that council for Spain.

This double appointment marked a watershed in Torquemada's career. By then forty-four years old, he had already spent more than half his life without leaving any notable impression on the developments of his time. Beyond his formal education and priorship of convents, little is known of him from that period, for none of the numerous works he produced was written before 1432. We may assume, however, that in the preceding years Torquemada enriched his store of knowledge, heightened his intellectual capacities, and further developed his literary skills, all of which later revealed themselves fully when given the proper forum and opportunity. In any case, the man who until the age of forty-four was virtually unknown outside his country, gained in Basle, within a brief time, international reputation. He would now affect the fortunes of the Church and, through the Church, the fortunes of Europe.

He arrived in Basle in August 1432 and in December delivered his first discourse, in which he stressed the need for overall reforms in the customs and morals of the Church's functionaries.[21] There was much of the conciliar reformer in Torquemada when he came to Basle in 1432. But the task of removing abuses in the Church soon receded in his thinking to the background as he found himself occupied more and more with the main issue that engaged the Council—i.e., its rights and functions versus those of the papacy. In June 1433 he undertook to defend the pope's prerogative in the appointment of bishops—a right which the Council wished to abrogate. And from then on, for the next seven years—that is, to the end of the Pope's conflict with the Council, he fought the latter's moves against the papacy every step of the way.[22] In the course of this period his pro-papal position became steadily more determined, more outspoken, and more extreme, and both the tracts and studies he wrote, as well as the public debates he conducted, established him in the eyes of one and all as the foremost champion of papal supremacy.

But apart from defending the papacy against the council in theological disputes, he was also the Pope's political emissary on various crucial missions. Thus he was sent in September 1437, together with Giovanni Aurispa, to Castile on a mission to persuade King Juan II to transfer the Castilian delegates to Ferrara.[23] In October 1438 he defended the Pope in the German Diet at Nuremberg,[24] and in March 1439, when the Diet met in Mainz, he addressed it again, vigorously upholding the principle of papal infallibility.[25] In August 1440 he spoke, as the Pope's legate, before the convention of French bishops and princes called by King Charles VII at Bourges. There Torquemada charged the conciliarists of Basle (who had elected the duke of Savoy as pope) with an attempt to create a new schism. He was confronted with the council's able representative Juan de Segovia (also a Spaniard), but the King, following Torquemada's presentations, recognized Eugene IV as the only lawful Pontiff.[26]

In all his utterances as debater and writer, Torquemada displayed his great powers as theologian and expert in Christian law and literature. No doubt his greatest achievements in these fields were his capital works on Gratian's *Decretum*[27] and the constitution of the Church.[28] But his fame was already established much earlier through his shorter discourses on papal rights.[29] It also gained much from his learned dissertations on various specific theological questions—such as the forgiveness of sins, the sacrament of the Eucharist, and the conception of the Virgin Mary[30]—as well as his judgments on various theories held or suspected to be heretical—such as his works against the Hussites and the Bosnian Manichaeans.[31] His struggle against heresies was part of his aim to bring about a united Christendom, cleared of all schism and internal divisions; and his effort to heal the historic breach in Christendom between the Catholic and Orthodox churches was basically another manifestation of that general aim.

Thus he became one of the chief architects of the unification of the two churches, which was finally expressed in the Decree of the Union issued in Florence on July 6, 1439. It was due, in fact, largely to Torquemada's tenacity, theological acumen and debating skills that Catholicism emerged victorious from its contest with the sharp-minded and obstinate Greek theologians on such complex issues as Purgatory and the Eucharist and, above all, the issue of the Primacy.[32] The Pope, who was watching that contest closely, was filled with admiration for Torquemada's great mastery in fencing with the crafty Greeks.

That Eugene IV duly appreciated Torquemada's contribution to the papal cause was evident almost from the latter's first appearance on the conciliar scene. Following his speech in December 1432, the Pope entrusted him with ever more difficult and more vital tasks. In 1434 he appointed Torquemada to the position of Master of the Sacred Palace, which meant the curia's official theologian and Rome's representative on outstanding matters.[33] Following Torquemada's discussions with the Greeks and his debate with Cardinal Cesarini,[34] Eugene named him Defender of the Faith, and in December of that year (1439) created him Cardinal-priest of St. Sixtus.[35] Subsequent popes bestowed upon him additional awards and still higher titles. In 1455 he was made bishop of Palestrina by Calixtus III,[36] and in 1463 he was raised (by Pius II) to the status of Cardinal-bishop of Sabina.[37] After the death of Pius II he was considered, together with Scarampo, one of the first two choices for the papacy. He declined the nomination for reasons of health, as did also Scarampo.[38]

III

This brief biographical sketch cannot by itself do justice to Torquemada, his public effort and creative achievement. Nor can it duly explain the influence he exerted upon the affairs of the Church. To reach such understanding, we must see him more fully and perceive more clearly both his literary work and the historical background against which it was produced.

"In regard to theology," says Pastor, the noted Catholic historian of the Church, "Torquemada was undoubtedly the most learned member of the Sacred College,"[39] while the Protestant church historian Georg Voigt does not hesitate to call Torquemada the "greatest theologian of his age."[40] Both Catholic and Protestant historians agree on the rare combination of high qualities that distinguishes Torquemada's writings, and, above all, on the uniqueness of his *Summa de Ecclesia,* which is generally recognized as "the most important work produced in the Middle Ages on the question of papal supremacy."[41] Moreover, these assessments reflect not only the conclusions of *modern* scholarship. In the twenty generations that have passed since Torquemada's time, his theological writings have aroused the admiration of many a scholar and erudite reader. Perhaps Hernando de Castillo, the historian of the Dominicans, has best expressed the high esteem for Torquemada shared by Spaniards in the 16th century,[42] while the attitude of premodern scholarship toward him is well indicated by Nicolás Antonio, who assures us that Torquemada will enjoy vast fame "as long as the love of letters and the zeal for learning dwell in the hearts of men."[43]

The thrust of Torquemada's literary effort—summarized in forty books and tracts[44]—aimed to establish, or reestablish, the old beliefs and views of the Church, as distinct from some of the deviating concepts that invaded its thinking in the preceding century. That he did not achieve all his objectives is clear from the subsequent events; but it is also clear that he achieved a great deal—indeed, enough to affect the course of history. In fact, it is remarkable that at a time when Europe's culture was following the lines of a revived classicism, and the Church was being swept by the tidal waves of a semi-democratic, Humanistic reformation, Torquemada could make such a historic impact by the sheer force of a scholastic theology which was, fundamentally, anti-revisionist, anti-Humanistic and, above all, anti-democratic.

He appeared on the scene of Church history at a time when the unsettled conflict in the Church threatened to tear it apart once again. It was when the Schism appeared to have been healed and the strife between pope and council subsided that the brewing quarrel broke out in full blast. The papacy was again sharply attacked by the surging conciliar movement, and allegiances were shifting from one side to the other, often according to the tide of battle. Compared with other leading churchmen of his time, such as Cesarini, Aeneas Sylvius, Nicholas de Cusa and Panormitanus, Torquemada distinguished himself by his constancy of policy and singleness of purpose—more precisely, by standing squarely and immovably on the traditional platform of Catholic Christianity.

Backed primarily by the authority of the Pope, which was by now much questioned and derided, and the papal party, which was semi-demoralized by repeated retreats and loss of face, Torquemada found himself in the Council of Basle on the side of what seemed a hopeless minority, and for a long time appeared to be trying to defend a doomed position. It was the courage, tenacity, zeal and idealism which he demonstrated in that defense that swayed the outcome of the uneven contest and saved the day for the papacy. Not for nothing did grateful popes confer upon him the title of "Defender of the Faith and Protector of the Church."[45]

The time of these developments, we should recall, was midway between Wyclif and Luther. The Church's foundations were shaken by the earthquakes that signaled the coming of the Reformation. Reduced in prestige and power by the Schism, and limited in its prerogatives by the Council of Constance, the renewed papacy was faced with a choice: should it yield further to the conciliar movement and finally become its servile agent, or should it break the shackles imposed on it at Constance and restore to itself its former independence?

The conciliarists were determined to hold on to their gains—the Constance decision of April 1415, which declared the pope subordinate to the council, and the series of "corrections" they managed to make in the administration and government of the Church.[46] These formed part of their Reform Program, which now, in Basle, they intended to complete. But standing in their way was the pope, Eugene IV, who not only opposed their planned changes, but had made up his mind to treat as dead letter the conciliar decision of April 1415. In fact, he tried to show by his very conduct that it was he, and not the council, who was in charge and laying down the rules for the Christian world. Thus began the contest over the Primacy which became the focus of the Council's interests. Torquemada staunchly defended the Pope, but the task he assumed seemed next to impossible. Against the strong conciliar case, which had been built for decades by such wise and brilliant men as Gerson, d'Ailly and Nieheim, Torquemada had to build a case for the Pope, or rather for the principle of papal Primacy, which was unpopular and seemed outmoded by the dominant current of thought in his time.

In the din of the great controversy, however, his voice was heard loud and clear, steadily gaining more attention and respect for the hitherto discarded point of view. But his only real ally in this battle was, for a considerable time, the pope, Eugene IV, a man of great courage and political astuteness, who was capable of fighting with dogged determination for what he considered his sacred rights. Yet these qualities alone, however helpful, would not have saved him from ignominious defeat, just as similar qualities did not save other popes who clashed head-on with the conciliar movement. In fact, all the popes who were deposed or abdicated (there had been five in the preceding two decades) clung to their office with extreme tenacity, even against overwhelming odds. The conciliarists, however, knew how to deal with them; they overpowered even the most stubborn popes; and they would doubtless have overcome Eugene IV too had it not been for two major factors that played in his favor. One was the reluctance of the Christian world to go through the agony of another schism, and the other was the papal counter-campaign that accompanied the pope's anticonciliar moves.

Heading that counter-campaign was Torquemada, and it is here that he made his greatest contribution to the papal cause. That campaign led many a conciliarist to doubt the very probity of deposing the pope, thus strengthening the general reluctance to depose him and weakening the moral appeal of the council. Seven years of fervent and persistent agitation were sufficient to turn the tide. When the conciliarists finally came down to the task of formally "removing" Eugene IV from his position, their cause was already lost.

IV

It has often been suggested that had the conciliar movement emerged victorious from the struggle at Basle, the Reformation would have been avoided and Europe would have been saved from the tragedies and horrors of the ensuing religious wars. This is possible, even likely. But no lesson can be gathered from such hindsight.

Nobody living in the middle of the fifteenth century could foresee the military consequences of a Reformation that had not yet come to pass. But assuming that such foresight could be had, it would not probably have deterred many partisans of the papacy from taking the course they pursued.

For the question that confronted both them and their adversaries was essentially as follows: Could the Church undergo such a drastic change as that proposed by the advocates of Reform without being ruined in the process? The conciliarists answered this question affirmatively. They were certain that the Church could take the strain, and they further believed that a reconstruction of its government was the only way to cure it of its ills. The answer of the conservative faction, however, was decidedly in the negative. As they saw it, the Church which the Reformists wished to fashion was destined to a short and miserable life. If the papal authority was to be reduced in both scope and degree as the Reformists planned, the Church would be robbed of its unifying principle, which had held it together for a thousand years. As a result, the various parts of Christendom—the restive, ambitious, and contentious powers—would press for greater independence of the pope and the right to resist his rulings and decisions. And where could all this ultimately lead if not to their total separation from the Church and, in consequence, to its disintegration? When the alternatives were seen in this light and considered in terms of "to be or not to be," every conceivable risk or hardship seemed worthwhile in the attempt to save the Church.

From the standpoint of the anti-Reformists, moreover, the danger to the Church was not limited to its dissolution by the loss of the unifying papal authority. Even if a Church based on conciliar principles could resist the various centrifugal pulls and manage to save itself from dismemberment, it could not continue as that powerful force which for more than a millennium had moved ceaselessly and relentlessly toward the attainment of its declared goals. The still unfulfilled destiny of Christendom—to conquer for Christ the whole of mankind—would remain forever unfulfilled, if the government of the Church was to be altered in the manner proposed by the spokesmen of conciliarism. In brief: If the Church triumphant could cope with such a change, it seemed certain that the Church militant could not. For only a Church that was undivided and unhampered by narrow nationalistic interests could launch a universal missionary effort or issue a call to the whole of Christendom to unite in a crusade against the infidels.

It was no mere coincidence, therefore, that Torquemada, the fighter for papal supremacy, was pushing hard for the union with the Greeks.[47] Fired by the vision of one monarchic Church, uniform in rule, faith and aspiration, he envisioned a Church striding forward to embrace the whole non-Christian world. The reconquest by Catholicism of Eastern Christendom, severed from the Church centuries before, was to him the first and foremost task to be accomplished in that direction. By 1440 he could see the triumph of his ideas in the consolidation of the Church's inner ranks and in the start of its expansion eastward. Granted that, for reasons beyond his control, the union with the Greeks was soon to prove chimerical. But the idea of restoring papal power in the Church appeared to have stood the test of time, and every passing day gave new evidence of the fact that papal authority was indeed reestablished.[48] The conciliar movement, to be sure, did not die, and the ideological battle was to be continued. But the last vestiges of organized conciliarism collapsed in 1449 with the abdication of Felix V (who was appointed pope by the Council of Basle). The schism in the Church and its gravest crisis seemed to be over.

It was at this moment, when Torquemada's prestige in the Roman curia was at its height, that the rebellion of Toledo broke out; and the cardinal was confronted with the converso persecution, gushing forth with volcanic force in the wake of a popular eruption.

V

What was going on in Castile? The question had been in the minds of the Pope's aides ever since news of the riots in Toledo arrived in the papal court. What caused the uncertainty was that, from the outset, Rome was swept by conflicting reports about the nature of the riots, their causes and their aims. The partisans of the junta that ruled Toledo described the outbreak as a popular reaction to a Judaic conspiracy that had engulfed Castile. On the other hand, the conversos portrayed the rebels as archcriminals, traitors and heretics; and the King, Juan II, who shared much of this view, demanded, as we have seen, that the rebels be denounced and excommunicated by the Pope.

Castile was virtually an ally of the papacy throughout the struggle with the Council of Basle, and Spain—in fact, the Iberian peninsula—knew none of the strong heretical movements that in the late Middle Ages appeared in such countries as France, England and Germany. Indeed, from the standpoint of Catholic orthodoxy, Spain was the healthiest spot in Christendom, and of course the papacy wished it to remain so. To allow it to fall prey to a spreading "heresy" and become a battleground of a divided nation was a prospect that the papacy did not welcome. But was this really what was happening in Spain? The picture that emerged from the conflicting accounts of the occurrences in Toledo was vague and equivocal, hardly capable of providing the Pope with a clear-cut answer.

Nicholas V obviously had to take a definite stand on these events. But the stand had to be based on full knowledge of the developments that had taken place in Castile. There was no doubt that a rebellion had broken out there which, politically, the Church had to oppose. The question that remained for the papacy to clarify was whether this rebellion could in any way be justified on moral and religious grounds.

It stands to reason that the Pope asked Torquemada to examine the matter and present his conclusions. Renowned as an expert on matters of faith and as an indefatigable fighter of heresies, Torquemada was indeed the most likely man to perform such a task. In addition, he was Castilian by birth and also by much of his education; he had lived in Castile until the age of forty-four; he knew Spanish society and knew Toledo, the city which was the scene of the disorders, for he had served there as Prior of the Convent of Pedro Mártir. Furthermore, Torquemada was generally considered to have been on friendly terms with Juan II ever since he was sent to Basle as Castile's royal representative. Nicholas V would obviously prefer to have his inquirer and adviser in this matter be amicably disposed toward the King, and consequently treat with as much respect as possible his testimony, counsels and wishes.

Torquemada tells us that he had before him not only the judgment against the conversos that was issued in Toledo by the rebels, accompanied by certain explanatory communications which the latter sent to the curia,[49] but also the letters that were sent by the King—no doubt to the Pope—and other trustworthy accounts of the riots in Toledo.[50] By these accounts he was probably referring to testimonies sent by some Castilian churchmen, including the foremost converso leaders who appealed to the Pope, the curia, or to him personally, to intervene in the deteriorating and intolerable situation. In all probability, most of these documents were given to him by the papal chancellery, so that he could examine the case and present a formal opinion. Judging by the evidence at our disposal concerning Torquemada's involvement in this matter, it is certain that he familiarized both the Pope and the curia with the view he formed of the Toledan events. What is more, we may assume that, in large measure, his opinions served as basis for the papal bulls of September 24, 1449.

VI

That Torquemada presented his views and recommendations on the Toledan conflict in a memorandum to the Pope may likewise be taken for granted. And we may also be sure that this memorandum was similar, in both content and approach, to the scathing critique he later penned against the rebels under the title "A Treatise against the Midianites and Ishmaelites." No doubt both works were part of the offensive then launched in Rome against the rebels by the conversos at the initiative—and, most likely, under the guidance—of their able emissary to the curia.[51] Torquemada, however, does not refer to this fact. All he says with respect to the treatise is that, roused by the foolhardy deeds of the Toledans and "fired by zeal for the divine honor," he wrote it "in defense of Jesus and Mary" against the "detractors of their race."[52] The statement can doubtless be taken as true; the writing of the treatise against the Toledans could well have its origin in Torquemada's own will. Yet it is certain that it was closely related to the function he fulfilled on behalf of the Pope and the tasks he undertook on behalf of the conversos. We may assume that Torquemada began to write the treatise upon completing his memorandum on the Toledan rebellion, making fuller use of the materials he had gathered for the purposes of that memorandum.

It is scarcely surprising that Torquemada made no mention of his assistance to the Pope in that matter. Nor need we wonder why the Pope, Nicholas V, left us no indication to this effect. It was not customary for the popes to disclose the names of those who counseled them in the preparation of their bulls, and obviously Torquemada would not embarrass the Pope by improper, uncalled-for revelations. What is more, in this instance there was a special reason for the Pope to keep his habitual silence. Nicholas V did not want it known—and even less, formally acknowledged—that his verdict concerning the Toledan conflict rested on Torquemada's judgments. He chose to have the role performed by the cardinal played down as much as possible; and Torquemada, of course, was aware of the reasons. The Pope sought to deny the Toledans an excuse to criticize him for his dependence on a man who, in their opinion, was a party to the quarrel and therefore unfit to be judge in the case. This they could say because it was widely known that the cardinal had Jewish blood in his veins.

VII

Spanish scholars have chosen to belittle or ignore, rather than investigate, the various allegations concerning Torquemada's Jewish origin. When they touched upon the question—and this happened rarely—they generally disqualified the available evidence attesting the cardinal's Jewish ancestry. For a long time this evidence consisted of one piece. It was a statement by Fernando de Pulgar.

In his sketch of the cardinal that he included in his collection "Famous Men of Castile," the well-known historian of the Catholic kings, who is generally considered a most reliable informant, says of Torquemada that his grandparents were "of the lineage of Jews who were converted to our holy Catholic faith."[53] Juan de la Cruz, the author of a *crónica* of the Dominican Order, treated Pulgar's statement as factual[54]; but other historians of the Dominican Order, such as Antonius of Siena[55] and Hernando de Castillo, as well as historians of broader scope, such as John Pontanus and Balthazar Porreño, categorically rejected Pulgar's assertion on grounds of genealogy and for other reasons, upon which we shall touch briefly.

Thus, Hernando de Castillo tried to show that Pulgar's account of Torquemada's origins was faulty in more than one respect. "He did not hail from Burgos, as Pulgar imagined, but from Valladolid, as Torquemada himself stated in his work on the *Decretum*. Nor did he descend from such ancestors as he [Pulgar] wished to give him in his fancy."[56] Castillo goes on to tell us that the great-grandfather of Juan de Torquemada—Lope Alonso de Torquemada—was knighted by King Alfonso XI of Castile on the day of his coronation in the city of Burgos,[57] and that his wife, Ana de Collaços, gave birth to a son, Pedro Fernández de Torquemada, the grandfather of the cardinal, who was married to Joana Fernández de Tovar. Pedro Fernández, he further tells us, was buried, at his request, in the Church of Santa Olalla de Torquemada, while his wife was buried in the cloister of San Francisco de Valladolid, in a chapel that was built for her by her elder son, Alvar Fernández de Torquemada, who was the father of Juan de Torquemada, the cardinal.[58]

It is strange that Castillo does not divulge the name of the cardinal's mother, even though he gives us the names of his grandmother and his great-grandmother and even though he mentions the burial place of his mother (the same chapel of San Francisco of Valladolid where his father and grandmother Joana were buried).[59] Was *she,* one might ask, of converso parenthood? Did Pulgar refer to *her* parents when he said that the grandparents of the cardinal were conversos? Did he know that they and she—i.e., the cardinal's mother—were natives of Burgos, thus providing the background for his assumption concerning the place of the cardinal's birth?

No firm answer, one way or the other, can be given to any of these questions. Yet the probabilities are that the correct reply should be in the affirmative. Pulgar was a younger contemporary of the cardinal, and it is difficult to assume that he would have made *such* a statement about *so* famous a man as Torquemada without being certain of the veracity of his assertion. Moreover, by stating that Juan de Torquemada was of Jewish origin, he related Tomás de Torquemada to Jews, and thus made the Inquisitor subject to the suspicion of having a partial Jewish ancestry. Would Pulgar, the converso, dare make such an allegation and present it to the reading public of Spain unless he was sure of his facts? It should be borne in mind that the first edition of the *Claros Varones,* which includes his study of the cardinal, appeared in 1486, when Pulgar was still alive and when Tomás de Torquemada, the Inquisitor-General, was at the height of his power and influence.

Porreño, the historian of the *limpieza* statutes, who was strongly anti-Marrano, claimed that Pulgar did not err, but lied in this particular instance. The reason: he wanted to avenge himself on a relative of the cardinal (presumably his nephew, Tomás de Torquemada) for some injury that the latter had inflicted upon him.[60] But apart from the fact that Porreño failed to indicate any basis for his conjecture, it is difficult to see in what way Pulgar could hurt Tomás de Torquemada if the statement was false. Rather, the falsehood would serve Tomás, the Inquisitor, as pretext to injure the chronicler further, in addition to the harm that he (or someone else) had allegedly caused him. Pulgar, of course, could have envisaged this development, from which he could gain nothing and lose much.

Even though these arguments suggest that Pulgar's assertion must have been true, it was difficult to settle the question definitely as long as Pulgar's statement was the only testimony supporting the disputed assumption. Today, however, we possess additional evidence in support of Pulgar's claim—evidence which makes it, in fact, apparent that the cardinal's Jewish—or rather partly Jewish—ancestry was common knowledge in Pulgar's time and that Pulgar therefore was revealing no secret when he spoke of the cardinal's Jewish forebears.

Such evidence is contained in the *Memorial* against the conversos, which was written by Marcos García de Mora toward the end of 1449. In this document, which dates from the cardinal's lifetime (the cardinal was then about sixty-two years old and in the prime of his literary and public activity), García says that Pope Nicholas V refused to grant an audience to the representatives of the Old Christians of Toledo under the influence of the "cunning Cardinal of St. Sixtus," whose position in this matter was obviously determined by the "Judaic persecution of his relatives"[61] (meaning that Torquemada's Jewish relatives—i.e., the conversos—were persecuted as Judaizers). To be sure, García would not hesitate to be untruthful in order to discredit his hated opponents; but his statements in such cases would appear plausible, or rather not easily proven false. However, his assertion about Torquemada, if deceptive, would not fit into this category. It would seem the height of folly for him to make such a charge against a famous cardinal, a leading figure in the Christian world, especially in a formal writ to the Pope and "all the princes of Christendom." Obviously, such a charge would be not only sensational, and to no lesser extent scandalous, but would soon be discredited as indefensible and stamp him as a slanderer and a liar. We must therefore conclude that he was absolutely certain that the cardinal was somehow related to conversos, and from the data we possess of this relationship, we may gather that this family tie was one of blood, and not the result of intermarriage between one or more of his Old Christian relatives with New Christians.

Additional evidence to this effect is offered by another contemporary document. In a "Note about Famous Jewish Converts to Christianity," which was written in the last third of the 15th century and appended to a manuscript of Pablo de Santa María's *Scrutinium Scripturarum,* Juan de Torquemada is mentioned among "the most learned, most devout and most religious" Christians who "descended from the people of Israel."[62] Since he wrote this note in Latin after he had read Paul of Burgos' Latin book, the author was obviously a well-educated person; and as such he also knew of the conversos' contribution to the Church in general and to Spain's ecclesiastical life in particular. In all probability, he was a converso who was proud of the achievements of certain members of his group and wanted to indicate to other readers of the *Scrutinium* that Pablo de Santa María was not an exception in his great learning and devotion to Christianity, and that other conversos in "exceedingly large numbers," as he put it, distinguished themselves as churchmen, Christian scholars and members of the monastic orders.[63] That the author was aware of Torquemada's activity, as he was of the others about whom he wrote, is evident from what he says of him: "There lived the Cardinal of St. Sixtus, known as Fray Juan of the Dominican order, who was most learned in Holy Writ and most useful to the Church of God in reducing the heresies of the Greeks, the Armenians, the Bohemians and others."[64] In view of this, there can be hardly any question that the celebrated fighter of those heresies was known in his time to be of Jewish origin, so that our author could not possibly have ignored him when he composed his list of the converso great.

All this makes it certain that the famous cardinal was partly of Jewish origin. At least one of his ancestors, most likely his mother, must have been of Jewish stock, and the matter was well known to the people of his own and the following generation. But in addition to the documentary proofs we have adduced, there is the internal evidence of his treatise on the Marranos, which, even without the testimonies cited, makes it abundantly and conclusively clear that Torquemada was a converso.

II. THE TRACTATUS

I

His tract on the statute against the Marranos in Toledo and its underlying socio-religious philosophy is called: "A Treatise against the Midianites and Ishmaelites, the adversaries and detractors of the Sons who draw their origin from the people of Israel."[65]

The title is revealing. By designating the opponents of the Marranos as Ishmaelites, Torquemada made it clear that he viewed them not only as foes of the conversos, but also as enemies of all Christians—indeed, as implacable and dangerous foes of Christendom as were the Moslems themselves. Consequently, the Church must move against them resolutely as it did against the Saracens and the Moors; certainly it cannot tolerate their existence *within* it, since, like the Moslems, they stand squarely opposed to everything dear and holy to the Church.

In contrast to this derogatory designation of the anti-Marrano party in Toledo, Torquemada calls the New Christians the "sons"—meaning the sons of the Church—a title by which he intends to signify their dutiful and complete devotion to Christianity, the filial affection they feel for the Church, and their readiness to protect it against any menace, such as is posed by the Ishmaelites. Yet implied in this title is not only an evaluation of the attitude of the New Christians toward the Church, but also of the attitude which the Church should take toward the New Christians. Mother Church should obviously embrace her sons, support and encourage them, and offer them every possible aid in their struggle against *their* adversaries, who are also the adversaries of the Church.

Also significant is the last phrase in the title, "who draw their origin from the people of Israel." Torquemada does not allude to the Marranos by such terms as "conversos" or "New Christians," which were common in Spanish literature of the time. By calling them "sons" he wanted to indicate—apart from what was suggested above—that they were full-fledged members of the Catholic Church, enjoying the same status as other faithful Christians, and that no vestige of any "conversion" was to be found in their religious life. In order to designate them as a group, however, Torquemada does not refer to their *religious* antecedents, but to their ethnic and national ones—that is, to the fact that they "draw their origin from the people of Israel," and not from Judaism as a religion.

This was a title which defined, he believed, the Marrano group in historical terms; but it also indicated the main feature of the group, as well as the way its enemies viewed it—for it alluded very clearly to the nature of the conflict that had erupted between the Marranos and their foes. As he saw it, the latter did *not* persecute the Marranos for any "religious" reasons (regardless of the excuses given to this effect) but because they "draw their origin from the people of Israel." In other words, the hatred and the persecution stemmed not from religious but from ethnic and racial motives.

Torquemada's treatise was aimed at exposing the *real* causes of the persecution and the fallacy of the most prevalent arguments that had been offered in its justification. In one way or another, all the arguments of the Toledans related to the nature of the Jewish race, and Torquemada's work was above all a rebuttal and refutation of the Toledans' race theories. As such, it is one of the most remarkable documents written in the Middle Ages.

The Jewish question as a question of race and as an inside problem of Christian society—this is the dilemma with which Torquemada grappled in his "Treatise against the Midianites." But it must be understood that Torquemada himself would have refrained from defining this dilemma in such terms. However central or crucial the racial issue appears in various parts of his discussion, the main problem involved, as he saw it, was still primarily religious. It was so because the race question in general, and what pertains to the Jewish race in particular, was viewed by him from the standpoint of Christian doctrine. What position should a *Christian* take toward the racial theory propounded by the Toledans? How should a *Christian* judge the Jewish race? And what place should Jewish converts to Christianity occupy in Christian society? These were some of the primary questions to which Torquemada addressed himself.

And the answers, like the questions, had to be "religious"—that is, based on Christian doctrine and authority. To prove his thesis, Torquemada brought to bear his great mastery of Christian literature, his expert knowledge of Christian law, and his lifelong studies of Christian dogma. But his treatise does not deal with the issues in a purely *abstract* manner. Throughout his exposition Torquemada touches upon events and circumstances of social import. Moreover, he describes what took place in Toledo and presents the causes of the hatred of the Old Christians for the New and the various manifestations of the anti-Marrano drive. Apart from being a theological tract, therefore, the work is a historical document.

To be sure, one may question the reliability of Torquemada's remarks on the grounds of his partly Jewish origin. Later on, we shall examine the validity of such questioning and seek to determine what measure of truth should be ascribed to Torquemada's testimony.[66] For now we can say that in Torquemada's work we find the Marranos' view—or, at least, a highly representative Marrano view—of the complex relationship that had evolved in Spain between Marranism, Judaism and Christianity.

II

Torquemada builds his argument on verses 3–5 of Psalm 83. He uses these verses as his *verba thematis* (the theme for his discussion), and he also treats them as a virtual summation of his thoughts on the Marranos and their opponents. We ought, therefore, to note what these verses say:

> For Thy enemies, O God, have made a tumult,
> And those who hate Thee have raised their heads;
> They took malicious counsel against Thy people,
> And conspired against Thy saints;
> They said: Come, let us destroy them as a nation
> And the name of Israel be remembered no more.[67]

Torquemada identifies the subject of these verses (i.e., the "enemies of God") with the "ancient foes of the people of Israel"—a people designated in the same verses as "*Thy* people" (i.e., the people of God). Such was Israel, Torquemada makes clear, because "the knowledge of the divine faith and worship flourished in that people," as is indicated by another verse in Psalms (76.2): "God is known in Judea, and His name is great in Israel."[68]

Chief among the "enemies" of the "people of God" were the Edomites, the descendants of Esau, who was also known by the name of Edom (Gen. 36.8). "And just as Esau hated his brother Jacob to the extent that he wanted to kill him (Gen. 27.41), so the Edomites, who descended from Esau, harbored *extreme hatred* for the sons of Israel who descended from Jacob."[69]

Other principal foes were the Ishmaelites, whose hatred followed a similar pattern. And here again: just as their ancestor Ishmael persecuted Isaac, the son of Abraham, as testified by the Apostle in his Epistle to the Galatians (4.29), so they, too, hated the sons of Israel who descended from Isaac. That these—i.e., Edom and Ishmael—were the major enemies of the Israelites is also mentioned in the same Psalm 83 from which the *verba thematis* are taken.[70]

This then is, according to Torquemada, the "literal" meaning of the verses. If we wish, however, to interpret them "symbolically"—that is, to unravel their "hidden" meaning—we may, he says, view them also as alluding to the conflict now evolving between some Old Christians and the New. For like the Edomites and Ishmaelites of antiquity, who were known for their intense animosity for the Israelites, certain "bad Christians and corrupt individuals" are filled with a "mortal hatred" *(odium mortale)* for Israel's descendants who are "Christ's faithful" (i.e., the conversos) in our own time.[71] So shorn are these people of any fear of God and so "inflated with the spirit of malice" that their hatred knows no moral restraint. It is expressed in numerous forms of persecution and it embraces all of "Christ's faithful," however "resplendent" they might be in their faith, their virtues, and "gifts of divine grace."[72] Indeed, these enemies of the conversos show every sign of being "ministers of the Devil" and "agents of his wickedness," for they seek both to obstruct the "divine glory," which glitters through the conversion of the people of Israel to Christ, and to impede the "human happiness" which was attained as a result. Therefore, it is reasonable to assume that Scripture also refers to them—i.e., the haters of the conversos—when it says about the Edomites and Ishmaelites, the most wicked of the ancient enemies of the Israelites: "Here are Thy enemies, O God."[73]

These opening passages of the *Tractatus* already indicate the tenor of Torquemada's thought. What we have before us is a "deadly hatred," which is inspired by evil inclinations ("inflated by the spirit of malice") and by no moral motives at all. Judging by Torquemada's overall presentation, we may assume that he attributed at least part of that "malice" to atavistic and hereditary factors, to a traditional attitude passed from father to son—or, more clearly, to a heritage of hate fanned for many generations, which goes back to the earliest ancestry of the groups. Yet what he wanted above all to make clear by comparing the converso-baiters of his time with the Edomites and Ishmaelites of antiquity was the untruth of the assumption that any backsliding from Christianity (on the part of the conversos), or any zeal for its purity (on the part of their opponents), lay at the bottom of the antagonism that evolved. Just as the hatred of the ancient foes of Israel was not caused by any religious crime or impropriety on the part of the people of Israel (on the contrary, "the divine faith and worship flourished in this people" and "God's name was great in Israel"), so the hatred of the Old Christians for the conversos did not arise, or gain intensity and fury, because of the conversos' religious faults. On the contrary, it is the *success* of the conversos in the religious field, their firm adherence to Christian beliefs, and their wholehearted adoption of the Christian way of life—in brief, it is the fact that the conversos are "Christ's faithful" that has outraged and infuriated their enemies to such a degree, just as the faithfulness of the ancient Israelites to God provoked the hostility of their enemies against them. Thus, as Torquemada saw it, it was not the alleged religious failure of the conversos, but rather their positive religious development, that alarmed the opposition.

Reflected in all this is Torquemada's conviction that the masses of Jews who went over to Christianity were indeed, by the time he wrote his treatise, converted to Christ's faith in the full sense of the word, and their attachment to Christianity was not fictitious but real. And a closer look at the theological terms that Torquemada employed in this instance will project this thought even more clearly.

We have seen that he calls the conversos "Christ's faithful" (*fideles Christi*), which in itself indicates this fact.[74] But in addition he speaks here of "the conversion of the People of Israel to the faith of Christ" (*conversio populi israelitici ad fidem Christi*).[75] Obviously, Torquemada refers here to a *true* conversion as well as to a conversion of a large body of Jews (the *people* of Israel). He further says that the Devil was roused to take action—to attempt to destroy the "faithful of Christ"—by his "jealousy" of the "divine splendor" that glitters from that conversion and of the "human happiness" which it brought about.[76] It is clear that both the "glittering" of the divine glory and the increase of human "happiness" could not come about except by a *true* conversion, and that only such a conversion, and not a false one, could arouse the envy of the Devil. Torquemada's view of the religious condition of the Marranos leaves therefore no room for doubt.

In view of this, Torquemada concluded that the assault upon the Marranos in Toledo by far transcended the interests of the conversos. It was a matter of grave concern to Christendom, because it harbored a threat to Christianity as a whole. That threat stemmed from two sources: the particular *tactics* employed by the rebels in their campaign against the conversos, and the particular *theory*—or, as Torquemada says: the heresy—which they disseminate in the course of their campaign. As agents of the Devil, says Torquemada, the enemies of the Marranos use the Devil's tactics, and their evil doings are cleverly masked. It is by such methods of falsehood and deceit—of the wolf appearing in sheep's clothing, of the wicked wearing the mask of the pious—that they also propagate their dangerous heresy. It is a heresy which "spreads slowly like a cancer" and which the evil-doers are now sparing no effort to push forward into all parts of Christendom.[77]

This brings Torquemada to point out another "symptom" in the activities of the "heretics." He elucidates it by a phrase from the verses which he chose to serve as his theme. "It was said about the persecutors of the faithful people of Israel that they *made a tumult.*" So do also the modern persecutors. What it means is that their evil agitation has reached a new stage and assumed a new form. "The hatred and malice which they carried in their hearts" and "the evil thoughts and blasphemies which they expressed against them secretly" they now do not fear to say publicly, sending moreover defamatory writings, designated as judgments [*sub nomine processuum*], to various parts of the world."[78]

The passage is revealing. We see from it that in Torquemada's opinion, the attack on the conversos in Toledo did not stem from a recent or casual provocation. Hatred for the conversos had been nurtured for a long time, but was not expressed in the open. It was kept underground out of fear. The change brought about by the Toledan outbreak was the surfacing of that hidden, ugly hatred; and the campaign, which was previously conducted underground, now became open and widespread.

"We have seen and read a certain judgment [*processus*] which was prepared in Toledo by certain impious people, rebels to their king and natural lord, and responsible for the crimes committed in Toledo. They sent it through one of their associates to Pope Nicholas V, together with certain letters to the Roman curia. We have carefully read and examined that judgment, and we regard it, from many standpoints, as impious, unjust, most scandalous and full of errors."[79]

The "errors" of which Torquemada speaks are, of course, errors of faith that, if stubbornly upheld, may turn into heretical beliefs. Errors like these cannot be ignored, for if ignored, they may be regarded as approved. As such they may soon "spread like a cancer" and "slip into the souls of the simpleminded."[80] To avert this danger, Torquemada tells us, he felt duty-bound to expose the Toledans' fallacies. Accordingly, "with the aid of our true God and man, our Lord Jesus Christ, and the most glorious Virgin His mother, whose own glory and *the nobility of whose progeny we undertook to defend against the detractors of their race,* we shall show that what the Midianites and Ishmaelites loudly criticized in their blasphemous and impious judgment is false, impious, scandalous, and full of error."[81]

Thus, already at the opening of his treatise Torquemada lets us know that he wrote the work in defense of the "noble" Jewish "race"—the race of Jesus and Mary—against the abuses heaped upon it by the enemies of the conversos. But this is not merely an apologetic writ. More than a "defense of the Jewish race" and an apology for the conversos, the tract is an attack upon the Toledan "heretics" and a severe denunciation of their views and actions. Indeed, Torquemada's aim in writing this tract was to mobilize the major forces of Christendom for an all-out effort to stamp out the "heresy"—i.e., the anti-Marrano race theory of the Toledans—and eliminate it from Christian life.

III

Following these introductory remarks, Torquemada proceeds to examine the *Sentencia* that was issued in Toledo against the conversos. Having studied all the documents relating to the case and having reflected upon the *circumstances* in which the sentence was pronounced—i.e., the rebellion and the related occurrences—Torquemada reached a verdict about the *Sentencia-Estatuto* which was so negative and indeed so damning that only the most scathing denunciation could duly fit its content. His treatise is, in fact, such a denunciation, expressed in the fiery language of the moralist, but backed by the cold reasoning of the scholastic and the hard-hitting arguments of an expert jurist.

The first objective of Torquemada's critique was to strike at the trials that the Toledans had conducted against some of the Marranos on religious grounds. As we have indicated, the findings of these trials served as formal and "factual" grounds to justify the issuance of the *Sentencia*. To determine the measure of the tribunals' reliability appeared therefore to Torquemada of prime importance. Accordingly, he first examined the trials from the standpoint of their rules and procedures; second, from that of the motives of their architects; and finally, from that of the main objectives which these architects sought to achieve. In all these respects he found the trials to have been so grossly illegal that any sentence rendered on their basis must, ipso facto, be null and void.

As for procedure, Torquemada avers, the worthlessness of the trials is evident—first of all, from the quality of the "judges." Psalm 83 refers to them in the words: "Here [O God] are Your enemies," which may well contain a triple allusion. For apart from being enemies of God, as will be proven in the course of the argument, and enemies of their king against whom they rebelled, these people were also *enemies of those on whom they passed judgment*. No fairness or justice could be expected for the indicted when their enemies sat in judgment upon them—a condition which is classed by the book of Deuteronomy among the worst misfortunes that may befall a group: "Our enemies are [our] judges" (32.31). This is why canon law expressly forbids persons suspected of enmity for the accused—let alone persons whose enmity is proven (that is, confirmed by acts of persecution)—to take any part in legal proceedings in which the objects of their animosity are involved. Not only, therefore, should enemies of the Marranos be prohibited from judging them; they should also be prohibited from serving as prosecutors or even bearing witness against the people they hate.[82]

The inadequacy of the judges cannot be questioned also for other weighty reasons. Says the book of Deuteronomy (1.13) about the qualities of those who should be appointed as judges: "Take from amongst yourselves learned and expert men, whose converse [with people] has been approved."[83] In other words, the judges should be both learned in the laws pertaining to the case under jurisdiction and distinguished for their moral way of life. Yet the judges of Toledo were manifestly deficient in both these requirements. Their moral depravity was attested by their actions in the course of the rebellion against the King (they all belonged to the party of the rebels), as well as by the testimonies of most reliable people who know them from their ordinary converse; and their judicial insufficiency is clearly evidenced by their actions in the course of the trials: "They knew thoroughly neither what canon law [*fides canonica*] dictates, nor when one should be judged a heretic."[84] Thus, they should have been disqualified as judges for three valid reasons: their animosity toward the accused, their immoral behavior, and their ignorance of the laws pertaining to the case.

Not unrelated to the quality of the judges was the *haste* which character-ized the proceedings in Toledo. Haste should be avoided in *any* trial, but particularly in one on matters of faith, where erring may involve the most dangerous consequences. Torquemada quotes Cicero in order to emphasize that "haste [in reaching verdicts] is the enemy of Justice."[85] He quotes Job to point out that "a case at law which I did not know, I have most *diligently* investigated" (Job 29:16)[86]; and he quotes Gregory's comment on that very verse that "for delivering sentence we should not ever be precipitate; that things not examined into we should not rashly judge; that *anything heard of a bad nature* should not affect us"; and "that *what is reported everywhere about* we should not credit without proving."[87]

These passages were, of course, carefully chosen by the author of the *Tractatus.* Evidently, what he sought to provide in them was not merely authoritative proof for his contention that judgment should be slow and cautious in the making, but also an answer to the possible claim that extra caution could perhaps be dispensed with in a case such as that of the conversos. For their crimes were "reported everywhere about," to use the language of Gregory the Great, and therefore were in the category of "com-mon knowledge." But "common knowledge," according to Torquemada, is not necessarily an established fact. *It all depends on the sources of that knowledge* and also on the manner of its dissemination. Torquemada was of course well aware of the widespread rumors about the "things of bad nature" that were allegedly committed by the conversos. He obviously believed, however, that these rumors were false, that if an honest and patient inquiry had been made, it would have exposed their malicious origin and, consequently, demon-strated the innocence of the accused. Yet such an inquiry was *not* held, indeed *could* not be held, when enemies of the Marranos were sitting in judgment or acting as their prosecutors.

These, however, were not the *only* improprieties that disqualified the proceedings, according to Torquemada. For enemies of the Marranos, he points out, were serving in these trials not only as judges but also as *witnesses;* and this was to him another reason to consider the proceedings null and void. Those who bore witness against the Marranos, he asserts, were people who only a short time before had attacked them viciously, subjected them to robbery, arson and massacre, and thus proved by their actions that they were not only "enemies" but also criminals of the worst kind. Yet canon law, following the ruling of Pope Eusebius, prohibits such criminals from being admitted as witnesses on the clear understanding that "their voice in such matters" may prove "fatal" to justice.[88]

Having exposed the flaws of the "judges" and "witnesses," Torquemada moves on to hit the Toledan trials from several other judicial angles. "We have read," he says, "that many were punished [following the conclusion of the trials], but we have not read that anyone was cited. No room was given [the accused] for defense, *nor was anyone convicted of heresy or* [*indeed of*] *any other error; nor has anyone confessed voluntarily that he entertained a feeling, or held a belief, which was against what the Church adhered to or preached.*"[89]

From the standpoint of the purposes of our present inquiry, these statements are extremely important, for they contain evidence of far-reaching import which has a direct bearing on our case. But some difficulties must be cleared away before we can determine their precise meaning. Obviously, Torquemada does not mean to suggest—as his statement indicates *prima facie*—that no *formal* convictions of heresy were made by the Toledan courts. For according to his own aforecited statement, a large number of Marranos were brought before these judges, and the very fact that "many" were "punished," and at least "some" were burned at the stake, indicates that such convictions were made and served as bases for punitive actions. What he probably meant was that no conviction declared by the court could be justified by the proceedings. Similarly, when Torquemada says that no voluntary confessions of guilt were made, he did not mean that *no* confessions of guilt of any kind were made in these trials. Since he limited his assertion to "voluntary" confessions, we may conclude that *non*-voluntary confessions were indeed obtained. And that this was so is further suggested by his citings from Augustine and Constantine the Great in support of his conclusion.[90]

Torquemada points out that according to these authorities, no judge is entitled to convict an accused person before the latter has either *voluntarily* confessed his guilt or been proven guilty by *innocent* witnesses.[91] The qualifying words "voluntarily" and "innocent" indicate what Torquemada had in mind. In the Toledan trials, there were of course witnesses who testified against the accused, but they were not "innocent"—they were hostile and criminal; and there must have been confessions, but they were not "voluntary" (i.e., they were made under torture, or threat of torture, or of some other severe harm). Hence, there was no basis for a conviction or, in fact, for any action against the accused; consequently, whatever verdict the judges issued against them was not a conviction in the judicial sense, but simply an arbitrary declaration of guilt, which is morally and legally of no value.

Torquemada, then, simply refuses to dignify the judgments issued in the Toledan trials with the awesome term "conviction of heresy." And he considers this position of his justified, not only by the procedures followed in these trials (which clearly did violence to the laws), but also—and this is necessary to stress—by the nature of the "sins" that were revealed in those procedures and seen by the judges as "heretical." Actually, those "sins," even if committed, had hardly anything to do with heresy. Nevertheless, the conversos who were charged with committing them were declared "heretics" by the Toledan judges. The latter could do this, we gather from Torquemada, because they did not know the laws referring to heresy and, moreover, did not know what heresy was.

"The learned theologians and canonists," says Torquemada, "know that it is one thing to err in matters of faith and another to be a heretic." For "heresy involves not only an error of the mind, but also a stubborn deviation of the will." This is why Augustine said, "I can err, but I am not a heretic."[92] The judges of Toledo did not make this distinction. To them, every irregularity in religious thought or action appeared as sure proof of heresy, or so they declared it to be. Actually, however, they confused errors of the mind, against which no person can be utterly immune, with errors compounded by a corrupt will. We may conclude, then, from Torquemada that some of the conversos displayed in their behavior, or in their expressed religious views, errors of the mind—namely, that some of them were wrong in their understanding of Christianity, or rather of some elements of the faith, because of certain misconceptions of theirs—but this does not mean that they were guilty of possessing a stubborn, deviative, sinful will—that is, of a determination to adhere to their errors even after they had been exposed. To translate the above into lay terms: no desire to get away from Christianity was shown to have existed among the prosecuted Marranos, and not even a single converso was found to have been a Judaizer or a heretic.

This, then, is the meaning of Torquemada's statement that "no convictions of heresy" occurred in the Toledan trials.[93] Coming from Torquemada, the leading canonist and zealous fighter of heresies in Christendom, such a testimony must be given the fullest and most careful consideration. It cannot be sidetracked or judged insignificant as some reckless or trivial pronouncement.

To be sure, it may be argued that Torquemada's sweeping statement is too extreme to be true, that it reflects an exaggerated, one-sided assessment aimed at exonerating the Marranos from guilt. Theoretically, such an assumption is legitimate; but what evidence do we have to support it? None, as far as we know. But other considerations may likewise undermine, if not nullify, that argument. For it is precisely the fact that Torquemada formulated his conclusion in such an unreserved manner—that is, in a way that left him no room for retreat—which lends his testimony the greatest weight. Habituated by his customary thinking and writing not to make statements which he could not prove, Torquemada must have had ample evidence at his disposal to demonstrate his contention, should the need arise. In addition, he must have realized that by making a declaration so extreme in form on so crucial an issue, he was laying on the line his hard-won reputation as a responsible Church leader, as "Defender of the Faith" and as the Church's foremost expert on heresy.

IV

These conclusions are markedly bolstered by Torquemada's further criticisms of the trials, which steadily become more emphatic, and his reiterated denials of the Toledan allegations about the Marranos' unfaithfulness. Since the criticisms and denials are interrelated, we shall cite them here together.

"The senselessness and injustice and, therefore, the nullity of the judgment [that was issued in Toledo] is demonstrated by the assumptions upon which it was founded, many of which are false, mendacious and malicious."[94] Such an assumption, according to Torquemada, was embodied in the claim that it was a matter of public knowledge (*publica fama*), presumably stemming from trustworthy individuals, that "most of the conversos practice circumcision, deny the true divinity of Christ, deny, in addition, the presence of His body in the sacrament of the Eucharist," et cetera. "It is strange," adds Torquemada, "that these wicked people did not fear to say that these things were 'notorious' when not even one of those converts could be shown, either by his own voluntary confession or by statements of innocent witnesses, ever to have said, after receiving baptism, that he believed in anything except what is believed by Mother Church herself."[95]

This statement is undoubtedly one of the most significant testimonies in the entire controversy (both old and new) over the Marranos' religious condition. One cannot help noting at this point that while the alleged findings against the Marranos by their enemies were repeatedly reported in scholarly literature, and generally treated as representing the "facts," not even once did anyone adduce the counterevidence of the cardinal in an attempt to arrive at the historical truth, or at least to present a balanced account of all available sources. Indeed, regardless of the variety of the approaches and objectives of the scholars involved, one is compelled to conclude that the treatment of the Marranos in the court of history was fundamentally not much different from that accorded them by the Toledan judges. Here as there, the evidence relied upon was fundamentally one-sided. Here as there, the accused party was not even given a chance at self-defense.

In the passage just cited, Torquemada, as we have seen, denounced in the most vehement language the contention of the Toledans that it was "notorious" that "most of the conversos" practiced circumcision, denied the divinity of Christ and other Christian dogmas; he branded this declaration "false, mendacious and malicious" and, in fact, considered it so palpably absurd as to demonstrate, by itself, the "nullity" of the whole trial. To be sure, by this denial of the claim that *most Marranos were Judaizers*, Torquemada does not tell us that, in his opinion, there were no Judaizers among them at all. Without contradicting his defense of the Marranos, he might have recognized the existence of "some" Judaizers, and if so, we should see whether, on the basis of his assertion regarding "most of the conversos," we can determine his view about the existence or proportion of the Judaizers in the Marrano group. It seems clear that had their number, in his opinion, comprised about 50 percent of the conversos, he would not have denounced the contention of the Toledans in such vehement terms; after all, the distance between 50 percent (a half), and 51 percent (a majority) is so small as to preclude any criticism of an assessment that replaced one figure with the other. We may further assume that Torquemada would have refrained from such harsh criticism of the Toledans had, in his judgment, the number of Judaizers amounted, say, to 49 percent, or generally approximated half their number. Again the slight difference between the figures mentioned and a "majority" of the conversos would have been too insignificant to matter, especially since the reference would necessarily be to *assessments* that could easily—and legitimately—differ. Hence, if Torquemada was so outraged by the assertion that the "*majority* of the Marranos were Judaizers"—so outraged as to denounce it as a vicious lie—the difference between this allegation and what he considered to be the truth must have been very large indeed; and consequently, we must conclude that if he recognized the existence of any Judaizers at all, they constituted, in his opinion, a distinct minority—so distinct and so limited that he could say with certainty that the great majority of the conversos were faithful to Christianity and the Church that represents it.

In fact, he said this much and more when time and again he designated the Marranos, taken as a whole, as "Christ's faithful"; and this repeated designation, together with his view of the findings of the Toledan inquiry, inescapably leads us to the conclusion that, in his opinion, the Judaizers—again, if he admitted their existence—did not constitute even a substantial minority; that they were in fact so scarce that the accusers, in their trials, could not prove the existence of even a single genuine Judaizer, however anxious they were to support their claims by some palpable example. Thus, the Toledan trials, in the cardinal's view, far from proving the Marranos' guilt, actually exonerated them from infidelity. This is what is implied in Torquemada's outcry: How remarkable it is that in view of this failure (this *total* failure of theirs to offer *legal* proof), the accusers still dare to refer to—and rely on—the "notoriety" of their assertions!

Torquemada thus strikes hard at the notion that Judaic practices were rampant among the Marranos, but he also tears apart the Toledan assertions concerning the Marranos' inward beliefs. Theoretically, the Marranos could have avoided (for fear, or other reasons) the practice of circumcision and other Jewish rites, and yet inwardly continue to believe in the Jewish articles of faith; or they could have performed all Christian ceremonies and inwardly deny all Christian dogmas. But what emerges from Torquemada's aforecited statement is that this was not the case at all. What we gather from it is that the Marranos, taken generally, were devoted to Christianity in thought as in deed; for he vehemently rejects the Toledans' charges that they did not believe in the divinity of Christ, in His bodily presence in the sacrament of the Eucharist, and in all other sacraments, tenets, and dogmas of Catholic Christianity. Hence, they were not *deniers* of Christianity or *indifferent* to it, or *disbelievers* in both religions (i.e., Judaism and Christianity), as their enemies had charged, but faithful and convinced followers of Christianity—and of Christianity alone.

We have dwelt at some length upon these passages because they contain Torquemada's rejection of the main religious charges leveled at the conversos, and also because to understand them properly, we ought to consider what they *imply* no less than what they explicitly say. For the same reasons, we shall now touch upon his view of the immediate source of these charges.

We have already seen him criticize the Toledans for basing their judgments on "rumors of bad nature"—a criticism we could gather from the statement to that effect which he quoted from Gregory the Great. Now he reverts to the same criticism, but in a far more outspoken and forceful manner. At this point he speaks clearly of the conversos' "public repute" (*publica fama*) on which their adversaries based their decisions—i.e., those reflected in their so-called legal actions. This is no doubt the same "notoriety" to which both the Petition and the *Sentencia* referred to justify their proposed treatment of the conversos.[96] Torquemada regards as plain nonsense the claim that the public rumor concerning the conversos stems from "honorable and trustworthy persons."[97] In fact, he suggests, such rumors could originate only in the minds of the most malicious individuals capable of the most outrageous lies. Moreover, Torquemada points out, the very judges who relied on that *fama* were among those who produced and spread it. They were indeed the architects and promoters of the campaign conducted against the conversos.

Can such a campaign, which is based on sheer lies, gain widespread credulity and mass support? Torquemada evidently had no doubt about it. This is why he said that the arrows of the accusers—i.e., the vilifications—were "wounding" arrows—that is, capable of undermining the reputation of the conversos—and furthermore, that these "wounds," unless "treated," may prove *mortal*—that is, pose a grave threat to the very existence of the New Christians in Spain. Torquemada alludes to this conviction of his by employing the verses from Psalms and Jeremiah: *"Their throat is an open sepulcher,"* while "their tongue is manipulated deceitfully,"[98] and he airs his feeling of lurking danger, and of the need for divine intervention, by the words of prayer found in the same psalm: "Judge them, O God!"[99]

This, then, is how Torquemada viewed the trials staged in Toledo against the conversos: Their injustice was evident from the standpoint of the rules, laws, and regulations established by the Holy Fathers to make a trial fair and respectable *(rationalis et honestus);* it was indicated by the haste, and also the lightheadedness, in which the trials were conducted; by the worthlessness of the witnesses; by the lack of proper judicial order; by the nature of the accusations, which were founded on mere rumor; by the quality of the judges, who were enemies of the accused and, in addition, ignorant of the laws; and above all, it was demonstrated by the crucial fact that none of the accused was proven guilty "either of heresy or of any other error."[100] To put it in a nutshell, Torquemada was convinced that the tribunal established by the rebels in Toledo to sentence Marranos on religious charges was nothing but a kangaroo court: its cases were prejudged; its evidence fabricated; its purpose was not to administer justice, but to punish enemies.

V

We have seen that in his treatise Torquemada pointed out two main reasons for the violent attack mounted against the conversos in Toledo. He defined them as (a) ethnic (or racial); and (b) moral (or religious), asserting that both reflect strong traditions that go back to ancient times. Now he added a third reason to explain the sudden burst of animosity at that particular time and place. He believed that while the old, historic enmity lay at the root of the outbreak in Toledo, the actual developments were triggered by motives originating in the city in January 1449.

"It is clear," says Torquemada, that the adversaries of the conversos "proceeded against them with robberies and murders after having turned, in their conspiracies and machinations, against their natural lord" [i.e., Juan II]. Then, "to give their crimes some semblance of virtue [*honestas*], they decided to stage a trial over invented heresies."[101]

In this explanation of the developments in Toledo, Torquemada shared the view which, as we shall see, was held by many conversos in Castile: There would have been no such outburst against the Marranos in Toledo if not for the antimonarchic rebellion. It was in the course of their rising against the King and his administration in the city that the rebels took action against the Marranos, who did not share their conspiratorial designs. While taking this action, they gave vent to their old hatred which, in turn, led them to commit more crimes; but the hatred was soon joined by fear of the punishments the King might inflict upon them for their crimes. In consequence, the evil-doers sought to "justify" their misdeeds—or rather cover up their criminal intentions—by claiming virtuous motives for their acts. Whence came the second phase of their activities: *They invented the fiction of an existing heresy, and proceeded to prove it by a formal trial.*

Motives are usually connected with goals; and the goals of the trials, as conceived by the Toledans, evolved from their motives as fruits from seeds. Torquemada did not view the rebels' actions, however, as proceeding without a conscious design. Carefully planned, the trial as a whole, and all its actions, procedures and objectives, were determined in a "council of iniquity and malice"[102]—just as the verse of Psalms says: "They have taken *counsel* against Thy people with a malignant scheme."[103]

The "malignant scheme" of the plotters of Toledo went far beyond their aim of merely justifying or covering up their criminal actions. It held out for them the promise of attaining two objectives: (a) to meet their immediate needs; and (b) to satisfy their deep-seated hatred. Thus, the immediate purpose of the trial was to cast a suspicion of heresy on the conversos—and thereby exonerate the rebels' misconduct, while the suspicion was also to serve as an excuse for a ruling which denied the conversos their rights. Nothing reveals the motive of that excuse, and thereby also its utter falsehood, as the *universality* of the ruling referred to—namely, that it was to apply to *all* conversos without any distinction whatever. If one might assume that the authors of the trial had doubts about the religious fidelity of *some* Marranos—that is, among the ordinary conversos *(mediocres personae)*—it is clear that they could not make such a mistake with respect to those leading conversos *(magnae personae)* who, thanks to "their known and numerous virtues, attained the highest distinction in the Church and the nobility, and [consequently] command outstanding authority, ecclesiastical as well as secular."[104] And yet the *Sentencia* applies to the elite no less than to conversos of a lower station. Psalm 83 alluded to such action in its saying: "They contrived against thy *saints*."[105] "Contrived"—for this ruling against people so highly reputed for their moral propriety and religious devotion was also deliberate and had a special purpose. The purpose was to undermine their great prestige and influence, to cast a slur upon their integrity, "to maculate them by their venomous blasphemies,"[106] and thus destroy the moral pillars on which the converso community relies.

Since no religious motive can be ascribed to their plan for prohibiting the Marranos to serve in public office, or even to testify in a court of law, it is clear that the real reasons for the *Sentencia-Estatuto* were of a different order. As Torquemada saw it, the main purpose of the enactment was not just to impose some sanctions on the Marranos, or even to reduce them to an inferior class. The main purpose was beyond all this. Just as the trials for heresy served as preparation for the issuance of the *Sentencia,* so was the *Sentencia* a preliminary step toward something far more sinister and destructive. What, then, were the enemies of the Marranos after? Torquemada's answer was unequivocal: the Marranos' total extermination.

Torquemada no doubt reached this conclusion on the basis of intelligence he received from many quarters; but the record of the trials held in Toledo might have served him as decisive evidence. Judging by his analysis of their proceedings, everything that occurred in those trials convinced him that a murderous drive was afoot and that it was too incendiary and too ferocious to be satisfied with the lives it had taken so far. Thus, the executions that took place in Toledo were meant to be merely a prelude to an action that was to be so large and so monstrous as to involve the liquidation of the whole Marrano group. Not in vain did the Toledan agitators class all Marranos as suspect of heresy. For it was only a step from such vilification to a full-fledged, brazen accusation of heresy, and thence to a conviction based on faulty evidence, which would be quite sufficient for these so-called judges to send more innocent victims to the stake. Indeed, so certain was Juan de Torquemada of the verity of this conclusion that he could declare without hesitance: *"This is their diabolical plan! This is their evil design!"*[107] It is the same plan that was followed by Haman: to exterminate the whole Jewish people—man, woman, and child. This is the plan that called forth the prayer of Mordecai: "Have pity, O Lord, on Thy people, as they want to destroy us and wipe out Thine inheritance."[108]

Thus Torquemada, at the conclusion of his discussion of the procedures, performers and goals of the trials, brings the reader back to the thesis he presented at the outset of his work. The heirs of Ishmael and Edom are again on the move. Those who sought to destroy the Jewish people—the People of God—in days gone by have made a new, all-out attempt to carry out their old design. In their struggle for existence, the Marranos have entered a phase which is most crucial and perilous—virtually a battle of life and death. They face the same danger that their forefathers did in the days of Haman, their most ruthless enemy, and once again they need Divine help to extricate themselves from the Satanic web.

III. CHRISTIANITY AND THE THEORIES OF RACE

I

In the preceding chapter we have seen Torquemada diagnosing the troubles that broke out in Toledo as a new manifestation of an old, and ever-latent social disease. He pinpointed its roots, described its course, and indicated the final goal of its thrust. Now we shall see him concentrate on a development which was hardly discerned in that disease before—an offshoot of the malady which threatened, in his opinion, to turn the disease into a universal plague.

This offshoot was the theory of race that was born, bred and nursed in Toledo, until it grew to its full proportions. It rested on the view that the Marranos belonged to a race predisposed to crime and evil, and therefore were naturally incapable of following a Christian way of life. On the strength of these charges, the Marranos could be prejudged—either as heretics or as potential heretics—before their trial began.

We have seen that the Relator viewed the race theory—and the racial persecution of the Marranos in Toledo—as the edge of a tide that, unless checked in time, would rise above the limits of the Marrano society, both in Toledo and Spain's other regions, and threaten to inundate the whole Christian world. This was Torquemada's view, too. He therefore decided to attack every part of that theory, reveal its full meaning, and expose its true face.

To support their thesis, Torquemada knew, the propagators of the race theory had presented many arguments, mostly of a legal and theological nature, by which they sought to show that it fully conformed to the teachings of Christianity. That they felt the need to prove this conformity was, of course, in no way surprising to him. No theory involving human relations, or issues of morality, society and religion, could be considered valid in medieval Christendom unless it was demonstrated to be "Christian"—that is, compatible with Christian law and dogma. Hence, Church approval, formal or informal, was considered vital for any doctrine, while Church rejection could be judged as fatal to any new or old idea. To the vast majority of the public, such rejection meant that the opinion in question was heretical, or otherwise anti-Christian, and hence untrue.

It was therefore for tactical as well as doctrinal reasons that Torquemada chose the allegations of the Toledans concerning the relationship between their race theory and Christianity as the major target of his counterattack. His task, as he saw it, was to show the falsehood of the contention that the race theory was a *Christian* doctrine; that the theory was, in fact, abhorrent to Christianity, opposed to its principles and practices throughout the ages; and furthermore that it constituted a dangerous stumbling block on the road of

Christian advancement. Once he proved this, Torquemada believed, the theory would be dealt a crushing blow; inevitably, it would invite the wrath, the opposition, and ultimately the anathema of the entire Church.

II

Noticing that the race theory of the Toledans consisted of two fundamental notions—one which assumed an inseparable relationship between the racial and moral qualities of man, and another which imputed to the Jewish race a predisposition to evil—Torquemada set out to demonstrate the falsehood of each of these propositions. Since the first notion was the cornerstone of the Toledans' race doctrine, Torquemada chose to attack it first. Undermining the major premise of a theory meant to him, as a logician, to shatter its foundations and thereby inevitably bring about the collapse of the entire structure.

Now, according to Torquemada, the Toledans' premise was that "anyone who is evil, or of an evil or damned stock, will always be rightly presumed to be evil and condemned on the grounds of that kind of evil for which he was originally pronounced bad, until [at least] four generations have passed [from the time of the original sinner]."[109] Even then the presumption of evil will remain until the descendant of evil stock demonstrates by his behavior that he is free of his ancestors' guilt. The racial doctrinaires of Toledo claimed that all this was embodied in canon law.[110]

Torquemada brands this claim, too, "false, blasphemous and erroneous."[111] Not only is such a view not found in any part of canon law, but canon law is expressly opposed to such thinking. Other Christian authorities also made it clear that they differed with that view; and the practices of the Church and Christian society corroborate this legal and ideological stand. To be sure, Pope Boniface VIII stated that "a bad seed is presumed to be *always* bad,"[112] but this must be understood in the same sense in which it was conceived by the Gloss[113]—namely, that the person designated as "bad seed" is presumed to be bad as long as he is not known to have repented.[114] This interpretation, of course, gives the law an entirely different complexion. "Seed" is understood by Torquemada to refer simply to a man of a certain "type," and not to one who provides a moral link in a chain of generations: "There is nothing in the decretals to bear witness to the effect that he who comes from an evil or damned stock is presumed to be always evil and condemned" for the crimes of his ancestors. There is nothing there about four generations either. Those who thus interpret the law, or so use it in support of their "heretical depravity," cannot be accused of mere incomprehension. They are deliberate "falsifiers of the law."[115]

That such a notion could never be accepted as a guiding principle by the

Christian religion is also evident, according to Torquemada, from the very history of Christianity. Since all Christians descended either from gentiles—of whom it was said: "Evil is their stock, and their wickedness is ingrained,"[116] as all of them were idolaters of the worst kind—or from Jews, whose race, "according to these malevolents," had also been condemned as evil—it follows that all Christians, including their supreme leaders (i.e., the emperors, kings and nobles) were to be suspected of the crime of infidelity and idol worship for at least four generations.[117] But this had never been the practice in Christendom; nor has the Church ever considered such a view either in the past or in the present. To illustrate this unchangeable conduct of the Church by an example from his own generation, Torquemada says:

> In our own time there were converted from paganism to Christianity the illustrious king of Poland, the father of the present king, with a large number of nobles and a countless multitude.[118] Later, in the days of Pope Eugene IV, the king of Bosnia, his Queen, and many other nobles were converted to Christianity from the Manichaean errors.[119] In addition, almost daily many of the Mohammedans are being convinced [of the Christian truth]. It would be a major scandal and intolerable sacrilege to say that all these people would have to be suspected, at least until the fourth generation, of idolatry and the errors which they and their fathers had upheld at some time.[120]

But the fallacy of the view embraced by the Toledans can be seen not only from the way the Church has treated all converts to Christianity throughout its existence; it can also be seen from the unreserved manner in which both Holy Writ and the sacred canons censured and condemned that view. Thus says the prophet Ezekiel: "The son shall not bear the iniquity of the father, nor shall the father bear the iniquity of the son; the soul that sinned, it shall die."[121] The lesson of the verse is quite clear: No ethnic relationship, however close, can transfer guilt in any direction. It is the individual alone, and in no way his stock, that is responsible for his actions.[122]

Torquemada points out that this biblical position, which clearly refutes the Toledans' view, was fully accepted by the Fathers of the Church and became an essential part of canon law. Accordingly, Augustine said: "The seed of man, from whatever kind of man, is the creation of God," and therefore "at no time shall be evil in itself." Hence, "from whatever source men be born, if they do not follow the vices of their parents, and worship God aright, they shall be honest and safe." Moreover, Augustine says in expounding the same principle, or rather its implications, in an opposite direction: "Just as the good sons of adulterers are no defense of adultery, so the evil sons of married persons are no charge against marriage."[123] The moral value of man, in brief, cannot be determined either by his progeny or by his ancestry; for it must be clear that, *unlike* ethnically, morally each man is a world unto himself.

This central point of prophetic morality was stressed, Torquemada points out, by other Church authorities as well. Quoting John Chrysostom, he shows that, like Augustine, this saint too clearly indicated the impossibility for anyone to inherit or bequeath moral worth. "For it cannot, nay, it cannot be that a man should be good or bad, obscure or glorious, either by the virtue or the vice of his forefathers."[124] Is there no limit to the evil of the parents wherein this rule no longer applies? Chrysostom's answer is unequivocal: There is no limit at all. "A man can have as a mother a prostitute, *or what you will*, and he can take no hurt thereby. For if the whoremonger himself, once changed, is no disgrace because of his former life, much more will the wickedness of his ancestry have no power to bring to shame an offspring of a harlot, if he be virtuous."[125] In brief, "the iniquity of the parents cannot hurt the good, just as the probity of the parents cannot help the wicked."[126]

Since these statements of Augustine and Chrysostom are incorporated in canon law, and since the law includes similar statements of such Church authorities as Pope Leo and others,[127] it is obvious that this is not only the theological, but also the legal position of Christianity. Consequently, any willful deviation from this position must be considered heretical.

III

We have seen that whereas, according to the racists, morality is based on the natural predilection of the group or stock to which a man belongs—and therefore it is, in a way, *predetermined*, according to Christianity it is founded on *individual* responsibility and, hence, on man's free will. This difference in itself is sufficient to indicate the depth of the chasm between the two views. Nevertheless, Torquemada noted, the antagonism between them goes even deeper. For not only is the race theory opposed to the major tenets of Christian *ethics;* it also conflicts with certain *dogmas* of Christianity on which the whole faith rests.

To prove this point, Torquemada presents a series of arguments that appear irrefutable. To begin with, he says, to assume that certain converts are not freed upon conversion from all their previous sins is contrary to the belief in Christ's *Passion* as upheld by all true Christians. According to that belief, the Passion is unlimited in its power to efface sin, regardless of the type of crime committed or the kind of individual involved. When the apostle Paul said: "Because God was in Christ, reconciling the *world* unto Himself, not imputing their trespasses unto them," he indicated that this reconciliation could embrace the whole of mankind (the "world") and all transgressions,

without any exception.[128] Yet this precious, universal and all-inclusive remedy, provided by Christ's Passion and death, the remedy that enables *anyone*
turning to Christ to come to Him clean of his past sins, these wicked people
try to "restrict" or deny, and thus to "empty" of its efficacy.[129] They do so
by claiming that Jewish converts to Christianity, no matter how sincere their
conversion was, must, by virtue of their descent, be held suspect as addicts
to their "past crimes"—that is, as devotees of the old religion and their
predecessors' way of life. This means that in their case, Christ's Passion and
death are powerless to effect the swift and radical change they can effect in
others.

But the race theory denies not only the full and true effectiveness of the
Passion; it also contradicts the teaching of the Church about the sacraments
deriving their power from the Passion. Referring to the sacraments of baptism and penitence, Torquemada first indicates the paramount importance
Christianity ascribes to baptism as a purgative of sin. Citing the words of
Ambrosius on baptism as the "transfer from earth to heaven,"[130] he adds that
this saying forms part of canon law, and quotes the remainder of that canonized statement to make clear what was meant by that "transfer." Indeed, the
Church holds, says Torquemada, that through baptism one passes "from sin
to life, from guilt to grace, from impurity to holiness"—in brief, one "rises
from the dead."[131] Nowhere does the Church make the slightest suggestion
that the power of the sacrament is nullified or lessened when administered
to converts of Israelitic origin. When Ezekiel said: "And I shall sprinkle clean
water upon you, and you shall be clean from *all* your filthiness," he indicated
what was to happen to anyone upon whom the holy water would be sprin-
kled.[132]

To show further how baptism was slighted by the race theorists and how
much their conception of this sacrament clashed with the most hallowed
beliefs of Christendom, Torquemada points out that according to the Toledans, baptism can have no effect on small children, for they say that such
children too must be "suspect of the sins of their parents."[133] But, says
Torquemada, the Church teaches that not only does baptism "blot out the
original guilt, and [thereby] removes damnation, but also all suspicion of [the
continued effect of] all ancestral transgressions *(delictorum priorum).*"[134] Thus,
the position of the Church on this issue is diametrically opposed to that of
the Toledans—so opposed, indeed, that canon law condemns as heretic any
Christian who questions the efficacy or usefulness of baptism administered to
small children.[135] It is thus heretical, blasphemous and foolish to insist that
any child who was properly baptized is still attached to his forefathers' crimes
when, according to Christianity, he enters the Christian world completely
sinless and free of guilt.

This theological discussion of baptism in relation to the Toledans' race theory was not merely of theoretical value. What was involved here was the perception and evaluation of the position of the conversos in the Christian world. By the time the racial ideology burst forth, the overwhelming majority of the conversos in Spain had been Christian as long as they could remember. They were baptized in their infancy or early childhood, and as such they could not be anything but Christian. We have seen how the Relator pointed this out and how he objected to the fact that people born in Christianity, or baptized in their infancy—as were, no doubt, most New Christians in his time—were regarded as *converts* to Christianity from Judaism.[136] As they had never been associated with the Jewish religion either spiritually or practically, they could not have been converted from it, and thus they must be seen as *originally* Christian as all other Christians are. Now, however, the Toledans' race theory disclaimed this contention. For no matter how early the date of his baptism and how Christian his entire education, a scion of Jews cannot become a true Christian because he carries the blight of Judaism in his blood. Hence, the whole converso group, even if all its members were baptized in their infancy, must be considered Jewish not only ethnically but religiously as well.

The struggle for the traditional view of Christianity insofar as baptism of children was concerned was therefore the struggle for the right of *most* conversos to be regarded as *non*converted Christians. Moreover, it was the struggle for the right of their future descendants, however remote, to be so regarded, and thus viewed as equal to all other Christians who were baptized in their infancy. Torquemada does not refer to this explicitly, but the implications of his argument are quite clear.

And equally clear are the implications of his statements on the contradiction between the race theory as propounded in Toledo and the dogma of penitence as upheld by Christianity. Penitence, as Jerome said, is the "second plank" we hold on to "after the shipwreck," and its effect may be as decisive and far-reaching as that of baptism itself.[137] Here again the questions at issue were not purely theological. The matter concerned a section of the conversos, though by that time only a small minority—i.e., the survivors in 1450 of the great conversions of 1391 and 1412. What had happened to these converts during those decades when they lived as Christians within Christendom? According to the Toledans, nothing had happened; these converts from Judaism had remained inwardly Jewish and opposed to Christianity as they were originally—that is, in 1391 and 1412. The reason: they were *organically* incapable of a real change of heart. But Torquemada did not subscribe to this view. The evidence he possessed led him to the conclusion that the views of the converts in the middle of the century were far different from those they held in 1412, let alone in 1391. By claiming that the verses concerning penitence in Ezekiel (18.21–22)[138] clearly prove that it is a *"very grave error"* to "hold under suspicion the converts to Christianity from the people of Israel,"[139] Torquemada reveals his view of the conversos in his time, who were not born to Christian parents but came over to Christianity themselves. He viewed them as true and honest Christians who had performed the penitence of which Ezekiel spoke: *They had turned from all their past sins*—namely, the Judaism to which they had adhered; *they had done all that is lawful and right*— namely, behaved as good Christians; and therefore *none of their former transgressions shall be remembered against them*. Had Torquemada thought that these converts were still Jews, or crypto-Jews opposed to Christianity, he would not have considered them "penitents," and consequently would not have applied to their case the cited verse and the lesson he derived from it. In brief, Torquemada's argument on penitence shows that, in his belief, the survivors of the original converts (or at least their great majority) had abandoned Judaism, de facto as de jure, and that their adherence to Christianity was by and large a conscious act of will as well as of mind.

It is obvious that Torquemada could not sanction the assumption that a sincere conversion from Judaism was "impossible," and his views on this question, perhaps more than anything else, made manifest his conviction of the unbridgeable gap between the doctrines of Christianity and the race theory of the Toledans. For if that theory is right—that is, if certain moral deficiencies are *inherited,* and are so deep-rooted that they may *never* be extirpated—then Christianity, with its insistence upon individual moral responsibility and its view that baptism, penitence and the Passion have unlimited powers of moral regeneration, is of course in the wrong. But since Christianity cannot be wrong, since it is the embodiment of all truth, it follows that the race theory is false, nonsensical, the product of misguided and perverted minds.

IV

Having thus destroyed, as he believed, the foundations of the race theory propounded by the Toledans, Torquemada proceeded to his second assignment—to demonstrate the fallacy of the Toledan views concerning the *Jewish* race. Ostensibly, it seemed a superfluous task. Since he had proved, as he was sure, that Christianity is opposed to the notion that moral corruption is inheritable—and that the road to salvation is barred to some people because of their, or their parents' sins—had he not also proven simultaneously the worthlessness of these views when they referred to the Jews? All that was necessary at this point, it seems, was to apply a simple syllogism, and reach the inescapable conclusion. Nevertheless, Torquemada devoted the next eight chapters of the treatise—about half of his work against the Midianites and Ishmaelites—to a detailed and exhaustive refutation of the contentions advanced by the Toledans concerning the Jewish race.

Why?

The reasons, which are reflected in the contents of the refutation, appear to have been the following. To begin with, Torquemada considered it improper to avoid discussing the main issue of the debate simply because the argument of the opponents could be quashed by means of a deduction. In view of the aspersions that were cast on the conversos and created such a furor of controversy, it was vital, he thought, for the converso cause to show that the race theory was wrong, not only on grounds of general principle but also—and especially—in its particular application to the conversos as a group. To prove this effectively, it was clear to him, one must go beyond the theoretical foundations; one must show specifically what the conversos were *not* and, even more important, what they actually *were* and how they should be seen and judged by Christians.

To achieve this, however, it was necessary to present the traditional, authentic Christian view of the Jews, their race, and their converts to Christ's faith. For Christianity indeed took a *special* position on what may be called the Jewish question; yet, as Torquemada saw it, it was not the position imputed to Christianity by the Toledans. In fact, it was the very opposite of theirs.

There is no doubt that Torquemada came to believe that his own view of the Jews coincided with the true, undiluted, and unperverted position of the Church toward the Jewish people. Nevertheless, taken as a whole, Christian literature of the preceding fourteen centuries must lead the unbiased, discerning student to question the validity of his belief. For in fact, there was a chasm between the conception of the Jews shared by almost all Christian authorities and Torquemada's perception of the Jews as a people in general historical perspective.

It would seem unnecessary here to go into a survey that would clearly demonstrate this point. But some remarks seem pertinent. From the earliest Gospels through the Fathers of the Church down to Torquemada's own period, Christian writers, with very few exceptions, had painted the Jew in ever darker colors, the emerging picture becoming ever more unpleasant and indeed more repulsive. What is more, this portrayal, in one way or another, was made to rely in all its details on the Bible—that is, on biblical statements about the Jews according to Christian interpretation. Now, this interpretation had never lost sight of the central act in the Christian historic drama—i.e., the Passion and the deicide, for which the Jews were held responsible; and when it touched upon the *reason* for their conduct, it did not, with rare exceptions, ascribe it to their ignorance (although this was indicated by Jesus

Himself) or to the frailness of man's self-control, but to a permanent, unrestrainable passion for evil which gushed forth repeatedly from the depth of their being. And so the image of the Jew as ultimately crystallized had the lasting features of the enemy of God—indeed, the enemy of all goodness—the sinister, "perfidious" and "treacherous" creature who was acting in the service of the devil.

Since this was the concept that pervaded Christian thinking, and since this very concept served as basis for the race theory, it is obvious that Torquemada, in contesting that theory, was from the outset at a disadvantage. What made the contest at all possible was that the above described view of the Jews, although dominant, was by no means uniform. In the great variety of attitudes and notions to be found in Christian biblical exegesis, there were here and there pro-Jewish strains and occasional expressions favorable to the Jews. These departures from tradition served Torquemada as points of reliance for his view of the Jews and, at least, as partial justification of it. But of course he could not ignore the fact that the major currents of Christian literature, no less than the tides of popular opinion, were running strongly against him; and it was, no doubt, this particular fact that determined his basic strategy.

That strategy is not hard to discern. To be able to claim the support of Christianity—or of Christian literature *as a whole*—Torquemada had to find in it a common denominator which, while not contrary to his own views, conflicted with those of his opponents. He came upon such a common denominator thanks to the tactical blunders of the racists who, for both psychological and ideological reasons, could not curb their tendency to go to extremes. In consequence, Torquemada could freely assert that all the theoretical armory he amassed and used in defense of his own views was aimed at achieving only one objective: to prove that the Jewish race *(genus iudeorum)* had never been and was not—as the adversaries claimed—totally rejected or "entirely condemned."[140]

This limited objective he could always attain, and essentially it met his primary need. Torquemada held fast to this position, from which he emerged from time to time to seize more ground. These moves resembled sallies into hostile territory which differed in the depth of their penetration, as well as in the measure of their attainments. But they were all anchored in Torquemada's awareness that he could always return to the safe haven—the limited base from which he set out.

It must be pointed out that Torquemada's tactic was to move to the positive from the negative. His plan of demonstration, therefore, included these steps: first, to make clear that the teachings of Christianity do not sanction the Toledans' view about the Jews; and second, to lay bare the fallacy of the proofs offered by the Toledans in support of their view.[141]

Bridge and gate of Alcántara and Castle of San Servando. Toledo.
Ministerio de Comercio y Turismo. Madrid.

Pedro IV of Aragón.
Museo de Arte de Cataluña, Barcelona. Mas.

Enrique II of Castile.
Capilla de los Reyes Nuevos. Toledo, Cathedral. Mas.

Pedro I of Castile.
Museo Arqueológico, Madrid.

Sepulcher of Juan II of Castile.
Cartuja de Miraflores, Burgos. Mas.

Saint Vincent Ferrer, attributed to
Juan Reixach.
Valencia, Cathedral. Mas.

Walls of the Palace of Pedro I (Alcázares Reales).   Seville.
Ministerio de Comercio y Turismo. Madrid.

Sepulcher of Alvaro de Luna.
Toledo, Cathedral. Mas.

Burgos on the River Arlanzón. An engraving by J. Carter after a drawing by Daniel Roberts. *Biblioteca Nacional, Madrid. Archivo Iconográfico, Barcelona.*

Battle of Higueruela, 1431. Sala de las batallas.
El Escorial. Mas.

Toledo on the River Tajo. A general view.

Thus, he not only managed to demolish the Toledans' basic positions. He also paved the way for the acceptance of his own view, however novel and controversial, of the Jewish people. We need not wonder at these methods of the cardinal, which remind us of tactics used in courts of law. Doubtless Torquemada saw himself standing before the court of public opinion and of history, and he also believed that the final judgment might depend on the success of his defense. Indeed, judging by his arguments, he was not only an apologist and a controversialist of a high order; he was also a great lawyer.

V

Turning at this point to Torquemada's demonstrations, we should start with his determined attempt to set forth the position of Christianity toward the Jewish people by adducing scriptural evidence on the Jews. Of this evidence he first presents a statement which seems to touch directly on the issue. It is from Psalm 94 (Verse 14):

> For the Lord will not cast off His people,
> Neither will he forsake His inheritance.

To a layman, especially a modern scholar, who understands correctly the meaning of the verse and has no doubts as to who was referred to by "His people" and "His inheritance," the verse offers, of course, a smashing denial of the Toledans' assertions. But as much as Torquemada might agree with this conclusion, he could not rely on that verse alone. He had to take into account the Christological interpretations that had been imposed upon the biblical text, and these gave quite a different meaning to the terms "His people" and "His inheritance." To present therefore the "true" meaning of the verse, he had to consult certain Christian commentaries, the common authoritative guides of all Christians who read the Bible in the 15th century—such as the Interlinear Gloss of Anselm of Laon, the Ordinary Gloss of Walafrid Strabo, and the *Postillae* of Nicholas de Lyra. These commentaries (especially the Ordinary Gloss) contain selections from the works of the Church Fathers that include interpretations of the biblical text. Yet none of these selections was exhaustive, and Christian students always felt free to roam the vast field of Christian literature in search of comments that could support their views or answer their specific queries.

We shall now take another look at the verse cited above from Psalm 94:

> For the Lord will not cast off his people,
> Neither will he forsake his inheritance.

"How this authority," says Torquemada, "should be understood as refer-ring to the Jewish people *(de populo iudeorum)*, thus proving the error of the calumniators," is shown by the comment of St. Augustine, the "outstanding light of the Church," on Psalm 79, 1–2.[142] That Psalm, too, speaks of the "Inheritance of God," and it says: "O God, the heathen have come into your inheritance; they have defiled your holy temple; they have laid Jerusalem in heaps," etc. Augustine inquires as to who was meant by that "inheritance," and he says, in reply, as follows: "From the people of Israel [came] all those who believed in Christ; all those *to whom the offer of Christ was made* and, in a manner, the salutary and fruitful fulfillment of the promise; all those concerning whom the Lord Himself said: *I was sent only to the lost sheep, the house of Israel.* They are those out of whom came the sons of promise; *they* are counted as the 'seed' (Rom. 9.8), they belong to the Inheritance of God."[143]

What can we gather from the above passage, which Torquemada cited from Augustine's comment? Did Augustine believe that by the "Inheritance of God" the *whole* "house of Israel" was indicated—that is, "the lost sheep" to whom Jesus "was sent" and *"out of whom* came the sons of promise"—or only the "sons of promise" themselves—i.e., "those *from* the people of Israel *who believed in Christ*"? One may readily assume that of the two possibilities, the former represents Augustine's thought. It likewise seems evident that Torquemada, too, relied on this understanding. Yet he does not comment on Augustine; he continues to quote him, and we too shall present here that quotation—or rather a brief summary of its contents—in attempting to get at what Torquemada had in mind and what he sought to express through Augustine's words.

In the continuation of the cited passage Augustine points out that all the believers in Jesus' divinity, both before His appearance and immediately thereafter, emerged from the ranks of the Jewish people. So did all the apostles and the first martyrs, and so did the "multitudes" who followed Jesus, or were baptized after His resurrection. It would seem that these Christians were inseparable from that "people" that Augustine had praised so much. However, when we come to the end of the passage, we encounter a different view. Here, in defining the early believers in Christ, Augustine says: "They were the inheritance of God out of that people."[144]

From this it is clear that Augustine arrived at the opposite conclusion from the one suggested earlier; for here he differentiates between the "people of Israel" taken as a whole and the "inheritance of God" that *came out of it.* Accordingly, the "inheritance," strictly speaking, consists only of the "*believers in Christ*," while the "people of Israel" taken as a whole, however distinguished it may be for having produced the "inheritance," is not the inheritance itself. We now seem to know what is referred to by the "inheritance of God" mentioned in Psalm 94. We are still not sure what is meant there by "*His* people." Torquemada does not touch upon this question, as on other questions that might arise in this connection. He continues to quote

Augustine, and as we shall see, the latter himself comes quickly to the point at issue.

Augustine relates to what he said on Psalm 94.14 the words of Paul in Romans II. 1–2: "I say, Has God cast off *his people?* Far be it! For I also am an Israelite, of the seed of Israel, of the tribe of Benjamin. God has not cast off his people, whom He has foreknown." There seems to be no better proof, then, that by "his people" the Apostle meant the *Jewish people as a whole*— the special national and tribal entity to which he, the Apostle himself, belonged; and thus we come back to our original concept of the "Inheritance of God," which, in the verse cited, seems to stand as an equivalent of "his people"[145]—i.e., the Jewish people. Moreover, Augustine, after stating the above, seems to offer support to this understanding. *"This people (plebs),"* he says, "which, out of that nation *(gens),* contributed to the body of Christ, *is* the inheritance of God. For what the Apostle says: 'God has not repelled his people whom He has foreknown,' corresponds to what that Psalm says, where it is written: 'The Lord shall not cast off his people,' and the following: 'and his inheritance he shall not forsake,' from which it evidently appears that such a people is the Inheritance of God."[146]

Torquemada does not try to elucidate this passage of Augustine, either; he makes no comment on it except to remark that it is evident from it "how foolish is what the impious people state in their reckless audacity—namely, that it is absolutely certain and notorious that the race of the Jews *(genus iudeorum)* had been damned."[147] Torquemada obviously here reaffirms what he gave us to understand at the opening of the discussion—namely, that Augustine identifies "His people" as well as "the inheritance of God" (both of which are mentioned in Psalm 94.14) with the Jewish people. But *did* Augustine do this?

VI

There is little doubt that when writing the above comment, Augustine was torn by two conflicting tendencies. On the one hand, he was somewhat carried away by his hidden enthusiasm for the phenomenon he was discussing: the emergence of Christianity from the ranks of the Jewish people—a phenomenon that kindled his secret admiration for the ancient people of Judea; and on the other hand, he wished to sustain the Christian doctrine about the *fall* of the Jewish people in the days of Christ; and this desire determined the goal and the meaning of his cited comments. That this was so is also evident (a) from Augustine's *introduction* to the passage quoted and (b) from his *concluding remarks.*

For in posing the question: What is meant by God's "inheritance" mentioned in Psalm 79, Augustine says in that *introduction:* "If anyone will assume that in this prophecy the laying waste of Jerusalem by Titus is indicated and, consequently, [that] it refers to the period in which the word of our Lord was already preached among the gentiles, *I do not see how that people could be called the inheritance of God*—a people that did not believe in Christ, whom having rejected and slain, they became reprobate; who refused to believe in Him even after His resurrection and who, in addition, killed His martyrs."[148] In presenting Augustine's comments on that verse (Psalms 79.1), Torquemada omits this introductory passage, which not only disparages the Jewish people but precludes its identification with that "inheritance" of which the Psalmist says that God will not forsake. He also omits Augustine's *conclusion* to his comments, which further clarifies the meaning he imputed to the terms in question. It is necessary to cite this passage, too, in order to see the difference between Augustine's thought on the subject and what was in Torquemada's mind.

Augustine tells his readers in his conclusion that the remarks of St. Paul which he quoted (from Rom. 11.1–2) came in the wake of the Apostle's reminder that to Israel it was said (Isa. 65.2): "All day long I have stretched forth my hands unto a disobedient and gainsaying people" (Rom. 10.21). This prophecy, says Augustine, relates to the future disbelief of that people of Israel (i.e., their disbelief in Christ), and it is in connection with *it*, and in this place, that Augustine says: "Should anyone judge wrongly that the whole of that people was condemned because of its unbelief and opposition to God, the Apostle found it necessary to add: *Had God cast off His people? Far be it. For I also am an Israelite, of the tribe of Benjamin.* Here he is showing what people *(plebs)* he spoke of—a people which certainly belonged to the former people *(populi prioris)*, the whole of which, if God had reproached and condemned, he himself would not have been Christ's apostle, being an Israelite of the seed of Abraham, of the tribe of Benjamin."[149]

If at this point we still adhere to the opinion that according to Augustine, the Apostle, by "His people," meant the people of Israel taken generally, and we just wonder about Augustine's differentiation between "His people" and the *former people* (for which we find no basis in Romans), we are soon led to abandon that opinion, and thereby also be freed of the perplexity. For Augustine himself moved to make it manifest that what, in his judgment, was signified by "His people" was identical with what was designated by "His inheritance." In both terms he understood Christ's followers, the "saved remnant," the Election by Grace, and by no means the Jewish people as a whole.[150]

The tortuous route that Augustine followed to arrive at his answer to the problem he posed is marked with ambiguities. But his final conclusion is nevertheless clear, and we can gather it also from his discussion of the same theme in his comments on Psalms 94.7. Referring there to those whom God has *not* rejected, and to whom the apostle Paul belonged, Augustine says patently and bluntly: "The people of God consists of *these;* not of all the Israelites, but as it is written: 'The remnant will be saved.' *Not of all the Israelites;* for the grain has been winnowed, the wheat garnered, and the thrash left on the outside. All you now see of the reprobate Jews is the thrash. The chosen wheat is already in the granaries. Let us see both and discern both."[151]

VII

There is no question that Torquemada was aware of the thrust of Augustine's argument and knew his conclusion. The fact that he chose precisely the passages where Augustine's idea is vague or obscured and omitted those where his intent is apparent testifies to this clearly. If despite this Torquemada dared to claim that from Augustine's comments one may gather that Psalm 94 signifies the Jewish people *(populus iudeorum)* by the terms "His people" and the "Inheritance of God," and that to *this* people, therefore, the promise was given of God's eternal care, it was because he knew that, at least at two points, Augustine's argument tended, unmistakably, toward this conclusion. That was (a) when Augustine defined "His people" (the People of God) as *"plebs iudaea"* and as "the people begotten according to the flesh from the seed of Abraham," and (b) when he presented Paul's question: "Has God cast off His People?" and answer: "Far be it. For I too am an Israelite," etc. "Here," said Augustine, as we have noticed, "the Apostle shows what people he spoke of." And what people *could* he possibly speak of if not the people of Israel as a whole, the people to which Paul had belonged, "the people which, if God had condemned *wholly,* he [Paul] would not have become Christ's apostle."

Torquemada's reliance on Augustine in this matter was, therefore, not entirely unjustified, even though he could with justice be criticized for having passed in silence over Augustine's *conclusion* as well as his *guiding* idea. Such criticism is especially apt from the standpoint of modern, formal scholarship, which seeks to determine theoretical positions by the totality of their varied expressions. But Torquemada was not a modern scholar or a critical historian of Church ideology. He was, above all, a medieval theologian who sought to establish the truth of Christianity—the one, irrefutable and all-embracing truth—in the maze of so often contradictory statements that were taken to represent the divine word. Surely he could not bring himself to think that Psalm 94 and the words of Paul in Romans about "His People" and "His inheritance" meant anything but the Jewish people, and he could see the difficulty in which Augustine involved himself when he tried to impose his own view—or the view developed by the earlier Church Fathers—on the related biblical sources. Indubitably, Torquemada could have made a strong case, from some statements that Augustine himself made, against what Augustine sought to prove. His purpose, however, was not to argue with Augustine, but to express his own thought through Augustine's words—or, if we are allowed to take a step forward, to express the inner truth of Christianity as it shone forth, in his opinion, from Augustine's pronouncements.

Yet Torquemada was not only a theologian; he was also a jurist; and as jurist he had to guard against making a wrong or refutable statement, and this brings us back to the "escape" which Torquemada prepared for himself. As he put it, all he wanted to prove was the falsehood of the allegation made by the Toledans that the Jewish people had been "*entirely* condemned," and this falsehood, he could claim, he proved, without violating the rules of proper demonstration. For does not Augustine himself say when referring to *His people:* "... the people which if God had condemned *wholly*, he, Paul, would not have been Christ's apostle?" And does not the Apostle, too, point out that after the Lord's Passion and Resurrection—that is, after the crime had been perpetrated against Him and most of the Jews continued to deny Him— thousands upon thousands of that very people became His faithful followers? So the Jews could not have been "absolutely" condemned, as many of them *were* "saved," including Paul, who was first the fierce persecutor of the Christians and later their greatest teacher and apostle.

From the standpoint of formal logic, then, Torquemada said nothing that could prejudice his position. Yet while holding on to his position, and while quoting Augustine as he did, he also attained another objective, which must have been uppermost in his mind. He projected an image of the Jewish people that was quite opposed to the Christian view. Obviously, no better way could be found to attain this than to let Augustine speak in his behalf— that is, to quote those passages of his works in which the Jews, regardless of what Augustine was driving at, emerge as a people whose religious history and achievements evoked the astonishment and awe of the great saint and, indeed, cannot fail to excite the admiration of anyone who has a sense for the wondrous and the divine. For this is the people (or the "nation") from whom came not only Christ in His human form (they "contributed to His human- ity"), but also all His apostles, all the first saints of Christianity, all its first martyrs, and, indeed, all the early followers of Christ who founded—and constituted—His renewed Church. That *such* a people was indeed "His people," "His inheritance," and that it could not possibly be "absolutely damned," seems to follow as a matter of course.

IV. THE BIBLICAL VIEW OF THE JEWS

I

This elusive treatment by Torquemada of Augustine's comments illustrates the problem he had to cope with in presenting the Christian position on the subject, as well as the lengths he was ready to go to in substantiating his own views of the Jewish people. Yet to appreciate more fully the complexity of the task and the various ways in which he performed it, we must note also his treatment of some other authorities which he adduced for the same purpose.[152] At this point, however, we shall turn our attention to his comments on the Prophecies of Redemption.

It would seem that these prophecies could serve Torquemada as the best means to attain his end; for these divine messages—which so clearly, and repeatedly, assured the Jewish people of a brilliant future—appeared to demolish the claims of the Toledans and conclusively prove Torquemada right. This is at least what many lay readers or critical scholars might assume today. As we have indicated, however, Torquemada could read the Bible only as a devout medieval Christian, which means that he had to take into account the views of the exegetical authorities of Christianity; and these authorities, beginning with the Church Fathers, interpreted most Prophecies of Redemption in an entirely different way. As a result, while the Bible assured the Jews a bright future, Christian theology more often than not transferred this assurance from the Jewish people to Christendom—that is, the Church and the future Christian world.

Thus, the problem Torquemada encountered in interpreting the biblical texts he had employed was not alleviated when he came to prove his case by "the divine promises given to the Jewish people." In a sense, it was compounded. For now he had to coordinate his aims not merely with the views of Christian exegesis, but also with his own dualistic view of the prophecies in question. For convinced as he was that these prophecies referred mainly and primarily to the Jewish people, he also believed that they spoke of Christ's faithful; and how could he combine these two concepts which seemed to represent a contradiction in terms? How could he identify the salvation of the Jews with what was assuredly promised the Christians? He could do so by interpreting the assured salvation in the only way a true Christian would. For what "salvation" could there be except through Christ, and how could the Jews be "saved" if not by Him—that is, by joining the faithful from the nations in a common universal Church?

Here Torquemada stood firmly on the ground of traditional Christian exegesis, and this materially facilitated his task. Yet so great were the differences between him and his predecessors in priority (of approaches), emphasis (of subjects) and, above all, the attitude toward the Jewish people that occasionally he had to resort to strenuous maneuvering to make the points he thought vital for his case.

To get a true notion of this particular effort, we must again take a look at his actual procedure. It is apparent in his comments on all the Prophecies of Redemption, but nowhere as clearly as in those he made on Micah 4.6–7. To illustrate that procedure, therefore, we shall note his explanation of these verses of Micah:

> On that day, says the Lord,
> I will assemble her that limps,
> And I will gather her that is rejected,
> And her that I have afflicted,
> And I will put the limping into a remnant,
> And her that was rejected into a mighty nation.

Nicholas de Lyra, the Christian commentator on the Bible, offers here two possible interpretations. According to the first, the prophecy refers to the *gentiles,* who were "deformed" (limping) because of their idolatry, and were in a way "rejected" by God when He refused to give them the Law and the Prophets. According to the second interpretation, it refers to the *Jews,* who "limped" (halted) between two worships—that of God and that of idols, as indicated by their behavior in the days of Elijah and, again, following the appearance of Christ (when some of them joined and the others denied Him). Also, the reference to "her that is rejected" fits the Jews, who were cast out—namely, allowed to "err through diverse vices"—while "her that I have afflicted" alludes to the afflictions the Jews had suffered at the hands of the nations—the Babylonians, the Greeks, and the Romans. Of them he also says: "I shall gather," meaning thereby "gather in the Church of Christ," but the prophet, de Lyra noted, found it necessary to add that not all the "afflicted" and the "limping"—namely, not *all* the Jews—will be "gathered" into the Church, i.e., the saving orbit of Christ. "I shall put the limping into a remnant," he says, "indicating thereby that only a few of the Jews will adhere to Christ compared to the other faithful."[153]

De Lyra says that the latter explanation appears to him superior, and thus he came close to the view of Jerome, who identified the "limping," the "rejected" and the "afflicted" with the Jews only and not with the gentiles.[154] The Interlinear Gloss, too, follows Jerome's interpretation. Torquemada, however, used portions of both interpretations, and by doing so he rejected their basic tendency and presented a view of his own.

Thus, in explaining "I shall gather the limping," he follows de Lyra's *first* interpretation (i.e., the one which was *not* de Lyra's choice), and repeats de Lyra's comment on that phrase: "meaning the gentiles who were limping because of their idolatry"[155]; but when he comes to the second part of the verse—"and I shall gather the rejected and the afflicted"—he follows de Lyra's other interpretation (which related that sentence to the *Jewish* people). He omits, however, de Lyra's remark about the meaning of "rejected" (i.e., that God left the Jews *to err in various vices*), as well as his comment that only "a few" of the "afflicted" will adhere to Christ.[156] In fact, at this point he abandons both of de Lyra's interpretations and uses the interpretation of the Ordinary Gloss: "These words [namely, 'I will gather,' etc.] fit the primitive Church of the Jews, of which the Apostle says that one day 5,000 believers joined it, another day 3,000, and later many thousands."[157]

Thus, by using different comments alternately and availing himself of several interpretations, Torquemada avoided a number of pitfalls. He eliminated the harsh criticism of the Jews as "limping" in the days of Elijah and the days of Christ and, furthermore, as having been "cast out" by God and allowed to remain in their "various vices" (which would come dangerously close to the Toledans' damnation theory); similarly, he removed the charge of idolatry from the Jews and laid it upon the gentiles, where, in his opinion, it truly belonged; and finally, he substituted for de Lyra's view that only "few" of the Jews would follow Christ the recorded fact that "many thousands" have joined Him, thereby suggesting that the prophecy assured salvation to *masses* of Jews—indeed, to the Jewish *people* as a whole—and not to a numerically insignificant "remnant."

This was certainly *Torquemada's* interpretation, and not that of traditional Christianity. But to render his comments compatible with the latter—or rather to lend them such an appearance—he chose those portions of the authoritative commentaries that did not compromise his thesis. To achieve this he moved from one commentary to another and used selected phrases and sentences from each, with little regard to their context. He used them as if they were isolated pieces of some old, ruined, or half-finished mosaic for the purpose of building a new mosaic according to his own design.

This kind of manipulation of sources violates modern scholarly norms, and even a medieval critical reader might question its propriety. Torquemada, however, seemed unconcerned, and apparently was sure of his rights. There was, after all, no uniformity in the Christian symbolic interpretations. Not only did Torquemada differ with some of them; their authors, too, often differed with each other; and Torquemada was in no way bound to consider them all of equal value. He *could* ignore comments he considered inferior, or certain portions of various comments, while pointing to some of their other portions as models of sound exegesis. He felt entitled to use passages that conformed to his view when convinced that his own or chosen interpretation fitted the contents of the text involved. Above all, he laid more stress on the literal meaning (of whose intent he had no doubt), and less on the symbolic meaning (which was open to speculation); and the basic verity of the literal import, plus Torquemada's implicit faith in it, was reflected in his words with special force. Hence the great cumulative effect of his comments on the Prophecies of Redemption. Altogether they added an important layer in the conceptual structure of the Jewish people which he attempted to build.

II

What we have before us is clearly an attempt to impute an entirely new trend and meaning to the bulk of Christian exegetical literature insofar as its view of the Jews was concerned. But apart from this, something else was involved which, fundamentally, was no less drastic. Two hundred years before the first results of Biblical Criticism appeared in Europe, Torquemada tried to bring the Bible closer to reality by removing much of the symbolic garb that covered virtually all of its parts. To be sure, Torquemada can hardly be compared with any of the biblical critics referred to, for the latter were generally freed from theology, while Torquemada was a theologian through and through. Inevitably, his moves were restricted to the paths historically followed by Christian theology, and his aims could not reach beyond the confines marked by its rigorous doctrines. And yet within these forbidding limitations, he pushed biblical exegesis forward—to be sure, not beyond the bounds of theology, but often to its extreme edges, dangerously close to the prohibited sphere, where symbolic interpretation is totally abandoned and historical truth is the sole guide.

Thus, we have seen him move to these borders in his comments on some biblical statements, wherein he parted ways with men like Augustine and Jerome,[158] because he saw in these statements a true expression of the Bible's attitude toward the Jews. We see it once again in his clear-cut expositions of the well-known biblical Prophecies of Redemption, where he thought that they referred to the *people of Israel*—and not only, or primarily, to *Christian* salvation, as Christological exegesis would have it.[159] And we see it even more so in his sharp refutations of the evidence the Toledans adduced from the Bible in support of their racial claims and notions.

This evidence appeared most damaging, indeed; for it did not derive, as some other charges did, from statements that were essentially *complimentary* to the Jews, but interpreted in an anti-Jewish spirit. This evidence relied on biblical passages that, by all appearances, were most *critical* of the Jews, containing harsh censures of their national conduct and severe denunciations of their social traits. It was clear to Torquemada that no matter what he argued or what proof he or others presented to the contrary, this evidence from the Bible, unless refuted, would greatly weaken the defense of the conversos. He therefore decided to rebut the conclusions drawn by the

Toledans from the passages they used, showing their interpretations to be based on false assumptions and offering instead his own explanations, which he felt were sustained by the sources.

As Torquemada was informed, the "proofs" of the opponents rested on *five* biblical statements, which seem sharply derogatory of the Jewish people and appear to indicate that it was indeed "condemned." Torquemada did not deny that these statements were disparaging; he merely rejected the Toledans' assertion that they refer to the *whole* Jewish people and imply eternal, irretrievable damnation. To be sure, he averred, Scripture contains passages which *seem* to reproach the *Jewish people as a whole*, and also speak of its rejection by God. Yet all this is *prima facie* only; and anyone who wishes to read the Bible correctly must bear in mind the basic rule of exegesis—the rule indicated by Nicholas de Lyra—that no scriptural statement chastising the Jews should be taken as referring to the entire Jewish people. Every such statement, without exception, refers to *a part of that people at a given time*— the time related to the statement at issue.

Using this criterion, Torquemada found it possible to repel the excessive claims of the Toledans. To be sure, here too he encountered obstacles— views expressed by some Christian authorities that, in some way, were opposed to his own; and in order to avoid an open clash with their assertions, Torquemada had to treat them in the same complex manner he treated similar Christian expositions. On the whole, however, he found it easier to rebut claims based on biblical censures of the Jews, simply because these claims were invariably denied by the Bible itself. Thus, he shows that Jesus' statements in Matthew—"This people pay me lip service, but their heart is far from me" (15.8–9), and "It is a wicked generation that asks for a sign" (16.4)—were not directed against the Jewish people as a whole, but only against specific elements of that people (i.e., the Pharisees and the Sadducees), as is stated in the openings of chapters 15 and 16 of Matthew. Similarly, the harsh rebukes of the Jews in Psalms 94.9–11 were not aimed at all the generations of the Jews, but solely at the generation of the desert—and, in fact, not at the entire generation, but only at those from the age of twenty up, as is stated in Numbers 14.29. Hence, only the older people were to die in the wilderness, while the younger were to enter the Promised Land; and this, too, is explicitly stated in Numbers 14.31. Likewise, the sharp castigations of the Jews in Deuteronomy 32. 5–6, etc. were directed at the same generation of the desert and not at the people in its entire lifespan, for Moses ends that prophecy of chastisement with a call upon the gentiles to sing the praises of His people (that is, Israel, as de Lyra understood) and with a stern warning to all its enemies that their attacks against that people would be avenged by God (Deut. 32.43).[160] Torquemada's answers to the Toledans on these points are generally terse, clear-cut and decisive. Less than elsewhere was he here

concerned with possible counter-arguments to his assertions, since no higher
or clearer authorities could be mustered than those he adduced from the
Scriptures.

This leaves us with Torquemada's rebuttal of the fifth Toledan claim of
the same category. It related to Paul's statements in Titus (I.1–10), which had
hardly evoked mystical comments, and it no doubt constitutes one of Torquemada's most effective and most brilliant strokes. Among other things, it
provides us with special insights into the Toledans' position toward the Jews,
and helps us understand Torquemada's view of the Jewish people as a racial
entity.

III

According to the Toledans, says Torquemada, the Apostle warned Titus,
his disciple, to be on guard against the circumcised (i.e., the Jews) "because
by nature they are bad and always unfaithful [*infideles*]," as is indicated by their
historical record; for even "while they were witnessing the miracles of God,
they worshiped a calf and idols and killed the prophets." Furthermore,
according to the Toledans, the Apostle ordered, in the same letter to Titus,
that *"the Christians separate themselves from any converse with the circumcised,"*
"for *by nature* [*naturaliter*] they are mendacious, false, deceptive, arrogant,
vainglorious, avaricious and sons of all iniquity." All this, the adversaries
claim, was said by the Apostle.[161]

To suggest that such a theory about the Jews was propounded, and such
a solution proposed, by St. Paul was to Torquemada the height of folly.
However, the folly, the way it was presented, agreed with the common
theory of damnation and the prevalent attitude toward the Jews. Hence,
Torquemada's thunderous reaction: "When these impudent people say that
the Apostle said all these matters, they are, first of all, lying. For nowhere did
the Apostle . . . the teacher of truth . . . say such things which are erroneous
and heretical. To those who have read his epistles this is a known matter."[162]

Torquemada then cites Titus I.9–10 to show what the Apostle really meant
by his reproofs. He points out that, as the Glosses indicate, the Apostle does
not *generally* speak there about the circumcised—i.e., converts from Judaism—as if he wished to brand with the same crimes *all* those who came from
the circumcision, including himself and the other apostles who were spreading the word of faith throughout the world.[163] As the Gloss explains, Paul
reproves there, first, the Cretans, who were gentiles . . . , and second, certain
false apostles who came from the circumcision (i.e., Judaism) and did not
become full-fledged Christians (*non pleni Christiani facti*).[164]

One need not stretch the point to show that Torquemada was right in interpreting as he did Paul's words in this place. Paul's sharp rebukes in Titus I

were obviously directed not against *all* Jews, or the Jewish people *as a whole*, but specifically against a small group of Jews—some of their converts to Christianity in Crete—and against the Cretan gentile population. It is about these gentiles, who were Greeks, that he said they were "liars, evil beasts, slow bellies" (Titus I.12), while his attack on the "vain talkers and deceivers" (I.10) was aimed at those *particular* Jewish converts. In misrepresenting the object of the Apostle's criticisms, however, the Toledans displayed something worse than ignorance; what was involved here was heresy; and to prove the heretical content of their assertions, Torquemada examines them point by point.

"The said impious people," says Torquemada, "stand convicted as heretics *(convincuntur heretici)*—first, for "having lyingly imputed to the Apostle the assertion that the circumcised are bad by nature *(quod circumcisi naturaliter sunt mali)*. Clearly, this is a most abominable error and an intolerable heresy *(nephandissimus error et heresis intollerabilis)*. For, if it is an error as well as a manifest heresy, which is ascribed to the Manichaeans and condemned by the Church, to say that the *demons* are [naturally] bad—since, as it is said in Gen. 1.31: *God saw all that he did, and it was very good;* and in Eccles. 3.11: *He has made all things good in his time*—how much more should be held as extremely bad heretics those who say that the circumcised are evil *by nature?* And what heretical pestilence could be more horrible than this, which weakens and defiles [*foedat*] the entire Christian faith?" For those who say that the circumcised are naturally evil, must agree, of necessity, that "all the saints from Abraham, who was the first to whom circumcision was administered, to Christ our Savior, who was also circumcised, were bad by nature and, consequently, were not saints at all. Christian ears can hear nothing more absurd or more offensive."[165]

Pressing this furious attack relentlessly, Torquemada scores point after point. "The said 'Ishmaelites,'" he argues, "prove to be heretics *(prefati Hysmalite heretici convincuntur)* also when they say that *the circumcised have always been unfaithful.* Surely in this matter the insanity of these people surpasses the error of the Manichaeans, for the latter condemned only the Fathers of the Old Testament, while these most accursed people condemn and reprove the Fathers of the Old and New Testament alike."[166]

To prove his point further, Torquemada refers to the words of the Apostle who, after lauding in an extensive discourse the faith of the Fathers of the Old Testament, "all of whom were circumcised," says this: "And what more shall I say? For the time would fail me to tell of Gideon, of Barak, of Samson, and of Jephthah, of David, and Samuel and of the Prophets."[167] Clearly, a large number of the circumcised *were* faithful. And to clinch the argument, Torquemada adds: "How can one explain that the Apostle Paul called Abraham, to whom circumcision was first given, the father of all believers (in

Romans 4.16), if all the circumcised who descended from him were infidels," as the Toledans claim?[168]

Torquemada then turns to the charge that the circumcised worshiped the golden calf and idols, stating that this charge is of no consequence, first, "because it is most foolish to assert such a thing about *all* the circumcised,"[169] and then, even if some of them did worship idols, it does not follow that their offspring did. Had such a sequence been inevitable, all "the faithful descendants of the gentiles—almost all of whom were prior to the advent of Christ extremely bad idolaters, cruel killers of the faithful, not only of the apostles, but also of innumerable other Christians—could be made subject to many other monstrous crimes, to which those nations were addicted."[170]

This was of course a most effective argument that cut the ground from under the charge in question. But harder blows were yet to come. Torquemada now strikes most forcefully and directly at the alleged biblical foundations of the race theory and its proposed solution for the Jewish question.

"The villainous people," he says, "do not fear to assert that the Apostle Paul instructed Titus and all the other faithful to separate themselves from any converse with the circumcised." This, however, is not only a false assertion, for the Apostle Paul never ordered such a thing; it is also an absurd one. "For who except one who is poor in mind and denied all power of reasoning could say that the Apostle Paul, who was, as one of the circumcised, *appointed by God as teacher of the nations* (I Timothy 2.7), ordered the faithful to separate themselves from any converse with the circumcised? This would mean to impede the divine arrangement, as he himself and the other apostles, all of whom belonged to the circumcised, were ordained as preachers and teachers of the world." Also, the apostle Paul says to his disciple Timothy, whom he had circumcised (I Timothy, 4.12): "Be an example to all believers in word, in converse, in charity . . . and in faith." Certainly this could not have been fulfilled if the Apostle had ordered all the faithful to separate themselves from the circumcised.[171]

Finally, when they say that the Apostle gave as reason for his "instruction" that the faithful dissociate themselves from the circumcised his alleged contention that the latter are *by nature* liars, etc., "they themselves become guilty of pronouncing a gross lie, for they ascribe to the Apostle a statement which he did not make—and one which he could not ever have made. For "whatever is natural is always common to all" who are of the same nature (*guod est naturale omnibus et semper commune est*); and had the apostle Paul made the statement ascribed to him, he would have declared himself to be mendacious by nature, being himself a member of the Jewish race and consequently sharing in the nature of the Jews. By claiming that the Apostle made the above statement, the Toledans have demonstrated not only their falsehood—

or, rather, the extent of their readiness to falsify—but also their almost unlimited folly; "for nothing seems more foolish than to think that the Apostle Paul, who was circumcised and who declared (Rom. IX.1): 'I do not lie,' said that the circumcised are by nature liars."[172]

What is worse, they have perpetrated an extreme blasphemy; because by saying that the Jews are liars by nature, they accuse of mendacity Christ, and all the Prophets, the Patriarchs, the Apostles, the Evangelists and all the other innumerable Saints of both the Old and New Testament. Worst of all, they expose themselves as heretical, because such assertions *tend* to empty *(eva-cuare)* and destroy *(destruere)* the whole of Holy Scripture. "For, since it had been edited by persons such as Prophets, or Apostles, or Evangelists, who were all circumcised, it clearly follows from the sayings of those individuals that Holy Scripture emanated from *naturally mendacious* people." Is there a thought that can be more ungodly and more detestable to any faithful Christian?[173]

It would seem that with this powerful argument, Torquemada's attack upon the Toledan race theory finally reached its summit. But this was not so. Beyond that high point there was a still higher peak.

IV

Fundamentally, throughout his work, Torquemada offers two kinds of proof—one by quotations from Scripture that state *directly* the view of Christianity about the Jewish people, and the other by scriptural quotations which state that view *indirectly*—i.e., they imply it, and thus we can arrive at it by the workings of reason. To this second category belong the proofs that Torquemada classed as "rational."[174]

In presenting his direct evidence from the Bible, Torquemada, as we have seen, had run into difficulties of a theological nature. In presenting his indirect proofs, however, his arguments hardly encountered a hitch and the deductions he made seem flawless. Perhaps the solid convictions he gained from these "rational" deductions helped him to interpret as he did the biblical passages of the first category, too.

For this and other reasons, it is important to note these inferences in some detail.

Christian dogma offered Torquemada several grounds for his deductions. According to John 6.55–54, Jesus said: "My flesh is real food and my blood is real drink. Whoever eats my flesh and drinks my blood has eternal life." On this is founded the sacrament of the Eucharist, which "enables every Christian to obtain vital nourishment for his soul, not only from Christ's salutary teachings," but also from His "real flesh and most precious blood." But this real flesh and blood were *Jewish*, and so it is impossible to believe that the human part of Christ was edifying and enlivening—indeed, possessed the power of eternal life—and simultaneously cling to the notion that the same human part belonged to a corrupt, sinful and condemned race. Such a notion is clearly repugnant to a Christian and insults the sacrament of the Eucharist.[175]

And a similar conclusion about the falseness of the race theory can be derived from the concept of the Virgin Mary, the Mother of Christ. Those who speak evil of the Jewish race inevitably vilify her, too, for implied in their criticisms against the Jews is the notion that she was the daughter of an "accursed" race. "What Christian," asks Torquemada, "can hear with equanimity these blasphemies about the Queen of heaven, the lady of the angels, the mother of the King of Kings and our Lord the Savior?"[176] Contrary to what these blasphemers suggest, Holy Church expresses its views and feelings concerning the origin of the Blessed Virgin when it sings about her on her birthday: "Mary was a maiden of *illustrious* birth, daughter of a *kingly race*"; and again: "This day was born the glorious Virgin Mary, a child of the *seed of Abraham*, a daughter of the *tribe of Judah*, a princess from the *line of David*."[177] Clearly, the Church could not be proud of Mary's lineage if that lineage was so sinful and so corrupt as to be ultimately repudiated by God.

Further illustrative of the absurdity of the doctrine that the Toledans propagate against the Jewish race is the fact that all the Holy Fathers of both the Old and New Testament belonged to the Jewish stock. How could the holiest of all people emerge from the most sinful of all races? Obviously, only an opposite premise—namely, that the Jewish people was the holiest group of men—can explain the extraordinary phenomenon that all the founders of true morality and religion exclusively belonged to it.[178]

And no other conclusion can be derived from the fact that the "saintliest humanity"—that of Jesus Christ—emerged from the Jewish people. For any other explanation would be offensive to plain logic, and no hair-splitting casuistry could make it stick. When God wished to appear in human form, He chose to be born to the race of the Jews—the same race to which were born the Virgin Mary, the Patriarchs, the Prophets, and the Apostles. Why? Because "no other race was more dignified, more noble, more saintly and more religious in the [whole] world."[179]

But not only Jesus' carnal origin proves this, according to Torquemada. Everything associated with His life on earth leads to the same conclusion. To prepare mankind for His appearance, His coming was prefigured by the Patriarchs, proclaimed by the Prophets, and heralded by John the Baptist— "all of whom were of the Jewish race," and it was the Jewish people that was first informed of His actual arrival on the scene. Having been born to a Jewish mother, he was also circumcised as a Jewish child (in accordance with the command of God) and thus He bore in His flesh the sign of the Jew, the sign of the son of Abraham. Then, again according to the law of Moses, He was presented at the Temple in Jerusalem—the Jewish Temple—and a sacrifice was offered on His behalf, in accordance with the law of Moses—the Jewish law—in the case of a firstborn son. In line with this, His mission of redemption—the redemption, first of all, of the Jewish people—was revealed by a Jewish saint (Simon) and a Jewish prophetess (Anna).[180] Above all, it was from the race of the Jews—and from that race only—that Jesus chose His martyrs, His disciples and His messengers, who, "like twelve rays of the sun, illumined the whole world." And finally, "When the presence of His humanity was about to depart from this world and He was to appoint deputies representing His authority, He chose, once again, these deputies of His from the ranks of the Jewish people. These were the Apostles, headed by Peter, to whom He said: "To you I shall give the keys of the kingdom of heaven; and whatever you shall bind on earth will be bound in heaven" (Matthew 16.9 and Matthew 18.18).[181]

"Certainly," concludes Torquemada, the granting of such an "awesome power" and the other "singular prerogatives of dignity," which are signs of love, not of rejection, "clearly proves as false and heretical what the most abominable people, the abovementioned Midianites, dare to assert in their impious sentence as the foundation of their errors."[182]

V. CHRISTIANITY AND CONVERTS FROM JUDAISM

I

Thus we come to the close of our survey of Torquemada's assaults upon the Toledan race theory. We have seen that he struck at this theory from many angles, with none of its points remaining untouched. He exposed what he considered the basic contradiction between the tenets of Christianity and the postulates of the racists; he showed how Christianity stands squarely opposed to the latter's view of the Jewish people; and he made it clear that each of their propositions is not only damaging to Christian interests but also amounts to a dangerous heresy, which has to be vigorously fought and stamped out. In support of his theses, Torquemada, as we have seen, presented a great array of proofs. He refuted, as he believed, the Toledans' assertions by contrary statements from the writings of the Church Fathers, by canon law and the traditions of the Church. He further disproved them by scriptural authorities that deny the Toledans' claims directly, and also by those that deny them indirectly—that is, by clear implication. He, moreover, demonstrated their glaring inconsistency with the divine assurances given the Jewish people and, above all, with the deeds of Christ from His birth to His ascension. In brief, Torquemada left no stone unturned in his effort to show the racial theory a fraud, and what emerged was a series of powerful arguments that even to us, after half a millennium, seem hard to resist.

With the completion of this difficult task, Torquemada felt free to approach the question that urgently called for a concrete answer and was indeed on everybody's lips: How should converts from Judaism to Christianity be treated in the Christian world? This brings us at last face to face with the issues that stood in the forefront of the conflict. Some of these issues had already been dealt with, especially by Fernán Díaz de Toledo. But Torquemada went far beyond the Relator. Not only did he broaden and deepen the foundations of Fernán Díaz' statements; he also changed the balance of the argument. For what interested him most, beyond the converts' rights, was their historic destiny in Christendom—not only the function they had fulfilled in the past, but the part they were to play in the future.

Torquemada incorporated all he had to say on these matters in the framework of answers to two questions: What stands are *prohibited,* and what attitudes are *recommended,* for Old Christians to take toward converts from Judaism? Altogether, he offered forty reasons in support of his various replies[183]; they all conform to major lines of traditional Christian theology and are all of interest to students of religion. Here, however, we shall deal only with those that bear directly on our discussion.

In presenting the traditional stand of Christianity toward converts from Judaism, Torquemada followed the same method he employed when he presented the Christian view of the Jewish people. Here, too, he begins from a minimum position, which he feels certain he can safely hold. His cardinal point is that converts from Judaism should not be abused in any manner by other Christians. That was supposedly all he wanted, and all he needed, to prove. But having achieved this limited aim, Torquemada moves on to expand his views in various other directions.

To prove his thesis that converts from Judaism should not be abused by other Christians, Torquemada draws first of all on the words of Paul in Romans XI. 2–5 and de Lyra's comments on that passage. In the days of Paul, he says, there were converts from gentilehood who sought to insult the converts from Judaism on the grounds of their Jewish origin. Abusively, they ascribed to these converts to Christianity the "traditional" Jewish *incredulity* (i.e., lack of faith in Jesus), "just *as many impious and carnal people do in our own times.*"[184]

The apostle Paul, however, Torquemada points out, censured these attempts for a variety of reasons. To begin with, he denied the claim of the abusers that the Jews generally should be charged with incredulity. That incredulity, the Apostle pointed out, affects only a *part* of the Jewish people, and even to this extent, it is not permanent. Indeed, Jews, in large numbers, have been "falling" from the faith; they fell before Christianity appeared, as well as after its inception, but at no time has this "fall" been general, nor is it destined to be everlasting. The matter can be gathered from the example of Elijah, who believed that the whole people was converted to idolatry and that he was the last prophet left. Nevertheless, it was not so at all, and this is why the Apostle pointed out:

> Don't you know what Scripture said of Elijah?
> How he makes intercession to God against Israel, saying:
> "Lord, they have killed your prophets,
> And destroyed your altars,
> And I am left alone and they seek my life."
> But what said the answer of God to him?
> "I have reserved to myself seven thousand men
> Who have not bowed the knee to Baal."
> Even so, then, at this present time,
> There is a remnant according to the election of Grace.
>
> (Romans XI. 2–5)

Torquemada follows here the text of Romans with the comment of de Lyra to the end of verse 4. Then, however, he turns to St. Thomas' interpretation for a reason that can be readily seen. "Seven thousand" represents a small minority, and de Lyra's remarks, like Paul's own words (in verse 5), indicate that only a "remnant" of the Jews was to be saved through conversion to Christ.[185] But the comments of St. Thomas and the Ordinary Gloss yield quite a different impression. Thus, Thomas says on the verse in question: *"I have left for myself* [i.e., saved through grace] *seven thousand people,"* this implies that "the *certain* replaces here the uncertain because of the perfection of the numbers seven and thousand,"[186] while the Ordinary Gloss says concerning this: "Generality is indicated by seven, perfection by thousand."[187] Obviously, Torquemada wanted to impress his reader with the "generality" of those who were destined to salvation. Hence, the Apostle's conclusion, according to St. Thomas: *"Thus also in this time,"* in which you see a multitude of Jews deviate [from the faith], "there is a remnant"—namely, the many who were left from the other destruction[188] and these will be or were saved, *"according to the election of grace"*—that is, according to the gratuitous[189] election of God. For as John said (XV.16): "It is not you who chose me, but it is I who chose you."[190]

The salvation of the Jews who were to be left after the "other destruction"—namely, after the destruction of Jerusalem by the Romans—is therefore not a disputable matter. It represents Israel's unalterable destiny, which is organically related to the divine "election," and consequently, whatever "falling" the Jews had or have must be viewed as merely temporary. But something else was pointed out here, and that was with respect to the number of the "fallen"—i.e., "damned"—and consequently of those who were to be "saved."

Torquemada made a strenuous effort to show that the reproaches of the Jewish people by the prophets referred to a minority rather than a majority, and that all those who were to survive the "destruction"—namely, all the Jews of the Diaspora or their descendants—were predestined to "salvation." When the prophet Elijah said that he alone remained of all the worshipers of God in Israel, he spoke without the spirit of God,[191] and when God said to him that He left for Himself "seven thousand who did not bow to Baal," He spoke symbolically, meaning thereby that the "generality" of the people—i.e., its majority—remained perfect in their faith. Thus, what Torquemada was driving at was to show that the prophecies of *damnation* did not refer to the whole Jewish people, but to a minority of it only, while the prophecies of *salvation*—which Christian theology interpreted as referring either to the Church or to a small "remnant" of the Jews who were to accept Christ—were actually directed to the Jewish people *generally,* and at least to its great majority. It was only through a careful selection and combination of excerpts from various Glosses—those of Anselm, Strabo, de Lyra, and St. Thomas—that Torquemada could arrive at this conclusion after having formally leaned all the way on recognized Christian exegesis.

II

With all this, Torquemada must have realized that he had not yet beaten the difficult problem. For thus far all he said related, in the main, to the remote past and the remote future. As to most of the era of Christian history, however, Torquemada had to admit that only a minority of the Jews were converted, even though he repeatedly tried to make it clear that this minority was substantial. The Glosses did not always permit even that, and at least on one occasion, in interpreting Romans II.12, he had to follow the position of the commentaries, which seemed to contradict what he sought to prove.[192] Yet viewed from another angle, Romans II.12 offered such a strong argument on behalf of the Jewish converts that Torquemada was prepared to use it in his apology together with the damaging comment.

Let us now note the crucial verse in Romans in which the Apostle says about the Jews:

> For if their diminution
> Is the riches of the Gentiles,
> How much more will be their fullness?[193]

Combining parts of the various Glosses, Torquemada comes up with the interpretation that if their "diminution," the few who were converted (namely, the apostles), were the "riches of the Nations"—that is, endowed the nations with spiritual wealth, illuminating them by their preaching and example—how much more will their "fullness" (namely, all the Jews, or most of them) when converted to God redound to the wealth of the world? As Ecclesiasticus 24.16 says: "In the fullness of Saints is my abode."[194]

Implicit in Torquemada's interpretation was the essence of his historical view of the Jews and his credo about the place that their converts to Christianity were to occupy in the future Christian world. A staunch belief in the spiritual strength of the Jewish people—a strength that can virtually move mountains of faithlessness, as well as of ignorance and indifference; pride over the fact that the achievement of Christianity was largely, and basically, a Jewish achievement; and a conviction that the final objectives of Christianity will be attained only after the bulk of the Jewish people will have joined the Church—all this reverberates in the above statements, which provide the commentary to the verse from Romans. An old crusader for the expansion of Christianity, Torquemada realized as only few did how enormous was the task that still lay before the Church—the task of converting the rest of mankind and sanctifying the whole of humanity. And whence will Christianity derive the huge force needed for the execution of that task? His gaze was fixed on an alluring prospect. Obviously, he thought, if a few Jews like the apostles could revolutionize mankind to the extent they did, if a minority of the Jews who followed Christ could offer the "gentiles" such wealth and such blessings, how much greater will be the Jews' contribution to the world when all or most of them will be converted? This was a conclusion which served not only as proof that Jewish converts should not be abused; it was not only a rebuttal of the boorish Toledan charges concocted against the Jews as bearers of faithlessness. It was a thought which reflected Torquemada's vision of Christendom and the outstanding position that the converted Jewish people was destined to hold in the ranks of the Church.

But there was something else of tremendous importance relating to the future of the Jews in Christendom that Torquemada found in the words of the Apostle. For there, in the same chapter of Romans, where he dwelt on the mystery of the Jewish attitude toward Christianity, the Apostle also made that famous puzzling statement:

> For if the casting away of them
> be the reconciling of the world,
> What shall the receiving of them be
> but life from the dead?[195]

What did the Apostle tell us by these words, which seem so enigmatic and so pregnant with meaning? According to de Lyra, the meaning is this: the Jews who know the Scriptures, when converted to the faith, could contribute more than other converts to the dissemination of Christianity. "Life from the dead," therefore, in de Lyra's opinion, means simply the conversion of the gentiles to the faith—their emergence from the "death" of pagan disbelief to the "life" of the Christian faith.[196] But according to St. Thomas, the reference is not—or at least not only—to the *unconverted* gentiles, but rather to the *converted* among them. In fact, Thomas explains, the conversion of the Jews will make these gentiles rise to life, for "the gentiles are believers whose ardor wanes,"[197] as is indicated in Matthew 24.12: "Because iniquity shall abound, the love of many shall wax cold"; and furthermore, "those who will entirely fall, deceived by the anti-Christ, will be restored to their pristine zeal [*pristinus fervor*] by the converted Jews."[198] It turns out, then, that the mass conversion of the Jews will not only be vital for the advancement of Christianity and its triumph over the rest of mankind; it will also help save the Christian camp from deterioration and dissolution. For the "gentiles are believers whose faith wanes"; they "wax cold," and therefore, to be restored to the faith, they need the warmth of conviction, the devotion and the fervor that only the Jews can provide. Only the latter can revive the "pristine zeal" that characterized Christianity in its initial stages.

This, again, was an idea that fitted Torquemada's inward thoughts. His view of the state of Christendom in his time, and the task which he himself had performed in the Church, seemed to substantiate that idea. Struck by the long Schism, by moral deterioration, and by such violent heresies as that of the Hussites, the Church was faced with a menacing situation precisely because the "faith of the gentiles waxed cold." And who labored harder to stem that retreat, who threw himself more ardently into the thick of the battle against all the followers of anti-Christ in his time, who did more for the restoration of that "pristine zeal" than he himself, the "Defender of the Faith"? His own experience, and his whole life achievement, seemed to offer a living testimony to the veracity of St. Thomas' concept.

III

From this position, which he thought he had established—namely, concerning the *roles* that Jewish converts played, and were to play, in the Christian world—Torquemada takes a big step forward when he indicates the *reasons* for these phenomena. But in so doing he again comes to grips with the racial problem—that is, the quality of the converts' race, which is the race of the Jews.

As in the previous discussion, Torquemada presents his views on this problem via a reply to his cardinal question (i.e., how Jewish converts to Christianity should be treated), which now, however, assumes a somewhat different form. Stressing that essentially *all* Christians are either converts or offspring of converts, either from gentilehood or from Judaism, Torquemada now formulates that crucial question in a way that brings it nearer to the one posed by Paul.

Why should converts from gentilehood to Christianity refrain from abusing converts from Judaism? One reason the Apostle gives, Torquemada points out, is that the "descendants of the Jews are disposed toward the good" and, consequently, "reparable for salvation."[199] Paul proves this first by the fact that all of the Apostles emerged from the Jews, and then by the fact that the Patriarchs were their fathers.[200] As to the Apostles, the proof is based on the result: "For if the first-fruit be holy"—that is, if the apostles and their disciples, who were like the first fruit offered by the Jewish people to Christ, were holy—"also the bulk *(massa)*"—i.e., the race as a whole—can be sanctified or repaired[201]; since, as the Gloss says, the first fruit shares its substance with the bulk from which it stems, the first fruit could not be holy if the bulk were foul.[202]

If in the case of the Apostles we gather the nature of the cause from that of the effect, in the case of the Patriarchs we can learn the nature of the effect from that of the cause. For "if the root"—namely, the Patriarchs from whom they [the Israelites] drew the moisture of the faith—"was holy, so are also the branches" (Romans, XI.16)—namely, "those who have descended, or descend, from their race, and were established in their faith." Torquemada here stresses the idea of *faith*, as he wishes to project the tendency of the Jews toward faithfulness rather than faithlessness; and he wants also to emphasize that the same principle applies not only to the Jews of St. Paul's time but also of later times; therefore, he adds to the words "who have descended," which are found in the Gloss, the words: "or who descend" (i.e., in all times). He could of course do so on the basis of the Gloss, which said earlier that the Jews (namely, *all* the Jews) *drew from the Patriarchs the moisture of their faith;* nevertheless, there is an intensification of the idea here via a more elaborate interpretation. "For just as a good root diffuses good fruit or juice in the branches where there is fruit of good taste, thus the Apostles and all the others, who drew their origin from the holy Patriarchs and imitated their faith, were good and holy."[203]

To be sure, says Torquemada (through the words of Paul and his commentators) "some of the branches"—namely, of the Jews who proceed, according to the flesh, from the Patriarchs—"were broken off" because of infidelity.[204] But that is no proof against the preceding argument. For it is not by the "broken" but by the "standing" branches that the race must be judged; and if there is anything that confirms this contention, it is the fact that the gentiles, to elevate their status, had to be "grafted" onto the "tree" of the Jews. As the Apostle said, "You, *the gentiles* (this word is added by Torquemada), who are an oleaster" (namely, a wild olive tree which cannot bear good fruit), you who had neither the Law nor the Prophets, nor even the worship of God, as you were dedicated to idolatry, ought to remember that you "were grafted in among them"—that is, among the standing branches *(ramis stantibus)*, which are the apostles and the other faithful Jews; "and with them you partake of the root"—that is, of the faith of the Patriarchs and the Prophets, *"and the fatness of the olive tree"*—that is, of the doctrine and grace of Christ which came from the Jews.[205]

It follows that the whole achievement of the gentiles was that they became associated with a *Jewish* faith; that whatever value they may have, they gained through that association; and thus there is no reason for them to be proud. Rather, they have every reason to be humble. For if any of the two parties should be reticent about its origin, it is certainly the gentile one; for they were a wild olive tree to begin with, which was raised to the status of a good olive tree only by sucking from the Jewish roots and trunk whatever health and goodness they now possess. For such a party to offend the Jewish stock is to pay with ingratitude the source that nourished it; moreover, it is to deny the essence of the change—the Christian change—which took place in the gentile nations. Indeed, only a denial of the blessings of Christianity, and a return to the basest forms of paganism, could be in keeping with the abuse which these modern pagans heap upon the Jewish race.

IV

However powerful this argument of Torquemada's against the gentiles' anti-Jewish attitude, it did not directly answer the question that spurred the whole discussion: What relations should exist in the Christian world between its two major components, the gentile and the Jewish—or, more precisely, between Christians of gentile origin and those of Jewish descent. The answer, to be sure, is implied in the foregoing; but Torquemada wished to make it explicit, and also to draw from it some final conclusions.

Nothing so symbolized the troubled relations between the two conflicting groups, Torquemada believed, as the arrogance with which the Old Christians treat the New. The Christians from gentilehood view the converts from Judaism as people who push themselves upward, without right, to the gentiles' elevated ranks. But in light of the historical evolution of Christianity, such a contention is grotesque. It was not the Jews who uplifted themselves to the status of the gentiles, but it was the gentiles who were uplifted to the status of the Jews; or as the Apostle put it, they were *promoted* to the society of the Jewish people—or, rather, of the Jewish people's faith *(gentiles promoti sunt ad societatem fidei populi iudayci).*[206] Moreover, this promotion did not come of itself; nor was it attained by the gentiles' own merits. They gained it through the efforts of great guides and teachers—namely, the Prophets and the Apostles, who were all Jews. It is they who raised the gentiles from the abyss of barbarism to the high level of faith that distinguished the Jewish people. Hence, Paul's purposeful, instructive words to the converts from gentilehood at Ephesus: "You are built upon the foundations of the Apostles and the Prophets" (Eph. 2.20)[207] Never should the gentiles forget this crucial fact when they approach a Jewish convert to Christianity.

Indeed, the Apostle warned the converts from gentilehood: "Do not boast against the branches" (Rom. 11.8)—namely, the Jews, who bore the fruits of Christianity. For, if either of these groups—i.e., the gentile and Jewish converts—has reason to boast over the other, it is obviously the latter, not the former. Torquemada does not suggest to the Jewish converts to assume an air of superiority or adopt a haughty attitude toward Old Christians; nor would such a thought enter his mind. But there is no doubt that his view of the Jewish convert—as the heir and bearer of the divine heritage, and as the transmitter of that heritage to mankind—was on his mind when he formed this argument against the converts from gentilehood.

Moving toward its preconceived climax, that argument appeared in its full, crushing weight when presented in the following words of the Apostle, accompanied by Torquemada's comments: "But if you boast"—despite this admonition of mine—against those who come to Christianity from Judaism, it is said there to you: O Gentile, "you do not bear the root, but the root bears you" (Rom. 11.18). And with these words Torquemada approaches what was perhaps the highest point in his countercharge, or what we may call the moment of truth in the whole bitter and crucial controversy. Clearly indicating what was implied in that statement, which he quoted from the words of the Apostle, Torquemada, in a spurt of courage and defiance, cries out, not only to his Toledan adversaries, but in fact to the whole Christian world: *"Judaea has received from you neither salvation nor anything else, but you have received from her your faith and, in addition, your salvation!"* As the Savior indicated in John 4.22: "Salvation comes from the Jews!" Hence the promise given to Abraham (Gen. 12.3): "In these shall be blessed all the families of the earth."[208]

The clear consciousness of the immense task fulfilled by the Jews in the history of religion filled Torquemada throughout the writing of his treatise, as was repeatedly indicated above; but perhaps nowhere was it so strongly expressed as in these challenging, ringing words. They reflect the author's unwavering conviction that the maligned Jewish people is the one group to whom mankind owes its greatest debt. But pulsating in them is also the pride of origin—of that divinely chosen "family of men" which constituted that particular people.

* * *

There remained, apparently, only one more claim that the opponents of the conversos had frequently advanced—namely, the alleged incapacity of the Jews to be assimilated to Christianity and its way of life. It was, to be sure, a marginal claim, and yet Torquemada could not let it go unchallenged, as it seemed to represent some hidden and possibly disturbing truth. Accordingly, he countered it briefly, but resolutely, with the following words of the Apostle explained by leading exegetes:

> For if you, the gentiles, *cut off from an olive tree which is wild by nature*—that is, born of the sterile gentilehood—*were grafted onto a good olive tree*—i.e., the faith of the Jews—*contrary to nature*—that is, against the common course of nature; for not only was the branch of the bad tree not accustomed to be grafted onto a good tree, but rather the opposite; if however this was done, *how much more shall these, . . . the natural branches,* who by their natural origin belong to the Jewish people, *be grafted onto their own olive tree*—that is, be brought back to the dignity of their own people [*gens*]—that of the Patriarchs and the Apostles.[209]

It follows that the integration of newcomers into Christianity is much easier and quicker in the case of Jewish rather than of gentile converts; and thus, the theory of the Toledans that the Jews find it difficult—or next to impossible—to adapt themselves to Christianity, its beliefs, and its rites[210] is rejected by Torquemada as so much nonsense with the rest of their "groundless" assertions. It is precisely because of the fundamental community of Judaism and Christianity, Torquemada asserts, that the convert from Judaism can find in Christianity the fulfillment of his highest ideals and the natural development of what is embodied in Judaism in embryonic form. It is absurd to assume therefore that the Jews, of all races, would fail to adopt the very religion which *naturally* suits them best.

Yet if this is so, the question must be raised—and Torquemada of course must consider it: Why did the conversion of the Jews proceed so slowly? Why was it not completed long ago? Torquemada admits there is a mystery here, and he points to the words of St. Paul: *For I would not, brethren, you should be ignorant of this mystery*—that is, according to the Interlinear Gloss: the secret judgment of God—*lest you should be wise in your own conceits; that blindness in part has happened in Israel until the fullness of the Gentiles come in. And so*—after it *will* come in[211]—*all of Israel shall be saved, as it is written* (Isa. 59.20): *There shall come out of Zion*—i.e., from the Jews according to the flesh—*the Deliverer who will remove wickedness*—i.e., infidelity—*from Jacob.*[212] *For this is my covenant unto them*—that is, as the Gloss says, this promise to them will be fulfilled, for I myself shall do what I have promised, *when I shall take away their sins* (Rom. XI.27); and this will be in the end, when the Jews will be converted to the preaching of Elijah and Enoch, as says the Ordinary Gloss.[213]

So there is a "mystery" in the manifestation of divine grace to the Jews and in the time of its appearance. But Torquemada also alludes to a solution. It may be hidden in God's will to demonstrate that *all* of mankind, including the Jews, will earn their redemption not by merit but by grace. Nobody could doubt, he points out, that the gentiles, who were pagans for thousands of years, did not earn their salvation by merit. But if the Jews, or most of them, had flocked to Christ shortly after His appearance in their midst, the matter *might* have been attributed to their merit. Such an attribution, however, would be impossible if they came to Him after centuries of estrangement. Thus, the mystery of the "late arrival" of the Jews may be related to this reason.[214]

III. Second Attack on the Conversos

I

If the Instruction of the Relator was intended as a rebuttal of the Petition and the *Sentencia-Estatuto,* the Memorial of Marcos García de Mora was intended as a rebuttal of the Instruction.[1] But this was not its only purpose. Written, like the Instruction, after the Pope's bulls against Sarmiento and the other rebels had reached Spain, the Memorial was to serve, above all, as a rejoinder to the Pope's charges. García, however, did not want this rejoinder to be directed at the Pope alone. According to his, or the rebels' plan, the Memorial was to present Toledo's case before the whole Christian world, and as such it was addressed not only to the Pope, but to King Juan II of Castile, Prince Enrique, the heir apparent of the kingdom, and all the kings and princes of Christendom, "both spiritual and temporal."

It is most unlikely, however, that the city's leadership approved the extant document, and in all probability the text before us is merely a proposal of an apology for Toledo which Marcos García composed on his own initiative or at the city's request. We are led to this opinion by a comparison of the Memorial with the *Sentencia* and the Petition, which may have been likewise drafted by García, but were carefully checked by a number of people who were influential in the city or in the rebels' group.[2] That is, we believe, why, in contrast to the *Memorial,* they are compact in content and terse in style, and why they contain reservations, or guarded formulations, on some points where the Memorial takes a more extreme position.[3] In brief, while the earlier two papers, which were issued by the city, betray some traces of collective thinking, the Memorial bears the stamp of García's own views, undiluted by Toledo's more moderate, or more cautious, politicians.

It is precisely this fact, however, that gives the Memorial its special significance as a historical document. For Marcos García was the moving spirit of the rebel movement in Toledo; he was its ideologue and foremost agitator, and also its major public spokesman and chief representative in the rebel government. Here in the Memorial we hear him speak freely, echoing the slogans of the campaign he conducted and voicing the opinions which not only his friends, his closest associates in steering the rebellion, but also no doubt many of their followers shared with him to the end. If, therefore, we wish to know the sentiments and views of the anti-Marrano movement in Toledo, we must turn to the Memorial, the only authentic writing left by its chief spokesman.

Seen in historical perspective, however, the value of the Memorial is not limited to this. For what we have before us is not only a document that faithfully represents the "popular spirit" of the period[4]—or, more precisely, the attitude toward the conversos that prevailed in large segments of the Spanish population—but one that also gives clear-cut expression to a particular theory about the Marranos—the theory of their racial inferiority—which hitherto was voiced, with some obfuscation, in certain limited circles only. To be sure, in the consciousness of the Spanish masses, that theory lived and exerted an influence long before the Toledan rebellion, and we have seen manifestations of that influence in both Castile and Aragon.[5] Yet judging by the forms of its outward expression, it was, more often than not, half suppressed. García was the first to express it fully and openly; and he also crystallized the theory in slogans and postulates, and launched a determined campaign on its behalf. Thus, a doctrine was born that was to arouse one of the stormiest public debates in Spanish history and to shape Spain's policies toward the conversos for two and a half centuries. Ideologically, politically and, more broadly, historically, its influence was incalculable.

The Memorial was no doubt meant, among other things, to serve as a vehicle of the racial campaign, even though it was utilized for this purpose on a much smaller scale than originally intended. If we are right in our assumption that its extant version was merely a draft unsanctioned by Toledo's leaders, it is certain that this document was never sent to its intended destinations. For the Memorial must have been one of the very last writings produced by García on the converso issue. As a rebuttal to the Pope's bulls of September 24 and the Relator's Instruction to Don Lope de Barrientos, it could not have been drafted before November.[6] This was a very short time before García was executed as a "traitor," and as such he could not of course be considered as author of the city's formal pronouncements. Even so, we have reason to believe that the Memorial was circulated by García's followers, agitating the minds of many Spaniards and gaining adherents to García's views.

The work consists mainly of three sections: its opening part presents the case of the Old Christians and the city of Toledo against Alvaro and the conversos; its middle part argues, on grounds of general principles, why the actions taken by the Pope and King Juan against the rebels and the city were both illegal and unjust; and the third and final part is devoted to a rebuttal of five specific accusations which were made against the rebels and which, García claims, were falsely conceived from the standpoint of both fact and law. Interpolated at one point in this final part are four passionate appeals to the Pope, the King, the Prince, and the people of Toledo, respectively.[7] They seem to belong at the end of the paper, and that is most likely where they would have been placed had the draft of the Memorial been duly revised either by its author or some of his associates who collaborated with him on the Petition and the Statute.

Within this framework, the Memorial deals sporadically with various subjects—social, political, legal, and religious—all related somehow to the converso problem. This problem is the main topic of the work, its backbone, and its recurring theme. The Memorial begins and ends with this theme—or, more precisely, with a violent attack on the conversos as well as their ancestors, the Jews.

Since this is the main issue discussed in the Memorial, we ought, it seems, to broach this subject first. In doing so, we shall try to provide answers to such questions as: What was García's view of the Marranos and the part they played in Spain's life? Wherein lay the core of the Marrano problem, as he saw it? And what measures, if any, did he propose for its solution?

Marcos García does not leave us long in doubt as to his answer to the first question. Already at the very beginning of his paper, when he presents the troubles that befell Castile in his time—or, as he put it, "the great cruelties and inhumanities that were committed by the evil tyrant Alvaro de Luna, who calls himself Constable of Castile"[8]—he discusses the conversos' share of responsibility for those atrocities. That share, in his opinion, was major—in fact, decisive. For it was they, the conversos, who "caused, promoted and incited" all the crimes perpetrated by the tyrant.[9] If not for the conversos, Alvaro, however evil, would not have perpetrated those crimes or even begun to commit them. The initiators were the conversos. Consequently, the partnership between Alvaro and the conversos, which, as we have seen, was already indicated in the Petition, now assumes a different aspect. The role of the partners is changed. According to Marcos García, the Marranos were not a tool of Alvaro; rather was Alvaro a tool of the Marranos. For they were not merely the *executors* of Alvaro's instructions; they were also the schemers of his actions, "their causers, promoters, and instigators."[10] Hence, not only do they *support and serve* the reign of tyranny and oppression in Castile; they manipulate, regulate and, in fact, *determine* it to the last detail.

Castile is in the hands of the conversos! That is the cry that rises from almost every page of the Memorial; and that is the alarm García sounds in the ears of all Christians. The assumed Judaeo-converso conspiracy, which allegedly pervaded the government of Castile and used its positions to destroy the Old Christians—that conspiracy which, as we have noticed, was emphasized both in the Petition and the Statute—is now no longer described as being in the making or even moving toward its goal; now it is portrayed as having *attained* its objective through the possession of the government of Castile and the virtual control of the administration's actions. For Alvaro de Luna, the head of the government, who had "imprisoned" the king, captured his administration, and thrown its doors open to the conversos, is in fact not the *real* ruler of the country. To be sure, he is a "tyrant" and of course a "traitor," who thinks he is "using" the conversos for his aims; actually, however, he is a puppet of the conspirators, who plan and dictate all his moves. Behind the formal government of Alvaro there is the real, secret government of the country, which is in the hands of the conversos.

It would be unreasonable to assume that such a clandestine organization, with the whole system of government in its toils, would lack a leader in whose mind would converge all its secret plans and designs. García does not hesitate to do what the Petition and the Statute refrained from doing. He points a finger at this man, indicates his position, and calls him by name. He is no other than Fernán Díaz de Toledo, the Relator (or, as García puts it, "who is called Relator"), who is mentioned in the Memorial almost as often as the Constable of Castile. García calls him by what may have been his own or his family's *Hebrew* designation[11]; and this, of course, should not be wondered at. For he is a man "most vile by his lineage, most lewd by his habits, damned and condemned as a heretic, a real Jew."[12] This is the great "spider" who contrives or master-minds all the Jewish schemes against Castile, and who spins all the threads of the deadly web that entangles the Old Christians of Spain.

It may be taken for granted that the "great spider" is crafty and cunning and vicious in the extreme; yet the power of evil that he represents is by no means limited to him alone, for it is shared in abundance by *all* the individuals of the collective body to which he belongs. When García describes in superlative terms the moral corruption and deceitfulness of the man—i.e., the conversos' clandestine leader—he really does not thereby mean to say that he is outstanding among the conversos in *these* respects. Essentially, his moral characteristics are the same as those of the rest of the conversos—of that "abhorred, damned and detested group, species and class of the baptized Jews and those who came from their lineage."[13] For *all* of them are "adulterous, sons of infidelity, fathers of all greed, sowers of all discord, rich in every malice and perversity, always ungrateful to God, opposed to his orders, and deviating from his ways."[14] It is that "group, species and class" as a whole—and not merely one or some of its members—which is responsible for the calamity that afflicts Castile.

García does not hesitate to admit that there are differences of opinion regarding the conversos. But what does that prove? Catholicism is certainly the highest form of religion, and as such it is honored by all faithful Christians; yet even concerning the evaluation of Catholicism there are differences of opinion in mankind. But who are the gainsayers? The Moors and the Jews! Similarly, there are some who dispute the fact that Spain is controlled and exploited by the conversos. But who are these discrepant people? Interested parties who—for the sake of their ambitions, or "for filthy lucre's sake," as

the Apostle said—are prepared to deny the simple truth or blind their eyes
to the facts. But all "good and noble" Christians believe in what "is believed,
declared and upheld by the noble and holy city of Toledo." Indeed, they
know what the culprits themselves (Alvaro, the Relator, and their partisans)
know—namely, that "the said kingdoms [of Castile and Leon] have been
subjected, subjugated and usurped under the tyrant and the Judaic yoke for
forty years"[15]; they know, as one knows a plain fact or axiom, that "Alvaro
de Luna with the said infidels have dilapidated, destroyed and wasted the
said kingdoms in detriment of the Catholic faith and the perdition of the
bodies and souls" of its followers who live within their borders.[16]

How do the conversos effect this destruction of the faith, the kingdoms,
and the Christian people? As García sees it, diverse means are used, but the
common denominator of all these means is their criminal character. In fact,
there is hardly a crime that the conversos shun in their efforts to achieve their
end. Thus, García tells us, "they are Judaizing, tyrannizing, simonizing,
hereticizing, adulterating, cheating, sowing discords, robbing, flattering, in-
triguing, demonstrating false theories against the Catholic faith, and sucking—through profiteering and usuries—the blood and sweat of the poor
Christian race."[17]

According to García, then, the crimes of the conversos embrace all spheres
of life. They are manifest in religion, economy, government, and of course
in all personal relationships between the conversos and the Old Christians.
Thus they gnaw at Christian society from all angles and undermine all its
institutions. Obviously, under the impact of such tyranny and maltreatment,
such perpetual and multifarious torment and irritation, the people are agitated, restless, fretful—in fact, convulsed with agony. No wonder that a
"painful and clamorous wail" is heard across Castile from one end of the
country to the other.[18]

We have thus far seen the end of the conversos' main endeavors, and we
have also seen the means by which they attain it. The end is the destruction
of the Christians in Spain, and the means are the various crimes they commit.
Yet we still lack the motive. The questions to be raised at this point are: Why
did the conversos set for themselves such a grim and dreadful goal? Why did
they assume the burden of this undertaking, which is as difficult as it is
heinous? And why do they pursue it with such stubbornness and determination—indeed, with such ferocious zeal—so as to devote to it all their efforts
and commit for its sake so many excesses? The answer we would expect to
receive from García—the answer which would fit the common view of the
Middle Ages—could be summarized in one word: hatred—or, more clearly,
the hatred which the conversos, as secret Jews, feel for the Christians, their
religious antagonists. In other words, we would expect an explanation from
which we might gather that it was a *religious* hatred that drove the conversos

to employ all the means they could possibly muster to strike deadly blows at the hostile religion. Yet this is not the answer we find in the Memorial.

To be sure, García does not ignore the religious aspect of the Marranos' alleged antagonism to the Christians. Repeatedly, he speaks of their "infidelity," their refusal to accept the truths of Christianity such as the "birth, Passion and resurrection of Christ."[19] He also speaks of the Marranos' violations of specific Christian laws and rites, as well as of their "heretical" performance of Jewish law and custom—all of which indicate the depth and determination of their opposition to Christianity.[20] Nevertheless, it is not in religion that García sees the root of the merciless war waged by the Marranos against the Old Christians. In fact, if we consider the sum total of his remarks, we come to the conclusion that, the way he saw it, it was not because of their opposition to Christianity that the Marranos behave so immorally toward the Christians; but it was because of their basic immorality that they developed their opposition to Christianity. Thus, all their crimes, whether religious or not, can be traced to one cause: their immoral disposition.

García does not fail to tell us what the origin of that disposition is. It is, according to him, the quality of the Jewish race, which is "base," "perverse," and inherently evil. Long before Christianity was born, he tells us, the psalmist David had recognized this when he defined the Jews, the conversos' ancestors, as a "perverse and adulterous" breed[21]; and long before that, following their wanderings in the desert, the Lord Himself declared that they are "a people that always err *in their heart*" (Psalms 95:10),[22] pointing thereby to their inward corruption. Such they were before the rise of Christianity, and such they remained after its birth. This is why St. Paul, in his "epistle to Emperor Titus, the avenger of the blood of Jesus Christ," cautioned him "not to appoint as bishops converts from the stock of the Jews, for *by nature* they are evil, vindictive, unfaithful, adulterous, arrogant, vainglorious—and skilled in the performance of all bad customs."[23]

St. Paul never issued a general prohibition to appoint converts from Judaism as bishops; nor, contrary to what one may gather from García, did he give any general advice to this effect.[24] Similarly, most of the negative epithets used by García to describe those converts—epithets presumably cited from St. Paul—are not to be found among the Apostle's words.[25] It is significant that in castigating converts from Judaism, Paul ascribed to them faults of doctrine (or such as are related to the teaching of their views),[26] while the flaws ascribed to them according to García are all related to moral defects. García painted a picture of the converso as he, and other Marrano haters, saw him in Castile or Aragon at the time—a picture that had hardly any relationship to the Judaizers in Crete of whom St. Paul wrote. Above all, nowhere in the aforementioned epistle—or, for that matter, anywhere else—does Paul say that the converts from Judaism were "evil by nature." These words, like the rest of the epithets, were García's, not St. Paul's; in fact, we may say that they were his "additions."[27] But it is precisely these additions which he attributed to Paul (or, at best, the wrong meanings he read into the text) that mark both his new approach and his new theory.

Briefly, the essence of this theory is that the source of all the troubles caused by the conversos is not their religion, or education, or training, but their nature, their mentality, their race. They do evil things—and only evil things—not because of external influences, but because they are constitutionally evil. They perpetrate all the "cruelties and inhumanities" they are guilty of because they are *by nature* cruel and inhuman. In fact, they should be called a "congregation of beasts," like all those "enclosed in the association of the synagogue."[28] Like beasts, they lack not only a moral sense, but also the higher faculties of perception. Hence also their dullness, their basic incapacity to grasp the inner meaning of Scripture and the higher truths of Christianity[29]; hence their disbelief, their doubts, their heresies. Hence, in brief, their Judaism.

From this point we can move directly to García's ultimate deduction. Since the moral and intellectual defects of the Jews stem from their natural constitution, they cannot be expected to change for the better. Conversion to Christianity cannot improve them either, because they cannot accept Christianity sincerely. Being what they are—the epitome of evil—they are opposed to Christianity—the epitome of goodness—more than to any other religion or any other way of life. Indeed, this is why they hate it so intensely and why they so ardently seek its destruction. Thus, there is no remedy for them in the present and no salvation in the future.

Scripture itself, García says, testifies to this in no uncertain terms. For even in ancient times God Almighty became so exasperated with the Jews' sinful conduct—or rather with their "obstinate persistence" in evil—that he "disinherited them from His eternal Glory" and doomed them to the "perpetual punishments of hell."[30] García also pinpoints the biblical statement in which "that condemnation of our Lord was made."[31] It is in Psalm 95, which reads, in its essential part, as follows:

> Forty years long I was grieved
> With this generation . . .
> Wherefore I swore in my wrath:
> They should not enter into my rest.[32]

This, then, is the theological basis of the theory about the eternal damnation of the Jews which is propagated by García. A passage in Psalms which clearly refers to the generation of the desert and to God's oath not to allow that generation to enter the Promised Land is taken to refer to *all* the generations of Jews, while the Land of Israel, the "rest" place from their wanderings, is construed as indicating the universal redemption. All this, of course, is contrary to the plain meaning of the text. And yet García cannot here be charged with false attribution or interpretation (as in his citation of Paul's words to Titus). For besides the literal meaning of the text, there was its so-called symbolic meaning, as accepted by Christian exegetical tradition; and from this standpoint, there can be no doubt, García stood on firm Christian ground.

The symbolic interpretation employed by García is found in the writings of St. Augustine, who was most likely its original author. In his comments on that verse, Augustine explained that it referred to the *Jewish people*—i.e., not only to the generation of the desert, but to all generations that followed.[33] Above all, the "rest" of which the Psalm speaks was understood by him, not as the Land of Promise in which the Jews expected to find peace, but as the true felicity and immortality that came with Christ's salvation.[34] God swore that these people would not "enter into His rest," which meant, in effect, that they were destined to "ruin"—i.e., the "ardor of eternal fire" and the "condemnation of the devil."[35] We touch here the heart of the Christian damnation theory insofar as it was associated with Psalm 95, and which, following Augustine, was embraced by such commentators as Cassiodorus[36] and others. García was no doubt influenced by this theory—or rather by that part of it which he used in the Memorial—while ignoring or narrowing the meaning of other parts which were not to his liking.[37] For Augustine, who was mystified by the fate of the Jews, the fathers of Christ the *man* and his rejecters, did not accept the aforesaid verdict as God's last word on the subject. Despite that "terrible oath," he stressed, God did allow some Jews to enter His "rest," just as he allowed "some gentiles" to do so, and furthermore, He assured all of the Jews salvation at the "end" of the world.[38] Puzzled by the strange fate of the Jews, Augustine left it to the mystery of the divine will; but of one thing he was sure: *God will not abandon His people;* and Jacob's dream, which signified to him the final happy phase of the Jewish destiny, was to be fulfilled. "A time will come," he said, "and that time will be at the end of the world's duration, when all of Israel will believe." Indeed, it will be then that Jacob will become Israel—the Israel who will see "the sky open and the angels of God ascending and descending toward the Son of Man."[39]

García paid little or no attention to this important aspect of Augustine's view, just as he failed to consider such commentaries as those of Nicholas de Lyra, who recognized the literal meaning of the text.[40] Perhaps he was unaware of them, or perhaps he thought that by pointing them out and giving due notice to what they implied, he would weaken or undermine his theory of race. And so, that single verse in Psalms, into which he read what he wished it to suggest, sufficed him to determine that, of all the races of mankind, the Jews alone were barred *forever* from the salvation of Christ.

II

It is obvious that a proponent of such views about the Jews, their past, present, and future, was confronted with a genuine dilemma when he considered the question of their conversion to Christianity. For centuries—in fact, since its inception—the Church had made every possible effort to induce the Jews to abandon their religion, and, moreover, saw in their conversion to Christianity the crowning of all its missionary efforts. Could García conscientiously and willingly support this traditional view of the Church? The answer, in our judgment, must be in the negative. What he said of the Jewish race and its qualities—that is, its inherent, ineradicable evil—and its exclusion, for that reason, from Christ's promise of salvation (albeit with some "exceptions"); what he said of the converts from Judaism to Christianity, their unquenchable desire to destroy Christian society, and the deadly designs they harbor for Christendom; in brief, what he said of the Jews and the conversos necessarily led him to one conclusion—namely, that Christianity should have refused, and should refuse, the acceptance of converts from that race. His sense of caution, however, warned him that, in saying this, he would place himself squarely, and dangerously, against the Church's dominant thinking and practice, both of which relied on strongly held traditions sanctified by age, custom, and authority. Therefore, to avoid the perilous confrontation, he hinted at his view only indirectly, leading the reader to conclude for himself that the whole policy of the Church on the conversion of the Jews was a great error which must be rectified.

He did this partly by replying to the argument of the Relator (and other conversos) that the Toledans' actions, if approved by Church or State, would have a negative effect upon the future conversion of the Jews. "The serpents" (namely, the conversos), he says, claim that the "persecution conducted against them [in Toledo], and their exclusion from public offices and benefices, will make the Jews cease to convert themselves to the faith of Jesus Christ."[41] But, says García, he who really wants to convert himself with a "holy and just intention to save himself," will not be prevented from carrying out his wish "either by privations or by denial of honors, offices, and benefices."[42] Both his presentation of the conversos' reasoning and his reply to their alleged contention indicate García's cunning and capacity to twist and distort a valid argument. The conversos, of course, did not suggest that the mere denial of public offices as such would prevent Jews from converting; what they referred to was the discrimination, the injustice, the suppression of rights, to which every person, by becoming Christian, is supposedly entitled by Christian law. What they referred to was the degradation, the humiliation and, consequently, the disgrace involved in that denial to every convert from Judaism for the sole reason that he belonged to the Jewish race.

What they referred to, in brief, was *the punishment for no crime* which the prospective convert is expected to accept.[43] And thus, what this argument of the conversos implied was that if Christianity tolerates "punishment for no crime," or if such a policy is pursued in its realm, Christianity cannot be considered by the Jews a worthy substitute for their own religion.

Disregarding these major reasons for the conversos' reaction to the Statute, García takes his argument further away from such considerations. Not only does he state that privation of office never prevented anyone from converting to Christianity if he really "wished to save himself"; he goes on to point out that the attainment of office was precisely the reason, or one of the main reasons, for which the Jews converted. Never were they moved to go over to Christianity by the need to "save their souls" or by "the love and charity" that should inspire all *true* conversions (witness St. Paul and all other saints!).[44] What motivated their conversion were the "*desire* to farm taxes," the "*appetite* to deceive," the *cupidity* expressed in usurious moneylending, the *ambition* to rule over Christians, and "carnal *lust* for nuns and [Christian] virgins."[45]

We see that these reasons as presented by García all constitute criminal passions, and all supposedly further the *aim* he ascribed to the Jews' conversion to Christianity (i.e., the destruction of the Spanish people). We have already shown the fanciful character of that "aim,"[46] but we should also consider his specific charges and see whether they contain a core of truth.

There can be no doubt that social aspirations (or, as García would have called them, "ambitions") were instrumental in the conversion of *some* Jews, who formed together a small minority that belonged mostly to the upper class. But it would be ludicrous to assume that these were the factors that determined the vast majority of the conversions. His listing of "carnal lust for nuns and virgins" as a typical cause of the Jews' conversion only shows how far he was prepared to take his extravagant accusations. García no doubt knew of conversos engaged in tax farming, moneylending and public offices—what he defined as "rule over Christians"; he must also have heard of amorous relations that developed between New Christians and Old Christian women (including perhaps, in some instances, nuns), and he identified what he saw in the *post*-conversion state with the *pre*-conversion intentions of the Jews. He ignored, however, the fact that the vast majority of the conversos were not tax farmers, moneylenders, and officeholders, but workers in a large variety of professions of quite a different order[47]; and he conveniently forgot that the mass conversions of the Jews (in 1391 and 1412) were not caused by any of the passions indicated, but by the desire to escape intolerable oppression and, above all, by the wish to escape death—by the sword or by starvation. Thus, we see wherein lay his main distortion. A condition of duress, compulsion, and choicelessness—in brief, a condition of "yield or die"—is presented by him as a normal situation in which plans were laid to gratify lusts and carried out in circumstances of completely free choice.

Whether García believed what he said is a complex question we shall touch on below; but whether he did or not, his claims were indefensible. The hollowness of his argument becomes strikingly apparent in the double standard he applies to the Old Christians and the New. "Our Savior Jesus Christ," he says, "did not attract or induce those who wished to come to Him with [promises of] temporal dignities and honors, but only with provisions of celestial things." On the contrary, He cautioned those who wished to follow Him that they would have to deny themselves these things.[48] How true; but such advice is not offered by García to the Old Christians. He does not tell them to be satisfied with "celestial provisions"; to stop seeking public offices and honors; or give up the goods of which they robbed the conversos and divide them all among the poor. On the contrary: rather than suggest to the Old Christians that they divest themselves of their earthly possessions, he says that they followed "Christ's doctrine" when they deprived the Jews of what they owned (or, as he put it, "of what the Jews vested themselves with by force, chicanery and cheating"). And then: "Jesus . . . told each of his followers to carry his cross on his shoulders as He did, and prepare himself to suffer martyrdom in defense of the faith and of justice as He did." And how can "martyrdom" be undergone and the faith defended, according to García? As he sees it, the Toledans showed the way. "The Catholic Christians trampled upon them [i.e., the conversos] and cut off their heads, and cast them under their feet, as is done to enemies of the law and the true faith of Jesus Christ."[49] For García's peculiar logic there was evidently no difficulty in arriving at such conclusions. Just as self-denial and self-dispossession are expressed in stealing other people's goods, so "martyrdom" is expressed by cutting off other people's heads.

Had García been clear about this matter, he would have had to eliminate this double approach; he would obviously have had to "coordinate" his stand with the Church's teaching about conversion. But García was neither clear nor outspoken, and nowhere does he make a real attempt to bridge the inconsistency between his own view of the conversos and the traditional Christian position on this issue. In one place, to be sure, he does admit that God, in His infinite goodness, compassion, and mercy, has exempted and *will* exempt *some* Jews from the eternal punishment which they surely deserve.[50] He even concedes that some of the converts, after a "diuturnal" living among Christians, may finally be purged of their Jewish blight and deserve full admission into Christian society.[51] Such concessions on his part, however, must be seen as mere bows to ruling Christian doctrine—bows prompted by political expediency and not by a conviction and a sincere desire that the

Jews convert to Christianity. In any case, they could not affect in the least the end result of the policy he recommended. García fully realized that laws preventing converts from admission to Christian society for *four generations*, as suggested by the *pesquisa*, would not hasten the free conversion of the Jews but, on the contrary, block it completely. And that is what he wanted to achieve. For it was not in conversion, but in quite different means, that he saw the solution to the Jewish problem.

III

We come closer to an understanding of his views when we review his defense of the Toledans' actions against the conversos during the rebellion. As he himself states, the rebels were accused of having committed crimes and excesses against the Marranos (a) by burning some of them to death; (b) by robbing many of them of their property; (c) by ousting them from the public offices they had held; and (d) by prohibiting them from occupying such offices in the future. García does not deny any of these actions, but he denies that they were taken against the law. And it is in the reasons he offers in their justification that he reveals not only his real attitude toward the conversos, but also the measures he wanted to be taken in dealing with the converso problem.

Why were some conversos killed and burned in Toledo? García's answer is plain and unqualified: because they were traitors and heretics. They were traitors because they conspired to deliver the city to the tyrant (i.e., Alvaro de Luna) and his servants (namely the converso officeholders), and they were heretics because they held Jewish beliefs and "guarded all the Jewish ceremonies."[52] García thus restates in the Memorial the charges made in the *Sentencia-Estatuto* regarding both the political and the religious crimes of the conversos in Toledo. Here, however, the same claims are presented not so much to demonstrate the Marranos' criminality as to justify the punishments they received from the Toledans. And to strengthen his case against the Marranos, García offers some additional arguments that afford us a better basis for judging the positions of the conflicting parties.

We have already indicated that the charge in the *Sentencia* that a converso conspiracy was organized in Toledo in order to kill "all the Old Christians in the city" and transfer the city to the hands of its enemies was a fabricated accusation aimed at justifying the outrages committed against the conversos by the rebel government. We have also presented our own reconstruction of what actually happened in Toledo.[53] The related data we find in the *Memorial* only fortify our conviction that this reconstruction is correct.

The conversos' plan of action, according to García, was to consist of three stages: first, to kill the Old Christians; then to steal their possessions; and finally, after putting these possessions at their disposal, to deliver the city, cleared of Old Christians, into the hands of Alvaro de Luna.[54] To the purposes of the plot as presented in the *Sentencia*, which includes the first and third stages, García then added the second stage—the planned robbery of the Old Christians. It would be really inconceivable, judging by García, that the conversos, so given to "filthy lucre," would fail to include in their program of action a plan to rob the Old Christians. That during attacks by Christians on Jews, or during armed conflicts between Old and New Christians, such robberies had been repeatedly committed by the Old Christians, but never by Jews or conversos, is of course a fact that throws a valuable sidelight upon the veracity of García's account. We can understand, however, why García felt the need to "fortify" his position by the charge that the conversos intended to "rob" the Old Christians. Since one of the purposes of his apology was to justify the expropriation of the conversos' goods, the charge of the intended robbery by the conversos would lend that expropriation a "moral" vindication. Thus, if García does not give us a truer account of the conversos' intentions, he does give us a fuller description of the rebels' "presentation" of the alleged plot.

Next he tells us that the conversos of the city, who armed themselves (which we know from the *Sentencia*) and got together ("were united") in their parishes, "remained for three days armed in their houses against the will and prohibition of Pero Sarmiento." Finally, they decided to implement their "plan." "They came out into the squares in two armed companies under the command of Juan de Cibdad and Arias de Silva. They would have in fact accomplished their evil purpose if not for the Old Christians who, by divine inspiration, killed the said Juan de Cibdad. With Juan dead, the others were terrified, which is always the case with those of a base race, who are used to conquer through cheating and profiteering rather than by armed struggle."[55] They fled in panic, thus bringing to an end their entire conspiracy.

These, then, are the "facts" that García offered in support of his charges about the conversos' plot. But his account makes no sense. If the conversos in Toledo could entertain any hope of capturing the city—and that meant, first of all, seizing the strong places—they could do it only by a surprise attack. But according to García, the conversos armed themselves and "remained armed in their homes" for three days "against the specific order of Pero Sarmiento," who doubtless demanded that they disarm. So the "sudden," unprecedented organization of the conversos (who "were united in their parishes") and their unprecedented decision to arm themselves were apparently no secret to the Old Christians. The fact that for three full days the conversos "stayed armed in their homes" and did not appear in the streets of the city could not remain, of course, unnoticed by the Old Christians and could not fail to arouse their suspicions to the point of preparing themselves against a surprise attack. But even if we assume that the Christians still knew nothing about the conversos' real plan, the charge of conspiracy is exploded by his narration that the conversos came to the squares of the city in two armed companies led by two commanders. So instead of launching a surprise attack on the fortresses, they came to the squares, which were filled with Old Christians and which had no strategic value at all. Surely they did not come there to capture the city, because the armed men in the alcazar and the other strongholds would have soon been alerted of their action, and their plan would have come to naught at the first stage of its implementation. We hear, in fact, of no aggressive action by the conversos either in the squares or elsewhere in the city. But we do gather from García that the conversos were greeted in the squares by the Old Christians with a shower of arrows and that, in that initial attack upon them, their leader, Juan de Cibdad, lost his life.[56] Surely, there must have been another explanation for the conversos' resolve to arm themselves, to "stay in their homes for three full days" and, ultimately, to venture into the squares "in armed companies," as García tells us.

What actually happened is not hard to imagine. The Marranos, sensing imminent danger, organized for self-defense. They armed themselves to protect their homes and their lives and did not venture out of their own neighborhoods. For several days things seemed to be quiet; no attack was launched against the Marranos and no excesses against them were committed. They decided, therefore, to end their isolation and try to restore relations to normality. Perhaps they went to the squares for provisions; but fearing a hostile encounter with their foes, they chose to come there in armed groups. This, however, did not save them from trouble. Aware of all their moves, their watchful enemies allowed them to reach the heart of the city, and there met them with a deadly attack. The conversos retreated with a dampened spirit, leaving behind them several casualties, including their leader, Juan de Cibdad.

If this reconstruction is more or less correct, the aftermath may likewise be easily guessed. The conversos were now accused of having formed a conspiracy to capture the city by force, and their coming to the squares, as well as their preceding moves (from the day they took up arms to defend themselves), was described as having aimed at that objective. These were not merely wild allegations designed to besmirch the Marranos as "traitors." These were *formal charges* made by the city for the purpose of bringing Marranos to *court* and "legally" subjecting them to death and confiscation. In portraying the related occurrences as he did, García simply followed the "official" accusation, one which he had doubtless helped construct in conformity with the rebels' "judicial" needs.

IV

If García thus justifies the killings and the gallows, he has another explanation of the lethal burnings. "For it is known that they were found to be
heretical, infidels and blasphemers of Christ and His Mother." Therefore,
"those of them who were burned as heretics were justly burned, for the
punishment of the heretic—according to divine, human and customary
law—is death by fire."[57]

It was certainly according to "human" and "customary" law in the case of
incurable heretics, but was it also according to "divine" law? García's answer
was, unhesitatingly, yes. And to prove it, he did what any other jurist in his
time would have done under the circumstances. Unable to point to a Church
decree that openly stipulated death for heretics, he turned to an expert on
canon law who interpreted certain canons in line with his thesis.[58] Then, to
prove that this interpretation was correct, he proceeded to show that it
agreed with God's orders. Such proof he found in Jesus' words (John 15.6):
"He who does not abide in me is cast off as a withered branch; men gather
these branches, throw them into the fire, and they are consumed." Can there
be more conclusive evidence that heretics should be burned to death? To
García, the argument was now sealed.

Jesus' words as cited by John may of course be comprehended quite
differently. Yet here, we should add, García's claims coincided with the
formal view of the Church—a view that was expressed in many legal pronouncements and adopted more than two centuries before. To be sure, canon
law had not explicitly demanded the death penalty for obstinate heretics, but
it had demanded, since the days of Gregory IX, the surrender of such heretics
to the secular arm, and this for the sole purpose of subjecting them to "due
punishment."[59] What "due punishment" meant was quite apparent from
certain implications of the canons themselves,[60] but one could gather it
directly from the secular laws that referred to this matter in unmistakable
terms.[61] It meant death by fire which, since the beginning of the 13th century,
had become increasingly common in the countries of the West. The Church
progressively encouraged this procedure[62]; and no less an authority than
Thomas Aquinas gave it his blessing and theological sanction.[63] Henry of
Segusio, better known as Hostiensis, the famous glossator of canon law,
further supported this approach,[64] and Giovanni d'Andrea, the later expert
in the field, buttressed the position by arguments of his own.[65] It was from
Hostiensis that García took his proof based on the words of Jesus in John,[66]
and he considered the glossator's interpretation as final, "regardless of what
some false commentators may say."[67] Indeed, he denounces these commentators as "false" because they claim that the "Church receives the penitent
heretic to its bosom after his first lapse into heresy, as is testified by the

stipulation to this effect in Canon Law."[68] This is not so, García declares. The truth is that even "according to canonic kindness," such a heretic is sentenced, after the first lapse, to perpetual prison; but "in cases of heresy where it is quite clear that such a punishment [of imprisonment] is not commensurate with the crime, one must follow the civil law, which advocates death by fire." Hence, says García, the burning of the Judaizers in Toledo was according to canon law. "For even this law does not recognize as penitents *all* those who regret their heresy after the first lapse. When it is presumed that the heretic repented, not out of true recognition of the faith but out of fear of punishment by fire, canon law judges the case as a relapse and orders delivery of the heretic to the flames."[69]

As authorities for these canonic decisions, he cites the decretal *excommunicamus,* and the comments of Hostiensis on this decretal.[70] But again his sources do not square with his claims. To be sure, canon law, as cited above, recommends perpetual prison for heretics who abjured their errors after having been arrested (presumably out of fear of death) and also expressed their willingness to do whatever penance might be imposed upon them. The law, however, does *not* demand the delivery of such heretics to the secular arm, which would amount to a death sentence, as García claims.[71] The commentator Hostiensis, on whom he relies, does not give him any basis for such a conclusion either.[72] Yet, this does not prevent García, as we have seen, from advocating in the name of canon law actions against heretics which are far more severe than the harshest canon law has ever recommended.

Did the Toledans, then, commit crimes when they killed, hanged, and burned conversos to death? Not only did these actions of theirs not constitute a crime, says García, but they were so justifiable that had they not been done, the Toledans *would* have been guilty of a crime.[73] Nevertheless, García adds, the Toledans are not guiltless in this matter. To be sure, they killed and executed *some* conversos as traitors to the city and as heretics, and to this extent they fulfilled their obligation. "For since they [i.e., the conversos of the city] rose with such great arrogance to kill Pero Sarmiento and the Old Christians [who reside in the city], they all deserve the punishment of traitors," and therefore the Toledans should have "finished [i.e., liquidated] also those of them who "remained alive after some of them were killed by arrows or on the gallows."[74] For, as he put it, "it is certainly a grave sin to tolerate people who are so infidel and so evil."[75] Therefore, if the Toledans did anything wrong, it was not in killing *some* of the Marranos, but in "tolerating" the remainder, whom they allowed to stay alive.[76]

Thus, according to García, what the Toledans should have done was to kill, hang, and burn all the conversos of the city. And there is no doubt that what he advocated for Toledo he wanted to see done in the whole country. Consequently, the solution he desired for the converso problem was the extermination of the whole Marrano group. Juan de Torquemada states, as we have noted, that *this*, and nothing less, was the purpose of the rebels, or rather of the anti-Marrano party; and judging by García, the cardinal was right. Thus, the race theory of García was inextricably bound up with the idea of genocide. And could it be otherwise? If a race was judged to be the epitome of evil, the source of all misfortune, and also incorrigible, there was obviously no other way to deal with it than to sentence it to death.

García realized that some people might consider his proposed solution too cruel, and therefore he tried to prove them wrong. To begin with, he says, the glossator Hostiensis shares and supports this thesis. Accordingly, "he who exults in cruelty against criminals for the sake of justice deserves a reward" for he carries out God's will ("he is the minister of God"), while he "who shows patience" to criminals is a sinner—in fact, "commits a mortal sin"[77]— for he invites upon society the worst calamities that can possibly befall the human race. Said the code of Justinian in its section on heretics: "Tolerance [of such people] corrupts the elements and the spheres, and as a result of this corruption there come deaths, wars, pestilences, hungers, persecutions and tribulations."[78] But let not one assume that in these calamities the reference is only to communal troubles which the sinful individual may escape. "The ire of God will fall [also] upon those who tolerate these criminals, beg clemency for them, and defend them."[79] Hence, no pity, no patience, and no consideration of any kind can be shown toward these evil men.

The remorseless, consuming hatred that dictated these passages of García informs and pervades also the rest of his apology for the Toledans. Thus, he regards as ludicrous the charge that the Toledans perpetrated crimes when they robbed the Marranos or expropriated their possessions. Since the latter are nothing but traitors and heretics, who deserve death, no wonder that both civil and canon law permit the taking of their possessions by force.[80] Further- more, both laws authorize such action against persons who acquired their property illegally—that is, by such means as usury, profiteering, and chica- nery[81]; and who would doubt that this is precisely how the conversos ac- quired what they own? Nevertheless, García must have felt that even those who would not question these assertions might still object to his argument. Granted, they might say, that the goods of such criminals can be confiscated by the authorities in due legal process; but does this mean that private individuals—any Old Christian of whatever standing—can appropriate Mar- rano property for himself as had been done in Toledo? García's answer is unreservedly positive. To be sure, he cannot cite any law that permits such action, but there are always biblical narratives to which one can turn for justification. Did not the Jews take, in like fashion, the possessions of the Egyptians? And did not this action please God? "When the Egyptians sought to recover the goods of which they were robbed . . . with God's permission, they were drowned in the sea. And this is what will happen to the said baptized Jews. For they will return to recover the goods which were taken from them, and they will lose their lives after the goods."[82]

Regardless of whether he intended to convey by this comparison of the Marranos (who were ousted from the city) with the Egyptians (who were drowned in the sea) a threat, a hope, or simply a prognosis, the comparison is both arbitrary and misleading, as are most of his biblical references. The reason he gives for the Egyptians' pursuit of the Jews is of course not the one given in the Bible (see Exodus 14:5), and consequently it could not be the cause of the Egyptians' drowning in the sea either. Yet beyond this, there is an overall idea that clarifies García's thought from another angle: that the property of such criminals as the conversos is outlawed, and that its seizure must be seen as the taking by soldiers of booty from an enemy at war. Moreover, such robberies are not only to God's liking, but they must be carried out in compliance with His will. Furthermore, it is God's wish that they be carried out *fully* and, indeed, unsparingly to the very end. "God was displeased with Saul," says García, "for the latter did not complete the robbing of His enemies. Because he pardoned some of them and left some of them their property, he was deprived of the kingship."[83] It follows that if the Toledans sinned, it was not in having stolen some converso property, but in not having stolen enough of it—in having, in their pity, left some of the possessions in the hands of the "enemy." Thus, the conclusion he derived from biblical accounts with respect to the Toledans' robberies is similar to the one he arrived at concerning their killings.[84] García, moreover, states openly: "It is not what was *done* in the taking of the possessions that ought to be considered a crime but what was *not* done. But for this there is a remedy: that we complete our persecution of them, and then our acts and motives will be pleasing in the eyes of God and the eyes of men."[85]

According to García, then, there was nothing wrong with the rebellion as such or with its declared aims and policies. If anything was wrong, it was the extent to which these aims were attained and the policies implemented. In other words, if the rebellion did not achieve its purpose, and difficulties piled up on its way, it was not because it went too far, but because it did not go far enough. This was also the cause of the controversy that ensued on the converso issue. For why, asks García, can the Marranos now press for the restoration of their rights, their properties and positions in the city? Because many of them still live in Toledo, as well as in the rest of Spain. But had the Toledan conversos been exterminated, all controversy about their rights would have ceased, as it would have become automatically senseless. Should the city, then, seek an accommodation with the King and try to save what it had gained from the conversos? Undoubtedly such proposals were then considered in Toledo, but there is also no doubt that García opposed them.

In his judgment, there was one way for the Toledans to emerge victorious from the struggle: *to finish what they had begun to do;* and we already know that, in his terminology, "to finish" meant to exterminate all the conversos and pillage or expropriate all their possessions. Thus, we hear in his apology for the rebels' actions an echo of the campaign he was conducting in the city—a campaign in which he urged the Toledans to remobilize for a final general assault on the conversos, which would be aimed at the goals indicated above. Only such a radical and decisive action, he claimed, could swing public opinion to the rebels' side. In García's words: "If we, the Toledans, wish to be victorious and wish to have our triumph declared by God to all men *(gentes),* we have to finish the persecution of that race, and then, by the Spirit of God, all will understand that our actions were just and holy as they are, whereas otherwise there will always be a diversity of opinion."[86]

Was García wrong? One hates to answer this question in the negative. But history is full of examples to prove him right. While a struggle rages, public opinion is divided on which of the parties is just or unjust. But such a controversy generally ends once the struggle is over. Then it is usually the victor who is acclaimed. For dead societies, tribes and nations there is no court of justice, or even a hearing, in the forums of public opinion. There is no real controversy about their case. Marcos García de Mora, it appears, sensed the veracity of this rule.

He knew, however, that meanwhile the city was not ready to go as far as he recommended and that a battle of public opinion was in progress over the city's treatment of the conversos. Few realized more acutely than García the importance of winning that battle; and hence, indeed, his detailed apology for the Toledans' past actions. We have seen how he defended the killings and the robberies. We shall now see how he defended the Statute.

V

No less concerned than Garcia and his followers about the outcome of the struggle over the *Sentencia* were of course the conversos who could not fail to notice that the discriminatory law was fulfilled without resentment by most if not all of Toledo's Old Christians. If originally one might think that the statute was *imposed* by the rebels' government on a voiceless citizenry, now it appeared to have been factually endorsed by the majority of the Old Christian population. As such, it could well remain in force even after the rebels' downfall. And should this happen, the conversos knew, their prospects of retaining equality with the Old Christians would be gravely jeopardized in the whole of Spain.

This is to put it mildly, of course. Actually, they knew that their social degradation and the reasons presented for its justification were merely first steps in a broader program which called for their total liquidation. To abolish the Statute was therefore the goal of all the conversos' public efforts. Conversely, to uphold it was a major objective of their determined adversaries.

The Statute was an act of law, and as we have seen, the conversos attacked it on the grounds that it negated the supreme laws of the Church and the overriding civil laws of the country. To use a modern term, we might say that the conversos saw the Statute as unconstitutional. Accordingly, the debate that evolved on this issue centered on the question of the Statute's "constitutionality."

From the standpoint of García and his view of the Jewish race, the whole discussion of the Statute was pointless. What need was there to prove that the conversos had no right to hold public office and give testimony in court once it was proven that they belonged to a race that was barred from Christian salvation? There was obviously no room to discuss even the possibility of granting *any* position of dignity to those who were condemned, because of their natural evil, to perpetual punishment in the world to come, and therefore, indisputably deserved to be consigned to the cruelest punishment in this world, too. Nevertheless, since the arguments of the opposition made a certain impact on Christian opinion (as was evident from the Pope's bull), García decided to answer them directly; and thus he set out to prove that the Statute, far from being in violation of the laws, was in full accord with all the "decrees and decretals," divine and human alike.

To substantiate his claims by biblical authority, he cites the words of Paul in his Epistle to Titus in the distorted manner we have indicated above[87] and follows this up by citing the Mosaic law, which supposedly confirms Paul's opinion.[88] According to García, this law stipulated that "if members of other nations and faiths convert themselves to the Mosaic law, they would have no offices or possessions until a certain generation."[89] But the law of Moses does not say this at all. There is no general provision there, as García would have it, governing all "*other* nations and faiths," only definite directives respecting *specific* nations who were regarded as historic enemies of the Israelites and bore deep hostility toward them[90]; there is no discussion there of "conversion to the faith," but of "entering the community of God"—i.e., intermarriage, and nothing is said about the denial of "offices and possessions" which, according to García's presentation, was the main aim of that law. It would be pointless to go here into a discussion of the motives and meaning of those laws. Our purpose is to reconstruct García's thinking, and this can be done by turning to a passage from another anti-Marrano paper, which was submitted by the rebels to the Roman curia only a few months before the *Memorial* was written. That passage read as follows:

All converts who belong to the Jewish race or who have descended from it—that is, who were born as Jews, or are sons, grandsons, great-grandsons, or great-great-grandsons of Jews who were baptized [to Christianity], including those [converts] who descended newly and recently from that most evil and damned stock, are presumed, according to the testimonies of Scriptures, to be infidels and suspect of the faith. From which follows that the vice of infidelity is not presumed to be purged until the fourth generation.[91]

Although allegedly relying on the "testimonies of Scriptures," the conclusion as cited cannot be supported by any biblical statement. The laws of Deuteronomy referred to by García indicate two periods during which four nations were prohibited from entering the community of God: one was of "ten generations" (meaning "forever"), which was specified for the Ammonites and the Moabites, and the other of "two generations," assigned for the Edomites and the Egyptians.[92] But the Toledan authors of the aforecited passage chose none of these alternatives. Why? Evidently, they did not dare to recommend the exclusion of the conversos from Christendom "forever" (as this would involve them in a quarrel with the Church which they realized they could not possibly win); yet, on the other hand, they could not agree to have the "suspicion" of Judaic infidelity limited to two generations only; this would have put the grandsons of converts—by then at least half of the converso population—beyond the date of two generations, and thus place them on equal footing with the Old Christians. Therefore, they came up with a time limit of their own (*four generations of life as Christians, besides that of the converts!*) which would push off the danger of converso equalization far into the future.

García, who may have shared in the writing of the paper in which this time limit was set up, or at least was consulted in its formulation, was of course aware of the difficulty involved in any attempt to reduce converso rights on the basis of biblical law. Nevertheless, he thought he could dodge the difficulty. By using the phrase "until a *certain* generation," which did not gainsay the language of the Bible, as well as of the paper submitted to the curia, he assumed he could offer a tacit defense, supposedly on the grounds of biblical law, for the limitation of "four generations." His argument, it seems, appeared valid to his partisans, and also to their followers in coming times. Considered from our own vantage point, however, it merely shows the callous disrespect with which he treated the laws of the Bible.

VI

But it was not only the Bible that García abused as a source of evidence for his assertions. No less distorted, arbitrary and misleading were the "testimonies" he adduced from canon law. According to him, there are four canon laws that specifically prohibit baptized Jews from holding offices or benefices in Christendom, and this, as he puts it, for the following two reasons which are presumably indicated in these laws: (1) because they (the baptized Jews) have always played false *(prevaricaron)* in the faith, and *under the guise of Christians* have always done evil and much harm to the *true* Christians; and (2) because it is a shady and ugly thing to allow him who yesterday recited prayers in the synagogue to sing today in the church.[93] Yet if we examine the four laws he mentions—those enacted in the Council of Agde (506) and in the Third and Fourth Toledan Councils—we find that he again exaggerates to the point of invalidating most of what he says.

To be sure, the law of the Third Toledan Council does entail a prohibition on holding public office—but it applies to Jews, not to converts from Judaism.[94] And as for the law of the Council of Agde, one has only to read it in its entirety to see how García plays havoc with its contents:

> Jews whose perfidy often leads them back to the vomit, if they wish to be converted to the Catholic faith, let them stay on the threshold as catechumen [for eight months], and, if they are known to have come in pure faith, then at last they deserve the grace of baptism. But if by some chance [they happen] to incur in the prescribed time a danger of sickness [i.e., a danger for their life as a result of sickness], and they become desperate—let them be baptized [at once].[95]

Again we see that this law was enacted only for *Jews* (in this instance, Jews who sought conversion to Christianity), but not for converts who had crossed the Christian threshold. In its opening derogatory remark, the law may indeed refer to converts—or rather to a negative, disappointing experience which Christians had with converts from Judaism. Yet it does not allude, even in a word, to a prohibition on granting them public offices and benefices, or to a limitation of any other kind.

The third of the laws referred to by García *(Plerique,* the fifty-ninth decree of the Fourth Toledan Council) does deal with converts from Judaism, but only with those who have relapsed. It offers no general ruling for Jewish converts and orders penal measures only for those of them who transgressed and resisted correction by persuasion. No indication is given in this law respecting the nature of these measures.[96] In any case, the issue of public offices is not mentioned in it at all.

Of the four laws García cites, therefore, only one offers support to his thesis. This is the sixty-fifth law of the Fourth Toledan Council, which prohibits "Jews, and those who are of Jews" from holding public office in Christian Spain.[97] The expression "those who are of Jews" may rightly be construed as referring to Jews who were converted to Christianity, and possibly also to their descendants. Yet as we have seen, this single law could in no way represent the legal, theoretical and practical position which Christianity took on this issue.[98]

Disregarding such inconveniences, however, García proceeds to prove that civil law also authorized the Toledan legislation. "King Receswinth," he says, "on the advice of his counselors, all the major nobles *(mayores caballeros)* and prelates of the kingdom, issued at Cortes many laws in which he invalidated baptized Jews as witnesses against Old Christians and as holders of public offices and benefices.[99] But King Receswinth issued only one law in this matter, and that law does not deal with offices or benefices, but only with the giving of testimony. It says: "Jews, either baptized or not, should be prohibited from giving testimony against Christians"[100]; and even this limitation is by no means universal, for the same law, as we have indicated, also enables "descendants of Jews" to testify among Christians, if a priest or a judge, let alone the King, "vouches for their morals and their beliefs."[101] García ignores this stipulation, and thus we see how an *incomplete* limitation in *one* area is turned by him into a *complete* one in *several* areas. The fact that he could find no law in any civil code (which applied to the whole country) that denied the rights of converts to receive offices and benefices did not prevent him from stating that there were "many" laws that provided such limitations.[102] This is another example of his habit to claim widespread authoritative support for his assertions when no such support existed.

Then he refers to the privilege of Alfonso, which, according to him, denied converts from Judaism the same rights which were denied them by the Statute.[103] García was not perturbed by the claim that this privilege was no longer in force owing to its replacement by contradictory decrees, laws and regulations of later kings.[104] He insists that the laws of the country and the city with respect to the status of converts from Judaism are those which he indicated, as cited above; and bluntly rejecting the criticisms on this score which were directed at the Toledans from many quarters, he declares in his usual bold manner: "Regardless of what the King and the Pope say of them," and despite the fact that the latter "dispense" with them, "the said rights *(derechos)*, decrees and laws cannot be abolished or repealed by any apostolic, imperial or royal law or constitution."[105]

Thus, the verses he cited from the Bible to "prove" the "perversion" of the Jewish race (and which, as we have shown, prove nothing of the kind) and the laws he referred to (which, upon analysis, contain only one canon law and one civil law dealing with the issues in question, apart from the above-mentioned privilege of Alfonso) are described by him—no more and no less—as representing the position of "all divine and human law"[106] on the converso issue. García, of course, was fully aware of the large body of civil and canon law that flatly contradicted his assertions; nor could he claim innocent ignorance in this matter, both because he was familiar with the sources and because the laws in question were distinctly and repeatedly pointed out by the opposition. But not only does he fail to deal with these laws; he refuses to admit their existence. To avoid such an admission and escape the charge that he failed to take into account the contradictory legislation, he refers to the latter in the following hypothetical manner: "If, therefore," he says, there are "some papal or royal letters or charters that qualify that damned race against all divine and human law, such letters should not be fulfilled or executed. Only the said laws and decrees must be obeyed."[107]

Conclusion

The first apparent lesson we draw from the Memorial is that Marcos García cannot be considered a reliable source for the evaluation of the Marranos or the reconstruction of Marrano history. Possessed with a deadly hatred for the Marranos, he must be disqualified as witness to anything related to converso life. His fury blurred his vision and crippled his judgment, and his violent desire to annihilate the Marranos virtually destroyed his sense of moral values.

We have seen how he presents his case without regard for truth or fairness; how he manufactures, or claims to possess, evidence which was unavailable to him; and how he ascribes to both canon and civil law, to prophets and apostles, to the Old and New Testaments, statements and ideas which are not to be found there and which no Christian commentator assumed were implied. It would certainly not be an overstatement to say that he did violence to the sources.

Yet apart from his arbitrary manipulation of the sources, he is disqualified by his manipulation of the facts. His facts, as we have seen, are frequently invented or distorted beyond recognition. For García had no more respect for facts—even for those he himself witnessed—than he had for legal and religious authority. He imposed his version of the occurrences upon the facts, just as he imposed his ideas upon the sources. And the resultant picture of the phenomena he portrayed was as imaginary as a work of fiction.

If, in view of the above, his statements on the conversos must be *generally* disqualified, his assertions about their religious behavior must be considered *especially* untrustworthy. Indeed, if García could go to such extremes as to claim that the conversos were inherently evil, of a devilish character, and beyond rehabilitation, either human or divine—claims which were unprovable and palpably wrong—he could easily make the far less extreme assertion that the conversos were religiously false.

It may be argued that a spurious testimony may contain some truth, too; and thus, while his claims about the morality of the conversos may have been fundamentally false, his assertions about their religious unfaithfulness may have been fundamentally true. Theoretically such a possibility exists, but practically the probabilities are against it. For it does not stand to reason that Marcos García, who throughout the Memorial exhibits a tendency to invent, distort and exaggerate, would radically alter his approach and habits when it came to the conversos' religious views. On the contrary, his predisposition to make extreme and false assertions when he thought they could help him to prove a point would indubitably be strengthened in his discussions and presentations of the Marranos' religious stand.

In fact, García *had* to exaggerate when he referred to the Marranos' religion, if he wished his view of the conversos' nature to be generally accepted. For it was only in conjunction with their alleged infidelity that their racial baseness could appear credible. Obviously, *true* Christians could not possibly be as low or evil as the Marranos were, according to García's description. But apart from these theoretical necessities, there were, evidently, practical requirements that moved him to take the same position. For only by portraying the *religious* behavior of the Marranos as shocking to every decent Christian could he hope to justify the shocking treatment to which they were subjected in Toledo. Otherwise, the rebels would inevitably be regarded as plain criminals and outlaws.

We must now revert to the question posed above: To what extent did García himself believe his own claims and charges? There is no doubt that he deliberately modified, exaggerated, or suppressed many accounts; and there is also no doubt that he was manufacturing "facts" that appeared to be suitable for his purpose. It is impossible to assume, for instance, that he did not know that the conversos in Toledo armed themselves in self-defense. Nevertheless, he declared that they were *all* involved in the plot to kill Sarmiento and capture the city; therefore all of them deserved the death penalty. We may assume of course that all the Toledan conversos *wished* to see Sarmiento overthrown and Toledo restored to the King's rule. But it is one thing to wish something politically and another to act upon it. To García, however, such a differentiation was unworthy of consideration. Like so many other extreme partisans, he viewed political opponents as enemies, whether or not they actually attempted to carry out their wishes. To him they were all either traitors to the regime or potential traitors, and therefore they all deserved to be eliminated by imprisonment, expulsion or, preferably, execution. If we compare his views and actions to those of revolutionaries such as Marat or Robespierre, or of totalitarian revolutionaries of our own time, we shall have a ready explanation for his charges and a correct assessment of their value.

For to such men, truth based on facts is of secondary importance. Far more important to them is *the* truth dictated by their views, attitudes and theories. To prove *their* truth it is sufficient for them to produce an argument hinging on some fact, however tenuously and loosely; and if there is nothing to hang it on, the necessary factual linkage is "supplied." To the unbiased mind, evidence like this would appear "fabricated," "fictitious" and "false." But that is not how it would seem to a man of García's cast.

For the existence of the truth of which he was sure did not depend on the availability of evidence to prove it. Hence, if nothing was proven about the conversos along the lines of his thinking and his accusations, it did not suggest to him that he might be wrong; all it meant was that the investigators charged with establishing the truth had failed to discover the real facts. For the "truth" he recognized was measured by one criterion: it had to justify his implacable hatred. Therefore, not only the Pope could not persuade him that he was wrong. If all the great teachers of Christendom in his time had come to him and pointed out his error, he would probably have said to them what he said to the Pope: your judgment is warped, you are deceived by the conversos, and the truth is as I have declared it.

We have noted the various reasons he gave for the conversion of the Jews, all of them apparently aimed at proving that their Christianity was feigned. We have shown that his reasons were mostly invented; but we should also ask why he turned to such ruses. After all, he well knew that most of Spain's Jews accepted Christianity at the point of the sword, and that *forced* conversion is *false* conversion. Why then employ invented "facts" when the true facts could serve him so well? But García must have realized that truth in this case was a trap. If the Jews were converted under duress, much of the blame for the plight he bemoaned would pass from the Jews to the Christians. And that, of course, would weaken his case. But even more important: if the conversions of the Jews were compelled, his theory of a Jewish plan to penetrate Christendom in the guise of Christians would obviously have to be given up, and the race theory, which is largely based on the assumption of a sinister Jewish mind, scheming havoc for Christianity, would suffer a shattering blow. Hence, to retain the myth of the Jewish conspiracy, and all the notions associated with it, the conversion of the Jews must be ascribed to their own will, and all the historic facts related to "compulsion" must be systematically ignored.

Thus we see how García's thinking worked and how his various statements were born. In essence, they were all subordinated to the ideas that he contributed to antisemitic thought; and these ideas formed the speculative constructions that were to play a great role in *his* time, and a still greater one in times to come. These were: the theory of the Jewish *conspiracy*, the theory of *race*, and the solution of the converso problem through *genocide*. Concerning this, we shall have more to say later.

That Marcos García's views of the Marranos were adopted or had originally been shared by many of his fellow rebels in Toledo, and perhaps also
by other critics of the Marranos both in Toledo and other places, is indicated,
in our judgment, by a satire about the Marranos written by an anonymous
Old Christian of Toledo within the first year following the outbreak of the
rebellion.[1] It is called "A Copy of a Letter of Privilege which King Juan II
gave to an *hijo dalgo*," and imitates, in its style, writs granting royal favors, so
that one may assume that its author was a lawyer or a member of some allied
profession (such as *escribano*), who was familiar with documents of this sort.
It is also possible that the author of this satire, who was an educated man and
an able writer, belonged to the low nobility, the caballeros, who were usually
part of the city's elite, though economically often hard-pressed.[2] But whether
or not the author belonged to any of these groups or classes, he certainly
wished to indicate that his own group was extremely unhappy with the state
of affairs in the kingdom of Castile, and particularly with its own lot in that
kingdom. He lays the causes of this unhappiness at the door of the Marranos,
all of whose gains, he claims, have been attained by a variety of criminal
means, obviously at the expense of the decent Old Christians. To correct this
situation, the king does not do what he would be expected to—i.e., order the
Marranos to change their conduct— but grants the hero of the satire, an Old
Christian hidalgo, a privilege permitting him to act like the Marranos and
follow the Marranos' way of life. And while enumerating the special rights
he gives him—the rights which had allegedly been granted the Marranos—
he presents what is supposed to be a true picture of the Marranos' social and
religious conditions.

Nicolás López Martínez was inclined to believe that the satire was composed in the days of Enrique IV,[3] but the late Professor Pflaum has correctly
concluded that "it was written by a Toledan citizen in 1449."[4] The Privilege
still speaks of Pero Sarmiento not only as the avowed enemy of the Marranos,
but also as the King's *repostero mayor* and *asistente* in Toledo (titles by which
Sarmiento styled himself during the rebellion). In the first half of Enrique
IV's reign, however, Pero Sarmiento was in disgrace, so that these titles, even
if remembered, would not have been taken seriously; and in the second half,
which was a stormy period, he could not possibly have commanded enough
attention to make the author present him as a leading figure. In addition, the
work is directed against Juan II, who is portrayed as a sworn protector of the
Marranos—a reputation which he had during the Toledan rebellion, but
which must have paled, or very much altered, during the reign of Enrique

IV. The reference to the "absolute royal power," on which the king relied in issuing his grants, may imply criticism of the King's unlimited authority—or rather claim of absolute power—and alludes to the rebels' political views as outlined in another chapter of this work.[5] Since none of this could be of interest in the days of Enrique IV, we assume that the satire was composed shortly before the collapse of the Toledan rebellion, in October or November 1449.

The satire begins with a complaint of an hidalgo about his inability to get ahead in life because, as a "pure Old Christian," he cannot compete with those of the Hebrew race who, "because of our sins," have recently been "hatched" (namely, converted) and became Marranos, that is, "legitimate" (Christians, or citizens), who are entitled to employ their "manipulations, chicaneries, subtleties and deceits, without fear of God and shame of the people." The hidalgo asks the king to treat him with clemency and "legitimize" him, too, to act like a Marrano for "in no other manner would he be able to live among them without being cheated." The king considers this request just and allows the hidalgo to employ and invent "whatever subtleties, evil deeds, deceits and falsehoods, of which all those of that race *(generación)* make use according to what they are inclined to by their constellation and birth . . . without suffering any punishment in this world."[6]

It is noteworthy that the author does not define these competitors as faked converts to Christianity, or as "recently *converted*," but as those of the "Hebrew race who became legitimized," or as Marranos who "have been recently *hatched* [like snakes?] because of our sins." It is evident that the author does not want to honor these Marranos with the title of converts of any degree, but to describe them as Jews who became "legitimized"—that is, permitted to live in a Christian society as Jews in the guise of Christians. By "constellation and birth" he refers of course to what was meant by these astrological terms, then in common use among the Marranos (although not among them alone): man's nature, dispositions, abilities, which cannot change under any circumstance. Since all Marranos were born under the same constellation, they *all* follow the same forms of conduct, and hence are guilty of the same deceits and chicaneries without incurring any punishment for them.

Following the grant of the *general* right to the Old Christian hidalgo to live like a Marrano (namely, like a criminal and a cheat), and thereby enjoy all the benefits of life, the satire goes on to mention the special fields in which the Marranos may exercise that right. These fields include religion, morality, law and economics; but the author does not deal with the misdeeds of the Marranos according to their categories, but at random, without any organizing principle. Here, however, we shall present his complaints according to their topics.

Of the Marranos' religious sins insofar as they relate to their fundamental concepts, the author speaks generally of the failure of the Marranos to "believe in what Holy Mother Church believes . . . and what is sung in our credo which is truly our faith"—namely, the dogmas of Christianity; he specifically refers to their view that "there is no other world except to be born and die, which the said Marranos hold and affirm against the truth."[7] This view was mentioned by the *pesquisa,* and the author, who probably composed his work during the Toledan rebellion, may have borrowed his charge from that source. The accusation was apparently of special importance to him. Having claimed that the Marranos arranged their lives so as not to fear punishment in this world, he went on to explain why, once they thus arranged it, they could commit their crimes without hesitation: they did not expect punishment in the other world either.

Apart from this reference to the alleged Marrano view about the world to come, the author mentions no converso belief. As for the conversos' religious *practices,* the author mentions only a few rites and customs, almost all related to the Sabbath, which, he claims, they observe meticulously, while they work on Sundays and other Christian holidays.[8] These charges were also made in the *pesquisa,* and are mentioned by García in the summary he offered of the findings of that inquiry.

As for the Marranos' social transgressions, the author first describes how the conversos commit frauds in their relations with the kings and nobles. They become their treasurers, managers of their estates, and members of their councils. In this capacity they induce them to overvalue the worth of their coins, thus enabling them to pay the workers less for their labor, while the latter and all who can afford little are unable to earn the barest living and are in consequence being destroyed. Thus, they arouse the greed and cupidity, and the inordinate desires, of the lords, who, because of this, become turbulent, fall into want *(menguas)* and earn the ill will of their subjects. In brief, the Marranos are responsible for the ruin of the national economy, the turbulence of the nobility, and the destruction of the lower classes.[9]

On the other hand, through the services they render the kings and nobles, they enrich themselves, for they "draw from the properties of their lords what they need for their [own] deals."[10] In brief, the Marranos are described as authors of evil designs and the great Old Christian lords as naive victims of their crafty manipulations, or as weak individuals who fall prey to the Marranos' fiendish incitements. Thus, they are induced and habituated to dedicate themselves to greed and excessive passions; to rely on the Marrano managers, who are expected to provide them with the funds they need for their lives of idleness and pleasure; and to use their free time to pursue their intrigues and warfare. Naturally, they frequently fall into debt, which compels them to put heavier burdens on their subjects, and these become steadily more impoverished and more embittered. Thus, the Marranos maneuver the kings, pervert the nobles, and ruin the lower-class hard-working groups from which the magnates derive their income.

With the wealth they acquire the Marranos increase both their social and economic power. Economically they use this power for profiteering and usury, and socially for attaining public offices, which are extremely important for their advancement; therefore, to gain these offices they employ every form of cunning, subtlety and flattery.[11] The offices they gain are those of judges, aldermen, jurors and public scribes, and by means of the facilities these offices offer them, they control the city, town, or place where they exercise their authority. Then this authority, and the subtleties they employ, enable them to ensnare the pure Old Christians in plots that provoke them to kill one another.[12] No punishment befalls the Marranos for having engineered these misfortunes. The privilege granted the hidalgo in the satire excuses him, as the Marranos are excused, from any penalty for "false oaths, lies and falsehoods he might say or make to deceive the Old Christians for his own interests and the interests of his relatives." In general, the Marrano is "entitled to use two faces, one for looking at a person's face to flatter him, and another for deceiving, bartering and lying."[13]

Following this description of the Marranos' social conduct, the author portrays their performance in the Church. They become priests and curates under false pretenses so that they may learn from the confessions of Old Christians the sins which the latter have secretly committed. Then either they or their Marrano partners blackmail these Christians for guarding their secrets and not exposing them to the public. Thus the Marrano priests, rather than serving their flock, form collectively a very important instrument in ruining the Old Christians and transferring their possessions to Marrano hands. Obviously, the author would advise all Old Christians never to confide in a Marrano priest or consider any Marrano a sincere religious teacher. They are false to the core, and their sole purpose is to bring harm and destruction upon the Old Christians, whom they hate.

But this is not all. The hidalgo is further authorized to make use of *every* secret sin committed by an Old Christian that became known to him, whether by the latter's confession or in any other way. Thus, the Marrano involved might accuse the Old Christian of the said crime or sin, and the latter, having confessed his crime and being unable to deny it, would have to beg mercy from the conversos, without gaining anything from this humiliation—for in the end he would lose all his possessions to the accusers, as happened on many occasions."[14]

Similar to the conduct of the Marrano priests is that of the Marrano physicians, surgeons and druggists. "Under the excuse of curing the sick Christians or of providing for their health," says the author of the satire, "they work and endeavor, as all those of their race do, to kill and humble the

Old Christians, both for the hate and enmity they feel for them" and for satisfying their desire to "marry the wives of the Old Christians they kill." Yet they enter these matrimonies not out of love, but—again—out of hatred for the Old Christians. Their purpose is to "take over the possessions and estates of their Christian spouses," defile and stain the "pure blood" *(sangre limpia)* of the Spaniards, and "get hold of the offices of the defunct Old Christians, so that they may pass to someone of the same race of the Hebrew Marranos or of a similar origin *(stirpe)* or stock."[15]

All these matters are usually not done privately. The author hints broadly that in order to advance in the Old Christian society, the Marranos have formed their "councils, unions, confederations, and mutual aid societies"[16]— in other words, the progress they made among the Old Christians was not just a product of individual efforts, but of a communal endeavor and perpetual planning by which they regulate their moves.

The satire is clearly in line with the racial views and social economic charges hurled at the Marranos by the Petition, the Memorial and the *Sentencia*. It recognizes no sincere Christians among the Marranos; it considers them all cheats and swindlers, men of evil nature, filled with hatred of Christianity, which they are determined to destroy. Thus, they corrupt the upper classes; impoverish the lower ones, kill any Old Christian they can lay their hands on, and studiously transfer the wealth of the country to their own hands. It is significant that this author does not mention any religious crime, such as host desecration or ritual murder. Evidently, he did not think that such accusations against the Marranos would be believed, and, as we have seen, they were not mentioned in the Petition and the *Sentencia* either. He copies some of the charges of the *pesquisa* to indicate the secret Judaism of the conversos, but compared to other medieval agitators against the Jews, he looks more like a modern antisemite.

IV. Conversos Bare Their Final Goals

I. ALONSO DE CARTAGENA

I. THE CLIMB TO EMINENCE

I

The spiritual leader of the conversos of Castile and their most famous spokesman from the mid-thirties to the mid-fifties was unquestionably Alonso de Cartagena, bishop of Burgos and second son of the convert Pablo de Santa María. Jurist, historian, philosopher and theologian, Alonso de Cartagena was also a great orator, a skillful diplomat and a Church leader of international renown. The excellence of his achievements was such that leading representatives in all these fields sang his praises in superlative terms. Some of these laudatory statements were often quoted by his biographers.[1] Others can be added to the same effect.

Thus, in assessing Cartagena's life work, Pérez de Guzmán, the famous poet and historian, saw in Cartagena an outstanding spokesman of ethics and jurisprudence, philosophy and theology, oratory and history, as well as poetry.[2] Guzmán compared the salutary influence exercised by Cartagena on his own life to that wielded by Seneca on Lucilius, and his influence on the intellectual life of Spain in general to that of Plato on Greece.[3] This encomium appears in a poetic eulogy written by Guzmán after Cartagena's death; and as such it may be viewed as an emotional expression, overflowing the bounds of objective truth. This may be so from our own standpoint, but not from the standpoint of Spain's intellectuals at the time. The carefully phrased stanzas and measured terms in which Guzmán stated his admiration for Don Alonso do not reflect a fleeting opinion, inspired by an outburst of grief, but an estimate formed in the course of a lifetime by close observation and intimate acquaintance. Moreover, they reflect not a *personal* opinion but that of many of his generation. Essentially, we find the same view of Cartagena in Lucena's *De Vita Beata,* where the author makes the marquis of Santillana, another known admirer of Don Alonso,[4] address the latter in the following words: "Philosophy was born in Greece. Socrates called it from Heaven.... Pythagoras sowed it in Italy; you [i.e., Alonso de Cartagena] have now transplanted it to Spain ... Blessed is she, happy Castile! It is for her, not only for yourself, that you were born when you were!"[5] Likewise, the poet Gómez Manrique, in assessing Don Alonso as a teacher of Christian doctrine, defines him as "another St. Paul," and says that "it is well known that, as far as learning is concerned, no one could be found equal to him since the days of St. Gregory."[6] This is of course a great exaggeration, but it speaks for the almost boundless admiration in which Alonso de Cartagena was generally held by the Spaniards of his time.[7]

The basis of his fame, which "fills the 15th century," as Menéndez y Pelayo put it succinctly, lay primarily in three areas: literature, diplomacy, and theology. In all these areas he provided leadership and inspiration, and helped shape the development of the drives and forces that determined in large measure the course of Spanish history. The positions he took in each of the above fields were by no means simple—in fact, they were complex; and we can understand their complexity only if we consider his motivation and education.

II

Alonso de Cartagena was born in Burgos in 1385[8] and was converted to Christianity by his father, Paul of Burgos, in 1391.[9] From then on his upbringing resembled that of other young converts who belonged to distinguished and well-to-do families. Unlike Jews who turned Christian in their maturity—as was the case with his father, Don Pablo—Alonso, like so many converts of his age, did not have to undergo a religious "crisis," a moral and intellectual transformation, to adjust himself to the life of a Christian. He was accustomed to that life from the tender age of six, with his memories of Jewish customs soon to be submerged by a flood of new impressions from his Christian experience. Alonso hardly needed to shed the "old man" and put on the "new," for he had scarcely lived as the "old man," or even gotten to know him. In effect, he was not aware, in himself, of any other man but the "new." He saw himself as a Christian and was one through and through—in culture and religion.

This does not mean, however, that certain views and attitudes originating in Jewish intellectual traditions did not enter his thinking from his converso environment, from converso literature and converso instruction, especially through his father, Don Pablo. Nor does it mean that certain positions of his group did not play a part in determining his views on a variety of public issues. Indeed, Jewish-converso strains of influence may be noticed in his cultural approaches, in the fabric of his theological ideas, in his political philosophy, and the policies he recommended to Church and state. Yet these strains in his thinking may be compared to narrow streamlets that wind their way through a broad countryside. The countryside itself—the main body of his thought—was provided by his formal, systematic education; and that was fundamentally Christian or, specifically, of the Old Christian brand.

One might conclude from this that his thought comprised some conflicting elements—Jewish and Christian—which could not be reconciled. But such a conclusion would be wrong. The part played by non-Christian ideas in the formation of his views was minor to begin with, and even these ideas merged in his thinking with principles of Christian religion and philosophy. They were not a discordant factor.

From the age of fourteen to his twentieth year, he was educated at the University of Salamanca, studying philosophy, theology and jurisprudence, and working toward the degree of doctor, which he attained about 1406.[10] This education gave him the tools to pursue his literary interests, and also prepared him for service in the administration of either Church or state. In fact, after leaving Salamanca, he tried his hand in three fields—literature, politics and ecclesiastical affairs—and for some time it was unclear which of the three would win him over. As it turned out, he entered simultaneously the service of both Church and state, and at the age of twenty-nine, in 1415, he became auditor of King Juan II and also Dean of Compostela.[11] Similarly, in 1419 he became a titular member of the Royal Council and also papal nuncio of Castile.[12] By 1428 he was known, on the one hand, as auditor, member of the Royal Council, and *referendario del rey* and, on the other hand, as *referendario* of the pope, dean of the churches of Compostela and Segovia, Canon of Burgos and the king's chaplain.[13] By that time he was also well known as an author, with several important works to his credit.[14]

But in 1428 he was already forty-two years old and his star was still far from its zenith. He occupied several honorable positions, none of which, however, was truly outstanding; he was respected in many circles, but it is doubtful whether anyone could then predict the heights of influence he was eventually to reach. By 1428, it appears, he was trying mainly for a Church career, even though whatever real distinction he had gained was in the world of secular politics. We must note this double trend of his career because it was by way of his political achievements that Don Alonso rose to high positions in the Church. In turn, his work in the ecclesiastical domain enhanced his prestige in the intellectual life of Spain.

III

It is evident that the son of Paul of Burgos felt indebted and bound to the Infantes of Aragon, especially to Juan, the eldest of them, because of the close ties between Paul and their father, Fernando de Antequera.[15] Nevertheless, despite these connections, and while he performed services for the Infantes, he managed to ingratiate himself with the Castilian court and gain the support of Alvaro de Luna. It was no doubt a difficult maneuver—to sail from the Scylla of the Constable to the Charybdis of the opposition without wrecking one's ship in the process. Few Castilians had the skill to do this. Alonso de Cartagena was one of them.

In the beginning of Alvaro de Luna's rule, following the failure of Don Enrique's coup d'état, he was a member of the council of the Infante Don Juan (1420).[16] In the following year, he sought, and obtained, the King's consent to the petitions addressed to him by that Infante and the nobles of his league.[17] Thereupon he was appointed, at the Infante's recommendation, member of Castile's Royal Council,[18] and shortly thereafter he endeavored, as the king's emissary, to induce Don Enrique to abandon his attempt to take over the marquisate of Villena.[19] The mission achieved only part of its aims,[20] but even so it may have been considered a success. In any case, it seems that Alvaro de Luna noticed Don Alonso's powers of persuasion, even mindedness and diplomatic skill, and was eager to use him in the diplomatic service of the state. Thus, toward the end of 1421, Cartagena was sent as royal ambassador to Portugal to negotiate a peace treaty with that country.[21] The negotiations lasted a whole year, and the peace which was attained through Don Alonso's efforts lasted almost thirty years.[22] He was sent again to Portugal in 1424 to settle some disagreements over the interpretation of that treaty, and this mission, too, he accomplished successfully after a year's stay in Lisbon.[23] His diplomatic achievements secured for him, no doubt, a place of honor in the Royal Council and helped cement more friendly relations between him and Alvaro de Luna. In any case, it appears that the Constable now regarded him as his partisan, actual or potential.[24]

This paved the way for the two appointments that were to prove the pinnacles of Don Alonso's career, both political and ecclesiastical. In 1434 he was appointed member of the Castilian delegation to the Council of Basle, together with his brother Gonzalo García, who was at the time bishop of Plasencia,[25] and in October 1435, while in Basle, Don Alonso was appointed bishop of Burgos, replacing his father, who had died that year.[26] None of these appointments could have come about had they not been proposed, or supported, by Alvaro de Luna.

IV

Basle gave Don Alonso the opportunity to rise to international fame, and also gain special renown in defending the interests of his own country. His eloquence, wisdom, skill and experience, both judicial and diplomatic, made him the ideal spokesman for Castile. He won the argument that developed with England over the seat of priority in the Council[27]; he won the important debate with Portugal on the issue of the Canary Islands[28]; and he made peace between the Emperor and the king of Poland at a time when their conflict seemed irreconcilable.[29] All this, of course, helped establish his authority in the field of international relations.

As for his activity in Church politics, it was even more impressive, and certainly more important in its results. For Don Alonso was trying to steer a middle course between the papacy and the conciliar movement, attempting to coordinate in some manner the legitimate interests of both. This was, to be sure, the formal policy of Castile, but in large measure it was, in all likelihood, inspired by Don Alonso. In any case, it fully agreed with his thinking, as well as his basic inclinations. For by disposition he was a compromiser and peacemaker. Just as he was trying to achieve equilibrium between the rival Infantes of Aragon, between the Infantes of Aragon and King Juan II, between Portugal and Castile, between the Empire and Poland, so was he trying to establish harmony between the Council and the Pope.

The latter attempt, however, was doomed. The opposing parties stuck to their guns—that is, to principles that were irreconcilable—and both were led by exceptionally able, strong, and stubborn men. In Basle the conciliar movement was determined to enforce the decision of the Council of Constance (1417), which established the supremacy of the council in Church affairs; on the other hand, the Pope was equally determined to bring the decision of Constance to nought and exercise what he considered his inalienable rights as the supreme leader of the Church. A violent clash of doctrines, interests and ambitions ensued.

Virtually from the opening of the Council in July 1431, both sides were on a collision course; and the moment of collision appeared imminent when, in April 1437, Pope Eugene IV urged the Council to move from Basle to Italy. The Council refused on the grounds that the Pope had no right to dictate such a transfer. A committee of three was agreed upon to examine the question. Two of the members represented the rival parties. The third, Don Alonso, was elected by the Council as the final arbiter between the two opposing views.[30] The papal party, it seems, counted on his support; but if so, they were rudely mistaken; for Don Alonso cast his decisive vote in favor of the conciliar position.

The Pope reacted with speed and vigor. He declared the Council of Basle prorogued and ordered it transferred to Ferrara. The Council, for its part, began to move systematically toward the final debate on the Pope's deposition.[31]

Don Alonso participated in this debate, and we have a detailed account of both the contents of his speech and the Council's general reaction to it. The author of this account was an outstanding man who was destined to become Pope himself, but at the time was still groping, pathetically and haltingly, toward an unknown future. This was Aeneas Sylvius Piccolominus, later Pope Pius II, one of the great popes of the Renaissance.

Aeneas Sylvius was a talented writer, an accomplished scholar, and an acute observer of men and affairs. The account referred to is included in the *Commentaries* he wrote on the Council of Basle, in which he weighed his words with great care; he was then forty-one years old, had been in the company of many famous men, and could tell the difference between prestige gained by position and that which was due to inherent qualities. One therefore ought not to underestimate the admiration shown in his *Commentaries* for Don Alonso.

That admiration was, in fact, so great that Aeneas Sylvius never mentions the bishop's name without a complimentary title or adjective. Thus on one occasion, he describes Don Alonso as the "delight of Spain" (*delitia Hispaniarum*),[32] on another as "ornament of the prelates" (*praelatorum decus*),[33] on a third, as "outstanding among *all* for his resourcefulness and eloquence" (*inter omnes consilio et fecundia praestans*),[34] and so on. Clearly, all these descriptions show how fascinated and captivated Aeneas Sylvius was by Don Alonso's talents and personality. We should also note that these remarks were written many months after the delivery of those speeches, when some of their impact may have been lost or weakened with the passage of time. Above all, we should recall that Aeneas Sylvius was then a strict conciliarist, while Don Alonso, as we have indicated, followed a middle course. So Aeneas Sylvius' great admiration for Don Alonso was sustained *despite* their basic differences concerning the policy that the Council should have followed toward the intransigent Eugene IV.

All this must be borne in mind in assessing the impression Don Alonso made, or the influence he wielded, in the Council of Basle—an assembly which included most of the leaders of Christendom in that generation. This also explains the special attention the Council paid to his speech on the proposal to depose the Pope. We may summarize this speech as follows:

While conceding that the Council was superior to the Pope and therefore could not be dissolved by the Pope—or transferred by him to another place without the Council's consent—he insisted that even if the Pope denied these propositions, he could not be charged for this denial with heresy and, in consequence, be deposed. Aeneas Sylvius could not hide his astonishment and disappointment that his idol, Don Alonso, took such a stand. In his opinion, it was directly opposed to the principles the prelate had so eloquently espoused. This is how he describes his own and the Council's reactions to Don Alonso's address:

> The Bishop of Burgos, a Spanish ambassador and particularly learned among the prelates, divided the resolutions into two groups, calling some general and others personal. He spoke excellently about the first three, stating that he had no doubts at all about them, except that the addition which made mention of the faith seemed doubtful to him. He wanted to dwell on this very much to show that the holy Council was superior to the Pope. After proving this by divine and human law he claimed it by scientific reasoning too, and bringing as witness the

greatest of all philosophers, Aristotle, he said that in every well-ordered kingdom it was particularly desirable that the kingdom should have more power than the king; if the opposite was found, it deserved the name not of kingdom but of tyranny. Similarly his own view about the Church was that it should have more power than its prince, that is the Pope. In this discourse he argued with such elegance, charm, learning and excellence that all hung eagerly on his words, not as in the case of other [speakers] longing for the end of the speech, but for a long continuation of it, and they proclaimed that he was the sole mirror of learning. When, however, he touched upon the other resolutions, and here wished to show opposition, he seemed for a while to go out of character and to cease to be the bishop of Burgos. For that charm of word, that dignity of utterance, that cheerfulness of countenance were all missing, and if he had been able to see himself, he would perhaps have felt surprised at the sight.[35]

Aeneas Sylvius thought that some outside force—a force which the bishop could not resist—compelled him to speak in the second part of his speech against his own convictions. He probably had in mind the policies of Castile, dictated from afar by Juan II. Actually, however, the dual position taken by Don Alonso on that occasion reflected his own views, formed under the impact of various influences, on the question of the Church.

V

These influences stemmed from theoretical as well as practical political sources, and it is necessary to consider them, at least briefly, in order to understand how they converged in Don Alonso's mind. As a student of Cicero, he disliked absolute authority, especially when exercised by one man. He opposed it in the State, the secular regime, and even more so in the Church, which, to his thinking, represented the highest ideals of government. Yet he did not believe that any large organization can be run effectively by councils and committees without being guided by a single man holding the reins of power in his hand. That applied, in his opinion, to secular governments, and all the more so to the ecclesiastic one, the Church, which was destined to embrace the whole of mankind and was potentially the largest government of all. The solution he envisioned, therefore, was a government of one, limited and controlled by councils of the elite—the political aristocracy in the secular state and the spiritual aristocracy in the Church.[36]

But if this was Don Alonso's view of the ideal government of mankind, he was certainly hesitant in presenting it fully to the delegates assembled at Basle. It is clear that he was considered a moderate conciliarist who showed much respect for the pope; otherwise, he would not have been chosen to cast the decisive vote in the three-member committee that would decide Eugene's right to transfer the council to Italy. When, by his vote, he tipped the scales in favor of the council against the papacy, he doubtless expected Eugene IV to submit to this decision, and thus have the crisis resolved. But the Pope, as we have indicated, acted differently, and this put Don Alonso in a difficult position—if not ideologically, at least tactically. Again he was compelled to take sides, and this time his position seemed to many inconsistent with his previous pronouncements.

There is no doubt that in this matter Don Alonso represented not only his own position, but also that of the state of Castile. Yet this does not mean that the policy he pursued was dictated by the Court against his convictions. In fact, he may well have been the architect of that policy rather than its subservient follower. His own considerations were not necessarily identical with those, say, of Alvaro de Luna. But both men came to the same conclusions, and that is what counted in this instance. Both the Court and Don Alonso had agreed to prevent the downfall of the Pope in case of a rift between him and the Council on whatever issue.[37]

For two tendencies were reflected in Castile's policy: a desire to sustain the ruling pope and an intent to cater to the conciliar movement, which formed the majority of the Council. Castile thus played the role of a neutral whose support was sought by both sides. Actually, Castile was determined that Eugene IV should stay in power—if possible, under the terms stipulated by the Council; if not—by sacrificing conciliar principles to the requirements of papal stability.

Accordingly, when the Council began to move toward the deposition of the Pope, Castile began to disengage itself from its previous position—a disengagement that had to be done gracefully, with as little loss of face as possible. Its goal, however, was virtually predetermined: to abandon the conciliar movement and go over to the pope's camp.

For the state of Castile, the act of disengagement was merely a tactical maneuver; for Don Alonso, it was a consequence of his political philosophy. It would be wrong to see the course he took in Basle, from March 1439 on, as the product of opportunism or political expediency. To be sure, his arguments against the deposition of the Pope sounded unconvincing to extreme conciliarists, as Aeneas Sylvius was in those days. They appeared to contradict the basic principles of conciliarism that were allegedly espoused by Don Alonso himself. This, however, was not precisely the case. For Don Alonso was not a full-fledged conciliarist as the radicals of Basle were. He wanted the Council to have the right to decide policy and be recognized as the supreme authority in the Church, but he did not want the Pope to be shorn of all his powers and become a mere official of the council. Practically, these positions were irreconcilable, but theoretically they were not.

As a student of both Aristotle and Cicero, Don Alonso embraced the theory of mixed government, and a mixed government means that no single element of the ruling body attains *complete* power. A council that can do with the pope as it wishes may be as ruthless and arbitrary as a tyrannical pope, just as a council of nobles that disregards the king may be as arbitrary and harmful as a cruel monarch. Clearly, for Don Alonso the council represented—or should have represented—the aristocracy of the Church, whose task was to guide the pope and aid him, just as the aristocracy of the secular state (represented in the Royal Council and Cortes) should, as he believed, guide the king. But this does not mean that in consequence the king must lose all his rights and powers. To be sure, a wise king ought ordinarily to follow the considered advice of his council, but that does not imply that, on occasion, he cannot prefer his own judgment. Should not the king—or, for that matter, the pope—possess such right of independent action, the king would be no king and the pope no pope; the government would be not mixed but autocratic, and could be subject to a tyranny of a different kind.

If we thus understand Don Alonso, we can better comprehend the positions he took. But beyond this, there was another consideration—no doubt, to him the most important: Was Christendom going to be split again? Was the Schism going to be revived? It was against this harrowing prospect that Don Alonso bent all his efforts.

It is clear that the policy pursued by Don Alonso gave the edge of power to the papacy and helped undermine the influence of the decisions adopted by the Council of Constance. Those decisions gave all power to the council, but this power amounted to very little if the council lacked the right to depose the pope when he chose to flout the council's wishes. By taking the council's side morally and the pope's side practically, Castile could hold both parties at bay and actually maintain the balance of power in the Council of Basle until the crucial moment. When that moment came, Castile made its move. It withdrew its delegates from Basle and went over to Eugene's side,[38] thereby dealing a decisive blow to the advocates of conciliarism.

Thus we see how at that critical stage in the history of the papacy—and indeed, of the Church—two leading conversos, Torquemada and Cartagena, performed vital tasks in the preservation and promotion of Christian unity and papal power. While Torquemada led a frontal attack on behalf of papal supremacy, Cartagena conducted a rear-guard defense, which delayed decisive action by the Council and gave the Pope time to make the most of his limited resources. There is no evidence of any collusion between Juan de Torquemada and Cartagena in this matter; and probably there was none. Their views were far apart, and their actions were in accord with their views. Yet both prepared the path, each in his own way, for the triumph of the Pope.

The reemergence of a strong papacy from the trial of Basle was, in large measure, their handiwork.

VI

Basle was the watershed of Don Alonso's career. When he left for Basle in May 1434, he was just the dean of Santiago. When he returned to Spain in December 1439,[39] he was bishop of Burgos and a leader of the Church on an international scale. In view of the great reputation he had acquired and the widespread admiration that his name evoked, some wondered why he was not created cardinal. It was suggested that his position in the Council, and especially his vote in Basle against the Pope, cost him the purple hat. There may be truth in this, but perhaps not the whole truth. Another reason could be Rome's reluctance to have a second converso in the College of Cardinals. In December 1439, we should recall, Juan de Torquemada was created cardinal—an appointment that seems to have been delayed, though it must have long been favored by the Pope.

For Rome was well aware of the tension that existed between the Old and the New Christians in Spain. Complaints against the conversos poured into the curia, and Don Alonso must have felt the impact of this agitation during the discussions in the Council on the decision concerning converts. To be sure, the decision was a victory for the conversos, especially insofar as it confirmed their rights to assume public offices and ecclesiastic benefices. But when he returned to Spain, Don Alonso must have realized that the decision had little if any effect on the actual situation in his country. The question of the conversos' place in Spain's society continued to simmer and disturb the public peace, and less than a decade after the Council's decree, the king, Juan II, had to warn the cities—through the famous cedula of 1444—to stop discrimination against the New Christians.[40]

Nevertheless, like most of the conversos, Don Alonso may have persuaded himself that matters were going the converso way. Converso penetration into the ecclesiastic hierarchy and the administration of the state and the cities continued, despite the steady resentment and obstruction exhibited by many Old Christians. And as far as his own position was concerned, his prestige had never been greater. In the years that followed his return to Castile, he became recognized as Castile's intellectual leader, its great authority in matters of literature, history, ethics and, of course, theology. He was one of the most respected men in the court of Juan II.

In the midst of this development, which seemed to have given him a sound basis for optimistic expectations, came the attack upon the conversos of Toledo, which called into question all his positive predictions. Who could believe that this kind of treatment could ever be accorded to New Christians in Spain? In its bloody ferocity and brutal destructiveness the outbreak recalled the great riots against the Jews. But in one respect it was even worse. For the members of the lower classes—who, now as then, did the killing, the looting, the burning, and the wrecking—were now joined by the city's formal authorities (that is, by the government led by Sarmiento) with their expropriations, imprisonments, and expulsions. Moreover, the latter engineered public trials in which conversos were charged with treason or heresy, and in the wake of which some of the accused were exiled or burned at the stake. On top of this, they enacted a new law—the *Sentencia-Estatuto*—which declared the conversos to be criminals and outlaws, unfit to be members of a Christian society. And what was even more ominous: they extended their campaign of hate and vilification to other cities and regions in the country, so that hardly a spot seemed free from the effects of their savage incitement. The danger that now threatened the New Christians could not be overestimated.

Alonso de Cartagena must have soon realized that like so many of his converso contemporaries he had failed to notice, or correctly estimate, the force of the gathering storm. What appeared on the surface as tolerable opposition actually stemmed from a deep-rooted hatred which had been constantly growing in intensity until it finally erupted. The immediate task was obviously to check the violent agitation against the conversos, which used racial slogans and catchwords. Don Alonso believed that this could be achieved by a series of powerful "answers" to the racists, exposing the sham of their theories, their motives, and the gross illegality of their actions. There was complete unanimity on this between him and other converso leaders, just as they all agreed that their answers should not have the character of mere apologies. What they really planned was a double-edged campaign: a determined defense of the conversos, on the one hand, and a sharp attack upon the Toledan hate-mongers and calumniators, on the other.

The strategy of this campaign is clearly seen in the writings of the converso leaders Fernán Díaz de Toledo and Juan de Torquemada, which we have discussed above, as well as in the work of Alonso de Cartagena, which we are about to examine. All of them are at once defensive and offensive; yet they differ from each other in the emphasis they place on each of their elements and approaches. In Torquemada's work, quite clearly, the spirit of attack predominates; in Fernán Díaz there is a balanced presentation of the aggressive and defensive arguments, while Cartagena's work is clearly more defensive, or at least more subdued in its offensive aspect. Its spirit is also reflected in its title: "A *Defense* of Christian Unity."

II. DEFENSORIUM UNITATIS CHRISTIANAE

I

As the title indicates, Cartagena did not wish to appear as an apologist for the conversos. It is a defense, to be sure, but a defense of the Church, not of the conversos per se, and it is a defense in the sense of protection against attack and not in the sense of an apology. Leading this attack are the new heretics, who, like other heretics, are also schismatics, and thus disrupt the Church's unity. Obviously, judging by the interests of Rome, the title "A Defense of Christian Unity" was bound to gain the work a receptive audience. There was nothing more objectionable to most Christians at the time than the specter of a new schism.

As we shall see, the schism referred to was not of the kind produced by an anti-pope, a split in Church government or the like, but one that was to come as an inevitable result of purely ideological deviations. It is not so much the *actions*, therefore, as the *theories* of the Toledans with which the *Defensorium* is concerned. And as a study of theories, it gives its author the opportunity to relate his subject, directly and indirectly, to his own long-established theoretical constructions. Written when Cartagena was sixty-four, the work is more than a rebuttal of the Toledans' doctrine. It is a summary of Cartagena's views, fashioned over many years, nurtured by almost ceaseless speculation, and supported by his lifelong studies of Christianity, Judaism and the converso problem. In effect, it presents his world outlook.

Divided into three sections, the *Defensorium* outlines in its first (and briefest) part its author's conception of the course of man's history inasmuch as it relates to his main topic. In describing this part in his preface to the work, Don Alonso says that it includes some "general considerations."[41] But these "general considerations" are in reality the author's specific views on the Jewish people in relation to other nations. All the major propositions that appear in the later parts are founded on these views.

It was no doubt for tactical reasons that Don Alonso refused to spell out in advance the content of this section in a few sentences (as was customary in those days) and left it for the reader to discover. Had he outlined his positions, unsupported by arguments, his conclusions might have appeared too pro-Jewish, too pro-converso, and perhaps even anti-Christian. If left with such impressions, many Christian readers might unfavorably prejudge the views and demonstrations he was to set forth.

II

Don Alonso begins with the Augustinian thesis that the final aim of mankind is to fashion a society firmly united by the bonds of love and free from any disruptive discord.[42] The destiny of man, like all the goals of history, is divinely ordained; therefore, that destiny is the aim of Christendom, which exists to attain the divine objectives. It is symbolized by the fact that, unlike other animals, man was not created in several pairs, or even in one pair, but as a single being, so that even his spouse, who was fashioned from his flesh, was actually part and parcel of him.[43] The purpose of this unique form of creation was, as St. Augustine pointed out, to serve as a constant reminder to all men that they came from the same source,[44] and thus be moved toward harmony and unity. But despite this fact the "vice of discord" appeared among man's first offspring. Abel was murdered, and following that crime, mankind has proceeded along the same disastrous course. The "race of men" *(hominum genus)* was split into different ways of life, accompanied by a variety of beliefs and superstitions, which deepened its divisions. Yet these divisions occurred within a single people and stock *(omnes sub unius populi et gentis unitate conclusi),* which is evident from what God said of them when they were building the Tower of Babel: "They are one people and one language."[45] There was not at the time any group among them that was distinguished by its carnal origin and which God favored over the others. Divine favor was then shown only to individuals, and only on the basis of individual merit.[46] Such persons were Noah and Job, who were "acceptable" to God because of their righteousness. But it must be understood that even the best of these men achieved only a partial knowledge of God. For all of them then lived under the law of Nature, with no written law to guide them. "*All of them were then gentiles,*" says Cartagena[47]; and only by employing the light of reason could some of them be led to a moral way of life, associated with some knowledge of God.[48]

Having begun with the Augustinian idea of the symbolic purpose of man's creation, he nevertheless parted company with Augustine when he described the diversity that developed in mankind. To St. Augustine, Cain and Abel represented the beginnings of two cities, the earthly and the heavenly, the society of men and the society of saints.[49] Each of these societies, according to St. Augustine, was represented in mankind by different groups, both in pre- and postdiluvial times, and their members were related to each other by their behavior—that is, by their knowledge and worship of God—and also by their ancestral origin. In prediluvial times, following the death of Abel, the City of God was represented by men from the family of Seth down to Noah, who was a son of the same family; in postdiluvial times it was the family of Shem down to Abraham that bore the same tradition.[50] On these Augustinian foundations, we should note, Juan de Torquemada built his view of the universal history of the Church.[51] Cartagena, however, found the theory unsupportable and, furthermore, contradicted by Scripture. As he saw it, there was no real knowledge of God prior to Abraham, no adherence to any divine law in the full and true sense of the word, and no society of believers in the divine truths that could constitute the City of God. There were isolated individuals who, through the law of nature, imperfect and general as it was, sensed (with God's Grace) the goodness of morality and therefore found favor in the eyes of God. But these represented no communion of faith, no continuity of a Church, and no hereditary relationship. Consequently, none of them could be distinguished by birthright. Differences arising from birth were introduced into mankind, according to Cartagena, only at the time of Abraham.[52]

For while differing with Augustine concerning the symptoms that indicate the existence of the divine city, Don Alonso adhered to the Saint's view of the relationship between faith and ethnic descent. As he saw it, mankind was originally *one people*[53]—i.e., one race—prior to the appearance of God's true worshipers, or—to use Augustine's terminology—prior to the appearance of the City of God. That single people was essentially pagan (or "gentile"), and only a few of its members, by perceiving the law of nature, managed to arrive at "some" conception of God. Mankind as a whole, therefore, in its primordial state, though living as one people and recognizing its unity, failed to grasp and attach itself to God. On the contrary, its moral behavior constantly deteriorated, leading to the punishment of the Flood, and then was again subject to deterioration until the generation of the tower of Babel. The punishment that followed the attempt to build the tower was usually seen as the splitting up of mankind into different "languages" and national groups. In Cartagena's opinion, however, that event was not crucial. As he saw it, the turning point in history occurred not with the division of mankind into "languages" or the formation of national societies, but with the appearance of a special group that was to carry the divine message to the world.

That group was united by a blood relationship whose origins went back to Abraham—and this fact, as we shall see, played a part in facilitating the performance of its historic task. Thus, whatever differences developed among the other groups, they were really of secondary importance, since the *common* features of these groups were more typical of them than the traits that *distinguished* them from each other; and so Cartagena lumps them together under the common heading of "gentiles." That was indeed the *mass of humanity*, the mass of gentilehood, from which the *particular* group had emerged. But once that group made its appearance, two distinct *peoples* became noticeable—the gentiles and the Israelites.[54]

The division of mankind into two different parts—one reverencing God and the other not—occurred therefore not in the days of Cain and Abel, but in the days of Abraham. Augustine's idea that the "Church of God" existed on earth from the beginning of mankind was obviously rejected by Cartagena. Prior to Abraham, according to him, there was no such "church," no "saintly society," and no "City of God." All these concepts may be related only to the people generated by the first of the Patriarchs. And thus, if we follow Augustine's terminology, the City of God made its earthly appearance only with the birth of the Jewish people.

That this people would define its spiritual identity by its hereditary ties with a certain family, no less than by its view and worship of God, did not come about as an automatic result of its special conditions of life or its history. In other words, it was not a "natural" development. It was by a special determination of God that Abraham, who became God's intimate friend *(amicus Dei),* was also chosen by Him to be the *father* of the people that would be dedicated to His service. To make that distinction universally apparent, and make the performance of that task possible, a closed body of men had to be created which was radically *different* from the rest of mankind, and also *detached* from it in certain ways. The detachment began by God's saying to Abraham: *"Go out of your country, and from your kindred* (cognatio), *and from your father's house, and come to the land which I will show you."*[55] It proceeded with the imposition of the duty of *circumcision* upon Abraham and his offspring—a sign to mark their distinction from all other peoples, and it culminated in the giving of the *Law* to that offspring—a special law that included unusual precepts, the like of which was not offered to any other people.[56] All these acts, however, were not aimed, as some believed, merely at isolating the people from all other groups; they were intended to raise it to a *high* status—higher than that of the rest of mankind—and this, too, to enable it to perform the task it was destined to fulfill in man's history.

That task was to establish a society fit for Christ to be born into, and it was in preparation for this great event that these descendants of Abraham were elevated to a rank compared by Cartagena to that of the nobility.[57] To be sure, not *all* of Abraham's offspring were privileged in this fashion, for among them, too, only certain men were selected to serve as progenitors of the noble people. Thus, from the seed of Abraham God chose Isaac, even though he was the younger, and out of the latter's seed he again preferred the younger (Jacob) to the older (Esau) to constitute the root of the special people from whom the Savior was to come. Indeed, Jacob, like his ancestors, was chosen "not only as bearer of the right of ancestry and paternal benediction, but also as heir of the singular prerogative of divine love" (which was granted to Abraham).[58] Said the prophet Malachi: "Esau was Jacob's brother; yet I loved Jacob and Esau I hated."[59] Why? "Surely, the hate of which he speaks here is not a human hate, which sometimes proceeds from unjust rancor, but should be understood as divine rejection according to His secret judgment."[60] But that judgment could not have been based on the actual behavior of the two brothers. As the Apostle said: "For the children being not yet born, neither having done any good or evil . . . it was said unto her [i.e., their mother]: " 'the elder will serve the younger' " (Rom. 9.11–12). The destiny of the brothers, therefore, was not based on their performance. On what was it based, then?

According to Christian theory from the days of St. Augustine—indeed, from the days of St. Paul—the Election was an act of pure grace, predetermined by God and not associated with merit.[61] Cartagena accepts this position; but he uses certain statements of Augustine to amplify the theory of "election for no merit" and thus render it more acceptable. Commenting on Romans 9.18, Augustine said: "But this will of God cannot be unjust, for it comes from hidden merits."[62] Cartagena recognized the difficulty of reconciling this statement with the view of Grace and Predestination as it developed in Christianity with respect to the Election. He agrees with Peter Lombard that merit would preclude Grace and also preempt Predestination, for it would seem as the cause of the Divine Will, while that will is eternal and preceded by nothing.[63] He believes, however, that when pondering a divine action like the Election, which is unique and full of mystery, we must assume that it stemmed from the most profound wisdom which we, human beings, cannot share.[64] Surely God had His reasons for it. For, as Job said, "Nothing on earth occurs without a reason."[65]

This statement again alludes to the question of the relationship between race and morality which formed, as we have seen, a central issue in the controversy on the Toledan race theory. There is no doubt that Christianity has dissociated man's moral conduct from his racial origin—at least, as the direct cause of that conduct. This was also the position of Augustine.[66] Yet his dominant, all-embracing view that mankind consists of two racial branches, representing two types of men, the good and the bad, inevitably suggested a causal relationship between man's ethnic origin and his moral constitution. By rejecting the Augustinian thesis of the two races, Cartagena freed himself from the problem it posed. Race could not be the source of man's morality—or rather determine his moral conduct—since there was only *one* human race, and the cause of the different forms of behavior observable in that single "human race" should therefore be sought in a different direction. But now, the rise of the Jewish people—the way it was conceived by Cartagena, and the evident connection between its hereditary ties and its moral character, growth and function—seemed to support the notion that race and morality are inseparable after all. Cartagena, however, overcame this difficulty by his theory of Election.

The theory of Election without prior merit—a theory supported by both

Augustine and Thomas[67]—enabled Cartagena to retain the view about the absolute ethnic unity of mankind. The Jews belonged to that general union, and thus no causal relationship existed between their ethnic origin and their moral achievements. For these achievements did not come as a result of the pristine powers of the Jewish people, but as a result of God's special care. It was part of the divine plan to fashion a people which would be acceptable to God as the carnal source of Christ, and that plan was implemented through certain divine actions. Not only was the Jewish people raised to the status of nobility in mankind—a fact symbolized by the sign of circumcision; it was also allotted the status of holiness, which was indicated by the *law* it received from God. For "laws which were established for the sanctification of some people are binding only on those they are intended for," and thus "clerics, who are assigned to the service of God, are obliged to keep certain special laws to which the laity are not bound. Likewise members of religious orders are committed by their profession to certain works of perfection to which laymen are not bound; and thus these [namely, the Jews] were obligated to perform [certain] laws from which other people were exempt.... For they were like members of religious orders among the other nations, following the written Law as a set of special rules that applied to their order."[68]

This passage from the *Defensorium,* except for the final explanatory sentence, was cited by Cartagena almost verbatim from St. Thomas' *Summa Theologica.*[69] And it was indeed on St. Thomas that Cartagena relied in the formation of his conception of the Jewish people. To understand this reliance more fully, however, we must take a closer look at both Augustine's and Thomas' views on the part played by the Jewish people in the history of the City of God.

Augustine agreed that from the days of Abraham on, the City of God, whose existence never ceased, concentrated in his offspring—the Jewish people—from whom Christ was to emerge in His carnal form; but the City of God was not to be identified with that people in its entirety, only with the saintly elements within it.[70] In addition, he believed that the particular era in which that concentration took place—namely, the era from Abraham to Christ—was marked by two things: clearer proof for the existence of the City of God, and more explicit indications of "the promises which we now see fulfilled in Christ."[71] Otherwise, no revolution was to be associated with Abraham and his descendants, the people of Israel, or rather—according to Augustine—with those individuals in the people of Israel who were dedicated to the divine worship. Ethnically, they continued the line of succession which started with Seth, and morally they continued the development of the Church which dates from Abel's time.

This view of Augustine's, which related the Jewish people to only *one* of the stages in the history of the Church—and not to that in which the Church was created—and which furthermore associated with the City of God only *part* of the Israelite succession of Abraham—but denied any valuable historical function to the people as a whole—conflicted with Cartagena's own reading of the Bible and his own understanding of the historic task fulfilled by the Jewish people. Fortunately, he could find in St. Thomas an authority to support a view similar to his own. According to Aquinas, there was no divine Church—or what Augustine called City of God—prior to its establishment by the Patriarch's offspring. There were only isolated individuals who performed good works (precisely as Cartagena said), and consequently there was no special people dedicated to the worship of God. Such a people was established only through and from the offspring of Abraham; and it was because no such people existed at the time that the Law could not be promulgated earlier, for it is the nature of all law, as Aquinas said, that it must apply to a public body.[72] The people of Israel, then, was fashioned to form the entity that could receive the Law, thus becoming the People of God, from whom Christ could emerge. This is why, as Aquinas made it clear, although Christ was born of a certain lineage, to a succession of families within the Jewish people, *He was also born to the people as a whole*—and therefore the people as a whole had to receive the prerogative of holiness.[73] This is also why, as Aquinas emphasized, all the signs of uniqueness we notice in Abraham[74] applied to the whole Jewish people, and why the whole people so arranged its life as to form a close religious order.[75] Thus, according to St. Thomas, it was the *whole* Jewish people, and not some group within it, that constituted the first society of men wholly devoted to the worship of God; and thus, if we use Augustine's language, it was the first Divine Church or City of God to be established on earth.

Forming as it did a fundamental part of Cartagena's historical outlook, the Thomistic view was more suitable than the Augustinian also for combatting the theory of race. Augustine claimed that only "a few" of the Jews shared in the succession of saintly humanity, while all the others belonged to the "sinners"; moreover, he claimed that the saintly part constituted, even in ancient times, the Church of Christ, while those who followed the "earthly," sinful path did not belong to that Church at all; and finally, he claimed that wherever "Israel" was praised or blessed anywhere in Scripture, the reference was rarely to the Jewish people but to the Church of Christ which was given that name.[76] In short, that whole part of Augustine's philosophy tended to support the view of the Toledans that those Jews who remained outside the Church, and were opposed to Christianity for so many centuries, must belong to the bulk of the Jewish people that traditionally followed the path of evil. Thomas' theory, on the other hand, placed the ancient Jewish people in its *entirety* within the orbit of morality; it insisted that the whole of it formed a sacred order, a "priesthood" dedicated to the service of God, and, what is more, it imputed to its *totality* the great privilege of constituting the carnal origin of Christ. Clearly, such a theory could not conform to any of the Toledans' assertions.

III

Having thus clarified his basic views on the special position of Israel among the nations, Cartagena turns to the intricate question of the unique relationship between the Jews and Christianity.[77] What was unique about it, as he saw it, was not only their share in the birth of Christ, in the rise of Christianity, its propagation and expansion, but also their whole attitude toward Christianity whenever and wherever they took it as their faith. To be sure, Cartagena readily agreed that the Bible is full of mystical allusions to the call of Christ to *both* peoples—i.e., the Jews *and* the gentiles[78]—and both of course have to convert to Christ, as many of them have done. But the conversion of the Jews is in no way similar to that of the gentiles. In fact, it is not a conversion at all. For when the gentiles are invited to join the faith, they are asked to accept a view which, to them, is entirely *new;* in fact, they are asked to adopt a law and a morality which are not only new, but also opposed to, or at least *at variance* with their own way of life, morals, and beliefs. To the gentiles, in brief, Christianity is foreign, and its acceptance means a *conversion.* Not so with the Jews. To them Christianity is merely a deepening of what they had known, a better understanding of their ancient teachings, and therefore its adoption does not mean to them conversion.[79] For *there is no basic difference between the Old law and the New;* they do not differ in *kind,* in their *tenor,* or in the *end* toward which they are directed; the difference is only in the *degree* of their perfection—that is, in the measure of clarity, lucidity, and fullness with which they proclaim their common ideas.[80] For many things pronounced by the New law explicitly are expressed by the Old law implicitly. They are presented by the latter as if under a veil, but they can be grasped through a spiritual explanation of those who reflect more deeply.[81] Thus, they differ merely in *form;* in content they are the same. "For not only did the Old law show God's existence, but also the trinity of the divine persons, as well as the incarnation of the Word of the Lord."[82] Also the creation of the world [out of nothing], and many doctrines and observances of religious duties,[83] as well as "the future advent of Christ, and the perfection which is to come in Him and through Him, all of which human reason could not attain," is indicated in the Law, the Prophets and the Psalms.[84] Hence the prophet says: "A candle to my feet is your word, and a light to my paths" (Psalms 119.105).[85] It follows that from the standpoint of religious thought, there was no real innovation in Christianity—that is, it presented no novelty for those who could read the Old Testament properly. Therefore when, following the appearance of Christ, many Jews grasped the true meaning of the Law, they could do so thanks to the special aid provided by Christianity. What Christianity offered them was, in fact, illumination—and that illumination was the essence of the promise which was given them to begin with. Hence, when the prophet says: "Arise, Jerusalem (the word *Jerusalem* is added by Cartagena), for thy light has come,"[86] we must pay special attention to the word "thy." "We must understand that the fullest illumination was to come to *Jerusalem* and that it was to be *hers*," according to the promises made to the Fathers and the predictions made by the Prophets.[87] Consequently, the "light," which was to illumine the whole world, was not only to come *from* Jerusalem; it was also "*of* the Jerusalemites; it came to them from the Law which was given *to* them and from the fulfillment of the law which was to take place *within* them."[88] The gentiles were, of course, invited to share it; but they were "invited to it not as to their *own* light, but as to a *foreign* light, in order to make it their own by their faith."[89]

All this of course was meant not only to show the extent of the Jewish contribution to Christendom, but also to refute the current claim that Jewish converts find it extremely hard to accommodate themselves to Christian teachings. What Cartagena tells us here by implication is that the opposite is true. It is the gentile converts who may face a problem of accommodating themselves to Christianity and its teachings since, unlike the Jews, they have to get used to something alien to their spiritual life.[90] That this is so, and the reverse is not true, is indicated by the cardinal facts of history, which Cartagena bluntly points out: *"It was not Jerusalem that turned to the gentiles, but it was the gentiles who turned to Jerusalem."*[91] And the result was of the same order: *"It was not Israel that received the Gods of the gentiles; it was the gentiles who received the God of Israel."*[92]

However momentous these challenging statements, they did not represent the ultimate conclusion Cartagena was driving at. For the acceptance by the gentiles of the God of Israel—or, as he believed, of true Judaism, or of Judaism in its fullest meaning—did not mean merely the adoption of a faith in the theoretical sense; it meant a radical change for all the followers of the faith (whether of Jewish or gentile origin) in their practical approaches to man's problems—a change which would lead to a total alteration in the structure of mankind and the course of history.

For, in Cartagena's view, the history of mankind was broadly divided into three periods: from Adam to Abraham, from Abraham to Christ, and from Christ to the end of the world. Each of these periods can be clearly discerned by the degree of unity or disunity in mankind, which reflect the measure of mankinds' faith in God and its adherence to His way of life. Thus, the first period was marked by splits and separations into various laws, custom, etc.;

the second by a continuation of these divisions, and on top of this, by the isolation of Israel from the gentiles, which, even though it had a salutary purpose, indicated a still deeper disunity in mankind; the third period is marked by the drive toward unity, whose achievement is the final aim of Christianity.

For in a truly Christian society no difference should be recognized between races, classes, even sexes. In such a society, as St. Paul said: "There is neither Jew nor Greek; there is neither bond nor free; there is neither male nor female; for you are all one in Jesus Christ."[93] The "separation" of Israel was made, as was indicated, when mankind was divided and dismembered; and it was made for one purpose only—to pave the way for man's moral elevation. Now that this end is to be achieved through Christendom, there is obviously no sense in any ethnic separation between Jew and non-Jew within its ranks. Consequently, explains Cartagena, what the Apostle meant by that statement of his (i.e., "there is neither Jew nor Greek") was that there was nothing in the differences indicated therein by which one of these groups—i.e., Jews and non-Jews—should be worthier in the eyes of God than the other.[94] Hence, no consideration should be given in Christendom to a difference of birth, of carnal generation, but only to the unity of spiritual generation, which is Christ's aim and achievement.[95] The carnal origins of the Jews, obviously, fall under the same category, and to point them out as a reason for differentiation is clearly to work against the unification of mankind, which is the essence of the Christian effort and the divine goal of history.

II. PROMISE AND FULFILLMENT

I

"I cannot think," says Cartagena at the beginning of the second part of his *Defensorium*, "that anyone will be so foolish as to dare doubt the fact that our Savior had both promised to save Israel and fulfilled the promise by His coming."[96] Nevertheless, he devotes the first of the four theorems making up the second part of his treatise to prove that "Israel is to be fully saved (*ad sufficientiam salvatus*) by the Redeemer of the world Jesus Christ our Lord."[97] What moved him to demonstrate this proposition was obviously the fact that the anti-conversos in Toledo not only "doubted" it, but denied it altogether. Moreover, they stressed the opposite assumption—namely, that Israel, as a people, was "damned"—and used this assumption as "proof" of the veracity of their race theory about the Jews. According to them, Israel was "damned" because its "nature" was so corrupt that it was "unredeemable"; even the Savior of the World could not save it.

Were, then, the Jews condemned by the Savior, or were they included in his plan of salvation?

Alonso de Cartagena clearly realized that the discussion was now entering a most delicate stage as it turned on a highly critical question. As long as it centered on the ancient Jewish past, on the ages of the Patriarchs, the Judges and the Prophets, he could speak unambiguously, and with unrestrained pride, of the Jewish people as the People of God. He could do so with equal clarity and vigor even when he spoke of the time of the Apostles, for there he could jubilantly point to the fact that the Jews were instrumental in launching Christianity and in defending it in its crucial early stages. But matters assumed quite a different aspect when the reference was to the later period—or rather to the long record of the Jews following the early history of Christianity. Christian thinking, he knew, used completely to isolate ancient Jewish history from the later period, as if two different peoples were involved with hardly any relationship between them. Accordingly, the Patriarchs, the Judges, and the Prophets seemed to belong to some legendary nation that was no longer extant, while the Jews seemed to have appeared out of the blue, on the eve of Christ's martyrdom, representing in their hypocritical Pharisees a malevolent and bloodthirsty breed. Even to more critical minds, Christ's Passion appeared, in one way or another, to have created such a split—or rather such a gulf—in the midst of Jewish history, as if it actually divided it into two different periods, with hardly any continuity between them. Such men would ask in all seriousness: Granted that the Jewish people produced saints and great teachers in the period that preceded Christ's appearance; but is it not evident that after His Passion a radical change took place in its spiritual as well as political condition? Has not a curse descended upon this people which no Christian could possibly explain, except as punishment for its unparalleled crime of delivering Him to death? And has not the protracted Jewish resistance to Christianity shown that, with the emergence of the Apostles and the other first Christians, all the good that inhered in the Jewish people was exhausted, and all that remained in it was the residue of that breed, low-grade and criminal, that produced the architects of Christ's crucifixion? Thus while the race theory might not fit the *first* (or pre-Christian) Jewish people, it could well fit the *second* (or later) Jewish people, whose very history since the days of Christ seemed to prove it unworthy of salvation.

It was this current view of the "second" Jewish people that Alonso de Cartagena sought to dispel, or rather to replace with another view which could serve the purpose of his thesis. His conception of the Jews in the Christian era was far removed from the popular conception, and yet, he believed, was in accord with Christian theory, Church policy, and the actual condition of the Jews in the world as seen through the eyes of a converso.

II

The strongest argument that could be made by Cartagena against the theory of damnation propagated by the Toledans was of course the proof that could be offered from Scriptures that the Jews were assured salvation. That this is actually what the prophets promised, Cartagena had no doubt whatsoever. Reading the Bible like other conversos (such as Juan de Torquemada, for instance), he clearly realized that the Jewish people stood at the core of all eschatological expectations. This was also how the Jews read the Bible. The main difference, however, between them and the conversos was that the Jews attributed their salvation to God, or to the Messiah who was to represent God, while the Christians imputed it to Jesus Christ, who was God and Messiah at one and the same time.

But apart from the difference in the identity of the *Savior*, there was the difference in the concept of the assured *salvation* that separated Jews from Christians. The Jews expected a national redemption, earthly and spiritual at the same time. They expected both the restoration of their statehood and the infusion of the Law in the heart of every Jew, envisioning their state to be thence everlasting and their Law an inspiration and a guide to all nations. The Christians, however, looked only for a spiritual redemption, inspired by Christ's teachings and enabled by His grace. And since, according to Christianity, this particular redemption was centered in no nation but applied to all men, the *third* difference between the views in question related to the *beneficiaries* of the expected salvation.

Were, then, these beneficiaries Jews, or at least *primarily* Jews, or were they Christians, and *only* Christians? It was obvious that to establish the Christian claims, the whole Bible had to be reinterpreted in opposition to the traditional Jewish affirmations.

In the foregoing we have discussed the sociological background of this exegetical development. Now we ought to remark on the theological precedents, which can be found already in Paul's writings. For every Christian who read the Pauline Epistles knew that the "sons of Abraham" or the "sons of promise" were not Abraham's carnal, but his spiritual descendants, and that the spiritual descendants of Abraham and the other Patriarchs were not the Jews but the Christians. Thus Paul gave the clue to solutions that Christians in later times offered to the prophecies of redemption. Accordingly, just as many references in the Bible to David, the Savior, the Redeemer, and the Son of Man were soon held to refer to Christ, so many references to "Israel," "Jacob" and "Judah," "Jerusalem," "Zion," and the "daughter of Zion" were interpreted as referring to the camp of Christ's faithful, to the Church, or to the "heavenly Jerusalem." How easy it would be, therefore, for any Christian theologian who would like to side with the Toledan party to reject all the evidence adduced from the Bible with respect to Israel's future salvation by claiming that the biblical promises of redemption were made in reality not to Israel the *people* but to "Israel" the followers of Christ.

As a Christian theologian, Cartagena, like Torquemada, could not disregard this Christological interpretation or consider it erroneous. From the standpoint of his immediate interest, however, it presented him with a special problem. We have seen how Torquemada found it difficult to avoid the pitfalls of the allegorical interpretation given by Christianity to the promises of redemption. We have noticed how, in search of Christian authorities who would support his own understanding of the prophecies, he had to skip from one commentator to another, take a portion from one and a sentence from another, and ignore whole bodies of Christian comment in order to present his case for Israel on the basis of the Bible. Cartagena, however, attacked the question in a straightforward manner.

Admitting that by the name of *Israel* and its synonyms the Bible often refers to *all* of Christ's faithful—including, of course, the faithful from Israel—he insists nevertheless that this is no reason to "tear asunder" the literal sense. The Scriptures, to be sure, may be interpreted in many senses, and each of them may be true and useful—that is, helpful to our understanding of the Bible; yet the literal sense must be held superior to the symbolic. "For out of it, as from a definite root, all the other meanings proceed."[98] It is from the literal sense, moreover, as Augustine has written against the Donatists, that solid arguments can be taken "in the faith, for the faith, and toward the faith."[99] Hence, whatever the Bible tells us about the salvation of "Israel," "Zion" and the like—which means, in plain language, the Jewish people—must be regarded as true and valid in the literal sense.

Having firmly established this principle, Cartagena could now offer scriptural proof that the prophets predicted that Jesus Christ would come and bring salvation to the Jewish people. To begin with, there is the famous statement in Deuteronomy containing God's assurance to Moses: "I shall raise for you a prophet out of your brethren *who will be similar to Me. To him you will listen.*"[100] And what prophet was raised out of the Jewish people who was *similar* to God except Jesus Christ, who was God and man, and assumed His humanity from the Jewish people? *And to this prophet the Jews were to listen*—namely, it is by Him that *they were to be saved.*[101] No wonder that Jeremiah, when he spoke of Jesus, called Him "the hope of Israel and its savior in time of trouble" (Jer. 14.8).[102] Similarly, when Isaiah said: "You are a hidden God, O God of Israel the Savior" (Isa. 45.15), had he not called the Savior of Israel, explicitly, a hidden God? And that could be no other than Jesus.[103]

The Christological explanations of these biblical phrases were of course not Cartagena's invention. He took them from the Christian commentaries on the Bible that since the earliest Church Fathers, indeed since the Gospels, had been engaged, as we have indicated, in reinterpreting the Bible, so that it might fit the events of Christian history and the Christian articles of faith. To be sure, from the standpoint of nonreligious scholarship, they offer none of the proofs suggested. From the standpoint of the Christian believer, however, they appear highly convincing. By the time Cartagena wrote his *Defensorium,* and also for many centuries before, the comments of the Church Fathers were themselves considered expressions of the Holy Spirit; and who would dare doubt their validity? They could also be found in the conversionist literature which converts of Jewish origin, including Paul of Burgos, had composed in Spain in the preceding centuries. Still, there was a novelty in Cartagena's presentation, in intent if not in content—or rather in its slant and basic thrust. For when the Church Fathers and the medieval commentators interpreted the Bible to fit Christian doctrine, they did so for the purpose of establishing Christianity as a divinely ordained religion. When converts from Judaism used the same passages, their main purpose was to offer proofs to *Jews* that the Savior to whom the prophets alluded was no other than Jesus Christ. Cartagena's interpretations supported these aims and yet had a purpose of their own. What he wanted to prove was a special point that related to the controversy in which he was engaged—namely, that Jesus was not only the Messiah, who was promised to *Israel* and *came* to save it, but also that he *would* save it in due course; that divine assurances were given to this effect; and that nothing that happened since the appearance of Christ was to divert the divine will from its aim. This was a new aspect and a new emphasis that could develop only as a result of the struggle in which the conversos were involved in fifteenth-century Spain.

If we bear in mind Cartagena's special purpose, we shall understand more clearly the many other arguments that he presented in this connection and why he had to offer so many proofs to substantiate seemingly the same point. *Seemingly,* indeed, but not *actually.* Thus, when he calls his readers' attention to what is written in Matthew 1.21—namely, that an Angel of God appeared to Joseph, Mary's husband, in a dream, and foretold the birth of Christ, and that he would be called Jesus—"for He will *save* his people from their sins"—Cartagena was not interested so much in pointing out the meaning of the name Jesus, which was lost on his readers who did not know Hebrew, as to lay bare the deep meaning of the prophecy: "He will save His people," with emphasis to be placed upon the words "His people" to fit the case which he sought to make, and also on he *will* save—namely, that salvation was not to be avoided or denied for any reason whatever. It is going to be a fact of history, as clear and simple as the prophecy of the Angel.[104] Similarly, when Zachariah, the father of John the Baptist, was filled with the Holy Spirit, he prophesied: "Blessed be the Lord, the *God of Israel,* who has visited and *redeemed His people.*" "Redeemed" is read of course by Cartagena in the sense of "will redeem," since "many prophecies speak of the future in the past tense"; and so the redemption, to be preceded by a "visit of God" (i.e., Jesus who is God), was regarded by the prophet as so definite and unquestionable that he could present it as an accomplished fact.[105]

That the "salvation" and "redemption" promised in those prophecies was to come to the *Jewish people* was likewise indicated by those very prophecies; for it was said of Jesus that He was to save *His* people—namely, the people to which He was born, or "those who descended, through the propagation of the flesh, from the house of Jacob"—i.e., Israel as a whole, and not a part of Israel.[106] And the same idea was also suggested by Jesus' title in the other prophecy: "The God of Israel," who was to save *His* people. For who was God's people except the people of Israel, who were known as His special people? Thus, there can be no misunderstanding about these assurances, which are further illuminated by the saying of Paul: "Jesus Christ was a *minister of the circumcision to confirm the promises made unto the fathers and the truth of God*" (Rom. 15.8). Not in vain does Cartagena precede the "promises made to the Fathers" (namely, the fathers of the circumcised Jews) to the words "the truth of God" which appear, in the original, in the reverse order.[107] For what he sought to emphasize was that the promises God gave the Fathers of the Jewish people remained unchangeable, and that Jesus Christ was sent to confirm the *validity of those eternal promises.*

Israel, then, was to be saved following the coming of Jesus Christ; this is the clear meaning of the prophecies; yet it is also clear that Israel as a whole was *not* saved during that coming, or shortly thereafter. Israel, however, was assured that it *would* be saved, and therefore saved it *will* be, and hence it must be understood that what the prophecies promised was that Israel's salvation should be effected through Christ—or more correctly, through the impact of Christianity. Indeed, it would *begin* with Christ's appearance and continue from then on until it is accomplished. This is why Peter, the first of the apostles, speaking to *the people of Judaea,* said: "The promise is unto *you,* and to your children, and to all that are afar off, even as many as the Lord our God shall call" (Acts 2.39). Now, "of whom," asks Cartagena, "does he speak when he refers to those who are 'afar off,' *except those who after many generations were to accept the faith?* All those of *Israelitic blood,* therefore, who were to receive the Catholic faith, even to the end of the world, he declared to be partaking in the promise."[108]

This interpretation of the words of the apostle came to substantiate Cartagena's view. The "call" of God to Israel was first heard when Jesus appeared to His people, but it was to be repeated until the end of the world, across many generations. To be sure, Christian commentators understood the cited verse in quite a different manner. Most of them believed that by "all who are far off" the reference was, apart from the Jews, "also" or "especially" to the gentiles, who were "far" from the speaker (the apostle Peter) either physically (by their distant locations) or spiritually (in the knowledge of God).[109] But Cartagena insists that the entire statement centers on the Jewish people alone, and that by "far off" the apostle referred both to those who were "remote" from him in space and those who were far removed from him in time. The prophets of Israel, adds Cartagena, foresaw that eventuality too, and that is why Hosea said: "For many days shall the children of Israel be without a king, and without a prince, and without sacrifice, and without altar, and without Ephod and without Teraphim; afterwards shall the children of Israel return and see the Lord their God and David their King."[110]

That by God and David the reference is to Christ who was both God and Messiah, the King from the seed of David; that the kingdom referred to was the kingdom of God, the Church triumphant which will ultimately embrace the People of Israel; and that by sacrifice, altar, ephod and teraphim the reference was to the divine ceremonies which were to be practiced by the Holy Church was already posited by many Christian commentators prior to Cartagena.[111] But there was innovation here, as we have seen, in the emphasis on the redemption of Israel, on the *scope* of the Israelitic redemption (which was to comprise the *whole* people) and, above all, on the length of time designated for Israel's salvation.

For what did the prophet mean when he said that "many days" would pass before salvation is effected? When will that predicted event take place? Traditional Christian commentators on the Bible delayed the absorption of the Jews by the Church to the "*end of days*," or the end of the world. Thus said Anselm of Laon; thus said Nicolas de Lyra; and thus said also many other commentators and theologians of renown.[112] Cartagena, on the other hand, does not object to the idea that "many days" *includes* the end of the world, but he insists that the conversion of the Jews—or most Jews—was not to be effected *only* at the end. It was not surprising to him that the abovementioned commentators postponed the Christianization of the Jews to the "end"—that is, to the latest possible date, or the time of Christ's second appearance. They were impressed by the Jews' strong resistance to Christianity and believed that, in the ordinary course of things, their conversion would not take place. But they all lived before the 15th century, when large masses of Jews, who joined the Church, were assimilated into Christendom. Cartagena, however, lived in those times, and therefore the return of the children of Israel to "their God and to David their King" was to him a much more realistic prophecy than it was to de Lyra and his predecessors. This "return," he said, "we witness with open eyes"[113]; and therefore he did not hesitate to introduce a correction in the prevailing conception about the conversion of the Jews. The return of Israel as a whole, he said accordingly, will not take place *at* the end of days but *up to* the end of days, when it will be completed.[114]

It follows that the redemption of the Jewish people was not only a matter of the distant future, but also of the past as well as the present. It was not a prophecy that was to be fulfilled; it was actually being materialized. For the conversion of the Jews was an ongoing process extending from the days of Christ on, and the mass conversion of the Jews in the Spanish kingdoms was merely a *part* of that process.

Yet despite this apparently acceptable interpretation, much remained to be explained, Cartagena felt. After all, the view that the Jews would "return" only at the "end of the world" was deeply rooted in Christian theology; it was stressed by both St. Augustine and St. Thomas, it was sanctified by tradition, and it could also be fitted into a theory of damnation which would cover the whole era from Christ's first to second coming. Above all, there seemed to be no compelling reason that it should be replaced by the theory of Cartagena, based as it was on *his* interpretation of Acts 2.39. To be sure, had there been since the days of Christ a continuous conversion of Jews to Christianity, a conversion in substantial or steadily growing numbers, the conversion in Spain could have been reasonably regarded as another stage in this development. But this was not what had happened. What had happened was that after many centuries during which Jews came to the faith in small numbers, actually in isolated trickles, there was suddenly this large influx of converts in the Spanish kingdoms. Could not the opponents conclude from this occurrence that this conversion was an *untrue* "return," as it did not fit any of the predicted schemes—and, in fact, any scheme at all? To answer this difficulty, Cartagena devoted the second theorem of the second part.

III

The novel argument implied in his answer is that in order to discern the scheme ordained by God, one must view—or review—the ancient prophecies in light of the historical developments. This is what Cartagena did; and what he came up with was a view of the past which appealed to him by its structural design, as well as by the use he could make of it in the crucial debate in which he was involved.

Christ's early life, according to Cartagena, indicates, by a series of symbolic events, the various stages in the expansion of Christianity. To begin with, on the very day of His birth His coming was proclaimed by the angel of God to the "shepherds who were then abiding in the field, keeping watch over their flocks by night" (Luke 2.8). Cartagena identifies the shepherds as Jews, adding that they "signified the Apostles and other Jews who believed [in Christ] in those times."[115] They were the first to adopt the faith and, as the Apostle says, "there were not many mighty or many noble among them" (I Cor. 1.26). Then, on the thirteenth day of his life, he became known to the adoring magi. These symbolize the acceptance of the faith by the gentile kings and the masses who followed them, as is indicated in Psalms: "And many kings will adore him and many nations will serve him" (Psalms 71.11). Finally, on the fortieth day he was brought to the Temple, where Simon the Just received the faith. The Temple symbolized the power, and hence the universality, of Jewry. Thus, these symbolic events hold the key to the future developments. "The firstlings of the Israelitic people, figured in the shepherds, came before the firstlings of the gentiles in receiving the Catholic faith, but the fullness of the gentiles represented by the Magi came before the fullness of the Israelitic people. Hence the apostle Paul said: "Blindness in part has happened to Israel, until the fullness of the Gentiles had come in. *And so all of Israel shall be saved*."[116]

Holy Scripture gives a clear indication of the various stages of the conversion to the faith to be passed through by both the Jews and the gentiles. But Cartagena believes that it also indicates the stretches of time that were to be involved. For "although thirteen days passed between the shepherds and the magi, twice as many days separated the magi from Simon. What else may be concluded from this fact except that while the plenitude of the gentiles was to come [to the faith] in the *near* future, *the full coming of the whole people of Israel* was to be awaited for a long time."[117]

This was of course a mystical interpretation and by no means of a compelling nature. But it was fascinating in more ways than one, and it was appealing to a true believer; for resorting to such mystical interpretations was not at all uncommon in those days. It was part of a long exegetical tradition followed in Christendom from the Church Fathers on, and this tradition was not slighted or abandoned even with the growth of classical studies. In any case, it was still believed in Christendom that the words of Scripture prefigure the future, just as it was generally believed by Jews that they contain allusions to the Messianic age. Above all, both Greek and Roman literature are full of indications of oracular knowledge and other ways of learning future events. As for Cartagena, who was heir to both traditions, the Christian and Jewish (through his converso background), there is no doubt that he *could* believe, in some measure, in the truth of his interpretation. In this he was a typical representative of his age. Mysticism and cold logic, blind faith and realism met in the thinking of this Christian humanist, this student of Seneca and Cicero on the one hand, and of Augustine and Jerome on the other, as they met in the minds of many of his contemporaries, Christian and Jewish alike.

What was the reason for the sequence of events thus established for the spread of Christianity? Cartagena dismisses the question as impudent. "Since, as the Jurists say, we cannot find the reasons for all the innovations made by our ancestors, it would be foolish to try to comprehend the profundity of the divine counsel by the limited powers of our thinking.[118] Such questions belong to the category of mysteries that must be regarded by man as insoluble, and therefore need not be inquired into. What is important—and sufficient—for us to know is not the *reason* for the developments but the *order* we can discern in them, so that we may be in a better position to relate the events to each other. For where there is order, there is a plan; and where there is a plan embracing the events that occurred across a long span of time, there is visible the hand of God. Implied in this of course was the dominant view that God is the architect of man's history, and that none of His structures is in any way whimsical, but based on the most perfect and harmonious plan. Obviously, the more God's plan in history is unfolded and revealed to us through its very execution, the more capable we are of grasping its outline, and that means discerning future events by the pattern of the past.

Now, to Cartagena's thinking, there was no doubt that much of God's plan for the expansion of Christianity, for its conquest of mankind and its conversion to God, had already been implemented. And it is by reflecting on the fate of the Jews, and their particular part in the advancement of the faith, that the outline of God's plan can be perceived. Especially does the plan become apparent when one ponders the developments in the Jewish camp in relatively recent times. God's outline suddenly emerges from the heavy, fleeting mist of the past, and a pattern can be observed in the seemingly chaotic events. What is obvious is that the great historic drama—that of the conversion of the world to God—begins with the conversion of the Israelites and ends with their conversion; first on a small scale, finally on a large scale, with a reversed order assigned for the gentiles. While the firstlings of the Jews preceded the firstlings of the gentiles, the multitude of the gentiles was to precede the multitude of the Jews. Of course, conversions from the Jews, like those from the gentiles, will continue throughout the period; and therefore when we say that their plenitude will come toward the end of the Christian era, it does not mean that this "coming" will be swift, accomplished in one swoop, or in a short spell. It is likely to take a considerable time, just as the conversion of the gentiles did—that is, of those who came in large numbers. "All this," says Cartagena, "shows with sufficient clarity to the devotedly contemplative person, and to one reflecting with a sincere heart, that inasmuch as the conversion of the Israelitic infidels becomes from time to time more general, so much closer approaches the time of which the Apostle said: 'All of Israel will be saved' and, in consequence, the end of this toilsome world."[119] And again: "The more frequent and abundant become the conversions of the Israelite infidels, the more probable it becomes that the day of universal judgment is approaching."[120]

The conversion of Israel is thus proceeding according to its divinely destined schedule. One should not be surprised that its "fullness" will come late, or doubt the soundness of the later conversions. Israel after the appearance of Christ, like Israel prior to His appearance, is acting according to the divine plan. It offered the "basis" for Christendom in the past; it will offer the "roof" for Christendom in the future. To speak of it as condemned in the second period of its existence is therefore no more foolish than to suggest that it was cursed in the pre-Christian times. This is Israel to whom the promise was given, and this is Israel in whom the same promise was being fulfilled as God wished it.

IV. THE CRUCIAL OBSTACLE

I

From the standpoint of the Church's general ideology, Cartagena's refutation of the racists' assertions was undoubtedly a masterpiece. From the standpoint of the Church's view of the Jews, however, it was still open to attack. For with all his arguments about Israel's election, its past glory and past services to Christendom, he did not cancel the effect of the notorious fact that Israel had committed deicide (a fact of which all Christians were certain), or of the prevalent view in Christendom that Israel was being "punished" for that crime. As long as these convictions remained unshaken, they could always give rise, Cartagena believed, to a race theory like that of the Toledans, and with it to the theory of damnation.

The likely developments in such circumstances were too grim to be ignored. The principle of racial equality could be upheld as a hallowed concept in Christendom; yet the Jewish race might be excluded from it as an "exception"—such as all rules have. The exclusion could be easily justified by pointing to two outstanding facts: The Jews formed an "exception" in mankind by the part they played in the Crucifixion; and they were an exception among all peoples by the fate that had befallen them ever since. What could be the reason for these two exceptions if not the Jews' exceptional nature—or rather their extraordinary evil? Obviously, we are again at the back door of the race theory and the theory of damnation. Thus, Cartagena felt that, unless he struck hard at the notion of the Passion which projects the Jew as a deicide, all his arguments and demonstrations on behalf of the Jews—and, indirectly, on behalf of the conversos—could be easily discarded.

There is no doubt that the question of the Passion was broached in converso circles many times.[121] To be sure, the main responsibility for the Passion was laid by the conversos at the door of the Jews, as was done by all other Christians; yet directly and indirectly, it cast a shadow also upon the conversos themselves. According to the Gospel of Matthew, the Jews declared prior to Jesus' execution: "Let his blood be on us and on our children,"[122] and this statement, understood as an oath, was taken as a "curse" on all the descendants of the Jews. Moreover, the "curse" could be interpreted to mean—as indeed it was on many occasions—that the "children" of the Jews were to pay with their blood for the spilled blood of Christ.[123] And were not the conversos descendants of the Jews and thus subject to the same curse? Very subtly, without appearing apologetic, Cartagena touches upon the subject of the Passion in several places in his book.

II

In all probability, Cartagena's thoughts on this subject, as we find them expressed in his *Defensorium,* took shape in the course of many years. But as far as we know, he had not exposed them earlier, either orally or in writing. If so, this was the first time that a strong attack was launched within Christendom upon the traditional Christian view of the Passion and Jewish responsibility for it.

Cartagena's argument is both theological and historical. Theologically, he remains firmly on Christian ground, and it is from an advanced Christian position that he attacks the prevailing concept. Historically, he appears equally sound, since his facts are taken from the Old and New Testaments, whose reported events were not questioned in the Middle Ages by any Christian student. He begins with the theological argument and proceeds with the historical. Here we shall present the latter first, as it will help us see the coherence of his thoughts.

Cartagena comes straight to the heart of the issue. The crime of the Crucifixion is laid at the door of the Jewish people *as a whole,* and it is assumed that all the Jews at the time of Jesus were directly involved in, or responsible for it; consequently, if their descendants have to pay for it, all the Jews of the succeeding generations are to bear the consequences of that crime. But this conclusion, Cartagena claims, is based on false premises. To begin with, he points out the fallacy of the notion that *the* Jews—namely, the people *as a whole*—were involved in Jesus' crucifixion. For "only few among the Jews participated in that crime"; and this was so for obvious reasons. First, the ten tribes, the largest part of the Israelites, were exiled from their land long before the Crucifixion, and obviously had nothing to do with anything that occurred in Judea during the time of Jesus. Second, of the tribes that remained in Palestine, most of their members lived outside Jerusalem and were not among those who assembled in the city during the events in question; therefore they, too, could in no way be responsible for the Crucifixion and the Passion. Third, among those who lived *near* Jerusalem, "who can say how many holy men and women were deeply pained by that most perverse act as, for instance, the Blessed Virgin, whose heart was pierced by a sword?" Fourth, also *in* Jerusalem we know that holy women grieved intensely over what was being done to Jesus, and the Savior himself confirms this fact by the words of compassion he addressed to them: "Daughters of Jerusalem, do not weep for me." Fifth, the sacred college of the apostles, and the devoted host of Jesus' disciples, such as Nicodemus and Joseph of Arimathaea, were of course opposed to the insane malice of those who committed that gruesome crime. Sixth, the pervert people themselves requested that the execution take place not on a holiday, "lest there be an uproar among the people." They feared, as is reported, that the assembled crowds, who believed Jesus to have been a prophet, would oppose their action by force. All this shows that only few among the Jews were involved in the crime of Crucifixion.[124]

But to what extent were these few really responsible for the crime? It is here that the theological argument comes in. Cartagena sees in the process of the Passion—in the share of the various culprits in the crime and the order of their participation in it—symbolic indications of forthcoming events, whose meaning may become intelligible only if we understand that the whole drama, in all its stages, with all its actors and witnesses to boot, was preordained by Christ himself. Rather than a result of human weakness, wickedness, and perverted desires, the Passion was a result of divine planning and an expression of divine will. In other words, the Passion was an act of Christ, and like all His other acts, as St. Thomas understood,[125] it was ordered and performed so as "to make the minds of the faithful rise in great admiration and devotion."[126] Why do Jews appear first among those who were responsible for Christ's execution? Why do gentiles appear later? For "in that manner was prefigured the effect of the Passion" upon mankind.[127] It was His will that under the impact of the Passion the Jews would be the first to be led to salvation; and after many of them had been baptized and began their preaching among the gentiles, the effect of the Passion would pass to the gentile world. "It was fitting therefore that Christ begin His Passion at the hands of the Jews, and that later, when these delivered Him to the gentiles, he complete His Passion at the hands of the Gentiles, so that thus all might participate in the guilt, just as they were to participate in the beneficence."[128] Since all this had been preordained, we must of course be very cautious in attributing extra guilt to the Jews. Nevertheless, *sub specie humanitatis,* we do see things in our human light; and since predestination does not cancel free will, or eliminate human responsibility, we do have the right, and even the duty, to define things from our own standpoint.

And what do we see from this standpoint? There were three human groups who shared in both the preparation and execution of the Passion: there were the Jewish priests and rulers; there were some common people from among the Jews; and there were the Roman leaders and soldiers (who stand for the gentiles). Cartagena attributes to each of these groups a different degree of guilt and, in agreement with Christian tradition, he admits that the guilt of the Jews was greater. Yet even among the Jews two degrees of guilt must be distinguished. Of these the guiltier were the Jewish leaders, who were called "princes" by the Apostle.[129] For even though they were ignorant of Christ's divinity, and even though, as the Apostle said, "*had they known this*, they would not have crucified Him,"[130] nevertheless "that ignorance does not excuse them from the crime." For they knew from the prophets, with whom they were familiar, the signs of the future coming of Christ; they *did* see these signs in Christ; and if they failed to recognize Him for what He was, it was because hate and envy had perverted their judgment and made them refuse to see Him in a true light. "Their guilt therefore was the heaviest, both because of the nature of the crime and the malice" which gave birth to it.[131] As for the common people among the Jews, their sin was also heavy, no doubt, though their guilt was somewhat diminished by the greater measure of their ignorance. Hence Bede's words on the verse: *Forgive them, Father, for they know not what they do.*[132] "He asks forgiveness for those who did not know what they were doing, namely, who did what they did out of zeal for God, but not out of their knowledge."[133] The gentiles, by whose hands Christ was crucified, also sinned of course, but they were much more excusable, as they did not have the knowledge of the Law.[134] Thus all people, both Israelite and gentile, leaders and commoners, participated in the crime and had a share in Christ's Passion, but divine clemency refused to forget its mercy even during the very perpetration of the crime, and hence the words of Jesus: "Father, forgive them for they know not what they do." In fact, in those who participated in the Passion—Jews and gentiles—the whole human race was represented, just as those who showed signs of repentance after it—and these were, again, Jews and gentiles—represented the whole mass of humanity. Moreover, salvation was offered not only to men of the generation then living, but to all those who were willing to follow in their footsteps for all time to come.[135]

Even though Cartagena attempts to present Jewish responsibility for the Passion in keeping with the traditional Christian view, the manner in which he presents it mitigates the accusation. For the degree of guilt, as he indicated clearly, depended heavily on the degree of *awareness* of who Christ was, and, as we have seen, he took pains to point out that none of the Jews, not even their leaders, realized that the man they condemned was Christ. In support of this thesis, he enlists St. Paul, whose authority would presumably preclude all opposition. To be sure, Cartagena also said that ignorance could not exonerate the Jews from the crime, for they *could* know who Jesus was if they truly *wanted* to know; and yet the fact remained that the Jewish leaders were ignorant of Jesus' divinity, and this fact cannot be minimized despite all explanations to the contrary. It was in this ignorance, shared by all the participants, Jews and gentiles, that Cartagena sees the reason for the divine clemency. Hence when Jesus said: "Forgive them, for they know not," etc., he referred to *all* the participants in the crime—since *all* of them, in effect, did not know.

This was of course a novel view in Christian theological literature. But novelty in a dogmatic faith is prohibited, unless it is implied or indicated in the words of recognized authorities. Cartagena, as we have seen, relied for his interpretation on what he found in the Gospels. Beyond the Gospels, however, he could refer only to Bede. But Bede's comment on Jesus' words: "Forgive them, etc." is far different from Cartagena's presentation. Here is Bede's full statement on the matter as it appears in his commentary on Luke:

> It should be soberly observed that not for those who, inflamed by the stimuli of envy and malice, *although they knew the son of God, but preferred to crucify rather than admit,* he offered prayers [of forgiveness] to the father, but surely for those who had the zeal for God, though not out of knowledge, and did not know what they were doing.[136]

Bede, then, clearly distinguishes between those who knew that Jesus was the Son of God but refused to admit it (and hence were not included in Jesus' prayer) and those who were ignorant of this fact (for whom Jesus indeed prayed), while according to Cartagena, *all* who were involved in the crime were *in fact* ignorant of Christ's divinity. To be sure, he too attributed envy and malice to the Jewish "priests and rulers," but the effect of these sinful attitudes was that their hearts and minds were shut to the light of the truth, but not that the knowledge of the truth reached them and they refused to admit it. The Jewish leaders, according to Cartagena, could not possibly admit Christ's divinity, because they were never aware of it, however deplorable were the causes of this unawareness; and therefore even though they were guilty of the crime, and even guiltier than the other participants in the Passion, they were not excluded from those who did not know (as is testified by the Apostle) and consequently they were not excluded from Christ's prayer of forgiveness either.[137]

If all this seemed quite clear to Cartagena, there could be no doubt about the implied conclusion either. That conclusion was that the doors of salvation were closed to none of the participants in the Passion (who, as we have noticed, represented symbolically *all* Jews and *all* gentiles—i.e., the whole human race). And this is really what that "forgiveness" meant. It meant that the crime of the Crucifixion precluded no one from salvation, which is attainable by repentance and recognition of Christ. This, too, is indicated in the story of the Passion, or rather in its immediate aftermath. For the Gospels tell us that the Roman centurion, and the others who represented the gentiles in the Crucifixion, recognized, after the act, what had been done and declared: "This was the Son of God!" (Matthew 27.54). Similarly, the whole crowd that "came to the sight"—namely, all the Jews who witnessed the Passion—"smote their breasts and returned" to the way of truth (Luke 23.48). Both these groups, the Jewish and the gentile, represented the totality of the future faithful from both the gentiles and the Jews. They were all "forgiven" because they were all qualified to be accepted to the Church of God.[138]

III

Cartagena no doubt felt that by this treatment of the Passion, he removed the only effective argument that could be made against accepting Jews into the Church on equal footing with all other Christians. And by doing so, he believed, he had dealt a fatal blow to the theory of "damnation" which was so stressed by the Toledans.

But his arguments did not serve only to uphold the principle of *equality*. Another principle, that of *unity*, was likewise given a great boost. To Cartagena this was self-evident. If in the society that emanated spiritually, through a spiritual birth, from the second Adam (Christ) all carnal differences were brought to nought, inevitably all the followers of Christ, from whatever tribe *(gens)*, or "whatever part of that ancient blood," constitute *one* people. Vividly to illustrate what he had in mind with respect to the sameness and equality of that people, Cartagena offers the following example, whose meaning and implications are beyond question.

According to him, all nations and races intermingle in Christianity as the rivers in the sea, and just as none of these rivers, however great, maintains its separate existence in the sea, "for all the waters, whencesoever they come, receive the maritime taste, and *retain neither the name nor the quality of their old origin*," so are the nations bound to disappear in the great sea of Christianity.[139]

It should not be assumed, of course, that Cartagena believed that this unification would occur instantly, or materialize in a short span of time. Obviously he realized that the process of this admixture—the intermingling of so many peoples to the point where their offspring lose their special characteristics and the awareness of their old origins—takes a long time; but to him that process was fixed and irreversible, and its outcome so distinctly foreseen that one could regard it as an accomplished fact. Moreover, the principle of one peoplehood, he believed, guides the policies of Christianity so clearly that all its followers must see themselves as members of one people even before the racial fusion is completed. For it is the spiritual unity, the unity of virtue, that gave birth to the society of the Church, and it is this very unity that dictates all other unions that are to be achieved in Christendom. Hence, by the laws of that unity, anyone who joins the society of Christ becomes, de jure and de facto, from the moment of his joining, an equal member of the Christian people.

That, in light of this, no racial division is permissible or tolerable in this people is to Cartagena self-evident. In fact, it can in no way be recognized—either practically or theoretically. Consequently, even nominal distinctions such as *Old* Christians and *New* Christians have no room whatever in Christendom and ought not to be tolerated. They mar the basic unity of the Church and represent, in effect, a contradiction in terms of the fundamental tenets of Christianity. Indeed, according to these tenets, there are no Christians who may be regarded as Old, for "there are no Catholics who did not come to the faith *recently*" (i.e., in this generation), since no Catholic, whatever his origin, is *born* a Christian.[140] Christianity can be received only through the sacrament of baptism, and this door must be entered by each initiate. "Hence," said Augustine, "if a pregnant mother is baptized, the child within her womb remains unbaptized for he does not belong to the maternal body."[141] And Isidore of Seville says: "Those who are in the maternal womb cannot be baptized with the mother; for he who is not yet born according to Adam cannot be reborn according to Christ. Regeneration cannot be said of him in whom generation has not preceded."[142]

Thus, since Christianity begins with every person at some moment of *his* own life, children of Jewish parents who were baptized at any time are no different from children of Christian parents, and no one can be considered an *older* Christian than another unless the date of his baptism precedes that of the baptism of some other person; but in this case many children of Jewish parents may be considered older than those of many Christians. Obviously, a differentiation between two distinct groups of Christians on the basis of some such principle is absurd, opposed to the sacrament of baptism, and calculated only to create division among Christians when absolute unity between them is called for.

V. CHRISTIANITY AND NOBILITY

I

Cartagena's views as presented thus far appear to form a solid front, strong enough to resist the Toledans' assaults. It is difficult to see in this front a weak spot at which an attack could be successfully launched. Cartagena, it seems, has secured all positions and fortified all vulnerable points. Had he now brought his *Defense* to its conclusion, it would appear entirely understandable. Yet precisely at this moment of assured victory, Cartagena abandons his impregnable position, opens another line of argument, and proceeds to attack the Toledans from another standpoint, which seems opposed to the first.

The reader's attention is now drawn to the subject of nobility in Christendom and its standing vis-à-vis the other groups. Judging by Cartagena's argument so far, nobility and Christianity seem mutually exclusive—that is, if nobility is defined as a class distinguished by its superior blood. For if it is assumed, as Cartagena maintained, that Christendom is a melting pot of all nations from which one *new* nation must emerge, how can a separate class of nobility arise or survive in this intermixture? If the big "rivers" flowing into Christendom—i.e., the big peoples which are to be amalgamated—are going to lose, as we have been assured, their distinctiveness and separate existence, how can the far smaller currents of "nobility" retain their identity within the vast sea? As for the desirability of such a development, it too, if we follow Cartagena, appears to go against the grain of Christianity. For how can a birthright of carnal nature be of any value whatever when men are to be spiritually regenerated and when this regeneration obliterates, in essence, any carnal division? And yet, despite his repeated affirmation that Christianity is heading toward the abolition of all birthrights, all carnal distinctions and ethnic differences, Cartagena voices unequivocal support for class differentiation based on hereditary rights.

Here we see again the kind of dichotomy we have noticed in his thinking on the race question—that is, when he emphasized the unity of man's origin, on the one hand, and the superiority of the Jewish nation, on the other. That dichotomy, as we noted, was founded theoretically on a combination of the Jewish idea of Election and the Christian idea of a universal Church. But what lay at the root of the present contradiction may have been the conflict between two opposite tendencies—the cosmopolitan and the nationalist—which were doubtless present in Cartagena's thinking but were never fully reconciled in his mind. Ultimately, however, the cosmopolitan tendency seemed to have gained the upper hand when he pressed vigorously for the idea of *one people* as a fusion of all ethnic elements. But this victory was by no means total. For the universalist equality from the standpoint of origin, dictated by the idea of "one people," now appears limited by an important reservation: the recognition of class differences based on heredity.

Thus, Cartagena's social ideal should be defined somewhat differently from what it appeared to be in light of his earlier statements. For now he insists that while the Church does not recognize the superiority of anyone on the basis of *national* origin, it does recognize different grades of standing on the basis of *social* origin. Hence, while the differences of the first sort should be disregarded by all Christians, the differences of the second kind must be respected and upheld.

To understand the significance of his subsequent discussion, we must consider the reasons that prompted him to open it. As we have seen, Cartagena presented a view which was as coherent as it was idealistic, and it also provided an effective answer to the racial theories espoused by the Toledans. This view was in full accord with the true, pristine doctrines of Christianity and, as such, stood on firm theological ground. Yet once the theory was developed to its limits, and its implications appeared in clear light, Cartagena could see that his final conclusions, while providing a smashing answer to the Toledans, also struck at the foundations of the social order as it existed in medieval Spain.

For if the Christian ideal is full unity and equality, to be achieved by the elimination of all ethnic differences, then obviously all class differences rooted in ancestry must be viewed as a defect that ought to be removed. And had Cartagena arrived at this conclusion and said nothing further on this subject, his theory would be regarded socially as revolutionary, anti-aristocratic and even anti-monarchic. Such a view, however, was far from his mind. Not only did he not wish to support it; he was actually opposed to it, as we shall see below. Hence an exposition of his thinking on this issue—that is, on the "rights" of the various classes—is a necessary corrective.

The dualism of his position is, in fact, indicated already at the start of his discussion. There he says that while the Church "rejects every consideration of carnal origin," it does not disavow respect for persons who "exceed others in virtue, in the fame of their lineage and other endowments."[143] We are struck by this apparent inconsistency between the Church's indifference to ethnic origin and the special respect it should show to some persons because of the "fame of their lineage." "Fame of lineage" may mean the high repute that one's ancestors gained for exceptional achievements, but it may also refer to some hidden qualities of the stock that produced the outstanding men. Clearly, according to the first meaning, respect is due to the ancestors only, and it extends to their descendants merely as a courtesy, or as consideration for the ancestral name. According to the second meaning, however, the progeny of famous families ought to be respected also for their own worth, as they are presumed to be not only successors of their forbears but also their *heirs* in a genetic sense—that is, to retain in some measure their qualities, which they had acquired through natural inheritance. Which of these two meanings did Cartagena have in mind when he associated "fame of ancestry" with virtues and other gifts? Clearly, the second meaning is farther than the first from the view that denies any value to "origin" in Christianity's social structure.

Some light is shed on this question by Cartagena's following statement. "Not all faithful," he says, "who descended from the gentiles should be equally honored; for some of them were emperors, kings, princes, and dukes, and of the different ranks of the most illustrious nobility, while others came from the plebeian multitude and rural ignobleness."[144] So against the *nobilitas* of the ruling class there stands the *ignobilitas* of the lower classes (the "plebeian multitude" and the rural elements)—who in medieval society were distinguished from the nobility, first of all, by their birthright. This gives us some clue as to what Cartagena may have meant when he referred to "fame of lineage." Another clue comes from the following statement: "Also among those who draw their origin from Israel, there is a great difference in this respect; for even during the time in which they lived in provinces which had been assigned to them by their fathers, and even though they descended from the same tribes, there was a huge difference in status between some of them and the others. For at that time, when no other people [except the Israelites] inhabited the land which they had conquered, it was unavoidable that the larger part of their multitude should be attached to the lowest works, while others became famous, as is the custom in the republics, in sacerdotal, royal and other ranks and honors."[145] Both the sacerdotal and royal families in Israel based their privileges on hereditary succession, and hence it is clear that in this instance too Cartagena was speaking of a "fame of lineage" that was inseparably associated with birthright.

It is hardly necessary to point out that Cartagena injected the values of his own society into the social system of ancient Israel, and that the latter system was built upon principles which were altogether different. But it is of interest to note that, according to his view, nobility and governance are synonymous terms. Nobility, judging by his remarks on Israel, originates in an act of conquest. The conquerors, then, become the nobility of the land, and the conquered the subjugated people, to whom the rulers relegate all the "mean tasks," which are essential, but not honorable. When no such possibility exists, as was the case with the people of Israel, the conquerors divide themselves into groups, of whom some assume the tasks of guidance and leadership, the others those which are necessary to provide for the people's material needs. We should refrain, however, from concluding that, according to Cartagena, it is the profession that makes men "plebeians" or "nobles";

rather it is the constitution of the person which determines his profession, and, hence, his status. To be sure, the division into classes, he believed, was prompted by the necessities of social life, but the association of each person with his particular class was determined, in large measure, by the person's qualities. The following passage from the *Defensorium* bears this out quite clearly:

Nature, as they say, works in a similar manner in the various parts of the same species. For all or most individuals of a species habitually follow those things which come as a result of nature's force. For we see that all animals follow in most matters certain things which are common to the species, and according to the diversity of their species are inclined to diverse ways of life. And although a few of their individuals follow something peculiar, this nevertheless is generally found on rare occasions only. But let us stop talking about brute animals, and turn our words to people, to whose species we belong, for although we, too, are animals, we are most excellent animals. Among people we see many, indeed almost an infinite number of things, which all share as a result of a certain general condition *(generalitas)*. But *some families are habitually inclined toward some things through a certain special quality,* a subject which to pursue in detail would take a long time and would not serve any purpose.

But this one thing I wish to say in relation to what I said before. *One of the differences found among people is that some are considered noble, others ignoble.* It is characteristic of the nobles to rise to higher pursuits, although they are difficult, and separate their actions from all mean activities. On the other hand, it is characteristic of the ignoble people to lead their lives under more tranquil and more laborious arts. Hence the fact that military exercise, which exceeds all other exercises in effort and danger, is nevertheless considered peculiar to the nobles because it is nearest to virtue, and also full of grace and courage. And although the common people sometimes use arms, and some of them brandish lances and swords both against the enemy and among themselves, they do it nevertheless in a rustic manner with both feet fixed on the ground. Nor do they dare resist the armed nobility. Military training, an equestrian charge, and doing battle under the standards of the princes, with head and breast shielded, and the shinbones covered with iron mixed with steel, and with trumpets blowing, is surely an action of the nobles; the rustics and plebeians, as long as they remain plebeians, do not use this manner of fighting. They are intent therefore upon *the cultivation of the fields and other occupations of rustic and urban care* which, although they are worthy professions, are nevertheless not of such beauty and fortitude as is the military art. *And although some of these [namely, the plebeians], driven by an impulse of courage, rise to perform acts of nobility, and fight to the finish with an armed hand,* and little by little join the fellowship of the nobles—*for nobility, like all other temporal goods can be acquired and lost*—few however who are born of rural or plebeian parents attain this station, compared to the multitude that are satisfied to remain within the rustic and plebeian, or popular and also technical, and other mean practices.[146]

To Cartagena, then, class division in society is indicated or expressed in occupation or, more precisely, in the *function* that each group fulfills in the totality of the social economy; but the fulfillment of these functions is related to certain talents, capacities and dispositions, which are hereditary. To be sure, "like all temporal things, nobility may be gained or lost," which would mean that the qualities making for nobility may be weakened or destroyed under certain circumstances, while, on the other hand, they may sprout and develop out of certain impulses, and thus appear among plebeians. This, however, happens in a small minority of cases and may be seen as the exception rather than the rule. Hence the occupations and pursuits of one's ancestors are generally an index to one's own qualities, as well as to the class to which one should belong.

We must, however, note one more point to define Cartagena's view correctly. What he considers natural qualities that make for social distinctions and divisions is not limited to one's talents and abilities to assume certain professions; they include also one's moral inclinations and capacity to live by moral standards. Thus, he considers the four cardinal virtues—prudence, justice, fortitude and temperance—to be based primarily on *natural* dispositions, or at least greatly assisted by the latter. In fact, he considers the part of man's nature in the possession of these and similar inclinations to be so great—and indeed so decisive—that he defines the nobility marked by their presence not only as "moral" but also as "natural."[147] Thus he seems to come close to the view that man's moral qualities are inheritable, which was the view held by the Toledans. Nevertheless, the differences between his view and theirs outweigh the similarities between them. For according to Cartagena, what are inheritable are not the virtues—which are each man's achievement—but the *dispositions* toward the virtues, and these dispositions are not stable assets; they can be bent by man's will one way or the other; they can be refined by training or deteriorate by habit; and they can all become subject to the influence of temptations or, contrarily, to that of faith. It follows that, in the final analysis, morally each man is his own master. Nevertheless, since the inclinations toward virtues may be helpful in their attainment, we may class men by their moral dispositions, which are not evenly distributed among them. In brief, the variety of the inclinations toward the virtues, no less than the variety of men's talents and abilities, can help place men on different social levels and in different grades of the social hierarchy.

That this was indeed Cartagena's view becomes further evident from the similarity he sees between the society sanctioned by the Church and the members of a living organism. In the society of the Church, which is a "body of Christ," all the members, he maintains, are expected to respect, love and support each other unsparingly; but it is inevitable that some of them be honored *more* because the functions they fulfill bear testimony to their excellence. For "just as the eye cannot say to the foot: 'do not be a member,' although, if we consider the function of the eye, it is more excellent, more delicate and more honorable, so it is also in the ecclesiastical body, in which the faithful members have different functions, some of which may be similar to the eye, others to the tongue, still others to the arms or the feet, etc., and thus one may have, by virtue of the fact that he fulfills a more excellent function, or possesses a more famous nobility, or whatever other particular eminence, more honor than the other. Nevertheless, every faithful [Christian], whencever he may come, is a full and qualified member [of the society] who is fittingly placed in his proper station under the guidance of the Church."[148]

The view that each member of the social body should fulfill the function to which he fits best, and that accordingly he should belong to the "class" of his peers, is of course Platonic in origin.[149] Yet in building his theory on the basic division between the two classes of men—the "noble" and the "ignoble"—Cartagena was following an Aristotelian rather than a Platonic principle. Thus, pointing to Aristotle as his authority, he says that "those who are inferior in their power of judgment should be governed by those who are wiser; and since they are ruled by the government of others, it is said that, in a certain manner, they are slaves."[150] To be sure, Don Alonso, it must be added, did not share Aristotle's justification of slavery—that is, slavery in the full sense of the word—since, as a student of the Roman jurists, he accepted their thesis that "all men are born free" and that slavery is of "social," not "natural," origin.[151] But as for the distinction between the two types of men with respect to their capacity to govern, he adopted that distinction, with the important addition that men also differ in their inclinations toward virtue, and that this is what lies at the root of the difference between "nobles" and "plebeians." It is obvious that in Don Alonso's view, this difference is often transmitted by heredity, which forms the basis for noble *families,* and more generally for the noble *class.* Thus we see in Don Alonso's theory the meeting of two diverse social theories—that of the Church Fathers and that of Aristotle, the one based on a religious ideal, the other on *nature* and its concrete manifestations; the one obviating all principal distinctions ("neither Greek nor Jew, neither bond nor free, neither male nor female"), the other admitting these distinctions, and considering their recognition, or even their promotion, as conducive to the good of society. One difference, however, the ethnic division, was singled out as superfluous and harmful, and therefore destined to be ignored.

But Cartagena's position differs from Plato's in another important respect as well. We have noted that the "classification" of each person, according to Cartagena, must be made "under the guidance of the Church," whose "wisdom" replaces, in Cartagena's concept, that of Plato's philosopher-king. Actually, however, this "guidance of the Church" was hardly viewed by him as a decisive factor. For more important in his eyes was, obviously, one's hereditary or actual class association, so much so that Cartagena felt it possible to state as a fact and a moral postulate: "The higher, more famous and more noble people [among those who come into the faith] retain in the Church their full preeminence and undiminished reverence for their persons and *families*."[152] Thus, class divisions are transferred into Christendom from the non-Christian world fully and automatically, with the "guidance" of the Church expressed in nothing but its preassured consent.[153]

Can the determination of a non-Christian group—whether pagan, Moslem or Jewish—with regard to one's position in society be binding upon the Church? We may take it for granted that Cartagena assumed that aptitudes and endowments—which determine one's vocation, and consequently also one's social class—are acquired by inheritance in the non-Christian world as they are in the Christian.[154] Just the same, one may ask, does not Christianity have its own evaluation of the various aptitudes and virtues, consistent with its different ideal of life? Cartagena does not ask this fundamental question, whose answer might conflict with his advocacy to accept the old social divisions—that is, as they existed in the non-Christian world. He simply proceeds to justify their acceptance on the basis of the facts as he knew them—that is, on the basis of Church practice and traditions, which, from the standpoint of Christian theology, were as valid and binding as any sacred doctrine.[155]

This reliance on the traditional stand of the Church with respect to the prevalent social structure was absolutely necessary for Cartagena, since theoretically, of course, he could not reconcile the two conflicting principles he espoused. The utopian world of amity and equality, toward which Christianity was heading, as he assured us, was poles apart from the world of feudal Europe in which inequality reigned supreme. In this latter world, class consciousness was rife, and the division of society into hereditary groupings was a fact of life, which nobody questioned and which dominated both politics and economy. In presenting this class-oriented society as fully acceptable to the Church, however, Cartagena did not justify the established order merely for its own sake. He did so also because some of the issues involved were closely related to the problem at hand—the one raised by the

Sentencia-Estatuto—and because the absence of racial discrimination, as he saw it, was insufficient by itself to solve that problem in a satisfactory manner.

II

In view of the above, the first question to determine was whether converts of Jewish origin had the right to join the Old Christian aristocracy. Cartagena begins his examination of this question by pointing to the fact mentioned above—namely, that pagan nobles who came over to Christianity retained their former status in Christendom. The Roman emperor Constantine, the Frankish king Chlodwig, the Gothic monarch Alaric are only a few illustrations of this well-known fact. Furthermore, they indicate that the pagan princes who were converted to Christianity in past ages "not only retained their badges of honor and the nobility of their origin" but were made in fact, following their conversion, more illustrious and prestigious.[156] A similar example from his own time Cartagena sees in the case of Jagiello, Duke of Lithuania, who was converted to Catholicism and became king of Poland.[157] So numerous indeed, he adds, were the Christian nobles who had been originally pagan—i.e., gentile—that in many languages, such as French and Spanish, gentilehood became synonymous with nobility.[158]

Now, if nobility attained in a pre-Christian status is upheld and respected also in Christendom when its bearers adopt the Christian faith, why should nobility attained among the Jews be less respected when they become Christian? Framed in such hypothetical terms, the question could be answered only positively. Yet Cartagena realized that objections could be raised, if not to the hypothesis itself, then to its practical applicability. For if, as we have seen, the status of nobility is related to control and government, the condition of the Jews with respect to nobility greatly differs from that of the pagans. Indeed, while the pagan nobles who converted to Christianity had been in possession of real power, the Jews, in their long period of exile, commanded no power at all. It is the fact of *holding power* in one degree or another that testifies to the capacity to hold it, and to one's belonging to the class of nobles that people are duty-bound to respect. In the case of the Jews, however, no such evidence was apparent, and therefore it would seem virtually impossible to associate their converts with the Christian aristocracy.

How to substantiate, in the face of these objections, the right of the conversos to join the noble classes? Obviously, the first thing to do was to examine the premises of the above objections. That meant to determine, first of all, whether the Jews possessed a noble class in the past; whether there is any evidence of its existence in the present; and whether privileges which were lost, or lost their effectiveness, in a pre-Christian condition could be restored to a person, a family or a class under the government of the Church.

The first question was not at all superfluous, as Cartagena realized too well. There is no hard evidence that the Jews at any time, including their periods of complete independence, had possessed a class of hereditary nobility of the kind that existed in medieval Europe. Nevertheless, groups of privileged families whose members controlled wealth and power doubtless existed in the kingdoms of Israel, as they did in all other ancient states. One may gather this from the biblical references to the *sarim, seganim* and *ḥorim,* even though, it seems, no common term was used to indicate the existence of a noble *class.* Probably unaware of the latter fact, Cartagena mentions the several cases where the word "nobles" is mentioned in the Bible—that is, in the Latin translation of the Vulgate.[159] Yet his conclusions, one should point out, were not based on such evidence alone.

In accordance with the view of the medieval jurists, Cartagena distinguished three kinds of nobility: the theological, the natural, and the civil.[160] Theological nobility rests on divine acceptance, and is expressed in excellence of thought and action that relate to divine worship and religious meditation; natural nobility may be called moral, as it relates to the basic virtues, such as prudence, justice, fortitude and temperance; whereas civil nobility inclines men to government and the military profession. It is closely related to moral or natural nobility, even though not in the same measure, since one cannot govern or fight properly without possessing the virtues indicated above. Now who can doubt that the Jews in ancient times possessed all three kinds of nobility? They had theological nobility of the highest order, as testified by the patriarchs and the prophets; they had moral nobility, which was abundantly displayed in many deeds of virtue by many individuals; and they had civil nobility, which was clearly manifested in the kings and their whole governing class.[161]

Actually, says Cartagena, civil nobility existed in Israel from the most ancient times, long before the period of the kings. It dates back to the days of Moses, who took "the chiefs of the tribes" and made them "heads over the people," "captains of thousands," etc. Of them it is said that they were "*the most noble* of the leaders of the people, *according to their tribes and families,* and the heads of the armies of Israel."[162] Thus, the nobility was engaged not only in the task of civil government, but also in military service, "with which civil nobility is usually associated." Moreover, as far as this service is concerned, the Jews have a long record of distinction. This is evident not only from the sacred canon, but also from the master of *Scholastic History*[163] and from the accounts of the historian Josephus who, both in his *Antiquities* and the *Wars of the Jews,* tells of many acts of unusual valor that were performed by the Israelites.[164] In fact, even the destruction of Jerusalem by the Romans bears sufficient testimony to that; for the conquest of no other city save Troy was preceded by such a great struggle and by so much shedding of blood.[165] Evidence of the military standing of the Jews can be adduced also directly from the Romans, the founders of the greatest empire on earth. For in the alliance they made with Judas Maccabaeus, they treated the Jews as equal partners, and no such alliance would have been concluded unless the Romans had reason to respect the Jews as a military factor.[166]

In brief, "where there is the highest form of kingship, there inheres the highest form of nobility,"[167] and this is indeed what we find in Israel. Therefore, "many Israelites, prior to their infidelity [i.e., prior to their denial of Christ], were distinguished by the "triple nobility," which in many of them appeared together.[168] Samuel was both prophet and ruler; David was king and prophet; and so was Solomon, his son, and many others. "I do not mean to say," concludes Cartagena, "that all the members of that people were nobles. There has not been, nor is there a nation that consists only of noblemen." It suffices to say that, "as in other nations, *some* individuals within the Jewish people were illumined by the splendor of nobility."[169]

III

The historical evidence adduced by Cartagena to prove the existence of nobility among the Jews in the past was not intended to illustrate a point of mere academic interest. The evidence was offered to lay the basis for a conclusion that had a bearing on the conversos' eligibility to the higher classes of the Spanish society. By demonstrating that for much of their past the Jews possessed nobility in all its forms to the fullest and highest degree, he established the possibility, if not the probability, that they possessed it in his own time as well. The question now was what happened to those aptitudes in the long period of exile and oppression that the Jews experienced since they lost their independence.

It has often been said that as a result of their sin—i.e., their outright rejection of Christ—the state of freedom the Jews had enjoyed was exchanged for that of servitude. Fundamentally, Cartagena avers, this is true; but one has to understand more clearly, he adds, what kind of servitude affects the Jews. For parallel to the three types of nobility, there are three types of servitude, and they may be designated by the same names: natural, civil, and theological. *Natural* servitude indicates the condition in which a person displays a low power of judgment—so low indeed that he should be governed by others.[170] The second kind of servitude—which Cartagena calls *civil*—emanates from human law. This is the condition of virtual slavery, which the victor imposes upon the vanquished and which some philosophers call "legal" because it was sanctioned by the *ius gentium.* Divine law, however, does not recognize such a servitude and nature does not know it either, for as the Roman jurist Ulpian said, according to nature, "*all men are born free.*"[171] Cartagena avoids further discussion of the subject, and merely points out that "he who is subject to this kind of slavery cannot appear in Court to enter a judicial dispute with his master or anyone else, nor can he be the possessor of any property. He is of no account."[172]

The third kind of servitude—the theological—is the servitude of sin. Says Scripture: "He who commits a sin is a slave of sin,"[173] and such, indeed, are all men, except those who *liberated* themselves from sin (that is, by adopting the faith of Christ). What distinguishes this type of slavery from the others is that liberation from it depends on the sinner's own will. Therefore theological slavery, which is the worst kind of servitude, is also the easiest to get rid of. "Once the slave wishes with his whole heart to be freed from his subjugation to sin, divine mercy immediately affords him liberty by means of the sacraments."[174]

If the Jews are enslaved, as is often said, what kind of slavery are they subject to? Surely they are not under natural servitude, for that stems from dullness of understanding; and "it is clear that not all of the infidels," whether Jews or non-Jews, even though they persist in their obscurancy, "are so stupid as to deserve subjection to others because of such a deficiency." In this respect the Jews, fundamentally, do not differ from other groups of men, for "no race or family can be found to exist, all of whose members possess a strong intelligence or, contrarily, an extremely feeble one."[175] Nor are the Jews in the category of civil slavery, for the main symptoms of this slavery are not evident among them. Accordingly, when the Apostle denounced them as "slaves," he could not refer to civil servitude, for the Jews then abounded in temporal possessions, and even Jerusalem was not yet destroyed. In fact, they have not been bereft of such possessions to this day in various parts of the world. "Also the Jews who live in our country [Castile], in full accordance with the quality of their status, possess temporal goods and have court litigations not only with common individuals, but also with the princes themselves." For "they sometimes conclude business agreements with the princes, and when disputes arise over the execution of these agreements, either they [the Jews] take legal action against the fiscal representatives of the princes or are subject to such action taken against them. All of this is contrary to civil servitude, for 'no man,' as the jurists say, 'can have action-at-law against a person whom he has in his *potestas.*' "[176]

If one therefore refers to *Jewish* servitude, one can speak only of the theological kind, and it is really this servitude that the Apostle had in mind when he compared the Jews to the sons of Hagar. For Hagar, the bondmaid, symbolizes the Synagogue and the legal ceremonies to which the Jews remained bound, just as Sarah, the free consort, symbolizes the Church and its adherents who were given the law of grace.[177] Now, the failure of the Jews to accept the latter law forced them to remain under the rule of sin; for it prevented them from being *reborn* as free men as all those who came to Christ were. But from this condition, into which they entered freely—that is, by their own free choice—they can be redeemed by another act of will in the opposite direction. For as soon as the Jew liberates himself from the shackles of the Old Law and is reborn in Christian freedom, the theological slavery, in which he finds himself, is entirely abolished. Can then such a Jew, when he joins the Church, also join any of the various classes that make up Christian society?

Judging by what was said before, it is clear that the possible obstacle of slavery does not apply in the case of the Jews. Since they were not subject to natural or civil slavery, it is clear that converted Jews enter Christendom as completely free men. Yet freedom in itself is only a prerequisite, not a qualification for them to join *any* class, and particularly that of the nobles. To determine this, a clear answer must be given to the second of the three questions posed above—namely, is there evidence for the existence of nobility among the Jews at the *present* time? More precisely, we should know whether any of the nobilities, in which the Jews once excelled, survived the ordeals of exile and dispersion and are still evident among them. If so, this evidence could provide some guidelines for "classing" their various converts in Christendom.

It would appear reasonable that, in discussing this subject, Cartagena should have first pointed out the fact that, despite all their wanderings and changes of fortune, the Jews strictly guarded all the lines of succession stemming from the tribe of Levi and the priesthood. As the single privileged class among the Jews whose prerogatives were recognized by law, the Priests and Levites formed, in a way, the only hereditary aristocracy among the Jews that was of a spiritual-religious nature. Paul of Burgos, who emphasized this fact, wanted to use it as a basis for his claim that members of *this* Jewish nobility could join the ecclesiastical leadership of the Church. Yet Cartagena seems to have ignored this claim, and for very obvious reasons.

For although the Priests and Levites belonged, as he saw it, to the theological nobility, that nobility disappeared among the Jews with the failure of its members to recognize Christ. As a result, the offspring of the Priests and Levites, though still recognized among the Jews, are, from the standpoint of theological nobility, an empty shell, a body without spirit. Yet this in itself does not present a problem for the Jews who were converted to Christianity. For theological nobility did not exist in any measure among the gentile nations either—and for the same reason: their infidelity. Consequently, in this respect, the Jews who join Christendom are on the same footing as the converts from the gentiles. Nor do they differ from the latter in their opportunity to join and rise in the ecclesiastical hierarchy; for the appointments to

positions in *this* hierarchy do not relate in any way to a hereditary class, as
was the case in Judaea. To be sure, when the pope ordains deacons, he
designates them as *Levites*, but by this he means to indicate their belonging
to the tribe of Levi, not according to the flesh, but according to the spirit.
"For the priesthood had been changed, so that it be offered . . . not to some
family in particular" but to everyone of the faithful who may deserve it,
"according to the rules of the church, with every difference of blood set far
aside."[178] It is clear, therefore, that insofar as *this* nobility is concerned, there
is no basis to look for its presence among the Jews who remained in their
Jewishness. We may only inquire whether the other kinds of nobility still
inhere among them.

IV

According to Cartagena, certain social phenomena prevalent among the
Jews of Spain and other countries provide a definite answer to this question.
If one observes the structure of Jewish society, its internal relationships and
its leading personalities, one can discover signs of nobility in the various
walks of Jewish life. To be sure, the total loss of their theological nobility,
which they suffered as a result of their infidelity, did not come about without
grievously affecting the Jews' natural and civil nobilities.[179] Yet vestiges of
both survived sufficiently for their owners to be identified as nobles. As for
natural nobility, which consists, as we have noted, of a high measure of
wisdom and morality, it is evident that some of the Jews in the dispersion
have retained a certain keenness of intellect which, because it does not tend
toward a proper end, cannot be called real wisdom *(prudentia)*; nevertheless,
it has a certain semblance of prudence.[180] And insofar as moral virtues are
concerned, although the Jews do not have them in their pure essence—since
they lack the virtue of true prudence, as well as the theological virtues—
nevertheless, some of them seem to have performed deeds not devoid of
moral value, and even such as give one the aptitude of ruling, which is
especially ascribed to natural nobility. This has been demonstrated by the
fact that some of them, having attached themselves to the rulers, instruct
them very often in matters of government *(agibilibus)*, from which it follows
that they retain certain vestiges of natural nobility.[181]

As for civil nobility among them, some remnants of it, too, are noticeable,
even though they are overshadowed by a heavy mist. "For among themselves, some are reputed as plebeians, some as noble people, and also among
those whom they consider noble, some are regarded as more noble than
others, to the point that they guard this difference most diligently in their
matrimonies and honors, so that the nobles among them will consider it
unworthy to receive the hand of a craftsman's daughter, or to enter marriage

with a plebeian, unless forced by extreme necessity."[182] This, adds Cartagena, is especially so in Spain, to which country, they say, came many of the noble Israelites after the destruction of Jerusalem in ancient times.[183]

There is then one sure way to determine which Jews stem from the old nobility. "Your royal Majesty, if he wishes, will be able to discern them by such eminences and reverences as they themselves, or their predecessors, under a thin semblance of nobility, observed toward each other."[184] Yet Cartagena stresses that by this yardstick alone—namely, the homage paid by Jews to some of their families—not all the instances of nobility among the Jews may be discerned. For under the harsh conditions of oppression in which the Jews had lived so long, many noble individuals were forced into the lower classes, and the signs of their nobility have been obscured or suppressed. It is only when the freedom of such individuals is restored upon their acceptance of Christianity that their basic tendencies can reappear and their noble traits be again revealed. Therefore, to "class" their converts to the faith, the converts themselves, even more than the Jews, have to be taken into consideration. In other words, from the occupations they engage in and the abilities they display (in the Christian society), one may gather to which kind of nobility their ancestors had belonged and which kind of nobility may be restored to them in their new condition.

In support of this position—which alone, as he saw it, could justify the rise of Marranos from the lower to the upper classes—Cartagena devotes a special discourse to prove that the traits of nobility revealed among the conversos must be taken as indications—indeed, as proof—that many of them belong to the noble class.

V

As we have seen, Cartagena believed that one's dominant disposition to certain pursuits is the factor that generally determines one's class; and this is what experience also tells us of the social divisions. For ordinarily, nobles are born to nobles, peasants to peasants, and plebeian citizens to plebeians. But what do we see among the converted Israelites? Unlike the rustic elements among the gentiles, of whom relatively few follow the military profession, among the faithful Israelites a disproportionately large number willingly undertake the exercise of arms and participate in the militias.[185] Moreover, they display competence and courage in warlike acts, which is as unique as was their well-known cowardice in their preconversion state. To be sure, people can exchange one or more of their vices for the contrasting virtues, but the process is usually difficult and slow, and it is *most* difficult where courage is concerned. Thus, people can abstain from excessive eating or illicit sexual intercourse, and they may even come to like this way of life, but they can achieve this only through a great effort exerted over a period of time. But what should be noted is that no danger is involved in the adoption of such virtues as abstinence or chastity; they require only the exercise of the will.[186] But this is not at all the case with courage. There is no time to get used to being bold in the midst of warlike actions, and "a sudden attack," as Jerome said, "frightens even the bravest of soldiers."[187] The need to make a decision is immediate, since there is no time for deliberation, and the decision to act with courage "involves a great danger which ordinary people shun." In brief, *it is most difficult to acquire fortitude in battle unless one is assisted in this by a natural disposition.* Hence, since so many of the "faithful Israelites" (that is, Jewish converts to Christianity) rise to the service of the armed militia, we must presume that nobility, which in ancient times distinguished so many of their forefathers, lay hidden and enclosed in their hearts. Therefore, if they join the nobility, one should not see in this an acquisition on their part of a new quality or status, but rather the return to a social condition which was originally theirs.[188]

The second question, then, as to whether there exist signs of nobility among the "faithful" Jews has thus been fully answered. There remains only the question of the propriety of revalidating privileges they lost in the pre-Christian state. Cartagena gives this question, too, a positive and unequivocal answer. The answer is offered by the example of *postliminium,* by means of which, according to Roman law, a person taken captive by the enemy in war is fully restored to his original status once he returns to his native country. So, says Cartagena, if according to *human law,* one who returns from the captivity of an enemy is treated as if he had never been captured—and therefore is restored to his original freedom, and also to all his former privileges—how much more must such a restoration be secured by a *postliminium* in accordance with divine law to the captives of the ancient enemy who managed to return to the society of God?[189] And just as no span of time, however long, can deny a person his right of *postliminium,* so no length of time can cancel that right—or even diminish it to any extent—for those who return after many generations from the captivity of sin to the land of faith. Those Israelites who come to Christianity today, therefore, are entitled to have all their rights restored as if they joined the faith near the time of the Passion, together with Paul and the other apostles, and to be received with all their dignities and prerogatives to the most perfect union.[190]

One may of course ask whether *postliminium* applies to the *offspring* of prisoners. But this question, too, can be answered positively on the basis of Roman law. Restitution of birthright is granted even to one who was *born* a slave; it bestows upon him, in abundant liberality, "*the purest and most innate freedom of primal natural law,* under which the misfortune of captivity and slavery had not yet been found."[191] Moreover, according to Roman law, the emperor can restore a person to his birthright—i.e., to his freedom—even if he had lost that status by committing some crime.[192] How much more can this be done by the *greatest* of all emperors and the king of kings? The emperor can say: I restore you to your honor, your order, and all the rest [of your original conditions].[193] Surely, this can be effected by Christianity, whose whole essence lies in forgiveness, redemption, and the restoration of man to his primal state.[194]

In brief, the *postliminium* of God restores the original rights most fully to those released from the bondage of evil, and as soon as they enter the Christian empire, once its doors are opened by baptism, they are regarded as if they had never been under any hostile power.

VI. HOW CAN TOLEDO BE RESTORED?

I

This completes Cartagena's argument on behalf of class division in Christendom and the right of the conversos to join the aristocracy. All that remained for him to do to conclude his treatise was to make some supplementary remarks on several points at issue.

Compared with the main thesis he unfolded, these remarks were possibly judged by Cartagena as merely of secondary value. Viewed from our own vantage-point, however, they are of major importance. For they touch on questions that, considered historically, should be uppermost in our minds. These are: (a) the attitude toward Christianity (and hence, toward Judaism) of the Marrano group taken as a whole; (b) the causes of the anti-marrano movement and the ultimate purpose of its violent campaign; and (c) the measures the Marranos considered necessary to suppress that movement and restore normality. Thus, these added remarks of Cartagena help us understand his total view of the converso situation at the time.

To clarify the trend of our forthcoming discussion we must note that Cartagena made some of these remarks via his refutation of the legal objections raised by the Toledans to Marrano "equality" in Spain—or, rather, of the legal evidence they adduced in support of the *Sentencia-Estatuto*. We shall therefore have to touch also on this refutation, which is of interest in itself; it embodies original, pointed criticisms of the Toledans' judicial position.

Cartagena's rebuttal was centered on the objections that were based on the laws of the Toledan Councils, and especially on that of the Fourth Toledan Council, which stipulated that "*those who are of Jews (ex Iudeis)*" were prohibited from holding public office. While examining these laws and determining their meaning, Cartagena consulted the glosses on the *Decretum*, as had been done by Juan de Torquemada and the Relator. Medieval jurists usually turned to these glosses when encountering some difficulty in Church law; and it is obvious that, to the converso jurists, the law on "*hi qui ex Iudeis sunt*" offered an especially hard nut to crack. We can see this also from their various approaches and various sources of reference. While the Relator relied mainly on Guido de Baysio, and Torquemada leaned chiefly on Huguccius, Cartagena was assisted primarily by Teutonicus. Yet as we shall see, his own position differed considerably from the latter's.

Teutonicus believed that the law which denied public office to *ex Iudeis* could not possibly refer to all converts from Judaism, let alone to their offspring who descended "from Jews." Hence, he concluded, it referred to "followers" of Jews, or to Jews who were converted to the faith recently *(de novo)*. Cartagena accepted the first interpretation as a possibly correct understanding of "ex Iudeis," but was dissatisfied with the second. The New Christians were often defined by their antagonists as those who were "recently converted," and if such converts were denied by canon law the right to hold public office in Christendom, the Toledans would have all the backing they needed and might consider their case won. Teutonicus's conjecture, therefore, appeared to Cartagena too dangerous to ignore. To defuse it, he points out that it is necessary to understand what may be meant by "recently."

The meaning is indicated, according to Cartagena, in the famous prohibition to appoint neophytes as bishops—a prohibition which Gratian included in canon law following the New Testament[195] and the Nicaean Council.[196] His reasoning is that offered by Jerome: "so that he who was yesterday *(heri)* a catechumen may not become today a bishop; who was yesterday *(heri)* in the theater may not sit today in the Church; who was yesterevening *(vespere)* in the circus may not minister today at the altar."[197] What was meant here by *heri* and *vespere* is of course not literally "yesterday" or "yesterevening"; what was meant is simply a very short time. But how short? The answer is indicated in another statement which Gratian includes in the same passage. He says: "A momentaneous priest—namely, one who became a priest a moment after his conversion—does not generally know what humility is."[198] Here, too, the term used for time (i.e., a moment) does not have to be taken in its literal sense; what it implies is a very short period, which, like the terms *yesterday* and *yestereve,* cannot possibly refer to a decade or two, or even to a year or two or the like. What it indicates are obviously shorter periods, limited only to months or weeks, even though the exact span required must be left in each case to the "judgment of good men."[199] But what should be further noted is that all this relates to *Church* positions. It does not relate to secular positions, concerning which no delay in appointment has ever been suggested on grounds of "newness" in Christianity.

It is clear, then, that by this definition of "recency" and those it applies to according to Church law, Cartagena disqualified Teutonicus' second explanation of the term *ex Iudeis* in the conciliar decree. For the sixty-fifth decision of the Fourth Toledan Council does not speak of ecclesiastical appointments in particular, but of public offices *(officia publica)* in general, with no specification of kind and degree. Above all, on the basis of the meaning of "newness" in apostolic and canonic writings, he showed that the law, if related to "New" Christians, could in no way apply to the Spanish conversos who, by any definition, are much "older" in the Church than such terminology might imply. The division of the Christians in Spain into the two camps of Old and New—a division which he dismissed as absurd—is now again revealed for what it is. Since no one becomes Christian before his baptism,[200] the conversos are neither "newer" nor "older" than any of the other Christians, and hence cannot be subject to special legislation. *Ex Iudeis* must therefore mean followers of Judaism, perhaps also "familiars" of the Jews, but not converts to Christianity from Judaism. If, however, one wishes to insist that *ex Iudeis* means converts from Judaism, one must read the decree not as universal— that is, valid for all places and all times—but as one which applied to a particular place and a particular time only—namely, to Spain of the seventh century. This was a period in which very many—in fact, almost all—Jews who received baptism were actually followers of Judaism, and the law, therefore, may have been considered fitting for those times, for that special situation and that special group of converts *(ex Iudeis)*[201]; but if so, it was not really a law, but a ruling to meet a certain emergency. Perhaps this is why this decree is presented as one that was commanded by the king and adopted by the council only at his order. It should be pointed out, says Cartagena, that of all the numerous decisions taken in all the thirteen Toledan councils, this is the only decree which is indicated as issued at the king's command.[202]

II

This interpretation of the sixty-fifth decision as a ruling directed against relapsed Jewish converts indicates quite clearly that Cartagena saw no resemblance between the situation in Spain in the 7th century and that of his own time. For all his arguments were so designed as to meet the possible objections of the Old Christians to his claim that the *Sentencia-Estatuto* was unjustified. Had he believed that the number of Judaizers among the Marranos was large enough to justify special measures against the group, his last interpretation of the sixty-fifth decision would have supplied the Toledans with the legal precedent they were seeking in support of their action. Cartagena, however, must have believed that his argument provided no such precedent, because he was sure that the New Christians of his time bore no resemblance to the converts of the 7th century—or, more precisely, that they were too Christianized to possibly fit into the latter's category.

But if the conversos were good Christians, two questions must still be answered: Why were severe charges to the contrary made so boisterously by their critics? And what is the reason for the burning hatred which the latter display for them without letup? Cartagena's answer to these questions consists of several parts. It offers the reasons for both the *hatred* and the *conduct* of the Marranos' opponents.

As far as the hatred of the Marranos is concerned, Cartagena ascribes it to a single motive: jealousy of the social and material successes attained by the conversos. No religious zeal, intention, or interest is ever suggested by him as motivating the Marrano haters, and this falls in with his repeated statement that the attacks on the conversos are directed against people who live a "clean" Christian life. The attempt to find fault with the Christianity of these people resembles that of Satan, who sought to find flaws in Job's devotion to God. Indeed, the very comparison of the Marranos to Job is further proof that Cartagena considered them innocent of the religious crimes with which they were charged.

Like Job, who was accused of having served God not because he truly believed in Him, but because of the blessings God bestowed upon him, the Marranos are accused of being Christian, not because they believe in Christianity, but because of the benefits they derive from it. Yet these accusations are based not on fact, but on the accusers' pretense of knowing what is in the conversos' hearts. Obviously, these words of Cartagena imply that no outside evidence was available to support the anti-converso charges; on the contrary, the evidence available, he was sure, indicates the opposite—namely, that the Marranos are good Christians, just as in the case of Job it indicated that he was an upright man. And these indications of human behavior are the only signs by which men *can* go—and hence, by which they are *permitted* to go. Of course, evil minds can raise and spread suspicions to the point where they may become believable, but if their assertions lack a factual basis, they must be rejected as libels and falsehoods. The purpose of such assertions is not to reveal some hidden truth, but to vilify and besmirch the object of the jealousy; to ruin his good name (the basis of all honor), which is one of the things that most violently stir the feeling of jealousy in the souls of men.[203] The Marranos, then, are faced with a campaign of lies, aimed at ruining the position of honor they attained in Christian society.

This, however, is only the first manifestation of diabolic envy. For what did Satan say to God next? "Extend a little your hand—he said—and touch all that he possesses, [and see] if he will not curse you to your face."[204] You already see, adds Cartagena, the manner of ascent of this detestable jealousy. *It proceeds from the denigration of the reputation to the destruction of the possessions.*

This is precisely what some of the people who have been following in Satan's footsteps have been doing in Toledo. "After having besmirched the reputation of their adversaries, they arranged for the seizure of their possessions *under false excuses*. They derive pleasure from the spoliation of their neighbors, even if they themselves do not partake in the booty. Some of them, however, add avarice to envy, exceeding in this even Satan himself, who, although he is envious of human happiness, does not grab for himself temporal goods."[205]

What Cartagena is here referring to are of course the robberies and expropriations of Marrano possessions perpetrated in Toledo under Sarmiento's guidance. These actions, too, had no justification, and no other cause but jealousy and greed. Yet "the diabolic envy does not quiet down even with these excesses. It proceeds with the most ardent hate to the rending of the victim's bodies."[206] This is why Satan smote Job with the death of his children, and this is why he wanted to kill Job himself. "Skin for skin and everything man has he will give for his soul," says the inciter to the Lord, who insisted on Job's innocence.[207] It was the warning God gave Satan not to dare take Job's life that prevented Satan from carrying out his wish; and in consequence, instead of killing Job, Satan smote him with the most horrible affliction. Yet these are the symptoms, and this is the process, of diabolic envy: first it seeks to destroy the reputation of the victim, then to take away his possessions, and finally to kill him. And all of these symptoms were manifest in the activities of García's followers.

This argument of Cartagena clearly shows his view of (a) the moral position of the conversos and (b) the motives of the opposition. As he saw it, then, the conversos were blameless—that is, innocent of the crimes imputed to them, which means that they were religiously sincere; the campaign against them was rooted in motives which were antithetical to that sincerity; it was nothing but evil opposing good and seeking its complete destruction. That was the whole story, according to Cartagena. And just as he defined the objective of the campaign, he identified its chief inspirer and architect. This was Marcos García, from whose morbid soul, sickened by ambition, frustration and failure, gushed forth the torrent of fiendish hatred that was now threatening to engulf the land.

III

Thus, the task Cartagena set himself in exposing the nullity of the Toledans' race theory, as well as the motives of their false charges, came to its assigned end. All the legal, doctrinal, and philosophical aspects pertaining to the rights of the conversos in Christendom had been duly clarified and related to the case he so carefully prepared against the Toledan rebels.

Theoretically, the case was now complete. But practically, something remained to be done. If on the basis of his presentation public opinion were to condemn the culprits, as Cartagena undoubtedly hoped, there still remained the important question of what punishment he should ask for the criminals. The answer, Cartagena sensed clearly, lay beyond the scope of legal justice. What he sought was a political remedy to the problem posed by the Toledan campaign.

In proposing this remedy, Cartagena bore in mind that the problem had two major aspects, ecclesiastical and secular—or, better, consisted of two separate problems which, though combined in the rebels' actions, had to be viewed and treated independently. For what was involved here was a religious heresy and a civil rebellion promoted by the same people at the same time. Cartagena addresses the heretical issue first. He warns García, the teacher of the new "dogma"—i.e., the dogma of race with respect to the New Christians—that unless he abandons his evil path and his stubborn clinging to the errors he propagates, he will incur the sin of heresy. He cautions him not to delude himself with the assumption that he may avoid being stamped as a heretic merely because what he preaches appears to him not explicitly contradictory to the articles of the faith. "Even civil law says that the term 'heretic' refers to anyone who was found to be deviating even by a slight argument from the Catholic religion." And is it not clear that Marcos García deviated from this religion not slightly, but to a very large extent? John XXII declared it fitting—and in agreement with Church law—that those who were regenerated by the font of baptism, having dismissed the Judaic blindness, should abound in favors and graces, and that all the officials of the lands of the Church should defend them from harm and molestation.[208] And does not García know that by denying these converts even the right of testimony alone he becomes a molester? For how would they abound in favors and graces when they are open to rejection by contumely of this kind?[209]

Yet the unjust attack upon the conversos is only one of the great evils perpetrated by García and his Toledan followers. Their very attempt to divide the members of the Church into two categories that must be kept apart is itself a vicious act that entails the gravest danger. Obviously, such a dogma cannot be introduced, let alone spread, without causing untold "dissensions among the faithful."[210] In fact, it cannot be advanced and upheld without tearing the Church apart.[211] But "he who rends the Church is a schismatic, and he who authors a schism and denies the unity of the Church is a heretic, especially when he adheres tenaciously to his divisive opinion."[212]

How should this heresy be treated? Cartagena has no doubt about it. The Spaniards are strong in faith and fidelity; but heresy, which is a most dangerous disease, can affect even the healthiest of people and therefore should never be taken lightly. The princes ought to exercise utmost vigilance in order to expunge, with the greatest speed possible, whatever error that appears against the faith, and thus avoid the peril of contagion. Even the smallest error should be combatted; for heresy is a fire which should be checked immediately. Jerome said: "Arius in Alexandria was a spark; but because it was not suppressed immediately, the blaze has spread across the whole world."[213] Yet however great the responsibility of the princes, the primary responsibility for checking the current heresy rests upon the shoulders of the Pope. "The Roman Pontiff, more than anyone else, should apply his mind to innovations of this kind, for it is to him, before all others, that the task belongs of both defending the faith and repelling what offends it. For it is in the power of the Roman Pontiff alone to determine questions relating to matters of faith. Consequently, the Pope is expected to do two things: First, inform all the faithful that the assertions of García and his followers are false—that is, unacceptable to the Catholic Church—so that the faithful are held in duty bound to act upon the warning and instructions of the highest Pontiff—the "supreme shepherd" of Christendom, the "vicar of Jesus Christ and his representative on earth."[214] Second, to proceed against the promoters of this error by means of ecclesiastical censure and other remedies provided by the law, so as to correct them if they are corrigible, and punish them if they are not.[215] A similar care is incumbent upon the lower prelates within their own dioceses. But the task to be fulfilled by the secular authorities is no less decisive. "For it is the duty of the secular judges, of whom the first are the kings, and below them the other princes, to uphold with the highest zeal, and with the temporal sword, the integrity of the faith and the unity of the Christian people."[216] Therefore, they should "attend with just severity to any stubborn and incorrigible error of heresy which has been revealed by a competent ecclesiastic judge and turned over to the secular court."[217]

Sensing the stubbornness of the "heretics" of Toledo and their strong determination to proceed with their plan, Cartagena, evidently, saw no way to stop them except by the use of fire and sword. Like the Relator, then, he advocates inquisitional measures; but to show his impartiality, he adds, again like the Relator, that the same measures should be used also in cases of other heretics whenever they are discovered and found to be incorrigible, be they Judaizers, paganizers, or any other kind.[218]

There remained the problem of the secular crimes perpetrated in Toledo during the rule of the schismatics. How should justice be served in *these* cases? Cartagena distinguishes two kinds of crimes among those he defined as secular: "individual" and "communal"—that is, crimes committed by individuals or by the community as such. Are all participants in the crimes of the first kind going to be tried and punished? Cartagena understood that such advice could never be accepted or, if accepted, followed. The number of the perpetrators of crimes of that kind was simply too great for the government to cope with, or for the city to tolerate their punishment. In this he had before him the example of what occurred following the great riots against the Jews of Spain in 1391. He proposed, therefore, that responsibility for crimes of this category be imputed not to *all* who were involved in the rebellion but rather to the movers of the disorders.

Similarly, he argued, Toledo as a polity cannot be seen as the author of the crimes he called "communal." The "major citizens" of this city, who are responsible for its government, were absent from the city during the disturbances, since they were expelled by the rebellious mob, and naturally cannot be held responsible for the criminal acts committed by the rebels.[219] It follows that although Toledo the *urbs* (the city per se) remained as it was, Toledo the *civitas,* the political entity, was no longer there. For its form of government has been so altered that it is no longer the same polity. The government that ruled Toledo before the rebellion was aristocratic, or, if you wish, oligarchic; it consisted of people reputed for their lineage, power and abundance of resources. As a whole, these were people who stood head and shoulders above the common men. "Under this form of government, not one man, as in a monarchy, nor the people, as in a timocracy or a democracy, but many—though few when compared with the popular multitude—have the authority of government."[220] But in the frenzy of the outbreak, the polity was broken apart and the multitude of the common people *(plebs)* assumed the power of government. And since this was done, the errors that ensued should not be ascribed to the same *civitas,* nor should any punishment be imposed upon the *civitas* as such. Only the arch-sinners, Cartagena maintained, should be gravely punished, while the crowd that sinned should be corrected; and even in this he counseled moderation. "For often the commotion of the people in some cities is occasioned by those whom the Greek called *demagogues,* and whom we call usually seditious, or popular orators, persuaders, or inciters of the people. These are the people who should be more severely punished when the common people commit a crime. For although all the participants in the crime are to blame, a greater share of blame should be assigned to the persuaders—i.e., those who incited the seditions with the promise of obtaining freedom from paying tributes, or of expelling the authorities from the city, so that the mutinous plebs may assume domination and illicit liberty. These persuaders duly deserve punishment because they deceive the simple people by their crafty persuasion. Them it is proper to accuse and punish with dutiful severity and severe dutifulness, according to the quality of the persons, so that some of them will regret the crimes they perpetrated, and others be prevented in the future from committing them."[221]

According to Cartagena, then, punishment should be meted out primarily to the demagogues, the agitators, and the architects of the mutiny, quite in parallel to the manner of treatment he suggested for the crimes against individuals. But he has more to say about Toledo and its future.

The Old Toledo died with the rebellion, but it can be revived; and the one who can revive it is the King ("who occupies the place of God on earth").[222] The democratic government should be abolished and the aristocratic one restored. All the present officials in the city who were involved in any crime should be removed, and others should be appointed in their stead—such who are "rightly reputed as standing above others in virtue, nobility, power and wealth of resources, so that in that city the splendor of aristocratic polity may always shine."[223]

What we have here is a clear indication of the other basic element of the conflict that evolved between the conversos and the rebels of Toledo. The latter sought to establish a democratic regime in the city in which the common people would have the major say. But a democratic government was the Marranos' nightmare. Such a government would reflect the sentiment of the plebs; it would necessarily be ruled by people like Marquillos, inspired by hate and jealousy for the Marranos and seeking their destruction. Under such a government, they would have no chance. Hence their determined support of the nobility and the wealthier classes. With them they could find a common language, and to them they could be of service.

II. DIEGO DE VALERA

Perhaps nothing so signified the conversos' determination to gain full social equality in Spain as their efforts to penetrate the ranks of the nobility, and nothing perhaps so irked their racist enemies as their steady expansion in those ranks. We have seen that Cartagena, in his *Defensorium*, attempted to prove the *right* of the conversos to join the Old Christian noble class—a right which was hotly contested by the racists—and he was not alone in making that attempt. About 1451, Diego de Valera, himself a nobleman and the son of a converso,[1] wrote his *Espejo de Verdadera Nobleza* ("A Mirror of True Nobility")—a treatise in which he sought to refute the arguments of the opposition.[2]

Knight, diplomat and administrator, Valera was also a poet, essayist, and historian; and while he made little headway in politics, he gained distinction in the field of letters. In fact, he became one of the better known figures of Castile's literature in the 15th century. His writings are marked by his down-to-earth approach, as well as his elegant and swift style. Valera liked to simplify issues, and left much of what he knew unsaid if he thought it did not touch the heart of the matter. Of his various works, his essays rank highest, and among these the treatise on nobility is no doubt one of the best.[3]

On the face of it, the treatise is not an apology, but an independent inquiry into the origins of nobility, its nature, structure, and obligations. We shall touch on these themes only to the extent that they relate to our present concern, which includes such questions dealt with by Valera as (a) whether converts to Christianity can retain the nobility they possessed in their former faith, and (b) whether converts who originally had *not* been nobles were entitled to enter the ranks of the nobility. Valera poses these questions toward the end of his treatise, but he may well have written the entire work for the sake of the answers he gave them.

Valera begins his inquiry by noting the three categories of nobles indicated by Bartolus, the leading medieval Italian jurist—the theological, the natural and the civil.[4] But of these categories he is mainly interested in the third—namely, the civil nobility—the class of the privileged masters and rulers that was the envy of the common people. Valera is not awed by this class, and the whole tenor of his discussion shows that he would like to reduce it to size, or at least to remove it from the high pedestal on which it stands in the eyes of the people. His view of this nobility, if not entirely negative, is certainly highly critical. Valera takes pains to stress its inherent flaws and the contrast it presents in real life to the ideal of its reputation.[5] What gave this relatively small group, he asks, the right to dominate the rest of the people and treat them as their serfs or vassals? Valera can find no moral justification for the origins of the process. Following Innocent III, he answers: "Nature created us free, but fortune made us slaves."[6] Fortune, then, was the real father of nobility that he actually defines as an enslaver. Fortune worked its way by means of individuals who, either by virtue or by force of arms, rose above the people and became its rulers. Then they appointed some who were close to them, or in whom they confided as their aides, for the sole purpose of assisting them in keeping the power they had gained. Thus was born the class of nobles, which was hierarchized, broadened, and ultimately institutionalized by both law and custom.[7]

The laws define the rights and duties of the noble and the qualities he should possess. But this does not mean that mere possession of these qualities makes a man automatically noble—or, more precisely, raises him from the camp of the plebeians to the ranks of civil nobility. What performs this radical change is only a specific grant of the prince. So it was in the past, and so it is in the present.[8]

Civil nobility, then, does not originate in the recipient but in the judgment, decision and, obviously, the interests of its grantor, who is the prince. It is not like theological nobility, which is God-given—i.e., a gift of divine grace—or like moral nobility, which consists of virtues that come to man by nature (and hence it is also called "natural"). In fact, civil nobility is not a virtue at all and one cannot say of it, as Dante did, that to be virtuous means to be noble and vice versa. Civil nobility is merely a *dignity,* a status conferred on some plebeian by a prince who wishes to favor him with a mark of honor. But this honor, though no virtue in itself, is nevertheless a "sign" of virtue; for according to the rules and conventions of nobility, the prince is supposed to confer it only on men known for their integrity and valor. If the noble lives up to the dignity bestowed on him, he may retain his nobility and bequeath it to his children; if he does not live up to expectations, he may lose both the nobility and its rights; for dignity cannot live with infamy.[9]

Nobility, then, is conditionally bestowed, with no guarantee of permanence. This is especially true of those who receive their nobility by inheritance, for their nobility is not based on their own virtues but on those of their forebears. Since moral virtues are not inheritable, what the nobles inherit is merely a status and a pattern of behavior provided by their fathers. This pattern they are expected to follow—if not by disposition, at least by self-interest—for they are assumed to be anxious to guard the reputation and the privileges they gained by their fathers' efforts. In any case, except for the lineages of the great lords, the succession of nobility generally lasts for no more than three or four generations.[10]

It follows that nobility is in a constant state of flux, and the prince often needs to replenish its ranks. He finds his new recruits in the plebeian camp,

which forms the storehouse of civil nobility. There he finds men distinguished by nature with the virtues that qualify them to be *hidalgos*.

That such men are found in all nations, and that therefore one is forced
to conclude that civil nobility does not stem from race, is proven by Valera
also from the presence of this type of nobility among the Moors. Pointing to
their numerous kings and princes and other men of universal renown, he
mentions among the latter the "false prophet" Mohammed, *an offspring of a
low and poor lineage*, who was an outstanding military leader; the great commander Musa, who conquered the whole of Spain; and Abdul Rahman, *the
son of a potter*, who subjected to his lordship the whole of Africa. "Who,"
Valera asks, "can deny these men civil nobility or *hidalguía*?"[11]

This brings us to the question raised above—namely, whether candidates
for civil nobility can be found among the converts. Valera's answer deals with
converts of all origins—i.e., from the *Jews*, the *Moors* and other gentiles. But
his discussion centers on the converts from Judaism, and here he seeks to
refute arguments based on racial grounds. Thus he says: "If anyone may think
that to come from the Jewish stock *(linaje)* is of lesser credit than to come
from any other nation, he can easily recognize how much he errs *if he wishes
to consider the truth*."[12] There are no racial differences between the groups of
men "since all of them came from that first father Adam." The separation of
mankind into different nations was due not to racial but to religious divisions,
and in this respect the nations indeed differ. Obviously, it is better to stem
from a nation that believed in the one true God than to come from a people
(i.e., the gentiles) that believed in many false divinities.[13] This is, he says, why
the apostle Paul, addressing himself to the converts from the gentiles, cautioned them not to boast over the converts from the Jews. After all, he
reminded them, they were merely disciples of the followers of Christ among
the Jews, and it was thanks to the latter, who founded the Church, that they
came to know Christianity.[14] We can see how Valera transferred the argument from the racial to the religious sphere, and turned Paul's apology for
the Jewish nation into a defense of the Jewish converts—and, by extension,
of the New Christians. The argument is supposed to suggest that the origins
of the Jewish converts to Christianity are superior to those of the gentile
converts, but it is a religious superiority, not a racial one.

This is also evident in his discussion of the share the Jewish converts had
in building the Church. The opponents of the conversos do not deny that the
first converts to Christianity came from the Jews and that it is *they* who laid
the Church's foundations. But against this they point out that only a few Jews
took part in this endeavor, and that the rest of the Church, apart from its
foundations, which is most of the Church's structure, was the work of converts from the gentiles. Valera's answer to this argument is aimed at establishing an equilibrium between the Jewish and the gentile converts.

Basing himself on Matthew (cap. 20), he says: "Our Lord does not receive those who were late in acknowledging Him in a lesser way than those who recognized Him earlier." For no one can receive Grace before it is given him, as the Apostle says in II Corinthians 12: "for anyone can allow himself to fall into a pit, but no one is strong enough to come out of it unaided. And thus the Jews who, because of their sins, fell into the [hole of] incredulity . . . cannot come out of it until they are called by the Grace of God." But "this call does not come to all people at the same time, but rather according to the marvelous order of divine providence," which baffles our understanding and remains a great mystery. "For the Gentiles, who had lived under the sin of idolatry before coming to the Lord," had already been called by Him, while "some of the Jews [who are not idolatrous] will be left in the sin of their disbelief [in Christ] until the coming of the Anti-Christ in the end of days . . . And thus in the sins of these as of the others, we see the manifestation of human weakness, and in the benefit of the calling of these as of the others the manifestation of divine kindness . . . For the Jews who still remain in their Jewishness will finally be called."[15]

Having thus divested the Jewish converts to Christianity of both racial and religious opprobrium, he comes to the paramount question in his discussion: Can they provide candidates for the nobility? Evidently, here too Valera had to reckon with the argument of the opposition, which denied this possibility on the grounds that the Jews, prior to their conversion, had no noblemen among them. This alleged fact was supposed to offer proof that the Jews lacked the fundamental qualities that entitled them to become nobles. Valera denies the validity of this argument by pointing to the nullity of the premise. For the Jews *did* possess the prerequisites of nobility, as is indicated by their life in ancient times. They then had all three types of nobles, and all in the highest degree. They had an abundance of *civil* nobility, as is evident from such kings as David and Solomon; they had many men of *natural* nobility, as is evidenced by such men of valor and virtue as Joshua bin Nun and Judas Maccabaeus; and as for *theological* nobility, they obviously surpassed any other nation in the number and greatness of the nobles of this kind. "For out of them came all the Prophets, all the Patriarchs and Holy Fathers, all the Apostles, and, above all, our most fortunate Lady, Holy Mary, and her blessed Son our Redeemer, God and true man."[16] By mentioning the great gallery of saints and heroes that emerged from the ranks of the Jewish people, Valera echoes a Torquemadan argument which, he thought, could fit into his thesis.[17]

Coming back to the subject of civil nobility, Valera also employs another argument to show that the conversos—the descendants of Jews—were entitled to join the Spanish noble class. As a matter of fact, he claims, this has been proven by the nobiliar record of the Christian nations. "For the Kings of England who reigned in that country shortly after the coming of Christ descended from Joseph Arimathaea; the kings of the Goths drew their origin from Abraham, whereas the first Duke of Austria, from whom stemmed many Emperors . . . was a Jew before he turned Christian."[18] The conclusion implied in all this is obvious. If the Jews had nobles who could provide kings and rulers to some of the mightiest nations on earth, there is no reason to assume that their Christian descendants could not join the Spanish nobility.

Valera, however, cannot ignore the fact that all the Jewish nobles he referred to belonged to the Jews in antiquity and that since then the condition of the Jews has worsened. They have lost the prerequisites for theological nobility which cannot be found among infidels, and they have lost the capacity for civil nobility under the punishment they took in their dispersion. The long servitude to which they were subjected has not only robbed them of their dignities and honors, but also harmed the natural dispositions by which they could be qualified to receive such dignities. The basic virtue essential for nobility—i.e., the virtue of courage—has especially been affected; for the "suffering of injuries for a long time naturally weakens the human heart, so that those who were by nature brave and strong turned weak, cowardly, and deficient."[19] Nevertheless, once converted to Christianity, the converts are bound to recover the qualities that prepared their forefathers to become nobles, and ultimately "return to the very state in which they [i.e., their ancestors] were in the beginning."[20] Since God's grace may no longer be denied them, they may again be endowed with theological nobility as were other converts from other infidelities, and they can fully recover the moral virtues that form the basis of civil nobility. But "one should not marvel at the fact," adds Valera, "that the converts are not so easily restored to the fortitude of their bodies and hearts," as well as their old honors, "for things lost for so long cannot be retrieved in a day."[21] But, he also says, "if we wish to respect the truth and consider it without malice, we shall find that Our Lord has restored many converts [from Judaism] to their [former] dignities not long after their conversion."[22] Here too we hear the voice of the apologist who was trying to offset the arguments of the adversaries—arguments which, as Valera hinted, were made in a spirit of hatred and malice, with little regard for the facts.

Valera's treatise was clearly a response to an attack on the conversos on the grounds of race, a response in which he moved the focus of the discussion from the field of race to that of religion. He could do so by denying that the racial factor determined either the rise of the different nations or the formation of their noble lineages—that is, the development of both their internal and international relationships. He placed the nobilities of the ancient Jewish people on a high—in fact, the highest—level, but did not hesitate to admit that it would take some time before the present Jewish converts recover from their injuries and reach the level of the ancient Jews. As we have seen, Valera's points of departure were identical with those of Torquemada and Cartagena, although the proofs he adduced to substantiate those points were often entirely his own. All in all, his treatise formed part of the counter-attack launched by the conversos against the racist offensive in the struggle for their right to full equality with all other Christians.

V. The Political Views of the Toledan Rebels

I

What we have gathered thus far from our review of the Old-New-Christian conflict in Castile is no less than astounding in more than one respect. The struggle against the conversos who, by virtue of their Christianity, sought entry into Spanish society, led to the development of a racial doctrine and a genocidal solution to the converso problem. Squarely opposed to religious concepts that had dominated Christian thinking for centuries, this development inevitably clashed with the *legal* traditions of both Church and State. As such, it was obvious that if allowed to run its course, it would threaten the established order with upheaval.

The question to ask now is whether this phenomenon, which touched upon so many vital areas, stemmed from one source—the hatred for the conversos—or owed its appearance to several currents that happened to merge at a given moment. We shall later revert to this question and consider some of its broader implications. But now we must ask whether the rise of the race theory was associated, at least in the minds of its sponsors, with other theoretical developments, political or religious, that may help explain its emergence at that time with such explosive force.

To begin with, we must ask: What was the political theory espoused by the Toledan rebels? In particular, what were the political principles upheld by García, their moving spirit? As we have seen, the rebels' utterances on the subject reflect a dual attitude. On the one hand, they recognize the principle of monarchy and indicate their willingness to submit to its authority; on the other hand, they threaten disobedience to the King and back that threat with concrete actions, including the overthrow of the royal government in the city and its replacement by a burghers' rule.[1] Was this dualism a result of duplicity, or did it express a theoretical position? In any case, their argument seemed self-contradictory; and struck by what appeared to be an inconsistency, some writers chose one, some the other of these antinomies to represent the real attitude of the rebels.

Thus, A. Sikroff believed that a "latent anti-monarchical sentiment" determined the views and actions of the Toledan rebels.[2] But Benito Ruano, a circumspect scholar who wrote a history of Toledo in the 15th century, disagrees, stating that "what cannot be concluded, nor could be conceivable for Castile of that period, is to see in this [Toledan] insurrection . . . a latent anti-monarchical sentiment."[3] Trying to weigh the various arguments that could offer support to either opinion, Nicholas Round, in a penetrating study of the ideological aspects of the Toledan rebellion, came to the conclusion that what was reflected in that rebellion was far more than a latent anti-monarchical feeling. It expressed a "revolutionary idea."[4]

The essence of that revolutionary idea lay, according to Round, in a new conception of the source of political authority. In his opinion, the rebels believed that this authority was "rooted in their own consciousness by divine inspiration."[5] In Marcos García's repeated references to the *Holy Spirit* as the rebels' guide, inspirer and protector, Round sees the reflection of a new concept about the "legitimacy" of man's actions—a legitimacy that gave rise to the "anarchical" tendencies which came to the fore in the Toledan insurrection.[6] Furthermore, he maintains that although these doctrines claimed to offer an answer to a *social* problem in a given political and economic situation, they fundamentally represented a "current of a popular religiosity."[7] In brief, Round believes that the Toledan uprising was an offshoot of the powerful millennial movement that stirred Europe from the beginning of the 14th century on; hence, it was essentially a *religious* insurrection—a striving for freedom from Church authority, or for self-directed religious activity, that was reflected in a political outburst and a parallel attack upon the monarchy.

Unlike the authors cited earlier, Round tries to link the Toledan movement, as far as its ideological manifestations are concerned, to a *general ideological development* which could better explain some of its phenomena, and provide a clearer historical perspective. Round sensed correctly that there was a problem here that required deeper probing than it had received. The essence of that problem may be summarized as follows.

No set of ideas, however novel, is free from older theoretical influences. In fact, to understand a new theory or doctrine means first of all to identify the "paternal" strain from which it stemmed or deviated. To say, therefore, that the Toledan rebellion reflected an anti-monarchical attitude cannot in itself tell us much, if anything, about the social and ideological origins of that attitude or its actual political content. To determine these matters, we must first inquire whether any other anti-monarchic movement—perhaps one of greater sweep and impact—was visible in Spain, or Europe, at the time. If, upon examination, we arrive at the conclusion that no such movement was apparent elsewhere, we must also conclude that the Toledan rebellion cannot be explained by a general trend of an anti-monarchical character. Then we should look for another trend to which we may relate the pertinent phenomena. Should we not find a broad current to which the Toledan movement belonged, we may perceive the latter in a dim or wrong light; we shall see neither its true similarities to other movements nor the real differences between it and the others. This means that we may fail to define it, and hence fail to understand it.

Round attempted to find the sources of the ideology of the Toledan rebellion and, in the process, made valuable observations. Nevertheless, the solution he arrived at does not appear right, primarily because his hypothesis does not fit the main facts of the case.

To begin with, there is no clear sign that "anarchic tendencies" dominated the activities and political thinking of the rebels of 1449. To be sure, the attack upon the houses of Cota, the converso financier and tax collector in Toledo, may be viewed as an instance of mob action, aimed at satisfying "anarchic" desires such as vengeance, robbery and looting. But attacks of this kind were no novelty in Spain; they had been repeatedly directed against the Jews, and the Toledans no doubt viewed the attack of 1449 as an anti-Jewish action. Moreover, the assault upon Cota's houses was, in all likelihood, a tactical move by which the rebels wished to register their protest against the rule of Alvaro and his Marrano agents. The rebels may also have sought by that move to inflame the anti-Marrano passions in the city, and thereby initiate the anti-Marrano policy which they wished to institute in Toledo. Nor can the attack upon the gates and castles of the city be seen as anarchical in character, as it was part of a calculated strategy swiftly to seize control of the city, and it was no doubt conducted, as we indicated above,[8] by the leaders of the rebellion, with Sarmiento at their head. After that, we see the rebels seeking the establishment of formal authority in the city and welcoming the leadership of Pero Sarmiento, the chief representative of the king in Toledo, who consistently claimed for himself the titles and authority derived from that representation.

There is no reason to doubt the report that Sarmiento accepted the leadership of the rebellion on condition that he receive full dictatorial powers[9]; and the fact that the rebels granted him such powers can hardly indicate addiction to anarchy. Furthermore, as head of the rebellious party, Sarmiento ruled the city with an iron hand, and as long as his rule continued, his followers seemed anxious to obey him.[10]

Moreover, we see the rebels earnestly seeking to legitimize their actions, and the new order they had established, by the consent of royal authority. They persistently attempted to obtain that consent from Juan II, king of Castile, or to secure for themselves another royal patron who might approve of their position. Their negotiations with Enrique (the hereditary prince) and Juan I, king of Navarre, were certainly moves in that direction, as were their appeals to the Pope and other princes and potentates of the Church. To be sure, through these moves they attempted to earn political or military support and turn public opinion against the King, yet their very approaches to these authorities show that they sought to be recognized by the established system, ecclesiastic and secular, and not to break away from it, as would have been the case had they been moved by anarchic aspirations.

Nor can any tendency toward anarchy be seen in the imprisonments and

executions of Marranos in Toledo during the rebels' rule. As integral parts
of a popular drive to reduce the power and influence of the Marranos, these
acts may be viewed as arbitrary and illegal; but they were based on governmental authority, and on some form of legal procedure which, however
faulty, indicates the importance the rebels attached to rule by law.[11] Furthermore, the rebels sought formally to legitimize at least some of their actions
against the conversos by issuing the anti-converso regulation—the *Sentencia-
Estatuto*—which they claimed was part of the city's law, granted and confirmed by the kings of Castile. We also note that García's Memorial is
addressed to "the very high and powerful King [i.e., Juan II of Castile], or
Prince [i.e., Enrique, heir apparent to the throne], or *administrator*, to whom,
according to God, law, right and reason, belong the administration and
governance of [these] kingdoms."[12] By *administrator* they referred to that
very authority which would substitute temporarily for the royal power if the
latter refused, or proved unable, to perform its duties according to their
notions. Administrators of this kind had appeared in Castile, and in many
other kingdoms, from time to time, especially during the king's minority, and
the rebels emphasized that such an administration must be authorized by the
existing laws.[13] Certainly, those who recognized the need for an administrator to govern their society in *all* circumstances and, furthermore, act in
accordance with the laws, were not preaching anarchy; nor can they be
assumed to have sought it.

Indeed, if anything differentiates the rebellion of 1449 from popular outbursts in Spain at other times (like those against the Jews in 1109) or in other
countries (like the Shepherds' persecution in France or the Black Death
persecutions in Germany), it is the remarkable absence of anarchic tendencies and the determined desire to establish, as soon as possible, a legitimized,
ordinary, firm government to carry out the policies demanded by the rebels
within the framework of a nationally recognized system.

Nor did an anti-monarchic spirit fire the "revolutionary" zeal of the
insurgents. Time and again, in all their documents, they emphasized their
devotion to the principle of monarchy, and even their faithfulness to the very
king with whom they found themselves in conflict. From this attitude they
did not budge. It is clearly indicated in the Petition they addressed to Juan
II on May 2, 1449, as well as in the *Sentencia-Estatuto*. Also, the *Memorial* of
Marcos García clearly manifests this solid adherence to the monarchic system as a form of government, and clearly expresses the rebels' preference that
their present King rule as king. They raise no question about the legitimacy
and desirability of his kingly government, provided he fulfill his royal duties.
"The rebellion in Toledo," says García, "was not directed, nor could it be
directed, against the person of the King [or the principle of monarchy].[14] For
the citizens of that city know very well that the said King is their king and

lord *by right;* They also [know that they] are his natural subjects, and such they want to remain."[15]

This is a cardinal statement, and we see no reason to suspect its sincerity in view of the whole trend of the rebels' argument, and especially in view of their repeated claim that it was not *they* who abandoned their king but rather the king who abandoned them—that is, by removing himself from the position of kingship when he allowed tyrants like Alvaro de Luna to usurp his powers and rule in his name.[16] Later we shall dwell upon this matter further; but it seems worthwhile to stress at this point that the statement of García cited above is in full accord with other expressions of his, as well as with statements found in the Petition, which leave no doubt as to where he stood on the question of kingship as a form of government. And in this connection one may note García's reference to "the most illustrious king and our Lord Don Juan who, *according to law, is* and *should be* the king of these kingdoms."[17] The rebels, moreover, indicated their recognition of royal rule as the optimal form of government by recognizing the *hereditary* principle of kingship; hence their justification for placing themselves under the rule of Enrique, the king's heir apparent, as long as the king failed, in their view, to fulfill the functions of his office.[18] Finally, the royal office was held by the rebels to be not only acceptable, legitimate and desirable, but (since it was of divine origin) also irreplaceable and unchangeable. "The honor of the royal Crown," says García, addressing himself to Juan II of Castile, "stems from Jesus Christ, and you represent Him."[19]

All this is obviously not anti-monarchism—and certainly not *revolutionary* anti-monarchism—and judging by this, Benito Ruano was right in making the statement we cited above. Nevertheless, it is also clear that a counter-argument could be made by pointing out that the same García, in the same Memorial, justifies the rebels' disobedience to the king, hails it as "a cause of great reformation of the administration of justice and a great recuperation of all the estates,"[20] does not show the slightest tendency to deviate from the rebels' course, and again makes it clear, as was done in the Petition, that unless the king followed the line of behavior prescribed for him by the rebels, the latter would "take defensive measures against him."[21] This is of course another way of saying that they would resist him even by force, and, in any case, withdraw their allegiance from him and refuse to pay him homage. In view of these insurrectionist statements, were not García's high-sounding assurances that he recognized royal authority mere lip service to the monarchy and monarchism, while in fact he and the other rebels hated both the principle and practice of kingship and aspired to rid themselves of its yoke?

We answer this question in the negative; but in order to justify this answer, we must present García's views more fully, and also identify the current of opinion from which these views sprang. This compels us to turn our attention to some of the medieval political traditions, including the theories concerning kingship that prevailed in Spain in the 14th and 15th centuries, and more particularly in the reign of Juan II.

II

The political tradition of the Middle Ages—at least since the times of Gregory the Great—embodied two conflicting principles of government relating to monarchic rule. According to one of these, the prince is the Vicar of God, the source of all authority and the fountain of law.[22] According to the other, the king is subject to the law, even though he is subject to no person, and the law that governs him is the law of justice, which is determined, first, by divine law and, second, by the customs and concepts of the community.[23] To be sure, the adherents of both principles agreed that the king alone had the right to promulgate laws, and it is with reference to the terms of that promulgation that much of the discussion about kingship revolved.

One or two more remarks are now needed to clarify the main issues of that discussion. Since the only limitation on the king's power could be found in the assumption that he was subject to the law, it was in the acceptance or rejection of this assumption by the king that the difference was seen between the two monarchic systems—the absolute and the limited—that had been in operation. The difference, however, was often merely theoretical, for the borders of the systems frequently overlapped, depending largely on the temper of the prince, as well as the general conditions of the kingdom. But confusion was also inherent in the definition and the very concept of each type of monarchy.

If the king is the Vicar of God, it was asked, is he not actually taking God's place in fulfilling His functions of government? And if so, is it not inevitable that the king be bound by the immutable laws of justice? On the other hand, if—as both sides agreed—the king alone is entitled to issue laws, how can he be prevented from issuing new laws if such be his will or fancy? It was further recognized that, with two exceptions—the laws of nature, which are immutable, and the divine laws, which are equally eternal—the law must be constantly revised or changed to suit new conditions and conceptions; it follows that even if one accepts the view that generally the king must be subject to the laws, including those enacted by himself, *both types of kings* should *not* be subject to the laws when these require change. Thus, both forms of kingship contain elements of limitation and—more than that—elements of freedom. It all depends on the measure of restraint that the king's caution or sagacity urges him to employ, or that the objective conditions impose upon the king, often against his inner inclination.

In Spain, as elsewhere, the conflict between these concepts marked the development of political theory as well as of the system of government; and the ups and downs of these conflicting doctrines are clearly reflected in the Spanish codes and the proceedings of the Cortes in both Castile and Aragon. In Aragon, the concept of a limited monarchy—limited by the will of the people's representatives—was more deeply rooted than elsewhere in the peninsula. In Castile, which bore the brunt of the battles of the Reconquest much longer, and more painfully, than the other Spanish provinces—and hence where strong leadership and complete obedience to the ruler were more often seen as the prerequisite of victory—the absolutist tendency gained the upper hand.

There is no doubt that Alfonso X of Castile spoke on behalf of absolute monarchy when he declared the king to be the sole rightful lawmaker, although he agreed that, for the king's own benefit, he should be the first to obey the laws he had enacted, and although, under the impact of traditional practice, he recommended that kings should seek the "advice and consent" of the great lords and the most learned persons in the kingdom.[24] There is a tendency in scholarship to emphasize the subservience of the Spanish (including Castilian) kings to the constitutional lawmaking processes, and consequently some see in these concessions of Alfonso X proof that he never claimed for himself the exclusive right to promulgate laws or abrogate them at his will, and that he merely wished to indicate in his legislation that laws could not be made without him.[25] But this is to read into the documents something they neither say nor imply.

For Alfonso's view of kingship is unequivocal. "Kings, each one in his kingdom, are vicars of God," he says; and that means that they were "placed on earth in the stead of God in order fully to dispense justice and give each one his rights."[26] And again: "The king occupies the position of God in order to dispense justice and law in the kingdom of which he is the Lord."[27] Moreover, "he is the soul and head of the kingdom," while all other persons in it are merely its members. And, "as from the head originate the feelings by which all the members of the body are controlled, so also from the king, who is the lord and head of all the people of his kingdom, originate the commands by which they should be directed and guided."[28] These were not mere academic formulae, as some scholars were prone to believe, but statements that meant to convey, in all seriousness, the convictions of Alfonso X regarding the nature of kingly rule. What is implied in them, from the standpoint of law, is that the king is the only source of law because he, as the "head," is the only one entitled to impose his decisions upon the people as commands. Royal commands, then, when they relate to *habitual* behavior, are what in common parlance is known as laws. Actually, however, each command of the king has the force of law; for it is incontrovertible and inviolable.

That this was indeed Alfonso's view—namely, that the king is the only source of law and that consequently no one else has the prerogative of lawmaking—is indicated clearly by Alfonso himself in his other, somewhat earlier law book, the *Especulo* or *Espejo*. There, almost at the beginning, he says: "No one can make laws except an emperor or a king, or someone else *by the latter's order*. And if others make them without such an order, they should not be called laws, nor should they be observed, or have the force of law at any time."[29] What is more, to eliminate any doubt whatever as to the scope or meaning of the king's prerogative of lawmaking, Alfonso included in the same book a stipulation clarifying that "making laws" by kings means mastery of the whole field of law, old as well as new. "Emperors and kings have the power to make laws, to add to them and subtract from them and change each of them as may be necessary."[30]

There could be no question, according to this philosophy, who decides what "may be necessary" or ultimately determines what is right and what is wrong. Consequently, both theoretically and practically, no law could have greater stability than one granted by the king's wish; but neither could it be guaranteed that the king would respect any of his own laws. Since the king could change any law at any time—or even abrogate it totally at his will— was there not truth in the old maxim: "What pleased the king had the force of law" *(Quod principi placuit legis habet vigorem)*? And, since the king could issue commands—i.e., orders or instructions that have the force of law—in accordance with his changing views and desires, or in accordance with his caprices and interests, did this not mean that, as far as he was concerned, he was "unbound by the laws" *(solutus legibus)*? Under the best of circumstances, this could mean that while a law might remain on the books, the king's commands could represent an "exception," which would take precedence over the written law. But since such exceptions could multiply, not only would the durability of the law be put in question, but also its universality. Yet the whole essence of law, qua law, lies in its durability and universality— that is, in its constant application as a standard of conduct to all whom it may concern.

III

To present even a brief outline of the problem, we must also touch upon several other points and, first of all, note that the Alfonsine codes provide some answers to the difficulty involved. To begin with, they say that the king, the lawmaker, should fear and love God and follow his commandments; and thus, while he is the maker of the law, he is bound by the principles of divine justice as expressed in the teachings of the Faith.[31] Second, he must obey his own laws, not less, but rather more than all other citizens, and therefore he should not on any occasion claim exemption from the law for himself.[32]

Third, in making laws the king should seek the counsel—and, if possible, the consent—of the best and most learned men in the country.[33] These are the assurances offered by this system against arbitrariness and frequent change.

The assurances, however, were insufficient. They left the king with the power to determine whether any new law he might wish to decree was in accordance with the divine ordinances or not; and they did not in the least affect the king's right to accept or reject any counsel he received. Nevertheless, they did appear as limitations of some sort, and much, of course, could be read into them. This is why the estates, both nobles and commoners, wished to use the above legal limitations as loopholes, through which they might breach the absolutist system and establish the durability and universality of the law. What they attempted to achieve, above all, was to abolish their dependence on the king's "interpretation" of the laws, which largely meant of course dependence on his will. In the voluminous *cuadernos* of the Castilian Cortes, we can see how this unceasing attempt was expressed in a tenacious and tortuous struggle, in which the kings endeavored as well as they could to hold on to their inherited prerogative of lawmaking.

Now, what was emphasized as a counter-principle, presumably derived from the above "limitations," was that while the king was admittedly above all persons, the law was nevertheless above the king. This meant, of course, reducing the king's status, bringing it closer to that of his subjects, for at least in one most important respect he was *not* above all other persons. Like anyone else, he was subject to the law, now presented as all-powerful, although—or because—it derived its authority from a principle superior to the law itself—namely, the principle of justice. Accordingly, *justice*, even more than *law*, was spoken of as a supreme factor, as something existing independently and objectively that could generally be recognized and agreed upon. Indeed, general agreement to any law was held to be a sign of its inherent justice. And what better way was there to secure such an agreement than having the estates share in its enactment—share, that is, not merely as advisers, but also as participants in the formulation? Thus, even if the laws were to be issued by the king and, in this sense, were the "king's laws," they still had to be "just" laws, and they could not be such unless they were regarded also as the "laws of the community."

Are the kings, then, to rule absolutely, with the prerogative of *making* laws, or are they to be *bound* by laws sanctioned by the people or changed only with the community's consent? In other words, is monarchy to be absolute or limited—or, more clearly, subject to the people's law? This was no doubt the crucial question around which the political struggle revolved, both overtly and covertly. Practical considerations, far more than theoretical ones, determined the course of that struggle. Whenever the kings felt strong enough to advance their absolutist theory of law, they would usually do so;

whenever they were weak, they made concessions to the estates and enacted laws petitioned at Cortes. As lords of the law, however, they often replaced these enactments by different directives, to which they demanded absolute obedience, "despite" *(non obstante)* the laws they had issued. Then, when the estates met again at Cortes, the kings often felt impelled, under their pressure, to assure them that in the future they would refrain from such practices. Yet as soon as they were relieved from that pressure, they invariably resumed the same practice, which meant to them the reassertion of the principle that the king's will is the supreme law. Alfonso XI, in 1348, had the strength to restate openly the views that had guided the legislation of Alfonso X when he said at the Cortes of Alcalá de Henares: "It is the king to whom belongs the power to make *fueros* [for the cities] and laws [for the country], and interpret them and declare them and correct them as he sees fit."[34] It was not without relation to this position that he imposed upon the country the *Siete Partidas,* with all its definitions of the rights of kings, based on the Vicar of God philosophy.

Things changed several decades later, after the monarchy had gone through a civil war and the initiative could again be seized by the estates. At the Cortes of Briviesca, 1387, Juan I laid down in the most explicit terms that "royal briefs, which were contrary to custom or law, were to be disregarded; that the royal officials were not to seal any briefs which contain "*non obstante*" clauses, and that laws, customs, and ordinances were not to be annulled except by ordinances made in Cortes."[35]

This was the most far-reaching concession that royalty in Castile made to the estates in the area of lawmaking; and it represented, of course, a great victory for the estates and for the theory of limited monarchy. But reversals were yet to come. When Alvaro de Luna, Constable of Castile, sought to establish an all-powerful monarchy, one of the first things he did was to repeal (in the Cortes of Palencia, 1431) the enactment of Briviesca.[36] In 1440, however, when he was out of office and the government was in the hands of the great nobles, the king had again to yield to the demand that briefs issued in his name which were contrary to the laws would be disregarded.[37] In 1442, Juan II, still in subjection to the great nobles, who sought the alliance of the cities, had to retreat further. Cortes then objected to the fact that briefs were still issued contrary to law, and furthermore that these briefs had the character of commands issued with the king's "certain knowledge and absolute royal power." It was the expressed wish of Cortes that such extravagant phrases should no longer appear in any royal brief, and if they did appear, the brief should be held null and void and the secretary who inserted them should be deprived of his office."[38] Again, the king yielded abjectly, accepting all the Cortes' demands and reaffirming that the law of Briviesca must be observed in full.[39] This was another leap for constitutionalism in Spain toward limited monarchy. That the phrase "absolute royal power" was to be forbidden, and that a secretary who used it was to be deprived of his office, were demands which had never been heard, let alone acceded to, in the history of Castilian kingship.

But this was not the end of the struggle between the kings who sought absolute power and Cortes or the estates who aspired to limit their rights and, if possible, make them mere executors of their will. In 1445, at the Cortes of Olmedo, Alvaro, the advocate of absolutism, was again in control of the situation.[40] He thought the moment propitious to regain lost ground after all the recent royal retreats, and finally establish, with due legality, the principle of absolute monarchy. Doubtless under his influence and insistence, the cities now submitted a "petition" to the king in which they made it clear that it was the king, and he alone, who was the arbiter of right and wrong and that any action against the king's expressed will, or even open criticism of it, amounted to an act of treason and violation of the king's divine right.[41] That the cities made this petition unwillingly—that it was imposed upon them by the crafty Constable, and most probably composed by his lawyers—[42]can hardly be doubted by anyone who has traced the struggle for their share in government. Yet regardless of the reasons for their surrender—whether they stemmed from fear or calculation—this is how matters stood in 1445. Juan II became absolute ruler by the declared will of Cortes itself.

The decree of Olmedo repeats all the statements in favor of unlimited monarchy that could be found in the law books of Spain—the laws of the *Partidas* cited above, of the *Fuero Real* (of Alfonso X) and of the *Ordenamiento* of Alcalá—and declares them to be the only foundation upon which the country's government should be based. Again it is emphasized, in all seriousness, that the king is the Vicar of God and hence occupies the place of God on earth; that he is the "head" and "heart" and "soul" of the people and that they are his "members"; that "naturally" they owe him by virtue of these facts "all loyalty and fidelity and subjection and obedience and reverence and service"; that his power is so great that he is above all law, customary and written, "for his power comes not from men, but from God, whose place he holds in all temporal matters"; that "the heart of the king is held in the hands of God, and that God guides him and inclines him to whatever He pleases," and consequently it would be "very abominable, and sacrilegious and absurd, and no less scandalous and harmful, and against God, as well as against divine and human law, and repugnant to every good policy and natural reason and to all law, both canon and civil, and inimical to all justice and loyalty . . . if the king . . . had to be subject to his vassals, subordinates and natural subjects and be judged by them."[43] Therefore, if there is anything in the former laws which is likely to lead people wrongly to understand their relationship with, and duties to their sovereign, the king is advised to revoke these laws by his "definite knowledge, and his own will, and absolute power."[44]

As Carlyle noted in referring to this statement, "It would be difficult to find a more emphatic assertion of the doctrine of Divine Right of the king, and of his absolute authority as above the law."[45] Yet this assertion became the law of the land and the guiding principle by which all other laws were measured. In practice this meant the loss of all the concessions gained by Cortes after two centuries of hard struggle; it meant the establishment of a virtual dictatorship, nominally royal but actually directed by the chief minister, Alvaro de Luna.

IV

It was unrealistic to assume that Castile, whose political tradition was opposed to such doctrines, would accept the new order without protest. Indeed, even if the king himself had been the real standard-bearer and enforcer of this principle, he would doubtless have encountered, sooner or later, stern opposition from some quarters. Now that the king's weak performance displayed the opposite of the powers ascribed to him, and the man who actually upheld the hated principle was not the king but his chief minister, it was easy to attack the new policy on the grounds that it was nothing but a maneuver by Alvaro de Luna to seize absolute power for himself. Having thus exonerated the king from blame, the struggle against the *absolute* monarchy could be presented as a struggle for the *legal* monarchy against a usurper who sought to augment the rights of kingship beyond what law and political tradition had ever permitted in Spain.

This was the argument that propelled the campaign of Alvaro's antagonists. In it lay their strength, but also their weakness. For Alvaro could counterclaim that the nobles' contentions were nothing but excuses to oust him from his post and thereby attain their real aim, which was not to protect the king from *him*, Alvaro, but rather to assume complete control of the government and render the king virtually helpless. Surely the cities would oppose such a prospect even more than they opposed a strong monarchy, and it was due to their stand on this issue that Alvaro could attain a political balance and maintain his position as ruler of Castile. It should be noted, however, that for many years Alvaro refrained from fully expressing the extreme parts of his political philosophy. Seeking to allay the fears of the opposition, he cautiously veiled his ultimate aims insofar as his formal stand was concerned. On the eve of the battle of Olmedo, however, he dropped all political caution. He forced Cortes to accept the doctrine of Divine Right and then proceeded to apply it to both the barons and the cities. His determination to apply the absolutist principle as a guiding rule for administrative action meant that all previous rights and privileges would be totally disregarded if the king found it necessary to override them. It meant taking harsh measures which more often than not appeared arbitrary and high-handed, and which the cities were not prepared to tolerate. This was Alvaro's great mistake. He went too fast and too far in his efforts to translate the principle of Olmedo into political reality. When it came to the actual test, Castile was not ready to take it; and the results were inevitable. New insurrectionist steps by the nobles were taken in 1448; and the cities became restive and more reproachful.[46] This brings us back to the chain of events that links Alvaro's policies with what occurred in Toledo in 1449.

Inasmuch as it touched the monarchic regime of Castile under Juan II, the outbreak in Toledo undoubtedly expressed the feelings of the great majority. Although the elite of Toledan society was prepared to give Alvaro the "loan" he demanded, it is clear that they did so unwillingly. When the lower classes broke out in revolt, the upper classes in Toledo and the country as a whole reacted with an ominous silence. If most of the elite failed to identify themselves with the rebels, they also failed to identify themselves with Alvaro and the king. They may have disliked Sarmiento, his tactics and his administration, but they approved of most of his declared goals, and rejoiced over the fact that Alvaro and the king were given a lesson to remember. Indubitably, they hoped that the occurrences in Toledo would lead to a change in the governmental system and prevent further attempts by the administration to ride roughshod over the cities' rights.

To this extent Marcos García de Mora was certainly the Toledans' spokesman. And he could be so precisely because he was not an anti-monarchist but a typical, though perhaps somewhat radical, representative of the party that argued for limited monarchy and the supremacy of the law based on old traditions, or newly created in a representative assembly by the mutual consent of the king and the people. This is why in his Memorial he so frequently cites the legal authorities that sustained his view,[47] and why he mentions, with great emphasis, the law adopted at the Cortes of Briviesca.[48] These citations indicate what the struggle was all about. It was a struggle not to abolish the monarchy, but to place it under the rule of law—and that meant to deny it the right to disregard or act inconsistently with the old laws, or those approved in Cortes. Again let us note the words of García: "The rebellion was not directed—nor could it be directed—against the person of the king. For the citizens of this city know very well that the said king is their king and lord by right; they also know that they are his natural subjects and *such they want to be.*"[49] It follows that if the city rebelled against the king (or, more broadly, against kingly rule), it should be "damned and reproached."[50]

But the city rebelled not against royal rule, which is legitimate, but against absolutism, which is illegitimate. Therefore, "those who say that the city of Toledo and its citizens perpetrated a *damned and reproached* rebellion do not tell the truth. They lie as traitors, flatterers, destroyers, and as those who, with their flattery, falsehoods and lies, make the king sin and *lead him to believe that he is entitled to use absolute power*."[51]

What Marcos García de Mora opposed, then, was absolute monarchy. Both his negative opinion of anti-monarchic rebellion and his justification of the Toledans' insurrection—or, rather, their resistance to Juan II's rule—help us understand his political thinking and define correctly the current of thought with which he should be identified. From the 12th century on, the political theorists kept stressing the difference between king and tyrant, and found it permissible, on a variety of grounds, to overthrow a tyrant by force. Tyranny, for these thinkers, was of course not synonymous with government by Divine Right; rather, was it seen as a government by *no* right, either divine or human. Indeed, both divine and human right as the foundations of the monarchic system could be recognized, it was believed, by the king's decrees, which aimed at the common or public good; and consequently, the nature of these decrees formed the test of a true and rightful king. This view was summarized by Aquinas as follows: "The rule of the tyrant is not directed to the common good, but to the private advantage of the ruler."[52] The definition was Aristotle's,[53] and before Aquinas, it was repeated in the Middle Ages by such leading churchmen as Isidore of Seville[54] and John of Salisbury.[55] But "private advantage" as the ruler's purpose ceased to be the real sign of tyranny. Essentially, the medieval jurists agreed that a king who puts himself *above* the law will ultimately act *against* the law, and hence against the interests of the community, which will inevitably render him tyrannical. "There is no King," said Bracton, the famed 13th century English jurist, "where merely will rules and not the law,"[56] and Bartolus, the foremost Italian lawyer, firmly supported this conclusion when he defined a tyrant as "one who rules *not* according to the law" (de jure).[57]

From the medieval political tradition, therefore, García could easily draw the conclusion that rebellion against tyrants is not a crime and, furthermore, that tyranny and absolute monarchy are virtually synonymous. But he could also gather something more radical—namely, that armed resistance to tyranny is not only permitted but commended by the law, and indeed even *required* by it. In fact, "when the citizens offer such resistance," he says, they not only defend themselves but "serve their lord the king, inasmuch as they do not allow him to act against God and against himself."[58]

In support of this argument, he cites a number of laws, both canon and civil, among them the extravagant *Ad reprimandam,* which condemns a rebellion made with hostile intent against the *person* of the king[59]—from which it is clear, in his opinion, that it does not condemn a rebellion made with no such intent, but simply for the purpose of preventing or curbing the abuse of royal power. He also refers to the laws of the *Partidas*, without indicating their identity or presenting their contents. We ought, however, to take cognizance of these laws, for it was around them that the controversy on rebellion revolved in Spain in the decade preceding the outburst in Toledo.

To begin with, the fifth title of the second part of the *Partidas* states that a king should be the first to obey the law[60]; and in the tenth law of title I part II—after describing the nature of a tyrant, generally according to Aristotle's definition[61]—it states that "if a king should make bad use of his power in any of the ways stated in this law, people can denounce him as a tyrant, and his government, which was lawful, will become wrongful." But it is the twenty-fifth law of title XIII, part II, that goes farthest in this respect. It speaks about the need of the people to watch over their king, and it reads as follows:

> This care should be manifested in two ways; first, through counsel, by giving the king reasons why something should *not* be done; second, through acts, by seeking ways which may cause him to detest something and abandon it, and also by throwing impediments in the way of those who advise him to do it. For since they know that bad conduct will appear worse in him than in any other person, it is expedient for them to *prevent* him from committing it. And in protecting him from himself, in the manner we have mentioned, they must know how to protect both his soul and body, proving that they are good and loyal men by desiring that their king *may be good, and perform his duties properly.* Wherefore those who have the power to protect him in these matters and are unwilling to do so, knowingly permitting him to err, and transact his affairs in an improper way so that men will be ashamed of him, commit open treason.

This law which speaks of the subjects' duty to protect their king against himself when he takes the wrong course; which commands them to "impede" the king's bad advisers so as to *prevent* him from committing wrong; which imposes this duty upon them to the point of imputing treason to those who ignore it—is one of the most remarkable pronouncements in the political literature of the Middle Ages. It is clear that in such a case the subjects, of whatever class—"the members of the body," so to speak—assume the function of the "head," which, supposedly, the members are in duty bound to obey. It is *they*—i.e., the members—who now determine what is right and wrong, proper and improper; and it is they who should use every means in their power, except for violating the king's person, to prevent him from accomplishing any act which they consider faulty. The law was cited by the rebel barons in justification of their acts,[62] and it was this law that Juan II opposed most forcefully at the Cortes of Olmedo when he established the principle of Divine Right.[63] There can be no doubt that this was the law that García had in mind when he referred, in this connection, to the *Partidas*.[64]

For while he emphasized that the rebellion of Toledo was, to begin with, not against the king but against the "scorpion" (Alvaro), who misrepresented the king, he added, nevertheless, that even when Alvaro's orders "emanate from the king's free will," they must be regarded as "nothing or iniquitous" and as "acts which the king committed against himself"; and in such a case, "not only are the subjects not duty-bound to fulfill them, but they ought to *resist* their implementation."[65] It is only by such "resistance" that they can serve their lord, the king,[66] whereas by complying with his orders, they commit a great sin not only against God, but also against the king himself.[67]

García relies on the law of Briviesca that is based on the *Partidas*. But he also derives the right to "rebellion" from the concept of kings by Divine Right, except that he imparts to this term an entirely new meaning. What are the rights and duties of monarchy, according to García? The answer is included in the following passage he addresses to Juan II:

> The honor of the royal crown stems from Jesus Christ, and you represent Him. Therefore, He wanted to be crowned with thorns that perforated the entrails of his head, giving to understand that the kings are kings for His sake, and [accordingly] wear His *crown*. For that crown, and with it, they have to suffer pains, afflictions and labors in order to serve Him, to avenge His injuries, to defend and shelter His people, and not to indulge in enjoyments and pleasures.[68]

It follows that the king is a "Vicar of Christ" not merely in the sense of the people's lord, of the highest governmental authority on earth, but also in the sense of Christ's moral image, in his selfless devotion to the people's welfare, and his ceaseless desire to do them good. The fulfillment of these tasks involves pains and hard labor, not pleasures and enjoyments—a direct jibe at Juan II, who was known for his love of feasts and holidays, and was inclined more to a life of leisure than to one of strenuous effort. Moreover, it involves martyrdom and self-sacrifice—indeed, a readiness by the king to give his life for the causes for which he was made king. All this is symbolized by Christ's crown of thorns, and not by the crowns of gold which are put on the kings' heads. It is a king who wears Christ's crown whom the people will "serve, obey and honor." But a king who represents the opposite of that image, who abandons his duties to Christ and His followers, and who turns a deaf ear to the complaints of his people, should not be honored, but resisted. The people should take "defensive remedies" against him—"remedies which are granted them by divine and human law, by the law of nature and the law of Scripture."[69]

It is not only a "tyrant," then, but also a king who neglects his duties, or fails to meet the standards of his office, who should be resisted by the people and deposed. Implicit in all this is the view that public office represents not only honors and privileges, but also difficult obligations; the higher the office, the greater the responsibilities and the heavier the burden upon its holder. Behind the high-sounding title of "Vicar of Christ," therefore, looms the idea of the people's king, who is responsible to no one but the people. Rather than their master, he appears as their servant, and he is entitled to their obedience only to the extent that he performs his service. This was certainly a concept of kingship far removed from that of the absolutists, but it had its predecessors in Europe and in Spain. Medieval political theory from the 12th century on repeatedly reflects the concept of the king as the people's servant,[70] and the image of the "king wearing the crown of thorns" is merely García's extension of that concept.

V

No less symptomatic of García's political position and the current of thought to which he belonged is his attitude toward the Pope. In fact, his ideas about papal prerogatives are closely related to his views on kingly rule. No wonder that his attack upon the Pope resembles, in more than one respect, his criticism of the King.

The Pope "closed his ears" and "hardened his heart" to the just appeals of the rebels, says García.[71] He denied the Toledans' request for an audience,[72] and thus refused to be confronted with the truth. Thus "against the Saints and against all justice, he qualified the Jewish race *(genero)* and those who came from it . . . to have public offices and benefits, and disqualified the Christians because . . . they burned the heretics."[73] "It is impossible to say that such judgments and apostolic letters emanated from the judicious or considered will of the Holy Father."[74] In fact, the Pope acted under Marrano influence, exerted upon him by the Cardinal of St. Sixtus, and under the influence of the constable of Castile. "He feared or favored the dismal face of Alvaro more than the Eternal Majesty."[75] Yet whether the Pope did what he did "out of love for, or out of fear of the tyrant," he acted like an idolater, "for it is idolatry to serve man rather than God."[76]

Such strong language by a commoner addressing the head of Christendom sounds impudent and, indeed, extraordinarily audacious. But even more offensive is García's declaration that *all* the Pope's orders against the city of Toledo, as well as against Sarmiento and himself, will be regarded as null and void; and topping the audacity is his open warning that, unless the Pope reconsiders his decisions and takes the course dictated by his duties, the city will take "defensive measures" against him.[77] It will present its case before a Council of the Church.[78]

Whence this daring language, this assault upon the Pope, with its open slight to the Pope's authority and flat refusal to accept his judgment? Was it merely a sign of stubborn adherence to the extreme position taken originally by the Toledans—a stubbornness that was part of García's tactics, a means of demonstrating his unshaken conviction of the righteousness of his and the Toledans' cause? Or do we have here a symptom of some general attitude that formed the background of this response? In other words, was it a revolutionary or an evolutionary factor that dictated his reaction to the papal bulls? As we see it, both these elements had a share in shaping García's criticism of the Pope.

García came of age, it must be recalled, during the great conflict that unfolded in the Church between the followers of the conciliar movement and the papalists. Central in this struggle was the question: Would the pope or the Council have the final say in the affairs of the Church? Or, to put it in political terms: was the pope the source of all authority in the Church and the final arbiter of right and wrong, and the Council had merely an advisory function; or did the Council, representing the community of the Church, possess decisive powers, and the pope was merely its obedient officer, subject to the Council's instructions? Viewed from a strictly legal standpoint, the question may also be framed thus: Was the pope the Vicar of Christ on earth (as had been claimed so frequently), and consequently his word was the ultimate law; or was he, like all other Christians, under the Church's law, whose interpretation lay in the hands of the Council, the highest authority in legal matters and the source of all final directives? In brief, was the pope in the position of king by Divine Right, or was he merely an executor of conciliar decisions expressing the views of the *demos* of the Church? It was around these issues that the struggle was waged in the Council of Basle throughout its duration, and a new schism developed in 1439 that was dissolved only in 1449—the very year of the Toledan rebellion. To be sure, several years before that dissolution the victory of the papal cause seemed assured. But the papacy was still gravely concerned with the possibility of a new flare-up of schismatism, and the views of the conciliar representatives were still popular in many parts of Europe.[79]

Spain, like all other European countries, was torn between the conflicting tendencies, and although Castile was more on the side of the Pope, it was by no means free from conciliar influences.[80] In Castile, as elsewhere, public opinion was divided between the pro- and antipapal school. Was the Pope to be what he wanted to be—emperor of the faithful in all spiritual matters— or was he to be the standard-bearer of the Church and the spokesman of its duly chosen representatives? Was the Church to be run like an absolute monarchy, or was it to be democratically controlled? This was the issue.

Figgis has shown the close relationship between the ideas that inspired the conciliar movement and the political theories about the nature of the best government that had developed in the preceding centuries. According to Figgis, the conciliar movement was fed by the currents of thought that urged a limited monarchy and gave increasingly stronger justification to a government of law—or rather of laws enacted by the people. Contrarily, the victory of papalist philosphy in the middle of the fifteenth century strengthened the current of absolute monarchism that established itself in Western Europe in the 16th and 17th centuries.[81] The thesis is of enormous breadth and depth, and requires further exploration. The probability of such a relationship, however, appears to border on certainty.

This does not mean of course that all who held the papalist view held a similar view about the king, or vice versa. This was not the case during the great conflict between the papacy and the Empire, and certainly not always the case in the period that followed the Pope's victory over conciliarism. But laymen who insisted on a limited monarchy were prone to sympathize with the conciliar movement. It was no mere accident that conciliarism drew its strength in the Council of Basle not so much from churchmen as from laymen, especially jurists; and these were, more often than not, advocates of limited monarchy.

Judging by some of his expressions on the papacy, Marcos García appears to have been a protagonist of the conciliar movement. We have seen that he threatens the Pope with calling a Council to determine the position the Church should take on the issue of the conversos, and accordingly react to the Pope's decision in this matter. He completely rejects the Pope's judgment, accusing him not only of improper treatment of the case from the standpoint of canon law, but also of partiality and favoritism to the strong. There is no question here of recognizing automatically the overall moral authority of the Pope and of treating his judgments as infallible, or even final. Above the Pope stands the Council, to which Christians can appeal for redress of grievances. But the spirit of Basle is especially reflected in the following passage of the Memorial, in which Marcos García states in no uncertain terms his theoretical position on the papacy.

> And let not the arrogant and dominant tyrants be confident; and let not the ambitious impetrators and surreptitious flatterers hope for assistance by broadening the divine authority that says: *all that you will bind will be bound,* etc. [Matth. xvi.19]. For by the very phrasing of the said declaration, the said authority is already limited, and truly understood [it means:] "If you bind *justly* [it will be bound] and if you do not miss [the keyhole, the door will be opened]," as is noted in the . . . decretals; and if that statement is understood in a different manner [i.e., as the aforesaid interpreters would have it], it would indicate a great obscurity and blindness—for then the delegated would have greater

power than the delegating, and the minor greater power than the major.[82]

By the "flatterers" and "impetrators" García referred of course to the leading conversos in the Council of Basle and especially to Juan de Torquemada, who fought for the supreme authority of the Pope, his complete independence and infallibility against the contrary position of the conciliarists. We see that García was well informed of what had happened in that council, and we can also see clearly what his own view of the rightful status of the papacy was.

To be sure, he too is prepared to grant the pope the highest honorary title; the pope is the Vicar of Christ, just as the king is the Vicar of God; but the *Vicar* of Christ is not Christ, just as the Vicar of God is not God. The authority granted the pope is *not* all-embracing; it is limited, as is the authority of the king; and the judge of the pope's behavior must be the Council, just as that of the king should be the Cortes. What determines the validity of his decisions is precisely what determines those of the king— i.e., the extent to which they conform to *justice,* which must guide all human decisions and is the yardstick for evaluating all human actions. "The Truth [that is, God]," says García, "does not hold condemned him whom a temporal tribunal or judge condemns *unjustly.*"[83] This is the view of Scripture and this is the position of the Holy Council, to which the Pope must yield and by which he must abide, for *his* tribunal is also "temporal."

What we see here is a clear challenge to the principle of papal infallibility. But the challenge also extends to the idea of the inherent *superiority* of the pope's judgments, and even more so to the basic *integrity* from which those judgments are supposed to stem. His criticisms of the Pope's reaction to the occurrences in Toledo, and of his attitude toward the rebels, reflect these positions clearly. Why did the Pope behave the way he did? García asks; why did he yield to Alvaro and the conversos? And as we have seen, he attributed this surrender to "fear" of, or "love" for Alvaro, the tyrant. But later on he admits or feigns ignorance of the reasons for the Pope's behavior. "It is not known," he says, "what cause moved his Holiness to qualify them" [i.e., the conversos] as good Christians, while "the decrees and decretals resist, impugn and contradict such qualification." But if he is perplexed by the Pope's conduct, he is certain about the reaction it deserves. "If there are some papal letters," he says, "that qualify that damned race against all divine and human law," the instructions they contain should not be fulfilled. Yet this was only the negative side of the reaction he recommended. As for the positive side, there remains his earlier conclusion: If the Pope reverts to the true course, the city will accept his orders; "if not, it will have to take 'defensive measures' to the extent that justice permits it."[84]

This is doubtless the lowest point in his devaluation of the papacy. The Pope may behave not only illegally, but also immorally. For, like the king, he is subject to human weakness and such influences as flattery, fear and interests, political as well as material, all of which lead him to flout and violate the just laws in favor of those whose favor he seeks. What is worse, he may be deprived of his own will and become the instrument of another will, as happened to Juan II, king of Castile. In such a case, the citizens of the Church need not respect his judgments; they have the rights to "defend" themselves against the Pope, as they have the right to take "defensive measures" against a misguided and tyrannical king.

Thus we see a remarkable similarity between his view of kingship and his view of the Pope; both were founded on the same principles, and both were related to the political position taken by the Toledan rebels. Marcos García de Mora, their leader, was a follower of the political tendency that advocated the curbing of the king's powers, and he was a follower of the conciliar movement, which advocated restriction of the Pope's rights. He did not seek abolition of the papacy any more than he did the annulment of kingly rule. Formally and ceremonially, he was ready to grant both king and pope the highest honors; but factually, he sought to narrow their powers and limit their prerogatives, so that they should be what their duties implied and what they ought to have been in the first place—that is, not rulers by Divine Right but rulers by the consent of the people.

VI

With the identification of the currents of thought in which García's political ideas had their origin, the question posed at the opening of this chapter may be considered, we believe, answered. The radical views of Church and State that reverberate in García's campaign were basically an extension of the ideologies of reformation, religious and political, which were agitating most of Europe in his lifetime, and not an offshoot of the millennialist movement, which arose at the time in Central Europe, but whose waves hardly reached the shores of Spain. The occasional appeals to the Holy Spirit that we find in García's *Memorial* provide no real evidence of the influence of a chiliastic tendency, since such appeals were typical of advocates of Church reform as they were of the believers in millennialism.[85] We may readily agree that García's references to the Holy Spirit point to a reliance upon the individual's own conscience as his supreme authority and final judge; but for this very reason, they do not indicate a deep, but a rather shallow religiosity. Stripped of their thin religious garb, his appeals to the Holy Spirit may be identified as appeals to the individual's convictions, illumined in some manner by divine inspiration, but tested in the final analysis for their truth in the assembly of the people. Essentially, in his opinion, it was not the voice of the individual, but *vox populi*—or rather the voice of the legal representation of the community—that should be, or in which should be vested, the supreme authority in both state and Church.

For García was, above all, a jurist, not a mystic; a political agitator, not an evangelist; a practical politician, not a dreamer; more particularly, he was a man of the people, who sought to broaden their rights and the scope of their power. In him we hear the call of the common man, the call of the lower classes (even the lowest!), whose spokesman and champion he wished to be. In him we hear the voice of burgeoning democracy—a democracy not yet properly defined, but arising out of repressed desires for justice and reform in many fields. For García, who emerged from the lowest classes, shared their deep yearnings for change as well as their bitter frustrations and resentments. Therefore, behind the political principles which he passionately advocated, and in which he firmly believed, there burned group hatreds and personal grudges; and these not only lent ferocity to his argument, but also led him away from his main purpose into the dark alleys of other theories that preached vengeance and bloodshed.

VI. Old Christian Apologies for the Conversos

I. FERNÁN PÉREZ DE GUZMÁN

Perhaps the earliest circumspect view of the conversos' religious attitudes and tendencies was expressed by Fernán Pérez de Guzmán, undoubtedly one of the brightest literary lights in the period of Juan II. As a member of the high nobility of Castile, he was involved in the political conflicts of his country at least until 1432, but he earned his fame not as statesman or politician but as poet, essayist and historian. Originally a partisan of the Infante Enrique, he remained all his life an adversary of Don Alvaro and a sharp critic of the latter's activities, but he clearly discerned the faults and vices also of many of Alvaro's opponents. His *Generaciones y Semblanzas*, which consists of brief portraits of many public figures of Castile, includes some of his opinions on social phenomena related in a way to the persons he discussed. His remarks on the converso problem occur in his sketch of Pablo de Santa María,[1] bishop of Burgos, whom he held in high regard, and for whose son, Alfonso de Cartagena, he felt both friendship and admiration.[2]

The article was written after Don Pablo's death (1435) and probably before the rebellion of Toledo (1449), because he makes no allusion to that event, which was intimately connected with the subject of the conversos and was still very much on the people's mind when he was about to complete his book.[3] We may gather this also from his assertion that none of the conversos rumored to be Judaizers had ever been brought before an ecclesiastic judge,[4] unless we assume that he denied the legitimacy of the judges who served in the Toledan tribunals of 1449 that condemned a number of conversos as Judaizers. Nor does he refer to any scandals or clashes produced by religious or other accusations leveled at the New Christians by the Old ones (as was the case in Toledo). Be that as it may, while discussing Don Pablo, Guzmán thought it fitting to express his view of the converso question.

Guzmán's observations constitute a moderate and guarded defense of the New Christians against those who considered them religious impostors. He had "several reasons," he says, to be opposed to those who "condemn or besmirch this *nation* of the New Christians ... without making any distinction and difference [among their members], claiming that they were [all] not Christians and that their conversion was neither good nor useful."[5] Guzmán cannot concur with these extreme assertions. To be sure, he does not doubt that people who lived all their lives in that religion (i.e., Judaism), who were born and reared in it, and especially grew old in it, if dragged by force to the New Law without admonitions and exhortations, would not be so faithful and

Catholic Christians as those born in Christianity and informed of its tenets by learned men and instructive writings.[6] Even the disciples of our Lord, who heard His holy sermons, and, what is more, saw His marvelous works, abandoned him and doubted His resurrection out of the weakness of their faith, until they became confirmed in their faith by the Holy Spirit. And even later, the apostles allowed the newly converted to practice some ceremonies of the Old Law until, little by little, they became firm in the faith. For all these reasons, Guzmán concludes, "I would not be surprised if some *(algunos)* of the newly converted in our time were not Catholic Christians, especially among the women and the dull and crude people *(groseros e torpes)*, who are not learned in the faith. For it is easier to draw to the knowledge of the truth an informed and learned man *(sabidor o letrado)* than an ignorant one who believes in the faith only because he inherited it from his father, but not for any other reason."[7]

This is of course a hypothetical statement. Guzmán does not tell us that he was actually not surprised to find some Judaizers among the Marranos, but that he *would* not be surprised if some delinquents *were* found among them. Obviously, the hypothesis does not lean on experience but on logical assumptions, supported by the example of the Jewish converts in the Apostle's generation. The logic is commonplace, and hardly disputable: it takes time for those born in a certain faith to be accustomed to and rooted in another faith. Obviously, this general assertion applies to the followers of *all* religions, including the Christian Spaniards (as we shall see below), and not only to the Jews who were converted to Christianity. On the other hand, what he knows from his own experience leads him to conclude that "there are among them [i.e., the conversos] *some [algunos] devoted and good people.*"

To begin with, he is acquainted with a number of converso friars who lead a hard and austere life in the convents, not because they are compelled to do so, but out of their own choice. Second, he sees some of them labor and spend much of their substance to improve the conditions in certain convents; and he has also seen others like Pablo de Santa María and his son Don Alfonso, both bishops of Burgos, who "wrote several works of great value to our faith."[8] These experiences corroborate his belief that the holy water of baptism has indeed great power and that it could not have touched so many people without having some positive result.

Thus, against *some* of the conversos who *may* not be true Catholics, Guzmán points out *some* others who *are* definitely good Christians; and while the former statement of his is grounded on assumptions, the second is based on fact—that is, on his own observation of converso friars, prelates, and reformers. It seems that Fernán Pérez de Guzmán did not know many conversos intimately and that he did not meet any Judaizers either. Nowhere does he indicate that he had close contacts with conversos other than ecclesiastics.

But what he saw was enough to disprove the *general* accusations against them; he would not be surprised if they were true *in part;* but he had no evidence of this.

Guzmán also rebuts another charge made against the converso theologians. It was said that they had composed their books out of fear of the kings and the prelates and in order to gain more favor with them. Guzmán cannot find any substance in this claim. "In our time," he says, "there is no such great zeal for the faith that they [i.e., the converso authors] would have to [compose their works] out of fear or hope. For today the hearts of the kings and the prelates can be gained by gifts and donations more than by virtues and devotions. Nor is the zeal for the faith so rigorous that fear would make one shun evil and do good." Therefore, he must adhere to his view that there are dedicated Christians among the conversos and that it is "not right to utter so absolute and definite a condemnation of a whole *nation*."[9]

What is the future of the conversos in Christendom? Guzmán does not deny that the newly grafted, tender plants require much care and labor before they become rooted in the faith.[10] In his opinion, the children of the first converts should have been separated from their parents and duly educated as Christians, for the precepts and counsels of the parents leave a strong impression on the hearts of small children. Yet although this was not done, he believes that their conversion was useful and beneficial, for the Apostle said: "I rejoice in the fact that the name of Jesus Christ is lauded either truthfully or feigningly." Above all, "assuming that the first converts would not be such good Christians, the second and third generation—and even more so the later ones—will be Catholic and firm in the faith."[11]

To prove this thesis Guzmán presents the case of the Christians who were converted to Islam after the Moslem conquest and whose offspring showed themselves so opposed to Christianity that they fought the Christians who sought to reconquer the land.[12] He also saw many Moors who went over to the Christian camp because of some disagreement with their king, and yet they remained faithful to their religion and not even one of them *converted* to Christianity, although they could do so freely—and all this "because they were so attached to, and so established in that error since childhood" that they could not abandon it.[13] Moreover, even those of them who died in Castile had remained so devoted to their ill-fated sect that, although they had no more reason to fear the Moors, they adhered tenaciously to their Islamic religion. This is what heritage and education do in matters of faith. "Why should I not believe about some of the conversos what I have noticed in all those Moslems?" Here, too, Guzmán seems to draw his conclusions about the conversos not from direct observation but from analogy; but actually he could rely on some experience also in the case of the conversos. After all, when he wrote his sketch of Paul (perhaps in the early 1440s), he had already met conversos of the second generation, and he could not help hearing their views and knowing where they stood toward Judaism and Christianity. One is inevitably led to assume that he based his moderate defense of the New Christians on analogies more than on evidence because he was hesitant to speak too favorably of the New Christians and thereby subject himself to the criticism of the converso haters. We can note his desire to protect himself against these critics when he opens his apology with a declaration of his reverence for those whose definite and unreserved opinions he was going to dispute.[14] "Why should I not think about some of the conversos what I have seen in all the Moslems?" Has he really seen *all* the Moslems who came to Castile, and only a few of the conversos who lived in it? "And thus, in my opinion, in all these matters we have to abandon the extremes and put limits and restraints on our judgments. Or, if people know that some conversos do not guard the [Christian] law, let them accuse them before the prelates in a manner that the punishment would serve as chastisement for the culprits and example to the others; but to condemn them all and accuse none seems to be more the result of a desire to malign than of a zeal to correct."[15]

Here at last Guzmán gives us an inkling of what he really thought of the criticisms so often uttered against the conversos. No proof has been proffered of their violations of the faith; no accusations have been brought forth; evil tongues, however, were busy besmirching and reviling them. Is not all this talk based on nothing but ill will? Theoretically, he could find some basis for the assumption that the first generation of converts were not "such good Christians," but he could not say this even theoretically of the second and third generation if we judge by what he says of the offspring of Christians who converted to Islam. He evidently believed that for a conversion to take root, time is an essential element and that, in all cases, the resistance of converts to their new religion must sooner or later break down and disappear under the force of habit and education.

II. LOPE DE BARRIENTOS

The bishop of Cuenca, Don Lope de Barrientos, was one of the most colorful figures in the entourage of Juan II. Friar, theologian, and author of tracts on such subjects as sleep, divination and fortune, Barrientos was also a statesman of stature and a first-rate political tactician.[16] A sincere patriot and confirmed royalist, he took a firm stand in support of Castile's kings and courageously opposed the rapacious nobles who endangered the country's stability and security. The signal services he rendered to the crown won him some high administrative positions. He was one of the two chief counselors of Castile (in the last months of Juan II) and, following that, chancellor of the kingdom (in the first years of Enrique IV). But on the whole, the kings made little use of Barrientos's great political potential, possibly because the ruling courtiers were reluctant to have in their company a man who, according to Mariana, was one of the "most upright and most saintly" men. Perhaps the term "saintly" does not fit Don Lope, who, in struggling with rebels, was prepared to use questionable diplomatic tactics. But he was certainly filled with a passion for justice and for what he considered the common good. Moreover, his acute sense of fairness and keen observation made him a superb judge of men and affairs. This is why the views he expressed on the conversos are so important in our eyes.

According to Padre Getino, Barrientos "boasted of having some blood of the Jewish race in his veins,"[17] and in proof of this assertion Getino quotes a statement from Barrientos' epistle to his nephew. The statement referred to, however, does not offer such proof. What it says is that the *family of the Barrientos* (not the bishop personally) should be glad and proud that "owing to *you* [i.e., the nephew] and other relatives of ours, we have them [i.e., the conversos of Jewish origin] in the ranks of the Barrientos family."[18] It is obvious that he would not have made such a statement had he himself been of Jewish or partly Jewish origin. He remembered, he said, talks that he had with his nephew on this matter, and that the latter told him that he (i.e., the nephew) felt within himself "both bloods *or* races, like a coat of mail with a tight-fitting jacket."[19] Commenting upon this recollection, Barrientos writes to his nephew: ". . . as indeed you are found to possess the qualities of both races, always well armed with courage [a gentile quality] and discretion [a Jewish quality], complementing each other."[20]

Barrientos, then, speaks clearly in this passage not of his own blood, but of that of his nephew and of the latter's characteristics, not of his; and if anything can be gathered from these statements about himself, it is that he was *not* of Jewish descent. But apart from these indications, we have Barrientos' direct testimony about himself, from which, in our judgment, we can definitely gather that he was of gentile stock. For in one place he says that "in the ecclesiastical histories the name *converso* is used in reference to *the gentiles, from whom we proceed* [*los gentiles do nos procedemos*], when they came to the faith."[21] The phrase "*do nos procedemos*" was not needed for his argument, which was taken from the Relator's work and which, in its original form, did not contain of course such a remark. It was supposedly introduced casually, in passing, but undoubtedly not without intent. Barrientos must have been looking for an opportunity to discredit the rumors that García and his followers were spreading about him—namely, that he belonged to a "Jewish family," which could mean that he had Jews among his ancestors.[22]

That such rumors were spread may be gathered from García's *Memorial*, where the author cautions Prince Enrique not to listen to the counsel of the "bad friar" *(el mal fraile)*[23]—a clear allusion to Barrientos (who was then the Prince's counselor), which served as prelude to the additional warning that if Enrique did follow that advice and violate the oath he gave the city of Toledo, he would not be absolved of his sin "by the *false bishop of Jewish descent* or by any other prelate."[24] Barrientos was both a friar and a bishop, and in the context of the argument it could appear that García referred to him by both titles, although by "false bishop" he might have meant another prelate—say, Alonso de Cartagena.[25] Allusions such as this, however ambiguous, about Barrientos' Jewish origin may have prompted the bishop to make the remark about his gentile ancestry.

But there is an additional statement of Barrientos in the same document that leads us to the conclusion that he was an Old Christian. He objects to designate as conversos the sons or grandsons of converts from Judaism for the following two reasons: first, because they "know nothing of Jewish customs" *(no sauen cosa alguna de los Judaicos usos)*—an argument which he borrowed from the Relator; and second, "they are as distinct [from the Jews] as we are" *(son en si tan diuersos [de los Judíos] como nos).*[26] It is clear that by "nos" he refers here to his own group, i.e., the Old Christians, presented as disparate from the New.

The work from which these passages are cited—i.e., Barrientos' letter to his nephew—was, in fact, a pamphlet entitled: *Against some sowers of discord with the nation of the converts from the people of Israel.*[27] It was written in Toledo, probably in November 1449, and there was little in it of Barrientos' creation. Basically, it was a revised edition of the paper submitted to Barrientos by the Relator with the aim of convincing the Prince and his advisers of their need to take action against the *Sentencia* and of their duty to avoid any settlement with the Toledans without restoring the conversos to their full rights. The paper, however, was so structured that it could be of interest to the average reader and suitable for general circulation; and it stands to reason that the

Relator, after learning of the bishop's favorable view of his paper, suggested to him that he publish it in his own name, or use any part of it as he saw fit. It was of course important to the Marranos that their defense be undertaken by the famous Old Christian churchman. Barrientos complied with this wish, and issued the paper in his own name in the form of a letter to his nephew, an offspring of Old and New Christian intermarriage.

But Barrientos introduced a number of changes in the Relator's Instruction. To be sure, he retained almost all the Relator's arguments, but occasionally gave them a different twist by omitting or adding a few words here and there, or by his revision of the style. Occasionally, he somewhat broadened the discussion, so as to make a point clearer or more forceful, and in some instances he added informative material which is not found in the Instruction. What interests us in the bishop's version are of course the changes he introduced in the original, and above all his omissions and additions. It is to the latter especially that the document owes its historical value.

From the outset Barrientos directs his criticism at García, to whom he attributes the major responsibility for the attacks upon the conversos. Whereas in the opening of his Instruction the Relator speaks, somewhat enigmatically, of the "second Haman" who persecuted the conversos, without indicating whether by that title he referred to Sarmiento or to García, the bishop applies that appellation specifically to the latter, while Sarmiento is not mentioned even once in the entire discussion. Similarly, in contrast to the Relator, who vigorously demanded in his Instruction the restitution of the property stolen from the conversos[28]—an action for which Sarmiento was held accountable—the bishop passes in silence over this matter. Indubitably, this silence did not result from oversight but from overriding political considerations. In all likelihood, Barrientos' revision of the Instruction was made after the Prince and his advisers had made up their minds that they should concentrate upon the elimination of the arch-inciter—Marquillos—whom they considered the spirit of the rebellious movement, and later try to get rid of Sarmiento by negotiations and concessions. One of these concessions, which should have served as inducement for Sarmiento to leave the city, was to let him depart with "all his possessions," without forcing him to give an account of the properties expropriated from the citizens during his rule. As a member of the team that was charged with the task of negotiating with the rebels and the city's leading circles, the bishop was no doubt bound by the strategy decided upon by the Prince.[29]

Accordingly, in the talk Barrientos had with Sarmiento prior to the latter's departure from Toledo, we see him repeatedly put stress on the robberies which the rebel leader perpetrated in the city, hoping perhaps to move Sarmiento to offer the return of the stolen goods. Evidently, such an offer was not made, and Barrientos presented no formal demand concerning this matter.[30] His paper reflects this avoidance of action, especially when it fiercely attacked Marquillos both for the persecutions he initiated in some cities and for the racial theory he propagated. In all this Barrientos followed the line of argument presented by the Relator, striving to make it clear that García's theory, while constituting a criminal perversion of Christianity, was doubly criminal when applied to the converts from Judaism in Spain.

Comparing the persecution conducted by the "second Haman" to that of the "bad Haman" in the days of King Ahasuerus,[31] the Relator saw the common denominator of these persecutions in the fact that both were directed at "our race" *(nuestro linaje)*. But the bishop was evidently thinking of another factor that triggered the attack in both cases: the high positions occupied by the Jews in the courts of the Persian kings and those held by the conversos in the administration of Juan II. However, to raise this issue now, he felt, would divert him from his main purpose, and therefore he made the following analogy, which merely hinted at his thoughts on the subject: King Darius, the son of Queen Esther, he said, "placed many of those Hebrews in many honorable positions *(oficios)* which, for divine reasons, they do not lack even today."[32] The analogy was obviously meant to imply that the issue of the public offices could not justify the actions of the "second Haman" anymore than it did those of the first. Marquillos, says the bishop, must have been blinded by the Devil when he failed to sense the groundlessness of his claims.[33] And having made this concluding remark, he goes over from the similarity to the difference, which was far more important in his eyes. For "Haman persecuted Jews, and he [Marquillos] persecutes Christians; and not only in his own land, but also in foreign ones" (namely, the territories of other cities)—a persecution which "resulted in many deaths, robberies and great destructions."[34]

Christians! This is how the bishop defines the conversos throughout the discussion, and, like the Relator, he too maintains that the grave persecution that had been launched against them threatens to undo the great work of conversion accomplished by the Church over many generations. But there is a broader approach here—a universal conception—which the Relator implied but did not state explicitly. We can readily notice these differences by comparing the remarks made on the subject by Fernán Díaz and the bishop:

The Relator	*Barrientos*
And whether from this [i.e., the persecution of the conversos] has followed ... a disservice to God our Lord, your grace can judge better than myself. For ... seeing how badly are treated those who came to	... for they [the persecutors] go not only against those *who are of God and came to His service,* and against those who aspire to come, but also against the Faith itself and against its orders. [For] what will say those who

our Holy Faith and those who descended from them, *the Jews and others who are outside the Faith* will stop to be converted to it, . . . and thus, there is no doubt that *some of them,* especially those who are of lesser knowledge and understanding, *who came to Christianity from Judaism* [*que fueron en tiempo de el Judaismo*], are [sometimes] stirred by the wish to go to the *land of the Moors* and to other kingdoms, *to become Jews,* saying that the faith is of no use to them, and that they cannot defend themselves with it against the evils . . .[35]

remain [outside the Faith] and desire [*esperan*] to come to it, when they see how maltreated are those who did come to it and those who descended from them? . . . I do not doubt that it occurs to *some* of them, and especially to those who little understand and know, to go to other kingdoms and regions. And not only to go [there], but also to leave the Faith, for through it they cannot fare well, and not even defend themselves against the evil doers. . . . [Indeed] I believe that the destruction of one race [*generación*] will cause the stumbling of the other, and so the world will come to its end [*acabaría*].[36]

We can see that the bishop used the Relator's argument precisely as the Relator wanted him to use it. He extracted the principle embodied in it by pointing out that the persecution of the conversos endangered the whole grand design of the Church to convert the world to Christianity. This, then, was not a Jewish issue, or one that concerned the conversos only. In fact, the words Jews and Jewish converts are not even mentioned in this connection. Clearly, Barrientos deliberately omitted here all the references to Jews which are found in the Instruction. Instead, he preferred to speak generally of those who *came* to God and *are* of God, and those who had *not yet* come and *will* not come, if converts will be so treated. Obviously, the bishop wanted to stress that the persecutions of the Marranos would have the most serious repercussions, not only among the Jews, but also among the Moslems and the rest of non-Christian humanity. "I believe that the destruction of one race *(generación)* will cause the stumbling of the other, and so the whole world would come to its end." In other words, the persecution of the conversos obstructs the Church militant and prevents it from becoming the Church triumphant; it may cause the Church to lose the battle, and thereby lose the world.

The warnings sounded by the Relator concerning the social upheaval that Spain could expect if García's racial theory were to be promoted hit the mark. Not only did Barrientos present fully the Relator's argument on this issue; he also strengthened it by indicating the force and speed with which

the defamation of the nobility may spread. Thus, after mentioning the famous houses of Spain, whom Marquillos harmed by his words and deeds, the
bishop adds: "And not only [by the words and deeds of] Marquillos, *but also
by those of his partisans, from whom emanate many poisons and slanders* both
against God and against all temperance and virtue."[37] Obviously, he considered the danger acute because the campaign of vilification was being carried
on not by one man, but by a whole group—that of his followers—and thus
the poisons which they spread may soon contaminate the entire social body
of Spain.

Barrientos accepts the Relator's view concerning the Christian faithfulness
of the conversos, but goes beyond him in his estimation of their religious
devotion. He regards the conversos' adherence to the faith in the face of the
persecutions they suffer not only as a product of strong will and great
patience (as does the Relator[38]), but as something bordering on the wondrous
and heroic. He cannot appraise (or, as he puts it, understand) "what willpower is needed for them *to be able* or *wish* to do what every good Christian
does."[39] It is not only their *capacity* to perform these deeds, but their *desire*
to perform them that amazes him. And not only the newly converted themselves, but also their offspring are to him a cause of great astonishment and
admiration. "I do not know," he says, "how the new convert and his descendants, when they see how they are treated by the Old Christians, can agree
to remain in our Holy Faith [even] for one hour!"[40] In this statement, too,
we find proof that he was not of Jewish descent: only a gentile could speak
like this! One sees here a greater preparedness to exonerate the deviators, the
backsliders, than we have in the words of the Relator.

That Barrientos was certain that the New Christians generally were
behaving religiously as the Old Christians do, and not as secret Jews, is also
indicated, among other things, by the changes he introduced in another
crucial statement of the Relator. In referring to the descendants of the
Marranos—"the sons and grandsons of converts" who "were born in Christianity"—the Relator says of them, as we have indicated above, that they
"know nothing of Judaism, or of its rites." Barrientos altered this statement—
first by deleting the Relator's assertion that they "know nothing of Judaism"
(he may have assumed, quite reasonably, that one may be a good Christian
and still know *something* of Judaism!), and then by exchanging the word "rite"
(rito) for the word "practices" *(usos)*, which embraced, besides the field of
worship, also that of custom.[41] It was here, he thought, that the real evidence
lay! For a large body of men may become familiar with the rites and customs
of *any* religion only by following them in practice; and thus by stating that
the Marranos were ignorant of the Jewish usages, he indicated that they did
not follow them either. However, to support this implication, and make
absolutely clear where the Marranos stood religiously, Barrientos added the

important observation that "they (namely, the conversos of the second and
third generations) are as diverse [from the Jews] as we [the Old Christians]
are."[42] Since there was no room for differentiation between the Old and New
Christians, there was obviously no room for religious persecution.

Of special interest are his remarks on the 65th decree of the Fourth
Toledan Council, which prohibits "those who are of the Jews" *(hi qui ex
Iudeis sunt)* from assuming public offices in Christendom. As we have noted,
the anti-conversos put much emphasis on this prohibition, which they interpreted as relating to *all* converts to Christianity from Jewish stock down to
the fourth or fifth generation, regardless of their religious behavior. According to Barrientos, however, the phrase *hi qui ex Iudeis sunt* referred, indeed,
to converts from Judaism, but only to those who relapsed into their former
faith. This, as we have seen, was also the interpretation given the decree by
Cartagena and most of the former authoritative commentators.[43] But Barrientos rendered this interpretation more precise by attaching to it an important limitation which is not present in the earlier comments. According to
him, *hi qui ex Iudeis sunt* (those who *are* of the Jews) meant those who *came*
from the Jews—i.e., who were converted *themselves*—and not their descendants, including their sons who, as he put it, "were born in the faith"—i.e., in
Christianity—and hence came from Christians.[44] But since the descendants
did *not come from Jews,* the 65th decree of the Fourth Toledan Council did
not refer to them at all. By making this distinction, Barrientos excluded the
sons and grandsons of the original converts—i.e., the great majority of the
group—from the application of that decree. Nor could it be automatically
applied to the rest of the conversos either. As indicated above, it referred only
to those who factually regretted their conversion.

How large was the number of such regretters among the conversos, according to Barrientos? Judging by his astonishment at the steadfastness in the
faith displayed by the "newly converted," it would seem that he considered
their number to be small. And this is also indicated by his remark that "some"
(algunos) of the conversos who "come to the faith" consider the proposition
of abandoning Christianity, because, as it appears to them, they can gain
nothing from it—"not even defend themselves against the evildoers."[45] But
to "consider" does not mean to have "decided," or to have actually "deviated" from the faith. It was inevitable, in Barrientos' opinion, that "considerations" of this nature should occur to "some" under the impact of the
persecution; yet he did not exclude the possibility that backsliders may exist
also in normal times. All Christian groups include "good, common and bad"
Christians[46]—namely, all grades of devotion to the faith—and he sees no
reason why the New Christians should be excepted from this rule. Consequently, wherever a sinner is found, he should be punished according to the
laws. But the laws do not say that this punishment "calls for insurrections on

the part of some Christians against others; nor do they sanction the activity of slanderers, plotters, seekers of robberies and deaths, and the depopulation of towns and cities."[47] This is a clear indication that, according to Barrientos, the rebels' religious accusations against the conversos were, in the main, false and libelous; they were "slanders," invented to serve their plots; for what the rebels sought, as Barrientos saw it, was not to provide defense of the faith, but to satisfy their criminal urges—i.e., to rob the Marranos, kill them, and oust them from their settlements, which in consequence would remain depopulated.

Barrientos adds emphasis, and penetrating insight, to the Relator's assertion about the main motive of the perpetrators of the aforesaid outrages. It is "vile greed, jealousy and ill will," the "wicked and bad roots of our life," which are nourished, in this case, by the wrong notion that "the world is being given more to those than to the others, and that the latter are imprisoned while the former are free."[48] In other words, the cause of the whole tumult was passion for earthly goods, coupled with the belief that these goods were not fairly divided. The New Christians attained a greater share of them than the Old because the latter were allegedly "imprisoned" (i.e., prevented from exercising their full capacities) while the Marranos were "free" to do so.

Here we have in a nutshell the anti-Marranos' view of the conversos' economic position and the obstacles they put in the way of the Old Christians to gain their rightful share. Barrientos considers the view preposterous. The world was not given to the New Christians more than to the Old ones, and the latter were not imprisoned and prevented from following their pursuits to the best of their ability. It is greed that distorts the judgment of the evil-doers. "In truth they are imprisoned," but not the way they think they are. "Imprisoned in the infernal chains," says Barrientos, "are those who cannot eat except from rapine, and those who cannot think except of robbery, and those who cannot conceive of being Christian except through evil talk, evil action and evil living (mal vivir.)"[49] "Like the Christians who became Moors and turned their lances against the faith" are these rabble-rousers who attack the conversos.[50] The Christian converts to Islam did not assail the Christians out of zeal for their new faith but out of their contempt for Christianity and their wrath over their former fellow Christians. They turn to the faith, from it and against it, like the shuttle of the weaver, as if the whole thing was a game. It is indeed a game of callousness and evil played by those "who make riots, call others Marranos, and justify themselves."[51] Barrientos clearly ascribes to the rebels not religious but the lowest kind of motives: callousness, rascality, and hypocrisy, which serve their attempt to cover their crimes by the sanctimoniousness of religious zeal.

Finally, it is proper to point out that unlike the Relator, Barrientos speaks openly in defense of the converso officials, praising the "temperance and disposition" [for their functions] that "many of them" exhibited in both the ecclesiastic and royal estates[52], and more than the Relator, he censures and condemns both Marquillos and his followers. As for Marquillos, he calls him not only a "prevaricator and public offender," but also a "man of low blood and the manners of a shepherd, notorious for his corrupt life and bad reputation, touched by a hundred thousand crimes,"[53] and altogether an "evil-doer and a heretic."[54] And as for his followers, he directs at them, apart from the harsh criticisms we have already cited, the accusation that they were the source of "many venomous sayings and maledictions against God and against every temperance and virtue." "It would have been better for such people," he adds, "to dig, plow, gather vine shoots and do similar work, just as their fathers, grandfathers and ancestors did, than to use their sacrilegious and wicked tongues against the divine lineage, and thereby injure and defile themselves with their envy and cupidity."[55] The impudence of the low classes, and the foul language they used in criticizing the conversos and their supporters, had evidently shocked and outraged the bishop. At the opening of his pamphlet, as we have seen, he attributed their conduct to the incitement of one man—Marquillos. Nevertheless, both he and the conversos could not fail to realize that, however great was the share of Marcos García in promoting the anti-converso movement, the ideas he espoused did not belong to him alone. This was one reason, we should add, why they did not die with him, but kept gaining followers and supporters among the country's population, and by no means in the low classes only.

Alonso Díaz de Montalvo, the well-known Castilian jurist, was another Old Christian who took the side of the conversos in their struggle against the *Sentencia*. Member of a family whose *hidalguía* could be traced back to the late 11th century,[56] Montalvo was born toward 1405 in Arévalo, where his family had lived since 1088, when the town was reconquered from the Moors. Early in his childhood, he moved with his parents to Huete (in the province of Cuenca),[57] and here Montalvo resided off and on for the greater part of his long life. Both in Arévalo and Huete his father was engaged as a legal consultant,[58] and it was probably from him that Montalvo inherited his interest in and gift for jurisprudence. He studied law and theology at Salamanca, where he may have met Lope de Barrientos, the incumbent professor of theology, and perhaps it was Barrientos who put him in touch with Fernán Díaz de Toledo, the Relator, who was one of the leading jurists of his time. Like Barrientos,[59] Díaz formed a high opinion of Montalvo's juridical abilities, while Montalvo's own attitude toward Fernán Díaz was one of lasting admiration.[60] It was no doubt thanks to these connections that Montalvo was appointed judge in several Castilian towns and *corregidor* in Baeza and Murcia[61]; and it was due to his reputation as jurist that the Relator asked him to join the group of counselors who met in Fuensalida in May 1453 to pass judgment on Alvaro de Luna.[62]

Following Alvaro's death and the appointment of Barrientos as first arbiter of the administration, Montalvo became governor of the Order of Santiago, *oidor* of the king and member of the Royal Council.[63] Retaining these positions during Enrique IV's reign, Montalvo also served in Enrique's administration as *asistente* of Toledo (in 1461 and again in 1463) and governor of the Order of Santiago.[64] In 1476, under the Catholic Kings, he resigned from his functions at Court and retired to his home in Huete, where he intended to devote himself to the completion of his studies on various juridical subjects. In 1480 he added to these undertakings the preparation of a corpus of the royal ordinances of Castile—a task with which he was entrusted by King Ferdinand and the Cortes of Toledo (1480) and which took him four years to complete.[65] He died in 1499. In the following year there appeared in Salamanca Montalvo's commentary on the *Fuero Real*, his most important juridical work, in which he incorporated his treatise on the converso question written in 1449.[66]

Both by virtue of its author and its date, the treatise must be of special interest to anyone pursuing the fortunes of the conversos in the middle of the 15th century. But before reviewing it, we must clear up a certain doubt raised by Fermín Caballero, Montalvo's learned biographer. Caballero believed that the name Díaz, which forms part of our jurist's surname, may have come to him, or rather to his father (Gonzalo Díaz de Montalvo), through marriage with the family of the Relator, Fernán Díaz de Toledo.[67] If this were true, it could help explain Montalvo's strong defense of the conversos and make the work he wrote on their behalf another converso apology. The conjecture, however, lacks a sound basis, and as Caballero himself admitted, he found no concrete evidence to support it.[68] It is certainly unnecessary and far-fetched to assume (in order to explain the name Díaz in his surname) that Montalvo's father married into the Relator's family, when Arevalo was the seat of the Díazes who, together with the Montalvos, were one of the six most illustrious noble families of that town. Also for another reason it is hard to accept Caballero's conjecture.

Montalvo tells us that he wrote his tract on the conversos at the order of King Juan II.[69] However, if he had been a converso, there would hardly have been any need for the King to impose on him such a task. An appeal by the Relator and the bishop of Burgos, it seems, would have been enough, in that state of emergency, to induce Montalvo to write the needed tract. Nor would his work appear so vital as to warrant the King's intervention. After all, New Christian opinions had already been written by Don Alonso de Cartagena and Don Alvarez de Toledo, and another one was being prepared at the time by Cardinal Torquemada.[70] Evidently, the Relator looked for a *non*-converso jurist who might substantiate the converso claims. It occurred to him that Montalvo, who in all probability revealed to him his views on the Toledan events, could offer that important public support; but apparently he was not at all certain that Montalvo would agree to be involved. In order not to risk a rejection, he asked the King to suggest to Montalvo that he write an opinion on the *Sentencia-Estatuto,* being sure that Montalvo would not decline the King's offer or procrastinate in fulfilling the assignment. This is, we believe, how the Old Christian Montalvo came to write the tract.[71]

It may be assumed that, when he wrote his opinion, Montalvo was not entirely a free agent. He was a royal official (in 1448 he was *corregidor* of Murcia) and he knew full well that his advancement in the administration depended on the goodwill of his friends at Court, among whom the Relator was perhaps the most important. One may further assume that as a practical man, who had never exhibited special courage,[72] Montalvo may have chosen to offer a judgment on the conversos that would please his royal patrons. This was, after all, the kind of stand he took during the trial of Alvaro de Luna. Nevertheless, it must be recognized that Montalvo was jealous of his reputation as a jurist and, when his vital interests were not jeopardized, protected it as much as he could. Thus, many years after the trial of Alvaro and after the death of the Relator and King Juan II, he sought to correct, or compensate for, the moral weakness and servility he had exhibited during that trial by expressing a sharp opinion against Alvaro's execution in his commentary on the *Partidas*.[73] He could as easily have shelved his statement on the conversos, rather than include it in his gloss on the *Fuero Real*, which appeared during the height of the Inquisition's activity and certainly could not add to his popularity.[74] He may have also revised his essay, so as to render it less offensive to the anti-converso point of view. Nevertheless, he did nothing of the kind. Consequently, we conclude that insofar as the conversos were concerned, Montalvo's published judgment agreed with his beliefs.

There is no doubt that before writing his paper, Montalvo discussed its theme and content with both the Relator and the bishop of Burgos. Several ideas in Montalvo's work are also found in the Instruction of the Relator and in Cartagena's *Defensorium*. Even the title of his tract, "The Unity of the Faithful,"[75] is similar to that of Cartagena's work: "A Defense of Christian Unity." It is possible, therefore, that some of his arguments were projections of the thinking of his converso counselors. On the whole, however, Montalvo's work is an independent creation, a product of his own inquiry into the subject and his own conclusions. It is highly technical in style and presentation, consisting for the most part of references and quotations; nevertheless, it conveys a clear message and a set of strong arguments.

Montalvo begins his criticism of the Toledans with sharp rebukes of their views on the conversos.[76] From his summary of these views, it appears clear that the Toledans considered all New Christians "damned forever"—that is, *incapable* of becoming true Christians and therefore utterly unqualified to assume public office or ecclesiastic authority.[77] In Montalvo's judgment, such a notion is grotesque since it is opposed to Christian doctrine and to the most evident facts. For the conversos are *sincere* Christians, truly converted to the faith of Christ; and any attempt, such as that of the Toledans, to make these "faithful" appear as "infidels" is "detestable" and, in fact, "heretical."[78]

As Montalvo sees it, the Toledan innovators, who seek to separate the Old Christians from the New, hark back to the enmity that in ancient times divided Jews from gentiles—an enmity for which there is no room in the Church. That enmity stemmed from the differences in worship and religious belief between the two peoples. But Christ called to Himself both the Jews and the gentiles, and those who came to Him accepted *His* teachings and abandoned their own faiths and forms of worship. With no religious barrier between them, the old enmity naturally disappeared, and all faithful were united under Christ's banner. This was, indeed, Christ's objective, and anyone who acts against it—who seeks to introduce, with brazen falsehoods, a religious division in Christian ranks—must be considered a schismatic.[79]

But not only religiously can no difference be maintained between converts to Christianity from the Israelites and the gentiles. Also when viewed from other standpoints, they cannot be seen as disparate. Thus, if their ancestry is conceived in a broad sense, they do not differ in their ancestry, either; for they are all "sons of Abraham," either from Ishmael, the son of the female slave, or from Esau, otherwise known as Edom, or from Jacob his brother, who is also called Israel."[80] Nor do they differ in blame for Christ's Passion. "For although the Jews unjustly accused Him, the Gentiles, who had jurisdiction and power *(jurisdictio et imperium),* condemned Christ to death perversely and wickedly." Moreover, both Jews and gentiles "derided and insulted Him, as one can read in the story of the Passion"; and it was because of the ignorance of both the Jews and gentiles that members of both groups crucified Him. Indeed, the Lord made this clear during His Passion when, hanging on the Cross, he prayed for his crucifiers: "Father, forgive them, for they know not what they do" (Luke 23.34).[81]

And just as Jews and gentiles do not differ in the responsibility for the Passion, they do not differ in the benefits which the Passion conferred on them. For Christ suffered for the whole of mankind and opened the doors of salvation to the entire human race. And what was meant by such terms as mankind or the human race was not only the generation of the Passion but all the generations to come. This is apparent from Acts 2.39: "For the promise is to you, and to your children, and to all that are afar off, even as many as the Lord our God shall call." And anyone who denies this major Christian postulate is clearly a heretic.[82]

Nor is there any difference between the converts from Judaism and those from gentilehood insofar as the impact of baptism is concerned. For they are all freed by baptism from their individual sins, and are all reborn and receive God's grace. Has not the Apostle said in I Corinthians (12.13): "For we are all baptized into one body, whether we be Jews or gentiles"? And has he not said the same in Galatians (3.27–29): "For as many of you as have been baptized into Christ have put on Christ. There is neither Greek, nor Jew etc."? It is groundless, therefore—and indeed nonsensical—to claim, as the Toledans do, that there are two kinds of baptism, one which was provided in ancient times and one which lost much of its original effect, such as was administered to the New Christians. The Apostle exposes this absurdity when he says in Ephesians (4.4–6): "There is one body, one spirit, one Lord, one faith, *one baptism.*"[83] Obviously, we are all called to the *same* baptism, just as we are called to the same faith and the same God. Hence, "the effect of the power of Holy baptism is as great today as it was in the time of Peter, the first of the Apostles . . . and to assert otherwise is a manifest heresy."[84]

Montalvo also touches on another reason given by the Toledans for their differentiation between the Old Christians and the New. They say that those who came recently to the faith cannot claim the same rights as those who joined it earlier, since the latter deserve a more elevated status. But that this argument is false is evident from the teaching of Christ Himself. For "the Lord gave the same amount of pay to those who came late to work in His vineyard as to those who came early." Hence, "the New are being saved equally with the Old without any difference."[85] The same is indicated also by the epistle that Peter addressed to the newcomers to the faith from the "strangers" who were scattered in various countries. They evidently came to Christ after many Jews had already come to Him and constituted the majority of the Church. And yet he designated those newcomers with the same titles that were used to describe the original members: "a chosen race, a royal priesthood and a holy nation" (I Peter 2.9–10), all of which indicates that they received equal faith with the Old believers, were raised to the latter's elevated status, and regarded as their equals in every other respect.[86]

But apart from refuting the above contention, which posits differences between the Jewish and gentile converts, Montalvo took up the more radical charge that Israel was under a divine damnation, which excludes it from Christian salvation altogether, and therefore its so-called converts to Christianity cannot be compared to true converts from the gentiles in any respect and in any degree. Those who argued thus made much of the passage in Deuteronomy 32, in which Moses spoke harshly of the Jews, of a passage in Paul's epistle to Titus (1.4–11), in which the Apostle rebuked Jewish converts, and, above all, of Psalm 95. 10–11, in which God swore never to bring Israel to "His rest." Montalvo confutes each of these contentions. Paul's castigations of Jewish converts to Christianity in Titus 1 were directed, says Montalvo, against those of their number who departed from the right way—i.e., who became *bad* converts—but he also highly praised the *good* ones among them, as one can see from his epistle to the Colossians (4.10–11), where he says of a number of converts from Judaism: "These only are my fellow workers unto the Kingdom of God which have been a comfort unto me." As for the passage in Psalm 95, Montalvo says that in his epistle to the Hebrews (caps. 3–4), the Apostle has already explained its true meaning when he said that it referred to those Hebrews who died in the desert because of their incredulity; it did *not* refer to the believers among them, either in that generation or in the coming ones. The believers *were* destined to enter God's "rest," as Paul himself states in that discussion. Finally, as for the chastisements of Moses (in Deut. 32), he indeed reproached the Jews for their sins, but he also made it known that God loved them as a father; and later, before his death, Moses blessed Israel, completing his blessing with the words: "Blessed are thou, Israel! What nation is like unto you, saved in God!" (Deut. 33.29).[87]

Thus, the authorities cited by the Toledans to prove that Israel was damned offer no evidence to that effect. On the contrary, both the Old and the New Testaments contain many definite and unambiguous assurances that Israel *will* be "saved," which means of course converted to Christ. Isaiah prophesied this when he said: "Israel has been saved in the Lord, with an eternal salvation" (45.17), and the Apostle said it in Romans 11.26. This is also the formal belief of the Church which is shared by all good Christians. When the Cortes of Alcalá de Henares (1348) decreed that the Jews could buy land in Spain, it justified that decree by referring to the prophecies that "the Jews were to be converted and be saved."[88] In fact, Montalvo states, the salvation of the Jews has not remained a mere promise. Many Israelites experienced it in the past, and it is being fulfilled daily in the present.[89]

Having settled these theological questions, Montalvo felt free to come to grips with the practical side of the problem that confronted him. Since the New Christians "do not differ from the Old ones either in faith or in salvation or in any other thing" that concerns their religious condition, wherein can possibly lie the justification for discriminating against them in civil life? Could their national or racial origin, which is different from that of the Old Christians, be the justifying cause? Montalvo rejects both possibilities as incompatible with Christian law and teachings. As for *nationhood*, Christianity does not see in national differences any reason for preference or rejection. God entrusted the keys of the Kingdom not to an ultramontane or citramontane person, but to a Galilean; and Pope Evaristus was the son of a Jew who belonged to the Greek nation. Similarly, *race* is not a yardstick for moral judgment to Christianity. "Jephthah," said Jerome, "who is counted by the Apostle among the holy men, was the son of a harlot," and Esau, the son of Rebecca and Isaac, who were obviously God-fearing people, was "rough in body and in soul, like good wheat which degenerated into wild oats and darnel." Moreover, Jerome makes a cardinal statement that negates the value of both race and nation. "Our Lord Jesus Christ," he says, "wanted to be born not only from an alien (i.e., the Moabite Ruth), but also from an adulterous mixture (i.e., Tamar and Judah),"[90] which shows that origins should not enter the evaluation of one's person. The obvious conclusion that must be drawn from all this with respect to the conversos is: the New Christians should not be rejected by the Old because they stem from the "Israelitic nation" and an unfaithful people. They should be judged on their own merits only.

As for the merits of the conversos, Montalvo's views are not subject to doubt. "These are people," he says, "who came from a great tribulation" and "washed their garments white with the blood of the lamb." Montalvo wishes to indicate by these words that the group he referred to (the converts from "that nation") is not only marked by its evident faithfulness, but also by its high moral standards. This is why there emerged from its ranks in "our times," as in the past, many "virtuous" and "pious" prelates, who were approved for their positions not only by their learning, but also by their way of life.[91] And why should such people be denied public offices? Could there be any other reason for this discrimination save the fact that they are considered aliens? But the "divine moral law, which is immutable" stipulates clearly in Exodus 12.48–49: "And when a stranger shall sojourn within thee . . . one law shall be to him that is home-born and unto the stranger that sojourns among you." The same is also stated in Exodus 22.20: "And if a stranger sojourn with thee in your land, ye shall not do him wrong." He "shall be unto you as the home-born among you, and thou shall love him as thyself." This agrees also with what the Lord said through Ezekiel (47.21–22) with regard to the division of the land: "The strangers that sojourn among you, who shall beget children among you, shall be unto you as the home-born among the children of Israel" and "they shall divide the inheritance with you in the midst of the tribes of Israel." Therefore, if the Lord wanted the alien and the stranger who comes to the faith to be received and be counted among the sons of Israel, why do these schismatics condemn him to be separated from the company of the faithful and thereby divide the unity of the faith; and why, "while God commanded that he be loved, they hate him, when they are to hate not people but their sins only?"[92]

This is of course a rhetorical question. Montalvo has no doubt about the answer; but before stating it *expressis verbis,* he finds it necessary to dispute the remaining reasons offered by the Toledans in justification of their stand. And first he touches on the question of the "Judaizers," which was made so much of by the Toledans. Like other apologists for the conversos, he admits that "some people of the Israelitic nation may fall into some heresy or superstition," but—again like those apologists—he argues that such lapses should not serve as reason to label the whole group as heretical. Had this been the right attitude to take, all Christian societies would have been viewed as heretical, since all of them contained heretics from time to time. "We should not abandon the Lord's threshing floor," he says, "because of the chaff; we should not break the divine net and lose all the fishes caught in it because some of those fishes were found to be bad."[93] The argument seems to indicate that the phenomenon he had in mind—or rather the development he considered possible—could involve only a fringe of the Marrano group (the "chaff," the occasional "bad fishes"), but it also indicates that he sought to refute the opposite view held by the Toledans. The Toledans "virtually assert," he says, "that if some part of the Israelitic race appears to have reverted to the Jewish rites, or relapsed into heresy," one may gather from it that "all the members of that race followed the same tendency."[94] It is here, in the attempt to stamp *all* new Christians as heretics and Judaizers, that Montalvo, like Torquemada, sees clear proof of the worthlessness of the Toledans' accusations. For what they claim is a manifest untruth, denied by all that is known and observed.

Montalvo then turns to the legal authorities on which the Toledans base their claims. The reference is to three enactments that deal specifically with converts from Judaism: one civil, one canonic, and the third—a royal privilege given to Toledo by King Alfonso VII.

The civil law is included in the 7th century Spanish code *(Liber Judicum)*, which states that "Jews, whether baptized or not, are forbidden to testify against Christians."[95] Montalvo objects to any reliance on this law, both because it is lacking in authority and because it is not observed in Spain; it has been superseded by a contrary law *(Partidas*, vii, tit. 24, 1.6.), which does not even mention it. But even if that law were authoritative, it means by "baptized Jews" false converts, who blaspheme God and guard the Jewish rites, which is clear when it says: "if he who lies" and "acts deceitfully against the faith."[96]

The canon law referred to is the sixty-fifth decree of the Fourth Toledan Council, which prohibits "Jews, or those who are of the Jews, to assume public office."[97] In Montalvo's judgment, any way it is interpreted, this law does not speak of Christians or sincere converts and therefore cannot apply to the conversos.[98] And as for the royal law—the Alfonsine privilege—it must be rejected, to begin with, because it leans on the civil and canon laws just mentioned, which are not applicable to the conversos at all; second, because it was contradicted by the laws of the *Partidas;* and third, because it was entirely annulled by the privilege granted by King Enrique III to the effect that "none of the faithful who has been recently converted be repelled under this kind of pretext [i.e., their Jewish origin] from public offices or from other privileges that are enjoyed by other Christians."[99]

It follows that the Toledans had nothing to rely on in advocating their policy against the conversos except heretical notions, inapplicable laws, and libelous accusations. It is with such means, however, that they are conducting a riotous, defamatory and ruinous campaign against a group which seeks only to live in peace and work hard for commendable objectives. What is it, then, that moves these unruly people to make such groundless claims, create such a turbulence, and provoke so much hostility against the conversos? Montalvo's answer is unequivocal: it is their great hatred of the conversos—a hatred kindled by jealousy of the gains, social and economic, made by the New Christians. "Blinded by cupidity and full of greed and avarice," they seek to destroy the conversos economically, so that they may have no partners in the country's mundane goods; and "inflamed by their desire for power" and by the "arrogance of domination," they oppose the conversos' occupancy of offices, so as to have no "partakers" in the governance of the republic.[100] They realize of course that there is no moral basis for either their intentions or their claims. But in a "sacrilegious and reckless daring" they cover their jealousy, hate and malice with a pretended zeal for the faith. In fact, they have no such zeal at all; "they lie when they claim to be Christians," for actually they are enemies of Christianity—"wolves" seeking to tear the faith apart and thrive on its torn pieces.[101]

Montalvo's opinion of the Toledans betrays no sign of doubt or ambiguity. In his book, the Toledans are plainly "wicked," "crooked," "ignorant," "corrupt," and "sick"—sick in their desire to destroy the conversos, whom they see as standing in their way. To him, they provide a spectacle of false Christians, who accuse sincere neophytes as false converts, and of heretics, who deny almost every Christian doctrine and accuse true believers of heresy. We have seen how, in his opening remarks on the Toledans, he presents each of their views as heretical; and this is what he stresses again and again in his summarized opinion about them. "They are heretics," he says, "because they understand Scripture in a sense different from what the Holy Spirit tells us and because they teach a perverse dogma against the faith." They are heretics because they persist in following "pestilential and deadly doctrines" and because they "try to defend their false and crooked judgments with pertinacious animosity and audacious presumption." Above all, they are heretics because they are schismatics. God, however, hates him who sows discord among brothers (Proverbs 6. 14–15), and "brothers are all Christians."[102]

Montalvo, however, does not limit his criticisms to these sharp denunciations. He also proposes a counteractivity to be undertaken by the leaders of the Church. "In order that the above detestable and execrable errors be not propagated further, and the hearts of the faithful be not perverted," the prelates, he says, are necessarily in duty bound to extirpate those errors from the orbit of the Church. He understands that this goal will not be reached easily, without undergoing a violent public storm. But he sees no way of avoiding this hardship. He communicates his thoughts about what should be done by citing Jeremiah 23. 19–20: "Behold, a whirlwind of the Lord is gone forth in fury; it shall fall grievously upon the head of the wicked; the anger of the Lord shall not pass until He have executed and performed the thoughts of his heart."[103]

When Montalvo wrote these words in the summer of 1449, he must have been sure that this was the course that Spain's ecclesiastic leadership *would* take—obviously, with the full support of the King. Things did not turn out as he expected. Fifty years later, just before his death, when his work was about to be submitted for publication, he evidently did not change his mind about the course his country *should* have taken in dealing with the anti-converso movement.

VII. The Historiographic Evidence: The Crónicas of Juan II

Except for the major converso apologies and the main anti-Marrano writings, the 15th-century Castilian chronicles produced before the founding of the Inquisition are no doubt the most important set of sources for the study of various fundamental aspects of the Marrano problem in Spain. Not only do they help remove doubts raised by the controversy over the Marranos' Christianity, but they clarify some crucial stages in the conflict between the conversos and their foes. Above all, they help establish the truth about the positions the Marranos took on many issues and understand the motives that impelled them to use the tactics they employed in repelling attacks.

Of the extant six chronicles of the period of Juan II, one mentions the conversos only in isolated places which have already been dealt with in the foregoing. We refer to the history of Juan II's reign written by Alvar García de Santa María. Another, the *Refundición de la Crónica del Halconero,* does not deal with the conversos at all. The following discussion, therefore, will be limited to the remarks concerning the Marranos in the remaining four chronicles, beginning with the *Crónica del Halconero,* which is the oldest of them all.

I. THE HALCONERO

I

The *Crónica del Halconero de Juan II*—or, as it is commonly called, the *Halconero*—was written by Pero Carrillo de Huete, official chronicler of the realm, who was also Chief Falconer *(Halconero mayor)* of Juan II. As a member of the King's inner circle, Carrillo was well informed on all major developments in the kingdom of Castile. For this reason the information he imparts must be considered firsthand, and his account gains added credence from his habit of recording events as they occurred.

The source of his strength was also that of his weakness. As Court chronicler and the king's confidant, Carrillo could not help giving an account which was slanted in favor of the King and his minister. Preceded by Alvar García de Santa María, who served as Court chronicler until 1435,[1] Carrillo was appointed to the post at the height of Alvaro de Luna's career. No such sensitive and vital position would have been entrusted at the time to *any* person without the consent, and probably the choice, of the powerful Constable. This leads us to the conclusion that Alvaro de Luna regarded Carrillo as his actual or potential partisan.

Nevertheless, within the bounds of his loyalties, Carrillo tried to stick to the facts and compose as truthful an account as possible. It was his habit to present both sides of a case and accompany each claim with supporting documents. He generally allowed the facts to speak for themselves, but occasionally felt impelled to express an opinion; and his judgment, on the whole, was fair and sound. He was a straightforward, common-sense man, not cunning but far from naive. He knew where evil and ambition lay, and he would not be deceived by the noble motives with which they were often camouflaged. Such is our impression of this man who left us his *Crónica de Juan II*.

Unfortunately, his work has not reached us in its original form. Each of its extant versions seems to differ greatly from the original because of editorial deletions and additions. The version that is the subject of this discussion seems to be closest to the original[2]; and the same goes for the evidence it contains about the conversos.

Although Carrillo's story of the reign includes the period covered by his predecessor, that is, the years 1420–1435, we find nothing in that part that seems to have any bearing upon the lives or problems of the conversos, save their mention (in a document cited by the author) as objects of a massacre (planned but not executed) in the aborted rebellion of Count Fadrique of Aragon.[3] In his annals of the period 1435–1448, Carrillo does not mention the conversos at all. But substantial data about them we encounter when we come to the rebellion of 1449.

The *Halconero*, however, presents these data in a peculiar manner. In describing Sarmiento's rule of Toledo, he tells us that the persecution then launched in the city was directed against those who were opposed to Sarmiento, his plans and his authority. It therefore appears as a personal persecution—i.e., motivated by Sarmiento's personal interests—although justified by a political excuse—namely, by the claim that the people he punished were averse to the city's struggle for its liberties and thus placed themselves in the position of traitors. Not by a single word does the *Crónica* suggest that the chief victims of Sarmiento's reign of terror were New Christians; nor does it hint in any way that a *religious* reason was behind the persecution. In discussing the expulsions that occurred later, when the King was approaching Toledo with his army, he says that Sarmiento "decided to oust from the city a large number of people who were suspect in his eyes"[4]—that is, suspect as liable to act for the King against the rebels' interests. Obviously, the chronicler suggests that by expelling them, Sarmiento sought to strengthen his hold on the city; and thus the expulsions, like the earlier punishments, stemmed from a political motive. Here, too, we have no inkling that most or any of the expelled were Marranos.

When the Marranos are at last mentioned in the *Halconero*, it is not in the chronicler's narrative of the events but in the text of Sarmiento's Petition to the King, which the chronicler reproduced in its entirety.[5] This document, as we have noted, is replete with complaints and accusations against the Marranos.[6] But it is strange, to say the least, that prior to presenting it, the chronicler does not give us even a hint as to the part that the Marrano issue played in the rebellion. Thus all the charges against the Marranos, which form a major part of the Petition, appear to the reader entirely unrelated to the chronicler's preceding account. Nor does the chronicler comment on these charges following the presentation of that document. He simply proceeds with his narration of events: the King's refusal to accept Sarmiento's demands; the approach of Prince Enrique, the King's son, to Toledo; the lifting of the siege by the royal army; and the agreement reached by Sarmiento and the Prince, according to which the latter and his men were allowed to enter the city.

The *Halconero* does not present the text of this agreement but a summary of its main terms. Four of these terms relate to the conversos, but their special place in the relevant events is more concealed than revealed.

According to the *Halconero*, the agreement stated that "all the goods which rightly or wrongly he [Sarmiento] has taken and robbed from the citizens of Toledo would remain in the possession of Pero Sarmiento and would not be demanded from him at any time."[7] Clearly, the agreement between the rebel and the Prince did not state that Sarmiento "robbed" the citizens of Toledo and that the Prince agreed to this blatant and admitted illegality. The word "robbed" was simply added here by the author, or editor, of this report.

Secondly, according to the *Halconero*, the agreement stipulated that "the deaths, expulsions, evils and harms that he [Sarmiento] caused the citizens of Toledo would be approved and at no time be called to account for."[8] Again, it is clear that the word "evils" *(males)* was not in the original formulation and that it, too, was inserted here by Carrillo or by the editor of his manuscript.

The third paragraph of those we referred to states that the conversos who had been ousted from the city must not be allowed to return to it; that never would they be restored to the offices (and positions of honor) they had occupied; and furthermore, that these offices and positions would be held by Sarmiento's appointees.[9] Outside Sarmiento's Petition to the King, this is the only place in this *crónica* where the conversos are explicitly mentioned as related to the Toledan affair.

Judging by Carrillo's habits of reporting, it is likely that, in the original version of his *crónica*, he presented the agreement between the city and the Prince in its full textual form. Had he chosen to summarize its contents, he would have followed the data he found in the original and would not have injected his own opinions into the summary of the text. Nor would he have any reason to omit all mention of the conversos in the rest of the narrative, as if they did not constitute a paramount issue in the Toledan quarrel, and as if they were not the main subject of the deaths, expulsions and expropriations he referred to. It is also most unlikely that he would totally ignore events that shook the country and were on everybody's lips, such as the enactment of the *Sentencia-Estatuto,* or the unprecedented trials of Judaizers in Toledo which ended with burnings at the stake. We must therefore conclude that the extant *Halconero,* or rather its account of the Toledan outbreak, was the work of a Marrano reviser or abbreviator who believed that it was in the interest of his group to summarize Carrillo's account as he did. Evidently, what he sought to emphasize was that Sarmiento was not only a rebel but a robber, and that the Marranos were persecuted not as Marranos, but simply as loyal subjects of the Crown among the other loyalist elements in the city. They were persecuted for their position in the *political* conflict, or rather for being opposed to Sarmiento, together with other Toledan citizens who were likewise persecuted for no other reason. Consequently, we might conclude from this presentation that there was no special movement or drive in the city against the conversos as such.

It cannot be assumed, of course, that the chronicler Carrillo, who knew very well what was happening in Toledo, wished to lead his reader to this conclusion. Yet this is briefly the position of the *Halconero,* or rather of its available text. We shall now see whether the same attitude prevails in another version of Carrillo's *crónica* that has come down to us in abridged form.

II. THE ABBREVIATION

I

This other version has been preserved in a single manuscript designated by Carriazo the *Abbreviation.*[10] A careful comparison between this manuscript and the *Halconero* leads us to the conclusion that, except for its three opening chapters, which deal with the period of Enrique III, the *Abbreviation* carefully followed the *Halconero,* even though it used a somewhat fuller version than the one at our disposal. Occasionally, therefore, it contains items of information that are not present in the extant *Halconero;* and this is the case with the account it gives us of the Toledan outbreak.

These additions are so minor, however, that they do not materially change the picture given by the extant *Halconero*. Where the picture does change noticeably, and the course of events becomes appreciably clearer, is in those few places where the Abbreviator interpolates data borrowed from other sources or based on his own firsthand knowledge. It is from these interpolations, no less than his deletions and the way he abridged certain relevant passages, that we learn of his own view—or the view he wished to communicate to his readers—about the causes of the Toledan outbreak and their relationship to the Marrano problem.

Thus while the *Halconero* gives us to understand that Pero Sarmiento remained on the fence during the revolutionary outbreak and did not show that his heart was with the rebels, the *Abbreviation* states that Sarmiento "gave the *común* aid" and that it was thanks to this aid that the *común* captured Alvaro's positions in the city.[11] It is possible of course that by this "aid" *(el fauor que les dio)* the author meant merely *moral* encouragement or mere intimation that he, the governor, would not oppose an assault on Alvaro's positions; but if this is what he meant, it is clear that, in his view, this encouragement was enough to make the *común* act. Thus, the author of the *Abbreviation* indicated his disagreement with the *Halconero*'s presentation of the "observer's role" that Sarmiento allegedly played in Toledo in the first stage of the disturbances. Far from being a passive onlooker, Sarmiento, in his opinion, had a major share in the perpetration of the outbreak.

To be sure, immediately following the above statement the Abbreviator reverts to the *Halconero*'s text, asserting that "at that time Sarmiento did not show himself clearly to be in favor" of rebellion,[12] and thus seems to contradict what he himself had just said. But this would be a wrong understanding of his assertions. It is evident that what he meant to say was that Sarmiento did not show himself *overtly and formally* in favor of the rebels (this is how he interpreted the word "clearly" [*claramente*]) in the *Halconero*, but that does not mean that *covertly* and *informally* he did not give them encouragement and aid. That this is indeed what he sought to convey is suggested by his second interpolation into the text. Sarmiento, he tells us, could not take an *open* stand in favor of the rebellion "because he did not have [as yet sufficient] time to accomplish his evil intention."[13] But from this it appears that his "evil intention" was—from the start of the rebellion, and perhaps even earlier—to join the rebels formally and become their leader. One may assume that his behavior in that period was in accord with that intention.

But now we come to the cardinal question: What did Sarmiento seek to accomplish by becoming the rebels' chief? In the answer to this question we again see a difference between the *Halconero* and the *Abbreviation*. According to the *Halconero*, Sarmiento had claims against the King and the Constable and he wanted to use the rebellious city as a means of exerting pressure upon the King to have those claims realized. But the Abbreviator believed that, apart from this, Sarmiento had other purposes. He wanted to rise with the city "in order to do all that he wanted to be done according to what he [actually] did."[14] In other words, what Sarmiento did during the rebellion was not only a means to attain some end that had long been fixed in his mind (the fulfillment of the King's pledge to him), but an end in itself.

Now, what precisely did the Abbreviator allude to when he made his carefully phrased statement about Sarmiento's aims? We shall answer this question with greater assurance if we take a look at the passages in which the *Abbreviation* and the *Halconero* address this point.

Halconero (p. 519)	*Abbreviation* (f. 283a)
. . . and some who wished to oppose this view [i.e., that it was necessary to rebel and persist in the rebellion], were made subject by Sarmiento to such cruel punishments as robberies and exiles, deaths and injuries, that all of those who remained in the city were frightened, so that, with some of them liking what he did and others afraid to express their objection, there was not a man [in the city] who dared utter a word against the will of Pero Sarmiento.	When Pero Sarmiento saw himself well in control of the city and the people *(pueblo),* he ordered the arrest of certain citizens [*ciudadanos*], honored and rich people, because of his great greed to take for himself what was theirs. And he ordered that they be subjected to certain torments, without these people having committed any sin—neither in deed nor in thought. And since the court scribe was of his party and he [himself] was the judge, he subjected some of those people to cruel punishment even though they merited no punishment at all. Then he took their possessions. He also persecuted and exiled other people, saying that they followed Alvaro's instructions. So it happened that while some did [what he ordered them to do] out of love and others out of fear, there was not a man who dared utter a word against the will of Pero Sarmiento.

So, according to the *Halconero,* Sarmiento used harsh measures against *one* segment of the population—i.e., those who opposed the rebellion—while according to the *Abbreviation*, there were *two* groups of people who were victimized by Sarmiento, and the group he mentions first was that of the "honored and rich people" whose properties Sarmiento sought to steal. "Honored and rich," as we know from other sources, is the title that was commonly used for *conversos* when the author did not wish to identify them. Sarmiento imprisoned them, put them to torture (which we also gather from other sources) and, finally, inflicted "cruel punishment" upon some of them (by which was no doubt meant death by fire), his sole motive in doing all this having been to satisfy his "great greed."

Then the Abbreviator mentions the second group, which was persecuted and arrested on the alleged grounds that its members "followed the orders" of Alvaro. Significantly, in this instance the Abbreviator indicates the nature of the charge raised against this group—i.e., the political charge which is also mentioned in the *Halconero*. In contrast, he gave no indication of the charges made against the *first* group, although he emphasized, time and again, that these charges were false, that the punishment was uncalled for, and that the people so penalized committed no sin—*either in deed or in thought* (referring, most likely, to the crimes of heresy, for which this exoneration—in deed and in thought—was especially fitting). Thus, the accusations leveled at the conversos were, according to the Abbreviator, artificially concocted, mendaciously presented by a crooked scribe who was Sarmiento's follower or aide, and determined juridically by Sarmiento himself—all for one reason only: to enable Sarmiento to confiscate for himself the possessions of his innocent victims.

We can now understand what the Abbreviator meant when he said that Sarmiento joined the rebels "in order to do all that he wanted to do according to what he [actually] did." One of the motives—and not the least weighty—that prompted him to take the road he followed was his desire to take for himself the conversos' enormous wealth. He could do so only if he became master of the city, and he could become its master only if he joined the rebels as their leader. This in fact he did. Then, to cover up his designs and justify his planned robberies, he launched a campaign against the conversos consisting of charges that were all groundless, but useful for him to attain his ends. Thus the Abbreviator bears witness to the worth—or rather worthlessness—of the accusations against the conversos with respect to their religious attitudes; but he does it in a roundabout way, in heavily veiled and guarded statements and without mentioning the conversos at all. In fact, had we to rely only on *him* to learn what happened in Toledo, we would be unable even to guess that there was a persecution of conversos in the city and that this persecution was based on pretexts (or, according to the author, sham accusations) that the conversos had committed not only political but also religious crimes.

II

This treatment of the converso issue is apparent also in other parts of the *Abbreviation,* and is especially evident in its presentation of the Petition that the rebels submitted to the King.

We have seen that the editor of the *Halconero* preserved the Petition in its original form, as he did not dare change a formal document. The Abbreviator was obviously more audacious and much less respectful of documentary truth. While he did not omit the Petition in its entirety, he deleted whole sentences and passages from it and added certain designations and phrases in order to conceal their true meaning. All of these changes, without exception, related to the conversos, and they show what this editor sought to accomplish by his arbitrary revisions.

Thus, he leaves almost untouched the statement in which Alvaro is accused by the petitioners of having placed "infidels and heretics" in the offices of government and administration of justice, but later on, when the petitioners state that he farmed the King's incomes, tributes and taxes to "the said *heretical and infidel people,*" the Abbreviator replaced this designation by "people who were to his liking."[15] There was obviously no reason to introduce this change in a document formally submitted to the King unless the Abbreviator was moved to do so by some overriding consideration. That consideration could only be this: he wished to blur the identification of the tax farmers with the "heretics and infidels"—an identification which, in this context, could leave no doubt as to the objects of the denunciation. As long as the accusation was general—i.e., that among the numerous officials of the government there were some "infidels and heretics"—the reader could not clearly identify these officials with a specific group. But when the denunciations of "heresy and infidelity" referred specifically to tax collectors—most of whom were Jews and conversos—any knowledgeable reader would easily conclude *who* those "infidels and heretics" were. This is what the *Abbreviation* sought to prevent.

That this was the sole intent of the Abbreviator, and that he was ready to go to any length to fulfil it by altering, mutilating and abbreviating the original, and also by deleting whole passages from the Petition, is evident from his whole revision of the manuscript and the careful thought he gave to every expression that might cast a shadow of disrepute on the conversos, especially as deviators from the Christian faith. A comparison of the revisions of the rebels' Petition in the *Halconero* and the *Abbreviation* will make this patently clear:

Halconero (p. 523)	*Abbreviation* (f. 283)
For it is notorious that the said Alvaro de Luna, your Constable, has publicly defended and received—and is defending and receiving—the conversos of the lineage of the Jews of your kingdoms, those who have been found to be for the most part infidels and heretics, have Judaized—and are Judaizing.	For it is notorious that the said Alvaro de Luna, your Constable, has publicly defended and received the conversos of the lineage of the Jews of your kingdoms and dominions, who are for the most part his partisans.

Thus, the passage in the Petition that defines the conversos as "Judaizers," "apostates," and "blasphemers of Christ[16]—and makes it appear that it is they who were the source of the heresies in the kingdom—is omitted by the Abbreviator and replaced by a brief assertion to the effect that the Master of Santiago supported the conversos "because they were for the most part his partisans."

In like manner he deleted the references to "heretics" and "infidels" which he found in other statements of the Petition or replaced the word "heretics" with the words "bad people," so that Alvaro, for instance, was described as a "receiver and protector of bad people" *(malos)* instead of a "receiver and protector of heretics *(ereges)*," as the text of the Petition actually says.[17] What led the Abbreviator to make this change was obviously his desire to protect the conversos against a dangerous accusation which, in all likelihood, he considered calumnious—a desire that made him overlook his own faults in trying to fight one falsehood with another.

Thus, in the whole *crónica* of Juan II, according to the version of the Abbreviator, the conversos are mentioned only twice: once in the Petition of the Toledans and once in the text of the town crier who announced the judgment of the conspirators in Seville in 1434.[18] Both cases occur in *formal* documents. In the latter instance (relating to Seville), no blame is attached to the conversos; they were singled out to be killed for no fault of their own, but to satisfy the desires of criminal conspirators who planned to rise against the King; in the former case (relating to Toledo) their fault was, again, according to the Abbreviator, simply their political support of Alvaro—i.e., of the King's administration; and this, of course, from the Abbreviator's standpoint, was no fault at all. But outside these two *official* documents, the conversos are not mentioned even once. And seeing that the Abbreviator did not hesitate to mutilate even large portions of official documents, we can safely conclude that he systematically obliterated the name of the conversos *wherever* they were mentioned in the *Halconero's own* account—that is, when the *Halconero* reported the events in his *own* words, or when he did not quote verbatim documents taken from the royal archives.

III

When was the *Abbreviation* composed? According to Juan de Mata Carriazo, not much before 1500. Carriazo arrived at this conclusion on the basis of one passage in the last chapter of the *Abbreviation*, which deals with the burial of Alvaro de Luna. It reads as follows:

> There [i.e., at the place of Alvaro's execution in Valladolid] his head and body remained for three days before they were interred by members of the *Misericordia* brotherhood in a church which is called . . .[19] After many days[20] the body was removed from that place and taken to the monastery of San Francisco of Valladolid. And after many [additional] days both the body and the head were transferred, most honorably, to the chapel which he ordered to be built in the Great Church of Santa María de Toledo.[21]

Now, says Carriazo, since that transfer took place after 1488–1489, "when the first duchess of the Infantado, Doña Maria de Luna, ordered new sepulchers to be built for her parents, the *Abbreviation* could have been completed only after that date."[22] This conclusion, however, would seem reasonable if we had to consider only the passage cited. As matters stand, it cannot be squared with some of the data we have cited above.

Carriazo concludes that the *Abbreviation* was prepared by a "Toledan Marrano."[23] That he was a Marrano is certain, that he was a Toledan is likely; but beyond that we cannot say anything. Carriazo, it seems, came to his conclusion because he believed that the Abbreviator showed great familiarity with what happened in Toledo in 1449. But such data and opinions as we find in the *Abbreviation* were doubtless shared by many Marranos, inside and outside Toledo. Informed conversos in the Court of Juan II, or intimates of Alonso de Cartagena, for instance, must have communicated to many other conversos what they knew and thought of these crucial events.

This, however, can apply only to contemporaries of the Toledan rebellion. Those who flourished about the year 1500 could not avail themselves of such sources. Carriazo, who no doubt considered this matter, thought therefore that only a Toledan, who derived his information from local traditions, could exhibit about the year 1500 such detailed knowledge of the events in question. But this assumption does not help much in explaining the Abbreviator's revisions.

For apart from the close familiarity with details (such as those touching the collection of the loan) which does not seem likely even for a Toledan writing about the year 1500, we must also ask what possible interest the writer and his audience could then have in such details. What, for instance, could induce an abbreviator in 1500, after so much water had flowed under the bridge, to state unequivocally—*quite unlike his source*—that Sarmiento aided the rebels from the outset and helped them capture the city's gates and towers?[24] And what could have possibly moved an abbreviator—assuming he wrote about 1500—to include in this summary such an item as that to get the loan, the rich citizens were required to pay ten doblas and the poor two—an item which is found in no other source dealing with the Toledan rebellion. Such details would be of no interest to an abbreviator who shared Carrillo's view that the rebellion was caused by the quarrel over the privileges—a quarrel which was of secondary importance in the face of the national emergency that Alvaro spoke of and would clearly put him in the right. On the other hand, the attention paid by the Abbreviator to the manner in which the loan was collected, and especially to the exaction of money from the poor, *"who could not pay"* and *"therefore rebelled,"*[25] suggests that he ascribed responsibility for the rebellion to Alvaro de Luna, whom he seems to have considered a ruthless ruler lacking in common sense and proper judgment. Such differences of opinion were of course of interest to the people who lived at the time of the disturbances and actively participated in the current controversy. To them the implications of the different data were almost self-evident. But fifty years after the events? Who would draw from those data the various deductions the Abbreviator wished his readers to draw and, above all, that the conversos, whom he does not even mention in his account, were not to blame for the rebellion?

To defend the conversos' religious reputation and remove from them the stigma of heresy would of course be of interest for a converso in 1500 (i.e., at the time of the Inquisition) no less, and even more, than in any preceding period. But would he go about it the way the Abbreviator did? He might have omitted some damaging passages from the *Halconero*'s text on the assumption that he did not consider them important enough to be included in an abridgment. But to make such omissions on so large a scale—and on top of this to falsify an official document that contains an all-out attack on the conversos, and one which accuses them of religious perversion—would be quite a different matter. A converso writing around the year 1500 would not be likely to commit an act of this kind. For by that time the misrepresentation of such charges as those enumerated in the Petition could be construed as an attempt to *conceal* a heresy, whose existence was attested not only by that document but also by the Inquisition. By easy deduction the Abbreviator could be accused of aiding and abetting the heresy movement, and thus his admittedly mendacious revision—and, in consequence, deceptive presentation—could serve as the core of a broader accusation that could possibly be built against him. Obviously, no abbreviator in the 1450s or 1460s would be exposed to dangers of this kind.

For all these reasons we believe that the *Abbreviation* was prepared within a decade or so after the Toledan riots. Replete with data, issues and allusions that could be known or understood only to contemporaries—and, more particularly, to those for whom the riots and their aftermath were a stirring personal experience—it could not have been composed at a time far removed from the events. Consequently, we conclude that the sentence referring to Alvaro's burial in Toledo was added by one of the later copyists, who was tempted to contribute something to the work.

III. THE CRÓNICA OF JUAN II

I

The largest and by far the most informative document we have about the period of Juan II is the *Crónica* of that reign generally attributed to the 15th-century historian Pérez de Guzmán. Actually, Guzmán was only *one* of the editors of this *Crónica,* which was shaped and reshaped by several revisers; and the problem of the editorship of this work calls for a special critical discussion. Here we shall confine ourselves to a few observations concerning the second part of the *Crónica,* covering the period of 1434–1453. For it is this part that includes all the references of the *Crónica* to the Marranos.

There is no reason to doubt the assertion, first made by Galíndez de Carvajal, that this part of the *Crónica de Juan II* is based on a version of the *Halconero*[26]; but the question is: which version?

Besides the abridgment of the original *Halconero* (known today plainly as *the Halconero*) and its *Abbreviation* (with which we have dealt), we possess also a *Refundición del Halconero*—a revised text of the original chroncile which came down to us incomplete: it ends in the year 1439. It is based on a broader account of the reign than the one reflected in the extant *Halconero;* and judging by the style, the order of chapters, and the sequence of the narrated events, it is apparent that the *Crónica* followed the *Refundición* from the beginning of 1433 to 1439.[27]

From the point at which the *Refundición* ends, however, we can compare the *Crónica* to the *Halconero* and the *Abbreviation,* and in this part too we find sections that bear the stamp of Carrillo's work. A number of chapters follow closely the *Halconero,* and some passages tally almost verbatim; but these are so frequently interrupted by chapters or passages that are formulated quite differently, or presented in a much more elaborate manner, or not found in the *Halconero* at all, that we must conclude that the editor of the *Crónica* used here another version of the *Halconero*—and why not assume that he used the same version that he followed for the earlier period (i.e., for 1433–1439)—namely, the *Refundición*?[28] If so, the *Crónica* followed the *Refundición* from 1433 to 1454 (i.e., the end of Juan II's reign), although additional documentary material was incorporated, some passages were replaced by others, and other editorial changes were made by various editors who revised the work, beginning with Pérez de Guzmán.[29]

II

In presenting the *beginnings* of the Toledan rebellion, the *Crónica* is very close to the *Halconero,* perhaps because the *Refundición,* which it probably followed, adhered in this place to the *Halconero*'s line. Accordingly, chapter 2 of the year 1449, in which these beginnings are described, is almost a replica of chapter 322 of the *Halconero,* except that it contains a few more details, which were possibly in the *Refundición.* Thus, it presents both conflicting opinions—that of Alvaro de Luna and that of the citizens—which clashed after Alvaro made his demand, and like the *Halconero,* it states clearly that it was the *común* whose indignation was aroused by the Constable's insistence on the loan, and it was the *común* that burst into rebellion and was responsible for the attack upon the houses of Cota and the seizure of Alvaro's strong points in the city. Then it touches briefly on the uproar caused by the wineskin maker who refused to pay the sum imposed on him by the assessors—an item that is found in the *Abbreviation* but not in the *Halconero.* It may have been taken, however, from the *Refundición,* and the editor of the *Refundición* (who was probably Barrientos) may have included it merely to explain a saying (common in his time) about the origins of the Toledan disturbances. On the other hand, it may have served to underline his view that the outbreak in Toledo sprang from the *común*—i.e., from the city's lower classes.

Similarly, the first part of chapter 5 of the year 1449 of the *Crónica,* in which Sarmiento's joining the rebels is related, follows on the whole the presentation of the *Halconero* in chapter 375, but the explanation of the considerations of both the *común* and Sarmiento for bringing about that union differs considerably in the *Crónica* from what we have in the *Halconero*—a difference which again indicates that the *Crónica* followed a different source here—namely, the text of the *Refundición.* This is how the *Crónica* presents this phase of the events:

> After Pero Sarmiento had seen that the *común* of the city was in such an uproar *(tan alborotada)* he joined it [in its rebellious stand]. And since they [i.e., the *común*] were very fearful [that they would be

severely punished] for the error they had committed in the disservice of the King; and since Pero Sarmiento held the alcazar and the position of the King's judge, when they saw that he wished to join them in order to carry forward what they had begun, they accepted him as leader and assured him that they would always carry out what he would order.[30]

As for Sarmiento, the *Crónica* tells us, he thought that joining the *común* on such terms was "a very good way" to take a stand against Alvaro *(para ser contra el maestre),* and thus, in his desire to push forward his plan, he began to talk to some of the city, who served as the city's deputies in this matter,[31] telling them that he wished to help defend their privileges, and that they should not permit the King to enter the city until he "removed from the Court the Master of Santiago who brought about the violation of such ancient privileges that the city received from the former kings."[32] Finally, the people,

> since they [belonged to the] *común* and had already been placed in the position of doing what Pero Sarmiento would order [them to do], agreed with him, and took an oath to stand for all that he would command.[33]

According to this, Sarmiento joined the rebels not *before* the first acts of violence were perpetrated (as suggested by the *Abbreviation*), but *after* the people had behaved as real rebels and were fearful of the prospect of the King's punishment. They realized they had committed an "error," but did not know how to rectify it.[34] Actually, they must have been afraid of Sarmiento, since "he was in charge of the alcazar and was also the King's judge"—namely, it was he who would be expected to punish them by virtue of both his judicial position and military control of the city. Now, when this man whom they feared most offered them his friendship and support, what could they do but persist in their rebellion and accept his proffered alliance and leadership?

But besides the untenable—indeed desperate—position in which the rebels of the city found themselves, there was another reason for their preparedness to carry out Sarmiento's orders and actually to appoint him as dictator. This was, according to the *Crónica*, the fact that the people with whom Sarmiento negotiated belonged to the *común*—i.e., the common folk. What is implied here is that these people had never been jealous for independence, and that it really made little difference to them whether they were subject to one kind of authority or another.

This presentation of the position of the *común* and the reasons that prompted it to continue in the rebellion under Sarmiento's leadership is offered neither by the *Halconero* nor by the *Abbreviation;* and similarly, it differs from both of them in the exposition of the motives that moved Pero Sarmiento to associate himself with the rebels. While the *Halconero* and the

Abbreviation tell us that Sarmiento was dissatisfied with both the King and Alvaro and sought to achieve through the rebellion "certain things" which were to put an end to his discontent, the *Crónica* states explicitly that his aim was to remove the Constable from his office and that he felt that by assuming control of Toledo he would obtain the means to achieve this end. To be sure, when he spoke to the *común* of Toledo he sought to appear only as jealous for their rights, and presented Alvaro solely as responsible for the violation of their privileges. But just as the *común* were really not interested in the defense of the city's "ancient" privileges, but rather in saving themselves from punishment, so was Sarmiento not interested in defending the city's rights, but in pursuing his own private goal, which was the overthrow of the Maestre. Thus, the city's case against the Constable became identified with his own case, although from quite different motives.

These, then, were the formal and actual reasons (and the formal, as we have seen, differed from the actual) for the formation of the alliance between Sarmiento and the rebels. Following this, the rebels "delivered to him the keys of the city, its gates and towers," which they had captured from Alvaro's men, and Sarmiento proceeded to rule the city as both dictator and tyrant. Moved by his "great malice and greed," he "ordered the seizure of certain citizens, honorable men and rich merchants in order to take from them what was theirs, and when he held them in prison, he put them to great tortures, claiming that they wished to deliver the city to the King and made them, under the extreme tortures they suffered, *admit to things they never did and never entered their minds.*"[35] Thus we see the *Crónica* share the same view, and take the same position toward the accused conversos, that we find in the *Abbreviation.* Then it adds:

> And since Pero Sarmiento held in his power the administration of justice and the court's scribe *(escribano)* was of his party, he imposed cruel punishment on some people, and after having done this he took their possessions, while from many others he took their estates, and others he exiled from the city, saying they were acting in behalf of the Master of Santiago.[36]

Hence, in discussing Sarmiento's reign of terror, the *Crónica,* like the *Abbreviation,* does not state that some people in the city were accused of crimes other than political; and in this respect it resembles the *Halconero,* which states that Sarmiento persecuted those who were opposed to the continuation of the rebellion. But apart from this ostensible reason for *all* the punishments inflicted on "some people," the *Crónica* offers another reason which is not pointed out—at least directly—by the *Halconero* but indicated rather clearly by the *Abbreviation.* This was Sarmiento's "malice and greed" *(gran maldad e cobdicia),*[37] which evidently moved him to pursue his tyranny far beyond his political goals and led him to accuse individuals of *crimes which they had never committed or thought of.* Accordingly, Sarmiento, whose original aim was to destroy the Constable's power, had another aim as well: to enrich himself at the expense of the wealthy citizens. Consequently, he added to his crime of rebellion the crime of further prostitution of justice by promoting additional false accusations that enabled him to sentence the accused to "cruel death" and expropriate their possessions, as he did. Essentially, then, it was a *personal* persecution, dictated by Sarmiento's political ambitions, and it became doubly personal when it became inspired by Sarmiento's insatiable greed. If the Marranos were the main victims, which the author does not indicate even by allusion, he evidently wanted us to believe that they had been involved not as Marranos, but as citizens who were (a) opposed to the rebellion and (b) were affluent, and therefore their wealth made them the target of Sarmiento's reign of terror.

The editor of the *Crónica* refrained from discussing the religious charges leveled at the Marranos probably because such a discussion could raise questions about the verity of his thesis; and thus, while assuming that many of his contemporaries, who were well aware of the occurrences in Toledo, would understand what he was alluding to,[38] he refused to spell out the contents of these allusions and left the uninformed reader of his time, and all the more so of future generations, with no way of gathering from his presentation that other accusations, besides political ones, were made in Toledo against a certain group of citizens, and that this group consisted of conversos—and of conversos only. Clearly, the same policy that, in our opinion, guided the editors of the *Halconero* and the *Abbreviation* in their treatment of the passages dealing with the conversos determined the manner in which the persecution of Toledo was presented by the *Crónica de Juan II.*

This policy becomes especially apparent in the way the *Crónica* deals with the Petition submitted by the Toledans to Juan II. The *Crónica* does not present the text of the Petition in its original form (as does the *Halconero*) or most of its passages—including some changes (as does the *Abbreviation*)—but offers a brief summary of its contents in the editor's own style. By freeing himself from the need to adhere in whatever measure to the text of the document, the editor made it easy for himself to project his own views through the summary he presented, without being guilty of direct falsification. His condensation is of course slanted. On the one hand, it broadens the scope of the complaints that the rebels voiced against the Maestre; on the other, it plays down, weakens, or conceals the complaints they made against the Marranos.

Thus, while the original document says merely that the Constable sowed enmity among the grandees in order that he might put an end to all of them,[39] the summary also says that he "killed, arrested and expelled the great nobles" and that he "sowed among them *as well as in the cities* . . . quarrels, divisions and dissensions, so that all of them would depend on him and all of them would have to serve him."[40] Similarly, while the Petition states that the Constable "violated the privileges, immunities . . . and exemptions of this city" (i.e., of Toledo),[41] the summary says that he "violated the exemptions, immunities, and liberties *(franquezas)* of *many cities*."[42] Finally, while the Petition decries the spoliation of the King's subjects by Alvaro's officials, the summary adds: "from which robbery he derives and had continually derived great benefits and services" for himself.[43]

These broadened and aggravated charges were obviously made by a man who agreed with this part of the Petition and, moreover, sought to emphasize the guilt of Alvaro de Luna. Evidently, he wanted to make it clear that while Sarmiento joined the rebels out of greed and ambition, *Alvaro was the one who turned the Toledan citizens into rebels against the regime*—not only by imposing an illegal tax, but also by his general behavior with the cities, as well as with the nobility. Alvaro provided the fuel for the fires of the rebellion by fomenting unrest, divisions and grievances—acts which included robberies, imprisonments, killings and expulsions.[44]

Yet while the summarizer felt it necessary to sharpen his attack upon Alvaro, he clearly sought to weaken the accusations which the Petition contained against Alvaro's officials. We have seen that he retained the charge of the Petition that Alvaro's officials "robbed" the country, but he deleted the more severe accusations that many "died" as a result of their actions. Likewise, he eliminated the claim that these officials "usurped the lordship that belonged to the great nobles,"[45] and also the epithets applied to these officials such as "heretics" and "enemies of the Christians," which appear repeatedly in the original document; instead of the word "heretics" he used (like the *Abbreviation*) the words "bad people" *(malos)*,[46] which is of course a much less pointed and definite designation.

It is clear that by deleting the appellation "heretics," the editor wished to prevent the identification of Alvaro's officials with the conversos whom the Petition described as "heretics." In agreement with this, the editor obliterated every trace of the accusations of heresy which the Petition carries against the conversos and suppressed all other anti-Marrano criticisms that abound in that document. What is more, *it avoided all mention of the conversos,* so that the reader might not even guess that the writ of complaints which the rebels of Toledo submitted to Juan II had, to any extent and in any way, to do with the conversos.

The *Crónica* follows the same line of suppression of the name of the conversos and the converso issue also when it presents the terms of the agreement reached between the rebels and Prince Enrique, under which the latter was permitted entry into Toledo. Thus, while the *Halconero* says that under those terms, "none of the conversos who had been ousted from the city was ever to be allowed to return to it," the *Crónica* says that it was agreed that "none or some of *those whom he had expelled*"[47] (without mentioning their Marrano identity) would be allowed to return to the city, adding, on top of this, the reason: "because they were following the orders of the Maestre"[48] (precisely as in the *Abbreviation!*). So again: "those who were deprived of the right to return" were so deprived, according to this *Crónica,* not because they were conversos, but because they were partisans of Alvaro—or, rather, foes of Sarmiento, his clique and his regime. Furthermore, while according to the *Halconero,* it was specified in the agreement that the banished conversos would never reoccupy the offices they had held in Toledo, the *Crónica de Juan II* does not say that offices were denied to *conversos* but to some unspecified supporters of Alvaro who had been ousted from the city. It follows that even when this *Crónica* touches the matter of public offices, it avoids mentioning the conversos, although they alone were excluded from the right to office in Toledo, and although a special law (the *Sentencia-Estatuto*) was enacted for this purpose against them.

Thus, the *Crónica de Juan II* went much farther than the *Halconero* and the *Abbreviation* in suppressing the name of the conversos and the converso issue, and was also more extreme than its related versions in attributing guilt to Alvaro de Luna for the outbreak of the Toledan rebellion. It is clear, then, that the editor of this *Crónica* of Juan II was both an ardent opponent of Alvaro and a staunch supporter of the conversos. Who was he?

That he was a converso is indicated by his endeavor to conceal any opinion, action, or relationship that could cast any aspersion upon the conversos; and this is also indicated by his attempt to put all the blame for the rebellion on Alvaro de Luna. As we shall see, the attitude toward Alvaro on the part of the conversos, and especially of their leaders, began to change shortly after the rebellion from extremely positive to extremely negative. Our author belonged to those Marranos who experienced this change of heart.

III

We have seen that thus far the *Crónica de Juan II* offers us no new information about the Marranos, except for what we may deduce from the manner in which the editor presents the occurrences in Toledo—or, rather, the rebellion of 1449—with the identity of the conversos completely hidden. Other new and more substantial data we encounter in the later part of the account, beginning with the agreement the Prince reached with Sarmiento concerning the latter's departure from the city.

This agreement was preceded by a talk between Sarmiento and Don Lope de Barrientos, Bishop of Cuenca, the Prince's counselor at the time. That such a talk took place we also know from the *Abbreviation,* and according to the latter, the Bishop reproached Sarmiento for the "great evils and disobedience he had committed against the King."[49] From this single remark in the *Abbreviation* about that talk we may conclude that Barrientos' chastisement of the rebel referred solely to Sarmiento's crimes against the *King*—i.e., to his political crimes, rather than to his offenses against any particular group of the Toledan population. From the report of this chastisement as presented in the *Crónica,* however, we gain quite a different impression.

For the *Crónica* recounts in great detail what the Bishop allegedly said, and it is here, in the presentation of the Bishop's words, that the chronicler gives us clues for reconstructing many of the Toledan events. This detailed account was *not* taken from the original *Halconero;* for had it been included in it, we believe, we would have found at least a brief summary of it in the *Abbreviation.* It stands to reason that at least a part of it was included in the *Refundición*—i.e., the text of the *Halconero* which was edited by Barrientos and which, in our opinion, served as the main source for the *Crónica de Juan II* (i.e., from the year 1435 on). Since the *Crónica* here quotes the very words the Bishop allegedly said to Sarmiento, the Bishop himself should be regarded as the person who most likely included them in the *Refundición.*

As we see it, therefore, things evolved as follows: When Barrientos read the *Halconero's* brief remark about his talk with the rebels' chief (perhaps the same remark we find in the *Abbreviation*), he felt the need to offer a fuller account of the final conversation he had with Sarmiento—a conversation to which he may have attributed some historical importance. As a result, he prepared an expanded statement about what had passed in that conversation, and that statement, incorporated in the *Refundición,* was copied into the *Crónica de Juan II.*

Thus, according to the *Crónica,* the Bishop said to the rebel:

> You, Pero Sarmiento, have committed grand treachery and disobedience against our Lord the King, who entrusted to you this city of Toledo. And having taken it, you have robbed and destroyed and killed many people, *honored citizens* of this city, and above all you have violated the Churches and monasteries, removing from them the possessions of the citizens *who put them there to be shielded and protected from you.*[50]

If by the term "honored citizens" the reference was solely or primarily to the conversos, as was undoubtedly the case, we may conclude that once the Marranos realized that Sarmiento was out to enrich himself at their expense, they tried to hide their most valuable possessions in churches and monasteries. Evidently, they hoped that Sarmiento would not dare to violate religious sanctuaries and remove from them goods entrusted to their care. That this was a vain hope is evident from the above statement. Sarmiento showed no more respect for Church institutions than for private individuals when it came to stealing property of conversos, whom he placed in effect outside the law.

In the following part of the Bishop's accusation, we find additional information about what occurred in Toledo, and particularly about what happened to the Marranos; and this, we believe, relates directly to the issue of their religious faithfulness. It reads as follows:

> And it was not sufficient for you to take their goods, but you also *executed honored citizens;* some of them you hanged, others you have *burnt to death,* without giving them a hearing and without having anything to justify their execution.[51]

Death by fire was a punishment assigned to convicted heretics, and the chronicler of course knew that some of the Marranos were charged with heresy. But even though he does not mention this charge, he vehemently denies it by his description of the sentences as a mockery of justice (the accused having been denied even a hearing) and as groundless from the point of view of evidence (as *there was nothing to justify the sentences issued*). The additional statement that the chronicler cites from the Bishop's denunciation of Sarmiento to his face makes these assertions even more emphatic:

> And since you had at your disposal the entire administration of justice, you sought out malefactory witnesses against the accused, and since all of them [i.e., the witnesses] feared you, they said what you had ordered them to say; and with these excuses you confiscated the properties [of those who were sentenced to death].[52]

Thus it is evident that, according to this author, the charges against the Marranos were trumped-up charges, supported by false witnesses. These witnesses were "malefactors"—i.e., people who were *capable* of giving false testimony; but even these people, however morally low, said what they said only out of fear—that is, because they felt *compelled* to do so. Thus, they imputed crimes to the Marranos that they had never committed, *and that had never even entered their minds*—a statement we have already found elsewhere in the *Crónica* and in the *Abbreviation*. Here, however, it comes from the Bishop's own lips—another denial, firm and unequivocal, of the charges of heresy leveled against the conversos during the disturbances of 1449.[53]

Furthermore, it is clear from the Bishop's statement that the charges of heresy, the trials, and the death sentences served Sarmiento merely as "excuses" to rob the conversos of their possessions. But Sarmiento also used another means to divest the conversos of their properties. Barrientos described it as follows:

And you have put behind bars and held in pits of the alcazar many *honored men and ladies* . . . where they could not see the sky, for in this manner you expected to receive ransom for them more quickly.[54]

This is probably how the above accusation was presented by the bishop also in the *Refundición*—i.e., his revised edition of the *Halconero* which served, in our opinion, as the major source of the *Crónica* edited by Guzmán. But the *Crónica* does not limit its account of the charge to the above scope and form. It also includes in Barrientos' chiding of the bishop a story of how a group of "honored men and ladies," incarcerated by Sarmiento in a pit to receive ransom, were ordered to be released by Prince Enrique, "resembling [in this] our Lord when he took out of limbo the Holy Fathers."[55] It is most improbable that the bishop told Sarmiento details of an occurrence that was of course known to him, and he would certainly not compare the Prince's order to Christ's liberation of the Saints from hell. Hence, this story was included in the account by a later editor of the *Crónica de Juan II*.

This editor must have been not only a Marrano, but also a Toledan. He was fully informed of what occurred in the city, and he may have also been personally involved in the Marranos' tale of anguish that he narrates. One can hear his personal reaction—an outburst of joy, relief and gratitude—which only people saved from such harsh imprisonment could utter and remember for a long time. And perhaps it is to him, the same editor, that we should also attribute the statement: "And when the bishop finished saying the above things to Sarmiento, the latter did not answer a single charge, because he knew that all those things were true."[56] This was supposed to have been Sarmiento's own admission of guilt, in addition to the testimony of the famous Barrientos—a most honorable Old Christian witness—and thus the case against Sarmiento as tyrant and robber could be considered complete.

IV

There is one more point we have to touch upon in our analysis of the various passages in the *Crónica* that deal with the Marranos in Toledo. We refer to Sarmiento's departure from the city with all the loot he took from its citizens. In enumerating the kinds of valuables looted, the *Crónica*, though hardly more detailed than the *Abbreviation*, adds the pointed remark: *"For a house that he ordered to be robbed, he would not leave until it was empty."*[57] The remark is of course calculated to prove that Sarmiento was nothing but a plunderer and that robbery was the main motive of the persecution he conducted against the conversos. The chronicler, moreover, does not pass in silence over the permission given that arch-criminal to get away with the proceeds of his crime. Expressing his views through the alleged protests that the robbed people voiced to the Prince, he thus presents their bitter complaint:

> Shall all the widows and citizens remain destitute and desolate while you consent that their belongings would thus be despoiled before your eyes and taken away by this cruel tyrant? ... More than thirty million [maravedis] has he robbed from this city, which can no longer be called noble but dissipated and destroyed; and *these citizens were not robbed for doing any evil*, but for listening to the order of the King our lord your father.[58]

Apart from informing us of the total scale of Sarmiento's robbery (which is indicated nowhere else), the *Crónica* again reasserts—and this time from the mouth of the robbed—that their only sin was their faithfulness to the King. The chronicler adds that the despoiled people appealed to the Prince and to his friends and favorites, the Master of Calatrava and the Marquis of Villena, but the Prince remained unmoved. He decided to keep the promise of safe-conduct that he had given to Sarmiento. And on this the *Crónica* remarks:

> It seems certain that the Prince Don Enrique had not read an imperial law which says: *we can do only those things that we can do legally.*[59] For had he known this law, he would have recognized his inability to give the protection he granted to Pero Sarmiento, to his family and his possessions. Nor was he in any manner obliged to observe that commitment after he had given it, for guarding it meant acting against his royal office and against all justice.[60]

This strong protest against the Prince—which was followed by a sharp attack on his advisers, who either did not know, according to the *Crónica*, what their obligations were, or else had debauched consciences (undoubtedly, an allusion to Pacheco and Girón)—is of course not at all typical of the style of Pero Carrillo. Nor could it have been written by Barrientos. The latter, as we know, negotiated with Sarmiento his departure from the city *on behalf of the Prince*; he no doubt attributed importance to the talk that he, Barrientos, had with Sarmiento, in which he influenced the arch-rebel to comply with the Prince's wishes. Furthermore, he indicated no disagreement when Sarmiento expressed his readiness to leave Toledo "together with all that he possessed."[61] Theoretically, Sarmiento's reference to "what he possessed" could be interpreted by the Bishop to mean "what he possessed *by right*"; and that only subsequently was this broadened to include also what he had gained by robbery. Yet even this is not very likely. For when Barrientos wrote his account, he already knew what Sarmiento had in mind and how the reader of that account would interpret his words. Yet on this occasion

Barrientos made no negative remark. The chances, therefore, are that he was well aware of the promises given to Sarmiento by the Prince, of the agreement reached regarding the "possessions," and that he, the Bishop, acquiesced in this agreement, even though he may not have been the one who counseled the Prince to make it. We are, therefore, again inclined to conclude that this passage, too—like the one we have just analyzed—was written by a later editor, probably by the one who wrote the story about the people imprisoned in the "pit." Indeed, here, too, we have not merely a record of related events, which, in the author's opinion, should not be forgotten, but also a poignant call for justice. So offended is the author by this behavior of the Prince, and so aggravated by his evasion of justice, that no discerning reader can fail to notice that he was directly concerned. In other words, he was a Marrano.

But what was expressed here was not only the author's personal shock over some glaringly immoral behavior, but a common political conviction of a group regarding the essentials of its life and the prerequisites for its security. The fact that Sarmiento could emerge from the affair not only unscathed, but with a prize of wealth, was to the conversos utterly unthinkable, and spelled evil for the days to come. If property seized by force from Marranos could be taken away by the robber in broad daylight, before the very eyes of the rulers, Marrano life and property were not worth much in Spain. The rulers' flagrant violation of their duties showed that the Marranos were treated in Spain as if they were outside the pale of law. This the author further indicates by the following words:

> Even less is it to be believed that the said Prince or the members of his Council, when they tolerated this thing, remembered that chapter that begins with the word *Error* in the eighty third distinction of the *Decretum* which begins thus: "An error which is not resisted, becomes approved; the truth, when not defended, is offended; to avoid the correction of evil when one can do so, is nothing but favoring that evil; he who does not denounce a manifest crime shares some of the thinking of a secret accomplice."[62]

A staunch and open advocate of the conversos, the author also has legal education. Such direct and harsh criticism—and such as is based repeatedly on laws—could come, indeed, from a Marrano jurist, or a Marrano writer who took his arguments from converso jurists. In fact, the thoughts expressed in the passage just cited, and the earlier passage about the "imperial law," could have originated with such men as the Relator.[63] In them we hear not only the clamor and complaint of the average Marrano—the man in the street—against the outrages of which he was victim, but the sharp protests that the leading conversos doubtless lodged with the Prince and King Juan II when they demanded justice for their people.

IV. THE CUARTA CRÓNICA GENERAL[64]

I.

Like all other "general" histories of Spain, the *Cuarta Crónica General* does not deal with a particular reign or period but presents the story of Spain from its ancient beginnings to the time of the writer. Thus, after a few introductory chapters, the *Cuarta* begins with the Gothic period and goes on to the end of Juan II's reign (1454). It exists in many 15th-century manuscripts and is believed to have been completed shortly after Juan II's death.

Nothing definite has been established about the authorship of this work except that its first part (up to 1243) is an amplified translation into Castilian of the Latin version of the chronicle of Rodrigo Jiménez de Rada, Archbishop of Toledo (d. 1247). As for the continuation from 1243, it is attributed in one manuscript to Gonzalo de Hinojosa, Bishop of Burgos and author of another *crónica* of Castile (up to the time of Alfonso XI), and in another to Pedro López de Ayala, Chancellor of Castile, who was also a historian of high repute. Since Hinojosa died in 1327 and Ayala in 1407, it is obvious that both aforesaid attributions are at least partly erroneous, since they relate to the entire period from 1243 to 1454; and the consensus of scholarly opinion is therefore that the author (or authors) of the *Cuarta Crónica General* must be considered anonymous. This is all the more true of the chapter on Juan II's time that is included in this chronicle, since none of the suggested authorships can apply to this period. Nevertheless, one important scholar had different thoughts on this matter. Fidel Fita, who believed that both Hinojosa and Ayala did participate in the writing of the *Cuarta* (the former to approximately 1325 and Ayala from that time to 1406), suggested that the chapter on the period of Juan II was composed by Alonso de Cartagena,[65] perhaps because, like two of the preceding authors, Cartagena was both bishop and historian. Fita mentions in reference to his suggestion Cartagena's *Arbol genealógico de los reyes de Castilla y de León,* but other arguments may be offered in support of his conjecture which is by no means without merit.[66]

Of the numerous extant manuscripts of the *Cuarta,* only two contain a chapter on Juan II's reign, their versions differing in scope, approach and contents. The more copious of the two is ms. 9559 of the Biblioteca Nacional, Madrid, which was published by the Marqués de la Fuensanta del Valle in the *Colección de Documentos Inéditos.*[67] It is the only one that covers the whole period of Juan II and contains an account of the Toledan events.[68] Our attention, therefore, will center on this version only.

The author of the chapter on Juan II, it may be noted, was well aware of the contents of the *Crónica de Juan II* but, at least in what he tells us about the Toledan rebellion, he does not seem to rely on that *crónica* or to have been in need of such reliance. He appears to have firsthand knowledge of what occurred in Toledo, and he also takes an independent view—certainly, more forthright and definite—about the personalities involved, their motives, and the causes of the developments.

Most critical of Alvaro de Luna, the author begins his account of the outbreak with an attack upon the Constable's role in the affair from a purely moral point of view. As he puts it, it was "because of the extraordinary greed of this Maestre" (the Master of Santiago), because of his desire to "amass treasures more than he had already amassed," that he advised the King to impose a loan upon Toledo, while he knew very well that that city was "exempt from the duty of paying tributes and granting loans" to the royal administration by virtue of the great privileges it had obtained from the former kings of Castile."[69] From this first cause of the rebellion the author proceeds to what he considers the second one: the imposition of payments upon the poor and the attempt to exact these payments by force. One of the poor people was arrested for having failed to pay his share of the loan, and "while he was being carried to the carcel, he shouted so much and made such a great noise that the whole city was outraged." As a result, "the people of the community declared rebelliously that they would neither grant the loan nor pay it." Then "they went and burned the houses of Alonso Cota, who was the King's appointed collector of the loan. In consequence there developed in the city great scandals, disturbances, and divisions between some of the people and the others."[70]

The author of the account thus places the responsibility for the outbreak in Toledo squarely upon the shoulders of Alvaro de Luna. Not only does he consider the demand which was addressed to the city of Toledo illegal—since it was in violation of the city's privileges—but he also considers it immoral and, in fact, criminal—since it stemmed solely from the Constable's desire to expand his own treasury. He completely ignores the Maestre's claim that the money was needed to meet the exigencies of war, with which the kingdom was confronted at the time, and clearly indicates that part of the money which Alvaro planned to collect in Toledo was to go, somehow, into the Constable's own coffers.[71] In all these charges the author echoes the severe accusations made against Alvaro by the Toledan rebels (and the nobles siding with the Infantes of Aragon), and he also gives some backing to their charges against the Constable with respect to the cruelty and harshness of his rule by pointing to the manner in which the loan was enforced: Poor people who could not pay their share were forcibly dragged to prison. It was natural, therefore, according to this author, that such acts would stir the common people to rebellion. And since Alfonso Cota happened to be the major official (or the tax collector) who was responsible for the execution of the order, they expressed their protest and wrath against Alvaro by attacking the houses of the collector of that impost. We understand why this author dropped the explanation that we find in the *Crónica de Juan II*—namely, that the people suspected Cota of having "induced" the Constable to impose the loan: He wished to place full responsibility upon the Constable himself, and therefore refused to mention the charge made against Cota. Thus, Alfonso Cota who, as we have noted, was one of Toledo's leading conversos, is presented in this account as merely an official who carried out orders of his superiors and had, in reality, nothing to do with the basic developments that led to the outbreak. What happened in Toledo was, to begin with, the result of a blunder committed by the Constable, and he was moved to commit it by no one but himself—that is, by his greed, his cruelty and his disregard for the people's rights.

II.

According to the *Cuarta Crónica General*, however, Alvaro's flaws and failures were not the only cause of what occurred in Toledo. There were other factors and tendencies involved, and this is how the *Crónica* describes them:

> And since Pero Sarmiento, a high born caballero, who was then the governor of the Alcazar of the said city, *was the inciter of these actions* which were thus done for the reason of that loan, [Don Alvaro de Luna] who was at that time in Ocaña, decided to go to Toledo and take from him the Alcazar and punish the culprits of that disorder." [But Pero Sarmiento,] having been informed [of this intent of the Constable], *seized all the gates of the city* and forcibly expelled from it the judges and caballeros who were citizens of Toledo and [also] the conversos. He despoiled the aforementioned of all their possessions,[72] and likewise robbed the majority of the abbots and beneficiaries in the city. In all these matters he was counseled and aided by the bachiller Marcos García de Mazarambroz who used to be called the bachiller Marquillos, and many others. These people killed and robbed and burned some conversos and conversas, bringing against them false testimonies by which they meant to provide an excuse for their own treason and heresy.[73]

It is quite evident from the above account that, next to Alvaro, the author holds Sarmiento responsible for the Toledan outbreak. Thus, while Alvaro de Luna *provoked* the people and worked them into a rebellious mood,

Sarmiento *incited them and urged them to translate that mood into action*. So the first disturbances, according to this author, were not spontaneous; they were the result of Sarmiento's incitement, which is quite in line with what we have gathered from the *Abbreviation*. As for the crimes that were committed later, the main responsibility passes to Sarmiento and his chief aide and counselor, Marcos García de Mazarambroz. To be sure, they were aided by "many" in the city, but it was the former's agitation, plans and orders that moved the latter to action. Implied in all this is the author's view—or the view that he sought to communicate to his readers—that despite the fact that the chief rebels were supported by a substantial number of citizens, the people of Toledo, taken as a whole, were not the main culprits in the disturbances. In fact, they were really not too much to blame. Those who were primarily to blame were several individuals who, pricked by their ambitions, brought the people to a state of exasperation and finally to the commission of all kinds of crime. Accordingly, the troubles did not stem from some rooted antagonism between one group of citizens and another—or, if we wish to come closer to our subject, by a widespread dislike for the conversos. They stemmed, to begin with, from the rule of Alvaro, and later from that of Pero Sarmiento, both of whom, each in his own way, sought to exploit the people of Toledo for their selfish designs.

And in contradistinction to the *Crónica de Juan II*, the author does not hide the fact that the conversos *did* constitute a target of persecution for Sarmiento, Marquillos, and their "many" aides. But he clearly seeks to leave us with the impression that the conversos *were not the only ones* against whom the acts of repression were directed. When he enumerates those who were expelled and robbed by Sarmiento and his henchmen, he mentions first the judges, then the nobles (caballeros) who were citizens of Toledo, and only then—i.e., in the third place—does he mention the conversos. Also when he refers to the properties robbed from some ecclesiastics in Toledo, he does not tell us what we gather from other sources—i.e., that these properties were deposited by *conversos* for safe keeping in monasteries and other Church institutions—but that, together with the properties of those he had expelled, Sarmiento robbed "*most* of the abbots and beneficiaries" in the city. As targets of spoliation and aggression, therefore, the conversos were in good company—with old Christian judges, nobles and ecclesiastics—all of whom were persecuted, quite obviously, not for religious but for political reasons, or more precisely—as we gather from this account—because the tyrant Sarmiento feared their objection to his continued control of the alcazar, and, more generally, his continued occupancy of the governorship of the city. Fundamentally, then, according to this author, the persecution that developed in Toledo did not constitute an exclusively anti-converso drive, but a drive against *all* elements in the city who were staunchly on the side of law and order. This is how this writer tries to interpret the events in Toledo, and, in this respect, he does not differ essentially from the other *crónicas* examined above.

Out of the aforementioned implications—i.e., (a) that the rulers, and not the masses, were responsible for the disorders, and (b) that the targets of the aggressors were not only the conversos but all individuals and groups in the city who openly took the side of the law—there emerges automatically the conclusion that the author no doubt wished us to draw—namely, that there was no general clash between Old and New Christians in the city; there was no background of hatred for the conversos that could possibly lead to such a clash; and there was no religious or social misconduct by the conversos that could serve as justification for such a hatred.

To be sure, after portraying the developments in a manner that must lead us to such conclusions, the author adds that "some conversos were robbed, killed and burned" on the basis of false charges that had been brought against them—charges supported by false witnesses.[74] But not a word is said about what we gather from other sources—namely, that the conversos were accused of heresy or, more precisely, of being Judaizers. Instead, the author says that false witnesses were brought against the conversos to give a semblance of justification to the treason and heresy which were committed by the accusers themselves.[75]

It is clear, then, that the author exonerates the conversos from any charge of heresy, just as he clears them of any charge of treason. On the other hand, we see that their adversaries were guilty, besides treason, of heresy; and to emphasize this claim of his, the author adds: "*And they raised several heresies which are against the faith and the Gospels of our Lord,* and they did other such great evils and ugly things that were not done at any time in any city of these kingdoms."[76] He defines Sarmiento not only as an "evil tyrant," but also as an "evil heretic" and similarly he calls one of his aides, Fernando de Avila, an "evil schismatic."[77] Finally, he points out what the other Chronicles do not, or rather what they cover up in silence—namely, that the Pope excommunicated Pero Sarmiento, Marquillos and all their company and ordered them to be tried as "Moors and rebels,"[78] thus indicating that they were not only adversaries of the state (rebels), but also enemies of the Christian faith (Moors).

Yet with all his emphasis upon the heresies of the rebels, he does not say a word about the nature of their heresies. Nor does he cite from the Pope's bull against the rebels even one sentence or phrase that would give us a clue as to what their heresy involved. Significantly, when the same author deals, in a preceding section, with the heretics of Durango, he gives us a clear intimation of at least one aspect of the religious deviations of that sect.[79] Why then does he not treat in the same manner the heretical deviations of Sarmiento and his group? The reason is not hard to see.

By revealing the contents of the latter's heresy the author would have to disclose the opinions which Sarmiento and Marquillos held of the conversos, and this he evidently refused to do. He no doubt was especially reluctant to mention the main point of the Toledan "heresy"—namely, that the conversos belonged to an inferior race which was evil and criminal by nature, and therefore condemned by God to everlasting suffering and disgrace. He would further have had to say that because of all this, most of the conversos were, according to the Toledans, incapable of accepting Christianity, and that therefore they remained even after their conversion secret Jews and enemies of the Christians; consequently, in the heretics' view, *all* of the conversos must be held suspect as unfaithful, and as such they should be categorically barred from every public office in Christian society. Clearly, the author was loath to present all these derogatory assertions about the conversos even as part of an *heretical* opinion—a fact which should have almost automatically branded these accusations as false. What is more, since he decided to conceal all this and avoid any discussion of the conversos' race, as well as the question of their religious faithfulness, he also refrained from mentioning the heresy trials organized by the rebels in Toledo against conversos, in which some of the latter were found guilty and burned as heretics at the stake (even though he alluded to this in his references to the "false witnesses" and the conversos who were "burned"). For that very reason, we may add, he did not mention the issuance of the *Sentencia-Estatuto*, which forbade all conversos to hold public office in the city, and for the same reason he failed to note the dismissal of the conversos from the public offices they had held in Toledo prior to the outbreak (even though he must have alluded, among other things, to these facts by his reference to the "evil and ugly acts which had never been committed in Spain before"). So even though this author, unlike some other chroniclers, does point out that the conversos were a target—and, in fact, a special target—of the rebels' persecution; even though he does indicate that Marquillos played a leading part in that persecution, and also that the Pope issued a bull against him, as well as those who were allied with him; nevertheless, he, too, like the authors of the *crónicas* we have discussed above, refuses to give us any concrete notion of what truly happened in Toledo.

Indeed, had we to derive our information only from what the *Cuarta* tells us about the outbreak and its aftermath, we would not know of the existence of a widespread antipathy, resentment and hatred for the conversos in the city; we would not know that the surge of these feelings was so strong that the government of Castile was incapable of suppressing it even after the downfall of Sarmiento and his clique; nor would we know about the charges of heresy that were leveled against the conversos during the rebellion, or the race theory that was propounded in support of these charges; finally, we would have no idea of the scope of the persecution that was conducted against the conversos, and of the city's legal enactments against them which were aimed at reducing them to an inferior caste. For the author of this chapter in the *Cuarta Crónica General* covers all these matters with a blanket of silence.

There can be no doubt, in our opinion, that this author, like the editors of the other *crónicas* we have reviewed, was a converso who was a contemporary of Alvaro, but one who viewed Alvaro not as a hero but as a villain[80] and an enemy. But not a word is uttered by him to suggest the real reason for the grudge the conversos held against Alvaro and for the change of the friendship they had felt for him to bitter hostility. Obviously, a policy was manifested here with respect to what should, and should not, be presented for public discussion. And the question that we ought to ask now is: why did the Marranos, who were in charge of these *crónicas,* choose to follow such a policy of concealment in presenting the story of the Toledan disturbances to their own and future generations in the histories of their country?

V. CONCLUSION

Having completed our survey of the chronicles dealing with Juan II's period, all of which were written before the age of the Inquisition, we notice immediately certain similarities in their treatment of the Marrano question. In fact, they display a uniform tendency in all that pertains to that treatment, and it is important for us to understand that tendency before we consider the evidence proper.

Regardless of who was the original author of each of the texts under review, and irrespective of the dates of the final revisions of the manuscripts that came down to us, it is clear, as we have seen, that all of them were partly edited, or written, by conversos within a few years after the Toledan outbreak. This, at least, is true with respect to the sections dealing with matters that relate to the Marranos. And thus what these documents reflect is a contemporary Marrano view and testimony—dating from the middle of the 15th century—of the developments that affected Marrano life in Spain, of the essential causes of the Marrano problem, and—what is no less important for us—of the means and methods that could be used for its solution.

We have seen that all four chronicles show, in varying degrees, a desire to suppress any religious accusation that had ever been leveled at the conversos by their opponents, and similarly all mention of any racial abuse that had ever been hurled against them. Both the issues of Marrano heresy (Judaism) and converso racial inferiority, which formed one of the stormiest controversies that had ever swept the kingdoms of Spain, were thus systematically forced into obscurity as if they had never been debated. Also issues of major practical significance that morally or legally hinged upon those theories— such as the Marranos' right to public office, or even their right to give testimony in court—were carefully evaded by these chronicles, as if they had never been raised in public and deeply affected the social life of Spain.

What were the reasons for the censorship imposed upon all the *crónicas* of Juan II by their converso authors and editors? The chief reason was no doubt this: The Marranos were faced with a campaign of vilification which clearly threatened their existence in Spain, and they were inevitably looking for the best method to quash that campaign, or reduce its effectiveness. As long as Toledo was the headquarters and center of the rebels' anti-Marrano agitation, the Marranos met the violent diatribes, which were directed against them from that source, with a counter-attack that soon put their enemies on the defensive. Determined to fight fire with fire, the Marranos placed in the forefront of their battle-line the strongest and ablest men they possessed— Torquemada, Cartagena, the Relator, and others; they enlisted in their support men of courage and brilliance, such as Lope de Barrientos and Alonso de Montalvo; they answered every charge, they exposed every lie, and they built a massive public opinion that was so adverse to Sarmiento and his followers that the latter came to be regarded as outlaws, not only politically, but also morally and religiously. Within one year after the Toledan outbreak, the Marranos saw their foes in retreat; the Pope had denounced and excommunicated them; their leaders had been executed or hunted down; and Toledo, like Ciudad Real before it, was clearly seeking accommodation with the Crown. To be sure, the struggle was by no means over, and the Marranos were still to suffer reverses, but the most dangerous and ruthless of their enemies had been silenced, and the anti-Marrano campaign had been checked.

What remained for them to do was to overcome the resistance of the Toledan Old Christians to the restoration of their status—that is, their right to full equality—and this, they thought, could be better achieved by quiet negotiations and diplomatic efforts than by noisy charges and counter-charges. More clearly, they expected to overcome the difficulties which they still faced in the Toledan area by inducing the King to act decisively in their favor, as he had done many times in the past. A frontal public campaign in their defense now appeared, in consequence, superfluous.

It also appeared risky or even harmful. It was obvious to them that if they pressed the attack, the problem of their discrimination in Toledo would be kept alive as a national issue—and what the Marranos wished was to isolate that problem, limit it geographically and reduce it thematically as much as they possibly could. Furthermore, a continued campaign in their behalf could lead to a strong counter-offensive, and to the renewal of the charges and recriminations that so besmirched the conversos' name. This might entangle them in a prolonged conflict, whose outcome could not be foreseen, and, in any case, might rekindle the fires which they had barely managed to extinguish. They knew that the embers of these fires were still glowing; there were still hot ashes and some isolated flames. But nothing should be done that might fan them, they thought. Instead, these flames might be dealt with individually until they were stifled.

This seems to have been the thinking of the Marranos—or at least of some of their foremost leaders—in the early 1450s. Fearing that by over-reacting to their opponents they might provoke a new outburst against them, they were quick to suspend that vigorous campaign—that straightforward, proud and passionate response which led to their notable achievements and triumphs. Their enemies' leaders were dead or anathematized; and they wanted to regard their enemies' ideas as dead and anathematized, too. In fact, they wished to see the whole Toledan outburst—that is, insofar as it related to them—as buried and erased from the memory of man. They wished to judge it as a mere episode that had no real roots in the social life of Spain, and therefore no lasting consequences and no baneful effect. In brief, they wished to judge it as a freak of history—the product of a few distorted minds, but not of general, deep-rooted tendencies. To be sure, these perverted criminal individuals had succeeded in turning reality into a nightmare, but their success was inevitably short-lived, as is usually that of all criminals, and the quicker the nightmare was forgotten, the sooner normality would be restored. That they were in error, that they indulged in wishful thinking, the subsequent developments proved. But this wishful thinking was, as we shall see, deeply imbedded in their assimilationist psychology, and it combined with more sober considerations to determine the policy they now pursued.

This policy is clearly reflected in the deletions and revisions made by Marrano editors in the chronicles of Juan II. They too wished to blot out the affairs of Toledo, insofar as they concerned the Marranos, from the memory of their countrymen, but they had to cope with the story of the rebellion which they found in the history books of the reign and which was too much connected—indeed, interwoven—with the general course of events. They could, therefore, revise it in some fashion and make it more acceptable to them, and it is obvious that, to attain this aim, they could follow one of two available courses. They could retain the accounts about the persecution of the conversos and the reasons offered by the rebels in its support, and add refutations of all these reasons, as well as denunciations of the persecutors, such as those enunciated by the Pope, Torquemada and other authorities of Church and State; this would not involve them in any falsification, but simply broaden the historical picture. Or they could eliminate all the censures of the conversos that had been aired in the *crónicas;* they could suppress the whole story of the converso persecution (which would inevitably be necessitated by the former action), and even go to the length of avoiding all mention of the conversos as connected with the whole affair. Obviously, such a form of revision would involve a flagrant distortion of truth. But historical truth was less important in their eyes than the consequences it entailed for the welfare of their group. They chose, as we have seen, the second course—and mainly, no doubt, for the aforesaid reasons.

Yet apart from the general reasons we have outlined, the Marrano editors were moved—we may assume—by other considerations which appeared to them valid, and which may be laid to their moral credit. Granted that they could present the charges against the conversos accompanied by their own— or others'—refutations. But what would be the result? They knew the secret that calumny and libel cannot be fought by mere denials, and that denials often have the opposite effect to the one which is generally expected. Doubtless the Marrano editors realized that, with the public mood as it was, the refutations might be less credible than the accusations to most or many of their readers, and that the very repetition of the charges through denials would only help defame the conversos further and serve the aims of their foes. Thus, if they chose the course of full exposure, they could easily see themselves as unwitting parties to the vilification of their own people. And since they were convinced, as we believe they were, in the total innocence of the Marranos, they might also view such action as a crime—the crime of subjecting innocent people to the ordeal of further abasement. In brief, as they saw it, the alternative they faced was between spreading a lie and suppressing it, and thus there could be no question as to the preferable course.

This could well be an additional consideration, if not the overriding one, of these historians; and supporting this conclusion was one more point which ought to be kept in mind. The facts in which these editors believed were not only that the Marranos, or their overwhelming majority, were free from the execrable crime of heresy, but that their accusers, too, were well aware of this, and that the motives that moved them to persecute the Marranos were not religious, but base and vile. So why tell the lie, and then deny it by the subsequent presentation of truth, instead of telling the truth only—and right from the outset? Why present the false religious excuse which the conspirators used to justify their crimes, instead of ascribing their crimes straightaway to their true motives—to greed, jealousy and political ambition and to the criminal intents of those adventurers? There was a redeeming feature in this kind of reasoning, which, one may assume, guided the Marrano editors—or, at least, some of them to some extent. Their "falsification" of the records could appear to them, in their overall considerations, as the presentation of the *inner* truth of history, while the fuller and ostensibly truthful presentation could be judged by them as leading to misunderstandings and hence to a distortion of the basic facts.

These were doubtless some of the considerations, practical and moral, that determined the general method or tendency that the Marrano editors followed in editing the *crónicas* of Juan II. That an ostrich policy was involved here can hardly be denied. For behind all these and other considerations there was the Marranos' almost intractable refusal to face the grim realities of their dangerous situation. By burying their heads in the sands of delusion, they could pretend that the storm which was blowing in their faces did not exist and that the hostile movement which was directed against them, and which emanated from the depths of the Spanish people, was merely the creation of political adventurers, fortune-seekers and traitors, and therefore destined to rapid decay. Thus their unwillingness to meet the challenge was coupled with their inability to assess the facts. Marrano reaction to the events of 1449—in that very year, and shortly thereafter—was the exception rather than the rule in the long, complex and tortuous history of Marrano life in Spain.

It would be wrong to assume that the above exhausts all the probable answers to the problem we have posed. Since the treatment of the Marranos by Marrano historians is symptomatic of the whole Marrano situation, it touches upon the Marranos' psychology, as well as on their social and religious aspirations. There is obviously more to this than what we have said, and the reader is referred for further discussion to other parts of this study.[81]

CHAPTER III

Reverses and Triumphs

I. The Aftermath of the Rebellion

I

If the story of the rebellion of 1449, as it appears in the chronicles of the time, is affected by distortions more than by omissions, the story of the aftermath in the same chronicles suffers from omissions more than from distortions. In fact, their authors have so managed to evade most of the pertinent events and developments that, had there not survived some related documents besides these semi-official accounts, we would be totally unable to form a clear notion of what actually occurred. And yet, these occurrences had a lasting effect on the history of the conversos and Castile.

From scraps of information pieced together from our sources, we may draw the rather surprising conclusion that Sarmiento's dismissal from his ruling positions, though it ended the rebels' control of Toledo, did not end Toledo's intransigence. Lasting for about another year, this intransigence now assumed a new form. Some of its goals were not quite the same as those proclaimed by Sarmiento and his aides. Yet it was insurgence nonetheless; for the city still refused to accept the King and serve him, except on its own special terms, and so continued in its defiance of the Crown, protected by none save the Prince.

But the Prince did more than protect the city. He also helped restore it to normality. Once Sarmiento was removed from his posts, the Prince revived the old city institutions, which soon resumed their former functions. No doubt the crucial tasks were entrusted to the same *regidores* and *omes buenos* (and other members of the upper middle class) whom the Prince invited to the meeting in December at which García and his friends were denounced.

It was with these citizens that the Prince now negotiated the terms of agreement between Toledo and the King.

One may wonder why there was need for such negotiations at all. It would seem that insofar as the council was concerned, the very restoration of the patrician leadership, which was not responsible for the insurrection, should automatically have cleared the way for the renewal of the king's rule in Toledo. Yet actually this was not so. The city leaders raised certain demands as prerequisites for making their peace with the King, and the Prince was no doubt aware of these demands even before he installed them in office. This brings us back to his agreement with Sarmiento, and the conversos' strong protests against the terms by which the rebel departed from the city.

The questions the New Christians raised on that occasion have remained unanswered to this day. Why did the Prince allow Pero Sarmiento to get out of Toledo scot-free? Why did he permit him to leave with the goods he had so brazenly stolen from its citizens? Ostensibly, the answer may lie in the commitment the Prince gave the rebel in June 1449—that is, never to punish or bring him to trial for any of his misdeeds as governor. Of course, the conversos were aware of this commitment, but claimed that such pledges, fundamentally illegal, were also morally void and invalid.[1] Quite apart from morality, however, certain political considerations were involved that motivated the Prince's stand. We should try to identify these motives before we proceed any further.

Enjoying the city's goodwill and obedience and, above all, its faith in his guardianship, the Prince regarded these attitudes as assets that could stand him well in his negotiations with the King. But, he may have thought, these assets would be lost if he treated Sarmiento as the conversos wished. Not only would he thereby violate the pledges he had given Sarmiento twice,[2] and thus impair his own credibility; he would also open a Pandora's box of fears, suspicions and desperate presumptions that might turn the city against him.

In the light of his immediate interests, therefore, the Prince's position is understandable. In fact, he had little choice. We shall see this more clearly when we take a closer look at the conflict then shaping between the King and the Toledans. Exacerbating this conflict were two issues which seemed to defy solution: (a) the punishment of those of the city inhabitants who had supported the rebels in one way or another; and (b) the conversos' future status in Toledo.

Regarding the first issue, the King, it was known, demanded the arrest and delivery into his hands of all Toledans who had aided Sarmiento, carried out his orders, or committed other crimes under his authority or during the rebellion. This, of course, would also apply to all those who had taken action

against the New Christians at Sarmiento's or his government's behest. The
Toledans were fiercely opposed to this demand. They knew that hundreds
of Toledans were involved in the first outbreak on January 27 and many more
in fighting the royal forces when the King besieged the city. In addition,
many, perhaps hundreds, took part in the robberies, tortures, killings, and
confiscations; and while most of these belonged to the *común,* some were no
doubt members of the middle class. To punish all these as the law required
would put half the city's population in mourning. The council members
could not accede to this. Their first condition, therefore, for their voluntary
acceptance of the King's renewed rule in Toledo was a full royal pardon for
all the crimes committed by the inhabitants in the rebellion.

The future status of the New Christians in the city was no lesser a cause
of disagreement. The King demanded that the conversos in Toledo be fully
restored to their former positions and that all discrimination against them
stop. This included of course admission to the city of all the conversos
expelled by Sarmiento, permission for conversos to resume the offices from
which they had been ousted by the rebels, and of course the abolition of the
Sentencia-Estatuto with all its degrading decrees. But the council would not
hear of any of these things. Its members stubbornly opposed the King's
demands as if their lives depended on it. Finally, the King and Alvaro must
have realized that, however unreasonable the council appeared, it could not
be ignored or discounted. It was a stumbling block on their road back to
Toledo; and it had to be removed.

We can now understand why the Prince handled the departure of Sarmiento as he did. He knew that the way he would treat Sarmiento would bear
directly on the two major issues that divided the Toledans and the King (i.e.,
how to treat the crimes of the rebels and how to judge converso rights). Had
the Prince followed the conversos' counsels and punished Sarmiento as they
wished, he would have signaled to the Toledans where he stood on the issues
that were uppermost in their minds. And he could foresee the result: the loss
of their amity and fidelity—a loss which he could then ill afford. For the
Prince did not expect plain sailing in his future negotiations with Alvaro on
Burgos, and he knew that his only chance of success rested on his firm grip
on Toledo. But the strength of this grip, he likewise realized, depended
considerably on the friendly relations he might cement with the Toledan
citizenry.

As the Prince saw it, sooner or later the administration would surrender
the castle of Burgos—if he could hold on to Toledo long enough. Toledo was
far more important than Burgos, and by any calculation the exchange he
proposed was in the King's favor, he believed. Alvaro, however, judged the
issue differently: the Prince wished to obtain a royal asset in return for
another royal asset he had seized and held illegally against the King's will.

Alvaro refused to satisfy that wish, which implied denial of the King's rights. In addition, his control of the castle of Burgos was vital, he thought, for the peace of the kingdom—not to speak of his security, which could be jeopardized by the surrender of that stronghold to his enemy.

Thus, to settle its Toledan problem, the administration had to contend with two factors that strongly opposed its plans—the council and the Prince. Resolving to deal with each independently, it chose to strike at the council first. It hoped to break the council's resistance by applying greater pressure to the city.

II

On April 18, 1450, the King ordered the republication of the bull against the rebels *(Si ad reprimandas)* that had been issued on September 24; and two weeks later, on May 4, he published the bull *Humani generis,* also dated September 24, against the persecutors of converts.[3] Both bulls were accompanied by the "sentences" of the bishops entrusted by the Pope with their "execution"—"sentences" that explained the intent of the Pope's orders, the procedures to be followed in carrying them out, and the punishments involved in their violation. Translated into Castilian, the bull against the rebels was published not only with the sentence of its "executor," Don Fernando de Luxán, bishop of Sigüenza[4]; it was also accompanied by an opening statement and a concluding declaration of King Juan II.[5] In this declaration the monarch made clear his determination to bring all the rebels to justice. This was the first public attack launched by the King against Toledo.

The sentence of Don Fernando, bishop of Sigüenza, was generally faithful to the Pope's scathing bull, but by emphasizing as it did the severity of the punishments decreed by the Pope for the Toledan rebels, as well as by its broadened definition of the culprits, it made the bull seem even harsher. As for the punishments, the sentence stressed the *perpetuity* of the "excommunications" that the bull had decreed,[6] and the total prohibition which this penalty implied on any association with the culprits.[7] And as for the range of the criminals involved, the sentence added to the categories of the transgressors (which were specified in the Pope's bull) the "messengers" and "agents" of the arch-criminal[8]—in all probability, to make it clear that not only those who shared his intentions, gave him counsel, or engineered his plans, but also those who carried out his instructions, were subject to the same punishment. Evidently, Alvaro and the King believed that by striking at everyone who took part in the rebellion, regardless of motive and personal condition, they would prove at last that rebellion does not pay and finally stamp out the insurrectionist movement.[9] The same aim and policy were also reflected in the King's declaration which was published, as we have indicated,

together with Don Fernando's sentence. The Pope instructed the lay authorities in Castile to arrest all the rebels and deliver them to the King, if the King
ordered them to do so.[10] Juan II now gave that order, coupling it with another
command. For in the same declaration he also instructed the authorities to
kill the rebels if they resisted arrest.[11]

The same determination of the royal administration to force the Toledans
to do its bidding is also reflected in the rigid sentence that accompanied the
bull on the conversos.[12] Pedro de Castilla, bishop of Palencia, who was
chosen by the King to "execute" the bull,[13] did his best to present the Pope's
directives in a way that fitted royal intentions. It is thanks to his sentence,
more than anything else, that we can see where the administration stood on
the converso issue—at least, until May 1450.

Addressing itself to all Christians, lay and ecclesiastic alike, but especially
to the Church leaders in Spain (patriarchs, archbishops and bishops), the
sentence orders them in the firmest manner "completely to desist from
separating" the conversos from all the "dignities, honors and offices, notaryships and depositions of witnesses,"[14] and also from "offending, attacking,
disquieting or molesting them by word or deed, by yourselves or by the
agency of any one of you."[15] It further enjoins them that "without deceit,"
they "revoke, undo and totally annul" such practices within their jurisdiction;
and it warns them not to contravene in any manner, "by your own action or
by any one else," these clear and stern prohibitions.[16] "Do not dare, nor let
anyone dare," the sentence states in clear-cut terms, "to dogmatize in the
future the opposite of the aforesaid," for "such attempts would only scandal-
ize all of you, or any one of you," who might be involved.[17]

Phrased throughout in such strong language, the sentence was calculated
to aid the conversos even more than the bull itself. Accordingly, it ignored
the issue of the "bad Christians," to which the bull paid considerable attention, thereby presumably taking for granted that all conversos were good
Christians and that the only problem the bull aimed at settling was their
mistreatment by some sinful men. No doubt by omitting the subject of the
"Judaizers" from the list of topics dealt with in his sentence, the author had
another purpose as well—i.e., to prevent the development of an *excuse* for
avoiding the fulfillment of the Pope's instructions. Indeed, in a sense, the
whole sentence was geared to attain that very purpose:

> And as for you, Patriarchs, Archbishops and Bishops, for whom we
> have special consideration due to your pontifical dignity, if you act by
> yourselves, or by the ministry of another person, *against* what has been
> stated above, or against any of this, publicly or privately, having made
> the canonic warning of six days, we are putting on you, through this
> script, an *interdict* to enter the Church. And if you remain in this

interdict six days beyond the six mentioned, with the same canonic warning issued through this script, we *suspend you from the sacred ministries*. And if you harden your heart another six days beyond the twelve mentioned ... we shall apply to you, through this script, the *sentence of excommunication*. And, in addition, we shall proceed against all of you, and against any of you or any others, more gravely, even up to *privation, inhabilitation, personal reclusion, and other pecuniary penalties,* as it will appear required by the nature of the transgression.[18]

Who formulated these sharp sentences which include such threats to the ecclesiastic leaders of so large a part of Christendom? It is obvious that the King and Alvaro approved of the general tenor and goal of the sentence, but it is also clear that special motivation was required to frame it in such strong language and fortify it with such exceptional provisions. It would seem that only a converso official entrusted to supervise the drafting of the sentence could have had such motivation. Who was that official? The King's declaration made public with the sentence of Fernando de Luxán bears the signature of the Relator[19]; and we may readily assume that it was the Relator who shared in the production of the other sentence, too. In any case, it is clear that the sentence was meant to impress the country with the royal resolve—not only to restore the *status quo ante,* but also to prevent any attempt by its opponents to disturb its speedy restoration. Above all, they sought to impress upon the Toledans, and especially their councillors and other leaders, that further resistance to the King's orders would only involve them in further crimes and hence in greater punishment. In short, the purpose of both episcopal sentences was to frighten the Toledans into submission.

But the Toledans were not frightened. They were outraged; and they may even have threatened to disrupt the negotiations if the terrible bulls were not withdrawn. In any case, the King could see that the sentences did not produce the results he had expected; rather than softening the Toledans' position, they stiffened their resistance to compromise. And yet, it seems, the King did not relax in pursuing his penal policy to the limit. He hunted down the rebels throughout the kingdom and punished them most cruelly wherever they were caught.[20] This of course related to the contents of the first bull, concerning which the King did not seem to yield an inch.

But different was the case of the second bull. To be sure, we do not know all that happened in this connection, but the documents tell us of the end result. Thus we are told that the King wrote the Pope (probably not later than August 1450) requesting the suspension of the bull *Humani generis* on the grounds that its execution might cause many scandals and, consequently, do more harm than good.[21] Perhaps the bull aroused tumultuous protests and the King found it necessary to make a conciliatory gesture to the irate Old Christians in Toledo. In any case, on October 28, the Pope granted the requested suspension, and this marked Alvaro's first retreat in his contest with the Toledans.[22]

It may have been of course just a tactical retreat, with plans to resume the attack later on. Even so, it is clear that the Toledans could see it as a sign of victory for their cause. At any rate, the King's friendly gesture toward Toledo did not evoke the response he had hoped for. The Toledans did not budge from their former position on either the question of pardoning the criminals or the future status of the conversos. And so, while the negotiations with them bogged down, those between the Prince and the King fared no better. The Prince refused to deliver Toledo to the King until the King gave up the castle of Burgos, while the King refused to surrender that castle to the Count of Plasencia, Alvaro's foe.

III

It is obvious that Alvaro saw no urgency in taking a final stand on the converso issue as long as he made no headway in his dispute with the Prince on the issue of Burgos. Perhaps he was hoping for an end of the stalemate, or rather for a breakthrough in his talks with the Prince, once he established peace with Navarre and thereby strengthened the kingdom's position. In all likelihood, he assumed that the military raids which Navarre was then conducting against Castile contributed in a way to the Prince's stubbornness; and this could be another reason why he sought to end, as soon as possible, the conflict with Navarre. Finally, Alvaro attained by negotiations what he could not achieve by military force. On December 18, 1450, Castile and Navarre signed a peace treaty, which granted the nobles who had fled to Navarre the right to be restored to their estates in Castile. It also provided for the resumption by Alfonso, natural son of Juan I of Navarre, of his position as master of Calatrava.[23]

This was a direct blow to the Prince, for the Order of Calatrava was under the command of Pedro Girón, Pacheco's brother; and by promising that Order to Alfonso, Juan's son, Alvaro no doubt sought to drive a wedge between Juan of Navarre and Prince Enrique. Alvaro knew, of course, that in this matter Pacheco and the Prince would refuse to yield, and that is why he hoped that the Order would become a bone of contention between them and Navarre and break up their dangerous alliance. In consequence, the Prince's position would be weakened, so that he might seek an accommodation with the King.

If this was part of Alvaro's plan, his stratagem did not work. He made his first move in this complex game by giving Navarre every indication that Castile would abide by its commitments. He accepted the fugitive nobles to the country and began to restore them to their estates. The King also

equipped Alfonso with letters, ordering all members of the Order of Calatrava to submit to Alfonso's command.[24] Alfonso, however, after entering
Castile at the head of a considerable body of troops, soon came to the
conclusion that the task was beyond him. He accepted, to be sure, one
position of the Order, but retreated from there to Navarre when he learned
that Girón was planning to take the field against him.[25] Alvaro must have
then informed Navarre that if Alfonso could not enforce his mastership,
Castile could not enforce it for him (except by a war between the King and
his son, which was of course unthinkable); and Navarre no doubt realized
that, under the circumstances, its plan for Calatrava had to be shelved. Also
for other reasons Navarre did not wish to make of this issue a *casus belli;* it
would have meant falling straight into the trap which the foxy Alvaro had so
carefully prepared. Juan of Navarre did not want to be placed squarely
against Prince Enrique and his allies (i.e., the nobles of the opposition), for
Navarre would then have lost in Castile all basis for its claims and maneuvers.

Alvaro thus resumed his negotiations with the Prince without having the
advantage he had hoped to derive from his peace with Navarre. To be sure,
the peace strengthened his position and, conversely, weakened that of the
Prince. Nevertheless, he was soon forced to recognize that the Prince was
holding fast to his position. His terms for agreement were not altered. Nor
were those of the Toledans.

Stuck by the firmness of both sides and their foiling of all his attempts at
revision, Alvaro could not be slow to perceive the core of the difficulty he
encountered. By aiding each other, the Prince and the Toledans simply
doubled each other's strength. With peace at last established with Navarre,
and with the exiled nobles readmitted to Castile, the Prince now needed the
Toledans' support more than at any other time. Therefore, if originally he
may have attempted to soften the city's rigid demands, he made no such
attempts any longer. He went over completely to the Council's side, gaining
thereby its unqualified loyalty and full support in his quarrel with the King.
With this kind of backing by the city's population, his hold on Toledo was
more secure than ever, while the Toledans, protected by the Prince, could
safely continue their intransigence. Thus it became apparent to Alvaro that
if he wished Toledo to return to the Crown, only one course was open to
him—to yield to both the Toledans and the Prince.

He concluded an agreement with both parties virtually on their terms. In
fact, he concluded two separate agreements, one with the Prince and another
with Toledo, and the latter consisted of two parts, one open and another
secret, as later developments make apparent.

IV

The open part was expressed, in the main, in the letter the King addressed to the Toledans on March 21, 1451—that is, ten days before his entry to the city. It is a letter of pardon to all the inhabitants of Toledo *(cavalleros, escuderos, pueblo, vecinos e moradores)* for all the "errors" they had committed against the "royal preeminence" and the laws of the kingdom during the rebellion.[26] Limited to this particular goal, the letter is tailored to suit its end. Even so, one can learn much from this letter about how the converso problem was settled in the negotiations between Alvaro and the Toledans.

In enumerating the crimes the Toledans had committed, the letter points out, apparently in the right sequence, that they had joined Pero Sarmiento in his rebellion; helped him to take over the city's government; executed and otherwise killed some men and women without any right and against the laws; illegally arrested and tormented others and seized and confiscated their possessions; ignored the king's orders and refused him entry into the city; bombarded the royal forces when the king laid siege to Toledo; dispatched many letters throughout the kingdom in which they described the king in foul terms, and "not as their king and natural lord"; laid hands on all the tributes and taxes which the city was in duty bound to pay the king, as well as on the revenues of certain churches and monasteries and the sums some people had deposited therein.[27]

The long list of crimes which, according to the letter, were committed in Toledo during the rebellion contains however nothing that pertains to the conversos. In fact, the conversos are not mentioned in the letter, as if they had not been a special target and not borne the brunt of the rebels' persecution. To be sure, in referring to the killings, the executions, the torments, the robberies and the confiscations, the king could be assumed to have meant the crimes perpetrated against the conversos, too; but there is no clear indication of this. Nor does the letter touch on the violations of justice committed by the so-called religious tribunals, under the leadership of Pero Galvez; these violations included atrocities perpetrated *only* against the conversos, and not against any other citizens; yet these crimes and their selected victims are not mentioned even in a word. Similarly, no mention is made of the expulsion of so many Toledans (mostly conversos) from the city; nothing is said about the peremptory removal of many officials from their public posts solely because they were conversos; and not a word is said about the enactment of the *Sentencia,* which established a regime of discrimination in the city—again, specifically against the conversos. In brief, the conversos' trials and tribulations seem to have been deliberately ignored, covered with a heavy blanket of silence as if they had not occurred.

To be sure, the letter adds that the citizens permitted or consented to the perpetration of many "other things" which deserve "great blame and repre-hension," and that these things are being done "to this day."[28] One may assume that under this category of "things" the king referred to the offenses committed against the conversos only; but if so, it is clear that *these* offenses, which were the gravest and most atrocious of all, were treated as secondary in importance compared to the others, which were conspicuously mentioned. What is worse, since these crimes were not even named, there was no indication that they were regarded as crimes and, consequently, that they should be discontinued. Thus, one cannot gather from the King's letter that the expulsion of conversos from their offices was a crime and that therefore those expelled should be reinstated; or that the prohibition on conversos' giving testimony at court was a crime and therefore should be abolished. In contrast, the letter makes it clear beyond doubt that the king forgave the citizens for all the crimes they had committed; that the goods they had stolen were to remain theirs; and that no one would have the right to call them to justice, or demand any compensation from them, at the request of any party:

> And it is my wish and order that at no time, nor for any other cause, or reason, or excuse, neither I, nor any other person, nor anyone of my governors and judges, nor any one else, be able to demand or proceed against your properties or against anyone of you, or against others who, at your order, committed such killings, burnings [*quemas*], acts of vio-lence, robberies and expropriations, and any other offenses, or misdeeds of whatever gravity, for I forgive it all and hold it as forgiven.[29]

What is more, the king revoked and declared of no effect all acts, processes, and sentences made or submitted against any inhabitant of Toledo, or against the possessions of any such inhabitant, in relation to the above[30]; and further-more, he cleared them of "*any infamy and blemish* that they incurred as a result of their crimes and misdeeds and as a result of the processes and sentences that were issued against you or anyone of you," and restored them to their "good reputation."[31] The citizens of Toledo therefore were cleared even of moral guilt for all the gross crimes they had committed; on the other hand, the conversos, who had been subjected by these citizens to a long and vicious campaign of vilification, who were blamed as heretics, Judaizers and apostates, remained in their infamy.

One can understand the feelings of consternation, distress and wrath that swept the camp of the conversos in Spain shortly after this cedula was published. It was obvious that in the final deal the king had made with the city of Toledo, the conversos' interests, needs and rights had been sacrificed to the wishes and demands of their enemies. Above all, we must conclude that the *Sentencia* remained in force; for not a word was said about its abolition; nor was any compensation offered the conversos for the losses and suffering they had endured; nor were those expelled allowed to return. All the appeals they had addressed to the rulers—such as the Instruction of the Relator (which was aimed at the Prince) or the *Defensorium* of Cartagena (which was aimed at the king)—seemed to have fallen on deaf ears.[32]

The King's letter to the Toledans was not issued by the Relator; it was processed by Pero Fernández de Lorca, doubtless an Old Christian.[33] To have the Relator prepare a royal letter that showed such disregard for the rights of his group, and such lack of consideration for his struggle in their behalf, was of course too much to ask. But the Relator did not need to prepare that letter to be informed of what was going on. There is no doubt that he, like other conversos who occupied high posts in the Court of Juan II, had long known which way the wind was blowing, and that the conflict between the Toledans and the King was being resolved at the conversos' expense. It is doubtful, however, whether they had known of *all* the concessions and promises given. Of some of these, it seems, they learned only later, when the course of events revealed to one and all the secret part of the agreement between Alvaro and the city.

V

On March 30, 1451, barely ten days after the publication of the pardon and more than a year after Sarmiento left Toledo—the King, accompanied by Prince Enrique, Don Alvaro and "other grandees then at Court," entered the city that had caused him more trouble than any other spot in his kingdom. His entry was to mark the restoration of his rule there, and this is indeed what it did. Juan II, his chronicler tells us, was received with great joy by "all" the townsmen of Toledo.[34]

It is of course unlikely that "all" these townsmen included all Toledan conversos. Nevertheless, despite the disappointment the King's letter to the city must have caused them, the conversos preferred the lordship of Juan II to that of the preceding rulers. They were well aware that they could expect no relief and no justice from the former city masters; but they still expected justice from the King. Especially did they count, we may assume, on the help of the King's first minister, Alvaro de Luna, who was known to be the conversos' friend; and many of them were probably pleased when they learned that day, March 30, of the special responsibilities that Alvaro had assumed in the administration of Toledo.

For what was made public on that occasion was that the alcazar and all the gates of the city were put under Alvaro's direct command[35]; that he likewise became the Chief Judge of Appeals,[36] while his son assumed the post of Toledo's *alguazil,* which meant the head of the city's police.[37] It was clear that the entire city of Toledo was now under Alvaro's personal control, even though Alvaro appointed deputies to fulfill his military and judicial tasks. Yet the conversos who were pleased with this news were ignorant of some crucial facts—that is, those related to the secret agreement concluded between the city and the King. To conversos who could judge things more critically, however, the news was no less than ominous.

For if the understanding between the King and the council included, as it seemed, the latter's consent to Alvaro's assumption of power in Toledo, then the city's enthusiastic reception of the King and, together with him, of Alvaro de Luna indicated some hitherto concealed developments which did not augur well for the converso cause. Did not Alvaro assure the city leaders that he had totally abandoned his pro-converso policy and would, from now on, be the city's friend? Soon the suspicion that this was the case turned into bitter certainty; for this is indeed what happened. By sacrificing the interests and rights of the conversos, the royal administration not only gained Toledo; it also succeeded in placing the city securely in the hands of Alvaro de Luna.

The formal responsibility for this negotiated deal is laid by the documents to the King and the Prince. No doubt the Prince supported the Toledans and strongly urged the King to accept their terms, and there is also no doubt that the King agreed; but behind the heir apparent stood Pacheco and behind the King stood Alvaro de Luna. Nothing that either Juan II or Enrique did in the field of political negotiation was done without the advice and consent of their chief guides and counselors. Thus the conversos were sold by Castile's two shrewdest and most pragmatic politicians—Pacheco and Alvaro de Luna.

The conversos of course could not put many hopes in Juan Pacheco, the Prince's favorite, although, as we have noted, the Relator tried to draw him, by some ingenious arguments, to the conversos' side. But the cold-blooded Pacheco was not impressed. He probably believed that it would be a mistake for him to link up with the hated group. He may have even thought that this was the time for him to gain the favor and trust of the Old Christians, and, accordingly, made himself their spokesman in the negotiations with the King.[38] No doubt the New Christians were informed of his stand by the bishop of Cuenca and others, and what they heard could hardly surprise them. It fitted the known image of the man.

But their feelings must have been quite different when they learned of Alvaro's final stand. Although he was reputed as a crafty manipulator, addicted to power and avid for wealth, he was also considered by many a statesman to whom the interests of the state were paramount. He could, it was assumed, shift his alliances with some nobles whose loyalty to him appeared questionable, but he would not change his basic policies at the expense of principles he was known to uphold. His position toward the conversos was believed to have been taken in full accord with these principles and to form an inseparable part of his governmental system; it had remained unaltered for thirty full years since the beginning of his rule and, naturally, was considered unalterable. That Alvaro would stand by the conversos in such conflicts as had arisen in Toledo during the rebellion appeared to the conversos unquestionable.

The facts, however, could not be misread. The King's letter of pardon to Toledo—in which converso interests were clearly disregarded—and the appointment of Alvaro as the city's master could mean only one thing: Alvaro had negotiated a deal with the Toledans by which he surrendered converso rights in exchange for Toledo's allegiance to the King and his personal control of the city. Once this view became widespread among the conversos, few of them could think of Alvaro de Luna except as traitor to their group and enemy of their cause.

VI

The verbal agreement concluded with the Toledans regarding the future of the conversos in the city no doubt conflicted with the previous assurances the administration had given to the converso leaders. Disclosure of its terms would have greatly embarrassed both King Juan II and the Constable, and this was one reason why it was decided to keep the agreement secret. The Toledans were allowed to go on treating the conversos as they had been doing under the Prince, with the royal administration neither formally approving nor offering objection to that treatment. It was probably assumed that the New Christians of Castile would in time accept their condition in Toledo as a fact of life that could not be changed and give up their struggle to change it.

But there was more to the secrecy that surrounded the agreement reached with the council concerning the conversos. Alvaro, as we shall see, promised the Toledans to take certain steps toward solving the converso problem in line with their demands and to their satisfaction; and he knew that this promise, if divulged, would provoke the strongest converso opposition. To prevent or at least delay this reaction, which was likely to hamper his moves, he chose to keep also this part of his commitments concealed as long as possible. But how long could a surreptitious deal like that remain hidden from the public eye? Inevitably the conversos soon came to suspect that some sinister deals had been made behind their backs; and by pressing for their rights, which were left undiscussed in the King's letter of pardon to Toledo, they uncovered the facts one by one.

To begin with, there was the matter of the New Christians who had been expelled from the city by Sarmiento. The conversos pressed for their return to the city, claiming that their expulsion was among the "crimes" committed by the rebels during the uprising; the King, to be sure, forgave the city for these crimes, but did not sanction their continuation. The Toledans, however, left matters as they were and forbade those expelled to return.

Similarly, the conversos must have asked to be allowed to resume the offices from which they had been ousted, claiming that their expulsion from those offices was illegal, an act of the criminal rebel government. They doubtless also insisted on their right to be appointed to any public office in the city, since the Statute enacted by the rebels was, obviously, in stark violation of the country's laws. Here again the Toledans disagreed, claiming no doubt that what was done was irreversible, relying on the fact that the enactment of the Statute was not denounced in the King's official pardon.

The conversos had no choice but to turn to the King, asking for his intervention and support. He procrastinated, avoiding a definite answer, thus forcing the conversos to come to him again. But he still refused to take a clear stand or reveal his true position. He was, however, under great pressure, and the Old Christians feared that he might retract. They decided therefore to put their case in writing, reminding the King of his agreement with them, of the promises he had given them on the matters in dispute, of his general assurance that he had changed his position with respect to the converso issue,[39] and asked him to stand firm by his pledges and not yield to the conversos' pleas.

The Old Christians sent their letter to the King through one of the city's *regidores*, perhaps to suggest that, with respect to the conversos, Toledo's leaders were all of one mind. The King could no longer avoid an answer, but his answer was hardly explicit. He stated that regarding the expelled conversos and their resumption of the public offices, "it is his will that matters be guarded according to what he had granted them" (i.e., to the Toledans).[40] The cryptic style of this communication, or rather the King's obvious refusal to state in clear terms what he had "granted"—again indicates the double-dealing that must have been going on for some time: the conspiratorial nature of the agreement made with the Toledans, on the one hand, and the contrasting assurances given the conversos in the course of the rebellion, on the other. Obviously, there was great need for face-saving toward all concerned, the conversos in particular. But the facts could no longer be concealed. The king did not deny the Toledans' claims concerning the commitments he had made to the city, nor did he correct their startling indication regarding his radical change of policy. Moreover, he fully confirmed their assertions by making them guardians of the "assurances" he had given them, and virtually authorized them to act in this matter according to their understanding.

The conversos now realized that the Old Christians' triumph was far more complete than they had thought. The Old Christians could now, by the King's authority, block the return of exiled conversos, and they also could, by the same authority, deny them public office. These rights were demanded from the King by Sarmiento in his Petition of May 1449, when the King did not agree even to consider them. But what a change had occurred since then! Sarmiento had left Toledo in disgrace; he was hunted down like a fugitive from justice; his closest aides, the leaders of the rebellion, had been cruelly executed or jailed for long terms. But the policies they had initiated regarding the conversos were very much in force, followed by the entire city of Toledo, and now upheld by the Crown.

VII

Gradually, more developments took place which further revealed the contents of the agreement made behind the conversos' back. We have seen that already in October 1450, the Pope suspended his interdict on Toledo,[41] and this suspension no doubt paved the way for energetic negotiations between the Toledans and Alvaro. But this was not all that the Toledans wanted. What they wanted was the lifting of the interdict and a retraction by the Pope of his bulls against Toledo of September 24, 1449. There is no doubt that in his agreement with the Toledans Alvaro promised them to do his utmost for the total cancellation of these bulls. He kept his word. Two royal messengers were sent to Rome to obtain the desired papal orders,[42] and on November 20, 1451, Nicholas V issued two new bulls, in which he nullified his previous pronouncements. In one of them he totally removed the interdict he had laid on Toledo and its territory, and in the other he absolved the city's inhabitants of all the crimes, wrongs, and excesses they had committed during the rebellion.[43]

The victory of the Toledans was now complete. They had received full pardon for all their crimes not only from the state but also from the Church, and their anti-converso policies were recognized by the royal administration itself. More than that, it seems, they could not ask. But the worst for the conversos was yet to come.

For on November 20, 1451, the Pope also issued a third bull, which called for the establishment of an inquisition in Castile.[44] According to the Pope, he issued this bull at the request of Juan II. But no such action would have been taken by the King without Alvaro's instigation. There is no doubt, therefore, that this bull too was a product of Alvaro's negotiations with the Toledans. He promised them to work hard for its attainment, and this was another reason why he and the Toledans preferred to keep the agreement under cover. Both sides wished to minimize or delay converso opposition both at home and abroad.

The worst part of the bull on the Inquisition was that it referred not only to Toledo but to the entire kingdom of Castile, and all other domains of Juan II. Furthermore, the bull authorized proceedings against any converso who might be put under suspicion, however high his status, rank or reputation. Specifically included in this elevated class were "men of pontifical rank"[45]— and this in opposition to a previous papal order (that of Boniface VIII in 1298) that exempted bishops from inquisitional proceedings.[46] The sphere of the suspect Marranos was thus widened to embrace *all* the conversos of Castile.

This was precisely what García in his Memorial, and the *Sentencia* in its supportive arguments, claimed: *All* conversos must be suspect as Judaizers and none of them therefore could hold public office. We have seen that Torquemada, in his "Treatise against the Midianites," considered this view so malicious and absurd that he used it as proof of the groundlessness of the Statute. Nevertheless, the Old Christians of Toledo adopted that very view and, furthermore, used it to justify their refusal to grant the conversos public offices. Alvaro obviously embraced that view, too, and thus it determined the letter and the spirit of the bull on the inquisition.

It need scarcely be said that every word in that bull was carefully weighed by its various authors—the secretaries of the Pope and the emissaries of Alvaro. In all probability, the mention of bishops as possible Judaizers was made at the insistence of the Constable himself. He could readily anticipate that the converso bishops would be in the forefront of the struggle against the inquisition; and he also knew that they would consider him an enemy and would not cease to obstruct him. Their inclusion among those suspect of heresy was intended to undermine their prestige and influence and deter them from taking any drastic action they might contemplate against him. Yet if these, as we assume, were Alvaro's considerations, he must have been rudely mistaken. The bull on the establishment of the Inquisition in Castile, and the mention of the converso bishops as its target, not only failed to intimidate those bishops; it actually roused them to intensify their activity against both Alvaro and the bull.

One may ask, of course, at this point: Why did Alvaro go so far as to agree to an inquisition in Castile? We can only suggest an explanation. If the bull on the inquisition, like the accompanying two bulls, emerged, as we believe, from the Toledan negotiations, it must have been promised to the Toledans for something they had granted Alvaro in return. But what could that something possibly have been? A correct reply to the second question might offer us an answer to the first.

As we have indicated, the Toledans obtained in exchange for their future obedience to the King, not only full pardon for their crimes, but also consent to the rules and policies they followed with respect to the conversos. But since this consent was given orally and secretly, they must have questioned the value of the commitment. After all, they had nothing in their hands to *prove* what was actually promised them by the King, and oral assurances, as they well knew, could easily be misinterpreted. These doubts must have greatly increased when they learned that Alvaro intended not only to resume his former posts in the city (the Chief Judgeship and control of the gates), but also to assume the command of the alcazar and virtually also of the royal police. This would make him complete master of Toledo, both militarily and judicially. And once this happened, who could assure them that he would not retreat from the promises he was giving and restore the *status quo ante?* Surely he would not lack pretexts to do so, and he *was* the conversos' patron. It stands to reason, therefore, that the Toledans demanded, as guarantee for the verbal assurances they had been offered, that the critical positions of Governor and Chief Judge be entrusted to men who shared their views and whom they could fully trust.

It was now Alvaro's task to move the Toledans to change their mind about his intentions. How could he persuade them to do so? Only by convincing them that he "understood" their position and had revised his entire view of the converso situation. He assured them that, as far as he was concerned, the converso problem had to be solved—not only in Toledo, but also nationally; and to earn their faith and goodwill, he appointed as his military deputy in Toledo Luis de la Çerda, who was the Prince's man.[47] But in addition, he offered them something which they may not even have dared to ask: he would solicit a bull for the establishment of an inquisition, which alone could justify the laws and rulings of the *Sentencia-Estatuto.* He swore that he would work for the issuance of this bull together with the other bulls they requested. This offer and oath may have broken the ice. Alvaro gained the Toledans' confidence; they dropped their objections to his rule of the city, and entered into their agreement with the King, in both its open and secret parts.

All this is of course conjecture. But what is not conjecture is the cardinal fact that a bull was issued by Nicholas V calling for the establishment of an inquisition in Castile; what is also not conjecture is that this bull was signed on November 20, the very date on which the Pope issued his other two bulls in behalf of the Toledans, thus indicating its connection with the Toledan case; and what is likewise not conjecture, but a safe assumption, is that this bull would never have been issued without Alvaro's urging and solicitation. And since none of this is conjecture, we must return to the reasons we have offered for the actions that Alvaro took in this matter.

For what other explanation, we may ask, can one give for Alvaro's radical change of course—to his sudden determination to establish an inquisition, and thereby jeopardize the conversos' position, and virtually abandon all the policies he had followed so consistently in this regard? Surely he did not turn to this course because, after thirty years of dealing with conversos—and presumably knowing them inside out—he now suddenly realized that they were all heretics; or because, although he knew that all along, he suddenly became a pious man, so pious indeed as to go to any length in defense of his religion. Since none of these assumptions appears reasonable, we must revert to the solution suggested above.

Alvaro, then, *changed* his position toward the New Christians; but he did so for political, not religious, reasons. Aware of the risks which the change involved, he thought nevertheless that they were outweighed by the assets that he was to gain in return. He saw the tide of popular hatred rising against the conversos in Castile, and he came to the conclusion that it was irresistible and that by further trying to protect them as he did, he was only tying his own fate to theirs and thereby ensuring his ultimate ruin. But other powerful reasons, too, induced him to come to the same conclusion. He needed to gain Toledo at all costs and he could not achieve this against the city's will. Also, it was vital for him to restore, as soon as possible, his popularity in the nation—a popularity which had been gravely damaged by the Toledans' campaign. And so, pragmatic as always and ruthless when necessary, he decided to cross the line.

VIII

The appearance of the bull on the inquisition indicates that Alvaro had his way. But his victory was not decisive. Silently, and out of the public eye—through negotiations *in camera* both in Rome and Castile, involving leading men in Spain and in the Curia—a strenuous contest was now waged between the powerful Constable and the converso leaders. The results of this contest could be seen, first of all, in another bull, which Nicholas V issued on November 29, 1451, only nine days after he had published his bull on the Inquisition and the other two bulls specifically directed to meet the Toledans' demands.[48]

In this latest bull *(Considerantes ab intimis)* the Pope reiterated the Christian position toward all converts to Christianity from Judaism, Islam, and any other sect—a position which dictates friendship for converts and their equality of status with that of the Old Christians. The bull specifies that no difference can be made between the converts to Christianity, recent or old, and any other Christian with respect to the assumption of honors, privileges, dignities and offices, both secular and ecclesiastic. It mentions the laws enacted to this effect by the kings of Castile and Leon—i.e., Juan II and Enrique III—but refers not at all to what had happened in Toledo or to the still unabolished *Sentencia*. It also orders no punishment for the violators of the bull and entrusts no one with its execution. It is simply a rehearsal of Catholic doctrine—which might be used by the conversos in their defense, but could hardly counterbalance the bull on the Inquisition, which virtually justified the policy of discrimination pursued by the Toledans against the conversos.

While the bull *Considerantes* must have been mainly the result of converso efforts in Rome, the efforts of the conversos in Castile were centered on preventing the publication of the inquisitional bull. It was a supremely difficult task—and yet it was accomplished with signal success. The bull was suppressed and never heard of again until archivists unearthed it in the seventeenth century. Indeed, except for those involved in its suppression, no one in Castile knew anything about it. That is why even a man like Espina, who looked for every possible reason or precedent for the establishment of an inquisition in Spain, made no mention of it. This is why it was never referred to by Alonso de Oropesa either, or by any of the other advocates of the inquisition in the periods of Enrique IV and the Catholic Kings.

How was this suppression achieved? Again we can only conjecture. The only man in Castile who could overrule Alvaro was the King, Juan II. We must therefore assume that at the crucial point, the King forbade the publication of the bull. The man closest to the King was the Relator, and hence we may presume that it was the Relator, possibly together with Alonso de Cartagena, who influenced the King to shelve the bull. Perhaps the extreme formulation of the bull worked in the conversos' favor and led the king to prevent a development that might plunge the kingdom into chaos. The King had just emerged from the Toledan conflict with a bad conscience toward the conversos; he had a good deal of face-saving to do, and was probably embarrassed by his own conduct and the gross injustice he was obliged to cover up; but the establishment of an inquisition—and the way the bull was phrased—may have been beyond anything he thought necessary, or had agreed upon with the Constable. In fact, it is possible that Juan II had no clear knowledge of the preparation of this bull, or at least of its crucial content.[49]

In any case, the total suppression of the bull must have been a result of stern instructions given by the King to Alvaro de Luna. Only such a decisive stand could make Alvaro abide by the monarch's wish and cooperate in the concealment of the bull. That he tried to change the King's position on this matter may be taken for granted, but he evidently failed. This confrontation between the King and Alvaro may have marked the first stage of the conflict between them—a conflict that was to end before long in the Constable's downfall.

II. End of Alvaro de Luna

I

The swift suppression of the bull on the Inquisition was doubtless the most vital and most urgent task the conversos had to accomplish at the time. But it did not provide an answer to the problem with which they had been grappling for years—the problem of the brazen discrimination against them which was instituted and practiced in Toledo. In a sense, rather than being assuaged, that problem was aggravated since the rebels' downfall. For now, the regime of discrimination was upheld not by such men as Sarmiento and García, rebels and usurpers of the city government, but by the legitimate authorities of the city, and, furthermore, was backed (at least de facto) by the powerful representatives of the Crown. The converso leaders were now at a loss as to how to continue their struggle. It seemed they had exhausted all possible means by which they might achieve their ends.

To be sure, they could make some use of the bull of November 29, 1451 on the right of converts to equality of status, and flaunt it as another clear indication of the Church's disavowal of the Toledans' policies. Yet what good could it possibly do? Their enemies had ready answers for them. Since the bull did not refer to the Toledan situation and did not denounce the *Sentencia-Estatuto*, the Toledans could claim that it was not aimed at *them* or did not apply to the conditions of their city. The bull, they could say, referred to *sincere* converts, and it was the rights of *such* converts that it came to guard, while the conversos were all suspect as Judaizers, and therefore the laws that would apply to *them* were those indicated in the *Sentencia-Estatuto*.

But also for another important reason was the impact of the bull of November 29 inevitably most limited, if not totally annulled. The effect of any bull in a western country, and especially in the Iberian peninsula, was usually commensurate with the support given it by the secular authorities. Hence, if the royal administration of Castile wanted to employ the bull *Considerantes* in defense of converso interests, the bull could have served it as an effective tool in the pursuit of that objective. But the royal administration lacked the moral resolve, let alone the political capacity, to do so. Only a few months before, as we have seen, the King had confirmed his agreement with the Toledans with respect to the treatment of the conversos in their city, and that agreement concurred, as we have noted, with the provisions of the *Sentencia-Estatuto*. Above all, it concurred with the secret assurances given the Toledans by the King and Alvaro, who was now not only chief minister of the state, but also virtual ruler of Toledo. What is more, he was head of the city's judiciary, the system that alone had the power to decide which laws (including bulls) were applicable to conversos within Toledo's jurisdiction. And since Alvaro had changed sides in the conflict, and wished to keep faith with his new allies, there was no chance that he would use the latest bull as an instrument to restore converso rights.

Under these circumstances, the conversos saw themselves locked in a dangerous stalemate. They had succeeded in heading off the worst—that is, the establishment of an Inquisition—but they had failed to make headway in their battle against the Statute. The results were ominous. In Spain's foremost center, ecclesiastic and otherwise, New Christians were treated as if they were Jews or—worse—heretical outcasts. Not for a single day could the conversos acquiesce in such a state of affairs.

For now more than ever the Statute threatened the existence of all conversos in Castile. Under Sarmiento they had reason to fear that Toledo might become a model for other cities; under Alvaro, evidently, that menacing prospect became far more real. There was no reason to believe that if the enemies of the conversos rose against them *now* in any other city, Alvaro would not grant them under slight pressure what he had granted the Toledans after a hard struggle. But the danger was not limited to the spread of discrimination. Once the legal bulwarks protecting the conversos were breached in several cities, it was realized, the whole nation could be swept by a flood of hatred that might radically change the royal stand as well. For such a situation could offer Alvaro the opportunity of "proving" to the King how right he was when, in the wake of the Toledan rebellion, he urged a reversal of their policy toward the conversos. That the King might then be swayed to agree with him seemed very likely. And what would follow, if this happened, was not hard to foresee. Alvaro might pull out the bull on the inquisition from the secret vault in which it was lodged and use it as a means to "pacify" the people and as a guideline for a new *national* policy. Few of the leading New Christians in Castile could doubt that Alvaro was capable of doing this; fewer could think of an answer to the problem. There seemed indeed but one way left to safeguard converso existence in Spain—and that was to remove Alvaro from his office as Sarmiento had been removed from his.

But to accomplish this task seemed next to impossible. No one had as yet managed to do it—that is, with real and lasting success. Those who tried it paid for their daring with their estates, their liberties, and sometimes with their lives. After all that had happened, it was hard to believe that enough bold spirits were left in Castile to make the attempt again.

II

At the start of the year 1453, Alvaro began to perceive, to his amazement, that he was the target of a deadly conspiracy in which the King himself was involved. To avoid scandal and embarrassment for Juan II, the plan was to kill Alvaro in such a manner that his death would appear accidental. Several attempts were made on his life which were calculated to produce that impression; but Alvaro, both cautious and suspicious, managed to escape them all.[1] He stubbornly remained with the King's Court, which then made its rounds in northern Castile (from Madrigal through Valladolid to Burgos) and from which were spun the webs of all the plots that had been contrived against him. It is difficult to explain Alvaro's persistence in exposing himself to lurking danger, unless we assume that by staying near the King, he hoped to get at the root of the conspiracy or find a moment of grace for a talk with the monarch in which he might regain his lost favor. Yet whatever the reasons for his conduct in those days, they were evidently based on idle assumptions. From the talks that he had with the King, he gained nothing except a clear indication of the monarch's desire to remove him from the Court as soon as possible; and as for the conspiracy, he never succeeded in discovering its source and its ramifications. By the time he came close to the heart of the matter, he was already hopelessly trapped. On April 15 he was arrested in Burgos, and six weeks later, on June 2, ended his life on the gallows in Valladolid.[2]

Who was behind that secret plan to destroy the all-powerful Constable? Who engineered the repeated attempts to ambush, seize, or assassinate him? And who designed the clever scheme that ultimately led to his capture and imprisonment? The sources are not too clear on these matters and leave much room for speculation. Most of them suggest that the King himself led the plot against his former favorite and was fully aware of the steps taken in the course of its execution.[3] But was the King the original author of the plan to do away with Alvaro, and was it he who took the first steps to have that plan implemented? Some authors ascribe the idea to the Queen, who fell out with the overweening chief minister and did not rest until the King, who loved her, had finally fulfilled her wish.[4] Others point to Alonso Pérez de Vivero as both the brain and arm of the conspiracy; he was Alvaro's "creature" and former friend, as well as a high official at Court, and he manipulated both the King and the Queen strictly for his own selfish designs.[5] The *Crónica de Don Alvaro de Luna* and other sources hint here and there at the involvement of conversos in the King's determined drive to rid himself of Alvaro, but nowhere do these sources present the conversos as the instigators of that drive or as its prime movers. The modern accounts of Alvaro's life—such as those of Quintana, Rizzo and Silió—have ignored even these restrained hints, and so have the historians of the Spanish kingdoms in their discussions of the Constable's career. Thus, Alvaro's fall of fortune is described without relating it in any way to the conversos.

Nevertheless, some scholars whose inquiries have centered on the history of the New Christians, on the annals of Spain's Jews and on the history of the Inquisition, differ on this matter from Alvaro's biographers and the general historians of Spain. According to those scholars, the conversos played a major—if not decisive—part in Alvaro's destruction; and while their views vary on some related points, taken together they offer strong arguments to support this extraordinary thesis.

It is obvious that this thesis, if substantiated, will throw new light on the history of Spain, as well as that of the Marranos in the 15th century, and will lead us, necessarily, to far-reaching conclusions on major aspects of both. We shall therefore attempt to evaluate the arguments of each of those scholars and examine the evidence on which they rest. Above all, we shall look into the two fundamental elements (of *motive* and *deed*) which must be considered in any inquiry of this sort. Then we shall see whether, in addition to the proofs and arguments offered by these scholars, we can find any other piece of evidence, and other reasons based on the sources, that may either support or invalidate the hypothesis we are about to examine.

III

The first to assert that the conversos of Castile sought Alvaro de Luna's destruction and were also instrumental in achieving it, was the first explorer of converso history in Spain, José Amador de los Ríos. According to Amador, they plotted his death, jointly with some of the Spanish nobility, while the leader of the conversos, Alonso de Cartagena, spearheaded the converso part of the plot.[6] Embodied in this thesis was the contention (which Amador also attempted to prove) that the conspiracy climaxed a protracted struggle between Alvaro and the conversos. That conflict, then, was at the root of the plot. But what was the root of the conflict?

As Amador saw it, that root was Alvaro's constant support of the Jews and his stern opposition to the conversos' plan to bring about an end to Spanish Jewry. This plan was, in Amador's opinion, the cherished dream of Paul of Burgos—a dream he endeavored to translate into reality by all the means at his disposal. His sons, and especially Alonso de Cartagena, inherited this ambition of his, and so did other leading conversos who followed in Paul's footsteps.[7] Amador had no doubt that the decrees of Basle (1434) and the bull of Eugene IV against the Jews (1442) were both inspired by Alonso de Cartagena and that, on the other hand, it was Alvaro de Luna who hampered or blocked the implementation of these laws.[8] Thus, he foiled the conversos' designs; and as a result, their dislike of him increased. After his reaction to the Basle decree, that dislike became "open enmity"[9] and, following the issuance of the *Pragmática* of Arévalo, the enmity turned into "a war unto death."[10] In consequence, they joined the subversive nobility in planning Alvaro's ruin. Thus triumphed the policy initiated by Paul of Burgos. "The death of Alvaro signified," says Amador, "the apotheosis of the *Ordenamiento* of Doña Catalina and the bull of Benedict XIII over the *Pragmática* of Arevalo."[11]

As we see it, Amador's theory represents a mixture of truth and fiction. Amador put forward three propositions which seemed to him incontrovertible: (a) the conversos participated in contriving the plot against Alvaro de Luna; (b) this participation emerged from a conflict that had long preceded that development; (c) the cause of that conflict was the disagreement between Alvaro and the conversos on the Jewish question. Later we shall touch on Amador's first two propositions, but now we shall deal only with the third, which relates to the conversos' main *motive* in contriving a plot against Alvaro. And concerning this, we can say from the outset that Amador followed a wrong line of inquiry, relied on a series of unproven assumptions, and built a theory that cannot withstand critical examination.

To fortify his view of the deep antagonism that existed between Alvaro and the conversos, Amador claimed that, besides the religious reasons, there were political considerations that tore the parties asunder. They stemmed from Paul of Burgos' friendship with Fernando, the Regent of Castile who became King of Aragon. According to Amador, Paul extended that friendship to the late Fernando's sons, the Infantes of Aragon—a fact that dictated opposition to Alvaro which was to be shared by his entire clan.[12]

What can be said about these conclusions?

It is possible of course that the bishop of Burgos had a latent affection for the Infantes of Aragon, but not for this would he start a quarrel with the powerful favorite of the king. Paul turned his back on Benedict XIII, to whom he owed his entire career, once he saw that his relations with that Pope could imperil or harm his interests.[13] Such a person would hardly keep faith with a dead man to the point of supporting his sons, once he realized that by taking their side, he might jeopardize the welfare of his own progeny. Nor would Paul have any reason to adopt an anti-Alvarian position. It was under Alvaro and due to his support that Paul's sons made their great careers in Spain; and not only they, but the conversos generally, benefited, as we have seen, from Alvaro's regime.[14] We have also seen that while Juan of Navarre, Don Fernando's son, controlled Castile's affairs, the conversos' position had palpably deteriorated; and that it was with Alvaro's resumption of power that the king could take measures in their defense.[15] In face of these realities, which clearly implied a factual alliance between Alvaro and the conversos, would

Paul's sons be moved by their father's infatuation with the late Don Fernando and his sons, the Infantes, to break that alliance and turn against Alvaro? The notion is both bizarre and unproven. We must judge it untenable.

And no more acceptable is Amador's view of the conversos' alleged hostility to the Jews as a factor that exacerbated their opposition to Alvaro to the point of becoming a "war unto death." Again, it is possible that Paul of Burgos—or his son Alonso de Cartagena, or some other converso leader in Castile—was helpful in moving the Council of Basle to adopt its radical decision against the Jews. But we have no evidence that, even if it were so, it adversely affected, as Amador claimed, the relations between Alvaro and the conversos. Certainly, the appointment in 1435 of Alonso de Cartagena as bishop of Burgos (an appointment that was, in fact, made by Alvaro) does not indicate that Alvaro considered him an enemy, anymore than he regarded him as such the year before, when he sent him to Basle as the King's legate.[16] As for Eugene IV's bull against the Jews, again we do not know who inspired it; but even if it was Alonso de Cartagena, we cannot see why the *Pragmática* of Arévalo should have made him Alvaro's mortal enemy. As we have indicated, the *Pragmática* was not issued by a government controlled by Alvaro de Luna, but by the government of Juan of Navarre (who was hardly inclined to take Alvaro's advice), and the *Pragmática,* moreover, did not offset Eugene's bull, as may be deduced from Amador's words.[17]

In addition, Amador, as we see it, misconceived the conversos' attitude toward the Jews at the time. By the middle of the century, the New Christians of Spain were not obsessed with the hatred for the Jews that had characterized some of their missionary ancestors. Their thoughts were centered on their own problems—political, social and intellectual—problems that related to their own life as Christians and to the sphere of their own interests. It is far-fetched to assume that they were ready to sacrifice these interests, or jeopardize their social and political gains, by entering a conflict so fraught with danger just to fulfill Paul of Burgos' "testament"—or rather his desire to "destroy" the Jews. Neither common sense nor the sources support such an assumption.

And now we shall turn to Amador's second proposition, which is closely related to the third. Amador understood that if the main motive for the plot which the conversos allegedly engineered against Alvaro was their thwarted hostility to the Jews, their conflict with Alvaro must have been of long standing and stretched across the whole period of his rule (since Alvaro had shown his friendliness toward the Jews already in 1420, and perhaps before). But Amador failed to prove this assumption, and the available evidence *denies* the existence of such a protracted conflict. This evidence derives from various sources and from all the three periods of Alvaro's reign.

The first of these testimonies comes from none other than a member of the family of Paul of Burgos—a family which, according to Amador, had constantly fomented ill will toward Alvaro. In 1431 Paul of Burgos's brother, Alvar García de Santa María, served as the royal chronicler of Castile, and in his work he devotes a lengthy chapter to Alvaro de Luna and his administration. This is one of the strongest apologies ever written on behalf of Alvaro; it rejects one by one all the accusations hurled at Alvaro by the opposition; and it extols all his efforts on behalf of the king, the country and the people.[18] To be sure, this was an official chronicle and Alvaro was then at the peak of his power; yet so convincing is the chronicler's presentation, and so cogent and moving are his arguments, that one feels certain that Alvar García truly believed what he wrote. In any case, it is clear that had Alvaro de Luna been hated or opposed by the bishop of Burgos, or generally disliked by the leading conversos, Alvar García would have used less fervent terms to describe the man and his performance.

From the second period of Alvaro's rule—more precisely, from 1440 on—we have the testimony of the nobles who opposed Alvaro and sought his expulsion from the Court. In the memorandum they then submitted to the King, in which they enumerated their complaints against his favorite, they referred, as we have indicated, to the special role which Fernán Díaz de Toledo, the converso Relator, played in upholding Alvaro's rule.[19] According to them, that role was decisive, and essentially, we believe their evaluation was correct; but if so, it does *not* square with Amador's assumption of the "enmity" between Alvaro and the conversos at the time. It is difficult to assume that, had there been such enmity, Fernán Díaz de Toledo could have cut the figure of so ardent a supporter of Alvaro de Luna; and, in consequence, the nobles of the opposition could not have believed that this was the case.

From quite a different source come similar testimonies that relate to the third stage of Alvaro's ministry. They are offered by statements of the Toledan rebels from the year of their uprising (1449). In all these documents, as we have clearly seen, the conversos are described as Alvaro's allies and the chief minister as their protector and promoter. To be sure, as we have indicated, the reasons for the alliance given in those documents must be judged groundless; but one can hardly question the basic fact that Alvaro's relations with the conversos were friendly and that his attitude toward them could be seen as protective.[20] In any case, it is certain that had those relations been marked by a "war unto death" (as Amador de los Ríos claimed), the whole line of campaign followed by the rebels would not have been adopted.

Amador's view of the conversos' motive for their alleged conspiracy against Alvaro de Luna, therefore, must be rejected in both its parts; for neither his theory about the cause of the conflict nor his view about its duration is corroborated by the sources.

IV

Despite its weaknesses, Amador's theory greatly influenced later historiographers, and among those who accepted it was Heinrich Graetz, the famous historian of the Jewish people. Like Amador, Graetz ascribed the conspiracy against Alvaro primarily to a number of leading New Christians who had long been bitter opponents of Alvaro because of his pro-Jewish policy. In the Basle decree of 1434 and Eugene IV's bull of 1442 (both of which he attributed, like Amador, to the influence of Alonso de Cartagena), he saw hard blows not only at the Jews, but also at Alvaro de Luna.[21] Graetz supported this assumption by new data, which he came upon in the course of his researches. For unlike Amador, Graetz was aware of Nicholas V's bull on the inquisition, and he was quick to realize that it must have been a product of Alvaro's determined efforts.[22] But as in the *Pragmática* of 1443, so in the bull on the inquisition, he saw merely Alvarian counterstrikes against his converso enemies. The enmity of the latter became mortal, Graetz believed, when Alvaro "failed to defend them," as he put it, during the rebellion of 1449[23]; and so they went all out to destroy him. They managed, in their plots, to get the better of him, and brought to the gallows the great statesman who was the defender of the Jews.

Since Graetz followed Amador's line of thought on the origins of the conversos' "enmity" toward Alvaro, we can apply our basic criticisms of Amador to the theory of Graetz as well. We shall only have to touch upon the new elements that Graetz introduced in his argumentation, and this we shall do later on.

Following in the footsteps of Graetz and Amador, Henry Charles Lea formed his own view of what caused the conspiracy against Alvaro. Like Graetz, Lea noticed the bull on the inquisition and attributed its appearance to Alvaro's efforts,[24] and like Amador, he saw in the conspiracy the final stage of a protracted struggle between Alvaro and the conversos.[25] But Lea does not touch on the causes of the struggle, leaving us to wonder whether he agreed with his predecessors or failed to arrive at a definite conclusion. As for the bull on the inquisition, he says that its object was merely the "destruction of de Luna's enemies, the converso bishops,"[26] for the constable "seems to have conceived the idea that if he could introduce the Inquisition in Castile, he might find in it a weapon wherewith to subdue them."[27] Why and when did the converso bishops become Alvaro de Luna's enemies? Lea did not explain. But it is clear that, in his view, that enmity was the cause of the bull which was produced by Alvaro in self-defense. In this Lea comes very close to Graetz, but he goes beyond Graetz in attributing to the bull the conversos' determination to destroy Alvaro, and the steps they took to achieve this goal. Now, says Lea, "the New Christians recognized that their safety depended on de Luna's downfall"[28]; they plotted his ruin with the discontented nobles, until the conspiracy against him won over the King.[29]

Our analysis of Lea's statements on this issue must also be postponed to a later stage—that is, following our presentation of the views of another scholar, who likewise inquired into the same problems. Without referring to Graetz and Lea, and perhaps altogether unaware of their positions, Beltrán de Heredia reached the same conclusion regarding the origins of the bull on the inquisition. More clearly, he maintained (like Graetz and Lea) that the architect of this decree was none other than Alvaro and, moreover, that Alvaro also solicited the bull of October 1450 (i.e., the one that suspended the bull *Humani generis* in defense of the conversos).[30] Both bulls, in Heredia's opinion, were instruments in the struggle between Alvaro and the conversos—"these two antagonistic forces which alternately dominated the national politics."[31] Heredia gives no clue to this antagonism, save what is implied in the sentence just cited. If we understand him correctly, he ascribed the origin of the conflict between Alvaro and the conversos to the desire of each of the "rival" parties to control the destinies of the Castilian state. Essentially, then, it was a struggle for power, and in procuring the abovementioned bulls from the Pope, Alvaro simply got an effective weapon to strike at his political adversaries.

But Heredia has more to say on this matter, thereby clarifying his perception of the problem. If Alvaro, as he believed, "conceived" the bull on the inquisition merely as a political "maneuver," the "conception" of the bull would have been impossible if it had not been based on a "reality." That "reality" was the "danger" posed by the conversos to the social and religious life of Spain. The social danger was expressed, as Heredia put it, in the conversos' "exploitation" and "oppression" of the Spanish people,[32] and the religious one in their adherence to the Mosaic faith.[33] Indeed, the action of procuring the bull on the inquisition was typical of Alvaro's tactics and procedures. For his "political wisdom" was characterized by his "ability to utilize an *objective* situation for his quite unrelated personal ends."[34]

Heredia's statements and terminology on this matter echo the partisan and biased charges that were voiced against the conversos in 15th century Castile and revived in large parts of the scholarly literature produced on this subject in the past century and a half.[35] The refrain is familiar. The conversos were secret followers of Judaism and as such were undermining the Christian faith; moreover, they persecuted the adherents of Christianity by ruthlessly "exploiting" and "oppressing" them. As the reader has seen, we have rejected these assertions as wild generalizations based on hateful attitudes; and Heredia, who presents them as "well-known" facts, offers nothing to prove them except this: if the bull on the inquisition had not been based on true claims, "the Pope would not have granted it."[36]

It is difficult to see how a scholar like Heredia could make such a statement in so definite a manner unless he believed in papal infallibility in *all* matters with which the Pope was concerned. But this sort of belief is clearly contradicted by Heredia's own indications that the same Pope changed his position on the converso problem two or three times in the course of two years, and this in accordance with the fluctuating influences wielded upon him from time to time. Similar instability has been noted also in the Pope's positions on other issues—and this condition, as is known, was often caused by changing political circumstances and considerations. Accordingly, when the Pope had to take a stand on any of Castile's internal problems (and the converso situation presented such a problem), he was moved by the wishes of the political authorities rather than by any moral suasion. Indeed, Heredia himself adduces evidence to this effect when he cites Juan II's public declaration on the death sentence issued against Alvaro de Luna.[37]

And just as Heredia's statements on the converso "danger" reflect the views of the Marrano haters of Toledo, and of their spiritual heirs in later times, so does his statement on the conversos' attempts to dominate Castilian politics. To be sure, in the 15th century, Marcos García de Mora who, as we have shown, was a violent antisemite, claimed that the Marranos were *partners* of Alvaro in their attempts to dominate the state of Castile,[38] while Heredia believed that they were his *opponents*, since, like him, they too sought that dominance. But the core of Heredia's views on the conversos was essentially that of García: both believed that the conversos' aim was to obtain full mastery of the Castilian government, and also that they achieved it to a large extent. This brings us back to Heredia's view that Alvaro and the conversos formed the "two antagonistic forces" that "alternately dominated the politics of the nation."

Heredia avoids a definite stand on the question of whether the conversos played a part in the death sentence issued against Alvaro de Luna. But he is clearly inclined to believe that they did. "Everything is possible and even probable," he says, "in that situation in which the King remained reduced to a mere decorative figure."[39] As the reader will see, we reject the notion that in the effort exerted in Alvaro's liquidation, the King acted as a "decorative figure," and similarly we must disagree with the view that the conversos competed and "alternated" with Alvaro in leading the state and determining its destinies. That Heredia should make such an assertion is to us hardly believable. There is no evidence whatever that at any time, at least during the period of 1420–1450, the conversos wished to replace Alvaro or compete with him for his position in the state. Nor do we have any evidence to the effect that the conversos rose against him in concert with his enemies. Serrano's statement that Alonso de Cartagena always displayed "absolute loyalty" to the King[40] could apply to almost all conversos; and for this reason alone the conversos should have been Alvaro's supporters, since the King was decidedly pro-Alvarian at least until the middle of 1451. Thus, if the conversos did take part in the plot against Alvaro in 1453, this action did not stem, as Heredia suggested, from a deep-seated political antagonism any more than it sprang from a protracted dispute on any "religious" issue. Both theories have no evidence to support them, and both rest on mere prejudice—in the case of Amador, prejudice against the converts, and in the case of Heredia, prejudice against the Jews (with whom he identified the New Christians).

It is obvious, then, that of all the scholars mentioned none had suggested an acceptable motive for the alleged converso plot against Alvaro. The view of Amador de los Ríos and Graetz that the motive lay in the conversos' opposition to Alvaro's treatment of the Jewish question had, as we have seen, no basis in fact, nor had their claim that a long-range conflict preceded the alleged conspiracy. Likewise, there is no evidence for Heredia's assertion that *political* strife bred the conspiracy against Alvaro, while Lea failed to offer any reason whatever for Alvaro's quarrel with the converso bishops, in which he saw the root cause of the plot. If we assume, therefore, as these scholars did, that the conversos conspired against Alvaro de Luna, we must revert to our description of the main events related to the Toledan negotiations.

For if there was anything that could provide a motive for such a radical converso action against Alvaro, it emerged from the agreement he reached with the Toledans concerning the solution of the converso problem. For that agreement not only secured for the Toledans royal and papal pardons for their rebellious actions, and other crimes committed during the rebellion; it also enabled them to continue their anti-converso discrimination which was, in converso eyes, the greatest crime of all. Even such royal concessions to the city as forbidding the conversos to claim their stolen property, to resume their services in the city's public offices, and even have their exiled return to Toledo (although they were its *citizens*, who were expelled by Sarmiento for their alleged support of Alvaro and the King!), were shocking indications of where Alvaro stood. Worst of all, that stand was fully confirmed by his support of the plan to establish an Inquisition in Castile and his ardent solicitation of the plan with the Pope. All this was not, as Graetz thought, mere "*failure to defend* the conversos *during* the rebellion" (in fact, during the rebellion, Alvaro *could not* defend them); this meant a direct attack on the conversos, aimed at denying them the protection of the laws—and not only for a limited period. For what was involved here, the conversos clearly realized, was not a temporary surrender to the Toledans, but a total reversal of Alvaro's policy—a reversal that threatened the rights, achievements and, indeed, the very lives of *all* the New Christians in Spain.

To be sure, the above-mentioned scholars have noticed the existence of a conflict between Alvaro and the conversos, but they could not give it a

credible explanation, because they failed to relate it to its true source—
Alvaro's negotiations with the Toledans. This is more understandable in the
case of Amador, who was not aware of the bull on the inquisition, but it is
less understandable in the case of the other scholars, who knew of that bull
but ascribed it to wrong reasons. This is also why most of them believed that
the conflict referred to was of long standing, while in reality it was of recent
origin. Hence the proximity of the two events—the issuance of the bulls of
November 20, 1451 and the emergence of the conspiracy about a year later.

Thus, all the pieces of the historical puzzle fall into their right place. The
conversos took radical steps against Alvaro not because of his pro-Jewish
attitude, but because of his anti-converso acts—and these acts were by no
means "counterstrikes" that the Constable made in self-defense, but direct
and unprovoked assaults on the conversos' most vital positions. Accordingly,
Alvaro was not—as Amador thought—a martyr to his *liberal* policy toward
the Jews, but a casualty of the *illiberal* policy he had adopted toward the
conversos—a policy which was, from the latter's standpoint, so harsh, so
cruel, and so fraught with danger that it forced them to take desperate
measures. And so, if the Marranos plotted against Alvaro, it was *they* who
made the counterstrikes in self-defense; and it was in one of those counterstrikes, which constituted the conspiracy, that Alvaro de Luna fell.

But the fact that we can see a logical motive for an alleged converso action
does not yet prove that the action took place. To prove it, we must offer
sufficient evidence. And thus we turn from the arguments offered regarding
the "motive" for the conspiracy to the evidence advanced concerning the
"deed."

V

Of all the scholars we have mentioned in connection with this thesis, the
only one who presented evidential data in support of the theory of the
converso conspiracy was the originator of that theory, Amador de los Ríos.
There is no doubt that it was primarily this evidence that moved men like
Graetz, Lea and Heredia to take seriously his claims about the plot.

Amador centered most of the evidence he assembled on what occurred in
Burgos before Alvaro's capture. In the case he built against the conversos of
Castile, Amador tried to show that they were at the heart of the conspiracy;
that they actively supported King Juan II in his efforts to destroy his first
minister, and that the man who played a leading role in all this was the bishop
of Burgos. According to Amador, Alonso de Cartagena "did not shun or spare
any means, however unusual or disloyal," to have the plan of the Constable's
ruin progress and finally "consummated."[41] But a later scholar, Francisco
Cantera, took quite a different stand on this issue.

In his biographical study of the Santa Marías, Cantera rejects the "grave accusations" which Amador de los Ríos "launched, without proof," against "one of our most distinguished prelates."[42] Contrary to Amador who, according to Cantera, "read the sources badly and interpreted them worse,"[43] Cantera finds no evidence for the assumption that the bishop was, together with the King, planning the death or imprisonment of Don Alvaro; and the only things the sources make clear, with regard to both the bishop and his family, are, according to Cantera, these: (a) their absolute and most faithful adhesion to the monarch; (b) their decided enthusiasm for Alvaro de Luna during the greater part of his government; and (c) a "discreet personal withdrawal [from Alvaro] when they came to believe that this was required by their loyalty to the King and the good of Castile."[44]

One can readily agree to the first proposition and, generally speaking, also to the second, but the third remains entirely unproven and, in fact, is contradicted by the major premise. If "faithful and absolute adhesion" to the King was the Santa Marías' first rule of conduct, how could they be satisfied in those crucial days, when the King so exerted himself to seize Alvaro and put an end to his power, with mere "discreet withdrawal from Alvaro," as Cantera so elegantly put it? Did not their "absolute loyalty to the King" require full cooperation with the monarch and active help in his determined attempt? Cantera seems to disregard all this, and above all he disregards the fact that, besides the causes of the "King" and "Castile," the conversos had also another cause to mind—that of their rights, freedom and safety, which were so imperiled by Alvaro's actions.

In all his discussions of what transpired in those days between the bishop of Burgos and Alvaro de Luna,[45] Cantera does not devote even a single word to the developments in Toledo. Nor does he touch on Alvaro's policy toward the conversos as it was reshaped in those days, or on the issuance of the bull on the Inquisition, which was a direct result of that policy. Cantera simply ignores all these facts as if they took place in some other country, or as if they had no influence at all on the evolving relations between Alvaro and the conversos. But they inevitably had much to do with that development! And therefore if we review what we know of those relations in light of all preceding events, we must arrive at the conclusion that the bishop of Burgos could not remain neutral, or passive, or withdrawn, in the crucial struggle that unfolded in Burgos in 1453.

What do we know of the relations between Alvaro and the bishop of Burgos in those days? What evidence do we have that the bishop was involved in the plot against the constable? And what testimony is there regarding the role that other conversos played in that affair?

Undoubtedly, the most important piece of information concerning the relations between Alvaro and the bishop is included in Alvaro's own statement as reported in the *Crónica de Don Alvaro de Luna*. He made that statement shortly before his arrest, when his enemies were closing in on him, in response to a proposal by a certain young man who volunteered to show him an escape route from the city. The young man's name was Alvaro de Cartagena, and he was the son of Pedro de Cartagena, the bishop's brother, at whose house in Burgos Alvaro lodged. To the Constable's friends who stayed in that house, the young man appeared trustworthy enough and his offer genuine and sound. They advised the Constable to accept his proposal; but Alvaro rejected their counsel, giving on that occasion the following reasons:

> You know that this Alvaro de Cartagena is of the stock of the Conversos, and you also know how much ill the members of this stock wish me. And in addition, this Alvaro de Cartagena is a nephew of the Bishop of Burgos who, I know well, is the greatest adversary I have in this matter.[46]

Cantera believed that no conclusions can be drawn from this statement about the bishop's attitude toward the Constable, and especially about the assumption that he was in collusion with the King in planning Alvaro's capture and imprisonment. He attributes no value to Alvaro's assertion that the bishop of Burgos was his major enemy when he, Alvaro, was harassed, confused and "suspicious of everything and everybody."[47] Cantera's view, however, of Alvaro's mood, and especially his capacity for clear judgment at the time, is based on no evidence at all and, in fact, is contradicted by our sources.

The *crónica* of Don Alvaro tells us of a row between the soldiers of the bishop Alonso de Cartagena and those of Juan de Luna, the Constable's son. It was deliberately provoked, the *crónica* says, by the conspirators, who expected the Constable to get involved in the skirmish, and thus enable them to capture and kill him. But the Constable avoided the trap. Recalling a similar clash in Madrigal which was contrived for the same purpose, he refrained from approaching the scene of the quarrel. "The prudent Master [of Santiago—i.e., Alvaro]," says the chronicler of Alvaro, "*recognized in his sagacity, or because God granted him this recognition,* or because his hour had not yet arrived, that that row was feigned and false."[48] Thus, the chronicler does not share Cantera's view of the Constable's state of mind. He considers him prudent and wise, endowed with a sharp grasp of events and something like a sixth sense.[49]

As for his suspicions at the time, we should add, they were fully justified under the circumstances, when he knew for certain that the King was involved in an effort to seize and kill him (as indeed he was), but these suspicions did not make him paranoiac. He did not suspect "everybody," as

Cantera says, but only those whom he had good reason to suspect. As it turned out, he suspected too few rather than too many.[50]

But let us come back to the case before us that gave occasion to Cantera's remarks.

One can understand why the Constable found it difficult to put his faith in Alvaro de Cartagena and suspected that his plan of rescue was a trap. Well might Alvaro de Luna wonder: Why should a converso—who, like most New Christians, was assumed to be loyal to the King—act against his group's basic attitude in violation of the king's wishes? Obviously, such a violation might incur punishment of the most severe kind, as Alvaro de Cartagena no doubt understood. And why should he risk his life for a man who had never done him a personal favor and whom his fellow conversos regarded as their enemy? Above all, such an act would implicate his father, Pedro de Cartagena, at whose house the Constable was lodging, and subject him to great agony and disgrace. And, again, why should the young man do it? It is obvious that Alvaro could find no answers to these questions—answers that might induce him to take his aides' advice.

We must conclude that Alvaro's suspicions in this case were not produced by an hallucinating mind. They were well founded; and it has never been proven that he was wrong. As for his remark about the bishop of Burgos, one cannot regard it as an expression of suspicion. It was a statement based on full conviction, on Alvaro's certain knowledge of the facts.

Let us note again what he said when he rejected Alvaro de Cartagena's offer. "You know," he pointed out to his aides, *"how much this stock* [i.e., the conversos] *wish me ill."* The hatred of the conversos for Alvaro de Luna and their desire to see him hurt or destroyed was common knowledge then, and required no proof. *"You know"*—he said to his men. On this basis, one might assume that the leader of the conversos, Alonso de Cartagena, shared his group's hostility to the constable. But Alvaro did not judge Cartagena by that general standard. "And *I know well,"* he added, *"that the Bishop of Burgos is the greatest adversary I have in this matter."* In other words, the bishop was not classed by Alvaro as just another converso opponent. He was involved in "this matter"—i.e., the attempt to seize him—more than anyone else. Accordingly, he was not just *one* of the conspirators but the "greatest adversary" of them all, which may mean, if not their leader, their chief instigator, main counselor, or their most determined member. Then, we must recall that this assessment was not made on the basis of guess or conjecture but, as he put it, from full knowledge. Alvaro did not use such indefinite expressions as "I fear," "I believe," or similar terms to express his thought of the bishop's stand. He said concerning this: "I know well," clearly indicating that in this matter he had no doubts whatsoever.

One may argue of course that Alvaro's "knowledge" is in itself no proof of truth. But on what grounds can it be discredited? Alvaro had known the bishop of Burgos for more than three decades. He knew where he stood on every issue that concerned the state, the Church and the conversos. He knew his moods, his manners and his reactions; and of course he knew how the bishop felt about him and his behavior in the Toledan crisis. He could hardly be mistaken as to the claim that the bishop belonged to the camp of his enemies; and his emphasis that he was the greatest of them all only indicates the firmness of his conviction.

To this reported statement of Alvaro de Luna we can add an important piece of evidence, which indicates that the bishop was indeed engaged in the effort to seize the Constable. In the final stage of the conspiracy and the hunt, when Alvaro was surrounded in Burgos by his foes and it was clear that he could not escape, the King wished to have him arrested and sentenced rather than killed in an attack. Accordingly, he sent to Alvaro emissaries whose aim was to persuade him that, rather than resist, he willingly surrender to the King. According to the *crónica* of Alvaro de Luna, the first of these emissaries were Alonso de Cartagena and Rui Díaz de Mendoza, the King's major *mayordomo*.[51]

They came to Alvaro, and Díaz de Mendoza communicated to the Constable the King's wish that he place himself willingly in the King's imprisonment, "inasmuch as this would be in the King's service and the good of his Kingdoms."[52] Alvaro answered that he was ready and willing to fulfill the King's wish; but he asked to be given a "security against his enemies," who are in the King's company and "knew how to turn the great love he had for him into a dislike and indignation against him."[53] To this the bishop responded:

"Señor, you ought not at this time to ask such things; for the King now certainly shows himself to be very annoyed with you, and if we come to him with such a demand, his anger will increase more."[54]

So far Alvaro had treated Cartagena with the customary civility and formal respect; but now, in reaction to the bishop's remark, he threw off his diplomatic mask, gave vent to his true feelings, and revealed what he thought of the bishop of Burgos and the "friendly advice" he gave him:

"Bishop," he said vehemently, "be silent now! And don't dare talk where *caballeros* speak! Speak where those who wear the long folds do. And don't dare interfere more in this [here], because I have spoken—and speak—with Rui Díaz, and not with you."[55]

One can understand what triggered this outburst against the King's messenger. For all its vehemence, it had a rational basis. Alvaro saw in the bishop an obstacle for him to achieve what he then needed most, the one thing that would give him a chance for survival—i.e., the King's safe-conduct. His violent reaction betrayed his resolve to remove that obstacle from his way.

Not for a moment did he believe that the bishop's advice was given for his own good, as its contents ostensibly suggested; it was meant, he was sure, to deny him, Alvaro, the only possible protection he could get—and thus secure his ruin. All the bishop wanted was to carry out his mission, which was to deliver Alvaro to the King with no strings attached—without safe-conducts or similar assurances. The King could then freely do with Alvaro what he wished and planned to do with him.

That the King's plan at that stage was to seize Alvaro, sentence him to death, and then confiscate his large estates can hardly be doubted. This is precisely what the King later did, and this is, most probably, what his trusted advisers (who, together with him, laid his schemes in those days) counseled and urged him to do. But even if we assume that, at that stage, the King had not yet arrived at the decision to send Alvaro to the gallows, it is clear that Alvaro's arrest at the time was meant not only to demote and disgrace him, but also to enable the King to impose heavy penalties on him and his estate. This was of course the minimal aim which the conspirators sought to achieve and without which there was no sense at all in the entire conspiracy. It would be unthinkable that this minimal aim, if not the plan as finally implemented, was unknown to the Kings' emissaries, who had to have this knowledge in order to perform their task.

The bishop was one of these emissaries; and hence his awareness of the mission's aim may be viewed as a foregone conclusion. He knew that the King would not want Alvaro to have the securities he asked for. Securities, to be sure, were occasionally broken, but their violation was likely to cause problems, moral and political, even for kings. Besides, there was no telling how this royal pledge might affect the King's ultimate position. And the bishop evidently wanted to be sure that Alvaro's surrender would this time lead to his political destruction. Hence his immediate negative reaction to Alvaro's logical and legitimate request. In any case, his participation in that mission, whose purpose was to bring Alvaro to prison, indicates his collusion with the King's plan, and not just a "discreet withdrawal" from Alvaro, as Francisco Cantera would have it.[56]

This cooperation of the bishop and the King continued up to the moment of Alvaro's arrest. From what the *crónica* of Alvaro de Luna tells us, it appears that Cartagena was with Juan II throughout the negotiations between Alvaro and the King concerning the securities demanded by the Constable. According to the same source, it is evident that all those who then surrounded the King, and whom he consulted on this matter, were adversaries of Alvaro and sought his downfall. It is virtually inconceivable that Alonso de Cartagena was the only exception.

The problem that now confronted them all was how to react to Alvaro's demand, which Alonso de Cartagena had tried to evade. But unlike Cartagena, the other counselors of the King did not take such a serious view of the matter. When they heard of Alvaro's condition for surrender, they urged the King to accept it. Consequently, Ruiz Díaz de Mendoza, this time accompanied by Afán de Rivera, returned to the Constable with a "security" for his life.[57] But Alvaro was not satisfied with it. He demanded a security which would assure him his life, his freedom, the inviolability of his body and the safety of his possessions, and he demanded the same guarantees from the King for his family and his closest friends. The *crónica* of Alvaro de Luna tells us that, after considerable consultation with his counselors, the King gave Alvaro these guarantees and swore to them before the bishop of Burgos.[58] According to the chronicler, all these guarantees were violated after Alvaro's arrest and treated as if they had never been given.[59] But this was not precisely the case.

The text of the security given to Alvaro seems to have been essentially the one found in the *Crónica de Juan II*. According to this *crónica*, the King gave Alvaro his "royal assurance" *(fe real)* that he would "receive neither damage nor injury either in his person or in his estates and that nothing would be done to him against justice."[60] This security, the *crónica* adds, could not have satisfied the Master; but "seeing that he was in no position to defend himself, and that his troops did not respond to his call, he surrendered himself to prison."[61]

We can well understand why the text of the security did not appeal to Alvaro. Its second part canceled in effect its first. The assurance that "*nothing would be done to him against justice*" implied that *everything* could be done to him if it was *not* against justice—and, in addition, what was just and unjust would of course be determined by the King. We see in the final, seemingly innocent clause, to which it was most difficult to object, the fine hand of an expert jurist such as the Relator or Alonso de Cartagena. With that escape clause, the bishop could accept formally, and without jeopardizing his honor, the King's oath (whose declared intent was false) and give the King the legal freedom he needed to act against the constable as he wished.

While the securities were being negotiated and "these matters, or rather these frauds," as the *crónica* of Alvaro puts it, were transacted, "the King was in the [public] square, and with him were the Bishop of Burgos, Don Alvaro de Estúñiga, and a large number of people, on horse and on foot."[62] Alvaro de Estúñiga was the commander of the force that was to attack Alvaro and seize him, dead or alive, if the negotiations for his voluntary surrender failed. He was the son of the Count of Plasencia, Alvaro's implacable enemy, and himself most anxious to carry out the attack. Besides him, in the King's company, the biographer of Alvaro refers only to Cartagena who, incidentally, is mentioned first in order, no doubt as the man closest to the King and the most prominent of his counselors. He stayed there with the King awaiting the news of Alvaro's consent to be imprisoned following his acceptance of the revised royal pledge, ready, if necessary, to advise the King what to do if Alvaro requested some other revision. In any case, he was there because *he had to be there until the conspiracy was fully consummated.* What can indicate more clearly the chronicler's view of Cartagena's complicity than his statement that the bishop was with the King while those "frauds"—i.e., false promises and deceptions—"were taking place"?

If we are to believe Cantera, the bishop of Burgos was dull and dumb and knew nothing of what was happening around him; or he was extremely naive and credulous, and unwittingly served as a pliant tool in the hands of the King and his collaborators. But the bishop of Burgos was neither dumb nor naive. He was subtle, discreet, extremely careful; but he did not succeed in fooling Alvaro, who "knew well" that he was working for his ruin; nor did he succeed in fooling us, though time has dimmed, and almost erased, the traces of his role in the "Alvaro affair." To Cantera it appeared "insidious" and "calumnious"[63] to suggest that this man, "one of our most distinguished prelates,"[64] was a leader in that nasty and bloody intrigue. But Cartagena was a son of his age; and he was not the only known author or bishop who engaged in such warfare. The Marquis of Santillana, bishop Lope de Barrientos, Alonso de Carrillo, archbishop of Toledo, Alonso de Fonseca, archbishop of Seville, and the historians Diego de Valera and Palencia are only few of his many known contemporaries who may be mentioned to illustrate that common rule.

If the *Crónica de Don Alvaro de Luna* supplies us with much or most of what we know of Alonso de Cartagena's share in the conspiracy, other sources contain valuable information about the parts played in it by other conversos. Thus the *Crónica de Enrique IV*, which was composed by Alonso de Palencia, preserved an important piece of evidence which confirms Amador's thesis— namely, that the conversos were involved in the promotion of the plot against Alvaro de Luna.

This evidence, which escaped the attention of our great Spanish investigator, relates to the major and final attempt to arrest Alvaro or kill him. Conceived or put in motion by Alonso Pérez de Vivero, Alvaro's former friend turned enemy, the plan was to induce the Count of Plasencia, the old and bitter foe of Alvaro, to dispatch to Burgos a military force that could overcome the Constable's troops in the city and thus bring about Alvaro's "end." Accordingly, Vivero informed the Count of the King's design concerning Alvaro de Luna and urgently asked him, in the King's name, to provide military help. But the Count, suspicious of Vivero's intentions, turned the offer down. In an effort to dispel the Count's suspicions, the King sent Castilla, chief of his couriers, to Diego López de Estúñiga, the Count's cousin, in the hope that the latter might help move the Count to offer his much needed aid. But this attempt, too, was to prove futile. The cousin, to be sure, tried to influence his uncle, but to no positive effect. The Count, now convinced that a conspiracy was afoot, turned down Castilla's request, too. "He did this," says Palencia, "because, not without reason, he feared the evil he could sustain from his adversary [namely, Alvaro] and the indolence and cowardliness of the King."[65] Then the King dispatched "with the same intent," a third messenger to the Count. He was Luis Díaz de Toledo, "son of the beloved Relator," and "once again the Count, moved by the same fear, gave the same answer."[66]

This extraordinary piece of evidence sheds much light on the problem before us. It forms a central link in the chain of testimonies that one can offer in support of the thesis first presented by Amador de los Ríos. Amador's argument suffered considerably from his failure to note and use this testimony. We shall now see what it implies.

Luis Díaz de Toledo, the son of Fernán Díaz, was not only distinguished by birth. He was doubtless endowed with no mean talents, since some Castilian leaders thought him worthy of occupying the office of his famous father. In May 1467 we find him acting as Relator in the government of Alfonso, Juan II's son, who was raised to kingship by Archbishop Carrillo and the nobles who rebelled against Enrique IV.[67] In the document testifying to this fact, he is also designated as *"oidor e referendario del Rey,"* as the King's "secretary" and "member of his Council," and *"notario mayor de los privilegios rodados"*[68]—in brief, by all the titles that adorned the name and defined the authority of Fernán Díaz de Toledo.[69] What concerns us at the moment is that in 1453, this able man enjoyed the full confidence of Juan II and was considered wise and persuasive enough to have a chance of succeeding where his predecessors had failed.

But especially important, from our standpoint, is the fact that he was the King's secret agent in the execution of the plan to seize Alvaro de Luna. This means that he was deeply involved in the plot—and of course not only he alone, but also his father, Fernán Díaz. As the son of the Relator, who was known as the King's most faithful and most influential servant, he could, it was hoped, assure the Count that the offer was genuine and the plan sound. For, from the very acceptance by Luis Díaz of that mission, the Count could infer that the Relator was behind it, and aware as he was of the Relator's sagacity, that inference should have led him to believe in the plan. And who indeed can doubt that this was the case—namely, that the Relator was a party to the plot? Surely if the Relator had not supported the attempts to seize Alvaro and divest him of his powers, he would not have let his son face the grave dangers which that mission entailed. No one knew better than the Relator what punishments he and his son could expect if Alvaro managed to weather the storm. In brief, Luis' role in the conspiracy at that phase makes it not just probable but absolutely certain that his father was deeply involved in it; and the measure of the risks the Relator then took indicates both the depth of his involvement and the fierceness of his determination.

But this, plus his closeness to the King as his most trusted confidant and most influential adviser, makes it evident that he was not just a collaborator, a theoretical supporter, or a member of the conspiracy, but one of its planners and prime movers.

VI

It seems that in the months preceding his arrest Alvaro never noticed that Fernán Díaz de Toledo was in collusion with his enemies; and this is why the latter was sent to him repeatedly in order to persuade him to surrender.[70] Other messengers the King sent to Alvaro were also involved in the plot, and Alvaro failed to realize their involvement, too. In any case we have no indication that he saw through Fernán Díaz.

It was only when the Constable was behind bars that the Relator took an open stand against him, clearly revealing where he stood in the attempt to destroy the powerful statesman. The facts related to this stand neatly tie up with the mission of his son to Estúñiga, the Count of Plasencia, as well as with his effort to induce Alvaro to surrender just before he was arrested. In this matter he worked hand in hand with Cartagena, and both of course were aiming at the same result.

But let us see what the Relator did after Alvaro's arrest.

In an anonymous document of the 15th century found in the archives of the Marquis de Villena, it is stated that "when King Juan II wished to have a judgment issued against the Master of Santiago, Alvaro de Luna, he invited nine jurists *(letrados)*, in whom he had confidence."[71] To these jurists, who were joined by two noblemen, he presented his charges against the Master and asked their advice as to what to do about it. The first of the eleven jurors listed in this document was Fernán Díaz de Toledo, and it was also he whom the King first requested, in the presence of all the others, to express his opinion.

The Relator then asked the King whether he was sure that all the things he said about the Constable were true. The King answered that he spoke with "certain knowledge" and that the assembled jurists could rely on what he said. In reaction to this, the Relator replied that, in this case, Alvaro deserved by right *(segund derecho)* the penalty of death and the loss of all his property to the chamber of the king.[72] "This answer pleased the King greatly. And since the other jurists saw what the King wanted, they all followed the counsel of the said Relator."[73]

Limited as it is to a few bare facts, this document conceals more than it reveals the Relator's great part in Alvaro's condemnation. One can hardly assume that it was then and there that the Relator first heard the King's accusations against Alvaro, and that the question he addressed to the King in response was meant to clarify certain things he wished to know. Actually, the question was purely rhetorical; it was directed to the audience rather than the King, and in all probability, it was orchestrated with the King before that meeting. Similarly, the "opinion" he expressed on that occasion as to how Alvaro ought to be sentenced was no novelty to the King. Indubitably, Juan II knew, from the many talks he had with Fernán Díaz, that the latter favored the death penalty for Alvaro, and the "opinion" he asked the Relator to voice was intended of course not for himself, but for the jurists whose support he sought. Thus, both the King and the Relator imposed, in a few minutes, the whole weight of their authority on the counselors assembled; they hardly gave them a chance for deliberation; and the Relator's opinion soon won over the whole group to the King's side.

Had not a hitch occurred soon thereafter, the verdict would have stood as given and the Relator's part in the affair might have been over. But two jurists, members of the King's Council, who were not present at this gathering (perhaps because they were absent from the town), expressed their wish to take part in the discussions concerning Alvaro's fate. The King, who did not want the sentence to look hurried, or issued by his own picked judges, had no choice but to call a second meeting. No doubt he suspected that the two councillors might object to the *contents* of the verdict; yet he said, as something he had taken for granted, that what they sought was to determine the *form* of its execution.[74] However, what took place in the second meeting was far from being in accord with his assertion. The two councillors, Franco and Zurbano, initiated a reconsideration of the judgment; and as the aforementioned document tells us, there developed, as a result, a sharp dispute among the jurists and the unanimity they had displayed in the first meeting could not be restored.[75] Finally, however, they agreed to confirm the sentence advocated by the Relator—not as judgment based on legal procedure *(por sentencia)*, but as a mere order of the King, whose directions they were in duty bound to obey.[76]

If we add the information included in that document to what we gather from the *Crónica de Juan II*, we may conclude that even this resolution was achieved with great difficulty. Shortly after presenting his case against Alvaro before the first meeting of the jurists, Juan II left for Maqueda and Escalona, the fortresses of Alvaro held by his captains which the King had to besiege.[77] He realized that as long as Alvaro was alive, his men would resist surrender, and this increased his desire to have Alvaro sentenced and executed as soon as possible. He must have been greatly disappointed upon learning of the disagreement that had developed among the jurists, but he ordered the discussions to be renewed, this time with the participation of additional

jurists and also of certain noblemen and prelates. We may assume that these
noblemen and prelates were all confirmed opponents of Alvaro. Nevertheless, the discussions lasted for two days, and it was only then that those
assembled subscribed to the death sentence against Alvaro—however, as
indicated, not as a court judgment but as a royal order.[78] When the King met
with them to hear their verdict, they asked the Relator to communicate their
decision, in the presence of all of them, to the King. He said:

> Señor, all the noblemen and doctors of your Council who are present
> here and I believe that also those who are absent will agree to join with
> us in this matter. Having seen and recognized all the deeds and things
> committed by the Master of Santiago Don Alvaro de Luna in your
> disservice and in harm of the public cause of your Kingdoms, and how
> he had usurped the Royal Crown, and how he tyrannized and robbed
> you of your rents, we find that it is right *(por derecho)* that he be
> decapitated, that his head be cut off and placed on a high pike on a
> scaffold for a number of days, so that his punishment may serve as an
> example for all the great of your kingdom.[79]

This declaration may appear to contradict what we said above about the
basis of the sentence issued against Alvaro de Luna. But it does not. When
the Relator said that the members of the council who considered Alvaro de
Luna's case found him to deserve the death penalty *"por derecho,"* he deliberately used here an ambiguous expression that could mean both *rightly* and
properly—i.e., according to proper procedure. By using this term, he not only
weakened the negative side of the decision made, but also brought up its
positive aspect, which we gather from his very formulation. For while the
councillors found it impossible to render judgment according to the requirements of the *law*, they could say that, in their studied opinion (and that meant
on the basis of what they knew), Alvaro *deserved* capital punishment, and
hence, if the king sentenced him to death, they would treat his decision as
a just order and accordingly subscribe to it as members of his Council.

It was of course a limited consent given on the basis of a hard-won
compromise, but it enabled the King to do by consent what otherwise he
would have had to do without it. There is no doubt that this achievement,
too, must be credited mainly to the Relator. Not in vain did the councillors
ask *him* to present their common decision to the King. By this they indicated
not only their recognition of his authority as jurist, but also of his leading part
in the debates that culminated in the above conclusion. And just as it was
his proposal that was unanimously accepted by the jurists in their *first*
meeting, it was probably again his formula—or one to which he gave his
consent—that was unanimously agreed upon in the final stage of the discussions on the verdict.

The conclusion we may draw from the data we have analyzed seems to us incontrovertible. The Relator's participation in the attempts to persuade Alvaro that he deliver himself voluntarily to the King; the fact that his son was sent by the King to enlist the Estúñigas in the plan to seize Alvaro; and above all, the role he played in the Council in order to obtain Alvaro's condemnation, all show that he was a leading force in the conspiracy and, as the Relator and the King's confidant, one of the guides and inspirers of the King's crucial anti-Alvarian drive. As far as the conversos were concerned, the Relator was undoubtedly their central figure in the plot, and he was joined in this with the bishop of Burgos, whose support he must have sought. It is indeed unthinkable that the Relator undertook such a critical and dangerous task—dangerous not only to him personally but also to the conversos, on whose behalf he worked—without receiving the consent and cooperation of the highest authority of the conversos in Castile. In fact, our knowledge—indeed our certainty—of the *Relator's* deep involvement in that affair confirms our interpretation of the various passages in the sources suggesting that the bishop was involved. Our conclusion therefore is that these two men, who jointly led the anti-Toledan campaign in their common struggle for converso rights, continued in that struggle throughout the Alvarian crisis until their objectives were achieved.

VII

This is not to say that all leading conversos had a share in, or were aware of the conspiracy (the number of these must have been very small), but all leading conversos—and the conversos generally—shared a strong desire to see Alvaro ruined. The growth of that desire no doubt coincided with the spread among their ranks of the definite news of Alvaro's deal with the Toledans. Thus, the conversos became known to one and all as part of Alvaro's political opposition. This must have happened in 1451, even before the Castilian public was informed of the bulls of November 20.

It is difficult, however, to pinpoint the time at which that opposition was galvanized into conspiracy. Presumably, it first manifested itself in cautious, controlled, but cutting criticisms, systematically expressed on every occasion when fault could be found with Alvaro's performance. The purpose of this campaign was common to all these critics and did not require a formal decision. The purpose was the same as that of the nobles who had sought Alvaro's removal from office: to cause a breach between Alvaro and the King, the source of Alvaro's power.

We have seen that during the dissension of 1440, the nobles demanded the dismissal of Fernán Díaz from the position of Relator. They declared him to be Alvaro's agent, advocate and shield in the King's Court. As we have indicated, there must have been truth in what they said regarding the Relator's special share in the promotion of the King's trust in Alvaro and, consequently, in Alvaro's omnipotent rule. But the nobles were powerless to effect their wish, because the King's faith in the Relator remained unbroken, as did the Relator's faith in Alvaro.

Now the conversos could finally accomplish what the nobles had sought in vain to achieve—and they accomplished it not by having Fernán Díaz removed from his position as Relator, but rather by his continued presence in that position as the man closest to the King. Alvaro's prestige with the King would suffer even if the Relator merely stopped defending him. All the more so if, on suitable occasions, he made critical remarks against the constable. Such censures by the Relator may have been sufficient to change the King's attitude toward Alvaro. But there is no doubt that the same procedure was repeated by other New Christians in the Court whose advice was highly regarded by the monarch. Alonso de Cartagena was surely one of these, as is indicated from all his relations with the King; but besides him there were other conversos who were high in the King's esteem (they comprised a large part of the royal Council).[80] It was sufficient for these councillors to stop defending Alvaro, and show dissatisfaction with his actions, to undermine the King's faith in the Constable and whatever affection he still felt for him.[81]

We say "still" because, judging by the sources, the King's former great affection for Alvaro had been gradually dwindling for some time. The change is attributed by many historians to the King's second wife, Isabel of Portugal, who fell out with Alvaro for a variety of reasons,[82] although it was thanks to Alvaro's insistence that the King married *her* and not the beautiful Regunda, daughter of the King of France.[83] That Isabel influenced the King's attitude toward Alvaro may be judged a reasonable assumption; but the claims that it was at her instigation that the King finally decided to destroy him are, most probably, exaggerated.[84] In our opinion, there were other motives (besides the insidious agitation referred to) for the King's total change of heart.

Since his early youth, King Juan II had been under Alvaro de Luna's spell both because of Alvaro's personal influence and his deeds on behalf of the Crown. These deeds spoke for themselves. The King cherished Alvaro as his "protector," as the one who assured his very survival against the predatory Infantes of Aragon. In time, however, this attitude changed; the fascination that Alvaro held for him decreased until finally, by 1452, it reached the vanishing point. Alvaro was now sixty-five years old, devoid of the charms of his youth and early manhood, as well as the brilliance that had characterized his thinking before he reached old age.[85] And as for the forces that threatened the King's rule, they had virtually been eliminated. Navarre was defeated, the Moslems were beaten, most of the rebellious nobles were subdued, and Toledo was pacified.[86] Never had the country been so internally peaceful and free from external danger. Alvaro had finally managed to achieve this, and now he no longer appeared indispensable. Yet this did not mark the end in the King's change of attitude.

For once Alvaro was not viewed as indispensable, he began to be seen as superfluous and, as time went on, actually harmful. Politically, Alvaro was now judged not an asset but a liability—a factor that prevented the achievement of real peace between the King and the nobility. And personally, too, he was felt as a disturbance. Alvaro's old habit of watching the King and interfering in his way of life was becoming more and more unbearable to the monarch. Inevitably, Juan II was eager to shake off Alvaro's oppressive burden.

But there was another important reason that ultimately combined all these considerations into a final decision.

For years the King was persuaded by Alvaro that he was the Vicar of God on earth and that he should demonstrate this in his government.[87] The Cortes of Olmedo (1445) gave him that right; but he never dared put it into effect except when Alvaro was there to support him. Eventually, however, these notions, oft-repeated, penetrated the King's thoughts and feelings and, when conditions appeared to him propitious, he came to believe that indeed he *was* "God's Vicar" and, furthermore, wished to act like one. Yet he was prevented from fulfilling his wish for the very reason that Alvaro was there, keeping tabs on all matters, internal and external, and assuming most functions of government. In fact, the very presence of Alvaro in the Court and the fame he had acquired as the King's "master," made a farce of any pretense by Juan to absolute rule and kingship by divine right. Alvaro therefore had to go; and nothing could prove the reality of the King's power, his total independence and supreme authority, more than Alvaro's removal from government and, above all, his death on the gallows.[88] Alvaro built the monster of the absolute king, and the monster finally destroyed him.

It was when all these factors converged in the King's desire to oust Alvaro from the Court that the conversos could move Juan II to translate that desire into action. Alvaro began his quarrel with the conversos when he was in an extremely perilous situation, but without realizing how vulnerable he was and how vital the conversos' help was for him. Had they backed him then as they did in the past, he would probably have escaped disaster. But rather than defending, he chose to attack them, and consequently lost the only solid friendship he had ever had in his political life. Thus he sealed his own fate.

This virtually explains what happened. But one or two more points must be touched upon to round off the picture. As we noted, Alvaro's power was broken by the combined efforts of the conversos and the King, with the aid of some Old Christian members of the bureaucracy that had been built up by Alvaro himself. But the great nobles, who for so many years had fought Alvaro in so many ways, had little to do with the attempt. They were so disheartened by their previous defeats, and so impressed by Alvaro's sagacity and proverbial ability to survive all dangers, that they would not even dare take determined action against the cunning and dangerous foe. This is why the King found it so difficult to enlist the Count of Plasencia for his plan. And when finally Estúñiga was persuaded to act, he placed the force he sent to Burgos under the command of two men in whose loyalty he could have absolute faith. One was his son Alvaro de Estúñiga and the other was Diego de Valera. The latter, to be sure, was in the service of Estúñiga, but he was also a converso.[89] This could give the Count added assurance that Valera would do everything in his power to see the mission through. And he did.

Thus we see the conversos present in every phase of the effort to destroy Alvaro. They were active in his seizure, his surrender to the King, and finally in sentencing him to death; and this without ignoring the great share of Pérez de Vivero in the conspiracy.[90] When Alvaro went over to the Toledans' side, he was sure that the conversos could not hurt him. That was so because he treated them as Jews; and no Jew in Spain had ever risen against a statesman of such great stature. But the conversos were not Jews; they were Christians; and they had a basis in Christian society that the Jews could never have. Thus they were able to act politically as the Christian Spaniards did. In fact, they followed Alvaro's example and fought him with the weapons he used so expertly—the weapons of intrigue, conspiracy and surprise, with which he defeated his foes.

It is not our intention at this point to judge the conversos' action against Alvaro by our own moral standards. But to understand that action, it is necessary, we believe, that we try to comprehend their own moral judgments.

It is difficult to see how the Marranos could blame themselves when they pondered their conspiracy against the Constable. As far as they were concerned, they were at *war* with Alvaro, for they considered his new policy against them tantamount to a declaration of war upon their group; and in such circumstances they felt entitled to fight him with the same methods employed by the nobles who were likewise at war with him. Moreover, morally they considered their own battle far more justified than that of the nobles. For the nobles fought for the preservation of their power, their wealth and all that went with it. The conversos had such goals in mind, too; yet what moved them to take the extreme steps they did was their need to protect more vital interests. What they fought for were their rights as citizens—in fact, their very survival. In such struggles, which are essentially defensive, and unavoidable in the face of the alternatives, hardly any means are ruled out. Any political and military measure that may seem helpful in defeating the enemy is rarely discarded for moral reasons. The Marranos could not see this otherwise.

But not only from the standpoint of wartime morality and the considerations of their self-defense, but also from the standpoint of peacetime morality, the Marranos no doubt saw themselves in the right. Amador de los Ríos viewed their conspiracy against Alvaro de Luna as an act of treason, ingratitude and moral perversity. But this was because he had not discerned the developments preceding the conflict and its causes. According to Amador, it was an evil intention that produced an evil design; and thus he portrayed the conversos as the villains and Alvaro as the innocent victim. Reality, however, was different. It was not the conversos who attacked the Constable but the Constable who attacked the conversos, and if any kind of betrayal was involved here, it was certainly not on the conversos' part, but rather on the part of Alvaro.

This is, we believe, how the conversos saw the case from their own vantage point. However deeply they probed their own conduct, political or religious, they could find nothing in it to justify the drastic change in Alvaro's stand toward their group. Consequently, they concluded that the only reason for it was his desire to control Toledo and thereby secure and promote his interests. Practically, it meant that he paid for his own gains with their rights, their possessions and their very lives. In their eyes he was guilty of a conduct that rendered him unfit for public office. And this, basically, dictated their position. They had seen themselves obliged to *serve* Alvaro and aid him as long as he behaved as the King's first minister—that is, as long as they could honestly believe that he was acting for the public good. But now that he had joined their enemies, who jeered at the laws that protected *all* citizens, and no longer served the interests of the country, but rather of one radical faction, such belief was no longer possible. Consequently, they saw themselves under no obligation to support him further. On the contrary, they saw themselves in duty bound to fight him.

This was no doubt the conversos' moral stand in their quarrel with Alvaro de Luna, and this was the position that their foremost leaders, like Alonso de Cartagena and Fernán Díaz de Toledo, could have publicly defended with great brilliance and conviction had they been in a position to do so. Such a position, however, was denied them by the very nature of the struggle they were waging—i.e., their clandestine method of warfare. In fact, so discreet were they in this matter that even many years after Alvaro's death, they thought it vital to guard their secret. This is why the chroniclers of the 15th century—and even those that remained uncensored—found little evidence to support the suspicions which their authors undoubtedly nurtured. This is also why today so much effort is required to recover the traces of some of the steps that led to that scaffold in Valladolid.

III. Closing the Circle

However illegal Alvaro's death sentence appeared to many of Castile's leading jurists, there can be no doubt that his public execution raised the prestige
of Juan II in the eyes of the populace, as well as the nobility. A monarch who
could send Alvaro to the gallows could no longer be viewed as the tool or
puppet of his famous all-powerful favorite. Juan II was now seen as a King
who could make hard decisions and enforce them, whatever the difficulties
involved. Inevitably, he was now judged capable of subduing anyone in the
kingdom whom he hated or opposed; and he came to be considered more
cruel and vindictive than he had generally been held before. Some of the
nobles who had long desired to take over Alvaro's position in the Court now
must have had second thoughts. Juan II, as it turned out, was not at all easy
to control; he was dangerous to collide with; and those who offended him
risked terrible retribution.

If this was the lesson drawn from Alvaro's fall by aspirants to the late
Constable's office, the lesson drawn by the urban oligarchies—especially by
their chiefs, who had dealings with the King—could not have been very
different. This must have been particularly the case with some, if not all, of
the leaders of Toledo—a city whose insubordination to the King had become
a mark of its identity. Having just emerged from a state of rebellion after long
and bitter negotiations, they knew that the king had agreed to pardon them,
and give them other important concessions, in return for their future obedience. But they also knew that this royal consent was of Alvaro de Luna's
making; and now that the powerful Constable was gone, his achievement
might go with him. The King could declare his consent null and void, a
product of deceit and misinformation given him by the fallen minister. In
fact, such a development seemed not merely likely but bound to happen—
and sooner rather than later.

For Alvaro's fall, they knew, coincided with the phenomenal rise of the
Relator's influence, and they could have no doubt that this clever man, now
virtually in the saddle of power, would soon move the King to dispatch them
new instructions concerning the conversos. It was not difficult for the Relator
to convince the King that the legal discrimination against the conversos in
Toledo, which went counter to the national law, was a festering wound in
Castile's body politic, and that the King's authority would inevitably suffer
if the Toledans were allowed to have their way. No argument could appeal
more to the King, who indubitably was thinking along the same lines.

But besides the position of the Relator on this issue, which in itself could
be decisive, there was another factor that made the Toledans realize the

precariousness of their situation. This was the role that Fray Lope de Barrientos, bishop of Cuenca, played in the new administration. The Toledans were of course aware that Fray Lope, now one of the King's two chief councillors,[1] was a staunch ally of the New Christians and unreservedly opposed to the *Sentencia* and the anti-converso policy it represented. And thus, faced with the combined force of the King, the Relator and the indomitable bishop, the Toledans understood that if they were ordered by the King to abandon their anti-converso policies, they would have no choice but to obey the order without further ado.

From a cedula issued by Enrique IV on June 10, 1471 we gather that converso rights denied by the "Sentencia" had been restored in Toledo—de facto and de jure—before 1465.[2] But we cannot determine from that cedula the year in which this happened. The question has never been broached by scholars, but bearing in mind that only ten months passed from Alvaro's death to that of Juan II, one might assume that the change took place during Enrique IV's reign. Definite proof, however, is available that converso equality in Toledo was restored in Juan II's lifetime. The evidence attesting this is included in Juan II's will, dated Valladolid, July 8, 1454. It reads as follows:

> Because certain Toledan citizens and residents were banished from Toledo during the time when the city was seized by Sarmiento, and because later I wanted to provide for the expelled the remedy of justice, I have restored them to their offices and possessions, and ordered that they be welcomed and received and well treated in Toledo, understanding that this would be necessary for the service of God and myself and for the discharge of [the duties of] my conscience.
>
> And since I wanted [when I made these provisions] that those who were banished from the city should serve me with a certain quantity of *doblas,* now, having qualms of conscience in this matter, I order that no one demand from the aforesaid the sum referred to above or any part thereof, or take from them any other thing due to the abovementioned matter. Especially [do I consider this regulation proper] since the aforesaid have already suffered exile and received many other harms for my service and for taking my side [against the rebels]. For this reason it is my wish and favor that these provisions be fully carried out and that for no cause or reason related to the above be anything demanded from those people or from others; nor would they have to pay for that matter anything at all.[3]

In the foregoing we have tried to reconstruct the struggle between the city and the King over the conversos' rights, and touched, among other things, on the city's refusal to readmit the conversos whom Sarmiento had expelled, robbed of their property and discharged from their positions, which were given to Old Christians. We have seen that the King had committed himself to the city's position in this matter, and that in taking this stand he was greatly embarrassed vis-à-vis the conversos. From the passage we have cited from his will, however, we see that he later reversed his position; he allowed the exiles to return to the city and also restored their offices and estates. What brought about this reversal?

The primary reason was undoubtedly the abolition of the *Sentencia-Estatuto*. Had the *Sentencia* remained in force, the King's order could not have been issued. It would have been ludicrous to permit the banished conversos to return and resume their offices in the city while denying the conversos who had not been banished the right to hold office. But apart from this self-evident deduction, there is another point we should bear in mind. The King says that he permitted the exiles to resume their former positions in Toledo in accord with the requirements of *justice,* which clearly means that the refusal to do so was against those requirements. But what was wrong for the *expelled* conversos was also wrong for those who stayed on; and it would seem unthinkable for the King to allow the same injustice to be practiced against one part of the group when it was forbidden to be inflicted on another. Thus we must conclude that *all* conversos were freed from the strictures of the Statute.

There remains the question of the reason for the fine that the expelled were ordered to pay the King. As we do not know what arguments were made in this connection, we cannot answer the question definitely. It is possible, however, that the expulsion was presented by some of the Toledans who opposed the repatriation not as an act against the conversos generally, but as punishment of those who had assailed Old Christians with the intent of causing them harm or death. The charge may have referred to what happened in Toledo during the skirmishes between the Old and New Christians shortly after the city was captured by the rebels.[4] And if this was indeed the Old Christians' argument, the King may have seen fit, while cancelling the expulsion verdict, to impose a fine on the accused New Christians. In consequence, the exiles were forced to commit themselves to make the stipulated payments.

Understandably, the conversos considered the imposition entirely uncalled for. They viewed it as a burden unjustly placed upon the shoulders of the returned exiles, and also as a potential reason for a future campaign by their adversaries. Referring to the exiles' payments to the King, these adversaries might claim that they returned to the city not by right, but in the usual converso way—through bribery and appeals to the cupidity of the rulers. To remove the basis from such a possible claim, it was necessary to change the King's ruling.

This brings us to the last phase of this unusual incident. By including the aforecited clause in his testament, no doubt at the request of the Relator or

Don Lope, the King, on his deathbed, admitted his error, recognized the injustice of his demand, and freed the exiles from any payment for their restored rights in Toledo. The final reason given for this revision may have hinted at the answer offered by the exiles to the charges advanced by their forces: If they were involved in skirmishes and hurt anyone, it was because they "took the King's side" against the rebels, and for that they should not be punished but praised. This was apparently the last point the conversos wished to win—and won—in their battle for legal equality.

BOOK THREE

ENRIQUE IV AND THE CATHOLIC KINGS

1454–1480

CHAPTER I

Enrique IV: His Aims and Tactics

1454–1474

I. The Baffling King

I

There can be no doubt that Juan II's death was seen at the time as a severe blow to converso hopes and interests. In the brief period of his post-Alvarian rule, Juan II did much for the conversos. He restored their legal equality in Toledo and brought their exiles back home. But full normalization of relations in the city could not follow as a matter of course. A few years of a resolute administration, imbued with a pro-converso attitude, were obviously needed for the state of affairs to resume its former shape. In the meantime, the conversos were still smarting from the wounds inflicted upon them by the Toledan persecution, and the anti-Marranos were still seething with rage over their recent political defeats. Both parties were evidently restless, and both must have speculated with no little anxiety over the new King's policies and forthcoming appointments.

In 1454, when he was enthroned, Don Enrique's political past could not offer any clue to the stand he was to take on the Marrano question. To be sure, in Toledo, on several occasions, he had shown his resentment over the brutal treatment of the conversos by Sarmiento's administration. On the other hand, the permit he gave Sarmiento to leave Toledo with his immense loot (mostly stolen from Marranos) seemed to indicate a lack of consideration for Marrano feelings and demands.[1] So also did his negotiations with the Toledans, during which he showed himself repeatedly prepared to trade Marrano rights for his own benefit.[2] The record of his behavior toward the conversos, therefore, was on balance more negative than positive. Yet since he was reputed to be acting under pressures imposed by his struggle against Alvaro de Luna, the question remained hanging in the air: Was Enrique the

King, who enjoyed full authority, going to act differently from Enrique the Prince, who, while groping for power, pursued vacillating policies and employed opportunistic tactics? Nobody could answer that question definitely at the moment of his coronation.

But the question seemed to be answered shortly after he was crowned king. When he finished appointing his first administration, it appeared to be tilted toward the conversos. Fernán Díaz de Toledo retained his post as Relator;[3] Barrientos became major chancellor of the kingdom[4]; and Alvar García de Villareal, a New Christian, was appointed personal secretary to the King.[5] Soon thereafter, the conversos in the administration were further strengthened by two appointments: the King made Diego Arias Dávila (the financial manager of his private estate) Treasurer and *Contador Mayor* of the kingdom, and Alvar García de Villareal was replaced by his relative Alvar Gómez de Cibdad Real.[6] According to Enríquez del Castillo, the King's chronicler, Enrique was to put "more faith in Alvar Gómez than he placed in any other secretary."[7]

The New Christians, therefore, had reason for optimism about the new regime. The King was evidently far from prejudiced, religiously or otherwise, against the conversos, and the fact that three key positions in the government—those of relator, treasurer, and secretary—were occupied by New Christians could suggest to some that Enrique's administration was a replica of Juan II's. Formally headed by Lope de Barrientos, it could be viewed by New Christians as a proconverso government. That it was so perceived by most Marrano-haters need scarcely be said. The latter doubtless saw in it proof of their theory that a secret Jewish clique had taken over the country and placed all the Christians at its mercy.

Both these New and Old Christian assessments were of course highly exaggerated. The most one can say in this connection is that Enrique's government did not discriminate against conversos and was not unmindful of converso rights. In any case, in the first eight years of his reign (that is, until 1462), we have no indication that Enrique's administration would permit anti-Marrano disturbances or allow them to pass with impunity. The conversos were thus given the government they needed for at least a few years after Juan II's death, so that their newly gained equality in Toledo could strike deeper roots. It is hard to overestimate the importance of this fact in view of the great influence that Toledo exercised, politically and ecclesiastically, on the rest of the country. The triumph of the conversos in this contested area reaffirmed the feeling they had nurtured for decades—namely, that they were in Castile to stay and that, protected by the laws and shielded by the kings, they could surmount all hostile opposition.

Reinforced, this feeling—or rather this conviction—stimulated the conversos to continue their advance in every possible direction. Accordingly, the first eight years of Enrique's reign were a period of expansion for converso activity, both economic and administrative. But it cannot be said that this expansion was matched by increasing political influence. The Relator may have retained his fame and authority as jurist, councillor and administrator, but we have no indication that, at any time, he enjoyed close relations with the King. In any case, he died in 1456, less than two years after Enrique's coronation; and one year later, in 1457, the New Christians suffered another great loss through the death of Alonso de Cartagena. The new generation of Castile's Marranos had produced no men of stature to match these leaders in civil courage and political astuteness. The conversos holding high positions at Court were career politicians of undoubted ability, but not of such stuff as men like Cartagena and Fernán Díaz de Toledo were made on. We must assume that the decline of converso leadership at court was paralleled by a decline in converso prestige.

We have referred to the Marrano courtiers of Enrique as the "converso leadership" of that period. Actually, however, we have no evidence that any of these courtiers performed any function on behalf of the conversos as a group. Nevertheless, we believe that by virtue of their positions, which made them prime targets of the Marranos' foes, they could hardly avoid taking an interest in their group, or being involved in some of its affairs, especially at crucial junctures. Yet whether there was a central leadership or not, there was a general converso policy that set guidelines for the conversos' conduct, which were usually accepted by them all.

II

Enrique IV was a complex man, tugged by conflicting ideas and ambitions. He considered kingship, rightly exercised, the highest and noblest form of government, but hated much of its paraphernalia and its routine administrative duties. He accepted pomp and ceremony as inevitable, but did not truly appreciate or like them, and consequently did not enjoy court life, with its many formalities and artificial restrictions. He was a man of simple tastes and habits, uncommon among the nobles of his time, but took up the nobles' sport of hunting, of which he became exceedingly fond. Bearing no bias against plebeians, he could enjoy their company, recognize their merits and readily raise them to high office. He demanded of his subjects loyalty and obedience, but rejected all manifestations of servility (such as kissing hands) and used the plural form of speech in addressing every man, even a child. He was also generous and liked to help the needy (often anonymously), without once mentioning any favor he did, or wishing to be reminded of any. His chronicler Castillo said of him: "A King without pride, a friend to the humble, disdainful of the arrogant."[8]

As a ruler, he hated to enforce his will and preferred the most wearisome negotiations to the use of violence and compulsion. His foreign policy was marked by a search for peace, but he did not exclude war, if he considered it "just" (like the war against Granada),[9] or highly beneficial to the security of the kingdom (like the battle of Aragon and Navarre[10]). He especially opposed the use of force as a means of settling internal conflicts, and preferred the least satisfactory compromise to the ravages of civil war. He showed great consideration for human weakness, often forgiving even confirmed traitors, and sometimes—when in straits—he even sought to win their loyalty by unconcealed appeals to their greed. If one may regard such attempts as dishonorable, one must also assume—in fairness to Enrique— that he gave some thought to the available alternatives and to what he considered the lesser evil. An honest Catholic, he was no fanatic, could feel sympathy for Jews and Moors (as could other kings in the peninsula), and even chose to entrust the safety of his person to a Moslem rather than a Christian bodyguard.[11] It need hardly be said that Enrique's habits, as well as some of his methods of government, occasionally aroused the consternation of friends and the criticism of antagonists.

The criticism, however, was largely subdued in the first decade (or half) of his reign, which Pulgar regarded as one of "peace," though it knew no respite from mounting frictions. It became caustic in its second decade, which started with rebellion and remained turbulent to the end. Deferring the discussion of the cause of this rebellion to a later point, we shall touch here only briefly on the major aim of the rebels' campaign. That aim was to ruin the King's reputation and thereby destroy his popular support. It was rightly said that, apart from Pedro I, no Castilian king was so defamed. Not only were all the kingdom's troubles (real and imagined) laid at his door, but they were also ascribed, in increasing measure, to his "criminal proclivities," his "cruelty" and his "perversion." In sum, Enrique was portrayed, publicly and personally, as a hideous misfit, alternately or simultaneously accused of tyranny, heresy and treason.

That these characterizations were plainly absurd, and incredible to anyone who knew him, need not lead us to assume that they were ineffective in mobilizing public opinion against him. Most people lack independent judgment, tend to deny altruistic motives, and often rely on repeated rumor more than on what they have seen with their own eyes. These common traits of human nature, which make every persistent vilification so dangerous, applied of course to Enrique too, so that the constant dragging of his name through the mud inevitably had its effect. What is surprising in his case is the firm faith that so many of his subjects retained in him throughout; but much of the dirt thrown at him stuck. The charge of impotence, of which his enemies accused him, was especially damaging and hard to rebut.

The difficulty, which was apparent from the outset, became compounded in Enrique's last years, when his half-sister Isabella claimed the right to succeed him on the grounds of his alleged impotence. In the last analysis, Isabella won the argument, not by the recognized rightness of her claim but by the power of the sword, or the victory of her armies over those of Juana, the king's daughter. But she also wished to win the moral battle—i.e., to "legitimize" her rule; and in compliance with this wish, her agents and admirers kept harping everywhere on Enrique's impotence. Skillful chroniclers, headed by Palencia, knew how to bequeath the notion to posterity.[12] In consequence, the scurrilous contemporary campaign was perpetuated by historiography. The prevailing view of Enrique in literature was summarized by a modern scholar who said: "They called him impotent, and this is what he was in every sense of the word."[13]

Of Spain's pre-modern leading historians it was only Mariana who rejected the claim concerning Enrique's impotence.[14] Of the modern scholars, it was J. B. Sitges who, in his study of Enrique (1912), first challenged that claim, subjected it to detailed critical analysis, and rebutted Palencia's judgment of the King.[15] Sitges was followed by Orestes Ferrara, who likewise centered his attack on Palencia, describing him as a "perfidious chronicler," a hireling serving the King's enemies.[16] Both made a determined effort to clear Enrique's name and sullied reputation, but their arguments hardly made a dent. Only most recently did Sitges and Ferrara finally receive the support they deserved. The documentary revelations of Tarsicio de Azcona[17] and the sound conclusions drawn from them by Hillgarth[18] laid to rest some wrong notions about Enrique and brought him closer to historical reality. As we see it, Lafuente's portrayal of Enrique as a "cowardly King, indolent and irresolute,"[19] or the picture of him presented by Ballesteros as a man of "weak will" and "scant energy,"[20] have little to do with historical truth. Enrique was no coward, as he often courted danger,[21] and he was not lazy, for he frequently pursued, with great exertion of body and mind, objectives he deemed to be vital for the state; nor was he irresolute or weak-willed but, as Valera indicated, "willful"; for he tenaciously followed his own will, while rejecting counsels with which he disagreed.[22] His failure to take action when urged to do so was not always due, as some thought, to "indecisiveness," but, in most cases, to his firm *decision*, often arrived at after much contemplation, to refrain from taking action in certain situations.

Yet while these observations may remove some of the obscurity that shrouds Enrique's life, there still remain elements in his behavior that are extremely hard to comprehend. We shall try to explain them at least in part, so as to clarify some of the events that characterized Enrique's ill-fated reign.

III

The enigmatic part of Enrique's biography belongs almost exclusively to the period of unrest that comprised the second half of his reign. There is hardly anything mysterious or inexplicable in his conduct as prince and heir apparent; and at least on the surface, there was nothing bizarre in his behavior as king in his first "peaceful" decade. But in the second decade, during which he had to cope with a series of betrayals and assaults upon his honor, he assumed a different appearance as ruler. Enrique of this period was generally misconceived, not only by historians, but also by contemporaries, including his most intimate associates. In fact, the more the treacheries multiplied, the stranger he seemed to his faithful servants and the more unlike the prince they recalled from bygone years and the king they had known heretofore.

There was undoubtedly an anomalous streak in Enrique's general behavior as ruler which ought not to be ignored (and on this we shall touch later). But there was also a perfectly normal factor influencing his position on a variety of issues—a factor reflected in many of his statements, which were faithfully reported by the chronicler Castillo. We refer to his particular view of kingship—a view to which his modern biographers have paid little or no attention.

Like most kings of his age, Enrique claimed that kingship is held by divine right—but unlike many other monarchs of his time, Enrique sincerely *believed* in that claim. The idea may have been implanted in his mind with special force by Alvaro de Luna, his adversary, who taught him that kings by divine right had absolute authority over their subjects. But this absolutism was not judged by Enrique to be what the term so often suggested. To be sure, it imposed on the subjects obedience to all the king's commands and instructions, but it did not allow the king to issue orders not viewed by him as necessary for the people's welfare. Enrique's concept of the king (so commonly upheld) as the representative of God's power on earth was merged in his thinking with the parallel concept—the one he could learn from Marcos García—that the king was essentially a vicar of Christ in guarding and promoting Christ's moral teachings. As such he must follow in Christ's footsteps, care for the people, show them mercy and compassion, and be ready to forgive them the injuries they had caused him by their folly, ignorance, or uncontrolled passions.[23] Enrique expressed the essence of this view in his coronation address when he said:

> It sometimes happens that great power moves rulers to do evil rather
> than good, and that absolute authority induces great princes to employ
> fury more than gracious kindness. It is therefore necessary that those
> who have reached such heights, if they wish to follow the true pattern

of nobility and be considered true nobles, be clothed in clemency and girded with pity. For the power and command of the royal person, the ruling and governing of the virtuous King, are placed in him only to make him magnanimous, gracious and benign, forgetful of the injuries he had suffered and grantor of rewards for services.[24]

Castillo included this statement in his chronicle along with other documentary material. It was not a statement composed by the chronicler on the model of those written by classical historians on appropriate occasions. It was a speech heard by many magnates and prelates, members of the chronicler's own generation, and confirmed by many other statements which the King uttered in other circumstances. Thus, touching on the subject of kingship from another angle, Enrique once said to one of his officials:

> If we consider properly the royal dignity, and how *God created it to rule the world for the universal good of all,* [we shall realize] that kings were not born to care for their own interests, or to do only those things which concern themselves, but to be useful to all and seek the benefit of the many . . . [Hence,] the good Kings should be such friends of their subjects and so partial to generosity, that they should aid them all and be happy in so doing.[25]

It need scarcely be said that a king holding such views, and so deeply concerned about his people's well-being, would be strongly disinclined to expose them to war, and especially to a war waged on his own behalf. Accordingly, in 1465, when he disbanded his large army then besieging Valladolid, where his enemies' forces were shut up, he addressed his troops in the following words, which reflect, perhaps more than his other pronouncements, his attitude toward war and his theory of kingship:

> All Christian Kings, because they rule on earth in the name of Jesus Christ, have to be fathers of their subjects, their guardians and protectors; [and therefore they have] to remove them from death and secure for them life. For this reason, having compassion over my subjects, and especially over so many noblemen, both men of high station [*hombres de estado*] and small *caballeros,* and the other people who are united in my service, I have decided to lift the siege without giving the enemies battle.[26]

This was certainly a remarkable statement, the like of which may not be found in the recorded utterances of any other king. Yet however far-reaching in its implications, it presented only part of Enrique's view of government. The other part was formed by his stand toward punishment, especially when related to antiroyal deeds. To one of the rebels who was caught by his men and confessed that he had intended to kill him, he said: "Juan Carrillo, it is not a great thing for me to forgive you the crimes you have committed against me, for it is incumbent upon Kings to pardon offenses that were perpetrated against them."[27] Indeed, as a king who wished to follow Christ, he could hardly see any other course before him. And thus forgiveness was one of the cornerstones of his internal policy. Castillo, who could not suppress his astonishment over the King's repeated demonstrations of forgiveness, came to the conclusion that "he was pleased more with pardon than with vengeance, with clemency more than with cruelty, with pity more than with rigor. Never did he find enjoyment in killing, nor did he like to ruin anyone."[28]

Castillo, then, attributed the King's habitual forbearance, as well as his abstention from violence and bloodshed, to his natural inclinations. If true, this attribution could provide an explanation of Enrique's conduct as king. However, as prince, we see him repeatedly display a willingness to engage in war, to plan, without qualms, violent conflicts, and also to attack and execute traitors without showing either hesitation or remorse.[29] He also joined Juan II's enemies and embarked on political moves and maneuvers which were likely to lead to bloody clashes with his father. Had his later attitudes been truly expressive of deeply ingrained personal tendencies, they would have appeared during his early manhood and would have left some traces in the records of the time. Since nothing of the sort had ever been reported, his behavior as king must have been the result not so much of his personal inclinations as of his political philosophy.

He no doubt embraced this philosophy a short time before he came to power, and it soon transformed his thinking and feelings, as well as his conduct as ruler. He began to declare his new views immediately after ascending the throne, and they no doubt affected his attitudes toward his subjects, as well as his position in foreign affairs. But for reasons that may be readily surmised, he was still seen by most people as the same man he had been before he was crowned king—a warlike prince, daring and ambitious, yet a careful strategist, who was aided and advised by the shrewdest politicians of Spain.

The new man that he became was finally exposed during the nobles' rebellion. By that time his views on kingship had matured and it was then that he put them to the test. But this does not mean that he entirely abandoned his previous habits as diplomat and governor, and all that he had learned from Pacheco in these fields. Time and again he was obliged to revert to the old forms of politics in which he was trained, and rely on his experiences as diplomat and negotiator operating with concealed designs and half-truths. Occasionally, he was also tempted to use force and settle by war menacing problems which otherwise seemed to him insoluble. But he regarded these moves as temporary retreats from the methods of government he considered proper (i.e., noble), and intended to resume the employment of these methods at the first available opportunity. He actually believed that his theory of kingship could work in real life, and he tried to the end to chart his course according to its principles.

This was Enrique's insurmountable difficulty, as well as his fatal mistake. *He thought he could act like a Christian king in a Machiavellian society*—that is, a society governed by principles diametrically opposed to his. Against the ideas of force, treachery, cruelty, cunning, vengeance, intimidation and death, which were believed to be the most effective means to achieve political ends, he pitted his own Christian ideas as measures of practical policy. Hence his love of peace, his forgiveness, his compassion, his clemency, his charity, his humanity and humility ("The humble," they called him, says his chronicler Escavias[30]). Hence also his tragic fate and, politically, his failure.

But besides the great difficulty stemming from his philosophy, or rather his political credo, his government was afflicted by a serious shortcoming that stemmed from his personal relationships. We refer in particular to his relations with Pacheco, who for many years had a strong grip on his life. Indeed, so powerful was Pacheco's influence on Enrique that it often curbed his freedom of movement, oppressed his thinking and vitiated his plans. Above all, it disrupted his efforts as statesman, and, among other things, was one of the factors that subverted his position on the converso issue.

II. The Delusive Peace

I

We have already briefly remarked on the character of the new converso courtiers and the decline of their status as converso spokesmen. Indeed, we are strongly inclined to believe that the conversos in the period of Enrique IV suffered from a serious failure of leadership which, in the circumstances, was in itself sufficient to assure their ultimate defeat. But what further contributed to their downfall was their adoption of a new policy that guided their political self-defense.

Undoubtedly, that policy was based on the lessons they drew from the struggle they waged for their rights in the last years of Juan II's reign. What impressed them especially were the final results of the two major stages of that struggle, the first of which was marked by their campaign against the *Sentencia* and the second by their drive to bring down Alvaro.

The purpose of the campaign against the *Sentencia*, let us recall, was to convince the people—and even more so the authorities—of the justice of the Marranos' position, and then to move the authorities to *act* in accordance with that conviction. This action was expected to take the form of clear-cut proclamations on the Marranos' innocence, coupled with strong denunciations—and severe punishment—of their detractors. About a year of such concerted agitation, in 1449–1450, against the views and claims of the conversos' enemies seemed to have justified these expectations. The Pope in his bulls of September 24, the bishops in the sentences they issued on these bulls, and the King in his ensuing orders and declarations all showed readiness to take decisive action along the envisaged course. But then the unexpected happened. Both king and pope began a gradual retreat from their declared pro-Marrano stand, until their positions differed only little from those of the Marranos' adversaries. Unavoidably, the New Christians wondered about the sense of their entire campaign, of the arguments they had advanced with such faith and fervor, and of the evidence they had assembled with such diligence and determination to prove the rightness of their cause. Evidently, there was no sense to it at all. Law, morality, and theological principles counted little when confronted with the interests and ambitions of the hard-boiled rulers of Church and state.

Thus, many Marranos came to view the campaign they had conducted in '49–'50 as useless or ineffective; and faced with a losing battle of survival, they could not help concluding that in order to survive, they had to change their tactics. Thus, they abandoned their public agitation and adopted different methods of warfare. They turned to *in camera* negotiations, political manipulations, and the formation of alignments that were likely to be in the Marranos' favor. This was how they had brought about Alvaro de Luna's downfall and, in consequence, the restoration of their rights.

Their changed conception of their best self-defense led the Marranos to change their position toward royal power. There can be no doubt that the failure of the hopes they put in the monarch, and the crisis of faith they experienced in their relations with both Juan II and his chief minister, was expressed in a breakdown of the solid front that united all the Marranos of Spain—a front that hinged on the traditional principle of "unqualified loyalty to the King." What followed was increased political maneuvering not only by New Christian courtiers, but also by Marrano notables in the cities—a maneuvering aimed at the formation of alliances on which they could hopefully rely. Inevitably, such alliances, once formed, loosened the Marranos' ties with the king, especially when the king was unable or unwilling to offer them the needed protection. Nevertheless, it must be noted that the majority of the conversos in Castile still preferred to rally around the monarch and lend him their support, though not at all costs and in all circumstances. Actually, the New Christian notables were now following the paths of the Old Christian nobles, and hence, when the king appeared to be slipping, some of them showed little hesitation in joining the camp of his opponents.

If the search for greater power by means of alliances now determined the Marranos' political conduct, another principle guided their behavior in the sphere of public opinion. That principle is indicated in their deliberate refusal to react to any written or oral diatribe against their rights, their activities and their reputation. It signified the beginning of a long-term policy of total avoidance of Marrano involvement in public debates on the Marrano issue. Thus, while in the year or two following the rebellion (1449–1450) there appeared at least six New Christian apologies,[31] in the two decades of Enrique IV not a single work of Marrano provenance appeared in defense of the converso cause. By the middle of 1451, when the failure of the campaign in their defense became apparent, many conversos must have come to believe that public agitation by Marranos on their behalf was more harmful than helpful. All their apologies had achieved, they thought, was to provoke greater hatred for the Marranos, rally more forces to their adversaries and, above all, bring the Marrano issue to the forefront of public attention and discussion. Indeed, this last result was, from their standpoint, the most detrimental to their cause.

These views, it need hardly be said, were part and parcel of their assimilationist thinking. As ardent assimilationists, they always wished to blend with the Old Christians as quickly as possible, and to attain this end, they sought to lower their profile as a separate group in the Christian society. To be sure, their campaign against the Toledan rebels made them stand out as a separate entity, but they conducted it on the assumption that it could not be helped if they wished to meet the emergency they faced. As soon as they realized, however, that these needs were not met, they not only hastened to terminate that campaign, but adopted a policy of strict non-involvement. In fact, they even sought to ignore or forget some of their bitter encounters with Old Christians and thereby try to cover up their cause—namely, the existence of a converso problem that disturbed the social peace.

The reader will find sufficient evidence of this policy in the general chronicles of Juan II's reign edited by Marranos in Enrique IV's time. A detailed analysis of this evidence is offered in one of the foregoing chapters.[32] What remains for us to note at this point is how the Marranos hoped to overcome by their silence their enemies' vociferous attacks upon them. We must assume they noticed that the arguments of their apologists led their opponents to produce counter-arguments, which broadened the discussion and kept it alive; and from this they could infer that it would be to their benefit to avoid any public response. They evidently thought that if they held their fire, the provocative dialogue would turn into a monologue, which inevitably would become repetitious and boring; both listeners and accusers would get tired of it and the campaign would gradually peter out.

It was wishful thinking. By withdrawing from public debate over their issue, the conversos did not silence the agitation against them but enabled it to grow louder and bolder. By abandoning the field of battle as they did, they left it wide open to their opponents, who knew how to use it to their full advantage. Libels, rebukes and reprobations multiplied; and while no converso arose to answer them, the anticonverso campaign was joined by new forceful agitators. The most eloquent and effective of these was undoubtedly the Franciscan friar Espina.

II

"To Fray Alonso de Espina," says Lea rightly, "may be ascribed a large share in hastening the development of organized persecution in Spain."[33] Like Marcos García, Espina was filled with a passionate hatred for Jews and conversos, and like the Toledan rebel, he was fired with the conviction that only by concerted action of the authorities (what Lea termed "organized persecution") could the Jewish question in Spain be solved. To be sure, the solution desired by Espina went far beyond the measures recommended by the Church; as a friar, however, he could not state it explicitly, but suggested it obliquely in some of his pronouncements. Nevertheless, it was clearly reflected in his agitation against both the Jews and the conversos.

As far as we can judge, Alonso de Espina was of Spanish origin and represented in his writings the ideological heritage of Iberian antisemitism. As such he was standard-bearer in the campaign against the Jews conducted by the cities since the middle of the 13th century, and chief spokesman of the anti-Jewish theories espoused by the Toledan rebels. But besides these two Spanish sources of influence, his antisemitism was fed by another current, which was ultra-Pyrenean and fundamentally non-Spanish. We refer to the views on, and attitudes toward the Jews that were rampant in Central and Western Europe, and especially to the particular form they assumed in the Observant branch of the Franciscan Order.

Compared to the Dominicans, who were generally known for their extreme hatred and censure of the Jews, the Franciscans—once again, generally speaking—adopted a somewhat milder attitude toward the Jews and the Jewish question. But things changed radically in this respect following the rise of the Observantine movement in the second half of the 14th century. The originator of this change was Bernardino da Siena, himself an Observant who, about 1405, met Vicente Ferrer, the Spanish Dominican whose indefatigable campaigns to convert Jews and Moslems made him the most famous missionary of his time.[34] Moved by Ferrer, and following his example, Bernardino began to devote his efforts to the conversion of the Jews and other infidels. But unlike Ferrer, he stressed the "dangers" the Jews posed to the Christian world far more than the reasons which, according to Christianity, should have moved them to convert.[35] As might be expected, such agitation, while bringing few, if any, converts to Christianity, gave rise to a new wave of anti-Jewish feeling, which was carried forward after Bernardino's death (1444) by his chief disciple, Giovanni da Capistrano. The latter, who assumed, following Bernardino, the mantle of leadership of the Observants, went far beyond his guide and mentor in his incitement against the Jews. Capistrano appeared to be convinced that the atrocities attributed to the Jews were no myths, and he knew how to communicate that conviction to the large crowds that listened to his sermons. In 1454, on a visit to Breslau, he outdid himself when he consigned to the flames forty-one Jews charged with desecration of the Host. He died two years later (in 1456), after setting an example, both in word and deed, to his followers in the Catholic world.[36]

Among his followers and disciples was another Italian, also an Observant, Bernardino da Feltre (1439–1494), who, in preaching hatred of the Jews, emphasized the charge of ritual murder. It was due to his violent agitation that the Jews were banished from Ravenna, Perugia, Brescia, and several other Italian towns. And more than anyone else, he was responsible for the infamous blood libel of Trent, in Tyrol, which ended with the execution of fourteen Jews (1475).[37]

Moving along the same lines and spewing out the same arguments, Espina began his campaign against the Jews several years before Capistrano's death and about a decade before da Feltre started his. The relationship between him and his brothers-in-spirit, the three aforementioned Italian friars, has never been inquired into, to my knowledge, and we do not know whether the latter influenced Espina's views and activities. It is not far-fetched, however, to assume that such influence, direct or indirect, was wielded. In any case, the four friars were linked to each other by both organizational and ideological ties. The four of them were Franciscans, Observants and leaders of the same mendicant faction, and the four of them dedicated their lives to spreading venomous hatred of Jews and Judaism by means of the most vicious accusations. Capistrano did it in Germany, the two Bernardinos in Italy, and Alonso de Espina in Castile.

III

If his fellow Observants considered the Jews a menace to Christendom in such countries as Italy, where the Jewish communities were relatively small, no wonder Espina considered Spanish Jewry—including the conversos, whom he counted as Jews—as the greatest threat ever faced by any Christian domain. He considered his task, therefore, far more vital than that of his fellow campaigners in Europe, and by the same token also more difficult. The difficulty, as he saw it, stemmed not only from the magnitude of the Jewish and converso forces involved, but also from their special social position and far-reaching public influence.

Most of Spain's Jews were Christianized, he knew, and although to him they were Jews in disguise, this is not how they were viewed by Spain's kings and most of the Spanish grandees. In addition, they were at the height of their power. When Espina was about to launch his campaign, the anti-Marrano party in Spain had just suffered a stunning defeat through the loss of all the gains it had made in Toledo and the restoration of the conversos' former status in the city. It was not easy to start a counter-attack after such a total surrender. Yet this is what Espina did. Defeats and retreats in the "battle of the faith" only spurred him to bolder action.

Espina realized that, compared to the conversos, the Jews were only a second-rate component of the problem he was confronted with. In the broad Jewish front which, to him, comprised two sectors—a smaller of "overt" Jews and a larger of "occult" ones—the conversos appeared to be the decisive factor and the force that would be harder to beat. Of the various reasons supporting this assessment, the following three were probably the foremost.

To begin with, there was the question of power. While the Jews relied on the goodwill of the rulers, which was undependable and could be withdrawn, the conversos formed part of the government and were strongly entrenched in the royal administration, as well as in the administration of the Church.

Second, while canon law, civil law and Christian custom discriminated against the Jews in almost every sphere, the conversos enjoyed the support of the laws, the teachings of Christianity and the policy of the Church. Finally, while an attack on Spanish Jewry could be spurred by analogies from other Christian countries, no such analogies could be applied to the conversos, since, except for Spain, no Christian country had such a large-scale converso community. For all these reasons Espina considered the position of the "overt" Jews far more vulnerable and, consequently, easier to hurt. He decided therefore to attack the Jews first, and then, once the people were aroused by his campaign, to strike at the conversos by labeling them Jews and, of course, by "proving" their Jewishness. None of this, to be sure, was a simple task; but it was infinitely easier than pinning on the conversos, right from the outset, all the crimes he could credibly ascribe to the Jews. This was Espina's strategy.

Espina, then, launched his attack upon the Jews along the lines of his Observantine teachers, describing the Jews as mythical vampires thirsting for Christian blood. Later we shall recount his fantastic accusations, which so many credulous Christians in the Middle Ages did not judge to be fantastic at all. Here we shall touch only on his charges relating to the Jews' social and economic activities. Based as they were on "realistic" grounds, these charges, though extreme, could be readily believed. In fact, they helped attune Espina's audiences to his far wilder claims.

IV

There is no adequate study of the condition of the Jews under the rule of Enrique IV. Nevertheless, it is safe to say that the first half of Enrique's reign was for Spain's Jews a quiet interval in the turbulent last century of their life in Spain. When the reign opened in 1454, there remained very few of the many disabilities imposed upon the Jews by Pope Eugene IV (in his bull of August 8, 1442) and largely accepted by the Infantes of Aragon. For, as we have indicated, when Alvaro resumed power, he paid no regard to the papal restrictions; and Enrique IV, who was tolerant of all minorities, and especially appreciative of the services of the Jews, saw no reason to upset that order. As a result, we find the Jews throughout the period occupying numerous positions of tax farming and tax collection in both the royal and nobiliar administrations. Likewise, they farmed the revenues of the churches and the incomes of monasteries, colleges, and townships. They also administered the estates of the great lords, temporal and spiritual, as treasurers, *contadores* and majordomos.[38]

There is no doubt that most Jews who engaged in these tasks belonged to prosperous, high-income groups, whose members also followed other pursuits which were equally profitable. Such pursuits included large-scale moneylending, international trade, and internal commerce in various precious commodities (such as spices), as well as medicine, pharmaceutics and law. Taken together, these groups did not form the majority of the Jewish community in Spain. But they did form a substantial minority, constituting the community's upper layers, from which flowed a considerable stream of money to the Jewish lower classes. The latter consisted primarily of artisans, shopkeepers, farmers, teachers, clerks, second-rate practitioners of the professions mentioned, and functionaries in the communal and religious fields. These, to be sure, were far from rich, but more often than not far from poor, too. In any case, opportunity was open to them, especially to those of the middle class; and pauperism in the Jewish community was rare.

Espina considered the Jews' situation a scandalous affront to Christian law and teaching. If Christianity permitted the existence of Jews in the countries under its dominion, it did so on the condition that they be perpetually enslaved as punishment for their deicide. But that enslavement, he emphasized, denied them forever not only all positions of authority (and hence all right to public office) among Christians; it also denied them all the essentials of life as free men, such as freedom of converse, settlement and movement, as well as choice of occupation. Moreover, it denied them the possibility of living in dignity even in their own communities; for the eternal captivity to which they are destined must consist of wretchedness, distress, humiliation and, above all, anxiety and fear. These conditions, according to Espina, were already assured to the Jews by Moses when he cursed them in his forecast of their great crime: "You will serve your enemy whom God will send against you in hunger, and in thirst, and in nakedness, and in want of all things; and he shall put a yoke of iron upon your neck until he have destroyed you" (Deut. 28.48). Espina, however, did not forget to add that the terrible agony to which the Jews were destined was meant not only to serve as their punishment, but also as a means of their salvation; for it is only through exceptional suffering and distress that the Jews may be induced to abandon their defiance.[39] However, if permitted to live in freedom, their condition will serve merely as incentive for them to continue in their rejection of Christianity; and, in consequence, the blight of Judaism will never depart from the land.[40]

To prove this point with all possible clarity, Espina enumerates many of the laws enacted against the Jews by Church and State, including the laws of Catalina of 1412, which subjected them to the harshest restrictions. There can be no question, then, what kind of life Christian law, divine and human, assigned to the Jews. But what do we see in reality? The Jews disregard all these laws, circumvent them, or treat them as nonexistent. Not only do they fail to wear the "sign"; they use Christian maids, employ Christian workers, lend money at interest to Christians of all classes, practice medicine among Christians, manage the estates of the great nobles and, by means of all these pursuits and positions, assume mastery over Christians. Thus, rather than being the Christians' slaves, they live in Spain like the Christians' lords. It need scarcely be said that these conditions (i.e., of freedom and mastery) encourage them to proceed along the path of sin. "They do not work the soil, nor do they defend it; but they devour the labor of the Christians by means of their evil and cunning arts, and thus they become the heirs of their possessions" and the owners of great wealth. As it is written about them in Jeremiah 5.27: "As a cage full of birds, so are their houses full of deceit—or, more clearly, of the yield of their chicaneries and criminal exploitation."[41]

In such statements, which present the Jews as "eating the fat and good of the land," without making any commensurate effort or any positive contribution, Espina echoes the social accusations leveled by García at the conversos. But unlike García, he centers his attacks on the "overt" rather than the "covert" Jews (for the reasons we have indicated above), and, again unlike García, he stresses the Jews' alleged religious crimes, which until then had gained little notoriety among the Spanish Christians. Only a few cases of Jews charged with perpetration of anti-Christian atrocities (like desecration of the Host) were recorded in Spain in the course of centuries, but they left their echoes in Spanish life and literature; and on the basis of these echoes, which Espina magnified by citing opinions of non-Spanish authorities, he felt safe in stating that "a book will not suffice to contain their crimes in this respect."[42] By means of such sweeping accusations Espina presented the Jews as hardened criminals who harm Christians and humiliate Christianity, without any regard to the laws of the country and without taking any punishment for their crimes. He realized of course that he had to explain how the Jews could manage to do all this; and here again he offered an answer that differed from that of García.

Espina moves straight in to lay the blame for this condition upon the "prelates and princes and all the other lords" who were charged with the execution of the laws and the prevention of their violation by the Jews. It is the "detested avarice of the Christian princes" and "the temporal gains which they get from the Jews" that bring them to let the Jewish crimes go unpunished. It is their excessive converse with the Jews, and the numerous gifts they receive from them, that lead them to permit the "ravenous wolves" who have entered the "flock" of God to continue their ravages without opposition.[43]

Only if we combine this description of the Jew as an unscrupulous economic exploiter with his portrayal as a religious criminal shall we grasp the full impact of Espina's campaign upon the Spanish public. Before long a movement was astir in many towns, calling for the elimination of the Jews from their territories. It did not urge the killing of the Jews, perhaps because it was assumed that threats of death might revive the movement of conversion (which was an undesirable prospect), but it called for robbing the Jews of their possessions and taking over their synagogues and graveyards.[44] Steps like these, it was believed, would be sufficient to force the Jews to abandon their neighborhoods and, if taken nationwide, to induce them to leave Spain—a consequence which was in full accord with Espina's objectives.

Judging by the information at our disposal, the plan gained not only the support of the lower classes but also the approval of some municipal councils and, within the hierarchy of the Church, of some friars and prelates. Moreover, some places hastened to issue special statutes against the Jews as a temporary measure, while in others preparations were approaching the point of carrying out the aforementioned program. The movement seemed so widespread and the attack so imminent that the royal administration found it necessary to issue, on May 28, 1455, a special warning to all the authorities in the country, forbidding them to countenance any attempt to rob the Jews of their private possessions or deprive them of their communal properties. The order placed all Jews under the King's protection and threatened violators with the "loss of royal favor, the privation of all offices and the confiscation of all goods." It also blocked any excuse for avoiding compliance because of ignorance of the law or inability to fulfill it.[45]

The King's stern order was a clear threat to all would-be aggressors. Enrique was then at the height of his prestige, "both feared and respected," and the order was issued by Fernán Díaz de Toledo, who now served as Enrique's Relator. Everyone could see that the administration meant business and that it would take drastic steps to prevent riots and disorders on a large scale. It stands to reason that Fernán Díaz de Toledo was involved in the planning of these steps which, we may assume, he considered imperative both as administrator and converso leader. Few could realize as clearly as he did whither the new winds were blowing. A repetition of the mass riots of 1391 would not only involve the whole country in trouble—indeed, in a turmoil of unforeseeable consequences. It would also place the Marrano community in unprecedented danger. In all likelihood, he viewed the planned attack upon the Jews as a prelude to an attack upon the conversos.

V

The royal administration may have exaggerated the strength of the anti-Jewish movement in 1455, or it may not have wished to take any chances with the riot preparations that came to its knowledge. In any case, it arrested the expansion of the movement, and little more was heard of it to the end of the reign. But this does not mean that the government succeeded in checking the growth of the anti-Jewish sentiment, or that Espina ceased his ferocious agitation. The numerous anti-Jewish accusations assembled in his copious work were doubtless first uttered by him in his sermons; and informed as we are of the impact of his preaching, we must assume that it contributed substantially to the rise of the anti-Jewish fever in Castile. Ultimately, his agitation produced in Castile the same results that da Feltre's had attained in Trent and Giovanni Capistrano's in Breslau. In 1468, the Jews of Sepulveda were subjected to the torment of a blood accusation, and in 1471, eight of them were sentenced to death. Following the execution, the Christians of Sepulveda attacked their Jewish neighbors, killing some of them and causing the rest to flee the town.[46]

This was the first time in Jewish history in Castile—indeed, in the whole of Christian Spain—that a court had issued a verdict of guilty against any Jew charged with ritual murder; and nothing illustrates more luridly the vehemence that the anti-Jewish feelings had reached in Spain. If pogroms and massacres may occasionally be attributed to a temporary upsurge of violent passions, blood libels stemmed only from deep-seated hatred, stoked by the belief that the Jews were capable of the vilest religious crimes. Nor would the ecclesiastical court in Segovia, which handed down the verdict against the position of the Church, have gone to that length unless compelled to do so by overwhelming public pressure.

The court responsible for that atrocious verdict was presided over by Juan Arias Dávila, bishop of Segovia and himself a New Christian, the son of Diego Arias Dávila, Enrique IV's *Contador Mayor*. Dávila's intent in rendering that judgment was no doubt to remove from himself the suspicion that, as a converso, he sided with the Jews; he wanted to demonstrate that, in religious matters, the New Christians did not differ from the Old. Indubitably, when Dávila was entrusted with the case, many enemies of the conversos wanted to believe that the converso bishop was hopelessly trapped. Would he issue a verdict against the accused and thereby confirm the veracity of the blood libel, or would he let them go free and thereby demonstrate that all conversos, including their bishops, were actually nothing but secret Jews? Dávila chose to condemn the Jews, of whose innocence he could have no doubt, thereby showing how great was his perversion, as well as the worries that beset his mind. He must have feared that, in the highly charged atmosphere in which the blood libel trial was held, a verdict in favor of the accused Jews could precipitate an attack on the conversos of Segovia, and perhaps of the whole of Castile.

Meanwhile, Espina kept propagating his claim, accompanied by his customary "proofs," that the New Christians were clandestine Jews, and the cry was frequently heard across Castile that the conversos were actually "heretics." In consequence, suspicion, distrust and ill will between the Old and

New Christians deepened, and the fabric of social relations between the groups was in many towns torn beyond repair. There inevitably followed quarrels and clashes between individual Old Christians and New, which often developed into lasting strife or expanded to engulf whole communities. By the turn of the fifties, a large part of Castile was seething with social unrest.

Now, having effectively aggravated an inherently tough and exasperating problem, Espina came forward with a solution. As we indicated, he advocated two solutions, one for the conversos and another for the Jews. His preferred way of dealing with the conversos would be to bring about their annihilation or expulsion—the same measures he favored for the Jews. But since he knew that the Church would reject both, he compromised by urging the application of a remedy tested by the Church time and again and always proved most effective. He recommended the establishment in Castile of an inquisition to root out the "Judaic heresy"—an inquisition of the kind that functioned in Languedoc and virtually destroyed the Albigenses. It was to be an institution subject to Rome, and thus immune to the influence of the converso bishops and the corruption of other Spanish prelates. All that was needed to establish such an institution was the consent of the King.

Espina tried to get that consent. He was Enrique's confessor, had easy access to him, and no doubt tried to induce the King to accept his plan for a Castilian inquisition. Evidently, he failed. Either he could not overcome the King's skepticism or negative attitude toward his arguments, or he was blocked by the counter-arguments of the conversos and their friends at Court. He therefore attempted to reinforce his appeal by enlisting the support of the leaders of his Order—i.e., the Franciscans in the Spanish province—and the latter agreed to follow him. They thought, however, that they stood a better chance with Enrique if they were joined in their appeal by the Hieronymites, who had become influential in Castile. Accordingly, they wrote to Alonso de Oropesa, the newly elected General of the Hieronymite Order, asking his help in petitioning the King to establish an inquisition.[47] Then something happened which the sources do not explain.

After having written to Oropesa, but apparently before sending their letter, the Franciscans decided to approach the King by themselves.[48] The reason for this change of plan is not known. Perhaps some of the Franciscans, Espina among them, doubted the possibility of uniting with the Hieronymites on a common plan of action. They no doubt were aware of Oropesa's deep interest in the Old-New Christian conflict, but they may also have heard that his view of the conversos was not precisely identical with theirs; thus, on second thought, they came to the conclusion that their chance to obtain king Enrique's support might be diminished rather than increased by a joint delegation.

There may of course have been other considerations that moved the Franciscans to change their plan. They may have been reluctant to share the credit for the establishment of an inquisition with another monastic order; or they may have wished to reserve the Hieronymites for a joint approach to Enrique, in case their own attempt proved abortive. Whatever their considerations, the decision seemed justified. For the King received the Franciscan delegation, appeared to be inclined to accept its arguments, and promised to act favorably on its request. Espina now expected to see some evidence that the King's promise was being fulfilled. But months passed and nothing happened. The Franciscans then decided to send their letter to the Hieronymites, with the aim of approaching the King together with the Hieronymites' leaders. But this move, too, turned out to be futile. For meanwhile the Hieronymites, no doubt offended by the shoddy way the Franciscans had treated them, decided to approach the King by themselves and acquaint him with their own views on the inquisition. In consequence a Hieronymite delegation, headed by Oropesa, saw Enrique in Madrid in April 1461.[49]

Oropesa pointed out to the King that the people, who view most conversos as Judaizers, were anxious to take the law into their own hands because they did not see the government act against the allegedly spreading heresy. If the royal administration, however, would agree to conduct a proper investigation into the matter and establish both guilt and innocence, the people would quiet down and the disturbances would stop. Hence, Oropesa concluded, there is need for an inquisition conducted in each diocese by Castile's Church leaders; and it should be aimed not only at the New Christians, but against all segments of the Christian population. Enrique IV was taken by the argument as well as by the proposal. He was also most favorably impressed by Oropesa. He expressed his agreement with the Hieronymite's ideas and promised him his full support, on the understanding that Oropesa himself would undertake the execution of his plan. He asked the General to write to all the bishops of the realm, asking them, in the King's name, to establish, each in his own see, an inquisition to investigate all deviations from the faith in all sections of the Christian population.

There was, however, no response.[50] Shortly thereafter, in Alcalá de Henares, Oropesa met Carrillo, the archbishop of Toledo, and urged him to take action in the direction he recommended. Since 1449 Toledo had been known as the center of tension between the Old and New Christians, and a successful inquisition there could serve as a model for all other cities. Carrillo refused to assume responsibility, but urged Oropesa to perform the task. He assured Oropesa that the bishop of Coria, Don Iñigo Manrique, would assist him in this matter, and Oropesa agreed to assume the main burden. But the bishop of Coria failed to cooperate, and Oropesa was left alone with the charge.[51]

For more than eight months he labored in Toledo, investigating rumors, establishing blame, punishing the guilty and exonerating the innocent. He came to the conclusion that, although some New Christians gave occasion for complaint against their religious behavior, the main root of the trouble lay in the jealousies which some Old Christians felt for the New. Using all his persuasive skill, his mastery of theology and his powers of preaching, he managed to reduce the most irritating differences and reconcile the quarreling parties. Sigüenza, his biographer, tells us that Oropesa left behind him a pacified city.[52] It is not certain, however, that Oropesa himself saw things in that light at the time. No doubt he realized that, although he had managed to extinguish some dangerous fires, many embers remained that could flare up again. What we may conclude from Sigüenza's report is that Oropesa was encouraged by the results of his efforts, that he became convinced of the rightness of his approach, and felt certain that if the work he had begun were to be continued, both in Toledo and in other cities, the dangerous malady might be controlled.

Upon completing his assignment in May 1462, he submitted his report to the King and the Archbishop on his inquisitional activities in Toledo and on what he had gathered from his experiences there.[53] No doubt the report was accompanied by his recommendations for future action in Castile, but no part of this account has reached us. We can only conjecture its general tenor on the basis of other evidence we possess, and we can safely assume that it led the King to cancel another plan he had considered and intended to implement in case Oropesa's approach failed.

VI

On December 1, 1461, Enrique IV's emissary to Rome submitted to Pope Pius II a request that he sanction the establishment of an Inquisition in Castile to deal with some heretical opinions which seem to have arisen in that kingdom. The King proposed to appoint four inquisitors, one of whom should be Jacobus de Veniero, the papal nuncio and general collector for Castile, who, together with the bishop of Cartagena, would nominate the other three inquisitors, whose appointment should be approved by the King. The petition further expressed the King's wish that the inquisitors should proceed in all matters in conformity with the directions of the common law (*juris communis*) and in line with the privileges conceded by the papacy to his predecessor concerning the establishment of an inquisition. The privileges referred to were probably those that had been granted to Juan II of Castile on November 20, 1451.

The first question to ask respecting this petition is: When did Enrique decide to submit it? And the second is: Why? Beltrán de Heredia assumed that the request to solicit the establishment of an inquisition in Castile was communicated by Enrique's representative in Rome in the last month of 1461; but this raises a certain difficulty. It would mean that Enrique began his move in Rome after having given Oropesa the right to establish episcopal inquisitions in all the sees of the kingdom. Moreover, it would mean that he began that action while Oropesa was conducting his inquisition in Toledo, on the assumption that his work would serve as a prelude to similar proceedings in other cities. Too much bad faith on the part of the King would be involved in such a move if it took place on the date suggested by Heredia.

The problem would be considerably lessened if we assume that Enrique sent his instructions to Rome prior to his meeting with the General of the Hieronymites. Enrique, we should recall, had promised the Franciscans to act in behalf of the establishment of an inquisition; and this is what he actually did. We can well understand why he kept the move secret. He wanted to avoid premature protest on the part of his converso courtiers, and he did not wish to give the fanatical Espina additional fodder for his campaign. Above all, he may have sought to prevent Espina from pressuring him on the terms of his petition; and when he turned to the Pope, he included in his appeal two provisions that could give cause for such pressure. The first was that the appointment of all inquisitors should be made with royal consent, and the second was that if the Dominicans had been promised that all the inquisitors would be members of their order, this promise would not hold good for Castile. The King, of course, may have included this provision at the request of the Franciscans; but he did not want the inquisition in his country to be managed by the Franciscans either. Especially would he object to have it fall into the hands of a man like Espina, who would certainly turn it into a lethal institution bent on the destruction of the conversos.

The preparation of the petition to the Pope, however, may have taken more time than expected. It may have passed through various revisions in Rome, and required a number of consultations with the King, before it was finally submitted to the papacy. In the meantime, Oropesa appeared before the King and presented his proposals. Oropesa's presentation made Enrique even more convinced that the establishment of an inquisition was a necessity. Therefore, he let his agents proceed to submit his petition to the Pope. After all, he did not know whether anything would come of Oropesa's plan—especially since the reaction of the bishops to that plan was, to put it mildly, disappointing. Nor could the King assess in November the results of Oropesa's activity in Toledo. It was at best a local experiment whose outcome could not yet be foreseen. The King, therefore, decided to submit his petition without informing Oropesa of the move.

On March 15, 1462, the Pope responded to Enrique's petition by his bull *Dum fidei catholicae*.[54] In this bull, the Pope authorized the establishment of an inquisition in Castile along the lines proposed by Enrique, but increased the prerogatives of his nuncio at the expense of the arrangement suggested by the King. The appointment of inquisitors, however, remained subject to the king's approval, and points in dispute could be renegotiated if Enrique wished to have them modified.[55] But by the time the bull came to the King's notice, or soon thereafter, Oropesa had completed his work in Toledo and submitted his report.

Judging by the views he expressed on the converso problem following his Toledan experience, it is clear that his report did not present that problem in the same light as it had generally been seen when he first met the King. Certainly, the converso group included some individuals who leaned toward Judaism in some of their conceptions, but neither in their number nor in their views did they constitute a truly heretical movement. There was nothing in what they did or said that reflected the position of the converso masses, and they hardly exhibited deviations from the faith that could not be corrected by proper instruction. He himself had offered such instruction in Toledo, and the results were extremely encouraging. The incidents of deviation he found among New Christians resulted from ignorance rather than ill will (that is, of errant notions stubbornly upheld that might be defined as heresies), and the deviators had readily accepted his corrections, together with the penalties he imposed upon them. Considering all this, Oropesa concluded, the converso group posed no danger to the faith.

But this was not the only conclusion Oropesa drew from his investigations. The other was no less radical and no less opposed to common opinion. As Oropesa now saw it, the core of the converso problem lay not in the converso camp but in the camp of the Old Christians—that is, in the basic unwillingness of the latter to recognize the conversos as equal citizens. It was this unwillingness that moved the Old Christians to view the conversos with constant suspicion and inclined them to accept every dark rumor about the conversos' religious behavior. The same unwillingness was also the root of most of their criticisms of the conversos' social conduct and their terrible jealousy of the conversos' achievements. It was simply a case of deep group hatred seeking justification in a nonexistent heresy, or of using the religious deviations of the few as an excuse to persecute the many. The Old Christians who partake in these persecutions deviate from the faith no less than any of the errant New Christians, and thus they, too, require instruction in true Christian behavior. To Alonso de Oropesa every moral sin constituted also a religious transgression; but viewed from a purely secular standpoint, his conclusion may be summarized thus: It was a social rather than a religious malady that Castile had to be cured of.[56]

According to Sigüenza, the Hieronymite friar who wrote a history of his Order, no party in Toledo, neither the New Christians nor the Old, complained of Oropesa's conduct of the Inquisition, and everyone, including those who were punished (according to Sigüenza, even severely), accepted his verdicts in a good spirit.[57] It is obvious, however, that the punishments he imposed were, for the most part, light. Had they included burnings at the stake, long-term incarcerations, excommunications, heavy financial exactions and the like, those affected would not have accepted these penalties calmly, or "without complaint," as Sigüenza put it. We must conclude, therefore, that the penalties consisted of penances of varying length and austerity and relatively tolerable financial fines. But this means that, in Oropesa's judgment, the deviations from Christianity among the conversos—and the moral digressions of the Old Christians—stemmed from ignorance, or temptation, or confusion of the mind, rather than from definite heretical notions, firmly believed and stubbornly upheld.

The reader who will acquaint himself with Oropesa's views of the anti-Marrano party in Castile, either by direct study of his work or through our survey in the following pages, will agree, we trust, that the above conclusions must have formed, more or less, the tenor of the report he submitted to the King on his findings in Toledo. But if this was the case, the King could see no sense in acting on the Pope's bull of March 15. To be sure, Oropesa did not abandon his plan for inquisitional activity throughout the realm; he still believed that the government had to demonstrate that it did not take lightly the Old Christians' complaints about the conversos' religious attitudes and would investigate any charge or suspicion touching the conversos' religious conduct. But in view of the results attained and expected, it was obvious that the function of such an inquisition was more educational than punitive, and its aim would be to heal rifts between the groups rather than dwell on their existence. Consequently, the officers of such an inquisition should be moralists rather than prosecutors, teachers rather than judges—in brief, they should be men like Oropesa, who would carry on the same kind of inquiry he had conducted in Toledo. To this task Oropesa assigned the bishops; and judging by the authority they commanded, they certainly were suitable for the task. Yet most bishops were more interested in politics than in the moral improvement of their flock, and Oropesa was not oblivious of the fact. Still, he believed, they would be better than most friars, who, rather than serving as the people's mentors, often became the people's spokesmen. He therefore stood by his previous recommendation, while Enrique, in the circumstances, saw no reason to set up a papal inquisition.

Thus, for the second time, a papal bull calling for the establishment of an inquisition in Castile to deal with the converso problem was shelved by the King without having been made public. Apart from the King, probably no one in the administration, except perhaps his secretary, Alvar Gómez de Cibdad Real, and one or two other officials, was informed of the bull and the King's decision to suppress it. Most probably, Oropesa knew nothing of it either, although his report, in all likelihood, was instrumental in moving the King to make that decision. This is why he never mentioned it in the book he wrote years later on the converso issue or in the records relating to his activity that he left in the Hieronymite archives.

VII

Espina no doubt learned before long of the report submitted by Oropesa to the King and of the King's decision to desist, as a result, from implementing the plan for a papal inquisition. He refused to give in. Oropesa, he knew, had concluded from his inquiries that those Marranos who misbehaved religiously—clearly, a minority of the group—were not guilty of heretical crimes, and therefore could be brought back to the fold by moderate corrective measures. Espina considered this conclusion wrong. He continued to propagate his own view that almost all Marranos were clandestine Jews and that if "there were made in our time a *true* Inquisition, countless numbers would have been delivered to the flames of those who would have been found to have really Judaized."[58] Presumably, by his reference to a "true" Inquisition and "really Judaized" conversos, Espina meant to criticize Oropesa's findings and the method of his investigation.

Espina thus continued to campaign across the land, hurling venom and virulence at the conversos as occult Jews and accusing them of secret performance of Jewish rites and other brazen affronts to Christianity. The social atmosphere became thick with discontent; and the fragile relations between Old and New Christians became strained to the breaking point in many places. It was only the strong hand of the authorities that enabled orderly life to go on, and there could be no doubt that should their vigilance cease, the conversos would soon become targets of assaults more furious and bloody than those of 1449.

That is precisely what happened in Carmona in 1462. In this central Andalusian town, a large and prosperous converso community had lived for decades in relative security until its governor, Beltrán de Pareja, chose to ignore the duties of his office. Instead of keeping the peace in accordance with these duties, he incited the anti-converso faction to mount an attack upon the conversos. We do not know what moved the governor to take this clearly illegal action, but it stands to reason that it served his interests. Thus, says Palencia, he "found it useful to his purpose" to deliver the

Marranos to the wrath of the "malevolent" who, "thirsty for their wealth," conspired to rob them, while urging the attack "in the name of religion, as if this [i.e., the religion] required pillage, assassination, and the violent perpetration of all sorts of infamies, as the evil-doers did before in Toledo, and as the thieves did later [in other places], following that harmful example."[59]

"Terrible and criminal was the riot in Carmona," says Palencia of the pogrom in that town, "and it necessitated speedy remedy; but since Don Enrique [the king] did not want to present it for consideration to [his minister] Don Beltrán de la Cueva, brother of the governor [of Carmona], he reverted to subterfuges such as a feigned punishment. This consisted of sending a certain Diego de Osorio, who called himself *corregidor,* with troops from Cordova and Écija, and some from Seville, in order to restrain the rebellious people—not to give each what was due to him, according to the true definition of justice. This iniquitous procedure was the cause of new misfortunes," which, says Palencia, "the city of Carmona suffered without interruption."[60]

Palencia, as we have noted, was a critic of the King and his criticism was often grossly exaggerated. In this case, however, his censure seems correct. It fits Enrique's treatment of the Marranos' enemies both before and after the Carmona outbreak. That the governor of Carmona was a brother of the king's minister may of course have affected Enrique's decisions; yet what mainly restricted his moves against the culprits must have been his conviction that they constituted a majority of the town's Old Christian population. In light of this conviction—and of what he had witnessed in Toledo in 1449 and 1450—he thought that, while punishing all the guilty was impossible, to punish some of them would be useless; it would be seen by their associates as a strike against them all, and raise the demand for a general pardon of *all* the residents involved. His father had no choice but to yield to this demand, and if he, Enrique, were now to act differently, he would only undermine his royal authority, create more bad blood, and make future reconciliation between the contending groups more difficult, if not impossible. The Marrano problem, he was convinced, could not be settled by punitive measures, but by solutions of the kind suggested by Oropesa. Therefore, he was interested in containing the riots and securing future order in the agitated city rather than "in giving each one his due, according to the true definition of justice." Palencia of course thought that avoidance of punishment would not only fail to pacify the town but rather encourage new disturbances, and his view was confirmed by experience. We may assume, however, that Enrique realized that danger; but he played for time, and was looking for an opportunity to put the city under proper controls.

In the meantime, Espina used the riots of Carmona as proof of the urgent national need to establish a special inquisition in Castile. The way he described them in his agitation, the riots in Carmona were not produced by envy, or by "thirst for the conversos' wealth," but by the people's refusal and inability further to tolerate the conversos' crimes. Most annoying and intolerable of these crimes were those committed in the religious sphere, and while repeatedly indicating these transgressions, he emphasized especially the crime of circumcision, which he claimed was rampant among the conversos. Nothing of course could prove the Jewishness of the New Christians more than their custom of circumcising their children, if indeed they followed this custom. Hence, Espina thought, if he could persuade the King of the prevalence of circumcision among the Marranos, he would prove the worthlessness of Oropesa's findings, as well as the propriety of his own demand to establish a "true" inquisition.

Toward the end of 1463, Espina believed that he was in a position to persuade the King to adopt his proposals. Heading a delegation of leading Observants, he came at the beginning of December to Madrid, where the King was staying at the time, and repeated his charges about the "great heresy" of the Marranos, who, feigning Christianity, circumcise their children and perform other Jewish rites. In addition to his own appeal to the King, some members of his delegation delivered sermons, in which they uttered the same charges and voiced their demand to establish an inquisition. One of them, Fernando de la Plaza, a guardian of the Franciscans, declared in a sermon that he had at his disposal one hundred foreskins of converso children who were circumcised by their parents. The statement caused a scandalous sensation, and many Old Christians in Madrid were shocked. The assertion reached the ears of the King, and what followed is related by his chronicler:

> Informed of the matter, the King ordered the members of the Franciscan delegation to come to him, and facing them, he told them that what they related about the circumcised New Christians was a grave insult to the Catholic Faith, and that he was in duty bound to have it punished. He then ordered them to have the foreskins brought to him and also let him know the names of the culprits, as he wished to be fully acquainted with everything pertaining to this matter. In response, Fray Fernando told the King that he did not have the foreskins in his possession, but that the matter was related to him by persons of authority. The King then asked him: Who were those persons? But Fernando refused to mention their names; so that it was all found to be a lie.[61]

Castillo tells us further that at that very time there came to Madrid Fray Alonso de Oropesa, together with some priors of his order, and that he "set himself in opposition to the Franciscans."[62] According to Sigüenza, it was Oropesa who proved the falsehood of the Franciscans' claim after "having examined it with great care" at the request of the King.[63] Then, to calm the aroused public, he delivered several sermons in Madrid in which he revealed the true facts, trying at the same time to save the face of the Franciscans by asserting that Fray Fernando was "misled in this matter and threw himself into it with little consideration."[64] But the Franciscans remained shamed and embarrassed. Espina's move boomeranged.

One cannot help asking certain questions about Oropesa's involvement in that incident. Was his presence in Madrid at the time coincidental, or was he asked by the King to come to Madrid and calm the irate populace? Of the two possibilities, the first is more likely; for early in December 1463 the King issued a privilege to Lupiana, site of the convent of San Bartolomé, which was under Oropesa's priorship.[65] It stands to reason that to obtain that privilege, a delegation of the Hieronymites, headed by Oropesa, appeared before the King in Madrid. The audience took place shortly after the King's arrival in the city, and he forthwith responded favorably to their request, so that the privilege bears the abovementioned date; but the Hieronymite delegation may have stayed in Madrid a few additional days until the document was processed, or specifically at the request of the King, who may have wished to consult Oropesa on some matters. In the meantime the scandal of la Plaza exploded, and the King was glad to have Oropesa on hand. As Sigüenza indicated, he asked the General to look into the matter and express his opinion.[66]

These occurrences further reduced Espina's declining prestige in the Court while strengthening the King's faith in Oropesa—his person, his judgement and proposed solutions. Oropesa gained the reputation of a wise, balanced, and extremely honest man, so much so that when the conflict between the King and the opposition stiffened and was submitted for arbitration to a five-member committee, including two representatives of each party, the General of the Hieronymites was chosen as the fifth member to cast the decisive vote in a stalemate. Oropesa was thus brought into the highest echelons of Castilian statesmanship.

Here, however, we must pause to look at the political situation that led to the appointment of the Committee of Arbitration, of which Oropesa was a member. This committee was to decide on the governance of the realm and the fate of Enrique's administration, and among other things, it cast a long shadow on the evolution of the converso problem in Spain.

III. Pacheco Undermines the Regime

I

None of the histories of the Spanish kingdoms attribute to Juan Pacheco any part in promoting the cause of the Holy Office and urging its establishment in Castile. Yet he undoubtedly influenced those developments, both directly and indirectly, to a large extent. As we indicated, we do not know precisely what occurred in the negotiations between Alvaro and the Toledans in 1450, and at what point he promised them to seek the Pope's consent to the introduction of the Inquisition in Castile. It is certain, however, that Alvaro gave that promise only when his negotiations with the Toledans were deadlocked and he saw no other way of having Toledo restored to Royal seignory. But who maneuvered him into that impasse? Who stood firmly behind the Toledans, counseling and authorizing their moves? It was Prince Enrique, who was then their guardian—or rather Pacheco, who was the Prince's guide.

If Pacheco's influence on the first royal attempt to establish an inquisition in Castile may be presumed, his strong support for the plan of the Inquisition submitted to King Enrique on January 15, 1465, must be taken for granted. The plan was included in the Reform Program that the Committee of Arbitration then recommended to the King, with a view to curing the ills of the realm; Pacheco masterminded the arbitrators' work and, as we shall see, was closely involved in shaping the inquisitional proposal. To be sure, the program was rejected by the king, and nothing came of it for the next few years; but not all its points were to remain a dead letter. Above all, the mere fact that a royal commission of the highest rank, prestige and authority advocated the establishment of a national inquisition could not but leave a lasting impression on Spain's public opinion. Even decades later that action was seen as the launching of the inquisitional project in Castile.[67]

But perhaps more important than Pacheco's direct influence on the formation of the plan for the Inquisition was the indirect impetus he gave that plan by his entire political activity. The second half of Enrique's reign was a period of disasters for Castile as a whole, and especially for the conversos; and the chief responsibility for many of their troubles must be laid at Pacheco's door. Indeed, it would hardly be an exaggeration to call that period *Pacheco's decade*; for few were the things of historical importance that occurred in Castile in those years that were not occasioned either by

Pacheco or in reaction to what he did. Obviously, Marrano history in that decade cannot be written without paying due attention to Pacheco's schemes and actions.

What kind of man was he? And what did he seek to achieve?

We have several descriptions of him by his contemporaries, all seasoned and acute observers, which together suggest a composite picture. Most instructive of these descriptions are no doubt those of Castillo and Palencia, the two chief historians of Enrique's reign, who closely followed Pacheco's career. Both left detailed accounts of his activities, accompanied by their unequivocal opinions; and though they radically differed in their views on the King and many other historical personages of their time, they were virtually in agreement in their evaluation of Pacheco, his character, and his motives. This agreement lends credibility to their judgments and allows us to feel safe in accepting them.

To Castillo, Pacheco was a "mirror of ingratitude, tyranny and insatiable greed."[68] To Palencia, who would doubtless subscribe to these epithets, he also appeared as a perpetual plotter and an "inimitable master of feigning."[69] Both considered him treacherous, unscrupulous, and capable of committing many a crime in pursuit of his ambitions. Their horrid descriptions of him would fit a legendary, rather than a real, villain; but the record of Pacheco's schemes and actions essentially confirms their accusations. In fact, their words pale before his deeds.

Pacheco owed his connection with Enrique to Alvaro de Luna, who chose him as companion to the adolescent prince. The choice proved calamitous— first to Alvaro, then to the Prince and, above all, to Castile's national fortunes. Pacheco was five years older than Enrique and knew how to win the young prince's trust. Since Enrique sided with his mother against Alvaro, whom she blamed for alienating the King's affections, Pacheco deepened the breach between the Prince and the minister in the hope of increasing Enrique's dependence on himself. The stratagem worked. Believing in Pacheco's sincere friendship, Enrique was accustomed to follow his counsels, especially since Pacheco's forecasts and analyses proved so often correct. Before long, he was deeply involved in politics, with Pacheco now known as his "favorite."

There is no doubt that Enrique learned from Pacheco the art of hunting in the political jungle that much of Castile resembled in those days. Pacheco had a genius for political negotiations, and before embarking on any affair of state, he "considered carefully," as Pulgar put it, "the quality of the subject matter, the time, the place, the person, and the other circumstances involved."[70] Thanks to Pacheco, Enrique became a considerable political factor in Castile, exploiting his position as heir apparent and causing much hardship to his father. Pacheco knew how to be rewarded. Enrique obtained from the

King, his father, the important marquisate of Villena for Pacheco and the mastership of Calatrava for Pacheco's brother, Pedro Girón. The brothers, however, saw in these gains only bases for further advancement.

All went well between the Prince and his favorite until some time after their entry into Toledo—or, rather, after the abolition of the rebels' government in the city. Then something happened that caused a break. The new situation called for new decisions, and the Prince and Pacheco may have strongly differed on what those decisions should be. By the middle of the century, we should recall, the Prince was already twenty-five years old; he knew Castile's politics from the inside, was a clever negotiator and expert tactician, and may have developed his own views on a number of major political issues. Above all, he learned to judge men's motives even when simulated or heavily disguised, and one day he perceived Pacheco as he was. The change of perception may have been produced by the cumulative effect of many impressions, or it may have come suddenly, like a flash. Perhaps it was stimulated by Lope de Barrientos, the Prince's former teacher, who was then in his company. Don Lope could see Pacheco's true face through the various veils of deception that covered it; he hated him and sought to undermine the influence he exercised on the young prince. In any case, once his eyes were opened, Enrique decided to part with Pacheco and have nothing more to do with him. He wanted him out of his life.

To his great dismay, however, Enrique soon discovered that it was not so easy to get rid of Pacheco. The brothers were quick to sense his intentions, especially when they noticed that Enrique spent much time with Rodrigo Portocarrero—Pacheco's brother-in-law, to whom Enrique took a fancy in those days—and little time with them, his alleged "favorites." Pacheco forced himself into the Prince's company. There can be no doubt that he used his sharp mind to clear up the "misunderstandings" between him and the Prince; but he did not succeed in restoring the affection that the Prince had felt for him before. He probably reduced Enrique's distrust to the point of giving him the benefit of the doubt, but this would not revive the old relationship. What prevented a break between Enrique and the brothers, and compelled the Prince to keep them as his "favorites," was his realization that he was in their hands much more than they were in his.

The brothers must have reminded Enrique that he had placed all his fortresses, including that of Segovia, which contained the Prince's personal treasure, under their command and that, unless he agreed to retain them in his service, they would treat these fortresses as their own. Enrique was then possessed by one thought: how to regain control of his castles, and, among other things, how to reduce the hold which the brothers had on Toledo. For in Toledo, too, he had put the alcazar under the command of Pedro Girón, though as yet he had not appointed the guardians of the various gates. Now

(in February 1450), before leaving Toledo, he took the precaution of placing
these positions in the hands of trusted friends, forbidding them to deliver to
"anyone" the gates of Alcántara and the alcazar. By "anyone" he meant, of
course, primarily Girón, but the guardians could not have known this. The
change in relations between the Prince and the brothers must still have been
kept to themselves; and under these circumstances, it was not difficult for
Girón to transfer to his hands, shortly thereafter, the control of these strongholds, too.[71]

Enrique must finally have gotten back the castles he had unwittingly
entrusted to the brothers, but not without giving them definite assurances,
which he was in duty bound to honor. The brothers had no doubt that
Enrique would honor those assurances, unless of course they gave him cause
to disregard them. They were very careful not to give him such a cause; and
so when Enrique was crowned King, both became members of his Royal
Council and occupants of high posts in his administration. Pedro Girón
became his *Camarero Mayor* and Juan Pacheco his Major Majordomo, but, in
fact, much more than what this title indicated. He was the "principal man of
his council," the main molder of the realm's policies, and the chief arbiter of
the kingdom's affairs.[72]

Although Enrique was now king, supreme in power, he was still uneasy in
his relationship with Pacheco. He could never free himself completely of the
suspicions he had developed about Pacheco early in 1450, and no longer
could he put implicit faith in him. To be sure, he would frequently seek his
advice, and benefit from it when he judged it useful, but he carefully watched
Pacheco's steps and did not entrust him with vital posts. When he appointed
Pacheco as Major Majordomo, he counterbalanced the move by raising Lope
de Barrientos from the position of first councillor to that of Major Chancellor.
Barrientos was a pillar of strength to Enrique; he realized the dangers Pacheco posed to the king—and to the tranquillity and welfare of the realm—
but failed to remove him from the administration; instead, Pacheco removed
him.

"Fearful of the noble audacity of a man of such great merit as Barrientos,"
says Palencia, "the Marquis took great care to make him leave the Court
shortly after Don Enrique was crowned King."[73] Barrientos, however, must
have stayed in his position longer than one may gather from Palencia, and
probably left the court a few years after Enrique had ascended the throne.[74]
Together with Barrientos, Enrique thought of moves to reduce Pacheco's
influence. Barrientos, though vigorous, had reached old age, and Enrique was
looking for younger men on whose shoulders he could lay the burden of
administration. He preferred to enlist them from the lower classes rather than
from the high nobility, who usually put their own interests before those of
the state and the Crown. He first had an eye on Juan de Valenzuela, whom

he later made prior of the Order of San Juan, and then on Gómez de Cáceres, whom he appointed Master of the Order of Alcántara. Finally, he pinned his hopes on Lucas de Iranzo, an honest commoner who was also a good soldier, and wanted to appoint him Constable of the kingdom, the position once held by Alvaro. Pacheco and his brother sensed real danger. They managed to terrorize Lucas to the point where, in fear of his life, he left for Aragon.[75] Barrientos, who supported the King's proposal, went to Aragon to persuade Lucas to return and take over the administration of the kingdom. But Lucas could not be persuaded. Regarding the brothers as potential assassins, he was sure that the Court would be his death trap. He finally accepted the title of Constable, but only on the understanding that he would, in fact, serve as governor of the outlying province of Jaén.[76]

These, however, were not the only steps Enrique took to solve his Pacheco problem. As he could neither trust Pacheco nor get rid of him, he looked for ways to control him. In 1457, and again in 1458, he signed special agreements with a few leading nobles who were supposed to form the King's inner council. None of the signatories to these agreements was allowed to enter into a league with any outsider or begin any undertaking without informing the others and obtaining their consent. Pacheco and Girón were parties to these pacts, which also included a high dignitary of the Church, Alfonso de Fonseca, archbishop of Seville, and Diego Arias Dávila, the King's *contador mayor*.

Obviously, these agreements were not to Pacheco's liking. If they were calculated to achieve anything, it was to curb his freedom of action. Enrique no longer wanted to face the crafty and dangerous politician by himself. He sought safety in numbers. Instead of standing alone against the two brothers, he changed the ratio. He increased his own side to four or five.

Pacheco, however, knew how to overcome the obstacles the King placed in his path. He violated the agreement first by entering with his brother into a secret league with Alonso Carrillo, the archbishop of Toledo, his uncle and rival, who, like Pacheco, aspired to supreme power. Later, he arranged for his brother and Carrillo to make (in 1460) a secret pact with Admiral Enríquez and the latter's son-in-law, Juan I of Navarre, who by then was also Juan II of Aragon, as well as with several leading nobles, among them the Manriques.[77] The second agreement was peculiarly treacherous as it gave Juan II of Aragon, the old enemy of Alvaro and Castile's Juan II, a new chance to interfere in Castile's affairs. In effect, Pacheco and Carrillo acted henceforth as agents of Aragon and Navarre.

The King heard of the latter agreement, which was so clearly directed against him, and of course could not help concluding that Pacheco had a hand in the matter. Pacheco feared arrest, ceased visiting the Court, but found an opportunity to have a talk with the King. Claiming ignorance of his brother's involvement, which he no doubt described as frivolous, he swore to make a determined effort to detach Girón from his league with Navarre and the ever-restive nobles associated with it. Girón supposedly recognized his error, and the King, reconciled, broadened his estates as a sign of his renewed faith in him, as well as in his brother Pacheco. The latter, indeed, soon resumed his position as first minister of the realm, and he also soon returned to contrive his schemes. Finally, Enrique obtained definite proof of Pacheco's faithlessness and treachery, and the resultant break between him and Pacheco now appeared irreparable.

What caused this break is directly related to our particular inquiry. In June 1462, the people of Catalonia, then locked in conflict with their king, Juan II, offered Enrique their fealty and allegiance and asked him to be their king.[78] Enrique was enchanted by the unexpected offer, which not only strengthened his prestige at home and checked the nobiliar attempts to control him, but also held the promise of his kingship's extension far beyond the borders of Catalonia—that is, to Aragon and Valencia as well. The Catalonians needed military aid, and Enrique hastened to invade Catalonia and attack the western parts of Navarre.[79] Had he pursued the war to its conclusion, the union of Castile and the eastern kingdoms might have been achieved twelve years earlier, with far different results for Spain and probably for large parts of Europe as well. But Enrique was deterred from fulfilling his wishes by the counsels of Pacheco, Carrillo and his secretary, Alvar Gómez de Cibdad Real. They all made strenuous efforts to convince him that the enterprise could not possibly succeed and, in fact, would end in dismal failure. Accordingly, they urged him to get out of the involvement as soon as possible, without loss of face. An honorable way out seemed to be offered by the preparedness of Louis XI, king of France, to arbitrate the dispute between Castile and Aragon, and Enrique was persuaded by his treacherous counselors to submit to France's arbitration. It is difficult to believe that Enrique did not realize that the French would prefer weak neighbors like Navarre, Catalonia and Aragon to a powerful Castile on their southern frontier. He therefore could not have been truly surprised by the results of the arbitration, which went against him, and accepted, without protest, Louis' verdict. He was, however, shocked to learn that Pacheco was rewarded by Louis for his efforts, and suddenly understood what happened. He was betrayed.[80]

Enrique's wrath matched his disappointment. The union of Castile and Aragon under his scepter, a union which was actually within his reach, had been snatched from his hands by the traitor Pacheco and his partner in treason Alonso Carrillo. He knew how to keep his thoughts to himself, but could not conceal his resentment. Pacheco and Carrillo must have soon realized that the King was aware of their treachery.

Sensing danger, they left the Court, and the administration was soon transferred to Beltrán de la Cueva, whom Enrique had created Count of Ledesma, and Pedro González de Mendoza, the bishop of Calahorra. Pacheco now realized that he had lost his place at the top of the royal administration, and began to think of how to gain by force what he could no longer get by consent. Lacking moral scruples, his fertile mind soon devised a scheme which may be termed diabolic. It turned Enrique's life into a veritable hell; it made a shambles of Castile's internal order; and, touching the subject of the present inquiry, it aggravated the Old-New Christian conflict to the verge of civil war. From this situation, as we shall see, a straight line led to the establishment of the Inquisition.

Indubitably, Pacheco saw clearly the obstacles that lay on his road to ultimate power. The biggest of them was of course the King, who had to be destroyed or reduced to insignificance if Pacheco was to attain his aim. But if the King were killed, he reasoned, Beltrán de la Cueva would no doubt become regent, perhaps jointly with Queen Juana. If Beltrán were removed too, there would still remain the Queen as the guardian of the Princess; and her wishes would probably play a major part in determining the regency. She would certainly not vote for Pacheco.

To achieve his goal he had to destroy them all: the King, the Count, the Queen and the heiress. But how could he do it, and on what pretext? He knew there was recurrent gossip in the Court about the Queen's special liking for Beltrán, and also some talk about the King's impotence dating from the days of his first marriage. No one had ever made much of these rumors and never had they been confirmed. Pacheco now decided to inflate and spread them as a way of building his political case. He would declare the King impotent, the Queen an adulteress, Beltrán faithless, and the heiress illegitimate. This would provide him with grounds to campaign for Alfonso, the King's half-brother, age eleven, as the legitimate successor. It would also provide him with a basis for the charge that Beltrán intended to kill the young Infantes (that is, Alfonso and his sister, Isabella) in order to secure the succession for Juana, his daughter from the unfaithful Queen.

It was a tissue of lies and slanders, but it appeared to make sense to many people, especially when stated without hesitation and repeated with growing emphasis. If Beltrán was indeed Juana's father, it stood to reason that the Infantes were in danger. Pacheco had no difficulty in getting Carrillo who, like himself, had lost favor with the King, to support his charges and plan of action. Both now played the role of guardians of the Infantes, of the true monarchy and its legitimate succession, and they had no difficulty in enlisting the cooperation of other magnates who, like themselves, sought more wealth and power.

Soon a dangerous conspiracy formed to strike a decisive blow. In April

1464, Pacheco and his allies worked out a plan to abduct Enrique, together with Beltrán de la Cueva and the Infantes, while the latter were staying in the alcazar of Madrid; but the attempt failed, and the King saw to it that Pacheco understood that his plan had been exposed. To show the traitor how little he feared him, he conferred upon Beltrán the Mastership of Santiago (May 23, 1464), for which Enrique had previously asked—and received— papal confirmation. The mastership of Santiago had long been Pacheco's most coveted prize, and the news that it had been awarded to Beltrán only doubled his determination to destroy his rival. Accordingly, he made another attempt to seize the King in his palace at Segovia, together with the Queen, the Infantes and Beltrán, who was to be killed on the spot. But Enrique's luck held again, and nothing came of this attempt either.[81]

Up to this point, it must be noted, the charges that allegedly motivated these attempts were still little discussed beyond the group of nobles enlisted by Pacheco for his plans. For reasons that are not hard to discern, the conspirators still thought it wise to refrain from involving the public in their quarrel with the King. We shall better understand their strategy in this conflict after noticing the following occurrence.

On May 16, 1464, archbishop Carrillo, Pacheco and his brother Pedro Girón signed a pact whose alleged purpose was to secure the Infantes' safety. In this document they assert that the Infantes Alfonso and Isabella—whom they call the "legitimate successors" to the throne—are in the hands of certain persons who wish to make sure that the "succession of these dominions" does not go to them, but to "whom it does not belong by right."[82] To accomplish their design, these plotters resolved to kill the Infante Alfonso and marry Isabella to someone of their choice, "against the welfare and honor of the royal Crown."[83] Accordingly, Pacheco, Girón and the archbishop committed themselves to save the Infantes from the peril that confronted them and "transfer them to our own power so that they be completely free" and duly guarded and served.[84] This commitment, the signatories claimed, was inspired by no other motive than their desire to discharge their patriotic duty—or, as they put it, to prevent any action which would entail a "disservice to God," and "irreparable damage" to the kingdom, and the "destruction of its public cause."[85]

What is peculiar about this document is that its authors do not mention by name anyone allegedly involved in the conspiracy against the Infantes. Nor does the document contain a word to suggest the causes of their intended action: the King's impotence, the Queen's adultery, and Beltrán de la Cueva's complicity in her crime. By the middle of May, it is clear, Pacheco and his associates still chose to keep their charges within their group, and they also wanted the King to know that they had refrained from causing a national scandal. Their ability to raise such a scandal at any moment was a threat they held over the King's head; and this was indeed what Enrique feared.

Rumors of the questionable succession, however, were heard here and there with increasing frequency; but as long as they were limited to small circles, Enrique preferred to ignore them. Rumors like these always fed the gossip that characterized the social life of the Court, and usually caused only little harm. But the case would be different if Pacheco and his allies made their allegations in a formal declaration, signed by leading magnates, addressed to the nation and circulated in all cities. Then, the King knew, he would be in trouble.

The publication of such a declaration, however, was avoided or delayed again and again. Pacheco must have thought it would ruin any chance of reconciliation with the King, which was, after all, what Pacheco really sought. Apart from this, he knew, it would be no easy task to persuade his associates to sign their names to such a libel. Mutual vilification was not uncommon in Castile among magnates, lay and ecclesiastic. But for leading nobles to besmirch their king, the queen and the heiress to the throne, to whom they had sworn allegiance, in addition to the King's chief minister, with the vilest calumnies for which they had no proof, was certainly no simple matter. It might be a cause for civil war. And the mere prospect of such a war could deter any grandee from lending his hand to anything that might provoke it. Pacheco thought it would certainly be simpler if the King were kidnapped and compelled to subscribe to terms that he, Pacheco, would dictate. He therefore devised a third plan to seize the King, which this time was supposed to be foolproof. Yet the execution of this plan, too, proved faulty, and the King was saved again.[86]

II

From this point on, the account of the developments presented by the fifteenth-century chroniclers is, as Sitges pointed out, confused,[87] and only with the aid of several documents preserved outside the official annals is it possible to reconstruct what happened. But before we come to consider these documents, we should note that the third attempt to abduct the King involved, unlike the previous ones, not a few selected individuals but hundreds of men from different places; and many people were indubitably involved also in the effort to foil it. Valladolid, where the plot was first discovered, was perhaps also the first urban center to hear that the conspirators stood for Don Alfonso.[88] The city was soon buzzing with rumors, which rapidly spread to other localities, and it became impossible for the nobles aligned with Don

Alfonso to avoid an explanation of what had prompted them to take such extreme measures.

No public declaration was made and no written statement was issued, but the oral campaign that Pacheco and his friends now had to conduct in justification of their action amounted to a moral attack upon the monarchy, though it formally centered on Beltrán de la Cueva and his alleged illicit relations with the queen. Before long various towns and cities, no doubt spurred on and guided by Pacheco, urged the King to dismiss Beltrán; and the administration, forced to defend itself, launched a far-flung counter-campaign. Royal letters were sent to all the places from which the damning proposals came, telling their citizens that the factious nobles were actively engaged in stirring up riots ("in the disservice of the King and the peace of his realm"), that they "seek war and scandals," and that all their vassals, and those who live in their territories, are forbidden, under pain of grave punishments, to respond to their calls to arms.[89] These communications were apparently repeated, and finally embraced the whole country, but the vilification continued, and constantly increased in both content and scope. Ultimately, it became so widespread and intense that the King, to abate it, decided on a move unprecedented in the annals of Spain.

The substance of the move is expressed in the cedula issued by the King in Cabezón (near Segovia) on September 4, 1464, at a meeting attended by some of his officials and several nobles of the opposition. Castillo tells us that before this meeting, King Enrique conferred with Pacheco in an effort to agree on the terms that might end the quarrel between the nobles and himself.[90] Both the contents of the cedula and its formal declaration in the presence of those who attended that meeting must have been decided by the two conferees after a great deal of wrangling.

Pacheco no doubt presented to the King his own and his group's conditions for peace: the transfer of the Infantes to the hands of the opposition; the formal denial of the succession to Juana; the removal of Beltrán and his associates from the Court; and the revision of the administration's practices and structure.[91] The King may have agreed to the transfer of the Infantes if all other demands were withdrawn, but Pacheco undoubtedly explained to the King that under no circumstances could the nobles be persuaded that Juana was his real daughter, and therefore their restlessness would inevitably persist until they were satisfied with the plan for the succession. Then the King produced the trump card he had prepared for precisely such an occasion. He would agree to transfer the succession to Alfonso provided that the nobles secured his marriage to Juana, whom they must recognize as his daughter and Princess, while all other demands of the opposition would be dropped. Pacheco, however, did not give up easily. He must have insisted on the other demands too, but the King was firm in his refusal, and Pacheco, recognizing the enormous gain involved in the King's new stand on the succession, accepted his proposal with some major amendments—i.e., that Juana should have the title of Princess, but not be referred to as the daughter of the King; that the king would make an immediate declaration regarding the transfer of the succession; and that the other demands the King had thus far rejected would be the subject of further consideration by him and the nobles of Pacheco's group. The final point must have been so framed as to give the King good grounds to believe that a real accord for peace had at last been reached, while Pacheco could apparently argue with some justice that major questions still remained unresolved.

Accordingly, in the cedula he issued in Cabezón on September 4, 1464, the king stated that

> to avoid any cause of scandal that might arise after our lifetime about the succession of my Kingdom, and wishing to provide for this in a manner that befits the service of God and my own service, I declare that the legitimate succession of my Kingdom and myself pertains, as it does, to my brother the Infante Don Alfonso and to no other person.[92]

Then he asked all prelates and nobles in attendance to swear allegiance and do homage to Alfonso in the manner due to the heirs of the kings of Castile and Leon; he expressed his wish for this performance to be followed by all the grandees and representatives of the cities, and wanted Alfonso to be titled and addressed, from that moment on, as the firstborn heir to his dominions and as prince. He assigned the month of December of that year for the completion of that procedure and stipulated that, following the oath of fidelity,

> all the said grandees and prelates, the *ricos ombres* and caballeros, and the procurators of the cities, towns and places, swear and promise to work and procure that the said Prince Don Alonso, my brother, marry the Princess Doña Juana[, and that] neither publicly nor secretly will they try to divert the marriage of Alfonso to another woman, or of Juana to another man.[93]

By this declaration, the King believed he had denied Pacheco any cause to espouse; secured his daughter's future as queen of his realms; defended her honor by calling her Princess (which meant that she was a legitimate heiress), and virtually compelled all the great of the kingdom to recognize her as such. But Pacheco thought otherwise. The King's announcement that a scandal might arise following his death with respect to the succession implied his admission that there were grounds for such a scandal; and his transfer of the right of succession from Juana to his brother the Infante Alfonso implied his recognition that she was not his daughter—or at least his belief that she might not be. For what king would rob his own child, against whom he was known to bear no grudge, of such a precious gift as the succession, unless he admitted in his own heart that the claim of the child's illegitimacy was true? No doubt Pacheco could further support this conclusion by the fact that, in referring to Juana, the King did not add to the title Princess (by which he designated her in the cedula) the words "our dear daughter" which were so customary in such announcements and which he would not have agreed to omit if he had really considered her his offspring. Pacheco, in brief, could see in the king's statement the most self-incriminating document he could hope for. And he knew to what use he could put it.

Shortly after the cedula was issued, Pacheco most likely saw the King again in order to induce him to meet the demands which the King had so far refused to accept. But Enrique remained stubbornly opposed to any additional concession. He especially objected to the proposals in which Pacheco was interested most—namely, the surrender of the Infantes to his care and the removal of Beltrán from the Court. The latter's dismissal was for Pacheco a prerequisite for the resumption of his own authority, while control of the Infantes would ultimately enable him to crown Alfonso king in case of need—that is, if Enrique persisted in his refusal to reappoint him as head of the administration. Alfonso's enthronement would of course be explained by the necessity to change Enrique's administration, which was allegedly both corrupt and inefficient, and hence the nobles' repeated call for a thorough overhaul of the royal regime. Enrique saw through Pacheco's schemes, and clearly understood why he so insisted on the fulfillment of each of his demands: they were all essential parts of his plan to secure his political restoration. But this was precisely what the King sought to prevent. In no circumstances would he agree to have Pacheco return to the Court.

Pacheco now realized, perhaps for the first time, how firm was Enrique's resolve not to let him come back into his life. He thought, however, that he now had the means of forcing the King to do what he wanted. He returned to the nobles with the King's refusal, pointing out that thus far they had achieved almost nothing by the King's declaration about the succession. For if the Infantes were not transferred to their hands, what would prevent the King and Beltrán from killing them at an opportune moment? The succession would then automatically return to Juana, and Castile would, in consequence, be ruled by an impostor and her fraudulent advisers. The only way to prevent this from happening was to intensify the campaign against the King. He must have reminded the nobles that, fortunately for them, they were now in a position to hit Enrique hard. For his declaration concerning the succession implied his admission that Juana was *not* his daughter, and if they duly explained this to the people, they could mobilize the whole country behind them. Carrillo supported Pacheco's plan of action. And so did the other magnates of their league.

On September 28 they met in Burgos (which had been their headquarters for some time) and addressed to the King a formal letter, in which they pointed out alleged disorders in the realm that urgently needed correction. Their complaints first centered on the religious depravity from which the whole kingdom, they claimed, gravely suffered; and they stressed what they said was "notorious in the Court"—namely, that the King had placed near his person "infidels," "enemies of the Catholic religion," and "others who, although Christians by name, are very suspect in the [Catholic] faith," especially since they "believe and affirm that there is no other world beyond the one in which we live, where people are born and die like beasts," which is a "heresy that destroys the Christian faith."[94] By "infidels" they meant the King's Moorish guards, and possibly also some Jews at Court who played a major part in the financial administration; "Christians by name" was their term for the New Christians, especially those grouped around Diego Arias Dávila, who was one of the King's most devoted servants and was accused of having denied the world to come.

In the main, however, this was not a personal attack but a new element in the anti-royal campaign—an element introduced by Pacheco and his friends in order to rouse, and attract to their side, the strong antisemitic and anti-converso factions of the Old Christian population. That is why they also sharply criticized the appointment of "unsuitable" individuals, who possessed "little knowledge" *(indotos)*, to pontifical and lower ecclesiastic posts, some of them by bribing associates of the King who could influence him to make such appointments. In this, too, the nobiliar critics no doubt alluded to the conversos, just as they undoubtedly alluded to them when they referred to the numerous appointments of judges, *veintiquatros* and *regidores* in the cities "to rob and oppress your subjects."[95]

They further complained of the devaluation of the coinage, which was known to be the work of Dávila's treasury and which caused "intolerable harm" to the people and brought about the destruction of the poor and the median classes.[96] They further complained of the excessive taxes extorted from the people by the "officials of your lordship" (who were known to be conversos and Jews) and of the lowering of the ceiling for the prices of goods sold by Christians to Jews and Moors. This reduction of prices, achieved by "gifts" which the Jews and Moors gave the King's officials, resulted in the "destruction of the poor laborers," on whose behalf the critics again raised their voice. It is clear that Pacheco and his nobiliar friends sought to draw the lower and middle classes to their side by feeding their enmity for the conversos, as well as the Jews and the Moslems. Hence their tirade against the King's Moorish guard, his alleged toleration of their violent crimes, and his general favoritism to the Moslems, which encouraged many Christians to convert to Islam.[97]

Playing the part of devoted subjects who sought nothing but the good of their lord, and of course also their country's welfare, they shifted all blame for the troubles of the kingdom, including those stemming from corruption and neglect, from Enrique to his minister, the Count of Ledesma. They accused the Count of having put the King's person under such intolerable oppression that he could no longer do by himself what "natural reason" commanded him to do; and from this they passed to the issue of the succession, which was of course uppermost in their minds. For the Count, they claimed, has "dishonored your person and your royal house, occupying things which belong only to your Highness" (a sharp allusion to Beltrán's relations with the Queen) and securing that the King move the nobles and the cities to swear allegiance to Doña Juana as heiress to the kingdom, "calling her Princess, which she is not, for it is clearly manifest to your Highness and to him that she is not the daughter of your Highness." Furthermore, he placed under his control the Infantes Don Alfonso and Doña Isabella, and "all the subjects of these kingdoms fear that he, and others who carry out his will, will procure the death of these Infantes, so that the succession of these kingdoms go to the said Doña Juana." Finally, they charged, he arranged to "disinherit Don Alfonso" of his right, "denying him the mastership of the Order of Santiago that your father Don Juan has left him," and transferring that inheritance to himself. Consequently, they demanded that the King order the arrest of the Count of Ledesma and his assistants, free the Infantes from their prison, restore the mastership of Santiago to Alfonso, and call a meeting of Cortes at which the Infante Alfonso would be proclaimed heir to the throne.[98]

In many ways, this harangue resembles the petitions that the anti-Alvarian nobles addressed to Juan II; but it was far more offensive to the King's honor and much more injurious to his interests. The powers that stood behind Pacheco now included eight counts (all leading nobles), two archbishops and two bishops, the admiral of Castile, the Master of Calatrava, and the lords of several towns (Murcia, Cañete, Monçon and Fromesta).[99] Militarily, the King may still have been superior. But what concerned Enrique now in particular was not the plotters' military strength but their capacity to do him moral harm. For what might have hitherto been presented as merely a villainous rumor became, through the letter of September 28, a formal charge backed by nobiliar authority and consequently of far greater credibility. How could he prove that Juana was his child and not the product of her mother's adultery? If he went to war, he might crush his enemies, but he could not crush the defamation. On the contrary, he would spread and reinforce it; for the people would now call him not only the "impotent" but the "murderer" of his subjects, whom he could not silence. Obviously, he had to answer the attack in a way that might contain the scandal. He called his council and sought their advice.

Invited to the meeting, among others, was Barrientos, his old teacher, friend and counselor. Barrientos urged war upon the traitors and strongly argued in support of his proposal. But Enrique, irritated, rejected his advice, claiming abhorrence of civil war. "This affair should be handled in a different manner, and not the way you suggest," he said. The Bishop did not remain in debt. "Since you do not wish to defend your honor, nor avenge your injuries, do not hope to reign with glorious fame," the Bishop said. "Of this I can assure you: from now on you will remain the most humiliated King that has ever been in Spain.[100] Barrientos' prognosis proved true.

But Enrique went his own way. In all probability, he now realized that he had committed a terrible blunder. Pacheco, the fox, had outwitted him. But he could not reverse the past or retract his statement of September 4 concerning the succession. The worst that he feared might happen had occurred: the rebels now possessed a deadly weapon with which they could bring about his ruin. He knew he was beaten and had no course open save war or further surrender. He chose surrender.

On October 25, he met Pacheco and accepted almost all the rebels' demands. He was to recognize Alfonso as the legitimate heir, presumably on the nobles' repeated assurance that they would have Alfonso marry Juana. He also promised to have the mastership of Santiago withdrawn from Beltrán and transferred to Alfonso and, finally, to have Alfonso given to the safekeeping of Pacheco. Then, on November 30, between Cabezón and Cigales, he met with a group of magnates much larger than the one he had encountered on September 4, again declared Alfonso as his legitimate heir to whom all those present swore allegiance, and once again ordered all the nobles and cities not represented on that occasion to express their allegiance to him as heir. Enrique also agreed to appoint a committee of arbitration that would recommend reforms in the management of the kingdom.[101]

Thus began the period of the "second decade"—a period of woes, troubles and tribulations that constituted the other half of Enrique's reign.

III

The committee of arbitration consisted of five members: two representing the King (Pedro de Velasco and Gonzalo de Saavedra) and two the opposition (Alvaro Destúñiga and Juan Pacheco). The choice of Oropesa to vote in a stalemate[102] was no doubt influenced by the friendly relations between him and the leaders of both parties (the King and Carrillo) and possibly also by the intention of the opposition to deal with the converso problem.

The committee accomplished its work in record time. On January 16, 1465, only six weeks after its appointment, it submitted its report on the state of the nation, together with its recommendations for improvements and revisions of the royal policies. The report, comprising some 60,000 words, included 129 paragraphs and touched on all the major issues relating to the governance of Castile. The administration of justice, the economic situation, the condition of the cities, the state of the army, the war with the Moors, and the function of the various departments of the government were all subjected to its scrutiny. The committee also devoted a lengthy section of its report to the Jewish question (paragraphs 96–119) and three paragraphs (in the opening section) to the problem of the conversos.[103]

The opening paragraphs of the report (1–3) deal with matters that Pacheco and his friends wished to play up for propaganda reasons. The first paragraph, which shows concern for Isabella, and touches on the services she was entitled to, was supposed to demonstrate the interest of the opposition in her rights and welfare. What they sought to indicate by that concern was the soundness of their political concept and the propriety of their corresponding actions. Isabella was not just an ordinary Infanta, but one who stood in line of succession immediately after Alfonso, her brother; and by referring to her other prerogatives, the opposition wanted to remind the King, as well as all the readers of its report, of the far-reaching change that had taken place in the condition of the royal house.

The second paragraph deals with the King's Moorish guard and calls for its total disbandment. The opposition had long harped on this theme, supposedly for religious and social reasons. There was much exaggeration, and much demagoguery, in its censures of the royal guard, but it all had a practical purpose: to denude Enrique of his protective shield. In a nation ridden with daring rebels who had tried to abduct him time and again, the abolition of his faithful Moslem guard would strip Enrique of the security he needed. A Christian guard, Pacheco knew well, would be far more open to blandishments of bribery and persuasions to betray the King.

The third paragraph calls for the prosecution of the war against Granada "until our enemies are totally destroyed."[104] It was another standard demand of the opposition, by which it meant to justify its own foreign policy and denounce that of the King, who chose, as they put it, to fight Christians (Navarre and Aragon) rather than Moslems (Granada).[105] Besides, it was a popular slogan: The war against Granada had long been regarded, at least formally, as the primary item on the national agenda of Castile.

Then came the paragraphs that deal with the "bad Christians," obviously to show that, apart from the war against the Moors, the state of the "bad Christians" ought to be considered the country's most urgent problem. Earlier, in their memorandum of September 28, they had criticized the King's tolerant attitude toward certain heretical conversos in his court, as well as toward some of their activities in the country. Now the censure of the conversos and their religious behavior appeared to be more detailed and thorough. The reason for this change is apparent. Pacheco wished to gain the support of the cities, and there was no better way for him to achieve this goal than to show sympathy for their views on the converso question. This is why the arbitrators were anxious to embrace the plan of the Inquisition as the solution to that question.

To be sure, the conversos are not mentioned by name. Alonso de Oropesa no doubt saw to that. He wanted the Inquisition to direct its inquest not against a particular group, but against individuals who "erred," or were accused of religious wrongdoing (or wrong thinking). This is why the document uses the term "bad Christians," and not conversos or New Christians, which would limit the inquiry concerning religious deviations to a specific part of Castile's population, and also cast suspicions of heresy on that part—all of which would be, to Oropesa's thinking, morally wrong and judicially unfounded. Second, the responsibility for the inquiries about the current heresies was placed in the hands of the archbishops and bishops—that is, in the hands of the Spanish Church, and no inquisition was to be instituted by the Pope or placed directly under papal control. Third, the inquisition in each diocese was to be local; there would be no national organization to supervise the activities of the local inquisitors. Fourth, those found guilty would be corrected or punished, but those judged blameless would be immune to defamation, maltreatment, or limitations of any sort. All these instructions were, of course, in the spirit of Oropesa's general plan.

Nevertheless, the recommendation of the arbitrators contained enough indications and allusions to show that the Inquisition was to be aimed at the New Christians and that by *"malos Christianos"* it meant primarily, or only, conversos of Jewish origin. To begin with, the Inquisition would direct its inquiries not only at those defined as "bad Christians" but also against all who may be "suspect in the faith" and "defamed by heresy"; these were terms commonly applied to designate the Judaizers among the conversos. Second, the suspects against whom the Inquisition was to act are described not merely as people who "do not live as Catholic Christians," but also as such who "guard the rites and ceremonies of the *infidels*," and this was again a description that could fit only the conversos. Third, the arbitrators wished to have it established that those who would not be found guilty by the Inquisition would not be subject "to riots *(robos)* and scandals in the cities, towns and places . . . where they reside." Riots and scandals caused by heresy accusations had broken out in some places only against conversos, and this was another clear indication that the Inquisition was to concentrate on the New Christians.

It is questionable of course whether Oropesa was satisfied with all the formulations in this proposal. But in documents composed by a number of parties with divergent views and interests, compromises in phrasing their summaries and decisions are common and almost unavoidable. Such compromises are doubtless found in the committee's proposal concerning the Inquisition. Nevertheless, it is easy to discern which passages or sentences were phrased by Oropesa and which by Pacheco or his aides. When we read, for instance, that the prelates should conduct the inquiries in absolute open-mindedness and complete objectivity, "subordinating to them all love, and affection, and hate, and partiality, and interest,"[106] we hear Oropesa's voice. On the other hand, the opening paragraph of the section under discussion was clearly phrased in Pacheco's spirit. It reads:

> Inasmuch as the aforesaid Prelates and nobles [i.e., those who belonged to the party of the opposition] have notified the King that there are in his Kingdoms *many* bad Christians and suspect in the faith from which are expected great evils and harms to the Christian religion; and inasmuch as they had requested his Highness to give them great power and aid, so that they might incarcerate and punish the individuals who may be found guilty of the above, and [also] that his lordship, with his own armed hand, aid and favor them in the aforesaid undertaking; and since the possessions of the said heretics are to be transferred to the treasury of his Highness, they asked him to assign ... part of the moneys thus attained for the release of Christian captives or for the prosecution of the war against the Moors.[107]

What may be gathered from this statement is that it was not men like Oropesa or Espina, or the Franciscans or the Hieronymites or King Enrique, who had called for an inquisition several years before (in 1461), that were responsible for the proposal in question, but the prelates and *caballeros*, who urged reforms in the kingdom. For according to their presentation, it is they—and only they—who "informed" the King of the presence in his kingdoms of a widespread heretical movement; so that one might assume that, without this information, the King was not even aware of the phenomenon. Furthermore, it was in response to *their* appeal that the King authorized the plan of the Inquisition (as is indicated in the continuation of that opening section). Above all, they discuss the existence of the heresy not in hypothetical but in realistic terms, as a fact that needs merely formal acknowledgment. Thus, before any inquiry was made, *they* determined that there were "many" bad Christians; *they* put special stress on the need to *punish* them and the great force (the "armed hand" of the King) which must be employed for that purpose. They speak with assurance of the prospects of confiscation which, judging by the above, would be quite large, and indicate the recipient of the confiscated properties (the royal exchequer) and the uses to be made of them (uses which are proposed here, it seems, for the first time). To be sure, the suggestion to use the confiscations for ransoming Christian captives and for the war against the Moors was no doubt readily subscribed to by Oropesa, but the stress on the *punishments* to be employed against the culprits, as well as on the *large number* of the heretics (with which the passage in question opens), cannot possibly be attributed to him. Oropesa would certainly begin that passage by stressing the need to "correct" the "erring," and he certainly would not have made the assertion that there were *many* "bad Christians" in the country. In fact, in the later parts of the discussion, the term "many" no longer appears; it is replaced by "some" *(algunos),* and the presence of heretics is discussed in hypothetical rather than in positive terms.[108]

However, regardless of the wrong attribution of credit, which we find in the section about the inquisition, the fact remains that this was the first time in the history of the Old-New Christian conflict that a committee sanctioned by royal authority and representing both the Crown and the nobility (and, in a way, also the mendicant orders) formally urged the establishment of an inquisition for the settlement of the religious problem in Castile. To be sure, the plan for an inquisition would not have been put forward had not the rebellious nobles been in need of popular support in their struggle with the King. But essentially the plan had been long in gestation; Spanish opinion had been pregnant with it (since 1449), and it had to be born sooner or later. The rebellious nobles merely served as its midwife.

What Pacheco hoped to achieve by the inquisition, therefore, was not an equitable solution of the problem produced by the alleged existence of a heresy, but an alliance with the anti-Marrano elements, whose support he sought for his future regiment. This is also evidenced by his attitude toward the Jews as reflected in the committee's proposals. Pacheco understood that, for the anti-converso movement, the Marrano question was inseparable from the Jewish problem, and that it was impossible to settle the first without taking care of the second. This is indeed what he intended to do. We have already mentioned that twenty-five paragraphs of the arbitrators' report (out of a total of 129) are devoted to the treatment of the minorities in Castile, and there can be no doubt that the committee's recommendations were made in response to demands of the majority respecting the Jews and Moslems in its midst. Obviously, in the main, the recommended treatment was aimed at the Jewish community in Castile, and it was in accord with the views of Oropesa as expounded in his *Lumen.*[109] But what was for Oropesa a religious requirement was for Pacheco another means of drawing the cities to his side.

What the Committee of Arbitration, therefore, recommended as the proper treatment of the Jewish minority was the opposite of the policy pursued by Spain's kings from the middle of the 11th century to the beginning of the 15th and then from 1420 to Enrique's own time. It was, in fact, a return to the laws of Catalina and those of Benedict XIII, except that the violation of these laws was to be punished even more severely. To illustrate this policy, it will suffice to present some of the measures referring to Jews that were recommended by the committee.

To begin with, it readopted the ruling advocated by Vicente Ferrer (1411) and Espina—namely, that all Jews and Moors should live in isolated quarters, in strict separation from the Christians. It further stipulated that this separation must take effect within one year (from February 1, 1465) and that the punishment for Christians who violated this law would be loss of offices and all possessions. The punishment for Jews and Moors who violated it was to be still graver: in addition to losing their entire property, they were to be reduced to the status of captives—that is, slaves of the King (in his domains) and of the various magnates (in theirs). What is more, if the king and the magnates failed to inflict these punishments, any person who charged infidels with violation of the order, and was in a position to prove his claim, would be able to take the accused Jews or Moors as his *own* slaves and captives. Other laws forbid Jews or Moors to act as managers and treasurers of the King, the Queen, the nobles, etc.; they also forbid them to serve as tax collectors, subcontractors, and *contadores*. Nor are they to be allowed to act as majordomos, tax farmers, and representatives of the king, the nobles, etc. Violation of these laws likewise involved the loss of all property for the Jews and the Moors, apart from imprisonment for a period of six months. Other laws forbid Jewish advocates to defend Christians, Jewish doctors to treat Christians as patients, and Jewish pharmacists to prepare drugs for Christians. Nor can Jews engage Christian labor and services or lend money at interest in any form. Dozens of other laws limit their occupations, their rights of inheritance, and their freedom of movement. They are also ordered to wear the sign.

It is not difficult to imagine the enormity of the calamity that would have befallen the Jews and Moors of Castile if even half of the committee's recommendations had been accepted. The conversos, too, would have been gravely affected by the establishment of an episcopal inquisition, however limited and controlled in its inquiries and punishments. But none of these plans materialized. The King rejected the entire report, with all its stipulations.

IV

During the proceedings of the Committee of Arbitration the King could notice from time to time some irregularities in its procedures. The committee would approach him occasionally to consult him or clarify his position on some issues, but, above all, to obtain his consent on matters that were especially important to Pacheco. Thus on December 12, 1464, it obtained Enrique's pledge to dismiss his secretaries, the brothers Badajoz (no doubt close friends of Beltrán), and what was far more important—to remove Beltrán himself from the Court (for a period of six months), as well as his associate the bishop of Calahorra (for a period unspecified in the extant document). From these meetings with the committee's members, from his contact man with the committee (his secretary Alvar Gómez), and possibly from some others involved in the work, the King got the impression that his two representatives agreed too often with Pacheco's views. Nevertheless, it was only a few days before the committee completed its work that the King could see how far it differed from his own views and policies. He ordered Alvar Gómez and Gonzalo de Saavedra, one of his appointees to the committee, to inform him fully of what was going on. They suspected, however, that the King had gotten wind of the part they had played in the preparation of the report; and fearing arrest and severe punishment, they fled the Court to the rebels' camp.[110]

The part Alvar Gómez and Gonzalo de Saavedra played in informing and counseling the King on the issues drawn up by the committee was not that of faithful servants of the Crown, but of traitors and allies of Pacheco and his associates. Early in the proceedings, Pacheco succeeded in persuading Saavedra and Pedro de Velasco, the King's two representatives on the committee, to go over to his side; and as for Alvar Gómez, he had been (since 1462) Pacheco's agent in the Court, regularly informing him of the King's intentions, so that Pacheco could always be prepared with effective counter-moves or answers.

Pacheco was sure that his way ahead was clear. By means of the arbitrators' decisions, he meant to complete the last phase of his complex and almost incredible scheme. He had managed to cancel the succession of Juana, to declare Alfonso the sole heir apparent, to place Alfonso in his own safekeeping, to have the mastership of Santiago taken from Beltrán, and then to have Beltrán removed from the Court. It now remained for him to place himself at the helm of the administration and make Enrique his puppet.

At this point, however, Pacheco was stopped. Enrique was prepared to retreat on many issues, but not on one: his rights as King. At the critical moment, his sense of danger moved him to inquire into the committee's doings, and thus he discovered the treachery of his men. In consequence, he now saw the committee as it was—not a body of arbitrators, but a clique of rebels, who abused the faith that Oropesa gave them and acted mostly behind his back.[111] The discovery freed him, of course, from his obligation to respect the committee's conclusions.

Pacheco was informed of the King's decision, as well as of the reasons that

moved him to make it. He understood that his renewed relations with the
King were again disrupted, and this time probably forever. He had failed to
kidnap the King politically just as he had failed to abduct him physically.
Pacheco concluded that the King was too smart or too cautious to be ensnared. He now realized that the only recourse left him was an open fight to
the finish.

V

Of the various losses suffered by Pacheco through the discovery of his plot,
the cessation of Gómez' services as his agent in the Court was no doubt the
heaviest. Since the matter bears directly on the main subject of our inquiry,
it deserves special attention.

Pacheco knew that without Gómez' help, he would not have gotten where
he did. It was Gómez who had helped him move the King to decline the
Crown of Catalonia, stop the war against Navarre, and agree to have his
conflict with Juan II arbitrated by the King of France; it was Gómez who had
counseled and urged Enrique, against the advice of all the King's friends, to
deliver the Infantes to Pacheco; and he may well have been the one who
devised the plan of transferring the succession to the Infante Alfonso. But the
damage he did was even greater. According to the royal chronicler Castillo,
he was the "inventor of all the evils [that befell the King] and the discoverer
of all the secrets of his Council, so that he followed in the footsteps of Judas
who sold his King and Lord."[112]

What could move a converso like Gómez to betray a monarch who treated
him so benevolently and raised him to such a high position? As the King's
secretary, he became rich and prosperous; purchased large estates; became
lord of Maqueda; and enjoyed much esteem and honor. No doubt he could
count on further remunerations and further advancement in his career. What,
then, could he gain from the betrayal? Castillo's answer was: nothing. But
"since his merits were few and his defects numerous, he fled loyalty, and
found treason attractive; so that not recalling who he was originally, and the
favors he received from the King, he put behind him shame and fear of God
for the sole purpose of destroying the King."[113]

If this description is correct, we have here a case of a perverted character.
But did Castillo recognize Gómez' true nature? There may have been more
weighty reasons for his moves than a treacherous disposition. If one tries to
relate his conduct to some concern for converso interests, one may assume
that the beginning of his betrayal started shortly after the King had submitted
in Rome a petition for the establishment of an inquisition. To be sure, a few
months later the King abandoned that idea in favor of Oropesa's much more
moderate plan, but once Gómez formed his link with Pacheco, the latter

knew how to cement it. Similarly, it may be argued that Enrique's failure to punish the organizers of the pogrom in Carmona could alienate a New Christian like Gómez from the monarch.[114] But such assumptions must remain sheer guesses, as we really know too little of the sequence of events. It is certain, however, that Enrique was generally well disposed toward the conversos and wanted to help rather than hurt them. Few knew this better than Gómez himself. Why then did he act so persistently and energetically against a king who was a friend of the New Christians in favor of a wily politician like Pacheco, who would turn out to be their open foe?

The answer, we believe, must be sought in the guidelines that determined the activities of the converso courtiers in the period of Enrique IV. These guidelines freed the converso courtiers from the principle of "loyalty to the King at all costs," which had virtually dictated the conduct of their predecessors. What meant more to them was the ruler's ability to impose his will and maintain order—an ability in which Enrique was deficient, as events in Carmona had shown.

Alvar Gómez no doubt agreed with this approach, but in addition, he may have considered Enrique, whose political philosophy was well known to him, a chronic and inevitable loser. He may also have concluded that no one else at Court could match Pacheco in astuteness, inventiveness and determination. He knew what Pacheco was driving at, and he did not believe that he could be stopped. Sooner or later, Gómez was sure, Pacheco would attain his political aims and become virtual master of Castile. If so, what we have here is simply the application of cold-blooded logic to the game of politics— Machiavellian tactics aimed at securing, first of all, the interest of the politician involved, and then, possibly, the interests of his group—that is, of the conversos—as well.

If the above hypothesis is correct, Gómez' conduct may have been symptomatic of many conversos of his class and standing. He was in fact not the only converso among Enrique's leading officials who betrayed the King and joined the rebels. At least four additional highly placed conversos followed in his footsteps.[115] Evidently, they were not too concerned about Pacheco's plans for the establishment of an inquisition as manifested in the decisions of the Arbitration Committee. Pacheco must have convinced them that these decisions were merely a device to attract the cities to the rebels, and that they should not be taken seriously; nothing would come of the present plan as nothing came of the former one, proposed years before by Oropesa; the bishops were not eager to establish an inquisition, and, unless pressed to do so, they would do nothing about it. Pacheco may actually have assured them that neither he nor his associates would exert such pressure.

Such assurances were given, we believe, even though Pacheco truly planned to act along the lines of the committee's decision. Events, however, could not prove his intentions one way or the other. Enrique's reaction to the committee's report canceled all the rebels' immediate plans. Gone was their hope to capture the administration by pacific means; unavoidably, both they and the King were moving toward a collision. More than that: they were moving toward civil war.

IV. The Civil War and the Second Toledan Outburst

I

On June 5, 1465, Archbishop Carrillo and Juan Pacheco arranged for a statue representing King Enrique to be placed on a platform in a field outside Avila. Hither they came, accompanied by such magnates as Alvaro Destúñiga, Count of Plasencia; Iñigo Manrique, Bishop of Coria; Gómez de Cáceres, Master of Alcántara; and other nobles, greater and lesser, in order to perform a strange ceremony that came to be known as the "farce of Avila." First, they lowered the statue to the ground at a considerable distance from the platform; next they read a paper which listed the reasons why Enrique could no longer be considered king; then they removed his crown and scepter, and finally demolished the statue altogether, showing great indignation in their movements and uttering in the process foul words. Alvar Gómez and Gonzalo de Saavedra, who had fled the court in the preceding January, were among those who attended this ceremony and took part in the proceedings.

The symbolic deposition, however, was only a preliminary to the main business in hand. For following the destruction of Enrique's effigy, they led his half-brother Alfonso to the platform, where they lifted him shoulder high and shouted in loud voices: "Castile for Don Alfonso!" The trumpets and drums made a great uproar, and the gentlemen assembled approached the young prince and, with great solemnity, kissed his hands in a demonstration of reverence and obedience. Alfonso was then eleven years old.[116]

The enthronement of Enrique's half-brother was greeted with outbursts of joy by at least half the kingdom. It was instantly followed by actions of support, and declarations of allegiance to the new king, by the councils of Toledo, Seville, Cordova, Burgos, Valladolid and other cities. In all these places nobles and plebeians wrested control of their local administrations from the hands of Enrique's officials and followers. In Toledo, the insurgents expelled from the city Don Enrique's assistant, Pedro de Guzmán, and also imprisoned a number of citizens suspected of siding with the deposed king. In the clamorous campaign in favor of Alfonso, only one dissenting voice spoke out. It was the voice of Don Francisco de Toledo, dean of the Toledan church.

Don Francisco, a converso, was a leading churchman. He was highly respected as theologian and preacher, and also as a diplomat of the first order. As such he was later employed by the Popes on important missions to various countries. In 1474, under Sixtus IV, he was invested with the see of Coria, and in 1479, at the age of fifty-five, was a candidate for the College of Cardinals.[117] But then death overtook him. According to Palencia, Don Francisco had been known as a sharp critic of King Enrique and even participated in the "public joy caused by D. Alfonso's exaltation to the throne"; but his "enthusiasm for the Alfonsine party cooled" when he recognized the "harmful intentions of the Marquis and the iniquitous ambition of some grandees," and because he believed the current rumor, "falsely disseminated in Toledo and other cities," according to which Don Alfonso was disposed (under the influence of the grandees referred to) to "persecute the conversos who were accused as prevaricators and abusers of the Christian cult and religion."[118] The rumor, however, was not utterly groundless as one might gather from Palencia's remarks. And the Marranos were to have additional reasons to fear a coming persecution of their group—not on the part of the child-King Don Alfonso, but of some of his leading supporters. In all likelihood, these forebodings of the conversos were shared by Don Francisco de Toledo, even though the chief New Christian officials associated with the royal administration, such as Alvar Gómez, did not seem to have anticipated any trouble for the conversos from the Alfonsine party.

Employing his great powers as preacher and logician and his great authority as theologian, Don Francisco now conducted a vigorous campaign in favor of Don Enrique. He delivered many sermons in which he tried to prove that no one has the right to depose a king, however incompetent or tyrannic, unless the king had been proven to be a heretic by a duly qualified court.[119] When the archbishop of Toledo, Don Alonso Carrillo, appealed to the Pope to support his actions, Enrique IV asked Don Francisco to set down in writing his refutation of the reasons advanced by the rebels for his deposition. It was of course important for Enrique in those days that the Pope reject the rebels' appeal, and he thought that a strong rebuttal of their claims could help him attain this end. It is noteworthy that it was the bishop of Calahorra, Pedro González de Mendoza, then chief arbiter of Enrique's administration, who advised the King to entrust Don Francisco with the preparation of the needed response.[120] The clever Mendoza must have been certain that no one could deal Carrillo, his rival, a harder polemical blow than Don Francisco; and he proved to be right. Don Francisco wrote the proposed paper, and the strong public impression it made may be judged by the fact that Don Alfonso's party hastened to publish two detailed "confutations," written by well-known theologians.[121] Pope Paul II, however, was not moved by their arguments, and if any party to that debate caught his fancy, it was assuredly Don Francisco.[122] The Pope remained a firm supporter of the King Don Enrique.

From Palencia's remarks on the attitude of the conversos toward Don

Alfonso's party, it appears that Don Francisco's position was shared by most leading conversos in the cities, as well as by most of their rank and file. But few had the courage openly to express their decisive preference for Don Enrique. Faced with the decisions adopted by the cities in which most of the conversos lived, the conversos had to take the stand of the majority if they wished to go on with their normal lives. Active support of Don Enrique and his camp, or even open sympathy with the King or his cause, would be seen as defiance of the urban authorities and might be punished by expulsions and confiscations. Don Alfonso's administration, for its part, chastened such offenders separately.

We must conclude, therefore, that in all the towns of Castile that fell under the rebels' sway, the conversos were either politically silenced or played the local political game. For several reasons, however, their constrained attitude became before long semi-voluntary. In the rebellious cities military controls were in the hands of one or more barons, and these were usually on good terms with the conversos and inclined to offer them protection. Likewise, the leaders of Don Alfonso's administration were interested in maintaining order in the realm; it would obviously be calamitous for their military plans to have their towns torn by dissension. Their policy toward the Marranos was indicated by their appointment of Luis Díaz de Toledo, Fernán Díaz' son, as the Relator of Don Alfonso.[123] They evidently wanted to draw to their side both the converso and Old Christian sections of the cities' population.

Under the rule of Don Alfonso, therefore, Marrano security seemed to be assured more or less to the conversos' satisfaction, and consequently they could not be suspected of looking to King Enrique for protection. In any case, this is how matters appeared in the first two years of Alfonso's reign. In fact, however, beneath the surface, Marrano security was steadily deteriorating. The division of the kingdom inevitably weakened King Enrique's authority in the areas he controlled, while Don Alfonso's party could not possibly establish an effective administration in its own domains. As was usual in Spain in such situations, the absence of a strong central government led to the emergence of subversive elements who sought to take the law into their own hands. Now they were particularly emboldened to act by the deep rift that was tearing Castile apart. The growing tension and the atmosphere of conflict permeating all parts of the kingdom increasingly endangered the balance of relations between the Old and New Christians; and in such a situation almost any provocation, accompanied by inflammatory agitation, was enough to upset the cities' social structure and make a shambles of the existing order. Such conditions appeared—again in Toledo—in the summer of 1467, and in consequence, the city soon became the scene of a second anti-Marrano outbreak which, in several respects, was more baneful to the conversos than that of 1449.

II

We possess three contemporary accounts of this event, all from Old Christian sources. As such they must all be considered one-sided and in fact are in parts clearly tendentious. Perhaps because of this they are also curtailed, for they evidently conceal more than reveal. One of them is included in Palencia's *Décadas,* his history of King Enrique's reign[124]; another is a letter which Pedro de Mesa, canon of the Cathedral Church of Toledo, wrote about a month after the riots to an unknown leading personality of that church[125]; the third is a casual sketch of the disturbances written by an anonymous Toledan eyewitness and preserved in two manuscriptal sources.[126] Of the three, the least objective is that of the canon, who is patently anti-converso; the least partisan is that of the anonymous Toledan; while that of Palencia seeks to strike a balance between the pro- and anti-converso approaches. In the main, however, Palencia, while writing his account, leaned on anti-converso sources, and this affected both the contents and the spirit of his entire presentation.

In discussing the causes and background of the outbreak, Palencia says that "at that time [i.e., 1467] there was revived among the inhabitants of Toledo the old enmity which was fomented by the fears of the New Christians and the indignation of the Old ones."[127] This was basically also the view of the anonymous author, who imputed the new outbreak to "no other causes . . . but the old enmity, which was deep rooted between them [i.e., the conversos] and the Old Christians—an enmity that had never been absent and was ever on the ascent."[128] The anonymous Toledan says nothing further on this matter. But Palencia, the historian, tried to explain the eruption at that particular moment. What contributed to the rise of the old tension at that time was, according to him, the faction of the New Christians who took the side of Don Enrique; they fell victim to the intrigues of ill-intentioned people and believed that victory of the Alfonsine party would mean the "extermination of the Jewish race."[129]

Thus, the view of the Marranos about Don Alfonso's followers and the plans which the latter harbored for their group was identical with that which Fernán Díaz and Torquemada had held about the followers of Sarmiento. Like the rebels of 1449, those of 1467 sought the "extermination of the Marrano race." Palencia, as we have indicated, disagreed with this assessment. He believed that what the followers of Don Alfonso were after differed from the aim of the antisemitic faction. In his opinion, the Marranos had simply been misled by false rumors, bred by intrigue and provocation.

According to Palencia, these rumors stemmed from "agents of discord," who not only "instilled fears in both parties, but also . . . convinced them, through certain intimations, of the hatred that one felt for the other." Owing to that excessive fear, they could, by the promise of help which they offered them, "inspire the conversos with unusual daring" in meeting the challenge they faced.[130]

Palencia does not tell us who those "agents" were. He may have had a general idea of their identity, or thought that they could be easily discerned by applying the rule of *cui prodest*. Since, in his opinion, the Alfonsine party had no intention of hurting the Marranos, those who were spreading rumors to the contrary must have been followers of Don Enrique. But what did they seek to achieve?

If we follow Palencia's line of thinking, we can reach the following conclusion. Toledo was an Alfonsine stronghold, but its Marranos were an important force. Once they were convinced that their lives depended on it, they could attack their enemies, wrest the city from their hands, and deliver it to King Enrique. Palencia believed that this was the claim of the Alfonsine agitators in the city, and indeed the aim of the Toledan Marranos. He assumed that when they spoke of the danger that confronted them and their need to prepare themselves for self-defense, the conversos were concealing their real intentions under a smoke screen of half-truths. The main purpose of their military preparations was not to improve their self-defense, he thought, but to enable them to capture Toledo; had they not been possessed with this idea, they could have kept calm and stayed unhurt.

The Marranos, however, could not remain calm. They were convinced that a storm was brewing, and they made elaborate preparations to meet it. They were determined not to allow a repetition of the disasters that had befallen them thrice (in 1449 in Toledo and Ciudad Real, and in 1462 in Carmona). This time, they decided, their enemies were to feel the mettle of their organized defense.

In line with this, the Toledan Marranos mobilized a clandestine paramilitary force which, according to the anonymous informer, numbered more than four thousand recruits.[131] They appointed as their chief one Fernando de la Torre, whom they regarded as a man of valor. They bought weapons with money they raised from their members and deposited them at la Torre's house. Their men in need of arms could resort to this arsenal as soon as an alarm was sounded. Moreover, the Marranos saw to it that their forces were supplied with all kinds of weapons, defensive and offensive, and the most modern and effective instruments of combat.[132] Yet while they thus armed themselves (according to Palencia, with "arrogant resolution"), they succeeded in gaining "by means of gifts and humble reverence" the support of a certain part of the nobility, so that they might not lack outside help "from the first moment of their encounter with their foes until the moment of declared victory."[133]

The nobiliar support referred to by Palencia was also mentioned by Pedro de Mesa and the anonymous reporter.[134] It was especially expressed in the alliance that the Marranos succeeded in forging with the Count of Cifuentes. This count, Don Alfonso de Silva, controlled almost half the city's population, and the conversos relied more on his help than on that of anyone else. "But *they did not reveal to him their secret intentions,*" says Palencia, "only presented their common complaints."[135] Thus, they pointed out to him the gross injustice with which the Old Christians of the city were treating them; for they "not only often calumniated them" for no cause save their "ill will and jealousy," but also "persecuted them with killings and expulsions." They further spoke of the "new outrages" which their enemies intended to add to the old ones, and stressed that this intention did not result from any crime "recently committed by the conversos." What moved the Old Christians to attack them again was "their covetousness of the wealth that was acquired by the conversos through their own labor and industry." There was no other motive; for "all the other accusations" the Old Christians voiced against them lacked validity or factual basis; they "were dictated by wickedness and arrogance."[136]

This passage, in which Palencia presents the Marranos' "common complaints," is an important piece of evidence, for it clearly contains the Marranos' answer to the charges leveled at them at the time. Since these, as he put it, were their "common" complaints, they did not present some new, special argument developed in those days to influence the Count. This rather was their fixed position, the claim they had made again and again—their protestation of innocence. What we heard the Marranos say in 1449, following the riots and inquisition in Toledo, we now hear in 1467, almost two decades later. They dismiss the accusations against them as false—in fact, as devoid of any vestige of truth, as vicious calumnies calculated to incite bloody assaults upon their communities. There is no new evidence that can support these calumnies, and no crime has been recently committed by the Marranos that could justify the charges leveled against them. What is it then that irritates the Old Christians to the point of resorting to such outrageous behavior? The Marranos could give only one answer, the answer given by the Relator, Torquemada and Cartagena, their advocates in 1449, and by anyone of them a hundred times since: It is the Old Christians' perverse desire to seize the Marranos' wealth. Jealousy is the root of the savage hatred that had been kindled against them in Castile's cities—jealousy, greed and malice—and none of the alleged religious, social and economic misdemeanors. The Marranos thus flatly rejected the accusations made by their Old Christian adversaries; they called them lies of men bent on robbery and murder and deterred by no legal prohibitions—lies produced to shield their foul intentions with the semblance of a moral pretext.

Thus, Palencia here presents what may be viewed as the "common" self-defense of the conversos. But did he consider that defense true? Palencia refrains from expressing an opinion in this particular case. Yet if we recall his statement on the motives of those who attacked the Marranos at Carmona, we must conclude that he concurred with the Marranos' argument. In discussing the riots in Carmona, as we have seen, Palencia spoke openly about the "rebellious conspiracy" which was organized against the Marranos of that city by those who, "thirsty for their wealth," did them harm "in the name of religion," even if the quenching of that thirst required "pillage, assassination, and the violent perpetration of all sorts of infamies." Palencia compared those infamies to the outrages perpetrated *"prior to that in Toledo"* (namely, during Sarmiento's rebellion) and to what "the *thieves* did later" in the same city in 1467.[137]

Here we do not hear the Marranos' self-defense as presented by Palencia on various occasions—a self-defense that one may consider tendentious and therefore at best only half true. Here we hear Palencia's own voice and can see that his view of the Marranos' foes was similar to, or almost identical with, that of the Marranos themselves. In Palencia's opinion, then, the Marranos were attacked not for religious or moral reasons, or concern for the common welfare, but because their attackers were essentially "thieves" who, possessed with a passion for gain and wealth, did not shrink from any kind of crime. Palencia, we may assume, did not include in this category *all* rabid anti-Marranos in Castile—all their agitators, spokesmen and leaders, who urged the elimination of the conversos from Spain. But he no doubt referred to many of these too and, above all, bore in mind the masses of their followers who did the robbing and the killing.

This, then, was the problem the Marranos faced, according to Palencia; and we have also seen some of the preparations made by the conversos to meet that problem. It is clear that they regarded a military clash between themselves and their foes as likely or probable, and did their utmost to meet the challenge. According to Palencia, they hoped to be victorious. But what kind of victory did they seek? What was it that Palencia meant when he referred to their "arrogant resolution," their "secret intention," their conspiracy, which they had not revealed to the Count of Cifuentes? Clearly, Palencia was here trying to tell us that the Marranos were no longer satisfied with repelling the Old Christian aggressors from their neighborhoods, or even with inflicting heavy casualties upon them while beating off their attacks. What the Marranos hoped for, according to Palencia, was not just a successful self-defense, but a crushing defeat of their enemies in battle, so that the latter would be placed at their mercy. Palencia does not say this in so many words, but his entire presentation leads us to the conclusion that this was indeed the Marranos' plan. In fact, Palencia gives the definite impression that the Marranos sought to *provoke* a conflict with their foes as soon as they completed their military preparations and their political and military alignments.

Where did Palencia find this information? No doubt in hostile anti-converso sources which, trying to blame the conversos for the disturbances, presented the Marranos' alleged intentions as the reason for the outbreak of the Toledan civil war. To support this claim, these sources pointed to the huge quantity of cords (more than ten thousand, according to one estimate) the Marranos had assembled to bind their captives. Palencia accepted all these data as factual and as proof of the conversos' grand design.[138] He probably considered the conversos' plan (as reported to him by their adversaries) unrealistic, a product of a gross exaggeration of their force; perhaps this is why he called it an "arrogant resolution." In any case, he averred that the Toledan Marranos were preparing a triumphant assault. What they needed was an excuse for their aggression, a mere spark to start the hostilities. According to Palencia, that spark, too, was provided by the Marranos.

"Finally," he tells us, "an occasion was offered for the execution of [their] plan. Alvar Gómez, former secretary of King Enrique, who was appointed extraordinary magistrate of Toledo, committed certain abuses shortly after he had begun the performance of his duties; as a result he was anathematized [by the Toledan Church]. But he, who knew that his friends of the same race [i.e., the conversos of Toledo] were plotting [an attack upon the Old Christians of the city], and perhaps he was also an accomplice of theirs, forced his way into the church during the divine services. These were instantly interrupted. Hard words were exchanged, and the followers of Alvar Gómez, without considering the sanctity of the place, put their hands on their swords and dispatched a clergyman who tried to repel the insolent. There arose a great uproar. The people responded to the sound of battle, shouting that the enemies have perpetrated that crime out of their hatred and contempt for the Religion and the holy temple."[139]

This is how Palencia describes the beginning of the battle that erupted in Toledo on June 19, 1467, between the Old and New Christians. It is easy to see that this description follows the same anti-converso line as the earlier part of his account. Palencia blames the New Christians for the outbreak, for, as he says, they were looking for an "occasion" to execute their "plan" of attack on the Old Christians. Again he speaks of the "plot" they contrived in which Alvar Gómez may have acted as "accomplice." Alvar Gómez is described as unquestionably guilty in the quarrel that erupted between him and the Church (he "committed certain abuses," says Palencia, and as a result was anathematized, apparently justly). It would seem that he deliberately provoked a great scandal (perhaps in collusion with some "friends of his race") in order to hasten the execution of the "plot," and thereby get rid of his Old Christian enemies and the humiliating judgment they issued against him.

All this, as we shall see, can hardly be substantiated by a careful analysis of what our other sources tell us about the development of the pertinent events. Indeed, to determine what actually happened, we must consider certain data touching the origin of the conflict between Alvar Gómez and the cathedral church—data that Palencia overlooked or suppressed.

III

The Alvar Gómez whom Palencia describes as "former secretary of King Enrique" is of course the Alvar Gómez de Cibdad Real, who had betrayed the King and gone over to the party of the rebellious nobles. His departure from the Court took place, as we have mentioned, in January 1465; and now, in July 1467, we find him in Toledo occupying the position of one of the chief judges. We may assume that the leadership of the rebel faction, especially Pacheco and the archbishop of Toledo, who appreciated the services Alvar Gómez had rendered them, were instrumental in having him installed in that office. But what were the "abuses" which, according to Palencia, he committed shortly after assuming his high post and which must have been so grave as to earn the anathema of the city's major church?

What we know of this conflict from other sources suggests that Alvar Gómez, in this instance, may not have committed any abuse at all. It turns out that the cathedral church of Toledo (the same church that anathematized Alvar Gómez) empowered a certain Jew to farm some debts due to the cathedral in the town of Maqueda. No permission to perform this task was given by Alvar Gómez, who was lord of the town, and the governor of Maqueda halted the collection and put the Jewish tax farmer in prison. The church made a great issue of the incident. Chief movers of its actions were its leader and patron, Fernán Pérez de Ayala, brother of Pero López, the leading nobleman of Toledo, and Juan Pérez de Treviño, vicar of the archbishopric, who was known as an enemy of the conversos. Apparently without questioning Alvar Gómez, who then happened to be in the villa of Velez, they put an interdict on Maqueda and excommunicated Alvar Gómez. Then they informed him of his excommunication and ordered him to come to Toledo.[140]

Alvar Gómez was deeply offended; in fact, he was outraged. He must have been a proud man, irritable and aggressive, and he returned to Toledo seething with anger. This was not the kind of insult he could take with equanimity. After all, he was not an ordinary citizen, but one of the two major judges of Toledo and a leader in the camp of the Infante Alfonso, who was recognized by the Toledans as their king. Surely the church could have found other means to satisfy its needs in Maqueda before turning to the extreme measures of interdict and excommunication. It is possible, of course, that Alvar Gómez claimed that the church had no right to collect taxes in Maqueda without clearing the matter with him or his official, the governor of the town. But whatever his claims, it is reasonable to assume that as lord of Maqueda, and as major judge, he must have known what his rights were. In any case, when he returned to Toledo and saw Fernán Pérez, he vehemently protested against the church's action and demanded its immediate cancellation. Ayala refused. Harsh and "indecent words" passed between the two; and the violent quarrel, which soon became known, shattered the public peace. From a dispute between two individuals (or, at most, between Alvar and the church) it became a quarrel between two camps. It assumed the character of a "great scandal between the conversos and the 'pure' Christians" (Christianos lindos).[141]

Some leading citizens (apparently Old Christians) fearing further dissension, tried to reach a reconciliation. But Ayala remained obstinate. His terms for a compromise were harsh. The governor of Maqueda, Fernando Escobedo, should be brought to Toledo to stand trial, he insisted, and Alvar Gómez should post ten thousand doblas as security for the losses caused the church by his official. In return, it seems, he was prepared to lift the interdict and cancel the excommunication. Alvar Gómez was prepared to yield. He delivered his governor to the authorities of Toledo and was about to post the guaranty.[142] But then the whole deal exploded.

At this point we are treading on unsafe ground, as we have only the decidedly biased account of the canon Pedro de Mesa to go by. Apparently, the conversos were dissatisfied with the terms agreed on by Alvar Gómez and Ayala. They must have felt that Alvar Gómez was treated shabbily and unjustly and that the measures against him constituted an affront not only to him, but to their entire community. From the start they had been anxious about the outcome of the conflict, and now that Alvar Gómez had yielded so abjectly, their concerns increased. They evidently saw in the church's terms a sinister design that could actually endanger their entire status in Toledo.

What was it in those terms that could lead the conversos to such extreme conclusions? Most likely, it was the forthcoming trial of the governor of Maqueda. The judge was to be Pedro de Treviño, nephew of the vicar Juan Pérez de Treviño (known, as we have indicated, for his enmity toward the conversos), who could be expected to press the governor to assert that he acted at the order of his lord, Alvar Gómez. Thus Gómez who, in all probability, had claimed never to have given such an order, could be accused not only of having lied to the church, but also of illegally withholding funds that belonged to the cathedral chapter. If found guilty, he would doubtless be deprived of his high office, and this was most likely what Fernán Pérez de Ayala had been aiming at from the outset. Fernán Pérez' interest in the matter was clear. Apart from being rabidly anti-Marrano, he sought to satisfy the wishes of his brother Pero López, the leading extraordinary judge of Toledo, to whom the presence of a converso in that high judicial office was a constant irritant and a blow to his prestige.[143]

Pero López de Ayala was the son of Pero López, whom Alvaro de Luna had dismissed from his posts as chief judge of Toledo and governor of its alcazar. Both from his opposition to King Enrique and the anti-converso stand he was to take, it appears that, like his brother, he was anti-Marrano—though perhaps for political reasons. For until the latest rebellion of the nobles, the conversos were known to have sided with the King, and locally they allied themselves, as we have noted, with the Count of Cifuentes, head of the second noble house in Toledo, which contested the city's control with the Ayalas. It stands to reason that Pero López de Ayala viewed Alvar Gómez, the converso and Cifuentes' man, as his political opponent, potential or actual, and sought to undermine his influence. The ultimate results could of course be attained if Alvar Gómez were to be dismissed from his post in compromising circumstances.

Thus, the conversos had reason to suspect that this was what Ayala and his brother Fernán sought to achieve by the trial of Escobedo; and they feared that Alvar Gómez' downfall might result in negative consequences for them all. The allegedly shameful career of the judge would be used as a pretext to block the path of all conversos aspiring to public office. Naturally, they wanted to forestall any move that might lead to such an outcome. But in this they were hampered by a *fait accompli:* Alvar Gómez had already delivered Escobedo into the hands of the church for trial.[144] It was a hasty and ill-thought-out move; and they now looked for ways to correct it.

They still had at their disposal one card to play: Alvar Gómez' unfulfilled promise to guarantee, by his signature or by deposited funds, the sum of ten thousand doblas; and they probably planned to have the trial quashed in exchange for Alvar Gómez' guarantee or settlement in cash. Apparently, they hoped that if the church were informed that it could not have both the trial and the payment, the church would prefer the payment. The leader of the conversos, Fernando de la Torre, impressed on Alvar Gómez the vital need for them all to reopen negotiations with the church. He also proposed to participate in these negotiations and to bear the brunt of the task.

They met Fernán Pérez in a side room of the church, and they tried, if our reconstruction is correct, to persuade him to cancel the interdict, the excommunication and the trial in exchange for a financial compensation. But Ayala would not yield. What he wanted was evidently not money or repair of the damage allegedly caused the church, but something else. The conversos no doubt thought they knew what he was after, and therefore (it seems likely) asked his permission to present their case to the chapter. But Ayala declined that request, too. The discussion became heated, and Fernando de la Torre lost his temper. He was heard to shout that he would not submit on any of these matters, but would break with both Ayala and the chapter. Alvar Gómez and Fernando left the church in a rage. Ayala returned to his regular seat. "The caballeros and others" (who were then in the church) "remained all confused," says Pedro de Mesa.

This happened on the morning of Sunday, July 19, during terce. About an hour later, there occurred, de Mesa tells us, an unprecedented incident. A group of "heavily armed" conversos, led by Alvar Gómez and Fernando de la Torre, entered the church through a side gate. Clad in armor and with swords drawn, they burst into the assembly of worshipers, shouting: "Let them die! Let them die! For this is not a church, but a congregation of villains." They struck the church's treasurer and left him dying; then they found the chaplain who had read the interdict and wounded him mortally, so that he too later died. Following this scandal caused by the conversos, the worshipers "went all to eat," the canon says.[145]

Little analysis is required to see that Pedro de Mesa's account of the occurrences is a gross distortion of the truth. According to de Mesa, what took place in the church was not a skirmish between Old and New Christians produced by an uncontrolled burst of emotion, but an organized assault by the converso leaders upon the Old Christian worshipers. The sole purpose of the conversos' assault was to perpetrate a massacre—a purpose which, according to de Mesa, was revealed by their violent entrance ("with drawn swords") and their battle cry ("Let them die!"). But why did they not accomplish that purpose when they were all, according to de Mesa, well armed, while most of the worshipers were apparently not? And what could they possibly hope to gain by such a brutal and unprecedented act? It seems that they could easily foresee what would happen if their plan was implemented—that is, if the massacre they sought to carry out materialized: they would raise against their group a storm of hostility on the part of *all* Old Christians in the country that would surely end in their destruction. Finally, one may ask, how could such an action help them achieve their immediate ends—that is, settle their quarrel with the church and free them from the interdict and the excommunication? Surely there must have been a different reason for their presence in the church that Sunday morning.

Judging by Palencia and the anonymous reporter, the sequence of events was quite different. The Marranos did not burst into the church with the cry "Let them die," for they did not come there with intent to kill the worshipers. Nor were they the first to pass from words to deeds (as is evident from the

anonymous account).[146] Their purpose in coming to the church that morning
was, in all likelihood, to present their case—this time not to Ayala and his
comrades, but to the whole body of the church's members. There is no doubt
that some of them came manifestly armed or that they included an armed
force, perhaps because they thought that in the presence of that force, no one
would dare prevent them from speaking. In any case, Alvar Gómez spoke.
According to Palencia, he directed to the audience "words of ire and threat,"
which were not well received.[147] Some of the officials reacted with abuses
while others tried to expel the intruders. The offended conversos reacted
violently; they used their weapons, and two church officials were mortally
wounded.[148] A heavy stone was thus thrown down a precipice; what happened later was determined by the pull of gravity.

What was the reaction of the church's rank and file to the encounter that
took place in their presence? Once the conversos left the church, we are told,
the worshipers "went all to eat."[149] They may have understood the reasons
for the conflict, or why it had gotten out of hand, and considered the
deplorable incident closed, however disgraceful or regrettable they judged it.
Yet this was not the reaction of the leaders. When they returned to the
church, they had their plans laid. One or two of them must have had the idea
of using the occurrences in the cathedral as a pretext to rally the people for
an assault on the conversos; they decided to present the violent encounter as
a deliberate converso attack upon the church—an attack which ought to be
duly met if the danger of far greater converso attacks was to be averted.

Events followed in rapid succession. Both Pedro de Mesa and the anonymous author tell us that Fernán Pérez de Ayala and his aides (the vicar
Treviño and the abbot of Medina) began to mobilize the Old Christians of
the city, allegedly for the "defense" of the cathedral.[150] They ordered all
churches to ring their bells and urge their men to assemble in the cathedral
church, which they fortified and turned into their headquarters. The response was not what they expected. Only three of the five parishes of the city
(those that were not controlled by Cifuentes) reacted positively to their call.
Therefore, to bolster their military force, Fernán Pérez and his friends issued
urgent appeals to all the villages in the neighborhood of Toledo to come to
the aid of the endangered church. The village of Ajofrin made a major
contribution by sending 150 volunteers. They were met at the church by a
thousand armed men,[151] who together with them planned an assault upon the
converso neighborhoods.

The conversos were aware, of course, of all these moves and realized that
an attack on their boroughs was imminent. They decided to preempt their
opponents' attack by striking at the church, their assembly place, before they
were properly organized. They aimed their artillery at the gates of the
cathedral, through which many of the would-be attackers were passing, and

they also set fire to a number of buildings in the vicinity of the church. "The assault and the burning lasted all night," says Palencia, and the action proved successful, at least in part, for the shooting caused the Christians "many casualties" and the fire destroyed several structures, although it did no damage to the church itself. Palencia ascribed the initial advantage gained by the conversos through this assault to their "premeditated design" of starting the war; and faithful to his thesis, he continued to claim that the conversos were not fighting in self-defense, but primarily to "hurt the Old Christians." They persisted in this "ardor" for two days, until they "slackened" in their determination. In consequence, the conversos returned to their homes. But at that moment, he says, the Old Christians gathered strength, and began earnestly to fight—not just to hurt the New Christians, but for "their liberty, their life, and their religion."[152] The battle soon took on a different cast.

Palencia, again reflecting the influence of his anti-converso sources, misrepresents not only the aims of the parties but also the whole course of the struggle as it evolved in those few crucial days. The deterioration of the Marranos' position, to be sure, took place on the third day of the fighting, but it resulted not from the altered goals or the decline in the "ardor" of the fighters,[153] but from a change in the fortunes of war, which Palencia failed to describe. We must here turn to our two other sources to get a clearer view of what occurred. And what occurred was in part due to sheer luck, and in part to the Old Christians' superior fighting skills and better military tactics.

To avert the concerted attack of the conversos from the front of the church and the adjacent areas, the Old Christians set fire to a few outlying buildings of the converso settlements, from where the wind carried it deep into the New Christian boroughs. A fierce conflagration soon developed which was impossible to control. Eight of the principal thoroughfares of the city—the richest, busiest and most thickly populated streets—went up in smoke. In this situation, our anonymous source says, the Old Christian assailants needed neither to fight nor to get help from other Old Christians.[154] In the heavy fumes and spreading flames that enveloped their streets and homes, most of the New Christians were now mainly engaged in saving their families and possessions from the holocaust. Only on the borders of the converso settlements did bitter fighting go on between the much diminished converso defense forces and their determined adversaries. The latter attempted to break through the conversos' well-fortified positions, but no such breakthrough was effected and, consequently, no massacre took place. The conversos managed to hold their ground.

The fortunes of war, however, were rapidly changing and positions were passing from hand to hand. Near the Church of Magdalena a band of New Christians, under the command of Alfonso Franco, broke through the lines of their enemies and caused them a number of losses. But a counter-attack of an Old Christian force, led by the dyer Anton Sánchez, pushed Franco's group into a corner, where Franco was captured by Sánchez' men. He was placed under the guardianship of Pedro de Córdoba, a *regidor* who belonged to Ayala's party and whose house served as headquarters for the political leadership of the anti-Marrano forces.[155]

Alfonso Franco was a well-known lawyer and an admired personality in Toledo.[156] He was doubtless one of the main converso leaders, and his capture by the enemy was a bitter blow to the conversos' prestige and morale. His being held prisoner by a *regidor,* however, encouraged them to believe that he could be freed if the Count of Cifuentes demanded his release. The Count, who fulfilled his promises to the conversos by fighting with them from the start of the battle, undertook the delicate and unpleasant mission. He went to the house of Pedro de Córdoba and asked that Franco be transferred to his hands. Met with refusal, he repeated his request until Pero López de Ayala, who happened to be there, sternly advised him to stop his entreaties if he did not wish to share Franco's fate. It was a rude insult and an ugly threat, and the Count left the place burning with rage. Determined to step up the pace of the fighting, he galloped at the head of some sixty cavalry to all the converso main battle stations and urged their men to resume the attack. The battle now thickened and seemed to be going in the conversos' favor, until the Old Christians under Sánchez' leadership bombarded the Count's positions so heavily that he was compelled to retreat. Dismayed by these results, the Count began to fear ultimate defeat and capture. He left the city for the monastery of San Bernardo, followed by many conversos seeking safety, among them Alvar Gómez.[157]

The fire lasted all Wednesday and through the following night. One thousand and six hundred pairs of houses, the residences of four thousand converso families, were laid waste by the conflagration, and enormous quantities of goods were destroyed. But much was still left to loot when the fire subsided. On Thursday the sack began of the neighborhoods evacuated by the conversos. It lasted through Friday and Saturday and left the ruined buildings clear of the remains of New Christian wealth. Topping their heavy property losses was the conversos long list of casualties (some 150 killed and hundreds of wounded). At this point, the anonymous author says, the Old Christians could have put all the conversos to the sword, and he marvels at the "great divine mercy which was responsible for their salvation."[158] He was probably right in not attributing their rescue to the compassion of the victors, but wrong in believing that the assailants in Toledo could massacre the conversos on such a large scale. What saved the majority of the conversos in the city, as well as many of their possessions, was, to begin with, the sanctuary they found among Old Christians who sympathized with their plight. Such sanctuary was offered especially in the parishes whose residents refused to participate in the war which the leaders of the church declared on the conversos. They evidently did not consider the conversos heretics, Judaizers, or enemies of the Old Christians; for not only did they accept them readily in their homes, but also repulsed any attempt to rob them.[159] In addition, the conversos found refuge in the strongholds of many of the nobles who lived in the city and, above all, in the monasteries and convents, where they also transferred some of their assets.[160] Thus, the great majority of the conversos remained within the city's confines, and much of their property was saved. What is more, almost all of them kept their arms, and this was another factor that no doubt accounted for their survival.

IV

The outcome of the battle caused a radical change not only in the state of the conversos in Toledo, but also in the city's Old Christian leadership. Before the outbreak, control of Toledo was divided between the houses of Cifuentes and Ayala, with the former commanding most military strongholds and supported by the larger part of the citizenry. After the battle, conditions were reversed. The Ayalas became sole masters of Toledo, thus recovering the influence they had wielded in the city during the rule of the Infantes of Aragon and becoming, more than ever, arbiters of its affairs.

In this situation the conversos were virtually at the mercy of Pero López de Ayala. They ceased being an organized force, and their leadership, to the extent that it remained in Toledo, was virtually paralyzed. Fernando de la Torre, their chief spokesman, was caught in the Church of Santa Leocadia when he was trying to flee the city. He was hanged, feet up, by his frenzied captors from the beams of the church's bell tower.[161] A similar fate was reserved for his brother, Alvaro de la Torre, the *regidor,* who was caught a day earlier in another neighborhood (that of St. Miguel).[162] Later, the corpses of both, laid on donkeys, were carried to the city's central square of Zodo-cover, accompanied by a large crowd and a town crier proclaiming:

> This is the justice which the community of Toledo ordered to be done to these traitors, captains of the heretical conversos, because they were against the Church. It ordered to have them hanged with feet up and head down. He who thus acts, thus pays.[163]

They hung there, feet up and head down, for four days, exposed to the vengeance of Old Christian passers-by, who cut them to pieces with knives and riddled them with gunshots. They were finally turned into shapeless bulbs of flesh, emitting an unbearable stench. The city then ordered the Jewish community to remove them from the gallows and bury them. They were interred near the Jewish cemetery.[164]

This treatment by the Toledan populace of the corpses of the Marrano leaders bespeaks the terrible, implacable hatred felt by many Old Christians for the New. It also explains the fate of Franco, who was transferred to the royal prison. The populace demanded his immediate execution, but the leadership of the city appeared hesitant to comply. They were faced with intercessions on Franco's behalf by the archbishop of Toledo and Juan Pacheco, who urged them to commute Franco's death sentence, and by a separate order of the King Don Alfonso to restore to him his freedom, estate and office.[165] The final say rested with Ayala who, in view of his rebuff to Cifuentes (when the latter intervened on Franco's behalf), seems to have sided with the Toledan populace rather than with the King and his ministers. Pedro de Mesa, however, tells us that the señores were inclined to "give Franco his life" but could not resist the crowds around the prison, who called for Franco's death. Finally, they ordered his execution, says de Mesa, "more under compulsion than for any other reasons."[166]

Under the impact of Franco's execution, the remaining converso notables in Toledo joined in an appeal to some leaders of the city (caballeros, *regidores* and *jurados*) that they move the council to allow all conversos who wished to leave Toledo to depart from it armed, together with their families and possessions, in peace, while those who wished to stay in the city be permitted to open their shops and offices.[167] The first request was fully accepted and, as a result, "many conversos," mostly members of the elite, left the city with their movable possessions.[168] As for the rest, the answer was given in a harsh and detailed order, forbidding all conversos of the Jewish race to assume any office or benefice. The regime of the *Sentencia-Estatuto* was restored.[169]

To justify this order, Pedro de Mesa gives all the reasons offered by the Toledans in the *Sentencia-Estatuto* and the report of the *pesquisa* made in 1449. But he also finds it necessary to point to some "facts" that justified the execution of Fernando de la Torre, the conversos' leader and military captain. Among these facts he mentions the discovery in his house of "many Hebrew books of devotion," and "Hebrew bulls absolving their recipients [from their sins] for a certain contribution to what they call pious works."[170] There is no reason to deny this assertion, although one may question its implied indication that the converso leader was a Judaizer. No evidence was offered that Fernando de la Torre had ever shown any leaning toward Judaism, contributed to any Jewish charity, or made use of the books found in his house. These books may have belonged to an old member of his household or to his deceased father or mother; they may have been lying there for years in an attic, with Fernando taking no interest in them or being unaware of their existence.

Nor do we hear that the find brought to mind any negative information about the religious behavior of Fernando de la Torre or his brother Alvaro.

As public figures, their conduct had been watched; and yet they apparently never gave cause to suspect their Christian sincerity. Nor could that find indicate in any measure the religious position of the New Christians generally. Hundreds of converso houses were ransacked and their covert places thoroughly searched in the hope of discovering hidden treasure. We do not hear, however, that any Hebrew books were found in any of these buildings. Indeed, we can imagine what a fuss would have been made by men like Pedro de Mesa if such books had been found in more converso houses.

Following the stipulations of the new order, all conversos holding any public office were immediately dismissed from their positions. All converso *regidores, jurados, escribanos* and jurists were prohibited from fulfilling their functions. Rights and privileges were denied to all conversos who had at any time earned Church prebends, canonries and stipends in Toledo. All leading and lucrative positions in the city were taken over by Ayala's men. Nobles who were considered opponents of Ayala, partisans of Cifuentes or friends of the conversos were forthwith removed from their posts. As was usual in such cases, the victors divided the spoils among their own men. Accordingly, the *alcaldía mayor* of Alvar Gómez was given to Pedro de Treviño, the abovementioned nephew of Juan Pérez de Treviño, who was among the chief instigators of the war, while the command of the alcazar was given to Anton Sánchez, who distinguished himself in the battle.[171] Thus the wheel of fortune turned full circle once more against the conversos of Toledo.

V

On August 20, three days after Pedro de Mesa sent his report about the riots and their outcome, there took place the second battle of Olmedo, this time between the forces of King Enrique and those of the rebels' king, Alfonso. In this encounter Enrique's army brought the enemy to the brink of defeat, but since the battle remained undecided, the Alfonsine leaders tried to claim victory. Toledo, which received an account to this effect, hastened to send Alfonso a delegation, ostensibly to congratulate him on his "triumph," but actually to get his formal approval of their anti-Marrano actions. Accordingly, they asked him to confirm the new laws they had issued against the conversos, to grant them the possession of all the offices and properties they had transferred from converso ownership to themselves, and also to pardon them for all the offenses they had committed during the riots.[172]

It can hardly be doubted that the Toledans knew the truth about the outcome of the battle of Olmedo. They probably knew that the casualties of Alfonso's forces were far greater than those of Enrique's and that it was only due to Enrique's refusal to press the war to its bitter end that Alfonso's army was saved from destruction. In this situation, the Toledans thought, King

Alfonso needed their support more than ever, and consequently would not refuse their request. They were, however, rudely mistaken.

The King told their delegation that he would never consent to a claim such as theirs, which was so iniquitous. And turning to the head of that delegation, Judge Fernando Sánchez Calderón, he expressed his astonishment that a man of his integrity undertook such an "infamous mission."[173] Though the judge appeared to support the King's position, he nevertheless continued with his plea, which he now sought to bolster by a new argument. He wished the King to know that he accepted the assignment, which went morally against his grain, because the Toledans threatened to join Enrique if Don Alfonso declined their petition. To this the King answered: "Let them do what they want. It is enough that matters are in such bad shape that they can pass the evil acts under dissimulation, but it would be dishonorable and shameful for me to confirm abominable and abhorred deeds."[174]

Palencia, who reported this conversation, was at the time in the King's company and expressed his astonishment over the sound thinking and sense of righteousness manifested in the young prince's words.[175] But Alfonso was then only thirteen years old, and while the cited statements may have reflected his vigor of mind and maturity of judgment, it is not likely that he uttered them spontaneously, without having been prepared for the occasion. But by whom? Who supplied him with such striking answers to the expected requests of the Toledans? Who inspired him to adopt such a forthright attitude reflecting so strong a moral conviction? In our opinion, it was Luis Díaz de Toledo, Fernán Díaz' son, who then served King Alfonso in the capacity of Relator.[176] He was the second converso of high standing who joined Don Alfonso's camp.

Nevertheless, several days later, on August 31, we find Don Alfonso sending the Toledans a clearly apologetic message. In this message he explained to them that when their ambassadors came to him and presented their request concerning the conversos, he could not properly consider their petition because, of all the grandees of the Royal Council, there was with him then only the archbishop of Toledo, and that now he was awaiting the arrival of other grandees who were expected to join him soon. He promised that as soon as they arrived, he would consult them, go into the matter of the Toledans' petition, and give them an answer which would be "suitable to his service and the good of the city."[177]

It is not hard to see what brought on this change in such a short time. When Carrillo learned of the tenor of the answer Alfonso had given the Toledan delegation, he thought that a blunder had been committed which required immediate correction. Evidently, he regarded the King's remarks as impolitic and, in view of the rebels' recent military reverses, even likely to produce unfavorable repercussions. The King's letter of August 31 was intended to avoid such a development. Its purpose was to calm the spirits of the Toledans and thereby prevent them from making overtures to the party of Don Enrique.

But despite Alfonso's promise to send the Toledans a carefully considered response to their petition, no further communication followed, and the Toledans' request remained unratified. Obviously, when the grandees of Alfonso's Council met and discussed both the contents of the petition and the implications of its approval, some of them expressed strong opinions against granting the Toledans their wish. Yet they did not dare send them a negative reply either, and so the matter was left in abeyance. Before long other problems commanded their attention, and the Toledan case was removed from the agenda. But developments in Toledo did not remain frozen. Quite unaware of what was going on there, Alfonso's aides and counselors one day realized that the city had slipped out of their control.

VI

Although Alfonso's government attached great importance to Toledo's allegiance and support, it could not approve of the Toledans' petition for a number of compelling reasons. To begin with, it realized that to pardon the Toledans for the crimes they had committed against the conversos, legalize their holding of stolen goods and, on top of this, sanction the regime of the *Sentencia* would encourage the enemies of the Marranos across the country to repeat the Toledan performance. The nobles, who almost to a man disapproved of any kind of attack on the conversos, would certainly not countenance additional assaults of the kind that took place in Toledo, let alone such as were likely to embrace all the towns and cities of the kingdom. They could easily foresee that in the prevailing circumstances, a popular outbreak on such a scale would virtually paralyze the malfunctioning organs of the country's security system and dangerously undermine whatever authority the Alfonsine government still enjoyed.

But apart from these and other considerations related to foreseeable developments, there was a matter of great urgency and importance that prevented the government from identifying itself with the enemies of the conversos in Toledo. This was the plan to conquer Segovia, whose implementation depended on the cooperation of the converso Pedro Arias (Pedrarias) Dávila, King Enrique's *contador mayor* and chief personage in that city, who had recently joined the rebels' ranks.

Pacheco and Carrillo had long been looking for a way to attract Pedrarias to their side and, with his assistance to gain control of Segovia and its castle, which housed the King's treasure. A direct approach by Pacheco to Pedrarias was rebuffed as an affront to the latter's sense of honor: Pedrarias was incapable of showing such ingratitude to the King, who had done so much good to his family. Pacheco appeared to drop the attempt, but resumed it surreptitiously. He devised a scheme by means of which his agents succeeded in persuading Enrique that Pedrarias, one of the King's most faithful officials, had embezzled royal funds entrusted to his care. Pedrarias was imprisoned at the King's order; but many of his friends hastened to intervene and showed the King where his error lay. Enrique was glad to admit his blunder, ordered Pedrarias' immediate release, and restored him to his position as *contador mayor*. But the former intimacy between Pedrarias and the King was never to be restored. Pedrarias could not forget—or forgive—the humiliation he had suffered through his incarceration. He contemplated vengeance.

Unaware that Pacheco was the author of the intrigue that had temporarily set the King against him, Pedrarias now informed the Marquis of Villena that he was ready to join the Alfonsine party. He also assured Pacheco that he would do his utmost to wrest Segovia from Enrique's control and transfer it to that of Alfonso. Soon detailed plans were worked out by the conspirators for the capture of the city with the aid of rebel troops. Pedrarias prepared his own men and enlisted the support of his brother Juan Arias, the bishop of Segovia, Perucho de Monjarrez, the governor of the castle, and other leading citizens on whom he could rely.[178] Some of them were no doubt conversos.

Before he left for the battle of Olmedo, Enrique was informed that the brothers Arias were planning to deliver the city to his enemies. He refused to believe it. Nevertheless, he thought he should call them for a meeting and bind them to him by new commitments. In the talk he had with them, Enrique must have surveyed his long relations with their family, stressed his trust in them at that critical moment, and accepted their oaths of fidelity and promises to guard Segovia against the rebels. The oaths, however, were not made in good faith. Shortly after Enrique left Segovia, Pedrarias got in touch with Pacheco and fixed a date for the invasion of the city.[179] It must have been early in September.

The rebels mobilized a large army, which lay in wait near Segovia until the signal was given that their men had already entered the castle through a postern gate left open for the purpose. Shortly thereafter Don Manuel Ponce de León, constable of Paredes, entered the city with his Sevillian cavalry; and the main body of the army, some three thousand men, quickly followed in their wake. The citizens of Segovia, faithful to Don Enrique, realized that treachery was afoot and that their city was being invaded. They seized whatever arms they could lay their hands on and resisted the invaders as best they could. They threw at the soldiers a hailstorm of stones, darts and logs from the upper windows of their houses. It was only a matter of a few hours, however, before the invading forces, aided by Pedrarias, crushed the opposition in the city. The governor of the alcazar then surrendered the fortress, seemingly under duress.[180]

Judged by the harm it did the King's cause, Pedrarias' betrayal was almost on a par with the treachery of Alvar Gómez. It denied the King his secure seat of power and robbed him of the financial resources which enabled him to mobilize and maintain a large army. Pacheco and Carrillo now had reason to believe that Enrique was virtually doomed.

Thus it would seem that two conversos, the King's most trusted and most favored officials, his secretary and his treasurer, brought on him the most unbearable hardships and indeed the greatest calamities. To be sure, they did not act on their own—both fell into the net of the cunning Pacheco. But had they not been steeped in a political philosophy that made light of treasonable acts against Kings; had they not been influenced by the example of the rebel barons—and instead been faithful to the policy of their ancestors, for whom loyalty to Kings was the first rule of conduct—the thought of such betrayals would not have entered their minds, and the course of Enrique IV's reign might have taken a different turn.

VII

The capture of Segovia by Alfonso's forces by far outweighed the partial defeat they had recently suffered at the battle of Olmedo. Apart from obtaining a military position of inestimable strategic value, they were now in possession of Enrique's great treasure, enabling them to go on with the war almost indefinitely, while Enrique's prospects to mobilize new funds appeared extremely poor. His ability to launch a military campaign would from now on depend on the readiness of his allies to carry by themselves the burden of the war; and under the pressure of the growing expenditure, these could be expected, sooner or later, to relinquish Enrique's camp.

No one perceived more clearly than Enrique the grim realities with which he was faced following his loss of Segovia. He seized therefore the opportunity of talking to the rebels when informed that they would be willing to meet with him to consider termination of the hostilities. The terms the rebels proposed for the meeting offered no security to his person. But Enrique hastened to accept the rebels' offer without even consulting any of his friends. He dismissed his army and informed its leaders that he was going to negotiate peace with the rebels; and to calm their concerns over his safety, he merely said he was assured that matters were now moving toward a favorable conclusion.[181]

Actually, Enrique was not sure of this at all. He only knew that to save the situation he must try to retrieve his stolen treasure, and that to achieve this goal he was prepared to risk his life and put in the balance his personal influence. Thus, mustering all the courage he possessed, he went to Segovia on the rebels' terms: without any military force and accompanied by only five of his men.

He opened the discussion in grave and measured words, which moved the Constable Rodrigo Manrique to respond in a rather friendly manner.[182] The reaction of Manrique, who spoke for the rebels, signaled their preparedness to come to terms with the King. In fact, the negotiations were concluded with an agreement that apparently meant to satisfy both sides. It stipulated that the King would place the alcazar of Segovia in the control of Pacheco, now Master of Santiago; that the royal treasure would be transferred to the alcazar of Madrid, after stripping it of many precious jewels, which would be put in the custody of the Count of Plasencia and the Archbishop of Seville; that Perucho, commander of the alcazar at Segovia, would be appointed governor of Madrid and its alcazar, and as such responsible for the royal treasure; that the Queen would be turned over as hostage to Alonso de Fonseca, Archbishop of Seville, to guarantee that the king would abide by the agreement[183]; and finally, the rebels "promised and assured that within six months from the date of the agreement they would restore to the King his entire estate." This meant that the King would resume his authority over the territories held by the rebels.[184]

It is evident that certain terms of the agreement were not intended for public disclosure. If the rebels really meant what they had promised, they had a serious problem to resolve: how to combine their new intentions with the allegiance they swore to Don Alfonso. We do not know how they planned to settle this problem and whether all of them were of one mind. It is, however, not hard to discern Pacheco's immediate interests. He sought to legalize, through Enrique's consent, his control of Segovia and its alcazar, and he also planned to gain control of Madrid, together with the treasure in its alcazar, with the aid of his henchman, the treacherous Perucho. Enrique, who read Pacheco's mind, could not fail to see his designs.

Nevertheless, when he left Segovia, he was not without a sense of achievement: He had removed his treasure from Pacheco's hands and stimulated some of the rebellious nobles to return to his obedience. As he put no faith in Pacheco, their leader, he did not know what would come of the promises he had received. And yet he must have entertained some hope that the path to peace had at last been opened. He ordered his men to watch Perucho's moves, while impatiently awaiting some positive news. No such news came from the rebels' headquarters; but a sign of a breakthrough suddenly appeared in an area where Enrique expected it least. Fortune began to smile on him again.

VIII

The citizens of Toledo had been much perturbed by the continued refusal of the Alfonsine government to grant them their requests concerning the conversos. They recalled the cruel punishments inflicted by the King on the chiefs of the rebellion of 1449, and wondered what fate awaited them all once the civil war was over and King Alfonso became the sole ruler of the country. They recalled that the losses in life and property suffered by the conversos in the recent outbreaks were many times larger than those they had endured during Sarmiento's rebellion, and they wondered whether their king, Alfonso, who showed himself so critical of their deeds, would not make them pay heavily for what he considered unforgivable crimes.

This growing anxiety among the Toledans, who wanted to enjoy the fruits of their crimes (or, as they saw it, of the victory they had gained over their sworn enemies), was put to use by two members of the de Silva family—i.e., the family of the Count of Cifuentes. They were Don Pedro de Silva, bishop of Badajoz, and his sister María de Silva, wife of Pero López de Ayala.[185] Harping on the danger that a victory by Don Alfonso would pose to all Toledans, Doña María, a clever woman who was deeply involved in Toledan politics, managed to influence some of the nobles, who upheld the cause of Don Alfonso in the city, to go over to King Enrique's side. Above all, she convinced her husband of their need to abandon their allegiance to the child-king and take the opposite course—that of following King Enrique—which she considered vital to their interests. She also got in touch with Don Enrique and acquainted him with her efforts and achievements. Soon Ayala and the King entered secret negotiations, which rapidly ended in agreement.

Enrique knew what price he had to pay to restore Toledo to his obedience. Recalling his experiences of eighteen years before, he took the same route then followed by his father and Alvaro de Luna. Thus, on June 16, 1468, he issued a total pardon to all residents of Toledo for their involvement in the rebellion against him, and confirmed their possession of all the properties and offices they had taken from the conversos.[186] Following the pardon, Enrique came to Toledo at Ayala's invitation and was received at Ayala's house as the city's recognized lord.

He was probably discussing with Ayala matters that still had to be thrashed out when a crowd gathered before Ayala's mansion and loudly demanded direct talks with the King. They evidently did not have much faith in Ayala's "protection" of their interests. Enrique received a delegation of three and signed a paper which they had prepared. But the following day they came back, demanding additional assurances. This time Ayala took action. He called the marshal, Hernando de Rivadeneyra, and together with the governor and chief of police, followed by a body of armed men, galloped into the rioting crowd, arrested its leaders, flogging some men, cutting off the ears of others, and sending a few of the protesters to the gallows.[187] Thus, order was restored in Toledo in the traditional Ayala manner. But the demonstration probably helped Ayala to get from the King what he wanted. On July 3, Enrique issued a cedula, in which he forbade the conversos to hold any offices and positions of government in the city, and the following day, on July 4, he formally entrusted Pero López de Ayala with the guardianship and government of Toledo.[188]

This, however, was not the end of the story. One day after Enrique authorized Ayala's military control of Toledo, Don Alfonso died unexpectedly and the political situation in the kingdom changed drastically in Enrique's favor. For the next three years, the Castilian ship of state was still plowing through rough waters, but on June 10, 1471, Enrique found it possible to issue a new cedula for Toledo, in which he ordered the restitution of the conversos to the offices from which they had been removed.[189] We shall now touch briefly on the occurrences that led to this important development.

IX

The restoration of Toledo to King Enrique and the death of his half-brother Alfonso seemed to have dealt devastating blows to the Alfonsine party, and these were soon followed by additional setbacks that the rebels must have found extremely hard to take. Burgos declared its allegiance to the King, and the national Hermandad, always favorable to Enrique, now formally took the King's side. In addition, four leading members of the opposition, the Counts of Plasencia, Benavente and Miranda, along with the Archbishop of Seville, gave a new oath of fidelity to Enrique and recognized him as their only lord.

At the advice of the grandees who returned to his obedience, Enrique issued a call to the rebels to cease their intransigence and return to his service. Pacheco, who saw which way the wind was blowing, hastened to respond that they would act on the King's offer if a person of authority were appointed to talk with them, so that the negotiations could be speedily concluded in "peace and concord." The person they chose as the King's representative was the Archbishop of Seville, Alfonso de Fonseca, who had repeatedly manifested his double-dealing and unfaithfulness to Enrique. After talking to the rebels, Fonseca came back with their terms for peace, all of which centered on one condition: that the King declare his half-sister Isabella his sole legitimate heiress to the throne; then they would all come with her to the King to kiss his hands as their one and only lord.[190]

After further negotiations, the King accepted that condition. On September 19, 1468, he formally declared, in los Toros de Guisando, in the presence of many leading nobles and prelates, his half-sister Isabella as his sole heiress, and demanded of all the attending grandees, as well as of all other authorities in the kingdom, to recognize her as such and swear allegiance to her as their future queen after his death. As for Juana, she now hardly counted. In the agreement reached between the King and Isabella she was defined merely as the "Queen's daughter"; she was forbidden to leave the country, and her future fate was to be decided by the King, with the "accord and consent" of Isabella, Pacheco, the Archbishop of Seville and the Count of Plasencia.[191] The agreement restricted Isabella in one matter only: she had no right to marry anyone without the consent of the king and the abovementioned grandees, who in turn had no right to force on her any suitor as husband against her will.[192] Shortly thereafter Enrique appointed Pacheco, who had become, under Alfonso, Master of Santiago, to his former position as chief minister of the kingdom.

The civil war was over.

V. Anti-Marrano Fury Engulfs the South

I

What was it that moved King Enrique to sacrifice the rights of his daughter as heiress to the throne and again entrust his administration to the man who had tried so hard to destroy him? Judging by the preceding developments, one might assume that these moves did not stem from a pessimistic evaluation of his condition. With Toledo and Burgos at his obedience, with the national Hermandad standing at his service, and with the nobles leaning more to his side, he should, it would seem, have had little doubt that the strength of the opposition would gradually wane until it was reduced to insignificance. What caused then his "agreement" at los Toros de Guisando which amounted to a total surrender?

Castillo, his chronicler, tells us that Enrique was very much disturbed by the very idea of having Isabella sworn as his heiress, but explained the King's surrender in this matter by his inability to suffer further "anguish," apparently from the issue of the succession. And as for his admission of Pacheco to his service, Castillo related it to the King's need of "rest," or more plainly: to his exhaustion.[193] According to that chronicler, the King expected Pacheco to take off his hands many pressing duties and give him the relief which he badly needed. But could these have been the true reasons for Enrique's conduct?

It is hard to believe that Enrique assumed that his "anguish" would disappear or be diminished by making his half-sister Isabella his heiress, very much against his will and sense of justice, and by disposing of his daughter's rights as princess in a manner more drastic than he did before—that is, when he recognized Alfonso as his heir. Nor is it conceivable that Enrique, who could have had no illusions about Pacheco, failed to foresee what was evident to all—namely, that by reintroducing that intriguer to his service, he would have no rest, but further trouble. We must conclude, therefore, that when he signed the agreement at los Toros de Guisando, Enrique did not expect it to enhance his position. What then led him to sign it?

To answer this question we must take another look at Enrique's conception of his role as monarch and at the nature of his connections with Pacheco. We have pointed out his political philosophy, which deeply influenced his royal governance, made him disinclined to shed his subjects' blood even at the cost of much damage to his interests and, conversely, inclined him to forgive his enemies even at the risk of his peace and safety. We saw these tendencies determine his behavior in the early stages of the rebellion, and we see them again dominate his conduct in the last stages of the civil war. He left the battle of Olmedo unfinished when the chances of victory were all on his side, perhaps because he was loath to turn the war into a carnage. Likewise, he adhered to his policy of forgiveness as if experience had taught him nothing in this matter. When, toward the end of 1467, he visited Madrid and learned that Perucho, governor of the alcazar, intended to deliver the fortress to his enemies just as he had done before in Segovia, Enrique ordered his arrest. But when Perucho was seized and brought before him, Enrique, addressing his attendants, said:

> Greater was the wickedness of Judas who sold our Lord and Savior [and yet was not sentenced by Christ to death[194]]; and had [Judas] done what this man did, He would have [certainly] forgiven and pitied him. Hence it is proper for me to do the same; for it *is the duty of the King to follow in the footsteps of our Redeemer in whose name we rule on earth.* . . . [And then, turning to Perucho, he said:] I pardon you so that God may pardon my soul when my time comes to part with this life. Go in a good hour to your land, and if you lack the means to go there, I shall order to give you what you need.[195]

Such an approach to the problems of government and the issues of war and peace seems sufficient to explain King Enrique's failure to press his advantage against his enemies at the moment of his superiority; but it cannot explain his total surrender on the question of the succession which concerned him so deeply. The only thing that can explain it, in our opinion, is his basic change of attitude toward his daughter Juana—a change that was occasioned by the following development.

In accordance with the terms of the Segovia agreement of October 1467, Enrique sent his wife as hostage to Alahejos, the castle fortress of Fonseca, archbishop of Seville, who was to hold her under his surveillance. There she stayed for almost a year, long beyond the period that the parties to the agreement assigned for the attainment of a final accord. Perhaps Enrique, engrossed in many problems and forced to be constantly on the move, believed that she found peace and safety there, especially after Alonso de Fonseca had left Pacheco and went over to his side. But following the death of his half-brother Alfonso and the change it occasioned in the political situation, Enrique sent messengers to the Queen in Alahejos expressing his wish that she return to the Court. The Queen, however, evaded his request and instead fled to Buitrago, to the Mendozas. It turned out that she had had a love affair with Fonseca's nephew (and, some said, with Fonseca, too), and when the king's messengers came to fetch her, she was heavy with child.[196] The revelation must have so shocked Enrique as to put in question some cherished positions to which he had hitherto adhered.

As long as he had no clear evidence that the Queen had broken her marital vows, he had paid little heed to the recurring rumors about her illicit relations with Beltrán de la Cueva. He attributed these rumors to her frivolous but innocent flirting with men of whom she was especially fond and, above all, to the evil tongues of his enemies who were looking for excuses to destroy him. But now that he had definite proof of the Queen's promiscuity, he must have seen what he was told about her unfaithfulness in a different light. Now at last he seriously considered the possibility that Juana was another man's child, and soon the possibility turned in his mind into a probability, if not a certainty. He shuddered at the thought that he, Enrique, who regarded kingship as a sacred trust, would place on the throne of Castile a person who had no right to occupy it. No doubt he mused that Pacheco, the rascal, must have known the truth all the time, but revealed it only when he could use it as a weapon in his campaign against him. Just the same, it was Pacheco and his allies who stood for the right cause, while he, the King, was in the wrong.

He no doubt pondered the senselessness of the efforts he had made to secure Juana's future as queen and concluded that now he would not risk for this purpose the life of even one man. To be sure, the present war was forced upon him by his rejection of Pacheco and his reform program, and especially by the rebels' declared intention to depose him. And yet he knew that, while fighting this war, he had on his mind the fate of his daughter and the future of the dynasty. Now these considerations vanished. There remained only the issue of Pacheco and his desire to regain his position in the Court.

Enrique knew of course that Pacheco had not changed: he remained what he was—a traitor and a troublemaker—and his return to the Court would mark, he was sure, the beginning of a new chain of intrigues and crises. It would be a boon for the country if he were out of office and no longer interfered in the affairs of state. But to achieve this aim, Enrique knew, would require a long, drawn-out war, and he questioned the justification of its cost in blood, especially since Pacheco had dropped his repellent Reform Program. As for his demand concerning the succession, Enrique could now find no fault in it; nor could he foresee any other solution. Lacking all motivation for battle, he must have felt weary and drained of energy; and reluctant as he was to attend to his duties, he allowed himself to sink into a deep depression formerly unobserved by his attendants. Thus, his "capitulation" at los Toros de Guisando appeared to Castillo a result of "fatigue," which was in a sense a correct observation. But it was fatigue caused largely by disappointment with himself, by a sorrowful recognition of his mistakes and failures, and, above all, by his assessment of the situation as he saw it—an assessment that virtually left him no choice but to accept the rebels' terms.

II

Back in his old seat of power, Pacheco started weaving a new web of intrigue with the aim of increasing his control. He saw to it that his friends were rewarded by the King, while the King's faithful servants remained disappointed. On one thing, however, he and the King agreed: that Isabella should not marry Ferdinand, the son of Juan II of Aragon. That is where Pacheco parted with Carrillo, the archbishop of Toledo, who continued as agent of Juan II of Aragon and concurred in this matter with the Princess' wishes. Isabella's evident defiance of Pacheco strengthened the latter in his determination never to allow her to become the mistress of Castile.

Isabella made his task easier. She decided to marry Ferdinand secretly, without the King's and Pacheco's consent, which she knew she would never obtain. Hillgarth may be right in assuming that Pacheco must have known for some time of her plan, but permitted her to carry it out in order to have a case against her.[197] In May 1469, when the King and Pacheco left for Andalusia, Isabella and Ferdinand were married in Valladolid. When the King returned and heard of her marriage, he saw himself free of the commitment he had made at los Toros de Guisando, since Isabella had violated the agreement. To his surprise, Pacheco now urged him not only to remove Isabella from the succession, but also to declare his daughter Juana as sole heiress to the throne. A question must have flashed through Enrique's mind: Was it possible that Pacheco was ready to put the daughter of an adulteress on the throne of Castile? However, if Pacheco was prepared to do *that*, he was certainly capable of libeling Juana as illegitimate; and thus the whole story of her being Beltrán's child was nothing but Pacheco's invention. If such thoughts, as we believe, then stirred Enrique, his belief that Juana was his own daughter must have been revived before long. Undoubtedly, he felt that he had done her a grave wrong and was anxious to rectify it in any way he could.

Both he and Pacheco were now engaged in finding the right suitor for Juana in order to secure that the succession would not fall into the hands of Isabella. And to protect himself further against such an eventuality, Pacheco took additional measures. He decided to get hold of all key cities in Castile so that he would actually control the kingdom. His first major targets were Cordova and Seville, and it was here that he again came face to face with the converso problem.

III

On the anti-converso riots in Cordova, which erupted in the spring of 1473, we have the detailed account of Palencia in his *Décadas,* which supplies vital information but is also questionable on more than one point.[198] His description of the riots in Toledo in 1467 was affected, as we have seen, by a shortage of data, misstatement of facts and tendentious views on the Toledan Marranos and the part they played in the disturbances. The veracity of that account, however, could be checked by comparing it with two other accounts, which in certain points complemented, and in others contradicted, some of Palencia's assertions. We do not have this advantage when we deal with his description of the course of the riots in Cordova; the auxiliary sources available in this case are extremely curt and deficient. Essentially, we remain here face to face with Palencia, and therefore we shall have to move most cautiously in our attempt to extract the truth from what he tells us.

The major cause of the riots in Cordova was, Palencia tells us, the violent hatred that many Old Christians felt for the conversos; and as a historian, he saw himself obliged to indicate the reasons for that hatred. These reasons, according to Palencia, were economic, social, political and religious (to list them in the order they are presented by Palencia), and all of them were products of the Marranos' moral flaws.[199] Later on we shall touch on Palencia's attitude toward the Marranos as displayed in his description of the Cordovan riots and the subsequent discussions of the Marranos in his work. It is a dual attitude, indefinite and contradictory, and markedly different from the one manifested in his earlier remarks on the Marrano question. We shall now refrain from touching on these differences insofar as they relate to the Cordovan conversos and proceed to other parts of his account, which describe the outbreak of the riots in that city. Here we stand on more solid ground.

The agency that was primarily responsible for kindling the fires against the Marranos in Cordova was, according to Palencia, Pedro de Córdoba y Solier, Bishop of Cordova and Cardinal of St. Angelus. "Trying to put an end to the scandals of the New Christians [allegedly arising from their religious behavior], he was accused by the conversos of being partisan and malevolent"—namely, that he took the side of the Old Christians and was not objective in his judgments, and furthermore that he harbored ill will toward the conversos, like the rest of their enemies. He was also accused of "being more inclined toward avarice than toward religion, and it was said that, forgetting his own lewdness and infamous corruption, he devoted himself to engineer harmful enmities." The Marranos, then, claimed that the bishop was leveling at them the same charges hurled at them by the opposing party, which were produced "not by evidence, but by ill will."[200] It is difficult to guess what else is hidden behind these cryptic words of the historian. Palencia evidently chose to present the Marranos' counter-accusations tersely; yet even from what he says it is clear that the conversos vehemently denied the bishop's charges and that there was more to these denials than meets the eye. Was the bishop censuring the Marranos in the hope of frightening them into buying his support as they had done with Alonso de Aguilar, Cordova's leading nobleman? Was this what the conversos referred to when they spoke of his "avarice"? "The bishop," says Palencia, "supplied sufficient grounds for the Marranos' accusations. For although he enjoyed fame and a better reputation before he had attained the dignity of Bishop, the increase of his honors caused his life and manners to begin to degenerate in his old age. His vanity was notorious, and frequently he acted without judgment. Thus he lost the respect of the nobles when he gained favor with the Old Christians."[201]

The bishop of course knew that his standing with the nobility had sharply deteriorated, and being ambitious and morally unscrupulous, he looked for followers among the plebeians. He decided to use the boiling hostility of the Old Christians for the New and fan the religious zeal of his flock by accusing the Marranos of religious crimes. He hoped that the people would respond to his incitement, and then the conversos, pressed to the wall, would turn to him for help with offers of payment. The first part of his plan seemed workable. The populace, influenced by his agitation, launched several attacks on the conversos, but apparently with little success. One of the attacks, it seems, was beaten off with considerable losses to the attackers. The enthusiasm of the warmongers cooled as a result, while the bishop himself was so abandoned by his partisans, and so harassed by his opponents, that Alonso de Aguilar declared him to be "worthy of being indignantly ousted from the city."[202]

The source that fed the animosity for the conversos was, then, according to Palencia, an impure, polluted source: a corrupt, greedy and frustrated clergyman, whose peers had lost all respect for him, and who sought to rebuild himself, politically and financially, at the expense of the hated conversos. Yet although he was unsuccessful in the beginning, the fires he fanned continued to burn. Palencia, faithful to his new approach, and trying to find fault with both sides, again blames the conversos for what happened. Their initial success in their encounters with their foes increased their "licentiousness," and this in turn "increased the jealousy of their opponents and encouraged their hopes for vengeance."[203]

But Palencia has something else to say about the development of the Cordovan conflict, and he ties this additional information to the conversos' religious behavior. The Cordovan Marranos, he tells us, struck a deal with Alonso de Aguilar; they supplied him with funds to meet the expenses of his household and the large salaries of his troops, including a cavalry of three hundred horse, which they themselves had recruited for him.[204] Then, emboldened by this arrangement, they no longer thought it necessary to perform their Jewish rites in a clandestine manner. "They were now boasting of public profanations of things that many of them had prior to that tried hard to execute secretly."[205]

The "public profanations" Palencia referred to were evidently the Marranos' alleged displays of disrespect for and disparagement of the Catholic faith by the open performance of Judaic ceremonies; and all this because they had the support of Alonso de Aguilar and his promise to protect them. Could this be true? At a time when the agitation against them reached new heights, and their security became so precarious that they had to spend huge sums of money for protection, would they dare to behave in so provocative a manner as to arouse greater hostility toward themselves and thereby increase the danger that threatened them? And all this after what had happened in Toledo only six years before, and after what had occurred in Carmona five years before that? Such assumptions make no sense. It is more plausible that here again we hear charges raised by the anti-Marrano faction to justify the bloodbath it was carefully preparing for the conversos in the city.

The terrible attack on the Marranos in Cordova took place on March 16, 1473.[206] It was stimulated, according to Palencia, by Pacheco, who "astutely used some Cordovese *caballeros* to throw dry wood into the fire" of discord. Pacheco's supporters, he tells us, contrived a plan by which to draw the majority of the Old Christians to the anti-Marrano side. They formed a nonpartisan charitable organization which included, nevertheless, the very partisan provision that no New Christian be accepted to its ranks. The provision, it seems, did not constitute an obstacle for many Old Christians to join the organization, while for others it clearly served as an inducement. "In a few days," Palencia tells us, "the organization gained a large membership," and he also relates that a certain blacksmith gained "singular authority among his fellow members by his reckless vehemence against the conversos," so much so that "what he praised was considered most worthy of praise; and what he censured was most vituperable."[207]

This, then, was an anti-converso organization—run by implacable foes of the Marranos, and undoubtedly motivated by a common desire to hurt the New Christians as painfully as possible. It stands to reason that the man who became so influential in its ranks only thanks to his impetuous anti-converso agitation would seek ways and means to increase his standing by some spectacular anti-converso action. He obviously looked for an opportunity to massacre or otherwise destroy the conversos of Cordova, and tried to produce provocative situations that would force the Old Christians to attack the New. For this purpose, he and his henchmen, who led the organization, arranged for a weekly procession of its members, carrying the image of the

Holy Virgin through several streets settled by conversos. The choice of the route may well have been made with a sinister design in mind. In any case, it proved helpful to the blacksmith and his friends.

One day, on the sixteenth of March 1473, when the procession was passing through the converso neighborhood, a dirty liquid was reportedly poured upon the statue of the Virgin from one of the houses. It was further reported that the liquid was urine and that it was poured by a converso girl eight to ten years old. None of these details can be taken as factual, since nobody could determine, in the commotion that ensued, what actually had occurred. Rumor fed by wild imagination was surely one of the chief sources of the accounts we possess of that incident. What we know for certain is that the blacksmith, without trying to make any investigation, declared the conversos to be responsible for the crime and urged the populace to avenge the Virgin's honor. The furious attack which immediately followed gives every indication of having been planned, and perhaps so was the incident that supposedly caused it.

Palencia, however, believed that what happened in Cordova that day was an unfortunate occurrence which the leaders of the procession made use of for their purpose. It was the blacksmith, he said, who declared that the liquid spilled on the Virgin was urine and that the "conversos" were responsible for the act.[208] Palencia, who chose his words carefully, wished to show how the mob, when led by plebeians, for whom he had almost limitless contempt, may be inflamed by false accusations to commit the most atrocious crimes. He wanted to show that for the blacksmith and his followers, there was no need to investigate what had happened—whether the liquid was urine or water or whether the incident was deliberate or accidental. They declared it to be what they wanted it to be: *a manifest contempt for the Holy religion* by the abhorred heretics. So an apparently innocent act was presented as a contemptible crime. If Palencia was right, this incident shows how also other acts, wrongly interpreted, seen through the eyes of suspicious men, were similarly interpreted as ugly crimes, so as to fit the image of the "abhorred heretics." But whatever the cause of the outbreak in Cordova, the voice of the blacksmith, Palencia tells us, was heard over the tumult: "Let us go and avenge the offense to the faith from these reprobate enemies of the faith and of charity!"[209]

Excited by their leader, the crowd surrounding him set fire to the converso houses when an unexpected disturbance occurred. A certain caballero by the name of Torreblanca, esteemed by both the Old and New Christians for "his humanity and purity of manners," tried to deter the crowd led by the blacksmith from carrying out their evil intent. He was immediately struck by the blacksmith or his followers and fell wounded to the ground; but many Old Christians came to his aid and opposed the blacksmith's partisans. What ensued, says Palencia, was "a fierce battle that soon extended through the whole city." In the end the blacksmith and his followers fled from the encounter and found refuge in the Church of San Francisco.[210]

What this encounter shows is that many Old Christians were not at all in favor of the aims of the "charity organization" that operated under the guise of "aid to the poor." What happened during the procession opened their eyes to its real goal, which was to provoke attacks on the conversos and use the membership of the organization for that purpose. That membership, which represented all classes and segments of the Old Christian population, would thus be misled into actions that were favored only by the extreme anti-Marranos and would appear to sanction their plans and misdeeds. All this was resented and opposed by the Old Christians who came to the aid of Torre-blanca and who undoubtedly belonged mostly to his social milieu (the lower nobility and upper middle class), and they gave an eloquent demonstration of their own attitude. Surely, if they had considered the New Christians heretics, who impudently practiced their Judaic rites, they would not have defended them so valiantly and so long even if they believed that the blacksmith invented the story about the urine poured over the Virgin's statue. We have noticed the same phenomenon in Toledo, where during Pero Sarmiento's rule a number of Old Christians tried to offer assistance to the harassed conversos, and again in 1467, when many of them came to the New Christians' aid and sheltered them during the riots. But as in Toledo, so now in Cordova, their resistance to the hatemongers was not massive or strong or determined enough to withstand the latter's relentless pressure. This explains what happened in the second stage of the Cordovan riots.

Accompanied by some horsemen, Alonso de Aguilar hastened to the Church of San Francisco. He knew that the core of the troublemakers was there and he wanted to speak to their leader, the blacksmith. The entrances to the church, however, were heavily guarded, and it was necessary for Don Alonso to lure the blacksmith out, so as to be able to rebuke him. When Don Alonso ordered him to disperse the people, the blacksmith gave him a rude answer. Offended, Aguilar struck him with his lance, and the blacksmith was carried, near death, to his home. The large crowd assembled there was given to understand that the blacksmith had died, but came back to life briefly, exhorting his followers to avenge his death. Infuriated by this tale, which spread across the city, Old Christian plebeians launched attacks on the conversos and sacked many of their houses. Don Alonso again rushed to their rescue at the head of a cavalry squadron; but when he came to the house of the dead blacksmith, he found that his authority counted for little. The crowd, undeterred, clashed with his horsemen. A shower of stones, lances and darts, which fell upon Don Alonso's soldiers, put their lives in danger and forced them to retreat.[211]

The way was now open for a general assault upon the Cordovan conversos who, expecting the worst, had armed themselves and fortified their most populous boroughs. The band of the original attackers was now joined by the "rural workers," who had come to Cordova to collect their wages, as well as by peasants from the neighboring villages, who were attracted by the expected sack. The Cordovan conversos, having to defend themselves not only against their enemies in the city but also in the countryside, must have fought well, perhaps even heroically, for the battle raged for two days. On the third day, however, most of the converso defenses collapsed, and wherever this occurred there commenced a massacre of the helpless survivors. "There was not a cruelty in the world," says Palencia, "that was not exhibited on those occasions. Maidens and matrons were not only violated," but "made to suffer a horrible death." Many old men were likewise slaughtered, thus increasing the toll of the carnage. This was soon followed by a general sack in which many houses were put to the torch.[212]

There is no record of the number of casualties among either the Old or the New Christians, but it must have been far greater than in the Toledan outbreaks, especially among the conversos. Nevertheless, the converso community of Cordova was not destroyed, although it was decimated by the battle, the massacre, and the ensuing flight. What saved it from total destruction was obviously the efficiency of its own defense. Palencia was merely echoing anti-Marrano sentiments when he described the Cordovan conversos as "timid by nature and by the consciousness of their evil deeds."[213] From what he himself tells us, it is apparent that they displayed great bravery in the fighting. They evidently received no support from Aguilar during the crucial attack upon their neighborhoods. Aguilar's troops fled to their fortress, and the whole burden of defense fell on the conversos. To be sure, some conversos escaped from the battle scene by following Aguilar or by fleeing from the city, but the "remaining multitude," as Palencia tells us, "attacked by the furious plebeians in their better-protected boroughs, could resist them only with great difficulty in the crossroads of the streets defended by old walls."[214] It is obvious that many places were not captured, that most of the houses were not burned, and that a large number of conversos remained in the city also after the riots. It is due to this fact that the city council found it necessary to issue a declaration to the effect that no New Christian was qualified to hold, from then on, any public office in Cordova.[215]

IV

The results of the attack on Cordova's New Christians boosted the desire of all anti-Marranos to follow the Cordovan example. The repercussions of that attack were felt throughout Spain, but especially across the length and breadth of Andalusia. Similar atrocities were soon committed in the small towns and villages neighboring Cordova—such as Montoro, Adamuz, Buja-lance, La Rambla and Santaella.[216] In Almodóvar, chief town of the Order of Calatrava, several conversos were killed by the peasants, but the Master of Calatrava, Don Rodrigo Girón, "made them pay on the gallows for their crime."[217] "Jerez and Écija freed themselves from disaster," says Palencia, "by the intervention of the Marquis of Cádiz and Don Fadrique Manrique."[218] Similarly, Baeza would have become a scene of riots had not the Count of Cabra protected the conversos by punishing the troublemakers.[219] In brief, it was only through the strong hand of the nobility, wherever it was shown, that the disturbances were halted.

That this was the case was also demonstrated in Jaén, where anti-converso feelings had run high for years and sought expression in violence. It was only the fear of Don Miguel Lucas de Iranzo, constable of Castile, who governed the town, that these desires were suppressed. He held constantly about him a thousand armed men ready to defend him and enforce his will, and he did not hesitate to impose harsh punishments on the violators of law and order. This of course made him all the more hated by the conversos' enemies, who missed no opportunity to undermine his authority and, if possible, destroy it. Such an opportunity seemed available to them after Lucas' retreat from his encounter with the Moors, who had raided the countryside of Ubeda and Baeza.[220]

Under the impact of these occurrences, Don Miguel lost some of his grip on the town, and the anti-Marranos soon gathered courage to plan his assassination. The assassins were "laborers," Pulgar tells us[221]; and having chosen to attack the Constable in the church, one of them struck him with an iron crossbow when Don Miguel was kneeling in prayer, and then his companions hastened to dispatch him with their swords and lances. Don Miguel's body was so riddled with wounds that it hardly resembled a human figure,[222] a reminder of the way the converso leaders of Toledo, the brothers de la Torre, were treated in 1467. In Jaén, as in Toledo, the treatment of the corpse reflected the immense hatred then felt for the conversos, as well as for their friends among the Old Christians who, no less than the conversos themselves, were viewed as enemies of the people. Don Miguel's death cleared the way for the long-desired assault on the Marranos and was immediately followed by a massacre and pillage of Jaén's New Christians.[223] We have no detailed account of what occurred there; but it is certain that, with no outside force to assist them, the conversos of Jaén could not fare any better than their brethren in Cordova.[224]

The wave of ferocious attacks on the conversos that engulfed large parts of Andalusia—and, above all, the events in Cordova and Jaén—did not pass without arousing the gravest concerns among all the conversos of Castile.

Especially concerned, according to Palencia, were the conversos of Seville, and apparently not without good reason. Seville lay at the heart of the area where the storm against the Marranos was raging, and its converso community was the largest and richest of all New Christian communities in Spain. As such it constituted the most coveted prize of the anti-Marrano faction. A violent strike against the Marranos in Seville, many of their foes no doubt thought at the time, could shatter the position of the conversos everywhere and precipitate the destruction of their national influence. The anti-conversos in Seville, therefore, were in no way inclined to miss the opportunity, and "many of them," as Palencia tells us, "began to plot, in the name of religion, something similar to the crimes committed in Cordova."[225]

The arrival in the city of Cordovan refugees, who first fled to Palma and then moved to Seville, believing that the metropolis could offer them more safety, gave the anti-Marranos in the city a new excuse for agitation. Seville was then hit by one of those "hungers" that visited Andalusia not infrequently, and they incited the people of Seville to protest the hospitality granted the "heretics" at a time of "such sterility and such scarcity of bread." These complaints, and fear of new outbreaks, induced the Duke of Medina Sidonia, who was then virtual master of Seville, to urge the conversos who came from Palma to return to that place. In compliance with his wishes, they departed from the city, but on their return to Palma, not far from Seville, they were attacked by country people, who butchered sixty of their men after having stripped and flogged them.[226] There can be little doubt that the attack was premeditated. As the preparations for the exodus were no secret, the villagers must have been fully informed of the refugees' planned moves. In any case, the Sevillian conversos had no doubts about the complicity of their own anti-Marranos in the crime, and the brutal murder of sixty conversos without the slightest provocation was to them a danger signal that could not be ignored. For nothing could demonstrate more clearly and effectively the fate their hostile neighbors had in store for them all.

No wonder that in this stormy social atmosphere a considerable number of Sevillian conversos were attracted to the plan of converso settlement in Gibraltar that some Cordovan conversos were promoting at the time. Wrested from the Moors in 1462, Gibraltar was then a small fortress town, inhabited by very few Christians, who held the place for its lord and owner, the Duke of Medina Sidonia. The Cordovan New Christians negotiated with the Duke the terms of converso settlement in Gibraltar, and after having concluded a satisfactory agreement, some two thousand Cordovan conversos, joined by several hundred from Seville, moved to Gibraltar with the aim of establishing a predominantly Marrano colony there. Elsewhere we shall deal in more detail with this venture which, as we shall see, ended in failure. Here it is necessary merely to add that the Sevillian conversos soon abandoned the project, apparently because of their objections to some rules laid down by the Cordovan majority. They returned to Seville, although they well realized that their hometown could no longer answer their need for security and orderly life.[227]

Palencia, however, tells us that while most of Seville's conversos were then thinking of migration, and many moved to other places and countries, "another large number remained quietly in their homes, *without fear of robbery or death*," even though they had reason to believe that an attack upon them was being planned, and possibly was imminent. In preparation for the onslaught, they "placed their valuables in cellars, arranged for safe refuge in case of sudden outbreaks, established guards and vigils, and shielded themselves within the walled zone of the old quarter which was built originally for the frightened Jews prior to their great disaster."[228]

So the specter of the calamity that befell their ancestors in Seville some eighty years before was now haunting the conversos, their descendants. They sought protection behind the same walls that had failed to shield their forebears in their day of trial. And yet they remained in their homes "without fear of robbery or death." Does not this deny Palencia's assertions concerning the "cowardice" of the conversos, in which he no doubt echoed the abuses of the anti-Marrano antisemites? It seems that he could not suppress his admiration for the courage of these Sevillian New Christians, their self-control in the face of danger, and their quiet preparations for self-defense in the stormy atmosphere in which they found themselves. "Those who wished to live with greater caution and security, divided among themselves the different tasks which the achievement of such aims required. Great care was taken to stifle every argument, the scuffles of the children, the quarrels of the older people, and all sorts of provocation. And in case all these precautions would not prove sufficient to curb the fierce hatreds of their enemies, the Sevillian conversos secretly mobilized among themselves a militia of three hundred horsemen and five thousand footmen, of them three thousand shieldbearers and the rest crossbowmen or users of shotguns, prepared to resist any attack."[229]

This shows that many of Seville's Marranos had received military training; and this explains in part why the Sevillian Marranos, despite the gravity of the danger that confronted them, were not fearful of an encounter with their foes. The events that were soon to take place in Seville fitted this conclusion.

"All the Sevillian conversos were manifestly inclined to suppress rather than provoke riots," says Palencia.[230] But the anti-converso elements in the city kept up their agitation against the conversos and sought opportunities to foment disorder. The example of Cordova raised in their hearts the inviting prospect of sack and loot. This is what Pacheco had originally counted on, and this is what actually happened. Accordingly, "some wicked people, always disposed to crime, began to feign a new religious fervor and accuse *all* the conversos of the city that they did not consecrate Sunday, but Saturday; that they not only shunned dealings with the Old Christians, but showed themselves hostile to them; and that at night they attended the synagogues to chant their Jewish psalmodies, or at least to bring oil for the constant feeding of the lamps."[231] So Palencia clearly states that the real motive for the incitement was the desire to commit *robbery* and other crimes and that the "religious fervor" of the conversos' critics was "feigned"—a cover for their real intentions. He further finds it necessary to reject their charge that *all* the conversos of the city were Judaizers, practicing Jewish ritual and following Jewish custom. "Surely," says Palencia, "there were *some* conversos at the time who were attached to such superstitious practices; but the intention of the accusers was manifest; *they wanted the sack and the shedding of blood, following the example of what happened in Cordova.*"[232]

It is clear, then, that according to Palencia, not all of the Sevillian conversos were Judaizers; only *some (algunos)* of them were, and it is obvious that by "some" he meant a minority of small, though unspecified, proportions. For Palencia would not have hesitated to state that "many" or "most" of the Marranos were Judaizers if he had believed this to be the case. But as a resident of Seville, who knew the city from the inside, he could not make such an assertion, and his cautious estimate at this point may be contrasted with the extravagant charges made by the conversos' enemies. It would indeed seem that these people *wished* to define all Marranos as heretics, "so that they might have a good excuse to attack them."[233] For what moved them, Palencia kept stressing, was not religious fervor but a "desire for robbery and spilling of blood." Hence, as Palencia saw it, criminals were those who were plotting these massacres, criminals posing as zealous Christians and avengers of religious wrongs, and not truly devoted Christians fired by religious zeal. It follows that in this as in other respects, the anti-Marrano agitators in Seville were true followers of their predecessors in Toledo of 1449 and 1467.

But not all the Old Christians of Seville participated in that campaign for robbery and murder. On the contrary, says Palencia, many Old Christians, who "were not contaminated by such perverse hopes, went from house to house, endeavoring to curb the madness of those assassins *(sicarios)* who wished to get hold of the possessions of peaceful citizens."[234] This fact in itself shows that the city as a whole perceived the real motives of the agitators and did not believe that all conversos, or even their majority, were secret Jews. Had most of the conversos really been Judaizers, the position of the accusers would have been so strong that no counter-agitation could have foiled their plans. It was only because it was known that the agitators were lying, that their charges were exaggerated and irresponsible, that the other

Old Christians acted as they did. In fact, Palencia tells us, "no person of means doubted that *those thieves would declare heretics all those whom they considered opulent;* and thus all men of means who saw the perverse intention of the Master [of Santiago] and the hopes of the assassins to heap harm on the city, paid attention with equal care to the question of security proper and to the destruction of the evil-doing."[235]

Did the counter-campaign of Seville's "honorable men" succeed in quieting the anti-Marrano faction? Palencia offers a definite answer: "The strong thirst of pillaging the wealth of others that devoured these men, who were licentious and of low breed, stirred them to provoke quarrels with the conversos,"[236] even through the pretext provided by scuffles between Old and New Christian children. "It is useless," says Palencia, "to look for means of temperance where, because of the corruption of the authorities, who had granted the *youth of the artisans* unbridled license for crime, the common people stopped recognizing the force of the laws, so that it became impossible to suppress their excesses."[237] As in other places, here too Palencia lays the burden of responsibility for the attacks on the conversos upon the low classes, the common people, the plebs. And indeed, it was by members of that group that all the acts of aggression against the Marranos, all the robberies, burnings and killings, were committed. These were the attackers of the conversos in 1449; these were the men who bore the brunt of the struggle against the Marranos in Toledo in 1467 and the battles against them in Cordova in 1473; from their ranks came the assassins of Lucas de Iranzo, protector of the conversos in Jaén, and it was these men who were now inciting Seville to attack the conversos of the city. This was the same *populo menudo,* men of the *low classes,* who assailed the Jews in 1391. Now their sons and grandsons took up the same war against the Jews' descendants who had become Christians.

Palencia's patrician disdain for the masses colors all his writings. He despised people of low extraction, engaged in low professions. He bemoaned the fact that respect for law and order, and for duly instituted authority, had deteriorated in these classes because of the "corruption" of the rulers. In the outbursts against the conversos he saw an expression of the lawlessness sweeping the country, and he had nothing but scorn for anyone who wished to ascribe to the perpetrators of these crimes noble motives such as religious devotion. It was folly to assume that these "thieves" and "assassins" were moved by any measure of religious idealism.

This then was the social arena in Seville after the Cordovan riots. The hostile plebs were there, as everywhere, ready for attack; from their midst sprang the rabid agitation against the conversos' religious infidelity; Pacheco's agents were fomenting trouble, pouring oil on the burning fires, and at least part of the young nobility was siding with Pacheco and the lower classes. The social atmosphere became so charged that any spark could start an explosion, and it was inevitable that sparks should fly. "Out of a very insignificant cause finally came a sudden outbreak. A young converso gave a knife slash to an Old Christian. It was summertime and the hour of the siesta, when few people came out of their homes. Nevertheless, on the pretext of avenging the injury of their co-religionist, a large number of *sicarios* ran to the house of the converso [who wounded the Old Christian], committed a thousand excesses there, and ended by starting a general sack in the quarter of the drug sellers, where a large part of the citizens have stores of perfumes. Soon the news of the sudden sack spread to the other quarters of the city, and thus the conversos, who at the beginning were frightened, prepared for themselves places of defense, while some of the nobles and honorable men came forth immediately, repelled the crowds, overcame some of the ringleaders of the uprising and, in order to disillusion the others, sent two of them to the gallows."[238]

Thus in Seville, as earlier in Cordova, the rioters were opposed and held back by some of the nobles and the urban aristocracy; and the riots in Seville were quelled. Only one quarter of the city was affected. The Marranos took up their defensive positions. No further disturbance occurred, and no resumption of hostilities took place in Seville as it did in other places, most probably because the attackers realized that the combined force they faced there—that of the authorities, the nobles and the Marranos—was too strong for them to overcome.

V

According to Palencia, the riots in Andalusia were engineered by Pacheco to gain control of its cities.[239] Palencia, however, does not clearly explain how that control could be attained. He believed, it seems, that Pacheco's plan was to undermine the oligarchic administrations through the riots and then take over the cities in the course of the disturbances with the aid of his anti-Marrano allies. But Pacheco's plans for Andalusia were thwarted. In Cordova, after the massacre of the conversos, the oligarchic authorities hastened to accept the program of the anti-Marrano party, which thus had no need to turn to Pacheco; and in Seville the nobility and the urban aristocracy managed to overcome the rioting mobs before the city was destabilized. Pacheco, however, was not deterred by these failures. He decided to try the same method in the north. The major objective was now the fortress of Segovia, governed at the time by Andrés Cabrera.

Cabrera was one of Enrique's officials who had joined Pacheco when the kingdom was split. Judging by certain indications we possess, Cabrera was most probably a New Christian,[240] and if so he was the fourth converso official—and the fifth of the leading conversos in Castile (if we include the bishop of Segovia)—who left the King's camp for that of the rebels. He took part in the enthronement of Alfonso in Avila and kept faith with Pacheco in all the vicissitudes that followed. When Pacheco returned to Enrique's service, Andrés Cabrera returned to it with him, and, having made peace with the forgiving King, was entrusted, at Pacheco's recommendation, with the government of the castles of Madrid and Segovia. Soon, however, Pacheco came to feel that Cabrera was beginning to assert his independence. Keen-sighted as he was, he could not fail to notice the unfolding friendship between Cabrera (and his wife Bobadilla) and Princess Isabella, and he likewise observed a growing trust and empathy in the relations between the governor and the King. If, in the case of conflict, Cabrera were faced with a choice of loyalty between Pacheco and Enrique, the results of such a choice, Pacheco suspected, would not be in his favor. In short, Pacheco could no longer consider Cabrera one of "his men."

In these circumstances, he devised a scheme for having the fortresses of Madrid and Segovia pass into his own control. He first tried to get hold of the fortress of Madrid, which was the easier target, without giving anyone the slightest indication of his ultimate aim. To obtain Madrid, he had to persuade the King to order Cabrera to give up the fortress, and Pacheco knew what arguments might move Enrique to follow his advice. The King was then possessed with one desire: to marry his daughter to his cousin Enrique (son of his uncle on his mother's side), believing that the marriage would strengthen her chances of succeeding to the throne. He wanted Pacheco to assist him in this effort, and Pacheco, who had other plans for Juana, pretended to share the King's wish, hoping that by taking this position he could get the castles he wanted. He stressed the dangers that Juana faced in Escalona and, consequently, that to secure her succession she must be guarded in the fortress of Madrid, which was the "most suitable place for the purpose." Accordingly, Cabrera was instructed by the King to deliver the castle of Madrid to Pacheco—an instruction which greatly dismayed Cabrera and whose fulfillment he repeatedly put off.[241] When he ultimately handed over the fortress, Pacheco presented the King with his request that the Segovian castle, too, be transferred to his hands, this time justifying his request by the danger posed by the friendship between Cabrera and Isabella. The King could not deny the validity of the argument, but having seen through Pacheco's design, he was not at all sure that the castle of Segovia, which housed the royal treasure, was safer in the hands of the treacherous Pacheco than in those of Cabrera, Isabella's friend.[242] Aware of the King's vacillation in the matter and uncertain of his final decision, Cabrera committed himself, on June 15, to Isabella, assuring her of his firm support both in negotiations and in military confrontations. Among other things, he promised her that, in the event of war between herself and her adversaries, he would

Auto-da-fé, by Francisco de Goya.
Museo de Bellas Artes de San Fernando, Madrid.

Avila. The Walls and the Cathedral.

Juan II of Aragón, by Felipe Ariosto.
Museo Militar, Barcelona. Mas.

Juan Pacheco, from his Sepulcher.
Monastery of El Parral. Segovia. Mas.

Monastery of Guadalupe, Cáceres,
Extremadura.

Queen Isabella of Castile, by Juan de Flandes.
Real Academia de la Historia, Madrid. Mas.

Jews desecrating a Host.
Hermitage of San Bartolomé, Villahermosa, Castellón. Mas.

The Alcázar, Segovia.

Castle of Cazorla, Jaén.

Ferdinand the Catholic, from his Sepulcher in Capilla Real,
Granada, by Domenico Fancelli.
Mas.

First page of the Decree of the Expulsion of the Jews from Spain. National Archive of Simancas.
Archivo Iconográfico, Barcelona.

A page from the Catholic Kings' proclamation (Sept. 27, 1480) about the establishment of the Inquisition.
Archivo Histórico Nacional, Madrid.

place at her disposal the castle of Segovia, together with the treasure it contained.[243] Although Cabrera stipulated in his commitment that Isabella and Ferdinand must treat the king "with awe," the assurances he gave her actually amounted to an act of withdrawal from the King's allegiance, if not of outright betrayal.

Sensing the King's reluctance to fulfill Pacheco's wish, and emboldened by his pact with Isabella, Cabrera did not hide his resolve never to relinquish the castle. Pacheco now realized that he had but one way to implement his plan for Segovia: He had to capture the castle by force. And it was then that he decided to advance his project by using the hatred for the New Christians which, he believed, was smoldering in Segovia as in other cities of the kingdom.

The conspiracy he organized moved fast toward its goal, which was not only to seize the alcazar of Segovia, but also to capture Cabrera and the King. Once they were imprisoned, Pacheco believed, the King would give Cabrera the necessary order and the latter would have no choice but to heed it. Pacheco wanted his violent coup to be formally sanctioned by the King and the governor, and thus have the force of a legal act that would also secure his possession.[244]

He got in touch with a few Segovian nobles, headed by one Diego de Tapia, who years before had been Enrique's *Maestresala*[245] and whom Pacheco no doubt knew from that time. Pacheco must also have been aware of his, and his friends', political ambitions and frustrations and, in all probability, of their anti-Marranism and their opposition to Cabrera. To these men Pacheco revealed his aim and appealed for aid in achieving it, while undoubtedly promising them high rewards for their determined cooperation. Having fallen in with Pacheco's proposals, they soon worked out a plan of action. Their first task was to sow discord and dissension between the Old and New Christians of Segovia by charging the conversos with the same offenses they had been accused of in other places. They should provoke quarrels between the two groups, so as to create an atmosphere of confrontation, and while the tension and unrest were rising, they were secretly to organize a military force that could launch an attack on the converso boroughs. Then, when the city was in an uproar and the forces of the governor tried to check the riots, Tapia and his men would take over the alcazar. The day and hour for the assault were fixed, the preparations for the outbreak were under way, and the secret was kept remarkably well.

The papal legate, however, learned of the conspiracy, and he communicated the information to King Enrique. The latter hastened to divulge it to Cabrera, whom he also asked to warn the conversos, so that they might not be caught unprepared.[246] This, then, was the condition to which the kingdom of Castile had deteriorated. The King had to serve as a secret agent, passing information to the side he favored, without daring to confront the culprits directly or take open action against them. Everything now depended on how the opposed factions fared in the coming contest.

It was only three days before the scheduled execution of the plot that Cabrera learned about it from the King. But in this brief time he did what was necessary to ward off the expected onslaught, probably in cooperation with the conversos in the city. Although many Old Christians joined Cabrera and the conversos, the secrecy of their moves seemed to remain unbroken, so when the attack was launched, the prospective victims were ready to meet the assailants. Surprised at the strong resistance they encountered, the attackers were easily defeated and, after suffering a number of casualties, fled. Among those killed was Diego de Tapia.[247]

Segovia was one of the few Castilian towns in which the armed conflict between the Marranos and their foes ended in the Marranos' favor. In Segovia, as in other places, what caused this result was the rulers' determined opposition to the rioters and the friendly attitude of the Old Christian aristocracy toward the conversos. But the part played by the Marranos themselves should not be disregarded. Had their forces not been equal to the task, the conversos in Segovia might have suffered heavy losses, and no guess need be made as to their fate in the wake of such an outcome.

VI

If in Segovia we have seen King Enrique acting behind the scenes to frustrate Pacheco's plans, and also warning the conversos of the impending attack upon their community, we have no record of his interference, whether overt or covert, in the events that took place in Andalusia. It seems, however, that he could not remain indifferent to the disturbing news from the South or to the demands for urgent intervention that must have reached him from many quarters. What, then, was King Enrique's reaction to the occurrences in the Andalusian cities? And especially, what was his public reaction to the bloody outbreaks in Cordova and Jaén?

There seems to have been no royal reaction to any of these events. "Although they caused the King sorrow," says Castillo, "he imposed no penalties."[248] This brief sentence aptly summarizes both Enrique's attitude and his policy. Recalling the pardon he urged his father to give to all the perpetrators of crimes against the conversos in Toledo (in 1450), and bearing in mind the pardon he himself gave to similar wrong-doers in Carmona and Toledo (1462; 1468), one must conclude that Enrique did not believe that punishment of the offenders in the internecine war between the Old and New Christians would do any good. Perhaps he even thought it might do harm. What purpose would be gained, he must have reasoned, if he hanged a few activists of the anti-converso faction? All he could attain by this was to add ferocity to the blood feud between the two camps. Enrique no doubt saw the Old-New Christian quarrel as a form of civil war; and he treated its factions in the same manner he had applied to his opponents in the civil war. Let us recall his statement to Barrientos: This was not "one of those things that could be handled by force."

The problem needed a basic solution, which he was unable to provide. He listened with sympathy to the counsels of Oropesa concerning the establishment of an episcopal inquisition, but he must also have noted the opinions of the bishops who found Oropesa's proposals unworkable; and he was no doubt impressed by the arguments of the conversos, who denied the need for any kind of inquisition. But if force could not be used and an inquisition was superfluous, what method, the King wondered, should be employed? He counted on patience, and on the change of circumstances that would ultimately show the way out. In the meantime, he was waiting for an opportune moment to correct some of the evil done.

But that moment never came. On December 11, 1474, Enrique died unexpectedly, in circumstances that gave room for suspicions of foul play.[249] His death left everything in midair, with none of the pressing problems resolved. It may perhaps be assumed that had he lived longer, with the disturbance of Pacheco, who died a month before him,[250] no longer present to disrupt his moves, Enrique might gradually have improved his administration, restored respect for it, and revived the faith of his subjects in his person. But such an assumption would be far-fetched. As we see it, Enrique allowed matters to go too far in the wrong direction and thereby reach the point of no return. The people of Castile became too demoralized, too restless, and too inclined to anarchy and revolution. Only a strong ruler or a great prophet could have possibly impeded, or temporarily arrested, that dangerous inclination. But Enrique was neither a strong ruler nor a prophet. He was therefore powerless to repair the social structure, which he himself helped damage by his conduct. The question of the conversos, like that of the succession, and that of his ill-functioning government, had to be tackled by the new sovereigns who inherited Enrique's throne.

CHAPTER II

Later Old Christian Controversy

I. Alonso de Espina

I

Little is known of Espina's youth and nothing definite about his old age.[1] We possess, however, a considerable amount of data for the period of 1450–1465, in which he reached the height of his literary activity, as well as the peak of his public influence. Thus we know that by 1452 he was recognized as expert in Christian theology, at least by the superiors of his order, for in that year he was regent of the theological *studium* of the Franciscans at Salamanca.[2] In view of this fact, it seems reasonable to assume that he was by then at least thirty years old and, accordingly, was born in the early 1420s, as was Alonso de Palencia. The famous historian comes to mind at this point because he and Espina may have shared the same birthplace.[3] According to some, Espina was born in Palencia and there assumed the Franciscan habit[4]; there, too, he was buried in a chapel which he built for his sepulcher toward the end of his life.[5]

In 1453 Espina retired to the convent of Abrojo, near Valladolid, and it was from there that he came out, with a fellow friar, to meet the condemned Alvaro de Luna, then on his way to the gallows in Valladolid.[6] This encounter helped no little to spread Espina's fame. Espina offered Alvaro his services as confessor, and it was reported that the friar so calmed the constable's spirit that Alvaro could offer at his death an example of Christian fortitude and piety.[7]

Espina's meeting with Alvaro on that occasion may of course be attributed to Espina's religiosity and the proximity of the convent of Abrojo to the place of Alvaro's execution. But much more than this may have been involved. It stands to reason that by 1453 Espina had already been a fiery Jew-baiter, and it is possible that the solicitude he showed Alvaro de Luna was not unrelated to his strong anti-Jewishness, and especially his anti-Marranism. It might have then been rumored that the famous statesman was a victim of a converso plot. Espina may have wished to show the doomed man, a fellow fighter in a common cause, sympathy and affection in his extremity.

In the following year we see Espina occupy two important positions: He became confessor of King Enrique IV and head of the Franciscan Observants in Spain.[8] In the latter capacity he participated in the convention of the Spanish Franciscans in Segovia (Feb. 1455), where he quarreled with the Conventual Franciscans over the possession of the Franciscan monastery. Espina wanted the Conventuals to leave the city and the monastery to be taken over by the Observants. The demand appeared unreasonable, if not outrageous, and King Enrique IV, to whom both sides appealed, sided with the Conventuals. He promised, however, to build a new monastery for the Observants and also endowed them with many gifts.[9] Perhaps the grants which the Observants then received were largely due to Espina's persuasions. Even so, the King's decision indicates that Espina's influence on him was not overbearing. Enrique IV appears to have retained his independent judgment in the face of his confessor.

By that time, or shortly later, Espina had changed his headquarters. He moved to the Franciscan convent in Valladolid, where he prepared his sermons on the Name of Jesus.[10] Espina became famous as a "great preacher," and his sermons drew large crowds, perhaps because Espina knew how to combine his themes with attacks upon the Jews, their religion and their customs.[11] In 1457, while in Valladolid, he also began his book, *Fortalitium Fidei*,[12] in whose chapters about the Jews he doubtless incorporated much of what he said in his sermons.

In 1459 he moved to Medina del Campo, where he preached on the Excellence of the Christian Faith.[13] Here again the title is misleading. Actually, these sermons were violent assaults upon Christian heretics of all sorts, but especially upon those who, according to Espina, were found among the converts of Jewish origin. Portions of these sermons, too, were no doubt included in the *Fortalitium*—or rather in its second part, devoted to heresies.

In 1459 we find him in Madrid, still serving as Confessor to Enrique IV and trying to persuade the cautious king to establish an inquisition against heretics in Castile. But again he must have failed to move Enrique to accept his views and his counsel. Espina, however, would not give up. He organized a Franciscan delegation to the King to appeal for his consent to establish an inquisition,[14] and he also arranged for the Spanish Franciscans to request the Hieronymites to join them in that appeal.[15] But all these efforts got Espina nowhere. As we have seen, it was Alonso de Oropesa, the General of the Hieronymites, who became Enrique's chief counselor on the question of the Inquisition.[16]

There must have been something in Espina's approaches that made the King distrust his judgment, or consider his plans too extreme or dangerous for him to give them royal sanction. The fact is that when, shortly thereafter, Alonso de Oropesa presented to the King *his* views on the conversos and the founding of an inquisition, he earned the King's unreserved support. Espina's proposals for solving the converso question were far different from Oropesa's, and the two vied for the King's favor. Espina lost, but continued to try to draw the King to his side. In December 1463, he made his last attempt; it, too, ended in failure.[17]

From this date onward nothing definite can be said about Espina's career, except that he continued to write his *Fortalitium,* which he probably finished in 1464. In later sources Alonso de Espina appears as a member of the Synod of Alcalá, which condemned the errors of Pedro de Osma (1479), and also as the Inquisitor for Catalonia who was sent by Torquemada to Barcelona (1487). But in both cases, especially the second, the identity of this Espina with the author of the *Fortalitium* may be open to doubt. So, at least, thought Menéndez y Pelayo and evidently also Henry Charles Lea—neither of whom gave reasons for their view, though they were probably right.[18] There is evidence that the Alonso de Espina who became Inquisitor of Barcelona in 1487 was "prior de San Domingo de Huete,"[19] while Espina was a known Franciscan and could not be prior of a Dominican convent. Furthermore, in an anonymous letter to Pulgar, written probably c. 1482, Espina is referred to as one *que dios tiene* ("who is with God"—i.e., deceased),[20] and consequently, he may not have been the Espina who attended the Synod of Alcalá, and certainly not the one sent as Inquisitor to Barcelona.

Nor was he, in this case, the Alonso de Espina who was appointed bishop of Thermopylae in 1491,[21] and who in that year built an altar for his burial in the Franciscan convent of Palencia.[22] These data, however, were reported not only by Franciscan encyclopedists, but also by historians of the city of Palencia. They are hard to deny; and in the last analysis we may have to conclude that the words *que dios tiene* in the letter to Pulgar were added by a scribe. This would suggest that Espina had virtually withdrawn from public life for at least twenty-five years—and for a man of his temper and public spirit such a withdrawal is rather astonishing. As there is no further evidence on this period of his life, one can only suggest a hypothetical explanation. Perhaps when the struggle for the establishment of the Inquisition was taken over by other protagonists (first by the Hieronymites and then by the Dominicans), Espina lost both the lead in the campaign and a place of honor in its front line. Dejected or rejected, he may have been fated to seclusion and, in consequence, also to silence.

II

Even if some of the above data did not belong to Espina's biography, his public record was sufficiently impressive to save his name from oblivion. What kept his memory alive to our own time was, above all, his *Fortalitium Fidei,* a Latin work of massive proportions. The pretentious title was thought appropriate by many of his own and later generations who considered Espina's *Fortalitium* a true "fortress" of the Faith.

Less than six years after its completion, its *editio princeps* appeared in Strasbourg (c. 1470), and between that year and 1525 seven more editions were published, all printed outside Spain, mostly in German-speaking centers.[23] Nevertheless, its Spanish reading audience, even though quantitatively rather limited, was qualitatively significant.

The book tapped a popular vein. Besides a large introductory chapter, it consists of four parts, which deal respectively with Heretics, Jews, Saracens, and Demons. Most of it is a vitriolic tirade against Jews and converts from Judaism to Christianity, and this was no doubt what especially attracted readers in Spain, Germany and France. It appealed to the prejudices of the Christian populations and their traditional hatred of the Jews.

It is difficult to gauge the effect of the *Fortalitium* on the development of antisemitism in the West.[24] At any rate, for Christians in Espina's time, and also for generations to come, the book had a twofold value: it contained a large body of anti-Jewish arguments—in fact, the largest ever assembled— and a variety of horror stories about the Jews that exceeded anything known before. Priests and members of the monastic orders found the book useful for their sermons. But even serious theologians and men of learning turned to it regularly for instruction. In vain did the humanists denounce the *Fortalitium* as a *liber mendosus quem nemo allegat, nisi stultus et fatuus.*[25] Even men like Mariana and Johann Christoph Wolf praised Espina for his great erudition[26]; and as late as the end of the 17th century the *Fortalitium* still served many a scholar as a respectable source of information about the Jews.

Today Espina's work is of historical interest only—and from the standpoint of the present inquiry, this interest centers on Castile's society in the third quarter of the 15th century. More particularly, we are interested in Spain's social attitudes as they are reflected in Espina's book. For as the first Spanish work that proposed the establishment of an inquisition against the conversos in Castile, the *Fortalitium* represents the climate of opinion in which the idea of the Inquisition grew. Moreover, it contains a large number of statements about Jewish and converso views and customs, and as such it has been generally regarded as a valuable source of information on these subjects. In fact, to many that information seemed sufficient to explain the founding of the Spanish Inquisition.[27] Yet whether it should be so seen or gauged depends on our opinion of the author's reliability, and this in turn depends no little on the view we take of his origin.

For more than three centuries, almost all scholars believed that Espina was a converso of Jewish stock.[28] On the basis of this belief, many modern scholars gave special credence to Espina's statements on the Marranos, which in turn led them to far-reaching conclusions about the Marranos' Jewishness. Since Espina claimed that virtually all conversos were secret practitioners of Jewish rites, his presumed Jewish origin led many scholars to accept his statements at their face value.

The question why Espina, if he was a convert, expressed himself so harshly against his fellow converts posed no special difficulty. Many Christians believed that Espina happened to be an extremely truthful person who told the world the inside story of Judaism, although he was aware of the dire consequences that his revelations might have for the "members of his race." Espina followed this course, they believed, because as one who became a *true* Christian, he felt the moral urge and pressing duty to alert Christendom to the danger it faced—not only from *overt* Jews, but also from *covert* ones. Others thought, however, that, like other converts, he was filled with hatred for everything Jewish, and that this was the cause—or the primary cause—of his acrid denunciations.

The notion that Espina was a converso became so rooted in world scholarship that only isolated scholars questioned it—and this, too, after a very long time. With no one to challenge that notion, it spread rapidly in all the countries of the West until its diffusion was somewhat checked by the appearance, in 1715, of Johann Christoph Wolf's *Bibliotheca Hebraea*, in which the supposition of Espina's Jewishness was first examined and attacked.[29] Wolf pointed out that Espina's book contains no admission that he had been a Jew and that nowhere did he refer to any experience from his alleged Jewish past. Impressed by Wolf's arguments, a number of scholars stopped identifying Espina as a convert.[30] Nevertheless, when Rodríguez de Castro published his *Biblioteca Española* (1781), he reverted to the old pre-Wolfian view and reintroduced into Spanish literature the vogue of defining Espina as a converso.[31] Among the many Spanish scholars who adhered to this view were Fidel Fita,[32] Amador de los Ríos[33] and Menéndez y Pelayo[34] and, in more recent times, Modesto Lafuente,[35] Sánchez Albornoz[36] and Américo Castro.[37] Outside Spain, too, among Jews and Christians those who held this view outnumbered by far those who doubted or opposed it. Critical inquiry had little to do with this. It is one of those instances that illustrate all too clearly the extent to which the study of history is susceptible to tradition and public opinion.

Nevertheless, it is no less than amazing how quickly Rodríguez de Castro's view was accepted by Spain's scholars, with the exception of one—Nicolás Antonio, who evidently questioned it, since he failed to follow it.[38] We consider it amazing because Espina's whole conduct and much of his anti-Jewish argumentation so differ from the patterns of convert thinking and behavior that this alone should have raised doubts about his "Jewishness" and prompted a probe into the matter. Granted that many converts, before Espina, denounced Judaism and the Jewish people; but no convert denounced them so viciously as he did, and no convert attacked his fellow converts along with the Jews—and this, too, so fiercely and so collectively. It was an anomaly, to say the least. But other anomalies, too, could be noticed and duly pointed out.

Fray Vicente Manuel Castaño, who disagreed with Rodríguez de Castro, was perhaps the only dissenting voice among the Spanish scholars; but his views on the subject, expressed in 1791, in two letters to Don Miguel y Rodríguez, remained unpublished until 1926.[39] Fray Vicente takes issue with Rodríguez de Castro for having followed the "foreigners" who have "Judaized" Espina, and pointed out that no other Spanish scholar had ever claimed that Espina was a Jew. Furthermore, even among the foreigners, he added, there appeared some who doubted or challenged that opinion. Ascribing to Espina a Jewish origin, he argued, casts an aspersion on the friar's good name; he found no justification for such an assumption, and accused Castro of scholarly incompetence, shallowness and irresponsibility.[40]

Padre Atanasio López, who published Castaño's letters, picked up the thread where Castaño left it and added a few arguments of his own. "If Espina had been a converted Jew," he says, "he would not have failed to indicate this in his work. Other converts did not hide their origin and confessed it publicly to give thanks to God for having made them see their errors." Furthermore, "Espina is supposed to have revealed in his book many secrets of Judaism, but never does he say that he knew any of these because he had been a Jew."[41] Both arguments echo Wolf's claims; they are of course sound; but they only add to the "anomalies" we may observe in Espina if one classes him as convert. In other words, they may serve as supportive evidence to the view that Espina was no convert, but not as conclusive proof. Atanasio realized the precariousness of his position. He himself believed that Espina knew Hebrew,[42] and had to reckon with the fact that all the greatest scholars of Spain insisted on Espina's Jewishness. "So it is, in effect," he says, "but it is also certain that no one until now has examined the foundations of Espina's Jewishness."[43] And right he was!

Unaware of Atanasio's remarks, I followed the same path of thinking; and prompted solely by the needs of my inquiry into the movement that fathered the Spanish Inquisition, I decided to examine the foundations of the notion concerning Espina's Jewishness. I presented the results of my inquiry in a study to which I have already referred the reader.[44] My definite conclusions were that Espina had nothing of the convert within him and that he was "as pure-blooded a Christian as ever was in Spain."[45]

Without going into the details of my investigation, I shall here only mention its upshot. I could find no reason for the rise of the notion that he was a convert from Judaism except for the belief generated in Christendom that he was a great rabbinic scholar; I have further established that this belief was groundless because, as I have shown, Espina knew *no* Hebrew, and all the Hebrew sources he cited were taken, without exception, from Latin (or Spanish) translations.[46] I also pointed out that he designates conversos as members of a race other than his own, and that he considered the ancestors of that race to have been half beast (snakes and asses) and half demon, descriptions which no convert, however self-degrading, would apply to the ancestry of the Jewish people.[47]

III

Insofar as his attack upon the Jews is concerned, Espina's work represents a culmination of medieval polemics against Judaism and its bearers. It seeks to demonstrate the folly of Judaism, its immorality, and the evil of its followers by offering a compendium of proofs to this effect from Christian and conversionist literature. He adopts the line of Raymond Martini's anti-Jewish campaign in his *Pugio Fidei* (c. 1280) that the best way of hitting Judaism is to expose it, and he shares Martini's views on the foulness of the Jews and the bleakness of their future. But Espina removes from his discussion all camouflage, all double-talk and all ambiguity; he speaks in much clearer language than Martini, so that his thoughts appear in sharp focus and his main intentions are fully revealed.

To his attack upon the Jews and Judaism he devotes the third and largest part of the book. There, after making some preliminary remarks on the "blindness" of the Jews, their subhuman origin, and the incoherence of their doctrine, which is a medley of contradictions, he goes into a systematic refutation of the arguments presented by the Jews against Christianity. He divides these arguments into three categories, according to the sources on which they rely (namely, the Old Testament, the Gospels, and the Law of Nature), and presents counter-arguments which, he maintains, expose the folly of the Jewish notions. He assumed to have left no stone unturned in disclosing the faults and fallacies of Judaism and believed that this task, however complex and toilsome, was necessary and essential for the good of mankind.[48]

His massive work therefore could seem all-inclusive and, to many, the last word on the subject; yet in reality it was based on fragmentary knowledge, secondhand sources and, in many cases, unfounded arguments, which he often presents as his own. For Espina was not an original thinker, and his work is essentially a patchwork of passages borrowed from various polemical writers, full of hatred and scorn for Judaism and, of course, for the Jews, its followers. Yet if Espina lacked ideas of his own, he knew how to employ the ideas of others. He knew how to fit each of his quotations into what seemed to be the most suitable place, so that they appear to support his thesis in the best possible manner. It was his skill as organizer and his cleverness as editor that led even men like Juan de Mariana to praise Espina as scholar.[49]

IV

If in striking at Jewish theoretical positions Espina remained within the bounds of Christian doctrine, in portraying the Jewish attitude toward Christians he generally left doctrine behind and let himself float on the popular currents of medieval legend and superstition. To be sure, he follows the Old Christian theory that the Jews were punished for their killing of Christ with universal dispersion and subjugation to the Christians, whose "perpetual slaves" they became and must remain[50]; but soon he makes the sharp turn to the notion that, seeking to avenge their condition of enslavement, they pour their blind rage upon their Christian masters by perpetrating horrible crimes against them. Thus, in the seventh "consideration" of the third part, Espina presents seventeen cruelties which the Jews had committed against Christians, hastening to assure us that these "famous" cruelties by no means exhaust all their great crimes. "There are no doubt many others that are concealed from us,"[51] he says, and this stands to reason since, according to Espina, all the Jews' evil deeds are done in darkness, and even the seventeen cruelties mentioned, or most of them, were discovered by accident, or rather by the limitless grace of God.

The cruelties he ascribes to the Jews most avidly are those related to the notorious accusation known in Jewish history as the blood libel. By the time Espina wrote his *Fortalitium,* this libel was more than three centuries old. Two famous popes of the 13th century—Innocent IV and Gregory X—and two popes close to Espina's time—Martin V and Nicholas V—had denounced the accusation as false and groundless; and the latest of these denunciations, dated November 1447, was made in relation to a Spanish occurrence and in consequence of a complaint lodged by Jews of Spain.[52]

The proximity in time of this papal blast to the date of Espina's writing on the subject and the fact that the papal declaration relied on previous positions taken by the papacy make it most probable that Espina was aware of the attitude toward the libel on the part of the popes. But he preferred to ignore their pronouncements on the subject, just as other monks had done before him. Consequently, the libel continued to spread and claim its victims in many parts of Europe, including those where it was least expected. Spain as a whole was such a part, for it was generally free from the scourge. Only three incidents of the deadly libel are known throughout the period in the kingdom of Aragon, and Castile had not known even one. Espina, however, sensed the mood of his time. He believed that Castile was ready for the myth. And he did what he could to implant it.

He looked for authorities to substantiate his charges and found them in the works of two well-known monks of apparently unblemished reputation. One was the French Vincent of Beauvais, also known as Vincent the Great (Vincentius Magnus); the other was Thomas of Cantimpré (Thomas Cantipratanus), also known as the Patriarch of Bavaria. Vincent wrote a *Speculum historiale,* an encyclopedic summary of the history of the world, and Thomas wrote a hagiological opus *(Bonum universale de apibus),* portraying the lives of contemporary saints. Both included in their books tales of miracles that saved Christians from the Jews' lethal schemes. Three of Espina's seventeen cruelties were taken from these sources.

Vincent did not include in his book an actual tale of ritual murder, but offered confirmation of the general belief that each year, on the Day of the Last Supper (or on another day in Holy Week), Jews, because of their hatred for Christians, kill a Christian, as if it were a sacrifice, and "having persevered in this kind of crime they were caught many times and burnt at the stake."[53] Vincent presented these allegations on the authority of Philip Augustus, King of France, who in turn heard them in his youth from his companions— boys of his own age, whose judgment and assertions could of course be questioned. Vincent, however, as is evident from his discourse, did not question them at all. On the contrary, he gave credit to those horrid allegations, for he adds: "Also St. Richard, whose body rests in the Church of St. Innocent in Paris, *was so killed by the Jews,* and having been nailed to the Cross by his killers, he happily went over to God, where, through his intercessions, many miracles were performed by divine work."[54] This unqualified statement by Vincent was sufficient for Espina. He presents it as a general confirmation of the libel, and thus makes his reader attuned to the tales he is about to narrate.

Like Vincent, so Thomas of Cantimpré assured Espina of the truth of the blood libel, which in Thomas' description assumed a different character. According to Thomas, Jews habitually kill Christians not out of hatred for them or their religion, but out of a pressing, ever-present need to remove the blight of a terrible curse. The curse was brought upon the Jews by themselves when they shouted: "His blood be upon us and our children." The guilt of the Deicide was thus passed to their descendants, and as a result their blood became afflicted with disease. When it courses through their veins they suffer torment, unless they admit their share in killing Christ. Now one of the Jews, whom they held to be a prophet, told them that they could be cured of this agony only by the use of Christian blood; and thus they decided to kill at least one Christian annually, and they cast lots among themselves to determine which province should supply the victim.[55]

The story, which was credible for a man like Cantimpré in the middle of the 13th century, is still credible for Espina in the middle of the 15th. We touch here upon one of the main factors that aggravated the Jewish question in the Middle Ages—the belief in the supernatural character of the forces that determined Jewish fate and behavior. We also touch here on one of the points at which the legend of the Jews' killing Christians out of *hate* branched out into a myth of *religious* murder, even though the original legend too continued to flourish for a considerable time before it faded into the background.

To Espina all the varieties of the myth are related to Jewish hatred of Christians, and all of them indicate, in one form or another, the excessive cruelty of the Jews. Thus, following Cantimpré as an authority, he presents not only the latter's theory as to *why* Jews annually kill Christians (this in itself he takes as indisputable), but also his tale about how such a murder was committed in Germany in his own time.

The incident, according to Cantimpré, occurred in Pforzheim, Bavaria, in 1261. An evil Christian woman sold a Christian girl, seven years old, to the Jews of Pforzheim, who proceeded to inflict wounds upon her and collect her blood in a piece of linen. When she died, they attached stones to her corpse and threw it into the river. But a few days later, fishermen found the body when they noticed a hand protruding from the water and pointing to the sky. The people of the town immediately suspected that the crime was perpetrated by Jews; and that it was indeed a crime of a religious nature was indicated by the miracles that followed. When the prince of the place came to see the body, the corpse sat up straight and extended an arm as if it begged vengeance or sought compassion, and after sitting in this posture for almost half an hour, it stretched itself out face-up. The same performance, moreover, was repeated when the Jews were brought before the dead child, except that in addition to what it did before, her face flushed and her wounds began to bleed. Following this the Jews were put to torture, and after having finally confessed to the crime (except for two of them, who strangled each other), they were hanged together with the bad Christian woman.[56]

The story is marked by all the features common to medieval tales of the blood libel: the crime is revealed in some outlandish manner; an abundance of miracles points to the guilty; the Jews ultimately confess under torture; sentence is passed on the grounds of the evidence provided by both miracle and "confession." From the standpoint of sound judicial procedure, both kinds of evidence are utterly worthless. From the standpoint of the credulous Christian of the Middle Ages, no further proof was needed or called for.

This was certainly the view of Cantimpré. He heard of the case from two Dominican friars, who in turn heard it when they came to Pforzheim several days after the event. Could there be any doubt of its veracity? A story like this, produced by wild imagination and carried on wings of hearsay and rumor, raised no questions in Espina's mind, as it did not in that of Cantimpré.

The other tales of blood libel narrated by Espina were not drawn from books or written records. They stemmed from circumstances in which he was involved or which he supposedly knew about. Such was the case of the ritual murder which was first imputed to the Jews of Castile. It was in Valladolid in 1454, when he delivered his sermons on the Name of Jesus, that Espina was told of a Christian infant murdered by Jews in the province of Zamora.[57] Espina was informed of all the details of the crime, of which he gives us a vivid account. The Jews took the child out of town, killed it in some field, extracted its heart, and then buried the body. But in their haste to depart from the scene of the crime, they did not bury it deep enough, and this accounted for what happened later. Meanwhile, the murderers got together with some of their fellow Jews of that vicinity to accomplish the purpose of their hideous deed. They burned the heart until it turned to ashes, mixed the ashes with wine, and then drank from the concoction. The crime, however, was discovered. Dogs passing the place of the child's burial unearthed the little body and gnawed away at it. One of them, carrying an arm in its mouth, was caught by Christian shepherds, and the death of the child, who had been missing for some time, was thus revealed to the public. A local knight, Rodrigo Díaz de Mendoza, made a determined inquiry into the matter and succeeded in identifying the guilty Jews. One of them, a red-bearded man, confessed under torture, and stuck to his confession even when he learned that he was about to be put to death. The Jews, however, came to his rescue. They managed to obtain an order from the king granting a stay of execution; the case was transferred to the king's court in Valladolid, and so was the good knight of Zamora "prevented from seeing justice done."[58]

"Possessed with this certain knowledge," says Espina, "I preached my sermon in the Church of St. Nicholas, which is located near the Jewish quarter." "The whole town," he adds, "came in procession, including many Jews; and there I bore heavily upon this cruelty, which was related to me a short time before. It has been said that the Jews who attended that meeting were not a little displeased by my statement, and that so were also many *of their race* (i.e., Marranos) who are favorably inclined toward them." The latter especially had reason to be displeased, for Espina accused them, no less than the Jews, of evasion of justice. The Jews managed to have the case transferred thanks to the assistance of their converso friends, who wielded great influence in the royal chancellery, and nothing has thus far been done by the new Court, because two of the magistrates who were appointed to the case are members of "that race" *(de genere illo)*—i.e., conversos. These two dragged the affair on endlessly under a variety of pretexts.[59]

We can readily understand why the king's magistrates were not hasty in pronouncing their verdict. Since the whole case was based on sheer libel, the evidence must have been shot through with lies; while the confession under torture was not viewed by them as valid, let alone as proof. Conversos knew of course from Jewish tradition the groundlessness of ritual-murder accusations; how could they give backing to such travesties? On the other hand, they knew the sentiment of the populace; they knew they were being watched carefully by the Old Christians, and they did not wish to show themselves a priori as arbitrary defenders of the Jews. Perhaps they were looking for some further developments that might help to reveal the real murderers (which, as is known, happened time and again), or perhaps they sought to prove more convincingly the inadmissibility of the evidence obtained. Espina, in any case, was satisfied with the evidence. To him, who heard the story, as he said, only a short time before delivering his sermon, it was clear that the accused were guilty as charged and should have been executed without delay. And so, without waiting for the outcome of the trial, he issued his *own* unqualified sentence, denouncing the procedure as a farce and the judges as parties to the crime. The unfinished case of the murder in Valladolid served him as an occasion to promote the blood libel and as a heaven-sent opportunity to "expose" the Jews as killers of Christian children.

That the Jews had always denied the accusation vehemently and without the slightest reservation, and that all confessions made in such cases were all made only under the most excruciating torture, evidently meant nothing to Espina. He must, however, have been troubled by the fact that converts offered hardly any cooperation in demonstrating the existence of the notorious rite. Moreover, the commission appointed by Emperor Frederick II to determine the truth about the blood accusations—a commission that consisted of the most famous converts in various European kingdoms—denounced the accusation as sheer fabrication.[60] And none of the well-known Spanish converts—from Petrus Alphonsi through Alfonso de Valladolid to Paul of Burgos and Jerónimo de Santa Fe, all of whom spoke so harshly of the Jews, their beliefs, their notions and their customs—uttered a word from which one could gain the slightest support for the rampant belief. Luck, however, played into Espina's hands. While writing the *Fortalitium* he could announce that he possessed evidence about the existence of the blood rite that no Christian before him had managed to obtain. He had at his disposal a statement of a convert—nay, of a *Jew* prior to his conversion—a statement made of the latter's own volition, testifying to his presence in a secret Jewish ceremony in which a Christian child was ritually killed. Was not this the ultimate proof that Christendom had needed so long? The matter deserved of course the closest attention, and Espina describes in minute detail how the evidence came into his hands.

"In the year 1456," he tells us, "when I stayed in the Convent of San Francisco in Valladolid, there came to me a Jew by the name of Emanuel, the son of a certain great physician in Genoa . . . and told me that he recognized the error of the Jewish people, and devotedly sought to be cleansed [of his sins] by being baptized to Christianity. In response to my question as to what had brought him to this double recognition—i.e., of the error of the Jews and the truth of Catholicism—he answered that it was the criminal practice which is often imputed to the Jews by Christians—namely, that they immolate Christian children whenever they can get them. And so, moved by his conscience and his zeal for Christianity, the Jew informed me of two such cruel deeds, one of which he heard from his parents and other Jews, and another which he saw with his own eyes."[61]

The case that he himself had witnessed, he said, occurred in Saona, in the territory of Genoa, some four years before—that is, in 1452—where he went to see how a Christian child was being slain by some fellow Jews. "My father," he related, "took me to a house where seven or eight Jews got together most secretly. Behind *closed doors* they took a strong oath to conceal what they were about to do, so that in no circumstances would they ever disclose what was to be done there; rather should they suffer death or kill themselves than relate what they would see there to any living being. Then they brought in a small Christian child, perhaps two years old, and placed it in the middle of the room; they also brought in a vessel which they use for receiving the blood of circumcised children. They put the child naked over the vessel, and four of those Jews proceeded to the slaughter in the following manner and order: One of them held the child in the right arm, and another in the left; the third held his head raised, so that together these three Jews held him stretched out in the form of a cross. A fourth man, who was to do the killing, put in the child's mouth, before it was stretched out, pieces of cotton filled with smoke to prevent it from crying. Then he received rather long iron needles *(ferreos aculeos)* which he stuck most cruelly into the child's stomach and lungs toward the innermost parts of the body, so that they might pass through the heart. When the wicked Jew was thus injuring the child time and again, quickly sticking and extracting the needles, a great quantity of running blood was shed into the vessel. As I shuddered when I saw the horrible crime and could not watch further, I moved away to another place in the house. My father then came to me and said many things, and among them he ordered me most *secretly* that I should not divulge to any living being what I saw and what I was about to see, and that I should prefer to suffer death, or kill myself, rather than reveal anything of this secret.

"When I returned with him to the scene of the ceremony, the child was already dead; they took his body and threw it into some deep, dark lavatory that was in that house. Then they mixed the blood in the vessel with tiny pieces of various fruits, apples, pears and nuts, and from that horrible concoction all those Jews ate. I too ate from that blood. After having tasted it I was so changed in my inner self that neither on that day nor on the following one could I eat anything at all. I felt as if I wanted, out of the horror I experienced, to pour out my inner entrails. Ecce, I have told you faithfully what I saw, and how I ate from the blood of the said Christian child."[62]

In a sane society, such an account would have been heard with a mixture of contempt and amazement—contempt for the person who tried by such means to gain the favor of men of influence, and amazement at the causes that could have brought him to such a low, perverted state of mind. But the society in which this perversion occurred was not sane but disordered—sick with an all-pervading hatred for the Jews and prepared to believe any calumny about them, however ludicrous and incredible it might ordinarily sound. So the vicious story of the degenerate Jew found eager hearers among most honorable Christians. As Espina tells us, the would-be convert repeated the same tale to Fray Pedro Vela, the guardian of his convent in Valladolid; he recounted it to Father García de Voamon, the bishop of Lugo (who was to act as godfather of that Emanuel when he was baptized into the Church); he told it to the venerable Lord Pedro Basques, the deacon of the Church of Compostela, and to many other notable men, ecclesiastic and lay, including the king's public notary and the secretary of the said bishop—namely, Pedro Martini de Guetaria, "by whom all that was said [about the two cruel acts] was put down in writing, and the signed statements were placed in the said convent of the Franciscans in memory of such a great crime."[63]

Yet however distempered the society, and however aware one may be of the grave and unusually complex nature of its malady, it is still astonishing to note the feebleness and credulity to which man's thinking can be reduced by prejudice and hostility. For like all feigned stories, however cleverly conceived, the story of the would-be convert from Genoa had its obvious flaw: it lacked contact with reality; it was a balloon that could explode at the first prick. But evidently, no pricking was done. The would-be convert claimed that he had been so disgusted with the religious crimes of the Jews that he decided to abandon his people and his faith and go over to Christianity. All is well and good. But why did he not reveal his "secret" close to home—if not in his native city, then in Rome, for instance, where his story would be heard by the foremost authorities, both ecclesiastic and civil, who could examine his assertions and establish the truth? Why did he have to remove himself to Spain? Was it because in Italy the authorities would have discovered the falsehood of his narrative, and also many things about him personally which would not be in his favor? This lack of a concrete tie to its origin, to the place of its occurrence and the people involved, is obviously the point where the story founders. Is it possible that Espina failed to notice this? To be sure, he tells us that he was careful to see to it that the account of the man, duly signed, was placed in the Franciscan convent of Valladolid, "in memory of the great crime committed." But is this all that had to be done with such a testimony? After all, we have here a terrible charge that had often outraged public opinion in the West, and this was the first voluntary admission by a Jew of his own participation in a ritual murder. Was it not incumbent upon Espina and his friends—the bishop of Lugo, the deacon of Santiago, and the other high officials and dignitaries mentioned—to send that testimony to Rome and Genoa for an investigation of the case? Only four years had passed from the reported crime, and it stands to reason that with the knowledge they possessed (about the man's father, a famous physician, and the place of the alleged murder), the authorities in Italy could still reconstruct all the phases of the horrid rite and bring the criminals to book. Surely it was worthwhile, even necessary, to bring the man back to Italy— that is, to Genoa and the scene of the crime—so that he might assist in the inquiry and serve as an unimpeachable witness. But none of these things was done. No attempt was made to avenge the blood of the Christian child and cleanse Genoa of its blood-eating vampires, and no use was made of the apparent opportunity to prove, once and for all, the truth about that rite, which the Jews kept denying and which many Christians too regarded as a mere legend. Why? Evidently, something bizarre, unreal, something which belonged to the world of fantasy, was associated with the story even in the eyes of its supporters. They left it where they found it, because they wanted to leave it there; they allowed the balloon to remain floating in the air, obviously because they feared that any real inquiry would soon cause it to explode.

V

The description of the blood rite in Saona, however, does not constitute the high point in Espina's portrayal of the Jews. For Espina does not depict the Jews merely as slayers of Christian children, but also as killers of Christian adults by various subtle and devious means, including the "cures" that Jewish physicians offer their Christian patients ("for every Christian they cure, they kill fifty others," he says).[64] Yet, in his opinion, the killing of individual Christians can in no way quench the Jews' hellish hatred for Christianity and their insatiable thirst for Christian blood. And thus from time to time, Espina tells us, they plot to wipe out whole Christian communities; they do not recoil, in fact, from planning to destroy the whole Christian world.

Espina has "proof" that attempts to this effect have actually been made. During the Black Death, he says, "it has been discovered" that "Jews had poisoned all the wells in Germany in order to kill all the Christians in that country."[65] How this was discovered was no secret to Espina. "Some of them [i.e., the Jews] confessed to the crime under torture," and, as we have seen, confessions under torture are for Espina foolproof evidence. So this is no longer a mere accusation that may be subject to doubt; this is a charge verified by the courts, and thereby raised to the level of fact. And having accepted the accusation as true, he naturally accepts the punishment as just. "Astonished at such a great cruelty, and fearing to have such traitors among them, the Germans burned the Jews throughout the country."[66] To Espina this mass annihilation of Jews appeared a reasonable punishment. It was a justifiable act of self-defense against deadly, unpredictable assailants.

But Espina has more to say about the large-scale criminal plans of the Jews. To implement these plans, he says, the Jews regard no means as improper or offensive, including the use of black magic, in which they are especially adept. This is indeed what happened in France. A very cruel Jew conceived a scheme to wreak vengeance upon the Christians. He made friends with a Christian executioner, an official of the administration of justice, whom one day he asked for a human heart. He pretended that he needed it for the preparation of a medicine without which a certain sickness could not be cured. He also said that the sick man would give him, the Jew, twenty golden crowns if he managed to cure him, and that half of this sum (plus many other things) the Jew would give his friend, the executioner, if the latter supplied him with the needed heart.

Out of either friendship or cupidity, the wretched man agreed to the arrangement and promised to give the Jew a man's heart; he then extracted a heart from the body of a Christian he had hanged and quartered. Giving the heart to his wife for safekeeping, he told her he expected to get for it ten crowns from the Jew, his friend, with whom she was acquainted. Since the woman knew the Jew to be a magician, she reproached her husband severely for his intent, but he chastised her by saying that she would cause him to lose ten golden crowns, apart from the other promised benefits. Finally, with the woman's counsel, this is what was done: they obtained the heart of a pig, delivered it to the Jew "in a most secret manner," and received from him ten golden crowns. The Jew used the heart for the preparation of his potion and then buried it in a certain field, believing that he had buried the heart of a Christian. A few days later a multitude of pigs, both wild and domestic, gathered in that field, and soon began to assail each other. So violent indeed was their strife that, in their rage, they tore each other to pieces, so that none of them remained alive. When the king of France learned of these occurrences, and the Jew was seized, it became apparent that what had happened to the pigs would have happened to the Christians of that province if the buried heart had been that of a Christian. For this reason all the Jews of that place were killed at the king's order.[67]

Espina does not doubt the veracity of the story or any of its bizarre and incredible parts. He does not doubt it because he heard it "frequently" from "many" people—people whom he considered "trustworthy"—and because he himself was a firm believer in the existence and efficacy of the occult powers. Nor did he doubt that the Jews, the Devil's sons, were in league with these powers. In fact, he was sure that they were not only sorcerers but expert in all magical arts. Among other things, as he put it, "the Jews are soothsayers, dream interpreters, augurs, diviners, enchanters, charmers, necromancers and pythons [i.e., such as consult ghosts and familiar spirits]. They practice all these arts although the Law [of Moses] expressly and sternly forbade them to do so."[68] Very shrewdly and with careful calculation, Espina presents his evidence. He cites Deuteronomy 18.10–11, which prohibits the Israelites from using all those arts, but omits the prologue and epilogue of that law, which make it clear that such practices were not "Jewish" but part of the "abomination of the gentiles" and that the Israelites were merely ordered to refrain from imitating their gentile neighbors. With these portions of the law suppressed, the reader may easily gather from Espina what Espina wanted him to gather and believe—namely, that the Jews had been addicted to witchcraft in all its forms before the Law was given them and remained so addicted thereafter. Obviously, divine law, with all its stern threats, was powerless to alter the bad habits of the Jews.[69]

VI

We are now in a position to offer a brief summary of Espina's view of the Jews as expressed in the *Fortalitium*. The Jew is not only cruel and sadistic by virtue of his nature or his mental makeup; he is also filled with a special hatred for Christianity and a desire to destroy the Christian world. This desire, or this urge to kill Christians, is not meant, however, just to satisfy his rancor; he must also kill them to quiet his sick blood and fulfill his religious needs. He is also ordered by his law—i.e., rabbinic law—to kill all Christians, let alone exploit them in every possible manner. Hence all the criminal chicanery that the Jews enact against the Christians. But they are not just most selfish and unscrupulous; they simply lack all sense of morality. They are, in fact, beyond the pale of morals. This is why they have always been "rebels against God," "idolaters" and "dealers in black magic." All this is explained by the Jews' origin—namely, by their ethnic structure and components. In Espina's view, the Jews are subhuman or, more precisely, they are only partly human, while the other parts are beastly and demonic—a direct result of their ancestors' cohabitation with monsters, beasts, and evil spirits.[70] From here it was only a small step to Espina's ultimate definition of the Jews: they are "sons of the Devil" (not only metaphorically, but in the full and real sense of the word), and as such they are a danger not only to their neighbors and to those who converse or come in touch with them, but to mankind as a whole.

What should be done to such a race living among the Christians? Or what should be the solution of the Jewish problem, according to Espina? The fanatical friar had no doubt about the answer. He expressed his opinion in no uncertain terms in describing the ways the Jews were treated in countries that no longer suffered from their presence. Such countries were England and France. He was fascinated by the fact that, of all the states of Europe, only those two had succeeded in ridding themselves of the Jews, and again and again he reverts to the question of the circumstances and the manner in which this was accomplished.

He presented Vincent's tale about the expulsion of the Jews from France; and like all such tales narrated by Espina, this too was intended to serve as a model of behavior to the Spanish kings and people. There was indeed much in Vincent's story that could offer an inducement to the rulers of Spain. Thus, Vincent tells us that the king of France seized one Saturday all "his" Jews in their synagogues and "first of all despoiled them of their precious garments, as well as of their gold and silver."[71] The implied lesson needs no elaboration. Spain's kings should not scruple to do such a thing (which some regard as robbery), even as the king of France (who "burned with the zeal of God"[72]) did not scruple to do so. Such despoilment would mean only to take back from the Jews a small part of what they have stolen from the Spaniards, just as the exactions of Philip II recovered a fraction of what they had stolen from the French. Expropriation of Jewish property therefore is morally permissible, just as it is profitable to the Crown. It would not be long before the Catholic Kings heeded Espina's counsel and expelled the Jews from Spain.

Vincent says further that when the King of France decided to expel the Jews from his kingdom, the Jews induced the barons and prelates (by gifts and promises of future favors) to attempt to change the King's mind about the expulsion, while the Jews, for their part, assured the King that if he did so, they would provide him with "infinite sums of money"; but the King was not persuaded by the Jewish bribes or by other "promises of temporal nature."[73]

Perhaps Espina expected that something of the kind would occur in Spain if an order of expulsion were ever issued there, and he wanted Spain's kings to learn from the French kings how true Christian monarchs should behave. If so, his sense of what was to happen in Spain with regard to both the interference of the nobles and the offer by the Jews of "infinite sums of money" was uncommonly acute. The Spanish sovereigns followed the French example (as was reported by Espina) to the letter. They not only issued an order of expulsion, but resisted all attempts of the nobility and the Jews to have the order annulled.[74]

This, however, does not exhaust Espina's thoughts about the solution of the Jewish problem. For with all the importance he attached to Vincent's story about the measures taken in France, he was not quite satisfied with it. So when several Cluniac monks came to Castile on a reformatory mission, Espina asked one of them to tell him the "real cause" of the expulsion of the Jews from France. In response the monk wrote him a long letter, which Espina reproduced in its entirety in his book; the gist of it was that the "real cause" was an attempt by a Jew to desecrate the Host.

It is necessary to turn to the Cluniac's tale about the expulsion of the Jews from France for us to see the working of Espina's mind and understand why he thought it important to present it. According to that tale, the expulsion resulted from an attempt made by a certain Parisian Jew to persuade a Christian woman to obtain a Host for him. Presumably believing what the Christians believed—namely, that the Host represents Christ's body—the Jew planned to torture the Host by submerging it in a kettle of boiling oil and water. However, when he threw the Host into the kettle, a handsome boy appeared walking over the liquid. The vicious Jew understood that the boy represented Jesus and, unperturbed by the great miracle, he endeavored to submerge the boy in the fluid with the aid of an iron instrument. But the boy could not be touched. When the Jew tried to strike him on the left side of the kettle, the boy appeared on the other side, and vice versa. Finally, the children of the Jew came in and, astonished by the sight, told first their mother, and later other townspeople, what they had witnessed. As a result, some Christians came to the place, and they too saw the miracle. Ultimately, the Parisian bishop, accompanied by his clergy, came to the Jew's house. They did not see the angelic boy, but they did see, in the midst of the boiling liquid, a very clean Host, wholesome and complete. The bishop took it with his own hands and, with all the people watching, carried it in a procession to the Church of St. John, where it was consecrated on that day. Naturally, the Jew was arrested, tried and, before long, sentenced to be burned. But the King of France was not satisfied with this punishment. He ordered all the Jews of France expelled.[75]

Today it is difficult to understand how such stories could so readily be accepted by learned masters of the medieval Church. The account illustrates the extreme credulity of even the most educated friars, who were supposed to be accustomed by their training to strict logical thinking. The Cluniac monk, Espina tells us, was a licenciate, a graduate in theology, and so, needless to say, was Espina. Both sought to reform society and knew much about its ills and follies; both had a reputation for devoutness, moral purity, even saintliness; and both used tales of divine miracles to justify the cruelest of all acts. How unfathomable is the heart of man! Under the cloak of piety, religiosity and compassion, Espina's heart was beating to a feverish rhythm dictated by prejudice, antipathy and hate.

Espina was certainly clever. Not a word was written in his book without a purpose. To justify such a cruel deed as the banishment of a great community from the land, some appalling religious crime, he thought, must be offered in justification. And what crime of such enormity could be imputed to the Jews of Spain? Vincent's reason for the expulsion from France was that the Jews killed Christian children—a suitable, convincing reason, to be sure. But the belief in that crime was not rampant in Spain. Despite Espina's efforts to disseminate the notion that the Jews of Castile, like those of other countries, were engaged in ritual murder, he knew that this was still a moot point. The accusation had not held up in the Spanish courts as it had in France (Blois) or in Germany (Fulda). On the other hand, court judgments *were* pronounced in Spain against Jews accused of desecrating the Host. But desecration of the Host was not indicated by Vincent, nor *could* it be mentioned in his account, since the myth was born *after* Philip Augustus had expelled the Jews from France. But Espina, no doubt unaware of all this, was bothered by the question: How could Vincent forget the desecrations of the Host? Or how could he pass over them in silence? Now came the account of the Cluniac monk to fill the lacuna. The Cluniac's story of course related not to the first expulsion of the Jews (by Philip Augustus) in 1189, but to the second (by Philip the Fair) in 1306, and by that time the Host libel was widespread in France, as it was in Germany and other countries. It seems, however, that Espina believed it related to the expulsion Vincent had referred to (i.e., that of 1189), since he gives no indication of knowing that the French Jews were expelled more than once. In any event, Espina thought that the Cluniac monk's story was a useful addition to Vincent's account. For however doubtful the Spaniards might be about the Jews' practicing ritual murder, few of them would deny Jewish involvement in desecration of Hosts. And such a crime could be sufficient to justify the expulsion of the Jews from Spain.

VII

However large this measure loomed to Espina as a way of solving the Jewish problem, it was not by any means his most favored solution. To his mind, the Jews, the arch-criminals of the world, the killers of Christ and of Christian children, the desecrators of Hosts and plotters of mass murders, deserved a penalty far more severe than mere removal from the countries of the West. Indeed, nothing short of death, Espina thought, even remotely approached the extreme punishment which these sons of the Devil deserved.

To attune his readers to this solution, he describes incidents in which it was applied, without showing the slightest doubt of the propriety of such a gruesome action. We recall his story of the raging pigs and how it ended happily from Espina's standpoint. For the alleged attempt of a Jewish sorcerer to destroy the Christians of a certain province, all the Jews of that province were put to death at the bishop's order. Espina apparently considered it right to have so many Jews pay with their lives for one person's criminal design, which, incidentally, did not materialize. In his eyes that Jew, the alleged criminal, was the representative and executor of the will of his community. No evidence was needed to demonstrate even partly the community's involvement in the planning of the crime—if indeed a crime like this had been contemplated—since all Jews are "known" to harbor such plans and do what they can to implement them. Thus they deserve to be put to death even before any crime is committed, just because they are what they are—namely, members of the accursed Jewish race.

That this was indeed Espina's view can also be seen from some of his other narratives that ended with mass killings of Jews. Typical of these is his tale of the nobleman who went from France to Spain and, on crossing the border, was asked by the tax gatherers, who were Jews, to pay a certain duty. Refusing to pay the tax, which he considered unjust, the nobleman quarreled with the tax collectors and gave one of them a box on the ear. When the beaten Jew returned the blow, the nobleman drew out his sword to dispatch him, but then he saw that he was not facing one man, but many armed Jews who were ready to oppose him, and this compelled him to suppress his desire. Later on, when he came to his senses, he began to wonder why God had so disgraced him and made him suffer such a great insult from the hands of these base and criminal people. He recalled that when the Jews were expelled from France, he alone of all the French princes refused to oust them from his domains and had remained their defender ever since. He concluded that God must have been angered by his conduct, and that was why he was offended so shamefully. Accordingly, he vowed that if the good God would bring him back safely to his land, he would not leave a single Jew in it. This promise he fulfilled to the letter. All the Jews he could find in his domains, he annihilated by the sword.[76]

On this occasion, too, Espina had nothing to say against the nobleman's action. On the contrary, he sees in it an expiation of the sin he had committed by his refusal to expel the Jews. In other words, to atone for that sin, he had to do something better than expel the Jews: he had to kill them. Let us note that the Jews who were killed on this occasion were not charged with a specific crime. Not one of them was accused even of an *attempt* to perpetrate a crime against any Christian. Nor did the incident that led to the mass killing constitute anything that could justify such a punishment; at most, it was a case of bad behavior by a Jew—one who forgot his "place" in the world and should have known better. Espina, of course, attaches no value to the fact that the Jews involved were official tax collectors, doing their duty on behalf of their king; that the nobleman was the first to use violence in the quarrel; and that the Jew merely reacted to an attack. All these circumstances, which he noticed and indicated, seemed to be of no importance to him. The crucial fact was that a Jew struck a nobleman; and naturally, the "most criminal people" in the world had to be taught a lesson to remember. Thus, the shame they caused was wiped out by the blood of the Jews of an entire French province—i.e., people who had nothing to do with the behavior of their brethren in another country.

But something else must be said in this connection which helps elucidate Espina's attitude. It is obvious that his position in this case was not determined by the nobleman's vow to "leave no Jew in his land." "To leave no Jew" did not necessarily mean to kill them all. The nobleman could have fulfilled his vow by ordering all the Jews expelled. And if, when he made his vow, he had in mind to kill them, Espina no doubt knew that a vow to commit a crime is ipso facto null and void. But here is the whole point: to Espina, the killing of Jews in *any* circumstances did not constitute a crime. In the case of the French nobleman, it was an act of piety, an expiation of a sin—the sin of tolerating the presence of Jews in his land and treating them humanely. It was here that the evil lay!

All these stories clearly show that Espina considered mass extermination a proper way to get rid of the Jews. For what was done to the Jews of a whole province could of course be done to the Jews of a whole kingdom. In fact, we may readily conclude that annihilation was Espina's preferred solution to the Jewish problem in all the countries of Christendom.

VIII

This conclusion is fully confirmed by the two stories Espina relates about the elimination of the Jews from England. The first may be called the story of the singing boy, the second, the narrative of the two tents. To understand Espina's thinking about the Jewish people, it is necessary that we consider both tales.

There was a boy in the town of Lincoln, the son of a poor woman, who was enchanted with the singing of a certain hymn in honor of the Virgin Mary. He used to sing it wherever he went, also while passing through the street of the Jews; but the Jews, enraged by his song, decided to kill him. So they cut out his tongue with which he praised the blessed Virgin; they also extracted his heart, with which he was meditating on that hymn; then they threw his body into a deep lavatory, which was of course dirty and full of bad odor. In this way they believed that not a sign of him would ever be found.

But the blessed Virgin did not forget her faithful servant. As soon as he was thrown in that stinking place, she immediately came near him and put in his mouth a certain precious stone that replaced his tongue; at once he began to sing the same antiphon, not stopping at any time during day or night. Four days passed, during which his mother was desperately looking for her son; in her search she came to the street where he was killed, and lo and behold, his familiar voice, singing that sweet song of the Virgin was ringing in her ears. When she heard it, she began to shout violently, and many people gathered about her, among them the magistrate of the city. They entered the house from which the voice came and found the youth in the lavatory. They brought him out, dressed him in new clothes, and carried him to the city's cathedral church. There the bishop preached a sermon, and instructed all those present to pray devoutly, so that by their prayers the Blessed Virgin would see fit to reveal this secret. When the sermon was finished, it pleased God the most High Jesus Christ and His Blessed Mother to have the treachery and cruelty of those wicked Jews revealed, for at that very moment the small boy stood up in the couch in which he lay, extracted from his mouth a very precious stone and, with a happy and cheerful face, told the assembled people what had happened to him. Then he informed them that he was rising to the sky, to the society of the glorious Virgin, and he gave the precious stone to the bishop, for him to put it together with other relics on the altar of the church. Following that, he signed himself with the sign of the cross and, adapting himself to the couch, gave up his soul to the Savior.[77]

When the King of England learned of that crime—and bearing in mind many other crimes that the Jews had committed (as has been established by a true inquisition)—he ordered all the Jews of his kingdom to be killed, with the exception of those who were not so vicious; the latter he ordered to be shorn of their properties and expelled from the kingdom of England. Since then no Jew has lived in that country; nor has any Jew dared to appear there, knowing that if he was recognized to be a Jew he would immediately be killed.[78]

In the story of the singing boy, as in that of the angelic child, the expulsion is ascribed to an ugly religious crime and its revelation by a miracle. But Espina was not fully satisfied with this account, perhaps because it had so little to do with the conditions in Spain. He therefore presented another story which, he said, was found in the old chronicles of England.[79] This story *could* remind his reader of the Spanish circumstances of his time, and held a clear message for the Spaniards.

According to this account, England was suffering from continuous wars, famines and pestilences. The king wondered whence came the trouble and why his realm was so heavily afflicted with such tribulations. He asked the saintly men of his kingdom to beseech God to reveal to them the cause of the great evil. This they did; they also mortified their flesh by fasts, and the merciful God finally answered their prayers. He informed them that those evils befell their country because of the crimes committed by the Jews.

When the king heard this, he called his Council to a meeting, wherein it was decided that all Jews must become Christians, believing that this would placate the wrath of God. The plan was put into effect, but the evils did not stop; on the contrary, they increased. So the servants of God were again consulted, and they told the king that the "Jews committed, under the name of Christians, worse crimes than they had under the name of Jews. For shortly after their fictitious conversion, they usurped, in their cunning ways and trickeries, almost all the offices of the kingdom, so that the true Christians in the country were seen almost as their captives."[80] This is what the "servants of God" had said, and the king, enlightened by God, proceeded to purge his kingdom of those serpents in the following manner.

On an assigned day, when all the people were going out to the field near the sea, he put up two pavilions—one on the seashore and another in some distance from it. In the first he put the *Torah* of the Jews, in the second the cross of Christ. The King, sitting in judgment between the pavilions, called the said *conversos* to appear before him, and with a clear voice and cheerful countenance said to them as follows: "I have made you all become Christians, and you have accepted my orders voluntarily; but after your conversion the evils in my kingdom have multiplied, and perhaps the cause of this was that you came to Christianity against your will. It is therefore my wish that you be left free. Behold, in that pavilion near the sea, there is the *Torah* of the Jews, in the other the cross of Christ; choose for yourself the lot you wish to have, and rush to it immediately." Rejoicing in the freedom granted them by the King, "the Jews ran at once, with their wives and children, to the pavilion of the *Torah;* and when they emerged from it on the other side they were slaughtered one after another and thrown into the sea. Thus was the said kingdom purged, and the plague ceased forthwith; nor has any Jew lived in that kingdom ever since. Let the Spaniards take note and see whether a similar plague is not flourishing among them!"[81]

The Spaniards, however, could not emulate England if they wished to follow the lines of conduct indicated in Espina's account. For never had there been a mass conversion in England and never had the Jews there been put to the sword at the order of the king. Espina's story is a Spanish concoction clearly alluding to Spanish conditions, or rather to *some* of these conditions as seen by the enemies of the Jews and the Marranos. It mirrors all the major claims and accusations leveled at both groups by their foes, and it clearly indicates the way the latter wished to see the conflict end. According to their claims, the Jews were the *source* of all the wars and plagues, calamities and misfortunes that befell the Christian lands. The kings favored their conversion to Christianity, believing that thereby the troubles would stop, but when the Jews were converted, the situation worsened. Why? Obviously, because although they converted "voluntarily," they inwardly remained what they were (i.e., Jews), and then, as formal Christians, they occupied high posts and made the Old Christians their slaves. Some Spaniards argued that if *all* the Jews had been converted, the Judaism of the Marranos would have disappeared. But the English "example" shows that this too was nothing but an idle hope. There, in England, *all* the Jews were converted (to all appearances "voluntarily"), but when they had real freedom of choice, all of them, without exception, returned to the religion in which they truly believed—i.e., Judaism. This of course reflects the anti-converso claim that *all* Marranos were Jews at heart and never would cease to be so. How then can the harm they inflict upon the land be ultimately averted? The King of England has shown the way. More precisely, Espina has shown the people of Spain how to settle their Jewish question.

There is good reason to believe that Espina omitted the beginning of this story about the Jews of England. The King, he tells us, decided "to have all the Jews converted" and "made" them fulfill his wish. How the King "had" them all converted—whether by persuasion, or coercion, or some other means—Espina does not say; but we are entitled to assume that behind the cryptic terms he used in his narrative, he concealed the explanation he found in his source: the King offered the Jews a "choice"—between conversion or expulsion—and the Jews "chose" conversion "of their own free will," thus giving grounds for the King's "reminder" that they accepted Christianity "voluntarily." Espina, who covered up the beginning of the story, as he wished to stress the "voluntary" conversion of the Jews, no doubt correctly reported the remainder; and he must have especially followed his source in asserting that the Jews occupied "all the offices" and thereby subjugated the true Christians.[82] For this agreed with the Toledan theory and served his particular purpose. And so, by removing compulsion from their conversion, he denied the conversos any excuse for their "Judaizers," and by indicating, as he did (implicitly, to be sure), that their conversion came to satisfy their lust for power, he made them look doubly deceptive and criminal. What should be the punishment for such multiple crimes, religious as well as social? Espina's answer is quite apparent. On the one hand, he does not have even a single word of reproach against the King of England for having put all the Jews of his country to the sword. On the other, he urges the Spaniards to take note of the English king's deed!

The last remark especially shows the "end" that Espina had in mind. He wanted Spain to draw a lesson from England as to how to treat the Jews who took over the offices and made the Spaniards look almost like their servants. And the lesson was evident. There is a way of ridding Spain of its Jews—a way both simple and direct. Kill them all—man, woman and child. This is the shrill genocidal cry that rises from Espina's work again and again. Kill them for violating a Host, for killing a Christian child, even for standing up against a Christian nobleman who offends them; kill them for converting disingenuously to Christianity; kill them when they live under the name of Jews, as well as when they live under the name of Christians!

But here we touch upon a different problem—Espina's attitude toward the conversos, which calls for a separate discussion.

ON THE MARRANOS

IX

The first part of Espina's book—i.e., the one following the introductory chapter—is devoted to the war against the heretics, indicating thereby that the *enemy from within* posed, in his opinion, a greater problem to Spain than the outside enemies—the Moslems and the Jews. He noted fourteen heresies that had arisen in Christendom, among which he included the errors of John Wyclif, of the "little fox" who followed him, John Huss of Bohemia, and of the "third viper," Jerome of Prague.[83] Some of these heresies he imputed to the Marranos; and with their "Judaic" heresies he opens and closes the chapter he devoted to all heresies in Christendom.

But before we touch on some of these "heresies," we should consider Espina's view of the conversos as followers of Judaism in the guise of Christians. This view is based largely on the Toledan inquiry, the *pesquisa,* whose findings Espina presents in detail. Since the text of the *pesquisa* has not reached us, and most of its "conclusions" are found only in the *Fortalitium*, our knowledge on some of the matters in question remains, regrettably, incomplete. Nevertheless, the data found in these "conclusions," joined with those we find in the *Sentencia*, gives us a fairly clear idea of the charges leveled at the "covert Jews."

The theoretical side of these charges can be subsumed under the following six headings: (1) A belief in the existence of a God and a Goddess; (2) a belief in idols; (3) a belief that the stars endowed Abraham and his heirs with the capacity of prophetical vision; (4) a belief that the powers of consecrated Hosts may be employed for anti-Christian ends; (5) a belief that "in this life there is nothing that matters except birth and death, and all the rest is vanity"; (6) a belief in soothsaying and other occult arts.[84]

We have already stressed the utter impossibility of attributing to Judaizers faith in idols or two Gods, and the same is true of points 3, 4 and 5: No Jew would ascribe the origin of prophecy to the influence of the constellations; no Jew could believe that the "Host" represents the body of Jesus in any form whatever; and no Jew could assume that it possesses any powers, either natural or supernatural. Similarly, the view of "this life" as a denial of the soul's Immortality, the World to Come and Reward and Punishment was as anti-Jewish as it was anti-Christian. And as for soothsaying and other occult arts, the *belief* in them was clearly antiprophetic (and as such fundamentally anti-Jewish), while in a sense it was closer to Christianity, which recognized the existence and power of the demons and their interference in human affairs.[85] To be sure, the *practice* of the occult arts was forbidden by Christian as well as Jewish law, but it was less common among Jews than among Christians in all the countries of the West; and if some conversos did practice magic, they might have been led to it by the influence of the society in which they lived—i.e., the Christian society—rather than by current Jewish thinking.

Thus, what is common to all these charges—or to all these heretical notions—is that they have nothing to do with Judaism as a doctrine or with the performance of any of its rites. And had we not been told that they were held by conversos who allegedly adhered to the Jewish faith, it would not occur to us that such opinions could possibly be related to Judaism at all. We might have attributed some of them to popular superstitions current among *many* peoples (Jews included) both before and during the medieval period, and some to esoteric or Averroistic circles, but not to the mainstream of Jewish opinion consisting of basic Jewish beliefs. Insofar as their speculative thought is concerned, the *pesquisa* had evidently discovered little or nothing about the Jewishness of the conversos.

This is also apparent from the quantitative aspect of the evidence offered by the *pesquisa*. Thus, its claim that the Marranos worshiped idols was supported by *one* Old Christian witness and allegedly involved *one* Marrano couple. Similarly, the assertion concerning the belief in the influence of the stars on Abraham and his offspring was based on the testimony of *one* Old Christian and allegedly involved *one* Marrano. The claim that the Marranos believed in the occult was based on hearsay evidence of *one* person, who reported that he heard it from *one* man (a Moor), who allegedly heard it from *one* converso. We have no information on the evidential basis of the assertion concerning the maltreatment of Hosts, but we know that it involved only *one* converso or, at most, *one* converso family—a priest(!) and his brothers.[86] As for the belief in two Gods, we have no data on its basis at all, but here our lack of information hardly matters, as the folly of the claim is self-evident. There remains only the question about the grounds for the view of the value of man's life as indicated above. Its evidential basis is likewise unknown, but it could not have been in any sense impressive, for García excluded it from the list of charges leveled against the conversos.

If the *theoretical* accusations of the *pesquisa* were at best flimsy or unreliable, its charges about the Judaic *practices* of the conversos were even less substantial. We have already touched on three of these "practices": the worship of idols, the mistreatment of Hosts and the practice of soothsaying (and other "evil arts"), which were related to the beliefs we have mentioned above. There remain, however, seven charges of the *pesquisa* that may indeed be associated with Jewish customs and precepts. Of these the most important were circumcision, observation of the Sabbath and celebration of the Passover. We shall therefore consider these charges first.

We have already shown that the *pesquisa*'s accusation that the conversos celebrated Passover is based on a worthless and self-negating testimony.[87] We may pass therefore straight to the second claim—i.e., concerning the observation of the Sabbath. Here we should confront the charge of the *pesquisa* with what we gather on this matter from the Hebrew sources. For if there is anything they reported regularly, it was the Marranos' attitude toward the Sabbath, and their statements on the subject leave no doubt whatever that this attitude became progressively more negative. Already from the fourth decade of the century, we have clear evidence that the Marranos violated the Sabbath, both publicly and privately, paying no regard to any of its laws.[88] If the *pesquisa* relied on some contrary evidence, that evidence could relate only to exceptions—a tiny minority.

Espina does not devote to those two practices—i.e., the Passover celebration and the observation of the Sabbath—more than the few lines he cited from the *pesquisa*. In contrast, he tried to build up by his own means—or rather by his own sources of information—the charge concerning the Marranos' circumcision. Indeed, of all the heresies he dealt with in this book, he first tackled the "heresy" of circumcision, "arising only among those who came from Judaism."[89] He wishes to assure us that the custom of circumcision was widespread among the conversos; and he presents two incidents to prove that they habitually circumcise their children. One relates to a converso father who claimed that his two circumcised sons were born like that, and the other to a converso mother who explained that her two sons had most uncommon accidents that necessitated surgery of their foreskins.[90] Espina does not question the veracity of these stories—anecdotes circulated at the time about the Marranos—although their folklorist, fanciful and hostile character is rather apparent. But realizing that they offered no proof for his claims, he tried to provide tangible evidence on which he could establish a case. So anxious was he to obtain such evidence that he came to rely on the absurd assertion of Fernando de la Plaza, his friend and follower, regarding the one hundred foreskins of circumcised Marrano children that he claimed to have in his possession.

Espina, however, would not limit his evidence on the important subject of Marrano circumcision to anecdotes touching children. "What is more painful," he says, "and what I cannot express without being bitter about it, is that some of their adults, who for such a long time enjoyed life on this side (i.e., in Christendom) under the name of Christians, have also been circumcised."[91]

From this remark one may gather that circumcision of adults was a new phenomenon, but if so, one must ask how widespread it was. Espina wished to show that the practice was common, and accordingly he tells us that in 1459, while he was preaching in Medina del Campo, he was informed by one "who knew their secrets" ("for there is no secret that does not become known") that "some thirty conversos who had been circumcised were hiding in a certain house in that town until their wounds of circumcision were healed."[92] But the story raises doubts that can hardly be dispelled. Since the matter was known to a faithful Christian, who not only "knew the Marranos' secrets" but also divulged that information to Espina; since the circumcised men were lodged in that house while Espina was preaching in the town of Medina, why did he not see to it that they be caught in the act and their Judaization exposed and punished? So this story too, like all his other stories, remains unsubstantiated, to say the least.

This, in any case, is the only incident that Espina can relate about the circumcision of adults. But reverting to the circumcision of Marranos later on, he seeks to throw some light on its origins. He tells us that the Marranos who deny the Gospels fell into this heresy under a special influence. A friar of their race who lived in Flanders taught the Bible secretly to certain conversos who visited that country as merchants. "He so impressed upon them the said error that some of them who returned to Spain perverted many others secretly. And these are those about whom I said above that they were hiding for about a month to cure their wounds of circumcision."[93]

According to Espina, then, the case of these people (who were circumcised in Medina del Campo) did not originate on Spanish soil; it was not at all an automatic result of the Marranos' alleged faithfulness to Judaism or of the influence of Spanish Jews, as we were so often led to believe; it was the product of some clandestine teaching that was transferred to Spain from another country and stemmed from a single converso friar, who was the teacher or founder of the group. Obviously, this was a new group of Marranos, who "for a long time," as Espina says, lived as Christians and then, suddenly, changed their ways. Under the circumstances, could such a group be large? To be sure, Espina tells us that the friar's disciples have perverted "many" of their brethren in Spain (which again shows that before that influence was exerted, the "perverted," too, lived as good Christians), but as no other source discusses or even mentions this Flemish friar and his new movement, we are entitled to doubt whether Espina's "many" were indeed so numerous. He further tells us that some members of the same group "expect shortly to transfer themselves to the Barbary States with a guide who awaits them secretly in Seville, so that when the transfer is accomplished they would freely become Jews."[94] Also in *haeresis I*,[95] when referring to this case, he tells us that many others are likewise reported to be "preparing themselves secretly to do a similar thing"—i.e., to follow the path of the doctor who secretly sold his possessions, departed to Jerusalem, and became a Jew. So what we have here are secret "preparations" and "expectations" reported by one person (or more) "who knew" and brought forth the evidence.

All this might have sounded quite realistic if it did not appear highly unreasonable for people who decided to emigrate from Spain to begin this move by being circumcised. One is tempted to ask why these people failed to do what that doctor did—namely, delay their circumcision until they reached another country, where they could join Judaism freely, without encumbering their plans by such an act as circumcision and, in addition, endangering themselves. But other considerations, too, prevent us from accepting Espina's account as given. Since he relates the occasion to a "past" event which took place in 1459, he must have written his story at a later date—say, at the beginning of the sixties. But we hear of no migration of conversos in the fifties either to Palestine or to the Barbary Coast, and very little of it (i.e., a few cases) in the early sixties; in fact, we have sufficient evidence to the effect that no such migration took place later on, or at least any that was considerable enough to leave any impression.[96] And so the "preparations" and "expectations" of the "many" were, at most, limited to isolated individuals (such may have existed), who prompted Espina's generalizations about the Judaizers or the practitioners of the "abominable" rite.

X

Espina's tendency to generalize and exaggerate when he referred to the Judaic heresies can be also shown from his other assertions concerning the same subject. When he presents the contents of the Toledan Inquiry, he informs us that according to its findings, "*some* of the conversos are not sound in the faith" *(aliqui eorum non sunt sani in fide)*[97]; but when he tells us of what he himself "heard," the number of the heretics changes rapidly to "many" *(multi)*[98] and later to "very many" *(plurimi)*.[99] We have seen that he spoke of "many" who "prepared" to leave Spain and return to Judaism, and on that occasion he mentioned a single case—that of a converso physician who sold all his possessions, departed for Jerusalem and became a Jew. But a few pages later he finds it possible to tell us that "of all the heresies that [of circumcision] spreads among the Marranos most, since *very many* are being circumcised, *and after having sold everything they have, they leave the realm and become Jews, as has been said.*"[100] So the "preparations" and "expectations" for departure became (after a few pages) a migration, and the single case of departure that has been reported became "very many" cases, "as has been said," although what "has been said" was quite different. But Espina is not satisfied even with that. He further extends his unfounded generalization, so that the "very many" becomes a "raging plague" *(pestis rabida)* that threatens to "destroy the faith of Christ." Hence it must be "vigorously resisted."[101]

And in addition to his tendency to exaggerate, we must note the sources of his information. Apart from the Toledan Inquiry, Espina depends on rumor or informants he considers "trustworthy." We have seen that Espina's accounts of the Jews' killing of Christian children, or their torture of Hosts, or their effective use of magic, were likewise based, according to Espina, on "trustworthy" witnesses; and this allows us to judge the trustworthiness of his witnesses regarding the "Judaizers" and the scope of their movement.

But Espina's exaggerations concerning the number of the "heretics" is not limited to assertions such as those we have cited. Skillfully, without saying so, he virtually identifies the conversos who allegedly follow Jewish law with the whole Marrano group. Thus, when he lists the Judaic sins of the conversos, he does not say, as the *Sentencia* did, that "*some* of them" committed those transgressions, but that, as the *pesquisa* "showed," "*they* circumcise their children," "*they* observe the Sabbath," "*they* send oil to the synagogues," and so on.

Moreover, in describing the heretics among the Marranos, he uses the invectives of Paul in Titus I. 10–12 against the Jewish converts to Christianity in Crete as if they referred to all converts from Judaism to Christianity in all places and at all times. Marcos García, too, used those invectives to depict *all* converts from Judaism, and thus we have here another example of Espina's following in the Toledans' footsteps. But Espina does not only repeat all of Paul's reprimands to the Cretan converts[102]; he also adds to them interpretations from the Ordinary Gloss, where he found more negative epithets to apply to the conversos. In fact, according to him, the conversos "who practice circumcision" and adhere to all other Jewish customs and beliefs indicated by the *pesquisa*[103] are even more iniquitous than what may be gathered from Paul's harsh words. For as Espina put it, they are "enemies of God," "idolaters" and "worse heretics than the Arians and all others who erred against the law of Christ."[104] Is there any wonder that the worst heretics in the world should be chastised in the most severe manner, even more severely than were the Arians and the other known heretical movements? Espina knew of course what treatment was accorded to the "other" heresies in Christendom. He knew that fire and the sword and every form of torture were employed to root them out. And this is indeed the treatment he thought proper and necessary to apply to the conversos.

For the conversos are a pest; and pests must be exterminated by all means available. "A republic can be corrupted even by one bad man, such as a thief, a homicide, an adulterer, etc.," he summarizes his view in the words of St. Bernard. But "if a sheep is sick, let not the herd perish." They "should be circumcised by justice and by death."[105]

It is obvious that Espina's preferred solution for the conversos was identical with the one he favored for the Jews—extermination. If he could devise a method by which all of them would be proven, formally and swiftly, to be what they were—namely, traitors to Christianity, secret Jews—and then do what the King of England did (according to the legend he related), he would have urged its immediate adoption. Espina was no doubt toying with such ideas and dreaming up from time to time such measures; but he had to abandon them as impractical. He lived in an age when heresies in Christendom were fought by means of an organized inquisition; and he had to be satisfied with that procedure. Thus, in this matter, too, he followed the Toledans and argued for the establishment of an inquisition against the Marranos in Castile.

This does not mean, of course, that he underestimated the impact an inquisition would have on the conversos. He realized that a "true" inquisition could destroy the conversos not only socially and economically but also physically. In the tenth "consideration," Espina specifies the four punishments meted out to heretics, which he expected to be imposed on the conversos: excommunication, dismissal (from offices), confiscation (of property) and prosecution (by the ecclesiastical authorities). "Any such person [who was found to have erred] ought to be surrendered to the secular authorities for due punishment, that is, by burning, unless immediately after the detection of the error, he expressed his wish to revert to the faith, to abjure his error and undergo penance; then the 'returners' should not be executed; they ought to be shut up in a perpetual prison."[106]

He also enumerates the penalties assured to a believer who supports or favors heretics. Abettors of heretics should be excommunicated, at least for one year.[107] During this entire time, all their ties to their society are severed. If the "abettor" is a *judge*, his decision is not enforced; if he is an *advocate*, his defense is not admitted; if he is a *notary*, his records are not honored; if he is a *cleric*, he should be removed forthwith from every ecclesiastic office and benefice.[108]

There is no need to indicate other rules related to the Inquisition (such as the seizure and torture of heretics) that Espina found necessary to present to his reader.[109] Espina took them all from Eymeric's *Directorium,* but it is clear that, at the time of his writing, these were generally unknown in Castile. As we see it, Espina presented these procedures in order to acquaint the Old Christians in Castile with the workings of an Inquisition. He must have believed that such a description of the Inquisition would excite the anti-Marranos in Castile to double their efforts toward its establishment, although he no doubt realized that it might also strengthen converso opposition to its introduction in that country. He must, however, have cared very little about what the conversos might think or do. His book was written to arouse the Old Christians to take action against the Jews and the conversos, and he probably believed that what he wrote on the Inquisition could be helpful in achieving this aim.

XI

We have already stated that Espina's data are, on the whole, grossly untrustworthy, that they bear the marks of fiction rather than fact, and further that they indicate no differentiation between the possible and the absurd, between truth and falsehood. This impression of stark unreliability is also generated by the hearsay evidence he included in his book and can be valued only by the standards of his prejudices. Espina was prepared to accept and publicize anything negative he heard about the conversos, anything that damaged their reputation and undermined their social or religious position. Never does he seem to have doubted such "information," however questionable or incredible it appears to us. Thus he accepted as "verified" findings all the conclusions of the Toledan Inquiry, although some of them were obviously based on nothing but foolish notions and groundless assertions; and similarly, he accepted all the folktales about the Marranos, although they bore the stamp of popular fabrications. No critical approach, no analysis, not even the slightest attempt at examination can we notice in his accounts about the conversos any more than we find in his tales about the Jews, and nothing good, commendable, or positive is ever related by him about either of these groups. When he occasionally refers to individual conversos, he always defines them as "members of their race"—i.e., the race of the Jews; and we already know from his discussions of the Jews his view of the Jewish race.

It is no less than amazing that such an uncritical author—to use the mildest term that could fit him—was taken so seriously by so many scholars. And this amazement is compounded by another puzzle. When we consider Espina's racial bias against the Jews and his wild hostility to everything Jewish, we cannot help asking: How could any historian ascribe validity to his charges against the conversos? Or perhaps we should phrase the question differently: How can one treat any of his assertions about the Marranos as true when we know that his statements about the Jews are so false? Since Espina could tell us with unwavering "assurance" that the Jews were "discovered" to be killers of children, desecrators of Hosts, poisoners of wells, and responsible for many attempted mass murders (as indicated in the case of the raging pigs), all of which have no grain of truth, can we assume that he stopped the working of his imagination when it came to his "discoveries" about the conversos? In brief, since one knows that Espina told us so many preposterous, vicious, false and groundless stories about the Jews, why should we not assume that he told us equally ludicrous, vicious, false, and groundless stories about the conversos, whom he judged to be Jews—and only Jews? To consider him mendacious in one field and truthful in another (which, we should remember, was to him the same field) is to treat his testimony in a manner unacceptable to any responsible inquirer.

Espina is simply not a credible witness. Filled as it is with distortions and inventions, his testimony about both the Jews and the conversos can rarely serve as basis for correct reconstruction. To be sure, here and there we may glean from his writings some true information about Jewish persecutions for which we have no other source. But this relates generally to the *background* of his stories, not to their main *content* and *thrust*. As far as these elements are concerned, what Espina tells us, one may say with assurance, belongs to the realm of popular fantasy, which means that historically it is usually worthless.[110] His testimony, however, has a side value which is *indirectly* related to its contents. It brings us face to face with the attitudes, feelings and claims of the Marranos' opponents. It helps us grasp the spirit of the times, and together with it the nature of the campaign that led to the founding of the Inquisition.

II. The Alboraique

The anti-Marrano satirical literature that first appeared in the days of Juan II of Castile continued to appear in the days of his successor, King Enrique IV, and included works, in both prose and verse, that furthered the anti-converso campaign. One of the surviving prose works of this kind, *El Libro del Alboraique,* pretends to offer a true description of the conversos in Castile, their habits and characteristics.[1] The picture it presents is generally revolting, undoubtedly reflecting the violent aversion which many Old Christians felt for the Marranos.

Isidore Loeb, and in his wake Fidel Fita and N. López Martínez, believed that the *Alboraique* was written in the 1480s.[2] Several indications in the work, however, convince us that it was composed about 1467. The first of them is the reference, in the opening of the satire, to the "conversos who became Christians *more than seventy years ago* as a result of the war then made throughout Spain," or rather "of the destruction of all Jewish communities."[3] It cannot be assumed that the author did not know that the "war on the Jewish communities" in Spain occurred in 1391[4]; and thus we must conclude that the *Alboraique* was written "more than seventy years" after 1391—and hence, a few years after 1461.

The work, furthermore, contains other indications of the date on which it was written. "It is more than fourteen hundred years," it says, since "the Herodians lost the kingdom, without ever regaining the staff of justice."[5] The last Herodian king who ruled over Israel (including Judea and Jerusalem) was Agrippa I, who died in 44 C.E. If the author had *him* in mind, then his statement: "It is more than fourteen hundred years since the Herodians lost the kingdom" may fall in line with the given date.

The third indication speaks of the Jews, the "infidel fathers" of the Marranos, who "came [to Spain] fourteen hundred years ago."[6] The reference is no doubt to the Jews who came to Spain following the destruction of the Second Temple (according to the tradition that prevailed among Spain's Jews). Thus, "fourteen hundred years ago," a round figure, brings us to the year 1470, which would seem to indicate the approximate time when the satire was written.

But the *Alboraique* contains a further clue to the date of its composition. It is found in its discussion of the conversos "who went to the Turk to shed the blood of Christians" and whom they burned in Valencia of Aragon *this* year" *(este año).*[7] We know of several conversos who planned to migrate to Palestine in order to return to Judaism there and were brought before the inquisition of Valencia in 1464. We do not know when and how the proceedings ended.[8]

However, if the group involved was identical with the one which, according to the *Alboraique*, volunteered to aid the Turks, we may conclude (if we rely on the satire) that some of its members were sentenced to be burned[9]; what is more, we may determine the year in which the inquisition issued its verdict. To be sure, according to the Madrid manuscript of the satire, the burning occurred "this year"—namely, the year in which the work was written; and this tells us nothing about the time of that occurrence. But the scribe of the Paris manuscript replaced the enigmatic indication "this year" with a definite date: 1467.[10] He deleted the words *"este año,"* which no doubt were part of the original version, because he copied the manuscript not in 1467 or 1468 but later, and "this year," he suspected, might be mistaken for the date of his own writing. The *Alboraique*, then, was written in 1467, probably after the Toledan riots of that year, whose impact was felt across the whole of Castile.

The author explains that the conversos were called Alboraiques after the animal which, according to the Koran, carried Mohammed to heaven.[11] Smaller than a horse and larger than a mule, it was of a kind not found in nature, nor mentioned in the written Law, nor indicated in Aristotle's work about the animals *(De natura animalium)*. It was a species in itself; and so is the converso who has something of the Moor and something of the Jew in him, but is neither a Jew nor a Moor—and certainly not a Christian.[12] As for the religious attitude of the Alboraiques, they resemble the Moors in their attitude toward the Christians, although they "do not believe in the sect of the Moors" either. "In their intention they are Jews," although they "do not keep the Talmud, nor all the ceremonies of the Jews"; nor do they treat any better Christian Law, in which they do not believe. Hence, they are neither Moors nor Jews, and Christians in name only.[13]

Borrowing a simile from the description of the Jews used by the Council of Agde (506),[14] the author of the *Alboraique* compares the conversos to "big whippets" who "return to their vomit in order to eat what they had spewed."[15] Like madmen who revert to their follies, so did "these dogs" (i.e., the conversos) resume the "observation of the Sabbath and circumcision and other ceremonies" they had solemnized before their conversion. "The Jews were insane to have guarded those rites" [after the coming of Jesus] to begin with; "now they return to them again after they had been baptized."[16]

In another place he says of the conversos: "You can recognize them by their public festivities *(fiestas)*, by their observance of the Sabbath . . . by their reciting *(meldar)* like Jews," and by their keeping the fasts and the passovers.[17] According to the Jewish sources, the conversos had stopped observing the Sabbath in the first third of the 15th century,[18] and as for circumcision, we have already pointed out that it was *not* practiced among them.[19] Isolated cases to the contrary had of course been reported and, true or not, were widely discussed. The author of the satire, however, did not hesitate to attribute the irregular behavior of *some* Marranos to *all* of them. He made a rule of the exception.

Referring to the dietary habits of the conversos, the author says that they eat all kinds of food. Thus, "they eat rabbits *(conejos)*, partridges killed by Christians and Moors, and fish; they eat little bacon *(tocino)* and other animals and fowls, like the Jews; and they eat them at all times, in the Forty [days] of the Christians, in the fast days of the Jews, and in the fast days of the Moors."[20]

The eating habits of the Marranos described by this author certainly indicate no respect for Jewish dietary laws. That they eat only "little" bacon may be attributed to custom, not to Jewish religious prohibition. They eat rabbits, which is forbidden by Jewish law, and partridges killed by Christians and Moors, which is also prohibited by Jewish law. They eat on Jewish fast days; so they desecrate the Jewish fast days, too. One may ask: How could people who eat on Jewish fast days—and on top of this, foods prohibited by Jewish law—be assumed to keep the Jewish fasts, as the author of the satire had stated? Obviously, if we follow his various assertions, we must conclude that most Marranos did not keep the Jewish fast days as they did not observe the Sabbath and practice circumcision. But if they did not keep the Sabbath and the Jewish fast days, it does not seem likely that most of them kept the other Jewish holidays (such as Passover).

But apart from imputing to the conversos the observance of certain Jewish rites and holidays, the author claims that they fail to follow Christian law and take part in Christian rites and ceremonies. Thus, he says, they eat meat on the forty days of Lent, they never confess or take communion, they do not keep Sundays, do not attend mass; nor do they praise the Virgin Mary or Jesus Christ, or read the Gospels.[21]

That all this is highly exaggerated seems evident from the plain facts that so many of the conversos were members of religious orders, occupied formal positions in the Church, and were associated with the activity of the chapters. We may suppose, however, that many Christian customs were not followed by many conversos with the regularity and steadfastness characteristic of Old Christians. We may further assume that some of the conversos were generally lax in their religious devotion, as undoubtedly were some Old Christians, too. It is also possible that the author describes here forms of behavior of a segment of Judaizers whom he identifies with all conversos. But even without bearing these possibilities in mind, we cannot give much credence to what the author of the satire says about the conversos' attitude toward Christianity when we know that what he says about their devotion to Judaism was highly inflated. Evidently, he is ready to ascribe to the conversos anything negative in the field of religion, whether it relates to Judaism and Christianity or to heresy in both religions.

The fierce animosity of the author for the conversos, and his virtual inability to judge them objectively, is displayed even more clearly when he speaks of their moral qualities and their social and economic activities. In his eyes, the conversos are terrible deceivers, for their appearance never suits their inward attitudes. Ostensibly they seem humane, merciful and friendly (falagüenos), but actually they are inhuman and cruel, wolves in sheep's clothing, but worse than wolves. They are human dogs, and mad dogs at that; this is why they bit the Lord with the madness of diabolic envy. Indeed, as Jews, they are what the Apocalypse says of them: a "synagogue of devils."[22]

And just as the conversos resemble large whippets, they also resemble a certain type of small horses fit neither for war nor for hard labor. "This is why the conversos are not used by us, the Christians, for acts of war or for hard work of laborers."[23] They are fit only to walk about the streets and the squares, where they deceive the people in many ways. This is why the prophet Isaiah said: Their works are of no use (59.6, according to the Vulgate). "They cannot be of use as speakers, because they are heretics; nor can they be of advantage as defenders, because they are cheats (and hence unreliable); nor can they be of any use as laborers because they are lazy."[24]

The author, however, is not satisfied with all these denunciations. The basic dishonesty of the conversos, he says, is manifested also in the way they talk and present their case. For "they sharpen their tongue like a snake (Psalms 140.4). Therefore, David said:[25] 'I shall send into them teeth of beasts, with the fury of serpents that will drag them across the land.' These are the devils who will bear their souls away."[26]

In view of all this, it is hardly surprising that the Marranos live among the Christians in fear; but, says the author, they know how to protect each other. If you touch one of them, all the others rush to his aid. "Like the cranes, they protect themselves with many vigils and guards." So "you can hardly kill an Alboraique through the process of justice, for he places over himself guardians, whom he gets by means of bribes and payments." Thus, "as the cranes come in the cold season, later wishing to return to their lands, and while they are here they cause us damage, so these came to us as captives [that is, after the conquest of Jerusalem], and since their arrival we received much harm from them; but now they wish to return to Judea."[27]

It is obvious that some of the Old Christians believed that the Marranos desired to return to Judea. The same accusation was leveled at them later by the advisers of the Duke of Medina Sidonia when the Marranos were preparing to settle in Gibraltar (1473). Palencia refers to Messianic hopes that were supposedly current among the Marranos, and he also tells us that the conversos were hoping that the Messiah would come to Seville.[28] No doubt there was *some* awakening of Messianic hopes among the Marranos—or, more precisely, in the small movement of "returners" that sprouted after the persecutions of 1449, 1462, and 1467. But there was no truth in the accusations of the duke's counselors regarding the intentions of the Marranos to migrate to Jerusalem.[29] If there was such a "movement" at all, it was undoubtedly very small, and like everything else that concerns Marrano Judaism, this tendency too was wildly exaggerated. Only in the wake of the establishment of the Inquisition, the persecutions in Portugal, the Expulsion from Spain, and the conquest of Palestine by the Turks (1516) do we see an actual movement of return not only to Judaism but to Palestine. But, as is known, even then its proportions were most limited. It represented a small minority of the "returners," who represented a small minority of the Marranos.[30]

The author completes his picture of the conversos with a number of bold strokes. Generally the Marranos, he tells us, are pompous and vainglorious, noted for their great pride, haughtiness and madness.[31] In their arrogance they wish to trample under their feet the Christians of the land in which they live. In fact, they prosper by theft and rapine. They rob the churches, buy the bishoprics, canonries, and other dignities of Holy Mother Church, assume positions of clerics, and do not believe in the holy Catholic faith or in the Mass which they say. Thus, in the tax collections and stewardships which were given them by the kings and the lords of the land, the rights of the true Christians are being encroached upon, because they raise the taxes *("pujen las rentas")* and rob widows and orphans and poor people and laborers. "They take from the income of the rich whatever they can, and from the poor more than they should, and in doing this they follow the ways of the wicked (Psalms 10.9) who "catches the poor by attracting him."[32] Thus, having indicated their qualities, dispositions and conduct, the author evidently feels justified in defining them as a "vile stock" and an "accursed race," despised by God, by the Christians and by the Moors.[33]

Nevertheless, bearing in mind that the Marranos, like most Christians, identified their race with that of the Prophets, the Apostles and Jesus Christ Himself, the author finds it necessary to explain that the conversos do not really belong to that race. When they returned to Judea from the captivity of Babylon, they married women of Edom, Moab, Ammon and Egypt, and of all the races of Babylon, and this they did also after the destruction of the Second Temple, when they came as captives to various countries and married women of all races. Thus, they became a mixed race, bad and reprobate, quite unlike the race of the tribe of Judah, which was originally good. As Jeremiah said: *argentum reprobum vocate eos.* He called them false silver. The Christians who intermarried with this race did so with honest intentions, believing that this was the purest race on earth *(la mas limpia generación)* that

God had chosen to be His people. They did not realize the vileness of the lineage with which they intermarried.[34]

But the harm caused to the Christians' "flesh" by intermixture with bad racial elements is paralleled by the even greater harm to their spirit caused by the infusion of wrong beliefs and heresies. The heresies of the conversos stem from ancient times; they inherited them from their ancestors, who came to Spain after the destruction of the Second Temple. Accordingly, some of them deny that there is any life beyond what we see between birth and death, while others among them adhere to false opinions held by some ancient Jewish sects. In stressing the Marranos' disbelief in the "other world" and in enumerating the ancient Jewish sects, the author indubitably followed Espina,[35] except that the latter refrained from ascribing the views of those sects to the New Christians. The author of the *Alboraique,* however, who identified the Marranos with the Jews, drew the conclusion implied in Espina's indication.[36]

The author concludes his discussion of the conversos with a reference to their end—or rather to the solution of the Marrano question. "Unless these people are restrained and stopped," he says, "they will cause even greater damage. But, as you can see, they now give them a rebuke which *must be followed by cruel death through the sword.* There should be fulfilled the prophecy of Moses (Deut. 32.42): 'My sword shall devour flesh,' which means: I shall avenge my devotees and harm those who hate me."[37] The author cites the words of St. Isidore: "There will arise in Spain a heresy among the people who crucified Christ. It will last seventy years, and on the seventieth year it will be destroyed by fire and sword."[38] Following the saint's prediction, the author urges that the Marranos be annihilated through "ignited fire" (the proposed inquisition) and "polished sword" (popular massacres). Here again he reminds us of Espina, with whose ideas he begins and ends his tract.

Having thus identified the author as a fanatical anti-converso racist of Espina's and García's brand, we are not surprised at any part of his portrayal of the New Christians, except for one passage in which he differentiates between the northern conversos and the other ones. For unspecified reasons, he decides that, unlike all other New Christians, the northern ones are *natural* (i.e., not forced) converts; and "just as in Old Castile, Burgos, Palencia, Valladolid, Zamora, Salamanca and Leon they will hardly find among these natural converts any heretic, so in the kingdom of Toledo, Murcia, Andalucia and Extremadura you will hardly find among them faithful Christians."[39] It was probably this passage that led Fidel Fita to assume that the author of the *Alboraique* was a Jew[40]—a notion that is not only untenable but incredible for a scholar of Fita's caliber. What we gather from the seemingly odd passage is that the author of the *Alboraique* was, apart from anything else, a clever tactician. His differentiation between the northern conversos and the others may reflect a desire to show impartiality, and thereby strengthen the credibility of the grave accusations he leveled at the great majority of the conversos, who lived in all other parts of the country. It would also soften his verdict of total annihilation, and thereby give it the aura of a just sentence. But the author must have known that the northern conversos were not shielded against his poisonous remarks any more than the southern ones. For what he said about their "mixed," vile race and their natural tendencies (such as their refusal to fight and do hard work) were characteristics applied to *all* converso groups, regardless of their geographical location.

III. Alonso de Oropesa

I

It would be impossible to offer a proper account of the positions taken by the Old Christians toward the conversos without considering in some detail the views of the man who, perhaps more than any other Old Christian in his time, took up the cudgels on behalf of the conversos. He was Alonso de Oropesa, General of the Hieronymite Order in Spain, some of whose activities in connection with the converso problem have been discussed in our survey of Enrique IV's reign.[1] Regrettably, beyond those reported activities, we know little of Oropesa's life. Only a few supplementary data, all more or less of a marginal nature, can be offered to help us form a somewhat fuller or less fragmentary biography.

No information is available on his family[2] or his place and date of birth, or the year of his admission to the Hieronymite Order. He must, however, have been a young man when he began his career as a full-fledged friar in the Hieronymite Convent of Our Lady of Guadalupe[3] after having studied arts and theology in the University of Salamanca.[4] Oropesa was known as a brilliant student and later as a dedicated friar. He was noted for his learning, his piety, his humility and, above all, his zeal for the faith. Before long he became also known as a preacher. Several years after having "professed," he was elected by the friars of Santa Catalina de Talavera as prior of their convent.[5] There, impelled by the requirements of his office, he expanded and improved his preaching,[6] so that he "became such a master in this profession as to be considered one of the most distinguished of his time."[7] His fame spread, and his prestige grew. Several years later, in October 1456, he was elected prior of the Convent of San Bartolomé de Lupiana, one of the oldest convents of the Hieronymites in Spain.

His interest in the converso problem dated from the time of the Toledan rebellion of 1449 and the publication of the *Sentencia-Estatuto*. Oropesa was then still a novice of Guadalupe but already a man of mature judgment, independent thinking and acute observation of men and affairs. In the bloody persecution of the conversos in Toledo, including the denial of their right to office, he saw nothing but the product of criminal passions that fired the ambitions of evil men, and consequently he judged it a terrible outrage that should shock the consciences of all honest Christians. Unable to suppress his thoughts and feelings in the face of the spreading violence and bloodshed, Oropesa decided to express them in public, and it was then that he began to preach.[8] He openly sided with the New Christians and fiercely attacked their opponents and persecutors as foes of Christian morality. The sermons gained Oropesa a following, and the prior of his convent, impressed by his arguments, urged Oropesa to summarize them in writing. It was in response to these urgings that Oropesa began to write his great work: *Lumen ad revelationem gentium et gloria plebis Dei Israel.*[9]

He intended to have the book comprise two parts, one covering the theoretical aspects of the Jewish-converso problem and another dealing with its practical aspects as they manifest themselves in the Spanish kingdoms.[10] Within several years he wrote some forty chapters, about two thirds of the first part, when his duties as prior of the convent of Talavera compelled him to interrupt the work. His election as General of the Hieronymite Order and as prior of San Bartolomé only added to the burden of his administrative duties, and in the coming years Oropesa could not find time to concentrate again on his writing. In fact, he says, the affairs of the order "absorbed both my mind and my spirit to the point that I forgot, as the saying goes, my own name."[11] But the converso problem evidently haunted him, for it required only a single public request that he lend a hand toward its solution to shake him out of his preoccupations and focus his attention upon it.

The event in question occurred in April 1460, when the leadership of the Franciscan order in Spain appealed to the Hieronymites to join them in an effort to establish an inquisition in Castile.[12] It started a chain of rapid reactions that led Oropesa to assume, with royal sanction, the responsibility for the conduct of an inquisition in Toledo, whose task was to inquire into the religious deviations of *all* sections of the city population, Old and New Christians alike. His performance of this task and the ensuing developments were already described in the foregoing. We shall now add to this description only a few points, mostly touching on subsequent occurrences.

After finishing his work as inquisitor in Toledo in April 1462, Oropesa set out to complete the book on the converso problem which he had begun to write twelve years before. He obviously thought that only a major work exposing all the facts relating to that problem could help dissipate the ignorance and malevolence that hampered its solution and poisoned the relations between the Old and New Christians. Oropesa may have started to implement his plan shortly after returning to the Convent of San Bartolomé, but the work progressed slowly, no doubt because of his monastic duties and his other public involvements. Finally, however, on December 24, 1465, Oropesa completed the first part, and shortly thereafter, perhaps early in 1466, he wrote a new introduction to the book, which he dedicated to Archbishop Carrillo.[13]

Oropesa was on friendly terms with Carrillo from the time he discussed with him in Alcalá his plan for the establishment of an inquisition in Toledo.

Undoubtedly, Carrillo was favorably impressed with the results of Oropesa's action as inquisitor, was well acquainted with his views on the converso problem and shared them at least to a large extent. This is why he urged Oropesa repeatedly to complete his unfinished *Lumen,* which was to include, among other things, a summary of his activities and findings in Toledo and the policies he recommended for the entire kingdom with respect to the religious situation.

When Oropesa wrote that introduction to his book, Carrillo was in confrontation with the King. He was the leader of the party that deposed Enrique and enthroned the King's half-brother Alfonso. Oropesa of course was not involved in all this and stayed away from the political conflict. He expressed no opinion of the rebels' actions and formally could be considered neutral.[14] Oropesa felt free therefore to remind Carrillo of the part he played in the completion of the book by the moral support he offered its author, and earnestly to request him that he defend the work against foreseeable attacks by "malevolent men." By this and other derogatory titles, Oropesa referred to the enemies of the conversos who, he knew, would be infuriated by his views and try to avenge themselves by maligning his work.[15] In fact, his appeal to Carrillo shows that Oropesa sensed what was in the making. He evidently suspected that the division of the kingdom and the weakened authority of the central powers would encourage the anti-converso elements to raise a new fury against the New Christians. For obvious reasons Oropesa refrained from signifying, in his address to Carrillo, the political situation as a definite source of further social contamination. Otherwise, however, he did not mince words; and for this reason, his introduction must be seen as a most important addition to the work. It helps us ascertain beyond a shadow of a doubt where Oropesa saw the root of the converso problem and the source of the troubles between the Old and New Christians.

Oropesa died on October 28, 1468, without ever writing the second part.[16] The loss to scholarship is irreplaceable. Had he written that part, we would have had today a clear and detailed picture of the religious condition of the conversos that might have precluded many of the doubts raised in this connection in later times. Nevertheless, Oropesa's first part provides numerous clues for reconstructing his thinking on the converso question in both its theoretical and practical aspects. Therefore, the importance of his work for any inquiry into what happened in Castile in those decades can hardly be overestimated.

It would seem that a work like the *Lumen*—a large-scale study of the converso problem, written by a religious leader of Spain who was the first to be appointed inquisitor in Castile, and as such was supposed to be intimately acquainted with all the aspects of the subject he dealt with, would attract the interest of all concerned, and that its evidence, opinions and conclusions would be eagerly examined by all students in the field. The history of scholarship, however, does not confirm this seemingly logical assumption.

From the standpoint of its impact on the Spanish people, the book was virtually stillborn. Compared to Espina's *Fortalitium Fidei*, which appeared in many editions, was widely discussed and frequently cited, Oropesa's work was never published, never cited and, in all probability, rarely read. Moreover, the fate of the author was similar to that of his work. For almost a century and a half after his death, Oropesa disappeared from the public eye, and he might have been destined for further oblivion had not José de Sigüenza, his fellow Hieronymite, revived his memory in his *Historia de la Orden de San Jerónimo* (1600). In addition to a sketch of Oropesa's life, Sigüenza offered a summary of the views expressed in Oropesa's unpublished work. Sigüenza, in a sense, put Oropesa back on the stage of Spain's history in the 15th century; yet he did not bring him back to life insofar as his true image was concerned. The picture Sigüenza drew of Oropesa both as a thinker and a man of action lacked some of Oropesa's distinctive features, and this may have been one of the reasons why interest in Oropesa remained slight.

It took an additional three and a half centuries before another scholar, also a Hieronymite, produced a work on Alonso de Oropesa based on a new examination of the sources. This was Luis A. Díaz y Díaz, who in 1973 published a sizeable article on Oropesa centering primarily on his work.[17] Six years later, Díaz y Díaz published a Spanish translation of the *Lumen*.[18] The translation is superb, but like all translations, it cannot fully replace the original. For scholarly purposes, the publication of the Latin version is still a desideratum.

II

Díaz y Díaz found Oropesa's work so similar to Alonso de Cartagena's that he came to believe that the *Lumen* and the *Defensorium* may have been "mutually dependent." If such dependence did not exist, "it seems necessary to assume," Díaz believed, "that, in some manner, both the *Lumen* and the *Defensorium* depended on an earlier author."[19] Such an author, Díaz suggested, could be Díaz de Montalvo.[20]

Both propositions are hard to accept. We might consider the possibility of mutual dependence if we had reason to assume that Oropesa and Cartagena consulted each other about the contents of their works and contributed to the formation of each other's views. There is no basis, however, for such an assumption. We have no evidence that such consultations took place and no knowledge whatever of any personal contact between the two authors. Nor is there any reason to assume that the famous Cartagena would consult the novice of Guadalupe on a subject to which he gave much thought throughout his life. Furthermore, chronological considerations incline us to discard Díaz' hypothesis. Cartagena, most probably, *completed* his work c. March 1450,[21] while Oropesa *began* writing the *Lumen* in June or July of that year.[22] Why then not follow the simpler line of thought and conclude that if the *Lumen* resembles the *Defensorium*, the resemblance was due to the influence of Cartagena's work upon that of Oropesa?

Nor can we assume that both authors followed a common literary model. We know of no work on the converso problem that resembles in its plan, contents and form either the *Lumen* or the *Defensorium*. To be sure, both support many principles and doctrines that were upheld by other apologists of the conversos such as Montalvo, Fernán Díaz and Cardinal Torquemada, but this can be explained by the fact that these authors, who were all Christian theologians and jurists, took the same position on many of the issues that formed the themes of their discussions.

That Oropesa had read Cartagena's *Defensorium* before or during the writing of his own work can be gathered from the following similarities. First, both authors, as Díaz pointed out, have a "common aim and purpose"—an aim and purpose which are clearly indicated in the very titles of their books[23]; accordingly, both authors insist that the unity of the Church is the supreme ideal of Christianity, and both seek to prove that by defending the conversos, they protect that cherished ideal. Second, both works discuss the converso problem from the standpoint of a vast historical panorama— from that of the whole history of Christianity and, in fact, of religion in general. And third, both works deal with many aspects, not only of converso, but also of Jewish life in the Spanish kingdoms in the fifteenth century.

But while we should note these common features of the *Lumen* and the *Defensorium*, we cannot share Díaz' opinion that the two works are also distinguished by an "extraordinary parallelism" in the *sources* they use, the *arguments* they employ, and the *points of view* that these arguments reveal.[24] Many (though not all) of the sources they rely on are, to be sure, the same; much less is the identity of the arguments; and frequently different, or even contradictory, are the viewpoints expressed by the authors. Indeed, had there been a complete parallelism in all these matters—had the works differed, as Díaz suggested, only in the "organization and systematization" of their materials[25]—we could scarcely explain why Oropesa deemed it necessary to write his book at all.

But the contents of the *Lumen* raise another problem which, we believe, ought to be answered before we can perceive the drift of the work and its author's true motives. Structurally, the *Lumen*, a large-scale composition comprising about 250,000 words, is not divided into "books" or "sections," but flows straight on, through fifty-one chapters, to its appointed end. Yet the reader will notice that the work is made up of two major parts of roughly equal length. While the first part deals primarily with the Jewish and the second with the converso problem, the connection between them is rather loose, and the entire first part appears non-essential for the subsequent discussion of the main subject. Why then did Oropesa write that "introduction," which seems as superfluous as it is copious, or at least does not seem to contribute materially to the understanding of his position on the converso problem?

In the following survey of Oropesa's work the reader may find an answer to this query. He may also find an adequate summary of the differences between the views of Oropesa and Cartagena who, in more ways than one, shared the position of other protagonists of the conversos. Above all, he will find a presentation of what constituted, according to Oropesa, the essentials of the converso problem and of the measures he regarded as indispensable for its alleviation and, ultimately, for its solution.

III

According to Oropesa, a single faith had inspired all believers since the Fall of Man, and this was the faith in Jesus Christ, the mediator between God and man. Without this faith ("in some manner" or degree) nobody could ever have saved himself,[26] just as nobody will be in a position to do so at any time in the future. Yet the prerequisite for salvation has never been absent, since groups of true believers existed in *all* periods, and from this we may also "analogically conclude that there has always been one universal Church that embraced all the faithful, the ancient and the new." Its name was the Church of Saints.[27]

This was fundamentally an Augustinian concept, which Oropesa accepted with some modifications. But he seems to have abandoned Augustine's view that (a) the faithful represented a carnal succession (from Seth to Abraham and then to Christ), and (b) that the Saints—i.e., the members of the Church—all shared a high standard of beliefs. Oropesa compared the Church to a vineyard that was planted gradually, little by little, and required in all the stages of its growth the care and attendance of a proper vinedresser.[28] The vinedresser of the Church was of course God, and it was He who tended it from its earliest time, when the faith of its few followers was limited to bare essentials, until its following encompassed large masses, whose faith was characterized by its fullness and perfection."[29] Accordingly, Oropesa saw the history of religion as consisting of three major periods: the period of the Natural Law, that of the Written Law, and finally, that of the Law of Grace.

Already at this point we can see a clear divergence of the views of Oropesa and those of Cartagena. For Cartagena identified the beginning of the faith—or at least its rise as a religious *movement*—with the appearance of Abraham on the scene of history. According to him, there were, prior to Abraham, only isolated individuals (such as Noah or Job) who were accepted by God for their right way of life, but there were no groups of followers and no church that carried the message of the faith in God. Such a following and such a church were formed by the Patriarchs, who raised the banner of the belief in God and, moreover, prepared, together with their offspring, the way of man's salvation through Christ.[30] To Abraham, therefore, credit is due that no man before or after him deserved. After long ages of general faithlessness, he opened the Age of Faith.

It is obvious that according to Oropesa's view of the history of religion (as outlined above), no such place could be assigned to Abraham or, for that matter, to any of the Patriarchs. According to Oropesa, both Abraham and his descendants lived in the period of Natural Law, a period which was not entirely faithless, but one in which the Church lived and grew. Abraham, like the other two patriarchs who followed him, were, to be sure, outstanding men, high above the common believers of their time in their religious devotion and comprehension. But besides them, there were in those days other men who were illumined by God with *a special knowledge of the faith*,[31] so that also in this important respect the Patriarchs were not unique. In any case, according to Oropesa, Abraham did not open the Age of Faith, or even a special *era* in that age (as was believed, for instance, by Augustine[32]). Consequently, his achievement did not constitute a turning point in the religious history of man. As Oropesa saw it, the first turning point in that history was marked by the giving of the Law; and the giving of the Law was not an act of man but purely an act of God.

In describing the growth of religious consciousness, Oropesa found it necessary to point out that the faithful in the various periods of the faith, although they all had some common beliefs, differed in the *number* of the beliefs they shared, and they also differed in the *clarity* of their perceptions and the *profundity* of the truths that they grasped and upheld. Thus, in the period of the Natural Law, most of the faithful believed in two principles—the existence of God and the workings of His Providence[33]—but they did not come to know the other principles, although the latter are implicit in the former, just as many truths of science are implicit in their axioms and other major propositions. We can understand the reasons for the partial obscurity that prevailed among the first believers. In science the implied truths may appear to our mind "through many deductions and a great deal of labor," while the truths implied in the first principles of faith can be revealed to man only through divine inspiration.[34] And thus, in the first period—that of Natural Law—only few individuals earned that inspiration and thereby gained knowledge of the implied truths.[35] In the period of the Written Law, that condition changed. Some of the implied truths were clearly revealed to all, while the others were also half revealed to many through numerous prophetic hints and allusions.[36] Finally, when the Law of Grace was proclaimed, all the truths of the faith were explicitly declared, and thus became known—or at least *could* be made known—not only to a few select individuals, or to a large group of saints, or even to a whole people, but to all the members of the human race.[37]

Insofar as the history of the faith is concerned, therefore, the Written Law occupied a midway position in the process of revelation of the divine truths to man. Its main value was in the method it employed to acquaint man gradually with the higher truths, thereby enabling him to grasp them fully when they were made public by Christ. Thus, though superior to the Law of Nature in the clarity, scope and level of its teachings, the Written Law was, in many respects, inferior to the Law of Grace, which replaced it.

Oropesa devotes five full chapters to what he calls the "imperfections" of the Old Law[38] compared to the New Law proclaimed by Christ. Thus, it was "imperfect" in its teachings about God (since it only *hinted* at the mysteries of His essence), as well as in its teachings about Providence (as it did not speak explicitly of the prerequisites of Redemption). Oropesa also censures the Law's system of worship, which was based on the old forms of sacrifice—forms which were not only improper in themselves, but virtually revolt our moral feelings. Oropesa then goes on to show various flaws of the Law in its three major fields: ceremonial, moral and judicial. He sees a great fault in the *summum bonum* (i.e., the attainment of material benefits) that the Law posited as man's final end, and an even greater shortcoming in its failure to be guided in all its rulings by the principle of Love. In consequence, many of its laws are too harsh, while others are plainly so wrong and immoral as to clash directly with the Law of Grace. Oropesa recognized that all these "imperfections" were unavoidable at the time when the Law was in force and were all designed for a good purpose. The Law had to educate a primitive people which was incapable of grasping the higher truths, and thus it had to suit that people's understanding, and also to make concessions to its passions.[39] It was not a law for man in a high religious state, and therefore, once its purpose was accomplished, it had to be abolished, as it actually was.[40] Oropesa's view of the Law is summarized in such expressions as "that crude and antiquated Mosaic Law" or "that coarse Old Testament" of which the Law was part.[41]

This was not the view of Cartagena. It is unthinkable that he could bring himself to speak of the Law, and the Old Testament in general, in such disparaging terms as those used by Oropesa, even though he too believed that the Old Law was "imperfect" in certain aspects, or rather from certain points of view. From these viewpoints, he agreed, one could see in it most of the "limitations" indicated by Oropesa, but he would sternly reject the under-tone of censure which so often accompanied Oropesa's assessment. Instead, he would remind us that the Old Law embodies the *wisdom of God*, which is above all reproach,[42] and that whatever it ordered was not merely necessary, but also moral in the highest degree. Moreover, he would, unlike Oropesa, stress the elements common to both laws (the Old and the New) rather than those in which they differ, and, above all, emphasize that what they have in common indicates, essentially, their identity. Accordingly, Cartagena says of the Old Law: "Here we do not speak of one of the laws which were born by the authority of men, such as those of Lycurgus, Phoroneus, or Numa Pompilius; here we speak of the divine law, which was not given to the gentiles before the advent of Christ."[43] And to show that Christ indeed gave the gentiles the same law God had given to the Jews, he presents Jesus' words in Matthew 5.17 that he "came not to destroy the Law but to fulfill it."[44] To be sure, he also offered Augustine's comment, making clear that what Jesus "fulfilled" was the Law in its *true* and *full* meaning (the meaning which the Old Law often covered with symbols),[45] but from this comment, too, he drew support for his view of the essential identity of the two laws. Thus, he emphasized that the Old Law prefigured what the new one fulfilled: it sometimes spoke tersely where the New one elaborated and cryptically where the New one was lucid, but actually it was the same law, given by the same God, having the same aim, and teaching the same things.[46]

How deeply Cartagena was imbued with the conviction of the essential unity of two laws, and how far he was removed from such a view as Oropesa's of the partial immorality of the Old Law, is evidenced by his discussion of the Old Law's moral principles. Granted, he said, that the Old Law did not shun the use of fear and the threat of punishment to "restrain hearts inclined to vice,"[47] but this does not mean that it ignored the law of Love, which, according to the Apostle, is the "bond of perfection."[48] In fact, he says, "under the Old Law, the ancient fathers observed, in many things, the Law of the Gospel,"[49] which meant that they followed the highest moral code that ordered us to love, not only our friends, but also our enemies and persecutors. To prove this he cites Origen's comments on Numbers 16: 20–23 which deal with Moses' and Aaron's prayer for their enemies, and concludes with Origen's far-reaching statement: "The truth of the Gospel, then, is found in the Law, and the Gospel is based on the foundation of the Law."[50] Then he adds that in other matters, too—matters that are generally hard to understand—it offered those capable of deeper reflection clear knowledge of the implied truths. "For not only did it show that God exists, but also the Trinity of the divine persons, as well as the Incarnation of the Word of the Lord. Also the question of the world's creation which Aristotle left undecided, and apart from this, many doctrines and observances of religious duties, and also the future advent of Christ, and the perfection which is to come in Him and with Him, all of which human reason could not attain, are explained in the Law correctly and lucidly. Hence the prophet says: "Thy word is a lamp unto my feet and a light unto my path."[51]

This verse from Psalms, which Cartagena cited here in support of his view of the Mosaic Law, shows perhaps more than anything else how far removed was his position on the Old Law from that of Oropesa.

IV

Oropesa's view of the Written Law was related, as we have seen, to his view of its recipients—i.e., to their moral and intellectual deficiencies, which rendered them incapable of adopting a higher law suitable to a nobler way of life. But this evaluation of the ancient Jews, in which he followed established opinion, represents only a small part of his reflections on the Jewish people. As we shall see, his idea of the Jews comprises various conflicting elements, and is far too complex to be reduced to a formula that would represent them all.

From the standpoint of man's religious development, Jewish history was divided, according to Oropesa, into two large periods—the same two periods into which the history of all mankind was divided *after the giving of the Law*— the *pre*-Christian and the *Christian*. But judged by its impact upon the lives of the people, the first of these periods—i.e., the *pre*-Christian—was of immeasurably greater significance to the Jews than to all other nations. For while to most members of the human race that period was a continuation of their past, an extension of their era of Natural Law as well as their former way of life, it was to the Jews the Age of the Law, a law that was novel and an age whose beginning coincided with the start of their national life. What is more, that beginning was marked by an act—a *divine* act relating only to them: the Election of the Jews as the People of God; and it implied a distinction which both Jews and Christians viewed as a prerequisite to the giving of the Law.

Any presentation of Oropesa's view of the Jews, as well as their moral and historical course, must therefore begin with his view of the Election—that unique event that seems to indicate at once the birth and the destiny of the Jewish people. What was it that made the Jews, of all nations, to be chosen to that highest standing and function? This was of course the first question Oropesa felt impelled to answer.

That the Election of the Jews as the People of God was based on no merit of the Chosen People was a view expressed both in the Law and the Prophets,[52] and as such it was upheld by some foremost Jewish thinkers, as well as by all Christians since the days of Paul.[53] The old biblical statements, however, attributed the Election to the merits of the Patriarchs, who earned it as a reward, and to God's faithfulness to the assurances he gave the Patriarchs and, hence, to His will to carry them out.[54] But Christian doctrine ignored this biblical explanation, and rejected the assumption that the merits of the Patriarchs played any part in determining the Election. Consequently, the Election, as viewed by Christian thinkers, was a pure act of divine grace.

Oropesa accepted this doctrine and also sharpened some of the arguments that had been offered in its behalf. Not only does he cite the Bible as evidence that the Election was not based on the *people*'s merit[55] but, following St. Thomas, he also dissociates the Election from any virtue of the Patriarchs.[56] In fact, even God's love for Abraham himself was not based on merits, as Augustine has shown[57]; and thus the love, the promise, and the Election itself stemmed from no consideration of merit; they were "free and gratuitous," says Oropesa[58]—or, in other words, pure acts of grace.

But Oropesa also expressed another idea which touched directly on the question of the Election and which should be given special attention. According to the prevalent view of the Election, the Jewish *people* was chosen by God to be His from *among all the peoples of the world*. This was the view propounded in the Bible, directly and indirectly, in many places[59]; and taken by themselves, such statements would suggest that the Jewish *people* was distinguished by some qualities that earned it that divine choice. Oropesa, however, struck at the heart of this notion by claiming that the Jews could *not* have been chosen from among all other peoples for the simple reason that prior to the Election, they did not constitute a people.

The idea was not his. It was borrowed from Augustine, who based it on a certain assertion of Cicero concerning the nature and rise of peoples. In Cicero's opinion, as set forth in his *Republic,* a people is not just an aggregate of individuals; it is an association based on a common moral sense which is embodied in a just order.[60] But a truly just order, Augustine explained, cannot be conceived without a just legislation.[61] And from this Oropesa could readily conclude that prior to the giving of the Mosaic Law, the Jews were a "multitude unworthy of the name 'people.' "[62] Their formation as a people followed the giving of the Law, and not vice versa, as Thomas thought. This was of course a "revolutionary" conclusion; and it could hardly be detached from Oropesa's thinking about the reasons for the Election.

For if the Jews were not a "people" prior to the Election, which must have preceded the giving of the Law, they evidently did not have any "national" qualities that could make them a subject of national distinction. They were just a group of men held together by descent, a kind of human herd bound by natural relationships, natural urges, instincts and interests. That such a herd should be "chosen" as God's people for its *merits*—i.e., its high moral achievements—appears not only far-fetched but untenable.

If we now turn to Alonso de Cartagena, we can see that he, too, like so many before him, accepted the doctrine of Election by Grace. In view of the support accorded this doctrine in Christian theological literature, he obviously had no choice in the matter. Nevertheless, he tried to weaken its foundations by cautiously hinting that the contrary view (i.e., of Election by merit) could not be utterly discounted. Thus, when he referred to Malachi's statement that God loved Jacob and hated Esau (Mal. 1. 2–3) and to Paul's words in Romans (9.11) that this attitude of God existed even before the brothers were born (and, hence, before they did good or evil), he also cites the Apostle's query and answer: "Is there unrighteousness with God? Forbid it!" which seem to contradict in unequivocal terms the idea of reward for no merit. Then, striking further at the roots of the notion that the Election resulted solely from Grace, Cartagena adds:

> The Holy doctors [of the Church] said that the love and hate of God originated in his foreknowledge of future events, *discerning by his judgment the future works of people,* for although God loved all the things he had created, he loved especially those that are enemies of vice, and hated those who are lovers of vice. Hence, Augustine, commenting on [the verse] "Therefore has He mercy on whom He will have mercy, and whom He will, he hardens" (Romans. 9.18), says: "But *this will of God cannot be unjust for it comes from hidden merits*" . . . whence, "I sanctified thee in the womb" (Jer. 1.5), and "I loved Jacob, and hated Esau."[63]

Cartagena realized of course that by citing these words of the "holy doctors" and of Augustine he deviated from the dominant Christian view on the subject. Therefore he hastened to correct himself by saying:

> I have not inserted these words as if to say that the merits of someone would be the cause of divine predestination; and in this too I follow the words of Augustine who, as the author of the *Sententiae* said,[64] changed his position—first, because if grace is granted for merits, it seems, in a way, to be emptied, and second, because nothing can precede the eternity of the divine will, and therefore it does not appear sound to indicate a cause as something that preceded the will of God.[65]

This, however, was not a complete retreat. For following this "explanation," Cartagena comes back to say that we may nevertheless "conjecture that the profound wisdom of God has ordained [everything] for a certain end, and when we designate something as the cause, we merely think that such gifts of God did not proceed without any reason." Yet if so, who can say that what we call the "reason" was not the merit foreseen by God? Cartagena does not say this explicitly, of course. But he seems to be leading us to this conclusion when he returns to the issue under discussion with the words: "Therefore, we should not think that that uniqueness of love [shown by God to Israel through the Election] came about without a reason. For, as Job said: 'Nothing on earth occurs without a reason.' "[66]

There can be no doubt that these speculative manipulations were aimed at establishing a foothold for the belief that the Election of the Jews as the People of God was not without relation to their merits. Oropesa, of course, would have none of this. And thus, on the Election as on the Law, the two thinkers differed—if not in their conclusions, at least in their attitudes toward the Jewish heritage and in their basic conceptions of the part the Jews played in the religious history of mankind.

V

Having clarified Oropesa's view of the Election and where it differed from that of Cartagena, we can now move to examine his view of the Jews, their conduct and their life in the *pre*-Christian era. This task, however, which seems easy at the outset, soon appears to be beset with difficulties. For Oropesa starts with a series of assertions which together form an evaluation of the Jews, and this evaluation is opposed to the views he expressed in the later part of his discussion.

The main contradictory statements we refer to appear in chapters 9–13.[67] Here we are informed that prior to Christ's coming, the Jews were the "only *true* people of God" and, further, that they *"served and obeyed only the true God,"* while all the other groups of men served idols.[68] Here we also hear that the Jews in those times constituted the only "authentic republic,"[69] since a true republic must be based on just laws and only the Jews, who received the divine Law, possessed equitable laws to guide them. Further, we hear that "mother synagogue" in those days "represented the image of the City of God, just as the Militant Holy Mother Church represents the Triumphant in its glory."[70] Accordingly, we are not surprised to hear that the Jews in that age—i.e., the *pre*-Christian era—were "the people, the republic and the Church of the faithful" at one and the same time.[71]

Moreover, the impact of this highly moral people was not limited to its own way of life. Thanks to their Law, priesthood and conduct, the Jews formed a "divine mirror" for the gentiles[72]; and indeed many gentiles, by divine inspiration, or "under the influence of their converse with the Jews," joined the divine cult and followed the Law, or became such upright and faithful persons that, although they remained under the Law of Nature, they were accepted by God and could be saved. And Oropesa concludes his assessment of the Jews by saying: "Thus was prepared by means of that Jewish people the salvation of all the gentiles," or, to use here another phrase of his, "the redemption of the whole human race."[73]

These were of course words of high praise that could match those of Juan de Torquemada. But as if he forgot his own words, or as if it mattered little or nothing, Oropesa, in his later discussion of the Jews, gives us quite a different appraisal—indeed, so different that it can remind us of the former only by its sharp contrast. For here we see him follow in the footsteps of Chrysostom, the most rabid Jew hater of the Church fathers, and present the latter's judgments of the Jews as the last word on the subject. Accordingly, the Jews in the *pre*-Christian era are now described by Oropesa as Chrysostom had portrayed them—namely, as a people that committed heinous crimes, practiced the most abominable profanities and showed flagrant disobedience to God. "They have worshiped idols, persecuted the prophets, murmured against God, risen against Moses, and sacrificed their sons and daughters to demons."[74] Indeed, asks Oropesa in Chrysostom's words: "What tragedy, what type of evil have they [i.e., the Jews] not surpassed in their lewdness? ... Have not the Prophets devoted to them all those long reproachful discourses?"[75] Yes, answers Oropesa, the Prophets denounced them, and God punished them, sometimes so severely that they almost broke under the whip, but only to make them come back to Him repeatedly, not wholeheartedly and not for long. For "neither by the influence of the oracles of the Prophets, nor by the harshness of the punishments they endured could they separate themselves from the idolatry of the gentiles, or maintain themselves in some manner in the observance of the Law. They have continually abandoned God and returned to the rites of the gentiles."[76]

There seems to be no way of coordinating this view of the Jewish people as compulsive criminals with his view of them as the People of God and the bearers of the divine truths to mankind. Oropesa, of course, does not fail to offer reasons for that "foul and infamous" conduct of the Jews, and these reasons, as we shall see, only deepen the gulf between his two assessments. Indeed, further consideration will leave us with no doubt as to what his dominant view was. It was the second, the negative, the condemnatory one, and it applied to the Jewish people *as a whole* and to the *general* course of its behavior.[77]

It need scarcely be said that this view of Oropesa was quite unlike that of Alonso de Cartagena. The latter would of course readily admit that Israel had repeatedly retreated from God and often deviated from the path of righteousness; but despite these retreats and deviations, he believed, the impact of the Law and the Prophets was decisive in shaping its character and way of life, so that Israel became a unique people, superior to all other peoples in the world. Thus Cartagena argued that when Isaiah says: "Arise, Jerusalem, for thy light has come," he indicated that "the light had belonged to the Jerusalemites, that it came *to* them from the Law which was given *them* and from the fulfillment of the Law which took place *within* them."[78] Granted, said Cartagena, that the prophets reproached Israel and sometimes even rebuked it sharply, but they also praised it in glowing terms, and *"praise has never ceased."*[79] Thus said Moses: "For the Lord's portion is his People, Jacob is the lot of his inheritance" (Deut. 32.9). And in another place: "Who is like unto thee, O people saved by the Lord, the shield of thy help, and the sword of thy excellency?" (Deut. 33.29). In such eulogies of the Jews Cartagena sees proof that "the vices of the bad could not harm the virtues of the righteous," and that neither will those vices be able to prevent the ultimate salvation of *"all the seed* of Israel." And while he admits that in many redemption prophecies "Israel" signified the "faithful" of all origins, he rejects the negation of the literal sense in which he sees the "root" of all other explanations—and the literal sense, he repeatedly asserts, refers to Israel the *people*. In fact, he sees in that symbolic meaning further proof of his basic thesis, for he does not hesitate to accept the implied assumption that "so great was the Israelitic purity (i.e., the purity of the Jews in the *pre*-Christian era) that *by this name of the people of Israel all the faithful were designated.*"[80]

VI

There is more to be said on Oropesa's view of the Jews in the *pre*-Christian era and where it differed from that of Cartagena. But the essential things have been said, we believe; and thus we shall now turn to Oropesa's thoughts on the Jews in the *Christian* era, beginning with their attitude toward the Passion—the event which stood on the threshold of the new age and which, according to Christian belief, served as the divide between man's past and future.

Were "the Jews" involved in Christ's crucifixion? Were they responsible for it in any degree? And if so, in what manner—and why? We have seen that until the thirteenth century, the opinions of Christian theologians on this question oscillated between two leading views: one that absolved the Jews of full guilt, since they were ignorant of Jesus' messiahship and divinity, and another that freed them from intentional deicide, since they did not know that Jesus was God, but not from the crime of killing the Messiah, who was recognized by many Jews. It was only in the thirteenth century, as we have noted, that the view of the Jews' full responsibility for the Passion began to dominate Christian thinking. Thus it was assumed that the Jews (or their leaders) murdered Jesus out of sheer malice, though they knew full well who and what He was—that is, both the Messiah and the Son of God.[81] There were, to be sure, deviations from this view, as well as variations of the main thesis, but taken as a whole Christian opinion veered toward the gravest incrimination of the Jews. What was Oropesa's stand on this question?

Oropesa ignores Cartagena's claim that only a few Jews favored the Crucifixion, while the rest of them were either unaware of it, or, if aware, opposed or bemoaned it. Insisting that the Jewish people as a whole was, in a way, responsible for the Passion, he seeks to prove this by statements from Scripture, including the one in which Peter, the Apostle, while addressing Jews, said of Jesus' crucifixion: "... whom *you* have delivered and denied in Pilate's presence, when Pilate was determined to let him go."[82] Curiously, he failed to cite in this connection Paul's more explicit and more damaging testimony—namely, that "the Jews killed our Lord Jesus"[83]—perhaps because he thought it to be too extreme. After all, the Jews did not "kill" Jesus; they only "delivered" and "denied" Him, as Peter said.

Similarly, he discards Cartagena's argument that none of the Jews, including their leaders, had any knowledge of Jesus' divinity—a fact that occasioned Jesus' own statement: "Forgive them, O Father, for they know not what they do."[84] He simply rejects the appeal to ignorance as an extenuating circumstance that may justify clemency, forgiveness, or mere reduction of punishment. His references to the Passion leave us with the impression that the entire Jewish people committed the deicide—knowingly, intentionally and even wantonly, and hence, it must bear full responsibility for the hideous crime.[85]

But this raises a most difficult question which appears *prima facie* inscrutable. If ignorance is excluded as a reason for the deicide, what *was* the reason? After all, we deal here with the most horrid crime ever perpetrated in the history of man, and the perpetrator was, according to Oropesa, no other than the people chosen by God. What could lead a people, so preferred and blessed, to commit such an atrocity?

The answer was again given by Chrysostom, Oropesa's mentor on most "Jewish" matters. Chrysostom related the Jews' crime against Jesus to their whole course of conduct under the Written Law. The deicide, as he saw it, was merely an extension of the numerous crimes they had committed before—i.e., "in the *pre*-Christian era—and it was also the crime by which they reached the climax of their continuous doing of evil. As Paul said of the Jews when he spoke to the Thessalonians: "All this time they have been making up the full measure of their guilt, and now retribution has overtaken them for good and all."[86]

This view of the Jews as incessant criminals whose crimes were steadily rising to their peak puts the deicide in line with their record—or rather their alleged immoral record—and brings it closer to our understanding. We are still, however, baffled by the record itself. What was the cause of that attachment to evil that had characterized the Jews since antiquity? Chrysostom had no doubt about it; nor had Oropesa.

It was the influence of the Ancient Serpent, he says, by whom the Jews have always been fascinated and who frequently managed to draw them to his side by his offers and persuasions.[87] Thus, the Ancient Serpent, the Devil, pulled them repeatedly away from God's path, to be recurringly saved from his clutches only by God's infinite mercy. Finally, however, when they committed the deicide, God removed his grace from the Jews. He left them to pursue their natural intents, and thus they fell completely under the Devil's sway, so that their evil ran its full circle. The Sons of Saints became Sons of Satans, and the People of God became the People of the Devil in the true and full sense of the word.

But the removal of God's grace did not mean only that God had abandoned the Jews. It was also accompanied with a frightful punishment—"a perpetual captivity" and a "wretched" desolation that was to "last forever without amnesty."[88] Considering the rule that "adversity discovers virtue"—a rule that was recognized by the Prophets and the Psalmists, as well as by so many saints of later times—one might assume that their harsh captivity would lead the Jewish culprits to regret their sins, or at least prevent them from doing further wrong. But nothing of the kind happened to the Jews. They neither repented nor stopped doing evil. In fact, they did the very opposite. They strengthened their resolve to go on sinning and stiffened their resistance to moral behavior.

According to Oropesa, "the Jews of today are more obnoxious and unfaithful than they have ever been, and they are also worse than the gentile idolaters who to this day worship images."[89] To be sure, the Jews boast of their faithfulness to the Law and their observance of all its precepts. But this is part of their problem. Like demented people, they flee salvation. They violated the Law when they had to observe it, and now, when it is abolished, they seek to fulfill it.[90] Today, as in the past, their conduct reflects their obstinacy, their blindness, and their rebelliousness against God.

What is the reason for this strange derangement which makes the Jews persist in their lust of evil under the most adverse conditions? Oropesa again points to the cause by which he explained their most tantalizing crime—i.e., the crime of the Deicide: "The Ancient Serpent drags them now to condemnation, hardening them in their infidelity, with the same cunning he used to push them to perdition when he drew them in a thousand manners to idolatry, and drove them away from the very laws which now they profess to observe with such zeal."[91]

So sure is Oropesa of the Devil's influence on the Jews, and consequently of their incurable blindness, that he has no doubt that "if Christ had reappeared and preached to them today, they would not have believed Him, but ambushed and crucified Him, precisely as their fathers did" when he addressed *them*.[92] Now that they cannot harm Christ, however, they merely "bark against Him like the mad dogs they are" and persecute His followers.[93]

In describing the Jewish persecution of the faithful, Oropesa does not mention such alleged atrocities as the killing of Christian children and the like, the kind of which we find in such abundance in Espina. As he saw it, what the Jews were really after was not the physical annihilation of Christians, but the spiritual destruction of Christianity. And at this, he believed, they ceaselessly labor. He realized that the Jews "cannot and dare not convert the faithful to their infidelity,"[94] but they can, he was sure, corrupt the Christians' morals, pervert their beliefs, and contaminate their faith. Thus, in his opinion, of all the enemies of Christendom—including the heretics, the schismatics and the Saracens—the Jews were by far the most dangerous.

But if so, one must ask: Why the toleration? Why does Christendom suffer them in its midst? Why does it not fight them with fire and sword as it fights the Saracens when "they invade our lands?" Why does it not treat them as it treats the heretics, whom it exterminates when they refuse to abjure? Oropesa offers a double answer, or an answer which is partly moral-religious and partly "practical"-utilitarian. On the moral part we shall touch later on. Here we shall refer to the "practical" part, which related to the great majority of the Jews. Oropesa took it from Augustine.

Augustine's explanation was not only known but also accepted by all Christian theologians, who did not find it in any way faulty or distasteful from an ethical standpoint. The Church does not kill the Jews, argued Augustine (in a famous passage in his *City of God*), for the following reason only: They are more useful to it alive than dead. As faithful guardians of the prophetic works, and at the same time as enemies of the Christians, they prevent the rise of the possible accusation that the Christians falsified the prophecies about Christ. Thus, by attesting the verity of the texts, which they fail to understand and commonly misinterpret, the Jews testify to the verity of Christ and the truth of His redemption. The upshot of this is that it is in the *interest* of Christianity that the Jews be present in every part of the world, including of course all the countries of Christendom.[95] Yet this means that Christians are strictly forbidden not only to kill the Jews but also to expel them, as well as to impose on them such hardships and coercions that would deny them the chance to live. And so Oropesa concludes: "We can neither persecute them nor exterminate them nor drag them by force to the faith. We have to suffer them among us."[96]

This then is the problem facing the Church: it must keep in its domains these implacable foes, who "look with viperish yearning to the heel of the faithful,"[97] and at the same time take every possible precaution against their lethal attacks. Oropesa knows no better precaution than the system of protection provided by the Church. He enumerates all the restrictive laws enacted by the Church against the Jews throughout the centuries, and he repeatedly reproaches the princes and the prelates for violating these restrictions by employing Jews and treating them amicably and honorably. Not only should Christians not socialize with Jews; they "should constantly avoid them with outmost care." And Oropesa's recommendation to all Christians is that they steadily refrain from speaking to Jews, or speak to them as little as possible; but even better than minimizing converse with the Jews is to "detest and abhor them like the pest."[98]

How the Jews can survive in a society from which they are almost totally ostracized, Oropesa did not say. Nor does he explain why he failed to define the treatment he recommended for the Jews as "persecution," or how he could view the repressive measures imposed upon the Jews by the Church's legislation as "humane" and indicative of Christian compassion. But all these contradictions are resolved when we recall that Oropesa was a man of his time, an ardent believer in the teachings of the Church, its moral code, and its policy toward the Jews. From all this he concluded, by logical deduction, that even the mere presence of Jews in Christendom was proof of Christian toleration and forbearance. We can understand this better when we cite some expressions by which he characterized the Jews or summarized his view of them: "mad dogs," "a race of vipers," "virulent serpents," creatures whose "souls are inhabited by demons," "servants of Satan" and "sons of the Devil."[99] What more can be expected of Christians in their dealings with so evil and dangerous a people?

VII

It need scarcely be said that these conceptions of the Jews in the second half of their historical existence—that is, in the Christian era—were far removed from those upheld by Cartagena. To be sure, Cartagena's view of the Jews in that era was likewise most critical, harsh and derogatory, but it was not as negative as that of Oropesa, and, in fact, it was mixed with positive elements, as we shall presently see.

We have already shown how Cartagena tried to exculpate the Jews (save a small minority) from the crime of the Passion and how he differed in this matter from Oropesa. But this does not mean that he thought the Jews blameless in their age-old, relentless quarrel with Christianity. As he saw it, the Jews, in their conduct with Christ, incurred heavy guilt that had to be expiated; but their crime—at least, the crime of their majority—was not the Crucifixion, but the denial of Christ, their rejection of the Savior and His message of salvation. To be sure, here too he tried to minimize the blame by stressing their ignorance of Jesus' divinity—an ignorance that could mitigate *their* guilt just as it diminished that of the gentiles. Nevertheless, he believed that in this particular respect—namely, their rejection of Christ—the Jews could not be compared to the gentiles. They, as the people of the Patriarchs and the Prophets, should have known better.

And precisely because Alonso de Cartagena so valued the Jews of the *pre-*

Christian era, he could not see their rejection of Christ and Christianity the way it was seen by Oropesa—as the culmination of a criminal trend that marked their life from its inception. Rather did he view their life under Christianity as a period of fall and decline—a precipitous fall from a high moral level and a steady decline ever since. The "fall" took place during Christ's earthly presence, with the Jews' disparaging treatment of Jesus, and the decline was expressed in the intellectual deterioration that paralleled their deepening social misery. Cartagena regarded the long captivity of the Jews as a gruesome punishment, political and social, but still worse in his eyes was the spiritual punishment that this condition entailed. For while through their long exile and dispersion the Jews lost most civil and natural nobilities, they lost, through their denial of Christ, the theological nobility by which they were distinguished. Moreover, they became *religiously* "slaves" (which devotion to the Law in the Christian era means), while in the "civil" or "natural" sense, they were never reduced to real slavery.

We do not really know what Cartagena's view was of the various restrictions placed upon the Jews, although we may assume that, like Oropesa, he supported the Church's formal policy. In any case, despite all those numerous restrictions, he saw the Jews in Christendom as *free men* from both the "civil" and "natural" standpoints, and unlike Oropesa, he was not morally incensed, nor did he fret or show discontent, when he spoke of the Jews who counseled Christian rulers or brought legal suits against their Christian lords.[100] Evidently, he considered it quite normal for the Jews, not only to retain their basic freedoms but also to exercise these freedoms in public. And what we may further conclude from the above is that he did not see the Jews as "satanic" beings who ought to be avoided by the Christians like a plague. Jews who speak freely to Christians, he believed, presented no danger to Christianity, while free talk of Christians with Jews could pose danger only to their Judaic faith. Experience has confirmed this in recent decades, and this was also part of his converso credo, which stood for a converso-Jewish dialogue aimed at converting the Jews to Christianity.

But there was something else in which the bishop of Burgos differed from the Hieronymite leader. Cartagena did not see in the condition of the Jews merely a result of the obstinate Jewish "blindness," but the latest stage in a "chain reaction" that brought about that blindness itself. What, however, started that strange "chain"? Already Paul had pondered the great "mystery" that "part of Israel was struck with blindness," but he left that mystery, in the main, unresolved. Oropesa and Cartagena, however, proposed answers. Oropesa attributed the Jewish attitude toward Christ to the influence of the Devil; Cartagena, to the historic design of God.

For according to this design, as Cartagena perceived it, the "fall" of the Jews was not a total fall and the "decline" was not endless and total either.

Thus, whenever he referred to the *beginning* of the Christian era, he stressed what the Apostles and other Jews did for the initiation and expansion of Christianity; and who can associate that activity with "falling"? And when he thought of the Jews in times to come, he foresaw them playing a leading role in the Church, both militant and triumphant. And who can regard this as a "decline"? Thus, when one considers his overall view of the Jewish people in the Christian era, one must conclude that he saw the Jews, despite their partial fall and earlier decline, as destined to rise to an even higher peak than the one they had reached under the Written Law. Obviously, to Cartagena, such a destiny was a fitting—indeed, the only fitting end for the history of the people that inaugurated, under Abraham, the Age of Faith in mankind and was elected as the People of God.

VIII

Our survey of the first part of the *Lumen* shows that Oropesa was not precisely a mouthpiece of Cartagenian ideas about the Jews, but followed his own line of thought, which occasionally coincided, but more often clashed, with that of Alonso de Cartagena. In fact, the antagonisms between the two thinkers were not only more numerous, but also more pronounced than the similarities we can discern in their evaluations of the Jews in both the *pre*-Christian and *Christian* era.

Yet by clarifying Oropesa's view of the Jews and wherein it differed from that of Cartagena, we have not yet answered the basic question that inevitably emerges from our exposition. For the *Lumen* was supposed to be devoted to a discussion of the converso, not the Jewish, problem, and the first part of the work, which deals with the Jews, should therefore be regarded as preliminary to its remainder, which deals with the conversos. Yet our survey of Oropesa's thinking of the Jews has shown no relationship to the converso situation. And this brings us back to our original query: Why this elaborate treatise on the Jews? Do we have here simply a structural flaw, a case of an author carried away by his thoughts on a subordinate, though related, subject? Or was it part of an elaborate plan which Oropesa conceived for his work from the outset? We ought to bear these questions in mind when we come to discuss Oropesa's position toward the converso problem in Spain.

IX

Oropesa's views on the Spanish conversos can be better understood if we first note his views on the *Jewish convert in general*—that is, on the convert from Judaism to Christianity as a historical phenomenon. Inevitably, his attitude toward this "historical" convert affected his stand toward the "concrete" convert—i.e., the one of his own country and time whom he met, observed and examined. To put both these attitudes in clearer perspective, we shall try to isolate them from each other. But this, of course, is not always attainable. Since the two phenomena of conversion are intertwined and have many aspects in common, it is sometimes impossible to discuss the one without touching upon the other.

In seeking to establish the view he should take toward the *Jewish convert in general*, Oropesa could tread a well-marked path. The subject had been discussed in Christian literature since the Gospels on many occasions and in considerable detail. Not that all authors shared the same view of the converts from Judaism. There were both positive and negative assessments, and one could find enough sources to draw on to form various opinions "on good authority." But any serious theologian could distinguish between the leading and second-rate masters, and on top of this, there was the Church law that indicated Christianity's formal position. Thus, it should not have been difficult for Oropesa to identify the true authoritative guidelines and follow them, if he wished, in his conclusions.

In fact, he did identify and follow them and, consequently, formed a favorable opinion of the Jewish converts to Christianity—so favorable, indeed, that it sharply contrasted with his critical view of the Jewish people. Moreover, his positive view of the *Jewish convert in general* forced him to soften or considerably limit some of his adverse judgments of the Jews. Thus, he was compelled to modify his assertion that "all the Jews were condemned forever without amnesty." Since the Jewish converts were saved from that fate, that verdict could not possibly stand unaltered. To retain it, Oropesa, more than once, had to explain it. He had to make it clear that he referred not to *all* Jews, but to a certain category among them. By "Jews" he meant those who remained in their Jewishness to the very end of their lives.

With the verdict of damnation so redefined, Oropesa could foresee that "God will always convert some Jews to the faith"—i.e., those whom "beforehand He wanted to convert, so that they pass to belong to his people." But this does not apply only to the future. For "some" Jews, he says, had been converted to Christianity also in the past, remote and recent—in fact, from the beginning of the Church down to our own time.[101] And that the term "some" did not mean a small number is clear from several other statements that Oropesa made on the subject. For what he says plainly in these statements is that the converts from Judaism were not few but numerous—if not in relative, at least in absolute numbers; they were by no means a *negligible quantity,* as some might be inclined to assume.

Indeed, says Oropesa, "many of the Jews who contemplated the prophecies" both before the Passion and after the Resurrection, "came to Christ," and, following His instructions, laid the foundations of the edifice of the faith.

They formed the membership of the nascent Church and at least the *majority* of the thousands of converts who were baptized in response to Peter's call. What is more, this "coming [of the Jews] to Christ" was not limited to certain occasions—to specific occurrences, periods and the like—but constituted an uninterrupted movement from the appearance of Christ on. For the Jews, says Oropesa, "have *always* converted themselves" (in the past), they keep converting themselves every day (in the present), and *many of them will continually convert themselves* (in the future), the process to persist "until the end of days, when all of them will convert to the last man."[102] In this exposition, which clearly spoke of the ceaseless flow of converts from Judaism to Christianity, of the major part they played in building the Church, of the large-scale conversion of the Jews and, above all, of the "end" as the culmination of this process, and not (as it had been commonly maintained) its main fulfillment, Oropesa shows clear traces of the influence wielded on his thinking by the converso apologists.

With all this, however, we should not ignore the difference between his and their position on this issue. We have seen how Torquemada sought to undermine the notion that only "few Jews" were converted to Christianity from its inception until his own generation, and that only a "remnant" of them would be saved with the second coming of Christ. We have also seen how Cartagena (and the Relator) revised the concept of the ultimate conversion by stressing that Jews would be converted in large numbers not just *at* but *until* the end, when *all* the remaining Jews would be converted. Oropesa, as we have noted, accepted these revisions. He admitted that Jews came in droves to the faith not only in ancient but also in later times, and that they keep coming to it daily. But unlike Torquemada, who stressed Paul's saying that "*All* of Israel will be saved," Oropesa could not make light of Paul's prediction that merely a *"remnant"* of Israel would be rescued. He obviously had to coordinate Paul's statement with his view of the current of Jewish conversion which, in its totality, was by no means insignificant, and he came up with an explanation that the word "remnant" was used by the Apostle in a figurative sense. Compared to the masses who remained unconverted (and, in consequence, unredeemed), the Jews who did convert to Christianity, however large their quantity in absolute numbers, *appeared* merely as a "remnant."[103] And there was of course a basis for this "appearance." For bearing in mind all the past generations, it is obvious that only a minority of the Jews—and, indeed, only a small minority—was saved by conversion to Christianity, whereas their great or overwhelming majority was doomed to eternal perdition. So while drawing near the conversos' stand at this particular point, Oropesa here too appeared to conform to the traditional Christian view.

Undoubtedly, his opinion of the Jewish converts and the great place they occupied in the structure of the Church could not have been formed if he had not considered them devoted Christians, imbued with the beliefs and ideals of the Faith. Yet when he comes to answer the question: What brought these former Jews to the Church?, he lets us understand that only the *first* converts—those who came to Christ before the "captivity" (i.e., before the destruction of Jerusalem by the Romans) joined the Church solely as a result of a revolution that took place in their spiritual life, while the Jews who turned Christian later on (namely, the great majority of the converts) were not moved to conversion without first being "vexed" by trials and tribulations.[104] Oropesa does not say that they joined Christianity *solely* to get rid of the troubles that had plagued them, and hence that their conversion was originally false. What he says is that it was due to their extraordinary suffering that they came to *consider* the meaning of Christianity, and that then they saw the light and were illumined by the faith.[105] Does this mean that the hardships of "captivity" were imposed upon the Jews not only as punishment, but to serve God's aim of rescuing those of them who were predestined to be saved?[106] Oropesa's statements may imply this idea, but only as an allusion to the divine will; there is no indication that he actually supported calculated "vexation" for the sake of conversion. When he urged the separation of the Jews from the Christians, he seriously believed in the gravity of the threat posed by the Jews to the Christian world. Obviously, he presents different considerations stemming from various Christian sources, but somehow converging into the same conclusions. But it was not Oropesa who combined these views or channeled them all into a common current. In this, as in other matters, he was clearly following the guidelines of Church policy and thinking, fixed after centuries of subtle speculation on the various aspects of the Jewish problem.

What kind of Christian does the Jewish convert make? In discussing this question, Oropesa again echoes Torquemada and Cartagena. "Those who are converted from the Jewish people," he says, "are more suitable and apt to benefit the Church than those who are converted from the gentiles," assuming that the Jews and the gentiles involved were converted "authentically on equal terms."[107] This is what the holy Doctors affirm, and especially the commentator Nicholas de Lyra; and the reasons for this are not hard to see. "Sustained by the discipline of the Law and the Prophets . . . they are more suited for the regimen of the Church and the government of the people of God than those who never had such experience." One can see this from Peter and Paul, whom de Lyra presents as examples of such converts, and "also from many others, ancient and modern (i.e., Jews "converted in our own time"), who benefited the Church by the examples of their lives, as well as by the doctrines they expounded in their writings."[108] No doubt when writing these words, Oropesa had in mind such men as Cartagena and Juan de Torquemada.

We now come to the practical question that had provoked the entire discussion. How should the converts from Judaism be treated by the rest of the faithful? Oropesa answers unequivocally: precisely as all other Christians are treated. God, he says, congregated the Jews "with the other faithful" in a single body—namely, the Church—"to live under the same laws which apply to the others, to enjoy the same benefits and graces like the others, receive the same rewards, and be castigated by the same penalties."[109]

Oropesa takes a leaf from Chrysostom's writings in clarifying what this implies. He relies on Chrysostom's general view of the structure of the Church and its supreme ideals. The structure of the Church is based on absolute equality of all its members in their basic rights, and its ideals are unity and brotherhood. Hence, "we should always take care of our brothers, that is, those who came to Christ from Judaism; we should not defame or scorn or molest them; we should not insult them in any form. If by chance they deviate from the right path, we should call them back to it with charity and gentleness, treating them fraternally with great care and perseverance"; and "if any of them sticks stubbornly to his error, he should be chastised peacefully as the law orders, without causing any blemish or infamy to other faithful who happen to belong to the same race."[110]

This brings us to the issue of race, which lay at the heart of the stormy conflict between the Old and New Christians. Oropesa's position on this issue is in line with that of Cartagena and Torquemada, and so are the principal arguments he offers in defense of that position. Considerations of race, Oropesa asserts as forcefully as did his converso predecessors, are opposed to the basic tenets of Christianity, which aims to save all parts of mankind and establish its equality and unity before God. "Those who come to Christ should not be excluded because of an improper class of blood," he says. "All that has to be proven," he stresses, "is whether their spirit is of God."[111] Like the converso theologians, he reminds his reader of Paul's exhortations in this regard, "for no one is excepted as unworthy or prejudiced, or favored in anything before God, for having been born to these or to the others."[112] And in further support of the same idea, he cites Jerome's letter to Celantia: "It is not important in what conditions one was born, when all of us are equally to be reborn in Christ. For if we forget that *all were born of one,* we ought at least to remember that *all of us are to be reborn of one.*"[113]

It follows that, like all other members of the Church, the Jewish converts should enjoy full equality with all other Christians in matters related to public functions, such as the occupation of offices, dignities and honors, both in the ecclesiastic and civil life of Christendom. This right operates from the moment of conversion, except in matters related to Church leadership, which require preparation and experience, but this limitation applies to gentile converts no less than to Jewish ones. Some interpret Paul's statements about the Jews being "first" (both in receiving honor and punishment) as indications that the Jewish convert to Christianity should be treated in a special manner. Oropesa opposes this interpretation. Jewish converts should not be treated preferentially, just as they should not be disparaged. The principle of complete equality must govern the Church's conduct toward all converts, Jewish or gentile, in all spheres of life.[114]

This principle, however, was sorely tested when challenged by the critics of the Marranos in Spain. For these critics did not deny the rule of equal treatment of all members in the Church; they only claimed that of all converts to Christianity, the Jewish convert forms an exception to which that rule cannot be applied. Oropesa had to prove their claim wrong if he wished his own to be considered right.

X

What were the arguments of the Marranos' opponents against the equalization of the converts from Judaism, and especially against granting them offices and dignities in the government of the Church? Oropesa presents these arguments straightforwardly, as if he were their advocate or proponent, adducing the evidence advanced in their support and making them appear as convincing as possible. Then he turns around to examine them, showing their complete groundlessness and hollowness. We shall have to consider Oropesa's rebuttal in order to comprehend his thinking and his stand in this crucial controversy.

The first reason offered by the foes of the conversos was supposed to be both historical and theological. It was based on the crime of killing Christ, a crime for which the Jews assumed responsibility and the punishment for which was extended to their sons (Matt. 27.25). Since the conversos, like the Jews, are the "sons" of those criminals, they too must bear the burden of that guilt, and certainly cannot share with the converts from the gentiles the blessings of Christianity in equal measure. As Oropesa put it, their argument ran like this: "Since the kingdom and the priesthood had been transferred by Christ to the people who received Him faithfully, as the Apocalypse says in Revelations: 'And with your blood you have brought for God men [i.e., followers] from every race, language, people and nation, and you have made of *them* a *kingdom of priests for our God*, they will reign over the earth'[115]; and also since in the first letter of Peter it is said about the Church of the gentiles: 'But you are an elected lineage, a *royal priesthood*, a holy nation, a peculiar people,'[116] it follows that they (i.e., the descendants of the Jews) were not included in that kingdom and priesthood and, needless to say, must be held inept for any office, honor and dignity in it. This is also confirmed by the words of Christ when He praised the faith of the gentile centurion. He said there: 'Many will come from the east and the west [i.e., from the gentiles] to sit down in the kingdom of Heaven with Abraham, Isaac and Jacob, while the children of the kingdom will be cast out of it into utter darkness.'[117] The argument implies that the conversos were unworthy not only to hold offices in the Church but also to be its members.

In replying to this argument, Oropesa says that it is based on a selected use of sources with the vicious intent to distort their true meaning and misrepresent their real contents. Oropesa, as we have seen, differed from Cartagena about the Jews' blame for the Passion; he did not claim, as Cartagena did, that only a fraction of the Jews was responsible in some measure for Jesus' death, while the overwhelming number of Jews—and hence, the Jewish people as a whole—had no share in it. He adopted the traditional Christian view that "the Jews"—namely, the entire Jewish people—had a major share in Jesus' crucifixion,[118] and therefore the curse which they put upon their children was in full accord with the punishment they took. The punishment was of course decreed by Christ according to His infallible judgment, and it included, as Oropesa had already indicated, dispersion, captivity and endless suffering. But it all related to the Jews qua Jews—i.e., to those who upheld the Jewish faith, rejected Christ and opposed His followers, as well as to their "children"—i.e., their descendants who "imitated" their fathers in adhering to their errors. Once, however, a Jew is converted to the faith and joins the Church through Holy Baptism, he "is freed from all the penalties" to which he had been subject, is vested with the freedom and grace of the Church, and is counted, like all its other members, as son and heir of equal standing.[119] Thus, if the Passion was the cause of the Jew's subjugation, Baptism is the cause of his liberation. And Oropesa explains why.

Conversion to Christianity, Oropesa says, is far more than a change of religious views or worship. Conversion is a total transformation of the man—a multiple miracle that can be effected not by adopting new views and beliefs, or even a new system of faith, but only by the sacrament of Baptism, in which the power of Christ is revealed. For whoever is baptized is incorporated in Christ, and as part of Christ he dies with Him, is buried with Him, and resurrected with Him to reappear as a morally pure person.[120] This is how the convert from Judaism is cleansed from all his past sins; and this is how he becomes also detached from the crime of the Passion.

But is there in all this anything unique to the Jewish convert? Oropesa reminds his reader at this point that the gentile convert is in need of baptism no less than the Jewish, for both "Jews and gentiles are children of wrath" (Ephes. 2. 3–5), and both must be cleansed of all their transgressions before they can become true Christians. To prove this, Oropesa finds it enough to mention the following two matters: first, all gentiles, no less than the Jews, are guilty of Original Sin, and second, no less than the Jews were they involved in Christ's crucifixion. And here, in discussing the gentiles' share in the Passion, Oropesa not only approaches Cartagena; he surpasses him in stressing the gentile responsibility for the Passion in all its stages.

To begin with, he points out, the conspiracy to kill Jesus was never a strictly Jewish affair: "For in this city [i.e., Jerusalem] both Herod and Pilate, the gentiles and the Jews, allied themselves against Jesus."[121] Then, Jews and gentiles vied with each other in inflicting suffering upon the Son of God in all phases of the Crucifixion. Thus the Jews, after having sentenced him to death, "spat in his face and struck Him with their fists," while others said, as they were beating Him, "Now, Messiah, if you are a prophet, tell us who hit you" (Matt. 67).[122] But the gentiles treated Him in a similar manner. For after having been sentenced to death, He was flogged, on Pilate's orders, by the soldiers, who also crowned Him with a crown of thorns. Then, like the Jews, the gentiles mocked Jesus, spat at him, and struck him on His head. Finally, it was they—i.e., the gentiles—who put Him to death on the cross.[123]

"And thus," says Oropesa, "in His holy crucifixion were all *equally* present, both the Jews and the gentiles, and these and the others, in one form and another, committed all the evil they could perpetrate against him. This may be gathered from all the Gospels, and the lesson implied in all this is that, just as He had suffered to save the whole world . . . , so He took that suffering from all mankind [i.e., from both Jews and gentiles], and finally was crucified, as it had been prophesied:

> The Kings of the earth [i.e., of the *Gentiles*] stand up,
> And the rulers [i.e., of the *Jews*] conspire
> Against the Lord and against His anointed."[124]

In this portrayal of the criminal part which the gentiles played in the Passion, we can note the strong influence of Cartagena. But Oropesa has more to say on this matter. He extended the charge of gentile criminality from attacks upon Jesus to assaults upon his followers. Accordingly, he rejects as false the claim that the Jews were the main, or most violent persecutors of the early Christians. Not the Jews alone, he says, but "Jews *and* gentiles sinned in the cruel persecution of the martyrs," and not only were the gentiles *partners* in these crimes; they also persevered in them much longer than the Jews. The persecution of the Christians by the pagans in the Roman world lasted almost four hundred years, and much may be read about this in Augustine; and today the gentiles (the Saracens and the Turks) do battle against the Church, invade its lands and violate its Holy Places. In fact, the gentiles' attacks upon Christianity were more violent and ferocious, and no less frequent than those of the Jews; for both groups hate the Church and seek to hurt it, and both will continue their harassment of Christendom, in a variety of forms, until the end of the world.[125]

In view of this history of persecution of Christianity, in which the gentiles were involved no less than the Jews, it is of course absurd to describe the gentile world as just and, in contrast, the society of the Jews as cruel. Similarly it is grotesque to claim, as some Christians do, that Christ built His Church *exclusively* with the gentiles, while he expelled all Jews from it as incorrigible sinners. Actually, Jesus built His Church on the foundation of the *Jews*, not of the gentiles, and following His Passion it was Jewish apostles who became "instruments of the election and the honor of the Church."[126] When Jesus said that many will come from the East and the West to the Kingdom of Heaven, while the sons of the kingdom will be ousted into the dark, he indeed referred by the former to gentiles and by the latter to Jews. But by these Jews we should not understand *all* the "sons of the Kingdom" of God, but only those who were "bad" or "abominable" to God because they remained in the darkness of their blindness; while those who emerged from that darkness—who at any time recognized the Son of God—were not excluded from the Kingdom. Similarly, it is clear that when Peter said: "You are an elected lineage, a royal priesthood, etc.," he did not refer only to the converted gentiles, but to *all* the members of the Church of God, which meant: the followers of Christ from both peoples. Likewise, the famous statement in Revelations (5.9): "With your blood you have purchased for God men from every race, etc.," rather than confirming, clearly denies the contentions of the conversos' enemies. Obviously, that verse did not refer to converts from the gentiles *only*; for he who says "every" does not exclude anyone, Jew or gentile.[127]

Thus has Oropesa confuted the argument against converso equality in Christendom which was based primarily on the Passion of Christ, the crime of the Crucifixion and the self-imposed curse of the Jews. The confutation seems clear and convincing; and yet one cannot help asking: If the gentiles sinned no less than the Jews in the Crucifixion and Passion of Christ, why were they not punished like the Jews? Why were the Jews alone singled out for that perpetual captivity and horrible suffering which befell no other nation on earth? Oropesa's answer is based on his conclusions concerning the Jews' special inclination to vice and their particular attraction to the Devil. It was their "abominable iniquity," as Oropesa put it, that led them to reject Christ, and it was because of that rejection, which was more total and determined than that of all other nations, that they were punished as they were.[128] But to this was added another consideration that cannot be ignored. The Jews alone of all the peoples of the world were benefited by God in a special manner; it was on them that He showered all His gifts and blessings;

and it was they alone who showed Him that "ingratitude" which typifies the most malicious of men. Therefore, *their* denial of Christ had a far more sinister character and, consequently, brought upon them alone that unparalleled disaster. God, who built them up as His people, ceased to tolerate them as He did; He punished them with His counter-rejection ("You are not my People," as Hosea said) and all the ensuing results.[129]

XI

If the first objection to converso equalization was based, according to Oropesa, on misinterpretations of certain statements in the *New* Testament, the second was founded, in his opinion, on inferences drawn wrongly from certain verses in the *Old* Testament. The verses in question are those of Deuteronomy, which prohibit the equalization of *some* gentiles with the Jews.[130] And the argument built on them against Marrano equalization ran more or less as follows: The Jews "viewed the gentiles who accepted their faith as outsiders and aliens" to their people; and "however sincere their conversion" to Judaism, the Jews did not admit them to their offices and dignities—at least, not on conditions of parity; for they either denied them such admission *forever*, as was the case with the Ammonites and Moabites, or accepted them only in the third generation, as was the case with the Idumeans and Egyptians. In the same manner, the argument continued, the Christians should now treat the Jews, so that "never, or very late, or with great difficulties, may they admit the Jewish convert to Christianity to offices and honors within the People of God."[131] Moreover, such treatment is fully supported not only by Scripture but by the current facts. For the Jews of today are more disagreeable to God than the gentiles were in ancient times, whereas on the other hand, the Christians of our time are far more agreeable to Him, and more united with Him, than the Jews were in those days."[132] And "if the amity and union of the Jewish people with God dictated harsh treatment of the gentiles (because of their past incredulity and errors), even when they wished to be converted to His faith, all the more so should the Christians treat harshly the Jews who wish to receive the faith of Christ."[133]

The gist of this argument against converso equalization is already found, as we have seen, in García's *Memorial*,[134] even though the reasons advanced by García were different from those offered by his partisans ten or fifteen years later. In any case, his claim that the Law ordered the Jews to discriminate against converts to their faith, or rather against *all* their converts from the gentiles, was manifestly false and could easily be confuted; but since no refutation, as it seems, was offered, it gained wide currency before long. Not only did the Marrano-baiters use it, but even a converso like Fernando de Pulgar accepted it as self-evident.[135] Oropesa was determined to expose the falsehood, but his attempt to do so was based, as we shall see, not on purely exegetical reasons, but rather on theological arguments, which dictated quite a different explanation of the biblical intent.

Oropesa shows that the particular laws on which the adversaries of the conversos rely belong precisely to the kind of laws that Christianity came to abolish, for they clearly indicate the imperfection of the Law to which the Jews were subject in those times. The Law was imperfect because the people it governed were incapable of following higher directives which treat with equality all human beings. Since the Law was given only to the Jews, the latter, says Oropesa, "arrogantly and contemptuously abhorred all other peoples." And not only did they thus offend those peoples while the latter were in their gentilehood; they also rebuffed and looked down upon them after they had been converted to Judaism. It was in opposition to that negative treatment—and in a clear attempt to improve their behavior—that the Law ordered the Jews to stop abhorring some nations (such as the Idumeans and the Egyptians) and accept them as equals, at least in the third generation, while in consideration of the Jews' crude nature, it permitted them to practice that discrimination indefinitely toward proselytes from other peoples. This, however, is Judaism; this is not Christianity. And it is precisely for such types of imperfection that the Old Law was abolished and the New proclaimed.[136]

Hence, concludes Oropesa, when the critics of the conversos seek to apply the same Jewish treatment to converts from Judaism to Christianity, they are actually reverting to an old evil, which the Old Law wished to limit as much as possible and Christianity had totally done away with. Indeed, in following such a course, these people, who pride themselves on fighting Judaization, are actually doing the very thing they pretend to avoid. For by adopting the above-mentioned principle *they are Judaizing*, and not even in accord with the intent of the Old Law, but in accord with the practices of the ancient Jews, which the Old Law sought to correct.[137] A modern lay scholar may question of course Oropesa's historical premises, but one can hardly question his deductions. Indeed, by the standards of medieval thinking, his rebuttal appears irrefutable.

In his effort to examine the theoretical foundations of the anti-Marrano faction, Oropesa presents also a third argument employed against converso equalization. It is based on two separate passages in Deuteronomy which Christian theology and exegesis combined by relating them both to Jesus Christ. The first passage, included in Deuteronomy 18, presents the promise God gave the Jewish people to raise up a prophet from among their brethren who would be "like myself" and "speak in my name." This promise is followed by a stern warning that the Jews would have to "listen" to that prophet, for otherwise God would "require it of them."[138] As is obvious from

the very content of this statement, and also as confirmed by the New Testament,[139] the God-like prophet of whom that passage spoke was none other
than Jesus Christ; and since the Jews did not "listen" to Him—nay, even
despised Him and delivered Him to death—they were evidently subject to
all the castigations indicated by the maledictions of Deuteronomy 28. One of
these maledictions, which, according to the Marrano-baiters, carries a message with respect to the converts, is included in the following verses:

> The alien who lives with you
> Will rise higher and higher,
> And you will sink lower and lower,
> He will lend you, and you will not lend him,
> He will be the head, and you will be the tail.
>   (Deut. 28.43–44)

This means that the Jews who, before Christ's advent, were religiously
"above" the "aliens"—i.e., the gentiles—would now become inferior to them.
They would be dominated by the gentiles who would "live with them"—i.e.,
by members of the same Church. And thus, in consequence of their crime
against Christ, they should not be allowed to assume positions of authority
over any other Christians.[140]

In reply to these assertions Oropesa seeks to show that the whole argument
has neither rhyme nor reason. The harsh servitude which the Jews were to
endure in punishment for their share in Christ's crucifixion was to last only
as long as they were *Jews*—that is, followers of their old infidelity. But once
they were converted to the faith of the Holy Church and entered it through
the sacred baptism, they are freed of all the "penalties of Judaism" and
clothed with the liberty and grace of Christianity. They are "counted among
all other Christians as sons of the Church and heirs of its possessions."[141] The
above-cited verses of Deuteronomy, therefore, could in no way refer to the
conversos.

There was also a fourth argument that the Marrano haters used against
New Christian equalization. It was based on the firm prohibition of the
Apostle against appointing neophytes as bishops and on the reasons he gave
for that prohibition: lest they be "lifted up with pride and fall into the
condemnation of the devil."[142] By these "neophytes" (i.e., new believers),
they said, the Apostle could mean only converts from Judaism, for the
gentiles came to Christ quickly in large numbers, and also accepted Him with
great devotion, while the Jews, who persisted in the blindness of their fathers,
came to Him in small numbers and much later (this is why they were
considered "new"); nor did they show the same devotion to the faith as did
the converts from gentilehood. Naturally, the Apostle considered it improper
for them to be put above the gentile converts.[143]

Oropesa devoted to the argument concerning neophytes one of the longest chapters in his book. He evidently considered the refutation of that argument of vital importance for winning the case against the Marranos' detractors. Like the converso apologists, he must have believed that as long as the conversos were distinguished from all other Christians by their very title (i.e., *New* Christians), and as long as that title was commonly identified with the "neophytes" of the Apostle, little could be done to defeat the opposition and heal the widening breach. Stopping the usage of that title, therefore, was to Oropesa an essential prerequisite for New-Old Christian reconciliation.

Oropesa apparently considered it possible to contribute materially toward this purpose by dispelling the confusion that reigned about the origin, meaning and application of the term "neophyte." The claim of the opposition was, as we have seen, that by "neophytes" the Apostle meant converts from Judaism, and that it was only to such converts that he forbade the assumption of high offices in the Church. But this whole claim, Oropesa insisted, was based on ignorance and misunderstanding. It is true that the Apostle, in his letter to Timothy, did not mean by "neophytes" converts of *all* origins, but of a *certain* origin only, except that the converts he signified by that term were not those indicated by the Marranos' critics. For the Apostle was against ordaining as bishops only those who were newly converted from the *gentiles,* but was not against appointing to that office anyone newly converted from the Jews. Indeed, those familiar with the history of Christianity know that, in that early period of the faith, the term "neophyte" was not applied to Jews who turned Christians, but to new converts from the gentiles.[144] This is how the Apostle's use of "neophyte" was understood by Saints Chrysostom and Ambrosius, and this is how it was understood by canon law.[145] Yet this is not the only consideration that makes a travesty of the detractors' claim. For if they insist that the Apostle's instruction was not given, as it was, in a *specific* situation, but was meant to be eternal in *all* its parts, they obviously must conclude that his prohibition on appointing bishops applies to this day to *all* gentile converts—and to them alone.[146]

The claim that the Apostle meant by "neophytes" *new* converts, and only such who came from gentilehood, was so firmly based in Christian theology that Oropesa considered it indisputable. It implied a *reductio ad absurdum* of the argument of the opposition and rendered irrelevant all the reasons and "proofs" that it tried to marshall in its support. The same claim, as we have seen, was already made by the Relator,[147] and likewise it implied the same *reductio.* But this in itself did not answer the question of *why* the Apostle excluded Jewish converts from the category of the "neophytes." Oropesa of course had to answer this question, as did, in fact, his famous predecessor; but his answer, as we shall see, differed fundamentally from that of the Relator.

According to the Relator, the Jews who came to Christ were not regarded by the Apostle as neophytes (or *new* converts) for the simple reason that they were not converts to begin with. When they became Christians, or believers in Christ, they did not pass from one religion to another (as was the case with the gentile converts) but remained in the same religion (or, as he put it, "in the same house"), except that now they understood far better what their own religion meant. Essentially, this was also the Relator's view of the converts from Judaism in later times—that is, following the time of the Apostle. Accordingly, he maintained that Jews who became Christians also in later generations (including his own), or were to become Christians at any time in the future, ought not to be designated as conversos (converts) any more than they ought to be considered *New* Christians—which is a reminder of "neophytes."[148]

But this was not at all the view of Oropesa. As he saw it, it was *only in the period of the Primitive Church* that the Apostle did not designate as neophytes the newcomers to Christ from among the Jews, for then the Gospel was not yet fully published and the Old Law was not yet abolished. For as long as the Law was not clearly *disproved,* it was still considered, as it had been, *approved;* and therefore the Jews did not have to abandon it when they recognized Christ to the extent they did. This, however, was not the case of the gentiles, who before they came to Christ had no *approved* faith and had to abandon all their beliefs, their forms of worship and their way of life. Since they "lived without God, without converse with Israel, and without any hope of the Promise," they came to God as "guests and strangers," as converts in the full sense of the word; therefore they were rightly called neophytes (i.e., *new* believers). Yet this distinction between the two kinds of converts (from gentilehood and Judaism) could last only until the Gospel was published. For once its contents became fully known, and the borders between the faiths were clearly drawn, no one could excuse himself by ignorance of Christianity, which called for the cessation of all Jewish worship and the total abolition of the Old Law. Consequently, the Jews who remained in their Judaism following the period of the Primitive Church, and later joined Christ when their eyes were opened, must be regarded, no less than the gentiles, as converts to the faith from an infidelity, and their newly converted must be viewed as neophytes, as are the new converts from the gentiles.[149]

One can readily note the root of the difference between the view of Oropesa and that of the Relator. While for Fernán Díaz Judaism and Christianity were essentially the same religion, for Oropesa Christianity was essentially another religion—to be sure, not different in *everything,* but different enough to *deny* Judaism, prohibit its practice, and come in its stead. His sharp distinction between the Old and the New Law did not allow him to combine both religions in the manner we find them combined by the Relator, although his distinction between the two religious eras—i.e., of the Written

Law and the Law of Grace—permitted him to consider a short period of transformation in which the Jews—who adhered to the Written Law—could uphold it together with the Law of Grace. The difference of opinion we notice at this point between the views of Oropesa and the Relator illustrates the cleavage that developed in Spain between the traditional Christian view and the view of the conversos concerning the true, fundamental relationship between the two religions.

But beyond this point, Oropesa's argument approached, or even merged with that of the conversos. Like Cartagena, he stressed the *brevity* of the period in which any convert may be considered a neophyte.[150] Similarly, he stressed that even in this period the convert is entitled to any office or benefice, except the prelacy and the priesthood. Likewise, he argued that these rights and limitations applied equally to *all* neophytes of whatever origin throughout the period of their neophytism. Since following that period all converts were equal, there was obviously no reason for any differentiation between "Old" and "New" Christians.

XII

It is noteworthy that all the above four arguments which, according to Oropesa, were used by the detractors and, moreover, formed the basis of their stand, are not to be found in the polemical literature written on the subject in 1449–1450. Both in the public debate of those years and in the positions rebutted by Oropesa, the Bible was claimed by the anti-conversos as the main foundation upon which they relied, but most of the biblical authorities they cited in the early stages of the controversy are not even mentioned by Oropesa, which shows that they stopped referring to them, and on the rare occasions when they used those authorities, they did not draw from them the same conclusions.

Apparently, in the fourteen years since the start of that debate, the opposition had abandoned some of its old arguments under the impact of converso criticism, and especially relinquished the biblical "proofs" that had spearheaded its first attacks. Thus, we see Oropesa grapple with new evidence, new reasons and new lines of demonstration; and it is, in fact, thanks to his detailed summaries of the arguments he found necessary to confute that we can see the development of the opposition's thinking and its stand in the middle of the sixties.

What is evident above all is that, while the foes of the conversos forsook most biblical foundations of their claims, they stubbornly adhered to the claims themselves. The core of these claims, as Oropesa put it, was that "those who came to the faith from the circumcision should be denied equality of rights with the faithful, *because of their bad works, because their hearts are not with Christ, and because they are always inclined toward evil and all the things which it is proper to object to.*"[151] Here we have in a nutshell the three main reasons—the moral, the religious and the racial—which the anti-conversos incessantly brought forth. In 1464 they were essentially the same as they were in 1449.

Oropesa's opinion of the anti-Marrano accusations is stated in clear and forceful language. He brands them repeatedly as false and malicious, and as calumnies that must be denounced.[152] If we add to these denunciations Oropesa's statements on the New Christians, we shall get a clear notion of his stand on the conflict between the two groups.

What is Oropesa's view of the conversos? Judging by the various assessments he made of both the converso masses and leadership, it is clear that he considered the conversos true Christians who were devoted to the faith and wished to promote it. He considered them full-fledged *"brethren in faith"*[153] no less than the other members of the Church, and designated them with the honorific titles of "co-inheritors and co-citizens of the Apostles and the Prophets" and "sons of promise and peace."[154]

Thus, in referring to the converts, he says: "We have seen—and see—in our own time *many* who were converted from among the Jews live righteously and walk in the faith of Christ, and some of them are bishops and prelates and serve very well the Church of God in its regimen and government."[155] But besides the converso prelates, whose number was necessarily limited, there were other conversos who gained great influence in the Church due to their moral and scholarly attainments. Of these Oropesa says: "What experience has taught us is that *many* of the Jewish race who were converted to the faith in our regions have become in a short time *great doctors on a grand scale* and also *outstanding in the customs of their lives*."[156] Both his general portrayal of these converts and the adjective "many" which he applies to them repeatedly (in fact, both to their masses and their spiritual leaders) indicate that he considered the group as a whole rooted in Christianity and integrated in the Church. Never does he use the adjective "many" when he refers to the backsliders among the conversos. Here he uses always the term "some."[157]

That these "some" were a small minority that could not change materially the character of the group is evident not only from his view of the conversos as reflected in the above-cited statements, but also from his various remarks on the "deviators," whose presence in the group he did not ignore. He says: "There have always been and always will be among the converts from Judaism 'good' and 'bad' Christians, just as there are—and will be—'good' and 'bad' Christians among the other faithful who have come to the Church from all parts of mankind and in all times."[158] This equalization of the general condition of faithfulness and unfaithfulness among the conversos with that obtaining among the other Christian groups shows that Oropesa did not see in deviation from Christianity among the conversos a phenomenon that called for special concern or for extraordinary treatment. He sees no necessity, and no justification, for issuing special laws for the conversos as a group, as was done in Toledo in the seventh century. When such legislation was enacted in Spain, it came to meet an emergency; for then it was found that the converts from Judaism included many feigned Christians, and there was *need* to take extreme measures in order to check the spreading heresy.[159] The tenor of the argument clearly shows that Oropesa saw no such need in his own time; he saw no similarity between the religious condition of most of the conversos in his generation and that of the converts in the Spanish kingdom in the period of the Toledan councils.

Obviously, when Oropesa speaks of "bad Christians" he does not necessarily refer to Judaizers. "Bad Christians," as he indicated, were found among the Old Christians (and these "bad" ones were clearly not Judaizers), and we may assume that "bad Christians" other than Judaizers were found, in his opinion, among the conversos, too. But he readily acknowledged the existence of Judaizers and discussed them in several places of his book.[160] He saw most of them as deficient either in the *understanding* of the faith or in the *fulfillment* of its instructions. Yet Christians who have such a view of a convert should not approach him in a hostile spirit. They should "admonish and support him, and induce and help him . . . to believe rightly and behave correctly." But they should avoid "discussions" that might lead the convert to believe that they consider him "guilty of hidden things." In saying all this, Oropesa relies on the Apostle in Romans 14.1 and the comments on that verse by the Ordinary Gloss. "It is not for us," he says in the words of the Gloss, "*to condemn him whose thought is not evident, or whom we do not know what he will be later on.*" In brief, we should accept, not reject him, and allow him to "enjoy all the privileges of the Christians." Of course, when "convicted" of some crime or error, he should be "corrected and chastised canonically," but even then "we must refrain from all rancor and defamation against both the one who ought to be chastised and the other faithful members of his race."[161]

This is of course not the kind of treatment that could suit convinced, stubborn heretics who were actually carrying the message of their heresy to the ranks of the faithful. And this is not, in fact, how Oropesa proposed to deal with heretics and schismatics. The lesson of his above-cited counsels, therefore, cannot be mistaken: just as he did not consider the Judaizers a real force in a quantitative sense, he did not consider them a threat from a qualitative point of view. Evidently, he regarded most of the Judaizers not as die-hard adherents of Judaism but as feeble believers in Christianity who may be inspired by proper instruction to become true followers of Christ. In any case, he saw the main problem they posed not in their own disbelief and misconduct, but rather in the excuse they supplied the Marrano-baiters for their anti-converso campaign. Indeed, it was to the presence of the Judaizers that he attributed the main slogans of that campaign—namely, that the conversos are a group of "apostates, feigned Christians and secret Jews."[162] Oropesa treats this accusation as outrageous, as "imputing the false under the appearance of truth."[163] In fact, he presents it as the very *opposite* of the truth, and in every respect as a crime befitting Judas. For these agitators against the conversos, he says, "did not sin out of weakness or ignorance"; they *knew* the truth. But like Judas they sought and found "the opportunity of substituting without evidence truth with lie and virtue with transgression."[164]

XIII

The focus of our attention has thus shifted from the conversos to their die-hard Old Christian adversaries, whose attitudes and activities against the Marranos pose difficult problems. If the conversos were, rather than miscreants, faithful followers of Christ and his teachings, and their portrayal as "heretics, feigned Christians and crypto-Jews" was not just a product of ignorance and prejudice, but a vicious lie deliberately concocted with the aim of replacing truth with falsehood, it is obvious that no religious motive was behind the anti-Marrano campaign. But if so, we must ask: What was the real motive? What turned the wheels of the anti-Marrano movement?

Like Cartagena, Torquemada and the Relator, Oropesa stressed that the troubles arose from the jealousy of the conversos felt by some evil Old Christians. This jealousy produced an implacable hatred that led to a terrible campaign of libels, which in turn gave birth to extreme violence, expressed in robbery, torture and bloodshed. But, adds Oropesa, all these evil actions did not stem only from rancor and ill will.[165] They were also propelled by certain wishes and ambitions that lurked in the hearts of the conversos' enemies. In Oropesa's words, "these men are moved by the anxiety of avarice, or by vainglory, or, which is certain, by their actual interests."[166] What they really want is by no means limited to the expulsion of the conversos from their positions; what they want is to *take over* these positions in order to enjoy the benefits they yield. These are the beasts in Ezekiel's prophecy (34.17–29) that do not merely wish to drive away God's flock from the green pastures in which they feed, but also to seize the whole pastureland and occupy it solely for their own use. In brief, what these people seek is plainly the usurpation of all the goods of the Church for themselves.[167]

This accusation of the conversos' foes matches in severity the criticisms which the Relator, Torquemada and Montalvo had hurled against them some twelve years before. But other censures and charges of Oropesa appear even more extreme. Touching upon the various "legal" measures which the anti-Marranos took and proposed, he says that to justify them, they amassed arguments allegedly based on law.[168] Oropesa did his utmost to demonstrate the falsehood, groundlessness, or absurdity of these arguments. But he did all this, he said, without hoping to convince the stubborn opponents. Since the latter know the truth and knowingly defy it, they will always circumvent any demonstration in order to reassert their mendacities. "You may vanquish or silence them," says Oropesa, "but you will never move them to confess their error," or even correct their wrong assertions. In vain may one point to canon law or to Catholic dogma, or even to the Holy Gospels themselves, in an attempt to show them that they are in the wrong. You may prove, for instance, by evidence as clear as daylight that the neophytes referred to by the apostle Paul were not converts from the Jews but from the gentiles; they will continue to shout and assert as they have done: "All those converted from Judaism to Christianity are those whom the Apostle designated as neophytes; to this category they should always belong, and as such they are subject to the decree of the Apostle, who forbade their being ordained to the Church."[169]

How to treat these enemies of truth, who so impudently reject any holy authority, any definite proof and any demonstrated claim? Oropesa offers concrete measures. To begin with, he says, *They must be silenced!*[170] Their agitation must be stopped by Church orders. "For as long as these ferocious beasts continue their campaign within the Church, it will be impossible to have peace, or end the quarrels, and stop the contentions" that arose within it. "Nor will there cease the jealousies and rivalries and the oppression of the simpleminded, the small and powerless"; nor will there disappear the dangerous errors which they disseminate in the ranks of the faithful—the errors which "disrupt the unity of the Church and destroy the charity of its believers."[171]

But Oropesa is not satisfied with a preemptory prohibition of the detractors' agitation. As long as they command authority in the Church, he says, they will always find ways to cause further damage, even if their campaign is formally suppressed. Therefore, he proposed to do to *them* what they wished to do to the conversos. They "must be thrown out of the pastures of the Church," and by this he means first of all Church offices and benefices held by these "bad men." These assets and positions "must be distributed to humble people . . . without showing any favor to persons . . . and without preference for any nation or race." But "those corrupted by the blight of envy and inflated by the wind of ambition should not be permitted to attain offices and benefices of pastorship or government of any sort, since they are thieves and robbers and also pestilent beasts that Christ expelled and removed from his flock."[172]

The last words indicate the ultimate measure that Oropesa had in mind. What he considered essential for the peace of the Church was to excommunicate the maligners of the Marranos and the advocates of their degradation. In this, too, he urged to do to *them* what the latter sought to do to the conversos—i.e., to oust them from Christian society. He proposed to ban any contact with them and anathematize them as heretics and schismatics who threaten the Church's very existence. And in accord with St. Chrysostom's counsel and exhortations, Oropesa says without mincing words:

> We have to destroy these pestiferous beasts and cut off their heads, because only then will those who dwell in the prairies of the Christian faith and the woodlands of its ministries sleep in security. For only then will calm down the riots, will end the oppressions, will disappear the errors, the rugged shall be made level and the rough shall become plain.[173]

XIV

According to Sigüenza, Oropesa found "much fault" with both the Old and New Christians; and summarizing Oropesa's view on both groups, he says: "These *(unos)* [i.e., the Old Christians] sinned as impudent, reckless and villainous; the others *(otros)* [i.e., the New Christians] sinned as malicious and inconstant in the faith. The latter suffered not without fault, and the others deserved grave punishment for their insolence and also for their ambition."[174] Sigüenza, as we can see, sought to find an equilibrium between the blame Oropesa ascribed to the conversos and that which he attributed to the Old Christians. We find no such equilibrium in Oropesa. Perhaps Sigüenza, who feared the censure of the Inquisition, did not wish to portray the great leader of his order as an ardent defender of the New Christians and as a harsh critic of their detractors; but this is precisely what Oropesa was. No other opinion can be formed about him when we carefully consider the contents of his book and the record of his involvement.[175]

While giving us a wrong impression of the contents and general thrust of Oropesa's argument, Sigüenza was careful in choosing his words. As we have noticed, he spoke of the New Christians in the same terms that he used for the Old ones ("unos" and "otros"), imputing much guilt to each group as a whole. Menéndez y Pelayo, who had not read the *Lumen*, accepted unquestioningly Sigüenza's judgments. Following the statement of the Hieronymite historian, he says that Oropesa's conclusion was this: "The Old Christians *(generally!)* sinned as impudent, reckless and villainous, and the New Christians (again, *generally!*) as malicious and inconstant in the faith."[176] But never did Oropesa accuse any of these bodies, taken as a whole, of any of the aforesaid attitudes.

Nor do we find in the *Lumen* a confirmation of *all* the defects which, according to Sigüenza, Oropesa found in the groups he criticized. It is true that he considered the Marrano-baiters "audacious," "reckless" and "villainous" (in fact, he described them in much more acrid terms), but nowhere did he define the faulty conversos as "malicious" and "inconstant in the faith." The latter term especially suggested heresy, steady backsliding and religious betrayal. But this is not at all how Oropesa judged at least most of the deviants among the conversos.

Thus, that whole presentation by Sigüenza was both erroneous and misleading. It suited those who sought to justify the Inquisition on the grounds of an allegedly existent heresy (a widespread Judaic movement that embraced most New Christians), but it did not fit the general view which Oropesa had of the assailed group. For Oropesa considered the conversos *as a whole* good and honest Christians, and he judged the accusations leveled against them to be calumnies and lies. Explicitly he says that his book was written to remove "the opprobrium and affront" from the conversos (our "faithful who came from Judaism to Christ"),[177] just as he says explicitly that he wrote it *against their detractors and accusers*.[178] This then was by no means a "neutral" study, a middle-of-the-road work that sought to strike a balance between two opposing sides; it was clearly a strong defense of the conversos and a furious attack upon their critics.

It should be recalled that Oropesa wrote these words after having served for a year as inquisitor in Toledo. And thus both his favorable view of the conversos and his sharp censures of their opponents assume the value of first-rate evidence based on personal observation, direct contact and intimate knowledge, and not on the common views and assessments offered by public opinion. Oropesa, Sigüenza tells us, had made a "diligent inquiry" into all the accusations brought to his attention, and he "left the city settled and quiet," after having "chastised the guilty as required."[179] But Oropesa himself would not be that positive in evaluating his achievement. He realized that the peace he attained was a truce, and he did not believe in its durability. As he himself wrote at the conclusion of his work, there could be no peace as long as the bad men, the ambitious self-seekers and the deniers of truth continue to operate in Old Christian society. Sooner or later they will find an excuse to break the peace and resume their attacks upon their hated New Christian neighbors (in fact, it took only one and a half years for this prognosis to come true). He had also no doubt that they would attack him, too, as fiercely and viciously as they possibly could, when his book made its way to the public.

For aware of the nature of the opponents he confronted, he did not delude himself for a moment that his proofs and arguments would make any dent in their views and attitudes, or change their methods of warfare. On the contrary, he was sure that, in assailing his work, they would not spare any lie, libel and falsehood that might undermine its influence. To forestall or limit their expected revilements, he first made it clear that he was no Jew. Since advocates of the conversos were usually accused of having Jewish blood in their veins, or, at least, some converso relatives, Oropesa found it necessary to stress that he had no blood relationship with conversos ("for I think that, ever since Noah, our races were so separated that never was there an occasion for anyone who knew me to suspect me in this respect").[180]

Second, he appealed to the archbishop of Toledo to "free me from the calumnies of the people, and defend, if it be necessary, with your noble and great authority this work, the product of so much labor, done with sincere intention" and "completed" at the archbishop's "order."[181] But, above all, to protect his integrity against the slanderers and defamers, he worked out the plan of the book as we see it and wrote it the way he did.

This, we believe, puts us in a position in which we can answer the rather puzzling question that was raised in the course of this survey: Why did Oropesa write his large-scale introduction, which dealt primarily with the Jewish people? He wrote it, as we see it, not in imitation of but in opposition to the converso apologies. Torquemada and Cartagena thought that the converso issue could not be judged apart from the Jewish problem, and in consequence of this, their defense of the conversos was somehow connected with a defense of the Jews. Oropesa believed that this was a mistake; it was wrong theologically and harmful tactically. To the extent the converso case should be related to the Jews, it should be presented, he thought, not as its extension, but as its direct antithesis.

In brief, to Oropesa's thinking, Cartagena's approach—and, for that matter, the approach of Torquemada—was too Jewish (in the ethnic sense), too Judaic (in the religious sense), and too tribal (in the nationalistic sense). His own approach, in contrast, was anti-Jewish, anti-Judaic and fundamentally anti-nationalistic—or, more precisely, it was universalistic. It seemed vital to Oropesa that at that point, when he came to express his view of the conversos—which was, as we have seen, strongly *pro*-converso—he should make it absolutely clear that he was no Jew lover, that he felt no sympathy for Judaism and the Jewish people, and that his position on the conversos was dictated strictly by the study of the facts, the laws and the teachings of traditional Christianity—the same Christianity which he likewise followed in his determined, unreserved opposition to Judaism and severe denunciation of the Jewish people.

CHAPTER III

The Chroniclers of Enrique IV

I. DIEGO DE VALERA

Unlike the *crónicas* of Juan II, those dealing with the period of Enrique IV and the succeeding years up to c. 1485 were not subject to that pro-Marrano revision which sought to ignore the existence of a Marrano question, and even to suppress all mention of the Marranos.[1] Responsible for the latter works were their authors alone, and this, together with the changing circumstances, made the conversos and their problem a recurrent theme in the *crónicas* of the second half of the fifteenth century.

Of the various chronicles of Enrique IV's reign, we shall deal here only with those of Diego de Valera, Fernando de Pulgar, and Alonso de Palencia. Of the other three chroniclers who wrote on that period, Rodrígo Sánchez de Arévalo does not mention the conversos at all, while Enríquez del Castillo refers to them twice—once in a positive vein (in censuring Espina) and once in a negative one (when he defines the conversos' travails in 1473 as a divine punishment for their religious sins). Only Pedro de Escavias adds something new to our knowledge of the converso situation. In discussing the assaults on the conversos in Andalusia in 1473, he says that the nobles in several places risked their lives in resisting the attackers and that the attacks were conducted everywhere under the slogan that the conversos were heretics and deicides. Escavias, who refused to endorse that slogan, marveled at the hatred, the insolence and the fury displayed by the lower classes toward the conversos, and in light of their sack of the converso borough in Cordova and their behavior in other places, he concluded that what moved these people was "more avidity to rob than zeal for the service of God."[2]

All the latter three chroniclers wrote in pre-Inquisitional times, and in this they differed from the other historians to whom we shall now turn our attention. Thus, Valera wrote his *Crónica* of Enrique IV, known as *Memorial de diversas Hazañas,* in 1486—that is, under the watchful eyes of the Inquisition. In this work he sought to clear the conversos of the charge of religious depravity, but he wished to do it in a manner that would not lay him open to unanswerable inquisitional questions. In describing the conversos, therefore, he used statements and phrases found in earlier sources, so that he might claim that his work was a product of a purely scholarly inquiry. It would obviously be a poor excuse as he could be accused of deliberately selecting almost exclusively pro-converso materials. But this was the only defense he could think of under the circumstances, without compromising his task as historian or betraying his conscience.

In his *Memorial* Valera relied largely on Palencia's *Décadas* and the *Crónica Castellana,* which is a vulgarized abbreviation of Palencia's work, and as such his *Memorial* may be regarded as devoid of real historical value. However, as a contemporary of Enrique IV familiar with the events of his time, and as an acute political observer, he shows by his remarks on the conversos in his *Memorial,* and by the materials of Palencia that he accepted and rejected, his stand on the converso issue. Furthermore, since this stand was opposed to prevalent anti-converso attitudes and, above all, to the inquisitional position, we must regard it as reflecting his own thinking and, more likely, as an expression of the views to which he had adhered during the events in question.

Valera ignores the anti-converso riots in Carmona, 1462 (probably because Palencia's description of these riots was too critical of the Old Christians), and the anti-converso outbreak in Toledo, 1467 (probably because Palencia is here too critical of the New Christians). He repeats, however, Palencia's tale of King Alfonso's rejection of the petition addressed to him by the Toledans to authorize their possession of the goods and offices they took from the conversos in the recent riots, defining the petitioners as *malvados robadores* (evildoing robbers).[3] Similarly, he presents the outbreak in Cordova in the wake of Palencia's account, but completely ignores Palencia's remarks about the Judaic practices of the conversos, which that chronicler presented as the chief cause of the outbreak. In Valera's opinion, the riots were provoked by the "great wealth of the Cordovan conversos that enabled them to buy public offices," and by the "arrogant" use of these offices by the conversos, which "the Old Christians could not tolerate."[4] Thus the causes of the Cordovan disturbances were, according to Valera, social and political; the religious aspect has completely disappeared.

He follows Palencia also in describing the attacks on the conversos in the other Andalusian cities, the assassination of Miguel Lucas in Jaén, and the ensuing pogrom on the conversos of that city. He weakens Palencia's criticism of the pogromists by attributing to them "a madness of cruelty" rather than a "mad thirst for blood," as did Palencia. But instead he incorporates the far-reaching statement (which he took from the *Cronica Castellana*) that the *conversos of Jaén were killed for no reason.*[5] It is evident, then, that with regard to both Cordova and Jaén, *Valera excluded the religious reason from the causes of the outbreaks.*

These were not minor assertions; and to make them under the inquisitional regime required considerable daring. To be sure, Valera was the King's *maestresala* and member of his Council; he was also favored by both the King and Queen; but to give the Inquisitors cause to attack him, by presenting himself as a defender of "heretics"—and to do so against the evidence of his main source (Palencia)—was to take chances that only morality could dictate and courage could permit.

His courage, however, was greatly diminished when he came to describe the founding of the Inquisition. The establishment of the Holy Office, he declares, resulted from the *"illumination by divine grace* of the most illustrious princes, Ferdinand and Isabella," who, in their desire to cleanse their kingdoms of all crimes, did not forget the heresies with which their subjects were infected.[6] According to Valera, the bearers of these heresies were not only "many of the newly converted," but also "some of the Old Christians, who deviated from the right path." Among the latter he mentions the heretics of Durango (who had already been wiped out decades before!), the doubters of all truths save man's birth and death, and those who interpret certain parts of Holy Scripture against the understanding of the holy doctors of the Church.[7] By including the above exegetes and skeptics, as well as the dead heresy of Durango, among the factors against which the Inquisition was created, Valera sought to present the Inquisition not as specifically anti-converso, but as generally anti-heretical, and thereby soften the blow against his group. No doubt for this reason he also stated that, in establishing the Inquisition, the Kings followed not only the advice of Tomás de Torquemada, the prior of Santa Cruz, but also that of the prior of Prado, Hernando de Talavera (who was a converso).[8] The statement led Zurita to remark: "He does not tell the truth. Hernando de Talavera did not share the intentions of Torquemada. He was *opposed* to the founding of the Inquisition."[9]

II. FERNANDO DE PULGAR

Like Valera, Pulgar, the son of a converso who must have been exceptionally well connected, was reared from his youth at the Court of Juan II.[10] His intellectual horizon was that of the early Renaissance, which by then had invaded Spain with great force, while his moral views were shaped by that particular blend of ideas, drawn from both Testaments and the Church

Fathers' teachings, which formed the converso social creed. That creed he was ready to defend. He may not have been trained as a fighter like Valera, but his pen was his sword, which he used with great skill and often with the artistry of a juggler. His eloquence as both writer and speaker, and his mastery of several languages (among them French), led to his appointment by Enrique IV as his secretary and chronicler (in 1458) and later as his ambassador to Rome and France. The same abilities must have earned him, under the Catholic Kings, the positions of the Queen's Secretary, member of the Royal Council, and ambassador to France (in 1475).

Since he was for many years the chronicler of Enrique IV, it stands to reason that he wrote the history of that reign. But if so, none of this work has survived, except perhaps some sections included in the chapters which precede his *Crónica of the Catholic Kings*. This *crónica* he began to write in 1482, possibly in 1481—i.e., after the establishment of the Inquisition—but what he writes on the conversos prior to that event reflects the views he held—and expressed—in the period of Enrique IV and the early years of the Catholic Kings.

In his extant chapters on Enrique, Pulgar does not refer to any of the attacks made upon the conversos during that reign (possibly because he dealt with these in his other *crónica*). But he discusses the converso problem after Enrique's time—that is, to the end of the seventies—both in his *Letters* and his *Crónica of the Catholic Kings*. Since his *Letters* are supposed to bear more distinctly the stamp of his own views, we shall first touch on them.

Of the letters in question, undoubtedly the most important is his epistle "To a Friend in Toledo."[11] "In this noble city," Pulgar writes, "it is not tolerated in good spirit that some who are believed not to belong to [the right] lineage have honors and governmental offices, since it is maintained that their defect of blood denies them the capacity of government. In the same way, some cannot agreeably see wealth possessed by men who are not believed to merit it, especially in those who had recently acquired it. These matters, which are considered grave and intolerable, give rise to an envy that torments men to the point of taking up arms and launching assaults."[12] As Pulgar sees it, these men seek to "correct the world *(emendar el mundo)* and redivide its goods and honors according to their own will" *(arbitrio)*. For it seems to them that "the world is in a bad way and its assets are not well distributed."[13]

One should not conclude from this that Pulgar refers here to a class struggle in the modern sense. What he has in mind is something more fundamental, more complex and more ancient. "This is a very old dispute," he says, "and a very old quarrel," whose deep roots go back to the beginning of mankind. What he is speaking of is the *racial* struggle, which no doubt has social and economic implications, but nevertheless stems from different urges, which the enemies of the conversos seek to exploit. By conditioning the right to wealth on lineage, these men, he says, err against the *law of nature,* for "all of us have been born of the same matter *(de una masa)* and had a noble beginning." They also err against *divine law,* which "wants us all to belong to one flock and be guided by one shepherd"; and especially do they act against the "virtue of charity," which illuminates the road to true felicity. Pulgar adds that many who are believed to be of "low origin" *(baja sangre)* become, by dint of their natural inclination, great scholars, or able fighters, or accomplished orators, or experts in governance and administration, while others who descend from kings and men of note remain obscure and forgotten, for being ["naturally"] incapable.[14] And this is so not only in mankind generally. "Even among brothers, of the same father and mother, we see that one is learned, the other ignorant; one is a coward, the other valiant; one is generous, the other avaricious."[15] And thus one should not be troubled by the fact that riches and honors are possessed by some who seemingly ought not to have them, and vice versa. "For this proceeds from a divine ordination" that *"cannot be obstructed on earth except by destroying the earth."* We have to believe, he adds, that "God created men, and not lineages, and that, when born, he made them all nobles." Baseness of blood and obscurity of lineage are acquired only by those who have left the way of virtue and inclined themselves toward the vices. Consequently, no natural force can secure the transfer of nobility from one to another, without the presence of the *"source of true nobility which is no other than virtue."*[16]

This summarizes Pulgar's credo about wealth, offices, honors and nobility. And the same views he puts into the mouth of Gómez Manrique, the governor of Toledo, when, in 1478, the city was threatened with new attacks upon the conversos. To calm the spirits of the incited citizens, the governor addressed them in a speech, which is included in Pulgar's *Crónica of the Catholic Kings* and which was no doubt prepared for him by Pulgar.[17] In that speech, Manrique surveyed the behavior of the Toledans in the preceding decades, showing how they rebelled against one king after another, believing that through these rebellions and robberies they would achieve wealth and honors. But what have they actually achieved? "Have those who incited you to rebel divided among you any goods or offices?" the governor asked his Toledan audience. "Or can anyone of you say that he possesses anything of the past robberies? Certainly nothing!" To be sure, the estates of the instigators were enlarged, and some of them attained "with your efforts and at your peril honors and offices of iniquity," but "you have remained the *deceived people,* without benefit, without honor, without authority, and with infamy, peril, and poverty"; and what is worse, "you have shown yourselves as rebels to your King, destroyers of your land, and subjects of the evil men who make war within the city, where it is forbidden to make it."[18]

Gómez concluded his address by saying that he refrained from continuing and extending the punishment he began to inflict on the evildoers "because the King and Queen, our lords, . . . do not enjoy shedding their subjects' blood" and because he believed that his arguments had influenced the troublemakers to abandon their mischief.[19] But this was not Pulgar's real position. "We may truly believe," he makes Gómez say at one point, "that if the first and second rebellions had been punished according to the gravity of the crimes they entailed, you would not have dared to commit the others."[20] But what appears in the speech as a passing remark represents only a small part of the program which he would recommend to the government as an effective way of pacifying the country. Those who "disturb the peace," and make themselves "principal guides" of the people, Pulgar says in the above-cited letter, are "moved primarily by arrogance and ambition; their means are envy and malice, and their ends death and destruction." Surely, such people do not deserve to have the authority of leaders, but as "men of scandal they *should be separated, not only from the people, but from the world,*" for so moved are they by their evil intentions that they will not be detained either by the fear of God, or the orders of the King, or the pangs of conscience, or the counsels of reason. They must suffer the ultimate penalty.[21]

Pulgar has thus made clear his view that the conflict between the Old and New Christians arose from envy of the conversos' wealth and jealousy of the honors they attained and the authority they exercised through the offices they controlled. The quarrel was therefore racial and social. It was not religious—a factor which Pulgar simply ignores as unworthy of mention. In the preceding generation this was the position of such converso leaders as the Relator and Torquemada, except that in the intervening decades the conversos must have been far more assimilated and their interest in the religious issue—or, more precisely, in the problem of the Judaizers—must have diminished accordingly. Also regarding the remedy for the conflict, Pulgar urged the same measures proposed by his converso predecessors and by Old Christian defenders of his group, such as Barrientos, Montalvo and Oropesa. He demanded extreme punishment of the conversos' enemies and *no* punishment for the conversos, who were in his eyes "not guilty" of the charges leveled against them by their adversaries. This, too, implies that he dismissed religious misconduct by the conversos as a problem requiring stern action to cure it.

This was Pulgar's position before the establishment of the Holy Office. But the Inquisition, and the war it declared on the conversos, must have shattered his outlook. The issue he considered fictitious or half-dead suddenly became all-important, and to deny the Inquisition's charges in this matter would place him in confrontation with the dreaded institution. Survival meant acceptance of the Inquisition's claims; and anxious to survive, he admitted them, persuading himself that by acknowledging the "problem" as presented by the Inquisition, he could dispute its applied solution. Thus he wrote his letter to Cardinal Mendoza, in which he argued, on the grounds of humanity, the impossibility of suppressing a large-scale heresy by mass extermination.[22] He soon learned that this was not the view of the Inquisitors, and that his tactical "admission" of the Inquisition's contentions had completely missed the mark. His letter was considered scandalous; he was even accused of heresy, and before long was compelled to leave the Court, since his arguments were regarded as inconsistent not only with the Inquisition but also with the policy of the Kings. When a year later he was invited by the Sovereigns to serve as chronicler of the realm, he knew he would have to be more cautious in presenting the Inquisition's case.

Thus in his early account of the Inquisition in his *Crónica of the Catholic Kings,* he tried to be as docile as possible and avoid any criticism of the Inquisition.[23] But soon thereafter he abandoned that stand. Evidently, he *could* not remain silent in the presence of the terrible atrocities he witnessed, and used his *Crónica* not only as a medium of information but also as an instrument of attack. Thus in the second account he included in the *Crónica* concerning the founding of the Inquisition in Seville, he speaks only of *"some* Christians of Jewish descent" who began to Judaize and did not "feel well about the faith"[24]; and after describing the actions of the Inquisition against them, he presents sharp criticisms of these actions as expressed by some "relatives of the prisoners and condemned." By means of these criticisms Pulgar publicly exposed the Inquisition's improper and illegal procedures, charging it with the infliction of punishments on the accused which were *"too grave for many reasons"* and therefore constituted a *"deviation from justice."* Above all, he here states that both the "ecclesiastic Inquisitors and the secular executors *behaved cruelly and showed great enmity, not only toward those they punished and tormented,* but also toward all [New Christians], with the aim of besmirching and defaming them with that horrible crime." What is more, this cruelty was clearly manifested in the entire range of the Inquisition's operations, beginning with the "acceptance of witnesses and information, through the tortures administered, to the execution of the sentences."[25] Pulgar could hardly have made a stronger case against the Inquisition. And this he did in the pages of the royal *crónica* itself!

He found another opportunity to assail the Inquisition when he touched on the beginning of its activity in Toledo, and then in Valladolid. In Toledo he speaks of *"some* men and women who performed secretly Jewish rites," among whom some were condemned for "perpetual incarceration and others were burned." It turned out, however, that these condemnations were based on testimonies given by Moors, Jews, servants and vile men, and especially by poor and iniquitous Jews who, due to their malice and enmity for the conversos, falsely accused them as Judaizers. Eight of these Jews were stoned, he reported.[26] The same thing happened in Valladolid, where "many vile

Jews" falsely accused "some conversos" in order to "carry them to death."
When the truth finally emerged, some of these Jews too were sentenced to
be stoned.[27]

Thus, Pulgar's accounts of the Inquisition turn into a grim accusation
against the Inquisition and against the Inquisitors as defenders of Christianity. In these accounts he totally forsakes the claim of the existence of a
widespread heresy, which he originally accepted for tactical reasons, and no
longer speaks of the Judaizers as a mass movement, or even as "many," but
only as *"algunos"* (some), which could of course suggest a small minority; nor
does he speak of the Inquisitors as men of pure intentions and proper
behavior, as he did in his first discussions of the Inquisition, but as cruel
agents, full of hate for the conversos, whom they subject to the worst evils.
However cleverly Pulgar conducted these attacks, it required exceptional
courage on his part thus to offend the Inquisition's performance and test the
patience of its severe functionaries—including the Inquisitor-General,
Tomás de Torquemada.

Adolfo de Castro said that "one voice alone in all Spain was heard in
defence of the victims" of the Inquisition.[28] That was Pulgar's. It must be
noted, however, that when he spoke in his name, he could not help lauding
the Inquisitors, and that when he attacked them, he did not speak in his name.
What we hear, then, clearly is his voice as reporter, who loudly, but indirectly, presented the charges which Pulgar, as accuser, had to suppress.

III. ALONSO DE PALENCIA

I

No other Spanish historian provides so much information about the evolution of the Old/New Christian conflict in the second half of the fifteenth
century as Alfonso Fernández de Palencia. Most of what we know about the
conversos of that period derives from his writings, and most of what he writes
about them was considered by him an inseparable part of Spain's history at
certain crucial junctures. Hence his extensive interest in this group. The
question is to what extent are his accounts about it true.

For no other Spanish historical narrative aroused so much controversy
about its credibility as Palencia's memoirs entitled *Three Decades of My Life*,
better known as the *Crónica of Enrique IV*.[29] The main cause of that controversy was Palencia's extreme criticism of King Enrique. According to Palencia, the King was not only a strange creature and a misfit, but a criminal
of the worst kind. That these characterizations do violence to the truth is
attested by all other contemporary portrayals of Enrique, such as those of
Valera, Pulgar and Escavias,[30] which resemble that of his official chronicler,

Carrillo, who often spoke of Enrique with genuine admiration. They are also denied by the Catalonians' repeated attempts to induce Enrique to become their king. When they made these attempts, Enrique was already thirty-seven years old and had been King of Castile for eight years. Had he been as perverse as Palencia described him, his crimes and misdeeds would have been public knowledge; and it is inconceivable that the legal-minded Catalonians would have wanted to put their country under his rule.

No wonder that Palencia's "image" of Enrique led many historians to denounce him. Said Gerónimo de la Cruz, the seventeenth-century biographer of Enrique: "Palencia was a historian of the worst intentions"; all he wrote against the King was "inspired with hatred and enmity"; he was a "salable person who hardly ever said even a single word of truth"[31]; and these denunciations were echoed by many authors, down to Orestes Ferrara, who called Palencia "a perfidious chronicler."[32] Against these critics, however, there stands the great authority of Zurita, who flourished only fifty years after Palencia and said of him: "Spain never had a more truthful chronicler."[33] He, too, was followed by a line of supporters, through Zúñiga, who wrote Seville's history,[34] to Palencia's modern biographer, Antonio Paz y Mélia, who praised Palencia's "valorous independence" and his courage in exposing the corruption of his time.[35]

Truth does not necessarily fall between two extremes. Even so, in the case of Palencia, some leading Spanish scholars of the nineteenth century tended to see him half-white and half-black. That is how Amador saw him[36]; and that is how he was seen by Ballester. The latter regarded Palencia as the most important historian of the time of Enrique IV; he also considered him an inexorable critic of his society, but—"more vengeful than just" (mas vengador que justiciero).[37] Similarly, Menéndez y Pelayo regarded Palencia as the Tacitus of Enrique IV, but flawed by the defect noted by Ballester.[38]

Was Palencia vengeful? Or was he mistaken? And if so, to what extent were these shortcomings reflected in his history? His attitude toward Enrique cannot be explained by the available sources; for his criticism of the King is not only partisan but irrational, reflecting a hatred that must have arisen from most humiliating confrontations between him and the King when Palencia served as his chronicler. This animus was extended by Palencia to many of Enrique's friends. Did it also determine Palencia's position in other related cases?

This raises the question of his alleged "independence," for which he was so praised by Paz y Mélia. Was Palencia really an independent judge? When he wrote his *Crónica* of Enrique, he was not a court historian who glosses over his master's errors and magnifies his achievements. But this does not mean that he was independent. For while he was free of Enrique's domination, he was in the service of the Catholic Sovereigns, especially of Queen Isabella.

To be sure, at least most of the *Décadas* were written after he had left the court of these Kings, but their powerful influence no doubt lingered in his mind, and he must have aspired to become royal chronicler. His *Décadas* were designed to serve the interests of Isabella, the legitimacy of whose succession clearly depended on the illegitimacy of Enrique's daughter, Juana. Like Valera and Pulgar, Palencia served the Queen by stressing Enrique's alleged impotence. But he went far beyond this. Perhaps he thought that by denigrating Enrique, he might win the Queen's greater affection and support. In fact, even after he had left the Court, he received a pension and grants from the Kings, among them the 60,000 maravedis given him in 1482.[39]

His apparent desire to please the Kings weakens the assumption of his "independence"; yet other facts seem to strengthen it. Virtually nothing is known of Palencia's social background, but we have a fair notion of his education, which was overseen by several strong personalities who stood firmly by their beliefs. These were famous men such as Alonso de Cartagena, Bessarion and George of Trebizond, with whom he was associated for decades; and it was their views of government and society, of war and peace, of the noble and the ignoble—together with the views of the Roman moralists and historians with whose works these men acquainted him—that taught him to judge things in a moral light and had a formative influence on his attitudes.

He remained faithful to the old Spanish political ideals: a strong monarchy, with the right of inheritance as conceived in the Middle Ages, but a monarchy governed by law—by the law of God and the law of nature, as it is inscribed in man's heart; he respected the social conventions of Spain, its social distinctions and class divisions, but he wanted the nobility to be true to its duties and, above all, to its code of honor. He was a Christian who believed in "true Catholicism," who wanted to see the Church purified and ennobled, less interfering in crude politics and devoting itself more, or wholly, to its religious principles. There was nevertheless none of the religious reformer in him, as there was none of the political innovator; and he had mixed feelings about the conversos.

II

These feelings raise the difficult question of his dominant attitude toward the New Christians—a question that is further complicated by the views expressed in modern historiography concerning his identity. Thus Juan Torres-Fontes, a Spanish scholar who studied the life of Enrique IV, wrote in 1953, referring to Palencia, that "his Jewish origin has been proven."[40] This assertion, however, was not supported by data as to when and by whom that proof was offered. Nor did Américo Castro supply such data when he wrote, in several of his works,[41] that Palencia was a New Christian. We can never-theless detect the source of these and several similar statements: Julio Puyol's *"Los cronistas de Enrique IV"* published in 1921.[42] In this work, which includes a chapter on Palencia, Puyol says: "He was born in Osma to a family of conversos on July 21, 1423," and in a note accompanying this statement, he says that the biographical data he presented in the text were drawn from the works referred to in the "preceding note."[43] In the preceding note Puyol mentions Amador, Fabié, Menéndez y Pelayo, Tomás Rodríguez and Paz y Mélia, all of whom indeed wrote of Palencia,[44] but none said a word about his Jewish ancestry. Nor do we find a statement to this effect in the works of Nicolás Antonio, Pellicer, Gallardo, Dormer, Clemencín,[45] or any of the other scholars and historians who had dealt with Palencia or his time before Puyol. On what grounds, then, did Puyol make his definite assertion?

Evidently, he made his claim solely on the basis of the reasons he presents in his work—reasons which both he and his followers must have found so convincing that they unhesitatingly ascribed a Jewish ancestry to Palencia. But are Puyol's reasons really flawless?

Puyol summarizes his main arguments in the following brief statement: "It is not to be forgotten," he says, "that the chronicler stemmed from Jewish stock *(de estirpe de Judíos)* and that, as such, he not only *retained the indelible characteristics of his race,* but also failed—despite his strong protestations of adherence to the Church—to hide his *profound affection for his congeners,* as well as his *hatred for the Old Christians."*[46] Logically, the statement is wrongly structured, for it rests on a *petitio principii,* assuming what it tries to prove. We shall, however, treat Puyol's arguments in due order and see whether we can derive from them the conclusion their author took for granted.

What are the "characteristics of the Jewish race" which Puyol considered "indelible" and which he evidently claimed to have discerned? "A reflection of his Jewish mentality," says Puyol, "is the superstitious background of his spirit and the credit he gives to omens—a belief which, especially in the Semitic peoples, presents the idea of the constant influence of the supernatu-ral in human affairs." Puyol finds evidence for this "belief" in Palencia's references to meteorological and astronomical phenomena, such as cyclones, storms, comets and eclipses, which form the overwhelming majority of his "signs" of irregular future events, and also in his incidental reporting (on five occasions) of other strange events of a seemingly miraculous nature.[47] But can any of these reflect what Puyol calls the "indelible characteristics of the Jewish race"?

The truth is that the belief in the occult generally, and in heavenly phenomena in particular, as instruments for predicting future events was not characteristic of the "Semitic peoples," or a particular trait of the "Jewish mentality," but a phenomenon common to almost all peoples at certain stages of their civilization. Semitic peoples, too, practiced the art of foretelling the future on the basis of various "signs"; but perhaps no other people had practiced them so regularly, and developed the belief in them into such a ramified study, as did the "non-Semitic" Greeks. There was hardly any form of divination known anywhere in antiquity (and later in the Middle Ages) that the Greeks had not adopted or invented and included in their general "science" of divination, which consisted of more than twenty branches. In contrast, the Jews were, in this respect, an exception among all ancient peoples, for they not only denied any value to the signs widely assumed as foretelling the future, but launched a crusade against the believers in such signs. Had Puyol forgotten the biblical injunctions against all occult practices,[48] or the prophetic scorn at those who "fear the signs of heaven" and follow the theories of the "nations" about them which are nothing but "nonsense"?[49]

This does not mean of course that the Jews of the Middle Ages were immune to the belief in miraculous signs and especially to astrology, but as believers in these methods of "forecast," the Jews were assuredly not an exception in mankind. The chapters "Comets and Courts" and "Astrological Predictions" in Lynn Thorndike's *History of Magic and Experimental Science* show clearly that astrology, and the prediction of events on the basis of heavenly signs, such as comets, eclipses and meteorological irregularities, was of common interest in fifteenth-century Europe, embracing the courts of France, Germany, Naples, Milan, Bohemia, Hungary, and Poland. The frequent appearance of comets in that century (and especially Halley's comet in 1456) was the subject of a whole literature, whose writers and sponsors included monks and bishops; and the astrological predictions from 1464 to the end of the century were more widespread and frequent than ever before.[50] Palencia was simply a representative of his age in following a tendency which, as we see it, had nothing to do with Jewish mentality, but with the state of European culture at the time. Moreover, as a student of Livy, Suetonius and other classical historians, whose works he took as models for his own, Palencia most likely also followed their example in frequently referring to omens of evil. That his readers might see in this a "Jewish" innovation would not, we assume, even enter his mind. The belief in miracles and their frequent occurrence was, after all, a feature of Christian, rather than Jewish life in the Europe of his time.

III

This, we believe, nullifies the main proof offered by Puyol for Palencia's Jewishness. But he offers, as we have noticed, two other proofs which on the surface seem reasonable. Palencia, Puyol claims, was imbued with "hatred for the Old Christians," presumably *all* Old Christians, or at least their great majority[51]; and to prove this contention, Puyol makes much of Palencia's attitude toward the popes. On the pretext of the corruption of the Roman Curia, says Puyol, he lashes its members severely for their avarice, accusing them of heaping evil upon evil when they succeed to the papacy, "as if it had been a point of honor for the successor to exceed all the others in the perpetration of detestable deeds."[52] In addition, Palencia laments that the popes hold the tiara "primarily for the arrogant ostentation of their power," and that "insignificant people who lack any merit" are "elevated to the grade of the pontifical throne"[53]; he accuses them of simony when they dispense all kinds of indulgences for money,[54] "always in a manner that the magnificence of the payment corresponds to the liberality of the grant."[55]

There is no doubt that Palencia's attacks on the popes (and, we may add, on the College of Cardinals) abound in offensive accusations and invective; but this is hardly evidence that he was a converso. These attacks reflect not a converso attitude, but an attitude then found in many parts of Christendom, especially in Italy and ultramontane countries. The "decades" he wrote about followed, we should recall, the long period of the Schism, which ended in 1449 and during which the sharpest denunciations and vilest criticisms were hurled against the popes. From these attacks on the occupants of St. Peter's chair the papacy did not recover for a long time; and the popes' positions following the Schism, in which principle was often sacrificed for expediency, their constant search for money to replenish their treasury (which could never keep up with their lavish expenses), and the moral shortcomings of some of the popes, fueled these continual reproaches, which finally culminated in the Reformation. Palencia expressed his view of the popes in the period between the Schism and the Reformation, and he wrote of them as one who had long lived in Italy, who had heard all the cynical and very worldly rumors that were circulated about them in that country, and who had noticed the complete lack of reverence with which critics of the Church in Italy often spoke of the popes and their activities. To be sure, sharp public censure of the papacy was not a common Spanish practice, but here too popes were harshly criticized by those whose interests they opposed; and Palencia, we should recall, was faced with popes who supported Enrique IV. Even so, his criticisms of the popes reflects an Italian rather than a Spanish attitude, and certainly not a converso attitude. For no other Catholic group produced more ardent and more effective defenders of the papacy than the conversos. Politically, too, it was important for the New Christians to generate respect for the popes; and despite their disappointment with the papacy's position in their quarrel with their enemies in 1451, they were careful to show it all homage and respect. After all, it was only the papacy they could turn to for aid when all other attempts and approaches failed.

It follows that Palencia's attacks upon the popes were not consistent with a converso policy any more than were other attacks upon the papacy during and after the great Schism. Indeed, as we see it, only an Old Christian would dare speak in those days against the papacy in such a vein. Had he been a New Christian, Palencia would have tended to moderate or disguise his opinion of the popes, if it were indeed so negative.

IV

There remains, then, the final "proof" that Puyol offers to Palencia's Jewish origin—the passages in which Palencia "defends and exculpates the conversos, especially those of Cordova and Seville."[56] According to Puyol, Palencia shows in these passages "profound affection" for his "congeners," the fellow members of his race. Puyol says nothing more on this subject, which apparently he considered self-evident. To us, however, his contention requires proof, especially since Palencia's attitude toward the conversos was likely to shape his views about them. Was then, we ask, that attitude marked by such a "profound affection" for the conversos as to be an unquestionable symptom of his belonging to their group?

The greatest attacks on the conversos in Enrique IV's time occurred in Toledo (1467) and Cordova (1473). Palencia used both occasions to express his opinion of the conversos and their share of responsibility for the outbreaks. In the case of Toledo, he puts the main blame on King Enrique's agents, who induced the conversos of the city to believe that King Alfonso's followers were their enemies who sought to exterminate all Marranos. That the conversos were agitated by such fears is possible, especially since the city, under Alfonso's regime, was seething with anti-converso agitation. The Toledan conversos' provision of arms and their attempts to secure the help of friendly nobles may be understood in the light of that situation. But this is not how Palencia explains their activity. According to him, these actions were not aimed at their self-defense, but formed part of a plan to attack the Old Christians and capture the city, apparently to deliver it to King Enrique. Naturally, their preparations were conducted in secrecy and thus, when they sought the Count of Cifuentes' aid, they pointed out to him only the dangers they had faced, but concealed from him the real purpose of their request, which was their "arrogant resolution" to take hold of the city.[57] But could such a position have been adopted by the conversos? Could they really have had the means and manpower to wrest all the fortified places in the city from the Old Christians' hands? Nothing that occurred in the course of the outbreak indicates that they had such a plan in mind or the capacity to implement it. What we have here, then, is merely a repetition of their enemies' claims in the days of Sarmiento that the conversos, who armed themselves in self-defense, planned to seize the city and deliver it to Alvaro—obviously, an excuse to blame the conversos for the casualties and other punishments they suffered. Yet no converso historian would have taken this excuse as an explanation of the pogrom. If Palencia was indeed "persuaded" to believe in the truth of this explanation, this in itself would show that he was an "outsider."

And no converso would have written as he did that the Count of Cifuentes supported the conversos during their military encounters with their enemies because he was *deceived* by them to believe that the *"conversos were fighting for their liberty and not [merely] to hurt the Old Christians."*[58] Nor would any converso write that the Old Christians, who were originally fighting "sluggishly," were "finally persuaded that they had to fight with determination for their *religion,* their freedom and their life."[59] For no converso writer would assume that the Old Christians, who initiated the battle to ruin the conversos, fought it for "their religion and liberty." One may conclude from Palencia's statement that the same interests also motivated the conversos. But then the "religion" they fought for would be *their* religion, different from that of the Old Christians. Could any New Christian author subscribe to such an assumption?

We have seen how in describing the quarrel that broke out in the Toledan Cathedral in 1467, Palencia showed a clearly anti-converso attitude; how he presented the conversos as deliberate aggressors, violating the "divine service," and responsible for the killing of Old Christian officials (against what we gather from another source).[60] What is more, he assumed that Alvar Gómez provoked the entire scandal because he was "aware of what his friends of the same race were planning [namely, the capture the city] and, being their accomplice [in the preparation of that plan]," he counted on their strength and their ultimate victory, and therefore behaved impudently and rudely.[61] Palencia here seems to forsake all logic in his attempt to prove the conversos' guilt. Alvar Gómez, who betrayed Enrique and was Pacheco's collaborator in the rebellion, wanted the city to be delivered to the man whom he fled in fear of his life! Everything is of course possible in politics; but Palencia has nothing to support his guess. He is simply trying to combine some glaring contradictions of fact to substantiate his case that the conversos of Toledo planned to take the city.

Coming to Cordova, he sees the main cause of the riots there in 1473 in the conversos' provocative religious behavior—that is, their "open" practice of Jewish rites which they had previously performed secretly.[62] To be sure, Palencia says that the bishop, who was corrupt, harped on their religious transgressions, and that the conversos accused him of being "factious and malevolent." Evidently, the conversos denied his charges, but Palencia does not bother to present their rebuttal. Instead, he says that the conversos performed their sacrilegious deeds in reliance on the military protection of Aguilar, whom they supplied with huge sums of money. But is this credible? Would a community so threatened that it had to pay so much for its protection behave in so provocative a manner—and this only five years after the great riots in Toledo, and five additional years after those of Carmona! Palencia does not seem to be disturbed by these questions, and in contrast to the conversos' contempt for Christianity, he stresses their opponents' "religious zeal."[63]

Nevertheless, to this initial cause of the conflict (i.e., the conversos' religious misdeeds) Palencia adds other reasons. "The conversos [of Cordova]," he says, "were extraordinarily enriched by rare arts, and puffed with pride, they aspired with insolent arrogance to dispose of the public offices."[64] What New Christian, we ask, would have expressed such criticism of the conversos' attempts to enter public service—attempts which, they believed, they had the full right to make as Christians and equal citizens of the republic? And what New Christian would see their efforts to attain such offices a display of *insolent arrogance* after they had been engaged in these offices for generations and served in all the country's administrations? These statements were framed in the style of the conversos' bitterest enemies, who never acquiesced in their entry into the administrative system, and Palencia seems to have taken them from a rabidly anti-Marrano document.

What is more, no converso would describe the efforts of the conversos in Cordova to protect themselves against the attacks of the Old Christians as Palencia did. "The conversos," he says, "*because of their natural timidity and the awareness of their evil deeds,* prepared defenses in their most populous precincts, armed themselves and hid *the treasures which they had accumulated, in most cases, by foul methods.*"[65] The readiness of the conversos to defend themselves with arms in hand is described by him as "timidity" (contrary to their "newborn valor," of which the conversos boasted) and that "timidity" (or cowardice) is not only *part of their nature* (just as Marcos García once said), but also stems from the knowledge of their crimes, whose discovery they feared. For their treasures were obtained not only through *rare* arts, as Palencia said earlier, but in *most cases,* through *"evil arts" (malas artes).* This, too, is part of the terminology of the converso racist enemies. If Palencia did not share the views they convey, he certainly copied them from anti-Marrano documents, which served him as sources for his Cordovan account. But his *readiness to use these sources and their extreme antisemitic language shows as clearly as any evidence could that he was no New Christian.*

His attitude toward the new Marrano nobles is also anti-converso. He considers them "men of low extraction, accustomed to the vilest trades," and accuses them of having attained the Order of the Cavalry only "by means of money and against any rule."[66] "Never did they attempt to take any part even in the least significant movement of liberty," he says; but once they joined the knighthood, they hastened to "rouse rebellions and form bands," which did not contribute of course to the country's welfare.[67] This passage bears the symptoms of Palencia's own thinking; he hated the upstart "intruders," who increased the tumult in the country; but in this instance too, we may safely assume, no converso would treat so critically the new converso nobility and so generalize its negative characteristics.

It follows that Puyol has misrepresented Palencia's attitude toward the New Christians. No one who drew such a bleak picture of the conversos' religious, social and economic conduct could be filled with such "profound affection" for them as Puyol claimed, and certainly not with such affection that could offer ground for identifying him as a member of their group. On the contrary, Palencia's negative descriptions of the conversos as analyzed above give every reason to believe that he was an Old Christian.

V

Nevertheless, it is true that on several occasions Palencia took the side of the conversos, and vehemently accused their persecutors. This happened in his discussion of the Marranos in Seville after the riots in Cordova, when he writes that while some of them sought to migrate, the majority remained in the city "without fear of death" (there is no mention here of their "timidity by nature"); in his description of the behavior of the settlers in Gibraltar, which was honorable religiously, too (if we go by the implications of Palencia's narrative); and especially in his portrayal of the riots in Carmona in 1462. Here, as we have seen, he calls the pogromists "evildoers" *(malvadores)*, who perpetrated their crimes against the conversos *"in the name of religion,"* but purely out of "thirst for their wealth," adding, after these crucial words, the cardinal remark *"as they had done before in Toledo and as the thieves had done later following their pernicious example."*[68]

Palencia wrote this during the reign of the Catholic Kings, and the crimes the "thieves" committed "later"—i.e., in Toledo, 1467, and Cordova, 1473— were already behind him, as were the events of Carmona. Yet here he judges the later occurrences as he does the Carmona massacre, quite differently from the way he treats them in later chapters, where he offered, as we have seen, his detailed account of what happened in Toledo in 1467 and Cordova in 1473. Obviously, we have here two conflicting attitudes toward both the conversos and their opponents. What caused the change in Palencia's position?

The only plausible explanation of this discrepancy must be related, as we see it, to the *time* in which Palencia wrote these chapters. The piece on Carmona was probably written in 1477, if not earlier, before the Sovereigns appealed to the Pope to authorize an Inquisition.[69] In contrast, the pieces on Toledo in 1467 and Cordova in 1473 were written, in all likelihood, *after* that appeal had been made, and possibly after the Sovereigns had received the Pope's positive response. Palencia must have been in touch with the Court and aware of the pertinent developments. He well realized the change that the Inquisition would effect in Spain's social life, and clearly understood that, under its authority, it would be utterly impossible to write on the conversos in the vein he had used when he described the pogrom in Carmona. If he tried to do so, Palencia was sure, he would sign his literary death warrant, and his literary survival may have been to him more precious than life itself. Once the Inquisition was established, he knew, all expressed views on men and events would have to be accommodated to its judgments. His portrayal of the Holy Office, which he wrote years later under the Inquisition, shows his moral collapse before the dread it inspired.[70] Like Valera and Pulgar, he too retreated from his previously expressed ideas and formally accepted the Inquisition's declarations about its findings, purposes and achievements.

Yet Valera and Pulgar retreated only after the Inquisition had been established, and even then conducted a kind of rear-guard action in the conversos' defense. Palencia, as an Old Christian, did not feel obliged to take such risks. He began his accommodation to the Inquisition as soon as he suspected its approaching establishment. This was not easy for a man who aspired to be a truthful historian and a just social critic. In the two years that passed between the authorization of the Inquisition and its establishment in Seville, there must have been moments when Palencia, like others, came to doubt the materialization of the plan. At such moments, he relaxed his vigilance and reduced his caution, and wrote on the conversos in a sympathetic spirit which reflected his true thoughts. But the panic that seized him when he prepared his accounts on Toledo in 1467 and Cordova in 1473 still left its imprint on his formulations, such as those he composed when he wrote about the plan to attack the Marranos in Segovia. In the anti-Marrano social atmosphere, which gave all the signs of a gathering storm, Palencia remained ever sensitive to what was said and done in the Court with regard to the inquisitional project. In consequence, he was often inclined to bend the truth, but, trying to retain his dignity as historian, he repeatedly attempted to restore what he mutilated even when least expected to do so. Thus while presenting the northern conversos' negative view of their southern brethren, he could not help incorporating his telling statement that *"the majority of the conversos of Spain follow the example of Pablo de Santa María and his son Alfonso in pursuing the right path."*[71]

CHAPTER IV

The Catholic Kings:
The Early Period

1474–1480

F ew kings came to power in a country more disorganized, more torn by dissension and more aching for good government than did the young Princes Isabella and Ferdinand when they ascended the throne of Castile. More than half a century of feverish unrest, of wars, rebellions, conspiracies and coups d'état, had left a residue of intrigue and turmoil so deeply ingrained in the life of the nation that Castile seemed always to have been on the eve of some social or political explosion. Such an explosion occurred a short time after the opening of the new reign.

Unexpectedly, Isabella's succession passed smoothly and quickly within only few weeks of the death of Enrique IV. Supported by Cabrera and Pedro González de Mendoza, Enrique's chief confidant and now Cardinal of Spain, she was recognized in Segovia as Queen of Castile first by the Segovians, and then by most cities and almost all grandees and prelates of the kingdom. As Isabella's husband, Ferdinand too was given the oath of allegiance as "King" and partner of the Queen in governing the realm. Thus, it appeared that the whole people stood united behind the young monarchs.

But this seeming harmony was not to last. Signs of a deep, irreparable rift became apparent before long.

Some aspirants for power were so embittered by their failure to obtain from Ferdinand and Isabella positions or estates they had considered theirs by right that they denied the legitimacy of Isabella's succession and claimed that the throne belonged rightly to Juana, King Enrique IV's daughter. The young sovereigns did their utmost to pacify the opposition and draw its ringleaders to their side. But the hard-core antagonists would not be won over, and before long the two princes found themselves embroiled in a war on two fronts, internal and external. Apart from their enemies within the nation, headed by the Marquis of Villena, Pacheco's son, and the stubborn, warlike archbishop of Toledo, they had to deal with Portugal's Alfonso V, who, as claimant to the throne, invaded Castile in the first half of May 1475.

In these circumstances, the attention of the nation centered on the shifting fortunes of war and the accompanying political developments. Other problems, including that of the conversos, were shelved for future attention. It was only in March 1476, when the Portuguese had suffered their most crushing defeat and the danger from without had almost vanished, that the sovereigns could attend to internal matters related to the major problem they were faced with—i.e., the establishment of law and order. Even then, however, the converso question received no priority on their agenda. Their first and foremost task, as they saw it, was to gain full control of the national police forces (the hermandades); to suppress some of the great nobles and cities whose loyalty had not yet been secured; and to reduce the remaining nuclei of rebellion still flickering or smoldering in the northwest. It was only when most of these tasks were accomplished that they took a hard look at the converso situation and came up with a radical solution.

The solution was the establishment of an inquisition, shaped according to their own design and calculated to serve their specific needs.

They took the first step toward realizing their decision when they secretly petitioned Pope Sixtus IV to authorize operations of an inquisition in Castile. Since they came to Seville in July–August 1477 and stayed there until September 1478, and since the papal bull approving their plan was issued only about six weeks later, it was obviously in Seville that they framed their petition to the Pope and, in all likelihood, it was also there that they had made up their minds to submit it. We shall dwell later on the major considerations that moved the sovereigns to decide on this step. At the moment we shall touch on some of the developments of that year (from mid-1477 to mid-1478) which had a share in influencing Ferdinand and Isabella to make that crucial decision.

The first of these developments was the return to Cordova of thousands of conversos who had left that city after the great riots (1473) and settled in the fortress town of Gibraltar, which belonged to the Duke of Medina Sidonia.[1] As we have indicated, they were expelled from Gibraltar by the Duke unexpectedly, for no fault of their own, after having done their utmost to build up the place and turn it into a safe Marrano haven.[2] Now, having nowhere else to go, the conversos returned to their old homes in Cordova, "to be confronted," as Palencia put it, "with the very dangers from which they had fled."[3]

Three and a half years had passed since the outbreak of the riots in Cordova. We do not know whether in this period the urban enactment which forbade all conversos to assume public office in the city was cancelled or modified in the conversos' favor. It is possible of course that on her own initiative, or moved by the highly placed conversos in her Court, the Queen instructed the authorities of Cordova to abolish their anti-converso ruling, which conflicted with the laws of the kingdom and the Church. But whether she had done so or not, it is clear that the conversos' condition in the city continued to be dismal. If the statute against them remained in force, they were obviously subject to discrimination and contempt. If it was abolished, hatred for them rose and showed in many other ways. One way or another, three and a half years was too short a time to alter substantially the hostile relations that had caused the assault of 1473.

Under these circumstances, the return to Cordova of thousands of New Christian émigrés undoubtedly roused popular discontent and raised bitter criticisms among the numerous Old Christians who belonged to the anti-Marrano party. To be sure, no mass attacks on the conversos were attempted. The firmness of the Queen, felt from afar, and that of Aguilar, close at hand, were sufficient to prevent such attempts at the time; but the social atmosphere in the city was feverish and was expressed, among other things, in a rising wave of crime. That this wave was directed especially at the conversos, who were also the target of constant vituperation, cannot be doubted, in our opinion; but it is also apparent that it hit many Old Christians, especially among the well-to-do. The city authorities in charge of law and order found it increasingly hard to meet their obligations, and security in Cordova had so deteriorated that at times it seemed that the administration of justice had ceased to function there altogether.[4]

The Kings were aware of this situation, especially since they had come to Andalusia, and they were also conscious of the close relations between the criminal upsurge in the city and the suppressed urge of so many of its residents to pour out their wrath on the conversos. Yet even more serious than the condition in Cordova appeared to them the situation in Seville. Here the conversos commanded great power—numerical, economic and political. Half the city's commerce was in their hands, and much of its administration. Thus both economic and political interests, enhanced by favorable social relations (in many cases, through intermarriage), moved large sections of the middle and upper classes to offer the conversos unqualified support[5]; but other large sections of the same groups, mostly competitors of the conversos, opposed them, while the low classes remained their sworn enemies and looked for excuses to attack them. As was usual in such situations, the friars sided with the conversos' foes, became their spokesmen, and conducted their campaign.

In Seville the anti-converso agitation was led by the Dominicans, who by then had taken over the advocacy of the Inquisition from the Observantine Franciscans. Indubitably, their anti-converso campaign made use of social and racial arguments, but as in the case of Espina and his followers, centered primarily on religious accusations and presented the Inquisition as the only solution to the converso religious problem. Rejecting the charges leveled against them as highly exaggerated or viciously made up, the conversos fiercely denied the need for the erection of inquisitional tribunals. They must have challenged their opponents for proof of their claims; and the Dominicans, like the Franciscans before them, found it hard to offer evidence. This, however, did not diminish the volume, extremism, and ferocity of their assertions.

Chief agitator of the Dominican camp was Alonso de Hojeda, prior of the convent of San Pablo in Seville. Both contemporary sources and modern historians of the Inquisition present him as the main influence that moved the sovereigns to adopt—after much reluctance—the inquisitional solution.[6] No doubt Alonso de Hojeda did his utmost to induce Ferdinand and Isabella to establish the Inquisition, and we may take it for granted that they listened to him respectfully and carefully noted his various arguments. But they must have accorded the same attention also to the chief critics and opponents of the plan. If they finally adopted the friar's proposal, it was not necessarily for the reasons he had offered. A study of their behavior in all that relates to the Inquisition leads us to the conclusion that they were moved to establish it by considerations of their own.

These considerations rested, above all, on the rising social tension they had noticed in Castile (and especially in Andalusia, where they stayed at the time) and on their assessment of the strength of the anti-Marrano party as opposed to that of the pro-converso faction. In measuring that strength, they no doubt considered not only the numerical factor, which must have been in the conversos' disfavor, but also the explosive revolutionary potential of each of the two groups. Riots, disorders and troubles on a large scale could come only from the anti-converso side, they knew; and this was true not only for Seville but for all Andalusian cities. Safe control of Andalusia obviously depended on finding a way to reduce the unrest.

No less disturbing than the developments in Seville was the news they received from Toledo. There, many citizens were aggrieved by the imposts they were required to pay for the Hermandades, recently reorganized by Ferdinand and Isabella as an effective peace-keeping force. It stands to reason that, in the ensuing debates, the conversos took the side of the Crown, both because they put their faith in the monarchs and wished to display their loyalty to them, and because, more than any other group in the country, they were interested in maximal security. This may have aroused the dormant hostility between the conversos and their opponents in the city, who could use the occasion to accuse the New Christians of another betrayal of their interests. In all probability, the charges and counter-charges developed into a bitter quarrel, so that by the middle of 1478 indications abounded that certain groups of Old Christians were planning an assault on the conversos.

The rising internal discontent in Toledo may have stimulated Archbishop Carrillo's hopes that he could move a large number of Toledans to join his pro-Portuguese plot against the Kings. According to Pulgar, certain elements in the city, "incited by the gifts and promises of the archbishop, joined in a conspiracy to kill, in an onslaught, the caballero who was the city's guardian [namely, Gómez Manrique, the *corregidor*] and declare the King of Portugal as their monarch." Pulgar also tells us that the conspirators conducted secret negotiations with those in Toledo "whom they considered ready for scandal" and gave them to understand that, "once the condition of the city changed, their fortunes would change, too," for "they would find *great interest* [i.e., much profit] *in the estates of the merchants and rich citizens, as they had on other occasions.*"[7] By the "merchants and rich citizens" (who were robbed in the past), only the conversos could be meant, and judging by Pulgar, it was Carrillo's incitement to rebellion against the Kings that aroused the lust for robbery among the conversos' foes. As is apparent from Pulgar's own statements, however, events happened in reverse order; the anti-converso ferment was not produced by Alonso Carrillo's agitation for rebellion, but preceded it and helped it spread. The conspirators, it seems, counted largely on the members of the anti-converso party, whom they considered "ready" for an assault, and this readiness was not created overnight; it was there, as a well-known phenomenon, before the development of Carrillo's plans. What is more, the speech which, according to Pulgar, Manrique made to Toledo's citizens at the time, dealt exclusively with the converso problem and clearly indicates that the menacing trouble was primarily of an anti-converso nature.[8] Carrillo's attempt in September of that year to organize an anti-royal conspiracy may, in fact, have helped Manrique to arrest the subversive movement. It gave him an opportunity to execute the ringleaders, not as fomenters of riots against the conversos, but as plotters of rebellion against the sovereigns, to which most of the citizens were no doubt opposed. It need hardly be said that these harsh measures did nothing to lessen and much to increase the animus for the New Christians.

Thus, hostility to the conversos, which the sovereigns saw growing in all the urban centers of Andalusia, including the great cities of Cordova and Seville, and the rising anti-converso fever in Toledo and its archbishopric, were no doubt the main factors that prompted the Kings to adopt the inquisitional solution. It was probably in June or July 1478 that they petitioned the Pope for authorization to establish inquisitional tribunals in Castile; and it was on November 1 of that year that he granted their request in his bull *Exigit sincere devotionis.*

It is unlikely that the receipt of the bull remained a secret to the anti-conversos. But most of them must have been very skeptical about the sovereigns' intention to use it. At any rate, the mood that was spreading in their ranks, especially among their followers in Toledo, was one of disillusionment with the sovereigns, if not of burgeoning defiance of their policy toward the conversos. Probably in reaction to the harsh punishments imposed by Manrique on their leaders in Toledo, some Old Christians, anxious to hurt the conversos, hit upon an anti-Marrano plan of action that might preclude governmental interference. Accordingly, several Old Christian fraternities adopted special statutes that excluded all conversos, purely on grounds of race, from their offices and membership. Their activity soon prompted imitation; and in the course of 1479 the groups and organizations committed to their principle mushroomed in all towns of the Toledan archbishopric. It was no doubt in response to urgent pleas of the conversos, who must have been concerned about that development, that Archbishop Carrillo convened in Alcalá, in early 1481, a special synod which condemned the movement of racial discrimination. It proclaimed all the statutes, rulings and regulations adopted by organizations that shared that movement's views as clearly anti-Christian, and therefore null and void, prohibiting their application on pain of excommunication.[9] Regardless of the impact of this proclamation (and that impact, we presume, must have been small), the events that prompted it could only strengthen the resolve of both sovereigns to go ahead with their inquisitional solution.

Like the anti-Marranos, the conversos were undoubtedly informed of the bull authorizing the establishment of an inquisition, and their leaders must also have become aware of the relevant petition the Kings submitted to the Pope. Like their adversaries, however, they too initially considered it unlikely that the sovereigns would actually use the bull. Accordingly, they must have viewed the petition for the bull as a mere propaganda ploy of the Crown to reduce the pressure of the anti-Marrano party. For the conversos had reason to trust both monarchs. Both had shown evidence of close relations with conversos before they ascended their thrones; and both expanded and cemented those relations after their assumption of power. Many of Isabella's high officials were New Christians, and so were those of Ferdinand. What is more, conversos were found in all the departments of government, in all the councils of state, and among the *personal* secretaries, advisers and associates of both the King and the Queen. The numerous and broadening functions of

these courtiers seemed so inconsistent with the establishment of an inquisition that the conversos must have found it hard to take the inquisitional
threat seriously. It is therefore probable that even in November 1478, when
the bull on the Inquisition reached the Kings, those conversos who were
informed of its arrival did not believe it would be enforced. In fact, almost
two more years passed before the kings took formal action on the bull. Why?

Most scholars attribute the delay to the influence exercised by the conversos at Court, but this is a conjecture with no evidence to lean on. One may
take it for granted that in the two years that passed from the receipt of the
bull to its publication, during which the Kings' intentions no doubt became
apparent, the converso courtiers made repeated attempts to change the
Kings' mind concerning the Inquisition; but it is almost equally certain, we
believe, that their reasoning and protestations did not move the Kings to
reconsider their decision. Before they submitted their petition to the Pope,
they had carefully weighed all the pros and cons of the Inquisitional plan. No
argument that the conversos could come up with months later could have
appeared so novel to the Kings as to make them postpone action on the bull.
What caused the long postponement was, in all likelihood, not the conversos'
pleas and arguments, but the country's social and political conditions in the
intervening period.

In November 1478, when the bull reached the Kings, Castile was still at war
with Portugal, and shortly thereafter preparations were made to meet the
second Portuguese invasion. It was only in February of the following year
that the conflict was decided in favor of Castile (in the battle of Albuera), but
peace with Portugal was not signed before September 1479. In the meantime
Ferdinand—the real architect of the Inquisition—had to attend to the affairs
of Aragon, which had fallen upon him since the death of his father in January
of that year. Apart from this, there still remained in Castile some unsettled
problems that could cause unrest, especially if supported by criticisms from
other quarters. The sovereigns suspected that the actions of the Inquisition
could provide grounds for such criticisms against them; they might throw the
country into a violent controversy, which the discontented elements could
use to stir up trouble; consequently, they did not wish those actions to start
before other disturbing problems had been settled and before the country had
been pacified, stabilized, and controlled to their satisfaction. It was only after
the Cortes of Toledo of 1480 concluded its activity on May 15 that they could
see all three vital tasks accomplished. And it was only then that they could
see their way clear to turn their inquisitional plan into a reality.

There was, in addition, one more matter that the sovereigns believed
should be taken care of before the start of the Inquisition's activity. It would
seem strange, and give room to much hostile comment, if so great an attack
is launched against the Judaizers while leaving the Jews, their inspirers,

undisturbed. In the Cortes of Toledo, therefore, it was decided that the Jews (and Moors) be transferred to localities completely separated from the Christian neighborhoods.[10] This was the first link in a long chain of actions, supposedly taken for a "religious" purpose, that made the sovereigns earn, after the expulsion of the Jews, the honorific title of "the Catholic Kings."

Thus, after removing all apparent obstacles, and taking all necessary precautions, the young monarchs, concerned about the outcome of their decision to establish an Inquisition in their realm, finally made the daring step and plunged into the unknown. And thus it happened that after six years of peace, which led the conversos to entertain sanguine hopes, they suddenly saw their entire world tumble before their eyes. What made the Kings cause that upheaval and assume such a changed attitude toward the conversos, which amounted to a declaration of war on their tribe? In the following chapters we shall tackle this question.

BOOK FOUR

THE ORIGINS
OF THE INQUISITION

CHAPTER I

The Major Causes

I. The Lesson of the Sources

I

O ur survey of the course of Marrano history in the century following the first mass conversion (1391) has thus reached its final stage. In this survey we have sought to describe the developments—political, social, economic and intellectual—that played a part in the gathering conflict between the Old Christians and the New. The conclusions we shall now draw from these developments will bear upon the principal aim of our inquiry, which is to determine the factors and drives that gave birth to the Spanish Inquisition.

What emerges from our survey is that the Spanish Inquisition was by no means the result of a fortuitous concourse of circumstances and events. It was the product of a *movement* that called for its creation and *labored for decades* to bring it about—a movement that reflected the will, the feelings and the attitudes of the majority of Spain's Christian population. Perhaps it was awareness of these facts that led Menéndez y Pelayo to say that the Inquisition was a genuine expression of the soul of the Spanish people.[1]

The *agitation* of that movement was no doubt the force that created the Spanish Inquisition, and in it we must look for the motives that impelled both the spokesmen of the movement and its rank and file. We must, however, take into account the fact that man's declared motives of his actions often differ from the real reasons that determine them. This is especially so when his needs and interests conflict with the ethical code of his society, which fact inclines him to camouflage his aims by arguments conforming to the prevailing moral system. Nevertheless, the real goals of movements, especially of those that endure for many years, are bound to be revealed in the end. Indeed, very often the truth is laid bare by the very arguments employed to obscure it. The campaign for the Inquisition was no exception to this rule.

What, then, can we learn from this campaign about the underlying causes of the Spanish Inquisition? In our search for an answer we should bear in mind that the forces calling for the establishment of the Inquisition formed part of an anti-Marrano drive propelled by arguments of three distinct kinds: religious, social-economic and racial. It is to the arguments of this three-pronged drive that we should first look for the answer to our question.

II

Of the various groups of sources dealing with the Marranos, we shall first turn to the Hebrew documents and consider some of the things they tell us about the Marranos' religious attitudes. As we have indicated, the contents of these documents were summarized by us in a special study,[2] and the testimonies it contains give us an account of the religious evolution of Spanish Marranism in the century that followed 1391. Ordinarily, we could have limited our task at this point by calling our readers' attention to this study. For the purposes of the present work, however, we shall have to cite here some of the evidence touching the *last* phase of that evolution. This will enable us to get a synoptic view of Marrano religious life as reflected in *all* our sources (Jewish, Marrano, and Old Christian) at the time the Inquisition was established. It will facilitate a comparison of the lessons we can draw from each of the above groups of documents, and help us arrive at definite conclusions regarding the questions at issue.

The problem discussed frequently in the Hebrew sources after the establishment of the Inquisition was how Jews should treat the converso fugitives who sought admission to the Jewish fold. In the few decades preceding the Inquisitional persecution, there was no "return" of Marranos to Judaism on any considerable scale.[3] To effect such a "return," the Marranos involved would have to leave Spain for a Moslem country. But except for isolated conversos who did this, we have no evidence of such migrations. The virtual cessation of Marrano emigration should not be attributed to economic considerations, lack of travel facilities, and the like. As we have demonstrated elsewhere, it was due primarily to the Marranos' loss of interest in Judaism—or, more precisely, to their Christianization. The Inquisition introduced a change in their attitudes. It revolutionized the thinking of some Christianized Marranos and led them to reexamine their relationship to Christianity, now that they were suffering torture and infamy at the hands of their fellow Christians. They decided to embrace their ancestral faith, from which they had been alienated so long; and to attain this end, they fled to Moslem countries, mostly to those that lay south of Spain. In brief, while no movement of Marrano "return" was responsible for the Inquisitional persecution, the Inquisitional persecution was responsible for the rise of a movement of Marrano "return."

Judging by our sources, the scope of that movement was far less than is commonly believed. It was too small to affect the main religious attitudes of the vast majority of the Marrano population, but large enough to stir the hopes of many Jews, who dreamed of a large-scale Marrano "revival." It is instructive that those who entertained such hopes were by and large not Castilian or Aragonese Jews, who knew the Marranos at first hand, but Jews who lived in countries to which the "returners" fled (such as Granada, Algiers and Morocco). Seeing in the newcomers lost brothers who were moved (or "awakened," as they put it) to "return" to God, the rabbis of those countries wished to encourage the "returners" by facilitating their admission to the fold. The acceptance of these Marranos as Jews, however, raised legal problems which had to be resolved; and it is from the discussions of these problems that we can see how the conversos were viewed by the Jews, and *what they actually had been religiously before the great persecution.*

What we first gather from these discussions is that the conversos were known to the Jews not as *forced* converts (i.e., secret Jews) but as *real* converts and *full-fledged Christians.* Indeed, if they had been viewed as *forced converts,* there would have been no problem about accepting them. Forced converts were regarded as full-fledged Jews in both the religious and the ethnic sense (that is, both as adherents of Judaism and members of the Jewish people), and therefore their return to open Jewish life involved no procedural difficulty. Moreover, even Jews who were converted *voluntarily* (and hence viewed as Jews in the ethnic sense only) could reembrace Judaism, if they chose to do so, without encountering any obstacle in their path. All that was required of the converts of *both kinds (forced and voluntary alike)* was formally to express their deep regret for their sin and perform the necessary penance.[4] But the case of the conversos was quite different. Since they had been Christians for *several generations* and behaved as such both religiously and socially (and, in part, also in their marriages), there arose the question of their authentic Jewishness; and this moved most rabbis to regard the Marranos not only as *real* converts but also as *gentiles*—i.e., non-Jews both religiously and ethnically. Accordingly, they decreed that the Marranos could be admitted to the Jewish fold not as penitent Jews, but as alien infidels who wished to *become* Jews—and hence, as *proselytes from the gentiles.* Obviously, to qualify for this title, they had to undergo proselytization.

This was the position of most rabbis in Spain who observed the Marranos from close range; this was the view of the rabbis in Morocco, as well as of most Spanish rabbis in the East (Egypt and Palestine).[5] The minority that objected to this decision argued only against the *gentilehood* of the Marranos, not against the view that they had been *real converts* (or, for that matter, true

Christians). No one claimed that they had been secret Jews, either in their behavior or in their thought; and no one who defended them presented any proof, or even partial evidence, to this effect.[6] Circumcision, for instance, could go a long way to demonstrate the Jewishness of the "returning" Marranos—or at least the Jewishness of their parents. But no one ever claimed that they had been circumcised—evidently, because no such claim could be made. The outcome of the debate on this question was that the "returning" Marranos were treated as gentiles and accepted into the Jewish fold only after proselytization.[7]

This was of course a far-reaching decision which could have, in effect, only one meaning. It meant that the majority of Spain's Jews viewed the Marranos (taken as a whole) not only as followers of another religion, but also as members of another people. To them the Marranos appeared as complete aliens, totally cut off from the body of Jewry—a view that could in no way have been formed if the ranks of the Marranos had been teeming with Judaizers or even contained a substantial number of them. Yet if this was the state of Judaism among the Marranos, the claim that the Inquisition was established to suppress a widespread crypto-Jewish movement in their midst must be regarded as untrue.

Moreover, this conclusion is not only *implied* in the evidence offered by the Jewish sources; it is *explicitly* stated by Hispano-Jewish scholars who wrote in the first decade of the Inquisition. Thus says Don Isaac Abravanel of the conversos:

> Even though they and their descendants will endeavor to be like *complete gentiles,* they will be unable to achieve this aim. For the native peoples of the lands [in which they live] will always call them "Jews," mark them as "Israelites" *against their will* and *falsely accuse them of Judaizing in secret*—a crime for which they pay with death by fire.[8]

Four times in his writings Abravanel stresses the falsehood of the accusations of heresy leveled at the New Christians,[9] and claims that it was on the grounds of this excuse that the Inquisition "burned them by the thousands." For our present purpose, which is to establish the *facts*—i.e., the Marranos' religious attitudes—we need not analyze *all* the utterances on the subject to appreciate the full meaning of his testimony; we can see it even if we dwell a little longer on the contents of the above cited statement.

Presenting the forecasts of the prophet Ezekiel (20.32), Abravanel speaks in this statement in the future tense, but he seeks to prove the veracity of those forecasts by *what was happening in his own time.*[10] And so we can gather clearly from his words that the conversos living in a Christian world were not merely *affected* by its culture and religion and *yielded* to the natural process of assimilation, but *consciously and willingly* participated in that process (they *"endeavored"* to be like their Christian neighbors); what is more, this endeavor was by no means "recent," but one that had persisted for generations without letup (for it was shared, as he said, by them and "their descendants"). Above all, the ultimate goal of that drive was not only to attain full Christianization, but also a state of complete gentilehood (they aspired to be like "complete gentiles"), which means also ethnic fusion with the non-Jews to the point of total disappearance. No wonder the conversos did not want to be designated either as "Jews" (religiously) or as "Israelites" (ethnically). These labels were attached to them coercively ("against their will"), as was the libel of their "heresy."[11]

In making this claim about the falsehood of the charges the Inquisition leveled against the Marranos, and in viewing the Marranos as determined bearers of anti-Jewish attitudes and aspirations, Abravanel is not alone among the Hebrew authors of the time. Thus Isaac Arama, one of the luminaries of Hispano-Jewish scholarship toward the end of the 15th century, confirms Abravanel's assessment in almost the same terms. Discussing the persecution of the conversos by the Inquisition during the 1480s, Arama says of the Marranos that

> although they *assimilated with those nations completely*, they will find no peace among them; for the nations will always revile and beshame them, *plot* against them and *falsely accuse them* in matters of faith. Indeed, they will always suspect them as Judaizers and subject them to tremendous dangers, as has been the case throughout this period of innovations, and especially in our time, when the smoke of the autos-da-fé has been rising toward the sky in all the kingdoms of Spain and the islands of the sea.[12]

This, then, was the view of the leading Jews of Spain concerning the Marranos persecuted by the Inquisition. They considered them *completely* assimilated and "removed from Judaism as far as one can be"[13] and in no way representatives of a secret Jewish movement that the Inquisition had uncovered and punished. But even more telling than all these statements portraying the Marranos' religious condition are the testimonies revealing the Jewish *attitudes* toward the Marranos at the height of the Inquisition's persecution. In the decade preceding their own expulsion, the Jews of Spain witnessed the horrors and calamities to which the conversos were then subjected. This was a time when thousands of Marranos were burned at the stake, incarcerated and tortured, and many other thousands, stricken with panic, abandoned their homes and fled the country. It would seem that the appalling misery of the Marranos, their dreadful suffering and terrible misfortunes should have evoked deep compassion for them by the Jews, their alleged "brethren in faith and in race." But this is not what the testimonies show.

What we find in the Jewish sources of the time are cold-blooded assertions that the Marranos got their due, or open manifestations of glee over their "fall." We find these attitudes and feelings expressed not only in the writings of such scholars as Caro, Saba, Jabez and Ibn Shuaib, but also in the works of Isaac Abravanel, whose judgment of the Marranos was more lenient and considerate than that of any other Jewish author of the time. This harshness in the face of overwhelming tragedy—and, even more so, that joy over its occurrence—can be explained only if the conversos were seen as *real* converts from Judaism and hence as renegades and traitors. Indeed, the writers mentioned define the Marranos, without reservation, as determined antagonists of the Jewish faith and as bitter enemies of the Jewish people.

The skeptical reader, who may find it hard to coordinate his own view of the Marranos (which may be akin to the traditional) with such an attitude toward them on the part of Spain's Jews, is asked to note carefully the following testimony, which relates to the same subject. To justify the Jews' happiness at the Marranos' plight, two great scholars, Jabez and Ibn Shuaib, sought to free the Jews of the prohibition "Rejoice not when your enemy be fallen" (Prov. 24.17). According to Jabez, the cited prohibition referred to *gentile* enemies of the *Jews* (such as Haman!), but not to *enemies of God* like the New Christians. Of such enemies, he claims, the Book of Proverbs says: *"When the wicked are lost, it is a cause for rejoicing"*[14]; and Ibn Shuaib reinforces the same interpretation by stressing that "the wickedness of these people [i.e., the conversos] is greater in our eyes than that of the gentiles."[15] The conclusion to be derived from all these testimonies with respect to the Marranos' religious state is incontestable. Such gladness at the Marranos' woes and such extreme hatred of *the group as a whole* could never have been expressed in the writings of these authors if most, or even a large part, of the Marranos were secret Jews.

It is necessary, however, to bore somewhat deeper into the statements of the Hebrew authors in order to understand what they truly meant. Indubitably, what these authors had in mind were two different categories of enmity: one aimed at human beings, at the Jews as members of a particular people—an enmity of the kind found among the *gentiles* (and, in extreme form, in men like Haman); another is a purely spiritual enmity, a hatred of a religion, a divine teaching, and as such it is an "enmity for God." Surely the conversos, however gentilized they appeared, and however inimical to the Jewish people, were not accused of seeking the extermination of all Jews, "both young and old," as did Haman, the arch-enemy of the Jews of all time. But they were accused of seeking the annihilation of Judaism as a set of beliefs that might be adopted by any people; and from this standpoint they were regarded by the Jews as "worse than the gentiles," including Haman himself, who were viewed as concerned primarily with satisfying their "human" animosity for the Jews. Accordingly, the Marranos were seen not merely as *real* converts, who religiously were identified with Christianity, but as people who sought to substitute Christianity for the Judaism in which many Jews still believed. Perhaps what stood before the Jewish writers was the image of converts like Alfonso de Valladolid, Paul of Burgos and Joshua ha-Lorki, the leading missionary, militant converts whose writings were filled with hatred of Judaism and whom the Jews regarded as teachers of apostasy and inspirers of all the conversos of Spain. In any case, from the standpoint of the *final aim*—i.e., the total extinction of Judaism—the Jews could see no fundamental difference between the New Christians of the seventies and eighties and the most zealous converts of earlier generations.

The Jews of Spain, who knew the Marranos from personal relations and close observation, had evidently no doubt then that the Spanish New Christians had reached in the seventies, on their road toward assimilation, as Arama put it, the "point of no return." The aforecited sources and many others that support them referred, as we have indicated, to the bulk of the Marranos, or rather the Marranos considered as a group. From this fact we concluded—inescapably, in our opinion—that the Judaizers among them were too feeble a minority to affect the overall picture. But let us try to be more precise in this matter, and also touch on another important point that bears directly on our conclusions.

That there were some Jewish pockets among the Marranos in the sixties, and probably in the seventies too, may be taken for granted. We have indicated this fact on the basis of the Hebrew sources that refer to them here and there; but from the same sources, coming mostly from the eighties, we can learn of their paucity in absolute numbers and, even more so, of their relative insignificance. The statements we have cited about the attitude of the Jews toward the Marranos punished by the Inquisition indicate that, in their assessment of the conversos, the group of the Judaizers made no difference. For whatever the strength of the Judaizers was, we must assume that proportionately they were more numerous among the victims of the Inquisition than in any other segment of the Spanish Marranos; hence, if their total number was substantial, they should have certainly constituted among those punished by the Inquisition a significant part that could not be overlooked. But this is not what we gather from the Jewish authors, who treat all those burned at the stake as renegades and enemies. Evidently, the Judaizers among them were too few to affect their general judgment.

We have to come back to Isaac Abravanel to confirm directly this far-reaching conclusion, which collides so violently with the claims of the

Inquisition and of all who rely on them as "confirmed facts." Obviously, if Abravanel had believed or assumed that a notable number of the victims of the Inquisition were secret Jews, and not Christians accused falsely, he would have expressed his admiration—or, at least, commiseration—for the martyrs who paid with their lives for their faith. He would certainly have treated them as a group apart. But we find no such reaction in Abravanel. The fires of the Inquisition move him only to observe that the fate of those burned confirms the verdict promised such people by Holy Writ: *"For the wicked will be cut off from the land and the traitors uprooted from its midst."*[16] Thus, all the Marranos burned at the stake were viewed by Abravanel not as crypto-Jews, as devotees of Judaism and martyrs for their faith, but as traitors to their religion like all *real* converts, and also betrayers and deserters of their people, since they wished to "intermingle" with the gentile nations and be cut off from the tribe of Israel. Hosea, he added, indicated in his prophecy how such assimilationists would end their career: *"they will be exposed to fire like a cake unturned."*[17] And this is what befell the Marranos.

It is futile to attempt to misinterpret these testimonies or take their clear message out of context or minimize their revolutionary impact upon our hitherto accepted views of the Marranos. Nor does it make sense to disregard them. Expressed in unmistakable terms by the foremost Jewish authorities of the period, they can neither be misconceived nor ignored. They show us not only the rise and progress of the trend toward Christianity among the Marranos, but also the climax it reached in their assimilation and alienation from the Jewish people. Accordingly, we must conclude that by 1480—i.e., when the Inquisition was established—the Marranos were by and large Christianized; and if a remnant of Judaizers still survived among them, it was steadily decreasing both in number and influence, and posed no danger to the Christianity of Spain, or of the New Christians. Hence, there was no justification whatever to label the whole group as tainted with Judaism, and certainly no need to launch against it the massive assault of the Inquisition.

III

Our attention will now turn to the documents produced by the conversos *themselves* on their religious condition, or rather on their position toward Judaism and Christianity. This should have been high on the agenda of all students of the conflict between Old and New Christians. After all, it is the conversos who formed the storm center of the controversy about their faithfulness to Christianity; it is *they* who were accused so long and so vehemently of harboring a festering Judaic heresy, and it would seem only natural—indeed essential—for scholars to find out what the accused Marranos had to say about the charges made against them. Yet strangely enough, no such interest was displayed for a very long time. In almost all the writings about the Marranos and the Inquisition, we can see how the assertions about the "Judaism" of the conversos were systematically repeated as gospel truth, without reference to even a single converso statement expressing the Marranos' view of those assertions. Indeed, it would seem as if the court of history judged the Marranos *in absentia*. It was a court in which only their enemies had a say. The Marranos' self-defense was never heard.

Did they have anything to say in their defense? For hundreds of years their testimonies lay buried in the archives of Spain, France and the Vatican, with no one bothering to examine or reveal them. And thus for centuries many histories were written about the struggle of the Inquisition against the Marrano heretics without taking those testimonies into account. Only in 1873 was one of these documents—the "Instruction of the Relator to the Bishop of Cuenca"—published for the first time by Fermín Caballero; but it does not seem that the crucial evidence it contains made a dent in scholarly opinion. Several years later (in 1876), there appeared the third volume of Amador de los Ríos' *History of the Jews in Spain and Portugal;* but we find no sign in it that he noticed the main thrust of that work, or that his views of the conversos were affected by it. So deep-rooted was the view of the Marranos held by all preceding historians that even the most original thinkers and researchers could not escape its influence. Even Henry Charles Lea, the great historian of the Inquisition, who knew the Relator's "Instruction" and cited it,[18] failed to discern its peculiar importance as testimony to the Marranos' religious condition, and the name of its author is not even mentioned in his great and copious work. And what is more amazing: F. I. Baer, who does mention Fernán Díaz in his book of Spanish documents (1930), refers to him only as signatory of royal papers and classes him as an Old Christian![19] To be sure, some twenty years later Baer recognized his error and wrote that "recently it had been discovered that the Relator was a Marrano," but even then he devoted to him only two lines.[20] Nor did the position of the historians change materially when Cartagena's *Defensorium de unitatis christianae* was published in 1943 and Juan de Torquemada's *Tractatus contra Madianitas* appeared in 1957. To be sure, certain aspects of some of these works were discussed in several scholarly studies; but the thrust of their arguments and the great message they contained for students of the history of the Marranos and the Inquisition remained in effect unnoticed, as if it were only of marginal relevance to the issues involved.

Curiously enough, the attempt to recognize the Marranos—not necessarily as portrayed by the Inquisition, but as reflected in their *own* writings—began from the historians of literature, who delved into Marrano belles-lettres, and especially into converso poetry. In this area, the contributions of Américo Castro, Francisco Márquez Villanueva, Cantera Burgos and other important scholars did much to unveil the true face of the converso who was culturally integrated into the Old Christian society and later lived in dread of the Inquisition. Yet Marrano poetry, though holding many clues to the image of the converso literary elite, could not by itself offer an answer to the question of *the religious posture of the group*. To obtain such an answer, the inquiry had to focus on direct Marrano testimonies concerning *this* question, and therefore to extend into the polemical and historical writings of the Marranos, where such testimonies are included. That is indeed what we have tried to do.

Of the two groups of sources just mentioned, the polemical works are by far the more important, for they deal exclusively with the converso problem, discuss it at length and in great detail and touch on many aspects of the converso situation, including the religious one which commands our attention. Unfortunately, only three of these works have come down to us, but they are all of outstanding importance.[21] They were all written by leading representatives of Spanish literature, law and theology; and their authors were also men of the world, who occupied high positions in the Church, as well as in the royal Court of Castile. Their testimonies therefore have not only the authority of great men of learning, but also of outstanding historical figures who took part in the battles of their time. These authors knew from their own experience what was happening in Spanish society, the forces that stirred its various movements, and the motives that drove its leaders and its masses to act as they did.

We have already analyzed the views, arguments and factual data included in these works, and shall now present a brief summary of what they say concerning the Marranos' religious attitudes. As we have seen, their authors are unanimous on the main question at issue. All of them agree that the converso community, taken as a whole, was devoutly Christian and happy to be so, until it became the object of vicious persecution and wild calumny by unscrupulous foes. So Christianized indeed were the Marranos in their own eyes that they failed to see why they should be called *New* Christians. Accordingly, they branded the charges of heresy leveled against their group as libelous concoctions produced by enemies who sought their ruin and wished to hurt their standing in the Christian world. They openly admitted that some followers of Judaism might still exist among them here and there, but insisted that they were so few and insignificant that in no way could they characterize their group. To label the whole converso camp *crypto-Jewish* because of such a small minority, they said, is tantamount to labeling a whole society "criminal" because some of its members have committed crimes.

To be sure, the conversos' apologists noted that a Toledan "Inquiry" into their alleged Jewishness found them guilty on many counts; but the apologists regarded this "Inquiry" too as an instrument of the campaign launched against their group. In the same light they saw the Toledan tribunals established to judge converso "heretics." The judges, they claimed, were hostile and unqualified, the witnesses false and their testimonies fraudulent; accordingly, the trials against the Marranos in Toledo were founded on no proof, no evidence, and no law. They were a travesty of justice.

The common position of the converso spokesmen, who declared the Marranos to be true Christians and denied that they harbored a large-scale heresy, is corroborated by other Marrano testimonies included in contemporary *historiographic* works. Produced in the first decade after the rebellion of '49, these works were written or edited by Marranos who, directly or indirectly, tell us what they knew of the rebels' persecution of the Marranos. According to these testimonies, the conversos were accused of crimes and transgressions that "had never entered their minds," and consequently, the conversos were "robbed, killed and burned" for no justifiable reason. They further tell us that in support of their charges, the accusers employed some perverse individuals (*"malefactores,"* as they are called in the sources) to bear false witness against the conversos; and thus they confirm the claims of the Marrano apologists regarding the criminal nature of the Toledan prosecution and the means employed by its promoters.

Thus, the religious charges leveled at the Marranos were exposed as false by the Marrano publicists and historians—first by presenting the actual situation, which was the opposite of what their enemies claimed, and second, by pointing to the origins of those charges, which were malice, jealousy and deep-rooted hatred. But besides this denial of the religious censures on the basis of the current facts, they rejected them on the basis of their conceptual grasp of their own religious position. This rejection helps us assess the depth and breadth of the Marranos' Christianity; it also sheds light on the Marranos' world outlook and enables us to see how the conversos viewed themselves as Christians in a Spanish society.

We have already touched on some of the reasons offered by the conversos of the middle of the century for their stern objection to being called *New* Christians, let alone *converts* to Christianity. Based on the dates of their ancestors' conversion and of their own baptism to Christianity, these reasons of course made sense. But the conversos advanced additional arguments in support of that objection—and not only for the purpose of removing a stigma which had long been attached to their name.

In our *Marranos of Spain* we have already referred to some of the sociopsychological problems with which the Spanish conversos were beset.[22] But perhaps the most irritating of these was created by the view that universally prevailed among the Jews, according to which no Jew in his right mind could abandon Judaism out of conviction that any other religion was superior to his own. Consequently, the Jews viewed the converts as perverts—as corrupt individuals who, for some reason, developed a grudge against their people and its faith, or as hunters for gain, opportunists and careerists, or, at best, as moral weaklings who could not withstand the stresses and storms of the "exile." This, in brief, was the general attitude that the Jewish convert faced from the *Jewish* side. But it ought to be pointed out with due emphasis that it was not limited to the Jewish side alone. The Christians, who noticed that most Jewish converts adopted Christianity under threat of death, could hardly consider such converts sincere; nor could they regard as genuine the converts who had been at loggerheads with the Jewish community (for financial or other non-religious reasons) before they crossed the line between the faiths. Indubitably, Jewish agitation, too, contributed to inculcate such views among the Christians; and the latter, reluctant to absorb the converts for powerful social and economic reasons, were quick to seize on the Jewish claims and call the converts "turncoats."

As we have indicated above, these descriptions did not fit the great majority of the Spanish conversos in the middle of the fifteenth century. They could be applied, on objective grounds, to most of the *voluntary converts among the Jews,* whose number was always very limited, but not to the *voluntary conversion movement that emerged from the masses of forced converts* in Spain, and certainly not to their children and grandchildren—i.e., their second and third generations—who were born or educated in Christendom. Yet regardless of truth, old labels, like libels, when backed by strong interest and nursed by ill will, are hard to remove, let alone destroy; and ultimately the conversos were forced to realize that they had here a problem to cope with.

In response to this problem the conversos fashioned an ideology that served them on two fronts: against the Jews and against the Old Christians. Their argument against the Jews was based on the claim that actually they were not converts at all; consequently, they were not traitors to their people or religion; nor were they "turncoats" or "newcomers" to Christianity. Essentially, as they put it, they remained "at home," still considering holy what the Jews considered holy—the same Patriarchs and Prophets, and even the same Law. Consequently, what differentiates them from the professing Jews is *not the Marranos' abandonment of the Law* (for, in fact, they have not abandoned it at all), but their better and clearer understanding of it (that is, of its covert and implied meaning). This is how they came to believe in Christ, who likewise did not abandon the Law, but adhered to it and came to fulfill it. Thus, it is not *they* who relinquished the true faith but the Jews, who, failing to grasp its allusions, distorted the meaning of the sacred prophecies. Hence it is *they,* the so-called converts, who have come to represent the true teachings of Judaism; yet by becoming real Jews, they automatically became real Christians.

The idea was fundamentally not new, of course. It was all of a piece with the theory of *true Israel,* propounded by Paul and propagated ever since. The *real Israel* consists of those people who grasp the full meaning of the prophetic teachings—who are *Israel* according to the spirit and not necessarily according to the flesh. Thus it is only *part* of the carnal Israelites (i.e., the part that came over to Christianity) that may likewise be so defined. What was nevertheless *new* in the concept of the Marranos was the emphasis that their group represented a continuity between "ethnic" Israel and "spiritual" Israel, and that the ethnic Israelites who accepted Christianity needed no "conversion" as the gentiles did, for they did not have to acquire the *foundations* of Christianity—the belief in one God, the Law and the Prophets—but only to extend these foundations somewhat further or, more correctly, grasp the full content of the writings which they had regarded as true and sacred. By virtue of this fact an Israelite in the flesh—who, like all such Israelites, is reared on Holy Writ—is always *potentially* a *true* Israelite; and when he becomes one *in fact,* it should be viewed as an outcome of a natural evolution, and not as a conversion (which is a revolution) of the kind that occurs among the gentiles.

Thus the conversos turned the tables on their Old Christian enemies, just as they did on their foes among the Jews. As "non-converts," who remained where they were—i.e., *in their own home*—they could not be viewed as "turncoats" and intruders but rather as old and most respected "citizens." The concept of converts, or sons of converts, is now attributed, conversely, to the gentiles, and it is *they* who are historically the "newcomers" to the "house"—i.e., the "home"—of the Israelites, the *real* Israelites, who are truly the Old Christians, and not *vice versa.*[23] But this was not all that this view conveyed. By portraying themselves as closer to the traditions of the older part of the Sacred Heritage than the gentiles who became Christians, they were, as de Lyra claimed, more prepared than the latter to grasp the full meaning of the ancient prophecies; and thus by better comprehending the Old Testament, they could better understand the New. Consequently, they belonged not to the lower ranks but to the intellectual elite of Christendom; and while most of their Christian friends described them as good Christians *despite* their Jewish past, they themselves claimed to be better Christians— better in the purely religious sense—precisely *because* of their Jewish background.

We have said that by means of this set of concepts the conversos sought to alter or erase their unfavorable image as religious impostors, which was created by their Jewish and Christian adversaries and accompanied them like a shadow. But that set of concepts, which they boldly proclaimed, was to them more than a means to an end. It was an ideology that sprang from their world outlook, from their deepest convictions and religious feelings and, curiously enough, was supported by their awareness of the low-quality religious beliefs of the vast majority of the Old Christians. The conversos certainly could not be impressed by criticisms of their religious sincerity—criticisms hurled at them by their foes—when they knew that the Old Christian masses around them were far less at home in Christian literature—and far less trained to understand Christian dogma, Christian symbolism and Christian philosophy—than many of their own members. In fact, they were certain that their own Christianity was far purer, nobler and more in accord with the letter and spirit of the teachings of Christ, of the Apostles and the Church Fathers than that upheld by their hate-filled enemies, who were besmirching their name and crying for their blood. Likewise, their references to the "great men" they had produced—to canonists like Torquemada, to theologians like Cartagena, to mendicant saints like Pedro Regalado[24]—were made not only to impress their adversaries, as well as their friends among the Old Christians, but also to assure and convince themselves that they could match the best that Christianity had created in their time and place.

If, therefore, we sum up the conversos' view of their own religious position, we can see that they not only denied as ludicrous the charges about their inclination toward Judaism, and vehemently rejected as libel the claim that they harbored a large-scale Jewish heresy; they also proclaimed their faith in Christianity as the one true religion that mankind must adopt and the one on whose expansion and triumph they pinned their most cherished hopes.

IV

If each of the two groups of sources just surveyed (the Jewish and the Marrano) leads fundamentally to *one* conclusion—namely, that the bulk of the Marrano group was *Christian*—the relevant evidence of the Old Christian sources does not suggest such uniformity. Rather does it reveal two distinct trends which are clearly opposed to each other: one exhibiting a pro-converso attitude, and the other an anti-converso one. As such they come up with different answers to the question with which we are concerned.

The testimonies of the first group comprise four important statements, three dating from the period of Juan II and one from that of Enrique IV. Their authors were all men of renown who attained great distinction in their respective fields. They were Lope de Barrientos, Díaz de Montalvo, Pérez de Guzmán and Alonso de Oropesa.

For an Old Christian to defend the conversos against their maligners on religious grounds must already have been an unenviable task at the beginning of the forties. It became increasingly difficult in the fifties and sixties, and in the seventies too risky—or too hopeless—to attempt. So charged with prejudice and hatred of the conversos had the social atmosphere in Castile become that any Old Christian, however respected, who took up the cudgels on their behalf soon became a target of slurs and aspersions, or even of rumors that he was a converso or of semi-converso descent. This is what happened to Lope de Barrientos, and later to Alonso de Oropesa, and both had to put matters straight to protect their integrity and their good name. Pérez de Guzmán, more cautious than the others, preempted the expected attacks against him by paying homage to the conversos' critics and by framing his positive evaluations of the conversos in moderate, low-key terms.

Guzmán did not deny the possibility that there were "some" non-Catholics among the conversos, but he objected to the tendency of their detractors to turn the possibility into a certainty and extend the existence of "some" heretics to the whole converso group. Guzmán had no doubt that converts to Christianity who grew up from infancy in another religion—and especially those who were *forced* to be baptized—could not cleave to their new religion like those who were born and bred in it. He was, however, certain that the young children of the converts, and all the more so their childrens' offspring, were bound to become "Catholic and firm in the faith." His own acquaintance with converso friars, prelates and reformers of religious orders could only confirm this conviction, as could the behavior of many children of Christians who were converted to Islam. Guzmán also noted that no actual charge of religious infidelity had thus far been brought against any converso, and he marveled at the audacity of the conversos' critics who, without concretely accusing any one, did not hesitate to condemn them all. Guzmán concluded his defense of the Marranos with the loaded remark that the anti-Marrano censures seemed to result from a "desire to malign rather than a zeal to correct."

Much more outspoken in his defense of the conversos and much sharper in reproaching their opponents was Lope de Barrientos, bishop of Cuenca, who witnessed the persecution of the Marranos in Toledo during Sarmiento's rebellion. Barrientos had been in close touch with the conversos and observed the growth of hostility against them long before that revolt took place. He no doubt heard that the Marranos were accused of harboring sympathizers or practitioners of Judaism, but his own assessment of their religious attitudes led him to say that their group "belonged to God" (i.e., Christ). What he saw of their behavior during the Toledan disturbances only confirmed him in this opinion and, in fact, excited his admiration for them. He marveled at their steadfastness in the Christian faith in the face of grim adversity, and he would not be surprised if, under the impact of their ordeal, "some" of the conversos were inclined to leave the faith. He believed, however, that such desertions would be few and only emphasize by their paucity the wholesomeness of the group.

Finally, Barrientos censured the attempt to discriminate against the conversos on the ground of their race. Theologically, he claimed, the racists' theory runs counter to the teachings of Christianity, and practically it is absurd because no part of the Spanish people is known to be free of Jewish blood. St. Isidore, in his *Etymologies*, Barrientos noted, said: *"All the Jews of Spain were Christians at the time of one of the Gothic Kings,"* and "who in our time can tell who is [or is not] of their descendants?"[25] But apart from all this, the racial view must be held as contemptible by all Christians, because it is steeped in scorn for the race that gave the world the Holy Virgin Mary and the incarnate Son of God. Barrientos exhorts the detractors of the conversos to stop using their "sacrilegious and vicious tongues" against the race of the Jews and the conversos, which he calls "divine."[26]

Díaz de Montalvo approached the defense of the conversos from a different angle. Starting from the premise that, generally speaking, the conversos were faithful and devoted Christians, Montalvo sought to establish the causes of the "hate and vengeance" that inspired their enemies. He concluded that these feelings were nourished by two sources—a yearning for the earthly goods of the conversos (which their enemies presumed could be wrested from their hands) and a growing thirst for exclusive power (which would exclude the Marranos from government). To satisfy these passions, the foes of the conversos proposed a series of anti-Marrano measures, which they tried to justify by various arguments. These arguments, however, are clearly anti-Christian; in fact, they are heretical.

The claim that the anti-Marranos are heretics is the recurrent theme of Montalvo's treatise. Thus he threw the charge hurled at the New Christians back in the face of the accusers. There is indeed a heretical movement in Spain; but it should not be looked for among the innocent conversos. The real heretics are the conversos' enemies, who deny every major tenet of Christianity and try to appear as guardians of the faith. In fact, they are the worst of all heretics; they are schismatics. And Montalvo sees no other way to deal with them except the one applied to all other schismatics: They must be "extirpated" from the ranks of the Church.

No less spirited in his defense of the Marranos and even more censorious of their detractors was Alonso de Oropesa, General of the Hieronymites, whose great work on the Old-New-Christian conflict contains the most reliable evaluation we possess of the religious condition of the conversos. To Oropesa, the Marranos taken as a whole are true and full-fledged "brethren in faith," worthy to be "co-inheritors and co-citizens of the Apostles and the Prophets." He considers them a fitting extension of the Jewish conversion movement to Christianity—a movement which, from the days of the Apostles, made an incalculable contribution to the faith. Oropesa rates the Jewish convert to Christianity higher than the gentile one insofar as his ability to aid the faith is concerned, but this, he asserts, does not give the Jewish convert the right to be treated preferentially. The Church's attitude toward all its members is based on the principle of complete equality, a principle from which it cannot depart.

The persecution of the conversos in Spain, says Oropesa, represents not only a departure from that principle but its reversal, and as such it is anti-Christian. Unlike Barrientos, who considered the presence of Judaizers in Castile only a "possibility," Oropesa regarded it as a reality. The conversos do include a minority of Judaizers, but it is too small to affect the character of the group and too indefinite in its beliefs to form a real heresy. Nevertheless, while the Judaizers in themselves do not pose a threat to Christianity, indirectly they have caused the faith great harm. For the anti-Marranos used the presence of the Judaizers as an excuse and a stimulus for their agitation. They have grossly inflated the Judaizers' numbers, exaggerated their influence, and identified them with the whole converso group—or at least with its vast majority.

Oropesa examined all the arguments advanced by the Marranos' foes in support of their position and found them all wanting or worthless. He presented his views with great clarity and precision, but had little faith in their possible impact on the anti-Marrano movement. No one knows better than the leaders of this movement that they operate with lies and falsehoods, he averred, and no one is as aware as they are of the criminal aims for which they invented them. Like virtually all other apologists of the conversos, Oropesa saw the roots of the anti-Marrano drive in the terrible jealousy of the conversos that agitated the minds of many Old Christians; and he believed that nothing that anyone might say could change the latter's course of action. Oropesa concluded that what could stop these miscreants was only the employment of repressive measures. And these must aim at the following three goals: (a) silencing the agitation; (b) ousting the agitators from all their offices; and (c) divesting them of all authority. But Oropesa went even further. He called for the excommunication of the agitators from the Church and their total exclusion from Christian society. Unless this is done, Oropesa warned, the terrible turbulence in Christendom will continue, and peace and quiet will never return to the ranks of the faithful.

Having summarized the evidence of these outstanding men, who represented different spheres of activity, we can see that their testimonies essentially tallied and that, in one way or another, their evidence concurred with that of the Jewish and converso sources. We have reason to believe that their statements reflect not only their personal views on the conversos, but also those of the circles to which they belonged and, to some extent, of the broader social spheres of which those circles formed a part. Thus Barrientos and Oropesa expressed, in all likelihood, the position of many of the Church's elite; Montalvo, the view of most leading jurists; and Guzmán, the attitude of most of Spain's nobles, especially of the intellectuals who belonged to the upper crust. Altogether, however, their opinions were upheld by a minority of the Spanish people. The vast majority remained open to the influences flowing from the camp of the Marranos' foes.

v

Our attention will now turn to the documents produced in the middle of the century by the anti-Marrano movement, and we shall focus, to begin with, on the statements that refer to the Marranos' religious stand. Here we have noted the recurring claim that the Spanish Marranos were mostly crypto-Jews who adhered to Jewish beliefs and rites. And here we also find that this claim was accompanied by a theory concerning the motives and beginnings of Marrano crypto-Judaism in Spain.

One assumes that there could be no division of opinion on this particular subject. Everyone seems to have known the reasons for the mass conversions of the Jews: the threat of being slaughtered by the pogromists (in 1391) and the danger of perishing from hunger and exposure (following the laws of 1412). Thus those who were converted under either of these threats were essentially *forced* converts, and they formed the vast majority of the Jews who went over to Christianity in those years (1391–1418). But even the minority, who could not be so classed, were mostly impelled by strong pressures. When some of the rich did not see any way to retain their wealth or great income as Jews, conversion was to them not a coveted goal, but a lesser evil than a life of poverty. Other Jews, too, who came to view the situation of the Jewish people as hopeless, took up Christianity not with relish, but like a defeated army that lays down its arms when it sees no sense in continued resistance. Thus, the minority of the converts not *truly* forced were not really voluntary either.

These were the causes of the movement of conversion that within some three decades transferred to Christianity hundreds of thousands of Spanish Jews. Elsewhere, we have spoken of the religious crisis that affected Jewish thinking at the time and no doubt facilitated that transfer.[27] But we have also made it clear that this religious crisis, insofar as the masses were concerned, resulted directly from the social situation, and could not in any case by itself bring about a large-scale conversion of Jews to Christianity. It played a part, as we have indicated, in accelerating the assimilation of the Jewish converts of 1391 and 1412. But it had nothing to do with the *major* causes of the original conversion.

Yet these causes, which the Spaniards of the time, both Jews and Christians, were presumably aware of, seem to have been conveniently ignored by the conversos' foes and detractors. Thus, if we go by the theories of García, chief critic of the Marranos in the middle of the fifteenth century, Spain had known neither the massacres of 1391 nor the laws of 1412; and so the Spanish Jews had never had to choose between death and conversion. Hence, those of them who asked to be baptized to Christianity were under no compulsion to do so; and thus they did it of their own free choice. But the choice was not made out of *preference* for Christianity, but rather out of their *hatred* for it and all its devoted followers.

García must have realized that the ascription of such a motive to the passing of masses of Jews to Christianity—and hence to the birth of Marranism in Spain—would be utterly incredible to all right-thinking people, and that his thesis would be met with the biting question: Why did Jews convert *voluntarily* to a religion they so deeply hated and abhorred? García's answer was, as we have seen, that the Jews became Christians to dominate Christendom. Their plan was to conquer Christian society from within by seizing all its positions of power and then, by means of those positions, to exploit the Christian masses to the point of exhaustion. Finally, when these masses collapse, their faith will expire with them, and this is how Judaism will achieve its triumph over the hated religion.

García found it easy to combine these claims with the charge that most of the Marranos were Judaizers. Since the Jews were converted for a purely Jewish purpose, their conversion was a strictly mechanical act that did not alter their religious attitudes. They remained devotees of Judaism *after* their conversion precisely as they had been *before* it, except that now they practiced Judaism secretly instead of following it openly. Their Christianity served them as a mask to hide their face—a prerequisite for the success of their scheme.

Every wrong theory that gains popularity contains elements whose falsity is hard to discern. García's theory was no exception; but one would think that the falsehood of at least one of its elements was glaringly obvious. For the claim that the Jews converted *willingly* to Christianity with the intent of living secretly as Jews contains a blatant contradiction in terms. To be sure, if the Marranos were *forced* converts who sought to perform the Commandments clandestinely, they *could* be regarded as true Jews, since Jewish tradition, law and custom would tolerate violation of the Law under duress; but if they converted of their own free will, and worshiped a "foreign God" voluntarily, they would be considered by the Jews as apostates, and no positive intention could justify their conduct and permit them to be regarded as Jews. Of course, the whole distinction was purely imaginary; for no Jew could be considered *faithful to the Law* and its *voluntary violator* at one and the same time. And if there was a Jew who so regarded himself, for whatever bizarre reason, certainly such a view could not be imposed, upheld and followed, by masses of people. Yet the converts from Judaism to Christianity in Spain numbered hundreds of thousands.

That such a theory, so brazenly inconsistent, so openly contradictory of Jewish law, and indeed nonsensical from every point of view, could be propounded by the enemies of the Marranos shows how distorted was their thinking and how perverted the attitude of the Christian audiences to whom their preposterous claims were addressed. For there is no doubt that the agitators believed that those audiences would accept their fanciful expositions of the anti-Christian goals of the Marranos, just as they believed they would accept their account of the genesis of Marranism in Christian Spain. Thus they often repeated these fables, embellishing them with additional absurdities which were likewise believed and upheld.

But absurdities related to public issues are usually invented to meet certain needs, and this was the case with the trumped-up tale about the root of Marranism in Spain. There was a need to relieve the Old Christians of responsibility for the massive conversions caused by coercion and at the same time assert with redoubled force that the Jews had converted not only insincerely, but with a vicious design. Thus, all moral scruples were removed from the path leading to the punishment of the accused. All that was now needed was to offer some data in support of the charge that the conversos were Jews, and such data could presumably be provided by the customs of the Judaizers still present among the conversos. That the number of these Judaizers was small and dwindling, that their customs were becoming more and more vestigial, did not matter very much in this instance. The aforementioned theories about the origins of Marranism, its aims, and, above all, its double life—namely, that the Marranos lived their Judaism underground—had prepared the way for the acceptance of the view that almost all Marranos were Judaizers.

If the theory propounded about the origins of Marranism, its immediate plans and ultimate aims, was based on nothing but an absurd myth, the evidence offered to prove its actual existence was based on no lesser absurdities. This is strikingly apparent from the religious views attributed to the Marranos by their opponents in the *Sentencia* (at the start of their campaign against the Marrano "heresy"). It is hard to believe that the authors of the *Sentencia* did not know that nothing was more alien to Judaism than any form of idolatry or any theory postulating the existence of two divinities. In presenting these views as typical or indicative of the Marranos' religious trends, the authors of the *Sentencia* had obviously relied on the ignorance of their audience and its blind hatred of the Marranos, which would lead it to believe anything against them, however ludicrous or grotesque.

Contributing to the spread of such beliefs was the violent campaign then conducted in Castile by the shrewd Franciscan agitator Alfonso de Espina. Espina, as we have seen, attacked the conversos both directly (by defining them as Jews) and indirectly (by ascribing to the Jews the most horrid practices). Yet while denigrating the Jews as he did, Espina made every possible effort to identify the conversos with the Jews. To prove this identification of the Jews and the conversos he pointed—on the authority of the Toledan Inquiry—to many customs common to both groups. He wanted, however, to bolster that authority by evidence (which he found hard to get), and concentrated on proving one charge of the Inquiry (namely, that the conversos practiced circumcision) which, more than all other charges, he thought, would demonstrate the Marranos' Jewishness.

We have shown that his claims on this score were denied not only by Jewish and converso sources, but also by unimpeachable Old Christian testimonies dealing with that particular accusation. Espina, however, kept repeating the charge, undoubtedly believing that the force of repetition would produce the effect of convincing evidence and finally implant in the public mind the notion that the conversos were practicing circumcision. Since this is the only charge against the Judaizers mounted by Espina on the basis of his *own* "findings," and since so much was made of his attestations, it is worthwhile to consider here the evidence adducible from the records of certain occurrences.

In 1449, during the rebellion of Sarmiento, the rebels hanged the bodies of several conversos they had killed in a skirmish with a New Christian force, exposing them to the public in the city's central square. Among those thus killed and hanged was the leader of the conversos in Toledo, Juan de Cibdad, of whose religious attitudes we hear nothing until many years after the rebellion. What we hear then is that, in the wake of Juan's death, some of his descendants left Spain for another land, where they lived openly as Jews. In view of the grueling experiences they had undergone, such an action by Juan's descendants is of course hardly surprising. But from this fact the Toledans deduced that not only Juan's relations had been crypto-Jews but also Juan de Cibdad himself. The deduction was of course faulty, but it shows how anxious the Toledans were to prove that the converso leader was a Judaizer. It need scarcely be said that if they could find on his body, and the bodies of his comrades who were hanged with him, any sign of circumcision, they would hasten to point out this fact as evidence of the Judaism of the hanged conversos (even though it could prove only the Judaism of their parents); but no such evidence could be found.

We may also note that in 1449 a number of Marranos were delivered to the stake by a Toledan ecclesiastical tribunal, and García, the rebel leader, sought to justify these executions by the Marranos' alleged devotion to

Judaism. He would use every sign and symptom he could think of to substantiate his allegation, but he could not tell us that the burned Marranos were found to have been circumcised.

Similarly, in 1467, Fernando de la Torre, the chief of the conversos, and his brother Alvaro, who was a *regidor*, were hanged in Toledo during the outbreak of that year, and their naked bodies, like those of their predecessors, were exposed for days in the central square. On that occasion, too, the Toledans were looking for some evidence that might prove that the hanged leaders were Judaizers, and consequently we may assume that if either of them had been circumcised, the Toledans would not have kept silent about it.

Nor could such a charge be made against the Marranos who were killed in Ciudad Real in 1449, in Toledo in 1467, or in Cordova in 1473. In Cordova especially, where the enemies of the Marranos loudly accused the Marranos of Judaism, the anti-Marranos were certainly interested in substantiating their charges. In the large-scale pogrom that broke out in that city, scores of Marranos were killed. Many of their bodies fell into the hands of their enemies, who would have been quick to point out that they were circumcised if this had been the case. But again, no mention was made of such evidence. For neither in Cordova nor in any other place where Marranos were killed, hanged, or stripped naked (like those murdered between Seville and Palma) could any evidence be offered that they were circumcised, as their detractors had claimed.

This, to be sure, is an argument *ex silentio*; but here, considering the circumstances involved, it is as valid and forceful as any evidence could be. What is more, it is in full accord with Jewish and converso testimonies that were uttered on this subject *expressis verbis*.[28] And thus we can safely dismiss the charge respecting the practice of Marrano circumcision. Our conclusion is that, rather than common, that practice was rare—so rare indeed that it fits the view we have formed of all other accusations made by the Toledan Inquiry concerning the Marrano heresy. For the sum total of our analysis of these accusations was that they were either absurd or based on feeble evidence or on no evidence at all (just on "notoriety") or flatly denied by other sources whose credibility cannot be questioned. Only few of them were gross exaggerations of facts that could be applied to small groups of Judaizers whose presence in Spain in the fifties, and even later, need not be denied.

If Espina, however, failed in his attempts to prove that the Marranos practiced Jewish law, he succeeded in spreading in Spain the belief that the Jews keep perpetuating devilish atrocities against their Old Christian neighbors, as well as in extending that accusation so as to apply it to the conversos too. We refer to the myths about Jewish religious crimes, such as ritual murder and Host desecration, and about Jewish attempts to kill masses of

Christians by a variety of means, including black magic. The *pesquisa*, we should note, found it difficult or impossible to include these libels among the Marranos' alleged crimes, and thus it only alluded to the *probability* that some conversos were involved in desecrating Hosts. Espina did not go beyond this allusion in so far as the conversos were concerned, but played up the crime of Host desecration to make it appear common among Jews, and ultimately also among the conversos, since he kept stressing that the latter are nothing but the Jews' identical twins. Thus he achieved his aim of striking at the entire "Jewish" conglomerate.

Espina's strategy proved highly effective. In 1465 the report submitted by the Arbitration Committee on the state of the nation to King Enrique IV claimed that the Jews were habitually desecrating Hosts and were assisted in this practice by some "bad Christians"—a title which broadly hinted at conversos. And a few years later, in 1468, the Jews of Sepúlveda were accused of ritual murder, the trial ending in 1471 in the conviction and execution of the accused (for the first time in Spanish history).[29] What is more, in 1490, the Inquisition charged both conversos and Jews with plotting together the annihilation of all Christians by performing a conjuration with a human heart and a consecrated Host. This time the conversos were alleged to have provided both the consecrated wafer and the heart of a Christian child crucified on a Good Friday.[30] One might think that such a libel could have been conceived, let alone insisted on, only by a group of madmen. Yet it was organized, worked out, and proclaimed as true by the highest ecclesiastical tribunal in Spain; eight people were executed for it; and a child from one of three alleged places, who was never missed and never identified, was declared to have been martyred near the town of La Guardia and soon recognized as saint by large sections of the people. How could such a thing happen in Castile, which had never fallen prey to such preposterous fatuities? It could happen because the social atmosphere of the country had been prepared for it by Espina's campaign.

That so many modern scholars and historians accepted Espina's assertions as valid, and as mirroring Marrano life, must partly be related to the anti-Jewish bias that lingered in the minds of more than a few researchers, however critical and sharp-sighted. But in part the explanation may lie in certain circumstances related to the inquiry under consideration: the Jewish sources on the Marranos were ignored or misread; the Marranos' testimonies were buried in the archives; and the most important documents of Espina's predecessors (that is, of hate-mongers like García) were likewise unknown to most historians. In such circumstances Espina's *Fortalitium*—or its sections dealing with the New Christians—appeared as a *rich* source of information and, since he was taken to be a converso, also as an *authentic* source. Today, of course, we know better. We know that Espina was no New Christian and had no inside knowledge of Marrano life; we know the real value of the *pesquisa,* on whose proceedings he drew so heavily; we also know that his other data were based on rumor, libel and myth—in fact, on the crudest myths spawned in the Middle Ages against the Jews and their beliefs. And above all, we know that he was filled with hate—the kind of hate that calls out constantly for vengeance and will stop at nothing to get what it wants. This is the hate that burned in García, that fired the authors of the *Petition* and the *Sentencia,* of the satires we have analyzed and the anonymous anti-converso *Coplas.*[31] We class them all as unreliable witnesses—the most generous, understated criticism we can apply to them.

Our summary of the 15th-century sources dealing with the religious position of the Marranos offers us, we believe, adequate ground for reaching definite conclusions. Two of the three bodies of literature produced by the groups involved in the controversy (i.e., those of Jewish and of Marrano origin) offer clear-cut evidence against the thesis that a widespread crypto-Jewish movement existed within the Marrano camp. The testimonies of both groups so harmonize with each other that one can hardly find a discrepancy between them. They agree that Marrano Christianization was a fact, both theoretically and practically, and they further agree that the midcentury generation was already so deeply imbued with Christianity that it had no knowledge of the Jewish religion and no interest in its precepts. Similarly, they agree that the Judaizers formed a shrinking remnant of little consequence and that the charges against the Marranos on this score were motivated by non-religious drives. The two groups of sources—the Jewish and New Christian—are not equally articulate on the *causes* of these drives, but both suggest clearly that there was no religious reason for establishing the Inquisition.

As for the works produced by Old Christians on the conversos' religious position, we have seen that some of them, authored by such men as Barrientos and Guzmán—men of great distinction in their respective fields—viewed the conversos in general as Christians and rejected as wild exaggeration the notion that all or most of them were heretics. Like the Marranos themselves, they freely recognized the possible existence of Judaizers in Spain, but did not believe that their number comprised more than a nonrepresentative fraction. Thus, in many respects, their position on the question was either identical with that of the conversos or else very close to it; and hence we can align the sum total of their evidence with that offered by the conversos and the Jews.

There remains, therefore, only one group of sources that supports the claim that the conversos were Judaizers, or harbored a Jewish underground so widespread that it might represent their majority. The authors of this single condemnatory group could not match in intellectual and moral stature those of the other three bodies of sources—an important consideration in choosing these sources as the foundation of our judgment. But as we have indicated, there is another reason that compels us to downgrade the anti-Marrano writings and virtually exclude them from the group of records that can help us determine the Marranos' religion. Because of the untruths they contain in such abundance—untruths both proven and self-evident—they are discredited by their own contents, and thus disqualified as bearers of witness. Inevitably, we remain with the information offered us by the other three sets of sources, whose clear-cut evidence is reinforced by the nature of the contrary assertions.

II. The Social-Economic Reasons

I

Since the charges concerning the Marranos' heresy proved so inflated and so imaginary, we must obviously look elsewhere for the sources of the movement that dictated the formation of the Inquisition. To be sure, false charges may often increase the force propelling movements of this sort; but to have a truly significant effect they must be accepted by great numbers of people; and such acceptance is conditioned by the presence of a widespread antipathy toward the maligned group. There can be no doubt that such an antipathy existed in Spain toward the conversos, but before going further we should determine its nature and the causes from which it sprang. We shall probably move closer to our goal if, from the outset, we view this antipathy as a veiled hostility which could be transformed, upon the slightest provocation, into open enmity. We are looking then for the roots of a genuine feeling, generating both discomfort and resentment, which would steadily become more irritating and disturbing until in the end it exploded. To identify that feeling we shall now turn our attention to the other complaints against the Marranos—or rather to the nonreligious censures of their conduct, which, as we have noticed, were repeatedly expressed in the anti-Marrano literature of the time.

Of these censures, we ought first to concentrate on the social-economic criticisms, because the Marranos themselves kept stressing, as we have seen, that the animosity toward them stemmed from the jealousy aroused by their social and economic successes. This is the view of the great apologists of the conversos—the Relator, Cartagena, and, in part, Torquemada[1]; and this is the view of the converso historians Diego de Valera and Fernando de Pulgar.[2] But not only conversos were of this opinion. The Old Christian historian Alonso de Palencia[3] seconded the views of Valera and Pulgar; and Old Christian ecclesiastics like Barrientos and Oropesa argued that social and economic jealousy was the root of the quarrel between the groups and the outrages perpetrated against the New Christians.[4]

According to these testimonies, then, it was social-economic, rather than religious factors that fueled the attacks upon the conversos. And the same conclusion may be drawn from virtually all anti-Marrano writings. For these writings criticize the conversos for their alleged social and economic crimes just as frequently as they scold them for their alleged religious faults. What is more, the social-economic charges exceed the religious ones in both ferocity and vengefulness.

We have already noted that until the middle of the 1460s, when Espina completed his *Fortalitium*, anti-Marrano literature rarely accused the conversos of religious crimes that had the nature of atrocities. Yet the crimes it attributed to them in the *economic* and *social* spheres were precisely of this nature. Accordingly, the charges in these fields are more sweeping and exaggerated than the religious accusations; and the invectives that accompany these charges are more vehement and scurrilous than any others in that literature. Unavoidably we are led to the conclusion that the social and economic activities of the conversos aroused a more passionate and implacable hatred than did their alleged religious transgressions; and thus we may have here some proof of the claim that "envy" was the root of the enmity.

To understand correctly what the claim implied and to what extent it conformed to the facts, we should go a little further into this matter. Obviously, the "envy" under consideration suggests deep feelings of ill will and rancor which the "success" of the conversos—or, rather, their achievements—stirred in some Old Christians toward the New. Yet similar or even greater successes of other Spanish groups (among the Old Christians) did not arouse such fierce jealousies, or any jealousies at all. It follows that in the case of the conversos, as in many other cases of economic envy, the ill will and rancor that met their achievements may have sprung from non-economic sources. We shall try to identify these sources—a difficult task in most cases of envy, whether individual or collective, but especially in cases of group jealousy, whose motives may be rooted in feelings and situations harking back to the remote past.

What, then, were the origins of the group jealousy that so many Old Christians felt for the New? And what made that jealousy swell into a torrent so violent that it swept almost everything before it? If we are right in relating it mainly to the conversos' social and economic achievements, the growth of the jealousy must have generally paralleled the greatness of those achievements. Inevitably, this gives rise to the question: What was it in the economic and social gains of the conversos that could generate such fierce hatred for their group? Obviously, in order to answer this query, we must look at those gains of the conversos against the background of the society of which they formed a part.

II

There is no doubt that of all the conversos' attainments in various social-economic fields, nothing so irked the Old Christians of Castile as their occupation of so many high offices in all four administrations of the country (the royal, nobiliar, clerical and urban), and there is also no doubt that the resulting irritation was felt most strongly in the cities. The conversos' growing influence in Castile's urban administrations became therefore the focus of Old Christian resentment and was increasingly felt as a festering wound in the unhealthy relationships that developed between the groups. Accordingly, our remarks on the social aspects of these relationships will first touch on what seems to have been the key issue in the conflict between the Old and New Christians in Spain.

The first thunderous evidence of the resentment referred to was given in Toledo in 1449, when the rebel party which then governed the city issued the notorious *Sentencia-Estatuto,* barring the conversos from all offices in the future and denying them the right to the offices they held. To be sure, the rebels relied mainly on the low classes, but the policy expressed in the *Sentencia,* as we have noted, was by no means favored by these classes only. It was also supported by the urban aristocracy when they took over the government of the city; in fact, their insistence on that policy was so strong that they were willing to put themselves, solely for its sake, in the compromising and menacing situation of both intransigence to the king and disobedience to the pope.[5]

This fierce determination of the Toledans to keep the conversos out of all offices surfaced again in 1467, when another quarrel with their New Christian neighbors offered them an excuse to readopt the *Sentencia,* which had in the meantime been rescinded. On this occasion, too, we have seen the Toledans violate their obligations to their royal lord—i.e., Alfonso, Enrique IV's brother (whom two years before they had proclaimed king)—because he refused to approve the requests they addressed to him with respect to the conversos. They abandoned his camp and rejoined King Enrique, who was now prepared to subscribe to their demands.

But Toledo, as we have seen, was not the only city that was so determined to uphold this position. Other cities, like Ciudad Real and Cordova, in which the New Christians were violently assailed, hastened to declare, following the outbreaks, that no converso could assume public office within their jurisdiction.[6] In making such rulings, these cities gave expression to a sentiment that embraced many urban communities. It was fast becoming nationwide when the new age approached, and in the following three centuries it fostered the view that the right to public office must be firmly held as the dividing line between Old and New Christians.

The resistance of Old Christians to the engagement of conversos in the public offices of their various administrations had deep roots in Spanish life. It stemmed from two traditional attitudes (which already dominated Spain's society in the 7th century): opposition to the holding of these offices by Jews and antagonism to having them controlled by Jewish converts. The former opposition was not unique to Spain. It accompanied Jewish life in many Christian countries from the beginning of the 5th century onward, although it did not always determine the policies pursued by the rulers on this particular issue. Occasionally, princes were moved by self-interest to employ certain Jews in an official capacity, but whenever this occurred with some regularity, it was invariably followed by an upsurge of Jew hatred and by vehement demands to oust the Jews from their positions. The same phenomena were witnessed in the Christian kingdoms that arose in Spain in the period of the Reconquest, except that the rulers of these kingdoms knew better how to cope with the forces of the opposition. Especially distinguished in this respect was Castile, which engaged Jews for a much longer time, and in more high offices, than any other kingdom; nor did any other country experience such a hostile popular reaction to this engagement of Jews on the part of the Christian populace.

But Castile was also unmatched in its antagonism to the holding of public offices by *converts*. And as in the case of the Jews, this antagonism assumed concrete political form in the cities. Toledo, as we have seen, took the lead in the drive against the appointment of both Jews and converts to office. We have noticed its opposition to Jews in high offices already before 1108 and to converts at least from 1118 on. Jews and converts, however, differed in their status, and we should distinguish the limits of the demands which Toledo (and, in its wake, many other cities) could present to the kings concerning the right of each group to occupy public posts.

Until the middle of the 13th century, no city in Castile had any say in the governance of the kingdom, and consequently no city could interfere in the appointment of officials on a *national* level. To be sure, relying on the Church's injunction prohibiting the appointment of Jews to high office, the cities protested with increasing vigor against any such appointments in Castile. For a long time, however, these protests fell on deaf ears. They could not alter the policies of the princes, who believed that the interests of the state took precedence over the pronouncements of the Church. But the case was different with regard to the appointment of holders of office in the *urban* administrations. Since most of these officials were appointed by the cities, their offices were hermetically closed to Jews—and often not to Jews alone. From 1118 to approximately 1250, we find one city after another insisting on its right to exclude Jewish *converts* from urban public offices, and it was only with great difficulty that the kings managed to engage Jewish converts as their treasurers in several Castilian cities.

From about 1250 the situation changed radically when the third estate became a permanent component of the Castilian Cortes—a change that reflected the growth of the cities' financial and military power. As regular participants in the Castilian Cortes, the cities had the right to petition the kings for revisions in their policies and methods of government, and they used this right to exert pressure on the kings to remove the Jews from the royal administration. It was long before this pressure bore fruit, because the services of the Jews were considered indispensable, especially in the management of the royal finances (the heads of the royal treasury were Jews). But in 1380 the kings finally yielded. They removed the Jews from their positions at Court—that is, from all the national offices—leaving them only in local positions as farmers and gatherers of their taxes. The cities thus gained a major victory, even though not yet a total one. The final battle was won only thirty years later—that is, with the issuance of the laws of 1412, when the Jews were removed from the tax-gathering system on the local levels, too.

The triumph of the cities now seemed complete. Yet it was accompanied by a revolutionary change that presented the cities with difficult problems with which they were hardly prepared to cope. For only one decade after the Jews were removed from their high offices in Castile, masses of Jews went over to Christianity under the impact of the riots of 1391; and in 1412, the very year in which they were ousted from their local posts too, the second mass conversion began, in the course of which additional myriads of Jews were brought into the Christian fold. These New Christians began to press for the financial and other offices vacated by the Jews. What is more, apart from the royal administration, they also sought entry into the municipal administrations, and thus the problem of Jews in public offices, which seemed to have been solved by the laws of 1412, was replaced for the cities by a far graver problem in precisely the same field. The restoration of the Jews to their former positions in the tax-gathering system (from 1420 on) naturally multiplied the difficulties they faced; but the issue of Jews in the royal administration, which had loomed so large decades before, now appeared minor compared to the converso problem. For while the cities could still oppose the entrance of *Jews* into their governing bodies on religious grounds, they had no answer to the problem posed by the penetration of *converts* into their officialdom.

The primary reason for the cities' objections to the presence of *conversos* in public office was essentially the same as their *real* reason for opposing *Jews* in the same positions. Although with respect to the Jews their religion was the reason given publicly for the objections, we have noted that religion, though related to the issue, was essentially a convenient pretext. In the case of the converts, the cities found it difficult, if not impossible, to use that pretext, and therefore they resorted to other excuses, which rarely proved convincing. We have seen that the conversos were not the only group that the cities opposed as potential officeholders. As in the 14th century, so in the 15th they refused to let nobles hold office in their administrations, just as they objected to the intervention of Church judges in their judicial procedures. All such intrusions were viewed by the cities as intolerable interference in their civic life. Yet the least tolerable intrusion of all was to them that of the conversos.

This opposition of the cities to the conversos appears, at first sight, less comprehensible than the antagonism they displayed toward the nobles, the clerics and the Jews. For the three latter groups belonged to different estates (or, in the Jews' case, to a different corporation); they were not subject to the cities' jurisdiction, and in many cases (such as those involving magnates) were not even residents of the cities. None of these conditions applied to the conversos. Almost all of them belonged to the third estate, were subject to the municipal laws, and resided within the very cities that sought to deny them the right to hold office. All this suggests that the struggle of the city oligarchies with the conversos over the control of the urban offices differed from their struggle with the nobles and prelates over the control of the national administration. For unlike their quarrel with the latter groups, the oligarchies' conflict with the conversos arose *within the municipal citizenry*, cut across the upper class of Old and New Christians, and placed both groups in a state of constant confrontation that increased competition and friction. No wonder the results of these contests differed, too. While the oligarchies were generally successful in repelling the magnates' attempts to usurp their functions, their efforts to ward off the New Christians often met with failure and defeat.

It was of course far harder for the cities of Castile to contend with the conversos in the 15th century than it had been in the 12th and the 13th. To begin with, while the number of Jewish converts in those centuries was comparatively small or even tiny, it was proportionately very large in the 15th century, during which the conversos came to comprise about a third of the cities' population. The weight of their numbers could not be ignored; and to this one must add the repute and high standing they acquired as officials in both Castile and Aragon. It was difficult for the oligarchies to charge the conversos with administrative incompetence or other inadequacies when conversos proved so suitable for all other administrations and, indeed, were so lauded for their services.

In addition, the highly important connections established by the conversos in all other bureaucracies could often exert sufficient influence on the oligarchies to determine appointments in their favor. These circumstances, too, did not exist earlier, when many high positions in the royal and nobiliar administrations were occupied by Jews, and not by converts. But even more significant than these differences was the radically changed legal condition in Castile, which worked to the converts' benefit. To be sure, in the earlier periods too the urban oligarchies encountered great difficulties in denying Jewish converts official appointments, since such denials went counter to the laws as well as the common practice of the Church. But in the 15th century they had to contend not only with canon law but with civil law as well. For the civil law of Castile, as represented in the *Partidas* (which became the nation's code in 1348), stated explicitly, as we have indicated, that converts from Judaism can freely enjoy *"all the offices and honors which other Christians have."* It was the clear-cut position on converso rights taken by the laws of *both* Church and state that paved the way for converso penetration into all the country's administrations, including the urban.

There was, however, an additional factor, more important than all others, without which the conversos would not have gone so far in their administrative achievements. This was the unwavering support they received for three decades from the Castilian Crown. We have seen the reasons for that support, which were all associated with the interests of the monarchy and its struggle for supreme power. Of course, the King's aims were not those of the conversos, who essentially wished to fulfill their duties as both efficient and honest officials of whatever administration they worked for. But they were dedicated to the concept of the king's supremacy and the idea that his orders should override the instructions of all other authorities. This attitude was, fundamentally, all that the Crown required; and the benefits the conversos derived from it followed as a matter of course. Just as their expansion in the royal administration resulted, in large part, from the King's conflict with the nobility and his desire to subdue the nobles to his will, so did their occupation of high offices in the cities result, to no little extent, from his contest with the cities and his wish to reduce them to complete obedience.

To be sure, the nobles correctly assessed the Marranos' stand and motives. But the reaction of the oligarchies was different. The presence of conversos in the urban administrations, anathema from the first, was now doubly resented by the Old Christian notables as a tyrannic imposition. While the king-city conflict somewhat abated during the reign of Enrique IV, the Old-New-Christian contest did not. In fact, the oligarchies' resistance to converso officials in their cities was constantly on the rise. The reason was the penetration of the conversos into most of the country's urban administrations, which became ever harder to reverse. Like other social drives, this drive, too, was largely propelled by the force of inertia; and the positions the conversos had gained in the preceding reign served them as springboards for further advance.

III

The quarrel over the offices, which split the cities' upper class into conflicting groups of Old and New Christians, embraced the farming and collection of the revenues, although these occupations belonged by their nature more to private enterprise and investment than to official appointment. Nevertheless, the tax farmers and collectors could perform their functions only when backed by an administrative power entitled to impose taxes. Thus, anyone invested by the royal treasury with the authority to gather the king's revenues was in fact a royal official.

In the 13th and 14th centuries, as we have noted, the cities opposed the engagement of Jews in the gathering of the revenues both as farmers and collectors, justifying their opposition by the same argument they had used in objecting to Jews in public office. As enemies of Christianity, the Jews, they said, should not be given positions of authority in which they might harm Christians. The reason may have been a mere excuse, but even if it was sincerely believed, it did not represent the sole or main motive of the cities' unwavering stand on this matter—for they were just as stubbornly opposed, as we have seen, to the gathering of their taxes by both nobles and prelates. Obviously, the absence of the "Jewish" shortcoming—or, conversely, the presence of devout Christianity—was considered by the cities insufficient to qualify any of these groups as their tax gatherers. The cities viewed all members of the high estates as unfit and ineligible for the task—to begin with, because their privileges freed them from the need to abide by the city's jurisdiction and thus rendered them unanswerable to its courts. Moreover, as "outsiders" from a civic standpoint—even when they lived within the city walls—they were presumed not to care about the city's condition or the welfare of its citizens. In one measure or another, these considerations applied also to the Jews.

Rejecting Jews, nobles and clerics, and of course also Moors, as tax gatherers for the crown in their territories, the cities proposed to place the gathering of the revenues in the hands of their *hombres buenos*, respectable men of their own upper class, who would presumably treat the towns' citizens fairly and also guard the rights of the crown. Never did they consider a compromise proposal, such as the appointment of trustworthy men from their own ranks *or* from the nobility and the clergy, by common consent of city and Crown. Nor did they consider the appointment of tax collectors from the middle or low classes by election or any other process. They insisted on the assignment of this task to *hombres buenos* chosen by the councils, or the oligarchies who virtually ruled the councils. We can see in this a clear sign of the desire—and indeed determination—of the Old Christian urban elite to make sure that the officials in this field, too, were members of their groups and subject to their control. And though they never said as much, they evidently wanted the income of these offices to go to their own men.

From the standpoint of the interests of the urban economy, it was hard to argue with this demand. Tax collection brought in considerable profits, and it seemed right for the city to try to keep these profits (which were derived from its own citizens) within the communal orbit. Nevertheless, it is difficult to believe that personal as well as oligarchic interests were not behind the cities' proposals. Undoubtedly, they wanted the profit to be made from the gathering of the royal revenues to go to their upper class and not to anyone else; but they wanted a profit that did not involve risk. Accordingly, they proposed that their *hombres buenos* be charged with the *collection* of the taxes and refused to let these collectors be subject to *tax farmers* even of their own chosen men.

It stands to reason that they based their case on the claim that tax farming was an evil system, because the tax farmer, to gain his contract from the king, was forced to assure the monarch an income far larger than was justified by the economic situation; and then, to secure his investment and expected profit, he had to squeeze taxpayers for high returns, which they were not duty-bound to pay. It is also possible that most *hombres buenos* were disinclined to be involved in such activities, which would inevitably lead their fellow citizens to disparage them or view them with ill will. It is even more likely that their inexperience in the field made them reluctant to risk the large outlay and commitments that tax farming usually required. But whatever the reasons for the cities' position, the arrangement they proposed, if accepted by the Crown, would have drastically reduced the king's income from the revenues, while giving him in fact no guarantee of any substantial income. Moreover, it would place the payment of the taxes virtually in the hands of those who were to pay them, and in consequence the king would financially become totally dependent on the cities. That is why the kings would not heed these demands and the Jews remained masters of the field— that is, they remained not only the tax collectors but also the farmers of the royal revenues. In the 14th and 15th centuries, it is obvious, Spain had not yet found a better way than farming to gather its taxes.

From 1380 onward, the records of the Cortes contain no more demands by the cities of Castile to abolish the farming system and transfer the tax collection to their own men. This suggests that the cities acquiesced in the king's methods of gathering the revenues. They did not cease, however, to complain about abuses of the laws and excessive impositions by the tax collectors of the king. But no indication was ever given of the personal identity of these tax collectors. In the fifteenth century, as we have noted, tax farming, which had been monopolized by the Jews, was gradually divided between them and the conversos. But even as late as 1469, the Jews held the "principal offices of the treasuries and *collections*" of the royal taxes in Castile *("rentas e pechos e derechos")*.[7] It would seem, then, that most of the complaints were directed against the *Jewish* gatherers of the revenues; but as we have no direct evidence of this, we must assume that at least some of the criticisms were aimed at the conversos, too. In any case, in the Petition which the rebels of Toledo addressed to the King in May 1449, the converso tax farmers are specifically mentioned as those entrusted with the gathering of the revenues and, furthermore, as responsible, together with Alvaro, for the "unjust and inhuman laws" enacted to raise the taxes above the needs of the Crown.[8] Moreover, in the *Sentencia* the converso tax gatherers are accused of having "taken, carried and robbed," by means of their "great tricks *(astucias)* and deceits *(engaños)*" large and innumerable quantities of maravedis and silver" from the king's "rents *(rentas)*, taxes *(pechos)*, and duties *(derechos)*."[9] Considering the rebels' intense hatred of the conversos and the wild accusations they often hurled at them, we can discount a great many of these charges. But even so, it is clear that the converso tax gatherers were not accused of actions that were formally illegal, but rather of managing to get their wealth (which the authors of the *Sentencia* regarded as "robbery") by employing their financial astuteness (in which those authors saw only "tricks and deceits") to obtain a larger portion than was due them from the royal taxes.

If we go by the rebels' statements, then, the tax-farming activities of the conversos raised bitter complaints and harsh criticisms from the Old Christians in Toledo and other cities, and especially from their upper classes. For according to the *Sentencia* they have "caused the [economic] ruin ... of many noble proprietresses *(dueñas)*, caballeros and *hijos-dalgo*," and have, in addition, "oppressed, destroyed, robbed and depraved ... most of the old houses and estates of the Old Christians" of Toledo ... and of "all the Kingdoms of Castile, as is notorious and accepted by us [i.e., by the authors of the *Sentencia*] to be true" *("y por tal lo habemos")*.[10] Based as it was largely on "notoriety," this charge of the rebels, like many of their other charges, must have been exaggerated. Surely not all or most estates of the lower nobility of Castile were bankrupt; and if many of them were, there must have been other causes, besides excessive taxation, that brought them to this condition. But since these accusations were made public in Toledo, we may assume that they were intended to appeal to many members of the Old Christian high classes in the city, and from this we may conclude that, like the occupation of the high offices of the urban administrations, the gathering of the taxes by the conversos generated much tension between Old and New Christians and was especially a source of friction and antagonism between the two constituent parts of the cities' upper class, the Old and New Christian elites.

IV

The steadily increasing strength of the conversos in the gathering of the revenues in Castile was in no small measure due to their hold on the royal office charged with the allotment of tax farming. This was the office of

Contador Mayor (the chief accountant or treasurer of the kingdom), which was occupied almost uninterruptedly by Jews from the days of Alfonso X to those of Juan I (1380). Faced with the violent anti-Jewish outcry that followed the murder of Joseph Pichon (1379), the King did not dare to reappoint a Jew to the office of *Contador Mayor*.[11] Nevertheless, no Christian, it seems, was to fill that position either. It would seem that the powerful Jewish tax farmers objected to having a Christian in that office, and as a result, the *contaduría mayor* continued to be run, though informally, by Jews.

Things, however, changed considerably in this respect after the conversions of 1391. Many of the converts must have been tax collectors who were anxious to resume their work in the field, and some of them no doubt were qualified to occupy the office of *Contador Mayor*. In any case, the Jewish monopoly in that area was broken or at least severely curtailed, and the Jewish tax farmers, with their number much diminished, could no longer object—as they may have done before—to the appointment of a convert to the contested office. Early in the reign of Enrique III, therefore, Juan Sánchez de Sevilla (the former Samuel Abravanel), probably the most famous convert of his time, became *contador mayor*.[12]

He served in this capacity until the end of the reign (1407) and possibly in the subsequent period of the Regency, and we find him still called *contador mayor* (obviously, by then an honorary title) when young Juan II succeeded to the throne (1419).[13] He was not, however, the only converso to occupy that office during the period of the Regency. Other *contadores mayores* in those days, perhaps already in the reign of Enrique III, were the New Christians Francisco Fernández Marmolejo and Diego Sánchez de Valladolid.[14] Their offspring, like those of Juan Sánchez de Sevilla, intermarried with Old Christian nobles—a sure sign of the fame and success they attained during their service.[15]

From 1416 the *contador mayor* was Fernán Alonso de Robles.[16] He was a man of low birth, probably from the middle class, who began his career as an aide to an *escribano* and rose to the high levels of the royal administration—only, we are told, "thanks to his abilities."[17] All this is typical of the career of a converso, though Robles may have been an Old Christian. In any case, as we have seen, in 1427, after he had broken faith with Alvaro, he lost his position, and his tasks were taken over by the New Christian Fernán López de Saldaña.[18] He, too, shared the job with another converso, who earned the same title. This was Diego González de Toledo (better known as Doctor Franco), who was held in high regard at Juan II's Court. Above or beside him served as *contador mayor* Alvaro's close friend and future antagonist Alonso Pérez de Vivero. Vivero's kinship in some degree with conversos cannot, in our opinion, be ruled out.[19]

In the following reign, that of Enrique IV, the chief *contador mayor* was again a converso. This was the famous Diego Arias Dávila, one of Castile's ablest treasurers in that century, even though he was the most reviled and most criticized by many Old Christians. We see no basis for the hostile charges that were leveled at him on the grounds of religion, but they no doubt reflected a popular reaction to the unconventional and sometimes ruthless methods he employed to keep the treasury well supplied. Enrique IV knew his value, and it was in grateful recognition of his services that he appointed his son Pedro Arias Dávila (Pedrarias) to the same position after Diego's death.

Thus we see that throughout the long period stretching from the first years of Enrique III to the last years of Enrique IV—and possibly even further— the Royal Treasury was almost exclusively in the hands of New Christians. Apart from facilitating the expansion of the conversos in the farming and collection of the revenues, it no doubt contributed to the growth of their activity in banking and money exchange, mining, and the management of royal finances in the provinces that were likewise under the Treasury's control.

Just as the conversos made large-scale advances in the fields related to the Royal Treasury, they also made notable progress in the spheres controlled by the administration of justice. The appointment of judges of all ranks in the cities was one of the functions of the royal chancellery, and it was no doubt thanks to their influence in the chancellery that conversos were given positions of judges in steadily increasing number. If we go by the list of the Toledan conversos ousted from their offices in 1449, Toledo had then only one converso judge (Diego González Jarada),[20] but later on we find conversos serving in Toledo in the capacity of both ordinary judges (such as Francisco de Cota[21] and Alonso Díaz de Toledo[22]) and extraordinary ones, alcaldes mayores (such as Diego Romero[23] and Alvar Gómez de Cibdad Real[24]). In Seville, we are told that Juan Fernández Albolasia, who was known as "a great jurist," served many times as alcalde de la justicia,[25] while Fernando de Rojas, the famous novelist, was alcalde mayor of Talavera.[26] From other indications in the sources we learn that conversos served as judges in many towns at various levels, as well as in special fields, such as the royal revenues in Seville or the Hermandad in Ciudad Real.[27]

Another part of the royal administration in which conversos attained a special place was the secretaryship of the king, which they held almost uninterruptedly from the beginning of Juan II's reign. The most prominent of these officials, who enjoyed special influence on the monarch, was no doubt Fernán Díaz de Toledo, who besides acting as Relator, served also as the king's chief secretary. In the subsequent reign, these functions of secretary were fulfilled by two other conversos, for the most part by Alvar Gómez de Cibdad Real, who was chief secretary of Enrique IV and his closest confidant in the first half of the reign. His betrayal of Enrique represented not the rule but the exception in the behavior of converso royal secretaries, and did not prevent Queen Isabella from appointing a New Christian to the same office. He was the famous Alvarez de Toledo, more commonly known as Zapata.[28]

There can be no doubt that the influence of the conversos in the royal secretaryship was one of the factors determining the appointments of the cities' chief authorities—the *regidores* and *corregidores*. Perhaps the first converso to function as *corregidor* was the one appointed for Orense in 1419[29]; and as in other offices, in this one, too, it was in the days of Juan II that more and more New Christians served as *regidores* and *corregidores*, despite the opposition that must have been shown by the local authorities. Thus in 1421, when Alvar Sánchez de Cartagena was sent by the king as corregidor to Toledo, he was refused entry into the city[30]; but few cities could show such disregard for royal wishes as did Toledo in that year; and in 1449 the Relator tells us that some of the descendants of Fernández Marmolejo (the *contador mayor*) served as *regidores* in Seville.[31] From the days of Enrique IV, there are clear indications that a steadily increasing number of conversos occupied these offices, and this was no doubt true also for the first years of the Catholic Kings—that is, until the founding of the Inquisition. This development is illustrated by the names of New Christian *regidores* and *corregidores* who, for one reason or another, gained special repute. Such were Juan González Pintado, the famous *regidor* of Ciudad Real (burned by the Inquisition in that city),[32] Alvaro de la Torre, *regidor* of Toledo (who was hanged by the populace in 1467),[33] and Diego de Susan, *regidor* of Seville, who, together with other leading Marranos, was accused of conspiring against the Inquisition in 1481 and was burned at the stake as an alleged Judaizer.[34] Not all of them, however, met such a tragic end. Other famous *regidores* were Fernando de la Torre, the well-known author (in Burgos),[35] Alonso Cota, the treasurer (in Toledo)[36] and Andrés de Cabrera, Enrique IV's mayordomo (in Cuenca).[37] The latter, who became governor of Segovia and promoter of Princess Isabella to the throne, secured for his brother Alfonso the office of *corregidor* of Segovia,[38] while Diego de Valera, the poet and historian, served as *corregidor* of Segovia and Palencia.[39]

But the crowning achievement of the conversos in government was attained through their membership in Castile's royal Council. Whereas throughout the history of the Jews in Christian Spain, only two Jewish courtiers are known for certain to have become members of the royal Council,[40] conversos seem to have joined this body from the beginning of the reign of Juan II. Toward the end of that reign they probably comprised no less than a third of its members,[41] reaching at that time the zenith of their influence in determining the actions and policies of the state. In subsequent reigns this influence was reduced either by the decline of the Council's participation in the governance of the kingdom or by the changes later introduced in both its structure and functions. Enrique IV relied more and more on isolated councillors, whom he chose from all estates, while Ferdinand the Catholic limited his council members to a small number of bureaucrats (almost all plebeians) chosen for their administrative expertise. Converso representation among these bureaucrats, however, was notable in the reigns of these kings too, until about the turn of the century.

In the 15th century New Christians often played a leading role in the hierarchy of the Church. Among the offices they occupied were those of bishop, archbishop, Master of the Sacred Palace, and cardinal. The first converso to gain high Church position was Pablo de Santa María, who became bishop of Cartagena (in 1401) and later of Burgos during the minority of Juan II (in 1415). Toward the end of the Regency's rule we meet with a second converso bishop—Gonsalvo de Santa María, Paul's eldest son, who acquired the see of Astorga in 1419. Under Juan II, when no bishop could be appointed in Castile without the king's consent, Alfonso de Cartagena, Paul's second son, replaced his aged father in the bishopric of Burgos. Among the sees occupied by New Christian prelates in the second half of the century were those of Segovia, Calahorra and Granada. Conversos were also appointed to other positions in the ecclesiastical hierarchy, such as those of archdeacons, deacons, abbots, canons, and chaplains of cathedral churches.

Paralleling their growing authority in the monarchic and ecclesiastical administrations was their rising status in the nobiliar estates. Here, too, they often served the great magnates as treasurers, *mayordomos, maestresalas,* and also as political counselors and emissaries. Their infiltration into the noble class was considerably facilitated by the numerous marriages contracted by their sons and daughters with nobles of high rank. All this often brought them in touch with the forces that shaped the policies of the kingdom, which also helped them advance their penetration into the royal and urban administrations.

These attainments of the conversos in Castile helped to spur a similar development in Aragon. Aragon did not have an Alvaro de Luna, who could overcome the entrenched opposition of the estates to the entrance of conversos into the different administrations. It was apparently only after 1458, when Juan II became king of Aragon, that the influx of conversos into the royal administration began. It markedly increased in the seventies and reached its climax in the following decade, under Ferdinand II. Suffice it to mention the following names to illustrate this fact: Alonso de la Caballería was Ferdinand's vice-chancellor; Luis de Santángel was *escribano de ración,* i.e., the King's financial secretary (apart from having served in other important posts), Gabriel Sánchez was General Treasurer of the kingdom,[42] Sancho de Paternoy was *maestre racional de Aragon* (chief controller of Aragon's finances),[43] and Gaspar de Barrachina, Ferdinand's private secretary.[44]

This summary is by no means exhaustive, even with respect to the *types* of positions occupied in that period. Thus we find in the royal administration conversos who served also as royal ambassadors, military commanders, and governors of castles, and in the urban sphere as treasurers, *mayordomos* and *procuradores* to Cortes. The list could be extended, of course; but the picture is clear. Conversos were among the occupants of positions in all four administrations of the country—the royal, nobiliar, clerical and urban—and at all levels. Above all, we should note, *most* of these positions carried with them, in varying degrees, governmental authority, social prestige, and a relatively high income. Thus, they all provided openings to achieve the three assets most desired by the great majority of men: honor, wealth and power. That is why the struggle for their control was characterized by such tenacity.

V

There is no doubt that the large amounts of money concentrated in the hands of the converso tax farmers enabled—and induced—some of them to engage in international commerce. In this field, the Genoese who had settled in Spain, Old Christian Spaniards and Spanish Jews had been active for a long time; and the New Christians, we may safely assume, met stiff competition. But in the 15th century, Spain's commercial horizons expanded toward both the Atlantic and the Mediterranean, thereby multiplying business opportunities. The strong merchant communities established by the conversos in such cities as Seville, Toledo and Barcelona must have been to some extent an outcome of their achievements in international trade.

Less competitive than the merchants of the upper classes were the middle-class Old and New Christians, who drew their income mainly from small industries and businesses serving local markets. Here New and Old Christians often dealt in different commodities, a fact that reduced competition between them. Of course, such division of economic activity was generally not found in the liberal professions, notably medicine and jurisprudence, in which members of both groups engaged. In these spheres, Old and New Christians may often have competed for the same positions in the bureaucracies, as well as for the same clients or patients.

Several remarks should be made at this point to clarify the essential elements involved. In the liberal professions no less than in commerce, conversos in the same field were not all of the same class. In medicine, for instance, their famous physicians, who were usually in the service of great lords, all belonged to the upper class; not so most of the beginning practitioners and many of those who served the common folk. These had to compete not only with Jewish but also with Old Christian physicians, most of whose patients were Old Christians. By income and status, all these competitors belonged to the middle class, but the conversos often had the edge over the others for the same reasons that caused their famous masters to outmatch their Jewish and Old Christian peers. In consequence, the Old Christian more than the Jewish doctors saw themselves increasingly deprived of their patients by the successes of their converso rivals. Nevertheless, they would not give up. In most communities Old Christian physicians were available besides the Jewish and converso ones, and many Old Christians preferred their services either for professional reasons or simply because they were Old Christians. The savage campaign against converso doctors, portraying them as killers of their Christian patients, no doubt contributed to this preference.[45] But the Old Christian doctors, it must be pointed out, probably had no hand in that campaign. They must have been asked by the propagators of the libels to express support for their accusations; but no evidence has emerged that any of them so acted. This not only attests the professional integrity of the Old Christian physicians, but also explains why, despite the frightening rumors, many Old Christians continued to seek the services of converso (and Jewish) doctors.

The contest between the Old and New Christians of the middle class in the other free professions—especially in jurisprudence—was, in all likelihood, no less determined. As indicated above, many young New Christians turned to the law,[46] which a considerable number of them later practiced, but compared to medicine, which had been dominated by Jews, competition in jurisprudence was much tougher. Toward the middle of the century, this competition sharpened to the point of bitter rivalry. At that time, Old Christian graduates from the colleges became too numerous to be easily absorbed by the frequently depressed Castilian economy. Soon they came to think that their problem arose from the partial occupation of the field by conversos and came to believe that their problem could be solved by laws forbidding their competitors to practice. It was not by mere chance, one may venture to suppose, that two of the main leaders of the revolt of '49 were bachelors of law[47] and that the *Sentencia* forbade the conversos to assume not only public but also private offices. By the latter, we believe, they meant primarily the offices of jurists and attorneys *(abogados)*.

Old and New Christians of the middle class also clashed over the *minor* public offices. For members of this class to gain *major* offices, talent and education rarely sufficed. They had, besides, to be well connected and—more often than not—well financed. Yet except for extraordinary cases, these conditions did not obtain in their ranks, and consequently they usually had to be satisfied with low-grade public positions. But even these were not to be had for the asking. Modest though the pay was, it was secure, and the jobs, though low, offered opportunities to rise in the bureaucracy. That is why many citizens of both groups who wished to enter the bureaucratic service were willing to compete for low-grade posts. The New Christians' chances of winning in these contests were, however, slimmer than those of the Old. For the second-grade officials were not appointed by the king, but either by the various departments of the councils or by the cities' highest officials. And since most of the council members were Old Christians, as were most of the high officials, their choice fell mostly on Old Christian candidates; and thus, the great majority of the low-grade officials belonged to the Old Christian camp. No other result, it seems, can be envisaged by anyone familiar with the tendencies of the age.

Combining some functions of public offices with some of the characteristics of the liberal professions were the posts of the *escribanías*. Scriveners were appointed by royal authority, but their professional success, reputation and income depended entirely on their personal abilities. In this respect, the scriveners resembled the physicians—and even more so the jurists, who, like themselves, dealt chiefly with judicial and economic matters. Like the famous physicians and jurists, some of the scriveners served the kings and great nobles, or otherwise managed a large amount of business; and these belonged of course to the upper class; but most of the *escribanos*, serving the urban populations, did not rise economically above the upper middle class. Nevertheless, both Old and New Christians eagerly sought to get hold of these positions; for apart from offering financial opportunities, they bestowed considerable prestige on their occupants, the scribe being regarded as an honorable person who could be entrusted with confidential matters. That is why they formed a bone of contention between Old and New Christians not only of the middle class, but of the upper classes, too.[48] When relations between Old and New Christians became tense, and certainly when they were openly hostile, members of neither group wished to share their secrets with *escribanos* of the opposition. In such times, of course, control of the *escribanías* was a matter of great interest to all residents of the cities, especially of the upper classes.

VI

More serious friction than the middle-class Old Christians experienced in their relations with New Christians of their *own* class may have developed in their contacts with conversos of the *upper* class, with whom they may often have had to deal. This was especially so when great converso merchants, doing business on a national scale, supplied town merchants with merchandise for their local markets. The town merchants may often have depended on credit, on loans they could not get from Old Christian sources, and it is here that the converso wholesale merchant would come to their rescue as financier. The middle-class merchant, however, was not always in a position to meet his contractual obligations, and thus he might occasionally get into debt, which ultimately landed him in deep trouble. In such situations the Old Christian merchant could be led to believe that he had been outmaneuvered by the converso supplier and financier, who practiced on him his "evil arts." If, in addition, he saw himself at the mercy of the converso tax assessor and tax collector, we can readily understand his distrust and even fear of the New Christians.

As for the relations between the Old and New Christians of the *lower* class, mostly artisans and suppliers of low-grade services, competition between them must have been considerably more limited than it was between the Old and New Christians of the middle class. To be sure, many Old Christian and converso craftsmen who shared the same skills and clientele often must have found that their interests conflicted, but the trades of many others, as indicated above, were peculiar to their collectivities; and this partial occupational differentiation, which naturally caused a separation of interests, tended of course to diminish competition as well as social friction between the groups. An illustration of this fact may be offered by pointing to the occupations of the Old Christian craftsmen who made a name for themselves in the anti-converso outbreaks. The Old Christian who raised the outcry in Toledo that started the rebellion of 1449 was a maker of wineskins; the Old Christian who led the assault on the conversos in the Cordovan riots of 1473 was a black-smith; the Old Christian who killed the Constable Lucas in Jaen, thereby unleashing an attack on the conversos, was a carpenter; while the Old Christian who distinguished himself in the battle of Toledo in 1467 belonged to a family of dyers. None of these professions was typical of *both* groups or practiced by them to a like extent. The first three crafts mentioned were dominated by Old Christians, while the fourth was almost monopolized by the New.[49] As for the crafts that were shared by both groups, we do not hear that this fact led to any troubles among the craftsmen involved. Nor do we have any evidence to the effect that Old Christians of the lower classes complained about conversos who worked in their own trades. If there was some competition there (and we assume that there was), it was certainly not so keenly felt as to fire the kind of red-hot animosity that the lower classes exhibited so frequently toward the conversos. It is also important to note in this connection that the *Sentencia-Estatuto* imposed no limitation on converso artisans, nor did it express any criticism of them. In *their* case, as in the case of the merchants, it disregarded the example of extreme discrimination offered by the laws of 1412.

But if the *internal* relations in the lower classes could not produce strong antagonism between the groups, the relations between the Old Christians of the lower class and the New Christians of the higher classes indubitably could. Like the middle-class merchant, the Old Christian artisan saw himself occasionally forced to resort to a New Christian with a request for aid or consideration of some sort. This happened especially in two situations: (a) when he was in financial straits and had to turn to his wholesaler, who was often a converso, for extension of his credit; and (b) when, faced with a converso tax assessor, he had to negotiate with him the terms of his payment. These contacts often made him tense, not only because of the ordinary worry that usually accompanied such encounters, but also because of his lurking suspicion that the converso would not treat him fairly. Imbued with dislike of conversos from childhood, it would not occur to him that the feeling of the converso for him would be any different. But besides this assumed mutuality of dislike, there was another reason for the special discomfort that he felt in his dealings with New Christians.

For in the consciousness of the lower classes there lingered the memory of the atrocities that their ancestors had committed against the conversos' forebears, and they could not shake off the belief that the conversos harbored a desire for vengeance. This belief fostered their suspicion that the conversos were somehow out to get them, and strengthened their ever-present distrust of the converso tax gatherer and financier. Naturally, when they thought they were overtaxed or that their converso creditors were unduly harsh, they were prepared (or even eager, if circumstances permitted) to apply to the converso the same solution that their forefathers had applied to his ancestors, the Jews—namely, to get rid of their debts by getting rid of their creditors.

What was said of the intentions ascribed to the converso who functioned as tax gatherer and financier could also be said of the intentions attributed to the converso official. The reason given for the old prohibition on appointing any Jew to public office in Christendom—namely, that the Jew might do harm to the Christians—appeared valid for the conversos, too. This was especially the dominant view among the members of the Old Christian lower classes, for whom the converso government official commonly formed an object of hate. What they hated in this official were not only his status and the powers he possessed and could exercise against them, but also his entire deportment which, they thought, breathed superiority and arrogance. It is possible of course that some converso officials were haughty, rude, or insensitive to the problems of the lower-class Old Christians with whom they had to deal. On the other hand, many of the complaints raised by the latter may have been imaginary or lacked sound basis, since the converso official, who was bound by the laws or by the instructions of his superiors, may have been compelled to act as he did. Just the same, to the needy Old Christians, whose appeals for special consideration he rejected, he may often have appeared cold-blooded and cruel, and sometimes even vengeful and humiliating. Indeed, humiliation, whether true or imagined, was the most irritating thing. The lower-class Old Christian could take patiently and obediently any sneer or abuse from an Old Christian nobleman, or from his Old Christian urban lord, but he could not tolerate similar treatment by a converso of whatever rank. In such cases, he felt the rage of rebellion dominate his entire being.

There were thus certain foci of irritation between the Old and New Christian communities, all connected to some degree with the social and economic activities of the conversos, and especially with their functions in the public offices. We discern the existence of social discomfort especially among members of the lower classes upon encountering conversos as collectors of revenues, as moneylenders, and as judges and officers of the law. We note the reluctance of the Old Christian middle class to yield to conversos the city's second-grade offices, as well as their competition with other conversos in the liberal professions; and finally, we see the hard struggle over the high offices, which actually amounted to rivalry for power between the higher Old Christian social strata and the upper crust of the converso community. The desire to disqualify the conversos from office was therefore shared, in varying degrees, by members of all the classes in the city; and this desire was heightened by the jurists of the middle class, as well as by some friars and their associates in the clergy, who served as spokesmen for the disgruntled elements and led the anti-converso agitation. They fired the hatred for the conversos of the lower classes, who merely needed an excuse to give it vent; and their campaign emboldened the upper classes in their attempts to remove the conversos from the offices. Economic, social and political urges thus combined to form a powerful front against the New Christians.

VII

It might seem, then, that the root cause of the troubled relations between Old and New Christians in the Spanish kingdoms lay in social-economic conditions, and especially in a number of acute irritants that evolved from those conditions and were never assuaged. One tends to attribute to this source both the hostility that was displayed toward the conversos and the various attempts to block their advancement in the social and economic spheres. For here we have conflicts that touched vital interests of considerable sections of the Old Christian population and reasons for emotional discomfort and concerns that could deeply disturb their peace of mind. And yet further analysis of the data relating to the social-economic relations between the Old and New Christians inevitably elicits a number of questions that put the above assumption in doubt.

If we consider the conflicts between the groups *within* the various urban classes, we are first of all puzzled by the attitude toward conversos of the Old Christians in the *upper* class. Granted that social-economic interests, and especially the desire to gain high office, could spur some ambitious members of the upper class to foil their converso rivals; but this fact in itself can in no way explain all the forms that that reaction assumed. After all, quarrels over offices and other social assets occurred among Old Christian burghers as well; they often grew from disputes between individuals into endless wrangling between their supporting bands, and the din of their squabbles, broils and battles often filled the streets of Castilian towns. But none of these quarrels, however violent, had the characteristics of the Old-New Christian feud. Nowhere did they expand beyond their native place to embrace vast areas and sections of the nation, and nowhere did they last for many generations, even centuries. And what is perhaps more significant: nowhere did any of the contending parties issue laws against the members of the other; nor did they deny them any basic right on account of their ethnic origin. To be sure, the frequent rise of these urban factions, fighting each other so acrimoniously, may help us understand the restless social atmosphere that prevailed in the Spanish cities at the time. Also, the fact that the goal of all these factions was to gain control of the city's public offices may throw a valuable sidelight on the quarrel then raging between the Old and New Christians. Yet although these matters admittedly belong to the background of the conflict, they do not fully explain it. They cannot account for its duration, expansion, and unique forms of warfare. Above all, they cannot account for its *end*.

The problem becomes even more perplexing when we consider the number of Old Christians who may have been hurt by the conversos in relation to the Old Christian population. To be sure, the conversos who gained administrative posts at the expense of Old Christian citizens formed numerically a considerable group, if all of them *throughout the nation* were counted. Nevertheless, they were a small minority in Castile's urban officialdom. For even at the peak of the conversos' expansion in the country's various administrations, the overwhelming majority of the cities' officials were Old Christians. Thus most *regidores* were Old Christians, and so were most *corregidores*. Likewise, the great majority of the *jurados,* the *veinticuatros,* and the *procuradores* in Cortes were Old Christians, and so were most of the *alcaldes, alcaides* and *alguaciles,* and undoubtedly most of the smaller officials, as we have indicated above. It was only in certain professions and places (like the *escribanías* in Toledo, for instance) that the conversos virtually monopolized the field. But this hardly affected the general picture. Real and overwhelming power in the cities lay in the hands of Old Christians.

The most apparent implication of this fact bears significantly on our subject. If the New Christian officials in the cities formed a fraction of the urban officialdom, the Old Christian burghers who resorted to their services were, correspondingly, a minority of the population. But obviously, not all the members of this minority were hurt by the converso officials; and thus, even under the worst of circumstances, the injured group must be further reduced. An opposite conclusion may be reached only by one who assumes that *all* converso officials were always negligent in their duties, or constantly trying to harm the Old Christians. But could this be true? Could they *all* have fulfilled their tasks so inefficiently? Could they have been so ill intentioned or so corrupt? We can see no grounds for such an opinion; nor are we alone in rejecting it. In one of his references to the conversos, the historian Jaime Vicens Vives said: "Continuing in the footsteps of their [Jewish] fathers, they became great financiers, good artisans and *excellent public officials*. All those who have studied 15th century life and society in Castile recognize this fact."[50]

By citing this statement we do not mean to suggest that *all* converso officials were "excellent." Nor was this suggested, we believe, by Vives. We may assume that some of the New Christian officials were incompetent or unreliable or ill-tempered or the like. Such elements were found in all administrations, and especially in those of medieval Castile, whose *royal* administrations were notorious for their shortcomings, both moral and organizational. Nevertheless, there are good reasons to believe that the proportion of dishonest or unfit officials was smaller among the New Christians than among the Old. One such reason must be related to the fact that the converso official was surrounded by Old Christians who wished him ill and hoped to see him fail; consequently, he had to watch his step and fulfill his duties as carefully and punctiliously as he could. In particular, he had to deal fairly with the Old Christians who resorted to his services, for he naturally wanted to forestall complaints that he treated any of them with bias. Thus we must conclude that the cases of Old Christians who were mistreated by converso officials were not numerous; in fact, they may have been exceptional.

In view of this, the question we should raise is: How did a small minority of New Christians who annoyed a small minority of Old Christians succeed in rousing great masses of Old Christians to such violent assaults on the whole converso camp? When we pose this question we do not disregard the feelings of the low classes against the converso officials. But these feelings, it seems, could breed only suspicion. They could not serve as real grounds for the enactment of laws like the *Sentencia-Estatuto*.

There seemed to be only one sphere of action to which the above situation did not apply—that of the gathering of the revenues. In this field, indeed, the New Christian officials greatly outnumbered the Old Christian ones, though they did not dominate most of the field, at least for most of the period. As we have noted, most of the collectors and treasurers of the revenues were

Jews, at least until a decade before the founding of the Inquisition—and this means that, with respect to tax impositions, the majority of the Old Christians were not under converso but under Jewish authority. The remaining minority, however, must have been large, both proportionately and in absolute numbers; and this, it seems, may give room for the assumption that it was the gathering of the revenues by the New Christians that was mainly responsible for the exceptional animosity that arose against the group.

We ought, however, to consider the following facts before we can make up our minds in this matter. The major complaint raised against the tax gatherers was their overassessment of the revenues. But the city councils knew that the main blame for this wrong lay not with the gatherers, but with the system of tax collection that was based on "farming." And they knew that direct responsibility for this system rested with the kings, who sought greater income, without paying due attention to their subjects' needs. The city councils, who were aware of this fact, could not blame the conversos for the consequences.

That this was indeed the councils' position may also be gathered from the following. If in the 14th century the cities pressed the kings to give up tax farming altogether, in the 15th century they did not raise this demand—either because they realized the hopelessness of such attempts, or because they ultimately came to the conclusion that they could not offer a workable alternative. The only occasion on which they touched the subject was at the Cortes of Ocaña, in 1469. Yet they did not then request that the system be abolished; they merely asked to have the Jews cleared out of it. No doubt, recalling Enrique II's claim (at the Cortes of Burgos in 1367) that no Christians were prepared to assume the tasks of tax farming,[51] they stressed that *if the king could agree to reduce the cost of farming to "reasonable prices,"* enough "Christians" would be available to replace the Jews in that field.[52] This shows that they clearly realized where the source of the trouble lay. Yet in 1469, when the *procuradores* referred to "Christians" who could replace the Jews as tax farmers, they did not exclude from those "Christians" the *New* Christians, for they used the term Christians without qualification—moral, social, or religious. What is more, they must have realized that if the Jews were removed from the gathering of taxes, the first to replace them would be the conversos, who possessed, besides the needed funds, the necessary organization, knowledge and experience. Thus we must conclude that the Old Christians of the cities did not loathe the conversos as tax farmers and tax collectors as much as we may gather from the criticisms on this score raised by the conversos' enemies.

Related to this is another testimony that must be borne in mind. In 1480 the *concejo* of Seville placed the gathering of the urban taxes in the hands of twenty-one converso tax farmers and two converso treasurers.[53] Could any fact be more revealing of the confidence the Old Christians had in the integrity and efficiency of the converso tax gatherers? Seville, which was known to be seething with animosity for its large New Christian population, entrusted the collection of its own taxes not to any of its Old Christian citizens but to conversos—and to conversos only. And this happened in the year 1480—the very year in which the Inquisition was founded! It is hard to believe, in view of the above, that opposition to converso tax farming activity, or abuse of the rights of Old Christian citizens committed by New Christian tax collectors, was the main cause of that hostility for the conversos which erupted in such violent outbreaks.

And let us also note this: besides the prohibition on assuming public offices (which included no doubt the offices of tax gathering) and on serving in private offices (which included, as we take it, those of lawyers and physicians), the conversos were not forbidden, even in the *Sentencia*, to engage in any other work. Thus, no converso craftsmen and industrialists are forbidden to go on with their work, or shopkeepers to sell their goods, or merchants to conduct their businesses, or financiers to invest their funds. The opposition seems to have centered on one issue—that of the public offices. Yet if this was the issue that fired the resentment of most Old Christians against the conversos, why did they not direct their fire at the high officials or gatherers of taxes, as they did in the case of Cota in Toledo?[54] Moreover, when we examine the list of conversos who were ousted from their posts by the rulings of the *Sentencia*, we find that it comprised only fourteen persons in all, of whom one was a municipal judge, while some of the others were *escribanos*. Is it possible that for such a small number of officials, at least half of whom were of median rank, the whole city was in an uproar and measures were taken as for civil war? Certainly, that list of fourteen persons cannot explain the fierce hatred of, and bloody attack upon *all* conversos of *all* classes and *all* ranks and the ardent desire to kill them all, or at least reduce them to third-rate residents denied even the right to testify in the courts.

We must get to the bottom of this situation if we wish to identify the true causes of the strife that broke out between the Old and the New Christians in Spain—a strife that lasted for more than four centuries and deeply affected the destinies of the peninsula and, through the Inquisition, of large parts of Europe and indeed of the whole world. Our exploration of the problem must therefore continue, but in the meantime we must recall the phenomena that were noted in the course of the present inquiry.

Each class of the Old Christians had individuals and small groups who clashed with conversos on a variety of matters of a social-economic nature. These clashes generated a resentment among the Old Christians which was first directed against the conversos involved, who were likewise either individuals or small groups. The fact, however, that this resentment often spread quickly to include the entire converso community shows that *beneath the economic grudges lay a deep feeling of antagonism to all conversos* which, in a sense, was lying in wait until triggered to rise to the surface by the social-economic conflicts.

Obviously, we are dealing here with a public sentiment which, in various degrees, was shared by *all* Old Christians and which, sooner or later, could be roused in them all, though in different degrees, against *all* conversos. Such a sentiment could of course be the root of the widespread hostility for the New Christians which evolved in Spain in the fifteenth century and reached its height with the establishment of the Inquisition—or rather in the course of its operations. Yet what was the nature of that sentiment, and what were its particular causes? Since no satisfactory answer to this question can be elicited from the religious accusations, and no adequate explanation is offered by the social censures of the New Christians, we shall turn to the third set of charges (the racial) embodied in the anti-converso literature of the time.

III. The Rise of Racism

I

Leopold Ranke, the first to notice the racial factor in the attacks on the conversos, attributed it to the natural, inherent antagonism between the Spaniards and the Jews. That this antagonism was openly expressed against the New Christians (and not against the Jews) was due, he believed, to the conversos' tendency to intermarry with the Old Christians. The "Germanic" and "Romanic" Spaniards, he maintained, could not bear to be amalgamated with Jews and Moors; and hence the vehement rejection of the conversos by means of a racial assault.[1]

Ranke's view appears to have been influenced by the German anti-Jewish racial movement of the first quarter of the 19th century; but insofar as Spain of the 15th century is concerned, it cannot be upheld. To begin with, the Spaniards, in their great majority, were not "Germanic," as one might gather from Ranke. Taken as a whole, they were not descendants of the Visigoths and Sueves who had settled in Spain, but a mixture of many ethnic elements that combined in the course of Spain's long history to produce the various Spanish "types." To the extent that "Germanic" features were still evident in the Spanish population of the 15th century, they were doubtless more commonly found in the nobility than among the plebeians. Yet it was with the nobility rather than the lower classes that the conversos intermarried; and it was *not* the nobility that spawned the theory of their evil, corrupt and inferior nature.

Looking for the origins of this theory, which he saw as the propelling force of Spanish racism, Menéndez y Pelayo, in one of his letters, expressed the rather startling opinion that the Spaniards may have borrowed their racism from the Jews.[2] The opinion, in effect, was mere conjecture, but it had a sequel in Spanish scholarship. Menéndez y Pelayo's brief remark may not have been lost on Américo Castro, who formed, perhaps under its stimulus, his theory about the Jewish origin of the *limpieza*[3]—the concept and advocacy of "purity of blood" that so influenced Spanish society from the middle of the 15th century on.

Américo Castro was puzzled by the emergence of so strong a racial bias in the Spanish people, which for many generations had been notable, in his opinion, for its racial tolerance. The appearance of that bias among the Old Christians following the mass conversions of the Jews led him to believe that the Jews were the source of the new racial attitude in Spain. The large-scale invasion of Spain's Christian society by Jews who had only recently been

Christianized inevitably brought into Spain's social life a number of dominant Jewish views, among which those related to race, Castro thought, were
perhaps the most contagious. Moreover, the Jews, who have always seen
themselves as God's "chosen people" (which to Castro meant the finest race),
treated the Spaniards as racially inferior. The Spaniards, however, reversed
the Jews' assessment, while adopting, in principle, a racial scale of values.
They came to view *themselves* as far superior to the Jews, and reacted to the
converts' scorn for their race with a fury of racial contempt and discrimination. Thus were born, according to Castro, the theory and policy of *limpieza
de sangre*.[4]

Castro was a scholar of vast erudition, original thinking, and a remarkable
ability to penetrate deep beneath the surface of documents that modern
research had salvaged from the past. Scholarship owes him much for his
studies on the conversos and the converso problem, and particularly on the
influence the conversos wielded in various spheres of Spanish culture. His
theory of the origins of the *limpieza,* however, was wrong in both its premises
and conclusions.

To be sure, to substantiate it Castro adduced certain statements from
ancient and medieval sources which, he believed, verified his claim regarding
the Jewish origin of the *limpieza.* Yet in a study I have devoted to the subject,
I have demonstrated that Castro's evidence was faulty, based on wrong
assumptions and, more often than not, on misinterpretations of the sources.[5]
Castro, in brief, could not prove his thesis that the Spanish racial attitudes
toward the conversos were merely a reflection of Jewish influences.

Nevertheless, considered more broadly, Castro's theory cannot be dismissed merely by disproving the evidence he adduced concerning the Jewish
origin of the *limpieza.* Curiously enough, Castro failed to investigate the
numerous utterances of the conversos on the race issue which certainly
belong to this sphere of inquiry. In this work we have dealt extensively with
these utterances, and as the reader can see, they unmistakably reflect a high
opinion of the Jewish *lineage.*[6] This may lead one to the conjecture that it is
here—in this opinion of the conversos—that one should look for the source
of the racial quarrel, and hence that Castro, although mistaken in his assumption that the racism of the Spaniards drew its inspiration from the *Jews,* may
have nevertheless been right in asserting that it was provoked by the *conversos.* Thus, we have to inquire into the following propositions: (a) that the race
theory was upheld by the conversos; (b) that they practiced it in their
relations with the Old Christians; and (c) that the latter, who had never been
racists, adopted it and expressed it in reverse form—in a counter-campaign
aimed at the conversos. Obviously, to determine whether these propositions
are true, we should examine them, among other things, in the light of the
utterances left us by the *conversos* on the racial question.

Yet before doing this, it is proper, we believe, to look at the works of Spanish Jews who were converted to Christianity before 1391. We refer primarily to the writings of such authors as Petrus Alphonsi and Alfonso de Valladolid, which exerted much influence on the converts of the 15th century. What we see is that they do not include any reference to the Jewish people's racial constitution as superior to that of any other people. In contrast, we find in them a great deal of reproach of the Jewish people's views, laws and customs. The total effect of their criticism is such that the Jews appear foolish, grossly unethical and, of course, unworthy of respect. Without using the term race, these converts portray the Jews as a human species that is clearly inferior, morally and intellectually, to the Christians.[7]

Nor do we find any statement or expression indicating the Jews' racial excellence or superiority in the writings of converts who went over to Christianity in 1391 and the subsequent six decades. Following in the footsteps of the earlier converts, Paul of Burgos launched acrimonious attacks against the views and morals of the Jewish people, not only in the time of Jesus but also in his own generation. He considers the Jews of his own time to belong to the old Pharisaic hypocrisy and calls them a "generation of vipers"—as Jesus called the Pharisees.[8] These denunciations of Paul of Burgos, moreover, pale when compared to those of Pedro de la Caballería, who applied to the Jews the most demeaning terms he could find about them in the Old and New Testaments, as well as in the literature of the Church Fathers. Thus, the Jews who denied Jesus are described by Pedro not only as "vipers," but also as an "accursed seed," "sons of the devil," a "perverse generation," and of course as people whose malice and pride blinded them to the apparent truth.[9] Jerónimo de Santa Fe is more controlled in his criticism of the Jews; but he too lashes out mercilessly at what he considers their follies, their blunders, and their distortions of the divine teachings.[10] None of these converts speaks anywhere in his writings of the racial excellence of the Jewish people, or of its racial superiority over the gentiles, even though Paul refers to the tribe of the Levites as constituting the spiritual elite among the Jews and the ancient bearers of the divine teachings.[11]

The first converso document referring to the race question as a factor in the relations between the Old and New Christians is the letter of complaint that the conversos of Aragon addressed to Pope Eugene IV in 1437. The complaint, as we have seen, centered on the discrimination practiced against the conversos by the Old Christians of Aragon, and above all on the refusal of the Old Christians to establish conjugal ties with the New, solely on the grounds of the latter's allegedly base and inferior race.[12] The mention by the conversos of their relationship to Christ was not meant to indicate their racial superiority, but their right to equality in a Christian society. Its purpose was to clinch the argument for that right by pointing to the bizarre and incredible fact that the people from whom Christ "took His flesh" were not considered good enough for marriage—indeed, even association—with other Christians. One can clearly deduce from that complaint that the originators of the racial attitude toward the converts were not the New Christians but the Old.

We also gather this from many other statements in various works produced by New Christians. There is not, in fact, a single converso document dealing with the race issue in one form or another that was not produced in response to an attack—that is, to an anti-converso disparaging argumentation or hostile legislation on racial grounds. This was what impelled Fernán Díaz de Toledo to write his Instruction in 1449; this again was what led Cardinal Torquemada and Alonso de Cartagena, the bishop of Burgos, to launch their counterattacks upon the Toledan racists; this was what induced Diego de Valera to express his favorable view of the Jewish race in the tract he wrote on the conversos' right to join the Spanish nobility; and this was also what prompted Pulgar to take his stand on the racial question (in 1478).[13] This fact in itself indicates clearly where the source of the trouble lay.

Yet not only the origins of these responses, but also their very tenor and contents testify to this quite clearly. As we noted in our survey of their views on the subject, the conversos stressed the *common origin* of mankind and essentially denied the existence of "races" in the true sense of the word. What appeared as racial differences, they argued, were merely reflections of the national divisions formed in mankind by its religious disunion, but Christianity does not recognize such distinctions and expects their total disappearance with its triumph—that is, when mankind is reunited under the banner of the one true faith. Obviously, such a view precluded the attribution of racial excellence to *any* group of men, and this applied also to the Jewish people, which was chosen by God to guide mankind to the truth and serve as the carnal origin of Christ. To be sure, the Jews became distinguished from all others by a set of moral attitudes and practices, but this distinction resulted from God's special care and His prophets' education, and not from any racial heritage. All this was of course in accord with Christian teachings as accepted by the Church for many generations. No Christian thinker had ever claimed that the Jews were "chosen" for racial reasons, and few denied that as *God's people* they were blessed with certain moral assets. The idea took root in all parts of Christian literature. Also the *Siete Partidas* writes: "In ancient times the Jews were held in great respect and they alone were known as the People of God."[14]

To be sure, in most of their writings on the subject (such as those of Valera, Cartagena and Torquemada), the conversos praised the Jewish people to high heaven, and even presented it as the noblest and saintliest of all the families of man. But what should be noted at this point is that, when they were *thus* lauding the Jews, they invariably referred to the Jews of antiquity, who were bent on fulfilling their extraordinary mission. In ancient times, they stressed, the Jews were the only people that possessed, besides the "natural" and "civil" nobilities, also the "theological" one, which is the highest; but then, because of their sins against Christ, they completely lost their theological nobility and also much of the other two nobilities, of which they preserved only certain traces in a poor or repressed condition. It follows that the Jews who are converted to Christianity come to Christendom not as a superior but rather as a deprived, crippled race, lacking the advantages of the three nobilities, which only the Christian nations possess. To be sure, they claimed that, once they are converted, their noble qualities are bound to reappear (without telling us precisely in what measure). Even so, they agreed that this might take time,[15] and thus, even in their Christian existence—at least, in the early phase of that existence—the conversos portrayed themselves not as superior, but as inferior to the other Christian nations. What they insisted on was only that *potentially* they had the capacity to rise to higher levels; and what they opposed was only the attempt—inconsistent as it was with the principles of Christianity—to prevent that potential from becoming actual.

Since I have discussed the conversos' views on race in several places in this volume, I shall touch here merely on a few points, which should help remove any doubt or obscurity that may still linger in connection with this matter. When the conversos expressed their belief that potentially they were still likely to achieve higher levels, both social and spiritual, they did not suggest that they wished to resume the position of the "chosen people." The "chosen people," they knew, were now the *Christians,* who had replaced ancient Israel as the people of God; and therefore all they *could* attain in Christendom was spiritual equality, not superiority. But they also knew that in a Christian society, which recognized "neither Greek nor Jew," there should be no discrimination against any person on grounds of racial or national origin, and instead there should be a complete equilibrium in the rights of all its members to exercise their abilities. It was in the name of this equilibrium that the conversos opposed the suppression of their potential and the denial of their right to rise to any level, including their accession to the noble classes, should their abilities, attested by performance, warrant such elevation.

The racial arguments presented by the conversos developed therefore in the course of *self-defense*—in their responses to racial affronts against them and their forbears, both recent and ancient. It was only the constant harping of their foes on their racial perversion and inferiority that forced them to come up with the opposite idea—namely, that of their *original racial excellence,* with which they defended not only their own but also their ancestors' honor. Actually, however, the conversos were interested not in superiority but in equality—or, more clearly, in equal opportunity. Accordingly, they had little regard for racial differentiation between social classes as well. They believed that differences among men should be based on individual talents, merits and achievements, rather than on lineages. The true nobility, they thought, was that of virtue, not of descent. This is the sum total of the opinion of Valera, of Pulgar, of Lucena, who puts in the mouth of the bishop of Burgos the words that "noble is he who owns virtue and not a parental heritage."[16] The whole discussion of their racial origin was indeed forced upon them by their opponents; had they not been attacked on racial grounds, they would certainly not have opened the debate.

Castro was therefore wrong in assuming that the racist movement which arose in Spain owed its origin to the conversos, who allegedly borrowed their ideas from the Jews. Consequently, he was also wrong in concluding that the racial agitation against the conversos was essentially a reaction to that of the New Christians, who allegedly started the racial quarrel. The truth was the opposite. And since he mistook the identity of the source, he could not possibly discern the historical causes that led to the rise of the racial theory in Spain and the functions it fulfilled in the evolving conflict between the Old and New Christians.

II

Turning to these questions, we must pointedly ask: What was the special need that impelled the Old Christians to produce their race theory and espouse it with such force when other grave charges (such as that of heresy) were leveled at the conversos at that very time—that is, in the middle of the 15th century? Above all, what function did the race theory fulfill in the evolution of the anti-converso campaign, and what made it so appealing to the Spanish masses that it served as the basis for their norms of behavior in many a sphere, both social and religious, for the next three hundred years?

To answer these questions we must go back to the early stages of the racial movement and the first documents expounding its ideas. As we have noted, many Old Christians, who were disadvantaged in their competition with the New, looked for ways to rid themselves of their converso rivals. They thought that an anti-converso legislation might be the best means to attain this end, and by this they meant the passing of laws forbidding the conversos to work in any field in which they might compete with Old Christians. In a sense, it was along the lines of this solution that the *Sentencia-Estatuto* was enacted.

Yet it was not a solution easy to attain, for it had to be accepted by a Christian society based on legal foundations. In such a society, no laws could be enacted against any of its groups, unless the members of the group considered for discrimination shared some special quality—a *common denomi-*

nator—which was supposed to justify that enactment. And what was the common denominator of the conversos that might serve as grounds for placing them *all* under social or economic disabilities? Surely the fact that *some* of them were involved in competition with Old Christians over certain *public posts* would not warrant the imposition of limitations on *all* conversos in that particular field. Similarly, the fact that some of the conversos competed with Old Christians in the sphere of *jurisprudence* could not call for barring *all* conversos from the legal profession. And the same would apply of course to their engagement in such areas as commerce, industry and finance. Obviously, the conversos' occupational division was an obstacle to any anti-Marrano legislation of a social-economic nature.

To be sure, in 1412 laws were issued in Castile—and in 1413, also in Aragon—forbidding *all* Jews to engage in professions which, in fact, were practiced only by *some* of them. But then it was not their professional activities but their religion that supplied the common denominator justifying legal discrimination against them. The conversos, however, were not Jews—they were Christians; and thus their religion could not provide the prerequisite for the issuance of laws against their group.

It would be of course a different matter if it could be proved that the Marranos were *false* Christians, or at least if this criminal imposture could be credibly imputed to most of them. This indeed was the claim that their enemies in Toledo set out to demonstrate in their Inquiry of 1449; and it was on the basis of the findings of that Inquiry that they hoped to be able to denounce *all* conversos as stubborn and irremediable religious sinners. In fact, when they submitted their Petition to the king, they expected this to be the outcome of their Inquiry, so that the incrimination of the conversos as heretics could rest on acceptable legal grounds. But upon examining the charges contained in the Statute, we could see that the conclusions arrived at by the Inquiry were far from fulfilling the Toledans' expectations. On the grounds of those conclusions, the Toledans could not claim that *all* or *most* Marranos were Judaizers—a claim that was further undermined by the fact that in the cases of "Judaizers" tried in their courts (and these cases were by no means numerous), the Toledans had to employ false witnesses; and thus, the most that might be gathered from their inquiries and judgments was that *some* of the conversos, a small minority, sympathized with Judaism or practiced Jewish rites, while their great majority followed Christianity and had no intent whatever to forsake it. This meant that in religion, as well as in economy, the Marranos were divided in their interests and performance; and hence, as in economy, so in their religion, they did not project a common denominator that might justify the enactment of laws against their group.

Faced with this difficulty, the opponents of the conversos came up with the claim that all New Christians, though not *proven* to be Judaizers, must nevertheless be held *suspect* of heresy, and thus their *being suspect* provided the prerequisite for a general anti-converso legislation. Nevertheless, even this limited claim was found to be inadequate to serve their purpose. For all that the Toledans could assert in this matter was that "very many" Marranos were suspect, from which one could conclude that they could not attach that suspicion of heresy to *most* Marranos. Yet on the grounds of mere suspicion of a minority, they could not issue the kind of laws they contemplated, or obtain the needed support for those laws. Inevitably the Toledans were led to the conclusion that they had to come up with a new accusation, another principle and a different argument to justify the legal degradation of the conversos and eventually their exclusion from the Christian society.

The racial doctrine set forth in 1449 supplied that need. Looking for a quality common to all conversos, and at the same time so negative as to support the issuance of harsh, restrictive laws against them, the racial theorists believed that such a quality should be sought not in what the Marranos *did* or *believed*, but in what they *were* as human beings. This did not seem to be a difficult task. For what they *were* was determined by their ethnic origin—or rather, as they put it, by their *race*. Since race, they maintained, formed man's qualities and indeed his entire mental constitution, the Marranos, who were all offspring of Jews, retained the racial makeup of their forbears. Hence ethnically they were what they (or their ancestors) had been before their conversion to Christianity; in other words, they were *Jews*.

This approach and conclusion of the racists were of extraordinary importance for the anti-Marrano movement. If it was difficult to prove the Jewishness of the Marranos on religious grounds, there was no difficulty—in fact, no need—to prove it on ethnic grounds. There was no denying the fact that ethnically the Marranos were Jews, and few could or would challenge the contention (or, from the racist standpoint, the implication) that they inherited many of the Jews' social attitudes, including their alleged hatred of Christians. Not only could such an argument be sufficient to stigmatize the Marranos as enemies of their neighbors, and thus disqualify them for Christian citizenship; it would also implant and sustain the notion of their *inseparability* from the Jews. In brief, the race theory identified the New Christians with the Jews much more than their religious origin might suggest, and by stressing that identity, their *Jewish* identity, one could mobilize against the Marranos all the antipathy and antagonism that were latent in Spanish society toward the Jews.

The *ethnicity* of the conversos was thus the *common quality* on the basis of which, the racists believed, they could take drastic measures against the conversos that would be sanctioned by *law*. Obviously, by having their anti-converso charges rest primarily on this quality, they transferred the center of gravity of their accusations from the sphere of religion to that of race; and this inevitably caused certain changes in the contents and emphases of their censures. But from this we ought not to infer that the racists relinquished the claims about the Jewish heresy of which the Marranos had been accused. In fact, they persisted in making these claims, as well as in stressing their importance; and they also asserted that they could prove them true by the postulates of their racial theory.

These postulates have already been discussed, and here we shall touch only on some of their ideas that relate to our present discussion. Race, they said, endows man, among other things, with his basic moral qualities and dispositions, which in turn dictate his religion. Hence the Jewish moral propensities, inherited by the Marranos from the Jews, must sooner or later determine their religion—which means that those who are *racially* Jews are also, or will be, *religiously* Jews. Obviously, this conclusion not only denied any immediate benefit from the Marranos' conversion, but also the possibility that the Marranos might at any time become true Christians. It was, in fact, only on the basis of this theory, which they attached to their charge of heresy, that they could issue their law (i.e., the *Sentencia-Estatuto*) denying *all* New Christians the right to public office for *all* time, present and future.

Nor did the racists abandon the charges leveled at the conversos in the social-economic field. Rather did they affirm, emphasize and broaden them by a multitude of new and even harsher charges, so that all the conversos' social-economic deeds appeared as one long sequence of offenses. Never did they suggest that any of these offenses stemmed from such circumstances as distress, or fear, or moral confusion, or provocation, or the like, which so often lead man to crime. All the Marranos' misdeeds, they stressed, had only one source: the converso's race, his mental constitution, his urge to do evil to all men of goodwill, and the ruthless egotism that unscrupulously commands him to use his victims' assets for his own profit. Thus we see how the racists grafted the social-economic crimes ascribed to the conversos onto the trunk of their racial theory, just as they grafted onto it the religious transgressions—i.e., the Judaic heresies—that were likewise attributed to the New Christians.

It was due to this absorption by racism of all the currents of the anti-Marrano movement that the racists gained from the outset a large following. But beyond this there was another factor contributing to the widespread acceptance of their message; and this was the affinity between the racial theory—or rather some elements of that theory—and the general view of the conversos as a *group* that prevailed among the Old Christians.

III

Our survey of the anti-Marrano works produced by Spain's racists in the 15th century has convinced us that they belonged to the category of writings called by the Germans "atrocity propaganda"—that is, agitation that ascribes to an opponent such loathsome improprieties and such deeds of horror that the general public is moved to view him as both despicable and frightful. It is senseless to look for levelheaded observation or desire for truth in such campaigns. Truth is the last thing that these campaigners seek. Their aim is to get popular support for the dreadful fate they have in store for their opponent; and to achieve this aim, they paint a picture of that opponent so hateful and repulsive, and indeed so shocking, that it must rouse people to condemn him.

Such was the anti-Marrano literature that denounced the conversos as heretics. Accordingly, there is hardly a vice, a crime, or an instance of foul play that is not attributed to the conversos. The epithets used to describe their qualities are: false, hypocritical, deceitful, treacherous, cowardly, shameless, pompous, boastful, arrogant and, above all, wicked, cruel, and merciless. Generally, they are defined as tyrants, oppressors, idol-worshipers, sodomites, false prophets, thieves, robbers, murderers and, needless to say, heretics and Judaizers. The picture has not a single redeeming feature. The Marranos are evil incarnate.

What is most ominous about these charges is that all of them, save one or two, were attributed to *all* conversos. Accordingly, a whole people, or at least a whole tribe, numbering hundreds of thousands of individuals, consisted of criminals and base, vile men. Not one of them was presumed to be decent. All of them, regardless of class or profession, were vicious, ruthless and villainous. Their officials were traitors, their doctors were killers, their druggists poisoners, their priests blackmailers, and all of them hardened, habitual criminals devoid of any moral sense. Could there be such a society of men? Were the Marranos such a society? Did none of them do a decent day's work, earn a living by honest toil, conscientiously fulfill the duties of office, or devote himself to higher ideals than robbery? The authors of this literature wanted people to believe that the answer to all these questions was no.

This, then, is the picture of the converso that the racists presented to the public. And in view of this picture we cannot be surprised that it generated so much hate of the New Christians—and also so much fear of their intentions—that many Old Christians came to treat the conversos as carriers of a lethal disease. Similar to this was the attitude toward the Jews that developed under the impact of ferocious campaigns in times such as those of the Black Death, and one might infer from the sameness of the effect the sameness of the cause that produced it. As we shall see, however, we should not be too hasty to draw such an inference.

Parkes, who studied the development of the conception of the Jew in Christian literature, came to the conclusion that as early as the fourth century the Jew was portrayed by Christian authors as a "monster"—not as a human being, but as a "theological abstraction of superhuman malice and cunning." The crimes imputed to him were rarely "human," and "little evidence" was drawn against him from "contemporary behavior" or from his part in "contemporary affairs."[17] The view of the Jew as described and disseminated by the Christian theologians of that time was of a creature whose mission in life was to serve the Devil and do his heinous work. In the last four centuries of the medieval era the outlines of this image were sharpened and deepened, while the crimes imputed to the Jews were multiplied and became steadily more appalling. They now included such ghastly atrocities as the murder of Christian children for religious rites, the torture of Hosts by piercing or boiling them, and the use of sorcery to inflict cruel death upon multitudes of Christians. To be sure, in a sense these crimes were "human" (for murder was after all a human crime), but essentially they were inhuman and demoniac, since they were committed at the devil's behest and frequently by means of magic. They were also inhuman because the Jew performed them without seeking to derive from them any benefit for himself. His sole interest in perpetrating these crimes was to vent the devil's wrath, which filled his soul, on Christ and His believers.

Was this image of the Jew as portrayed by the friars identical with that of the Spanish Marrano as depicted by his racist foes? One must answer this question in the negative. To be sure, the image the racists drew of the converso was likewise of a monstrous being; but it was a *human* monster that the racists were thinking of, whose qualities and tendencies, however repellent, were *human* qualities and tendencies. Also, his crimes, however malicious, were not effected by means of sorcery and, unlike the great crimes imputed to the Jews, were aimed at achieving some advantage for himself. Rarely do we find in the literature of these racists a reference to an atrocity of a "religious" nature for which a converso was held responsible,[18] and unlike the crimes attributed to the Jews, those ascribed to the conversos were intimately connected with their "contemporary behavior," or rather with their action in "contemporary affairs." Evidently, the hatred of the converso, which the racists fomented, was such as could be related to his daily activities, and hence to his "human" side, to his "nature," or his "race," and not to his relations with supernatural forces.

This was the main difference between the image of the New Christian presented by the racists in 15th century Spain and that of the Jew portrayed by the spokesmen of Christian antisemitism in the Middle Ages. It is necessary for us to note this difference in order to understand the social attitude toward the conversos and the rise of the myth about the deadly plans they devised to destroy the Old Christians. Indeed, one may note the peculiarity of these plans when one compares the secret anti-Christian schemes attributed to the Jews of Europe in the middle of the 14th century (in connection with the Black Death) and those imputed to the conversos by the Spanish racists in the middle of the 15th. For here one may readily discern the distinction between the "devilish" and the "human" crimes allegedly contrived—and, in part, carried out—by the different perpetrators. Whereas the alleged Jewish schemes were said to be invented to annihilate whole Christian populations—and this without promising the Jews any profit—the plan ascribed to the conversos was aimed, apart from wreaking vengeance on the Old Christians, at bringing the conversos massive wealth and power. But in addition, it had the characteristic of being connected with a *real* issue—a "contemporary" development in which the conversos were involved—that kept agitating the public mind.

That issue was the expansion of the conversos into virtually all the administrations of the country and the opposition which that expansion encountered, especially in the larger cities. The racists of course encouraged that opposition with every argument they could muster. But as in other cases, in this case too they stretched their arguments so as to extend from the sphere of reality to that of fiction, and ultimately have their imaginary parts substitute for the factual elements. Thus, the racists considered it puerile to assume, as many Old Christians had undoubtedly done, that all that the conversos were trying to achieve in their effort to occupy additional offices were so many more positions for their people or so many more income-yielding posts. According to the racists, what the conversos were after was to capture the country's government; in consequence, the Old Christians would be subject to their rule, their ruthless exploitation and, finally, their enslavement.

From our foregoing discussions of the issue of the offices, we could see how the struggle for power in Castile reached such extremes of passion and violence, and gave birth to so many devious designs, that people kept wondering what plots were being hatched and what subversive actions were being prepared for the immediate future. Especially mysterious seemed to some Castilians the role of the conversos in those struggles; for while on some occasions they appeared uninvolved, on others they were seen in the thick of the conflicts. One should also bear in mind that this was the time when the Relator Fernán Díaz was believed by many to be the real head, the guiding force of the royal bureaucracy of Castile, and when the influence of the conversos in the royal Council was such as to enable them, within a few years, to terminate Alvaro de Luna's career. Moreover, the strength of the conversos' drive for the offices was attested by their expansion into all the country's administrations in the days of Enrique IV, too—and this despite the incessant campaign conducted against them since the forties. Could this expansion be merely the result of fortuitous endeavors of converso individuals? Inevitably, there were many Old Christians who hesitated to answer this question in the affirmative. And thus the rise of the conversos to so many high positions and the growth of their influence, seemingly irresistible, could not pass without causing occasional tremors in various Old Christian circles. It produced a certain feeling of uneasiness, which was in the beginning dim and obscure, but ultimately became a source of real anxiety in more than a few quarters. It was this feeling that the racists depended on, cultivated, and made use of in their agitation.

But the question of the offices and the controls they involved was not the only "contemporary issue" that supplied fodder for the racists' campaign. Another was the steady process of intermarriage between the Old and New Christians. The Church, as we have seen, favored this process and unstintingly urged both sides to follow it. The conversos, too, were anxious to advance it, and Alfonso de Cartagena was looking forward to the day when the converso "river" would merge with and disappear in the waters of the great Christian "sea." Yet from the racists' point of view, intermarriage between the groups—that is, the Old and New Christians—confronted Christian Spain with a peril even greater than all the other threats posed by the conversos. For not only would intermarriage help the conversos take over Christian offices and possessions; it would also infect the Spanish people with a malady from which it might never recover. What they meant by this was that by marrying Old Christians, the conversos would "contaminate" the latter's blood; and if this contamination became widespread, it would corrupt the Spanish character beyond repair and eventually cause its disappearance. Thus, from the standpoint of the anti-Marrano racists, their conflict with the conversos was infinitely more crucial than their struggle against the Jews; for while the Jews were opposed for what they *were*, the conversos were opposed for both what they *were* and what they wanted to *become*—namely, an integral, indistinguishable part of the Spanish people.

If the charge that the conversos were steadily engaged in taking over the government was a myth, the claim that their intermarriage with Old Christians was motivated by their desire to *rob* the latter of their assets was not much closer to reality. To be sure, both sides, Old and New Christians, married each other for a variety of reasons, but so far as material gain was concerned, it could probably be attributed as a leading motive much more to the Old Christians than to the New.[19] In any case, the racists saw the conversos steadily increase their rate of intermarriage, just as they noted the converso advances in the sphere of public offices. Hence, the stand the racists took on intermarriage did not reflect opposition to an abstract *principle*, advocated by the Church at the Marranos' instigation, or to a *plan* urged by the Marranos in their preachings and writings. It was an objection to something visible and concrete—to an aspiration that was daily being translated into reality.

Says the Relator in 1449 about the state of intermarriage at that time: "There are many houses in Castile, both of laymen and clerics, of the lineages of nobles as well as of caballeros, and of townsmen [of the middle and high classes[20]], whose members are sons, grandsons, and great-grandsons of people who came from the stock of Israel."[21] This shows that when the Relator wrote these words, intermarriage had spread to all estates and classes of the Spanish people (save the peasants and low-class laborers). Yet this should in no way surprise us. The growing penetration of the conversos into the nobility and the example set by the nobility for intermarriage; the greatly increased wealth of the conversos and the wider dissemination of that wealth among their ranks; and, above all, the full-fledged Christianization of numerous conversos, which brought them much closer to the Christian way of life, were major factors that helped open for the conversos the doors of ethnic fusion.

To be sure, by the middle of the 15th century the movement of intermarriage between Old and New Christians was still limited and of moderate proportions. Yet it was the steady *progress* of that movement that alarmed the opposition and roused it to action. No doubt many of its members believed that Spain was on the eve of a flood of mixed marriages which would sweep away much of the nation; and this was, in our judgment, the second reason why racism arose at that particular time. By virtue of its view of the Jewish race and the function of the conversos in Spanish society, racism saw itself as the only force capable of averting the "menace of intermarriage." In any case, the widespread acceptance of its message shows where most Spaniards stood on this issue. Spain reacted to the absorption of the Jews as an organism reacts to a foreign element; and the antibody it produced to that absorption was the racial theory.

Thus we touch upon the other inducement for the racists to hurl the harshest racial criticisms against the Jews and their kinsmen, the conversos. For the theory that aimed at blocking ethnic fusion between the Old and New Christians could be truly effective only if the conversos were described as inferior, base and unworthy. It was especially vital, from the racists' standpoint, to besmirch the conversos and blacken their name at a time when their general prestige was rising, owing to their achievements in various walks of life and the high reputation that some of them attained in the governments of Church and state. The racist campaign warned the nation not to be dazzled by these "misleading lights," for behind the glittering facade of their fame, there lay corruption, depravity and evil. Obviously, the purpose of this defamation was to erect a new, impassable division between the conversos and their fellow Spaniards, when the old barriers that had kept them apart—i.e., the religious and cultural differences—were crumbling and had almost disappeared. And they *could* expect this division to be impassable because it related to man's innermost qualities, his basic constitution—and indeed his very being. In the language of the time, there was no better way of expressing this newly conceived difference than by using the term *pure blood* as completely distinct from, and indeed antithetic to the polluted blood of the Jews.

That such a distinction was capable of attracting many an Old Christian to the racial theory is manifest for other reasons, too. It flattered his ego and raised him automatically, without requiring any effort on his part, to a higher level than that of any converso, however famous or successful. This is why the race theory appealed especially to the lower classes and those of the middle class and lower nobility, whose ambitions remained unfulfilled. The phenomenal rise of the conversos in all spheres puzzled these groups no less than it dismayed them. How did it happen, they inevitably asked themselves, that they who were yesterday despised Jews, and most of them, upon their conversion, destitute, became overnight so rich and influential? That this happened largely as a result of the freedom the conversos were given to exercise their powers—and that, in addition, it was due to their industry, their learning, their ingenuity, their frugality, their driving force and, perhaps above all, their talents, was an answer which these groups refused to accept. To accept it would mean to ascribe their low condition to their lack of the qualities that make for success. It would mean an admission of the conversos' superiority, or even worse, of their own inferiority—an admission which their self-respect could not permit. Consequently, they looked for another explanation, one that would heal their wounded pride and restore their shaken faith in themselves.

Such an explanation was offered them by the racists, according to whose theories the attainments of the conversos were not due to any virtues, which they never owned, but to the vices and defects which they had in abundance. Above all, it was due to their falsehood and deception, which enabled them quickly to obtain by fraud what no honest man could attain by fair means. Hence, if the Old Christians were overtaken by the conversos in the race for social and economic achievements, it was not because they lacked talent or initiative, but because they would not use such devious methods as those employed by the conversos. Moreover, by claiming that the conversos had ensnared by their wiles whole sections of the Spanish people, the racist theoreticians freed many Old Christians from any responsibility for their misfortunes. Accordingly, they should view their poor attainments and low station not as the result of personal deficiencies, but as so many incidents of the *general calamity* that had befallen the nation. Thus we can see that what the racists achieved was not only to bolster the ego of the deprived; they also justified their individual envies, combining them into a multiple force—a common grudge that had to be satisfied, a collective wrong that had to be avenged, and a national cause to fight for.

We should now be in a better position to understand the favorable reaction of the Spanish populace to the answer given by the racists to their question: What should be done to such a vile group, which caused so much damage to the Old Christians and threatened them with such terrible dangers? Obviously, the racists were not satisfied at all with the methods of resistance employed by the burghers. They were far from being satisfied with denying the conversos further occupation of official positions. What was necessary, in their opinion, was to oust the conversos from all the offices they held, since each such office was an enemy outpost from which the adversary might resume his attack. Nor were they satisfied with the anti-converso laws that were—or could be—adopted in the cities. They knew that the conversos would subvert these laws or influence the kings to abolish them. They also saw no way to stop intermarriage as long as the conversos were present in the country, and they knew that expulsion was not a solution the kings would ever accept. The only way to avert the disasters with which the New Christians threatened the Old ones was, therefore, a large-scale massacre of the conversos—a massacre that could be effected across the country if the people were sufficiently aroused and inflamed. What the racists proposed, then, was a large-scale bloodbath, mass extermination or, to use the language of our time, genocide.

The genocidal solution of the converso problem no doubt drew upon medieval methods of dealing with the Jews in the West; but in recognizing this we cannot insist on the exclusiveness of this influence. The genocidal proposition we are here considering developed out of the racial theory about the conversos just as fruit develops form a kernel. It was obvious that the extreme, irreparable evil which allegedly inhered in the Jewish nature had to be treated in an extreme manner: since it was incorrigible, it had to be annihilated—for the good of Christianity and mankind as a whole.

Thus we see how, in the midst of a people whose Christian zeal could in no way be doubted, a theory based on racism appeared whose three major articles of faith were: the existence of a *conspiracy* to seize the government of Spain; the ongoing "contamination" of the "blood" of the Spanish people; and the need to do away with these frightful dangers through a genocidal solution of the converso problem. No less than racism itself, these three postulates were alien to everything Christianity stood for or had ever taught about the Jews. That such a theory could hold its own and, moreover, gain ground against the doctrines of the Church, until it finally overcame the Church's opposition and became an established social principle in Spain, indicates that it was driven by a far stronger force than any obstacle the Church could put in its way. It remains for us to clarify the nature of that force and identify the source from which it sprang.

IV

There is a major problem posed by Spanish racism that has not been tackled or even raised by scholars. It can be formulated in two or three questions, each related to the rise of racism and the early stages of its theoretical evolution. When was it born? And what prompted its emergence? In 1449, when the Toledan racists launched their first violent assault on the conversos, racism had the marks of a complete theory, whose postulates were set and arguments prepared on almost every question involved. Such a theory must have required a considerable time to develop—a requirement which would preclude the assumption that it was shaped during the Toledan rebellion or only several months before it. Indeed, in our survey of various phenomena that may be viewed as antecedents of 1449, we have noticed a clear racist trend leading to the outbreak of 1449. We could discern it in the various anti-Marrano programs *openly proposed on the grounds of race* from 1414 on—programs which, among other things, denied the conversos the right to enter college, or serve in public offices or intermarry with Old Christians. To be sure, the documents we have traced present no reasons for that racial discrimination; they do not tell us, for instance, that the conversos' race was "inferior," or "corrupt," or "polluting," or the like; nor do they suggest that the required disabilities were indicated in Scripture, or agreed to by Christianity; nevertheless, it is certain that *some* reasons were given in justification of the proposed measures and that these reasons formed in due time the basis of the theory espoused in 1449. The silence surrounding the racist arguments in the documents antedating the Toledan rebellion makes us wonder, of course. Perhaps it testifies to the strong opposition which those arguments were expected to provoke, and thus they were not expounded publicly, though they were uttered, discussed and elaborated in the inner circles of their protagonists. In fact, in 1449 Cardinal Torquemada tells us that for a long time the racist agitators did not dare preach their gospel publicly, that they moved about in "corners," as he put it. This suggests that for a considerable period racism was a semi-underground movement that did not dare to come out in the open. When it did come out, however, its theory was full-fledged and its various circles were combined and organized into a substantial faction.

It is clear, then, that both as a theory and as a movement, racism grew at least for several decades in the sixty years that followed the great riots (1391–1449), and it is also evident that throughout this period it fostered increasing hate for the New Christians and built up the image of moral monstrosity that finally was openly related to the conversos. It is evident that these three elements of racism—the concept, the image, and the ferocious hatred—were geared to achieve, as their primary aim, the expulsion of the conversos from all the spheres they had entered as equal citizens in Christian Spain. Essentially, the racists expressed in all this the same attitude that had guided their ancestors in 1392, when they sought to drive out the converts from their cities by means of "injuries, disgraces and damages." To be sure, the measures then taken by the Old Christians could still be considered in a sense *preventive*, aiming at blocking or hindering a development in which they did not want to acquiesce, whereas those proposed later by the racists were *revocative*, as they tended to repeal established laws and abolish a given situation. Yet they all rested on the same idea and were inspired by the same principle: *the inadmissibility of the conversos into Spain's Christian society.*

It was from the adherence of so many Old Christians to that principle of inadmissibility that their long, bitter conflict with the conversos emerged. And thus, to determine the causes of this conflict, we must recognize the roots of that potent attitude and the elemental feelings with which it was imbued. What was it in the New Christian, the convert from Judaism, that moved the Old Christians to reject him so adamantly? Or more broadly: What was it in the Old Christian view of the converso that made him so disliked and opposed?

What we must first note about this view is the function that religion fulfilled in its formation as a dominant opinion in the Christian world. To the Christians, the Jews represented, above all, a *religious* entity, the followers of a faith, or the adherents of a law (the Mosaic Law), with which they were involved in a bitter quarrel. But they also appeared as members of a *people* which, owing to its unique historic course (bizarre and perverse, according to Christianity), remained attached to its old faith. In the evolution of Judaism, as seen in Christian eyes, the people and the faith became coextensive.

But apart from the Christian interpretation of history, these two forms of Jewish existence no doubt reflected an objective reality for most of the periods of Jewish life. In the Middle Ages, certainly, the two elements referred to—i.e., the Jews' peoplehood and religion—were so intertwined and indeed so blended that they seemed to be an indissoluble whole. It was only when the Jew was converted to another faith that the seemingly indivisible union was disrupted and its two major elements were laid bare.

To be sure, the Church maintained that conversion to Christianity obliterated the components of that union, for the Jew, upon conversion, left not only his faith, but also his people. But this was not the view of Jewish law. Distinguishing between the Jew's religion and his peoplehood, Jewish law insisted that the convert from Judaism, though he renounced his faith, remained a member of his people, thereby retaining also some of the rights which that status conferred upon him. What is more, it attributed the same membership to his offspring, provided their mothers were of Jewish descent, even when these offspring were, like himself, religiously non-Jewish. Curiously enough, the view of the Jewish convert that prevailed among the Old Christians, or at least among the members of the anti-Marrano party, was closer to that of Jewish law than to the view upheld by the Church.

The position of the Church was dictated, we must note, not only by its view of the Jews and Jewish history but also by its concepts of the structure of mankind and the destiny of Christianity. Its stand on the issues raised by these concepts was determined by its abstract and cosmopolitan approach. It divided men into Christian and non-Christian and was little concerned with national differences or differences stemming from ethnic origin. Its ideal was to see all mankind as one flock led by one shepherd—the Vicar of Christ. But historical reality conflicted with that ideal and often put Church ideology to the test. It was essentially this conflict between the Church's political theory—or rather its universalist outlook—and the living feelings of Europe's rising nations that placed Church policies under severe strain and ultimately led to the Reformation. The same kind of strain was experienced by the Church in the wake of the struggle that developed in Spain between the Old and New Christians.

By 1435, during the Council of Basle, forty-five years after the first great conversion and more than twenty years after the second, the Church must have realized that something had gone wrong with the Jewish converts' assimilation in Spain. Judging by the decree issued in the Council, it is evident that the Church sought to counteract the opposition displayed by Spain's Old Christians to the converts, but it is also apparent that it failed to diagnose the underlying causes of that opposition. Hence its proposed palliatives.

There was of course much truth in the Church's belief that the Jew, upon his conversion to Christianity, abandoned his people together with his religion; and judging by the converts' communal relationships, that belief was factually confirmed. Yet while the convert abandoned his people, his peoplehood did not abandon him. It was reflected in many of his characteristics, the

product of numerous factors—ethnic, social, environmental and educational—that had influenced Jewish life for centuries. These were essentially
Jewish characteristics; and although assimilation had somewhat dimmed
them, they could still be discerned in the Jewish convert even decades after
his conversion.

But this leads us to the following observation. If the above was true of
individual converts, or small groups of converts from Judaism to Christianity
(and, for that matter, to any other religion), it was doubly true in cases of mass
conversion of the kind that occurred in 1391. To be sure, the desertion of the
Jewish people by the convert could still be considered factual in these cases
when viewed from the standpoint of its final outcome, or judged by his ties
with the Jewish community, but it was not concrete if seen from the standpoint of his collective position following the conversion. For when masses of
Jews were converted at the same time, each of them saw himself *within his
people* and by no means as one who had forsaken it. In Spain, where these
converts, or their great majority, lived for many years in boroughs of their
own, this feeling of communion was kept alive as long as the process of
assimilation had not destroyed, or seriously affected, the collective fabric.
Also many characteristics of the Jew and his life-style, which even isolated
converts retained for many years, were guarded for much larger periods in
the converso communities. As a result, the converso could still be recognized—even several generations after his ancestors' conversion—by his Jewish appearance, his habits and mannerisms, his attitudes and reactions, as well
as his views on a variety of issues. In consequence, in the middle of the 15th
century (and no doubt in many cases even later) the great majority of the
New Christians in Spain had not yet shaken off the shadow of their past; and
the result of this fact was the consciousness of their "otherness" that determined the attitude of their neighbors.

What precisely constituted the *core* of that "otherness" was of course not
easy to determine. After decades of life in Christendom, one may assume, the
convert appeared different from the Jew; yet this difference did not efface his
basic Jewish features, and his otherness from Christians was felt just as keenly
and generated the same hostile attitudes. For the Christian, who hated the
Jew to the point of being anxious or prepared to kill him, *disliked his whole
being* and not merely his religion, even when religion was claimed by the
Christians to be the sole or major cause of their aversion. And therefore
when, following the Jew's conversion, his *non*-religious features continued to
be manifest, they also continued to feed the hatred which the Old Christians
had felt for him before his conversion. In vain did the Church exhort the
Christians to remember that the Jew, once converted, was spiritually reborn,
that the "New man" he put on had replaced the "Old" one, and that therefore
they ought to show him brotherly affection and aid him in case of need. The

Christian masses would not be convinced. What they saw before them was
the same "Old man" whose Christianity did not change his overall image, but
equipped him with rights and facilities that enabled him to interfere with
their own lives. In consequence, that *otherness* of the converso, which was
reflected by the *non*-religious side of his being, soon stamped him not only
as "different" from the Old Christians but also as a "foreigner" and, as such,
as an "intruder." This brought out the Jewishness of the Marranos from
another standpoint—that of the relations between an alien minority and the
majority within which it lives.

Thus we touch again the direct cause, or the major root, of the deep-seated
antipathy underlying the antagonism of the Old Christians toward the New.
Essentially, it was the antagonism to the Jewish *peoplehood* that survived
among the Marranos in the state of their conversion, and it is here that we
find the point of affinity between the hatred of the Marranos by the Christian
masses and the theoretical approaches of the racist movement.

To comprehend more fully what this implied, we should note that the
conception of the Marranos as a *people*—the same people to which the Jews
belonged—was expressed not only in the feelings and attitudes exhibited
toward them by the Old Christians, but also in terms which testify clearly
that the Marranos were viewed as a distinct *nationality* which, in more ways
than one, was related to the Jews. Indeed, not only did their enemies so
regard them, but also their friends among the Old Christians; and, what is
more, they were so regarded by the Marranos themselves. The latter, who
insisted that religiously they were Christians and had nothing to do with
Judaism and its followers, could not help admitting their actual belonging to
a separate entity, which they clearly defined.

Three times does the Relator, in his *Instruction,* refer to the Marranos as
a *nation.*[22] Similarly, when Pulgar, in his letter to Cardinal Mendoza, suggests
that Marranos inclined toward Judaism be educated in Christianity by members of their own group, he designates that group by the term *nation.*[23] Also
the anonymous Old Christian who polemicized with Pulgar says to him:
"someone of your *nation* was appointed to instruct them" [i.e., the conver-
sos].[24] Likewise, Pérez de Guzmán, in his discussion of the New Christians,
defines them twice as a *nation*[25]; and opposing the detraction of the Marranos
as a group, he says: "It is improper to condemn a whole *nation.*"[26] Also
Palencia, in describing the conversos as viewed by the Old Christian critics,
alludes to them as to a separate *nation*[27]; while Barrientos, speaking of
the many Old Christians who have converso blood in their veins, says that
almost all the "noble houses of Castile or their greater part are of the
Israelitic *nation.*"[28] Naturally, when Valera refers to the *Jews,* the ancestors

of the conversos, he describes them in the words of Deuteronomy, according to the Vulgate: "Is there another *nation* so noble?"[29]; and when he comes to the subject of theological nobility, he asks: "In which *nation* could be found so many nobles as in that of the Jews?"[30] The Marranos, then, were identified as descendants of the Jewish nation—and, although converted, still as members of that nation—by themselves, their friends and their enemies alike.

That their stock was now the major, or one of the major, components of their nationality was admitted by all concerned, the conversos included. When the Relator speaks of the converso "nation," he defines it as belonging to the "stock" *(linaje)* of our lord Jesus Christ."[31] In like manner does Diego de Valera speak of the Jewish people as the cradle of Christ and says that the Son of God "chose this *lineage*—of the Patriarchs, the Prophets and the Apostles—for himself as the most noble."[32] Accordingly, when the conversos of Aragon complain about the refusal of the Aragonese to intermarry with them, they point out that Jesus took His flesh from their own people— namely, that they, the conversos, are of the same race as that of the ancient Jews. Similarly, Juan de Torquemada identifies the conversos as Christians who *descended* from the *people* of Israel[33]; and when the Relator refers, in his letter to Barrientos, to Haman, he says that the bishop knew of the great persecutions that he, Haman, conducted against "our race" *(nuestro linaje)*.[34] Espina called them both "race" *(genus)* and "people" *(gens)*,[35] while García saw them as a special human "kind," a stock and a "breed."[36] Descent, racial origin, their *linaje*, was now therefore one of the hallmarks of the Marranos; and it was indeed their main collective symptom, as indicated above.

As a "nation apart," despite their conversion, as a nation united by common origin or race, the Marranos were thus exposed to the evaluation of their group as an *alien national entity*, whose fellowship with the *people of the country* must be questioned, and whose preparedness to betray it could be taken as likely even by moderate adversaries. When the chronicler Castillo criticizes the arch-rebels against King Enrique IV, and wishes to explain the reason for their readiness to enter such treacherous designs, he explains it by the fact that they belong to foreign *nations*,[37] referring no doubt to Archbishop Carrillo and Juan Pacheco, who were of Portuguese origin, and to their converso allies, like Alvar Gómez and Pedrarias, who belonged, according to the common concept, to the *judáica nación*. This view of the conversos is also reflected in Palencia's report on the Old Christians' belief that the conversos were "secretly plotting infamous conspiracies" against them.[38] Palencia apparently shared this belief, for a plot like those "infamous conspiracies" was contrived, he tells us, by the Toledan conversos, and it was largely to that imaginary scheme that he ascribed the outbreak of the conflict between them and the Old Christians in Toledo in 1467. It was also because of the prevalence of this view that the rebels of 1449 felt safe in declaring, against common sense and against the known facts, that the conversos were planning to seize Toledo in order to deliver it to Alvaro, their ally. And it was indeed the same view of the New Christians that sustained the belief in the still larger plot—the grand conspiracy of the conversos of Castile to capture the government of the country.

Such suspicions and beliefs could be spun about the conversos because they were considered not only an *alien* but also an *enemy alien* group, one that belonged to a different *nation,* which was ostensibly at peace with the Spaniards but actually at incessant war with them, as it was with all other Christian nations. But at this point, we must ask whether the term "nacio" (or "natio") when applied to the Marranos meant *nation* or *nationality* in the modern sense, or perhaps something else which has to be defined. The question is legitimate, but also difficult and complex. We shall try, however, to answer it as briefly as possible without deviating far from our purpose.

V

The history of the growth of nationalism in the Middle Ages, including the growth of nationalism in Spain, is still one of the least studied subjects of the humanities, although its importance for understanding the medieval era, as well as the era that followed, can hardly be exaggerated. But the cardinal question "What is a nation?" was asked not only in the nineteenth century. It was asked already at the beginning of the fifteenth and, in all probability, even before; and in dealing with this query, we shall have to confine ourselves to the inferences we can draw from what was said about this matter in the period with which we are concerned.

At the Council of Constance (1417) a discussion arose on the subject of nationhood, or rather on what constitutes a *real* nation as differing from the artificial political formations that were recognized as *nationes* in that Council.[39] On that occasion the English delegation expressed the view that the essential elements or signs of nationhood were either a *"blood relationship marking a people off from the others,"* coupled with a "habit of unity," or a "peculiar language," or a "territory," which serves as the people's dwelling place or homeland.[40] We are mentioning these "signs" in the order they appear in the original statement of that delegation, from which it is evident that only two of those "signs," or even one of them, sufficed to determine national distinction. Perhaps most remarkable in that definition is the fact that its "signs" of nationhood do *not* include common obedience to a prince, or anything related to government. A nation is recognized by its *substantial* qualities and not by the shifting identity of its rulers. It is evidently not the same as a kingdom, and it exists quite apart from the royal dominion.

This was not an isolated opinion. A few months earlier, the Portuguese embassy to the Council of Constance protested "against the inclusion of prelates from Sicily and Corsica with the Aragonese in the Spanish nation on the ground that, although subjects of the king of Aragon, they spoke another language and were "truly of a different nation."[41] Similarly, in a speech he delivered in the Council of Basle (1434) on the priority of Castile's seating rights in that Council, Alonso de Cartagena said that in "the dominion of my lord the king [of Castile] there exist diverse nations and different languages," mentioning by way of demonstration the fact that the "Castilians, the Galicians and the Basques are different nations and use different languages."[42] It is apparent that, according to Cartagena, nationhood was not identical with language, although he evidently regarded language as one of its most significant signs. We shall probably not be far off the mark if we assume that, in Cartagena's view, "blood relationship and a habit of unity" constituted, as it did for the English in Constance, a nation's primary attributes.

Thus, when the Relator, or Barrientos, or Pérez de Guzmán spoke of the Marranos as a separate "nation," they had a clear notion of what they referred to. They referred to an entity which could be "marked off" by the "signs" mentioned by the English in Constance. But what "sign" could be attributed to the conversos? They had neither a special territory of their own nor a language that differed from the others'. What remained to distinguish them as a separate nation was their "blood relationship and their habit of unity." Hence the importance that "race" assumed for their "national" distinction; and hence the intermixture of race and nation as terms designating their identity.

This brings us to the heart of the problem that inevitably emerges from this discussion. If the nations of the peninsula were divided from each other not only by their shifting dynasties and rulers (which were often imposed upon them from the outside), but also by inherent, natural differences (such as their stock, language, etc.), and if the conversos, too, were viewed (by themselves, as well as by their friends and foes) as an entity with special national characteristics, may we not assume that the conflict between them and the other national entities of Spain stemmed primarily from *national* differences rather than from any other source? Or if it did originate in some other source, such as those we have pointed out above (i.e., religious, economic, or social), was it not exacerbated by a *national* antagonism to the point of becoming as acute as it did? The question, to our knowledge, has thus far not been broached in the historical literature related to the Marranos. It must, however, be raised and considered if we wish to do justice to our subject.

When Alonso de Cartagena spoke of the *nations* that lived under Castilian dominion, he no doubt echoed the argument of the English at Constance, who saw in a group's "peculiar language" a major sign of a nation, and he may also have ascribed to certain Castilian groups some of the other signs in which the English saw evidence of national qualities. But these qualities in themselves (such as homeland, ethnic origin), like other common attributes of nationhood (such as statehood, government, legal system, etc.), are no signs of a *national* existence any more than the limbs of a body testify to the presence of a functioning organism. As is well known, for a nation to exist and function, it must have, in addition to the above properties, that particular asset which students of nationalism have designated *national consciousness*— an asset which comprises *memory* and *outlook* (i.e., awareness of a common past, as well as a common concern for the future); a *will* which consists of a common determination to prolong and protect the community's life; a generally understood or declared *consent* to regard the interests of the community as superior to other interests; and above all, an *aspiration* to retain, or attain, a state of political independence. To be sure, these elements, as scholars have noted, are not found in all nations in the same degree, nor do they appear together at a given moment. They grow and develop from small beginnings until they (or some of them) reach maturity and are capable of motivating the nation's actions. But they ought to be present at least in a form considerably beyond the embryonic stage for any collectivity to possess nationhood. And so, if the groups in Spain of the 15th century that were called by some of their members "nations" possessed these elements to a notable extent, then they were indeed half- or full-fledged nations in the modern sense of the word, and the laws applying to the lives of nations were valid for them, too. If not, what was meant by the term *nation*, when they were referred to by this designation, was something else, which still has to be defined.

Spain had gone through such terrible convulsions in the eight hundred years of the Reconquest that it could offer ground for a variety of theories about the fate of Spanish nationalism in that period. Thus, according to Américo Castro, the Spaniards of ancient times virtually disappeared in the storms and stresses of the wars with the Moors, and the nation that ultimately replaced the old one was molded in the last centuries of the Middle Ages, assuming final shape only at the dawn, or on the eve of the new era. As Castro saw it, the new nation emerged as the product of the particular social structure that characterized Spanish life until the 12th century and beyond—a structure that comprised three religious castes: Christian, Moslem and Jewish. "What is called today 'fatherland,' 'nation,'" he says, "in terms of defining the people as a whole, was felt in the 12th century as a conglomerate of believers in distinct faiths—that is, each in his own religious code."[43] This situation, according to Castro, persisted until the turn of the 15th century, when finally, out of the castes' *convivencia*, first as collaborators and then as contenders, emerged the "Spaniards as we know them." Obviously, according to this conception, there was hardly any room in the medieval Christian kingdoms for national life in the modern sense, let alone for a variety of national experiences.

Yet there *was* such a variety. However one may assess Castro's view that, in the first several centuries of the Reconquest, "religious affiliation served to delimit the national form of a whole people,"[44] it is clear that already in those early times foundations were laid for the rise and development of a number of distinct national entities, and that other factors besides religion played a major part in fashioning their "form." Castro, in our opinion, overrates the congeniality in the relationship between the castes in the earlier period and underrates their antagonism in the later. The so-called Christian caste was not, as we see it, just one of three components of Spain's society, but *always* the ruling and controlling factor, to which the other two were markedly subservient. If the attitude of the "Christian caste" toward the other groups changed, the change was not from cooperation to domination, but from domination, which was constant, to suppression and exclusion. Above all, it was the Christian caste—and it alone—that provided the roots, the trunk and the main branches of the new Spanish nation.

Different was the view of Menéndez Pidal, who perceived Christian Spain as a national rock split by the hammer blows of the Moslem conquest and then reunited by Spanish forces who worked for the cementation of the scattered fragments. In these fragments, Menéndez Pidal believed, the national spirit continued to live. Accordingly, he said that since 1035, the "unifying impulse continually asserted itself . . . until [Spain's] final unity was achieved by the Catholic Monarchs."[45] These are of course far-reaching statements which their author has not duly proven. In view of the jealousy for their separate independence which the Spanish Christian kingdoms have perennially manifested; in view of the zeal which they steadily displayed in protecting their interests and pursuing their goals; and, above all, in view of the ruinous wars which they frequently waged against each other throughout the era, it is hard for us to see them as part of *one* nation, or even agree that the "impulse for unity" asserted itself *continually* in their lives. To be sure, certain memories, laws and customs were commonly retained by all Christian kingdoms; but the centrifugal forces were on the whole stronger than the centripetal ones, and the new conditions changed the face of their societies so that eventually they were seen by themselves, and by others, as different national entities.

It is not our purpose to be drawn here into the controversy about the "origin and identity" of the Spaniards. But the subject bears directly on the question that concerns us—namely, the relationship between the Old and New Christians—and therefore we find it necessary to remark that we find ourselves considerably removed from the views of both Castro and Pidal, while, on the other hand, we feel considerably closer to those of Ortega y Gasset. In the words of Ortega in *Invertebrate Spain:* "It would be an error to believe that, when Castile took Aragon, Catalonia and the Basque country and welded them into the unit that was Spain, they lost their character as peoples distinct from each other and from the whole of which they now formed a part."[46] "There was none of this," Ortega emphasized. "Submission, unification, amalgamation, did not mean the death of these groups as groups. Their innate force of independence persisted even though they were conquered."[47] But peoples whose "distinction" is so pronounced that it cannot be blurred even when "amalgamated," and whose "innate independence" is so strong as to persist even in a state of submission, could not have attained those qualities except by the factors that shape nations. And indeed Navarre, Aragon and Catalonia had been nations long before they united with Castile, although Ortega y Gasset reserves the title "nation" for Spain, their combined unit.

That Castile was no less a nation than its partners in what we may call the Spanish Union need scarcely be said. To be sure, the growth of its national consciousness was slowed down by the drastic changes (dynastic, territorial and demographic) it had undergone during the first centuries of its existence. But in 1230 its dynasty was solidified; in 1266 its border was stabilized[48]; demographic changes were subsequently minimized; one law was established for the whole country; and some national representation was secured through Cortes. In the following two centuries (1250–1450) Castile also became far more united ethnically, so that by 1450 it seemed to have all the essential attributes of nationhood, including a government of its own, a tradition of independence, and a past rich in heroic deeds, which was kept alive by its literature.

That this was indeed the situation at the time is also attested by some special studies. In three short but incisive works, Gifford Davis showed how the national sentiment was manifested in both Castile's politics and literature in the 13th, 14th and 15th centuries,[49] and María Rosa Lida de Malkiel demonstrated how, in the first half of the 15th century, the concepts of Castile and *España* merged in the minds of most poets of the period, and especially how the view of a united Spain animated their works as an ideal.[50] To be sure, Rosa Lida assumed that she had noticed two important exceptions to this rule: the Marquis de Santillana and Fernán Pérez de Guzmán[51]; but in this she was rather in error, and the error only strengthens her correct generalization. Santillana calls his homeland *(patria),* which was Castile, also by the name of *España*[52]; and Guzmán considers not only Castile and Leon, but also Portugal and Aragon, *"kingdoms of that nation"*—namely, the same nation (Spain), whose glories he sings in his famous poem *Loores de los claros varones de España.*[53] Also the very fact that Guzmán dedicated that poem to the great of the whole of Spain, and not only of Castile, shows that his political and national horizon encompassed the entire peninsula, and that he viewed all Christian kingdoms of the peninsula as members of one historical unit.

It would be wrong to assume that these sentiments and perceptions were shared in equal measure by all the sections of the people. Those who upheld and promoted them first were intellectuals (primarily poets and historians), who belonged to the upper classes. But they gradually sifted down to the lower classes, especially their educated, "learned" elements. By the middle of the century this extended attitude gave rise to a development which is related to our subject.

The growing awareness by a people of its "self," or rather of its national identity, is always paralleled by its growing desire to share in the management of its affairs. And Castile, of all the countries of the peninsula, had the least representative government. The attempts made toward the end of the 14th century to involve Castile's cities in the central administration were completely abandoned in the 15th, when the Crown's dictatorship excluded from the government not only the cities but also most grandees. Supported by some of the urban oligarchies, the nobles reacted with rebellious protests, only to be repeatedly crushed. In 1445 the Cortes of Olmedo authorized an absolutist regime, and all hope of popular representation seemed lost. But then four years later, in the rebellion of Toledo, the lower classes made their voice heard, asserting their right to determine and shape (together with the nobles) the government of the nation and the *nature* of its officialdom.

Accordingly, we can see the national spirit surge in the demands put forth in the Petition they addressed to the king in May 1449 and in the Memorial written later in that year by their spokesman, Marcos García. What they wanted was a regime based on the people's *expressed will,* announced through its representatives in Cortes; they wanted Cortes to represent the *whole kingdom,* including *all the cities, towns and places* (and not only the *nobles* and the *principal* cities, as had been the case hitherto); and they wanted a monarchy that would recognize its duty to serve the people, care for its needs and, above all, abide by the people's wishes. Otherwise, they (i.e., the people) threatened to withdraw their allegiance from the king and thereby overthrow his government.

In all this we can see indications of nationhood, or of an advanced national consciousness, or of a nation in the making. Moreover, since the rebels of Toledo spoke, as we have seen, not only for their own city, or for a particular class or estate, but for all cities, classes and estates, their position assumed a *national* character, thereby adding another indication to the presence of a national sentiment in their ranks. Nevertheless, the term *nation* is not to be found in their writings. Instead they used the term *republic,* or other terms signifying national existence, as we shall presently see.

Cartagena, as we have noted, saw Castile's population as comprising three *nations* (Castilians, Galicians and Basques), and it was indubitably these nations that the rebels referred to when they spoke of the king's *peoples.*[54] They viewed these peoples as representing three *generos*—three ethnic *types* (the marks of nationhood) whose common denominator lay in the fact that their members were all *naturales.* These *naturales*—i.e., the natives, the *authentic* or indigenous sons of the country—comprised as a whole what we might today call the national body or unit: they alone were entitled to represent the *republic* and occupy its public posts. The conversos, whom they called the "fourth ethnic type" *(el quarto genero),* the type that descended from the Jews,[55] were obviously excluded from this category. They were not *naturales* but *extranjeros* ("aliens"); hence, they were not part of the national conglomerate and shared none of its rights.

That as non-*naturales* they could not be *entrusted* with the task of representing the republic was taken as a matter of course; and in consequence, they were not entitled to the authority and privileges which go with that task. The denial to the conversos of the right to public office was a direct deduction from that general premise, and so was the disqualification of the conversos as recipients of benefices from the Church. When we recall the cities' stubborn resistance, so firmly and repeatedly displayed in Cortes, to the granting of benefices to foreigners *(extranjeros),* we can better understand the Toledans' insistence that conversos be forbidden to assume benefices of the Church.

We have seen that the rebels refrained from applying the term "nation" not only to the conversos but also to the other Castilian groups, which Cartagena has defined as "nations." Instead, they described them by ethnic epithets, and those whom they regarded as legitimate components of their country's population, they also occasionally designated as *peoples.* But they had a clear conception of the *inherent unity* of what they viewed as the authentic peoples of Castile,[56] and that conception further suggests an advanced stage of national consciousness. Perhaps they did not employ the term "nation" because it was not yet in common use, but they managed to communicate what they had in mind; and what they had in mind was, though not identical with, close to what we now call "national identity."

The rebellion of Toledo was, we should recall, a political uprising directed against the regime—including its conversos, who were viewed as its alien and illegitimate agents. When the revolt failed to attain its end, which was to overthrow the dictatorial government and replace it by a "democratic" regime, the masses were persuaded to continue their fight against the conversos alone, perhaps believing that by ousting the conversos from their posts they would secure these posts for themselves. Thus, the continued assault on the Marranos resulted from a frustrated revolution. To be sure, the racial form of that assault owed its appearance to a *variety* of causes, mainly to those we have indicated above, but there is no doubt that the assailants gained much strength from additional forces then rising to the surface. For besides hatred of the Jew, the racist drive harnessed the energy and dynamism of a revolutionary movement, which was already *national* in essence and could find at that time no other outlet. That is why the struggle against the Jewish "race" was felt as a struggle against a foreign *nation* which had usurped the positions of the nation's true sons and must therefore be vanquished or destroyed.

IV. Ferdinand of Aragon

I

In the foregoing chapters we have summarized what we gathered about the general circumstances, tendencies and interests that combined to form the powerful drive that led to the establishment of the Inquisition. It should be obvious by now that without this drive the Spanish Inquisition would not have been created; but it is also certain that this drive alone would not have created it either. For although general tendencies, interests and circumstances can produce *movements* demanding change, they cannot produce the complex *organizations* that translate these demands into reality. Such organizations are fashioned by individuals who can channel the forces of popular movements, just as the builder of a power station at the edge of a cataract can harness the energy of the current.

The creation of the Spanish Inquisition was no exception to this rule. It happened thanks to its architect and builder who was, without question, King Ferdinand of Aragon. He was aided to be sure by his spirited wife, Queen Isabella of Castile, especially in the various stages of planning; and the momentous resolution to establish the Inquisition must be imputed to both. This decision was the final link in the chain of causes that generated the Inquisition. What led Ferdinand and Isabella to make it?

In the three decades after 1449, the racists made repeated attempts to implement the main parts of their program. Their bloody attacks on the converso communities were meant to be a prelude to the Marranos' extermination, or to their expulsion from Spanish society, while their enactment of statutes against the Marranos in cities that succumbed to their policy of discrimination was intended to spur the rest of the kingdom to reduce the Marranos' status.

In the final analysis, none of these projects was accomplished to the racists' satisfaction. Their physical assaults no doubt caused the Marranos considerable loss of life and treasure. But they could not bring about the extermination of most conversos even in a single locality; nor could they cause the expulsion of the conversos from even a single Castilian town, or otherwise effect the complete liquidation of any Marrano community. More successful were the racists' attempts at damaging the Marranos' civil status. They managed to set up discriminatory regimes in Toledo, Ciudad Real, Cordova and other places, thereby causing dangerous breaches in the legal defense line of the

New Christians. But before long these breaches were repaired by the Kings, who acted under converso influence. Thus here, too, the racists failed to achieve their ultimate objectives.

Yet while in the actual fulfillment of their program the racists gained only partial victories, and the curve of their attainments rose and fell, in two respects the course of their activities showed a constantly upward trend. To begin with, their movement kept growing steadily, attracting more people of almost all classes, and second, they fostered hatred of the conversos to an ever more threatening degree. Both developments increased the pressure on the authorities and both hurt the relations between Old and New Christians. In fact, in some places these relations became so tense that they could be disrupted by the slightest provocation, and mutual toleration would give way to civil war.

When Ferdinand and Isabella came to power, they were well acquainted with this situation. They had seen the ravages it produced in Cordova, in Jaén and other towns in Andalusia, and they knew of the havoc it had caused in Toledo, Ciudad Real and elsewhere. They noticed the hatred growing and spreading; and they realized that its growth and spread must be arrested before it produced new, powerful explosions that might rock the whole kingdom.

The question was: What could be done?

Two courses of action seemed open to the kings to avert the danger of new disorders. One was to follow the advice of the conversos; the other, the demands of their opponents.

The advice of the conversos in 1474, when the Catholic Kings came to power, was indubitably the same they had offered Juan II (in 1449) and, most probably, Enrique IV (in 1462, 1467, and 1473): the administration should act promptly and vigorously in full conformity with the laws of the kingdom, and this meant, of course, to punish the lawbreakers, and especially the inciters of riots. No concessions should be made to the criminals, because every concession would only encourage them to resume and increase their intolerable mischief. On the other hand, if the monarchs treated them as the laws require, they would earn the respect of the great majority of the citizenry who are seriously hurt by the incessant turmoil; the agitators would understand that there was no chance for their criminal wishes to come true and would ultimately abandon their insane hopes of seeing the New Christians destroyed. The result would be the restoration of public peace.

The Catholic Kings were of course aware that this method had never been tried. It is true that in 1450–51 some of the chief assailants of the Marranos were cruelly executed or otherwise punished, but the public was somehow given to understand that they suffered this fate for their betrayal of the Prince, or for their rebellion against the King (Juan II), and not for their excesses against the conversos. In fact, both Juan II and Enrique IV pardoned all robbers and killers of the New Christians, so that the public might form the conclusion that crimes against conversos go unpunished. But the Catholic Kings also knew *why* their predecessors had taken a soft line against the Marranos' foes. They had taken such a line because a policy of reprisals was opposed by almost *all* Old Christians in the cities, and they feared that by pursuing such a policy they might harden the opposition and ignite a popular resistance that would be beyond their power to put down.

Ferdinand and Isabella were well aware that the general respect for law they had established, and the fear they had instilled in potential lawbreakers, had much to do with the peace that prevailed between the Old and New Christians in the first years of their reign. They erected a strong wall against anarchy and revolution for the benefit of all their subjects, but they also saw the anti-converso forces battering dangerously against it at many points. The Kings must have wondered what they would do if, at some point, their defense system cracked. They were especially concerned about the realistic prospect that rioting against the Marranos might erupt in many towns. If such general outbreaks, they reasoned, were possible in the 1460s and 1470s, they were even more likely in the 1480s. For the movement against the Marranos had grown, hatred of the conversos ran much higher, and the problem of containing such a movement had become correspondingly more difficult. It would be impossible, they realized, to punish masses of lawbreakers, while selective punishments against the ringleaders might swell the rising waves of disorder. They must have considered also their military potential in foreseeable situations. If two or three great cities revolted at the same time, could the Kings put down such a multiple insurrection? It was obviously a prospect they could not ignore, nor was it farfetched. When many small fires were burning in many places, nobody could tell how many of them might turn into conflagrations.

But apart from the question whether the anti-Marrano movement could be suppressed by force, there was another question that Ferdinand and Isabella considered of primary importance. This was the question of their standing in the country as admired rulers. Would not a campaign of suppression cost them the great popularity they were enjoying—a popularity which to them was one of the main assets they had got out of the War of Succession? Having determined to subdue the nobility, which had caused so much trouble to their predecessors, they could hardly afford to fight the commoners, too—for if they did so, on whom would they rely? To keep the commoners' unreserved support was therefore a task which, in their judgment, had priority over anything else; but the fulfillment of this task would be utterly impossible if they protected the conversos against the commoners' demands.

They had no choice but to take sides, and it was clear which side they would take. If they wished to have the support of the majority *and* the preservation of peace and order, they had to come to terms with the anti-Marrano party and demonstrate their sympathy with its position and its goals; otherwise they would lose the goodwill of that party and, before long, its help and obedience. But they also knew that this display of sympathy could not be limited to mere words; if they wished it to have the desired effect, it had to be expressed in concrete actions, which meant that they would have to adopt at least *part* of the anti-Marrano program. But what point of that program could they possibly accept? It was here that the Kings faced a crucial difficulty in the policy they intended to pursue.

For almost all the anti-Marranos' demands involved a violation of the country's laws and posed a direct threat to the existing social system. The Kings, however, believed that respect for the law was the primary condition of an orderly government and in no circumstances would they countenance or contribute to an open disregard of legal prohibitions. Nor would they support a brazen disregard of traditionally accepted morality and thus throw the country into moral confusion, which would sooner or later lead to social chaos. Consequently, they could not approve of a bloodbath as a way of settling the Marrano question. Nor could they agree to banish the conversos or degrade them socially because of their race, for such moves would likewise violate the laws and contradict hallowed policies of church and state. Similarly, they could not officially prohibit the assumption by conversos of public offices or benefices; for the issuance of orders to this effect would be equally opposed to the existing laws and, in addition, would be objectively devoid of any justifiable reason. Despite the violent campaign against the converso officials, the latter were known to have performed dutifully, and it would be a travesty of justice to repay them for their services in so offensive and humiliating a manner. Similarly, to restrict the rights of *all* conversos because some of them were rumored to be Judaizers would be grossly illegal, since heresy could not be punished collectively, and certainly not on the grounds of hearsay. What then could the sovereigns do if they wished to draw the anti-Marranos to their side and remain within the laws on which the Kingdom rested? The only thing they could do was to adopt the measure demanded by all the critics of the Marranos—that is, establish an inquisition.

To accept this demand would not breach the legal system, or require laws against the conversos as a group, or a policy of discrimination against any of their members. The task of the inquisition was only to investigate—that is, to determine the validity of accusations leveled against individual suspects—and then pronounce sentences of guilt or innocence. Such inquisitions, controlled by the Church, operated in several Western countries; Aragon had had one since 1237; why should not one be established in Castile? There seemed to be no reason to oppose such a proposal. Castile, after all, had been long swept with rumors that Judaism was rampant among the conversos, and it was hard to believe that so much smoke was generated without any fire. In any case, it was the duty of the Sovereigns to check the veracity of such rumors and eradicate the scourge of heresy from their land, if indeed such a scourge existed, and nobody could blame them if they decided to conduct a searching inquiry in the matter.

The Inquisition was not one of the plans initially most favored by the Spanish racists, especially by their secular wing. They had tried it in Toledo—with little success (in 1449)—and, judging by their various public proclamations, they were not eager to renew it.[1] They preferred to take social and economic measures, and accordingly issued their *Sentencia-Estatuto*. Nor did the Inquisition appear to them necessary for the attainment of their objectives. By definition, the Inquisition was merely an instrument of inquiry into suspicions of heresy, aimed at determining the guilt or innocence of suspects. The racists were not eager to resort to such procedures; nor were they really in need of them. Their theory assured them that all conversos were heretics—an assurance which was to them an article of faith. It justified the extreme measures they had proposed against the conversos; and these measures did not necessarily include an inquisition.

The inquisition that first appeared in Toledo (in 1449) was probably introduced at the prodding of the ecclesiastic racists, headed by the vicar of the Toledan church. The latter perceived that charges of heresy were an effective means of humiliating the New Christians and could serve as lethal weapons if properly handled by an ecclesiastical inquisition. By this they meant an inquisition whose main functionaries were enemies of the New Christians like themselves. Accordingly, they believed that if such an inquisition was allowed to operate throughout Spain, it would spell the end of the Marranos' existence. Their view must finally have been adopted by the elite of Toledo's Old Christians who negotiated the terms of their reconciliation with the King. It is difficult to see why the royal administration solicited a papal bull to establish an inquisition, unless the Toledans made such solicitation a condition for the resumption of their obedience to the King.[2]

Under the conversos' counter-pressure, however, the plan for the inquisition was then shelved, as we have seen; but the ecclesiastic racists kept urging its adoption, while proclaiming that most conversos were heretics. It was especially Espina, who paid little regard to the social-economic criticism of the Marranos and concentrated on the charge of their infidelity, who argued tirelessly for the establishment of an inquisition as a useful (though not the most effective) tool for dealing with the Marrano problem. His campaign was taken up, in one form or another, by all three monastic orders in Spain (the Franciscans, the Hieronymites and the Dominicans); and reechoed as it was by the secular racists, who claimed that the conversos were indeed secret

Jews, it seemed that all the factions of the anti-Marrano party would back the Inquisitional plan.

What made that plan steadily more popular was the increased currency of the notion that the conversos were false Christians, secretly devoted to their ancestors' faith. In consequence, the terms *Marrano, Jew* and *heretic* came to be regarded more and more as synonymous, and the influence of this synonymity was so strong that not only ordinary uninformed people, who generally follow the prevailing views, but also critical observers, researchers and historians could not escape its pervasive spell. We can see this in the changed attitudes toward the conversos of chroniclers like Enríquez del Castillo and Palencia, who from sharp critics of the Marranos' enemies became supporters of the latter's charges. The change was also seen in the contents and extremism of the defamations heaped upon the New Christians. If in 1449 the authors of the *Sentencia* limited their religious criticism of the Marranos to *suspicions* touching a *minority* of the New Christians, in the sixties the suspicions turned to *certainties* about their *overwhelming majority*. The wildest accusations about their heretical practices were now circulated as ascertained facts, and the rising popular fury against them soon made new outbreaks seem inevitable. In the seventies the pressure became so disturbing that the sovereigns had to find some way to relieve it. As we have indicated, they examined all possibilities and, by a process of elimination, arrived at the conclusion that the establishment of the Inquisition was the only way.

From the standpoint of the immediate goal of the Crown to secure its own endurance and stability, it was hard to find fault with that conclusion. Of the various potential solutions offered, the solution they chose appeared most likely to succeed. Both logic and interest pointed in that direction—and not for the first time. In fact, the three sharpest politicians of Castile in the 15th century made the same calculation and reached the same conclusion. They were Alvaro de Luna, Juan Pacheco, and Ferdinand of Aragon. All three understood that of the two conflicting forces (i.e., the conversos and their enemies), one would eventually have to give way; and all three of them, apparently, were certain which of the two that would be. Of the three, however, it was only Ferdinand who had the power to translate his conclusion into reality. Accordingly, he abandoned the Crown's support of the conversos, established the Inquisition, and thereby assumed the unofficial sponsorship of the anti-Marrano party—that is, the party which was likely to triumph and which he considered too risky to oppose.

II

On January 2, 1481, two Dominican friars published in Seville the letter of their appointment as Inquisitorial judges for Castile by Ferdinand and Isabella.[3] Included in this letter, which was signed by the Kings on September 27, 1480, was Pope Sixtus IV's bull of November 1, 1478 *(Exigit sincere devotionis)*, which authorized the Kings to appoint Inquisitors in Castile for extirpating the heresy that had been spreading in their land.[4] According to both the bull and the letter, the heresy consisted of a "Judaic" deviation by certain "Christians in name and appearance" who, after having been duly baptized, "converted and returned" to the Jewish "superstition," "guarding the ceremonies, rites and customs" of the Jews, and "turning away from the true faith."[5] This reversion, however, was not limited to those people. Since the measures provided by law for such cases were not employed against any of the culprits, the latter not only remained in their "blindness," but also "infected" with it "their sons and daughters and others with whom they had conversed."[6] In consequence, the Sovereigns, "zealous for the faith" and seeking to "protect their subjects against evil," appointed as Inquisitors two "venerable fathers"—Fray Juan de San Martín, bachelor of theology and prior of the monastery of San Pablo in Burgos, and Miguel de Morillo, master of theology and vicar of the Dominican Order in Spain—and instructed them to proceed against the aforesaid "infidels" with all the means and methods provided by the laws. The Kings expressed their confidence that the two appointees would carry out their duties faithfully and diligently "until the achievement of the proper end"; but they also warned them that "action to the contrary" would result in the loss of the temporalities they enjoyed and in the forfeiture of their "natural" citizenship (which would render them "strangers" in their native land).[7] Then, in an apparent demonstration of their lordship and actual control of the Inquisition, the monarchs added that they could *dismiss* the two Inquisitors and *appoint* others in their stead, in accordance with the rights granted them by the Pope.[8]

There is a marked difference between the portrayal of the "heretics" in the bull of Sixtus IV of Nov. 1, 1478, and their description in preceding papal bulls on the Inquisition, just as there is between the delineation of the heretics in the Kings' letter of Sept. 27, 1480, and that in the report of Enrique's Arbitration Committee of January 15, 1465. Noting these differences will help us realize the change that had occurred in the Kings' policy toward the conversos and the ultimate goal they sought to achieve by means of the Inquisition.

In Pope Nicholas V's bull of November 20, 1451 *(Cum sicut ad nostrum)*, addressed to Juan II of Castile, the heretics are spoken of merely as people who "observe the ceremonies of the Jews and Saracens."[9] In Pius II's bull of March 15, 1462 *(Dum fidei catholicae)*, they are referred to as "some sons of iniquity" who "disseminate various heresies, superstitions and fallacies."[10] In Sixtus IV's bull of August 1, 1475 *(Cum sicut non sine displicencia),* they are defined as "keepers of the Hebrew customs" and "imitators of the rites of the Jews."[11] Finally, in the report of the Arbitration Committee, submitted to the king in January 1465, they are branded as people "suspect of heresy" who "do not live as Christian Catholics and guard the rites and ceremonies of the infidels"; they are also designated "bad Christians."[12]

What is common to all these formulations is their failure to mention the conversos (or any other group) as the bearers of the "heretical depravity." Judged by the terms used in these statements, the heretics might belong to *any* part of Christendom, or to *several* segments of Spain's Christian population, so that one might assume that Christians of *all* origins had fallen, in some circumstances, under the influence of Jewish views. What is more, in none of the pertinent documents, save one, was the heresy even marked as specifically "Jewish." In Nicholas V's bull it is either *Jewish* or *Moslem;* in the Arbitration Committee's report (of 1465) it is still less definite, being associated with the ceremonies of the *infidels;* and in Pius II's bull it is even vaguer, as the bull speaks of *"various heresies, superstitions and fallacies."* Quite different is the Pope's description of the heresy in his bull of November 1, 1478, and so is the Kings' in the letter they made public on January 2, 1481.

For both these documents indicate unmistakably not only the identity of the heretics involved, but also the group to which they belonged. Both refer to them as *converts* to Christianity and both say that, following their conversion, they *returned to their Jewish sect*[13]; thus it becomes clear that the heretics referred to were all *converts from Judaism*—namely, Marranos or New Christians.

There can be no doubt that the description of the heretics in the latest papal bull (as in the royal letter) was made in accordance with the Kings' instructions; and the Kings knew full well what it all meant. They knew that by this portrayal of the heretics they stigmatized the Marrano group as heretical and each of its members as a potential heretic. This was, in fact, almost identical with what the conversos' foes had been claiming for three decades, and this was the message which the two monarchs wished to communicate to them at that point. They wanted the anti-Marranos to know that the Kings had come close to their view of the conversos and signaled to them that the Crown had approved their position with respect to the "remedy"— namely, that the Kings, too, thought that the heresy could be extirpated only by a campaign against the whole New Christian camp.

As in other fields of life, so in politics, signals are given by means of certain code words or allusive actions that the parties involved clearly comprehend. The orders issued on January 2, 1481, contain three such signals, indicating what the Kings had in mind when they launched their inquisitional project.

The most telling of these signals was the Kings' description of how the conversos had become Christians. We refer especially to the clause in that description which says that the conversos (or rather their ancestors) were baptized "without pressure or force" *(sin premio ni fuerza)*.[14] Evidently, this formula came to dispose of the claim that the conversions of 1391 resulted from a death threat and hence were "forced," and that those of 1412–1418 were effected under duress *(intolerable pressure)* and hence were also forced. Judging by the Kings' declaration, then, all these conversions were voluntary.

To appreciate more fully the Kings' aim in this contention, we have to compare it to the description of the conversions as given in Sixtus IV's bull. According to the Pope, the New Christians (or their ancestors) who converted to Christianity were "not absolutely forced" *(non ad id precise coacti)*. No previous papal bull concerning the Inquisition includes such an assertion, and it would not have appeared in this bull either had not (as we see it) the Kings of Spain asked the Pope to present the baptism of the conversos as voluntary. The Pope, however, could not go so far, and limited himself to Boniface VIII's formulation, which is included in canon law.[15] It was close to what the sovereigns requested, but not good enough for public consumption.

"Not absolutely forced," the Kings realized, would not be understood and might raise disturbing questions. In their own letter, therefore, the Kings avoided this difficulty and wrote in plain, unequivocal language that the converts were baptized "without pressure or force." According to common opinion, this meant that *no* threat of death was involved, which was not precisely what the Pope's bull suggested, and of course contradicted the facts of history related to the Jewish conversions in Spain. The Kings were well aware of these facts. If, however, when arguing for the establishment of the Inquisition, they substituted a wrong assertion for the truth, they must have had powerful reasons to do so. What could those reasons have been?

So secret were the moves preceding the creation of the Inquisition that no documents survived to give even an inkling of the opinions voiced in the Kings' closest circles concerning the propriety of petitioning the Pope to authorize the establishment of an Inquisition. Evidently, such opinions were expressed; they were voiced also after the arrival of the Pope's bull and echoed in later recorded discussions, from which they might be inferred. The following conjecture, which offers, we believe, a plausible answer to the question posed above, leans on such inferences from a later source.

The source we are referring to is the *Tratado*, which Alonso Ortiz, one of the Court chaplains, wrote in response to a tract against the Inquisition by the converso Juan Ramírez de Lucena, "Apostolic protonotary, Ambassador, and member of the King's Council."[16] In Tarsicio de Azcona's view, this literary debate probably took place at the commencement of the Inquisition,[17] and although Lucena's work has not come down to us, its main points may be gathered from Ortiz's citations. If we are right in our assumption that such exchanges of opinion occurred in the Court not only in 1481, but also shortly after the King had received the Pope's bull authorizing the establishment of an inquisition, we can better understand why the Marranos were described in terms that do such violence to truth.

It is reasonable to assume that in the debates held at Court concerning the Inquisition in the first half of 1478, a strong case was made *against* its establishment on the ground that an inquisition was, constitutionally, not the proper instrument to deal with the Judaizers. By the terms of its constitution, it could be argued, an inquisition could deal with heretics and apostates, but the Judaizers were neither heretics nor apostates. Since their parents were *forced* into Christianity without ever believing in any of its tenets, their infants and small children could not become Christians by being "baptized in the faith of their parents" which was what it had been—i.e., Judaism. Thus, since these children had never been Christians, they could not have *deviated* from Christianity (i.e., become heretics) or *depart* from it (and thus turn apostates). Like their parents, they were forced into Christianity and kept in it against their will out of fear, and thus they, too, must be seen as *forced converts,* who should be outside the inquisition's jurisdiction. Those who so argued of course rejected the view of *forced conversion* held by Boniface VIII, who maintained that forced conversion was effected only when physical compulsion was applied (specifically excluding "threat of death"); but they also differed from the views of famed authorities like Isidore of Seville and the Fourth Toledan Council, who recognized conversion under fear of death as forced (and hence forbidden by Christian law), but considered it valid *after the fact*.[18] The argument in favor of this conclusion might be viewed by many as casuistic, and those of the Kings' counselors who firmly opposed it could lean on the opinions of other great authorities, such as Gregory the Great, Thomas Aquinas and Duns Scotus, who were either disinclined to approve forced conversion, or specifically denied the validity of conversions of the kind produced in Spain in 1391.[19] What is more, they could rely on the fact that, with rare exceptions, all Christian authorities denounced forced conversion and canon law explicitly forbade it. It would be against the basic rules of logic, they could argue, if the victims of the grim crime of forced conversion were made to acknowledge it as a blessing and be punished if they tried to get rid of its consequences. Undoubtedly, they added that the problem of the Judaizers should not be left untreated; it should be addressed—but not by an institution like the Inquisition, which was not designed to settle it.

What conclusion could the Sovereigns draw from such a chain of ideas? Certainly, they could not rely on the theory that recognized the validity of forced conversion *after the fact,* since it was neither unchallengeable nor convincing. Nor could they rely on the acceptability of the sentences the

Inquisition would hand down on the basis of such a theory. Many people, they knew, would question these sentences on the ground of the arguments presented above, and such questioning could ultimately end in confusion and undermine the Inquisition's moral foundations. It appeared, then, that the Inquisition could proceed safely only if the Judaizers were classed as heretics; yet this could be done if the New Christians were defined as voluntary converts who had relapsed into Judaism. The sovereigns could find no other solid basis on which to build their projected tribunal.

This was the first reason for the Sovereigns' declaration that the Marranos were baptized without coercion. But there was also another reason; and this brings us back to the Sovereigns' use of "code words" as a means of maneuvering public opinion. The Kings, as we have noted, sought to inform the anti-Marrano party that they had adopted its basic view of the conversos, and there was no better way to do so, without saying it in so many words, than by asserting that the Marranos' conversion was effected "without force or pressure." For the foes of the conversos had also claimed that the conversion of the Marranos was *voluntary*, even *designed*. According to them, the aim of that design was to hurt and ruin the Old Christians; and this part of their claim the Sovereigns dropped, as it would unnecessarily complicate their position. But by adopting the anti-Marrano view about the basic nature of the New Christians' conversion (namely, that it was voluntary), they cleared the way for the Inquisition to treat the Marranos the way the anti-Marranos wanted it to treat them—that is, as outright heretics.

The second signal to the anti-Marranos is found in the order the Inquisitors appended to the Kings' declaration of Sept. 27, 1480. This order, which was published on Jan. 2, 1481, recalled the proclamation the Kings issued in Seville about the beginning of December 1480, forbidding *any person* in the archbishopric to leave his place of residence during the Inquisition's operations.[20] The term *any person* was another code word indicating the Kings' real intentions. The Old Christians understood that by "any person" the proclamation really meant "any converso." They realized that the Kings would not unnecessarily immobilize the great city of Seville and other towns in the archbishopric, and therefore had no doubt that the decree did not apply to Old Christians. They were sure that if any Old Christian asked for an exit permit, he would get it immediately, while a similar request by any New Christian would be denied. All this was obvious to the conversos, too. And this is what caused their exodus.

It was partly because they wanted to prevent this exodus that the sovereigns formulated their proclamation as they did. They realized that if the conversos *alone* were formally forbidden to leave the city, they would suspect that the Inquisition was planning to inflict some appalling blow upon them, and their rising fears would spur their escape from the Inquisition's sphere of jurisdiction. The change of formula from "any converso" to "any person" was meant to allay those fears; but the conversos were not soothed. They easily discerned the Kings' stratagem, and more and more of them sought safety in flight.

But the main coded message communicated by "any person" (which actually meant "any Marrano") was that the Inquisition was to deal with *all* conversos, whatever their fame or social status. This meant that for the Inquisition no converso was above suspicion of heresy. And this in turn suggested the fate that lay in store for the whole Marrano group.

Perhaps nothing could so win for Ferdinand and Isabella the sympathy of wide sections of the populace as the above instruction, with its evident implications concerning the *scope* of the intended persecution. But no less significant was the third signal, which clearly indicated what *kind* of inquisition the Sovereigns intended to have. It was given by their announcement that they had appointed two Dominicans as chief Inquisitors for Seville and its archbishopric. The Dominicans were then steering the anti-converso movement and led the campaign to establish the Inquisition. There was no anti-converso calumny or libel they were not ready to seize on and exploit, and it could be easily foreseen with what temper and disposition they would perform their Inquisitional assignments. The Kings exhorted them most earnestly to fulfill their duties until their assignment was accomplished, and also warned them of the punishments they could expect if they failed in their mission. Both the exhortations and the warnings were superfluous, as the two Inquisitors were only too anxious to display their fierce dedication to their task. We must conclude that these exhortations and warnings were, like other words in their letter, intended to let the anti-Marranos know with what seriousness and determination the Sovereigns were to act in all that concerned the conduct of the Inquisition. There was certainly no need to urge the two Dominicans that they faithfully perform their duties. When they were chosen as the first Inquisitors, the Sovereigns must have known of their hatred of the conversos and their desire to reduce them to the lowest level possible. There could therefore be no question about their devotion to their task, just as there could be little doubt about the manner of their procedure. In fact, they may have exceeded the expectations. So harsh and cruel, and so palpably unjust, were the sentences they rendered against the alleged Judaizers that their treatment of the accused caused violent protests that stirred the courts of both the Kings and the Pope.[21] There is no need to go here into the pertinent documents. The Pope took the side of the conversos. The Kings, on the other hand, supported the Inquisition, and thereby showed where they stood.

G. G. Coulton wrote in dealing with the Inquisition that "to ignore the question of human responsibility would make all history meaningless."[22]

Here is a case in which human responsibility—or, more precisely, moral responsibility—is the key issue we cannot ignore if we seek to understand what truly happened. When certain cautious historians and diplomatic authors, who wish to appear impartial in the controversy about the Inquisition, merely tell us that the Holy Office, in the first stage of its activity, displayed "excessive rigor," they avoid the element of "human responsibility" and consequently tell us little or nothing. For "excessive rigor" could stem from a sincere conviction as to how best to deal with the problem at hand, or from honest zeal for the faith, or, conversely, from partisan interests or uncontrollable bias. Obviously, we would like to know the main motive of that "rigor" and the attitude that inspired it. And, as we see it, there should be no difficulty in supplying answers to these questions, provided we use less ambiguous language.

Ferdinand was of course aware of the views, tendencies and attitudes of the Inquisitors he appointed, and was not at all surprised at the way they treated the conversos. Yet if he allowed the Inquisitors to go on committing their atrocities undisturbed, it was because he realized that, by their treatment of the conversos, they were giving vent not only to their own feelings, but also to those of large masses of Spaniards, and thereby satisfied the latter's desire to *smite* the Marranos as hard as possible. By saying "satisfied" we touch the key reason for the establishment of the Inquisition.

For the purpose of the Inquisition was, first of all, to *satisfy* the anti-Marrano movement—emotionally, socially and politically. A mild inquisition would not achieve this aim, and Ferdinand understood this. Since his purpose in establishing the Inquisition was to draw the masses of the people to his side, it was senseless to have it function in a manner that would ultimately draw them away from him. The choice was therefore clear. It was either to create a real instrument of persecution, or not create one at all.

The Marranos were now placed in a position resembling that of a flock in a sheepfold, from which a number of sheep were often chosen to be thrown to the wolves roaming around. The destruction was to proceed piecemeal, and there was no telling how long, or at what rate it would continue. It all depended on the King's final aims, which, it seems, he revealed to no one. Just the same, he sought—and managed—to instill in the antisemitic masses the belief that the hopes they entertained with respect to the conversos would eventually be realized.

But this does not mean that these hopes and plans were identical with his own—or, to put it plainly, that he ever contemplated the extermination of the whole Marrano community. He was not a racist and could befriend New Christians no less than Old ones, provided they earned his absolute trust. In fact, no one appreciated more than he did the talents of the conversos in administration, diplomacy, finance and the liberal professions (his personal physician in the last years of his life was the famous converso doctor Villa-lobos). However paradoxical and unrealistic it may appear, he intended to make use of these abilities despite the storm of persecution he unleashed against the conversos; and this also suggests that he meant to preserve a large part of the group intact. In time, he may have thought, he would scale down the attack. When he founded the Inquisition, however, he no doubt saw it moving, for a few years at least, in the opposite direction—that is, of expansion and escalation.

III

It would be incredible if such a widespread operation, based as it was on the false assumption that all or most of the conversos were Judaizers, did not rouse the consternation of some critical minds and lead them to propose different explanations from those officially given for the founding of the Inquisition. Since Ferdinand was considered by one and all the architect and head of the Holy Office, it was inevitable that these explanations be connected with assessments of his motives and his character. We may safely assume that Machiavelli's famous statement that religion served Ferdinand merely as a mask for the concealment of his political designs[23] was based, among other things, on the conduct of the Inquisition, which was known to have been controlled by Ferdinand. Guicciardini, too, asserted that Ferdinand employed religion as a cover for his ambitions, which he generally defined as "greed."[24] Then Bernardo Segni, Guicciardini's disciple, speaking explicitly about the Spanish Inquisition, combined his master's view with that of Machiavelli when he concluded that Ferdinand established that tribunal for both financial gain and political domination.[25]

It was no accident that such views were expressed in Italy, where the Pope and his officials were well acquainted with the performance of the Spanish Inquisition and where the critical opinions stemming from their circles were supported by the numerous accounts of the Marranos who flocked to Rome in search of refuge. No Spaniard in Ferdinand's Spain would dare say openly that politics and finance motivated the King's "religious zeal"; and no one could, under the Inquisition's censorship, relate such motives to its establishment. It was only after Spain's conquest by Napoleon and the abolition of the Inquisition by the Cortes of Cádiz (1813) that such views were expressed by Spanish authors both at home and abroad.

The first—and still the most influential—of these authors was Juan Antonio Llorente, whose *Critical History of the Spanish Inquisition* (1817) opened the modern historiography of the subject. Llorente asserted that, apart from political considerations, the financial motive was the main factor impelling Ferdinand to set up the new tribunal. According to Llorente, the few verified cases (or "examples," as he put it) of crypto-Jews living among the conversos were sufficient to give Ferdinand the "religious pretext" he needed to implement his plan.[26] This was a charge of the utmost gravity that impugned the reputation of both Ferdinand and the Inquisition and, consequently, was suppressed in Spain following the restoration of the old regime. It was therefore only after the second abolition of the Inquisition (in 1834) that Castillo y Mayone, in his *Tribunal de la Inquisición* (1835), could renew the charge that "Judaism served [merely] as a *pretext* to establish the Inquisition in Spain, but the real object [of its establishment] was [Ferdinand's] cupidity of the confiscations."[27] "Superstition and despotism," said Castillo, "converted that tribunal into a ministry of Police and a major customhouse" for the properties of those who were declared heretics. These were of course Llorente's ideas, more trenchantly expressed.

Twelve years later Castillo's assertions were echoed in Spain by another scholar, whose vast erudition and intellectual courage matched his penetrating insights. In his memorable *History of the Jews of Spain* (1847), Adolfo de Castro minced no words in assailing Ferdinand's policies and tactics, and exposed what he saw as the background conditions that impelled the king to establish the Inquisition. Ferdinand, he said, had "exhausted his treasury" in the wars he waged to secure his dominion, and unable to "extricate himself from his troubles, . . . he looked to the Inquisition as the sole means of augmenting the royal revenues." This was, he emphasized, *'the true reason why he consented to the proposals of the Dominican Friars.'* Later on, Castro added, the war with Granada and his warlike enterprises overseas further taxed his depleted treasury and made him rely on the Inquisition to replenish his vanishing resources. Hence, Castro concluded, "it was on the confiscation of the possessions of the condemned conversos that all his zeal for the exaltation of the Christian faith in his land and seigniories depended."[28]

These theories, according to which financial or political (and not religious) motives induced the Kings of Spain to establish the Inquisition, appeared also to other scholars preferable to the old view that religion—or, more precisely, the Judaic heresy—lay at the heart of the Inquisitional undertaking. What truth was there in these explanations?

A. Domínguez Ortiz, an eminent scholar whose works on the conversos offer notable contributions to the study of their life and problem, is one of the many modern authors who stick to the old ("religious") view. Accordingly, in his most recent work on the subject, he concludes that financial considerations played no part in the decision to establish the Inquisition.[29] On the contrary, he maintains, the Kings took that measure despite their realization of the grave damage and injury that the Inquisition was to cause to Spain's economy. As evidence he presents Isabella's statement on the subject, according to the testimony of Pulgar.[30] We may add to this Ferdinand's own assertion on a different occasion.[31]

That financial considerations were not the *prime* motive for the Catholic Kings to establish the Inquisition is a view to which we can readily subscribe: it agrees with the conclusion that emerged from our analysis of the various issues involved. If other considerations of major importance had not moved them toward the inquisitional solution, they would not have come to think of the Inquisition in terms of financial gain. It is difficult to say when, or whether, Isabella came to assess the Inquisition in such terms.[32] But Ferdinand was a different case. Once he was persuaded that the Inquisition was the only means of settling the converso problem, he decided to make every possible use of it as a financial resource.[33]

Domínguez Ortiz, however, does not share this opinion. "The Inquisition," he says, "does not seem to have been good business" for the Spanish Kings. In the first period of its activity, he agrees, the Crown benefited from the confiscations "to an extent we cannot fix," but "a few years later the Inquisition became a burden," because the income it derived from the confiscations it had made "did not suffice to cover its expenses."[34] Domínguez, moreover, seems to doubt that the Crown had any financial interest in the Inquisition even in the "first stage of the abundant confiscations." His evidence: "A part of the income was assigned for works of piety or for the erection of sumptuous constructions" (such as the Church of St. Thomas in Avila or St. John in Guadalupe). "Some quantities," he concedes, "were spent on the war with Granada, and others were included in the royal treasury," but these sums must have been smaller than the losses incurred through the "economic breakdown caused by the persecution [of the conversos] and later by the expulsion of the Jews."[35]

All this, however, in no way affects our position on the problem before us. The erection of sumptuous buildings with the funds of the Inquisition suggests an abundance, rather than a scarcity, of the resources obtained through the confiscations; and we really do not know the size of the "sums" drawn from the Inquisition for the war with Granada or for other needs of the royal treasury. In any case, conjecture on this matter would be besides the point. For even if the income of the Holy Office proved small or illusory after the first years of its activity, it does not mean that the expectations were not high when the Inquisition was founded; hence, these expectations may have served the King as an inducement to establish the tribunal. The conversos were held to be extremely rich, and Ferdinand may well have shared this notion. When, in 1478, following the War of Succession, he was faced with an empty treasury and a financially exhausted country, the fabled treasures of the conversos could have strengthened his inclination to establish the

Inquisition. Finance was not the *major* factor, but it further tilted the weighted scales of his various calculations.

It can hardly be doubted that the Sovereigns *foresaw* the economic harm the Inquisition would do and took it into account. But other interests, more crucial in their eyes, overrode that important consideration. Essentially, Domínguez agrees with us on this, except that in his opinion these interests were religious, while in ours they were social and political.

The question, then, comes down to Ferdinand's material expectations from the Inquisition within the limits of the liabilities it entailed. Like other rulers in financial straits, he could ordinarily be expected to exchange long-range advantages for immediate gains. But Ferdinand did not face that kind of dilemma. He had anyway sacrificed the greater part of the conversos' long-term economic value for his kingdoms, and was prepared to suffer the economic losses to be caused by their persecution through the Inquisition. Extreme financial pressures concentrated his mind on the alternative left him—namely, to try, as best he could, to turn the liability into an asset.

That asset was of course the profit he hoped to reap from the Inquisition's operations, and this in turn depended entirely on his assessment of the conversos' wealth. Indubitably, Ferdinand could obtain sound estimates of the conversos' fortunes from his tax farmers and treasurers, and on the basis of these estimates he could more or less envisage the possible income of the Inquisition. As we do not possess this information, we can try to get at his thinking from the other end—that is, through what we know or may conjecture about the *income* of the Inquisition from the New Christians in Spain.

Domínguez is far off the mark in his attempt to minimize the income of the Holy Office throughout the period of its operation. It is true that in certain times and places the income of the Inquisition did not cover its costs, but this does not mean that at most times and places its income did not exceed its costs by far. To assess the income of the Inquisition through its exactions from New Christians, we must bear in mind its *total* intake in at least its first five decades. Today, however, we cannot compute this total on the basis of authentic, adequate data, simply because we lack vital information for many years, places, and types of exaction. The excellent work done in this field by Tarsicio de Azcona in his *Isabel la Católica* (1964) has certainly broadened our knowledge of the subject,[36] but still too many blanks remain in his chart to make an overall calculation possible.

Fortunately, we possess some general figures that give us an idea of the sums involved. On June 5, 1522, Don Juan Manuel, lord of Belmonte and Charles V's ambassador to the court of the Pope, wrote the Emperor that the conversos of Aragon and Catalonia were endeavoring to get a judgment from the Rota, the papal Appellate Court, against the confiscations of goods from those of them who confessed voluntarily to their heresies. The ambassador cautioned the King that, if such a judgment were obtained, he would have to return "more than a million ducats of the sums he had acquired in this manner."[37] This indication may serve as key to an assessment. It is hard to believe that the ambassador referred to the sums exacted by Charles *himself* from the voluntary confessors in the two provinces within the first five years of his reign; on the other hand, it is no more plausible that he referred to the exactions of the same category made in those provinces since the *beginning* of the Inquisition. Be that as it may, the fortunes confiscated from the *condemned* conversos in the kingdom of Aragon (including Valencia) in thirty-five years of the Inquisition's activity must have been far larger than those received from the conversos who *confessed voluntarily*; and therefore it could hardly be considered an exaggeration to assess the total of the confiscations in Aragon at 2.5 million ducats. The amounts extracted from the conversos in Castile would surely treble this estimate, so that the total confiscations in both countries would rise to 10 million ducats. This is indeed the very estimate indicated in another source.

"In 1524," says Henry Charles Lea, "the licenciado Tristan de León, in an elaborate memorial addressed to Charles V, asserted that Ferdinand and Isabella obtained from this source [i.e., the amounts wrung from the victims of the Inquisition] the enormous amount of more than 10,000,000 ducats, which greatly assisted them in their war against the Moors."[38] This was certainly an enormous amount, but not excessive compared to the sum mentioned in Juan Manuel's letter and when the various sources from which it was gathered are duly taken into account. Nor was it evidently too great a share of the conversos' wealth. Tarsicio de Azcona was certainly right when he said: "Against one case like that of the father of the bishop of Segovia, Juan Arias Dávila, in which . . . a fortune of 300,000 ducats was involved, we might find dozens of culprits with small fortunes, sufficient only for their maintenance."[39] But the Dávilas were not the only converso millionaires; there were scores of extremely rich New Christians who could boast huge treasures and estates, and there were of course the numerous members of the middle class and the small earners of the lower classes. The income derived from the fines and confiscations extracted from these groups was not despised by the Inquisition, either. The small sums, too, were eagerly gathered and combined with the large ones to form the grand total.

Llorente did not know of the 10 million ducats that Tristan de León mentioned as the income of the Inquisition in the period of the Catholic Kings; but bearing in mind what he gathered from Manuel, and no doubt from many other data, he reached the conclusion that financial considerations were Ferdinand's main motive in establishing the Inquisition. Similarly, Ranke was unaware of the total quoted by Tristan de León in his memorial, but the datum mentioned by Juan Manuel sufficed for him to conclude that the financial factor played a great role in Ferdinand's decision.[40] And on similar grounds did Castillo and Castro form their own opinions on the subject.

Nevertheless, we do not go as far as Llorente and his followers. We believe that Ferdinand's *main* motive in establishing the Inquisition was his need to act on the converso problem in such a way as to secure internal stability and retain his people's support. But the prospect of supplying his hard-pressed treasury by means that could be considered legal did not form a *minor* element in his careful calculations. It never became the decisive factor, but it was a *major* inducement for Ferdinand's resolve to embark on that extreme anti-converso course.

IV

In attempting to determine the various reasons for the establishment of the Inquisition, we should also examine the more controversial view that the Inquisition was conceived, from the very start, as a means of attaining monarchic absolutism. The idea may have first occurred to the Florentine historians mentioned above. In modern times it was enunciated by Ranke, in his *Princes and Peoples of Southern Europe* (1827),[41] and supported by such leading scholars as Hefele[42] and François Guizot.[43]

The historical foundations of the theory are apparent. For more than two centuries since Alfonso X, Castile's kings had endeavored to transform their rule into a government by divine right, but were repeatedly frustrated in this effort by a nobility no less determined to increase its own powers. In the 15th century, the absolutist drive reached its peak under Juan II and then fell to its lowest ebb under Enrique IV. In these circumstances, Ferdinand may have concluded that by ordinary means, military or political, royalty in Spain would never achieve its goal, and that only an inquisition controlled by the Kings could force the nobility to surrender to the monarch and make an absolute regime possible.

The core of this theory, then, is the assumption that the Kings despaired of the political process as a possible means of achieving their ends. But the facts at our disposal do not support this assumption. When the Kings asked the pope to authorize the Inquisition (1478), and even more so when the tribunal was established (1480), most rebellious nobles had already been subdued, while the power of others was severely curtailed by the reduction of their incomes and estates.[44] There remained only the comparatively minor problem of the small piratic nobles in the northwest (Galicia), whom the Kings planned to crush by military action—a plan they implemented in 1480. Thus, when the Spanish Inquisition was established, the nobility posed no threat to the Kings, while the latter were constantly strengthening their authority, so that one could believe that—in the not too distant future—it might serve as a basis for absolute rule.

Nor was it for the sake of absolutism that Ferdinand attempted to subject the Spanish prelates to the jurisdiction of the Inquisition. For what he meant to achieve by that attempt was the subjugation of the *converso* bishops, whose exemption from the Inquisition's prosecution served to undermine the prestige of the Holy Office and the campaign it was conducting against the conversos. Innocent VIII refused to grant him that privilege, which Nicholas V (in 1451) had granted Juan II, and allowed the Inquisition only to collect data in evidence against "suspected" bishops, and then submit that evidence to Rome for consideration and decision.[45] This limited right allowed the Inquisition to embarrass, humiliate and otherwise embitter the life of any bishop it chose to "investigate," and from the choices it made for this purpose we can see that, under Ferdinand, it was only converso prelates that the Inquisition sought to bring down. Two New Christian bishops—Arias Dávila of Segovia and Pedro Aranda of Calahorra—and an archbishop, Hernando de Talavera of Granada, were selected as targets of the Inquisition's inquiry during Ferdinand's reign; and the reasons for this selection are not hard to see. Arias Dávila incurred the wrath of the Inquisition when he threw its agents out of Segovia, and he no doubt also aroused its cupidity by the enormous family fortunes he possessed. Pedro de Aranda served in Rome as Master of the Sacred Palace, a key position in the papal administration, in which, it was believed, he could do much damage to the Inquisition; and Hernando de Talavera, who was revered for his saintliness, gave too much honor to the converso name for the Inquisition not to try to destroy him. Above all, it was important for the Inquisition to prove that no converso, however honored, or reputed for his faithfulness and piety, could not be a secret heretic. And thus even someone like the bishop of Segovia, who *condemned Jews to death on a charge of ritual murder*,[46] or Talavera, who *wrote a long tract against the Judaizers*,[47] or one like Pedro de Aranda, who *sat at the heart of the Church organization*, could be, in effect, a heretic in disguise.

We may conclude therefore that the subjugation of the prelates by the Inquisition was not sought by Ferdinand to promote absolutism any more than was the subjugation of the nobles. As a matter of fact, the unruly prelates (including Carrillo, the most restive of them) were subdued before the Inquisition was established, and there was certainly no need to establish an inquisition to bring about their suppression.

Lea, moreover, dismissed Ranke's theory on the basis of the whole Inquisitional record.[48] Neither Ferdinand nor his successors until the ascent of the Bourbon kings, he claimed, employed the Inquisition as a means of oppressing lay or clerical magnates. To be sure, Lea mentioned the famous trials of Carranza, Antonio Pérez, and Villanueva as notable exceptions to this "rule."

But since none of these cases occurred in Ferdinand's reign, we may perhaps take the record as an index of Ferdinand's original intentions.

One wonders, of course, at the uninterrupted peace that prevailed between Ferdinand and the great magnates. Part of the answer may lie in the fact that Ferdinand knew, as Lea pointed out, how to divert the interests of the nobility to the military, diplomatic and administrative tasks in his broadened dominions; but many Spanish nobles remained on their estates, and the lasting peace between the nobility and the monarchy during the reign of Ferdinand and his successors cannot therefore be explained solely by the reason suggested by Lea. We do know that at least some of the nobles were extremely unhappy with their role in the state. Is it, then, possible that the "peace" between the grandees and the sovereigns resulted, after all, from the perturbing fear the Inquisition instilled in the hearts of many nobles?

To be sure, if we examine the behavior of the nobility toward Ferdinand and his successors, we shall have to conclude that fear *was* the cause of their usual submission to the monarch's will. Yet while fear was the cause, it was not so much the Inquisition that the nobles feared as the power behind it, which was that of the King.

This is clearly attested by the fact that no attack on the Inquisition by any noble took place throughout the first period of Ferdinand's reign, which lasted more than twenty-five years (January 1481–June 1506), nor during the second period of his rule, which lasted for almost a decade (1507–1516). Only in the short interval between these periods, several months after Ferdinand had left Castile (in the wake of his resignation from Castile's regency), did two Cordovan nobles lead an assault on the Inquisition which disrupted its activity in their city; and shortly after Ferdinand's death, some nobles rose in revolt against Jiménez, then both Regent and Inquisitor-General. Jiménez, however, used his army to suppress them. No inquisitional order or threat would have brought about this result, and Jiménez, no doubt, would have considered such a move both useless and impolitic.

Ferdinand, like Jiménez, clearly understood that the Inquisition was not an effective instrument to reduce the nobility to obedience, if it rose as a concerted force. It would be ridiculous to declare the great nobles heretics, or suspect them of Judaic tendencies; and if such attempts were made against *some* of them, they would all before long rise against the King. When Philip IV made such a move against one nobleman (the Marquis of Villanueva), it proved to be a blunder too costly to repeat, and it could serve to demonstrate Ferdinand's sagacity in avoiding such hazardous ventures. Yet the case of the Marquis could also prove that no single noble, however popular or innocent, could emerge victorious from a clash with the Inquisition. The conflict ended with the surrender of Villanueva, or of what was left of him—a broken reed.

The peace between the nobility and the monarchy, therefore, was actually based on a tacit understanding that the King would not employ the Inquisition against the nobility in any disagreement he might have with its members. But there was no ironclad guarantee that, in exceptional cases, the cohorts of the Inquisition would not be directed against some isolated magnate, lay or ecclesiastic, and persecute him to the bitter end. In fact, every nobleman was likely to suspect that *he* might be that exceptional case; and in many instances such suspicions could increase a noble's subservience to the monarch.

We ought, however, to mention another factor, likewise connected with the Inquisition, which probably played a greater part in subjugating the Spanish nobility to the Crown. We have pointed out that by 1478, most of the restless nobles of Castile had been vanquished or reduced to obedience, and the Kings could feel no urgent need to set up an inquisition to aid in their suppression. But that does not mean that the problem of the relations between the Crown and the nobility ceased to occupy their minds. Never could they forget the gloomy history of Castile in the reigns of the two kings who preceded them—reigns in which the nobles' attacks on the Crown were interrupted only by brief intervals of peace, and they could of course suspect that their own peace with the nobility was no more than a truce—a part of the same cycle. Determined to prevent further assaults upon the Crown, they carefully weighed every plan of action, every major measure, and every policy proposed from the standpoint of the impact it might have on the nobles—that is, whether it would add to the strength of the nobility or weaken its potential for disturbance.

The plan to set up an inquisition in Castile must likewise have been subject to this test. If in contemplating it the Kings had concluded that the Inquisition would increase the power of the nobility, they would doubtless have withdrawn from the project altogether. But their examination of the possibilities involved convinced them that they could expect the opposite. What they wanted to gain through the Inquisition, let us recall, was the sympathy and support of the urban masses; and this meant to get the support of the cities. But from this point a straight line of thinking must have led them to consider the impact of that goal upon the conduct of the nobility. If the Crown forged ties of friendship with the cities (or, more precisely, their Old Christian populations), the cities would inevitably be prevented from becoming allies of the nobles against the Crown. And thus, once the cities were neutralized, the nobility would be neutralized too, for no nobiliary revolt could be expected to succeed without urban support. This, then, was another way in which the Inquisition could help the Kings tame the nobility—not by inspiring the nobles with dread, but simply by denying them the main bases of power on which they could rely in a conflict with the King.

The above observations, therefore, may be summarized as follows. The Inquisition was not established as a vehicle for royal absolutism in Spain. But when the sovereigns considered the possible effect it might have on the relations between the cities and the nobles, they could not fail to realize that the Inquisition would weaken the nobility by depriving it of the cities' assistance. This must have encouraged them to proceed with their plan to set up the Inquisition, though it was not a major factor in determining their position. It was only an added argument, an auxiliary reason that helped them make up their mind in that direction.

V

Associated with the question whether the Inquisition was established to serve Spanish absolutism is the oft-repeated query whether, rather than a papal, it was a royal institution. The first to have answered this query affirmatively included leading Catholic scholars in Germany of the 19th century, such as Hefele, Gams and Hergenröther. The gist of their view was that the Spanish Inquisition, though it assumed the *forms* of an ecclesiastic tribunal and worked within the framework of canon law, was actually an instrument of secular authority that served primarily the interests of the state.[49]

In a frontal attack on these Catholic scholars, Lea accused them of having taken their position in order to "relieve the Church from the responsibility" for the Inquisition's disreputable acts. By attributing this motive to the above scholars, without evidence or argument, Lea seems to have abandoned the rules of fairness to which he normally adhered, and exposed himself to the equally unfair charge that his own definition of the Inquisition as a religious court stemmed from the fact that, as a non-Catholic, he wished to relate the faults of the Inquisition to the Catholic Church. Nor did Lea strengthen his case when he noted that "in the Catholic reaction since the time of Hefele, the most advanced writers of that faith no longer seek to apologize for the Inquisition and to put forward *royal* predominance to relieve it from responsibility. They rightly represent it as an ecclesiastical tribunal which discharged the duty of preserving the religious purity for which it was created."[50]

The writers who, in Lea's opinion, "rightly" presented the case of the Holy Office, and to whom he referred as reliable authorities for the opposite view of the Inquisition, were Orti y Lara, García Rodrigo and Ricardo Cappa. That these writers did not "apologize" for the Inquisition, as Lea put it, is true enough, but this was because they saw no reason for an apology, having found nothing wrong in its performance. For them the activities of the Spanish Inquisition were all just and holy, dedicated to the noble and vital task, which was the extirpation of heresy from the land; and it would not occur to any of them that the activities of the Inquisition implemented any plan formed for non-religious reasons. Likewise, it would not occur to them that Ferdinand was anything but a devout Catholic, carrying out his religious duties under the supreme guidance of the pope.

No one should have known better than Lea that the Inquisition was not a Church tribunal in the ordinary sense of the word. To be sure, the popes authorized the aims of the Inquisition and allowed the Inquisitors to act in their name as formal apostolic messengers. In addition, they could supervise the activities of the Inquisition, insist on revising them, or suspend them altogether. To them was also reserved the right of sentencing prelates suspected of heresy, and it was to the sphere of papal authority that the highest court of appeals belonged. Theoretically, therefore, the popes' power was great, and if one wishes to charge them, as many authors did, with *moral* responsibility for the Inquisition, one may find grounds for such a charge. Practically, however, the popes were rarely capable of challenging the might of Spain's kings, and although they tried repeatedly to do so, they usually retreated before a crucial test. The reason was that the papacy headed not only a religious but also a political organization, and seeking to play both ends, it often sacrificed, as is well known, religious principle for political expediency.

Nevertheless, there was frequent tension between the papacy and the Crown respecting the conduct of the Spanish Inquisition, and this tension occasionally generated clashes, which strained the relations between the two powers. In these clashes, both sides sometimes stretched their antagonisms almost to the point of a break, without, however, allowing a break to take place. The popes, to be sure, displayed in most cases less stamina than the kings, and in consequence gradually surrendered to the latter more and more of their prerogatives. Nevertheless, they never gave up their ultimate authority over the Inquisition. Nor did the kings want them to do so. It was in their interest that the Inquisition appear to be the highest ecclesiastic tribunal.

Thus, it is impossible to answer the question whether the Inquisition was papal or royal in absolute terms. Considering its ties to and dependence on the pope, which were by no means merely formal, the Inquisition was *in part* papal; but bearing in mind the real power behind it, the one that determined its policies and actions, it must be admitted that the papal part was minor, and hence that the Inquisition was *mainly* royal. For it was the king who nominated and virtually appointed the chief Inquisitors and also dismissed them,[51] determined the salaries of the Inquisitors, received their reports, and gave them orders. Furthermore, it was the king who supervised the confiscations, instructed the receivers, scolded or encouraged them, and it was solely in accord with *his* wishes that the officials of the Inquisition, who were *his* officials, made financial deals with sons of condemned persons and freed them

from disabilities imposed by canon law against payments to the royal exchequer. More than the pope, the king bent Church laws for profits whose size
he himself determined, without giving the Church any of the income, or even
seeking its consent or counsel. To be sure, from time to time the popes tried
to interfere with the practices and procedures of the Spanish Inquisition, but
more often than not they were rudely defied, and on the few occasions that
they had their way, they had it on matters, in a manner and to an extent that
the king considered necessary, or unavoidable.

The Spanish Inquisition, then, was a royal tribunal for all its *major* purposes—almost as Gams and Hegenröther claimed, even though it was mod-
eled according to the patterns, rules and guidelines of the medieval
inquisition. It is surprising that Lea did not recognize this fact, which is so
incontestably demonstrated by the evidence which he himself had so diligently assembled. Indeed, since it is apparent from this evidence that the
pope's authority over the Inquisition was minimal—that is, confined to the
extremely narrow limits which the Kings of Spain assigned to him from
the outset—one might have expected Lea to pose the question why, to begin
with, the Kings turned to the *Pope* with the request to authorize the establishment of the Inquisition, and did not create an *episcopal* inquisition (of the kind
proposed by Oropesa and Pacheco), and thus be less exposed to papal
interference and the requirement of papal consent. As we see it, the answer
to this question reveals both Ferdinand's expectations from the Inquisition
and his political prudence.

It was not difficult for Ferdinand to foresee that the Inquisition, as he
planned and envisaged its activities, would generate harsh criticisms, bitter
complaints and severe charges on the part of the conversos and others who
might take their side; and he wanted to divert such censures to the Pope, who
could shield the Inquisition against such attacks. One of the documents
published by Lea reflects this intention clearly. Speaking of the massive
confiscations by the Inquisition of the property of its victims and their
children, Lea says that there was evidently "popular repugnance to this
spoliation and no one wished to be responsible for it. Ferdinand, in a proclamation of October 29, 1485, declared that *the confiscations were made by order
of the Pope, in discharge of his* [i.e., Ferdinand's] *conscience and by virtue of his
obedience to Holy Mother Church.*"[52] Of course, all confiscations of heretics'
possessions were in a sense made at the pope's order, since it was he who
authorized the proceedings of the Inquisition in accordance with canon law;
but the pope did not order the *specific* confiscations carried out by the
Inquisition, or confirm that the instructions of canon law were correctly
applied to the cases in question. Ferdinand's reliance on the pope in this
instance was merely a clever ruse, a move in his battle of public opinion, and
it contained no more evidence of his sincerity than his claims regarding his

"obedience" to Holy Mother Church and the "discharge of his conscience."

We should, however, note two more reasons for the preference Ferdinand gave to a papal inquisition over an episcopal one. To begin with, an episcopal inquisition would have made him depend too much on the bishops, whose stand as a group was unpredictable and some of whom could be reasonably expected to take different positions on the converso question. In case of disagreements he might have with these bishops, they could be expected to seek assistance from the pope, and thus the king might be faced with a two-front opposition, domestic and external, at the same time. This was of course an important consideration based on what he could easily foresee. But the second reason was even more important. It hinged upon Ferdinand's clear understanding that, to run the Inquisition, he would need moral backing of a kind that episcopal support could not provide. For the bishops were known to depend on the Crown for the attainment of promotions and preferred positions, and even if they all cooperated with the king, their cooperation was likely to be often perceived as a mere manifestation of self-interest. Ferdinand's eyes, therefore, turned to Rome. If formally sanctioned and supervised by the pope, the highest religious authority in Christendom, the Inquisition, he realized, would assume credibility that no ordinary bishop could give it. Royal support of such an inquisition would be viewed as compliance with papal instructions, while its being backed by both pope and king—i.e., the spiritual and temporal powers—would make it hard to question its motives and resist its decisions. For this double gain of augmented authority and increased guarantee against possible trouble, Ferdinand was willing to pay the price of minimal papal interference.

VI

Such were the public or monarchic motives that impelled King Ferdinand to establish the Inquisition and also determined, to a large extent, the nature and scope of its operation. But besides these motives, which we called "public," because they all related to the governance of the state, there was a personal factor that played a major part in producing the above results. It consisted of the character and abilities of King Ferdinand, without whom the Inquisition might not have been launched—and if it had, it might not have assumed those special *forms* by which it exerted so powerful an influence. Hence, to comprehend the Spanish Inquisition, it is necessary to understand the man who created it, conceived its design, molded its structure, guided and controlled it, and infused it with his spirit throughout the first three decades of its eventful existence.

We have already indicated our departure from Lea's definition of the Spanish Inquisition as an "ecclesiastical tribunal." Now we must part even more completely from his view of the real master of that institution. In Lea's opinion, Ferdinand of Aragon was "sincere in his religious convictions,"[53] or as he put it elsewhere in his work, a "sincerely bigoted" man.[54] Accordingly, he saw in the Inquisition not merely a "financial or political instrument" but "a means of defending and advancing the faith."[55] Proof of this Lea sees in Ferdinand's letter of September 30, 1509, to the Inquisitor Juan Alonso de Navia, after witnessing an auto-da-fe in Valladolid, in which he expressed the "great pleasure that it had given him as a means of advancing the honor and glory of God and the exaltation of the Holy Catholic faith."[56] Lea also presents as evidence of Ferdinand's devoutness his responses to Inquisitors who reported on the autos they had celebrated, responses phrased "in terms of high satisfaction, urging them to increased zeal."[57] As we shall show further on, we cannot see in these expressions either indications of sincere belief or strong religious motivation. Taken together with other evidence of Ferdinand's religious attitudes, they appear quite different from how Lea perceived them.

Nor do we see in the concessions Ferdinand made to some of the sufferers from the Inquisition's confiscations—or in the occasional orders he issued in support of some "honest claims" of its victims—a manifestation of "kindliness" or a "spirit of justice," which Lea saw in them.[58] Since Ferdinand gave these orders to his officials in confidential correspondence, they could not have possibly reflected, Lea believed, "a hypocritical affectation of fairness."[59] Lea appears right when these orders are considered within the limited scope of the incidents involved. When viewed in conjunction with Ferdinand's policies, however, they assume quite a different meaning. Lea, in fact, makes a major error in reading Ferdinand's intentions.

For Ferdinand was possessed with *one* desire, which was to strengthen and expand his power; and to attain this end, he knew no other means save the art of politics. Indeed, rather than an art, politics was to him a science—the science of gaining and expanding power, which to him was not only "beyond good and evil," but also beyond man's deepest emotions. His political conduct reflects his belief that the statesman must not only learn how to overcome, or at least how to control, his feelings, but also how to suppress his moral judgments. Apparently, Ferdinand was never much troubled by his personal moral and religious requirements, and Prudencio de Sandoval may have sensed this when he noted how the King, in the last days of his life, kept avoiding his confessor. "I came here," he said to him, "to negotiate state affairs, not to discharge my conscience."[60]

Yet this is not to say that he was a Cesare Borgia, ostentatiously displaying contempt for moral values. Ferdinand, in contrast, sought to appear ethical and religious; for he accurately assessed the crucial part played by ethics and religion in human affairs. Instead of openly defying morality, he sought to employ it for his own ends. He knew how to evaluate mass feelings as a factor in social life, and used the force of popular passions (to borrow a metaphor from later times) as steam to move his ship of state. Thus he harnessed the hatred for the conversos and the laws of the Church concerning heresy to advance his political interests, all the while trying to appear as Holy Mother Church's true son, whose eagerness to guard religious law even exceeded his desire to guard the civil one.

In civil life the task involved no problem, since it fully agreed with his political aims (for a state could be governed well, he believed, only when duly governed by law). In the case of the Inquisition, however, where Church law was often flouted, he acted *as if* he knew little or nothing about the abuses referred to by the critics, and *as if* he had implicit faith in the legal and moral propriety of the Inquisitors. To implant this belief in his country and beyond it, he had to rely on his talents for simulation, persuasion and manipulation of public opinion. Few statesmen surpassed him in these capacities.

In his relations with his officials, including the Inquisitors, Ferdinand tried to project the same image that he displayed to the general public. He clearly understood that his public image would be much affected by the rumors and reports emanating from his inner circles. Accordingly, he refrained from formally inquiring into the Inquisition's judicial proceedings, so as to avoid responsibility for its verdicts and prevent anyone from disputing his claim that he had full confidence in the Inquisitors' judgments. But he often interfered in the gathering and division of the Inquisition's spoils, on which occasions he could show the "receivers" his interest in their work, as well as his insistence on the fulfillment of the laws when they were in favor of the victims. He wanted the receivers of compensations to know that they must respect the law just as he did (which would enhance his reputation as a lawful king), and he wanted to accustom them to keep the laws and thereby check their inclination to theft and embezzlement (which would of course increase the Crown's income). He could show largess in small matters, and occasionally appear even magnanimous, when he knew that most of the great confiscations were to go to his exchequer; but there was no fairness in his conduct for fairness' sake and no real magnanimity of the heart. Lea says that Ferdinand was not "naturally cruel" and "took no pleasure in human suffering"[61] (which appears to be a correct observation); but Lea forgot to add that neither could "human suffering" stir sympathy or pain in him, or deter him from implementing his plans. He could coldly sacrifice throngs of civilians for political ends, just as he could sacrifice battalions of soldiers to win a contest on the battlefield. Essentially, he viewed both civilians and soldiers as peons in his game of power; but he did his best to conceal the fact.

To consider such a morally unprincipled man "religiously sincere" is to us unthinkable; nor can we regard him as a "*sincere* bigot"; for a "sincere bigot" fiercely *believes* in the notions that dictate his actions. Ferdinand, for his part, did not wish to be regarded as bigoted in any sense. Had he been a bigot, or wished to be considered one, he would not have filled his court with Marranos when the Inquisition sought to make every Marrano appear potentially guilty of heresy—i.e., of the gravest religious crime in the world. Bigotry would have precluded such conduct, but the laws permitted it—and this is what counted with Ferdinand. He labored to present himself as a *stickler for the law,* both civil and canon.

This simulated faithfulness to the laws of the Church, which were frequently violated by the Inquisition, must be extended to his attitude toward the popes. While publicly he spoke reverently of papal authority and presented himself as the pope's loyal servant, he actually held the popes in contempt, defied their instructions when they displeased him and vehemently demanded that they be revoked and that the popes do his bidding. He viewed the papacy as a political tool which could be useful to him in attaining his ends, and he could hardly contain his wrath and impatience when it did not live up to his expectations. When he addressed the pope in polite or measured terms, it was either because he feared his resistance, or because he thought that a friendly approach would serve him better than a rude one; but he never felt for the pope the reverence due to the head of the Catholic Church. In fact, he viewed the popes as crafty politicians who cared for their interests precisely as he did, except that he considered them much beneath himself, and seemed to have frothed at the need to ask them favors, as if he were a beggar and they the benefactors. He appears to have developed a hatred for the popes, as Adolfo de Castro correctly observed.

Although, said Castro, that hatred was "often on the very verge of bursting upon the court of Rome, it remained locked up in the prison of his own breast"[62] until "at last it came to an open exhibition" on the occasion of some action of Pope Julius II, which he regarded as prejudicial to his rights. Since this action took place in Naples, he wrote to Count Ribagorza, his viceroy, a letter in which he not only chided him severely for yielding to the Pope's instructions, but also indicated to him, in "intemperate expressions," what he should have done to earn his [i.e., Ferdinand's] approval. *"Why,"* he asked, *"did you not comply with our wishes and strangle the legate who presented the brief to you?* It is quite clear that the Pope will . . . do the same in other kingdoms, for the sake of extending his jurisdiction. *But good viceroys proceed in a summary way with such fellows,* and by the infliction of a single punishment, prevent others from making similar attempts."[63]

That this outburst was not spontaneous but calculated, reflecting latent feelings and long-pondered behavior, is indicated by the contents and spirit of the letter he addressed to the Pope through his ambassador to the curia.

The letter presented a vile threat to the papacy, a threat that could hardly be expected from a king who claimed to be an executor of the pope's orders and a guardian of the Church's laws. He communicated that threat to his viceroy, too, and also stated, in that communication that he was "*positively determined, should his Holiness refuse to revoke the brief, as well as the acts performed by its authority, to deprive him of the obedience now paid him by the realms of Castile and Aragon,* and to take such other steps and make such other provisions as a case of such gravity and emergency requires."[64]

The "gravity" and "emergency" referred to by the King concerned, surprisingly, only several excommunications, which the Pope declared in Naples without consulting the King—a step which may not have been common but which was certainly within the Pope's prerogatives. Without even seeking an explanation for that step, Ferdinand reacted with the grim ultimatum that the papal brief be immediately revoked if the Pope did not wish to lose the allegiance of both Castile and Aragon. This was how Ferdinand displayed his care for the unity and glory of the Catholic Church, in the name of which he so often claimed to act. In fact, his oft-declared devotion to religion masked an essentially cynical attitude toward the ideals of Christianity and the interests of the Church.

To overlook these elements in Ferdinand's tactics obscures the reasons for his behavior, and particularly his behavior with respect to the Inquisition. Lea, who discerned and correctly noted several important features of his character, missed (or misinterpreted) other characteristics which would have required him to change his portrait of Ferdinand. Yet it is only the *true* portrait that can help explain his motives in establishing the Inquisition and determining its course of action.

To justify the portrait he drew of Ferdinand, Lea tried to reduce as much as possible the King's responsibility for the excesses of the Inquisition and instead blamed the "corrupt officials" in whom he, the King, placed his confidence. That argument, however, must be judged untenable on the grounds of Lea's own assembled evidence of Ferdinand's part in running the Inquisition and defending its methods and operations. For Ferdinand was not only the supreme head of the Inquisition and its overall supervisor; he was also its firm controller. To assume that he was not aware of the atrocities that many of the Inquisitors had committed—and this *for a period of thirty-five years!*—is to defy all probability and all reasonable judgment. Nevertheless, it is only on the basis of such an assumption that one can say that Ferdinand, in shielding the Inquisition, was sincerely cleaving to the laws of the Church.

VI

A wrong hypothesis must sooner or later bring its follower to an impasse, and this is what happened also to Lea when faced with the case of Lucero. The ghastly story of this fiendish creature and the Inquisitional excesses he had committed has been told by scholars several times. Here we shall refer to it only insofar as it relates to the present discussion.

Diego Rodríguez Lucero, chief Inquisitor in Cordova from 1499 to 1508, was an arch-criminal in whom Lea sees the "incarnation of the evils" resulting from the powers lodged in the Inquisitional tribunals. The terrible crimes and atrocities he perpetrated were only brought to light by the resistance they had provoked, which led to a formal investigation of his performance and the issuance of a guilty verdict against him. This investigation began, we should note, during the absence of Ferdinand from Castile—that is, during the reign of Philip of Austria and the subsequent brief interregnum. According to Lea, the shocking revelations made in the case of Lucero and his accomplices "afford us the only opportunity of obtaining an inside view of what was possible under the usually impenetrable mantle of secrecy characteristic of inquisitional procedure."[65]

Lea's statement stands in need of correction. By no means can we agree to his assertion that the Lucero affair offered the *only* window through which we can see what went on inside the Inquisition. Lea himself provided us with many such "windows," among them the case of Brianda de Bardaxi, one of a multitude of obscure sufferers, whose "commonplace story" he minutely investigated and skillfully presented in a special study.[66] No other case can offer a clearer "inside view" of the proceedings of the Holy Office, or better illustrate how the agonies of the torture chamber, long years of incarceration, and the testimonies of false witnesses were employed to extract from innocent New Christians confessions of crimes they had never committed. Other aspects of the same persecution are revealed with equal clarity in the partly extant records, not only of the "common" but also celebrated cases of the Inquisition, such as that of the Holy Child of La Guardia. Indeed, this case—which relied on several gross myths drawn from medieval superstition, resting on the subsoil of another crude myth involving the murder of Christian children by Jews—could be rightly called, as one of the accused put it, "the greatest lie in the world." Yet on the basis of this lie, in which the "murdered child" was no more than a phantom (as it was never identified, was nowhere missed, and its body was never produced), six conversos and five Jews were sentenced to death.[67] Does not this trial, which was engineered by the Inquisition (including its leaders on the highest level), offer a clear "inside view" of the performance of the Holy Office?

What is more, we believe that we can gain such a view not only from *individual* cases, but also from available testimonies on the *general* activity of the Inquisition. According to these testimonies, the Inquisitors and their aides, inspired by hate and desire for vengeance, tormented, robbed, and delivered to the stake numerous conversos who were sincere Christians. And these attestations cannot be questioned. They were held to be true not only by Fernando de Pulgar, who was well informed and extremely cautious,[68] but also by Pope Sixtus IV[69]—and not by this pope alone. As late as May 20, 1520, Don Juan Manuel, Charles V's ambassador to the court of Pope Leo X, informed the Emperor of the Pope's accusation that *"terribly evil things were being done by the Inquisition,"* and that the Pope insisted on the truth of this accusation despite all the ambassador's efforts to rebut it.[70] *Rome knew what the Inquisition was and clearly saw its true face.* And cannot *we* too discern its features? Is not the abundant information we possess—besides the cases singled out by Lea—sufficient to make us fully aware of what was going on in the dungeons of the Inquisition? We certainly know enough to judge correctly what kind of tribunal the Inquisition was—unless we make up our minds in advance to believe the Inquisitors more than their victims and the torturers more than the tortured. But let us return to Lucero.

From September 7, 1499, when he became Inquisitor in Cordova, until May 18, 1508, Lucero's persecution of the New Christians in the city left a trail of blood to match anything left by the Inquisition elsewhere. But then he expanded his persecution to include *Old* Christians. It happened that early in his Cordovan career he quarreled with some Old Christian officials, and in his rage conducted a personal vendetta, which soon developed into a general attack upon Cordova's Old Christian community. The apparent helplessness of this community in the face of Lucero's machinations opened for him new, almost incredible opportunities. He discovered that what was done to the New Christians could be done with impunity to the Old Christians, too; and it occurred to him that he could take massive actions against *both* groups on the basis of the old charge that the conversos engaged in a nationwide campaign to Judaize Spain. By means of torture, he extracted "evidence" that this campaign had gained many Old Christian converts who had turned their homes into synagogues and meeting places for the preaching of Judaic missionaries. On the basis of such charges and such "evidence," Lucero and his associates condemned many Old Christians, citizens of Cordova, to the stake, among them "nobles and gentlemen and Church dignitaries . . . of unblemished reputation and *limpios de sangre*."[71] But the tentacles of Lucero and his colleagues spread beyond Cordova to embrace—or throttle—much of the country, so that "they were able," as one contemporary wrote, "to defame the whole Kingdom; to destroy without God and justice, a great part of it, slaying and robbing and violating maids and wives to the great dishonor of the Christian religion."[72] The Old Christians of the country were shocked and puzzled, but the Cordovans, who were in the eye of the storm, knew precisely what had caused it. Moreover, it took a number of years before they gathered enough courage to express their protests to Diego de Deza, the Inquisitor-General, who was in close touch with King Ferdinand. And this brings us back to Lea's assertion that Ferdinand was primarily interested in the Inquisition "as a means of defending and advancing the faith."

To be sure, in Lea's opinion Lucero was an *exceptional* "monster,"[73] but he recognized that, fundamentally, he represented an institution, a system of operations and a body of officials who were "wicked" and "perverse" in the extreme. Referring to the excesses of Lucero and his associates, Lea said, quite sensibly, that "when a horde of rapacious officials, clothed in virtual inviolability, was let loose upon a defenseless population, such violence and rapine were inevitable incidents"[74]; and further: since "such wickedness could be safely perpetrated for years and only be exposed and ended through the accidental intervention of Philip [of Austria] and Juana [his wife]," during their brief rule of Castile, "it may safely be assumed that the temptations of secrecy and irresponsibility render frightful abuses, if not universal, at least frequent."[75] But these true statements absolutely contradict Lea's view of Ferdinand. For if these "frightful abuses" were *inevitable*, if on top of this they were *frequent*, how can one explain Ferdinand's failure to take action against them for six whole years; and how can one reconcile Lea's view of Ferdinand with the "unswerving support" the King offered that "monster," notwithstanding all the clamors and complaints which undoubtedly reached the King's ears? Lea, who could not ignore these questions, but still sought to uphold his view of Ferdinand, tried to explain the King's support of Lucero by the "complicity of Juan Róiz de Calcena, a corrupt and mercenary official, who was Ferdinand's secretary in inquisitional affairs."[76] But this explanation is untenable. Ferdinand was no Enrique IV, who could be fooled for many years by a devious secretary. Even if he did not suspect Calcena of complicity with Lucero, he could have assumed that Calcena was misled, and the numerous accusations leveled at the Inquisitor should have moved him to open an investigation of his conduct, which would surely have revealed to him the deceptions of Lucero and of Calcena, his accomplice. But this is not what Ferdinand did. He continued to engage his corrupt secretary and allowed Lucero to go on with his activity; and what is even more astonishing: he continued to care for Lucero's welfare even after his gruesome crimes were revealed and confirmed by a formal investigation. Such conduct on the part of Ferdinand cannot be explained by a regard for fairness, or honesty, or justice, or any moral principle. It can be explained only by self-interest.

This conclusion becomes inescapable when we note the peculiarity of Lucero's drive. For what was unique about him was not the magnitude of the crimes he committed or the scope of the excesses he perpetrated—namely, that he burned so many innocent people, or violated so many maidens and matrons, or confiscated such enormous amounts of property—but the fact that he persecuted, apart from conversos, many Old Christians of all urban classes. In doing so, Lucero diverted the Inquisition from its original course of activity to a path which the King had consistently avoided; and it is clear that Ferdinand would not have tolerated this diversion unless he considered it *useful* to his purposes. But what could that usefulness be?

As we see it, the King felt that Lucero's persecution could counteract the campaign waged by the New Christians against him and the Inquisition in Spain and abroad. This campaign portrayed Ferdinand as an arch-hypocrite and his Inquisition as an engine of tyranny and extortion that had nothing to do with the real condition of the faith, which they falsely claimed to protect. Not only in the kingdoms of the Iberian peninsula, but in Italy and France—and, in fact, all over Christendom—his reputation was tarnished by the rampant accusation that he used the myth of Judaic heresy for his political and financial ends, and that Judaism posed no danger to Spain since almost all conversos were sincere Christians, as they were actually seen by the popes and their officials. The strongest evidence in support of these claims was of course the fact that, unlike all other heresies, the so-called Jewish one had never drawn Old Christians to its ranks. The implied question which must have been asked was: How could this happen if for more than a century a cunning and powerful converso underground was secretly preaching Judaism in Spain? Surely such an underground should have left some traces among the Old Christians! Ferdinand was anxious to meet this argument which, he feared, might ultimately make a travesty of the Inquisition and his honorific title as Catholic King. He did not know, however, how to go about it until Lucero showed him the way.

Lucero demonstrated that the Inquisition, with its methods, with its garrots and its racks, could achieve much more than anyone had imagined. Just as it "proved" that there were myriads of Judaizers among the New Christians, it could "prove" that there were thousands of Judaizers among the Old ones. Who could assume that the Holy Office would burn good Old Christians as heretics? And who would believe that Ferdinand would allow Old Christians to be persecuted without sufficient reason? Obviously, if the new myth could spread and be sustained, the Inquisition's campaign against the conversos would be seen in a different light. His claims about the converso "danger" would be vindicated, and he would be hailed as the deliverer of Christendom from a heresy that could subvert even a Christian nation like Spain.

It is hard to know how long and how far he intended this persecution to go on, but it is evident that five years after it started, he did not yet believe that its aims had been achieved. Lucero was in the midst of constructing his grand edifice of deadly libel when he was surprised by the spirited attacks which the Cordovans launched against him and his associates. Despairing of the King·and his Inquisitor-General, who would not institute an inquiry into Lucero's conduct, the Cordovans finally turned to the Pope, and Ferdinand now saw himself threatened. He feared that Lucero might not only be denounced, but also drag down with him the reputation of the Inquisition, as well as of its head and architect, the King. Thus, stepping into the dangerous breach that had opened in the Inquisition's wall of secrecy, he wrote on November 17, 1505, to Pope Julius II, urging him to reject the Cordovans' petitions. The Pope, he claimed, should accept the punishments imposed on Lucero's accused prisoners, not only as just but also as indispens- able. "For if I or any other prince," he wrote, "had declined to inflict" these punishments, "*there would have been created such a great schism and heresy in the Church of God as would be greater than that of Arius,* and Your Holiness ought to thank God that it was discovered in my time to have it punished and repressed."[77] Here is the indirect confession of the motive that moved him to support Lucero. He wanted to present the persecution of the New Chris- tians as a means of averting a grave danger to Christendom. Thus, he would not only justify that persecution and the part that he (and the Inquisition) played in it. He would also appear as the savior of Christianity from the threat of a terrible heresy and schism which, according to his own assertion, was "greater than that of Arius."

The threat, however, was not averted by his letter. Pressing for their rights, the Cordovans in Rome were assisted by the ambassador of Philip of Austria, who was unreservedly on their side, while Ferdinand continued his strenu- ous efforts to block the acceptance of their petitions. On April 22, 1506, he wrote to Loaysa, his Roman agent for the Inquisition, ordering him to do whatever he could to foil the attempt to "destroy the Inquisition," which was now "more necessary than ever."[78] "Minute instructions were given as for the influence" that he must bring to bear, and he was reminded that *"Holy Writ permits the use of craft and cunning to perform the work of God."*[79] Craft and cunning were indeed Ferdinand's weapons, and no more typical instruction, written in his spirit, could have issued from his chancellery.

If the truth of the affair was eventually discovered and Ferdinand failed to achieve his goal, it was because, at the crucial moment in the struggle against Lucero, Ferdinand was forced to abandon the regency of Castile in favor of his son-in-law, Philip of Austria, and also because Lucero, Deza and Ferdi- nand himself miscalculated the extent to which they could stretch the big lie when it was applied to Old Christians. The numerous bitter complaints of the New Christians against their persecution by the Inquisition remained voices crying in the wilderness, but those of the Old Christians were ultimately heard and led to a formal inquiry, to Deza's resignation as Inquisitor-

General, and to an unreserved verdict of "guilty" against Lucero, the arch-criminal. Were it not for this, many good scholars would have pored over the documents of the Cordovan Inquisition, studied the accusations so convincingly presented by the clever scribes and censors of the Holy Office, and been astonished at the breadth and strength of the "Judaic" movement that could subvert so many Old Christians in Spain. Said Lafuente in his discussion of the Lucero case: "It would certainly have been hard for us to believe in the enormities of the crimes committed by Lucero and his associates, had we not in our hands the data which the Cordovans instructed their deputies to submit to King Philip, Queen Juana and the members of their Council, in the name of the Church and the city of Cordova, about the excesses of the Inquisitors."[80] The New Christians were not so fortunate. They did not have Old Christian prelates like Juan de Daza to raise their voices in their defense, or a city like Cordova to send its deputies to represent them, or noblemen like the Marquis of Priego to liberate their prisoners from the carcels of the Inquisition. The accounts of their own protests and appeals were suppressed and destined to oblivion. And thus, in dealing with *their* cases, even great and insightful scholars like Lafuente would have before them only the records of the Inquisition, and in using them they would find it "hard to believe" that they conceal behind them a story far more sinister, and atrocities far greater, even than those that may be gathered from the censored reports of the Holy Office.

V. Conclusions

Our survey of the conflict between the Old and New Christians in the Spanish kingdoms of the fifteenth century has come to its appointed end, and with this we have also completed our search for the origins of the Spanish Inquisition. What we have gathered from our various investigations can now be summarized as follows.

We have seen that Ferdinand established the Inquisition as a means of appeasing the anti-Marrano party in order to impair, if not thwart, its capacity to cause new riots and disorders. He could no doubt foresee the damage and disruption that the Inquisition would cause the social fabric of the nation and the harm it would do to the country's economy, but he hoped to minimize the unavoidable losses by allowing all conversos not condemned by the Inquisition to retain their positions and proceed with their activities, and also by using the income of the Inquisition to further the monarchy's favorite projects. That he generally succeeded in achieving these aims cannot, in our judgment, be denied. But while the Inquisition served him as a tool, he remained in a sense a tool of the Inquisition, or rather of the movement from which it emerged. Never did Ferdinand lose sight of his need to be on good terms with the popular force that stood behind the Holy Office.

This force was of course the anticonvert movement that followed all large-scale Jewish conversions in Spain in the period of the Reconquest. The antagonism displayed by that movement to the converts varied from time to time in its manifestations, but its source was always the same: an aversion to the converts *prior* to their conversion—that is, as members of the Jewish people. The inseparable link between the Jewish and the converso problems as they evolved on the Spanish scene is thus indicated by the very sequence of events. The question that has remained for posterity to grapple with is: What was the nature of that link?

The weight of the evidence has led us to the assumption that Old Christian hatred of the Spanish Marranos was basically an extension of Christian hatred for the Jews—an extension that apparently could not be prevented by a mere change of religion. But this assumption has not been explored. None of the scholars who have dealt with the Marrano question has considered it worthy of investigation; for following the Inquisition, they relied on its claim that Old Christian antagonism toward the Marranos sprang primarily from their religious misconduct—namely, their overt unfaithfulness to Christianity and their covert practice of Jewish rites. Upon examination, however, this claim proved unfounded. That it is not valid for the later period—from 1449 on—is evident from the fact that the contemporary Marranos had already been overwhelmingly Christianized; and that it is inapplicable to the earlier period is attested, among other things, by the absence of such terms as *Judaizers* and *crypto-Jews* from the slurs hurled at the Marranos at that time. The rapid Christianization of the conversos was no doubt so generally recognized that reviling them on that particular score seemed to have been pointless.

The same conclusion will be reached by observing Christian attitudes toward the converts from another angle. When in 1109, in 1367, and in 1391 the Christian Spaniards arose to slay the Jews in their towns, it was not only religion that fired their hatred. The avowed "desire to avenge Christ's blood" may have served both as pretext and stimulant, but sociological factors, such as those we have indicated, were without doubt the dominant cause. That is why the pogromists paid little heed to Church prohibitions on killing and robbing the Jews and went on with their work of murder and spoliation as if no such orders existed. To be sure, they spared Jews who consented to be baptized, but in doing so they yielded to a widely held taboo on taking the lives of *would-be Christians*. The self-restraint they exhibited on such occasions sprang, as with every other taboo, from awe for a custom considered inviolable rather than from obedience to religious law. In 1391, it also stemmed in large measure from their obedience to Martínez' instructions. It did not stem, in any case, from a *revolution in the feelings* of the pogromist assailants toward their potential victims, or from a newborn, genuine desire to welcome the converts wholeheartedly to the fold. Therefore, when on the morrow of the conversion the assailants were instructed to treat the converts "amicably," to assist them as "brothers" and regard them as "equals," they defied that instruction (which was—again!—a *Church* instruction!) and made it clear that they would not fulfill it.

It was of course unrealistic to expect a different reaction on their part. Human emotions are not so flexible as to change swiftly from revulsion to affection, and from long-lasting hate to sustained toleration, merely in response to outside authority. Least of all could such a change be expected in the attitude toward Jewish converts. As indicated above, the hatred of the Jews that pervaded the West from the first two centuries of the medieval era did not stem solely from a religious disagreement, but also from a variety of social-economic conflicts that evolved from the particular condition of the Jews. Conversion, therefore, could at best eliminate one of the components— the religious element—from the aggregate of factors producing that hostility; it could not prevent the remaining components—and especially the perception of the Jew as alien—from keeping the fires of hatred burning. Diagnosing the growth of anti-Marranism in Spain, Fernán Díaz de Toledo said that "hatred of the stranger" was the main source of the anti-Marrano movement. And Alonso Díaz de Montalvo, a no less keen observer and profound analyst of the same phenomenon, stated—after examining all possible explanations for the hateful discrimination against the Spanish conversos—that he could see no other reason for that discrimination save the fact that the Marranos were regarded as "strangers."

To be sure, for a short time after the conversion, most Old Christians displayed self-control; the general level of aggression was reduced, and the active hatred became passive or dormant. But as soon as the convert showed the Old Christians that he intended to take his Christianity seriously—that he wished to fulfill all the duties it placed on him, while benefiting from the rights it entitled him to; when he approached the Old Christians with concrete demands to regard him as a full-fledged citizen; above all, when he offered his candidacy for the offices that were open to all other followers of the faith, the Old Christian soon lost his composure, and his passive aversion once again became active. For these demands of the converts immediately touched off the *non*-religious causes of the conflict with the Jews, and the winds of hatred which kept blowing toward the latter engulfed in their sweep the converts, too. Soon the Old Christians began to look for ways to reverse the laws of both Church and state that granted the converts equality of status; and their determination to achieve this reversal was not weakened by their realization that the converts were becoming more and more attached to Christian customs and beliefs. In fact, the more Christianized the conversos became, the less the Old Christians agreed to put them on an equal footing with themselves.

It follows that the aversion of the Old Christians for the New did not arise from the latter's religious misconduct but was actually an extension of the antisemitic tendencies that had already troubled Spain in the 11th century. More precisely, in one measure or another, Spanish anti-Judaism became anti-Marranism the moment the Jew became a converso, regardless of whether his conversion was fictitious, doubtful, halfhearted, or sincere. It was the same old hatred aimed at the same group, which was no longer Jewish religiously, to be sure, but remained the same historical entity, whose members continued to be recognized as such so long as their life in Christendom did not obliterate all the signs of their identity.

Here, then, in this transfer of hatred from the Jews to the converts, lay the primary cause of the great struggle that evolved between the Old and New Christians in Spain, and with it the final outcome of the struggle—the Spanish Inquisition. Yet to understand the meaning of that transfer, we must note that it was not a precise replacement of one hated object by another. Since the social and political demands of the conversos were much greater than those of the Jews, and the possibilities of denying them much smaller (based as they were on the laws of Church and State), hatred for the Marranos was much stronger from the start, and its growth, which paralleled the Marranos' attainments, proved to be likewise much faster. These observations, we believe, suffice to indicate the upward curve of hatred toward the Marranos which began, as we have noted, at a high point. But to grasp more fully the evolution of this hatred, we must bear in mind its various stages, together with the major factors involved. These stages and factors were discussed in previous chapters. I shall now present them briefly together, so that we may get a summary view of the causes of the Inquisition.

1. The first factor to note is the rising influence of the Spanish cities since the reconquest of Toledo in 1085 and *their ability to wrest from the Crown special laws that denied the converts a status of equality.* These laws, to begin with, denied the converts the right to hold office in the urban domains (1118) and fostered a tradition of discrimination against them, which came to be regarded as legal and just. This tradition persisted and, in fact, remained dominant also after the middle of the 14th century, when certain civil and canon laws pronounced the converts equal to all other Christians, and it militated against the translation of these laws into realities of the cities' social life. Even when the cities, under royal pressure, were formally forced to recognize these laws, their resistance to convert equality continued by means of a series of local measures, including sabotage and arbitrary segregation, accompanied by a vituperative campaign. It was only thanks to the pressures built up by the great influx of converts into Spanish Christendom (from 1367 on) that the converts broke through the walls of resistance and, aided by the kings, gained their first footholds in urban Old Christian societies.

2. Indubitably, the factor that first put much strain on the relations between the Old Christians and the New was the growth of converso economic power. Though, unlike the Jewish, the converso economy was not centered on the two occupations (moneylending and tax farming) that always gave rise to numerous complaints, it nevertheless produced a variety of grievances for quite different reasons. As the converso economy expanded in many fields (such as commerce, the crafts, and the liberal professions), it involved more deeply many more sections of the Old Christian population. The points of contact between the Old and New Christians became, as a result, much more numerous, and this multiplied of course the points of friction and inevitably also economic strife. At the same time the conversos, as Christian citizens, were generally in a better position than the Jews to defend successfully their rights and interests, and thus they could gain, more frequently than the Jews, the upper hand in their economic struggles. Naturally, the defeats of the Old Christians in these contests increased the latter's animus for the conversos; and therefore, much more than in the case of the Jews, economic clashes served to exacerbate the relations between the Old Christians and the New.

3. Supplementing the growing economic competition was the political rivalry between the two groups, which formed another major source of hatred toward the New Christians in Spain. For various reasons the political problem was far more acute than the economic, and consequently also far more disturbing. We have seen that, after a long and bitter struggle, the cities succeeded in removing the *Jews* from their high positions in the *central* government, but they could not bar these positions to the *converts,* who kept invading them in increasing numbers. What is more, while *locally* the Jews functioned only as officials and agents of the *Crown* (primarily in the gathering of the revenues), the conversos occupied more and more posts in the cities' *administrations.* Politically, therefore, the New Christians seemed to undermine the national standing of the urban oligarchies and, together with this, their prestige and influence in the cities' populations.

4. Paralleling the growth of the conversos' attainments in the fields of economy and politics was the rise of their general *social* standing on both the urban and national levels. In the cities, not few of their upper social classes formed segments of the urban elite, and nationally they became an integral part of the highest social and intellectual circles. Since the members of these circles belonged, for the most part, to the nobility and the clergy, the conversos were not slow to realize their hope of joining these estates themselves. Thanks to their wealth, education and connections, some of them entered the hierarchy of the Church, while others married into families of great nobles and, many more, of the lower nobility. Nothing, however, could so hurt and aggravate the Old Christian plebeians of all strata as the emergence of a converso nobility. Resentful as they were of the conversos' equality as citizens of the urban domains, they doubly begrudged the latter's place in a class that would elevate them above the mass of the people. But this social development aroused their opposition also for another reason. The rise of the conversos to the higher estates obviously had political implications. On the urban level, nobles of low rank had a stronger claim for positions of authority, and on the national level, nobles of high rank often determined the destinies of the nation. Viewing the conversos as dangerous competitors in the political arena, the urban elites would prefer to see none of them in any of the grades of the higher estates.

5. It was unfortunate for the conversos that the long-standing conflict between the Crown and the oligarchies of the Castilian cities over the latter's share in the national administration came to a head at the time when the conversos were expanding their power both politically and economically. To secure his mastery over the cities' governments, King Juan II inclined, as we have seen, to appoint more and more New Christians (whom he trusted) to key positions of the urban administrations and deny such positions to Old Christians of the cities (in whose loyalty he put little faith). Naturally, the

latter saw themselves threatened. Fearing that the alien minority was heading toward transforming its condition vis-à-vis the oligarchies from political rivals to political superiors, they came to believe that if the Crown had its way, the entire Old Christian urban population would come before long under the New Christians' thumb. It was an ominous expectation that could provoke only rage and arouse the desire actively to resist the conversos' expansion in all walks of life.

6. The opportunity for such active resistance came in the wake of the great rebellion that broke out in Toledo in 1449 and brought to the surface a new fount of hatred that had long been building up underground. We refer to the anti-Marrano bias which, from 1449 on, was promoted by a race theory that radically affected the character of the struggle. For according to that theory, all conversos by their *nature* were so malicious and criminally in-clined that they could not abide by the rules of societies based on moral principles. Least of all could they fit into the Christian society, whose moral-ity was taken to be the highest; and being, as they were, *immoral by nature,* they could not truly convert to Christianity, which is inseparable from its moral doctrines. From this point the racists moved straight to their conclu-sion that neither canon nor civil law could bar anti-converso legislation. Since these laws, which stipulated convert equality, were meant only for *real* converts, which the conversos could never become, they obviously did not apply to the Marranos; hence the racists would not override the laws of Church or state if they enacted harsh restrictions against them. Thus the way was opened for a violent campaign which stressed that the conversos had no right to public office and urged their elimination from Spanish society.

7. It would be hard to understand the rapid spread of racism and its enormous impact on the Spanish mind had it not emerged at the very time when the national sentiment was rising and stirring every vital part of the Spanish people. To be sure, in the middle of the 15th century, Spain's national consciousness was still half awake and most of its objectives were still dimly perceived. Nevertheless, it was groping for national identity and the forma-tion of a single entity out of the various Spanish elements that showed inclination to unite. Lending their support to this general tendency, and pretending to speak on behalf of the whole nation, the racists signified the various groups which, in their judgment, were fit to join the union and indicated those which ought to be excluded. Spain was not the only country in Europe in which national galvanization produced a drive toward unifica-tion, along with demands for separation and exclusion; and the call of the racists to isolate the conversos—together with the Jews—from the national conglomerate fell on attentive ears.

These seven causes of antagonism to the conversos became sources of new streams of hostility that flowed, like seven powerful tributaries, into the mainstream of animosity toward the Marranos, which was formed by the old, unmitigated hatred that in modern times became known as antisemitism. Violent waves of that gushing current, now vastly broadened and strengthened, were relentlessly hitting the Marranos' shores and yet could not make any deep inroads, because they were blocked by a dike. By the dike we mean the conversos' Christianity and the powerful system of laws that sustained it and prevented a breakthrough.

Things began to change radically, however, when in the middle of the 15th century the great current of Spain's anti-Marranism was joined by another flow of hostility which burst forth at that time. We refer to the enmity produced by the campaign charging the conversos with a Judaic heresy—a charge hurled into the public domain with overwhelming force by the rebels of '49. It must have occurred to some foes of the conversos, perhaps for some time before 1449, that a campaign based on such an accusation was likely to have a powerful effect, as it might deny the conversos their protective shield—i.e., their Christian identity. But it was only during the Toledan rebellion that the idea found attentive ears. Looking for excuses that might justify the crimes they had perpetrated against the Toledan New Christians, the rebels thought it helpful to seize on the rumor that some conversos still practiced Jewish rites; and demonstrating unsurpassed insolence and readiness to go all the way with the employment of "big lies," they labeled *all* conversos "heretics" and "Judaizers" who actively sought the destruction of Christendom. No doubt the rebels' success in combining this wild accusation with their racist postulates contributed to their rapid acceptance. In any case, the accusation caught fire, steadily gaining both in following and in credence. Thus the conversos were now attacked from every angle: socially, economically, politically, racially, morally, and religiously. But the religious charge—i.e., that of heresy—was of special significance. It is hardly conceivable that without this charge the monastic orders would have joined in the attack, and it is certainly inconceivable that, without its wide dissemination, anyone could have proposed the establishment of the Inquisition.

CHAPTER II

Sidelights and Afterthoughts

I. Conceptions and Realities

Did the conversos have a clear idea of the nature of the movement that rose against them? Did they understand its underlying causes and assess correctly its inner force? It is hard to give positive answers to these questions. Obviously they gave much thought to the subject. But their situation was too complex, and too perplexing, for them to come up with the right explanation. And adding to these difficulties were their preconceived notions about their place, as Jewish converts, in the Christian world. These notions were long in the making; they were the product of their historical background, and therefore deep-rooted and hardly eradicable. We ought to say a word on this subject if we wish to understand their state of mind.

What must be first remarked in this connection can be summarized briefly as follows. For centuries the Jews, the conversos' ancestors, believed that their unique sufferings among the nations stemmed from their unique religious position—that is, their devotion to their Law, and that if they had agreed to abandon their religion, they would have escaped all persecution. This was also the position of the Church, which promoted, and kept stressing, the view that the discrimination against the Jews, and all their consequent miseries, resulted from their stubborn adherence to their faith, and therefore, once they were converted to Christianity, all discrimination against them would cease, and they could live happily ever after like all other Christians. Similarly, this was the belief of the New Christians, who inherited it from both their Jewish ancestors and the Church that had so persistently urged them to convert. It took them decades of living in Christendom—in fact, more than two generations—to realize that something was wrong with the theory. For even when their conversion was complete, and religiously they saw themselves as Christian, they could notice that this was not at all the way they were seen by their fellow Christians.

In fact, what they noticed was the very opposite of what they had expected: the more their faith in Christianity deepened and the more they assimilated to Christian life, the more sinister and unfriendly became the attitude of the Old Christians—or rather of a growing body of Old Christians—toward their entire group; and they could also see how that attitude was crystallized in ever more disturbing acts. Whereas in the beginning the Old Christians put stumbling blocks in the way of their possible advancement, later, when these means proved ineffective, their ill will turned into bitter hatred, implacable and aimed at their destruction. It was difficult for the New Christians to assume that the view that had been hammered into their minds by their Jewish forefathers, and confirmed with such emphasis by the Catholic Church, indeed by all its teachers, saints and lawmakers, was based on wrong assumptions or misconceptions. Nor could they believe that all their ancestors had misread the lessons of their own history or that the promises given them by the Church were insincere, or based on wishful thinking. The fact, however, remained that the conditions they were faced with were a far cry from the conceptions they grew up on.

What then was happening in Spain's Christian society? What was the cause of the growing animosity, the spreading vilification and the ominous wave of bloody persecution that was rising against them? Had they been Jews and faced such persecution, they would have related their troubles to their faith in Judaism. But the conversos were not Jews; they were Christians, and could not avail themselves of such an explanation. The only answer they could offer to these questions which would be in accord with their basic conceptions was that they faced an *anomalous* development, a deviation from Christianity caused by evil men, who were jealous of their achievements.

We have seen that jealously was indeed there, that it triggered and fueled the attack on the conversos; but we have also seen that underlying that jealousy was the Jewishness of the Marranos which was well recognized—their identity as members of a different people rather than devotees of a different religion. This *non*-religious Jewishness, as we have seen, kept them distinct, apart and disliked, and it was this dislike of the people as such that assumed the form of race hatred. The Marranos, who were trying to explain the phenomenon, and rightly denounced it as a deviation from Christianity, could not possibly see its deeper causes, and if they could, it would have shattered their whole outlook and the framework of the world in which they lived.

Since they failed to understand the causes of their condition, they could not comprehend the chain reaction against them which developed before their very eyes, nor could they discern the links of that chain or the relationships among them. Cardinal Torquemada was perhaps the only New Christian who understood that the attack on the conversos in 1449 was not a freakish, disconnected happening, but one that was deeply rooted in the past and inseparably linked to the hatred of the Jews, which had stirred the gentile world since antiquity. Most conversos, however, believed that the bitter animosity with which they were confronted sprang solely from social-economic motives. There was truth in this as we have seen, but not the whole truth. For behind the social-economic factor there was the racial, and behind the racial the national.

That the conversos did not see in the assaults upon them an expression of a national will is not surprising. Although they recognized the existence of "nations" in the "natural" sense, and even regarded themselves as constituting one, they did not view nationalism, unless conceived politically (that is, as a *state* organization), as an actual cause of hostility between groups. To be sure, some of their Old Christian foes claimed that they spoke in behalf of the whole "nation"—or rather in behalf of the *state,* or the *Republic,* which comprised several *peoples,* or "nations," in the natural historic sense; and we have also seen that they excluded the conversos from that national collectivity. But the conversos could see no ground for that exclusion, which they considered arbitrary and absurd. They rejected the two reasons offered by their enemies—their "religious insincerity" and "racial inferiority"—as malicious accusations, fundamentally false, and they did not take seriously the claim of their foes that they spoke for the Republic and for most Old Christians.[1] They found it hard to believe that the party of their enemies would ever comprise the majority of the people, and we cannot regard this assessment as groundless when we bear in mind that even in the middle of the seventies—that is, several years before the founding of the Inquisition—the Old Christians of Spain were sharply divided on the attitude to be taken toward the Marranos.[2] What is more, the Marranos categorically denied that any faction, or even all factions combined, had the right to speak on behalf of the *people.* This right, they maintained, belonged only to the king or to his appointed spokesmen; and the king, they were sure, despite contrary pressures, was ultimately bound to take their side. To take an opposite view and agree that the *people* was entitled to speak in its own behalf would require a stage of political development from which Castile as a whole was still far at the time, despite the stirrings of national consciousness that was groping for emergence and self-assertion.

That the Marranos did not feel these stirrings, or failed to interpret them correctly, may be taken for granted. But the kings indubitably *felt* them keenly, and although they, too, may have missed their true meaning, they realized what the Marranos did not—namely, that they were faced with an elemental force which was most difficult to suppress and most dangerous to ignore. To be sure, from the standpoint of Spain's political direction, the Marranos judged correctly when they emphasized and upheld the overall superiority of the king. In this they clung to a political principle which was cultivated in Castile throughout the century and served as basis for the absolutist regime that was to be erected within the coming decades. But from the standpoint of their own interests, they committed a grave error when they relied on that royal superiority as a factor that would ensure their safety and their rights. Their error lay in their failure to understand that for the king to attain absolute power, it was necessary first to gain the people's sympathy by various concessions which were to serve as "baits." Still less did it occur to them that they, the conversos, would be first—and indeed the main— "bait" to be sacrificed by the kings to achieve that end.

II. The Racial Substitute

If the genocidal solution to the converso question may serve as an index to the boundless hatred that filled the thinking of the Spanish racists, the rise of the theory about the conversos' vile stock indicates that the claim of their secret Judaism could *not* at the time serve as valid reason for prohibiting their occupation of offices and their intermarriage with Old Christians. Obviously, if the public could have been easily convinced that most of the Marranos were secret Jews (i.e., heretics), this fact alone would have been quite sufficient to justify the above prohibitions, and there would have been no need to go to the length of inventing such bizarre and outlandish theories as those of "blood contamination" (to block intermarriage) and the "conspiracy to capture the government" (to block converso bureaucratic expansion). It was the very life of the conversos as Christians, and the difficulty of finding fault with their Christianity, that prevented the use of the heresy argument as sufficient basis for the desired sanctions and forced their opponents to look for excuses that might appear more acceptable. In fact, if there was any need for further proof that the great majority of the conversos were Christian, it was the emergence of the race theory against them at that particular time.

Never had such an anti-Jewish theory been anywhere espoused in the Middle Ages, evidently because there was no need for one; the Judaism of the Jews—their religious beliefs—was to the Christians reason enough to molest them and limit their rights. Racism as a theory, however, reappeared in full force with the rise of antisemitism in the 19th century. It is necessary to note this development and compare it to its medieval counterpart in order to understand more fully what happened in 15th century Spain.

The external similarities are easily observable. In both cases the campaign focused on denigrating and vilifying the Jewish *race;* in both the theme was stressed that the members of this race were conspiring to exploit, socially and economically, the majority of the nation in which they lived; in both we hear of their secret endeavors to take over the vital positions of government and thereby control the nation's destinies; in both the charge was raised that intercourse with Jews will "pollute" and corrupt the nation's "pure" blood; and in both the final solutions preferred were expulsion and mass extermination. Elements of this theory appeared in the 19th century in several European countries (including France), but they first appeared in Germany, where they had their strongest impact.

German racism arose at the beginning of the 19th century and was triggered by causes similar to those that brought it to the fore in Spain. In Spain it was the legal and factual equalization of the converts from Judaism with the Old Christians. In Germany it was the drive toward social equalization of the Jewish minority with the Christian Germans, aided by waves of conversion to Christianity by Jews who despaired of attaining that goal. There appeared what was known as the "plague of conversion"; and the converts, making use of their rights and freedoms, invaded certain spheres of German culture and society, while many of them intermarried with Germans. The racist movement arose in response to both processes, long before the world heard the word *Nazism.*

Throughout the first half of the 19th century the drive to equalize the Jews of Germany with the Germans continued nevertheless with undiminished vigor, and in parallel there continued (with no less fervor) the drive against their equalization. Unlike earlier anti-Jewish campaigns, that of the Germans in the 19th century relied less and less on religious arguments and more and more on racial reasons, as well as other considerations related to the nation's social and economic interests. Toward the end of the century, when the Jews of Germany, who had been emancipated since 1860, were rapidly making their presence felt in many vital areas of the nation's life, the racial arguments became increasingly dominant in the ever growing agitation against them. At the same time, the religious argument reached a low point in both frequency and influence.

Thus, in Germany as in Spain four centuries earlier, racial theory largely replaced religious doctrine in justifying discrimination against the Jews and, quite evidently, for the same reason. In both countries religion no longer sustained impassable divisions between groups. In Spain it stopped fulfilling this function because of the Jews' Christianization; in Germany, because of the general decline of religious influence in the country. Though the causes differed, the result was the same. Hence in both nations, which were fiercely antisemitic, another obstacle had to be raised to the expansion of the Jews in social fields and to their intermarriage with the majority.

One may find enough reasons to suppose that if the Spanish racists had come to power, the fate of the Marranos would not have differed greatly from that of the Jews of Europe under Hitler. But Spanish racism did not come to power; the instruments of the state were not at its command; and the state permitted persecution of the Marranos only through the Inquisition. Could the Inquisition carry out the plans that the racial movement conceived for the conversos? If some of its members were skeptical from the start, most of them believed that the Inquisition would realize the hope they entertained with respect to the conversos. Said Bernáldez, one of their spokesmen: "Once the fire has been ignited, it will be necessary for it to go on burning until all the Judaizers are consumed and dead, and none of them remains."[1]

Bernáldez left no room for doubt as to what he meant by this prognostication. For the Inquisition, he tells us, has learned from the "confessions" of the

Sevillian Marranos and those in other places that not only in Seville, but also in Cordova, Toledo, Burgos, Valencia, Segovia, and the whole of Spain, "*all of them were Jews.*" And thus it "was made clear and confessed that *the whole race (linage) was defamed (infamado)* and infected with this infirmity" (i.e., the heresy of Judaism).[2] It is obvious, therefore, that when Bernáldez said that all the *Judaizers* would have to be "consumed," he had in mind all *conversos*.

III. The Parallel Drive

There can be little doubt that this statement of Bernáldez reflected not only the sentiments of most racists but also their conviction that the Inquisition was heading toward the extermination of the Marrano group. By the turn of the eighties, however, when Bernáldez made that statement, there were also many racists who, while hailing the Inquisition, were displeased with its progress and consequently skeptical about Bernáldez' forecast. They were evidently dissatisfied with the pace of its proceedings, which resulted, from their standpoint, in too few condemnations, and also disturbed by its failure to reduce the legal status of the converso community. Faithful to their principle which called for the exclusion of *all* conversos from the ranks of the Old Christians, they thought that the Inquisition had provided ample grounds, judicial and propagandistic, for such exclusion and, consequently, for the issuance of laws and regulations forbidding *all* conversos to take part in any function that might affect the fortunes of the Old Christians. Inevitably, they were baffled by the policy of the kings, which left all Marranos who had not been proved guilty (let alone accused) of heresy by the Inquisition all their rights, possessions, offices, and honors; and they were especially dismayed by the sight of New Christians in the highest offices of the royal administration. Thus, to these racists some aspects of the regime were not only puzzling and disconcerting; they were clearly pernicious and intolerable.

They would not dare openly criticize the Kings, who were viewed by one and all as above reproach, but they would not leave matters where they stood either. They thought they could outflank the royal policy by inducing Church organizations which were subject, at least formally, not to royal, but to ecclesiastic control, to enact statutes forbidding all conversos, solely on racial grounds, to join them and assume any position in their midst. If many such organizations adopted the same principles, the government, they assumed, would have to follow suit. Thus, they thought, they could establish from below—i.e., through the Spanish people itself—a regime of anti-converso discrimination which the Kings had failed to impose from above.

This was the basic idea or plan that inspired the racial movement under the Inquisition and formed, in the 1480s, that relentless drive which, after a century of agitation, covered Spain with a network of organizations committed to the *limpieza* principle and urging its institution in all the spheres of Spanish life. In that general plan lay the basic difference between the new *limpieza* thrust of the eighties and the earlier attempts to excommunicate the conversos through similar organizational enactments. The earlier attempts, such as those made in Toledo (by many "fraternities, chapters and Herman-dades"), against which Carrillo took action in his synod (1481),[1] were spontaneous demonstrations of popular dissatisfaction with the government's toleration of converso equality; they were also expressions of the strong desire felt by racist groups in various places to do away with that equality in their own circles. It is hard to detect in their activities, however, any planned drive on a national scale, of the kind we can notice in the ideas of the racists who campaigned under the Inquisition.

It need hardly be said that the proponents of these ideas did not belong to one organized body, acting on the instructions of its governing authorities. What united them were the views they inherited from their forerunners (i.e., the authors of their racist theory), their common reactions to major developments bearing directly on the Marrano situation, and their common temper as political critics anxious to take some independent action. Dispersed as they were in various places, they were moved by those affinities to meet or correspond, and finally agree on a general plan. Before long, cells of activists were formed in many ecclesiastical associations across the country with the aim of inducing the majority of their members to enact anti-converso statutes. If we judge by the results, a good number of those activists must have been persuasive speakers and able organizers, although few of their names were transmitted to posterity. On the other hand, we know the names of many of the organizations that joined the racist drive in the course of time.

Of these organizations, it was the Hieronymite Order that gave the *limpieza* movement the strongest push and put it on Spain's national agenda. The part played by this Order in that evolution has been discerned by a number of scholars,[2] but several aspects and phases of its activity still require exploration.

From various indications in the sources, it appears that the adoption of the *limpieza* principle by the Order was carefully prepared by a group of racist friars who were led by one Gonzalo de Toro, prior of the monastery of Montamarta. It was doubtless especially to the members of this group that Sigüenza, the historian of the Order, referred when he spoke of the friars who watched prudently, "like serpents," the behavior of the "enemy" (i.e., the "heretical" Judaizers) in order to strike him at the proper opportunity.[3]

The opportunity came when the persecution of the Inquisition moved many young conversos to seek admission to the Order in the hope of finding safety in monastic life. Apparently, most of those who took this step chose the Hieronymite Order because it was believed (since the days of Oropesa) to be friendly toward the New Christians. The Hieronymite racists, however, who had always looked askance at the presence of converso friars among them, and especially at those who held positions of authority, were naturally alarmed by the influx of conversos, who might, they feared, upset the Old

Christians' superiority in the Order's membership and leadership. Under their influence, some Old Christian friars, though far from sharing their racial approach, came nevertheless to accept their view that the newcomers' sole aim in joining the Order was to avoid the Inquisition's inquiries and judgments.[4] Thus, together with the racists, they urged the Order's authorities to refrain from accepting more New Christians to their ranks, but apparently without success. Some proof of their claims, it was realized, was needed for the Order to follow their counsel. But where could such proof be obtained?

Under these circumstances, it stands to reason, the racists turned secretly to the Inquisition, called its attention to what was happening in the Order (its admission of conversos fleeing the judgment of the Inquisition and the refusal of the Order's authorities to take counter-measures), and asked its active intervention. Before long the Inquisition took several actions which gave the racists the excuse they needed to introduce their racial policy into the Order.

The precise scheme then worked out by the Inquisition in collusion with the racist friars of the Order will probably remain unknown. But that such a collusion existed is indubitable, and it is indicated, to begin with, by the Inquisition's attempt to induce the General of the Hiéronymites, fray Rodrigo de Orense, to exchange his position as General of the Order with that of Inquisitor of Toledo.[5] Rodrigo was an inert, reserved man who neither by his views nor by his temper fitted the task of Inquisitor,[6] and the offer was no doubt intended merely to remove him from his office as General, so that he could not interfere with plans which the Hieronymite racists had contrived. Rodrigo, however, refused the offer, and it was probably for this reason that the Inquisition assailed the converso friars in the Order the way it did. Rather than proceeding against them directly, it thought it wiser to proceed against the community of New Christians clustering around the monastery of Guadalupe (one of the chief Hieronymite convents), with the aim of entangling the converso friars of that convent in its inquiries against the lay New Christians. This was, in fact, the plan that the Inquisition followed. It erected a "temporary tribunal" in Guadalupe, and appointed as Inquisitor the prior of the convent, Fray Nuño de Arévalo,[7] who must have been known as a fierce enemy of the conversos and as an impetuous racist.

The Inquisition attacked the small community of Guadalupe with a vengeance rarely evinced in other places. Besides many who were sentenced to perpetual imprisonment, to the galleys, or to penance for life, fifty-two Judaizers were burned alive, together with the bones of forty-eight dead and twenty-five effigies of fugitive conversos which were consumed in seven autos within one year.[8] Held before the gates of the convent, these autos served as an accusing finger at its friars, who could not be believed to have seen or heard nothing of the rampant heresy that was raging about them. The large number of sentences (perhaps more than two hundred) rendered in

such a short time showed how little evidence the tribunal needed to pronounce its harsh judgments against the New Christians; and indeed its
performance, which virtually wiped out the whole converso community of
Guadalupe, resembled more a massacre or a series of executions, carried out
rapidly by enemy court-martials, than punitive actions decided on and ordered by a conscientious court of law. It is evident that only a racist Inquisitor, eager to destroy all conversos root and branch, could carry out such a
murderous campaign. As expected, his inquiries into the conduct of the
townsmen soon involved some friars of his own convent, who were likewise
found to have been Judaizers and accordingly sentenced to be burned at the
stake.[9] The racists made much of these condemnations, seeking to shame the
Order to the point that it would be compelled to accept their plan. And it was
no doubt also for this very purpose that the spotlights of their propaganda
were focused on a friar (a member of the same monastery of Guadalupe) who
was "discovered" never to have been baptized, although he had lived in the
convent for forty years.[10] Obviously, they wanted to present his case not as
a bizarre, anomalous exception, but as a model of the "scandalous things" that
take place in the Order's ranks.

We do not know what truth that "discovery" contained and what were its
factual grounds. The account of this case has not reached us, and in the
atmosphere of terror that gripped the Order, false testimonies abounded also
among monks who were non-racist in their views and dispositions, or even
New Christian.[11] Nor do we know whether the condemned friars of Guadalupe were veterans or newcomers to the Order. The racists could have
implicated converts of both types by giving false testimony against any of
them—especially since their testimonies remained secret. But regardless of
how we evaluate those judgments, they were generally held to be above
question; as such they provided ample ground for the racists to stir up the
Order by a violent campaign on behalf of their racial program.

The Twenty-third Conference of the Spanish Hieronymites, which met in
April 1486, stood entirely under the impact of that campaign, which was
conducted by Gonzalo de Toro. He now emerged as a leading figure of a
stature befitting a General of the Order, and under his and his fellow racists'
pressure, the Order adopted three resolutions that show the decisive influence of the racists, although they preserve some traces of the opposition they
had encountered in advancing their proposals. Thus, the first resolution calls
upon the Order to establish an Inquisition of the "heretical depravity" in all
the monasteries of the Order; the second commands the Order to avoid the
acceptance of New Christians into its ranks "so long as the Inquisition
operates in these Kingdoms" and the expurgation of heresy is under way.[12]
The third goes much further: it empowers the prior of the Convent of
Guadalupe, the one who so distinguished himself as Inquisitor, to appeal to

the Pope (Innocent VIII) that he forbid *forever* the acceptance of New Christians to all the monasteries of the Order, and especially to his own convent (where Judaizers had been found),[13] and explicitly disqualify them as holders of offices such as priors, vicars, confessors, and the like.[14] An edict by the Pope to this effect, it was believed, would not only establish the *limpieza* policy in the Order, but also pave the way for the introduction of that policy into many other Church organizations. Yet this was not all that this conference resolved. For practical purposes on the internal level, perhaps the most important decision made was to appoint the racist leader, Gonzalo de Toro, as the first of the two Hieronymite Inquisitors whose task was to uncover the lurking heresy in the Order and take care of its extirpation.[15]

We have already indicated that these resolutions were probably not passed by unanimous consent and that traces of opposition to more extreme proposals can be detected in the resolutions themselves. It is evident, however, that the opposition was weak and could not halt or change the current of opinion that dominated the April convention. One reason for this weakness was the absence from that gathering of García de Madrid, a courageous and astute converso friar who commanded special influence on the Hieronymite authorities. When García heard of the Order's decisions, he sprang to action to have them revoked. As a close friend and confidant of Rodrigo de Orense, it was not difficult for him to convince the General of both the religious and political errors he committed by lending his support to Gonzalo and the proposals of his party. Religiously, he pointed out, the resolutions adopted conflict with the decrees of Pope Nicholas V (in his bull *Humani generis* of 1449) and the Synod of Alcalá in 1481, both of which forbade, under pain of excommunication, any differentiation between Old and New Christians; and politically they came to serve the interests of the racists, and especially of their leader, Gonzalo de Toro, who intended to prevent, by his rising influence, the reelection of Rodrigo as General of the Order and instead secure his own election to that office.[16] Convinced that he had been misled and abused, Rodrigo who had generally been a modest man and reluctant to shoulder any public responsibility, was now filled with a fervid desire to defeat the racist party and stop its leader. He issued orders to all the priors of the order that they disregard the statute adopted at the last conference and obey the bull of Nicholas V.[17] The prior of the Convent of Guadalupe (to whose services as Inquisitor we have referred above) and that of the Convent of Sisla in Toledo (another major monastery of the Hieronymites) refused to accept the General's judgment and replied that the decisions were well taken, claiming that since they expressed the Order's will, they could not possibly contradict the will of the Pope. The General's reaction was unequivocal. He decided to excommunicate both priors, cancel their membership in the Private Chapter, which was charged with the election of the General, and appoint two other friars in their stead.[18] He also sent to Rome two Burgensian conversos for the purpose of obtaining a bull from the Pope securing his reelection as General for three additional years. And "not satisfied with all this," Sigüenza tells us, "he went to Guadalajara to consult converso jurists about the legal aspects of the controversy;" then he "proceeded to the Royal Court to gain the favor of the Catholic Kings, as well as the support of Cardinal Mendoza and other prelates and great nobles, informing them of what was occurring in the Order and presenting the position taken by his opponents as abhorred and prohibited by our laws."[19] The conflict now became a national scandal, while the order split into two factions that denounced each other vehemently and sought each other's ruin.

On August 26 of the same year (1486) the private chapter met in the Convent of San Bartolomé to elect a General for the following three years. As prior of the Convent of Montamarta, Gonzalo de Toro, and his two chief supporters, the priors of Guadalupe and Sisla, came to the crucial gathering; but shortly thereafter, and only three hours before the expiration of his term of office, Rodrigo, relying on the bull of Nicolas V, disqualified their membership in the elective body and appointed others to replace them. Gonzalo, however, was prepared for this. He had gotten in touch with the bishop of Palencia, who was one of the executors of Pope Nicolas' bull, and obtained absolution from excommunication.[20] He and his friends therefore could participate in the meeting and exercise their full influence on the voters. Both sides strained all their efforts, Rodrigo benefiting from the open support given him by the cardinal of Spain (Mendoza) and the Duke of the Infantado. The Kings, however, instructed the two magnates to stay away from the election process, which they viewed as an internal affair of the Order, and both the Cardinal and the Duke complied.[21] But the Kings' order worked against the conversos, as it soon became evident that the majority of the delegates favored the racists' side. Gonzalo was elected as the new General, and the question touching the previous resolutions was not placed on the agenda.[22]

Nevertheless, it could not be shelved. For while the Kings refused to interfere in the election, they took a clear stand on the issue of the *limpieza* statute. In letters they sent to the Order's definitors, they strongly urged the revocation of the statute "until the arrival of the proper time to settle this matter."[23] They also sent their chaplain Diego de Daza to represent them before the Hieronymite leaders and see to it that their will be done.[24] In consequence, Gonzalo saw himself compelled to present the Kings' letter to the Conference, and a long discussion ensued. Some of the attendants, opposing revocation, suggested that a delegation should be sent to the Kings in order to inform them fully of their reasons for seeking to keep the statute in force, but this, as well as other suggestions, could not offset the royal appeal and Daza's strong arguments. "So forcefully did Daza present the disgust which the kings would feel if their request were denied," says Sigüenza, that the Hieronymites had no choice but to yield. Above all, Gonzalo realized that Ferdinand was determined to have the statute revoked, and he did not wish to start his career as General with a dispute that would spoil the friendly relations that had hitherto existed between the Crown and the Order. He therefore saw to it that the conference resolve to inform all the institutions of the Order that the statute must be considered revoked. It stressed that the reason for the new resolution was neither fear of excommunication (which was allegedly threatened by Pope Nicolas' bull) nor a change of view on the issues involved, but solely consideration of the Kings' wishes and the Order's desire to be of service to the Kings. It explained that what moved the Kings to "request very insistently" and, in fact, "order the revocation of the Statute" both by means of their letters and their chaplain, was *their fear that if the statute remained in force, many churches and cities would like to follow suit*—namely, enact similar statutes for their members or citizens.[25]

The cited words, which have been ignored by all the scholars who have dealt with this development, represent the crux of the problem Ferdinand had to cope with when he was confronted with the Hieronymite plan; and they also reveal a major element of his policy toward the conversos. What he wanted was (a) to have the Inquisition, which he guided, serve as the sole agency for "punishing" the conversos, and (b) to let the conversos who were *not* punished by the Inquisition proceed with their usual businesses and occupations, and thereby contribute to Spain's economy. In any case, he was categorically opposed to the development of another anti-converso drive supplementing the Inquisitional activity. Insofar as the persecution of the conversos was concerned, *he intended to be its only determinant and to let no other factor interfere in its regulation.*

Ferdinand, however, could not fail to realize that in openly taking a stand against the racists, he was treading on shaky ground. He did not wish to appear as defender of the conversos, which would spoil his image as their oppressor and persecutor—the image he had acquired through his sponsorship of the Inquisition—and preferred to avoid direct action against the racists when they enacted their *limpieza* statutes. This, however, was not possible in the present case. The issuance of a racial decree against the conversos by a large religious order like the Hieronymites' was clearly different from a similar ruling adopted by a college or a small fraternity. Such an enactment could have far-reaching consequences that might affect adversely the economic situation, and therefore he thought that he should intervene. Thus, we have here the first confrontation between the monarchy and the racists on the issue of the *limpieza*, whose application the racists wanted to expand despite monarchic disagreement.

If Ferdinand believed that by the results of that encounter he averted a threat to his dual policy, he evidently did not duly consider the nature of the man who led the other side. Gonzalo de Toro was a harsh and ruthless person, obstinate and cunning, and not in the habit of accepting defeat.[26] Nor did he intend to give King Ferdinand the last word on the conversos in his Order—a matter that was to him of utmost significance and aroused his fiercest passions. The revocation of the decision excluding the conversos from the Order's offices and from admission to its ranks did not abolish the resolution to establish an inquisition, which was to cleanse the Order of its "hidden heretics." Gonzalo now intended to use that resolution as a stepping-stone for his new plan. He resigned the position of Inquisitor he had assumed in the preceding conference of the Order, leaving for himself only the task of "inquiring" into the wholesomeness of the Convent of San Bartolomé, which was one of the chief monasteries of the Hieronymites and the seat of their new General. He appointed a larger inquisitional tribunal which was to take care of the Order as a whole, and reserved for himself the right to join it in cases necessitating his interference.[27] Soon a violent persecution was launched against all converso friars in the order. According to Sigüenza, "some were burned at the *quemaderos,* others were sentenced to perpetual imprisonment, while others were denied the exercise of any function."[28] No doubt Gonzalo attempted to prove that the racists' charges of a Judaic heresy lingering in his Order were no invention and, therefore, the *limpieza* statute was a necessity and ought not to have been revoked.

Perhaps on the assumption that he had proven his case, Gonzalo finally gathered courage to make a dangerous move. In 1491 he appealed secretly to the Pope to issue a bull approving his *limpieza* policy.[29] But Innocent VIII could not see his way clear to give a positive answer, and when he died (in July 1492), he left Gonzalo's appeal to his successor, Alexander VI. The latter dilly-dallied a long time, his generally unfriendly relations with King Ferdinand no doubt causing him repeated hesitations; but at last, in December 1495, he issued his brief *Intelleximus non animi,* which responded favorably to Gonzalo's request. As long as the Inquisition functions, the Pope stated, no descendant of conversos to the fourth generation shall be admitted to the order, save by special consent of the General and the Private Chapter; nor will any converso friar be appointed to any of the order's offices, under pain of excommunication.

Gonzalo knew that Ferdinand would not take up the cudgels for the conversos against a papal decree. And indeed Ferdinand did not. But the failure of the monarch to act at that point meant only that he was biding his time. Meanwhile, however, the order had its effect, and so did the procedures followed by the Hieronymites who carried it out. It was probably in response to the growing demands that the kings sanction new appeals for *limpieza* that they issued in September 1500 two laws demonstrating their approval of the racial principle in treating persons sentenced by the Inquisition. According to these laws, both all "reconciled" and all descendants of people condemned by the Inquisition were denied the right to any public office or the exercise of any public function.[30] The professions they were forbidden to practice included those of surgeons, physicians, druggists, *escribanos* and notaries— professions that were originally permitted to penitents who were not even reconciled. Nevertheless, though they went to these extremes in restricting the offspring of convicted Judaizers, the kings did not limit to any extent the rights or activities of other conversos. Indeed, as far as this group was concerned—the group which was the chief target of the racists—the kings stuck to their guns.

In August 1503 Alexander VI died, and Julius II replaced him as pope. This was the opportunity Ferdinand was waiting for. Julius II was known to have hated Alexander VI and opposed almost everything he did or stood for. It was no surprise, therefore, that shortly after his enthronement, Julius II issued a bull which sharply denounced the *limpieza* practice and decreed its total abolition. In this bull he said that information had reached him that "in Spain and other places, the [Christian] descendants of the Jews and other non-believers were not admitted to religious Orders, fraternities and other Christian congregations, religious or secular." He condemned these acts as sheer manifestations of "detestable customs and real corruption" and declared "null and void all the rules, regulations, constitutions, and laws, etc., which were enacted for this purpose, including those confirmed by the Papal See."[31] This bull, directed at Spain (though formally it referred to other countries, too), would not have been issued without Ferdinand's consent and secret collaboration. It dealt a harsh blow to the *limpieza* movement and its interference with Ferdinand's policies. For the following ten years, until the end of Julius' reign—and, in fact, to the end of Ferdinand's lifetime—we hear of virtually no new enactments of *limpieza* statutes in Spain.[32] It was only after Ferdinand's death (in January 1516) that Spanish racism again raised its head. In 1519 the Major College of Ildefonso adopted an extreme *limpieza* statute,[33] and in 1522 the Inquisition forbade the universities of Salamanca, Valladolid and Toledo to confer degrees upon New Christians.[34] From then on the *limpieza* movement progressed, despite the numerous obstacles it encountered, until it dominated all Spanish ecclesiastical organizations—and, through them, also a major part of Spain's public opinion.

IV. The Unchanged Goal

Since the drive of the *limpieza* spanned more than three centuries—that is, the whole period of the Inquisition, the conversos were attacked through most of that period by *two* instruments of persecution—the Inquisition and the race movement. In the foregoing we have touched on the immediate reasons for the rise of that movement in the middle of the fifteenth century and noticed the principles of Spanish racism in the early stages of the Inquisition. We would now like to determine whether the same principles propelled the racist drive in later times, too, or whether they were significantly altered or replaced by other guidelines. This would help us assess the influence of the *original motives* of Spanish racism—the motives that more than any other factor were responsible for the birth of the Spanish Inquisition.

To arrive at such a determination it is necessary to compare the racist literature in its early stages with its manifestations in later times. For our present purpose, however, we may limit our examination to one particular phase of that literature—the one associated with the racist campaign in the middle of the 16th century—that is, a century after Spanish racism had proclaimed its beliefs and plan of action.

The foremost representative of the mid-16th-century phase was Cardinal Juan Martínez Pedernales, better known as Siliceo, who was archbishop of Toledo from 1546. The cardinal was a man of peasant stock who inherited from his ancestors their hatred of the Jews and their prejudices against the conversos. By the time he appeared on the scene with his ideas, the *limpieza* movement had already gained much ground. All of Spain's military orders, most of its religious orders, and nearly all its major colleges and universities had by then been closed to New Christians. The only group of ecclesiastical organizations still generally open to them were the churches, and many young New Christians, who sought a Church career, tried to become priests or other Church ministrants of both higher and lower ranks. Now Siliceo tried to bar the conversos from these institutions, too. Thus, after becoming archbishop, he had the cathedral chapter of Toledo adopt an extreme *limpieza* statute which excluded from the church all its converso functionaries, including many canons and well-known theologians. But the statute required papal confirmation, and Paul III was disinclined to sanction the racial policy in the Church's institutions. Siliceo, to be sure, finally induced the pope to act favorably on his appeal. But the opposition put up by the conversos to his plan brought the case before the Royal Council, and Siliceo found himself again compelled to defend his propositions. Accordingly, he composed several memoranda in support of his position, and these are our best sources of information about the views and aspirations of the racist movement at the time.[1]

A curious documentation bearing on our subject, which has been made public by various authors, ought to be considered at this point. It consists of an alleged exchange of letters between the heads of the Jews of Spain and those of Constantinople that supposedly took place on the eve of the expulsion of Spanish Jewry in 1492. In this correspondence the leader of Spain's Jews asks his Eastern counterpart to give him advice on how his community should conduct itself in the face of its current difficulties. The king of Spain, he says in his letter, has ordered them to convert or leave the country, and, in addition, the king destroys their synagogues, kills many of their members, robs them of their property, and subjects them to numerous intolerable vexations.[2] In response, the head of the Jews of Constantinople offers Spain's Jews the considered opinion of the "great satraps and rabbis" of the Jews of the East.

According to that opinion, Spain's Jews would do well to meet the assaults of the "Spanish King and the Christians" upon their lives, possessions, freedoms and religion in the following manner. They should train their sons as merchants and financiers so that they may strip the Christians of their wealth; they should equip them with the skills of government officials so that they may subjugate the Christians and oppress them; they should educate them in the disciplines of the priesthood so that, as priests, they may destroy the Christian temples; and they should teach them the arts of medicine and surgery so that they may freely kill Christian patients. By so acting they will "avenge" themselves on the Christians "for what they have done and intend to do" to them. Yet they would be able to accomplish all this only if the Christians come to view them as their own—namely, if they convert to Christianity. Indeed, they should be converted in any case, since they are given no choice in the matter; but this conversion should of course be feigned. They should "baptize their bodies" but not their souls, which should continue steadfast in their faithfulness to the Law.[3] Thus, false conversion was the fifth measure that the Jews of Constantinople urged Spain's Jews to take. Anyone who believed that the other four counsels (in business, officialdom, medicine and priesthood) were given to the Jews of Spain would have no difficulty in believing that the fifth counsel was advanced as well.

Siliceo claimed to have found copies of this correspondence in the archives of the Toledan church and submitted them to the pope as authentic documents.[4] These documents, we are told, convinced the pope of the "malice and evil" of the conversos, and in contrast to his previous stand, he responded favorably to the archbishop's request concerning the statute he had enacted in Toledo.[5] The correspondence, however, offers no evidence that Spain's Jews had followed their brethren's counsel; nor do we have direct evidence that Siliceo claimed that they did. To be sure, his petition to the pope is not extant, but in the memoranda he addressed to the king, he asserted that the conversos were wreaking death and destruction upon all classes of the Old Christian population—and thus actually implementing the plan proposed by the Jews of Constantinople.[6] What the "correspondence" added to these assertions was the allegedly "inside" information which shows that this destructive activity had been planned by the leadership of world Jewry as an act of vengeance against the Christians. Consequently, there can be no doubt as to the function the aforesaid letters were designed to fulfill in Siliceo's campaign.

That the letters were apocryphal hardly needs proof, and it is not at all impossible that it was Siliceo (or one of his aides) who perpetrated the fabrication.[7] But this is really of secondary importance. What is truly significant, and historically illuminating, is that a cardinal of the Church could present such myths and such preposterous charges to both pope and emperor in a formal exposition of the conversos' "crimes." Nothing represents more striking evidence of the depth of the anti-converso bias that dominated Spain's public opinion. But what is even more meaningful for assessing that bias is the particular sphere of human interests on which the above correspondence dwells.

By the time Siliceo began his campaign, no converso served as bishop, archbishop, or cardinal[8]; nor, with rare exceptions, could conversos be found in high posts of the royal administration, such as those of royal councillors, major judges, governors, or *corregidores*. The absence of common educational prerequisites (such as graduation from a major college), coupled with the pressure of the racialist movement, had led the kings to abstain from appointing or even nominating conversos for such high posts. By then they also avoided interference in the management of all or most Church organizations against dominant anti-converso trends.[9] But they would still not permit the removal of conversos from their major sources of livelihood. Thus, in the middle of the 16th century, we find conversos still engaged in their main traditional occupations (commerce, tax farming and banking), as well as in the free professions (law and medicine) and the public offices in the cities (as judges, *regidores*, deputies and *escribanos*).[10] The presence of conversos in these professions and occupations aroused the antagonism of the Old Christian burghers as had their presence in the higher royal offices. It is not surprising, therefore, that in the middle of the 16th century, when the churches (the last converso strongholds in the *ecclesiastic* system) were about to fall into the racists' hands, the latter launched their strongest attacks on the remaining social and economic positions still held by the conversos.

The apocryphal letter of the Jews of Constantinople directs the racist fire at these positions and shows that, as in the middle of the fifteenth century, so a hundred years later, the main interest of the racists in attacking the conversos was social and economic rather than religious. The fierce denunciations of the Jewish *merchants* and *physicians* which we find in that "letter" spearheaded a broader attack on the conversos in the fields of finance, city administration, and the liberal professions. Indeed, in his appeals to the Royal Council, Siliceo lashes out against converso participation in all those occupations, thereby indicating clearly what was meant by the charges included in the "letter from Constantinople." To be sure, he assails the converso priests as well (just as the apocryphal letter does), for the conversos still retained these positions in the churches; but here, too, while referring, as his cardinal's duty commanded, to the "spiritual" damage those priests "caused" the Christians, he harps on the managerial offices they occupied, on the benefices and other advantages they gained, and thereby denied to the Old Christians.[11]

Thus we see Siliceo take the same position adopted by the racists of 1449, who aspired to destroy the conversos' social status and used the conversos' alleged religious deviations only as a means to that end. As in the fabricated letter, so in Siliceo's memoranda, the religious crime is relegated to the background and serves only as an auxiliary factor in the execution of the racists' plan. Above all, the idea of the converso conspiracy, which is explicitly presented in the letter, is also suggested in Siliceo's memoranda, so that in this too there is full conformity between the apocryphal document and his own presentation. In all these matters, both the "letter" and the memoranda repeat the accusation leveled at the conversos by the racists in 1449. The only element which is missing in the "letter," and which the cardinal did not ignore, is the issue of intermarriage between New and Old Christians. Siliceo assails the phenomenon, and thus completes the cycle of the principal arguments voiced by the racists in their earlier campaigns.[12]

The spurious letter of the Jews of Constantinople is therefore not just a literary curiosity or a mark of ignominy on the cardinal who used it. It is rather a document of major significance, as it presents in a nutshell the main racists' charges in 1548, thereby showing the extent to which they repeated the views first enunciated in 1449. It tells us that the racists' main sphere of interest was secular rather than religious, and that in 1548 they were still fighting a social, economic and racial battle disguised in religious arguments, precisely as they had done a century before. What is more, Siliceo repeats these arguments not only in content but also in style. When he says that the conversos became the "masters of the Old Christian estates" as well as the "lords of the Old Christians' lives,"[13] he echoes the voice of Marcos García; and when he asserts that the converso physicians *took their offices for no other purpose than killing the Old Christians,*"[14] he is plainly quoting Espina. It is the identity of the racists' style in the various stages of their campaign that helps convince us that their aims remained the same, as does the overall thrust of their arguments and the fierce hatred that fired them.

It would be impossible to separate this ferocious hostility, and the lines of argument that supported it, from the long evolution of the Inquisition and its sustained assaults upon the conversos. The Inquisition was essentially a child of the racist movement, and in both its thinking and feeling it tended toward the racist point of view. Under Ferdinand this tendency was curbed, and the Inquisition had to act, at least formally, within the limits of a strictly religious persecution. But under his successors it was given greater freedom, and with the advancement of the *limpieza* drive, the Inquisition could give more vent to its desire to act in full accord with the racists' aims. It became, in fact, more and more a formal spokesman, advocate and champion of the racist movement, and in the days of Siliceo its racist language was plain and unmistakable.

Thus in its appeal to Pope Julius III to confirm a *limpieza* statute of the Observantine Franciscans, the *Suprema* (i.e., the leading council of the Inquisition) referred to "the *crafty and unscrupulous ways in which that unquiet race* [*i.e., the conversos*] *disturbed the peace of all bodies to which it found entrance*,"[15] thus describing the conversos in the same language applied to them by Siliceo in his own appeals for the confirmation of similar statutes.[16] What is more, we can see the Inquisition's growing tendency to subscribe to the four racist arguments we have noted (with respect to commerce, offices, priesthood, and medicine). To be sure, insofar as commerce was concerned the Inquisition could not urge, freely and openly, the suppression of all trading activities of the conversos, as the kings were firmly opposed to such demands. But on all other issues it expressed its position (which was in effect the racists' position) with little or no restraint. Thus, in urging that the conversos be barred from offices in a religious order, it speaks of all New Christians as *"aspiring to rule, with the object of ruining the Old Christians."*[17] At the same time it burned converso priests as Judaizers who sought to "profane and capture the churches," as we know from a variety of sources[18]; and as for its view of the converso physicians, we have the testimony of Siliceo, which speaks for itself:

> For not many years ago there was burned in Valencia a [converso] physician, to whom his sons used to say when he returned from work: "Welcome, the avenger!" [*Bien benga el bengador*]. And in Ciudad Real another was burned who used to put poison under one of his fingernails, which he allowed to grow [excessively] for this purpose, and with that finger he would stir the purgatives, which he administered to his Old Christian patients, until the poison was absorbed in the purging substance, so that the Old Christians who took it died. And a few days ago they reconciled in Toledo a surgeon who would throw into the wounds

of Old Christians a certain poisonous powder of which they died. And to bring [more] examples of these [atrocities] would mean never to finish.[19]

These were not charges drawn from propaganda pieces, written by unknown vilifiers and calumniators, but charges that served the tribunals of the Inquisition to condemn men to death, perpetual imprisonment, torture, infamy and loss of all possessions. Lea, who was flabbergasted by these accusations, said: "Wild as this may seem to us, it gives us a valuable insight into the impulses that governed Spain in its dealings with the alien races within its borders."[20] In the whole great work of this great scholar, there is no other statement in which he comes closer to diagnosing the converso problem. For the above statement shows that the conversos were not persecuted as bearers of a heresy—that is, of a different religious creed—but rather as members of a different *race*—and even more important, an *alien* race. No other connotation can be associated with this expression save that of a group foreign to the Spaniards, and as such hated and subjected by them to libels of the vilest nature. Moreover, Lea tells us that the purpose of those libels (and the policy they initiated) was "brute repression and extermination,"[21] without adducing any religious aim such as "correction," "penitence," or "purity." Here we see Lea, in one of the few moments in which he freed himself from the prevalent conceptions and let his own insights define what he observed—namely, the *real* "impulses that governed Spain"—approaching a correct interpretation of the problem, its symptoms and manifestations.

We cannot, however, end our remarks on this point without expressing disagreement with Lea's implied concept of Spain's attitudes toward its "alien races" (in the plural!), as if those attitudes were of the same order. Lea seems to equate Spain's policy toward the conversos with the one it pursued toward the Moriscos, and he seems also to consider identical the motives that determined those policies. But this identity was only partial, or rather limited to specific issues. Like the conversos, the Moriscos were viewed by the Old Christians as an alien minority group, and no doubt there was a racial-national irritant in Spain's persistent drive against them. In all the rest, however, the two drives differed. In the case of the Moriscos, Spain had to deal with a basically anti-Christian, anti-assimilationist and anti-Spanish element that could hardly merge with Spain's culture and society. In the case of the conversos, the opposite was the case. The problem of the conversos belonged to a different category, stemmed from different sources (in addition to the common ones), and was governed therefore by different impulses. It is to solve *their* problem, and theirs alone, that the Spanish Inquisition was erected.

V. Struggling Assimilation

No less important than the impact of the above changes in limiting the Inquisition's persecution of the Marranos was the steady transformation that was taking place in the conversos' ethnic condition. In 1548 Cardinal Siliceo complained that the conversos ("these people who descended from the Jews") kept marrying their sons and daughters to nobles of high rank (in his words: to the "most illustrious people of Spain") in order to "shield themselves from the Inquisition and raise themselves above the Old Christians."[1] Like all other statements of Siliceo on the conversos, this one, too, is affected by his hatred, and although there is truth in it, it is coached in phrases that misrepresent the actual development. One may gather from his assertions that the conversos' sole interest in marrying nobles was to find shelter from the Inquisition. But this was certainly not the case. The process of intermarriage between the two groups was, as we have seen, already well advanced by the middle of the 15th century,[2] and thus it began at least two generations before the founding of the Inquisition. What prompted it was the conversos' desire to rise to the highest social level (what Siliceo called "to raise themselves above the *Old Christians*"—as if the nobles were *not* Old Christians!) and profit from its social and economic advantages. What motivated the nobles to enter such wedlocks were no doubt primarily financial interests, which always counted heavily in nobiliar marriages; but utilitarian considerations were not always the main stimulant of intermarriage among either the nobles or the conversos. Indubitably, some members of the great nobility and the higher ranks of the converso aristocracy developed ties of comradeship, friendship and affection, which provided incentives for marital unions. For all these reasons, we may take it for granted that if the Inquisition had not been created, the progress of intermarriage between nobles and conversos would have continued at its former—if not quickened—pace.

The establishment of the Inquisition, however, moved the Marranos to accelerate and expand the process of intermarriage for the very reason indicated by Siliceo—that is, because intermarriage with the nobles offered them protection from Inquisitional persecution. The kings would refrain from involving the nobility in heretical charges, which would have roused the nobles against the Crown and turned them into its sworn enemies; and the Inquisition would not dare challenge royal policies of such high significance. Consequently, intermarriage between nobles and conversos proceeded with little or no disturbance. As a result, about 1535 (more than half a century after the founding of the Inquisition) the famous doctor López Villalobos could state that speaking evil of the converso stock touches *"the majority of the Spanish nobility,*"[3] and in 1560 Cardinal Bobadilla could go beyond this when, in a memorandum to the king, he asserted that no part of the Spanish nobility was clear of admixture with Jewish blood.[4]

But intermarriage between New and Old Christians was not limited to the nobility. By 1449, as we have noted, it included commoners in the cities, too[5]; and we may safely assume that as time went on, the number of such marriages increased. They must have especially involved members of the upper classes of both the Old and New Christians in the cities, and ultimately, in growing proportions, members of their middle classes, too. Out of these marital unions emerged most of the urban merchant communities that dominated a large part of Spain's commerce, such as the one that became prominent in Toledo in the first half of the 16th century.[6] What prompted intermarriage within these classes was basically what started it in the 15th century—the common pragmatic and emotional factors that make for marital unions, as well as the desire of many conversos to live a full Christian life in a Christian society. Their need to find some protection from the Inquisition can obviously not be excluded from their motives, since marital association with Old Christian commoners could usually screen them against the Inquisition almost as effectively as their marriages with the nobles. In fact, almost every mixed Old-New Christian family, especially of the urban upper classes, formed the nucleus of a web of kinships, economic interests and other relationships that were interwoven in Spain's social fabric. To touch it might stir a wave of protest that could prove too strong or too risky to repress.

But besides the social obstacles posed by intermarriage to the activity of the Holy Office, the moral obstruction it presented to that activity was likewise of no minor importance. For the very idea that a faithful Old Christian would give his son or daughter in marriage to a heretic was considered incredible if not absurd, and thus it was assumed that every Old Christian who entered such a union had ascertained beforehand that the converso involved was a true Christian. Moreover, the charges leveled at the Judaizers as performers of Jewish rites were based on the assumption that they had perpetrated their crimes in the privacy of their homes or in secret gatherings enabled by the support of their families; but when a Judaizer married an Old Christian, he lost that sanctuary and the facilities it offered him. Such a marriage brought him into a Christian environment—that of his spouse's family and society, which would obviously prevent him from conducting a concealed or double religious life. This meant that a converso who married an Old Christian, even if he had been a Judaizer, had resolved to abandon his former faith and ritual and raise his children as Christians. These obvious conclusions denied the Inquisition any reasonable excuse to attack him.

It need scarcely be said that not all Spanish racists accepted these conclusions as guidelines for their conduct. To most of them, followers of men like Siliceo, *all* conversos, including those married to Old Christians, carried their Judaism in the recesses of their minds and, if they did not actually perform Jewish rites, remained "mentally steadfast in [their] conformity with the Law."[7] Siliceo, of course, could not prove this claim. On the other hand, however, it would be wrong to assume that the bulk of the Old Christians who took conversos as their consorts made that step after careful consideration of the arguments we have outlined above. What we ought to bear in mind is that on both sides of the fence very large numbers of people were involved and that the personal solutions to their various problems were shaped by group attitudes and beliefs, by general observations and common impressions, which were partly inherited and partly formed by themselves in accord with their social inclinations. To explain more clearly what this implied, a few remarks must be added to what has been said about the attitude of the Spanish people toward the conversos.

In the foregoing we have centered our attention on the racists and, more broadly, on the antisemitic movement which drove Spain, from the middle of the 15th century, toward the creation of the Inquisition. Our special interest in this movement stemmed from our conviction that it constituted a dynamic and aggressive force which, more than any other segment of the people, determined the course of Spain's history at the time. We also believe that in the eighties and the nineties, it came to comprise the majority of the people, though we do not believe that at any time it constituted an overwhelming majority. Those who opposed it or differed from its views were never numerically insignificant. To be sure, under the reign of the Catholic Kings (and the crushing regime of the Inquisition), they were forced into political passivity, but this does not mean that they were totally submerged, or frightened into social passivity as well. Undoubtedly, most of them were sons and grandsons of the Old Christians who had sheltered the conversos and defended them in Toledo during the outbreak of 1467, who battled on their behalf in the streets of Cordova in 1473, who fought with them against their enemies in Segovia in 1474, and who prevented attacks upon them in Seville in both 1473 and 1474. These Old Christians, we may safely assume, bequeathed this attitude to many of their descendants, and the friendliness of the latter toward the conversos increased, rather than waned, under the persecution. They considered the conversos sincere Christians, believed that they were gravely wronged by the Inquisition, retained their business and social contacts with them, and rendered them whatever help they could offer within the limitations of the existing laws (and occasionally no doubt also beyond them). It is this section of both nobles and commoners with whom the conversos intermarried, and it must have been a large section indeed; for if it did not represent a silent majority, it certainly constituted an important minority, at least a quarter of the Spanish people. *Otherwise it is utterly impossible to explain the ethnic absorption of such large masses of Marranos into the Old Christian population.* This is how it happened that within only one century after Siliceo's attacks on Spain's Marranos, their demographic picture had radically changed, and in 1670 Spinoza could write that they "became so intermingled with the Spaniards as to leave of themselves no relic or remembrance."[8]

To be sure, Spinoza, in making this statement, relied on information obtained in Amsterdam from Marrano sources regarded as reliable. Yet what these sources conveyed was the general impression which any visitor to Spain, or any resident in that country, would gain from his contacts and relations with the Spaniards.[9] Judging by the latter's general attitudes, nobody seemed to distinguish any longer between Old and New Christians. But that does not mean that all Spanish racists and the Holy Office, their faithful representative, lost all interest in the subject. Although the mass of the conversos was no longer recognizable, a few of them could still be discovered and "identified" as secret followers of Judaism. And thus it took more than half a century after 1670—the date of Spinoza's aforecited statement—before the last fires of the Inquisition were extinguished, and more than another century before all search was abandoned for remnants of Marranism among candidates for office.

Thus was finally achieved the goal that Alonso de Cartagena, the converso bishop, proclaimed in the middle of the 15th century as the ultimate objective of Marrano life in Spain. The goal was racial merger, fusion, disappearance; and from the standpoint of the ardent Marrano assimilationists, they triumphed over the racists who sought to prevent its achievement. It seems certain, however, that had their early protagonists imagined the way in which their objective would be gained or the cost that was to be entailed in its attainment, they would have been much more reserved, and more reticent, in the advocacy of their cause. For the cost was staggering by any calculation. Not only did it involve enormous bloodshed, indescribable suffering on a tremendous scale, and myriads of lives turned into nightmares; it involved also the massive spoliation and destruction of the products of the labor of many generations; the abandonment of numerous hard-won positions, and the loss of influence, honor and prestige; it meant indeed not only retreat from power, but also retreat from fame. Moreover, it meant the sacrifice of identity, not only in collective but in personal terms—as it implied the suppression of thousands of talents and the choking of the hopes, strivings, and aspirations that make any man's life worth living. Marranism died hard, praying for its end, its suicide being prevented not by friend but by foe, and its death throes lasting four hundred years—a terrible way for assimilation to be effected and for the light of a creative group to be put out.

VI. The Insidious Pretext

Never did cunning, hypocrisy and deception make greater use of sanc-
timonious contentions than did the Inquisition in its attack on the conversos.
Nor was any similar operation crowned with such phenomenal success. What
doubtless contributed much to this success was the Inquisition's skillful
presentation of its verdicts as the judgments of wise and righteous men who
had but one purpose: the establishment of truth. Vested with the authority
of the Holy Office, their sentences were regarded as "holy," too—the final
word of Spain's highest tribunal entrusted to deal with the gravest of all
crimes—that of "heretical depravity." Only king and pope could outweigh
that authority (the former practically, and the latter also formally), and it was
indeed only through these channels that the conversos could, on rare occasions, gain some relief from the Inquisition's pressure.

The notion that many of the conversos were heretics had, as we have seen,
become widespread in Spain already in the middle of the 15th century, owing
to the relentless and unscrupulous campaign conducted by the conversos'
foes at the time. But shortly after the establishment of the Inquisition, it was
on virtually everybody's lips. This was largely due to the numerous confessions made by New Christians in Seville and other places in response to the
Inquisition's Edicts of Grace. To critical minds these confessions proved
nothing except that the Inquisition inspired great fear from the very beginning of its operations, and that many conversos, in their desperation, took the
promises of the Inquisition at face value and hoped that by admitting minor
sins they might escape major tribulations. They were soon to discover,
however, that these hopes were delusive; that their "confessions," which they
thought would end their worries, started a long chain of troubles for them;
and that in fact they had fallen into a terrible trap cleverly laid for them by
the Inquisition. But before the Inquisition made use of their confessions as a
foolproof net to catch more "culprits," it used them as evidence for the
existence of Judaizers in immense numbers. If before this "discovery" the
charges of heresy appeared to many doubtful or exaggerated, many more
now joined the racist claim that "all" conversos were heretics.

That this claim became so deeply entrenched in the thinking of large
masses of Spaniards; that it withstood the objections, criticisms and denials
of its numerous opponents among the Old Christians, was due in large
measure to the Inquisition's ability to turn its campaign into a crusade—into
a perpetual call upon the Spanish people to join it in hunting down the
heretics. When such a hue and cry engulfs a nation, very few can withstand
its impact. The herd instinct in man then has its heyday, and even the most

independent spirits tend to follow the great majority. This happens often even in societies that do not use harsh measures against dissidents. In societies that use such measures, conformity is virtually universal. Spain under the Inquisition was such a society. Hence, any public defense of the conversos would be instantly met with a crushing denunciation, and the defender would be marked as a fautor of heretics, if not as a secret heretic himself. In such circumstances, the Inquisition's verdicts enjoyed immediate public acceptance. Nobody dared dispute its "facts," just as nobody ventured to question its motives.

Armed with terror, espionage and propaganda, the Inquisition proceeded to capture Spain's opinion and control it almost flawlessly for three centuries and more. But the impact of its agitation was not confined to Spain. The notions it instilled in the Spanish public spread abroad and were accepted in Europe, especially those that concerned the conversos and their "secret Judaic practices." Nor was the triumph of its claims and assertions limited to the period of its reign; it is visible also in most scholarly works written by truth-seeking, eminent historians from the beginning of modern historiography on the Inquisition down to the present time.

Thus we see the old apologists of the Inquisition matched by many modern authors who describe its actions not only as just, but also as considerate and humane. Similarly, the charge that the Spanish Inquisition was a cause of Spain's cultural regression and decline has been met by strong denials from scholars who claim that the Inquisition in no way retarded Spain's scientific and intellectual development. And as for its general social impact, it may suffice to cite the learned Vacandard to illustrate one of the major opinions that infuse modern studies of the Inquisition. "Taking everything into consideration," he wrote, "we may say that the Institution and working of the tribunals of the Inquisition were the means of real social progress."[1]

It is questionable whether the scholarly apologists of the Inquisition have at any time been outnumbered by its critics. But if many pointed out the atrocities of the Inquisition, the cruelties and inhumanities it practiced on its victims, only few historians considered the possibility that this great organization designed to fight heresy was actually created for a different purpose, and was exclusively devoted to the attainment of that purpose for decades after its inception. If this possibility had been carefully weighed, it would have led researchers to quite different conclusions. But this was not to be the course of historiography. That the Inquisition operated under false pretenses; that religion served it merely as a mask and an excuse for its basically *anti*-religious persecution; that it abused the authority of the Pope and his aides by pursuing objectives they had never approved—indeed, that had never entered their minds; that it attempted genocide of a Christian people on the pretext of its alleged anti-Christianity—in brief, that it perpetrated a terrible crime against humanity, against religion and against the Catholic Church itself by deceiving it in a manner, on a scale and for a goal that was radically opposed to anything it stood for, only isolated researchers came to see and admit.

When Lord Acton described the Inquisition as founded on a "murderous" principle, as an "appalling edifice of intolerance, tyranny, cruelty, which believers in Christ built up to perpetuate their belief,"[2] he actually referred to all inquisitions that operated under papal auspices—the Medieval, Spanish and Roman. He did not single out the Spanish Inquisition as an organization *sui generis*. And to the extent that his description relates to the Inquisition *in general*, one can readily agree with it. It cannot, however, serve as an adequate characterization of the Spanish Inquisition at its inception, as well as in the first forty years of its activity, during which it dealt almost exclusively with conversos. Inasmuch as that early period is concerned, it was clearly distinct from all other inquisitions, and therefore what applies to the category as a whole does not cover its distinctiveness.

Scholars, to be sure, have pointed out certain matters related to the authority, procedure and severity in which the Spanish Inquisition differed from its predecessors, and thereby seemed to justify its special designation. It is hard, however, to see in any of these matters a true mark of its uniqueness. There was not really much innovation in its procedures, or the rules it applied to the treatment of suspects, or the guidelines it followed in its investigations, or in the issuance of its judgments. Nor can we say that the Spanish Holy Office exceeded all previous inquisitions in ruthlessness, cruelty, and bloodshed. It was certainly an awesome instrument of persecution, the like of which the world had seldom seen, but it is questionable whether the Inquisition of Languedoc could not match it in the aforementioned aspects. Even the fact that the kings, and not the popes, were its real guides, protectors and masters, would not have made it so different from the others, had it not been for other factors closely associated with its royal control.

As we see it, the Spanish Inquisition was distinguished not by greater tyranny, intolerance and cruelty—the qualities Lord Acton found in all Inquisitions—but by the cynicism, hypocrisy and false pretenses it employed in the first four decades of its existence (and also later insofar as the conversos were concerned). For the Spanish Inquisition was not created by "believers in Christ" in order to "perpetuate their belief," but by Christians who wished to deny other Christians their rightful share in Spain's Christian society. It was an institution based mostly on false pretenses, sham pretexts and invented accusations. For its purpose was not the exaltation of religion, but the suppression of a people that could not be reduced save by pinning on it the charge of heresy. It was an onerous task, but the Inquisition could perform it because social conditions and political interests combined to provide it with the necessary tools, as well as with a suitable setting—i.e., a surrealistic theater of war, in which a religious weapon like the Holy Office could be used to attain a secular aim. It is here that the real difference lay between the Spanish and all other Inquisitions, and it is because of *this* difference that the Spanish Inquisition did indeed occupy a special place in the history of persecution.

VII. The Destructive Urge

It was inevitable that the Inquisition's attitude toward the conversos and the special way in which it treated them would affect its treatment of other groups that fell under its broadened jurisdiction. This touches the problem of what brought about the extension of the Inquisition in so many directions and so many spheres. As we shall see, the solution to this problem is closely related to the theme of this work.

Viewed politically, the explanations so far given for the spread of the Inquisition may appear satisfactory. The extension of the Inquisition, we are usually told, resulted from the expansion of the Spanish empire, from the rise of the Reformation and the Counterreformation, and from the growth of Spain's monarchic absolutism, which used the Inquisition to buttress its power and spearhead its territorial conquests. Historians have repeatedly noted these facts, which doubtless had much to do with the phenomenon. The one major fact they have failed to consider, however, is the evolution of the expansionist impulse of the Inquisition in the course of its long, obsessive engrossment in the Jewish question and its "solution."

European historiography has been noted for its tendency to relegate the fate and fortunes of the Jews—including the major catastrophes that befell them—to some remote corner on the stage of history, without imputing to them any real influence on the general course of events. The result on more than one occasion has been a misconception of the general course which was often affected by the Jewish factor. The scholarly treatment of the Inquisitional expansion is a case in point.

The misconception in this particular case stemmed largely from the view of the Spanish Inquisition as a uniform, monolithic, and unaltered entity throughout the course of its existence. The Inquisition, however, was no mere machinery, an instrument in the hands of kings and popes. It was a living organism, with its own views and attitudes, as well as its own plans and aspirations. Scholars have agreed that it fought for its interests, promoted its schemes, canvassed its projects and, more particularly, represented a movement that it was anxious to support and defend. What has hitherto not been fully realized, or taken duly into account, is that changes were wrought in the Inquisitors' dispositions, in their tendencies and frame of mind. These changes evolved under the influence of practice, habits, traditions, gains and losses, and, needless to say, of certain developments in the general state of affairs. We ought to dwell on these changes for a moment before our study draws to a close.

As we have shown, the functionaries of the Inquisition, all or most of

whom were ardent racists, were bent upon achieving the aim of their movement, which was to ruin the conversos. Denied as they were by the Inquisition's own rules and, above all, by Spain's royal policy, the right to take
measures of mass extermination, they nonetheless believed that, with the
means at their disposal, they could destroy the conversos by degrees. This
expectation, however, was not realized. Despite the terrible punishment they
had taken, the conversos as a group were not crushed. What is more, they
stubbornly resisted the Inquisition and threw more and more obstacles in its
path. In consequence, the Inquisition came to feel a sense of failure. If in forty
years of ceaseless effort it could not vanquish the conversos, it had to look
for other, more effective means to beat them.

To apply more sweeping measures, however, the Inquisition had to gain
greater independence. But this meant challenging the king, and often the
pope, who insisted on supervising its activities. As none of them would grant
it greater powers, the Inquisition was forced to change its strategy. The
essence of that strategy was to achieve by width—that is, by broadening its
jurisdiction—what it could not gain by height—that is, by raising the level
of its prerogatives. It was not at all far-fetched to assume that once its
jurisdiction extended to encompass larger spheres than that of the conversos,
its increased influence would at length force the kings to give it greater
independence. This was the so-called political consideration that started the
expansion of the Inquisition in Spain (apart from the psychological causes,
to which we shall refer); and under these circumstances, it was inevitable that
the Inquisition would cast covetous eyes on the Moriscos—that large body
of infidels, about the size of the converso group, who had recently been
coerced to join the faith.

The forced conversion of the Moors, which began in Granada in 1501,
continued, under the prodding of the Inquisition, until it embraced both
Castile and Aragon.[1] What moved Ferdinand and Isabella to subscribe to
measures that directly contradicted both the terms of capitulation they
signed in Granada and the solemn assurances for freedom of religion they
repeatedly gave the Moors of their kingdoms? Unlike the conversos, it should
be noted, the Moors, both before and after their conversion, were not faced
with a powerful popular movement that demanded their punishment and
subjugation; consequently, the Kings were under no pressure to meet such
demands, which, unless satisfied, might threaten the country's stability. Nor
was there any other group in Spain, either in the nobility or the third estate,
that had a real interest in persecuting the Moors and later the Moriscos. It
was only the Inquisition and its closest associates that urged, incited and
persuaded the Kings first to consent to the Moors' forced conversion and
later to turn the whole Morisco camp into a hunting ground for the pursuit
of heretics. In both circumstances, the alluring argument was the opportunity

to realize a great goal—unity of faith in all the Spanish Kingdoms—an argument that was not even vaguely considered when the Spanish Inquisition was established.[2] Such an idea could occur to Jiménez only after the expulsion of the Jews and the capture of Granada, which placed all Moors in the Iberian peninsula at the Christians' mercy. For various reasons, which are not hard to guess, the idea could appear attractive to the Kings. But realizing the hardships and economic losses that its materialization was bound to entail, they naturally hesitated to give it flat approval and hampered its materialization.

That the Inquisition would seize on the "unity of faith" slogan to further its objectives could of course be readily envisioned. To be sure, the Moors, on their conversion to Christianity, were promised by the Crown immunity from the Inquisition for a period of forty years; but the Holy Office knew how to remove such an obstacle by some flimsy excuse it invented for the purpose, and the Moriscos soon fell under its sway. It also managed, by adroit maneuvers, to free itself from the various restraints which the Kings sought to place on its Morisco persecution. Following that, it saw its way clear to apply to the Moriscos the brutal treatment it had designed for them all.

William Lecky, the well-known inquirer into the evolution of European morals, believed that the persecutors' faith in a doctrine and their absolute devotion to its realization made them "indifferent" to the suffering of the victims and removed their "reluctance to inflict pain" upon them.[3] This may be true of some doctrinaires who urged stern measures against dissenters, but were personally detached from the scene of action. It can hardly be true of their followers and agents, who carried out the persecutory measures. In any case, Lecky's view does not square with the evidence offered by the Inquisition. What moved the Inquisitors (with a few exceptions, of course) to apply their dreadful techniques to the Moriscos was not devotion to this or that principle, but the desire to extend their controls and powers and demonstrate that extension in fact. They were certainly not enthusiastic at the prospect of making the Unity of Faith come true insofar as the Moriscos were concerned; for the ruthless persecution they launched against the latter was not calculated to bring them closer to Christianity but to keep them as far from it as possible. To assume that the Inquisitors did not realize all this is, to say the least, naive.

This brings us to the psychological factors involved in the expansion of the Inquisition. Indeed, in the long period (almost a whole century) during which the persecution of the Moriscos unfolded, the Inquisition used every outrageous act, every cruelty, intrigue and plot imaginable to provoke the Moriscos to rebellious resistance, and thereby justify their extermination. For the genocidal impulse of the Inquisition against the conversos (which was checked in mid-course, as we have indicated above) sought to find fulfillment in its struggle with the Moriscos; and it was not only that general impulse that drove them toward the new target. Associated with it was the habit of tormenting, robbing and humiliating their hapless victims, which sought exhibition in broader domains. And the extension of their habit of thus treating "culprits" from the camp of the conversos to that of the Moriscos cannot be explained by their "indifference to suffering" (as may be gathered from Lecky's theory) but rather by the anomalous, ghastly pleasure they derived from their hideous actions. The excesses to which they subjected the conversos did not satisfy, it appears, their ferocious urges, which grew with every brutal act. For such practices have the effect of drugs; they compel their addicts to seek further sources and means of intoxication. Only if we take this factor into account can we explain the twin phenomena that lie at the heart of the Inquisition's history: its endless search for new groups of victims and its perpetual attempt to reach higher stages of potency and repression.

It was, in all likelihood, not by accident that the start of a large-scale Morisco persecution nearly coincided with the Inquisition's campaign for the *limpieza*, when it forbade the universities of Toledo, Valladolid and Salamanca to issue graduate diplomas to converso students purely on the basis of their Jewish stock.[4] This decree should not be viewed as indication that the Inquisition then decided gradually to limit its ruthless, bloody war against the conversos, and henceforward to carry on that war primarily on a social-racial front. The racial measures it took were not meant to serve as substitute, but as supplement to its previous assaults; they formed a flank attack by which it sought to destroy the social ground on which the conversos stood when they wrestled with the Inquisition. For throughout the 16th and 17th centuries, the Holy Office kept sending conversos to the flames, although the number of those burned had gradually diminished due to the conversos' intermarriage with Old Christians. The Morisco heretics were to compensate the Inquisition for the decrease in the total of its heretical victims, which had previously been supplied entirely by conversos. The new victims provided an important source of income, which had been heretofore untapped,[5] and they offered justification for the Inquisition's claim that heresy in Spain was more widespread than it seemed. Nevertheless, the causes of the Morisco persecution must be looked for not only in the Inquisition's search for funds and its need to demonstrate its *raison d'être*, but also in the psychological reasons we have indicated above.

In fact, for the same reasons, we may safely conclude, the Holy Office did not plan to limit its operations to the two "foreign" groups (the conversos and Moriscos), and from the beginning of the century it repeatedly exhibited a growing desire to spread its net of terror over the broad masses of the Spanish people. Lucero's attacks on the Old Christians in Cordova indubitably reflected this tendency, which in his case was brought to an abrupt halt by the furious protest of the Spanish public. In no way could the Spaniards fall for the notion so audaciously advanced by the Inquisition—namely, that Old Christians became Jewish converts and, on top of this, missionaries of the Jewish faith. The bitter lesson of that dismal failure was not forgotten by the Holy Office. Never did it repeat that costly experiment, which almost endangered its very existence; but the inclination to penetrate Old Christian ranks was nonetheless not abandoned.

Thus in the mid-1520s, at the very time when it started its drive against the Moriscos, the Inquisition also opened a new route aimed at invading the Old Christian population. The new route was marked by a series of raids on marginal groups known to hold opinions which, though not tainted with Judaism, were disfavored or opposed by the majority of the people. Both by simple arguments and subtle twists, some of these opinions could easily be presented as squarely contradicting Christian law and doctrine, and as such condemned as heretical. Obviously, the consequences of these condemnations could be as fatal to their followers as those of any heresy, but the general public would be denied any means of judging the propriety of the Inquisition's procedures. For rarely did the bearers of these opinions have a way of making their views widely known, though their various theories covered the whole spectrum of European thought in the coming centuries. Accordingly, their adherents in Spain included mystics like the Illuminists, Quietists like the Molinists, rationalists like the Erasmists, spiritualists like the Jansenists, free thinkers like the Philosophists, and of course outright religious dissenters like the Protestants. Though each of these groups was numerically small, relatively and in absolute numbers, their combined persecution by the Inquisition left in its train enough bloodshed and ruin to terrorize large sections of the Old Christian camp.

It would have been anomalous if this quenchless thirst for power and its exercise by torture and terror had not overflowed the borders of Spain into the countries that fell under its sway. It was in the nature of things that in dealing with non-Spaniards, the Inquisition would give more free rein to its urges and its frequently checked or half-restrained schemes. The symptoms of this development were noticed in many places, but perhaps nowhere so markedly as in the Netherlands. Here the Inquisition (established in 1522), though formally distinct from Spain's Holy Office, was actually governed by the Spanish authorities, guided by their policies and abided by their orders, while these in turn were counseled and inspired by the chief leaders of the Inquisition in Spain. The following brief passage from Motley's famous work on the rise of the Dutch Republic should suffice to give us a clear idea of the Inquisition's performance in that country.

Upon the 16th of February, 1568, a sentence of the Holy Office *condemned all the inhabitants of the Netherlands to death as heretics.* From this universal doom only a few persons especially named were excepted. The proclamation of the King [Philip II], dated ten days later, confirmed this decree of the Inquisition and *ordered it to be carried into instant execution, without regard to age, sex, or condition.* This is probably the most concise death-warrant that was ever framed. Three million people, men, women, and children, were sentenced to the scaffold in three lines, and as it was well known that these were not harmless thunders, like some bulls of the Vatican, but serious and practical measures which were to be enforced, the horror which they produced can be easily imagined.[6]

Motley, who wrote this in 1856, long before World War II, could not believe that it was the purpose of the government actually to carry out the "wholesale plan in all its length and breadth," but he adds that the Netherlanders—who, needless to say, knew both Philip and his Inquisition—believed that for them nothing was "too monstrous" to be carried into effect. But the king's approval of the Inquisition's decree[7]—an approval given without any limitation—and his *unreserved* order to carry that death sentence into instant execution, leave no doubt to his intent. Above all, the *actions* taken by the authorities confirm the Netherlanders' grim expectations. Thus, the same author says that, following that decree, "men in the highest and humblest positions were daily and hourly," at a mere moment's warning, carried to the scaffold. Then he adds that Alva, in a letter to Philip,

> coolly estimated the number of executions which were to take place immediately after Holy Week, "at eight hundred heads." Many a citizen, convicted of possessing a hundred thousand florins and of no other crime, saw himself suddenly tied to a horse's tail, with his hands fastened behind him, and so dragged to the gallows. But although wealth was an unpardonable sin, poverty proved rarely a protection.[8]

That the Inquisition was inclined toward genocidal plans is also evident from other developments. In 1566 (less than two years before mass extermination was decreed for Holland) Philip entertained various plans for the settlement of the Morisco question; and some of these plans, which were most seriously considered, wavered between extermination and expulsion.[9] They were urged on him again in 1588; and if he refrained from adopting fully any of these courses, it was perhaps not so much because of moral scruples as because of his fear that implementation might provoke resistance that could be hard to quell. Similarly, if the death warrant on the Dutch people was not executed in full as announced, it was because that people broke out in a revolt that ultimately released them from the grip of Spanish rule. But the order as given was no idle threat. It reflected the intense wishes of its framers, and especially of Philip's Inquisitional counselors, to give, in that terrible punishment of the Netherlanders, free vent to their deep and intense desire—i.e., to that genocidal impulse they were forced to restrain in dealing with the Marranos and the Moriscos in Spain.

We may better understand the expansion of the Inquisition, and the peculiar compound of feelings that impelled it, if we consider the case of Nazi Germany and the evolution of the movement that created it. The rise of Nazism is commonly attributed to the military humiliation and economic distress which Germany suffered through its defeat in World War I, to the excessive indemnities the victors imposed on it, and to Germany's refusal to abandon all hope of becoming a leading power in the world. There is of course much truth in all these contentions, but they should not serve to underrate the fact that Nazism came to power in Germany on the gales of a furious antisemitic outburst. Indeed, anyone who treats this fact as marginal or as a freak phenomenon in German affairs is ignoring a key factor which determined not only the rise of Nazism to its peak of influence, but also some crucial stages of its history both before and during World War II. Like the Spanish antisemites' hatred of the conversos, the German Nazis' hatred of the Jews so affected their thinking, their policies and decisions that all their activities, in virtually all fields, were influenced in varying measures by that hate. Not only did that odium obsess them, but it overflowed their souls to the point where it needed more objects of torture, exploitation and destruction than the Jewish people could possibly provide. This explains why, while so strenuously engaged in the extermination of millions of Jews, they also exterminated millions of non-Jews and why they planned to annihilate more masses of non-Jews once their hold on Europe became secure. In both cases persecution overreached itself, so that from a means it became an end. Persecution was conducted for its own sake, and if allowed, it would expand in new directions, without any limit of space or time.

It is scarcely astonishing that those possessed by such desires lost not only the common capacity to distinguish between what is morally permissible and what is not, but also the ordinary ability to differentiate between what is feasible and what is not. This was very likely one of the factors leading to the fatal misjudgments they made. It would not be too far-fetched to suggest that Hitler's glaring, all-too-obvious errors in drawing America and Russia into the War, and Philip's bungled conduct of his own compulsive war against the Netherlands and England stemmed both from minds unhinged at least partly by the maddening urges to which we have referred.

Thus we see how both these developments—the Spanish and the German—which so drastically affected the history of Europe and had their beginnings in those torrents of hate which stemmed from ancient and later antisemitism, managed to produce anti-social forces which, driven as they were by their fierce animosities, proved almost impossible to restrain. Social psychologists are known to differentiate between animosity toward *opinions* or *beliefs* (and, because of this, toward their adherents too), and animosities toward *persons* as such, regardless of their views or behavior. The former animosities may decrease or disappear with the surrender of the hated views, but the latter hold fast under any circumstance in which the persons involved may find themselves. The hatred of the Inquisition for the *conversos* and that of the Nazis for the *Jews* belonged to the second type of hostility. It was a naked enmity for *persons* or *groups,* regardless of their social or ideological position. This is why both Spanish antisemitism (which was the real author of the Spanish Inquisition) and German Jew-hatred (which gave birth to Nazism) produced *race* theories about the Jewish *persons* aimed at their annihilation.

But having thus touched on the similarity of these movements, we ought also to note an important difference, which has a special bearing on the present study. Whereas Nazism openly proclaimed its goals and advocated total war to achieve them, the Inquisition never revealed its true aims and instead veiled its motives with arguments designed to justify its actions on moral grounds, as well as to give them an air of sanctity. The reason for the difference is evident. While Nazism grew out of a nihilistic culture which could openly value naked power, the Inquisition operated in a social climate imbued with religious concepts and principles. Hence, whereas Nazism could treat with contempt the demands of traditional morality, the Inquisition had to present its brutal acts as necessary, and indeed unavoidable means for the exaltation of the Catholic faith.

That the Inquisition succeeded, under the smokescreen of its claims, in concealing its real motives and intentions seems to be one of its most remarkable feats. But carefully examined, it is not a cause for wonder. Said the prophet Jeremiah:

> The heart of man is the most deceitful of all things,
> And deep is its perversion.
> Who can fathom it?[10]

As we see it, the "hearts" of the Inquisitors—i.e., their mental constitutions—were incurably perverted by the various influences that shaped their thinking and their tendencies. Apart from religious interests (which no doubt motivated some of its leaders), these tendencies were expressed by the officials of the Inquisition, down to its lowest functionaries and agents, in a blatant disregard for human life; a fervid desire to flaunt power and exercise control over life and death; a capacity for repression that could crush any spirit; a morbid passion for inflicting torture and causing pain that could break all resistance; and apart from all this, a shameless rapacity designed to render the torturer also the inheritor of his victim's goods. Could the Spanish Inquisition cover all this up?

It could; for the "heart of man is the most deceitful of all things." Clever persons can always find ways to present a base action as a noble deed; and the Inquisition's campaigners were very clever indeed. They were crafty agitators who knew how to argue, persuade and convince, and their task was facilitated by the long and bitter conflict between the Catholic Church and the Reformation. In the course of this conflict the rival camps fought and destroyed each other in a wholesale manner—all this allegedly because of differences in faith, for which they were ready to kill and be killed. Under such circumstances it was not hard to assume that all the actions of the Inquisition, however dreadful, were nevertheless motivated by religious interests.

So deeply was this notion implanted by the Inquisition in the public opinion of most European nations that even in the 19th and our own century most scholars had agreed that the Inquisitors *believed* in the validity of their reasons, as well as in the morality of their deeds. Hence, in appraising the functionaries of the Inquisition, most scholars did not question the sincerity of the Inquisitors, and differed only in appraising their characters. Thus, while conservatives viewed the Inquisitors as devout Christians who fulfilled their hard duties, the liberals considered them bigoted fanatics who acted as emissaries of a ruthless Church. This was also the position of the Commission on the Constitution, which the Cortes of Cádiz (1812) appointed to report, among other things, on the Inquisition. It goes without saying that it could not differentiate between the nature of the Inquisition's persecution of the conversos and that of its assaults upon other groups. Yet when referring to the passion that Fray Luis de León suffered at the hands of the Inquisition, the commission was so "overwhelmed with horror and amazement" that its members could not find words to express their feelings. "It is inconceivable," they said, "how far prejudice can fascinate, and false zeal can lead astray."[11]

But it was not only "prejudice" and "false zeal" that moved the Inquisition and its racist cohorts to act against the conversos as they did. What moved them above all was a deep-seated hatred—fierce, implacable, and infernal hatred—for everything related to anything Jewish, be it ethnic or religious, social or intellectual—that hatred which stemmed from prejudice and a tradition rooted in the peculiar condition of the Jews. Without bearing in mind this special hatred and the various sources from which it sprang, one cannot understand its volcanic outburst through the birth of the Inquisition and its early operations, or its outpouring of burning lava for more than three and a half centuries.

VIII. Expulsion

It would have been strange—indeed, incredible—if the Inquisition had not tried to extend its authority over the Jews of Spain. Both the fierce hatred of its functionaries for the Jews and their obsessive desire to increase their powers would seem to dictate such an extension; and in fact the Inquisition acted accordingly. Spanish Jewry was the first non-Marrano group that the Inquisition sought to get into its clutches. But its efforts in that direction were hindered by two factors—one constitutional and the other political.

Constitutionally, the Inquisition was designed to deal with Christians who consciously and stubbornly deviated from the faith[1]; it had no authority over Jews any more than over any other infidels. Politically, it encountered the opposition of the Kings, who wanted the Jews to remain unmolested and their services to the Crown to continue undisturbed. There was only one way in which the Inquisition could legally entangle Jews in its net: if it charged them as fautors and abettors of heretics. But these charges had to be well founded; for the Kings would not allow the Inquisition to unleash a massive persecution against the Spanish Jews of the kind it had mounted against the conversos (i.e., on the basis of inadequate evidence). Here the Inquisition encountered an obstacle that it could not easily overcome. Since the number of Judaizers was small, and the number of their Jewish "assistants" still smaller, the Inquisition could show the Kings only a few cases in which Jews were involved as aides of heretics. Thus it was faced with the inescapable necessity of adopting new tactics in attacking the Jews.

Espina, whose ideas guided the Inquisition, had advocated, as we have seen, two possible ways to eliminate the Jews from Spain: extermination or expulsion.[2] In its violent campaign against the conversos, the Inquisition tried Espina's first solution: it subjected the conversos to a *gradual* extermination, which it intended to accelerate and extend. To solve the Jewish question it had no choice but to apply Espina's second method: expulsion.

Expulsion, however, could be carried out only by direct order of the Kings, and the problem of the Inquisition was how to move the Kings to take an action they were known to oppose. It is in addressing this problem, perhaps more than elsewhere, that the Inquisition revealed its ingenuity, perseverance, and dogged determination. As it could not prove *judicially* that the Jews of Spain hampered its activity by aiding the Judaizers, it sought to implant the idea by propaganda—i.e., by constant repetition of the charge. As far as the populace was concerned, the Inquisition knew that it would not have to prove the charge by many *real* cases of Jews who had helped Judaizers. Its mere assertion that such cases were numerous would be taken by the masses as proof. In fact, the Inquisition could inflate its claim further by accusing the Jews of having been responsible for the very emergence of the Judaic heresy, and then of steadily nursing and sustaining it so as to prevent its extirpation.[3] It was inevitable that such a campaign, if prolonged, would stir the populace to attack the Jews, and the realization of this eventuality by the Kings was, in fact, all the Inquisition needed. It counted on the great sensitivity of the Sovereigns to Spanish public opinion and on their interest in law and order. Especially, it knew, they would fear unrest while fighting the Granadan war.

Faced with the Inquisition's prodding and agitation, the Sovereigns felt that they had better yield. But they looked for an honorable way out. They knew of course that the presence of the Jews did not impede the Inquisition's anti-converso operations, but they gave the appearance of believing that it did, and consequently that the "solution" proposed by the Inquisition was an absolute necessity. Thus, on January 1, 1483, the Kings informed the Inquisitors of their decision to expel the Jews from the archbishopric of Seville and the bishoprics of Cordova and Jaén. The three sees made up most of Christian Andalusia, which was then the sphere of the Inquisition's activity. And so that region, which for more than six centuries had been the great center of Spanish Jewry, was at last cleared of the Jews who still lived there after the upheaval of 1391.

"It is beyond any doubt," says Baer, "that the Inquisition's influence on the royal resolution to expel the Jews of Andalusia was *decisive*."[4] Extreme as it is, this assessment is correct, and it can be extended also to what happened a few years later in Aragon. The introduction of the Inquisition into that kingdom was strongly opposed by the Aragonese conversos, as well as by many leading Old Christians. The resistance was especially formidable in two cities: Teruel and Saragossa, and persisted even after inquisitional tribunals had been set up there and begun their work. The Inquisition no doubt argued that this powerful resistance was largely inspired by the Jews, and that the Jews must be removed from the kingdom if the Inquisition was to accomplish its task. Once again the King yielded to the Inquisition. On May 12, 1486, he informed the Inquisitors in Saragossa of his decision to expel the Jews from their archbishopric and the bishopric of Sancta María de Albarrazin, which included the town of Teruel.[5]

The Inquisition's influence on this second decree of expulsion is evident from the fact that the Inquisitors of Aragon, like their predecessors in Andalusia, were empowered to carry out the edict. It is apparent also from Ferdinand's letter of July 22, 1486, to Tomás de Torquemada, the Inquisitor-General, in which the King begs, rather than orders the Inquisitor to postpone the departure of the Jews from Teruel for six months, "in addition to the three that the Inquisitors had given them."[6] The King, who admitted that this delay was granted in accordance with his own expressed wishes (evidently, without first consulting Torquemada), now argued for the additional postponement by claiming that the Jews would be unable to sell their houses and pay their debts in the time allotted them. He concludes by saying to the Inquisitor-General: "Look into this, and if it is agreeable to you, let it be done."[7]

The order of expulsion from Teruel and its bishopric and, what is more, from the archbishopric of Saragossa, was in all likelihood ultimately rescinded. But this does not mean that the original decree did not stem mainly from the Inquisition's pressure. The King had of course "the last word" on the subject as on other matters that related to the Inquisition. But he would not retract an order of this nature unless moved to do so by overriding reasons. In this case we may take it for granted that the Jews of Aragon gave him a huge sum to withdraw the edict; and the King, who was then in the midst of a campaign aimed at reducing Granada's strongholds (and was, as usual, hard-pressed for funds), no doubt considered the offer too valuable— and too timely—to be turned down. He was of course sure that the requirements of the war would be regarded even by the most extreme Inquisitors as sufficient to justify the revocation of the order. And yet he could not slight the commitment he had made to the Holy Office and the Inquisitor-General, whose granitelike hardness and relentless ferocity made him virtually indomitable. If indeed Ferdinand canceled the order, he did it no doubt with the consent of Torquemada, who may have been compensated by a solemn promise that, as soon as Granada was conquered, all the Jews of Spain would be expelled.

We believe that such a promise was given, and if it was, the Inquisition, rather than retreating, came closer to its goal with respect to the Jews. But "closer" is no final achievement; and the Inquisition could not yet rest on its laurels. To secure the fulfillment of the royal promise, it thought it vital to exert public pressure on the Kings; and this time the pressure, the Inquisition realized, had to be exceptionally strong, so as to overcome the great counterinfluence that the Jews would undoubtedly bring to bear. Accordingly, the Inquisition determined to fan the anti-Jewish feelings rampant in Spain into a popular fury that would make the Kings comply. But what could possibly create such a fury? It evidently took the Inquisition some time before it formed its plan.

The plan was to prepare a monstrous trial against the Jews for conspiring with conversos to paralyze the Inquisition and kill all Christians by a magic conjuration. The terrible incantation was to be pronounced by Jews over a consecrated Host and the heart of a Christian child whom Jews and conversos would crucify for the purpose. A number of Jews, among them leading figures, together with an equal number of conversos, would be "caught" and forced by torture to admit to the crime. Their confessions, once publicized, would inflame the populace; attacks on the Jews would break out in many places, and these would be followed by the King's decision to expel the Jews from the country.

Thus was born the case of the "Holy Child of La Guardia," to which we have already referred. It is hard to believe that such a crude charge, concocted on the basis of Espina's sordid tales, could serve as adequate grounds for the Inquisition to conduct for sixteen months such a ramified "investigation" involving many agents and two tribunals, and supervised by the Inquisitor-General himself. Yet *this* was the charge which the Inquisition tried to prove by "confessions" extracted from Jews and conversos by means of the most appalling tortures. Not all the details of the "crime" as conceived by the Inquisition could be elicited from the "confessions," and no coherent story emerged.[8] The Inquisitors would undoubtedly have continued their attempts to eliminate the most glaring contradictions from the "testimonies;" but the fall of Granada was impending and the Inquisition decided to issue its verdict on the basis of the evidence it had procured.

Thus on November 14, 1491, only two weeks before Granada's capitulation, the Inquisition made public in Avila its sentence condemning five Jews and six conversos to the stake for desecrating the Host and crucifying a Christian child, whose heart was ripped out for the purpose of a conjuration aimed at neutralizing the Inquisition and sending all Christians raving mad to their deaths. The punishments by the secular authorities soon followed. They burned effigies of three of the condemned Jews, who had died before judgment was pronounced, and tore the flesh of two others, an old man and his son, with hot pincers before burning them alive. The conversos, who professed repentance and asked for readmission to the Church, were strangled before their corpses were burned. In Avila, where the sentence was issued, one Jew was stoned to death by the populace, and preparations to attack the Jewish community were halted only by the timely intervention of the Kings. At the same time the Inquisition made public its sentence in all the cities of Castile and Aragon, with the obvious intent of arousing the people and moving the Sovereigns to proceed against the Jews in the manner the Inquisition had urged.[9] It was not long before the Kings responded. On March 31, 1492, three months after they had entered Granada, they ordered the banishment of the Jews from their kingdoms.[10]

Lea, who clearly saw the connection between the trial of the Holy Child of La Guardia and the expulsion of the Jews from Spain, tried nevertheless to present the accusations as having some basis in fact, thus suggesting that the trial as a whole was not fabricated by the Inquisition. He wrote:

> Possibly some conversos may have sought to procure by means of sorcery immunity from the threatening dangers of the Inquisition, for

it is not easy to set bounds to the superstitious credulity of the period, but it is extremely improbable, as Juce Franco pointed out in his defense, that Jews, who were not subject to inquisitorial jurisdiction, would have dabbled in such dangerous practice to shield conversos with whom they had no sympathy.[11]

It is not, however, "extremely improbable," but utterly impossible for any Jew to have been associated with conversos in a magic conjuration wrought with a wafer and the heart of a Christian child. For no Jew attributed any power to the Host, whether consecrated or not, and no Jew would use it for a conjuration of any kind, with or without hearts of Christian children. Consequently, the assertions of conversos under torture that Jews had performed a conjuration with a Host to neutralize the Inquisition or to kill many Christians had no basis in fact, and could be made by them only in response to their torturers in order to end their intolerable pain. And since the evidence was fabricated regarding the Jews, it was inevitably fabricated regarding the conversos, too. Since no Jews made such a conjuration, no conversos could "assist" them in making it. Hence the outcry of one of the Jewish martyrs of that trial that the whole thing was the "greatest lie in the world."[12] Yet such a great lie could not have appeared of itself. Its structure was too large, too complex and too functional—that is, designed to serve a certain end—to have been built without an architect. That architect was the Inquisition.

The Inquisitors naturally knew the truth, and so did the Sovereigns; so also did many others in Spain, like the historians Bernáldez and Alonso de Palencia, who chose to ignore the trial in their histories. No wonder the Kings acted like their chroniclers and refrained from including the "revelations" of the La Guardia trial among the reasons they gave for their order of expulsion. If the trial of the Holy Child of La Guardia influenced their decision to issue the order, the influence must be related to other aspects of that gruesome affair.

The expulsion of the Jews from Spain was brought about by essentially the same factors that caused their expulsion from England and France and other places in Europe. It was caused by the completion of a historical development that began with the Kings' support of the Jews against a popular opposition, which was originally minor, and ended with the withdrawal of the royal support when that opposition became intense and widespread, and assumed a revolutionary character. In Spain the kings' support of the Jews lasted longer than anywhere else, but when Ferdinand and Isabella came to power, Jewish history in Spain had run its course. If the Kings listened to the Inquisition's counsels and paid high regard to Torquemada, it was because they knew that Torquemada and the Inquisition represented a movement too strong to ignore and a popular sentiment too deep to trifle with. That sentiment, they felt, was ineradicable; it was bound to grow, with or without the Inquisition, and persistently demand satisfaction. Sooner or later, the Sovereigns realized, they would yield to this relentless demand if they did not wish to affront the masses and lose the popularity they enjoyed among them. Especially now, after the conquest of Granada, when they stood at the height of their prestige, content with their people's unbounded admiration, they would not undermine that hard-won achievement by their continued protection of the Jews. Thus, they concluded that the best possible time to perform the unavoidable operation was the *present;* delay might cause them harm, and therefore should be avoided.

Needless to say, none of these considerations appear in their "justification" of the edict of expulsion. In fact, the only reason they gave for this edict was that the Jews had been aiding the Judaizers and there was no other way to extirpate the heresy save the expulsion of the Jews from Spain. The reason bears the stamp of the Inquisition's agitation, which provided the Sovereigns with a "noble" excuse for an ignoble action, and one finds it hard to take it seriously. Yet many historians accepted it unquestioningly as a valid explanation for the expulsion, and thus attributed the Sovereigns' move to purely religious motives. Scholarship has often been misled by authority, but rarely to so large an extent. For what greater delusion could penetrate and distort the annals of mankind?

APPENDICES

APPENDICES

A

The Number of the
Marranos in Spain

How many Jews went over to Christianity in the mass conversions of 1391 and 1412? Scholars differ widely in answering this question, and their estimates range from some tens of thousands[1] to three hundred thousand "in the 15th century."[2] In *The Marranos of Spain* I presented the reasons for my conclusion that toward the end of that century, the number of New Christians in Castile and Aragon was approximately twice as large as the latter figure.[3] Among other things, I assessed the Marrano community in Seville in 1391 at some 25,000 souls and in Seville's archbishopric at some 20,000 more[4]; and in the second edition of that work, I answered the arguments advanced by S. W. Baron against these estimates. I also added proofs to support my belief that ninety years later, when the Inquisition was founded, the Marrano community in the city of Seville was 40–45,000 strong, while in the archbishopric it reached about 70,000.[5]

My starting point in assessing the number of Seville's Marranos was the testimony left us by Hasdai Crescas, the famous leader of the Jews of Aragon. According to Crescas, "the majority of Seville's Jews who numbered six to seven thousand households" (i.e., 30–35,000 souls) were converted during the riots of 1391.[6] Crescas did not refer to the Jews of the archbishopric but to those of the city of Seville alone, and his statement seems valid for a number of reasons, including the great caution and accuracy he showed in all his other reports about the conversions of 1391. What is more, in response to the criticism of Baron, I cited an additional dozen sources in support of my conclusions concerning Seville. They have never been disproved, and it is hard for me to see how they can be confuted.

Nevertheless, J. N. Hillgarth seems to have ignored these testimonies and, referring to the evidence I cited from Crescas, dismissed it by asserting that "Crescas had no knowledge of . . . the number of Jews" in Seville.[7] How the leader of the Jews of Aragon could be so uninformed about Sevillian Jewry, or so callous as to impart to the Jews of France worthless information on its "massive" conversion (which allegedly never occurred), Hillgarth does not explain. Perhaps in making the above remark he relied on Isidore Loeb, who questioned Crescas' statement on the ground that the latter's place of residence (Saragossa) was "far" from Seville, and therefore he could have been unaware of the number of Seville's Jews.[8] Such an argument, however, might be considered valid for some small place in Castile, but not for such a great and famous community as Seville's, with which the Jews of Aragon had many contacts, or for a man like Crescas, who must have been in touch with Castile's Jewish leaders. Indeed Crescas, we may assume, had many sources at his disposal, from which he could acquire definite knowledge about the number of Jews in the chief Castilian cities.

But I think we can bypass Loeb's argument, and also refute Hillgarth's assertion, by presenting the testimony of a Sevillian author who was undoubtedly well informed of the size of Seville's Marrano community. This was the historian Alonso de Palencia who, in one of his statements about the conversos, casts clear light on the question before us. In his *Guerra de Granada*, he writes:

> In 1481 the conversos began to flee from Seville as a result of the Inquisition. Among other excuses they used was the terrible plague which at the time was ravaging the city. The plague was such that it caused *about 16,000 victims* among them. *Another such number escaped the punishment [of the Inquisition] through flight,* so that the aspect of the city was the saddest and it appeared almost uninhabited.[9]

Palencia's figures for the Marrano *plague victims* in Seville and the *refugees* from the harassed city form together an approximate total of 32,000 souls. Assuming that one third of Seville's Marranos *remained* in the city despite the plague and the persecution (an assumption that would not be far-fetched), the Sevillian Marrano community at the time would have comprised about 48,000 people. But if so, my estimate of 40–45,000 for the Marrano population of Seville in 1481 appears to be fully confirmed, as does my conclusion that Seville's converts in 1391 numbered some 25,000. Surely we cannot suppose that Palencia's figures, too, were groundless or remote from reality. Unlike Crescas, it cannot be said of him that he lived "far" from Seville; for he lived in Seville for many years, and consequently there is no reason to assume that he did not know the number of Seville's Marranos. Similarly, my assessment of the number of conversos who *fled* Seville in 1482–83 (14,000),[10] based on the number of deserted houses in Andalusia in the wake of their flight as indicated by Pulgar,[11] is fully confirmed by Palencia's account. Finally, Palencia's statement that, following that exodus, the city of Seville looked "almost uninhabited" suggests that the Marrano community in Seville formed a very large part of its population, probably some 40 to 45 percent of its total.[12]

But the question of the number of Seville's Marranos is only part of a far broader problem. Much more important is the question of the size of the Marrano population in Spain as a whole, and here again my estimate is based, to begin with, on an item of information found in the sources—the 15th century chronicles of Zacuto and Arévalo, both of which give us the same number for the converts of 1391: "more than two hundred thousand." To be sure, Loeb and Baer considered this number highly exaggerated and tried to reduce it to several thousands by suggesting corrections in the texts of the above chronicles.[13] But, as I have shown, their emendations were arbitrary, conflict with certain indisputable data, and therefore cannot support their theory about the scope of the conversions of 1391.[14] The theory, in any case, was virtually exploded when support for the numbers of Zacuto and Arévalo came from a newly discovered document: the estimate of the converts of 1391 given by Reuben ben Nissim Gerundi in September of that year.[15] Gerundi speaks of 140,000 converts, a figure considerably lower than Zacuto's, but as I pointed out, in September 1391 (only three months after the beginning of the riots), the author most likely did not possess all the relevant information and, in any case, "could not take into account those who left Judaism *in the wake of the riots* and therefore came also to be regarded as converts of '1391'."[16] Baron seems to have come close to this view. "Reuben's figure," he says, "probably was but part of the larger total of 200,000 converts cited by Abraham Zacuto in his *Sefer Yuhasin*."[17]

The problem is thus really limited to the figure given by Zacuto and Arevalo for the converts of 1412. It is the identical figure: "more than 200,000"[18]; and because of this identity it of course appears questionable. Loeb avoided dealing with this estimate, while Graetz concluded that the persecution of 1412 resulted in "at least 20,000 forced converts."[19] Yet this conclusion cannot be accepted for a very simple reason. If we compare the lists of taxes the Jews of Castile paid the Crown in 1474 or 1482 with those they paid in 1291, we can see that the total sum for the later years was reduced to about a fourth of the earlier figure.[20] What could have caused this great reduction? Obviously, either a drastic deterioration in the Jews' economic condition or a sharp decline in their numbers through conversions. But if we rely on Abravanel's statement regarding the wealth of Spain's Jewry on the eve of the Expulsion,[21] the former possibility must be excluded; and thus we must conclude that it was their massive conversion that brought about that great reduction of their taxes.

Now, since the taxes had fallen to approximately a fourth of what they had been and since the number of Spain's Jews during the Expulsion amounted to approximately 225,000, we might assume that the number of Spain's Jews in 1290 was at least several times larger. Indeed, according to Graetz, the Jews of Castile alone comprised in 1290 over 800,000 souls,[22] and although this assessment may appear to us excessive, his computation could not be altogether wrong. In addition, we ought to take into account the natural increase of Spain's Jews between 1290 and 1391, as well as in the century following the great riots (i.e., between 1391 and 1492). Hence, even if the number of Castile's Jews toward the end of the 13th century was considerably smaller than that indicated by Graetz, it seems obvious that a figure of 200,000 or 230,000 for the converts of both 1391 and 1412 would not cover the difference between the number of Spain's Jews during the Expulsion and their number in 1290. Obviously, some other large figure, such as the one given by Arévalo and Zacuto for the conversions of 1412, could fill the gap.

Yet the identity of the figure they give for 1412 with the one they indicate for 1391 stands in the way of its acceptance. Offhand, it would seem that Zacuto, who completed his chronicle in 1504, may have borrowed the information for 1412 from Arévalo, who composed his work c. 1487, and that the latter's text was corrupted in the section dealing with the conversions in 1412. But this assumption must be rejected. A comparison of the parallel passages shows that Zacuto's account contains data not found in Arévalo's, and this leads us to the conclusion that Zacuto, like Arévalo, relied on an *earlier* source. If a copyist's error must therefore be considered here, it ought to be related to the *original* version and not to Arévalo's manuscript. Two questions, therefore, seem to be involved: (a) Was the text used by the chroniclers corrupt or, conversely, presented the original version? and (b) Was that version based on reliable information? To answer this question, we must first summarize what we know about the conversions of 1412 *besides* what was copied by Zacuto and Arévalo from their common source.

The only additional figures we possess relate to the converts made by Ferrer in the course of his missionary campaign among the Jews in both Castile and Aragon. Contemporary estimates of the total of his conversions range from 15–100 thousand; and these include not only Jewish but also Moslem converts, as well as reformed Christian sinners.[23] Thus, we cannot gather from these estimates how many Jews were converted by Ferrer. But what is important to note in this connection is that most of his campaign in Castile was over before the promulgation of the laws of 1412. And these laws no doubt caused an influx of Jewish converts far larger than that caused by the preaching of Ferrer.

The same may be said about Aragon. Ferrer's missionary campaign in that country lasted much longer than it did in Castile; it was also assisted directly by the agitation conducted by the anti-Pope Benedict XIII, and it undoubtedly had a more notable effect. But as in Castile, most conversions in Aragon must have resulted from the harsh anti-Jewish laws which were enacted in that kingdom, too (1413).[24] Especially conducive to many conversions was the law that stipulated the removal of the Jews from mixed neighborhoods to boroughs of their own. Since no houses were provided for the expelled, many of them were driven out to the fields. The execution of the order was thorough and ruthless, and caused intolerable agonies to many of the expelled. Solomon Alami, a contemporary author, described their condition in vivid terms:

> People who had been well protected in their homes were ousted from their dwellings to find shelter in caves. Others live in huts in summer and in winter, with hungry infants crying in the bosoms of their mothers, and with boys and girls dying from exposure to the cold and the snow.[25]

Alami wrote these words in 1415, more than three years after the laws of Catalina had been issued in Castile. The ordeal therefore remained unrelieved for a long time, and Zacuto tells us that these conditions persisted for seven years (i.e., from the beginning of 1412 to the end of 1418).[26] We may wonder at the endurance of the expelled Jews who saw their children undergo such torments and still refused to surrender their faith. But we should also bear in mind that a whole people cannot consist of martyrs and heroes, and that the resistance of many must have broken down in the face of the continued hardships and tragedies. It would not be unreasonable to assume therefore that with the increase of the distress among the homeless Jews, the number of conversions also increased.

In fact, the conversions produced by the law of 1412 forbidding Jews to live in mixed boroughs began shortly after the publication of that law, and even *before* it was actually enforced, as is evidenced by the testimony of Alvar García de Santa María, the official chronicler of Juan II. Writing in his survey for the year 1411 about the results produced by the laws of Catalina, he tells us that "many Moors and Jews were converted to Christianity in order *not to have to leave their homes*"; that except for Seville, where the Jews got a reprieve with respect to their immediate departure, "many" of them turned Christian in *"all the cities and towns of the Kingdom"* (apparently before enforcement took place), while the enforcement of the segregation accelerated, in some places, the process of conversion, and because of this, as Alvar García states, *"every day there were converted to Christianity both Jews and Moors."*[27]

But conversions were produced also for another reason—perhaps no less compelling. While García speaks of the housing problem as a major cause of the immediate conversions, Alami refers also to the economic strangulation effected by the laws of 1412. As he puts it: "The majority of the tax gatherers were converted when denied the right to farm and collect taxes; they knew no other profession from which they could derive a living."[28] But the upper social strata of the Jews were not the only groups that felt the crunch of the new order. "On account of the dryness [i.e., because all the sources of income were dried up], and the [resultant] pressing needs," says Alami, "a part of the artisans were also converted; . . . they were cast down by these trials and tribulations and could not rise again."[29] Alami does not tell us how large that "part" was. But judging by the restrictions the laws of 1412 placed on Jewish industry and the sale of its products,[30] we may readily assume that the "part" referred to was very large indeed.

We must bear in mind also a third factor that undoubtedly swelled the wave of conversions. This was the hopelessness felt by Spain's Jews in the wake of the enactments of 1412. In previous persecutions they had been able to turn for help to the king or the pope; but now both royal and papal governments appeared solidly united to effect their conversion. Apart from this, in other cases of repression, Jews had been allowed to depart from the country; the laws of Valladolid, however, forbade them to leave Spain, or even move from the king's areas to those of the nobles. Appeal and escape seeming equally impossible, many Jewish communities, large and small, saw no sense in further resistance and capitulated almost to a man.

Expressing the desperation pervading Spain's Jewry, a Hebrew dirge written in those days says: *"In 1412, the sky was covered with a cloud [so heavy] that it blocked the passage of any prayer to God."*[31] And the same lament, which was probably composed somewhere in northwestern Castile, describes the havoc produced in the Jewish communities of that region following the issuance of Catalina's laws. It mentions the calumnies, the agitation and the threats that accompanied the execution of those decrees *"which were adamantly enforced until the Jews were converted."*[32] Among the communities affected, the elegy mentions those of Zamora, Salamanca, Valladolid, Toro, Segovia, Avila, Benavente, León, Valencia,[33] Astorga, Mayorga,[34] Palencia, Paredes and Burgos.[35] And what was true with regard to the communities of that region no doubt applied also to the other communities of Castile and, in large measure, of Aragon as well. Hence, judged by the number of conversions they caused, the laws of 1412 may have been demographically not much less disastrous to the Jews of Spain than the pogroms of 1391. For while most of the conversions of 1391 occurred in the places hit by the riots, those that followed the laws of 1412–1413 occurred in *all* areas where these laws were in force, and this meant actually throughout Spain. No wonder Zacuto described the calamity of 1412 as the *"greatest* shemad [persecution accompanied by mass conversion] *that had ever taken place."*[36]

Thus, it seems clear that the figures given in some Christian sources for the number of Jews converted by Ferrer are too small to reflect the scope of the conversion that took place in that period among the Jews. Those figures referred only to the Jews (and Moors) who were converted under the influence of *Ferrer's preaching during his visits in certain cities;* they did not embrace the conversions effected in the numerous localities he did *not* visit or during the entire period of the persecution (1411–1418), which by far exceeded the short terms of his agitation even when put all together. Obviously, a much larger number, closer to the one suggested by Zacuto and Arevalo, would appear more realistic. There remains, however, the question of the precise identity of their figure for 1412 with the one they cite for 1391. Can this identity be explained by anything save a copyist's error?

Before we attempt to answer this question, we must carefully consider certain facts and probabilities.

Despite the criticism justifiably leveled at medieval statistics, the Jewish communities of Castile and Aragon were constantly aware of their actual size. The collective taxes they had to pay annually necessitated frequent recounting of their members and reassessment of their possessions, and the strictness developed in this regard is attested by the decisions adopted in Saragossa c. 1280 and in Valladolid in 1432.[37] Thus, while establishing its numerical strength, each community would occasionally calculate the losses it suffered from conversion. It transmitted this information to the country's Jewish leadership (i.e., the Rab de la Corte and his officials), even if for no other reason than to explain its inability to meet a tax quota; and this information, assembled and combined, may have served that leadership in computing the conversion losses throughout the period of 1391–1418. Such a computation could be made, in our opinion, c. 1422 (that is, after the termination of the persecution), or perhaps as late as 1432 (when the Castilian Jewish communities met in Valladolid and took stock of the situation).

We must assume, however, that their calculations were not based solely on official communications. For their records must have been incomplete and marked by great lacunae. Many communities, whose public functions were disrupted by the massacres, the flight of their members and the conversions, could not supply the Jewish leadership of Spain more than scanty data, to begin with; and to fill the gaps in their information, the calculators unavoidably relied in many cases on unconfirmed notions and assessments. What was known for sure, however, about these communities was the number of their

Jews prior to 1391 and their number at the time of the computation. And taking these data into account, the calculators could make a reasonable assessment of the *total number of Jews who went over to Christianity throughout the persecution of 1391 to 1418.*

It would seem that by means of such an assessment, they came up with a total of over 400,000, while the number of converts in each of the conversion periods of 1391–1398 and 1412–1418 remained inevitably unresolved. Consequently, they decided to divide the grand total into two equal halves, intending thereby to give a general idea of the enormous scope of the disasters, and probably believing that by doing so they would not make too big an error. It was of course a rough and ready division, obviously inaccurate, but it may not have been too far from the truth.

This is how the equality of the figures for "1391" and "1412" can possibly be explained. But much more important than these figures is, in our opinion, their total of "over 400,000." Apart from the reasons indicated above, it gains credibility by its basic conformity to the figure given by Isaac Abravanel for the conversos in the 1490s: "over 600,000."[38] It conforms to this latter number because Abravanel's figure no doubt included the natural increase of the conversos since 1391—that is, in the course of three generations.[39] It also agrees with the high percentage of the Marranos in Spain's city populations, as indicated by accounts such as those of Quirini, the Venetian ambassador to Spain in 1506,[40] and the Polish traveler Nicholas Popielovo in 1485.[41]

Of course, the paucity of our data on the developments under review inevitably leads us to question the few we have. But questioning need not imply rejection. It should be noted that prior to the discovery of Gerundi's figure for the converts of 1391,[42] scholarly opinion was generally most skeptical—indeed, censorious—of Zacuto's estimate for that year. In view of this, we should not be surprised if a similar discovery at some future date will likewise support a more positive evaluation of his figure for "1412."

B

Diego de Anaya and His
Advocacy of Limpieza

The question of the beginnings of the racial policy of the College of San
Bartolomé in Salamanca cannot be settled without taking into consideration the printed versions of the bulls of Bendict XIII and Martin V authorizing the founding of the college. Both bulls were published by Ruiz de
Vergara in his biography of Anaya[1] and later in the second edition of this
work by the Marqués de Alventos in his three-volume history of the college.[2]
Both bulls prohibit the acceptance of collegians who are not of "pure
blood"—a definition that allegedly referred to Christians of Jewish origin.

A. Domínguez Ortiz, who rightly judged the undated *limpieza* statute of
the college to belong to Don Diego de Anaya, also took as genuine the papal
confirmation of the *limpieza* policy as suggested in the two published bulls.[3]
This opinion, however, cannot be accepted for the following reasons:

1) The printed version of Benedict XIII's bull (dated Oct. 2, 1414) contains
the instruction that the collegians should be *integrae famae et opinionis ex puro
sanguine procedentes,* and the printed version of Martin V's bull (dated May 4,
1418) likewise required the collegians to be *puri sanguinis.*[4] Registered copies
of these bulls are preserved in the Vatican archives[5]; and doubting the
genuineness of the aforesaid Latin phrases, I examined those copies and can
state with full assurance that they do *not* contain those phrases; nor do they
include any other reference to "purity of blood." Obviously, the versions
reproduced by Vergara were not those of the original documents but copies
to which the phrases in question were added (probably in the 16th century)
by officials of the college.

2) It would have been unthinkable for Benedict XIII to endorse discrimi-

nation against converts from Judaism at a time when Paul of Burgos was his mainstay in Castile and one of his chief aides and counselors in all major matters relating to the papacy. It is likewise extremely hard to believe that Martin V would adopt such a policy when he felt indebted to Gonzalvo, Paul's son, for his position on his election as pope and when he, Martin V, knew that Gonzalvo, Paul of Burgos, and other conversos wielded an influence not to be slighted in the kingdoms of Castile and Aragon. And why should these popes have issued such instructions? At the very time when Benedict XIII signed his bull concerning the College of San Bartolomé, he was in the midst of a major effort to convert the Jews of Castile and Aragon and doing everything he possibly could to attract them to Christianity. We have no indication that either he or his successor, Martin V, departed, or was inclined to depart, from the age-old policy of the Church concerning converts, which called for their full and complete equality with all other Christians.

3) Albert A. Sicroff thought that when the bulls were issued (i.e., in 1414 and 1418), the "purity of blood" phrases referred to did not convey the racial meaning that they came to signify in later generations. In this, as we shall see, he was right. But Sicroff also believed that in the latter sense, the term was not employed before the 16th century[6]; and in this he was doubtless wrong. The satire composed in 1449, farcically discussing an imaginary privilege given by Juan II to an Old Christian hidalgo, speaks of Marrano physicians who kill their Old Christian patients and then marry the latter's widows "para ensuciar y mancillar la *sangre limpia*." And when Marcos García de Mora says of himself that he has the "appearance of a *pure* Old Christian" (gesto de christiano viexo, *limpio*), he too may have referred to his "purity of blood."[7] Nevertheless, it is true that for most of the century the common term used for "pure Old Christians" was "Christianos viejos *lindos*" (not *limpios*).[8]

Sicroff thought that the "purity of blood" phrases found in the printed texts of the bulls *were* included in the original documents, but that in the 16th century, with the growth of the *limpieza* movement, the *bartolomicos,* who wished to show their priority in practicing *limpieza* in the colleges of Spain, "attached themselves" to the aforementioned expressions in the bulls, to which they ascribed the meaning which they had in their time (that is, in the 16th century).[9] The popes of the early 15th century, however, had something else in mind.

Sicroff conjectures that by "pure blood" the popes indicated legitimate birth,[10] and believes to have found support for this conjecture in José de Rújula's assertion that the *colegios mayores* were established exclusively for poor students.[11] On the basis of this, Sicroff assumes that the colleges were inclined to admit as collegians also "foundlings or children of uncertain parents" and that the popes (i.e., Benedict XIII and Martin V) were opposed to that tendency.[12]

Sicroff's conjecture may be rejected, first, on the grounds that the term in question is missing in the registered copies of *both* bulls (thereby excluding the possibility of an error). But it is untenable for other reasons, too. In the beginning of the 15th century, *limpio sangre* signified noble descent, or rather noble blood that remained unaffected by plebeian or other deleterious admixtures.[13] Benedict XIII, who was a Spaniard, certainly knew that the people in Spain would understand by "pure blood" noble origin, and Martin V knew that, too. It does not seem likely that they wished to establish a school for sons of nobles only. However, if they had something else in mind—such as refusing college admission to those who lacked legitimate birth—they would have said so in terms precluding misconception.[14]

In brief, Sicroff is probably right in assuming that in the 16th century, with the growth of the *limpieza* movement, the *bartolomicos* were anxious to demonstrate the "antiquity" of the statute they had enacted against the conversos; but to prove this they did not "attach themselves," as he suggests, to the term *puri sanguinis* (or *ex puro sanguine*), allegedly found in the bulls, which could not possibly contain it, but added these terms to the original texts (as indicated above, § 1).

It seems exceptionally audacious for the authorities of a school devoted to religious studies to make such interpolations in papal bulls; and it is certainly an unwelcome task to suggest that this is just what they did. Perhaps this is why Sala Balust[15] and Gaztambide,[16] who no doubt noticed that the crucial phrases were absent in the copies of the Vatican register, pass in silence over their presence in the texts printed by Ruiz de Vergara. But the facts we have pointed out, and the arguments we have presented, cannot, in our judgment, be disregarded. They force us to acknowledge the unpleasant truth.

C

When Did Sarmiento
Leave Toledo?

The date of Sarmiento's departure from Toledo raises a question that so far has not been satisfactorily settled. The annals of the period suggest two dates: November 1449 and February 1450. Is either of them correct, and if so, which?

The date of November 1449 is clearly indicated by the *Crónica de Juan II.* Here we are told that Prince Enrique came to Toledo at the "beginning of November" (1449) and that, after the welcome celebrations, which lasted eight to ten days, he "requested" Sarmiento to give up both his command of the alcazar and his position as chief judge.[1] Sarmiento, according to this account, consented, and shortly thereafter the alcazar passed, at the Prince's order, to Pedro Girón. Then, the same *crónica* adds, a "few days later," Don Lope de Barrientos informed Sarmiento of the Prince's "will" that he also *leave* Toledo, to which Sarmiento reluctantly agreed, after some argument.[2] He would ask the Prince, he said, for an exit license and "leave this night *(esta noche)* with all my possessions." This is indeed what he did.[3]

It is clear that, according to the timetable of events recorded in the *Crónica de Juan II,* Sarmiento left Toledo about the middle of November. Can we find support for this timetable in any other source?

The compiler (or editor) of the *Crónica de Juan II* probably based his conclusion on the *Halconero,* whose account he followed at the *beginning* of his narrative—that is, from the Prince's departure from Segovia to Sarmiento's surrender of his Toledan positions. But the *Halconero*'s account of the "surrender" is curtailed. It begins with the first approach to Sarmiento immediately after the welcome celebrations, and proceeds to report Sarmiento's consent to relinquish his military and judicial posts; it omits the intermediate occurrences, including the Prince's departure from Toledo for Requena, his return to the city after a few days, and his actions against García and his friends. Thus the reader may assume that Sarmiento "surrendered" his positions immediately after the Prince had first approached him in this matter—or, more precisely, soon after the welcome celebrations.[4] No doubt the compiler (or editor) of the *crónica* believed this to have been the case.

This misunderstanding by the author (or editor) of the *Crónica de Juan II* led to misconceptions concerning the date of Sarmiento's departure from Toledo. The *Halconero*, who notes very briefly, as indicated, Sarmiento's "resignation" from his posts, says nothing about the order the Prince gave him (following that resignation) to leave the city, or about the talk that Lope de Barrientos had with him on this matter. The *Crónica de Juan II*, which gave a detailed account of that talk,[5] must have taken that information from some other source—perhaps an ampler version of the *Halconero*, or the one that was revised by Barrientos and is known as the *Refundición*.[6] In any case, the *Abreviación* of the *Halconero* touches briefly on these facts (i.e., the order of expulsion and Barrientos' talk), and one may gather from it that these occurrences followed closely Sarmiento's transfer of his authority to the Prince. What is more, the *Abreviación* alludes to the date of the talk between Barrientos and Sarmiento: "Wednesday, the 17th of the month of . . . 1449."[7] Since the *month* was not specified, the compiler (or editor) of the *Crónica de Juan II* concluded that it must have been the month of November. After all, the talk took place "a few days" after Sarmiento gave up his positions, and the latter event happened, as he came to believe, in the month of November.

Now, Benito Ruano, who noticed the above data concerning the date of Barriento's talk with Sarmiento, established that these data could only fit the month of *December,* and thus departed from the *Crónica*'s view that Sarmiento left Toledo about the middle of November.[8] In this departure he was of course right. On the other hand, he accepted the *Crónica*'s assertion that Sarmiento left Toledo, as he put it, *esta noche*—i.e., on the night of the day of his talk with Barrientos; and so he concluded that the date of Sarmiento's exit from the city was December 17, 1449.[9]

That conclusion, however, appears to us erroneous for the following reasons:

1. The *Halconero* states that Sarmiento left Toledo in February 1450.[10] We see no reason to dispute this information in favor of the indications given in the *Crónica*, especially since the dates here offered by this document are clearly distorted and confused.

2. The detailed account given in the *Crónica* of the talk between the bishop and Sarmiento has all the earmarks of a tendentious story, which might have been produced by some admirer of Barrientos (in all likelihood,

a converso author), if not by Barrientos himself, who may have been the editor of the *revised Halconero*—i.e., the *Refundición*.[11] The purpose of the story was to show the great effect that Barrientos' talk had on the rebel, and the compiler of the *Crónica* may have read in his source that Sarmiento was prepared to leave Toledo "that night," provided that the necessary arrangements were made. From this the compiler (or the editor) concluded that he actually left "that night," which was another wrong conclusion he drew from the sources that were at his disposal.

3. The *Crónica* says that Sarmiento left "that night" *with all the possessions he "stole" from the citizens packed on some two hundred beasts of burden*.[12] This does not seem possible. The dismantling of his large house in Toledo and the massing of his belongings in such a huge caravan would have required more than a few hours—i.e., the time between the conclusion of his talk with the Prince and his departure from the city (according to the *Crónica*).

4. Sarmiento could not give the bishop of Cuenca a definite promise to depart "that night" before he knew where he might find refuge. Evidently, he did not wish to see the Prince simply to get a permit to leave the city (such a permit was implied in the *order* to leave which was communicated to him through Barrientos), but also to obtain permission (1) to take with him all the possessions he had in Toledo, and (2) to settle in Segovia.

Also, from what the *Halconero* tells us about the compensation the Prince promised Sarmiento and the conditions attached to that compensation,[13] it is obvious that these conditions were negotiated; and such negotiations required some time. No doubt there were also other matters that could not be taken care of in a rush. Sarmiento must have asked the Prince for the right to stay in Toledo a few more weeks in order to settle his affairs in the city. He must have also asked the Prince for the right to join him on his return to Segovia, so that he might be protected on the road from the King's agents.

This was the origin of the *Halconero*'s statement that "in the month of February, the Prince left Toledo for Segovia, and *took with him the said Pero Sarmiento*, his wife and sons, as well as his entire *fazienda*."[14] The *Halconero* no doubt heard that the Prince had agreed to this arrangement, which was proposed by Sarmiento, and believed that it materialized. Actually, however, it did not.

5. On February 6, 1450, Don Fernando de Luxán, bishop of Sigüenza, published his "sentence" regarding the execution of Pope Nicholas V's bull against the rebels. In it he directs all the cities of the kingdom, and *especially the city of Toledo*, that within a month of the publication of the bull, they take up arms against Pero Sarmiento, seize him and his associates, and keep them imprisoned "until the Lord king and the others who were hurt by them, receive due satisfaction."[15] Benito Ruano, who noticed this instruction, might have considered it strange that it was made public after Sarmiento "had been

absent from Toledo for months."[16] The formulation of this instruction, how-
ever, may appear strange only if we assume that Sarmiento left Toledo on
December 17 (as was assumed by Benito Ruano). It is *not* strange at all if on
February 6 Sarmiento was still in Toledo. In fact, the sentence of Don
Fernando may serve as another indication that Sarmiento did *not* leave
Toledo on December 17.

6. He left Toledo in February, but not with the Prince—although judging
by the *Halconero,* he had been assured of this. The reason for the change in
the original plan was, in all likelihood, the publication of the "sentence" on
the pope's bull by Don Fernando de Luxán. The sentence made it most
embarrassing for the Prince to associate with Sarmiento. He did not withdraw the safe-conduct he granted him and the promises he gave him regarding his possessions and his right to settle in Segovia, but he ordered him to
leave Toledo at once, and go wherever he wished *by himself.* He did not want
to appear as Sarmiento's protector on the long road to Segovia.[17]

7. On February 20, 1450, a letter was received by the municipality of
Burgos from the *corregidor* of Miranda de Ebro, requesting military aid to
confront Sarmiento who, according to rumor, was approaching Miranda
(where Sarmiento had one of his estates).[18] Benito Ruano believes that the
rumor was spread in wake of the departure of Sarmiento's wife from Segovia
to Miranda prior to his own flight from the city.[19] This explanation appears
reasonable. However, according to Benito Ruano, Sarmiento sent his wife to
Miranda some two months after his arrival at Segovia (if he left Toledo on
December 17), whereas according to *our* understanding, he sent her there
shortly after they had reached Segovia, perhaps even before the Prince
returned to the city. The reason for his decision to do so was, most likely,
the change he noticed in the Prince's attitude after the publication of Don
Fernando's sentence. Sarmiento was again seized with fear for his life, as the
Crónica de Juan II attests.[20] The Prince, it occurred to him, may one day
arrest him in compliance with Don Fernando's sentence, or in conformity
with his agreement with the King, toward which he was ceaselessly working.
Accordingly, he decided to send his wife, without much delay, to Miranda,
and leave Segovia at the earliest opportunity. In any case, the date of
February 20, on which news reached Burgos about his approach to Miranda,
would tally with the information of the *Halconero* that he left Toledo in
February.

D
Juan de Torquemada

I. RACE AND THE JEWISH PEOPLE

We have seen that Torquemada systematically rebutted all the tenets of the Toledans' race theory, culminating with his emphasis that the Christian religion, for which "there is neither Greek nor Jew," recognizes no difference of race among its followers, whatever their source. These rebuttals seem consistent with each other, as well as with the guiding principles of his thought; and had his reactions to the Toledans' claims been limited to them alone, they would seem to form a cohesive counter-theory to that of the Toledans. Yet while censuring the Toledans' views, Torquemada also argues that "no other race was more dignified, more noble, more saintly and more religious" than that of the Jewish people[1]; and while asserting that the Jews formed the holiest group of men, he also says that their tendency toward goodness was natural, while that of the gentiles was "unnatural" (or against their nature); and hence to attain the faith of Christ, the gentiles had to be grafted upon the Jewish trunk.[2] It appears, then, that in contrast to the Toledan race theory, Torquemada presents a race theory of his own, in which moral inclinations are conceived as "natural," and hence as inheritable dispositions (just as they are in the Toledans' view), except that in *his* theory it is the Jews, and not the gentiles who are the source of real goodness and true faith.

If Torquemada had been a superficial thinker, such contradictions might be understandable. But Torquemada was a meticulous logician, and the issue was central to his theological position and his view of the history of the Church; we cannot believe therefore that his statements on this subject were made lightly. Consequently, we assume that, in his own thinking, they were harmonized, or at least coordinated to the point of avoiding a blatant incon-sistency. Indeed, a careful study of his expressions on the subject will soon eliminate some of the discrepancies.

To begin with, we should note that nowhere in his treatise does Tor-quemada say that moral qualities or tendencies were inherited in Israel through a biological process, such as is attributed to a racial transmission. When he says, for instance, that the Apostles "imitated" the faith of the Fathers,[3] he obviously refers to a *spiritual* influence, which comes by instruc-tion or example. For had they received the faith by inheritance, they would not have had to "imitate" it; it would have sprung from *within* them. Simi-larly, when he said that the gentiles could adopt the moral and religious approaches of the Jews, he did not think of any other means of influence than instruction and inspiration, despite the "racial" terms he used. Obviously, the "grafting of the oleaster onto the good olive tree" was only a symbolic way of speech, for nobody suggested that the gentiles became Christian by racial intermingling with the Jews.

It follows that when he says that the "Jews are more suited *(habiles)* for the good" and therefore more reparable for the faith,[4] he referred to a condition acquired not by racial but by moral conditions, not by biological inheritance but by a spiritual heritage. The Prophets propagated their beliefs within their people, and thus the predilection toward good struck roots; it became "habit-ual" to the Jews, not as an innate quality, but as something deeply ingrained and entwined, hallowed by a long educational tradition and resembling in its impact a "second nature."

The moral inclination of the Jewish people, therefore, was not a racial property, which is inherited or inheritable; it was not a *natural* phenomenon, which, as such, is unchangeable. Torquemada must have realized this, for he recognized that certain sections of the Jewish people often deviated from the faith, were idolatrous, etc. But he also insisted that devotion to goodness was stronger in Israel than in all other peoples. And in this connection we must again touch on his view of the Jewish people as a race.

For according to Torquemada, it was not only the inspiration of the Patriarchs, the Prophets and other holy men that was responsible for the Jews' superior morality. The other cause was the Election. To be sure, Scripture attributes the Election to God's special love for the Fathers; but there must have been more to it than this alone, so that the full explanation of the Election remained, as the Apostle said, a mystery. Certainly, it was not the moral qualities or the conduct of the Patriarchs' descendants—i.e., their merit—that earned them the *choice* and the title of *God's people;* for their moral behavior was often deficient and, in any case, below that elevated status. Nevertheless, the very fact of the *choice* had greatly affected the people's state of mind, for it made moral behavior and faith in their ranks incumbent upon them far more than in other nations. This is why it was from the midst of this people that the "most sanctified humanity"—i.e., that of Jesus Christ—was destined to emerge; and it is in relation to the birth of Christ and the Election that Torquemada says that "no other race *(generatio)* was more dignified, more noble, more saintly and more religious in the world" than the Jewish people.[5]

Thus all these qualities, it must be clearly perceived, did not stem from the people's original nature, but from God's special will and imposition. "God has chosen you today"—Torquemada quotes Moses—"to be his peculiar people so that you should follow all His commandments and be holy to the Lord your God."[6] This thunderous moral imposition, together with the impact of the Law and the Prophets, had their expected effects. Israel became superior to all nations "in praise, and in name, and in glory."[7] But although it was superiority *of* the race, it was not a *racial* superiority. It was a *divine* prerogative, which earned the Jews far more respect than they might have gained if they had been endowed *by nature*.

This is how Torquemada's view of Israel's position among the nations of mankind should be understood. Any other explanation, it seems, would lead us into insoluble contradictions and complications which would merely confuse his clear-cut statements as we have presented them above.

I

In addition to his basic statements on the Judaizers which were cited and discussed above, Torquemada made other pertinent remarks which can help us, we believe, gain clearer insights into his view on that issue. Exploring the subject from various angles and touching both actual and potential conditions, Torquemada offers us in these remarks a more rounded picture of the "Judaic" situation as it appeared to him in his time. Above all, he provides us with more direct answers to two crucial questions which he was no doubt asked: Are there any Judaizers among the conversos? And if so, do they reflect the *inward* attitude of the majority of the converts from Judaism?

"Surely," Torquemada says, "if those people [i.e., the Toledans] had spoken of particular cases, they could have been supported [in their claims], for *we judge it to be true* that some *(aliqui)* of the Jewish race who were converted to the faith *were not, or are not, good Christians (non bonos fuisse aut esse christianos)*, but bad and even suspected in the faith, observing among themselves some ceremonies of the old law."[1] Any other judgment would indeed be unreasonable. "For the descendants of the Jewish race are not more privileged than the descendants of the races of the pagans, the Ishmaelites, the Saracens, or even the ancient Christians, among whom, under the name of Christians, were found the most criminal people: robbers *(raptores)*, blasphemers, sodomites, homicides, infidels, practitioners of simony, usurers and heretics."[2]

From the types of the wrong-doers mentioned by Torquemada, and the word *aliqui* which he uses in this instance, we can gather that he believed the number of the Judaizers, whom he assumed to have existed among the conversos, to have been small, or rather insignificant. They were the freaks, the misfits, the scum of humanity, such as exist in every society and which no human group has ever been free of, even the early Christians. But this should not lead anyone to believe that the society in which they happened to be found—i.e., the society as a whole—consists of such elements. Especially should Christians who descended from pagans beware of such generalizations. Their own histories, past and present, are full of examples of backsliders and heretics who have been punished and burned. "Even last year, in Fabriano, in the Marches [of central Italy], among 22 suspects of heresy who were caught, 9 were burned, and the others incarcerated, according to the measure of their iniquity."[3]

Thus, while noting deviations from the faith that appeared in Christian

Europe in his time, he fails to indicate anything similar among the Spanish conversos. Evidently, no heretical movement has left a trail of activity among them to the point that it could not be ignored. Yet, he adds, "with these things occurring in different parts of Christendom (*diversis hiis ergo sic se habentibus*), we should not be astonished if some of the descendants of the Jewish race (again: *aliqui de genere iudeorum descendentes*), passing under the name of Christians, are in reality bad Christians, and should be deservedly so regarded judging by their deeds."[4]

All this, we must note, is stated by Torquemada not on the basis of established facts, but simply on the grounds of logical assumption. His trend of argument is clearly hypothetical: "If some of the conversos should be found to have transgressed, it should not surprise us." But thus far, we must conclude from his own words, no demonstration has been proffered. Only *general* accusations have been advanced by the Toledans against the group as a whole, while the specific charges of Judaic practices, leveled against individual conversos, were not substantiated in legal proceedings, properly followed in a court of law.

This conclusion, which is clearly implied in all he said on this matter thus far, is further substantiated by the following remarks, with which he concluded this discussion. "If the said impious people," he asked, "heard that some of the converts blasphemed Christ, or were observing Jewish rites, or exercising the abominable circumcision, why did they not proceed against them in accordance with the royal advice and the decision of the holy council, so that converts, censured by pontifical authority, might be called back to the dignity of Christian worship, and wherever they refused to emend themselves, be restrained by sacredotal chastisement?"[5] The answer is that the accusers failed to do so—that is, to follow the "just procedures"—because they "were not moved by the spirit of God, or by zeal for the faith, but by an evil spirit." They were "violently incensed by the flame of cupidity, which is the root of all evil," so that "without prior admonition, without any judiciary order, with false attestations, supported by no authority, against the will of the king, and against the prohibition of their bishop, they proceeded not to recall the converts to the faith, but to exterminate and destroy them."[6]

It is obvious that in Torquemada's opinion, no judgment at all can be made about the Judaizers on the basis of the charges brought by such people. These charges must be held to be unproven; and it is doubtful that they had any basis to begin with. It stands to reason that the accusers had no evidence at all; for otherwise why did they use false witnesses and violate *all* the proper procedures? And how can one trust the statements of people with such base motives and such vile conduct? No wonder Torquemada preceded the questioning that led him to his conclusion with an "if" that implied a negation.

II

Yet, while we cannot find in his treatise any evidence of the actual existence of Judaizers in Spain (except the "general judgment" mentioned), we find in it evidence of the negative influence which the Toledan persecution had on the conversos—in particular, on their attitude toward Christianity.

Torquemada compares that persecution to "a scorching wind which damages the flowers in the garden."[7] "It is clear," adds Torquemada (to leave no doubt in this matter), "that many who flourished in devotion to the faith from about the beginning of the conversion" are not strong enough to endure trials of this sort in the storm of such a persecution. Agitated and perplexed, and, above all, astonished that Christians could inflict such sufferings upon Christians, they fall down from the flower of the faith *(a fidei flore decidunt)* and lose the pleasantness of the devotion to Christianity, while they are in danger of being condemned by those who persist in causing their ruin."[8]

The above embodies an important testimony concerning the religious state of the conversos both before and after the Toledan riots. Torquemada speaks here of the "*devotion* to the faith" which could be seen almost since the beginning of the conversions, and he describes the religious condition of the conversos, prior to the Toledan outbreaks, as "flourishing." But following these outbreaks, he does not hesitate to admit, their religious attitude underwent a change. Vexed by the fears, doubts and disappointments generated in their minds by the persecution, "many" of the conversos who had been ardent Christians "fell off from the flower of the faith," which in no way means that they parted with Christianity, but it does mean that they lost their enthusiasm for being Christians (or, in his words, "the pleasantness of the devotion to the Christian religion"). This shows that a process of some unhealthy feeling, of some discomfiture and bewilderment, had begun to be noticed among the conversos under the impact of the Toledan occurrences. It also stands to reason that such a development might lead some conversos to desert Christianity and return to their former religion. This is, in fact, what Torquemada alludes to in a forecast of events under a protracted persecution. "Not only will many [outside the faith] be restrained from receiving the Christian religion, but many also of the newly converted will regret [their conversion], or become tepid in their love of the faith they had received."[9]

So what we have here is a description of the present coupled with a prediction of the future—a prediction which was meant to serve as a warning and a summons for the Church to take preventive action. In essence, this warning of Juan de Torquemada regarding the impact of a protracted persecution is identical with that voiced by the Relator in his "Instruction" to Barrientos. Both foresaw a halt to conversion from Judaism and considerable defection among the harassed conversos, but both made it clear that the Toledan outrages had so far not produced a movement of Judaizers, or even the beginning of such a movement. Regardless of what happened, both were still certain that the conversos remained, as they were, "Christ's faithful," "believers in the Gospel and its obeyers,"[10] and that their camp, while shaken, was still distinguished by its religious purity and devotion to the faith.

A Spanish scholar, Nicolás López Martínez, who seeks to justify the activities of the Inquisition on the grounds that it came to uproot a widespread heresy, finds it difficult to accommodate this view of his with the evidence offered by Torquemada. An admirer of Torquemada the scholar, the canonist and the fighter for pristine Christian values, López can in no way assume that the Cardinal was saying what he knew to be untrue. Is it not impossible, then, López asks, that Torquemada was ignorant of the true facts because of his long absence from Castile and that the information he received while writing his treatise was defective and misleading?[1] López is obviously attempting to explain the Cardinal's statements about the Marranos in a way that would not hurt the position which he, like so many other scholars, took on the issue in question. His proposed explanation, however, cannot be supported for the following reasons.

Except for the seven years of his stay abroad (mostly in Paris), Torquemada lived in Spain until 1431—that is, until he was 43 years old. His life until then practically coincided with the first four decades of converso existence (1391–1431). If we assume that Torquemada judged the Marrano situation in 1449 (when he wrote his treatise) on the basis of what he knew it to have been in 1431 (when he left Spain), we must conclude that, in the first 40 years that passed since their conversion (1391–1431), the conversos have reached the state of assimilation that he ascribes to them in his cited treatise. It may be reasonably assumed that the longer the conversos stayed Christian, the deeper their assimilation became, and therefore what happened in the subsequent years—from 1431 to 1449—was not likely to have moved the clock back. In fact, all the evidence we possess shows that converso assimilation proceeded at the same or a quicker pace at the time, and we may also conclude that converso Christianization increased rather than diminished in that period.[2] If so, Torquemada's view of the conversos' Christianity—as expressed in his treatise against the Midianites—may be taken as moderate rather than exaggerated, and consequently there is no basis to suggest that his statements were not well founded.

It would similarly be wrong to assume that Torquemada (considering his stature, position and connections) was so completely detached from Spain that he lacked reliable information on what was going on there (especially respecting the Marrano situation, which was of interest to him and concerned him personally). No doubt he was in touch with old friends, who kept him abreast of the developments in his homeland, and particularly in Toledo,

where for many years he held his last position in Spain as prior of a leading
Dominican convent. Furthermore, in the Council of Basle he must often have
met with members of the Spanish delegation (who included both Old and
New Christians) and probably discussed with them the converso problem, at
least prior to the Council's decision on converts of September 15, 1434. Then,
two years later (in 1436) he visited Castile as papal legate, and on that
occasion he could get a direct glimpse of the conditions that obtained there,
which are pertinent to our problem. In brief, there is no reason to assume that
Torquemada was unaware of the Marrano situation when he wrote his
treatise. Indeed, his statements and analyses show that he spoke of that
situation with the certainty of one who was fully aware of all its aspects.

Seeking to explain Torquemada's statements on the Marranos by another
extraneous cause, López advanced another hypothesis: "Was it merely a
desire to please the king or to attend to certain recommendations?"[3] But such
an explanation appears no more plausible than the one we have just discarded. Would a man like Torquemada have so fiercely attacked the Toledan
rebels for their views on the Marranos merely to please the king or support
some recommendations, even if he was not at all sure that these recommendations were correct? Could his passionate refutation of the Toledan claims,
and the depth of conviction which it clearly reflects, be explained by such
external reasons? Had his work been written merely to please the king or
some other friendly and respected individuals, it would no doubt have a
different character in content as well as in form.

López, who realizes that the above conjectures cannot "duly" explain
Torquemada's position—that is, his strong and unqualified objections
("*cerrada opposición*") to the anti-Marrano party's point of view—falls back,
reluctantly, on the last alternative: "Perhaps we shall gain more light if we
revise the genealogy of the famous Cardinal?"[4] López, who, in his admiration
for Torquemada, calls him "one of the glories of our race"[5] (i.e., the Spanish
race), is obviously reluctant to follow this line of research. He would certainly regret to arrive at a conclusion by which the "glory" would have to be
shared with another race, which is not particularly admired by him. As we
have indicated, we fully agree with López' latter assumption; we see it
sufficiently attested by the documents; and we cannot conceive of Torquemada's treatise except as one composed by a converso author.

But this would not explain what López would regard as Torquemada's
"*erroneous* view" of the Marranos. It would explain his wrath over what
happened in Toledo and his ire against those who were responsible for those
happenings; it would explain certain parts of his theological position and his
defense of the besmirched Jewish people—a defense which no Old Christian
of that century would be prepared to shoulder; and it would explain his view
of the outstanding role which the Jews had played in the history of man-

kind—a role which Old Christians of his and later times would tend to overlook or minimize; but it would not explain a contravention of the facts with respect to the conversos' religious probity.

For dedicated as he was to the cause of Christianity and to the struggle against heresies wherever he found them, Torquemada would not have minimized the scope of a Judaizing movement among the conversos, if such a movement had indeed existed to any appreciable extent; nor would he have shown that firm opposition to the claims of the Marranos' critics. However apologetic he would have liked to be in favor of his attacked kinsmen, he would not have ignored the heretical crimes, as well as the faults and failures of his group. Rather would he have courageously exposed the conversos' shortcomings and failures, and demanded their return to the right path, while he might have chided the opposition for its excessive zeal and lack of consideration for the conversos, who might have needed more time to be integrated in Christendom. Torquemada, however, not only vindicated the Marrano group as a whole, but fiercely denounced its opponents, without giving them the slightest justification. Far from being a professional apologist, Torquemada would not have taken such an attitude unless he was completely certain of his facts.

The value of any testimony depends on the extent to which its bearer can discern and present the truth; and this depends on his capacity to make correct judgments and his courage to pronounce these judgments in public, especially when they are unpopular. It involves the measure of his respect for truth and, above all, his *self*-respect—that is, the extent to which he cared about how he would be judged by his own and future generations. By these standards, Torquemada's testimony must be given the highest credibility.

When he wrote his paper on the outbreak against the conversos, he was Cardinal of St. Sixtus and a member of the Roman curia. Behind him was a most distinguished record of battles against religious deviations in Christendom which earned him the reputation of an expert in these matters, as well as of a dauntless fighter for truth—the truth of Christianity as he understood it. Was he going to risk this hard-won reputation and involve himself in the defense of "Jewish" heretics, who could be found, according to their critics, in almost every corner in Spain? Would he pass in silence over such a *widespread* evil, or look for excuses to defend the heretics against the infuriated Old Christians who, even if they had followed wrong procedures, were right in their *main* accusation? And would he commit such a great blunder as to praise the culprits to high heaven while furiously attacking the true defenders of Christianity? And even if he had been tempted to do so, whom would he have fooled by such behavior? Would not the facts, and the contrary evidence, fly in his face and expose his folly, prove him to be untruthful, irresponsible, and unconcerned with the harms done to the faith?

It seems, therefore, that unless Torquemada was *convinced* of the plain righteousness of his position, he would not have taken the stand he took. Self-interest, if nothing else, would have kept him from making such a wrong move.

But this brings us to the next question that must be tackled in this connection. Assuming that Torquemada thought he knew the facts and was certain of his statements, could he not have been mistaken? What, after all, was the nature of the information at his disposal? There were no reliable statistics in Spain at the time; there were no public polls, secret or open; there were no probes made by the conversos to establish the attitudes of the members of their group toward either Judaism or Christianity. On what then could he rely? The only possible answer is, of course: on the views prevalent among the conversos. But this raises another question. Torquemada, as we have seen, sharply denounced the "notoriety" of the conversos' unfaithfulness—the "notoriety" on which the Old Christians relied. He insisted that no bad reputation spread about an individual or a group can replace facts proven by reliable witnesses in a properly conducted court of law. Yet did he not himself base his judgments in this matter on some general opinion, some *publica fama*, except that this opinion stemmed from different sources and was favorable rather than disparaging? To what extent can we rely then on *his* assertions—not from the standpoint of what *he* believed in, but from the standpoint of objective truth?

Here we come to the crux of the problem that confronts us in assessing such a testimony on the conversos as the one offered by Torquemada. How could Torquemada *know* what he said about the Marranos, about their religious views, attitudes and preferences? The answer is: *He knew it because he was one of them*, because he lived with them and communicated with them and had direct knowledge of their views and tendencies. No outsider can judge with such certainty a group's stand on any of its crucial issues as one who belongs to the group himself, especially when the group involved is surrounded by a hostile environment. This is that particular awareness of things which comes from within, from being part of the community, from contact with its members and admired leaders in whom one develops implicit trust. No Jew has investigated the activities of all his fellow Jews and established, by his own inquiry, that Jews do not use the blood of Christian children for religious purposes. Yet every Jew would instantly be ready to swear, whenever such accusations were made, that they were groundless lies, without a shred of truth, concocted by evil or foolish people. That is the knowledge that comes from one's belonging to the party involved, from having been *inside* that party—a knowledge more reliable than all the hundreds of inquiries that can be conducted by outsiders. It was the certitude created by that kind of knowledge that inspired Torquemada's statements.

Because of these considerations, we ought not to take the view that had the evidence we find in the *Treatise* been given by an *Old* Christian cardinal, we might regard it as more reliable. Had Torquemada been a full-fledged Old Christian, the question "How did he know?" could be asked with greater justice. He might have been influenced by some of his Marrano friends, who misled him with erroneous information, or he could have been inclined to act upon the information of some other people whom he considered trustworthy, and yet could be wrong in this particular instance. Such criticisms could be leveled against him, and rightly so, because he would have lacked the *intimate* knowledge that comes from *direct* experience and *inward* group awareness of the facts. In brief, we believe that Torquemada's evidence is *more* reliable precisely because he was, and considered himself, a converso, and not just a "friend" of the Marranos at court.

E

The Gibraltar Project

In the first half of August 1474, only four months before the death of King Enrique and the assumption of power by Isabella and Ferdinand, several thousand conversos left Seville for Gibraltar with the aim of settling in that newly captured place.[1] Most of them were refugees from Cordova, the others Sevillians who, fearing outbreaks against their group, sought safety for themselves and their families. Their hope of finding safety in Gibraltar was based on a plan for Marrano settlement in that town which was negotiated, and agreed on, with the lord of the place, the Duke of Medina Sidonia.

The idea was born among the Cordovan conversos after the riots of 1473 and was sponsored by one of their leading members, Don Pedro de Cordova, who was distinguished, as Palencia put it, by his "dignified countenance, charming conversation and affability in dealing with people."[2] Searching for a place where they could live in peace, free from the threats of hostile neighbors, they thought of Gibraltar, recently captured from the Moors. Sparsely populated, the town could be settled by thousands of conversos, who might soon become the overwhelming majority there and thus be masters of their own fate. To get the Duke to agree to their plan, the conversos offered to cover the cost of a garrison and to participate in the town's defense. But they insisted that the governor of the fortress should be their own Pedro de Cordova.

Palencia tells us that the counselors of the duke advised him to decline the conversos' offer. "They claimed," he said, "that the New Christians are inept to maintain the security of such a great town, and pointed out the necessity that those who wish to live there be well qualified to organize and participate in terrestrial and maritime expeditions, indispensable for the defense of a city so exposed to the dangers of war." They added that those "timid people, accustomed to soft life and generally dedicated to low occupations such as those of shoemakers or moneylenders, would be of no use to garrison the place." Moreover, the "Andalusian conversos," they argued, "are rightly considered infamous, because, dedicated as they are to their Judaic rites, they rarely follow loyally the Catholic religion, which fact was the cause of their main misfortunes. Nor would it be reasonable to hope for a favorable change [in their attitudes] if they came to dwell in such a fortified city, because, once separated from the Old Christians, they would dedicate themselves to the most depraved lawlessness which they would consider licit whenever they desired it. He who will give occasion for such license will, therefore, not be free of guilt."[3]

These opinions of the Duke's counselors echoed the notions that were shared at the time by numerous Old Christians of all classes, especially of the South, which, following the riots in so many towns, was swept by anti-converso agitation. The Duke, however, ignored his counselors' advice and entered into serious negotiations with the conversos concerning their settlement project. According to Palencia, what moved him so to act was the expectation of the funds he was to get from the conversos; but he may also have been impressed with the plan presented to him by Pedro de Cordova. According to Pedro's plan, the fortress of Gibraltar, then a mere military outpost, was to become a great, prosperous town thanks to the many thousands of conversos who would flock to it from all parts of the country. As such it would become also a more powerful defense position and a great source of revenues. As for the anti-converso charges, Pedro dismissed them as mere fabrications. If the conversos were to settle in Gibraltar, he said, "they would palpably demonstrate there, with their honorable conduct and Catholic practices, that the Catholic religion is observed among the conversos much better [than among others]; that their being judged timid was merely a result of their natural inclination toward peace; yet if some danger threatened Gibraltar, soon would the Old Christians see how strong was their loyalty to the [Catholic] faith and how well they knew to face the risks of war."[4]

Thus, like the Relator facing the charges of the Toledans, Pedro de Cordova, facing the charges of the Andalusians, insists on the conversos' loyalty to Christianity, their honorable attachment to the Catholic religion, and their steady observance of its rites. Such definite, unqualified statements could be made by the conversos, when such damaging accusations were leveled against them, only if they had a strong basis in fact. There is not a trace of an apology here for any religious misconduct or transgression, or the slightest admission that any group of conversos deviated from the right path. Instead we note in Don Pedro's assertions a firm denial of guilt, an unreserved declaration of faith, and an emphasis on the error the Old Christians were making in judging the conversos to be infidels. We shall see to what extent this position can be justified by the additional evidence provided by Palencia concerning the Gibraltar project.

Despite all of Pedro's arguments, however, the Duke withheld his decision. Perhaps he was angling for better terms, or perhaps he was, at last, influenced by his counselors, who kept producing arguments against the venture. Thus, they claimed, the Marranos may have planned to use Gibraltar as a station on the way to Egypt and Jerusalem.[5] The Duke no doubt presented all these arguments to Pedro, who knew how to refute them.

According to the agreement that was finally concluded, the Marranos were to maintain a cavalry force in Gibraltar at their own expense and at no cost to the Duke. While the Duke was to collect annually 5,000 doblas from the ship captains and the royal tax collectors of Seville, he would have to pay in the first two years only 1,000 doblas a year for "guarding the place and sustaining the Christians who reside near the walls [of Gibraltar]." The governor of the town was to be Don Pedro, "certainly a man of an ingenious mind *(vivo ingenio)* and recognized skill"; and, in the early period of the settlement, he was to manage the town's public affairs and elect its council-men *(regidores)*.[6] Palencia calls the agreement "dishonorable" because in his opinion, the Duke, who was moved only by avarice, sold the conversos his "false humanitarianism at a very high price."[7] He took advantage of unfortunate men, who yielded to exorbitant financial demands and other unfair exactions, only because they were struck with fear, were in desperate need of a haven, and had no choice but to yield to his rapacity. Nevertheless, the Marranos obtained two important concessions: the Governor of the fortress was to be their man, and it was he who would elect the councilmen. They assumed that they were going to lay the basis for their future control of the government of a city—of course, under the overlordship of the Duke.

It is evident that the settlers in Gibraltar had abandoned the old Marrano dream of *convivencia* with the Old Christians under the existing conditions. To live in the Christian cities as minorities—however numerically strong and influential—meant to expose themselves to the constant danger of massacre and spoliation. They could live with the Old Christians only in places where they were the overwhelming majority, as they would be in Gibraltar, and even there they would not be safe from molestation unless the government was in their hands. These, then, were the two essential conditions for the solution of the Marrano problem—majority and self-government. The Gibraltar settlement was to serve as a pioneer project—a model for that envisaged solution.

There can be no doubt that these ideas, as well as the prospect of unmolested life, lured not only the Cordovans to Gibraltar but also many Sevillian conversos who had not experienced the ordeal of mass massacre, pillage and destruction. Thus, a considerable number of them, especially among their wealthier members, decided to move to Gibraltar together with the Cordovans. Many families went by ship; the majority went on foot (2,000) and others on horseback (350). On August 15, 1474, most of them entered the city, which was in "great need of seasoned soldiers as well as of shoemakers and other artisans."[8]

Plans did not work out as expected. The first setback took place when a maritime expedition sent by the Marranos against an enemy position was beaten back with considerable losses. The second resulted from internal disagreements that developed among the settlers. The Sevillians fell out with the Cordovan Marranos and returned to Seville. But the Cordovans stuck it out.[9] After overcoming the initial difficulties, Palencia tells us, they "persuaded themselves of the need to accommodate themselves to the new circumstances, and from day to day added more courage under the sure direction of the governor, who incessantly advised them of the practice of the good."[10] No practice could be hailed by Palencia as "good" if it did not include observance of Christianity. Had a practice of, or a tendency toward Judaism been noticed among the conversos in Gibraltar, and had reports to this effect been circulated by Christians (to begin with, by those who lived in the fortress), it would have undoubtedly been made much of, and Palencia would have mentioned it as proof that the Duke's counselors had been right. Palencia's detailed account, however, contains only indications to the contrary.

Despite this, the converso settlers in Gibraltar continued to be censured by the Duke's counselors. As no evidence was offered of their alleged Judaic practices or of their intention to go to Jerusalem, the counselors of the Duke felt the need to explain why their prognostications had not materialized. Now they said that both the passage to Jerusalem and the performance of Jewish rites would come later—that is, "once they [i.e., the conversos] become masters of free navigation."[11] In other words, if the conversos had thus far failed to go to Jerusalem and, in addition, concealed their Judaism, it was because they were not yet in control of the sea lanes—presumably because of the war between Portugal and Spain. When passage from Gibraltar became easy, they would doubtless follow their two nefarious goals. For then they would be able to escape.

It is hardly necessary to point out the groundlessness of these charges. Palencia tells us that the converso settlers of Gibraltar had spent all their savings there, so that their remaining means could barely suffice for their sustenance. Apart from having been "obliged to cover the cost of building new homes, as well as the expense of maritime expeditions and the transport of expensive provisions," they had to pay for the maintenance of a cavalry force, and consequently "their resources were exhausted."[12] Would any person in his right mind make such investments in a place he planned to leave at the first opportunity? Obviously, the Marranos had come to Gibraltar to stay. Relying on the promises of the Duke, they invested in the place all they had with the aim of establishing a home there for themselves; and they were already beginning to reap the fruit of that investment (or, as Palencia said, "to recompense themselves") when the Duke, as we shall see, ordered them out.

Thus, the charges leveled at the Cordovan settlers remained, to say the least, unproven. This is why the Duke's friends had to revise their accusations against them from time to time, or exchange them for new accusations. Indeed, this is what they did during the last phase of the conversos' stay in Gibraltar. The main objection they then raised against the settlers was that now, after the conversos had struck roots in Gibraltar, the "place could be considered as sold to Don Ferdinand" [i.e., the King] if the Cordovans will retain control of it; for "since they are so clearly inclined to his obedience, they would surely try to introduce—on the pretext that they owe fidelity to the Crown—some innovation that would be harmful to the Duke."[13] If we follow Palencia's tale to its conclusion, we can clearly see that this political argument had no more merit than the religious ones.

Far from having in mind any thought of betraying the Duke, Pedro de Cordova was then working on a plan whose materialization would have greatly enhanced the Duke's power. He proposed the organization of a military expedition to capture Ceuta from the Portuguese. The Duke accepted the proposal, sent five thousand troops to seize Ceuta, and while these were engaged in investing the place, he used the ongoing fighting as excuse to visit Gibraltar with a unit of choice cavalry, as if he were on his way to the battleground. Upon his arrival in Gibraltar, he insulted Don Pedro, who had obediently fulfilled all his wishes, stripped him of his rights, and ordered all conversos to leave town.[14] What moved the Duke to behave so inhumanely was, according to Palencia, only his conviction that the Marranos were impoverished, and that for a considerable time to come they would probably be unable to support his treasury.[15] But in addition, it is not impossible that the suspicion planted in his mind by his counselors—namely, that he might lose the place to King Ferdinand—had much to do with his behavior. This was a prospect which he could consider plausible and may have frightened him to take the action he did.

And what did the Cordovan conversos do when they were ordered to leave Gibraltar? Like the Sevillians who preceded them, they returned to their former homes.[16] Not a single one of them was reported to have gone to Jerusalem.

F

The Death of Enrique IV

Did King Enrique die a natural death, or was he a victim of foul play—more precisely, of poisoning? The question arises in the light of certain hints in Castillo's account (which are otherwise hard to explain) and in view of the closeness of the King's death to that of Pacheco. As if to dissipate such a suspicion, Palencia, Enrique's enemy and critic, ascribes the King's death to his "incontinent" eating and to "several intestinal attacks" he had suffered before the one that killed him.[1] Castillo, however, in speaking of such "attacks" presents them clearly as irregular and as products of a condition that affected the King since the meal he had in the Palace of Cabrera on the Feast of Epiphany—that is, in the last year of his life.[2] The last attack, which lasted two hours, also occurred after he had a meal[3]—a fact which may likewise have been mentioned by the chronicler as an allusion to repeated poisoning.

But a stronger indication to this effect is given in Castillo's loaded remarks on the visit that Ferdinand and Isabella paid the King during his first sickness. They pressed him, he tells us, to acknowledge his commitment regarding Isabella's succession, but no peace could be established between them, as on both sides "many things were alleged which are dangerous to put down in writing."[4] What were the things which Castillo considered so perilous to reveal? Did the King accuse the Princes or their "friends" of an attempt to poison him? Did Castillo, who may have written the above words after the King had died, decline to expose himself to the new rulers' wrath, and possibly to their punishment? In any case, it appears that Enrique then considered himself gravely threatened by the Princes, for Castillo further tells us that Pacheco, who "knew *from what the King had informed him of all that had occurred*,"[5] tried secretly with the King to organize one night the capture of the Princes and their ally, Mayordomo Cabrera.[6]

G.-H. Gaillard, the 18th-century French historian, noted that "those who put obstacles to the satisfaction of Isabella's fortune always died at a time very opportune for her."[7] This statement cannot be dismissed as a "malicious remark of a hysterical critic," as some admirers of Isabella defined it, for it fits the relevant facts too well. King Enrique indeed died at an opportune moment for the Princess, when he was known to have been making every effort to marry his daughter Juana to the king of Portugal—an effort which, if crowned with success, would have ruined Isabella's chances of succession. But this alone would not have provided a sufficient basis for the suspicion indicated. Enrique's demise, however, occurred less than a month after Pacheco expired under "mysterious" circumstances—or at least in circumstances too "opportune" for Isabella to be readily regarded as sheer luck. He was then in Simancas, on his way back from Portugal, where he tried to persuade King Alfonso V to consent to marry Juana, and, as Palencia put it, he died "like his brother, the Master of Calatrava . . . of the same infirmity—a repugnant and deadly abscess in the throat."[8] Pacheco's sudden death at the most critical moment, coupled with the similarity of his final sickness to that of his brother, cannot fail of course to raise the suspicion of foul play in his case, too. Since he and the King worked closely together on the project of Juana's marriage, the materialization of that project would not have been prevented had not the King been removed from the scene shortly after Pacheco's death.

Pedro Girón, Pacheco's brother, died on May 2, 1466, on his way to Madrid, where he planned to force Isabella into marriage. He passed away, according to Palencia, "at a time when no pestilence took place; and among a multitude of healthy people, he alone suffered miserable death in consequence of an abscess in his throat."[9] According to the *Crónica Castellana*, he died as a result of *esquinencia* (i.e., quinsy), but the *Crónica de Calatrava* states that his physicians *"could not diagnose the cause of his sickness"* and that *"great suspicion"* was astir that certain grandees of the kingdom, who were discontented with that marriage, saw to it that he got some deadly poison."[10]

And suspicion of poison also accompanied the demise of Alfonso, Enrique's foster brother, whose death paved the way for Isabella's assumption of the position of heiress to the throne. In this case, poisoning is hinted by Castillo, indicated by Valera, and unequivocally asserted by Palencia. According to the latter, Alfonso fell ill on his way from Arévalo to the "lands of Toledo" after he had eaten a certain dish of which he was particularly fond. Following that he went to his bed without saying a word, and without getting out of it even once until he died five days later (on July 5, 1468).

Palencia stresses that he had none of the symptoms of the pestilence which was rampant at the time, while several signs (such as his loss of speech and the black color of his mouth) indicated clearly that he was poisoned.[11] But who was interested in thus terminating his life in that particular time?

Palencia had no doubt that it was Pacheco who schemed and carried out the assassination.[12] The strength, honesty, and independence of character displayed by young Alfonso, Palencia thought, convinced Pacheco that he would never be able to use him as his tool; therefore he decided to replace him with Isabella. It is hard to believe, however, that Pacheco would enter such a venture in the midst of the civil war, when Alfonso's death was sure to strengthen Enrique's royal position and when he could not be at all sure that Enrique would agree to repeat the disgrace of surrendering the rights of his daughter, Juana, to a new pretender (in this case, Isabella) who could not even promise Juana, as did Alfonso, a position of partnership in the throne. To be sure, Pacheco was not beyond contriving intricate and long-range plans; nor was he incapable of plotting murder—after all, he plotted to kill King Enrique—but in this case, the risks involved in such a plan must have outweighed its promise.

A person more likely to contemplate that assassination, and thereby open the way for Isabella to the throne, would seem to be Juan II of Aragon, who could lose nothing from the failure of the attempt, whereas, if successful, it could bring him much closer to his cherished goal. He, too, was a long-range planner, and he could figure out that, under the circumstances, Pacheco would be forced to exert all his efforts to secure Isabella's right as heiress, and also that if he made such efforts, he stood a good chance of attaining that end.

Thus, Isabella's marriage to Ferdinand as well as her succession to the throne were saved by four "opportune" deaths, all of which took place in circumstances that gave room to suspicion of foul play. No open-minded scholar, it seems, can fail to consider this possibility, and Balaguer's censure of Gaillard's statement as the "malicious note of a hysterical critic" must be viewed as the exaggerated reaction of a patriotic admirer. So must be judged also his remark that "nobody had ever had the slightest suspicion" of Isabella's involvement, or "dared to hurt with it the venerated record of that august princess."[13] But this is not the point. Nobody had ever suggested that young Isabella (at the age of sixteen or seventeen) had anything to do with the poisoning of her brother or her unwanted suitor, Pedro Girón.

If there is substance to the above suspicions (and we are inclined to believe that there is), the finger of accusation must be pointed not at Isabella, but at Juan II of Aragon. We have seen that he could be considered a schemer of the death of the anti-King Alfonso (if the latter was indeed poisoned), and certainly he was the only likely suspect of the probably contrived death of Pedro Girón. Obviously, Girón's marriage to Isabella would have nullified all of Juan's past efforts to get hold of Castile's government, as it would kill his dream that his son would marry the future heiress to Castile's throne. His interest in destroying both Pacheco and the King at the most crucial moment of his son's fortunes is even less in question. And that Juan II of Aragon was considered capable of such crimes is attested by the *vox populi* of Catalonia that accused him of poisoning his son Don Carlos.

Yet if one assumes that Juan II of Aragon was the secret assassin in all the above cases, if it was he who was responsible not only for the deaths of Alfonso and Girón, but also of Enrique and his minister, one cannot avoid asking the crucial question: Was Ferdinand ignorant of his father's deeds at least with respect to the latter cases? A credible answer to this question could of course throw added light on Ferdinand's image.

G

Espina's Source for the
"Tale of the Two Tents"

The question of the origin of Espina's tale of the two tents, which is related to the expulsion of the Jews from England (*Fortalitium*, lib. 3, tertia expulsio, 219b–219a), cannot be easily settled. Baer says that Espina claimed to have read it in the English chronicles (*History*, II, p.289). But Espina made no such claim. In fact, he was careful to assert that *it is said* to be found in the "old chronicles of the English [people]" *(alia causa)* [for the expulsion of the Jews from England] *in cronicis anglorum antiquis ut fertur asignatur; Fort.* lib. III, nona consideratio, teria expulsio, f. *219 a*), without telling us from whom he got this information or where he read it. In any case, as John Selden pointed out (in his *De Jure naturali et Gentium iuxta disciplinam Ebraeorum*, 1665, lib. II, cap. 6, f. 190), the story in question does not appear either in the English chronicles dealing with the expulsion or in other old documents related to it.

Selden made the above remark in connection with the version of the same story found in Gedalia ibn Yahya's *Shalshelet ha-Qabbala* (Venice, 1586, ff. 112–113; Jerusalem, 1962, pp. 265–266). Gedalia, however, took the story from Joseph ha-Kohen (*Emeq ha-Bakha*, completed 1663; ed. Letteris, Vienna, 1852, pp. 53–54), who in turn borrowed it from Samuel Usque (*Consolaçam as tribualçoens de Israel*, 1533, ff. 174ʳ–178ᵛ). According to Usque, his version of the narrative was based on two sources; Espina's *Fortalitium* and a work he indicated as *Li. eb*. Could this *Li. eb* have been composed *before* the *Fortalitium* and thus serve, directly or indirectly, as Espina's source, too?

Graetz suggested, with some reservations, that *Li. eb* could mean *libro ebraico* and that the reference was to Efodi's *Zikhron ha-Shemadot*, which may

1131

have been written at the turn of the 14th century or in the beginning of the 15th (*Geschichte*, VIII, 3rd ed., p. 397). Isidore Loeb, on the other hand, believed that Usque referred by the above initials to Ibn Verga, the author of *Shevet Yehuda (Liber Iehuda Ebn Berga)*.[1] But Martin A. Cohen, in the study he appended to his English translation of Usque's work, had convincingly shown both identifications wrong[2] and, in addition, advanced the notion that, in *Li eb.* the reference was to Leone Iehuda Ebreo, whom for some reason Usque mistook as the author of Isaac Abravanel's *Yemot Olam*[3] (a history of the Jews which was designed to include an account of all the troubles and persecutions that befell them). Cohen's hypothesis has merit. It leans on the only work that could possibly serve as source for *all* the narratives under consideration (i.e., those whose source is marked by Usque as *L. eb*), although we cannot be sure that *Yemot Olam* (or most of it) had actually been written. All we know of this work is that Abravanel *planned* to write it, *began* to compose it, and *intended* to finish it.[4] We do not know, however, to what point he advanced in writing it.

If Usque indeed referred to *Yemot Olam*, as conjectured by Cohen, its author (namely, Isaac Abravanel) could have borrowed the story under discussion from the *Fortalitium*. But then we come back to our original question: Where did Espina find it? Baer was convinced that the story was a fable invented by Espina, since a converso problem, the way he described it there, did not exist in any country but Spain. I cannot share Baer's conviction. Espina was a man rich in credulity, but poor in imagination, and the story has too much of a folkloric flavor to it to have been created by an author like him. Nor can his failure to mention his direct source offer support for Baer's contention. Espina does not mention the direct source of his other tale about England (that of the singing boy) either; nevertheless we know that he did not invent it.[5]

That a folkloric tale about the expulsion of Jewish converts from England could be produced in part in England (of the 14th century) and in part in Spain (in the first half of the 15th), *where it might have been circulated orally*, is not entirely excluded. An unspecified number of Jews remained in England as converts after the expulsion, and their presence was resented by the general population and caused a variety of problems (see on this A. Neubauer, "Notes on the Jews of Oxford," in the Oxford Historical Society's *Collectanea Franciscana*, second series, p. 314, and Cecil Roth, *History of the Jews of England*, 1942, pp. 86, 132, 274). The story, therefore, may have reached Espina from an oral Spanish source. Hence perhaps his phrasing: *fertur* ("it is said").[6]

H

The Abuse of the Conversos as "Judaizers": When Did It Begin?

In asking this question, we ought first to note that the anti-convert laws in both Castile and Aragon tended to avoid, from the very outset, any clear reliance on religious grounds. Thus, the law denying converts from Judaism the right to public office in Toledo, which Alfonso VII enacted in 1118, does not indicate any religious transgression or impropriety on their part. To be sure, the law offers in its justification the king's wish to follow the "instructions of the Holy Fathers" (thereby meaning no doubt the sixty-fifth decree of the Fourth Toledan Council).[1] Yet while those "instructions" could be interpreted to refer to *converts who remained Jews at heart or followed the Jews' ways* (thereby implying that *true* converts were not subject to their limitations), the law of 1118 leaves no room for such an interpretation as it clearly refers to *all* converts of Jewish origin, regardless of their religious attitudes. Nor does it make any exceptions in cases of *proven* devotion to Christianity, or of flawless adherence to its laws and regulations for some specific period of time. Evidently, the authors of the law of 1118 interpreted the "instructions" of the Fourth Toledan Council as referring to *all* converts of *Jewish origin*, without touching on any other qualification; in other words, they interpreted those "instructions" in a racial sense—and a *strictly* racial one—as later did the authors of the *Sentencia-Estatuto*.

The same description of the Jewish converts employed by the law of 1118 *(nuper renati)*, which is total and prevents any exception—above all, exceptions on religious grounds—also appears in the laws of the other cities that followed the aforesaid Toledan decree.[2] It was only in the middle of the 13th century that we find in one of these urban laws an attempt at some religious

1133

justification for the anti-convert discrimination it proposed. In the *fuero* of Carmona (1247), the converts in question are presented as *tornadizos* (turncoats), no doubt in response to the determined campaign then being conducted by the Dominicans in Spain against convert discrimination. Yet the implied "justification" in no way alludes to the converts as "Jewish" in any way, for "turncoats" who abandoned Judaism for base motives, related only to their personal interests, were obviously not likely to return to the religion on which they had turned their backs. It is also significant that no other title such as would suggest any contact with Judaism was used to denigrate the converts in that period. This would seem to indicate that the converts of that time were generally not believed to be "secret Jews."

We get the same impression also from the reactions to the conversions that occurred during the Civil War (1368). By that time the cities could no longer prevent Jewish converts from occupying public offices, for both canon law and the civil code of Spain were now explicit in their demand that converts and Old Christians be treated as equals. Since popular reception of the new converts, however, was as hostile as ever, the old hostility had to be given new forms of expression. With legislative discrimination now denied, an anti-convert campaign was mounted which was of a vituperative nature. Once again, however, the most common invective was the term *tornadizo* (turncoat), although, as we gather from the Cortes of Soria (1380), "many" other terms of abuse were used as well. We would not be surprised if one of these terms related to the convert's Jewish feelings or attitudes, for it stands to reason that in 1380, only twelve years after the civil war and its accompanying persecution of the Jews, a number of crypto-Jews were still present among the converts produced by that persecution. Yet the fact that no such charge had surfaced, and that the dominant denunciation was still *tornadizo*, suggests that Judaism, whatever strength it still retained among the converts of the Civil War, was not the most typical feature of those converts, evidently because their religious assimilation had proceeded apace. Indeed, it took only another fifteen years for that assimilation to be so advanced as to move, in all likelihood, some of these converts to help Christianize the forced converts of 1391.[3] Thus, it is not astonishing that the converts of 1367 were not called Judaizers. What *is* rather astonishing is that they were berated—obviously, by their enemies—as "turncoats" and not as converts who went over to Christianity against their will. We therefore judge that abuse to be a libelous insult chosen for lack of a better one.

We have seen that also after 1391 the converts were given a hostile reception, expressed, in addition to brutal acts, in a more virulent campaign of defamation. To the old invective, a new term was added (*Marrano*— "swine"), which soon became the most pervasive insult. But even then we do not hear that the converts were abused as crypto-Jews or "Judaizers" or

"Judaic heretics," although the number of secret Jews among them must still have been considerable. No doubt the rapid transformation of many "forced" converts into voluntary ones after 1391 had to do with the absence of the "Jewish insult," or with its limited public use, so that it left no imprint in the records; and we may also assume that the same transformation was responsible for another related phenomenon. When in 1416, and in later years, Archbishop Anaya sought to bar all conversos from entry to the college he had founded in Salamanca, he did not base the statutes he recommended for the purpose on the possible faithlessness of the New Christians, but solely on their Jewish descent. He rejected converts of Jewish stock, without paying any regard to the question of their fidelity—in all likelihood, because he believed that the applicants to the school would prove to be good Christians. It stands to reason that such applicants in 1418 were expected to be mostly sons of veteran converts (i.e., those converted in 1391). Had many of them been known as secret Jews, Anaya would undoubtedly have mentioned this fact in support of his proposed statutes.

A parallel indication of this situation may be observed in Aragon. The first and only time that we hear any complaints about the Jewish converts' religious behavior is at the Council of Tortosa (1429). There the charge was raised against many New Christians that they had not baptized their children in due time; but even then *they were not accused by the Council as followers of Jewish rites or beliefs*. The Council of Tortosa met about one decade after the persecutions of 1412–1418, which resulted, as we have indicated, in a massive conversion. Indubitably, by that time the immense group of converts still contained many believers in Judaism; but practicing Jews among them must already have been few, and since their activity had rarely surfaced, they may hardly have been noticed. To be sure, their neglect to baptize their children showed that their attachment to Christianity was still frail, but the failure of their overwhelming majority to perform any—or many—Jewish rites (as attested by the council's silence on this matter) indicates that their actual detachment from Judaism was, by the end of the twenties, far advanced. Under these circumstances, the Council's warning to the converts that it would take drastic measures to enforce their children's baptism was probably sufficient to move the negligent among them to fulfill their Christian duties.[4]

But even more illustrative of the religious condition of the Jews in the kingdom of Aragon is the letter they wrote eight years later to Pope Eugene IV. In this letter they pointed out, as we have mentioned, the attitude of outright rejection and discrimination they experienced in their relations with the Old Christians—an attitude they considered extremely unjust and which they were really unable to explain. What is apparent from this account is that their adversaries did not justify their hostile attitude on *religious* grounds—that is, by some religious misconduct of the conversos—for if such accusations had been publicly voiced, the conversos would not have found it possible to ignore them upon presenting their grievances to the pope. What we gather from their letter is that the rejection they experienced was of a purely racial character, and that no one had abused them as "Judaizers" or "crypto-Jews," for no complaint was made by them on this score.

In fact, for the whole period of almost three and a half centuries from the opening of converso history in Spain (1109) until the Toledan insurrection of 1449, there is not a single indication in the sources that the conversos were reviled as clandestine Jews. It was only in 1449, during the Toledan rebellion that we hear them denounced for the first time as "Judaizers,"⁵ and hence also as "heretics" and "apostates." The phenomenon appears especially odd as it occurred some 60 years after 1391, and more than 30 years after 1412, when most New Christians were converts' sons or grandsons and when the over-whelming majority of the Marranos were Christianized. Obviously, an explanation is called for.

The explanation is not far to find. The sudden burst of "Judaic" accusations was part of the great gush of charges that made up the anti-Marrano barrage of the time. In this violent agitation, every speck of a flaw ever found in the conversos in any sphere of life—be it religious, social, economic, or political—was inflated to monstrous proportions and boldly presented to the people as a truth that had been ascertained and could not be denied. As we have noted, *all* of these charges—and not only the religious—struck deep roots in the people's thinking and served as common ground for the rising demand to oust the conversos from Spain's society. If ultimately the religious charges came to play a larger part in the anti-Marrano campaign, it was not because of their greater veracity, but because religious law offered a better opportunity to use them as destructive weapons.

I

Bernáldez on the Conversos' Occupations

ndrés Bernáldez, who is known for his *Memoirs from the Reign of the Catholic Kings,* devoted several passages of his work to the New Christians.[1] A native of Fuentes, a small town near León, Bernáldez became in 1488, at about the age of 34, a curate of another small town, Los Palacios, in the territory of Seville.[2] He began his service there, when Diego de Deza (later Inquisitor-General) served as archbishop of Seville, and his chapters on the New Christians appear to have been written at the height of the Inquisition's persecution of the Marranos. Bernáldez, as we have seen, was heart and soul with the Inquisition's methods and operations.[3] He was a follower of the extreme racists, sharing their fierce hatred of the conversos and their ardent desire to destroy them.

Thus, one might assume that what Bernáldez tells us about the economic life of the conversos would be consistent with what we find in the writings of his predecessors. This is indeed generally the case. Bernáldez added only a few details to those offered by his forerunners; and his description differs from theirs more in his omissions than in his additions. For Bernáldez was a clever writer. Avoiding making charges that could be easily disputed, he refrained from supporting fantastic accusations of the kind we find in Espina's *Fortalitium* or in the satires we have analyzed. This made his statements about the New Christians appear credible, and consequently some scholars considered them sound and even endowed them with special insights. Such assessments were made especially of Bernáldez' comments on the conversos' social and economic life.

Bernáldez begins his remarks on the subject with the judgment of the conversos which was held by their enemies, but which he accentuates with a few comments of his own. Thus, he informs us that the conversos were generally, or in their majority, a people of profiteers *(logreros)* who use in their dealings "many tricks and deceptions" and "live from comfortable occupations" *(oficios holgados)*.[4] "Never did they want," adds Bernáldez, "to undertake such tasks as plowing or digging or walking through the fields raising cattle. All they taught their sons were urban professions." More precisely, they taught them, he explains, how to "earn their living with little work."[5]

Nevertheless, Bernáldez adds, though they did little work, "*many* of them" not only "earned their living" but attained in a *short time* great fortunes and estates." They accomplished this feat because they "had no moral scruples" in "taking their usuries" and "exercising their profiteering,"[6] great evils in themselves, which bred another evil. In the wake of the great riches they had accumulated, there developed their "haughtiness and pride"—characteristics which, Bernáldez says, were formed by another cause as well. This was the presence in their ranks of "many scholars and learned men, and bishops and canons, and friars and abbots, and majordomos, and *contadores,* and secretaries, and agents of the king and the great lords."[7]

When one sees things through a distorting mirror of intense hate and prejudice, one can see only a caricature of reality and not its true face. This is what Bernáldez saw and presented—a caricature of the conversos that includes some true elements and many exaggerated, false features, all of which were aimed at producing a distasteful and repellent image. What is probably true in Bernáldez' description is the "haughtiness" that was common to very rich conversos, their nobiliar elements and top officials, and the general "pride" of the conversos over the fact that so many of them distinguished themselves in the scholastic life of Spain, in its religious life, and in their services to the monarchic and nobiliar administrations. But he is utterly misleading when he tries to convince us that the bulk of the conversos was comprised of profiteers who made their great wealth "quickly," with little or no effort—and this due to frauds, tricks and chicaneries they practiced on the Old Christians.

For it is clear that most wealthy conversos could not possibly have made their fortunes overnight, and certainly not through ensnaring all Old Christians with whom they did business. What brought them wealth were their undertakings in the fields of tax farming, international commerce and large-scale banking and financing; and these undertakings required, besides know-how, professional skill and much ingenuity, and a great deal of energy and driving force. Not in vain did Don Isaac Abravanel, who was experienced in precisely this sort of business, tell us that those who acquire great wealth were born under the star that endows men with energy.[8] And we must of course note also the following: most of the fortunes made by the conversos resulted from their dealings with the kings and great magnates, the owners of vast estates or the lords of the Mesta, and with great Christian merchants in Spain and overseas; and these people were surrounded by their lawyers, *contadores* and experts in the fields involved, who were no less aware than the conversos they dealt with of all the intricacies of their undertakings. The "frauds and deceptions" referred to by Bernáldez, therefore, reflect only his provincial notions—notions typical of a small-town priest whose thinking was saturated with the slogans and charges of the antisemitic propaganda of his time. He had no conception of what was involved in the making of the immense fortunes he referred to, and did not understand that if the converso financiers, tax farmers and businessmen had been fraudulent as he assumed, they would not have been engaged again and again by both the kings and the great nobles. Nor did he realize that these fortunes were, in most cases, amassed in generations, and not "in a short time," as he was led to believe by his informants.

But even more misleading is his attempt to convince us that most conversos were opulent individuals who hated hard work and spent their time idling. Granted that as city people they aspired that their sons would master professions that may be called "urban," but in this they could not possibly have differed from most Old Christian burghers, their neighbors. Nor did the urban professions of the New Christians generally involve "little work." What is reflected in this assessment of Bernáldez is the old, primitive view of labor, which identifies hard work with physical exertion and not with any effort of the mind. If, however, strenuous mental activity may likewise be rightfully considered hard work, then the conversos engaged in the professions which Bernáldez classed as "easy" and "comfortable" were not "idlers" or lazy at all. Success in the tasks involved in these professions, which often meant settlement of intricate problems, called for alertness, attention to detail and laborious application of one's mind. Hence, if the conversos not only held their ground but also made progress in these competitive undertakings, as one must conclude from Bernáldez' own words, one must also assume that they were not "idle," but rather heavily engaged in providing the requisites for guarding and advancing their varied enterprises. Thus they were usually in a state of strain, rather than of blissful indolence or heedlessness, as Bernáldez would like us to believe. But apart from this, his whole portrayal of the conversos as a group, or rather as a sociological entity, is plainly a gross distortion of the truth and far removed from the historical reality, of which he seems strangely to have been unaware.

For, in fact, the conversos, viewed as a *group*, were not plutocrats who could live a carefree life, but men who had to work for their livelihood and whose income was generally rather limited. Despite everything that was said of their great wealth, as if it had been shared evenly by them all, their great majority were artisans (of various trades), shopkeepers or manufacturers (on a small scale), physicians and lawyers (of the median level), and holders of second-rate public offices. Their canons and friars were certainly not rich, or richer than most of the other low-rank clerics; and this applies also to most clerks and agents of the leading converso entrepreneurs. It was only their famous physicians and high officials, and above all their great merchants, tax farmers and bankers, who could boast of real wealth. But those who belonged to these categories of earners comprised a minority of the converso population, probably no more than a tenth.

It would seem proper to pay special attention to Bernáldez' aforecited statement on the conversos: "Never did they want to undertake occupations such as plowing and digging, or walking through the fields raising cattle, nor did they teach these occupations to their children." Domínguez Ortiz sees in the above statement an "acute observation" which betrays the "aversion of the worker on the land against the exploiting city."[9] Possibly Bernáldez came to notice this fact in his search for evidence of the conversos' inclination to live on the "hard work" of others, or perhaps he was led to the thought by some other reasons.[10] But the movement against the conversos cannot be described in terms of the well-known, ancient conflict between the village and the town. After all, the assaults upon the conversos were conducted mostly by *urban* elements, and if, on one occasion, people from the countryside came to Toledo to attack the conversos, they came there to assist other *city dwellers* and in response to the latter's call.[11] Nor do we see them at any time assail other urban elements save the conversos. The hatred of the peasant for the converso, which is indeed repeatedly attested by our documents, drew its inspiration from other sources than the one suggested by Domínguez.

J
Racism in Germany and Spain

In his "Nationalism and Race in Medieval Law,"[1] Guido Kisch, the distinguished scholar, known especially for his studies on Jewish law in the Middle Ages, dismissed the notion that the *Sentencia-Estatuto* was fundamentally a racial, not a religious document. Seeking to confirm his thesis that *all* anti-Jewish legislation in the Middle Ages was based solely on religious principles, Kisch tried to prove that the Toledan *Sentencia* was no exception to this rule. It, too, he claimed, stemmed from religious considerations, as is evidenced by its reference to the *pesquisa* (Inquiry) that listed "no less than twenty-five transgressions against the Christian religion, with which the New Christians were charged."[2] According to Kisch, then, the Toledan *Sentencia* emerged from the "suspicion of religious infidelity" which was raised against the converts from Judaism in Spain, and apparently with good reason. For "these converts remained at heart attached to the ideals of their former brethren in faith" and "baptism had not affected them spiritually." To infer from this, Kisch said, that "the prejudice which had previously been ostensibly religious became 'racial' " means "reading modern racist conceptions into medieval sources where no justification can be found for such interpretation."[3]

Kisch, however, is mistaken. He shows no awareness of the racial literature that preceded and succeeded the *Sentencia-Estatuto*, or due attention to what is contained in the *Sentencia* itself. "In medieval sources," he rightly points out, "converts from Judaism are, as a rule, explicitly designated as former adherents of the Jewish faith."[4] And this fact, he says, does not "permit an interpretation of the relevant sources in racial terms." But the *Sentencia-*

Estatuto speaks of the conversos not as descendants of "adherents of the Jewish *faith*," but as "descendants of the perverse *race* of the Jews."[5] And thus if the designation of the converts in the sources is an index to their meaning and interpretation, then their designation in the *Sentencia-Estatuto* must be interpreted not religiously, but racially. To be sure, Kisch mentions the reference of the *Sentencia* to the *pesquisa*'s indications of the Marranos' "Judaism" (which led some of them to be burned as heretics), but he fails to mention that, besides referring to their heresies, the *Sentencia* speaks repeatedly, plainly, and emphatically about their "*other* transgressions, insults, seditions and crimes which were committed and perpetrated by them to this day."[6] Evidently, Kisch did not ask himself what part was played by those *other* alleged crimes in the formation of the *Sentencia-Estatuto*; and thus he could conveniently define this ruling as a purely religious legislation.

One who tries to accept Kisch's thesis cannot, obviously, avoid asking: How could a policy that was essentially *religious* lead in fifteenth century Spain to "results corresponding to those aimed at by modern racial legislation in Europe?" Kisch, who acknowledges the legitimacy of the question, evades it by asserting that this is "a different story."[7] Yet in our opinion, this is *not* a different story. Rather do we believe that it is the same story, for the "results" of that policy in fifteenth century Spain emerged from racial, not religious conceptions.

Kisch's argument was directed against Cecil Roth, who noticed the "correspondence" between what happened in Spain in the 15th century and what occurred in Germany in the 20th.[8] In both countries, Roth claimed, "the prejudice which had previously been ostensibly religious became 'racial.'"[9] This observation is on the whole correct and, with some modification, we can subscribe to it. Where Roth erred, however, was in his assessment of the reasons for that passage from religion to race, or rather of the causes of the change in the thrust of the anti-Jewish agitation.

According to Roth, the rise of the race movement in both Germany and Spain resulted from the same cause—i.e., the removal of the disabilities against the Jews (in Spain, to be sure, when the latter were converted). What ensued was the release of the "pent-up genius" of the Jews, which "rushed forwards" with an overwhelming force. The sudden "pre-eminence of a fraction of the population," which had been previously considered inferior, "not unnaturally . . . gave rise to jealousy"; and the jealousy sought its justification, "not as hitherto in the religious beliefs of the hated element, but in their ethnic origin."[10]

Roth seems to believe that in both countries the remarkable expansion of that "fraction of the population" in all the spheres of the nation's life took place after "segregation was broken down," and that in reaction to that expansion the race theory evolved. This description of the evolution of racism is obviously inaccurate when it comes to Germany. For German racism appeared long *before* the "pent-up genius" of German Jewry was released and "rushed forward" in all directions; hence, "jealousy" could hardly be the cause of the birth and rise of the racial theory in Germany. What made it appear there was obviously the *weakening of the religious factor as a barrier to the Jews' social equalization* and the fear of many Germans that this equalization would lead to full assimilation of the Jews in German culture and ultimately to their ethnic fusion with the Germans. That this fear was not altogether groundless was indicated by the progress of Jewish cultural assimilation and the "plague of conversion" to Christianity among the Jews which broke out early in the century (c. 1805).

Following the anti-Jewish riots in Germany, Boerne wrote in 1919 that "even the most vicious hypocrite does not dare say that he persecutes the Jew because of his religion."[11] This was largely so because of the decline in the influence of religion in Germany and because the anti-Jewish forces in that country had to count with Europe's strong liberal movement that declared religious distinctions inadequate to justify the continued discrimination against the Jews. The German anti-Jewish agitators of the time, such as Ruehs, Scheuring, Fries and others, sought therefore to fortify the religious distinction with another barrier which to them appeared impassable—i.e., the alleged inferior race of the Jews, which should prevent their equalization with the Germans. This is how racism came to serve in Germany as a stumbling block on the path of the Jews' equalization and—more broadly— of their determined attempts to enter German society.

The German racist campaign against the Jews that evolved in the first half of the 19th century could not stop the progress toward Jewish emancipation. But the more this progress became apparent, the more acrid the racist agitation became, expanding in the forties into broader and higher spheres of German scholarship, art and science.[12] "National Socialism," says E. Sterling, "took most of its slogans from the teachings of the Germanomania and the fanatic wing of [German] conservatism in the early part of the nineteenth century."[13] This is on the whole a correct observation (although it requires some clarification[14]), but one should not deduce from it that the influence of those teachings was constantly on the rise. For in the period just mentioned, Germany was also swept by international currents (social, intellectual and political) which were predominantly anti-racial, and the first racist assault upon the Jews of Germany (i.e., that of 1815–1850) failed therefore to attain its prime objective.

Moreover, thanks to those anti-racial forces, the Jews of Germany achieved their emancipation (1860), and between 1860 and 1880 Jewish penetration into German society proceeded in all directions. It was then that the *second* racist campaign was launched, which, although checked in various areas, managed on the whole to cut new ground and prepare the way for the third—and final—racial attack upon German Jewry (the one that began following World War I). What is important for us to note at this point is that in Germany the racial campaign was marked by a constant and progressive disengagement from religion, or rather from religious considerations. Accordingly, while in its *first* stage that campaign still used theological Christian arguments, and in the *second* it employed them much less, in the *third* it detached itself from Christianity almost completely. It was then that it achieved its destination.

If the above remarks of Roth cannot explain the rise of racism in Germany, his supplementary remarks (referred to below) cannot explain its appearance in mid-15th-century Spain. True, when racism was launched there (as a theory), the Marrano "expansion" had already been effected and the reaction of "jealousy" was no doubt apparent. Still, we do not see why this should have called for a change in the "justification" of that jealousy—namely, why that justification ceased to rest mainly on religion—or rather on the Marranos' religious misconduct—and centered on their "ethnic origin" as a major reason for the persecution. After all, unlike Germany in the 19th century, Spain in the 15th was a deeply religious country; and, if we go by Roth, the conversos were believed to have remained "attached to the ideals of their former brethren in faith," that "their *nominal* change of faith was meaningless," and therefore "it was considered right for the Old Christians to behave as though it had never taken place."[15] But if so, the antagonism and persecution could have safely continued on the grounds of religion only, as they did in the past. In fact, given the above allegations, we can readily understand why the anti-Marranos demanded the establishment of an Inquisition in Castile; for the Inquisition was a *religious* instrument designed to wreak havoc upon Christian heretics, and many expected it to be strong enough to destroy the "Jewish heresy" root and branch. Why then did racism arise in Spain— and this against the hallowed principles of Christianity and the clear-cut original opposition of the Church? Roth fails to offer an answer to this question. Having noticed the similarity between Germany and Spain with respect to some *facts* of the racial persecution, he failed to notice the dissimilarity with respect to its deep, underlying *causes*.

For the development in Spain was both similar and dissimilar to the one that occurred in Germany. It was similar inasmuch as there, too, as we have indicated, the religious argument alone was *inadequate* to meet the needs of the converso haters, who aspired to what the German antisemites did— namely, the elimination of the object of their hate. It was dissimilar, however, in the *cause* of that inadequacy. To be sure, in both countries the inadequacy was caused by the diminution of the possibility to employ or rely on the religious difference. But while in Germany that diminution resulted from the general *reduction of the religious influence,* in Spain, where Christianity was at its acme, it resulted from quite a different development. One could not rely very well on the *religious* difference when this difference had almost disappeared; and it almost disappeared because most of the Marranos—or rather their overwhelming majority—had been Christianized. In consequence, the anti-Marrano elements, seeking to strengthen the basis of their campaign, had to turn to the theory of race—a theory that provided them with another distinction which they badly needed to attain their goal: to block the "Jews' " invasion of the Spanish society and their amalgamation with the Spanish people.

Indeed, nothing demonstrates more convincingly the weakness of the so-called Judaic heresy in Spain than the rise of the strong racial movement against the conversos at the very time when converso Christianization was pushing the Marranos toward final assimilation. It was indeed here, at that stage of the developments, that the racist movement saw its historic mission. Its purpose was not to protect the Spanish people from the fictitious "danger" of a Judaic heresy, but from the real danger of full-fledged Christianization, which was bound to bring about, as the racists believed, the Jews' domination of the Spaniards and their increasing ethnic fusion with the latter. Out of their fierce hatred of the Jews, they viewed that fusion as "contamination"— that is, as infecting the Spanish blood with the vile tendencies of the Jewish race—and by describing the conversos, in full accordance with that view, as *naturally* and *unalterably* immoral, they planned to disturb their merger with the Spaniards not only ethnically, but also socially. Racism, as we have said elsewhere respecting both Germany and Spain, is the "last obstacle that antisemitism can put up to the assimilation of the Jews into the majority of the people."[16]

One final remark is called for about the conclusion of these historical struggles. In Germany racism gained total power, and could therefore steer its course toward its aims. But in Spain it never became fully independent, and therefore its advance was often hampered by the sanctions of the Church and the restrictions of the Crown. Hence the importance the racists ascribed to the Inquisition, whose manipulation was, at least partly, in their hands, even though it had to abide by the Church's rulings and the King's commands. Hence also the difference in the final outcome. Thus, while in Germany racism achieved its goal, in Spain it fell short of its mark. To be sure, it managed for long periods to segregate most New Christians from the majority of the Spanish people; it inflicted great losses on the Marrano population and caused it terrible damages and hardships. But in the long run it failed in its effort. It could not prevent the final fusion of most conversos with the rest of the Spaniards. In Spain, therefore, it was not the racist movement but the Catholic Church that won the ultimate battle—the Catholic Church and the majority of the conversos, who sought assimilation into the Spanish people.

K

The Converso Conspiracies
Against the Inquisition

How can one explain the general credulity displayed by so many eminent historians toward the claims and accusations of the Spanish Inquisition? What could bring men otherwise distinguished for their critical faculties and keen sense of truth to accept so readily almost all the information imparted by the Inquisition, as well as by its agents, "familiars" and promoters? Who can doubt that most, if not all of the Inquisitors were mortal enemies of the conversos and therefore were anxious to prove them guilty?[1] But even if some of the Inquisitors were neutral, Spanish society was not. It so seethed with hatred toward the conversos that the judges of the Inquisition were in no position to issue honest verdicts. Where would the witnesses of their cases come from if not from that society? And what integrity and courage would they need to withstand the pressures of public opinion from all sides? Even if the functionaries were more or less impartial, we would have to suspect every decision and sentence handed down by a court like the Spanish Inquisition. How much more, then, should we question its accounts and verdicts when both the functionaries of the Inquisition and the society in which they worked were howling for converso blood? Can one rely on documents produced in a spirit of malice and vengeance and a desire to consign the accused to the flames? The hatred of the Inquisitors for the conversos, of which we have incontestable evidence, should be grounds enough to doubt their records and judgments to the point of making them scarcely usable. In addition, the Inquisition regularly used torture to extract "confessions" to the crimes it ascribed to the accused. How can one take seriously any information obtained under torture or threat of torture when not corroborated by trustworthy evidence? Such corroboration was hardly possible under the Inquisition, for its witnesses were never cross-examined by the accused; even their names remained a secret to the defendants; and this secrecy afforded many vile characters an opportunity to gratify their grudges against the accused or satisfy their desire to serve the Inquisitors. If we add to these facts the Inquisition's reign of terror, which deterred everyone from defending the accused, and the eagerness of both the Crown and the Inquisitors to confiscate the possessions of the condemned men, what other conclusion can we arrive at except that the documents of the Inquisition do not deserve the credit that is usually given them?

Nevertheless, we do not suggest that these documents should be disregarded. Of course, they contain some genealogical items, data concerning family relationships, as well as the professions engaged in by the accused, and such information may prove helpful to us in reconstructing some elements of the past. But insofar as the substance of the cases is concerned—the events they relate and the charges they contain—we must approach them all with the utmost caution and a low degree of credulity.

But not only the documents of the Inquisition itself must be so treated when it comes to the conversos. Also statements on the conversos made by neutral individuals who lived under the Inquisition must be suspect as untrue. Rarely can they be taken at face value, for paralyzing fear dictated every word. Incriminating documents were systematically destroyed, including those that contained references or allusions to the Marranos' true Christianity. Any such allusions, if made at all, were usually so heavily camouflaged that one might often wonder whether their author was defending the conversos or detracting them. It is easy to see the motives of a Bernáldez, who was a sworn enemy of the conversos, but not easy to discern the precise attitude toward the Marranos—or toward specific charges leveled against them—when we come to authors like Palencia or Mariana, or even to conversos like Valera or Pulgar. None of them tells us a straight story, let alone the whole story, or even a good part of it. And rarely do they make clear statements asserting the Marranos' innocence.

Needless to say, one must question the veracity of anonymous papers from that period, especially when they appear to have emanated from the Inquisition or pro-Inquisitional circles. That they were not so treated by many great scholars, but regarded as highly reliable documents, becomes apparent from a study of the scholarly literature concerning the conspiracies allegedly organized by the conversos against the Inquisition.

SEVILLE, 1481

One such document is an anonymous paper touching the reaction of Seville's conversos to the establishment of the Inquisition in their city. Preserved in two copies, one from the 18th century and another from the 17th, in the Biblioteca Colombina of Seville, it is entitled: "An Account of the Reunion and Conspiracy Organized in Seville by the Jewish Conversos Against the Inquisitors who Came [to that city] to Establish the Holy Office of the Inquisition." Amador de los Ríos was the first to make use of this document, presenting its contents as verified fact, without seeing any reason to question it.[2] Later, Fidel Fita published it fully,[3] defining it as a "most precious document" which "attests and briefly describes" the "celebrated conspiracy" which the Sevillian conversos organized against the Inquisition.[4] According to Fita, the paper was extracted from a work compiled by Cristobal Núñez, "chaplain of the Catholic kings and librarian of the Sevillian Church, c. 1500, when Núñez was already an old man."[5] Although Fita presented the extraction as factual, his claim was based merely on conjecture. The paper, we should note, makes no mention of either Don Cristobal Núñez or his work. What, then, led Fita to make his above attribution?

A *Códice de Apuntamientos,* edited by Juan de Torres y Alarcón in 1616, contains a number of passages from Núñez' lost work, one of which is similar to the passage about the conspiracy found in the anonymous paper. On the basis of that similarity Fita concluded that the Colombina paper was drawn from Núñez's work.[6] A careful examination of the pertinent documents, however, does not warrant that conclusion.

Fita also published the relevant text from Juan de Torres' *Apuntamientos,*[7] so that one may compare the accounts in question. For most of their parts, the two passages, of Núñez and of the anonymous manuscript, are identical in style and contents. Both refer to a meeting held by the conspirators shortly after the arrival of the first Inquisitors in Seville; both indicate that those who attended included some of the most important conversos of Seville (judges, lawyers, rich merchants, council members, high Church officials) and some leading New Christians from Otrera and Carmona; and both describe what occurred at that meeting. But the anonymous account is somewhat longer and raises some doubts about its authenticity. We shall therefore present it here together with the extract drawn by Torres from Núñez' work:

Version A
Extracted by Juan de Torres from Núñez *Cosas Notables*

Version B
From vol. LXXX of various papers in the Biblioteca Colombina, Seville

They* said to each other:

"What do you think? How did they dare come against us? We are the principal men of this city and are well liked by the people. Let us gather men. You, so and so, have so many of your men ready *(a punto)* and you, so and so, have so many, etc. And if they come to seize us, we shall cause a scuffle *(meteremos la cossa a braja)* together with the men [we shall mobilize] and the people [of Seville].

A Jew by the name of Foronda who was present there, then said: "To have people ready appears to me a good idea . . . But how? Where are the hearts."[8]

They* said to each other:

"What do you think? How do these regulars *(regulares)* [dare] come against us? Are we not the principal men of this city? Are we not well liked by the people? Let us gather men. You, so and so, have so many of your men ready *(a punto)*, and you, so and so, have so many ready, etc. And thus they divided among the heads *(cabeças)* arms, people, and money, as well as other things necessary for the purpose. And if they came to seize us, we shall cause a brawl *(meteremos en bollicio la cossa)* with the men [we shall mobilize] and the people [of Seville]; and thus we shall kill them all and avenge ourselves of our enemies.

An Old Jew by the name of Foronda, who was present there, then said: "To have people ready appears to be a good idea . . . But how? Where are the hearts? Give me hearts."[9]

*Namely, the conversos attending the meeting.

Version A suggests that the assembled conversos planned to resist the Inquisition by force, but offers no evidence that they took any step toward materializing their plan. In fact, if we go by this document, we must conclude that the meeting ended on a pessimistic note, without a decision by those assembled.

Version B, in contrast, tells us that the assembled conversos not only talked about their plan, but also passed from words to action. They divided among their leaders arms, men and money and other provisions called for by the conspiracy. Version B also informs us that the aim of the scuffle they intended to cause was to "kill all the Inquisitors and take vengeance on their enemies."

It is easy to see that version A constitutes one organic whole. It presents the assembled leaders' discussion of the proposal to resist the Inquisitors, and then the skeptical reaction of a "Jew" called Foronda (no doubt a converso) to that proposal. Version B does not impress us that way at all. The account of the discussion is interrupted by the statement: *"And thus they divided among the[ir] heads arms, men, and money,"* etc.; and what follows this sentence (i.e., *"and if they come to seize us,"* etc.) does not represent its natural sequence, but a continuation of the story about the discussion (which was interrupted, as indicated above). We must conclude that the statement about the division of arms, etc. was interpolated in the original account by an editor who wanted to show that the assembled conversos not only contemplated rebellion, but were also engaged in carrying it out. He wanted to prove them guilty both of conspiratorial thought and rebellious deed.

Moreover, from version A one may gather that the point of causing a brawl was to prevent the Inquisitors from making the arrests and proceeding with their planned work. It was therefore basically a *defensive* action, with no real harm meant for the Inquisitors. But according to version B, the assembled conversos had in mind an *aggressive* action, extremely criminal and inspired with a *vicious intent*. They wanted to kill all the Inquisitors and avenge themselves on their enemies. The concluding sentence in the reported discussion, therefore, may have likewise been interpolated by the same editor, who wanted to prove the conversos guilty by deed as well as by design.

It is very likely therefore that the longer version was not identical with the one drawn by Torres from Núñez' work (and allegedly abridged by Torres). Accordingly, it did *not* emanate from Núñez' *Cosas Notables,* as surmised by Fita (but from another source). It is also likely that the paper used by Núñez included that account in its earlier form—that is, *before* it was amplified, as indicated above; yet it too—and this must be understood—originated from Inquisitional sources or from circles close to the Inquisition. It is possible that the two versions represented two stages in the Inquisition's investigations into this matter. In the first stage it limited its accusations to a charge of organizing resistance to arrests; in the second it went further and charged the accused with a plot to kill the Inquisitors.

Let us now consider the plot itself as presented in these sources. Obviously, the first question to ask about it is: Were there any grounds for any reasonable expectation that *any* of the plans described, if implemented, could stop the Inquisition's activity in Seville? The account of the meeting is supposed to acquaint us with the thinking of the conspirators on this matter and point out the reasons that moved them to believe that their action might end in success. But a careful reading of this account (in both its forms) shows clearly that it did *not* present the actual discussion of those assembled, but arguments ascribed to them that hardly make sense. According to this report, the assembled conversos asked: "How [dare] these regulars come against us? Are we not the principal men of this city?" As if they did not know that those "regulars" of the Inquisition represented the Pope and the Kings and acted under strict and explicit orders. But the question appears strange also for another reason: "How [dare] these regulars proceed against *us?*"—i.e., against the people who attended the meeting. It would seem that the authors of the alleged report wished to indicate that those particular conversos organized the conspiracy for purely personal reasons—that is, because they were some-how informed that the Inquisitors intended to proceed against *them.* But could this possibly have been the case? Were not communal purposes in-volved? The inquisitional accusers clearly tried to play on the common notion about the conversos' selfishness, pomposity, and self-assurance. "Are we not the principal men in this city? Are we not well liked by the people?" Both arguments suggest that the conspirators believed that the Inquisitors' decision to proceed against them was foolhardy because the conspirators' position in the city was so strong as to be impregnable. But could the assembled converso leaders see their position in that light?

Judging by our source (in both its versions), the conspirators had no doubt that the "people" (i.e., the Old Christians of Seville) "liked" them so much that they would rush to their defense if they were actually threatened, or to the defense of the New Christians generally. But no one knew better than the converso leaders that such an expectation had nothing to rely on. Only seven years before, the conversos of Seville had been seized by such fear of their Old Christian neighbors that they mobilized all their men for self-defense, migrated by the hundreds to Gibraltar, while many of them sought refuge in Niebla, the stronghold of the Duke of Medina Sidonia, and many others considered leaving Spain and going to Flanders or Italy.[10] Certainly the relations between the Old and New Christians had not so improved in those seven years that the Marranos' fear of the Old Christians' enmity was re-placed by their reliance on Old Christian amity. To be sure, a large section of Seville's population deeply resented the coming of the Inquisition and was on rather friendly terms with the conversos (on this, see further below), but they certainly were not the majority of the Old Christians; and their opposi-tion to the Inquisition, like their friendship for the conversos, was not so strong as to lead them to endanger their lives or freedoms in a rebellion against the Crown. The authors of our account, who presented this argument, wanted to explain why the conversos pinned their hopes on an armed assault against the Inquisition: The New Christians, who realized that their own forces would not suffice to shoulder such a venture, commenced the conspiracy on the assumption that they would be assisted by the "people." But the conversos could not possibly be so naive as to put their trust in the "people's" assistance. Nor could they expect aid from any nobleman within the city of Seville or outside it.[11] Thus, they must have realized that, in a test of arms, they would have to face the Inquisition by themselves. And what were their chances in such a situation? Surrounded by the majority of the Old Christians who hated them, they would ultimately have to face the royal forces who, together with the hostile elements of the population, would cut them to pieces or seize and imprison them, only to subject them to the most excruciating tortures. As men of the world who could assess realities, the converso leaders cannot be assumed to have failed to foresee this end.

Says Fidel Fita: "That there was a certain plan or danger *(amago)* of a conspiracy appears credible from the edict of January 2."[12] He also says that "the Cura de los Palacios [i.e., Bernáldez] alludes to it in his assertion that Pedro Fernández Benadeva (*veintiquatro* of Seville and *jurado* of San Salvador, who was one of the alleged conspirators) had at his home sufficient weapons to arm a hundred people."[13] But the proclamation of January 2 does not indicate that a conspiracy was afoot, and Bernáldez does not say it, either. To be sure, he asserts that Benadeva had gathered a considerable quantity of arms in his house, but nowhere does he state that a conspiracy was revealed. Had he possessed such information he would certainly not have passed it over. He further says that Diego de Susan and other conversos (mentioned in the documents we have cited above) were burned as Judaizers, not as conspirators.[14] Nor does Palencia refer to the "Sevillian conspiracy" (he, too, would not have ignored such an event); and neither do Pulgar and Valera. They all no doubt heard the rumor about the plot, but they evidently all came to the conclusion that there was nothing in it. Nevertheless, most modern historians have found it possible to assert, on the basis of the senseless account we have presented, that a converso conspiracy was organized in Seville and that it was revealed by the Holy Office in an uncanny—indeed almost miraculous—manner by the voluntary delation of Susan's daughter against her Judaizing father.[15]

What actually happened? The key to the occurrences under consideration should be looked for in the preamble to the story about the conspiracy which is included in the anonymous account. There we are told that "after the Inquisitors and the officials of the Holy Office entered Seville, the city was divided into two factions or opinions about this matter. Some took the side of the Inquisition, and these were of course the good Christians . . . both among the descendants of the ancient Christians, as well as among the new converts, who were truly devoted Christians. [But others took the opposite position,] and what caused great scandal and astonishment was the fact that this party included the powerful [men of the city] and those placed in [high] offices and ecclesiastic dignities; they favored the worst part of this opinion."[16]

There was, then, a strong body of citizens in Seville that included many influential men and high officials in both the lay and ecclesiastic administrations of the city who sided with the party opposed to the Inquisition. These were no doubt the "people" to whom our documents referred. They were not planning to oppose the Inquisition by force (for our source does not hint at this even in a word), but they expressed sharp criticism of its entire plan and created a division of opinion in the city that was obviously against the Inquisition's interests. Under such circumstances, the Inquisitors felt, they were not likely to get the full cooperation of the citizens, and the work of the Inquisition would be hampered as a result. Something had to be done, they thought, to foment a frenzy against the conversos and build up popular support of the Inquisition; and the fabrication of a charge about a converso plot to kill all the Inquisitors and the conversos' enemies (i.e., the Old Christians who supported the Inquisition) could be most helpful for that purpose.

As for the conversos, they must have realized the gravity of their situation. That their leaders met to consider their extremity may be taken for granted; that various measures were proposed to meet it may likewise be considered certain; but it is also certain that if they could agree on anything, it was to reject any idea of forcible resistance to the Inquisition or of killing the Inquisitors. Nevertheless, when information about their meeting reached the ears of the Inquisitors, they decided to treat it as a conspiratorial gathering. Thus they arrested the chief converso leaders, charged them with planning resistance to the Inquisition, and appointed Alfonso de Hojeda, Prior of the Dominican Convent of San Pablo and the conversos' arch-enemy in Seville, as prosecutor against the accused.[17] There is no doubt that in the beginning the inquiry aimed at showing that the conversos attempted to put into operation a murderous design against the Inquisition and its functionaries; but it is also apparent that the Inquisitors found it difficult to prove the conversos guilty of that attempt. Although they undoubtedly used torture for that purpose,[18] they probably could not exact confessions of details that might be coordinated to build up a case. Much time was needed to obtain such a result, and the Inquisitors were anxious to begin their work. In the meantime, the rumors they spread about the plot accomplished much of their desired purpose; and once the intended victims were in their hands, they could not fail to force them, by means of torture, to confess to the crime of Judaizing. The charge of conspiracy was therefore abandoned, and the accused conversos were burned as Judaizers, not as plotters against the Inquisition. That is why the historians of the time failed to mention the alleged conspiracy of Seville.

TOLEDO, 1485

No less questionable than the aforecited accounts of the converso conspiracy in Seville is the one that relates to a similar conspiracy allegedly organized by the conversos in Toledo. It comes from a mid-16th-century manuscript of Sebastián de Orozco, a Toledan jurist and poet, consisting of passages copied from an "old book" dealing, among other things, with the Toledan Inquisition in 1485–1502.[19] According to Orozco, the author of that book was a citizen of Toledo, who habitually wrote down what came to his knowledge about current events he considered of importance. From Orozco's failure to divulge the author's name, and from his description of the latter as a "curious person,"[20] we may gather that the author was not a well-known man—that is, a lay or ecclesiastic leader, one of the so-called "makers of history," who had inside information about the developments he described, but rather "one of the people," who recorded events that he himself witnessed, or were known to his contemporaries, or assumed by some of them to have taken place. His assertions may be generally regarded as true when they refer to the bare facts of the occurrences; however, when they touch the interpretation of these facts, or the motives for the actions he narrates, he seems often more believing than believable.

Thus we can benefit from most of the data he imparts about the beginning of the Inquisition in Toledo, some of which are directly related to our subject. Of these we shall first mention the items touching the sermon that Pero Díaz de la Costana, one of the two Inquisitors who came to Toledo in May 1485, preached, presumably in the Major Church of the city, on the third day of Passover (which, in that year, fell on May 24). Díaz de la Costaña, licensed in theology and canon of the church of Burgos, spoke on the theme of the Holy Spirit, but naturally devoted a good part of his sermon to the forthcoming work of the Inquisition in Toledo. He reminded his audience that he and his co-Inquisitor, and the other functionaries of the Inquisition in the city, represented both the Pope and the Kings; and then and there, he imposed *major excommunication* on anyone who would proceed against the Inquisition in word, or deed, or counsel. All those present in the church took an oath to "defend and shelter the administrators" of the Holy Office and to urge all Judaizers to return to the faith and appear before the Inquisition for reconciliation.[21]

The issuance of a warning against any person who might desire to take action against the Inquisition was part of common inquisitional procedure, but in view of what was soon to happen in Toledo, the advance excommunication of any such person, coupled with the peremptory demand that the Judaizers come to the Inquisition for reconciliation, must have sounded ominous. In any case, by May 24, the date of the sermon, the Inquisitors already knew that they had a problem in Toledo. For about a week earlier they published their Edict of Grace, allowing all heretics to confess their sins within 40 days from the date of publication, and thereby be reconciled with the Church without incurring the customary punishments. But up to the date of the sermon (May 24) no converso had appeared before the Inquisition in response to the Edict. Another week or so passed after that, and still no New Christian came for reconciliation.[22] It was obvious that the Toledan conversos were boycotting the Inquisition's offer of reconciliation and that they were doing it by a communal decision. What could be their purpose?

The anonymous author cited by Orozco, our sole contemporary source for these occurrences, had no doubt about the answer. The holy day of Corpus Christi fell fifteen days after the publication of the Inquisition's Edict. On that day a solemn procession was to pass through the city, carrying an effigy of Jesus Christ. The procession, which undoubtedly was to be headed by the Inquisitors and the notables of the city, was expected to pass through the converso neighborhood, and at that point, when it reached the "four streets," the conversos were to emerge from their hideouts and launch a sudden assault upon it. According to our source, they planned to "kill the Inquisitors and all the other *señores* and caballeros and all the Christian people." They also intended to "seize the city gates and the tower of the Major Church, and then rise with the city against the king." It was only on the eve of Corpus Christi, hours before the scheduled execution of the plan, that the conspiracy was discovered and quashed.[23]

This, then, according to the anonymous author, was the reason for the conversos' failure to seek reconciliation and thereby save many of them from the stake and avoid confiscation of their properties. They did not have to come to terms with the Toledan Inquisition because they planned to abolish it altogether, and they expected to attain this objective by killing the Inquisitors and capturing the city. Our author makes no comment on this venture, which he evidently considered feasible and credible. But can we assume that the conversos of Toledo actually harbored such a plan?

If the alleged conspiracy of the Sevillian conversos amounted to folly, the one ascribed to the conversos of Toledo was sheer lunacy. For according to the sources at our disposal, in 1481 the conversos of Seville had counted on the support of their Old Christian friends, whereas in 1485 the conversos of Toledo could rely only on their own strength. But their own strength was quite insufficient to undertake such a task as the capture of Toledo, supposedly the goal of their conspiracy. The Toledan conversos, it seems, could have learned how to assess their military potential from the lessons of the disturbances of June 1467. Not only did they then lack the capacity to take over the city from the hands of the Old Christians, but they could not even properly defend themselves against the latter's determined assaults—and this at a time when their forces were all mobilized, when they were exceptionally well armed and when, in addition, they were supported militarily by the Count of Cifuentes. In fact, if they had not found shelter among many Old Christians who refused to side with their adversaries, the struggle might have ended with the destruction of their community.[24] It is most unlikely that the conversos had forgotten that frightful experience.

But let us assume that they had forgotten it and really intended to attack the Old Christians and seize control of the city. What could they expect to gain as a result? In 1449, if they got hold of the city, they could deliver it to Alvaro de Luna. In 1467, they could deliver it to King Enrique. But there was no friendly potentate to whom they could deliver it in 1485. Now, in 1485, they could expect no relief or aid from any quarter, nobiliar or monarchic. All they could do was to try to hold the city against the King, precisely as the anonymous author stated. But who could doubt the hopelessness of such an attempt? Ferdinand, unlike the previous monarchs, had full control over Castile's nobility, was in command of a powerful army, and had behind him a united nation. He certainly had the power speedily to crush a rebellion in Toledo or anywhere else in his kingdoms, and there was indeed every reason to assume that he would do so without delay. Accordingly, there was nothing for the conversos to expect but that he would soon besiege the city, force them to unconditional surrender, and then subject them, as rebels and traitors, to the horrible punishments customary at the time.

Were there any grounds for the conversos to hope that if they managed to capture the city, the King would prefer to negotiate with them rather than go to war against their city—a war that would involve him in considerable expense and the diversion of forces from the Granadan front? After all, all the Kings had to do, it might be argued, to bring the city back to their obedience would be to keep the Inquisition out of Toledo. But this could have occurred only to those who did not realize what royal prestige and the operation of the Inquisition meant to the Kings. The conversos of Toledo in 1485, however, must have realized all that. They understood that the Kings of Spain would not jeopardize their authority by surrendering to the converso community in Toledo, or to any community in the country, whatever the cost or effort involved; and by 1485 they no doubt also recognized what Seville's conversos in 1481 may not have clearly perceived—namely, the determination of the sovereigns to put into practice their plan for the Inquisition. What is more, by the middle of May 1485, they already knew of the collapse of Teruel's resistance to the introduction of the Inquisition into its domain, and they must have also known of Ferdinand's preparations to invade that city with his military forces if Teruel persisted in its opposition.[25] Also, by May 1485 they must have learned of the total failure of all the efforts of the Aragonese to ameliorate or modify the Inquisition's practices in their country. Ferdinand was reported not to have budged an inch. Consequently, they could have developed no delusion that the King would be less severe in their own case. On the contrary, any compromise on his part in that central city would signal a retreat from his inquisitional plans for Spain as a whole; and this was plainly unthinkable.

The insurrectionist plot presented above appears therefore to be nothing but a libelous accusation; and this is also suggested by the attribution to the conversos of another vicious design. According to the manuscript copied by Orozco, the conversos intended to kill not only the Inquisitors, but also "all the *señores* and caballeros" and "all the Christian people" (presumably, those who were to form the procession of Corpus Christi). This reminds us of the accusation leveled at the Sevillian conversos, who allegedly planned to *avenge themselves on their enemies* on the occasion of their assault upon the Inquisitors. But considering the intention ascribed by our author to the conversos of Toledo in 1485, those of Seville in 1481 appear in a much better light. For the Sevillians were reported to have at least differentiated between friend and foe among the local Old Christians; they wanted to rise against the Inquisitors in their city together with their Old Christian supporters, whereas the Toledan conversos were assumed to have planned an indiscriminate massacre of all Old Christians who were to participate in the procession, thereby showing that they hated *all* Old Christians and had no concern for the lives of any of them. This is of course what the Inquisitors, their accusers, wished to communicate to the Old Christian population in Toledo.

But let us also consider what such an attack would do to the relations between the Old and New Christians both in Toledo and in Spain as a whole. There is no doubt that the conversos had friends in Toledo and were interested in preserving that friendship. We have already noted that in 1467 they found shelter in two boroughs of Old Christians, who also defended them against their assailants; and there is no doubt that this friendship enabled the conversos to restore their community after the debacle of 1467. What is more, we know that in 1484, Gómez Manrique, the *corregidor* of Toledo, appealed on behalf of the city to Queen Isabel, to delay the installation of the Inquisition in Toledo because such a move would inevitably lead to the flight of many conversos from the city and cause irreparable damage to the city's economy. Palencia, the author of this report, tells us that the Queen consented to this request,[26] although, as we know, she later changed her mind, probably under the influence of her husband or the Inquisition. Manrique's appeal, however, would not have been made unless supported by the majority of the Old Christian upper classes, and these must have included many Old Christians who were genuinely friendly toward the conversos. But had the allegedly planned attack on the Corpus Christi procession materialized and the indiscriminate massacre of Old Christians been carried out, the friendships the conversos still enjoyed in Toledo would have been lost forever. They would have been replaced by implacable hatred, fiercer than any the conversos had encountered, and it would have overrun the frontiers of Toledo to engulf all Old Christians of Spain. We assume therefore that self-interest, if nothing else, would force the conversos to avoid such a move.

It may perhaps be assumed that our manuscript's assertion about the killing of "all the *señores* and caballeros," as well as "all the Old Christians" etc., was added by the author on the grounds of gossip, but formed no part of the conversos' plan. But such an assumption would not fit the rest of the account. The very task of killing all the Inquisitors while they were walking in the holy-day procession involved encounters with all those in the procession who would rush to their defense, and the outcome of these encounters would inevitably be a battle to the end of all against the all. This was especially so if the conversos also planned to seize the city gates and the tower of the church, and ultimately capture the entire city. Hence, if one accepts the charge that they planned that assault upon the Corpus Christi procession, one must also accept the claim that they planned to kill "all the *señores* and caballeros," etc. To be sure, the conversos might later argue that the conditions of battle were such as to prevent them from distinguishing between friend and foe; but this would not relieve them from responsibility for the results which, it would be argued, could be easily foreseen.

We have paid close attention to the implications of the conspiracy ascribed to the conversos of Toledo in 1485, as these implications may not be evident to the modern reader. They would have been plain, however, to the Toledan conversos. The latter could not have failed to realize that an assault upon the Inquisition of the kind described by our author had no chance of alleviating their hardships and every chance of making them insufferable. What is more, it would have denied the New Christians even escape through flight, which was their best means of survival, because once they adopted such a plan as indicated, the conversos themselves would prevent their members from depleting their defense forces by desertion. In brief, it was a prescription for suicide, and this was certainly not in the conversos' minds, or at least in the minds of their majority. Whatever, therefore, may have been the expectations of some hot-headed members of their group, one cannot doubt that many of them had foreseen the fearful consequences of the above-mentioned venture (assuming that it was ever proposed) and sternly opposed it. Yet such a plan could have never been implemented without the unanimous, or *almost* unanimous consent of the converso community; and since no such consent could possibly have been obtained, the plan could not have been undertaken. This is another reason that leads us to conclude that the conversos' alleged conspiracy was nothing but a figment of their accusers' imagination. It was a libelous invention disseminated by the Inquisition for its own special reasons; and it remains for us to consider what those reasons were, or what purpose that libel could possibly serve in that particular time and place.

This purpose is indicated in the first part of the account, which refers to the refusal of the Toledan conversos to appear before the Inquisition for reconciliation. This was undoubtedly a new tactic adopted by the New Christians in their struggle against the Inquisition. By 1485 all conversos knew that the Edicts of Grace, which were supposedly proclaimed to offer them security from burning and confiscation, provided them with no such security at all. For the Inquisition would first exact fines from the conversos in the course of the reconciliation, and then often return to the reconciled with charges that they had failed to confess *all* their sins—and consequently, judge and punish them as heretics. Often it also accused their deceased parents of adherence to Judaism or to its rites, condemned them as heretics and, on this basis, robbed their heirs (i.e., the reconciled conversos) of their inherited possessions. But what was perhaps worst of all was the pressure exerted by the Inquisitors on the reconciled to act as informers of any deviation from the faith by any family member, friend or acquaintance. Under this pressure and the threats that accompanied it, many of those who came for reconciliation supplied the Inquisition with pieces of information sufficient for it to drag to its dungeons many innocent New Christians. These provided the Inquisitors with the first group of "culprits," with whom they could start their investigations. Indubitably, the conversos of Toledo came to think that they would gain rather than lose if they avoided the reconciliations. In any case, they could hope that by taking that stand they might hamper or forestall the Inquisition's operations. On this they evidently all agreed and acted with remarkable uniformity.

The new policy adopted by the conversos and their sullen rejection of the Inquisition's "graces" had evidently worried the Inquisitors greatly. They now had to rely only on items of information culled from Old Christian informants, and these apparently were not too plentiful. Consequently, they had to think of ways to arouse the Old Christians to testify against the New and force the conversos to remove the fence they had placed around themselves by their collective silence. The fabricated charge that the New Christians were plotting to attack the procession on the day of Corpus Christi was designed to serve the double purpose. But to make it truly credible to the Old Christians and sufficiently threatening for the New, the alleged plot had to be "discovered," publicized and denounced, and a number of conversos formally accused and condemned to death on the gallows.

We do not know precisely the role that Manrique, Toledo's *corregidor,* played in this affair. But there can be no doubt that his role was vital for the success of the Inquisition's ploy. Gómez Manrique indubitably received clear orders from the Kings to welcome the Inquisitors and lend them every

possible assistance, and it is certain that, as a loyal official, he did his utmost
to follow these instructions. Thus, we may assume, he allowed the Inquisitors
to conduct the inquiries about the alleged plot, relied on the evidence they
extracted by torture, and hastily carried out their first verdicts, which no
doubt rested on religious accusations. On the day of Corpus Christi, before
the start of the procession, he hanged one of the condemned conversos, and
in the following few days he hanged four more. Then he suddenly stopped
the executions and substituted the death sentences with rather moderate fines
imposed on every converso in Toledo. His excuse for doing that, our manuscript tells us, was that if he punished all the culprits as they deserved (i.e.,
if he executed them all), the city would be depopulated.[27]

Manrique's conduct is certainly puzzling. If the conspiracy was so wide as
to implicate all or most of the conversos in Toledo, and if the aims of the
conspirators were as described—to kill the Inquisitors and rise against the
King (and, judging by our source, they presumably were, because so many
of them deserved execution)—it seems strange that so few of the guilty paid
the ultimate price for their crime. What is more, the executed consisted of
four artisans and one member of the higher classes, a jurist by the name of
de la Torre.[28] Surely the artisans could not possibly have been among the
architects and inspirers of the conspiracy (and therefore were the last to
deserve capital punishment), whereas de la Tore, whom our manuscript
describes merely as "*one* of the captains," may have been presented as its *chief*
leader. Why were the other authors of the conspiracy allowed to get away
with a mere fine? We assume that the conversos were assured by the Inquisitors that the executions would be terminated and replaced with fines if they
reversed their stand toward the Inquisition, and especially toward the Edict
of Grace. The conversos were persuaded that they had no alternative but to
yield to the Inquisition's will.

The above description of the "attempt at insurrection" by the Toledan
conversos in 1485 was based on our analysis of the one related source that has
come down to us from those days. There is, however, a later source which
none of the historians of the Inquisition has employed and which, in our
judgment, throws valuable light on some of the occurrences we have discussed. This is the account of the Toledan conspiracy as presented in the
memorial that Cardinal Siliceo, archbishop of Toledo, submitted to Emperor
Charles V in 1548.

The purpose of this memorial was to justify the *limpieza* statute which the
Cardinal had enacted in the preceding year, denying all conversos the right
to assume office in the Cathedral Church of Toledo. In line with that
purpose, Siliceo sought to show the criminal anti-Christian attitude of the

conversos—an attitude which, he claimed, was displayed throughout their history; and to attain that aim he raked up all the libels against the New Christians that he found in anti-converso sources. He concentrated especially on stories about the harm they had contrived to cause to the Old Christians in Toledo; and thus he tells us that "in the days of Juan II, when Pedro Sarmiento was *corregidor* of Toledo," the conversos stirred up and aroused the whole city against the said *corregidor* and the Old Christians [of Toledo] in an attempt to become masters of the city, so that they might [continue to] Judaize and persist more freely in their perfidy."[29] These descriptions of Sarmiento's function in Toledo and of the causes of the disturbances of 1449 are sufficient to demonstrate Siliceo's "truthfulness" in reporting well-known historic events; but we can gain the same impression also from other incidents he narrates in support of his thesis. Thus he tells us that "in a village called La Guardia, nine leagues from Toledo, the conversos of that place crucified a child, known today as the Holy Innocent, and subjected him to all the torments that their ancestors had inflicted on Christ."[30] In view of this, it is hardly surprising that he included the tale about the "conspiracy of 1485" in the list of testimonies he adduced to demonstrate the insatiable hatred of the conversos for the Old Christians and their repeated designs to capture Toledo and massacre its Old Christian citizens.

According to Siliceo, the "conspiracy" was organized under the leadership of the converso Bachiller de la Torre, who served as *alcalde mayor* (chief judge) of Toledo when Gómez Manrique was *corregidor*. De la Torre, together with other conversos, contrived a plan which would enable them to "put to the knife *all* the Old Christians of Toledo, as well as the Inquisitors and the officials of the Holy Office who had recently come to the city." They chose to execute their plan on the day of Corpus Christi because the Old Christians would be then in a carefree mood and therefore vulnerable to an attack. Accordingly, the chief judge issued an order that nobody in Toledo should bear arms on that day, supposedly for the sake of avoiding clashes, and that the laborers of the villages who come to town on Corpus Christi to perform their customary sword dances would this time dance with sticks. "All this was discovered," Siliceo tells us, "in due time, so that the *corregidor,* and the caballeros who aided him, seized and punished many of the conversos, including the *alcalde mayor.* The latter was hanged and later burned as a Judaizer; his *sanbenito* is preserved in the Church of San Vicente."

What we gather, then, from this account is that de la Torre was not just a "jurist" but the city's *alcalde mayor.* He probably belonged to the famous de la Torre family, which had provided the Toledan converso community with distinguished leaders, two of whom were hanged during the disturbances of 1467. In all likelihood, the *alcalde mayor* was head of Toledo's conversos, and we may assume that it was under his guidance, or at his counsel, that they decided to defy the Inquisition's Edict of Grace. Thus, he became the chief target of the Inquisition in its planned offensive against the conversos.

Other data in Siliceo's account may lift the fog from other phases in the invention of the libel. It appears that the Inquisition's agitation in Toledo created a tense atmosphere in the city and, in consequence, we may assume, the conversos feared that a riot could break out against them on Corpus Christi, when many laborers from the countryside—known as foes of the conversos—would crowd into the city and fall for the incitement of its pogromist elements. To reduce their temptation to attack the conversos, the chief judge may indeed have used his authority to issue the instructions mentioned by Siliceo.

It also stands to reason that the Inquisitors or their counselors among the Old Christians in Toledo saw in these irregular instructions an opportunity to pin on the conversos the charge of planning an assault upon the forthcoming procession. The judge was accused as the "leader" of the conspiracy, and it was of course no superhuman task to make him "confess" under torture.

That such a thought never entered his mind may be taken for certain. Even less than any other converso notable would the chief judge of Toledo undertake such a venture, which would endanger the lives of all conversos in the city, without the consent and cooperation of all other leading members of the converso community. To be sure, Siliceo tells us that the judge "joined the other conversos" in their "secret" planning of the massacre. But we know that none of the "others" paid with his life for the crime, which certainly would have been the case if they had been parties to the conspiracy. Siliceo's statement that "many" of the seized conspirators were "punished" is obviously misleading by its failure to indicate who these conspirators were and what kind of punishment was imposed upon them. As we have gathered from our contemporary source, however, only four additional conversos, all members of the lower class, were executed by Manrique. But these, as we have indicated, could not be among the planners.

That the Inquisition was the chief author of the inquiry, as well as of the aforesaid verdicts, is also apparent from Siliceo's statement that de la Torre, after having been hanged, was "burned as a Judaizer." Thus we have here a precise repetition of the tactics employed by the Inquisition of Seville when it punished the converso "conspirators" in that city in 1481. They too were brought to trial as rebels but sentenced and executed as heretics—obviously, because a civil crime would be outside the Inquisition's jurisdiction. Had the charge been brought before a civil tribunal, where witnesses could be examined by the accused, and where one of the accused was a trained lawyer like de la Torre (the *alcalde mayor*), the fraudulent nature of the accusation would probably have been exposed.

There is no doubt that, aware of these developments, Palencia gave no credit to the tale of the conspiracy and, therefore, while pointing out Isabella's consent to postpone the installation of the Holy Office in Toledo (in 1484), he passed in silence over the subsequent events (of 1485), for which he realized the Inquisition was responsible. He did not dare to tell the true story of these events because he knew it would expose him to the wrath of the Inquisition, and he was also no doubt loath to criticize Manrique (whom he greatly esteemed) for his "callous" cooperation with the Holy Office. Pulgar, unlike Palencia, did discuss the beginnings of the Inquisition in Toledo, but he too refrained from mentioning the "converso conspiracy" and treated it as a "non-event." Evidently, he too did not dare accuse the Inquisition of having fabricated the gross libel, and therefore, like Palencia, chose to remain silent.

SARAGOSSA, 1485

At the very time that the New Christians in Toledo struggled with the persecution we have just described, a far more harrowing persecution, based on a similar accusation, was being prepared against them in Aragon. The blow was to descend upon them primarily in Saragossa on the charge that the Aragonese conversos plotted and perpetrated the murder of Pedro Arbués, chief Inquisitor for Saragossa, on the night of September 5, 1485, as he knelt in prayer at the Cathedral Church (the Seo). Like the previous accusations of this category, this one too developed against a background of opposition to the Inquisition—not only on the part of the New Christians but also of considerable segments of the Old. But in Saragossa this opposition was much more entrenched, more influential and more disturbing to the Inquisition than it was in Seville or Toledo. Hence in Saragossa, more than in the other cities, the Inquisition felt the need to enlist the support of the Old Christian population. To do so it had to divert the attention of that population from the campaign conducted by the conversos and their friends against the Inquisition's encroachment on the people's rights and direct it at the conversos' alleged criminal intent to hurt the Inquisition and the Old Christians generally. The news about the murder of Arbués by the New Christians was calculated to achieve this end.

That Arbués was assassinated by the conversos has been accepted by all historians as fact. For our part, we question it. We apply to the case of this murder the old question which is posed in connection with every crime: *cui prodest?* What could the conversos expect to gain from the killing of that Inquisitor? The answer, as we see it, is: Nothing. If in Seville and Toledo the dispatch of *all* the Inquisitors (in the alleged conspiracies) could conceivably disrupt the activity of the Inquisition, the killing of one Inquisitor in Saragossa would not stop that activity for even one day. The organization as a whole could continue to function, and the murder of one of its members would only spur the others to greater zeal.

Lea says that what prompted the assassination of Arbués by the New Christians was the growing desperation of the conversos in Saragossa and the belief of the "bolder spirits" among them that, if "one or two Inquisitors were killed," the warning would "deter others from incurring the hazard."[31] But the assumptions underlying these assertions are, as we see it, hard to accept. To begin with, one may question the degree of desperation of the Saragossa conversos in September 1485—that is, at the time of the assassination. There is no doubt, of course, that the conversos realized the precariousness of their situation and feared that Ferdinand would ultimately enforce his plans for the Inquisition in Saragossa, as he had done in Teruel and other cities. But if there was a place and a time in which they might still cling to the hope that they could avert disaster by political pressure, it was Saragossa in September 1485. So strong was the moral, judicial and political pressure they exercised upon the Inquisition in Saragossa that it virtually ceased its activities for more than 13 months. Would it not be senseless to abandon the political process that had brought such positive results and undertake a terroristic venture which, any way one looked at it, was fraught with danger?

Second, it is extremely unlikely that the conversos ever thought that the killing of "one or two" Inquisitors would deter the others from "incurring the hazard." Such thoughts could perhaps occur to some conversos, if they could believe that the activity of the Inquisition depended merely on the will and decision of the Inquisitors. But the conversos knew that the prime movers of the Inquisition were not its functionaries but the Kings of Spain, and that the Kings would always be able to find substitutes for anyone who might withdraw from the Inquisition out of fear. In addition, they must also have realized that the mendicant orders were thronged with zealous men who would not shirk but rather seize the opportunity to serve the Holy Office in the face of threats. Says Lea: "The conspirators miscalculated when they imagined that his murder [i.e., the murder of Arbués] would deter others from taking his place."[32] In our view, the alleged conspirators never "miscalculated" because, in all likelihood, they never had such calculations. As we see it, they could never have conceived of such an unrealistic outcome as the one ascribed to them by Lea and other historians.

Finally, the assertion that the assassination was the result of incitement by the "bolder spirits" of the conversos cannot stand critical examination. That some impetuous individuals could embrace such a scheme, especially in a mood of desperation, is possible. But the assassination of Arbués was not undertaken by a few audacious men driven to that act by temporarily uncontrollable passions. According to the claims of the Inquisition, it was carefully prepared for a long time by the leadership of the Aragonese conversos; and thus we have to consider what could have been the position of that leadership and whether it could really have subscribed to such a plan.

Lea, who relies on the reports of the Inquisition (actually, of Juan de Anchias, secretary of the tribunal and author of the *Libro Verde de Aragon*), says that when the conspirators in Saragossa consulted their friends at the royal court, including Gabriel Sánchez, Ferdinand's treasurer, the latter approved of the conspirators' idea and wrote to them that "if an Inquisitor was murdered it would put an end to the Inquisition."[33] Here we note one of those incredible phenomena that we encounter so often in the historiography of the Inquisition. As we see it, it is extremely unlikely that a man like Gabriel Sánchez, who was so close to Ferdinand and knew him so well, misjudged so badly the character of the King and was so unaware of his fierce resolution to establish the Inquisition in Aragon. Could Sánchez believe that the murder of one Inquisitor would induce Ferdinand to relinquish his plan? Even if we assume that Gabriel Sánchez thought so, it is impossible to suppose that all other converso courtiers, who were likewise close to Ferdinand and knew him well, were also so mistaken about the possible impact that the killing of the Inquisitor would have on Ferdinand. Did they too so misjudge Ferdinand's character and the value he placed on the Inquisition in Aragon? Yet our sources (i.e., those left us by the Inquisition) tell us that this was not only the view of Gabriel Sánchez but of almost all converso leaders and courtiers who were consulted by the plotters of Arbués' murder.

It is also worthwhile to consider the following. The alleged conspiracies to kill inquisitors in Seville and Toledo had at least one element in their favor: they demonstrated the preparedness of the conversos to rise against the Inquisition and confront it with the force of arms. However futile the outcome of that resistance might have been, it reflected the pressure of a large group and a public problem that had to be coped with. But the Saragossa murder was allegedly committed by hired assassins; the assumption was that the converso connection would not be discovered; and the conversos as a group would seem to have had no hand in the murder. What then could impress the government to change its policy with respect to the Inquisition? Surely a criminal act by some individual, vengeful or deranged, would not change the government's policy. In brief, the only advantageous element that could possibly be involved in the murder of the Inquisitor—namely, that it was the act of a public body—was missing in the alleged Saragossa conspiracy, when considered from the standpoint of the conversos and their assumed expectations from its impact.

Says Baer, another historian who believed in the veracity of the Arbués murder charge: "In this as in other scandalous trials held in those days, the indictment was based on confessions extracted under torture and on mutual slanders which were often contradictory in point of details."[34] This fact, however, does not lead Baer to suspect that the whole affair was the outcome of a grand manipulation by the Inquisition to whip up public feeling against the conversos, put an end to the criticism of inquisitional procedures, and enable the Inquisition to reap a large harvest from the charges it would level at many conversos, whom it would accuse of complicity in the crime. Here, Baer thought, the process of conviction would be much simpler. For "in this case," he says, "the prosecution did not base its charges on such evidence alone"—namely, evidence extracted by torture. "The murder and body of the murdered man," he says, "were matters of public knowledge!" What an astonishing revelation, coupled with an exclamation mark, which is supposed to convince us that we are dealing here after all with a case of proven guilt, and not with a possibly false charge. Adds Baer: "All other matters taken for granted by the Inquisitors must be regarded by the modern historian as unproven, especially since few of the original documents have been found and only extracts from those documents have seen the light of print." This is a correct statement, with the exception of the assertion about the "matters taken for granted by the Inquisitors." The matters taken by them for granted, Baer believed, were the identity of the murderers and the conversos' plot, which is further indicated by Baer's remark: "It is unlikely that the material would mislead the historian regarding the Jewish background" of the con-spiracy.[35]

So despite the fact that the evidence we possess consists of shreds of "confessions" extracted under torture, and despite the numerous contradic-tions it contains, Baer accepts the charge that the conversos organized the murder of Arbués, and he also knows the reasons why. The arch-conspirator, he knows, was of course the leader of the conversos (precisely as was the case in Seville and Toledo), Jaime de Montesa, an aged and distinguished jurist and deputy of the chief justice of the municipality. "Speaking by and large," says Baer, "the allegations of the witnesses for the prosecution were definitely not unfounded in *Montesa*'s case." We would like to hear what they testified regarding his share in the plot to kill Arbués. But the testimonies we possess deal with his habit of secretly following Jewish customs. A few witnesses could be "persuaded" to attest that this was Montesa's usual practice, and then a "confession" to this effect could be extracted from him by means of torture. "He was *suspected* of keeping to his room on Saturdays so as to be able to recite the Jewish prayers in private."[36] The value of this accusation can be judged by its contents, as well as by the vagueness of its formulation. He "was said to have consorted intimately with Jews in his home." This was certainly not the kind of crime recognized by the law books. All the other accusations against the judge were quite as preposterous. "The physicians who examined Montesa were unable to determine whether or not he had been circumcised," as if that could possibly mean anything! Assuming that he had been circumcised by his father seventy or eighty years before he was examined, was it supposed to reflect on his Judaism? But the physicians were unable to determine even this. "Montesa was also alleged to have repeatedly quoted the skeptical saying: 'In this world you will not see me in trouble, and in the other you will not see me in torment.'" We do not know why Baer says here "alleged" when in other cases he presents the evidence as definite. Obviously, if a man repeatedly said that he did not believe in the world to come, he could not possibly have believed in Judaism any more than in Christianity. Certainly, such a man would not have attached any value to the performance of Jewish rites. For what these words conveyed was no mere skepticism, but a denial of a principal tenet of Judaism, no less than of Christianity. Why then does Baer use in this connection such terms as "alleged" and "skeptical?" Is it only to fit his conclusion that Montesa was "on the whole deeply attached to Judaism," although he was a "skeptic in some minor respects?"[37] The denial of faith in the world to come, which he was said to have expressed "repeatedly," was no minor matter! "Montesa's brother, a monk, reproved him for behaving like a Jew behaved."[38] Baer takes seriously this testimony, too.

The same kind of evidence is offered in the case of the other accused. The Inquisition wanted to prove that they were not only murderers but also Judaizers. Luis de Santángel, nephew of the famous courtier, was reported to have kept a scroll of the Law in his home and to have recited the prayers in Hebrew. His brother, the prior of the monastery in Daroca, had to do penance for having tried to persuade witnesses to testify in Luis' favor. Francisco de Santa Fe, *assessor* (legal counselor) of the Governor of Aragon and son of the famous Jerónimo de Santa Fe (Joshua ha-Lorki), was likewise condemned as a Judaizer.[39] Thus leading conversos, Christian to the core, whose brothers were monks and priors, and who were sons or grandsons of missionary converts like Pedro de la Caballería and Jerónimo de Santa Fe, fiery agitators against Judaism and fervent enemies of everything Jewish—all men deeply involved in Christian life, without which involvement they could not have risen to their high positions in state or Church—were deliberately dragged by the Inquisition to their doom—obviously, to prove that there was no converso, however high in the royal or ecclesiastic administration, who was not likely to be a Judaizer.

This is what Baer calls the "Jewish background" of the conspiracy which he considered proven and which we regard as not proven at all, since it relies only on evidence extracted under torture with the clear purpose of demonstrating the viciousness of the Jewish killers of the dedicated servant of Christ. But to come back to the "conspiracy": having demonstrated the total uselessness of the plan to kill Arbués, which must have been evident to the converso notables, and concluded that there was no reason for them to hire assassins to dispatch the Inquisitor, we must of course pose the cardinal question: Who, then, killed Arbués? Or rather, who was behind the plot to murder him?

According to the information that has reached us, more than fifteen individuals contributed funds to hire the assassin and more than thirty were implicated in the conspiracy. In an excellent work recently published on the subject, Ángel Alcalá Galve writes: "In the small Saragossa of those days, where every circumstance came to be noticed, it is improbable that the plot was not detected in time and that, if desired, it could not have been prevented."[40] Moreover, we know that the authorities not only *suspected* that a plot to kill Arbués was being contrived; they seem to have had no doubt about it. In the letter of Ferdinand to the Governor of Aragon, Juan Hernández de Heredia, dated Jan. 29, 1485—i.e., seven and a half months before the murder—he states in unequivocal terms that a "conspiracy to kill Arbués was afoot" and that money was being collected to hire assassins.[41] If the authorities knew that much, is it possible that they could not find out who were the contributors of the funds and who were the masterminds of the plot? The fact is that *after* the assassination they discovered all who were allegedly involved in it in record time. Why did they not do it earlier? It is especially hard to explain this failure—or rather, this inactivity of the authorities—in view of the fact that Arbués had been subject to an earlier attempt on his life. We unavoidably come close to Alcalá's conclusion that "the King or the Council of the Supreme Inquisition, or those who helped the King to shape his policies, incited the assassination of the first Aragonese Inquisitor"—that is, encouraged it by their failure to interfere with the preparations for his assassination.[42] But this does not yet answer all the questions involved.

Alcalá's view is that "Arbués served unconsciously as a *peón de brega* in realizing a policy which was, according to all indications, unknown to him personally." He was considered "a necessary martyr," whose martyrdom was not only utilized, but "perhaps permitted, and even secretly desired by the ruling power, and, of course, magnified by the inquisitorial machinery for its own interests, as an opportune sacrifice."[43]

According to this theory, then, the Inquisition knew that a plot was being hatched; it may also have known who its organizers were; and yet it allowed it to take place because a martyr would help it promote its cause in the circumstances prevailing in Aragon at the time. The theory, as we have seen, is anchored in evidence; but an analysis of the arguments supporting it permits us to make a step further. If the Inquisition was badly in need of a martyr, and agreed that Arbués should be sacrificed for its purposes, it would not rely too long on the chance that the conversos would supply it with the required martyr. The Inquisition would create the martyr by its own agents, and then put the blame on the conversos. Furthermore, since our analysis leads us to the conclusion that the conversos could not possibly have foreseen any benefit from the assassination of Arbués, and hence had no reason to plot his murder, the question "who killed Arbués?" can be given only one answer: the Inquisition itself.

But if the agents of the Inquisition killed Arbués, they did not do it without Ferdinand's consent. We have pointed out the general interest that the Inquisition had in attributing Arbués' murder to the conversos of Saragossa, just as it had an interest in ascribing similar plots to the conversos of Seville and Toledo. The motives of the Inquisition must of course be identified in this case with those of Ferdinand. But it stands to reason that in the case of Saragossa, he was moved to take the extreme step of pinning a murder charge upon the conversos for a special reason. He was fully aware that the strong resistance he encountered to the Inquisition in Aragon sprang from the converso leadership in that kingdom, as well as from some of the conversos in his court. It was they, he knew, who pulled all the strings of that resistance and raised one obstacle after another to block the materialization of his plans. In consequence, he grew steadily more wrathful and vengeful toward these converso magnates and came to see in their conduct an act of ingratitude for the numerous favors he had granted them. After all, it was thanks to him and his father that these conversos were raised to their high positions, became courtiers and men of renown, and it was due to the prestige they had gained through their positions that they could influence the Old Christians in the country. Now they were using this influence to work against him and frustrate his plans. There seemed to be only one way to put an end to this evil influence: to destroy its source; and the murder of Pedro Arbués offered him the vehicle for his scheme. The cream of the converso community in Aragon, including its highest officials in the country, was almost entirely wiped out on the grounds of the charge that they had plotted Arbués' murder, and the great speed and ruthlessness with which that purge was effected displayed not only Ferdinand's determination to do away with the New Christian elite in his country; it also betrayed his personal vindictiveness against his "treacherous" converso officials.

Manuel Serrano y Sanz gathered a wealth of data about the leading converso families in Aragon and wrote a thorough and comprehensive study of the proceedings of the Inquisition in the case of Arbués.[44] He had no doubt about the truth and accuracy of the inquisitional records and, accordingly, based his account of that case on the documents of the Inquisition. This is where his enormous research and otherwise admirable study failed.

Serrano of course noticed that the Inquisition tried to implicate in the assassination of Arbués the most important conversos in the Aragonese administration, including men of high standing like Alfonso de la Caballería, Vice-Chancellor of Aragon, and Luis de Santángel, Secretary of the Royal Household; and he realized that these men were spared only because of Ferdinand's intervention. But he was puzzled by the fact that Gabriel Sánchez, the famous Treasurer of Aragon, was not even brought for questioning before the Inquisition, although two leading conversos who were condemned by the Inquisition, Jaime de Montesa and Sancho de Paternoy, declared "without vacillation," as Serrano put it, that Gabriel Sánchez "proposed" the murder of an Inquisitor and conducted for this purpose a coded correspondence with his brothers Juan, Alfonso and Guillén.[45] In fact, according to Montesa's testimony, Gabriel Sánchez advocated the killing not of one Inquisitor but of three, and also chided his brothers for having postponed so long the execution of their common plan.[46] Moreover, in the words of Paternoy, "nothing was done in that undertaking [i.e., the killing of Arbués] without [the knowledge and approval] of Gabriel Sánchez."[47] And yet Sánchez emerged from the whole affair unscathed as if he had nothing to do with it.

Surely the Inquisition had enough grounds, Serrano thought, to subject Sánchez to a thorough inquiry and obtain from him whatever information it required. But nothing was done to that effect. On the contrary, the Inquisition suppressed all the data it had concerning the Treasurer's alleged guilt. Even in the sentence it issued against Montesa, it failed to mention the incriminating assertions made by Montesa against Sánchez.[48]

Serrano felt that these irregularities posed a "grave problem,"[49] but he tried to solve it in accordance with his view of the rectitude of the Inquisition and its procedures. "The involvement of Gabriel Sánchez in the tragedy of the Seo," he said, "must remain a doubtful and unproven fact."[50] He suggested that the "testimonies of Montesa and Paternoy, who were submitted to the hardest torment of the cord," probably could not convince the Inquisition. But this does not begin to solve the "grave problem" pointed out by Serrano. If certain doubts were raised about the evidence obtained by the Inquisition concerning Sánchez, the best way for it to clarify those doubts would obviously have been to seek Sánchez' explanations. It should also be noted that Montesa and Paternoy could not anticipate all the questions the Inquisitors would put to them, and certainly could not coordinate their replies under torture.[51] If their testimonies, therefore, were not "guided" by the Inquisition, if they were not produced by its hints and allusions, there should have been no reason to doubt them. Indeed, if one shares Serrano's view of the Inquisition, one must find it hard to explain why it failed to bring Sánchez to trial.

As we see it, Sánchez was spared the agony of an inquiry not because of the Inquisition's scruples but because Ferdinand, who must have known that Sánchez had never taken any part in the campaign against the Inquisition, ordered the Inquisitors to leave him alone. We cannot of course guess all of Ferdinand's motives, but we may confidently assume that he considered Sánchez' services of extraordinary importance. Otherwise he would not have retained him in his post or appointed his son as his successor. Sánchez, however, did not come to the Court for most of the remaining period of his service and performed his various tasks through a deputy. Serrano explains Sánchez' strange behavior, which was against both rule and custom, by his great "sorrow" and "perhaps his shame"[52]—the shame he felt over the terrible crimes committed by his brothers and relatives. We, for our part, venture another explanation: Sánchez could not stand the company of the man who had subjected so many members of his family, whose only fault was their objection to the Inquisition, to excruciating torture, exile and ignominy, as well as to life-long incarceration and death.[53]

The three alleged conspiracies discussed have several things in common. They are all related to the beginning of the Inquisition's actions in major urban centers where the conversos were strong; they all occurred in places where opposition to the Inquisition existed in large sections of the Old Christian population; they were all speedily "discovered" and mercilessly put down; and they all served as an opening for a massive persecution accompanied by a large-scale spoliation. These common features help elucidate our conclusion that the accusations were libelous, not factual. We have presented our thoughts on the subject in some detail, partly in reaction to the inexplicable credibility given so readily by most historians to almost everything the Inquisition tells us.

NOTES

ABBREVIATIONS

AAJR	American Academy for Jewish Research
AEM	Anuario de Estudios Medievales
AHDE	Anuario de la Historia del Derecho Español
AHR	American Historical Review
APHK	Abhandlungen der philologisch-historischen Klasse der sächsischen Akademie der Wissenschaften, Leipzig
AST	Analecta Sacra Tarraconensia
BAC	Biblioteca de Autores Cristianos
BAE	Biblioteca de Autores Españoles
BH	Bulletin Hispanique
BIFAO	Bulletin de l'Institute Francaise d'Archéologie Orientale
BNM	Biblioteca Nacional, Madrid
CIC	Corpus Iuris Civilis
CICa	Corpus Iuris Canonici
CLC	Córtes de León y de Castilla
CODOIN	Colección de Documentos Inéditos para la Historia de España
HF	Historia Francorum, *PL,* 71
HUCA	Hebrew Union College Annual
IEC	Institut des Études Centrafricaines
JAOS	Journal of the American Oriental Society
JESHO	Journal of the Economic and Social History of the Orient
JPOS	Journal of the Palestine Oriental Society
JQR	Jewish Quarterly Review
JST	Jewish Social Studies
LCL	Loeb Classical Library
MGH, LV	Monumenta Germaniae Historica, Leges Visigothorum
MGH, Concilia	Monumenta Germaniae Historica, Concilia
MGWJ	Monatsschrift für Geschichte und Wissenschaft des Judentums
MIOG	Mitteilungen. Institut für Oesterreichische Geschichtsforschung
PAAJR	Proceedings of American Academy for Jewish Research
PG	Migne, Patrologia Graeca
PL	Migne, Patrologia Latina
RABM	Revista de Archivos, Bibliotecas y Museos
RAH	Real Academia de la Historia, Madrid
REJ	Revue des Etudes Juives
RHCHO	Recueil des historiens des croisades: Historiens occidentaux
ZfRP	Zeitschrift für romanische Philologie
ZfWT	Zeitschrift für wissenschaftliche Theologie
WHJP	World History of the Jewish People

AUTHORS

Alvar García, *Crónica*—Alvar García de Santa María, *Crónica de Don Juan II,* in *CODOIN,* 99, 100

Amador, *Historia*—J. Amador de los Ríos, *Historia Social, Política y Religiosa de los Judíos de España y Portugal,* 1875–1876

———*Estudios*—*Estudios históricos, políticos y literarios sobre los Judíos de España,* 1848

———*Historia crítica*—*Historia crítica de la literatura española,* 7 vols., 1861–1865

Baer, *History*—Y. F. Baer, *A History of the Jews in Christian Spain,* Hebrew ed. 1959; English transl., 1961

———*Die Juden*—*Die Juden im christlichen Spanien,* I–II, 1929–1936 (indicated also merely by *Baer*)

Baron, *History*—S. W. Baron, *A Social and Religious History of the Jews* (2nd ed.)

Boletín—Real Academia de la Historia, Madrid, *Boletín*

Cod. Theod.—*Codex Theodosianus*

Códigos Españoles—*Códigos Españoles Concordados y Anotados,* 12 vols., 1872–1873

CODOIN—RAH, Colección de documentos ineditos para la historia de España

Crónica Castellana—*Crónica Castellana de Enrique IV*

Crónica de Juan II (or: *Crónica*)—ed. F. Pérez de Guzmán, *Crónica de Juan II,* in *BAE,* 68

González-Tejada—*Colección de Cánones de la Iglesia Española,* publicada en latin por F. Antonio González, traducida al castellano con notas e ilustraciones por J. Tejada y Ramiro, I–IV, 1849–1855

Graetz, *Geschichte*—H. Graetz, *Geschichte der Juden,* 10 vols., 1866–1888

Historia de España—ed. Menéndez Pidal, Ramón, *Historia de España,* IV, V, XIV, XV

Josephus, *Against Apion; The Jewish War; Antiquities*—*Works,* ed. Loeb Classical Library, 9 vols.

Lea, *History*—H. C. Lea, *A History of the Inquisition of Spain,* I–IV, 1905

Memorias or *Colección Diplomática*—RAH, Memorias de Don Enrique IV de Castilla, II, 1835–1913

Palencia, *Crónica*—Palencia, Alfonso de, *Crónica de Enrique IV,* transl. by A. Paz y Mélia, I–IV, 1904–1908

Philo, Works—ed. Loeb Classical Library, 10 vols.

Pulgar, *Crónica*—Fernando de Pulgar, *Crónica de los Reyes Católicos,* ed. J. de M. Carriazo, 1943

Valera, *Memorial*—Diego de Valera, *Memorial de diversas hazañas,* ed. Juan de M. Carriazo, 1941

Zúñiga, *Annales*—Diego Ortiz de Zúñiga, *Annales eclesiásticos y seculares de . . . Sevilla,* 1617

Zurita, *Anales*—Gerónimo Zurita y Castro, *Anales de la Corona de Aragon,* 1646

BOOK ONE

Historical Background

The Jewish Question

1. See the text of the decree published by F. Fita, "La Inquisición anormal ó anticanónica, planteada en Sevilla," in RAH, *Boletín*, XV (1889), 448–453.

2. The approximate date given above is based on the first Inquisitors' declaration dated Jan. 2, 1481, according to which they were informed about a month earlier, after they had begun their activity in Seville, that some men and women had fled their places of residence for fear of the Inquisition's judgments *(ibid.)*. No precise date is available for the commencement of the Inquisition's operations.

3. See the Kings' decree of September 27 *(ibid.,* p. 448) and the bull of Pope Sixtus IV of Nov. 1, 1478 (authorizing the establishment of an inquisition in Castile) which was incorporated in that decree *(ibid.,* p. 450).

4. For the anti-Jewish persecutions in that period, see below, pp. 116, 142–164, 191–196. For the number of the Jews converted as a result, see my *Marranos of Spain*, 1973², pp. 238–248, 255–270, and below, pp. 1095ff.

5. See T. Mommsen, *Römische Geschichte*, V, 1909, p. 519.

6. That Assyria's deportations and exchanges of population served it not only to pacify rebel countries, but also bolster its rule in other conquered territories (with the aid of the exiles who needed its protection) was first pointed out by H. Winckler *(Alttestamentliche Untersuchungen*, 1892, pp. 97–107) and G. Maspero *(The Passing of the Empires*, 1900, pp. 200–201). Following the same methods of control and subjugation, Babylonia also used deportees to colonize undeveloped lands in its dominions, and hence the tolerable terms of settlement it granted to many of the Judean exiles (see Jer. 29. 4–7).

Under the cosmopolitan rule of Persia, the condition of these exiles must have further improved, as indicated by S. Daiches (*The Jews in Babylonia in the Time of Ezra and Nehemiah According to the Babylonian Inscriptions,* 1910, p. 30 ff.), though Daiches' description of the exiles' status ("The Jews were free citizens in a free land," p. 30), which might have fitted Persia of the fifth century, was clearly an exaggeration for Babylonia of the sixth. More realistic was the summary of E. Klamroth who pointed out the special burdens and restrictions to which various groups of deportees were subject (*Die jüdische Exulanten in Babylonien,* 1912, pp. 32–41). Of the later scholars who dealt with this subject, see E. Kaufmann (*History of Israel's Religion* [Hebrew], IV-i, 1967, pp. 12–14), J. Klausner (*History of the Second Temple* [Hebrew], I, p. 65–74), and the more recent researches mentioned in *WHJP, The Restoration: The Persian Period,* ed. H. Tadmor, 1983, pp. 18–20, 256–257.

7. See Ezra, 1.6, 2.65–69, 8.25–29.

8. We may gather this from the presence of Jewish courtiers or otherwise influential Jews in the courts of the Persian Kings as reflected in Ezra (7.14, 21–22, 26), Nehemiah (2.1, 6–8; 13.6) and Esther (2.19, 21; 3.2; 8.2); and see below, n. 9.

9. Echoing these conflicts is the brief passage of Hecataeus of Abdera (cited by Josephus, *Against Apion,* I. 22) which speaks of religious persecutions of the Jews [by the Persians] and the note preserved by Eusebius in his chronicles (Migne, *PG,* 19, p. 486; and E. Schöne's edition *Eusebii Chronicorum Canonum,* 1866, pp. 112–113, about the deportation of Jewish captives to Hyrcania on the Caspian Sea. The religious persecutions are generally associated with the reign of Artaxerxes II (404–358 B.C.E.), and the deportations with that of Artaxerxes III (358–338), as is indeed stated by Eusebius. The latter troubles suggest political conflict

(perhaps echoed in the book of Judith), the former—social and religious tension (probably reflected in the book of Esther). The religious tension may have been aggravated by the establishment in Persia of the cult of Anahita, concerning which see A. T. Olmstead, *History of the Persian Empire,* 1948, pp. 471–472, and J. Hoschander, *The Book of Esther in the Light of History,* 1923, pp. 119–120, 130–135. Though working on an erroneous hypothesis that the book of Esther was an historical account, Hoschander helped establish its Persian origin against theories such as those of Graetz ("Der historische Hintergrund ... des Buches Esther, etc.," *MGWJ,* XXXV [1886], especially pp. 473–503), who related the book to the final stages of Greek rule in Judaea.

10. Supporting this reconstruction is the information offered by the Letter of Aristeas (M. Hadas' translation, 1951, pp. 99–100) that Judea sent military auxiliaries to Psametich for his war against Ethiopia, and the well established fact (through Herodotus II. 161 and the inscriptions on the Ramses colossus at Abu Simbel) that Psametich II (594–589 B.C.E.) invaded Ethiopia in 591. In the wake of G. Rawlinson (*History of Ancient Egypt,* II, 1882, p. 497), many historians considered it plausible that King Zedekiah, planning rebellion against Babylonia, sent Psametich II a contingent of troops to "strengthen his claim for a return in kind when the fitting hour came." Following the publication (in 1903 and 1911) of the documents discovered at Jeb (Elephantine), most scholars ascribed to Psametich II the delivery of this important fortress to the guardianship of a Judean force. Other scholars (among them Ed. Meyer, *Der Papyrusfund von Elephantine,* 1912), related this fact to Psametich I (663–609), who is likewise known to have fortified Jeb and employed

mercenaries of foreign nations (Herodotus, II. 30). Meyer's suggested date was based on evidence he found in the Jeb documents for customs conflicting with the laws proclaimed during the religious reform under King Josiah. It is obvious, however, that in the short time that elapsed from Josiah to Psametich II not all the old customs could be abandoned.

Recently the argument advanced by Rawlinson was contested on the grounds that Zedekiah, who reaffirmed his allegiance to Nebuchadnezzar in 594/3, was unlikely to offer within the following two years military aid to Egypt, Babylonia's rival (see Sauneron and Yoyotte, in *VT*, II [1952], pp. 131–136, and B. Porten, *Archives from Elephantine*, 1968, p. 11). The argument cannot be considered conclusive, however. It must be questioned in the light of Zedekiah's instability, fluctuating policy and ultimate capitulation to the pro-Egyptian party in his country, as well as in view of the formal peace that prevailed at the time between Egypt and Babylonia and might have permitted the dispatch of limited Judean aid to Egypt against Ethiopia. Nor do we know that Psametich I had ever entrusted Jeb to foreign guards (his original garrison consisted only of Egyptians; see Herodotus, II. 30). Above all, there is no clear evidence that Psametich I had ever launched a military campaign against Ethiopia (see Sauneron and Yoyotte, "La campagne nubienne de Psametique II," in *BIFAO*, 50 [1952], p. 201, n. 4, and Freedy and Redford, in *JAOS*, 90 [1970], pp. 476–477, n. 69).

If therefore the testimony of Aristeas' Letter is accepted as essentially historical, the balance of the controversy on this matter seems to tilt to the side of Psametich II, although recruits to his army from Judean fugitives to Egypt may have assumed in the sources of Aristeas' Letter the form of auxiliaries sent from Judea.

11. Jeremiah, 44.1. Isaiah's prophecy about the "five cities in Egypt that would speak the language of Canaan" (19.18–20) might have been influenced by the presence of Judean communities in Egypt, established by fugitives from the Assyrian invasion in 701. His reference *(ibid.)* to an "altar to the Lord in the midst of Egypt and a pillar to Him at the border thereof" may have alluded to one of these communities, possibly on the eastern border. Also, Jeremiah, speaking of "the residue of Jerusalem ... that dwell in Egypt" (Jer. 24.8) may have referred to these communities, and not only to fugitives from the Babylonian invasion of Judea in 597.

12. Cf. A. E. Cowley, *Aramaic Papyri of the 5th Century B.C.*, 1923, p. xvi.

13. See the letter of the Jews of Jeb to Bagohi, governor of Judea, *ibid.*, pp. 111–114.

14. The first indications of the impression the Jews made on highly cultured Greeks may be deduced from Clearchus and Theophrastus (both disciples of Aristotle) and from authors such as Megasthenes and Hecataeus of Abdera, contemporaries of Alexander's successors. See their statements in Reinach, *Textes d'auteurs grecs et romains relatifs au Judaïsme*, 1895, nos. 5, 7, 8, 9, and M. Stern, *Greek and Latin Authors on Jews and Judaism*, I, 1974, pp. 8–17, 20–44, 45–52; see also Y. Gutman, *The Beginnings of Jewish-Hellenistic Literature* (Hebrew), 1958, pp. 49–58, 63–71, 77–82, 91–102.

15. Josephus' claim (*Against Apion*, II.35–37, and *War*, II.287) that the Jews were invited to Alexandria by Alexander the Great, founder of the city, is generally disputed. They must have settled there, however, in the "very earliest times," as stated by Emperor Claudius

(see his edict to Alexandria and Syria in Josephus, *Antiquities*, XIX. 280), probably not later than the days of Ptolemy I (cf. *Letter of Aristeas*, ed. cited above [n. 10], p. 101). On their settlement in Cyrene and other Libyan cities, see Josephus, *Against Apion*, II. 44.

16. For the settlement of the Jews in Antioch at the invitation of its founder, Seleucus I Nicator, see *ibid.*, II. 39. That they garrisoned strategically important places in Phrygia and Lydia is attested by Josephus, *Antiquities*, XII, 148–53. See on this A. Schalit, "The Letter of Antiochus III to Zeuxis etc.," in *JQR*, 50 (1959–1960), pp. 289–318.

17. That the social status of the Jews under the Ptolemies was *de facto*, if not *de jure*, far above that of the Egyptians is indicated by both Philo (*Flaccus*, X.78–80) and Josephus (*Against Apion*, II, 71–72); and see below, n. 35.

18. See *ibid.*, I, 73–90, 227–287.

19. *Ibid.*, II, 69.

20. On the various components of Greek immigration to Alexandria, see M. Rostovtzeff, *The Social and Economic History of the Hellenistic World*, II, 1967, pp. 887 ff., 1054ff, 1076–1095, and other places.

21. *Against Apion*, II, 49.

22. *Ibid.*, 49–50.

23. According to Josephus (*ibid.*, 53–54), Ptolemy IX Euergetes II sought to destroy the Jews of Alexandria by exposing them all to an attack of drunken elephants, but the elephants turned against Euergetes' men. It is hard to reconstruct what actually happened. Perhaps the planned punishment of the king was not aimed at *all* the Jews of Alexandria, but at their leaders only, and popular imagination inflated the King's plan. In any case, the Jews of Egypt must have escaped a grave threat, since they marked the event by an annual celebration. There remains also the question as to the time of that event, for another source (III Maccabees VI. 6) relates the same "miracle" to the reign of Ptolemy IV Philopator. The correct answer, we believe, was given by Tcherikover who relies in this matter on Josephus. "What was impossible in the period of Philopator," he says, "assumes historical credibility under Euergetes II;" Ptolemy IX "hated the Jews because he viewed them as his political opponents" (*Jews and Greeks in the Hellenistic Period*, 1930 [Hebrew], p. 289).

24. Josephus, *Antiquities*, XIII, 284–287, 348–351.

25. *Id., Against Apion*, II, 49.

26. The definite forecasts about the ultimate struggle between the heathen and Jewish worlds, as well as the expressions of boundless hatred of Greek morals and beliefs, which we find in the Third Sibylline Oracle (see R. H. Charles, *Apocrypha and Pseudepigrapha of the Old Testament*, 1913, II, pp. 379ff), indicate that certain Jewish circles in Egypt were convinced that the conflict between Greek and Jewish civilizations was irreconcilable and that a decisive clash between them was in the making.

27. Josephus, *Antiquities*, XIX, 290.

28. *Against Apion*, II, 80–124.

29. See H. A. Wolfson, *Philo*, I, pp. 164–194; II, 405–426. Philo's fervent belief that Jewish religious and moral ideas were far superior to those of the Greeks is clearly presented by E. R. Goodenough in his *Introduction to Philo Judaeus*, 1962, pp. 75–90, although Goodenough, like many others, maintained that Philo's Judaism was mixed or saturated with Greek philosophical concepts. Related to this is Y. F. Baer's view that Philo drew some of his major concepts from Hebrew sources, representing a

coordination between Jewish and Greek ideas (see his *Israel Among the Nations* [Hebrew], 1955, pp. 81–98).

30. Numbers 15.15.

31. See *Antiquities*, XIV, 98–99. Josephus, we may assume, follows the pro-Herodian Nicolaus of Damascus when he says that "Antipater won over the Jews above Pelusium to his side" (*ibid.*, 99). Antipater may indeed have tried to win them over, but it is most unlikely that it was his argument that moved them to take such a decisive step. And see below, n. 32.

32. Josephus, *War*, I, 187–192; *Antiquities* XIV, 128–132. Here too Antipater is claimed to have "persuaded" the Jews to offer assistance to the invading army against their original intention to resist it. Antipater is reported to have shown the Jewish commanders in the Land of Onias a letter from Hyrcanus, the Hasmonean ruler of Judea, urging them to take the course he recommended "on the ground of their common nationality" (*ibid.*). It is most questionable that this approach could have moved these forces, committed to Egypt's defense, to take an anti-Egyptian stand. What influenced them primarily was no doubt their awareness that the Romans were supporting Queen Cleopatra, who was opposed by her chief ministers (one of whom was an Egyptian) and the Alexandrian populace, their avowed enemy.

33. See Caesar's decrees in Josephus, *Antiquities*, XIV, 190–216.

34. Concerning Augustus' letters and decrees see Philo, *Flaccus*, 50, and Josephus, *Against Apion*, II, 61. Noteworthy is also Tcherikover's conjecture that Augustus installed in Alexandria the slab which, according to Josephus (*ibid.*, II, 37), recorded the "rights bestowed upon the Jews of Egypt by Caesar" (see *Corpus Papyrorum Judaicarum*, p. 56, n. 20).

35. The long lasting controversy over the question of the rights in Alexandria under the Ptolemies cannot be decided in the Jews' disfavor in line with the seemingly dominant tendency. The repeated statements of Josephus that the Jews were in possession of documents attesting their full civic equality cannot be brushed aside as meaningless assertions based on Jewish forgeries or exaggerations, as H. Willrich ("Caligula," in *KLIO*, III [1903], 403–407), Ulrich Wilcken ("Zum alexandrinischen Antisemitismus," *APHK*, XXVII [1909], pp. 787–788), F. Stähelin (*Der Antisemitismus des Altertums*, 1905, p. 35) and others would have it. Josephus would not have dared to define Apion as a "knave" or a "fool" for having ignored the orders concerning the Jews issued by various Greek kings (*Against Apion*, II, 37) unless he was sure of his facts.

Similarly, one cannot disregard Josephus' statement: "Not a single king, it appears, not a single emperor in our times, ever conferred citizen rights upon Egyptians" (*Against Apion*, II, 72). To be sure, this statement was imprecise since individual Egyptians *could*, in rare conditions, obtain Roman citizenship (see *ibid.*, II, 41, n. c). Josephus, however, no doubt wished to point out that the Egyptians *as a people* had not gained rights of citizens, whereas the Jews of Egypt received such rights *as a group* from both Greeks and Romans. Obviously, the presentation of this contrast, too, attests Josephus' certainty in the matter—a certainty that could hardly be acquired without reliance on well-known or confirmed data.

Finally, one cannot ignore Philo's statement that the Jews of Alexandria were robbed (by Flaccus) not only of their *civic*, but also of their *political* rights (*Flaccus*, VIII.53) before one embraces the notion that the Jews of

Alexandria as a *community* lacked a rather elevated status. Supporting this questionable view were Wilcken (*op. cit.*, 786ff); I. Bell, *Jews and Christians in Egypt*, 1924, 12ff, and others; among those who opposed it were Juster, *Les Juifs*, II, 1ff, and Schürer, *Geschichte*, III (fourth ed.), pp. 133–134 (and cf. Klausner, in *Kirjath Sepher*, IX [1932], pp. 163–164). Distanced from both contrasting views, but closer to that of the latter scholars, is H. A. Wolfson's position on the question which is based on his analysis of the terms used to designate the main parts of Egypt's population (*op. cit.*, II, pp. 398–400).

36. See on this Tcherikover, *Corpus Papyrorum Judaicarum*, I, pp. 62–74.

37. *Against Apion*, II, 69.

38. Tcherikover, *Jews and Greeks in the Hellenistic Period* (Hebrew), 1930, p. 364.

39. James Parkes, *The Jew in the Medieval Community*, 1938, pp. 4–5.

40. *Id., Antisemitism*, 1963, p. 60

41. *Ibid., ibid.*

42. Philo, *Flaccus*, IX, 59.

43. *Ibid.*, IX, 66.

44. Philo, *Embassy to Gaius*, XIX, 131.

45. *Ibid.*

46. *The Anguish of the Jew*, 1965, p. 14.

47. Josephus, *Against Apion*, I, 70.

48. For the pogrom in Alexandria in 66, in which the Greeks were joined by the Romans, see Josephus, *War*, II, 487–498. According to this account, the number of Jewish dead amounted to fifty thousand.

49. On the massacres of the Jews in Syria and Palestine in towns of mixed Greek-Jewish population, see *ibid.*, II, 457–480, 559–561.

50. See Eusebius, *Historia Ecclesiastica*, 4.2 (Migne, *PG*, 20, 304–307); *id., Chronica*, in *PG*, 19, 553–554, and Jerome's translation and amplification (*PG*, 8, 609, for the years 115–116); Cassius Dio, *Roman History*, 68.32. Of the modern literature on the subject, see Y.

Gutman, "The Wars of the Jews in the Days of Trajan," in *Sefer Asaf* (Hebrew), 1953, pp. 149–184; A. Fuks, "The Jewish Revolt in Egypt etc.", in *Aegyptus*, XXXIII (1953), 131–158; V. Tcherikover, *The Jews in Egypt in the Hellenistic Roman Age in the Light of the Papyri* (Hebr.), 1945, pp. 206–229; *id., Corpus Papyrorum Judaicarum*, pp. 86–93.

Tcherikover assumed that the main cause of the outbreak was neither political nor social, but the growth of messianic hopes among the Jews to the point of inspiring them with the belief that they could vanquish the entire heathen world (see his *Jews and Greeks in Egypt* [Hebrew], pp. 226–228). But a messianic movement leading to a war of such unsurpassed ferocity, and encompassing such large masses of Jews, could not have been produced without having been nursed by intolerable social conditions. Given the background of Greek-Jewish relations, there is every reason to believe that such conditions existed in the decades preceding the war of 115. That the movement had no messianic pretensions is evident from the fact that the Jewish assaults were originally directed not against the Romans, but only against the Greeks and the other gentiles who co-inhabited with the Jews the countries involved (see Eusebius, *Hist. Ecclesiastica*, IV.2; *PG*, 20, 304: *Judaei adversus Graecos et gentiles qui una cum ipsis habitabant, tumultum excitare coeperunt*); Paulus Orosius, *Historiarum adversum paganos libri VII*, ed. Zangemeister, 1882, 7.12, p. 467; and see on this further Gutman, "The Wars of the Jews Under Trajan," *loc. cit.*, pp. 177–179).

51. See Cassius Dio, *Roman History*, 68.32.

52. Such as that the Jews would eat the flesh of their victims (*ibid.*), which is prohibited by Jewish law, while

"ceremonial cannibalism [during war] was typically Egyptian" (see J. Grafton Milne, *Egypt under Roman Rule*, 1898, p. 63).

53. According to Dio *(ibid.)*, two hundred and twenty thousand persons perished in Cyrenaica and two hundred and forty thousand in Cyprus. These numbers, though probably exaggerated, indicate the enormous scope of the upheavals even beyond Egypt, the main sphere of conflict.

54. Reflecting this outcome is Eusebius' statement that "Hadrian rebuilt Alexandria which had been destroyed" [by the Jews] (*Cronica*, ed. Hieronymus, in Migne, *PL*, 27, 611–612, for the year 119) and the assertion of Orosius (*op. cit.*, lib. vii, 12, p. 253) that Libya, which had been struck by the Jewish rebellion, would have remained a wasteland, if it had not been repopulated by Hadrian. And see S. Applebaum, "A note on the work of Hadrian in Cyrene," in *Journal of Roman Studies*, XL (1950), 87–90.

55. The discovery in Egypt, in 1936, of a fragment of the Gospel of John, written, according to paleographic experts, in the first half of the second century (see C. H. Roberts, *An Unpublished Fragment of the Fourth Gospel*, 1935, p. 16), and the fact that the Gospel is first mentioned by Justin Martyr in his *Dialogue with Trypho* (c. 155) offer support to the view that this gospel was composed about 120–125—shortly after the war of 115–117. There seems to be no compelling reason to advance the composition of this gospel to the turn of the first century or the beginning of the second as suggested by recent Christian theologians (see W. G. Kümmel, *Introduction to the New Testament*, transl. H. C. Kee, 1975, p. 246). If this date is proven right, however, it in no way contradicts our view that the gospel was the product of a growing hostility between Greeks

and Jews, such as prevailed at the time in which Josephus wrote his *Against Apion* and which preceded the war of 115–117.

56. See John's repeated allusions to the identity of the Father and the Son (1.13–14; 8.19; 10.30, 33; 12.45; 14.9, 24–25) and his conception of the Holy Spirit as a distinct personality representing both the Son and the Father (14.25; 15.26)—a conception which led, after centuries of speculation, to the identification of the essence of the Holy Spirit with that of the Father and Christ.

57. Matthew, 10.5; 15.24, 26; Mark 7.26–27.

58. See his long talk with the Samaritan woman (John 4. 7–26) and his response to those who told him that some Greeks wished to see him (*ibid.*, 12. 23–26: "If *any* man serve me, let him follow me"), as well as his statement in John 10. 16: "Other sheep I have, which are not of this fold" etc.).

59. John, 8.17.

60. In fact, the Gospel of John systematically shows that "the Jews" schemed to do away with Jesus from their first encounter with him and that their determination to kill him steadily increased (see John 5.16, 18; 7.1; 8.37, 40, 59; 10.31; 11.8, 53). From this description the impression was created, as F. Ch. Baur rightly pointed out, that "the death of Jesus [was] the work of the Jews alone." Baur further stressed that the view of the Jews' desire to kill Jesus was associated with the Jews' unbelief, and thus "this unbelief, in which the whole power of darkness [was] revealed," and which appeared as "the expression of the character of a whole nation," invested the "crisis which followed in the death of Jesus with the deepest significance." See Baur's *History of Christianity in the First Three Centuries*, I, 1878, p. 156.

61. John, 8.44.

62. A. Harnack, *The Expansion of Christianity in the First Three Centuries*, I, 1904, p. 77.
63. *Ibid., ibid.*
64. *Ibid.*, p. 81.
65. See J. Starr, "Byzantine Jewry on the Eve of the Arab Conquest (565–638)," in *JPOS*, XV (1935), p. 281.
66. *Cod. Theod.*, XVI, 8.22.
67. *Ibid.*, XVI, 8.24.
68. *Ibid.*, XVI, 8.16 and 8.24.
69. See Juster, *Les Juifs*, II, pp. 263, n. 6; 245; Nov. Theod. 3.2.
70. For the sources of the conversion order, see Baron, *History*, III, pp. 236–237, nn. 19, 20, 22, and M. Avi-Yonah, *The Jews Under Roman and Byzantine Rule*, 1976, pp. 254–256. One of the sources in question is the eighth century chronicler Pseudo-Dionysius of Tell-Mahre, who proved to be mistaken with respect to some items, especially dates. It is difficult, however, to assume that his basic information on such major events as the war of Antiochian Jewry and Phocas' reaction was the product of sheer invention. Nor is it likely that anyone would attribute the first forced conversion of the Jews to Phocas, if it occurred under Heraclius, a famous emperor (as suggested by some scholars, among them Starr, *ibid.*, p. 284, n. 20, and p. 288, n. 43). See on this J.-B. Chabot, "Trois épisodes concernant les Juifs," in *REJ*, XXVIII (1894), 290–294, and S. Krauss, *Studien zur byzantinisch-jüdischen Geschichte*, 1914, pp. 22–23; see also Krauss' article in *Zion* (organ of Israel's Historical and Ethnographic Society), II (1927), pp. 28–37, which deals with a disputation between Jacob a "recent convert," and Justus, a Jew. Jacob was probably converted under Heraclius (in 634), but the translator of the Disputation into Ethiopian ascribed his conversion to the time of Phocas (*ibid.*, p. 29). This seems to indicate

that a large-scale conversion did indeed take place under Phocas and furthermore that it left a lasting impression on the minds of Jews and non-Jews. See also C. H. Kraeling, *The Jewish Community at Antioch*, 1932, pp. 159–160.
71. Kraeling, *ibid.*, p. 160.

The Spanish Scene

1. No direct information is available on the causes and beginnings of anti-Judaism in Spain, though we may assume with reasonable assurance that it stemmed from both pagan and Christian sources. Evidence of the pagan influences may be adduced from the antisemitic expressions of Hispanic-Latin authors like Seneca and Quintilian, and it may be worth mentioning that Seneca in his youth spent some time in Egypt. Christian anti-Jewishness must have begun in Spain with the spread of Christian propaganda, but the early history of the Christian campaign in Spain is mostly veiled in obscurity. Perhaps the strength of Christianity in Baetica (Andalusia), attested by the membership of the Council of Elvira, suggests, geographically, a North African extension; and contacts between the Christians in North Africa (Carthage) and Spain are known from the middle of the third century (St. Cyprian, Tertullian). Osius, no doubt the most forceful personality among those who took part in the Council of Elvira, may suggest similar connections.

Osius, who was bishop of Cordova, the birthplace of Seneca, may have had, like the latter, some juvenile relationship with Egypt. His name was probably Greek (meaning "saint"), and he was known as "an Egyptian from Iberia," according to Zosimus, the pagan Greek historian of the 5th century (see his *Historia Nova*, ed. Mendelssohn, 1887,

p. 86, and n. 1, for line 5). Menéndez Pelayo, like other Christian authors, interpreted the appelation "Egyptian" as "magician," or "sacerdote" or "learned" (*Historia de los Heterodoxos Españoles,* ed. E. Sánchez Reyes, I, 1963², p. 143). But this explanation is far-fetched. As Menéndez saw it, Osius "belonged to the Hispanic-Latin race" because, according to the Acts of the Nicean Council, statements made by Osius in that assembly had to be "interpreted" to the audience, thereby suggesting that he did not know Greek (*ibid.*). Whatever his familiarity with the Greek tongue, however, it cannot serve as proof of his origin. Osius may have come to Spain in early childhood and inherited from his Greek-Egyptian parents some of their views and attitudes, even though he may have forgotten his Greek and become accustomed to speak Latin. Gams, moreover, argued strongly against the notion that Osius, who presided over the Council of Nicaea, could perform his task as chairman without commanding adequate knowledge of Greek (see *Die Kirchengeschichte Spaniens,* II/I, 1956, pp. 138–141). The same arguments may apply also to his visit to Alexandria in 324 as Constantine's emissary charged with the mission of settling the theological controversies that raged there.

That Osius was most likely of Egyptian origin is a view shared by several historians of Christianity, such as Ph. Schaff and A. Harnack. But V. C. De Clercq, who wrote a thorough and most comprehensive study of Osius, believed that he was of Spanish stock since in several old documents his name is spelled Ossius, which would indicate, in his opinion, a Roman ancestry. Different forms of spelling, however, may owe their origin to different causes, which are usually hard to determine. On the other hand, De Clercq cannot explain why Zosimus described Osius as "Egyptian" and admits that in no other instance does this appellation stand for "magician" or "priest" (*Ossius of Cordova,* 1954, p. 54). Nor does he consider it likely that Osius did not master Greek (*ibid.,* pp. 70–74).

2. Scholars differ on the date of the Council of Elvira. It is generally agreed, however, that it took place after the Diocletian anti-Christian persecution (303–305) and before 313—the year in which Osius was known to have been present at the Court of Emperor Constantine (see Gams, *ibid.,* pp. 4–9). See Hefele's summation of the controversy regarding the Council's date and his conclusion that it convened in 305–306 (*History of the Councils,* transl. W. R. Clark, I, 1894, pp. 131–137).

3. Guided by the principle that "*no association is possible between the faithful and the infidel*", the Council of Elvira went as far as imposing the penalty of excommunication on Christians who accepted Jewish blessings on their agricultural yield (canon 49) or took meals in common with Jews (canon 50). This was the first time that the prohibition to eat in the company of Jews was decreed in Christendom, and only after a century and a half (from 465 on) was it enacted by other Christian Councils. For the canons of Elvira, see González-Tejada, II, pp. 18ff.

4. For the anti-Jewish laws in the Theodosian Code that passed into Alarich's *Breviarium* (the Gothic code assigned for the conquered population), compiled in 506, see J. Juster, "The Legal Condition of the Jews under the Visigothic Kings" (transl. from the French edition, 1912, with an updated annotation by A. M. Rabello), in *Israel Law Review,* XI (1976), pp. 259–261. Juster noted that the number of statutes concerning Jews in the Theodosian

Code was reduced in the *Breviarium*, due to omissions and condensation, from 53 to 10 (see *ibid.*, p. 260, n. 5). Among the anti-Jewish restrictions it retains, most notable are those touching the purchase of slaves and the assumption of public offices (*ibid.*, n. 5, §1,2). That most of these restrictions fell into abeyance is evident from their repeated reenactment by the Church Councils of both Gaul and Spain in the sixth and seventh centuries. See on this below, pp. 30–32, 34, 38.

5. MGH, *Concilia aevi Merovingici*, ed. F. Maasen, 1893, p. 78 (canon 14 or 13).
6. *Ibid., ibid.*, 94 (canon 30).
7. *Ibid.*, 159 (canon 16).
8. *Ibid.*, 204 (canon 11).
9. *Ibid.*, 210 (canon 9).
10. *Ibid.*, 67, (canon 9).
11. *Ibid.*, 158 (canon 13).
12. *Ibid.*, 190, (canon 17 or 15).
13. MGH, *Leges*, I (ed. Pertz), 15 (Chlothacharii II. edictum, anni 614, c. 10).
14. See above, p. 29.
15. This may be gathered from S. Dill's description of the Gallo-Roman and Frankish societies in the sixth century and beyond it (see his *Roman Society in Gaul in the Merovingian Age*, 1926, especially pp. 235–307). More definite about this is L. Sergeant, *The Franks*, 1898, pp. 154–155, 252–256, and other places.
16. MGH, *Scriptores rerum Merovingicarum*, II, ed. Bruno Krusch, 1888; see *ibid.*, Fredegarius, *Chronica*, lib. IV, cap. 65, p. 153, and *Gesta Dagoberti*, lib. I, cap. 24, p. 409. According to these sources, Dagobert took the move under the influence of Heraclius who, in turn, was impressed by an astrological prediction that his empire would be destroyed by a circumcised people. Discounting the astrological detail as legendary, but considering Heraclius' counsel likely, Baron (*History*, III, pp. 54, 254, n. 68) tends to postpone that

counsel (and Dagobert's edict) for several years when the Emperor came to realize the danger posed to the Empire by the Moslems (the circumcised people). Since Heraclius decreed, in 632–34, forced conversion for all the Jews of the empire, Dagobert's move, Baron believed, would be better understood against such a background.

Despite the apparent plausibility of the argument, it cannot, as we see it, disqualify the data offered by the chapter of the *Gesta Dagoberti* (I, cap. 24), which deals with this matter. These data tell us (a) that Dagobert decreed conversion or expulsion for all the Jews of his Kingdom; (b) that the decree was issued in the eighth year of his reign (629); and (c) that in that year he also sent a delegation to Constantinople to negotiate a concord with the Empire. These are data of historical significance, which the Chronicler must have drawn from reliable sources, and we see no reason why they should be superseded by the only questionable item in that account—Heraclius' counsel offered on the ground of an astrological prediction. In 629, we should further note, the Jews of Palestine, then reconquered by Heraclius, were strongly pressured to convert to Christianity, and in that year the Arabs launched their first assaults on the Byzantine forces in Palestine. Years later these events may have been echoed in the story of the astrological prediction, which was somehow attached to the sources dealing with Dagobert's decree.

17. See E. A. Thompson, *The Goths in Spain*, 1969, p. 87ff.
18. *Ibid., op. cit.*, pp. 58–59. The prohibition on Catholics marrying heretics was first decreed in the Council of Elvira (canon 16); it was reenacted in the Council of Laodicea (in Phrygia), which was held between 341 and 381,

and in the Fourth General Council at Chalcedon. See Hefele, *History of the Councils,* I, pp. 11, 31, 144; II, pp. 305, 316; III, p. 400.

19. *Ibid.,* p. 84.
20. Gregory of Tours, *HF,* VI. 18.
21. Thompson, *op cit.,* p. 85.
22. Gregory of Tours, *HF,* IX. 15.
23. See below, nn. 50, 51.
24. On Reccared's secret conversion, see Fredegarius, *Chronica,* lib. IV, cap. 8; on the conspiracies organized by Arian bishops and the Counts of Narbonne, see E. A. Thompson, "The conversion of the Visigoths to Catholicism," in *Nottingham Medieval Studies,* IV (1960), p. 26, and *id., The Goths,* pp. 102–104. On the existence of a tendency among the Visigoths to convert to Catholicism already at the time of Leovigild, see J. N. Hillgarth, "La conversión de los Visigodos,", in *AST,* XXXIV (1961), pp. 21–35.
25. See MGH, *LV* (ed. Zeumer), lib. XII, tit. 3, law 13: "The depravity of the Jews" (meaning thereby their bribery) has "corrupted the minds of princes." The law is here presented in S. P. Scott's translation (*The Visigothic Code,* 1910, p. 369).
26. See *ibid.,* laws 13 and 14. Law 13 repeats Sisebut's prohibition on Jews' owning Christian slaves. Law 14 further orders: "Slaves who are known to be the issue of marriages between Christians and Jews . . . shall be made Christians." In marital unions between Jews and Christians the infidel party must become Christian; if objection is offered, the marriage is dissolved and the recalcitrant person shall be driven into exile. If a Hebrew circumcises a Christian or induces one to join his sect, or performs any of his rites, he shall be beheaded.
27. For Sisebut's order of forced conversion, see Isidore of Seville, *Historia Gothorum,* cap. 60 (MGH, *Chronica Minora* (saec. IV–VII), II (ed.

Mommsen), p. 291), *Chronica maiora,* c. 416, *ibid.,* p. 480, and *Continuatio Hispana,* c. 15. (*ibid.,* p. 339). For the date of Sisebut's decree, see Isidore's *Etymologiae,* lib. V, 39.42, and Thompson's remarks, *op. cit.,* p. 166, n. 2. See, however, also F. Görres, "Das Judenthum im westgotischen Spanien von König Sisebut bis Roderich (612–711)," in *ZfWT,* 48 (1905), p. 356, who believes that Sisebut's original harsh laws were sufficient to lead many Jews to conversion or exile, thus explaining Isidore's statement (in his *Historia Gothorum*) that Sisebut's forced conversion was begun *in initio regni.*

28. See H. Graetz, "Die westgothische Gesetzgebung in Betreff der Juden," in *Jahresbericht des jüdisch-theologischen Seminars,* Breslau, 1858, p. 2.
29. See his "Legal Condition" etc., *loc. cit.,* p. 261.
30. For Pope Gregory's view that the Jews should not be forced to convert but be attracted to the faith by humane approaches, see, among other places, MGH, *Gregorii I Papae Registrum Epistolarum,* I, 1957 (ed. Ewald and Hartmann), epist. I. 45 and XIII. 15.
31. See above, p. 26.
32. *Additamenta ad Chron. Maiora,* I. 2, in MGH, *Chronica Minora* (saec. IV-VII), II, p. 490.
33. There is no contemporary source for this information, and the first to offer it was Alfonso de Espina, in his *Fortalitium Fidei* (lib. III, nona consid., quarta expulsio, ed. Lyon, 1511, f. 219ᵛ), from which it passed to a Hebrew work which served as source to Samuel Usque (*Consolaçam as Tribulaçoens de Israel,* III, Coimbra, 1906, pp. iᵛ–iiʳ; Engl. transl. by Martin A. Cohen, *Consolation for the Tribulations of Israel,* 1965, pp. 167–168; and see Cohen's discussion of the related sources, *ibid.,* pp. 277–287, and below, appendix G, pp. 1131–1132). In *Emeq ha-Bakha,* a Hebrew chronicle completed in 1575,

however, we read that many of the Jews who fled from Sisebut's coercion to Gaul returned to Spain under King Swinthila—and not under Witiza, as stated by Espina and Usque. The correction shows familiarity with Gothic history and suggests that the author, Joseph ha-Hakohen, used some Christian source, now lost—perhaps the same source reflected, in distorted form, in the Christian documents used by Espina which are likewise no longer extant (see conclusion of his passage on the *quarta expulsio* cited above: *Hec ex cronicis hyspanie et ex archivo fratris johannis egydii zamorensis*).

34. Canons 65 and 66 (see González-Tejada, II, p. 308).
35. Graetz, *loc. cit.*, p. II; Hefele, *op. cit.*, IV, 1895, p. 461, c. 3.
36. Attesting this is the *placitum*—the forced declaration of faithfulness to Catholicism—addressed by the Converted Jews to the King which was published by Fidel Fita ("Placitum de los judíos en tiempo de Chintila") in *Suplementos al Concilio nacional Toledano VI*, 1881, pp. 43–49.
37. *LV*, III, 1, 2.
38. *LV*, II, 1, 9.
39. See González-Tejada, II, p. 366; *LV*, XII, 2, 3.
40. See *LV*, lib. XII, tit. II, laws 5, 6, 7, 8; Jews were also prohibited from testifying against Christians, prosecuting a Christian or suing him upon any written contract (laws 9–10).
41. "Die Westgothische Gesetzgebung," *loc. cit.*, 19–20.
42. "The Legal Condition," *loc. cit.*, pp. 269–71.
43. González-Tejada, *op. cit.*, II, p. 366.
44. LV, XII, 2, 15.
45. LV, XII, 3, 16. This is according to Zeumer's edition of *LV*; in the *Fuero Juzgo* (the 13th century Spanish version of *LV*) this law appears as c. 17 of lib. XII, tit. 2, and is erroneously

attributed to King Egica.
46. This commitment is included in the new *placitum* addressed to him by the converts which he incorporated in his Code (LV, XII, 2, 17; in the *Fuero Juzgo*, the *placitum* appears as law 16).
47. Thompson, *op. cit.*, p. 207.
48. See F. Dahn, *Urgeschichte der romanischen und germanischen Völker*, I, 1881, p. 396; see also pp. 510–511, 531–532.
49. See above, p. 29.
50. See González-Tejada, II, pp. 245–246 (Third Toledan Council, canon XIV).
51. *Ibid.*, p. 245.
52. *Ibid., ibid.*
53. LV, XII. 2, 13–14.
54. González-Tejada, II, p. 307, canon 63.
55. *Ibid.*, p. 308, canon 66.
56. *Ibid., ibid.*, canon 65.
57. *Ibid.*, p. 304, canon 57.
58. *Ibid.*, p. 305, canon 57.
59. *Ibid.*, p. 307, canon 63.
60. *Ibid.*, p. 306, canon 60, which speaks of *Judei* but is no doubt an extension of canon 59 as pointed out correctly by Tejada, in his introductory remark to canon 60, *ibid.*
61. There is no direct evidence of the number of Jews in Spain toward the end of the 6th century. We may safely assume, however, that the tolerant treatment of the Jews by the Visigoths in the fifth and sixth centuries attracted to Spain many Jewish immigrants from North Africa and other regions governed by the Byzantines, who discriminated against the Jews. Also the great financial strength the Jews of Spain displayed during the later persecutions (see on this below, pp. 48–49) suggests that it was sustained by a larger rather than by a smaller group.
62. *Ibid.*, p. 308, canon 65.
63. *Ibid., ibid.*
64. Such as those that might come from children of mixed marriages; see above, n. 60.

65. See the King's opening address at the Eighth Toledan Council, in González-Tejada, II, p. 366.

66. *Ibid.*, p. 383, canon 12.

67. See C. H. Lynch and P. Galindo, *San Braulio, Obispo de Zaragoza,* 1950, p. 363 ff.; F. Dahn, *Die Könige der Germanen,* VI, 1885, pp. 404–405, 644–650; and F. Fita's elaborate study: "El papa Honorio primero y San Braulio de Zaragoza," in *La Ciudad de Dios,* IV (1870), V (1871) and VI (1871).

68. Lynch and Galindo, *op. cit.,* pp. 363–364.

69. *Ibid.,* p. 363.

70. A. K. Ziegler, *Church and State in Visigothic Spain,* 1930, p. 198.

71. *Ibid.,* p. 197.

72. *Ibid.*

73. *Ibid.,* p. 198.

74. See R. Altamira, "Spain under the Visigoths," *Cambridge Medieval History,* II, 1980, p. 172; S. McKenna, *Paganism and Pagan Survival in Spain up to the Fall of the Visigothic Kingdom,* 1958, especially pp. 121–122, 125–134.

75. *LV,* XII, 2. 13.

76. Had the Jews provided a basis for the charge that they were promotors of rebellion, the kings would have used this as decisive argument for the Church Councils to decree their doom. But none of the royal laws or conciliar canons even hint at such an accusation. Also in Narbonne, in 673, the Jews were not among the plotters of the uprising, but were probably moved to join the insurgents as residents of the mutinous province (as may be gathered from the references to the Jews in this connection by Julian, *Historia Wambae regis,* c. 6, in MGH, *Scriptores rerum merovinigicarum,* V, 504, and Lucas of Tuy, *Historia Galliae,* in Migne, *PL,* 96, 767—both markedly anti-Jewish sources). King Wamba who, after he had crushed the rebellion, expelled the Jews from the city of Narbonne, would hardly have permitted their return if this had not been the case.

77. Bernard S. Bachrach ("A Reassessment of Visigothic Jewish Policy, 589–71," *American Historical Review,* LXXVIII [Feb.-Dec. 1973], pp. 11–34) attempted to portray the Visigothic-Jewish struggle against the background of the kings' conflict with the nobility. The attempt, a step in the right direction, was flawed, however, by the author's misconceptions. Bachrach ignored the kings' drive for total union and the complex reaction of the Church Councils (a mere "tool of the monarchy," in his opinion) and consequently replaced the original cause of the quarrel by the ensuing political antagonism. Above all, he expanded the Jewish involvement in the conflict far beyond its real aims and confines, perhaps because he wrongly viewed the Jews as a "formidable political faction" (pp. 33, 34), which the nobles courted (pp. 22, 26) and which threw its great weight behind those on whose aid it could count. Indeed, if we go by Bachrach's assertions, the Jews played a direct and important role in both the making and unmaking of kings—a view which takes the picture entirely out of focus and beyond the sphere of historical reality.

78. The anti-Jewish laws which the Third Toledan Council (589) enacted at Reccared's "order," were "proposed," it should be noted, to the King by the Council (see opening of canon 14—González-Tejada, II, p. 245).

79. *LV,* XII, 3, 1.

80. González-Tejada, II, p. 455 (the King's opening speech at the 12th Toledan Council).

81. *LV,* XII, 3, 23–24. Bishops were also to be present at the legal proceedings against followers of Judaism, and if they could not attend any of the sessions, they were obliged to appoint a priest as their deputy (*ibid.,* law 25). The Church, moreover, was ordered

to punish bishops who evaded any of these duties (*ibid.,* law 24).

82. *LV,* XII, 3, 3; González-Tejada, II, pp. 476–478 (canon 9).

83. Thompson, who thus summarized these laws (*The Goths,* p. 206), attributed them to Receswinth; the summary, however, better fits Erwig's legislation (see *LV,* XII, 3, 1–2).

84. *Ibid.,* law 11.

85. *Ibid.,* law 4. The same law adds: "Should any woman presume to practice the operation of circumcision, or should present anyone to another person to be circumcised, she shall have her nose cut off, and all her property shall be given to the King."

86. *LV,* XII, II, 18.

87. *Ibid., ibid.*

88. See the King's address to the 17th Council of Toledo in González-Tejada, II, p. 593, and his recommendations to the Council as summarized in its decisions (*ibid.,* p. 603).

89. *Ibid.,* pp. 603–604.

90. *Ibid.*

91. Menéndez y Pelayo, *Historia de los Heterodoxos Españoles,* I, pp. 372–373. Among those who shared Pelayo's view were Dozy (*Spanish Islam,* 1913, p. 227), Graetz (*Geschichte,* V², 1870, p. 148), Juster ("The Legal Condition, etc.," *loc cit.,* pp. 282–283), and other well-known historians. In our judgment, however, the contention is not only far-fetched, but utterly indefensible, since the converts could not envisage, even in their wildest dreams, the overthrow of the Visigothic power with the forces at their disposal. Some substance might have been lent to King Egica's charges had he claimed that certain Hispano-Jewish converts tried to induce the *Moslems* in North Africa to invade Spain and promised them the help of their Spanish brethren if such an invasion took place. But in 693 the Moslems were not yet established in western

North Africa, and evidently no such claim could be made. Egica, therefore, had to limit his assertions regarding the alleged foreign allies of the converts to the Jews of North Africa only, and this reveals the groundlessness of the conspiracy he portrayed and the absurdity of his charge. Moreover, Egica accused the converts not only of planning the "ruin of the fatherland and the entire people" *(conati sunt ruinam partiae ac populo universo),* but also of the whole of Christendom, their plans having actually extended to other Christian countries besides Spain (see González-Tejada, II, p. 593, and p. 603, canon 8 of 17th Toledan Council). Thus he further exposed the fictitious nature of his charge, which foreshadowed similar antisemitic libels of much later times.

92. See concerning this Franz Görres, "Charakter und Religionspolitik des vorletzten spanischen Westgotenkönigs Witiza," *ZfWT,* 48 (1905), pp. 96–111.

The Second Cycle

1. RAH, *Memorias,* VII (1852), p. 93.

2. Evidence of the existence of a Jewish community in Barcelona in the third quarter of the 9th century comes from both Christian and Jewish sources. In 876, Charles the Bald, King of the Western Franks, whose reign included the Spanish March, expresses his gratitude to the Barcelonians for their faithfulness to him (Charles' kingdom had been beset by attacks from all sides), of which he had heard much from the Jew Judah *(fidelis noster)* who may have dealt with the King as the city's representative (see *España Sagrada,* XXIX, p. 185: *de vestra fidelitate multa nobis designavit*). From about the same time comes the letter which Amram Gaon sent the Jews of Barcelona (see Responsa of the Geonim [Hebrew], Lyck, 1864, p. 21b). The letter,

addressed to "all the Rabbis and their students" in Barcelona, seems to suggest a sizable community whose growth had required several decades.

Evidence of the presence of the Jews in Coimbra (twenty-five miles east of the Atlantic), which was conquered by the Christians in 866, comes from the year 900 (see Baer, II, p. 1) and in Castrojeriz from 974, when the Count of Castile granted the inhabitants of the place a privilege equalizing Jews and Christians in wergild (Baer, I, p. 1, §2).

3. R. Dozy even goes to the extreme of presenting the alleged Jewish "betrayal" as an unquestionable historical fact (*op. cit.*, p. 232).

4. For the source of the legend and its refutation, see E. Ashtor, *The Jews of Moslem Spain*, I, 1973, pp. 407–408 (n. 5) and P. Leon Tello, *Los Judíos de Toledo*, I, 1979, pp. 20–21. See also Norman Roth, "The Jews and the Moslem Conquest of Spain," in *JST*, 37 (1976), pp. 145–158.

5. For the Arabic sources see C. Sánchez-Albornoz, *La España Musulmana*, I, 1960², pp. 35–45; R. Dozy, *Recherches sur l'histoire et la littérature de l'Espagne pendant le moyen âge*, 1881, pp. 49, 52–54; and see Rodrigo Jiménez de Rada, *Rerum in Hispania gestarum chronicon*, Granada, 1545, lib. III, cap. 23.

6. This factual alliance, which existed during the Arab conquest, continued, despite some disturbing interruptions, throughout the period of Omayyad rule (see Ashtor, *op. cit.*, I, pp. 26, 56, 93, 100–101).

7. Ashtor, *ibid.*, p. 93.

8. *Ibid., ibid.*

9. *Ibid.*, pp. 30–31, 60 and other places on the reasons for Jewish immigration into Spain in the Moslem period.

10. For the prolonged struggle between the Moslems and the Franks, see F. Codera, "Narbona, Gerona y Barcelona bajo la dominación Musulmana," in IEC, *Anuari*, III (1909–1910), pp. 178–202, and J. Reinaud, *Invasions de Sarrazins en France, et de France en Savoie, en Piemont et en Suisse*, 1836, pp. 1–153.

11. In his *Mohammed and Charlemagne*, 1937, pp. 164–174, 183–185.

12. Especially by R. S. López in *Speculum*, XVIII (1943), pp. 14–38.

13. Cf. Archibald R. Lewis, *Naval Power and Trade in the Mediterranean*, 1954, p. 126. Lewis who, unlike Pirenne, maintained that the main commercial hardships experienced by the Carolingians were originally caused by the Byzantines, and not by the Moslems, nevertheless describes the conditions in Southern France of the 9th century in the same manner as they are portrayed by Pirenne (see *ibid.*, pp. 146, 177).

14. J. Régné, "Étude sur la condition des juifs de Narbonne du Vᵉ au XIVᵉ siècle," in *REJ*, 55 (1908), p. 12.

15. The primary source is the *Routes and Kingdoms* of the ninth century Iraqi-Persian author ibn Khurdadhbeh. The relevant passage was first translated into English by A. Sprenger in the *Journal of the Asiatic Society of Bengal*, 1844, p. 519ff, and, translated into French, was later published by C. Babbier de Meynard in *Journal Asiatique*, Sixth Series, vol. V (1865), pp. 512–515. On the Radhanites see J. Jacobs, *Jewish Contribution to Civilization*, 1919, 194–204; L. Rabinowitz, *Jewish Merchant Adventurers*, 1948; C. Cahen, in *REJ*, 123 (1964), pp. 499–505, who questioned some of Ibn Khurdadhbeh's data, and E. Ashtor, *JESHO*, XIII (1970), 182ff, who put to rest Cahen's questioning (pp. 184–186) and stressed the importance of the Radhanites' connections with Spain.

16. M. Lombard was one of the few scholars who viewed Narbonne as the key port of Gaul's shipping both

southward along Catalonia and the Spanish littoral to North Africa and eastward along the shores of Provence and Italy toward the eastern Mediterranean up to Antioch (see his "La route de la Meuse et les relations lointaines de pays mosans entre le VIIIe et le XIe siècle," in *L'Art Mosan*, 1953, pp. 1–28). "It is from Narbonne that the Jewish merchants, the 'Radhanites,' started their itinerary to Egypt and Syria," says Lombard, who also indicates Barcelona as the first major station of Gaul's maritime merchants who travelled southward toward Africa along the Spanish coast (see *ibid.*, p. 18, n. 42, and map following p. 28). In view of Narbonne's Jewish and commercial history and the precarious condition of the coastal cities of Provence in the 9th century (they were frequently raided by Moslem pirates), Narbonne appears as the only safe haven and most likely center for the Radhanites' activity. That it was from this city that the Radhanites departed on their journeys to the East (both through North Africa and the Tyrrhenian sea) was also the view of Cecil Roth (*WHJP, The Dark Ages*, 1966, pp. 23–29, 386; and see map, p. 26).

17. Pirenne, *op. cit.*, p. 258.
18. *Ibid.*, p. 260.
19. On the Carolingians' policy toward the Jews of Narbonne, see Régné's work mentioned above, *loc. cit.*, pp. 242–243.
20. It is from his days that we have the news of Jewish presence in Coimbra; see above, n. 2.
21. C. Sánchez-Albornoz, *España, un Enigma histórico*, 1950, II, p. 177.
22. *Ibid., ibid.*
23. This is why Jews were invited to settle in Seville, Murcia and other cities; see Baer, *History*, I, pp. 111–114.
24. On fortresses in the hands of Jews, see below, p. 1211b.
25. See below, p. 1211ab.
26. "I shall not deny," says Sánchez-Albornoz (*op. cit.*, II, p. 178), "that there were many Jewish craftsmen in the Spanish cities in the Middle Ages," but at all times, he contends, they formed a minority in the "industrious and industrial masses" of those cities. As proof of this contention, he presents evidence from Avila in the early 14th century (*ibid.*)—evidence that cannot contradict our claims, which relate to much earlier periods—i.e., the 11th and 12th centuries.

27. Américo Castro was no doubt close to truth when he asserted that trade, like craftsmanship and money-lending (the "equivalent of banking institutions") were almost the "exclusive *birthright*" of the Jews in Christian Spain in the early period of the Reconquest (italics are mine, B.N.). Castro, however, failed to pay due attention to the changes wrought in Spanish economy in the course of the following centuries and wrongly applied the initial situation to the rest of the medieval era (see his *Structure of Spanish History*, 1954, p. 499).

More balanced is Sánchez-Albornoz' view of the Jewish share in Spain's medieval commerce. "Nobody," he says, "can dispute the mercantile activities of the Jews in the urban centers of the peninsula. But as the decades passed, there increased with intensity the parallel activities of the Christians, who finally came to control international commerce including the Castilian trade" (Sánchez-Albornoz, *España, un Enigma Histórico*, II, p. 179).

28. Which led to Castro's ultimate conclusion: "The history of Spain has risen on the basis of a Jewish economy" (see his *Structure of Spanish History*, 1954, p. 502).

29. W. Roscher, "The Status of the Jews in the Middle Ages Considered from the Standpoint of Commercial Policy," in *Historia Judaica*, VI (1944), p. 26.

30. *Ibid.*
31. Fr. de Bofarull y Sans, *Los Judíos en el territorio de Barcelona (siglos X al XIII),* 1910, pp. 4–22; and see also J. Miret y Sans and M. Schwab, "Documents sur les Juifs Catalans aux XIᵉ, XIIᵉ et XIIIᵉ Siècles," *REJ,* 68 (1914), pp. 49–83, 174–197.
32. Sánchez-Albornoz, *op. cit.,* II, p. 177.
33. *Ibid.*
34. On the rise of Jewish officialdom in Aragon during the reign of Jaime I, see Bofarull, *op. cit.,* pp. 15–22.
35. S. W. Baron, "The Jewish Factor in Medieval Civilization," in AAJR, *Proceedings,* XII (1942), p. 36.
36. This, too, is implied in Baron's emphasis *(ibid.)* that the Jew, because of his religious position, could never expect to be regarded as a native.
37. *Ibid.*
38. *Córtes de León y de Castilla,* I, 1861, p. 99 (§15).
39. M. Colmeiro, *Historia de la Economía Política de España,* I, 1965, p. 473, refers to the "desenfrenada codicia" the Jews allegedly displayed in their money-lending activities, and says that because of it "inventaron fraudes y corrieron el riesgo de perder sus caudales e incurrir en pena, buscando la compensación de estos daños y peligros en prestar con sórdida ganancia" (p. 476).
40. See the testimony of Samuel Zarza, contemporary of the civil war of 1367, about the attacks of Christian townsmen in Segovia, Avila and *many other towns* upon the Jews, in which the latter were robbed of their pledges and notes indicating the debts of Christian borrowers (see appendix to *Shevet Yehudah,* ed. Wiener, p. 132).
41. See below, pp. 159–160.
42. Baer, *History* (Hebrew), p. 120.
43. J. Vicens Vives, *An Economic History of Spain,* transl. F. M. López-Morillas, 1969, p. 284.
44. See below, p. 95; and see Cortes of Alcalá, 1348, §57 (cf. below, p. 1205, n. 29).
45. Baer, *History,* I, p. 361.
46. A. Ballesteros, "Don Yuçaf de Ecija," in *Sefarad,* VI (1946), p. 253.
47. We refer to the grave danger faced by Spanish Jewry in the days of Alfonso XI, when Gonzalo Martínez, commander of his army, urged the king to despoil and destroy all the Jews of Spain (see *Shevet Yehudah,* ed. Baer-Shohat, 1947, pp. 52–55; and Baer's *History,* I, pp. 354–359).

The Castilian Cities

1. See RAH, *Córtes de León y de Castilla* (below: CLC), I, 1861, pp. 104–105 (Cortes of Haro, 1288, §21).
2. *Ibid., ibid.,* p. 104 (§20).
3. Cortes of Valladolid, 1293, §9 (CLC, I, p. 110).
4. *Ibid., ibid.*
5. Cortes of Burgos, 1301, §16 (CLC, I, p. 149); Cortes of Zamora, 1301, §14 (CLC, I, pp. 155–156).
6. Cortes of Medina del Campo, 1305 §§9–10 (CLC, I, pp. 175–176).
7. *Ibid.,* §10, p. 176: *por esta razon se hermava le tierra.*
8. *Ibid., ibid.,* p. 175.
9. Cortes of Valladolid, 1307, §16 (CLC, I, p. 191).
10. Cortes of Palencia, 1313, §7 (CLC, I, p. 224). However, the crux of their request at the Cortes of Medina del Campo, 1305 (§10, p. 175)—i.e., *que los cojan los cogedores que nos (i.e., the cities) pusieremos en las villas*—was not accepted.
11. Cortes of Burgos, 1315, §6 (CLC, I, p. 275).
12. *Ibid., ibid.,:* . . . *e que non ssean cogedores nin recabdadores cauallero ninguno . . . e ni andar en las cogetas clerigos nin judios nin otros omes rreboltosos, e las cogetas que non ssean arrendadas.*
13. Cortes of Carrión, 1317, §8 (CLC, I, p. 305).

14. Cortes of Valladolid, 1322, §18 (CLC, I, p. 342).

15. *Ibid., ibid.*

16. Except for the towns of Extremadura and León which are excluded from the limitation. There, the petition states *(ibid., ibid.)*, the taxes should be gathered by both *omes buenos* and caballeros who reside in the towns and are their citizens *(vecinos)*.

17. Cortes of Madrid, 1329, §37 (CLC, I, pp. 415–416).

18. *Ibid., ibid.*

19. *Ibid.*, p. 416: lo tengo por mio seruicio, saluo en aquellos logares do me lo pidieren. Nor did the King include the *arrendadores* (tax farmers) among those whose services he promised to forgo in the gathering of his revenues *(ibid.)*.

20. Cortes of Burgos, 1367, §11 (CLC, II, p. 151).

21. *Ibid., ibid.*

22. Cortes of Toro, 1371, §2 (CLC, II, p. 203).

23. See below, p. 256.

24. See Baer, II, p. 5 (§12).

25. Cortes of Valladolid, 1293, §4 (CLC, I, p. 131).

26. *Ibid., ibid.*, §3.

27. *Ibid.*

28. Cortes of Valladolid, 1312, §73 (CLC, I, p. 214).

29. Cortes of Palencia, 1313, I, §25 (CLC, I, p. 241).

30. *Ibid., ibid.*, §§2–3 (CLC, I, p. 222).

31. *Ibid.*, §20 (CLC, I, p. 226).

32. *Ibid.*, §§19, 21 (CLC, I, p. 226).

33. Cortes of Valladolid, 1322, §4 (CLC, I, p. 338).

34. *Ibid.*, §§7, 10 (CLC, I, p. 339–340).

35. *Ibid.*, §37 (CLC, I, p. 347).

36. *Ibid.*, §5 (CLC, I, p. 338).

37. *Ibid.*, §6.

38. *Ibid., ibid.*, p. 339.

39. *Ibid., ibid.*

40. Cortes of Burgos, 1367, §6 (CLC, II, pp. 148–149).

41. *Ibid.*, §10 (CLC, II, pp. 150–151).

42. *Ibid., ibid.* (CLC, II, p. 151).

43. Cortes of Toro, 1371, §13 (CLC, II, p. 208).

44. *Ibid.*, §2 (CLC, II, p. 203).

45. Cortes of Burgos, 1377, §11 (CLC, II, pp. 281–282).

46. Baer, II, p. 62 (§81); cf. Amador de los Ríos, *Historia*, I, p. 486; see RAH, *Colección de Fueros y Cartas Pueblas de España*, 1852, pp. 156–157; Fuero de Sevilla, June 15, 1250, Zúñiga, *Annales de Sevilla*, 1677, p. 24; *Memorial Histórico Español*, I, p. 207.

47. Cortes of Palencia, 1286, §15 (CLC, I, p. 99).

48. Cortes of Valladolid, 1351, §68 (CLC, II, p. 40).

49. Cortes of Valladolid, 1385, §16; (CLC, II, pp. 328–329).

50. See Amador de los Ríos, *Historia*, II, p. 621, law 7. According to this law, Jews and Moors could no longer have their internal litigation (both civil and criminal) decided by their own judges, but only by the municipal magistrates. This seems to imply that their conflicts with Christians were not to be treated differently. The law directs the municipal judges to consider, in their treatment of *civil* litigation among Jews (or Moors), the latter's customs and ordinances. No such consideration is suggested for internal *criminal* litigation, or for disputes involving Christians.

51. See for instance, Cortes of Valladolid, 1322, §51 (CLC, I, p. 351); Cortes of Toro, 1371, §8 (CLC, II, p. 207).

52. Cortes of Valladolid, 1322, §48 (CLC, I, p. 350).

53. Cortes of Valladolid, 1293, §22 (CLC, I, p. 114).

54. See *Crónica de Alfonso X*, caps. 23–24 (ed. BAE, vol. 66, pp. 20a–21a).

55. Cortes of Valladolid 1322, §94 (CLC, I, p. 365).

56. Cortes of Zamora, 1301, §21; (CLC, I, p. 157)

57. *Ibid., ibid.*

58. Cortes of Burgos, 1301, §17 (CLC, I, p.

149); Cortes of Zamora, 1301, §5 (CLC, I, p. 152).

59. Cortes of Medina del Campo, 1305, §6 (CLC, I, p. 175); *ibid.*, §5 (I, p. 181); Cortes of Valladolid, 1307, §20 (I, p. 192); Cortes of Valladolid, 1322, §93 (CLC, I, p. 364).

60. Cortes of Valladolid, 1293, §26 (CLC, I, p. 115).

61. Cortes of Palencia, 1286, §2 (CLC, I, p. 95); Cortes of Zamora, 1301, §13 (CLC, I, p. 155).

62. Cortes of Valladolid, 1312, §102; (CLC, I, p. 220).

63. Cortes of Palencia, 1313, §33; (CLC, I, p. 230).

64. Cortes of Burgos, 1373, §1, 15 (CLC, II, pp. 257, 264).

65. Cortes of Zamora, 1432, §30 (CLC, III, p. 141).

66. *Ibid.*, §34, p. 144.

67. The petitioners included in this category of caballeros also *escribanos* and officials of the King, Queen and Prince. See Cortes of Valladolid, 1442, §23 (CLC, III, pp. 422–423); Cortes of Valladolid, 1447, §36 (CLC, III, p. 539); Cortes of Valladolid, 1451, §29 (CLC, III, p. 611 ff).

68. Cortes of Alcalá de Henares, 1348, §2 (CLC, I, pp. 594–595). In this petition the procuradores demanded the cancellation of the usury which Christian borrowers were committed to pay to nobles, clerics and other Christian money-lenders.

Debacle and Transition

1. Pedro I still appears inscrutable to many researchers who find it hard to determine what is true and untrue in the account of his reign written by his opponent, Pedro López de Ayala (*Crónica del rey Don Pedro*, BAE, vol. 66). Ayala's judgments, shared by some subsequent Spanish historians (among them Zurita), have been subjected to a variety of criticisms since the appearance in the 17th century of various apologies for the King, among them that of J. Antonio de Vera y Figueroa, *El Rei Don Pedro defendido*, 1648. Opinions of Pedro have since fluctuated in both directions, with most writers taking a more positive view of Pedro than that expressed in the earlier historiography. The most thorough study of Pedro and his reign, which unequivocally takes the king's side, is that of J. B. Sitges, *Las mujeres del Rey Don Pedro I de Castilla*, 1910. The most recent work on this ruler and his times, which strikes a balance between the conflicting views, is· that of L. Suárez Fernández in *Historia de España*, XIV, pp. 1–158. For the sources on Pedro, see especially Sitges, *op. cit.*, pp. 7–48.

2. Ayala, *op. cit.*, año 1351, .cap. 3 (BAE, 66, p. 412b).

3. *Ibid.*, cap. 20.

4. *Ibid.*, caps. 5 and 6; año 1353, cap. 1.

5. *Ibid.*, año 1350, cap. xiv (p. 410b). Don Samuel is here designated as the "King's *Tesorero Mayor*" (see *ibid.*, año 1353, cap. xvi, p. 434b; año 1354, cap. 38, p. 459b, and the many documents published by Baer, II, pp. 177–180). This does not mean, however, that Don Samuel was not made *Tesorero Mayor* upon his appointment as "Treasurer" in 1350. Thus in a document of October 18, 1353, he is referred to as both "*thesorero mayor* de nuestro sennor el rey" and "*thesorero* de nuestro ... rey" (see Baer, *ibid.*, p. 178).

6. Ayala, *op. cit.*, año 1353, cap. 16, p. 434b (*era muy privado del rey e su consejero*).

7. This is stated explicitly by Ayala in his concluding remarks about Don Samuel's career (*ibid.*, año 1360, cap. XXII, p. 510b), where the King's Chief Treasurer is described as "*su privado e del su consejo.*"

8. The inscription preserved on the walls of the synagogue built by Don Samuel in Toledo in 1357 asserts that "throughout the history of the Exile no one in Israel has reached the height of his influence"

(see photograph of the inscription in F. Cantera, *Sinagogas de Toledo, Segovia y Córdoba*, 1973, following p. 106). This assertion may be taken as factual if one bears in mind the other part of the inscription, according to which Don Samuel's position was not only "higher than that of any other minister," but also such as made him "the ruler of the country" without whose consent "nobody in the Kingdom would dare make a move" *(ibid.)*. However highflown in defining Don Samuel's powers, such pronouncements could not have been made during King Pedro I's reign unless they were substantially true.

9. On the plague in Spain see R. D'Abadal i de Vinyals, in his prologue to the *Historia de España*, XIV, pp. xxvii–xxxv; J. Sobrequés Callicó, "La pesta negra en la península Ibérica," in *Anuario de Estudios Medievales*, 7 (1970–1971), pp. 67–101; A. López de Meneses, "Una consecuencia de la peste negra en Cataluña: el pogrom de 1348," in *Sefarad*, 19 (1959), pp. 92–131, 321–364.

10. See Baer, I, pp. 324–328, 337 (§§230–232, 243), referring to an attack upon the Jews of Barcelona. Bloody assaults occurred in other places, too; see *ibid.*, p. 350, the introduction to the decisions adopted by the representatives of the Jews of Aragon meeting in Barcelona in December 1354. Other documents *(ibid.*, §§238 and 241, pp. 331–332, 334–335) refer to the losses caused by the plague to the Jewish communities in Saragossa and Calatayud. In Saragossa barely a fifth of the community survived *(ibid.*, p. 332).

11. As did the outbreak against the Jews of Seville (1354), stimulated by a charge of Host desecration (see Baer, I, §187).

12. Cortes of Valladolid, 1351, §§31, 32 (CLC, II, p. 19).

13. *Ibid., ibid.*, §1, p. 2.

14. *Ibid.*, §66, p. 39.

15. *Ibid., ibid.*

16. *Ibid.*

17. Ayala, *op. cit.*, año 2, cap. xii (BAE, 66, p.417a).

18. See Cortes of Alcalá de Henares, Feb. 28, 1348, §55. (CLC, I, p. 613).

19. See Cortes of Burgos 1345, §5 (CLC, I, p. 486); Cortes of Alcalá de Henares, 1348, §55 (CLC, I, p. 613); Cortes of León, 1349, §22 (CLC, II, p. 634).

20. Cortes of Valladolid, 1351, §§75, 76 (CLC, II, p. 44).

21. Ayala, *op. cit.*, año 4, caps. xi–xii, pp. 432b–433ab.

22. *Ibid.*, año 6, cap. 5 (p. 450ab).

23. *Ibid.*, cap. 6, pp. 461b–462a.

24. *Ibid.*, p. 462ab.

25. *Ibid.*, p. 462b.

26. This is in fact confirmed by Ayala's statement: "Estaban con el Conde é con el Maestre algunos Caballeros é Escuderos de Toledo que eran sus vasallos, é venian con ellos de Talavera; e otros estaban dentro de la cibdad de Toledo, que magüer non eran sus vasallos, los querian bien, é tenian ese dia su parte é su voluntad" *(ibid.*, p. 462a).

27. *Ibid.*, cap. vii, p. 462b.

28. *Ibid.*, pp. 462b–463a.

29. *Ibid., ibid.* (p. 463a).

30. *Ibid.*, cap. ix, p. 464a.

31. *Ibid.*, cap. x, p. 464a (por quanto fueron en aquel consejo de se alzar la ciudad).

32. Baer, II, 185–186, §190.

33. See Eusebio Ramírez, "Perdón a Cuenca por haber seguido a doña Blanca de Borbón," in *RABM*, 27 (1923), 341–351.

34. Baer, II, p. 186 (§191).

35. Ayala, *op. cit.*, año 7, 1356, cap. ii, p. 470ab.

36. *Ibid., ibid.*, cap. 5, pp. 472b–473a.

37. *Ibid.*, cap. 2, p. 471b.

38. *Ibid.*, año 6, cap.xv, pp. 466b–467a.

39. P. E. Russell, *The English Intervention in Spain and Portugal in the Time of Edward III and Richard II*, 1955, pp. 14–15.

40. Ayala, *op. cit.*, año 1356, cap. viii (p. 474a), cap. x (pp. 474b–475a).

41. See Suárez Fernández, in *Historia de España*, xiv, 1966, pp. 43–46.
42. Ayala, *op. cit.*, año 1356, cap. 8, p. 474.
43. V. Balaguer, *Historia de Cataluña*, III, 1862, pp. 221–222.
44. *Ibid.*, p. 222.
45. Zurita, *Anales de la Corona de Aragón*, II, 1668, lib. IX, 268.
46. Ayala, *op. cit.*, año 1361, caps. i and 2 (p. 511).
47. Zurita, *op. cit.*, II, p. 297f.
48. See *Historia de España*, XIV, p. 39, n. 5.
49. Ayala, *op. cit.*, año 1460, cap. 7, p. 503ab.
50. *Ibid.*, cap 8, p. 504a.
51. *Ibid.*, p. 504a, n. 1.
52. *Ibid., ibid.,*
53. Valuable observations on this subject are found in the works of Julio Valdeón Baruque, *Enrique II de Castilla: La Guerra Civil y la consolidación del Régimen* (1366–1371), 1966, pp. 326–334; *Los Judíos de Castilla y la Revolución Trastamara*, 1968, pp. 37–50.
54. According to Catalina García, *Castilla y León durante los reinados de Pedro I, Enrique II . . .*, I, 1891, p. 227.
55. Amador, *Historia*, II, p. 247.
56. For the Hebrew evidence of his activity in the field of foreign relations, see the synagogue inscription mentioned above (n. 8): "He stands before Kings . . . [representatives of] nations come to him from all parts of the world." For the Portuguese source, see Fernão Lopes, *Cronica de D. Pedro*, ed. G. Macchi, 1966, p. 147–148. According to this *cronica*, Don Samuel came to Portugal in January 1358 to conclude a friendship treaty between Portugal and Castile.
57. See above, p. 94, and Baer, *History*, I, p. 363, on his confiscation of nobiliar estates.
58. See above, n. 8.
59. On the rivalry between Joseph Nasi and Samuel Aben Huacar (ben Wakar), see A. Ballesteros, "Don Juçaf de Écija," in *Sefarad*, VI, pp. 274–279.
60. See the *Compendio*—i.e., the inter-

polation in the *Sumario de los Reyes de España*, ed. Eugenio de Llaguno Amirola, 1781, pp. 72b–73a; Amador, *Historia*, II, pp. 244–245. A different version of the same story is found in the *Continuación de la Crónica de España* (of Rodrigo Jiménez de Rada) by Gonzalo de Hinojosa (and his successor or successors, whose contribution is commonly entitled *La Cuarta Crónica General*), *CODOIN*, 106 (1893), pp. 92–93.
61. Ayala, *op. cit.*, año 1360, cap. xxii, p. 510b.
62. See *ibid.*, cap. XVIII, pp. 507b–508b, on the imprisonment of the family of the condemned Gómez Carrillo.
63. Amador, *Historia*, II, pp. 244–245.
64. This is indicated in the "Cuarta Crónica General," *loc. cit.*, p. 92: *estando el rey en Toledo, quejauase que estaua muy gastado de las guerras que en su tiempo avia avido.*
65. This appears to be another true item in the *Sumario*'s narrative which clearly reflects antisemitic bias. It is unlikely that this kind of a story involving accusations of Jews against a Jew (contrasting with the common antisemitic notion that the Jews were united against Christians) would be produced out of thin air. Similarly, the account of Don Samuel's behavior under torture, attesting his courage and self-respect, could not have been invented.
66. Ayala, *op. cit.*, año 1360, cap. 22, p. 510b.
67. According to the *Cuarta Crónica General*, the King was distressed by Don Samuel's death (*CODOIN*, 106, p. 93: y al rey pesóle mucho dello desque lo sopo).
68. Baer, *History*, I, p. 364.
69. Ayala, *op. cit.*, año 1360, cap. 22, p. 510b.
70. Sitges, *op. cit.*, pp. 137, 201.
71. Russell, *op. cit.*, p.
72. Ayala, *op. cit.*, año 1361, cap. 2, p. 511b and cap. 5, p. 513b.

73. See the text of the treaty in Sitges, *op. cit.*, pp. 240–241.
74. *Ibid.*, p. 249.
75. Zurita, *Anales de Aragón*, lib. IX, cap. 43; cf. Sitges, *op. cit.*, p. 265.
76. See on this Russell, *op. cit.*, p. 28.
77. Balaguer, *op. cit.*, III, p. 234 (on the basis of Zurita, *Anales*, lib. ix, cap. 44).
78. Balaguer, *op. cit.*, III, p. 235.
79. Samuel Zarza, appendix to *Schevet Jehuda*, ed. Wiener, 1855, p. 131.
80. Russell, *op. cit.*, p. 51.
81. In Ayala, *op. cit.*, año 1366, cap. 7, p. 541a; cf. T. López Mata, "Morería y Judería," *loc. cit.*, p. 335; F. Cantera, *op. cit.*, p. 18; *id.*, *Sefarad*, xii (1952), p. 77.
82. *Ibid.*, Samuel Zarza, *loc. cit.*, p. 131.
83. *Ibid.*
84. See Ayala, *op. cit.*, año 1366, cap. 8, p. 542a; cf. Graetz, *Geschichte*, VII, 367f.
85. Ayala, *op. cit.*, año 1366, cap. 9, p. 542b; cap. 14 p. 545a; año 1367, cap. 27, p. 573b.
86. Cortes of Burgos, 1317, §10 (CLC, II, pp. 150–151).
87. *Ibid.*, §3 (CLC, II, p. 146).
88. *Ibid.*, §2 (CLC, II, pp. 145–146).
89. See Baer, II, p. 205 (§215), and Samuel Zarza, *loc. cit.*, p. 131.
90. *Ibid.*, *ibid.*
91. See below, p. 1208, n. 11.
92. See Ayala, *op. cit.*, año 1367, cap. XXIII, pp. 570b–571b.
93. See Russell, *op. cit.*, pp. 122–137.
94. Ayala, *op. cit.*, año 1367, cap. 35, p. 578b.
95. See Enrique's order of June 6, 1369 for the sale of Toledo's Jews into slavery in Baer, II, pp. 201–203 (§210), and Menaḥem ben Zerah, *Zēdah la-Derekh*, introduction. Toledo surrendered by the end of April, 1369, six weeks after the King's murder and almost a year after it was besieged.
96. Samuel Zarza, *loc. cit.*, p. 132.
97. Baer, I, p. 397.
98. Cortes of Toro, 1371, §2 (CLC, II, p. 203).
99. Cortes of Burgos, 1377, §1 (CLC, II, pp. 275–276). Enrique reduced their debts

by a third and gave them short moratoria for payment of the rest; he also forbade the Jews to lend money at interest. See *ibid.*, §2 (CLC, II, pp. 276–277).
100. *Ibid.*, §11 (CLC, II, pp. 281–282); §10 (CLC, II, p. 281).
101. Ayala, *Crónica de Juan I*, año I, cap. 3; BAE, 66, p. 66a; Amador, *Historia*, II, pp. 333–336; Catalina García, *op. cit.*, II, p. 211, n. 1.
102. Ayala, *Crónica de Juan I*, año I, cap. 3, p. 66a.
103. *Ibid.*, p. 66b. The *Crónica Abreviada* gives the names of two of these conspirators: Don Zuleman and Don Zag (*ibid.*, n. 2) and the *Cuarta Crónica General* mentions a third associate: Don Mayr (*CODOIN*, 106, p. 105).
104. Ayala, *Crónica de Juan I*, año I, cap. 3, p. 66b.
105. Cortes of Soria, September 3, §2 (CLC, II, pp. 311–312); Lindo, *op. cit.*, p. 162.
106. Cortes of Soria, September 18, §23 (CLC, II, p. 310).
107. Baer, *History*, II, pp. 367, 450 (n. 53).
108. Alami, *Iggeret Musar*, ed. Habermann, 1946, p. 44.
109. *Ibid.*, p. 45.
110. *Ibid.*
111. The title "justiciero" was suggested by Philip II; see Suárez Fernández, in *Historia de España*, XIV, p. 39, n. 2.

Ferrán Martínez

1. Among the sources referring to him with these titles, see those published by J. Amador de los Ríos in appendix XI to volume II of his *Historia*, p. 579.
2. See Paul of Burgos, *Scrutinium Scripturarum*, 1591, p. 523.
3. See above, pp. 117–120.
4. See the order of Enrique II, dated August 25, 1378, published by Amador, *Historia*, II, p. 581 (appendix XI).
5. *Ibid.*, p. 582.

6. *Ibid.*, p. 581. The *albala* of August 25, 1378 was therefore the second order that the King directed to Martínez on the same matter. And see the later instruction of Juan I which refers to the *albalas* (in the plural) addressed by Enrique II to Martínez (*ibid.*, p. 584).

7. *Ibid.*, pp. 582–583.

8. *Ibid., ibid.*

9. See above, pp. 121–122.

10. See *Ordenamiento sobre Judíos hecho en las Cortes de Soria*, Sept. 3, 1380, §2 (CLC, II, pp. 311–312).

11. *Cortes of Soria*, Sept. 23, 1380, §23 (CLC, II, p. 310).

12. See the *albala* of Juan I, dated March 3, 1382, in Amador, *Historia*, II, p. 583.

13. See Juan I's *albala*, in Amador, *Historia*, II, pp. 583–584.

14. *Ibid., ibid.*, p. 584.

15. *Ibid.*, p. 585.

16. CLC, II, p. 322 (§3).

17. *Ibid.*, p. 325 (§9). It is noteworthy that while the King assured Cortes that no Jew or Moor would serve as treasurer to the King or any member of the royal family, he failed to respond to the request that Jews and Moors be excluded from the tax-farming system.

18. *Ibid.*, p. 326 (§10).

19. Amador, *Historia*, II, pp. 588–589.

20. *Ibid.*, p. 580.

21. *Ibid.*, p. 586–589.

22. Concerning the number of synagogues in Seville, see my *Marranos of Spain*, 1973², p. 259.

23. See Amador, *Historia*, II, p. 589.

24. See Zúñiga, *Annales eclesiásticos y seculares de Sevilla*, 1677, lib. 8, año 1388, p. 249a.

25. Amador, *Historia*, II, p. 345.

26. See the archbishop's sentence against Martínez published by Amador, *op. cit.*, II, pp. 592–593 (appendix XIII).

27. *Ibid.* p. 593.

28. *Ibid., ibid.*

29. *Ibid.*, pp. 593–594.

30. See the text of Martínez' order in Amador, *op. cit.*, II, p. 613 (appendix

XVII), and the letter of Castile's Regency to the Dean and Chapter of the Church of Seville dated December 2, 1390, published by Lea in *American Historical Review*, I (1895), pp. 220–222.

31. See *ibid., ibid.*, p. 221 (*que estan en punto de se dispoblar et yr et fuir de los mis reynos a morar et a vebir a otrtas partes*).

32. See *ibid.*, p. 222.

33. See the record of the meeting of the chapter's leadership, published by Lea in the *American Historical Review*, I (1895), pp. 222–223.

34. *Ibid.*, pp. 223–225.

35. Zúñiga, *op. cit.*, año 1391, p. 252; *Cuarta Crónica General*, CODOIN, 106, p. 105.

36. *Ibid., ibid.*

37. *Crónica de Enrique III*, cap. 21 (BAE, v. 68, p. 177b).

38. The prohibition on converting Jews by force was part of Church official doctrine since Gregory I and Isidore of Seville. See on this above, p. 37 and n. 30.

39. Ayala, *op. cit.*, p. 177b.

40. The date of the Sevillian outbreak is indicated by two Hebrew sources: Crescas' letter to the Jews of Avignon (printed by Wiener in his edition of *Schevet Jehuda*, 1855, p. 129) and the lament published by Schirmann (in *Kobez al Jad*, 1939, p. 66). Both state that the riots began on the first of Tamuz (*rosh hodesh* Tamuz, *rosh* Tamuz)—i.e., on June 4, 1391.

41. Amador, *op. cit.*, II, p. 358.

42. On the number of Sevillian Jews converted during the riots, see my *Marranos of Spain*, 1973², pp. 255–270.

43. See Zúñiga, *op. cit.*, p. 252.

44. Amador, *op. cit.*, II, p. 359.

45. See the statement quoted by Amador (without indicating source), *ibid.*, p. 355; and see the letter sent by Enrique III's Regency to Burgos on June 16 (i.e., twelve days after the riots in Seville) in which Cordova is mentioned together

with Seville among the places attacked by Martínez' followers; see Baer, II, p. 232 (§24).

46. *Cuarta Crónica General, CODOIN,* 106, p. 105.

47. Amador, *op. cit.,* II, p. 362.

48. See Rafael Ramírez de Arellano, "Matanza de Judíos en Córdoba. 1391" in RAH, *Boletín,* xxxviii (1901), p. 297; and see Ramírez de Arellano and Díaz de Morales, *Historia de Córdoba,* IV, 1919, pp. 143–145.

49. Amador, *op. cit.,* II, 362.

50. On the fate of the Toledan Jews attacked during the riots, see the dirge published by C. Roth in *JQR,* xxxix (1948), 129ff, and the lament published by S. Bernstein in *Sinai,* xxix (1951). According to Crescas, the Toledan rabbis "sanctified the Name together with their sons and students" (*loc. cit.,* p. 129). The dirge published by Roth likewise stresses the martyrdom undergone by the leaders of the community. Otherwise, it refers to an indefinite (possibly limited) number of "pious" Jews who fell into the hands of the pogromists. On the basis of this, Roth remarked: "Perhaps, after all, these were the only martyrs" (*loc. cit.,* p. 127, n. 11a). But the lament on the suffering of Toledo's Jews in 1391 (published in *Sinai,* 29, pp. 209–214) suggests that the martyred represented a considerable part of Toledan Jewry. "Some of them," it says, "were killed by the sword; some were thrown into the river; some were taken captive to be sold as slaves, while others were forcibly converted." From this description one may gather that the forced converts did not constitute the majority of the community's losses, though their number may well have been large. This is also indicated by Crescas ("Letter to the Jews of Avignon" cited above, n. 40) who says: "many" of Toledo's Jews were converted.

51. According to Amador, *op. cit.,* II, 378, n. 1 (without an indication of the source).

52. Concerning Madrid, see Fidel Fita, in RAH, *Boletín,* VIII (1886), p. 443–444; the officials of this town could still speak of *el destruymiento e muerte e robo que se fizo de la aljama de la dicha villa* (*ibid.,* p. 451). Of those who refused to convert, some were killed, but the overwhelming majority were no doubt baptized. Hence the summary account that *"todos los judios desta dicha villa de Madrid se bolvieron christianos"* (*ibid.,* p. 455). And see the dirge on the victims of 1391 published by J. Schirmann in *Kobez al Jad,* New Series, vol. III-i (1939), p. 66.

53. This is apparent from the order issued on September 9, 1391 by the Council of Burgos forbidding the Jews to "give, sell, lend, or barter arms" to anyone who might come to the city to attend the Cortes which was about to convene there; and see Anselmo Salva, *Las Cortes de 1392 en Burgos,* 1891, pp. 56, 61.

54. See Baer I, p. 655: *Car en tan enorme crim tota cuyta es triga, e tota severitat es leniment e dolçor de justicia.*

55. See F. Danvila, "El robo de la judería de Valencia en 1391," in RAH, *Boletín,* VIII (1886), pp. 369–370.

56. *Ibid.,* p. 371.

57. *Ibid.,* p. 374.

58. *Ibid.,* p. 372.

59. *Ibid.,* pp. 372–373; cf. the Acts of the City Council's session of July 10, 1391, *ibid.,* p. 21, no. 23.

60. *Ibid.,* pp. 373–374.

61. See Caspar Escolano, *Decada primera de la historia de Valencia,* 1610, I, lib. 5, cap. 10, col. 958; cf. Crescas' letter to the Jews of Avignon, *loc. cit.,* p. 128; and see my *Marranos of Spain,* 1973², p. 241.

62. F. Fita, "Estrago de las juderías catalanas," in RAH, *Boletín,* XVI (1890), p. 439.

63. *Ibid.,* pp. 437–438.

64. *Ibid.,* p. 438.

65. *Ibid.,* p. 440; cf. Villaneuva, *Viaje literario,* XVIII, pp. 21–22.
66. *Boletín,* XVI, p. 438.
67. *Ibid.,* p. 441.
68. *Ibid.,* p. 438.
69. See Crescas' letter to the Jews of Avignon about the riots of 1391, *loc. cit.,* p. 128. Crescas says there: "The state leader[s] were not involved in the crime; they did everything in their power to save them [the attacked Jews]; they supported them with bread and water and endeavored to inflict severe punishment on the criminals."
70. Baer, I, pp. 699–700.
71. *Ibid., ibid.*
72. *Ibid., ibid.*
73. J. Parkes (*The Jew in the Medieval Community,* 1930, p. 70) saw the uniqueness of the Jewish conduct in its "rarely equalled" manifestation of the "power of the spirit over the weakness of the flesh." This "power," however, was displayed many times by individuals and groups committed to some cause. As we see it, the uniqueness of the Jews' behavior in the Rhineland lay in the particular motives that inspired it.

　Those motives did not spring from rigid adherence to Jewish law or from the kind of excessive zeal that makes men fanatics. Had fanaticism determined the Rhineland Jews' stand, they would have viewed any convert under duress as a weakling or traitor deserving contempt. But this was not their attitude. When a group of Jews in Worms were converted under circumstances that could be defined as only semi-compulsory, the unconverted Jews comforted and aided them, assuring them support "even unto death." This shows that they considered forced conversion "humanly" understandable—and even tolerable, despite the contrary directive of behavior that Jewish law dictated on this issue.

Nevertheless, their overwhelming majority preferred suicide to baptism. Hence, what they held "tolerable" for others was unendurable for themselves. Publicly to declare their true faith false meant to them not only to offend and profane it, but also to attest—against their own conviction—that life as such was worthier in their eyes than the honor of their divine heritage. Thus, from their standpoint, forced conversion represented so base and shameful an act that they could not possibly go through with it; and hence their suicide resulted, above all, from a moral *non-possumus* of the highest order.

74. See on this my *Marranos of Spain,* pp. 13–15.
75. I find it hard to accept R. Chazan's view (in his *European Jewry and the First Crusade,* 1987) that the "goal of the Crusaders was *certainly* not plunder" (p. 68), that their "violence was inspired *primarily* by ideas and ideals" (p. 64), and that "of the two alternative modes of destroying Judaism [i.e., death and conversion], the crusaders *much* preferred conversion" (pp. 72, 100; emphases added). There are testimonies in which deeds speak louder than words, although I find no definite statements contradicting what I intend to say. Thus the ghastly unending tortures inflicted by the crusaders on the wounded and the dying reflect more a wild and bestial hatred than the inspiration of ideas and ideals, while the stripping of the victims in all places of their clothes shows an insatiable thirst for plunder which would not give up the slightest spoil. The Jews of the Rhineland knew from the outset that they could save their lives through conversion, but this does not mean that the Jews' conversion was the crusaders' main interest. Had conversion been their "*much* preferred" aim, they would not

have failed to agitate for it in some impressive manner (a failure noticed by Parkes, *op. cit.*, p. 67), or at least to proclaim their demand for conversion prior to launching their major attacks. We have no evidence, however, of such proclamations in Worms or Mainz, or in smaller places such as Neus, or Xanten, or Eller. In Mehr the effort to convert the Jews was made by the mayor and in Trier by the bishop. In Speyer a warning appears to have been issued, but it may be ascribed to some of the townsmen who, while joining the crusaders, must have feared their upright bishop, and sought to "justify" their intended crimes by a display of some religious motive (later the bishop cut off the hands of burghers found guilty of pogromizing the Jews of Speyer).

The above, I should add, fits to a great extent the desciption of the pogromists of 1096 as given by Albert of Aachen (see his *Historia hierosolymitana* in RHCHO, IV, 1879, pp. 289–295, especially cap. xxix: *pecuniae avaritia magis quam pro justitia Dei gravi caede mactaverant*), except that Albert fails to mention the extreme *hatred* for the Jews which largely motivated the pogromists' behavior.

76. See the King's letter to his brother, Duke Martín, in Baer, I, § 409, p. 656.

77. See the royal order to the governor of Roussillon of Sept. 5, 1391 in Baer, I, p. 683, §432.

78. Baer, *History*, II, pp. 102–103.

79. See F. Fita, in RAH, *Boletín*, XVI (1890), p. 435, and see *ibid.*, p. 441 (the report of Guillermo Mascaró).

80. See Julián de Chía, *Bandos y Bandoleros in Gerona*, I, 1888, p. 184; and cf. E. C. Girbal, *Los Judíos de Gerona*, 1870, p. 25.

81. See Ramírez de Arellano, in RAH, *Boletín*, XXXVIII (1901), p. 297.

82. Danvila, "El robo de la judería de Valencia," *loc. cit.*, p. 372.

83. Zúñiga, *op. cit.*, p. 252a.

Paul of Burgos

1. This was also how he designated himself shortly after his conversion. See the conclusion of his letter to Lorki in *Ozar Nechmad*, II (1857), p. 21.

2. His approximate date of birth may be established by the epitaph inscribed on his sepulcher stating that he died on August 29, 1435 at the age of 83 (aetatis vero suae LXXXIII); see *España Sagrada*, XXVI, 1771, p. 387. On his family origin and conditions, see Christophorus Sanctotis, "Vita D. D. Pauli Episcopi Burgensis," published as introduction to a new edition of Paul's *Scrutinium Scripturarum*, 1591, p. 14a; and see also Luciano Serrano, *Los Conversos D. Pablo de Santa María y D. Alfonso de Cartegena*, 1942, pp. 9–10; and F. Cantera Burgos, *Alvar García de Santa María*, 1952, pp. 287–288. For his literary work, see Amador, *Historia crítica de la literatura española*, V (1865), pp. 333–337; *id.*, *Estudios*, pp. 337–355, and Manuel Martínez Añibarro, *Intento de un Diccionario Biográfico y Bibliográfico de autores de la Provincia de Burgos*, 1889, pp. 470–489.

3. According to Bonet Bongiorn, one of Paul's converts to Christianity, Paul distinguished himself in various fields of science, especially in astronomy and geometry, to which he seems to have made some original contributions (see Profiat Duran's epistle, "Don't be like thy Fathers," ms. 8° 757 of the National and University Library, Jerusalem, edited by A. Posnanski, f. 71). Besides these disciplines and philosophy, he studied Latin and Castilian, in both of which (judging by his writings) he attained a high degree of knowledge. It is noteworthy that compared to his Latin and Castilian works which are notable for their fluency and clarity, his two extant Hebrew pieces are written in a cumbersome, profuse and unnatural style. See especially his letter to Meir Alguades, published by A. Neubauer in

Israelitische Letterbode, X (1884–1885), p. 81ff and by I. Abrahams in *JQR,* XII (1900), p. 258ff.

4. See V. J. Antist, *Vida de San Vicente Ferrer,* 1575, cap. xix, p. 174 (in the edition cited below, n. 49); and Sanctotis, *loc. cit.,* p. 21ab.

5. From Lorki's expectation that Paul write a "new work" (and not "*a* work") on the Christian-Jewish controversy (see L. Landau, *Das apologetische Schreiben des Josua Lorki an den Abtrünnigen Don Salomon ha-Lewi,* 1906, p. 18) Cantera concluded that Paul had written several tracts in refutation of Christianity (see his "La conversión del célebre talmudista Salomón Levi," in *Boletín de la biblioteca Menéndez Pelayo,* XV [1933], p. 425, n.1). The conclusion appears self-evident. Nevertheless, it is hard to believe that if Paul had produced even one work in defense of Judaism, Lorki would have failed to cite it in his elaborate argument against Paul's conversion. It is more likely therefore that by "a new work" Lorki meant a composition of a *new kind* that would differ from all other polemical writings in its more thorough treatment of the problems involved.

6. On the Jewish community in Burgos of the 14th century both before and after the riots of 1391, see López Mata, "Morería y Judería," in RAH, *Boletín,* 129 (1951), pp. 357–377; Cantera, *Alvar García,* pp. 16–22; *id.,* "La Judería de Burgos," in *Sefarad,* XII (1952), pp. 105–124; L. Serrano, *op. cit.,* pp. 11–12.

7. See on this Ayala, *Crónica de Don Juan I de Castilla,* año 1388, cap. 2 (BAE 68, pp. 118a–120b), and Cantera, *Alvar García,* p. 292ff. Baer (*History,* II, p. 437, n. 38) disagrees with Cantera's reading of the Hebrew letters h.r.e.i.n.s.i (in Paul's letter to Alguades) as *arrehenes* (or *rehenes*), which would indicate that he was one of the *arrehenes* (hostages)

referred to by Ayala (*ibid.,* pp. 119a and 120a). According to Baer, Paul was a member of a diplomatic mission sent by the King of Castile to Aquitaine to take part in the negotiations for a truce between England and France, Castile's ally. However, Paul's statement (in the same letter) that he was kept in a "pit with the other prisoners of the King" (see *JQR,* XII, [1900], p. 258) can in no way refer to a member of such a mission, while it may allude (in Paul's highfalutin Hebrew style) to a hostage who, though not treated as an ordinary prisoner, was watched and denied complete freedom of movement.

8. This is suggested by Lorki's remark that, after becoming a functionary of the King, Paul provided for himself a "carriage, horses, and a retinue prepared to fulfill his wishes" (see Landau, *op. cit.,* p. 2).

9. Paul speaks there of the religious reasons that moved him and his "colleagues" *(haveray)* to convert to Christianity (see *ibid.,* p. 19; and cf. *Ozar Nechmad,* II, p. 5).

10. See the dirge on the losses the Jews suffered as a result of the catastrophe of 1391 (published by Schirmann in *Kobez al Jad,* New Series, III-i [1939], p. 67), in which the leaders of the community of Burgos are described not only as "erring" *(to'im)* but also as "misleading" *(mat'im)*—in fact, as "enemies of the Jewish people" who, like Jeroboam of old, drove the community into the path of betrayal. As for the rabbi of Burgos (namely, Paul), he is described not only as an "enemy," but as one who smote the community hardest *(ve-harav hoveli),* and the simile of Jeroboam must have been applied especially to him. From all this we may conclude that the move toward Christianity by Paul and the other notables *(sarim)* was accompanied by an active campaign for conversion aimed at convincing the faithful Jews

that what appeared to them as a gross misfortune was actually a blessing in disguise.

11. That most Burgensian Jews opposed the trend toward conversion is evident from the fact that so many of them were ready, while fleeing the pogromists, to leave behind them most of their possessions and pay large sums of money to Christian neighbors who provided them shelter from the rioters. See below, n. 14.

12. Relying on Sanctotis (*loc. cit.*, p. 24b), Cantera, "La conversión," *loc. cit.*, p. 19, and L. Serrano (*op. cit.*, p. 21) believed that Paul converted on July 21, 1390. But Graetz (*Geschichte*, viii, [1890], p. 78, n. 2) has demonstrated, on the basis of Lorki's letter, that Paul converted during the period of the riots. Baer believed that the change of date was made unintentionally, since "various authors used to ascribe the riots to 1390 instead of 1391" (*History*, II, p. 474, n. 40). It can hardly be doubted, however, that Paul and his family chose to show in their records that their conversion took place in 1390 (a year before the riots), thereby seeking to prove that they should not be counted among the forced converts of 1391. Sanctotis must have had such records before him.

13. No source is available for the date of the pogrom in Burgos. It may be assumed, however, that Amador de los Ríos who stated unreservedly that the community of Burgos was attacked on August 12 (see above, p. 1200, n. 51) did so on the basis of some reliable source. That the assault on the Jews of Burgos resulted in large-scale destruction is indicated by Ayala's inclusion of the Burgos community among the aljamas reduced to shambles by the riots (*Crónica de Enrique III*, año 1, cap. 5; ed. BAE 68, p. 167a) and by King Enrique's letters to the Council of Burgos dated July 20 and 30, 1392 (see López Mata,

"Morería y Judería," *loc. cit.*, pp. 361–365).

14. See Ayala, *Crónica de Enrique III*, año 1391, cap. 5 (p. 167ab), where he attributes the extreme poverty of the unconverted Jews in various cities (including Burgos) to the "great gifts they gave the señores who sheltered them in that extreme tribulation."

15. According to L. Serrano (*op. cit.*, p. 29), he was graduated as "doctor." However, according to Serrano's source (Feret, *La faculté de Théologie de Paris*, III, p. 8), Paul gained upon his graduation the title of "master." This is also what is stated by his biographer Sanctotis in his introduction to Paul's *Scrutinium*, ed. 1591, p. 31a, and on the title page of that edition.

16. See L. Serrano, *op. cit.*, p. 31.

17. See *ibid.*, and *España Sagrada*, XXVI, p. 376a; and cf. Sanctotis, *loc. cit.*, pp. 31–32.

18. See on this my *Marranos of Spain*, 1973², pp. 223–224.

19. See Profiat Duran's Epistle, "Don't be like thy Fathers", *loc. cit.*, f. 71.

20. Judging by the date of Duran's epistle (see my *Marranos of Spain*, pp. 225–226).

21. Duran's Epistle, *loc. cit.*, f. 72.

22. *Generaciones y Semblanzas*, ed. Domínguez Bordona, 1954, p. 89.

23. See Duran's Epistle, in P. M. Heilpern's ed. of *Even Bohan*, II, 1946, p. 24, and my remarks on this point in my *Marranos of Spain*, 1973², p. 225.

24. See L. Serrano, *op. cit.*, p. 42, and L. Suárez Fernández, *Castilla, el cisma y la crisis conciliar (1378–1440)*, 1960, p. 47.

25. See *ibid.*, p. 48.

26. See Ayala, *Crónica de Enrique III*, cap. 20 (pp. 265b, 266b).

27. Suárez Fernández, *op. cit.*, p. 64.

28. For the long list of Jewish functionaries and officials in Enrique III's financial administration, see Baer, II, pp. 257–259.

29. See Cortes of Alcalá de Henares, 1348, §57 (CLC, I, pp. 532–534); Cortes of Burgos, 1377, §2 (CLC, II, pp. 276–277).

30. See Baer, II, pp. 111–112, §121.

31. Cortes of Valladolid, 1405, §1 (CLC, II, p. 547).

32. Cortes of Burgos, 1367, §2 (CLC, I, p. 532).

33. Cortes of Burgos, 1367, §2 (CLC, II, p. 146), and Cortes of Burgos, 1377, §1 (CLC, II, pp. 275–276).

34. Cortes of Valladolid, 1385, §10 (CLC, II, pp. 326).

35. Cortes of Valladolid, 1405, §7 (CLC, II, pp. 550–551).

36. *Ibid., ibid.,* p. 551.

37. *Ibid.,* §4 (CLC, II, p. 549).

38. *Ibid., ibid.,* §5 (CLC, II, pp. 549–550).

39. It is included in the *Siete Partidas* (lib. VII, tit. 24, law 11), which was adopted as the country's law in 1348.

40. Cortes of Valladolid, 1405, §9 (CLC, II, pp. 552–553).

41. See Baer, II, pp. 260–261; English translation of the same law in E. H. Lindo, *The History of the Jews of Spain and Portugal,* 1848, pp. 186–188.

42. See *ibid.,* and Baer, II, p. 261.

43. See Serrano, *op. cit.,* p. 54; Sebastián Puig y Puig, *Pedro de Luna,* 1920, pp. 175–187; Suárez Fernández, *op. cit.,* p. 64.

44. See L. Serrano, *op. cit.,* p. 55.

45. See Baer, II, p. 261 (§273), at the conclusion of the decree.

46. Espina, *Fortalitium Fidei,* lib. 3, De bello judeorum, mirabile undecimum, ff. 223ʳ–223ᵛ; Colmenares, *Historia de Segovia,* 1640, año 1410, cap. 28, §§VI, VII, VIII, especially p. 324a (new critical and annotated edition: I, 1969, pp. 557–559).

47. *Ibid., ibid.*

48. This may be gathered from Paul's letter to Don Meir, which reflects an intimate association (see above, note 7).

49. Of the literature dealing with Vicente Ferrer, mention must be made of H. Fages, *Histoire de Saint Vincent Ferrier,* 1892–1894, and *Biografía y Escritos de San Vicente Ferrer,* ed. J. M. de Garganta and V. Forcada, 1956. See also B. Llorca, "San Vicente Ferrer y su labor en la conversión de los Judíos," in *Razón y Fe,* CLII (1955), pp. 277–296, and F. Vendrell, "La actividad proselitista de san Vicente Ferrer durante el reinado de Fernando I de Aragon," in *Sefarad,* XIII (1953), pp. 87–104.

50. On his schooling see V. J. Antist, *Vida de San Vicente Ferrer,* cap. 2, in *Biografía y Escritos* (cited above, n. 49), pp. 102–106.

51. See J. M. Millas, "San Vicente Ferrer y el antisemitismo," in *Sefarad,* x (1950), pp. 182–184, and R. Chabas, in RABM, VIII (1903), p. 111ff.

52. See Baer, II, p. 62, §81.

53. See RAH, *Colección de fueros y cartas-pueblas de España,* 1852, pp. 156–157.

54. See Cortes of Valladolid, 1351, §31 (CLC, II, p. 19); cf. Baer, II, §181.

55. See González-Tejada, III, p. 617 (Council of Palencia, canon 5).

56. *Ibid., ibid.*

57. *Ibid.,* p. 610.

58. Amador, *Historia,* I, pp. 425–426.

59. *Crónica de Juan II,* año 1411, cap. vii, p. 336a; año 1410, cap. 45, pp. 333b–334a.

60. *Ibid.,* año 1411, cap. ix, p. 336b.

61. *Crónica de Juan II,* año 1411, cap. xxii, p. 340ab.

62. Amador, *op. cit.,* II, pp. 494–496.

63. Graetz, *Geschichte,* viii (1890), p. 108.

64. Lea, *History,* I, pp. 78–79.

65. Baer, *History,* II, p. 166.

66. *Ibid.,* p. 169.

67. J. Parkes, *The Jews in the Medieval Community,* 1938, p. 135.

68. L. Serrano, *op. cit.,* p. 58.

69. Baer, II, p. 265 (law 1).

70. *Ibid., ibid.*

71. *Ibid.,* p. 266.

72. *Ibid., ibid.* (law 5).

73. *Ibid.,* p. 269 (law 20).

74. *Ibid.*, pp. 265, 266, 269 (laws 2, 6, and 20).

75. *Ibid.*, p. 265 (law 2). Baer believed that the law of 1412 merely forbade Jewish physicians, surgeons and druggists to serve *Christians*, but the law does not contain this specification. It plainly says that no Jew or Moor was entitled to act as apothecary, etc. (nin algun judio o judia nin moro nin mora no sean especieros nin boticarios nin cirugianos nin fisycos).

76. *Ibid.*, p. 267 (law 10).

77. *Ibid.*, p. 266 (law 4); Lindo includes this prohibition in law 5 (*op. cit.* p. 197).

78. Cf. the laws of the Council of Elvira (above, p. 29 and p. 1185, n. 3.).

79. Baer, II, p. 269 (law 18).

80. *Ibid.*, p. 268 (law 11).

81. *Ibid.*, p. 269 (law 19: No Jew or Moor shall hire any Christian to cultivate or work on their lands, vineyards, houses or other buildings).

82. See above, p. 1205, n. 31.

83. Baer, II, p. 267 (law 9).

84. *Ibid.*, p. 264.

85. *Ibid.*, p. 270.

86. *Ibid.*, pp. 266–267 (law 7).

87. The same effect was noted in Aragon (see Manuel Serrano y Sanz, *Orígenes de la dominación Española en America*, 1913, p. 68), although the laws issued there by Fernando were somewhat less severe.

　　In a subsequent discussion of the laws of 1412, Lea (*History*, I, pp. 116–117) said that these laws built a "wall" around the Jews and Moors from which they could escape only through baptism. In the area surrounded by that wall, however, Lea assumed that survival was possible—an assumption that seems to us most questionable, especially with respect to the Jews.

88. *Sefer Yuhasin*, ed. Filipowski, p. 225b.

89. Amador, *Historia*, II, p. 493.

90. Graetz, *op. cit.*, VIII (1890), p. 108; Lea,

History, I, p. 116. Lea, in fact, believed that this entire legislation was drawn up by Paul.

91. L. Serrano, *op. cit.*, p. 57.

92. Cantera, *Alvar García*, p. 308.

93. *Ibid.*, p. 238.

94. *Crónica de Juan II*, año 1411, cap. 22 (BAE 68, p. 340ab).

95. See Baer, II, p. 270.

96. See above, pp. 194, 197.

97. Completed in 1434, it first appeared in print in 1470; and see below, pp. 206, 1207, n. 127.

98. See *Scrutinium*, 1591, distinctio VI, cap. 1, ff. 495a–498a.

99. *Ibid.*, *ibid.*, f. 532a. Evidence of this desire of the Jews is seen by Paul in the dominant position assumed by Samuel Halevi under Pedro the Cruel.

100. *Ibid.*, f. 523b; Paul identifies Martínez as "quidam Diaconus" of the Metropolitan Church of Seville.

101. *Ibid.*, f. 524b.

102. *Ibid.*, *ibid.*

103. *Ibid.*, f. 523b–524b.

104. *Ibid.*, f. 49a.

105. See Fages, *op. cit.*, pp. 303–348.

106. *Ibid.*, p. 296: a la fin d'un sermon de jour de Saint Antoine, il pouvait dire: "Sachez une bonne nouvelle: les juifs et les moures se convertisse tous a Valladolid."

107. For the list of the communities in north-west Castile that suffered great losses as a result of the conversions, see the lament published by Graetz, *Geshichte*, VIII (1890), pp. 110–111, n. 2.

108. On the severity of the enforcement, see *ibid.*, p. 111 *(ve-hehemiru ad kĕmiru)*, and Alami's statements cited below in Appendix A, p. 1099.

109. See R. Menéndez Pidal, "El Compromiso de Caspe," in *Historia de España*, XV, pp. cxiii–cxxcii.

110. The laws issued by Fernando in Cifuentes for the part of Castile he governed as regent were published by T. Minguella y Arnedo (*Historia de la*

diocesis de Sigüenza, II, 1912, p. 620f.); those for Aragon were included by J. L. Villanueva in his *Viaje literario en las Iglesias de España*, v. 22, pp. 258ff. For an English translation of the latter laws, see Lindo, *op. cit.* pp. 210ff; cf. Baer, I, p. 790.

III. See B. Llorca, "San Vicente Ferrer y su labor en la conversión de los Judíos," in *Razón y Fe*, 152 (1955), p. 293. On Ferrer in Majorca, see Antist, *op. cit.*, pp. 181–183. We should not be surprised that most of the converts he gained there were from among the Moslems. In December, 1412, when he visited Majorca, Fernando had not yet published in Barcelona his own version of Catalina's laws.

112. On Lorki, see Amador, *Historia*, II, pp. 432–433, 446–448.

113. On the disputation of Barcelona, see Baer, *History*, I, pp. 152–155 and *Tarbiz*, II (1931), pp. 177–187; C. Roth, "The Disputation of Barcelona (1263)," *Harvard Theological Review*, XLIII (1950), pp. 117–144; Martin A. Cohen, "Reflections on the text and context of the Disputation of Barcelona," HUCA, xxxv (1964), pp. 157–192; and J. Cohen, *The Friars and the Jews*, 1982, pp. 108–128.

114. *Jeschurun*, ed. Joseph Kobak, VI (1868) p. 47.

115. Ibn Verga, Solomon, *Shevet Yehuda*, ed. Baer-Schohat, 1947, p. 96; J. Kobak, ed., *Jeschurun*, VI (1868), p. 47.

116. See *Shevet Yehuda*, pp. 97–98, 105 (lines 26–32); and the detailed summary of A. Pacios López, *La Disputa de Tortosa*, I, 1957, pp. 253–290.

117. For the entire proceedings of the Disputation (in Latin), see A. Pacios López, *La Disputa de Tortosa*, II, 1957.

118. See Amador, *Historia*, II, pp. 434–446, and Lorki's summaries of the Tortosa debates concerning the coming of the Messiah and the validity of the Talmud in Pacios López, *op. cit.*, II, pp. 549–556, 589–593. See also the submissive admission of Astruch, the Jewish spokesman, of his inability to explain Talmudic statements which, on the face of it, are offensive and embarassing, though he attributed his inability to intellectual inadequacy, and not to the impropriety of the Sages involved.

119. On the tendency to convert among the Jewish notables who came to Tortosa, see the testimony of the contemporary poet Bonafed in my *Marranos of Spain*, p. 107, n. 62.

120. Published by Amador in his *Historia*, II, pp. 627–653 (appendix 20). On the contents of the bull, see *ibid.*, pp. 506–510.

121. Cantera, *op. cit.*, pp. 410–411; Zurita, *Anales*, lib. XII, cap. 45.

122. See L. Serrano, *op. cit.*, p. 63.

123. *Crónica de Juan II*, año 1415, cap. 20 (BAE 68, p. 367b).

124. L. Serrano, *op. cit.*, pp. 65–66.

125. See Suárez Fernández, *Castilla, el cisma y la crisis conciliar*, 1960, pp. 77–79, L. Serrano, *op. cit.*, pp. 65–67.

126. See Sanctotis, "Vita Pauli," *loc. cit.*, p. 53a.

127. *Ibid.*, p. 70b.

The Conversos Enter Spanish Society

1. Diego Ortiz de Zúñiga, *Annales eclesiásticos y seculares de Sevilla*, 1677, p. 252a, says that, following the riots of 1391, "most of the Judería remained a wasteland," while according to Ayala, *Crónica de Enrique III*, cap. 20 (BAE, 68, p. 177b), "most of the Jews who had been there [i.e., in the Judería] turned Christian." Thus, the conversions during the assault did not prevent (in most cases) large-scale robbery and destruction of property. The plunder of Jewish possessions was, in fact, so massive that it led Ayala to state that the desire to rob the Jews was the main motive of the attackers (*ibid.*, cap. 5, p. 166a).

2. A clear testimony of this is offered by the Jews of Aragon in their letter to Pope Eugene IV (see below, p. 279).

3. For the misery of the Jews after the riots see Ayala, *op. cit.*, cap. 5, pp. 166–167 (even those who "escaped" the outrages of the pogroms remained "very poor owing to the great gifts they gave to the Señores for guarding them in so great a tribulation"); and see the letter of Enrique III to the city of Burgos (dated July 20, 1392) which freed the remaining Jews of the community from payment of all debts and taxes to the Crown on the ground that "los non poder pagar, pues fincaron muy pobres despues del dicho robo;" see Cantera, *Alvar García*, p. 24.

4. See on this my *Marranos of Spain*, index, v. Marranos.

5. See *ibid.* p. 92, and n. 23; and see Profiat Duran, *Ma'asē Efod*, 1865, p. 195.

6. *Ibid.*, and *The Marranos of Spain*, p. 92 and n. 24.

7. See *ibid.* pp. 87–88; and see Profiat Duran, "Kĕlimat ha-Goyim," in *Hazofe mē-Erez Hagar*, III (1914), p. 102.

8. *Ibid.*, p. 103; cf. *The Marranos of Spain*, pp. 90–91.

9. See *ibid.*, pp. 84–87.

10. Such as Juan de Valladolid, who confronted Moses ha-Kohen of Tordesillas in a public disputation in Avila in 1375. See the latter's *Ēzer ha-Emuna* (written in 1379), introduction, ms. 659/353 of the National and University Library, Jerusalem.

11. See for this, too, Duran's testimony cited in my *Marranos of Spain*, p. 90; the increased number of the missionary converts, which is already indicated by Moses of Tordesillas (1379), may be attributed also to agitators for Christianity who came from the converts of the civil war (see above, p. 116).

12. And see concerning this my work on the books of *Haqanah* and *Hapeliah*, in *S. W. Baron Jubilee Volume, III,* 1975, p. 260.

13. See his *Magēn va-Romah*, ms. no. 787 of the National and University Library of Jerusalem, introduction, p. 1.

14. E. Renan, *Averroès et l'Averroïsme*, 1861, p. 183.

15. Baer, I, p. 350: *va-asher heēmiru hēmiru.*

16. See above, pp. 171 and 1203, n. 10.

17. See my citations from Bonafed in *The Marranos of Spain*, p. 107.

18. Baer, *History*, II, pp. 162ff; 253ff, and other places indicated in the index, v. Averroism.

19. See my *Marranos of Spain*, pp. 110–121.

20. See *ibid.*, p. 105.

21. See his *Iggeret Musar*, ed. Jellinek, 1872, pp. 45–46.

BOOK TWO
The Reign of Juan II

The King and His Minister

1. Cf. the studies of Alvaro by Manuel José Quintana, *Vidas de los Españoles Celebres*, III, 1833; José Rizzo y Ramírez, *Juicio crítico y significacción política de Don Alvaro de Luna*, 1963; César Silió, *Alvaro de Luna y su Tiempo*, 1935, and the latest and most detailed work on Alvaro and his time by L. Suárez Fernández, *Historia de España* (dirigida por R. Menéndez Pidal), XV, 1964, pp. 30–217. An important study of Alvaro's downfall is Nicholas G. Round's *The Greatest Man Uncrowned*, 1986.

2. See on this José Amador de los Ríos, in *Revista de España*, XIX (1871), p. 245.

3. *Crónica de Juan II*, año 1419, cap. 1 (BAE, 68, p. 377b).

4. *Ibid., ibid.*

5. *Ibid.*

6. *Ibid.*, cap. 2, p. 378a

7. *Ibid.*, cap. 5, p. 378b.

8. See *Crónica del Halconero de Juan II*, ed. Carriazo, 1946, p. 17 (cap. 58).

9. *Crónica de Juan II,* año 1420, cap. 43, p. 396b.

10. We may safely conclude this from Alvar García's remark on Don Abraham: *que era de Juan Furtado* (see his *Crónica de Don Juan II de Castilla,* in *CODOIN,* 99, p. 90). Don Abraham would not have been regarded as "Mendoza's man" unless he had steadily served the Major Majordomo in some high financial capacity.

11. *Crónica de Juan II,* año 1419, cap. 10, p. 380a.

12. *Ibid.,* p. 380b.

13. *Ibid.,* año 1420, cap. 2, p. 380ab.

14. *Ibid., ibid.,* p. 381b; and cf. Alvar García's *Crónica,* in *CODOIN,* 99, pp. 89–90.

15. *Crónica de Juan II,* año 1420, cap. 2, p. 381b.

16. *Ibid., ibid.,* cap. 3, p. 381b.

17. See his account of Juan II's reign in *Historia de España,* XV, p. 75.

18. *Generaciones y Semblanzas,* 1954, pp. 103–104.

19. *Crónica de Juan II,* año 1420, cap. 17, p. 387ab; cf. Alvar García's *Crónica,* in *CODOIN,* 99, pp. 130–131.

20. *Crónica de Juan II,* año 1420, cap. 17, p. 387b.

21. *Refundición de la Crónica del Halconero,* ed. Carriazo, 1946, pp. 37–38.

22. *Crónica de Juan II,* año 1420, cap. 29, p. 391ab.

23. *Ibid.,* pp. 391b–392a.

24. *Ibid.,* p. 391b; Alvar García's *Crónica, CODOIN,* 99, cap. 42, p. 154.

25. *Crónica de Juan II,* año 1420, cap. 37, p. 394b.

26. *Ibid., ibid.*

27. *Ibid.,* cap. 38, p. 395a.

28. *Ibid.,* cap. 40, p. 395b.

29. *Ibid.,* pp. 395b–396a; and cf. *Crónica del Halconero,* p. 14.

30. *Crónica de Juan II,* p. 398b (cap. 47).

31. Alvaro's activities on behalf of the Jews have to this day received no adequate treatment by the historians of the Jews of Spain. Amador de los Ríos, and in his wake Graetz, who correctly pointed out the great part he played in the restoration of Spanish Jewry, did not as yet possess the necessary documents to prove their contention. On the other hand, they attributed to Alvaro's influence the pragmática issued by Juan II on April 6, 1443 in reaction to Pope Eugene IV's bull of August 8, 1442, which reaffirmed many of the laws of 1412 (see Amador, *Historia,* III, pp. 44, 583–589; Graetz, *Geschichte,* VIII³, p. 148). This attribution is an error. In April 1443 Alvaro was out of office and the administration was in the hands of his adversary, Juan I of Navarre, without whose explicit consent and instructions the pragmática would not have been issued. It is also wrong to see in this order a strong pro-Jewish position. Juan of Navarre, who needed the support of both the Pope and Castile's cities (undoubtedly the inspirers of the papal bull), accepted all the Pope's severe restrictions, but sought to reduce their apparent rigor in an effort to placate and encourage the Jews. This, and the administration's long delay in formally adopting the bull's decrees, merely show that he was extremely reluctant to part with the system of Jewish tax-collection (and other services) established by his predecessor.

32. See Quintana, *op. cit.,* p. 45 *(El era criador de aquel partido que podía llamarse del Rey);* Rizzo, *op. cit.,* p. 222.

33. *Ibid.,* appendix 3, p. 326.

34. *Crónica del Halconero,* pp. 327–328.

35. Alvar García, *Crónica,* in *CODOIN,* 100, p. 309.

36. *Ibid.,* pp. 309–310.

37. *Ibid.,* p. 311.

38. Cortes of Toro, 1371, §13 (CLC, II, 1863, p. 208).

39. Cortes of Madrid, 1419, §18 (CLC, III, pp. 20–21).

40. Cortes of Palenzuela, 1425, §10 (CLC, III, p. 56).

41. Cortes of Zamora, 1432, §5 (CLC, III, pp. 120–121): *Aesto vos respondo que está asaz bien por mi rrespondido e proueydo.*

42. See Cortes of Madrid, 1419, §5 (CLC, III, p. 14); Cortes of Palenzuela, 1425, §30 (CLC, III, pp. 69–70); Cortes of Zamora, 1432, §11 (CLC, III, pp. 125–128). In the latter Cortes the King undertook not to send corregidores to any city unless all the members of the city council or their majority requested it (*ibid.,* p. 127). That the King reneged on his promise, however, is evident from the renewed petition on this matter in the Cortes of Madrid, 1435, §17 (CLC, III, pp. 205–206) as well as from his response to that petition, in which he did not reiterate the promise he gave in Zamora.

43. Cortes of Burgos, 1430, §13 (CLC, III, p. 85); Cortes of Zamora, 1432, §2 (CLC, III, p. 118); Cortes of Valladolid, 1442, §12 (CLC, III, p. 407).

44. Manuel Colmeiro, *Córtes de León y de Castilla,* I, 1883, p. 514.

45. *Crónica del Halconero,* p. 327.

46. *Ibid.,* pp. 521–522; and below, pp. 354–355, 375–377.

47. Cortes of Valladolid, 1447, §23 (CLC, III, p. 525).

Precursors of Toledo, 1449

1. See especially M. Menéndez y Pelayo, *Historia de los Heterodoxos Españoles,* ed. E. Sánchez Reyes, 1963[2], II, pp. 470–471; also L. Delgado Merchán, *Historia documentada de Ciudad Real,* 2nd ed., 1907, p. 148; and more recently, Manuel Alonso, in his introduction to Alonso de Cartagena's *Defensorium unitatis christianae,* 1943, p. 22. The latter two writers, it should be noted, adopted Menéndez Pelayo's view.

2. *Historia de los Heterodoxos Españoles,* (ed. cited above), II, p. 471.

3. *Ibid.,* p. 470.

4. See on this below, pp. 354–355.

5. The conversions in the Gothic period,

which were dealt with above (pp. 35–53), obviously form a distinct line of evolution, though they often parallel in important respects the course of developments we are about to survey.

6. On the Christian and Jewish sources for these events, see my study "Did the Toledans in 1449 Rely on a Real Royal Privilege?," in *PAAJR,* XLIV (1977), p. 123, notes 64–65.

7. See Tomás Muñoz y Romero, *Colección de Fueros Municipales,* etc., I. 1847, pp. 363–367.

8. *Ibid.,* p. 365. The original version of the law reads: . . . *nullus judeus, nullus nuper renatus habeat mandamentum super nullum christianum in Toleto, nec in suo territorio.*

9. *Cod. Theod.,* XVI, 8. 16, 22, 25, 27, and especially *Nov. Theod.,* III, 2, from the year 438 (declaring *all* Jews ineligible for *any* public office), which was followed by *Cod. Just.,* lib. I, tit. 5, law 12, and lib. I, tit. 9, law 19. See also the Church Councils' decrees in Gaul in the 5th, 6th and 7th centuries (Council of Clermont [535], canon 9; of Mâcon [581], c. 13; of Paris [614], c. 17) and in Spain in the 6th and 7th centuries (3rd Toledan Council, canon 14; 4th Tol. Council, c. 65; 8th Tol. Council, c. 12).

10. On Jews in Alfonso's diplomatic service, see *Primera Crónica General de España,* ed. R. Menéndez Pidal, II, 1955, p. 552b, 568a; Amador, *Historia,* I, 183–184; R. Dozy, *Histoire des Musulmans d'Espagne,* ed. E. Lévi-Provençal, III, 1932, p. 119; Baer, *Die Juden,* II, p. 14 (§29).

11. *Ibid.,* II, p. 5 (§12).

12. See Baer, *History,* I, pp. 50–51. A dirge on his death was composed by Yehuda Halevi; see his *Diwan,* ed. Brody, II (1909), pp. 92–99. According to Halevi, the assassination occurred on May 3, 1108; see *ibid.,* p. 99, lines 141–142.

13. For this date see Fidel Fita, in RAH, *Boletín,* VII (1885), p. 75, n. 2.

14. See above, p. 68.

15. According to Amador, the left wing of Alfonso's army consisted almost entirely of Jews who were suspected to have shown irresolution in the face of the enemy's attack, thereby causing the collapse of the entire Christian front (*Historia de los Judíos,* I, p. 189). F. Cantera (in WHJP, *The Dark Ages,* ed. Cecil Roth, 1966, p. 377) accepts the gist of Amador's contention, although, as Baer has pointed out (*Die Juden,* II, p. 10), no evidence is available to support it. This, however, does not invalidate the assumption that (at least since the time of Alfonso VI) Jews fought with the armies of the Reconquest, or otherwise with forces of the kings of Castile—an assumption to which a variety of sources (Moslem, Christian and Jewish) lend considerable credence.

The Moslem sources relate to the battle of Zalaca (1086) and sound highly exaggerated or legendary. Moreover, they are included in works written more than two and a half centuries after the event (such as *Kitab al-Ihata* and *El-Hulal*), which further reduces their credibility. Nevertheless, at least one of them *(Kitab al-Ihata)* relies on a much earlier source (that of Yahya ben Mohammad ben As-Seirafi, who died in 1174), and the very exaggeration that 40,000 Jews (!) fought on the Christian side (see Amador, *Historia de los Judíos,* I, p. 185, n. 2) suggests that the statement had a factual core. Likewise, the probably fictional account that, prior to the battle, King Alfonso proposed that, considering the many Jews in his army, Saturday (like Friday and Sunday) be declared a day of rest for all contending forces (see Ambrosio Huici Miranda, *Las Grandes batallas de la Reconquista durante las invasiones Africanas,* 1956, p. 46; and see also Dozy, *Histoire,* III, p. 127, n. 2) indicates that Jews, in no mean number, participated in that battle on the Christian side.

Other sources, Christian and Jewish, also lead us to the same conclusion. Of the latter, most significant in our judgment is Yehuda Halevi's poem, "I shall bemoan my bitter troubles" (*Diwan,* ed. Brody, IV, 1930, pp. 131–133), whose meaning has escaped the scholars who have dealt with it. Yehuda Halevi, who lived in Toledo during the battle of Uclés (1108) and the massacres that followed, describes these massacres as an "act of vengeance" and relates them to the preceding war. He says:

Between the armies
of the Christians and the Moslems
My own army was lost,
So that now there are no more in Israel
Soldiers fit to serve in battle.

(p. 131, lines 7–8)

It is difficult to understand these verses by reading symbolic meaning into the words "our army was lost" in conjunction with the phrase *bein ziv'ot sē'ir vĕ-kēdar* and the sentence *vĕne'edar yozē za'va be-yisrael*. Most probably, what they indicate is that all Jews trained and prepared for war were mobilized for the battle of Uclés and that the Jewish force was virtually wiped out. Yehuda Halevi seems to reject the claim that the great defeat at Uclés resulted from a Jewish retreat. He says: "When they [namely, the Christians] fight their wars, we fall when they fall" (*ibid.,* line 9), suggesting that the defeat of the Jewish units resulted from the failure of the *Christian,* not the *Jewish* forces, to hold off the enemy.

Another poem of Yehuda Halevi ("The Philistines are Gathered," *ibid.,* p. 134), written most probably *before* the battle of Uclés, describes the poet's concern over the fate of the Jews who were to take part in that violent clash. Comparing the Jews among the other combatants to "the youngest of lambs among rams and bulls" (lines 12–13), he asks: "How can a flock be saved when it is led by Lions?" His answer is: "Only by amazing deeds, heroic acts and miracles" (lines 14–15). The poet realized the great danger in which the Jews (whom he judged much inferior to the other combatants in both military skill and numbers) were put when the "lions" were leading them to battle. He relied on a miracle to save them, but also on their innate heroism and ability to perform "amazing deeds."

The other Jewish testimony needs no interpretation, for its meaning is as apparent as its value. It comes from the German rabbinic authority Eliezer ben Yoel Halevi of Bonn who, in one of his responsa, states unreservedly: "It is still a general practice in Spain for the Jews to go out to war together with the King" (see *Sefer Rabiah*, Jerusalem, 1965, IV, p. 98, no. 900 [and *not* no. 820, as printed erroneously in Aptowitzer's *Introduction*, 1938, p. 464]; see also Isaac ben Moses of Vienna, *Or Zaru'a*, I, 1862, p. 194b, no. 693; and cf. S. W. Baron, *A Social and Religious History of the Jews*, IV, pp. 36 and 43). The testimony dates from c. 1200 (*ibid.*, p. 448, n. 2), but apparently refers to an old custom.

This brings us to the related Christian sources; and of these mention should first be made of the *fuero* granted by Alfonso VII to Guadalajara in 1139. In this *fuero* Alfonso imposed upon the Jews of that town the duty to go with the King to battle in the same proportion that was obligatory to the Knights, and also to the Moors of that town (Cavalleros vayan en hueste con el rey las dos partes, et la tercera parte finque en la cibdat . . . mientras jodios et moros en Guadafayara non fagan aqui menos; cf. Amador, *Historia*, I, p. 194, n. 3).

Of the other Christian testimonies to this effect priority should be given, in our opinion, to the *Cronica Adefonsi Imperatoris* (ed. L. Sánchez Belda, 1950),

written by a contemporary of Alfonso VII (*ibid.*, pp. ix–xvii). It tells us that when the commander of the castle of Burgos (which was held in behalf of the King of Aragon) refused to surrender it to the King of Castile, the Jews and Christians who sided with the latter took the castle by storm (a iudaeis et christianis expugnatus est) and delivered it to the king (*ibid.*, p. 8). Luis G. de Valdeavellano, *Historia de España*, I (2), 1955, p. 425, believed that the reference was not to Alfonso's troops, but to the citizens of Burgos and its neighborhood. The conjecture is reasonable. Even so, the *Crónica* testifies to the Jews' military participation in the battles of the time. Especially notable is the fact that among the assailants of the castle (Jews and Christians) the Jews are mentioned first.

That the Jews were also militarily responsible for castles placed exclusively in their hands we learn from a number of documents dating from the time of Alfonso VIII (see Julio González, *El Reino de Castilla en la época de Alfonso VIII*, I, 1950, pp. 131, 132, 133, 719; II, p. 440 [doc. number 267, dated Aug. 25, 1178]; on the castle of Haro: III, p. 660 [doc. number 962, undated]; on that of Zorita: III, 710 [doc. number 991, Dec. 20, 1215]. On castles held by Jews in later times see Baer, *Die Juden*, II, doc. 205 from 1376 (p. 196) and two documents relating to the castle of Soria: no. 319 from 1465 (p. 331) and no. 342 from 1484 (p. 355).

We ought to mention also another piece of evidence (dating from the middle of the 14th century) that bears significantly on our subject. When Alfonso XI asked Pope Clement VI for a permit to build a new synagogue in Seville, he supported his request by the claim *qui iudei sunt summe necessarii, quia contribuunt in necessitatibus civitatis necnon aliquotiens exeunt una cum christianis adversus saracenos, et se exponere morti non formidant* (Baer, II, p. 163, doc. no. 167).

16. That the pogroms in Spain were mainly or entirely the work of the residents of the towns involved is stated in the *fueros* of Castrojeriz and Toledo, as confirmed by Alfonso I *el Batallador* (Muñoz, *op. cit.,* p. 41) and Alfonso VII (*ibid.,* p. 366), as well as in the *Carta condonationis* (letter of forgiveness) which the latter king gave Saldaña, Carrión and other places for the outrages they had committed against the Jews (*Indice . . . de Sahagún,* ed. V. Vignau, 1874, pp. 24–25).

17. Evidence of this attitude had already been provided in 1035, when the Christians of Castrojeriz attacked the Jewish community and killed 60 of its members (see Muñoz, *op. cit.,* pp. 39–40). Like the disturbances of 1109, this outbreak too occurred shortly after the death of the king (Sancho *el Mayor* of Navarre), before one of his heirs, Fernando I, established his authority in Castile (see *ibid.,* p. 39). How anxious the citizens of Castro were to clear their town of the remaining Jews we can gather from the fact that shortly thereafter (*regnante Rex Fernandus*) they evicted all the surviving Jews from their houses and estates and transferred them to Castrillo, probably a half-abandoned castle in the vicinity of the town. Seventy-five years later, during the riots of 1109, the people of Castrojeriz attacked the Jews of Castrillo, "killing some of them, taking others captive, and putting all of them to the sack" (*ibid.,* p. 41). Baer's reconstruction of the events of 1035, in which he identified Castrillo with Castrojeriz (*History,* I, p. 43), is clearly misconceived. See L. Huidoboro y Sena, "La judería de Castrojeriz," in *Sefarad,* VII (1947), pp. 137–145.

18. See Muñoz, *op. cit.,* p. 366; and see further, for the date of the Toledan *fuero,* my study in *PAAJR,* XLIV (1977), p. 124, n. 66.

According to A. M. Burriel, *Informe de la Imperial Ciudad de Toledo,* 1780, pp. 287–288, Escalona received, on the same date, the identical *fuero* given to Toledo and possessed the original text of that *fuero* at the time of Burriel's writing. Disregarding this clear-cut evidence, A. García-Gallo (in his study "Los Fueros de Toledo," in *AHDE,* XLV [1975], pp. 390–398) claimed that Escalona received its fuero on Jan. 4, 1130, as is indicated by the text of the fuero for that town, first published by J. A. Llorente in his *Noticias históricas de las tres Provincias Vascongadas,* 1808, IV, pp. 39–43. It is difficult to accept this claim in view of the fact that Burriel, who had seen the text indicated by Llorente, related it to a special (i.e., second) *fuero* which Alfonso VII granted that town (see Burriel, *op. cit.,* number 105, and Muñoz, *op. cit.,* p. 485, n. 1).

19. Literally, "recently *reborn,*" conveying the essence of conversion to Christianity according to Christian doctrine; and see above, n. 8.

20. Only high *ecclesiastic* offices were barred to neophytes, generally within a year from their conversion. See on this below, pp. 570–571.

21. See on this my above-cited work in *PAAJR,* XLIV (1977), pp. 99–100, 104ff., 122–125.

22. See *ibid.,* especially p. 125.

23. They evidently took the "recently" of *nuper renati* to mean *a very short time ago,* while some of their descendants could then claim with good reason that they had never been converts to begin with. It stands to reason that such arguments found supporters among the Old Christians as well. And cf. above, n. 20.

24. Cf. A. Díaz de Montalvo's comments on the *Fuero Real de España,* lib. IV, tit. 3, ley 2 (ed. 1781, II, p. 352a).

25. This might have also contributed to the fact that the Privilege fell into desuetude (see above, n. 24).

26. See Muñoz, *op. cit.,* p. 382.

27. See Fernando III's extensions of the *fuero* of Toledo for Cordova (1241) and Carmona (1252) in *Memorias de Don Fernando III,* ed. Miguel de Manuel Rodríguez, 1800, pp. 460, 542. The relevant text in the *fuero* of Cordova reads: *ningun judio, nin ninguno de nuevamente cristiano,* and in that of Carmona: *ningunt judio nin tornadizo.*

28. Thus, in the privilege given Alicante (1252), the reference is not to recent converts *generally,* but specifically to the recently converted among Jews *(ningun judio, que nuevamente sea tornado cristiano);* see *Colección de Privilegios de la Corona de Castilla,* VI, 1833, p. 97.

29. Several generations after the conversions of 1391, the descendants of these converts were still defined as "recently converted." See the discussion of this issue below, pp. 553, 570–571, 887–889.

30. In view of the inclusion of the anti-convert clause in the *fueros* of Cordova (1241) and Carmona (1247), it is difficult to see why Fernando III should have excluded it from his *fuero* of Seville (1250), especially since all these *fueros* supposedly followed the Toledan *fuero* of 1118 as confirmed by Fernando III in 1222. Yet it is a fact that the Sevillian *fuero* contains no stipulation about converts, and instead it says "que ningun Iudio, *ni ningun Moro* ayan ningun mandamyento sobre ningun Christiano en Toledo, ni en su termino daqui adelante" (see Zúñiga's *Annales eclesiasticos,* p. 27). The extant version, however, is not the original of either the Toledan or the Sevillian grants. The text of the *fuero* given to Seville was lost c. 1285, and the Sevillians, wishing to have at their disposal the *fuero* of Toledo that had served as model for their own,

obtained from the Toledans a copy of that *fuero,* and soon thereafter, it seems, translated it (see the Romance version, which alone was preserved, in Zúñiga, *op. cit.,* pp. 26–29). Muñoz, who considered the translation faulty and the contents "very incorrect," did not include it in his collection (see his cited work, p. 363, n. 1). The clause about the Moors, then, may have been a product of these "errors," while, on the other hand, it could be deliberate. Possibly by means of the Toledan document (i.e., the *fuero* of 1118), and with the aid of their memory, the Sevillians tried to restore the text of *their* fuero (which must have differed in some points from the Toledan), and this work of restoration was "supervised," in all likelihood, by officials of Sancho IV (significantly, even the copy of the Latin text referred to was entrusted, at Sancho's order, to his alcalde; see Zúñiga, *op. cit.,* p. 26b). This could have given rise to departures from the original in accordance with the current royal policy, which by then, as we know, was already opposed to discrimination against converts (see on this below, pp. 260–262).

31. See above, notes 27–28.

32. See above, n. 27.

33. *Fuero Real,* lib. IV, tit. iii, ley 2.

34. Concerning this date see Pedro Gómez de la Serna, introd. to the *Partidas,* in *Códigos Españoles,* II, 1872[2], pp. xviii–xix.

35. *Las Siete Partidas,* VII, tit. xxv, ley 3.

36. On the contrary, the law indicates that the converts viewed Christianity as superior to their previous faith *(. . . despues que han entendimiento, e conoscen la mejoria de nuestra fe, la resciben), ibid., ibid.*

37. *Ibid., ibid.:* mandamos que todos los cristianos e christianas de nuestro Señorio fagan honrra e bien en todas las maneras que pudieren a todos

quantos de las creencias estranas vinieren a nuestra fe, *bien assi como farian a otro qualquier que de sus padres o de sus auuelos ouiesse uenido o seydo christiano.* The italicized words clearly convey the importance of the ethnic factor in the anti-convert agitation. And cf. below, n. 39.

38. See above, n. 37.

39. *Las Siete Partidas,* VII, tit. 25, ley 3: E si alguno contra esto fuere, mandamos que reciba pena de escarmiento por ende, a bien vista de los judgadores del lugar, e dengela mas crudamente que si lo fiziesse a otro ome, o muger, que todo su linaje de abuelos, o de visauuelos, ouiessen seydo christianos.

40. *Ibid., ibid.*

41. *Ibid.,* tit. 24, ley 6. Note the expression: ninguno non sea osado de retraer a ellos, *nin a su linaje,* de como fueron judios en manera de denuesto.

42. It may be argued that the reminder of the "Jewish lineage" and the convert's former religion implied the charge that the converts from Judaism were secretly devoted to their ancestral faith. If so, the lawmaker rejected this charge (obviously because he found nothing to support it), as is evident from his unqualified order to "honor" them and treat them "as all other Christians" *(ibid., ibid.).*

43. See above, n. 41.

44. *Las Siete Partidas,* VII, tit. 24, ley 3.

45. On Peñafort and his missionary effort in Spain, see Jeremy Cohen, *The Friars and the Jews,* 1981, pp. 104–108. Concerning his influence on Jaime I, King of Aragon, see F. Valls Taberner, *San Ramón de Peñafort,* 1936, pp. 98, 123–131. On his particular position in the Disputation of Barcelona (1263), see *Kitvei R. Moshe ben Nahman,* ed. Ch. Chavel, 1971², I, pp. 302–303, 319–320 (Hebrew); Amador, *Historia,* I, 433–436; and Graetz, *Geschichte,* VII (2nd ed.), 130–131, 135. On his actions following the disputation, see the

documents published by H. Denifle in *Historisches Jahrbuch,* Munich, VIII (1887), 234–244; I. Loeb, "La Contraverse de 1263 a Barcelona," in *REJ,* XV (1887), pp. 16–17; Martin Cohen, in *HUCA,* xxxv (1964), pp. 180–181.

46. Besides the stipulation against taunting converts "under the pain of a fine to be determined by the judge"—a stipulation directed against the attitude of the *Christians* toward "converts from Judaism or paganism" (i.e., Islam), the decree also sought to remove obstacles to conversion stemming from the attitudes of the converts' former brethren. Thus it secured the convert's rights to possessions which were denied him under Moslem law and the inheritance rights of his children (and relatives), who may receive "what they would have been able to claim reasonably if he had died a Jew or a pagan" (see on this L. Ginzberg, *Genizah Studies,* II, 1929, p. 122; M. B. Lewin, *Otzar Hageonim,* IX [Qiddushin], pp. 30–34; 7–8, part IV, 61–62; Baron, *op. cit.,* III, pp. 143–144; and cf. my *Marranos of Spain,* 1973², p. 17, n. 45, and below, n. 52). In addition, the law compelled Jews and Saracens to attend missionary sermons, "whenever an archbishop, bishop, or friar, Dominican or Franciscan . . . wishes to preach the word of God." The decree, included in Innocent IV's letter to the archbishop of Tarragona, was reproduced and translated by S. Grayzel in his *The Church and the Jews in the 13th Century,* 1966 (revised ed.), pp. 254–257.

47. On the strong probability that Peñafort influenced the legislative work of Alfonso X, see José Giménez y Martínez de Carvajal, "San Raimundo de Peñafort y las Partidas de Alfonso X el Sabio," in *Anthologica annua,* Rome, III (1955), especially pp. 329–338.

48. The preamble to the general law reads, as we have noted: "Many people live and die in foreign faiths who would prefer to become Christians, etc.". The opening of the law concerning converts from Judaism likewise broaches the same question: "Since some Jews may be converted to Christianity," etc.; see above, p. 261.

49. For a detailed description of Alfonso's attempt and the papal reactions to it, see Antonio Ballesteros Beretta, *Alfonso X el Sabio*, 1963, pp. 153–160, 177–189, 213–224, 240–243, 332–345, 409–416, 536–544, 674–677, and 706–732; see also H. Otto, "Alexander IV. und der deutsche Thronstreit," *Mittheilungen des Instituts für Oesterreichische Geschichtsforschung*, XIX (1898), pp. 75–91.

50. This explains why both Ferdinand III (in the *fuero* for Cordova, 1241) and Alfonso X (in the *fuero* for Alicante, 1252) insisted that their *almojarife*, if he was a convert, should be excluded from the prohibition on converts from Judaism occupying public office. See Baer, *Die Juden*, II, p. 9.

51. Although convert cooperation with the Dominicans in Aragon is documented since 1263 (in connection with the Barcelona disputation of that year), there is no doubt that it began much earlier, probably not later than the end of the forties, when Raymond de Peñafort embarked on his plan to provide Arabic and Hebrew training for prospective Dominican missionaries. Obviously, insofar as Hebrew was concerned, such training could be greatly assisted by the collaboration of Jewish converts. Cf. J. Cohen, *op. cit.*, pp. 107–109; Balme and Taben, in *Raymundiana*, I. 32.

52. Amplifying the decree of James I of Aragon of 1242 which secured for the convert the ownership of his property (see above, n. 46), the law of the *Partidas* assured him also full rights of inheritance. The converts, says the law, "ayan sus bienes, e de todas sus cosas partiendo con sus hermanos, heredando de los sus padres e de sus madres, e de los otros sus parientes, bien assi como si fuessen judios" (*Partidas*, VII, tit. xxiv, ley vi). Jewish law is generally in accord with this ruling, but many Jewish authorities maintained that Jewish Courts could confiscate what the converts inherited from their Jewish fathers (see Rashba, *Responsa*, VII, 282; Maimonides, Hilkhot Nehalot, VI.2; and cf. my *Marranos of Spain*, 1973², p. 17, n. 45, p. 18, n. 49, and p. 20, n. 50).

53. For the conversions during the civil war of the 1360s see the testimony of Samuel Zarza, in *Schevet Jehuda*, ed. Wiener, p. 132. That the number of converts was large is indicated not only by that author, but also by a Christian source (see *Córtes de León y de Castilla*, 1863, II, 309).

54. *Marrano* as a designation for Jewish converts is known since 1220; as a term of abuse, meaning swine or pig, it is known since 1380. On this, and the original meaning of the word, see my *Marranos of Spain*, 1973², p. 59, n. 153.

55. See *Córtes de León y de Castilla*, II, p. 309 (§21).

56. See above, p. 260. This seems to have been the case despite the repeated devaluation of the currency in Castile from 1255 to 1380. Cf. M. Colmeiro, *Historia de la economía política en España*, 1965², I, pp. 504–505.

57. See *Córtes de León y de Castilla*, II, p. 309 (§21).

58. See F. Cantera Burgos, *Alvar García de Santa María y su familia de Conversos*, 1952, p. 55, n. 52, where the whole document, taken from the Municipal Archives of Burgos, is reproduced, together with the related bibliography. For the date of the document (Oct. 14, 1392), see *ibid.*, n. 27.

59. *Ibid., ibid.*

60. Amador, *Historia,* II, p. 378, n. 1. According to Amador, the community of Burgos was finally "annihilated," but Cantera, *op. cit.,* p. 22, considering all available documents, rightly termed the statement "exaggerated." Nevertheless, from the dirge published by Schirmann (*Kobez al Jad,* III [13], Jerusalem, 1939, p. 67), it is evident that most of the community was converted.

61. Cantera, *op. cit.,* p. 24; and see Baer, II, p. 237. According to this document, the movement to renew the attack upon the Jews was organized by "some vile people of low station" (algunos omes rafezes de pequeno estado).

62. Cantera, *op. cit.,* p. 25; Baer, *Die Juden,* II, p. 239. See the king's letter to the Council of Burgos dated July 30, 1392, which points to some of the most recent converts as instigators of actions against the Jews: que algunos judios que *agora se tornaron christianos* lo prosiguen e les fasen muchos males. See Baer, *ibid.,* II, p. 239.

63. See the letter dated October 14, 1392, part of which was cited above, note 58.

64. See Juan de Torquemada, *Tractatus contra Madianitas et Ismaelitas,* ed. N. López Martínez y V. Proaño Gil, 1957, p. 127.

65. *Ibid., ibid.*

66. *Ibid.,* pp. 127–128. The gist of Enrique III's law is also presented briefly by Alonso de Cartagena in his *Defensorium Unitatis Christianae,* ed. Manuel Alonso, 1943, pp. 207–208.

67. See the Instruction which Fernán Díaz de Toledo addressed to Don Lope de Barrientos in 1449 (appended to Cartagena's *Defensorium,* p. 346).

68. See *ibid., ibid.* Also Enrique's letters cited above state that they were issued "con leçençia e avtoridat de los mis tutores e regidores de los mis regnos" (Cantera, *op. cit.,* p. 55, n. 52).

69. See *Cortes de León y de Castilla,* II, p. 310 (§23).

70. On conversos in the King's municipal offices, see above, pp. 247–250.

71. See Garibay, *Compendio Historial,* II, lib. xv, cap. 48. And cf. Amador, *Historia,* II, pp. 493–494, n. 3.

72. See L. Serrano, *Los Conversos D. Pablo de Santa María y D. Alfonso de Cartagena,* 1942, pp. 33, 49, 51.

73. Juan de Torquemada, *op. cit.,* p. 128. The editors of Torquemada's *Tractatus* state that this privilege of Juan II was given in Valladolid in 1412, and cite in evidence the *Códigos Españoles,* X (Madrid, 1850), 1 *(ibid.).* The law referred to in the *Códigos,* however, is paragraph 3 of the *pragmática* against the Jews which was issued by Queen Catalina on Jan. 10, 1412 of that year (see Amador, *Historia,* II, p. 620), and does not contain any part of the privilege under discussion. It is possible, of course, that the privilege was issued not in Catalina's time, but shortly thereafter—that is, when Juan II (and Alvaro de Luna) assumed the reins of power. And see above, pp. 238–239.

74. See on him F. Ruiz de Vergara y Alava, *Vida de Don Diego de Anaya Maldonado, arzobispo de Sevilla, fundador del Colegio Viejo de San Bartolomé,* 1661.

75. See Joseph de Roxas y Contreras (Marqués de Alventos), *Historia del Colegio Viejo de San Bartolomé,* part 2, vol. III, 1770, p. 44; cf. A. Domínguez Ortiz, *La Clase social de los conversos en Castilla en la Edad Moderna,* 1955, p. 57, note. 13.

76. See L. Sala Balust, *Constituciones, estatutos y ceremonias de los antiguos colegios seculares de la Universidad de Salamanca,* III, 1964, p. 9.

77. See Roxas y Contreras, *op. cit.,* II (vol. 3), pp. 41–45; and cf. Sala Balust, *op. cit.,* III, pp. 73–77.

78. *Ibid.,* p. 10.

79. See P. B. Gams, *Series Episcoporum Ecclesiae Catholicae,* 1957, p. 73a.

80. The *Statuta Rectoris et Collegialium* (which in Roxas' edition, *ibid.*, p. 41, are entitled: *Statuta Reverendissimi Archiepiscopi juranda per Collegiales*) open with the following statement: *Didacus, miserationae divina et Apostolicae sedis gratia Archiepiscopus Hispalensis, circa nostrum Collegium sequentia statuta ordinamus* (see Roxas, *ibid., ibid.*).

81. See Sala Balust, *op. cit.*, pp. 100–101.

82. See above, p. 272.

83. There is good reason to assume that this statute was adopted not later than the 1480s. A sentence issued by the Catholic Kings on October 18, 1491 permitted the Rector and Councillors of the College to expel from it a certain collegiate who was found to be of "infected blood" (see Rújula, *Indice* etc., p. xxx). It is most unlikely that the College authorities would have sought, or received, such a verdict, if their claim had not rested on a supportive ruling, which formed part of the College's constitution. This leads to the conclusion that the *limpieza* statute of the College of Santa Cruz de Valladolid (1488), like that of the College of San Antonio in Sigüenza (1497), was enacted under the influence of the example of San Bartolomé, the oldest of Spain's *Colegios Mayores* (see *ibid.*, pp. xxx, xxxiv).

84. See Ruiz de Vergara, *Vida de D. Diego de Anaya*, p. 52, n. 13.

85. *Ibid., ibid.*

86. See above, p. 272.

87. *Ibid.*

88. See Ruiz de Vergara, *op. cit.*, pp. 37–41. R. Sicart, however, maintains that Anaya's demotion occurred in 1422 (see his article on Anaya in *Dictionaire d'histoire et de geographie ecclesiastiques*, II, col. 1503), while J. Goñi Gaztambide believes that it took place in 1421 (see his study "Recompensas de Martín V a sus electores Españoles," in *Hispania Sacra*, xi [1958], p. 18).

89. See Sicart's article on Anaya, *loc. cit.*

90. See below, appendix B.

91. J. Hardouin, *Acta Conciliorum et Epistolae decretales, ac constitutiones summorum pontificum*, VIII (1409–1442), Paris, 1714, §v, p. 1191.

92. *Ibid.*, § vi, p. 1191. The decree refers to *bona ex usure aut illicito quaesitu fuerint aquisita*. Since Church jurisdiction against the taking of usury by Christians did not apply to Jews, it may at first glance appear strange that the church associated the taking of usury by Jews with "illicit profits," and even ordered the gains the Jews made by usury to be returned to the Christian borrowers. Earlier church decrees on this subject, however, could offer at least a partial basis for this particular order. Thus, in 1215 the Fourth Lateran Council, in its 67th chapter, forbade Jews to take excessive usury from Christians and ordered them to make "sufficient amends" for their "exorbitant exactions," under pain of forfeiting all commerce with Christians (see S. Grayzel, *The Church and the Jews in the 13th Century*, 1966², pp. 306–307). The Council of Narbonne in 1227 echoed this decision by decreeing that "the Jews shall never receive any immoderate usury from Christians," and also: "should they continue to do so, the Church shall compel them to restore it by excommunicating the Christians who enter into any relations with them" (*ibid.*, p. 317). Similarly, in 1246, the Council of Béziers adopted the same law (§ 37; *ibid.*, p. 333). Since these decisions were rarely enforced, the Church could claim that the Jewish gains were made by excessive usury and therefore had to be returned. Moreover, Church legislation could provide examples of broader or less qualified rulings. Thus Innocent III, in his letter to the Province of Cologne in 1213, ordered

that the Jews be "compelled by the secular power to restore to their Christian borrowers the usury taken" (*ibid.*, p. 137).

93. *Ibid., ibid.*, p. 1192.

94. *Ibid., ibid.*

95. *Ibid., ibid.*

96. See above, n. 77.

97. See above, n. 52.

98. Although Alfonso de Cartagena arrived in Basle on Aug. 26, less than three weeks before the enactment of the law (Sept. 15), and therefore, most likely, was not involved in the *original* work on its formulation, we may nevertheless assume that, shortly after his arrival, he was informed of the contemplated law and perhaps also shown a proposed draft, in which he may have made some changes. See also below, p. 526.

99. Bearing in mind the deep penetration of the Marranos into the hierarchy of the Spanish Church, the advocates of the Inquisition may have sincerely believed that most Spanish bishops would be disinclined to declare any of the conversos guilty of judaization. See on this below, p. 740. The same fact may also have been offered as explanation for the paucity, or absence, of "proven" heresy cases among the conversos in Spain.

100. The testimony of the petitioners on this point is in full accord with the statements to this effect that we find in the Responsa of the Rabbis of the time concerning the "second generation." See my *Marranos of Spain*, pp. 44–50, and see below, p. 410.

101. The identical figure is mentioned in Benedict XIII's bull on the Jewish question, issued on May 20, 1415, with reference to the Jews who were converted under the influence of the Tortosa Disputation. See Amador, *Historia*, II, p. 630.

102. See V. Beltrán de Heredia, "Las bulas

de Nicolás V acerca de los conversos de Castilla," in *Sefarad*, XXI (1961), p. 37.

103. *Ibid.*, p. 37: *consilia et regimen universitatum.* The term *universitas* was used in Aragon to designate "city."

104. *Ibid.*, pp. 37–39.

105. *Ibid.*, p. 38.

106. *Ibid., ibid.*

107. The *Crónica* of Alvar García is divided into sections according to the calendar years.

108. *CODOIN*, 100, Madrid, 1891, año 1434, cap. I, pp. 387–388.

109. *Ibid.*, pp. 388–389.

110. See on this below, pp. 290, 639.

111. *Crónica de D. Juan II*, in *Crónicas de los Reyes de Castilla*, ed. Cayetano Rosell, II, Madrid, 1953, BAE, 68, p. 515a (año 1434, cap. I).

112. See *Refundición de la Crónica del Halconero de Juan II*, ed. J. de Mata Carriazo, 1956, p. 148.

113. *Ibid.*, p. 149.

114. On the Genoese economic activity in Seville, see M. Angel Ladero Quesada, *La Ciudad Medieval (1248–1491)*, 1976, pp. 93–99. For additional bibliography, see R. Pike, *Enterprise and Adventure*, 1966, pp. 213–226.

115. We say, "the *citizens* of the *towns*" because the rebels could not rely on the great nobles of Seville or of Andalusia, none of whom, in fact, was involved in the conspiracy.

116. See *Crónica del Halconero de Juan II*, ed. Carriazo, 1946, p. 152; the identical version of the proclamation appears also in the *Abreviación del Halconero*, MS. 434, Biblioteca de Santa Cruz, Universidad de Valladolid, f. 62a.

117. See above, p. 285.

118. This of course conflicts with Ladero Quesada's assumption that the purpose of the conspiracy of 1434 was to raise Seville to the status of an "independent urban republic, according to the example of its Italian

contemporaries" (*op. cit.*, p. 37). There were no such urban plans or aspirations in 15th century Castile, and Ladero's conclusion must have been drawn solely from his reading of the *Crónica de Juan II,* and the Halconero's version on which it relied, which conceal the real motives of the conspiracy.

That the conspiracy was much broader and more ramified than it appears from its description in the *Refundición,* we can gather also from the Halconero's remark about the range of the punishments that followed it. After mentioning those who were executed, he says: "many others involved in the [conspiratorial] deals were imprisoned and exiled [from their places] ("Otrosy fueron presos otros muchos que en los tratos eran, e desterrados"; see *Crónica del Halconero,* p. 152).

119. In the modern histories of Castile or Seville which deal with the abortive revolt of D. Fadrique, such as those of J. Guichot, *Historia de la Ciudad de Sevilla,* III, Seville, 1898, p. 342–345, this aspect of the conspiracy is completely ignored. Zúñiga, on the other hand, mentions the plan "to rob the houses of the richer merchants of the city, among whom were many Genoese;" see *Annales Eclesiásticos y seculares de . . . Sevilla,* II, Madrid, 1795, p. 1390, año 1433. Of the post medieval historians Zurita is the only one who speaks of the conspirators' double intention "to put to sack the merchants and *kill the conversos*" (*Anales de Aragon,* 2nd part, lib. XIV—tomo tercero, p. 222, Saragossa, 1669). Zurita, as is known, used the *Abreviación* of the Halconero.

120. This is why he devoted so much space to disparaging descriptions of Don Fadrique, to his wastefulness and need of money, and so few words to his associates. He does not even mention the social positions and the parts played by Fadrique's chief allies in the affairs of Seville. Cf. above, p. 285.

121. See Amador, *Historia,* III, p. 121, n. 2. The same formulation is included in the description of this privilege in the catalog of the Archivo Histórico Nacional, Madrid (Libro 83 de Matriculas del Archivo de la Casa de Osuna), and Amador may have taken the above quotation from this source. The original or a copy of the cedula, which was addressed to the town of Guadalajara, was once found in the Archivo de los Duques del Infantado, Legajo III, n. 2, but my colleague, Prof. Ciriaco M. Arroyo, who examined that *legajo* at my request, informed me that the document was not there.

With the text of the cedula remaining unknown, I had of course to consider the possibility that the document in question was identical with Juan II's letter cited by Torquemada and Alonso de Cartagena (see above, p. 271 and notes 57 and 59). My conclusion that we are dealing here with two separate statements rests on the following two reasons: (a) The document reproduced by Juan de Torquemada (which declares the right of converts from Judaism "to have the same offices and honors as other Christians") does not include the specific phrase preserved from the letter of 1444 ("as if they were born Christians"); (b) in discussing the attitudes of the kings of Castile toward converts to Christianity from Judaism, the Relator refers to the position of Juan II in the following words: "*y aun assi lo tiene ordernado el Rey nuestro señor en sus Leyes*" ("and thus has also ordered the King our Lord in his laws"; see Appendices to Cartagena's *Defensorium,* p. 345). It seems that if the Relator had in mind *one* order only (and an order of the King was *law*), he would not have added to his statement the phrase "en sus leyes." By speaking in that juncture of the king's "laws" (in the plural), the Relator, it seems, wished to inform his readers that the King issued more than one law concerning the converso question. And cf. Lope de Barrientos' statement on this subject which leads to the same conclusion ("E aun el Rey Nuestro Señor don Juan . . . lo tiene por sus ordenamientos e leyes"). See Luis G. A. Getino, *Vida y obras de Fr. Lope de Barrientos*, 1927, p. 186.

122. *Crónica de Juan II*, pp. 623–624.

123. See Amador, *op. cit.*, III, p. 121, n. 2: las principales villas y ciudades de todo el reino.

124. Barrientos was instrumental in organizing the alliance that made the King's liberation possible, and his influence in the administration was then at its peak. The Bishop was a staunch friend of the conversos, and several years later, the Relator called him "father and protector of our nation" (i.e., the conversos), doubtless for great services rendered by Barrientos to the converso cause (see Cartagena, *Defensorium*, Appendix II, p. 343). The Relator may have had in mind the Bishop's share in moving the government of Juan II to issue the aforesaid cedula.

125. The scathing denunciation of the Infantes' rule included in the cedula of Prince Enrique, dated May 22, 1444 (see *Memorias de Don Enrique IV de Castilla*, II, pp. 9b–10a), must have reflected an objective situation, as well as a widespread view. No doubt most cities then wished to get rid of the Infantes' yoke, which they came to see as "foreign," and believed that this end was attainable, and perhaps unavoidable.

126. See on this below, p. 594.

The Outbreak of the Rebellion

1. This framework was provided by the terms of surrender he agreed on with the Moors before entering Toledo. See on this Rafael Altamira, *Historia de España*, I, 1900, pp. 350–351, and R. Menéndez Pidal, *La España del Cid*, I, 1947[4], p. 306. No documents are extant to indicate the policy pursued by Alfonso toward the Jews of Toledo immediately after the reconquest of the city, but it seems they were treated as a privileged group, in accordance with the *fuero* Alfonso gave Nájera (in 976) which equalized the penalty for the killing of a Jew with that of an *infanzon* or a monk (see Baer, *Die Juden*, II, p. 4, doc. 11). In the *fuero* given Miranda de Ebro in 1099, the Jews, like the Moors, appear equal to the Christians (*ibid.*, II, p. 8, doc. 15). In the *fuero* granted the Mozarabs of Toledo (in 1101), the Christians are given a privileged position, but not when it referred to the killing or wounding of a Jew or a Moor (see *ibid., ibid.*, doc. 16).

2. A major breach of the king's agreement with the Moors had already been made in the second month of the Christians' renewed rule in Toledo (July, 1085) when the Cluniac monk Bernardo, Abbot of Sahagún, took over the chief mosque of the city and turned it into a church (see E. Lévi-Provençal, "Alphonse VI et la prise de Tolede [1085]," in *Hesperis*, XII [1931], pp. 48–49). This action infuriated the king, but Bernardo was elected Archbishop of Toledo that very year (against the king's will) by an assembly of prelates and nobles (see A. González Palencia, *Los Mozárabes de Toledo en los siglos XII y XIII*, IV, 1930, p. 155).

3. The migration of the Moslems which started with the departure of most of their political leaders from the city during the siege and after the surrender was followed by the migration of the wealthy and the learned. The poor

condition of the Moslem community from the middle of the 12th century onward is reflected in the documents published by González (*ibid.,* pp. 151–153 and the related sources).

4. That Toledo became, after the reconquest, a major center for the Jews of Castile is indicated by the fact that it counted among its residents men like Yehuda Halevi and Cidellus. On the important Jewish community in Toledo prior to the reconquest, see E. Ashtor, *History of the Jews in Moslem Spain* (Hebrew), II, 1966, pp. 139–142.

5. See above, pp. 256–257.

6. See Ayala, *Crónica del Rey D. Pedro,* año sexto (1355), cap. 7 (BAE, t. 66, p. 462b); Menahem ben Zerah, *Zēda La-derekh,* Sabionetta, 1567, p. 16b; see also J. Valdeón Baruque, "La Judería Toledana en la guerra civil de Pedro I y Enrique II," in *Simposio, 'Toledo Judáico,'* I, 1972, pp. 107–131.

7. See the lament of Yehiel ben Asher, in *Sinai,* XIX (1951), p. 211 (claimed by S. Bernstein with good reason to refer to the Jewish community of Toledo); and the anonymous elegy, first published by A. Neubauer in *Israel. Letterbode,* VI (1880–1881), p. 33ff. (with notes by D. Kaufmann, *Ibid.,* pp. 80–84; also *id.,* in *REJ,* 38 [1899], p. 251ff.), then by H. G. Enelow, in his edition of *Menorat ha-Maor,* 1930, pp. 445–450, and finally by C. Roth in *JQR,* 39 (1948), pp. 129–150.

8. Concerning Vicente Ferrer's visit to Toledo in 1411, we know that his preaching there was climaxed by a violent action he took against the synagogue, which he transformed into a church (see above, p.187). There is no reason to assume that the fate of Toledo's Jews differed materially from that of the other cities where the friar conducted his fierce agitation and which, following that agitation, were subject to the laws of 1412.

9. See above, p. 258.

10. See Juan de Torquemada, *Tractatus contra Madianitas et Ismaelitas,* ed. N. López Martínez and V. Proaño Gil, 1957, p. 127; and see above, pp. 266–269.

11. See above, p. 258.

12. For the pro-converso decree of King Enrique III which was directed especially against the Toledans, see above, pp. 268–269, notes 65, 66.

13. The numerical strength of the converso community in Toledo may be gathered, among other things, from its military capacity in 1467. See my *Marranos of Spain,* 1973², pp. 263–264. Some notion of its wealth may be formed from Sarmiento's huge robberies in 1449; see below, p. 649.

14. Although a distinct anti-Jewish streak may be detected in the attitude of the Ayalas toward the Jews (see the "Rimado de Palacio" in *Poesías del canciller Pero López de Ayala,* 1920, I, verses 244ff., 463ff.), nevertheless, like all other nobles, their foremost concern was to advance their own interests; and this dictated a policy of restraint first toward the Jews and later toward the conversos (at least, until 1449). In 1467, we see the Ayalas take a clearly anti-converso stand. See below, p. 782.

15. See below, p. 1228, n. 12.

16. See below, p. 302.

17. *Crónica,* año 1420, cap. 28, p. 391a.

18. *Halconero,* cap. 262, pp. 319–320, 334; 358–362; *Crónica,* año 1440, caps. 8–9; BAE, 68, p. 563ab; año 1441, cap. 1, pp. 570–571.

19. *Abreviación,* caps. 153–154, ff. 243–244a; *Refundición,* pp. clxxxix–cxci; *Crónica,* año 1444, caps. 16–17 (pp. 623ab–624a).

20. See Benito Ruano, *op. cit.,* pp. 23–24, and doc. 6, pp. 174–175.

21. See *Crónica,* año 1445, cap. 6, p. 628, where mention is made of all the participants in the battle of Olmedo; and cf. *Halconero,* cap. 337, pp. 463–464. Ayala, however, was present in the

Cortes which assembled in the king's camp outside Olmedo just a few days before the battle. See *Córtes de León y de Castilla,* III, 1966, p. 458.

22. *Crónica,* año 1445, cap. 25, pp. 638–639a. Complaints of his misconduct as Chief Judge, however, had already been lodged against him in 1411. See Emilio Sáez, "Ordenamiento dado a Toledo por el Infante don Fernando de Antequera . . . en 1411," in *Anuario de Historia del Derecho Español,* XV (1944), pp. 517, 519; cf. Benito Ruano, *op. cit.,* p. 28, n. 45.

23. *Crónica,* año 1445, cap. 25, pp. 638b–639a; *Halconero,* cap. 341, pp. 468–469.

24. *Ibid.,* cap. 24, p. 638ab.

25. This we gather from the subsequent agreement between the King and Prince Enrique about the restoration of this office to Ayala (*Crónica,* año 1446, cap. 5, p. 647a) and from all other related sources (see below, notes 26, 32).

26. *Halconero,* cap. 342, p. 469; *Crónica,* año 1445, cap. 24, p. 638b.

27. See *Crónica,* año 1446, cap. 5, p. 647a; concerning the office of chief judge it was agreed "quel Alcaldia Mayor . . . quel dicho Pero López tiene, non le sea perturbada, nin sea fecha ninguna inovaçión de como siempre la touo" (Benito Ruano, *op. cit.,* doc. no. 8, p. 177).

28. See on him and his ancestry, Benito Ruano, "Don Pero Sarmiento, Repostero Mayor de don Juan II de Castilla," in *Hispania,* XVII (1957), pp. 484–490.

29. See, for instance, *Crónica,* pp. 628a, 630. See also *Memorias de D. Enrique IV de Castilla,* II, 1835–1913, p. 12a, where, in a cedula issued by Prince Enrique, Sarmiento is mentioned *first* among the captains of Juan II to whom the subjects of the kingdom should turn in case of a Navarrian invasion.

30. See King Juan II's statement of September 10, 1444 (preserved in the Archivo de la Corona de Aragon, Reg. 2934, f. 114), which is cited by Benito Ruano, *op. cit.,* 26, n. 39.

31. For his estates and income, see *id.,* "Don Pero Sarmiento," *loc. cit.,* pp. 498–499; see also *id.,* "El Origen del Condado de Salinas," in *Hidalguía,* V (1957), pp. 41–48.

32. On his appointment as commander of the Alcazar, see *Crónica,* año 1445, cap. 24, p. 638b, and *Halconero,* cap. 341, p. 468; on his appointment as chief judge of appeals, see above, n. 26, and below, n. 32.

33. Benito Ruano, *op. cit.,* doc. 8, p. 177. From both the agreement between the King and the Prince and the King's letter to Sarmiento of June 28 it is obvious that, while the Alcaldía Mayor was *promised* by the King to Sarmiento, not only orally, but also in *writing* (non embargantes qualesquier *mis cartas e poderes* que en contrario desto de mi tengades; *ibid.,* doc. n. 10, p. 180), the position was not yet actually transferred to Sarmiento's hands. In both cases the king says that Ayala was still in possession of the post. In the letter the King says of the Alcaldía "quel dicho Pero Lopez por mi *tiene* en la dicha ciudad," and in the agreement with the Prince it is likewise stated: "el Alcaldía . . . quel dicho Pero Lopez [de Ayala] *tiene*" (*Crónica,* año 1446, cap. 5, p. 647a). It seems, however, that Sarmiento already took, with the king's consent, certain steps toward the transfer of that office to his possession. The king's letter to him of May 15 says: "si algunas inovaciones son fechas contra ello, que sean tornadas al primero estado . . . non embargante qualesquier *mis cartas e poderes* que . . . yo aya dado fasta aqui" (Benito Ruano, *op. cit.,* doc. 8, p. 177). The same is indicated in the king's agreement with the Prince (*Crónica,* año 1446, cap. 5; BAE, 68, p. 647a).

34. See pertinent documents in Benito Ruano, *op. cit.*, pp. 176–179 (doc. 9).

35. *Ibid.*, doc. 10, pp. 180–181. In this new order, punishment for violation increased from 10,000 maravedis (*ibid.*, p. 177) to loss of offices and confiscation of property for the King's Chamber (*ibid.*, p. 180).

36. From a royal document dated February 23, 1447 it appears that the matter was not settled even then, i.e., nine months after the order was given. See *ibid.*, p. 29, n. 51.

37. See concerning these positions Emilio Sáez, "El Libro del juramento del Ayuntamiento de Toledo," *AHDE*, XVI (1945), pp. 530–624; and cf. Benito Ruano, *op. cit.*, p. 30, n. 54.

38. That the gates were taken over by Alvaro is evident from subsequent events; see below, p. 312.

39. *Halconero*, cap. 355, p. 519; *Abreviación*, cap. 171, f. 283.

40. See above, p. 301 and notes 35 and 36.

41. The story of Ayala's dismissal, as presented by the *Halconero*, cap. 341, p. 468, gives an idea of the king's method of combining cunning and surprise in the performance of such acts. According to this story, the King, before coming to Toledo, asked Ayala to prepare the Alcazar for his lodging. Upon his arrival, the king walked through the Alcazar as if to inspect the suitability of the place for his needs, and then told Ayala that he should transfer himself to his home since his stay in the Alcazar would make the place too crowded for the king's offices and retinue. Pero López tried to counter-argue, but the King persisted in his demand, and in the end Ayala complied. Then the King delivered the fortress to Pero Sarmiento, and informed Ayala that he removed him from his post as governor. See also the same in the *Crónica*, año 1445, cap. 24, p. 638ab.

42. *Crónica*, año 1448, cap. 2, pp. 656b–657ab; *Halconero*, cap. 364, pp. 499–500.

43. *Crónica*, cap. 4, 658a; *Halconero*, cap. 368, p. 505.

44. See below, p. 312.

45. *Crónica*, año 1446, cap. 7, pp. 650b–651a; *Halconero*, cap. 348, p. 475.

46. *Ibid.*, cap. 349, p. 477; *Crónica*, año 1446, cap. 8, p. 651a; año 1447, cap. 4, 654b.

47. *Halconero*, cap. 361, pp. 494–495.

48. *Crónica*, año 1447, cap. 2, p. 654a; *Halconero*, cap. 354, pp. 487–488.

49. *Ibid., ibid.*, p. 487; *Crónica*, año 1447, cap. 2, p. 654a.

50. *Ibid.*, año 1448, cap. 2, 657b; *Halconero*, cap. 364, pp. 500–501.

51. *Ibid.*, cap. 370, pp. 508–509; *Crónica*, año 1448, cap. 4, p. 660b.

52. *Ibid., ibid.*, p. 658b; *Halconero*, cap. 369, pp. 507–508.

53. *Crónica*, año 1449, cap. 1, p. 661ab; *Halconero*, cap. 371, pp. 510–511.

54. See "El Memorial contra los conversos del bachiller Marcos García de Mora," published by E. Benito Ruano, in *Sefarad*, XVII (1957), p. 346.

55. See "Instrucción del Relator para el obispo de Cuenca," first published by Fermín Caballero in his *Doctor Montalvo*, 1873, pp. 243–254, and again by Manuel Alonso as appendix to his edition of Alonso de Cartagena, *Defensorium Unitatis Christianae*, 1943, pp. 343–356. I am citing according to the later edition. See *ibid.*, p. 354, where the Relator describes García as a man of "villano linaje de la aldea de Maçarambros . . . e mejor fuera de tornarse a arar, como los fizo su padre e sus abuelos e lo fazen oy dia sus hermanos e parientes."

56. See "Instrucción," *loc. cit.*, p. 344: "hombre prevaricador e infamado de mala vida y acusado de muchos crímenes e delitos."

57. *Halconero*, cap. 372, p. 511; *Crónica*, año 1449, cap. 2, p. 661b. According to Higuera, however, the course of development was more complicated.

Faced with the necessity of meeting the danger of an Aragonese invasion, Alvaro first "sent a request" to the Toledans, among whom he had "many friends and allies," to give the King a grant of a million maravedis. The request was refused by the Council on the grounds that its fulfillment would change Toledo's status from a free to a tributary city. Alvaro repeated his request a second and third time, and only when all these appeals bore no fruit did he come to Toledo and suggest that the Toledans lend him the money, rather than contribute it. Alonso Cota, the treasurer of the city, gave or promised Alvaro the loan, and even began to collect it from the citizens; but he evidently did this without securing the city council's consent. Resistance continued; there was disagreement with Alonso Cota; and the citizens sent a delegation to Alvaro, who was then in Ocaña, requesting him to abandon his proposition, but he insisted on the fulfillment of his demand. See Higuera's *Historia eclesiástica*, lib. 28, cap. 5, Ms. 1290, Bibl. Nacional, Madrid, f. 222ʳ.

58. *Crónica*, año 1449, cap. 2, p. 661b; *Halconero*, cap. 372, p. 511; *Abreviación*, cap. 17, f. 283a.

59. On Alonso Cota see E. Cotarelo, "Algunas noticias nuevas acerca de Rodrigo de Cota", in *Boletín de la Real Academia Española*, XIII (1926), pp. 11–17; and recently F. Cantera Burgos, *La Familia Judeoconversa de los Cota de Toledo*, 1969, pp. 11–18.

60. Rather than supporting the administration's request, which he was expected to do as its official, he gave clear notice of his negative reaction to Alvaro's appeal. This may have been his first public indication of his desire to provoke a conflict between the city and the king and ally himself with the citizens (see Higuera, *op. cit.*, f. 222ʳ).

61. Higuera, *op. cit.*, lib. 28, cap. 5, f. 222ᵛ, says that the *común* suspected Cota to have been the originator of the idea of the loan and that he influenced Alvaro to accept it. See *Crónica*, año 1449, cap. 2, pp. 661b–662a; *Halconero*, cap. 372, pp. 511–512.

62. *Crónica*, p. 662a; *Abreviación*, cap. 171, f. 283.

63. *Crónica*, año 1449, cap. 2, p. 662a; *Halconero*, cap. 372, p. 512.

64. According to the *Halconero* (cap. 372, pp. 511–512) and the *Abreviación* (cap. 169, f.278a), the rebellion broke out on Sunday, January 26. This date was accepted by many authors, including Mariana (*Historia de España*, lib. 22, cap. 8, *BAE*, vol. 31, p. 130a) and Garibay (*Compendio Historial*, vol. II, 1628, lib. xvi, cap. 40, p. 485a). But the *Crónica*, whose editors noted the data indicated by the *Halconero* (they even included it in the beginning of their account), changed it to Monday, January 27 (año 1449, cap. 2, p. 662a: el lunes, que fueron veinte y siete de Enero). Also Higuera, whose account of the events preceding the rebellion is much more detailed, fixes the outbreak of the rebellion on *Lunes, 27 del mismo mes (ibid.)*. And so does the *Cronicón de Valladolid* (see *CODOIN*, XIII [1848], p. 19). This is no doubt the correct date.

According to both the *Halconero* and the *Crónica*, Alvaro visited Toledo on Saturday, January 25. According to Higuera, the city sent its delegation to Ocaña on Sunday, January 26; it was only after it had returned to Toledo that the Council decided to yield to Alvaro's demand, and when the outbreak took place the collection was almost completed (see *Abreviación*, cap. 171, f. 283). It is hard to assume that all these occurrences (Alvaro's visit, the meeting of the Council, the delegation to Ocaña, its return to Toledo, the Council's second meeting, and the implementation of most of the collection plan) took place within only 24 hours. Nor can we agree with Benito Ruano who assumes that, while the rebellion broke out on Monday (Jan. 27), the scandal with the *ordero* took place on Sunday (*op. cit.,* p. 35). Is it possible that on that very day Cota's agents completed the collection among the rich and also began the collection among the poor? The sources indicate no separation between the scandal caused by the *ordero* and the calling of the mass-meeting. In fact, it is likely that the whole conduct of the *ordero*, serving as an excuse for the agitation and the meeting, was planned by the rebels' chiefs.

65. See, for instance, the *Abreviación* (cap. 171, p. 283) which clearly attributes the outbreak to the inability of the lower classes to pay the sums allotted to them, and the *Cuarta Crónica General, CODOIN* 106, p. 138, which seems to take a similar view. On the particular reasons offered for the rebellion by these *crónicas,* see below, pp. 638, 652.

66. See below, p. 347. According to Mariana, *Historia de España,* lib. 22, cap. 8 (BAE, 31, p. 130a), the two canons were the first to stir the populace to take rebellious actions.

67. Zurita, *Anales de Aragon,* lib. xv, cap. 56, Saragossa, 1669, p. 317²b. This was also the view of the *Cuarta Crónica General* which said explicitly that "Pero Sarmiento was *the inciter of these actions* which were thus done for the reason of loan"—namely, the attack upon the houses of Cota, etc. (*loc. cit.,* p. 139).

68. Zurita, *op. cit.,* p. 371b.

69. Mariana, *op. cit.,* BAE, 31, p. 130a, says that the rioters, following their attack upon the houses of Cota, sacked and burned the suburb of Magdalena, the dwelling place of many of the city's rich merchants (i.e., conversos), and, "unsatisfied with this, they threw into prison those whom they found there,

miserable people, without having respect for women, old men and children." We have no confirmation of this by any other source, and it is most unlikely that such major occurrences would have left no trace in any contemporary record, or any chronicle of the following generation. Mariana seems to have erred in this as he did in other data concerning the rebellion; and Martín Gamero followed Mariana (without referring to him as his source). According to the former (*op. cit.,* p. 766), what was done to Cota's houses was done also to the houses of "many other citizens" *(vecinos),* especially of the "rich converso merchants who lived in the suburb of Magdalena."

Higuera (*op. cit.,* lib. 28, cap. 5, ms. 1290, f. 222ᵛ), for his part, offers at this point quite a different story. He tells us that following the attack on Cota's houses, the regidor Arias de Silva tried to pacify the populace, but the rioters killed some of his men, including Juan de la Cibdad. This account, however, conflicts with what we gather about the involvement of de Silva and the death of Juan de la Cibdad from García's "Memorial," whose account of these events appears more coherent and far more reliable (see below, p. 498).

Amador (*Historia,* III, pp. 118–119) here followed Mariana, Higuera and Martín Gamero (without referring to any of them), and L. Delgado Merchán (*Historia documentada de Ciudad Real,* 1907, p. 159) just followed Amador.

70. See "Memorial," *loc. cit.,* p. 329: lo hiçieron (namely, the seizure of the gates) *con authoridad o liçençia del dicho señor Pero Sarmiento,* el cual tenia poder e *authoridad plenaria* del dicho señor Rey *para mandar e haçer semejantas cosas e mayores."* The *Cuarta Crónica General,* too, states that it was *Sarmiento who seized the gates* (*loc. cit.,* p. 139) although it erroneously claims that

this action was taken not *during,* but *after* the outbreak (see on this below, p. 653).

71. See *Abreviación,* cap. 171, f. 282a: "Luego el común *con el favor que les dio Pero Sarmiento* apoderaronse en las puertas e puentes e torres."

While this evidence attests Sarmiento's involvement in the first stages of the rebellion, it also throws light on another testimony which bears directly on this subject. In a statement made by King Juan II on April 18, 1450 with reference to the origins and beginnings of the rebellion, he said: "Having forgotten the fear of God . . . and the loyalty that he [Sarmiento] owed me . . . as his King and natural lord, he rose and rebelled (se alsó, e rebeló, e levantó) together with some of my disloyal individuals *(singulares)* of the common people *(pueblo común)* of that city (i.e., Toledo)—his partisans, and accomplices, and satellites, and participants, and abettors, and adherents, *conspiring with them,* and *making with them a conspiracy and sworn allegiances* (juramentos), *and deals and homages, and fraternities* (confradias), against me and the royal crown of my Kingdoms, *in order to rebel against me and disobey me, and take over the* [*control of the*] *said city, and rise with her against me,* as he [actually] did with her and my alcazar" (see the King's introduction to the "process" issued by Fernando de Luxán, Bishop of Sigüenza, with reference to Nicholas V's bull *Si ad reprimandas* of September 24, 1449 (*Colección Diplomática,* p. 27ab).

Nowhere does the king's statement suggest that the first author of the rebellion was the *común* and that Sarmiento joined them *after* they had rebelled and achieved their first objective. Instead it clearly says that *he,* Sarmiento, rose against the king *together* with some individuals of the common people (say, men like García and some of his friends), and that *he conspired* with them *to rebel* against the king. Thus, not only was Sarmiento with these men from the start; he was also their leader; for they were defined as *his* partisans, *his* accomplices, *his* satellites, *his* adherents, etc., with whom *he* made a *conspiracy* against the king. There was no need for a conspiracy *in order to rebel* (as the statement put it) *after* the rebellion had broken out, and similarly there was no need for *confradías* and *juramentos* (secret oaths), which are an inevitable part of any conspiracy.

72. *Crónica de Juan II,* año 1449, cap. 2, p. 662a.

73. *Ibid., ibid.,* cap. 5, p. 664a.

74. *Ibid.*

75. Higuera, *Historia eclesiástica,* BNM, ms. 1290, vol. VI, f. 232.

Toledo Under the Rebels

1. Palencia, *Crónica de Enrique IV,* transl. by A. Paz y Mélia, I, 1904, p. 16; Pulgar, *Letras,* ed. J. Domínguez Bordona, 1949, p. 89.

2. *Ibid., ibid.*

3. See his "Memorial," in *Sefarad,* 17 (1957), p. 325.

4. *Halconero,* cap. 375, p. 519.

5. For the use of torture, see *Abreviación del Halconero,* ms. 434, Bibl. de Santa Cruz, University of Valladolid, f. 283a, and Román de la Higuera, *Historia Eclesiástica de la imperial ciudad de Toledo,* lib. 28, cap. 8, ms. 1290, Bibl. Nacional, Madrid, f. 233^r: "fue tan grande la fuerça de la violençia y de los tormentos que les dieron, que confesaron los cuytados lo que ni por pensamiento ni por obra jamas passaron." Both these sources say that the arrested and tortured were "homes honrados y ricos" *(Abreviación)* or "hombres ricos y caudalosos mercaderes" (Higuera), titles which were

often used in the historiography of the period as synonyms for conversos.

6. Higuera, *op. cit.*, ms. 1290, f. 233ʳ.

7. Thus, Arias de Silva, who headed a company defending the conversos, was a member of the influential Silva family which, unlike the Ayalas, distinguished itself in its faithfulness to the King. He was no doubt the same Arias de Sylba, described by the *Halconero* as "cavallero, hombre fijodalgo," before whom Ayala made his sworn commitments to Juan II (cap. 285, p. 359; see also cap. 268, p. 340), and whom Higuera (*op. cit.*, lib. 28, cap. 5; ms. 1290, f. 222ᵛ) called "Regidor y Cauallero principal de esta ciudad" and "cauallero leal y del servicio del Rey" (*ibid.*, f. 225ᵛ). His high position in Toledo's leadership is also indicated by Higuera's listing him as second in order among Toledo's *regidores* (see *ibid.*, lib. 28, cap. 6; ms. 1290, f. 226ᵛ).

8. See Marcos García, "Memorial," *loc. cit.*, p. 330; *Cronicón de Valladolid, loc. cit.*, p. 19; *Crónica de D. Alvaro de Luna*, p. 241; Higuera, *op. cit.*, lib. 28, cap. 5, f. 222ᵛ; and see below, p. 945.

9. See on this below, n. 12.

10. For this inquiry (*pesquisa*) see the "Sentencia-Estatuto," in Martín Gamero, *Historia de Toledo*, 1862, pp. 1037–1038.

11. See the entire list of these practices in Espina, *Fortalitium Fidei*, ed. Lyon, 1511, ff. 75ᵛ–77ʳ (lib. II, consideratio vi, heresis 1).

12. Pero López de Galvez was one of the four Toledan delegates who submitted Sarmiento's Petition to the King (see *Abreviación*, cap. 171, f. 270a), and he must have been close to Marcos García, judging by their common line of action in the last phase of the rebellion (see below, p. 347). Pero Sarmiento described him in the Petition as "nuestro promotor" (*Abreviación*, f. 270a), and he no doubt exercised, under Sarmiento, his authority as chief

ecclesiastical judge. In this capacity he dismissed Fernando de Cerezuela, the Archdeacon of the Cathedral Church, from his position and deprived him of his benefits (see on this below, p. 1231, n. 30), and issued death sentences against "Judaic heretics." Cardinal Juan de Torquemada, who denounced these sentences, declared that Galvez not only lacked the right to sit in judgment in such cases, but was explicitly prohibited from doing so (see his *Tractatus contra Madianitas et Ismaelitas*, ed. N. López Martínez and V. Proaño Gil, 1957, pp. 49–50), no doubt by the Archbishop, Alonso Carrillo. This prohibition, however, must have been addressed to Galvez from outside the city. For Carrillo was absent from Toledo not only during the outbreak of the rebellion, but throughout the period of the rebels' (and probably also of the Prince's) rule. We have a precise record of his whereabouts from November 1448 to June 1449. He was constantly in Juan II's court, and followed the King also when the latter went with his army on his way to Benavente (Jan. 1449) in pursuit of Count Alfonso Pimentel who had escaped from his imprisonment (see *Crónica de Don Alvaro de Luna*, cap. 75, p. 222; and see *ibid.*, pp. 219, 216). He must have been with the army that fought in Benavente and later beleaguered Toledo. It was only in the beginning of June 1449, when the King left Illescas (Carrillo's town) in the course of his retreat from Toledo, that Carrillo parted company with the King (see *ibid.*, p. 245).

13. For the burning of "heretical" conversos, see Marcos García, "Memorial," *loc. cit.*, p. 331; *Crónica*, año 1450, cap. 1; BAE, 68, p. 670b; *Cuarta Crónica General*, in *CODOIN*, 106, 1893, ed. Marqués de la Fuensanta del Valle, p. 139 (here the burnings are referred to *conversos e conversas*).

14. *Halconero*, cap. 375, pp. 519–520; *Crónica*, año 1449, cap. 5, p. 663b.
15. See below, n. 18.
16. *Halconero*, cap. 375, p. 520; *Crónica*, año 1449, cap. 5, p. 664a.
17. *Ibid., ibid.; Halconero*, cap. 375, p. 520.
18. The Petition was submitted on behalf of the city by four individuals who, like the bearers of the former message, were all members of the city's upper classes. See *Abreviación*, p. 290a; *Crónica*, año 1449, cap. 5, p. 664b.
19. *Halconero*, cap. 376, p. 525–526.
20. *Ibid.*, p. 526; *Refundición*, p. cxciv; *Crónica*, año 1449, cap. 5, p. 665a.
21. *Ibid., ibid.*, cap. 6.
22. See Zurita, *Anales de Aragon*, vol. III, 1699, pp. 317ᵇ–317ᵃ.
23. *Halconero*, cap. 369, p. 507; *Crónica*, año 1448, cap. 2, p. 657b.
24. *Crónica*, año 1449, cap. 6, p. 665a; *Refundición*, p. cxciv.
25. *Ibid.*, pp. cxciv–cxcv; *Crónica*, año 1449, cap. 6, p. 665b.
26. *Crónica*, año 1449, cap. 9, p. 667b; *Halconero*, cap. 379, p. 531. According to both these sources, the Prince granted Sarmiento the right to hold the two positions *perpetuamente*.
27. *Halconero, ibid.; Crónica*, año 1449, cap. 9, p. 667b.
28. *Halconero*, cap. 379, p. 531.
29. See on all this in detail, below, p. 381.

The Rebels Under the Prince

1. *Halconero*, p. 532.
2. This concurs with the view of Benito Ruano, *op. cit.*, p. 50, who, however, offers no reasons to support it. For our own reasons, see above, pp. 322–327.
3. *Crónica*, año 1449, cap. 6, p. 665a; *Halconero*, cap. 379, p. 532; *Abreviación*, cap. 173, f. 294a (this source repeatedly mentions the caballeros in the Prince's entourage).
4. *Halconero*, cap. 379, p. 532; *Abreviación*, cap. 173, f. 295 (the same in *Refundición*, p. cxcvi).

5. *Halconero*, cap. 379, p. 532; *Crónica*, año 1449, cap. 9, p. 667b.
6. See above, pp. 315–326. That the Prince intended right from the start not to tolerate violence against the conversos in Toledo may be gathered from the following incident which is related by the *Halconero*. Several of those expelled from the city (undoubtedly conversos), returned to it with the Prince's men. They were, however, recognized and maltreated by the populace. Don Enrique, says the *Halconero*, could "not consent that such things be done in his city," and he explains the Prince's failure to intervene on that occasion by sheer practical necessity. The Prince realized that he had first to get hold of the city before he could take action against such abuses (see *Abreviación*, cap. 173, f. 294ᵃ–295; printed in the *Refundición*, p. cxcv). The same narrative also makes it apparent that those responsible for the maltreatment of the returners were all low-class people (esto non lo facían salvo homes de poca manera, *Ibid.*,) and hence, that the administration was not involved in any way, even though the agreement between the Prince and Sarmiento stipulated that those expelled should not return.
7. In describing the persecution of the conversos in Castile in the wake of the Toledan rebellion, Alonso de Oropesa says that they were "robbed, wounded, flogged, and even carried to violent death, as is evident from their blood which, less than a year ago, was shed in *various cities, towns and places in this kingdom*" (see his *Lumen ad revelationem gentium*, cap. 2, ms. Ambrosiana, f. 25r; cf. Spanish translation by L. Díaz y Díaz: *Luz para conocimiento de los Gentiles*, 1979, p. 90). Likewise, the Relator Fernán Díaz de Toledo says that the organizer of the persecution in Toledo "incited *several cities* to do the same, and in *some of them* carried out his

design" (see the "Instrucción del Relator," appendix 3 to Alonso de Cartagena's *Defensorium Unitatis Christianae*,
1943, p. 343). Similarly, Bishop Lope de
Barrientos says that the "new Haman"
of Toledo "persigue cristianos [i.e.,
conversos] no solamente en su tierra,
mas *en las tierras agenas*" (see L.G.A.
Getino, *Vida y Obras de Fray Lope de
Barrientos*, 1927, p. 182). The scope of the
anti-converso persecutions is also
indicated by Pope Nicholas V in his
Bull of Sept. 24, 1449 (see on this
below, p. 339).

8. See L. Delgado Merchán, *Historia
documentada de Ciudad Real*, 1907², pp.
161–162.

9. Despite the attempt made by the City
Council, in its report to the King of
September 5, 1449, to place the main
responsibility for the riots on the
conversos, it is clear that no small part
of the blame rested on Fray Gonzalo Manuento, Commander of the
neighboring town of Almagro (then
controlled by the Order of Calatrava),
who had apparently acted in collusion
with the Toledans in inciting the Old
Christians of Ciudad Real against the
New. See *ibid.*, pp. 399–404.

10. Perhaps symptomatic of this line of
thought was the reconciliation reached
between the conversos and the other
groups involved in the riots in Ciudad
Real (i.e., the Old Christians and the
Calatravans), all of whom petitioned
the King to pardon the city for the
offenses committed during the disorders. See *ibid.*, pp. 162, 404.

11. Cartagena, *op. cit.*, p. 61.

12. According to Mariana, *Historia General
de España*, lib. 22, cap. viii (BAE, vol. 31,
p. 131), this notable was the "dean of
Toledo" who later became Bishop of
Coria. Following the publication of the
Sentencia, says Mariana, he retired to
the village of Santa Olalla (near
Toledo), where he wrote a seven-point
refutation of the Statute and offered to

defend it in a public disputation. José
Sabau y Blanco, editor of Mariana's
Historia (vol. xii, 1819, p. 48, n. 1),
identified that dean as Don Francisco
de Toledo, and Benito Ruano, *op. cit.*, p.
52, accepted this identification (see his
study "La Sentencia-Estatuto de Pero
Sarmiento," in *Revista de la Universidad
de Madrid*, VI [1952], pp. 285–286). This
identification, however, is wrong.
According to Benito Ruano, Gil
González Dávila says (in his *Teatro
eclesiástico de las Iglesias Metropolitanas y
Catedrales de los Reinos de las dos
Castillas*, II, pp. 450–451) that Don
Francisco became Dean of the
Toledan Cathedral in 1447; but
González Dávila says no such thing.
Like Fernando de Pulgar, whom he
closely follows, he avers that the
Deanship of Toledo was conferred on
Don Francisco by Pius II, who became
Pope in 1458 (see *ibid.*; and cf. Pulgar,
Claros Varones de Castilla, ed. J.
Domínguez Bordona, 1954, p. 131).
Mariana, we must conclude, was
misinformed about the identity of the
converso notable in question just as he
was misinformed about the contents of
his work. Thus he says: "sobre el
mismo caso enderezó una disputa ... a
don Lope de Barrientos, obispo de
Cuenca, en que señala por sus nombres
muchas familias nobilisimas con
parientes del mismo y otros de seme-
jante ralea emparentadas" *(Historia,
ibid.)*. But all this clearly relates to the
Instrucción of the Relator (see below, p.
416), and not to Don Francisco! We
cannot therefore dismiss as groundless
Román de la Higuera's detailed
assertions that the converso who wrote
in "Santo Lalla" (sic!) an anti-Statute
paper ("un apologetico contra Pedro
Sarmiento") and then went to Rome
was García Alvarez de Toledo who
had been Abbot of Santa María de
Atocha (Madrid) and later, in the days
of Enrique IV, Bishop of Astorga (see

Higuera, *op. cit.*, lib. 28, cap. 7; ms. 1290, ff. 231ᵛ–232ʳ). In another place (*ibid.*, cap. 8, f. 235ᵛ) Higuera says explicitly that "don Garci Alvarez de Toledo por medio del Cardinal Juan de Torquemada alcanzo una bula del papa Nicolás V en que repruaba la division y distincion de pueblos." The reference is to the bull *Humani generis* (see below, p. 336f).

13. Higuera, *ibid., ibid:* and see below, p. 430.

14. According to the *Cuarta Crónica General*, in *CODOIN*, 106, pp. 139–140, the King, following his retreat from Toledo, *embió notificar toda lo susodicho* [about the rebellion] *al Santo Padre Eugenio*. It stands to reason that by "embió notificar" the chronicler meant to indicate that the King (or Alvaro) sent to Rome one or two emissaries, not only to inform the Pope of the rebellion, but also to negotiate the issuance of a bull against the Toledan rebels.

15. See Higuera, *op. cit.*, cap. 7, ms. 1290, f. 232ʳ. The licenciado Rui García de Villalpando, who prior to the rebellion was Alvaro's Deputy Chief Judge of Appeals in Toledo (see *ibid.*, cap. 6, f. 225ʳ), went over to the rebels' side and placed himself at Sarmiento's service. He had been a member of the King's Council and a jurist of high standing (Higuera calls him "gran letrado," *ibid.*). Both his record and legal training seemed to make him highly suitable to represent the city to the Pope.

16. See García, "Memorial," *loc. cit.*, p. 341; Higuera, *op. cit.*, lib. 22, cap. 7, ms. 1290, f. 232ʳ.

17. See below, p. 340.

18. *Crónica*, año 1440, cap. 7, pp. 665ᵇ–666ᵉ; *Halconero*, cap. 377, pp. 527–528.

19. *Halconero*, cap. 377, p. 528; *Crónica*, cap. 7, p. 666a.

20. Halconero, p. 528; *Crónica*, p. 666a.

21. *Ibid., ibid.*

22. *Ibid.*, año 1449, cap. 7, p. 666ab; *Halconero*, cap. 377, p. 528.

23. *Crónica*, año 1449, cap. 7, p. 666a; *Halconero*, cap. 377, p. 529.

24. *Crónica*, año 1449, cap. 11, p. 669a; *Halconero*, cap. 382, pp. 535–536.

25. *Halconero*, cap. 380, p. 533.

26. *Ibid., ibid.*

27. *Crónica*, año 1449, cap. 16, p. 665b.

28. In his bull against the rebels of September 24, the Pope says that he heard about the outbreaks in Toledo *nuper* (recently) from the King's letters *(regis illustris litteris)* and the clamorous report of many others *(multorum aliorum clamosa insumatione)*. The word *nuper* could not be construed to mean "the other day" *(este otro dia)*, as the official Spanish translation of the bull has it (see *Colección Diplomática*, p. 29a), no doubt with intent to show the immediate attention paid by the Pope to the King's appeal. The word *nuper* may of course easily mean two or three months, and the indication that the Pope heard about the events in Toledo from the bitter complaints of *many* people (also "recently") shows that the matter had been referred to the Pope not just before he issued his bull, but a considerable time earlier. It need hardly be added that bulls such as *Si ad reprimandas* and *Humani generis* (both dated September 24) called for lengthy deliberation and careful drafting; they could not be prepared within a day or two. And see above, n. 13.

29. *Crónica*, año 1449, cap. 11, p. 669a; *Halconero*, cap. 383, p. 536.

30. More specifically, the bull is directed against Pero Galvez, Vicar of the Toledan Cathedral Church, who deprived the Archdeacon of Toledo Fernando de Cerezuela of his office and benefices because of the latter's failure to keep the oath of allegiance he had given, out of fear, to Pero Sarmiento. See Benito Ruano, *op. cit.*,

doc. 20, pp. 203–205; and see concerning this further below, n. 45.

31. For the Latin text of the bull, see Benito Ruano, *op. cit.,* doc. 19, pp. 201–203; for the Spanish translation (which may have been the one prepared by the Relator or under his supervision, see below, p. 393), see *Collección Diplomática,* pp. 29a–31b.

32. Benito Ruano, *op. cit.,* doc. 19, p. 202.

33. *Ibid.,* p. 201: *dominum et iura interventere conatus est.*

34. *Ibid.,* pp. 201–202.

35. *Ibid.,* p. 202.

36. *Ibid., ibid.*

37. *Ibid., ibid.*

38. *Ibid., ibid.*

39. *Ibid., ibid.*

40. The bull was published (with some abbreviations) by Manuel Alonso as an appendix to Cartagena's *Defensorium Unitatis Christianae,* 1943, pp. 367–370; in Benito Ruano, *op. cit.,* doc. 12, pp. 198–201; in Higuera's *Historia,* lib. 28, cap. 9, ms. 1290, ff. 236ᵛ–238ʳ, and in Alonso de Oropesa, *Lumen ad Revelationem Gentium,* ms. Ambrosiana, ff. 302ʳ–307ʳ. Oropesa's version, which differs in some details from the others, is found also in Spanish translation (see *Luz para conocimiento de los gentiles,* pp. 536–542; and cf. above, n. 7).

41. Benito Ruano, *op. cit.,* doc. 18, pp. 198–199.

42. *Ibid.,* p. 199.

43. *Ibid., ibid.*

44. See above, note 36.

45. For this reason, we believe, the Pope avoided censuring Pero López de Galvez for the death sentences he had issued against alleged Marrano heretics, although the Pope knew that López had no right to serve as judge in those cases (see above, n. 30). And this is why, in canceling his verdict against the Archdeacon of Toledo (see above, n. 30), he only *alluded* to his false claim as judge, but did not expose it explicitly.

46. Benito Ruano, *op. cit.,* doc. no. 18, p. 199.

47. *Ibid.,* pp. 199–200.

48. The statement, incidentally, does not indicate that such relapses had actually been noted.

49. See on this decree, above, p. 45.

50. *Halconero,* cap. 382, p. 536; *Crónica,* año 1449, cap. 11, p. 669a.

51. *Ibid., ibid.,* p. 669b; *Halconero,* cap. 382, p. 536.

52. See *Crónica,* año 1450, cap. 1, p. 670a. This visit lasted until November 28, when the Prince left Toledo to go hunting near Requena (see *ibid.,* año 1449, cap. 9, p. 667b, and the *Abreviación,* cap. 173, f. 295ʳ). The relevant passage in the ms. of the *Abreviación* (as cited by Carriazo in his introduction to the *Refundición,* p. cxcvi) reads here: "salió el Principe para la dehesa de Requena," omitting in error the words "de Toledo" which appear in the manuscript.

53. This despite the fact that at the opening of the talks the King presumed that an agreement was at hand. See his letter dated October 9 to the Count of Arcos, in *Colección Diplomática,* p. 24 (doc. no. 13).

54. This is indicated by the presence of the mariscal Payo de Ribera in the Prince's entourage and the arrival, a few days later, of Juan de Silva, the Prince's alférez (*Halconero,* cap. 383, p. 538; *Crónica,* p. 670a).

55. Thus Higuera says (*op. cit.* v. VI, cap. 12, ms. 1290, f. 243a) that Barrientos joined the Prince because he was very dissatisfied with the King "for not having given him the archbishopric of Toledo which he, the King, had promised him." Barrientos, however, must have been aware that the appointment of Alfonso Carrillo for that position was made at the insistence of Alvaro de Luna, and against the King's will (see *Halconero,* cap. 343, p. 470).

56. On Don Lope's absolute faithfulness

to the Crown at that very time, see *Halconero,* cap. 385, p. 541.

57. All these arguments are implied in the complaint addressed to the Prince by Marcos García in his "Memorial." Cf. below, n. 61.

58. *Ibid.,* p. 343: . . . no aparten vuestras voluntades temores vanos . . . ni *apetito banaglorioso de señorear ni sobrar unos a otros.* Most probably, in trying to get the support of some of the leading citizens of Toledo, the Prince assured them positions in the new administration which would be established in the city with the change of the regime.

59. The reference is of course to Fray Lope de Barrientos.

60. Either Barrientos or Cartagena, who was among the chief leaders of the struggle against the anti-Marrano movement. On him, see below, p. 517ff.

61. See "Memorial," *loc. cit.,* pp. 342–343. The reference is to the anti-royal threats which García directed against Juan II (see *ibid.,* p. 342) and the anti-royal steps which he actually took.

62. We may gather this from the findings of the investigation which the Prince conducted against the rebels shortly thereafter. See below, p. 346.

63. See *Cuarta Crónica General, loc. cit.,* p. 140: Fernando de Avila, un malo cismatico . . . el cual tenia las torres de la puerta de Alcántara por este malo eretico de Pero Sarmiento.

64. The story of the conspiracy is related briefly in the *Abreviación,* cap. 172, ff. 295a–296. A much more detailed account, taken probably from the unabridged *Halconero,* is found in the *Crónica,* año 1449, cap. 9, 667b–668a. According to the *Crónica,* the plot was first revealed to a certain friar through a confession he took from a dying man. Since the friar was informed of the identity of the people whom the conspirators intended to kill, he felt he

could not keep such knowledge secret, and decided to "impart it immediately to the caballeros of the Prince who were on guard in the city" (*ibid.,* p. 668a). From this, one is led to conclude that the conspirators planned to capture the gates held by Prince Enrique's men.

65. See *ibid., ibid.* According to the *Cuarta Crónica General,* it was the King who revealed to the Prince the plan of the conspiracy (see *CODOIN,* 106, p. 140), but this conflicts with everything the *Abreviación* (cap. 178, f. 296) and the *Crónica* tell us about the way the Prince learned of the matter (beginning with the letters he received from Toledo and ending with the findings of his *pesquisa*), and above all with the significant datum we possess that the discovery of the conspiracy and the end of the conspirators caused the King great annoyance (*Crónica,* p. 668a; *Abreviación,* cap. 178 [end], f. 296: De todo esto, desque el Rey lo supo, ovo dello grande enojo). There was no reason for the king to be annoyed over the failure of the conspiracy if it was he who had revealed to the Prince the plan of the conspirators.

66. *Crónica,* p. 668a.

67. *Ibid., ibid.*

68. *Ibid., ibid.*

69. *Ibid., ibid.*

70. *Ibid., ibid.*

71. *Ibid., ibid.*

72. *Ibid., ibid.*

73. *Ibid., ibid; Abreviación,* f. 296.

74. *Ibid.; Crónica,* p. 668a; Higuera, *op. cit.,* cap. 10, f. 240ᵛ. That the execution was ordered by the Prince is stated in the *Cuarta Crónica General. loc. cit.,* p. 140.

75. *Crónica,* año 1450, cap. 1, p. 670a; *Halconero,* cap. 383, p. 538.

76. *Ibid., ibid.*

77. *Ibid., ibid.; Halconero,* cap. 383,. p. 538.

78. *Ibid., ibid.; Crónica,* p. 670a.

79. *Ibid., ibid.*

80. *Ibid., ibid; Abreviación,* cap. 175, f. 299.

81. *Crónica*, p. 670a.

82. *Ibid.*, p. 671a.

83. *Halconero*, cap. 383, p. 538.

84. We can gather this from the *Halconero*'s statement that when the Prince left Toledo for Segovia, "traxo consigo al dicho Pero Sarmiento, e a su muger e fijos, con toda su fazienda" (*ibid.*, p. 539). This must have been the original understanding, of which the *Halconero* was informed and which, he thought, was carried into effect.

85. See *Colección Diplomática*, pp. 28ff; and see below, pp. 665–666.

86. See *Halconero*, cap. 383, p. 539; *Crónica*, p. 671a; and see below, appendix C.

87. *Ibid.*, *ibid.*; and see Higuera, *op. cit.*, ms. 1290, f. 295.

The Petition

1. Concerning this date see above, pp. 342, 344, 393.

2. See above, p. 321. The Petition (under the title of *soplicación e rrequerimiento*) is included in the *Crónica del Halconero de Juan II*, ed. Carriazo, 1946, pp. 520–526. The final part of this document, which is missing in the *Halconero*, appears (with some revisions) in the abridgment of the *Halconero*, ms. 434, Biblioteca de Santa Cruz, University of Valladolid, ff. 289–290ª (Carriazo printed this missing part in his introduction to the *Refundición de la Crónica del Halconero*, 1946, pp. cxciii–cxciv); from the concluding section we can see that the rebels entitled their presentation a *Petition*, see *ibid.*, p. cxciv. See also the ms. in the Archives of Simancas, which deals with Toledan events of 1448–1449 (cf. Julian Paz, *Archivo general de Simancas, Catálogo I; Diversos de Castilla*, Madrid, 1904, p. 26, no. 112, Fragmento de Historia, etc.).

3. *Halconero*, p. 521: "*en nombre . . . de la rrepública de vuestros rreynos*"; *Refundición*, p. cxciii: "*e en nombre de todas las otras ciudades de vuestros reinos.*"

4. See below, p. 510.

5. According to the Petition, "son fechos pobres todos los vuestros naturales" (*Halconero*, p. 521), "e es perdido todo el estado de los oficiales e labradores" (*ibid.*, p. 522). Also, Alvaro de Luna "a desaforado las cibdades e villas e logares de vuestros rreynos, e los grandes dellos" (*ibid.*, p. 523).

6. See below, pp. 364–365, 509–511.

7. See RAH, *Memorias de Don Enrique IV de Castilla*, pp. 1–4; see also Juan Rizzo de Ramírez, *Juicio crítico y significación política de D. Álvaro de Luna*, 1965, pp. 324–331.

8. See *Halconero*, pp. 320–334; cf. *Crónica de Juan II*, año 1440, cap. v, pp. 560–562b. Judging by the *Halconero*, the document was dated between Feb. 18, 1440 (p. 313) and March 22, 1440 (p. 333).

9. See Rizzo, *op. cit.*, pp. 325, 326, 327; *Halconero*, pp. 323, 327; the Petition, *ibid.*, pp. 521, 524.

10. *Halconero*, p. 324 (*desordenada cobdicia*); see Petition, *ibid.*, p. 521 (*cobdicia desordenada*).

11. Rizzo, *op. cit.*, pp. 325–326; *Halconero*, pp. 326–327; the Petition, *ibid.*, pp. 523–524.

12. Rizzo, *op. cit.*, p. 327; *Halconero*, p. 325; the Petition, *ibid.*, pp. 523–524.

13. Rizzo, *op. cit.*, p. 327; *Halconero*, p. 325; the Petition, *ibid.*, p. 522.

14. Rizzo, *op. cit.*, pp. 327–328; *Halconero*, p. 325; the Petition, *ibid.*, pp. 522–523.

15. *Halconero*, p. 326.

16. *Ibid.*, p. 521.

17. *Ibid.*, pp. 324–325.

18. *Ibid.*, p. 522.

19. *Ibid.*, p. 326.

20. *Ibid.*, p. 524: . . . e rrobadas las tierras e vasallos, asy de los propios de la dicha cibdad como de su juridición, e de las otras; and cf. above, n. 5.

21. *Ibid.*, pp. 329–330.

22. *Ibid.*, p. 522 (. . . *al fin que con el poder vuestro acavase a todos los grandes de vuestros rreynos*).

23. *Ibid.*, p. 332.

24. *Ibid.*, p. 522 (asy por nombre como por efeto).

25. See also *ibid.*, p. 524: porque vuestra señoria [i.e., the King] . . . non quiera dar logar que el dicho vuestro condestable quiera ser rrey e señor dellos.

26. *Ibid.*, p. 521.

27. *Ibid., ibid.*

28. *Ibid.*, p. 523: los quales por la mayor parte son fallados ser ynfieles e herejes, e han judayzado e judayzan, e han guardado e guardan los más dellos los rritos e cerimonias de los judíos.

29. *Ibid., ibid.*

30. See *ibid.*, p. 521 (vuestros naturales) and p. 523 (vuestros subditos).

31. *Ibid.*, pp. 521–522.

32. *Ibid.*, p. 523.

33. *Ibid.*, pp. 521–522.

34. *Halconero*, p. 523: "so color e nombre de cristianos, prebaricando, estroxesen las animas e cuerpos e faziendas de los cristianos viejos en la fee catolica."

35. *Ibid., ibid.*

36. See above, pp. 353–354.

37. Concerning the views on the conversos of K. J. von Hefele and Menéndez Pelayo, see my article "La razón de la Inquisición," in *Inquisición Española y Mentalidad Inquisitorial*, ed. Ángel Alcalá, 1984, pp. 26–28, 32–33. Similar views were expressed by many authors, such as E. Schäfer, *Beiträge zur Geschichte des spanischen Protestantismus und der Inquisition im XVI. Jahrhundert*, I, 1902, p. 41; C. Sánchez-Albornoz, *España, un enigma histórico*, 1962, II, pp. 253, 255, 288; B. Llorca, "La Inquisición española y los conversos judíos o Marranos," in *Sefarad*, VIII (1948), pp. 113–151; N. López Martínez, *Los Judaizantes Castellanos y la Inquisición*, 1954, pp. 187–213; and others.

38. See below, p. 391.

39. See his *Fortalitium Fidei*, lib. II, Consideratio VI, heresis I (ed. Lyons,

1511, f. 76ʳᵛ). And see below, pp. 839–841.

40. We refer of course to the trial of the Holy Child of La Guardia in which the alleged plot to destroy the Spanish people occupies a central position (see on this below, pp. 1089–1090).

41. See above, pp. 191–196.

42. See above, pp. 11–14, 42–43, 66–68, 127–128.

43. See Espina, *op. cit.*, ff. 75ᵛ–76ʳᵛ.

44. *Ibid., ibid.*, f. 76ʳᵛ.

45. *Halconero*, p. 523: otros de ellos an adorado e adoran ydolos.

46. *Ibid., ibid.*: "los conversos de linaje de los judíos de vuestros señoríos e rreynos, los quales *por la mayor parte* son fallados ser ynfieles e herejes."

47. *Ibid., ibid.*: "E otros muchos dellos án blasfemado muy áspera e grauemente de nuestro Salvador de Jesucristo, e de la gloriosa Virgén María su madre."

48. See above, n. 46.

The *Sentencia*

1. See above, pp. 324–327.

2. See Marcos García's "Memorial," in *Sefarad*, *XVII* (1957), pp. 326–328, 332–333, and other places.

3. The text of the Sentencia-Estatuto, in Martín Gamero's *Historia de Toledo*, p. 1037, reads: en la qual frecuentemente bomitan de ligero judaizando. This recalls but also distorts the known phrase of the Council of Agde (c. 34): *Judaei quorum perfidia frequenter ad vomitum redit* (cf. Prov. 26.11).

4. Martín Gamero, *op. cit.*, p. 1037.

5. See González-Tejada, II, p. 308.

6. *Corpus Iuris Canonici*, c. 31, C. 17, q. 4, cap. *constituit* (ed. Aemilius Friedberg, *Decreti Secunda Pars*, v. I, p. 823).

7. *Forum Judicum*, lib. xii, tit. II, lex 18.

8. *Ibid., ibid.*: Whenever a Jew . . . renounces the perfidy of his religion and is converted to the profession of the true Catholic faith and, repudiating the errors of his rites and ceremonies, lives his life according to the customs of the

Christians, he shall be free from every burden or disability, which formerly, when attached to the Jewish faith, he would have been subject to for the public benefit (see *The Visigothic Code,* translated by S. P. Scott, 1910, p. 377).

9. Significantly, the *Fuero Juzgo* (lib. xii, tit. 2, ley 19) omitted the general statement about the removal of all disabilities from sincere converts from Judaism to Christianity, as indicated in the *Forum Judicum* (see above, n. 8), and limited itself to stating that such converts will have freedom of commerce with Christians. See *Códigos Españoles,* I, 1872, p. 189a.

10. *Forum Judicum,* lib. xii, tit. 2, ley x.

11. Seemingly supporting this understanding is the law's exemption of converts' offspring, whose "good customs and good faith" were vouched for by "a priest, the King or a judge" *(ibid., ibid.),* from the general prohibition it imposes on converts of the first generation. Notable is also the similarity between this law and the 64th law of the Fourth Toledan Council that denied the right of giving testimony not to *all* converts from Judaism to Christianity, but explicitly to those who "became Christians some time ago, and later transgressed against the faith of Christ" *(judaei . . . qui dudum christiani effecti sunt et nunc in Christi fidem praevaricati sunt, ad testimonium dicendum admitti non debent).* See González-Tejada, II, p. 307a.

12. Such as Fernán Díaz de Toledo (see below, p. 400) and Diaz de Montalvo in his comment on the *Fuero Real de España,* lib. IV, tit. iii, ley 2 (ed. 1781, v. II, p. 349ab). That the law refers only to *insincere* converts is proven, says Montalvo, from the law itself which speaks explicitly of those who *hace[n] engaño contra la Fé.* Montalvo here cites (in his Latin work) the law as given in the *Fuero Juzgo* which not always corresponds precisely to the laws in

the *Forum Judicum.* In this instance, however, the Spanish version correctly transmits the Latin original; see *Leges Visigothorum,* ed. K. Zeumer, 1902, p. 416 (in *Monumenta Germaniae Historica,* Legum Sectio I, v. I).

13. With this, it should be noted that, while the law considers *all* converts from Judaism *false* converts, it does not hold the same view of their descendants who (it admits) *may* be of good morals and true adherents of the faith. To qualify for testimony among Christians, however, their religious sincerity must be attested by highly credible persons (cf. above, n. 11).

14. See below, p 400.

15. Most probably, because they could not find a canon supporting the prohibition on testimony, and a civil law supporting the one on public offices, the authors of the Statute preferred not to indicate the precise laws which they had in mind and referred to the canon and civil laws generally (Martín Gamero, *op. cit.,* p. 1038); and see below, n. 16.

16. See the *Sentencia-Estatuto* in Martín Gamero, *op. cit.,* 1036, 1037, 1039; and Marcos García's "Memorial," *loc. cit.,* p. 319. For the correct text of García's statement on this matter, see my article, "Did the Toledans in 1449 Rely on a Real Royal Privilege?" in *PAAJR,* XLIV (1977), pp. 104–105.

It should be noted that the reference to the prohibition on testimony allegedly decreed in Alfonso's privilege is indicated in the *Memorial* (see *loc. cit.,* p. 102, 105), but not in the *Sentencia,* which lumps together canon law, civil law and Alfonso's privilege as a common basis for denying converts the rights to office and testimony, without indicating which of these laws denies specifically any of these rights (Martín Gamero, *op. cit.,* pp. 1038–1039). Specifically related to King Alfonso's privilege is only the prohibition on offices and benefices (see *ibid.*, pp. 1036, 1037, 1039).

17. See Amador, *Historia*, III, p. 120, and E. Benito Ruano, "La Sentencia-Estatuto . . ." in *Revista de la Universidad de Madrid*, VI (1957), p. 279.

18. See my detailed discussion of this issue in my article, "Did the Toledans in 1449 Rely on a Real Royal Privilege?", *loc. cit.*, pp. 93–125.

19. Cf. Montalvo's comment on the *Fuero Real*, ed. cited, p. 352a.

20. See below, p. 626.

21. See Martín Gamero, *op. cit.*, p. 1036 (por ser sospechosos en la fe de nuestro señor).

22. *Ibid.*, p. 1037: ". . . e por quanto contra muy gran parte de conversos de esta ciudad, descendientes del linaje de los judios de ella, se prueba, é parecio é parece evidentemente, ser personas muy sospechosas en la santa fe catholica."

23. *Ibid., ibid.*

24. *Ibid., ibid.*

25. *Ibid., ibid.* (procedieron contra algunos de ellos a fuego); and cf. Higuera, *op. cit.*, lib. 28, cap. 6, ms. 1290, f. 225: y quemaron a algunos con titulo que judaiçavan.

26. Martín Gamero, *op. cit.*, p. 1037; cf. above, nn. 22, 23.

27. See above, pp. 370–372.

28. See above, pp. 362–363.

29. Grammatically feminine in Hebrew, the *Shekhina* (divine presence) is conceived in the Cabbala as the last of the ten *Sephirot* and as the feminine element of the divine essence. On the *Shekhina* see especially G. Scholem, *Elements of the Kabbalah and its Symbolism* (Hebrew), Jerusalem, 1976, chapter 8.

30. See *id.*, *Major Trends in Jewish Mysticism*, 1941, p. 229f.

31. *Ibid.*, p. 30; and see my article "On the Composition Date of the Cabbalistic Books of *Hapeliah* and *Haqanah*," in *S. W. Baron Jubilee Volume*, 1975 (III, Hebrew part), especially p. 258.

32. See Martín Gamero, *op. cit.*, p. 1037: En el Jueves Santo mientras se consagra en la Santa Iglesia de Toledo el santíssimo óleo y chrisma, é se pone el Cuerpo de nuestro Redemptor en el Monumento, los dichos conversos degüellan corderos, é los comen é facen otros géneros de olocaustos e sacrificios judaizando, segun más largamente se contiene en la pesquisa sobre esta razon fecha por los vicarios de la dicha Santa Iglesia de Toledo.

33. The word used in the *Sentencia* for this description is *judaizando*; see above, n. 32.

34. See Mishna, Moēd, Pesaḥim, 5.1; Tosefta (ed. Lieberman), Moēd, Pasḥa, v. 2–3; Maimonides, Korbanot, Hilkhot korban Pesaḥ, I. 1, 8.3, 10.12–13.

35. *Ibid.*, Hilkhot Ḥagiga, I. 1, 1.3.

36. See Numbers 28, 11; Maimonides, 'Avodah, Hilkhot temidin u-Musafin, VII, 3. On the second day of Passover an added burnt offering was made *(ibid.)*.

37. The reason: sacrifices could be offered only in the Temple court (see Mishna, Zevaḥim, chapter V; concerning the Passover sacrifice, see *ibid.*, v. 8); Maimonides, Hilkhot korban Pesaḥ, 1.3). The prohibition was treated with such gravity that, following the destruction of the Second Temple, it was forbidden for Jews to prepare for the Passover feast a whole roasted kid lest it might be regarded as a substitute for the Passover sacrifice. See Caro, *Oraḥ Hayyim*, siman 469.

38. According to the Jewish calendar, the 14th of Nisan fell that year on a Friday. The problem of the date of the Last Supper which, according to Christian tradition, took place on a Thursday, was therefore a subject of ramified scholarly inquiry and controversy. Among the various views on this subject see Joseph Klausner, *Jesus of Nazareth*, 1929, p. 326; W.O.E. Oesterley, *The Jewish Background of the Christian Liturgy*, 1925, pp. 154–165; and

Ch. C. Torrey, "The Date of the
Crucifixion According to the Fourth
Gospel," in *Journal of Biblical Liter-
ature*, L(1931), pp. 227–241.

39. Martín Gamero, *op. cit.*, p. 1037: ". . . o
de alli, porque los santos decretos lo
presumen, resulta la major parte de los
dichos conversos no sentir bien de la
santa fé catholica."

40. See below, pp. 441–442.

41. See below, p. 443.

42. See M. Orti y Lara, *La Inquisisción*,
1932, pp. 41–43, 53–54, following St.
Thomas' *Summa Theologica* (IIª, IIªᵉ, Q.
XI, art. 4) and *Las Siete Partidas* (VII,
tit. 26, ley 2).

43. See below, pp. 442–443.

44. See below, p. 443.

45. See below, p. 616.

46. See above, p. 1115.

47. See above, n. 22 of this chapter and n.
28 of chapter on Petition.

48. See above, n. 39.

49. See Martín Gamero, *op. cit.*, p. 1038.

50. *Ibid.*, pp. 1036–1037.

51. *Ibid.*, p. 1038: han oprimido, destruido,
robado é estragado (in Higuera:
tragado) todas las más de las casas
antiguas é faciendas de los christianos
viejos de esta cibdad . . . é de todos los
reinos de Castilla; . . . todos los bienes
y honras de la patria son consumidos
y destruidos.

52. See above, n. 51.

53. See Martín Gamero, *op. cit.*, p. 1038: la
tierra é lugares de los proprios de la
dicha cibdad son despoblados é destruidos; cf. Higuera, *op. cit.*, lib. 28, cap.
7—ms. 1290, f. 230ʳ: e la tierra e logares
e proprios de la dicha ciudad etc.

54. Martín Gamero, *Ibid., ibid.*

55. *Ibid., ibid.:* para destruir la santa fé
cathólica y á los christianos viejos en
ella creyentes.

56. *Ibid., ibid.:* segun es notorio, é por tal
los habemos; and further on: como
segun es dicho, es público é notorio, é
por tal los habemos é tenemos; and on
several other occasions.

57. *Ibid., ibid.*

58. See Lucas' *Chronicon Mundi*, III, era
748, in Andreas Schottus, *Hispaniae
Illustratae*, IV, 1608, 70–71 (Spanish
translation: *Crónica de España por
Lucas, etc.*, ed. Julio Puyol, 1926, p. 270).
According to Lucas, the Christians of
Toledo went on Palm Sunday to the
Church of Santa Leocadia, which was
located outside the city, a cir-
cumstance which gave the Jews the
opportunity to carry out their
treacherous design. And cf. *Primera
Crónica General de España*, ed. R.
Menéndez Pidal, I, 1955, p. 316a.

59. See Norman Roth's convincing
arguments in his article "The Jews
and the Muslim Conquest of Spain,"
in *Jewish Social Studies*, XXXVII (1976),
pp. 156–158, and Pilar Leon Tello,
Judíos de Toledo, I, 1979, pp. 20–21. Leon
Tello points to the practical
impossibility (and illogical assumption) that the Christians would
abandon the city during the siege (p.
20); she also refers (*ibid.*, p. 21) to the
treaty of surrender allegedly signed
between the Moslems and the
Toledans, according to which the
latter, if they wished, could leave
the city freely with their movable
possessions (according to *Chronicon de
Petri Juliani archipresbyteri S. Iustae*,
Paris, 1628, p. 90).

60. The numbers given by the *Sentencia*
for the victims (killed and captured),
segun se falla por chrónicas antiguas (see
Martín Gamero, *op. cit.*, p. 1038), however, are not found in Lucas or in any
of the other extant chronicles of Spain.

61. See *Primera Crónica General* (cited
above, n. 58), especially chapter 557,
pp. 309–310. On the historical reality of
the Moslem conquest of Toledo, see
E. Lévi-Provençal, *España Musulmana,
711–1031*, in *Historia de España*, IV, 1950,
pp. 5–15; E. Saavedra, *Estudio sobre la
Invasión de los Árabes en España*, 1892,
pp. 70–73.

62. Martín Gamero, *op. cit.*, p. 1038.
63. *Ibid., ibid.*
64. *Ibid., ibid.*
65. *Halconero*, p. 519.
66. *Ibid., ibid.*
67. Martín Gamero, *op. cit.*, p. 1038: los dichos conversos descendientes de los judíos.
68. *Ibid., ibid.*
69. *Ibid., ibid.:* los dichos conversos descendientes del perverso linaje de los judíos.
70. *Ibid.*, p. 1039: sean habidos é tenidos como el derecho los há é tiene por infames, inhabiles, incapaces é indignos para haber todo oficio é beneficio público y privado en la dicha cibdad de Toledo.
71. *Ibid.*, p. 1040.
72. *Ibid.*, pp. 1037, 1039, 1040.
73. *Ibid.*, p. 1039: *linaje y ralea de los judíos.* According to R. Menéndez Pidal and others (see *Revista de Filología Española,* xxxiv [1950], pp. 4–5), *lindo* is a derivation from *limpidus* (clean). Cf. A. Domínguez Ortiz *Los Judeoconversos en España y America*, 1978, p. 25, n. 14.

The title *lindos* (in the original sense of *limpios*), as qualifying the Old Christians against the "dirty" New Christians, must have been a common description toward the middle of the century (note the expression "*sucios judíos*" as designating the conversos against "e yo … christiano viejo, *limpio,*" in the "Memorial" of Marcos García, in *Sefarad,* XVII [1957], pp. 346, 347). It reappears in the letter of Pedro de Mesa, canon of the Church of Toledo, about the Toledan riots of 1467. He uses the term "christianos lindos" as meaning "Christianos viejos" (see Martín Gamero, *op. cit.*, p. 1040). Ms. 2041 of BNM, however, which was probably composed c. 1470, describes the Old Christians as "limpios."

74. Although, as we have seen, conversos in Aragon were excluded from certain Old Christian associations for reasons which were undoubtedly racial (see above, pp. 281–282), we have no evidence that these reasons were explicitly declared.

75. *Halconero*, p. 526.
76. Martín Gamero, *op. cit.*, p. 1037.

The Relator

1. Several aspects of the work were examined by Nicholas G. Round, "Politics, Style and Group Attitudes in the *Instrucción del Relator,*" in *Bulletin of Hispanic Studies,* XLVI (1969), pp. 289–319. Apart from this, the *Instrucción* has been dealt with only briefly by several writers; see J. Amador de los Ríos, *Historia de los Judíos,* III, pp. 62–63, 121–123; A. A. Sicroff, *Les controverses des Status de "Purete de Sang" en Espagne,* 1960, pp. 38–41; Tarsicio de Azcona, *Isabel la Católica,* 1964, pp. 373, 374, 378; E. Benito Ruano, "La 'Sentencia Estatuto' de Pero Sarmiento," in *Revista de la Universidad de Madrid,* VI (1957, pp. 286–289).

The Instruction was first printed by Fermín Caballero, *Doctor Montalvo,* 1873, pp. 243–254, and reprinted from the same source by Manuel Alonso, as appendix to Alonso de Cartagena's *Defensorium Unitatis Christianae,* 1943, pp. 343–356. In our citations from the Instruction, we shall refer to the latter edition.

2. It was preceded by at least two works on the subject, which have not come down to us: 1. Alfonso de Cartagena's rebuttal of the Toledans which was written in Castilian and addressed to the King (see his *Defensorium unitatis christianae,* ed. Manuel Alonso, 1943, p. 61); 2. A seven point paper against the Statute, which, in all likelihood, was composed by the converso García Alvarez de Toledo who later became bishop of Astorga (see concerning this above, pp. 1230–1231, n. 12). Alvarez' father, Alonso Alvarez de Toledo (see Higuera, *op. cit.,* ms. 1290,

f. 231ᵛ), may be identified with Alfonso Alvarez who is mentioned by the Relator as his cousin (see his "Instrucción", *loc. cit.*, p. 352).

It is questionable whether either of the aforesaid two papers was meant for public consumption. Nor, as we shall see, was the Relator's Instruction intended for wide circulation. Its excellence, however, overcame that intent. And so it was made public—first, by Lope de Barrientos (in a revised form; see below, pp. 610–618), and later, most likely, in the original version. This may account for its survival.

3. Amador, *Historia*, III, p. 121.

4. See Marcos García's "Memorial," in *Sefarad*, XVII, p. 346. Marcos García says of him that he was notoriously a Jew and one who descended from the "vilest and dirtiest Jews *(los mas viles et sucios judios)* of Alcalá de Henares."

I see no reason to speak of the "*possible* Hebrew ancestry" of the Relator as does Benito Ruano (see *Sefarad*, xvii, p. 346, n. 15), as if there were the slightest doubt about his origin. In his appeal to the Bishop of Cuenca, the Relator identifies himself as a converso (see pp. 343, 356) and speaks of his *own* and his cousin's grandchildren who intermarried with Old Christians (see p. 352). In addition, he is mentioned among the most illustrious converts in a note written c. 1470 (see López Martínez, *Los judaizantes Castellanos*, p. 389); and see also the note (from the end of the 15th century) found in a margin of the proceedings of the Cortes of Cordova, 1455, in which he is defined as *neophitus* (see *Cronicón de Valladolid*, in *CODOIN*, XIII [1848], pp. 32–33).

That he was a native of Alcalá, as stated by García, is also indicated by the fact that one of the town's Churches (the Parroquia de Santa María la Mayor) contained a chapel known as *La*

Capilla del Relator which served as a place of interment for himself and members of his family (see on this Rodrigo Amador de los Ríos, "La parroquia de Santa María la Mayor de Alcalá de Henares, etc.", in *Boletín de la Real Academia de Bellas Artes de San Fernando*, Madrid, XVIII [1898], pp. 231, 249–252, 255, 279–284; and see also Luis Mª. Cabello y Lapiedra's work, *La Capilla del Relator ó del Oidor*, etc., Madrid, 1905). That he was *born* a Jew may be indicated by the fact that Marcos García, in his *Memorial*, calls him repeatedly by his alleged Hebrew name: *Mose Hamomo, loc. cit.*, pp. 332, 323, 326, and other places. The surname *Hamomo* is included in the list of Jewish family names assembled by the Inquisition (see Fidel Fita, "La inquisición toledana," in RAH, *Boletín*, XI (1887), p. 310, and cf. José Gómez-Menor, *Cristianos Nuevos y Marcaderes de Toledo*, 1970, pp. xxx–xxxi).

According to Pedro de Salazar y de Mendoça, *Crónica de el Gran Cardenal de España*, 1625, lib. ii, cap. 54, p. 385, Fernán Díaz de Toledo was physician to Juan II of Castile and later holder of various church offices, having been in succession Archdeacon of Niebla, Canon of Toledo, and Major Chaplain of the New Kings (Reyes Nuevos). On the other hand, he does not mention Fernán Díaz as Relator, the title by which he became famous *(ibid.)*. Rodrigo Amador de los Ríos (*loc. cit.*, p. 251), however, attributes the positions mentioned by Mendoza to the Relator who, accordingly, had medical and ecclesiastical careers in addition to his political and administrative ones. Yet this is virtually impossible. No doubt the reference in Mendoza's *Crónica* is to another Fernán Díaz de Toledo—i.e., the Archdeacon of Niebla, who was referred to in the *Instrucción* (*loc. cit.*, p. 356) as *cousin* of the Relator (see on him Benito Ruano, "La Sentencia etc.," *loc. cit.,* p. 289, n. 41, and N. G. Round, "Politics, Style, etc.," *loc. cit.,* p. 296).

5. According to a cedula issued in Avila on October 4 of that year (see F. Layna Serrano, *Historia de Guadalajara y sus Mendozas,* Madrid, 1942, I, p. 175). Likewise he is mentioned as the King's secretary and *referendario* (as well as notary of the *Privilegios Rodados*) in almost all the cedulas, privileges and grants issued in behalf of Alvaro de Luna from Jan. 4, 1421 to August 1445. See the summaries of the relevant documents in the *Crónica de Alvaro de Luna,* ed. Josef Miguel de Flores, 1784, pp. 399ff. (Appendices).

6. In the epitaph on her tomb, his mother is described as "mater praeclari Doctoris, D. Frnandi Didaci, in Regnis Castellae *Primi Relatoris."* See Miguel de Portilla y Esquivel, *Historia de la Ciudad de Compluto etc.,* Alcalá, 1725, I, p. 568. Cf. Rodrigo Amador de los Ríos, "La parroquia etc.," *loc. cit.,* p. 250, n. 1.

7. See *Crónica de Juan II de Castilla* of Alvar García de Santa María for the year 1423, in *CODOIN,* 99, pp. 326, 433.

8. *Ibid.,* v. 100, p. 310.

9. *Ibid., ibid.*

10. *Ibid., ibid.*

11. *Ibid., ibid.*

12. *Ibid., ibid.*

13. *Ibid.,* pp. 310–311.

14. Not unrelated to this fact is the assertion of the author of the *Centón Epistolario* that Fernán Díaz refused to share in the possessions of the condemned Infantes, Juan and Enrique, which were divided by the King among his favorites (see Fernán Gómez de Cibdareal, *Centón Epistolario,* Madrid, 1775, pp. 74–75, letter 44). The *Centón Epistolario* may have been a spurious work as some outstanding scholars have argued (see especially Adolfo de Castro, *Sobre el Centón Epistolario, etc.,* 1875, and before

him George Ticknor, *History of Spanish Literature,* III, 1965 [6th ed.], pp. 486–494), but the author of the *Centón* correctly sensed the uniqueness of Fernán Díaz' attitude toward gain in that avaricious society.

15. *CODOIN,* 100, p. 310.

16. See *Crónica del Halconero de Juan II,* ed. Juan de Mata Carriazo, 1946, p. 327.

17. *Ibid.,* pp. 362–364, 376.

18. One of them, Iñigo Ortiz de Stúñiga, assured the Infante under solemn oath that he would "go to his land" and remain neutral in the quarrel; the other, the adelantado Parafán de Ribera, gave the Infante the same assurance, but made it conditional on the King's failure to call him to his service. See *ibid.,* p. 379.

19. *Crónica de Juan II,* año 1441, cap. xi, p. 577a; *Halconero,* cap. 293, p. 379.

20. See the documents included in the *Crónica de Juan II,* año 1441, cap. 30, and note Fernán Díaz' name attached to documents of Sept. 2 and 20, 1441 (*ibid.,* pp. 592ᵃ, 592ᵇ, and 594ᵇ), not as Relator, but as *oidor, referendario y secretario* of the King. The title "Relator," however, appears at the end of the King's letter to Alvaro de Luna (dated Aug. 21, 1441) informing him of the Sentence pronounced against him (*ibid.,* p. 595a).

21. See *Halconero,* cap. 312, p. 421; *Crónica de Juan II,* año 1441, cap. 30, p. 599a.

22. According to the demand of the Queen and Prince Enrique (see *ibid.,* p. 587a; *Halconero,* p. 419), and the verdict against Alvaro (*ibid.,* cap. 318, p. 426; *Crónica de Juan II,* p. 601a). Some of them, however, like Doctor Periáñez and Alonso Pérez de Vivero, were restored before long to their former positions by the new administration (see *ibid.,* año 1442, cap. 7, p. 609a).

23. As is evidenced by certain documents prepared by him in that period, such as the Pragmatica of April 6, 1443 (see

Amador, *Historia,* III, p. 589). On the response of Juan II to the petitions made in Cortes (July 20, 1442) he is signed with the titles of "oydor e referendario del Rey e su secretario"—the same titles with which he countersigned the King's response in the Cortes of Valladolid of September 10, 1440, and earlier responses in Cortes which he processed (see *Córtes . . . de León y de Castilla,* III, 1866, pp. 184, 250, 392, 451).

24. Possibly also his release from the prison in which he was held by the Admiral of Castile occurred after the nobles were given to understand that, unless the Relator returned to the Court and was allowed to resume all his former positions, the king would refuse all negotiations with the nobles concerning the future of his administration. In fact, in documents related to the Sentence against Alvaro, dated Sept. 1441, Fernán Díaz appears as the King's *Oidor, referendario e secretario* (*Crónica de Juan II,* año 1441, cap. 30, pp. 592ª, 592ᵇ and 594ᵇ), while the King's letter to Alvaro of Aug. 21, 1441, is signed "por mandado del Rey. Relator" (*ibid.,* p. 595a).

Likewise we should note that, apart from the esteem in which he was held by the king for his abilities, he also earned the latter's affection, as testified by at least one chronicler. Referring to Fernán Díaz de Toledo, Palencia calls him the King's "beloved *(amado)* Relator" (see *Crónica de Enrique IV,* transl. Paz y Mélia, I, 1904, p. 111).

25. A grudge of this kind may have been held by Sarmiento, who most likely believed to have been denied adequate royal grants; see above, p. 301.

26. Memorial, *loc. cit.,* p. 348: ". . . e aun por quanto de un año a esta parte el dicho Mose Hamomo fue e esta condempnado por herege e sedicioso a pena de fuego e a pena de muerte de aleuoso, como aquel que a sido e es

proditor e traydor a su Dios e a su Rey e a su tierra."

27. See above, p. 1235, n. 28.

28. Nicolás López Martínez, *Los Judaizantes Castellanos,* etc., 1954, p. 389.

29. *Crónica de Alvaro de Luna,* p. 244.

30. See *ibid.,* p. 431; cf. *Crónica de Juan II,* año 1452, cap. 2, p. 682b; and see below, pp. 701 and 1279, n. 3.

31. All he said about him in connection with the death sentence issued against Alvaro was: "el qual por cierto era un hombre muy agudo e de sotil ingenio"; *Crónica de Don Alvaro de Luna,* p. 431.

32. Related to this is Fernán Diaz' statement on the marriages of some of his grandchildren with noble Old Christian families (*Defensorium,* p. 352). No Judaizer would speak of such marriages in such a positive vein as does the Relator. Echoing his assertions on this subject is the affirmation of the bishop Lope de Barrientos: "E algunos de los nietos del Relator son de Peñasola e de Barrionuevo e de Sotomayor e Mendoza, que descienden de Juan Hurtado de Mendoza el uiejo, mayordomo mayor del Rey" (see Luis G. A. Getino, *Vida y obras de Fray Lope de Barrientos,* 1927, p. 199).

33. He continued to occupy the position of Relator at the beginning of Enrique IV's reign (see *Memorias de D. Enrique IV de Castilla,* II, 1835–1913, document dated Feb. 1455, p. 140b), but his duties were soon to shrink, perhaps because of sickness or old age. In any case, later documents which appear over his signature do not bear the title of Relator. Thus, in a document of June 12, 1455, he is described as "oidor, y referendario del Rey y de su consejo y su secretario y notario mayor de los privillejos rodados" (*ibid.,* p. 143b). The last document that bears his signature (as "oidor, referendario and secretario" of the King) is dated Feb. 22, 1456 (see *ibid.,* p. 148b). He died on

May 2, 1457 (see *Cronicón de Valladolid,* in *CODOIN,* XIII (1848), p. 32; and cf. *Annales Complutenses* (cited by R. Amador de los Ríos, *loc. cit.,* pp. 231, n. 1, and 252, n. 1).

34. See below, p. 489.

35. Manuscripts of the "Instruction" are found in the libraries of the University of Salamanca, the Biblioteca Nacional, Madrid, the library of the Academia de la Historia, Madrid, and other places. For the two available editions of the "Instruction," see above, n. 1. A critical edition based on all extant manuscripts is still a desideratum.

36. See *ibid.,* pp. 346, 355.

37. *Ibid.,* p. 346.

38. See below, notes 46, 47, 48.

39. See "Instrucción," *loc. cit.,* pp. 346, 355–356.

40. See the Latin text of the Pope's bull in Benito Ruano, *op. cit.,* p. 202, and its Spanish translation in *Memorias de Don Enrique IV,* II, p. 30.

41. See above, pp. 323–324.

42. See Lope de Barrientos, "Contra algunos zizañadores," etc., in Luis A. Getino, *Vida y obras de Fray Lope de Barrientos,* pp. 202–203, and N. Round's work, "Politics, Style, etc.", *loc. cit.,* p. 294, n. 1.

43. See Getino, *op. cit.,* p. 191; and see below, pp. 610–611.

44. It is possible that in speaking of "el falso obispo de linaje de judios" ("Memorial," *loc. cit.,* p. 343), Marcos García refers to Lope de Barrientos and not to Alonso de Cartagena. Prior to this, however, he twice called Barrientos *el mal fraile* (*ibid.,* p. 342), denouncing the bad counsels he gave the Prince, but without referring to his origin. And see concerning this below, p. 611.

45. See Round, *loc. cit.,* p. 294, n. 1.

46. "Instrucción," *loc. cit.,* p. 356.

47. *Ibid., ibid.* (printed: "de obligado," but should be, in my opinion, "el abogado."

48. *Ibid.,* p. 343 (todos lo tenemos por Padre y Protector de ella"—namely, the *nación* of the conversos).

49. *Ibid.,* p. 356.

50. *Ibid.,* p. 343.

51. *Ibid.,* p. 344.

52. *Ibid.,* pp. 343–344.

53. *Ibid.,* p. 344: no tanto entienden ni saben [lo] *que* fueron en tiempo de judaizmo. The ms. of Salamanca, No. 455, f. 42, which reads: que tanto no entienden ni saben *e* fueron en tiempo del judaismo, may be here more in agreement with the original version.

54. *Ibid., ibid.*

55. *Ibid.,* p. 343.

56. *Ibid.,* p. 344: que dice que es canonizado y fecho decreto de ello.

57. See González-Tejada, II, p. 308.

58. *Fuero Juzgo,* lib. xii, tit. 2, ley 10 (*Códigos antíguos de España,* ed. M. Martínez Alcubilla, I, 1892, p. 64b).

59. Guido de Baysio, *Rosarium decretorum,* on causa 17, q. 4, c. 31.

60. This would be in accord with c. 64 of the Fourth Toledan Council which forbids testimony not to *any* convert from Judaism to Christianity, but specifically to those who, after their conversion, "played false with the faith of Christ" (see González-Tejada, II, p. 307: judaei ergo, qui dudum christiani effecti sunt et nunc in christi fidem praevaricati sunt, ad testimonium dicendum admitti non debent).

61. "Instrucción," *loc. cit.,* p. 344.

62. *Ibid.,* p. 345.

63. *Ibid., ibid.: Decretales Gregorii IX,* lib. I, tit. II, cap. 7 (*Eam te* in *De rescriptis*); see *Corpus Iuris Canonici,* ed. Friedberg, II, pp. 18–19.

64. *Ibid., ibid.:* sobre aquel paso dicen los doctores, que no solo no deben ser desdeñados, mas que deben ser favorescidos.

65. *Ibid.,* p. 345; cf. Romans II. 10.

66. *Ibid., ibid.*

67. *Ibid., ibid.*

68. *Ibid.*, p. 346.
69. See above, p. 292.
70. See *Partidas*, I, tit. II, leyes 17 and 19.
71. "Instrucción," *loc. cit.*, p. 346.
72. *Ibid.*, pp. 346–347.
73. *Ibid.*, p. 350. From the Relator's discussion of this point it is clear that by "those who come to the faith" he refers to the *gērim* of the Old Testament who had been regarded, prior to their adoption of Judaism, as "strangers" both ethnically and religiously. In the conversion of Jews ("the descendants of the Israelitic stock") to Christianity, the Relator evidently saw a solution to the problem of their alienship in the Christian world.
74. *Ibid.*, pp. 347–348.
75. *Ibid.*, p. 347.
76. *Ibid.*, pp. 345, 349 (gradne heregia; notoria heregia).
77. *Ibid.*, p. 345.
78. *Ibid.*, ibid.
79. *Ibid.*, p. 349.
80. *Ibid.*, ibid.
81. *Ibid.*, ibid.
82. *Ibid.*, ibid.
83. Ostensibly, "kill those of his race" may refer to the *converts* of the Jewish race; but the conclusion of the sentence (the Church prays ... that he bring *them* to the faith) indicates that the reference was to the Jews generally, and not only to converts.
84. *Ibid.*, ibid.: "Despues que *oiga* Marquillos tan grande heregia como dice, no see quales orejas Christianas e piadosas lo puedan oir, nin qual corazon fiel e Catholico lo pueda sufrir." The word *oiga* in the beginning of this sentence (as printed by both Caballero and Alonso) makes no sense. It should be replaced by *diga*, in accordance with mss. 721, f. 87, and 2041, f. 14ʳ, of the Biblioteca Nacional, Madrid.
85. *Ibid.*, ibid.

86. *Ibid.*, p. 350.
87. Romans 2.9. The Relator here seems to have followed Ambrosius who said: "Just as the faithful Jew should be more honored [see Romans 2.10] because of Abraham, the dissenting one should be treated worse because he refuted the promises given to the fathers" (see Glossa Ordinaria on Romans 2.9). Ambrosius, however, had to coordinate this view with the principle of equality of all men before God, and therefore, in commenting on Romans 2.12, added that "God does not follow the prerogative of race so as to accept the dissident for the sake of his fathers, or reject the faithful because of the fathers' unworthiness." Hence the "greater honor" is merely an indication of the special respect due to Abraham, or a sign of recognition of the promises given him (Gen. 22.18 and 26.4). Jerome thought that "*primum* pro *quidem* ponit," but considered the possibility that the "Jew first in honor" indicated merely a chronological precedence (the Jew was "first in time" to believe in God), and therefore it applied to the pre-Christian period when the gentiles were still living by the law of Nature. To the Christian period, in any case, related the rule that the "Jew was first in punishment," for, unlike the gentiles, he was instructed by the written Law (in addition to the Law of Nature), and thus was supposed to know better (see his *Commentaria in Epistolam ad Romanos*, 2.9, ML 30, 654–655).
88. *Ibid.*, p. 344: ". . . de los quales creo que hay muy pocos ahora, ca dudo que en todo Toledo de estos haya dies".
89. See above, n. 53.
90. *Ibid.*, p. 348.
91. See his Responsa, no. 89, ed. Livorno, p. 17ab, and my *Marranos of Spain*, 1973², pp. 45–46.

92. *Ibid.*, p. 350.

93. *Ibid.*, *ibid.*

94. See below, pp. 634, 654.

95. See below, p. 572 (for the view of Cartagena).

96. *Ibid.*, p. 351: E si en Castilla se levantara alguna Heregia, no por eso se sigue que sean en ella todos los Castellanos.

97. Ezekiel 18.20; "Instrucción," *loc. cit.*, p. 351.

98. *Ibid.*, *ibid.*

99. See *Tizón de España* (or: *Tizón de la Nobleza*), ed. 1871, pp. 2, 3, 4, 5, 6, 33, 34, 40 (reprinted by Caro Baroja, *Los Judíos en la España moderna e contemporánea*, 1961, III, pp. 288–289).

100. See below, p. 506.

101. "Instrucción," *loc. cit.*, pp. 352–354.

102. *Ibid.*, p. 354: . . . a los quales todos no fase poca injuria el herege malvado de Marquillos el poner contra ellos esta mancilla.

103. *Ibid.*, *ibid.*

104. *Ibid.*, *ibid.:* lo que mas malo e peor es a sabiendas dogmatizar con grande error una fee; and p. 355: Marquillos ha dogmatizado esta heregia.

105. *Ibid.*, p. 354.

106. *Ibid.*, p. 355: es cierto que continuando su costumbre Diabolica, querra ir por ella adelante.

107. *Ibid.*, *ibid.*, p. 353.

108. *Ibid.*, p. 346: bien creo . . . que estos señores, que cerca de su merced son, acatando su virtud, y sus personas, y dignidades, y Linajes, [no] quieran ser en cosas de tan mal exemplo.— Note the word *linajes*, which we translated as *origins*, but which means, to be precise, *lineages*, or the ancestral lines of descent.

109. *Ibid.*, p. 351.

110. *Ibid.*, *ibid.*

111. *Ibid.*, *ibid.*

112. *Ibid.*, p. 348.

113. *Ibid.*

114. *Ibid.*, pp. 348–349.

115. Cf. Paul of Burgos' letter to Lorki in

L. Landau, *Das apologetische Schreiben des Josua Lorki*, 1906, p. 19.

116. See below, pp. 935–937.

Juan de Torquemada

1. The first modern biography of Torquemada by Stephan Lederer (*Der Spanische Cardinal Johann von Torquemada*, 1879), although still of value, has been somewhat outdated by the many new data that have come to light since its publication. Partly meeting our present-day needs are the shorter studies of Torquemada's life that appeared as introductions to some of his works, which were published or republished in the past four decades (such as J. F. Stockmann's introduction to T.'s *De corpore Christi mystico*, 1951, and Nicolás López Martínez' introduction to Torquemada's *Tractatus contra Madianitas et Ismaelitas*, Burgos, 1957). Documentarily important are V. Beltrán de Heredia's collections of documents related to Torquemada's life, published in *Archivum Fratrum Praedicatorum*, VII (1937), 210–245, and XXX (1960), 53–148, and bibliographically (for Torquemada's own writings), J. M. Garrastachu, "Los manuscritos del Cardinal Torquemada en la Biblioteca Vaticana," in *Ciencia Tomista*, XLI (1930), 188–217, 291–322 (in addition to the list of Torquemada's works, published and unpublished, in Quétif-Echard, *Scriptores Ordinis Praedicatorum*, I, 1719, 839–842). Concerning Torquemada's general view of the Church, see Karl Binder, *Wesen und Eigenschaften der Kirche bei Kardinal Juan de Torquemada*, 1955; Thomas M. Izbicki, *Protector of the Faith*, 1981, 31–119; and W. E. Maguire, *John of Torquemada: The Antiquity of the Church*, 1957. For T.'s position on the critical questions of papal primacy and infallibility, see especially Emmanuel Candal, introduction to Torquemada's *Apparatus super decretum Florentinum*

unionis Graecorum, 1942; August Langhorst, "Der Cardinal Turrecremata und das Vaticanum über die Jurisdictionsgewalt der Bischöfe," in *Stimmen aus Maria-Laach,* XVII (1879), pp. 447–462; Joseph Hergenröther, *Anti-Janus* (transl. by J. B. Robertson), 1870; and V. Proaño Gil, "Doctrina de Juan de Torquemada sobre el Concilio," in *Burgense,* I (1960), pp. 73–96.—On T.'s historical influence, see K. Binder, *op. cit.,* pp. 196–207.

2. 1450; see the very end of Torquemada's work mentioned below, n. 4.

3. See below, pp. 724–725, on the change of Marrano tactics of self-defense.

4. J. de Torquemada, *Symbolum pro informatione Manichaeorum,* ed. N. López Martínez y Proaño Gil, 1958, prolog, p. 5.

5. *Tractatus contra Madianitas et Ismaelitas,* ed. N. López Martínez y V. Proaño Gil, 1957.

6. See Hernando de Castillo, *Primera Parte de la Historia General de Santo Domingo y de su Orden,* etc., Valencia, 1587, lib. iii, cap. 32, p. 488b.

7. See the discussion concerning this by Stockmann, *loc. cit.,* p. 16.

8. See Castillo, *op. cit.,* p. 488b.

9. *Coronica de Don Alfonso el Onceno,* cap. 101 (ed. BAE, vol. 66, p. 236ab), and *Crónica del Rey Don Pedro,* año 1366, caps. 4 & 5 (ed. BAE, vol. 66, pp. 539b, 540a).

10. *Crónica del Rey Don Pedro,* año 1367, cap. 37 (ed. cited: p. 579b), and año 1368, cap. 3, p. 581b.

11. Beltrán de Heredia, "Colección de documentos inéditos para ilustrar la vida del Cardinal Juan de Torquemada," in *Archivum Fratrum Praedicatorum,* VII (1937), pp. 230–232.

12. Stockmann, *loc, cit.,* p. 16.

13. A. Touron, *Histoire des hommes illustres,* III, 1746, p. 396; Beltrán de Heredia, *Ciencia Tomista,* LXXIII (1948), p. 335.

14. Emmanuel Candal, *loc. cit.,* p. viii,

n. 2.

15. Stockmann, *loc. cit.,* p. 17.

16. See López Martínez, *loc. cit.,* p. 100, n. 8, and J. Goñi Gaztambide, "Recompensas de Martín V a sus electores españoles," in *Hispania Sacra,* XI (1958), pp. 15–20.

17. His constitution to this effect, which he made public on March 10, 1418 (see Creighton, *History of the Papacy,* II, p. 109), was preceded by his refusal to accept the Council's view (expressed in its decree of October 30, 1417) concerning the "causes for which a Pope could be admonished or deposed" (see *ibid.,* p. 107). His plan to act as supreme arbiter in Christendom in all matters related to the faith was also indicated in his announcement (on April 22) that he would "approve and ratify" all the decrees made "*in materias fidei per praesens sacrum concilium conciliariter*" (*ibid.,* p. 116), thereby leaving the door open for himself to reject any decision of the Council, which was *not* made *conciliariter*—that is to say, which, in his judgment, was not within the Council's rights (otherwise there was no sense in adding the word *conciliariter* to the phrase *per sacrum concilium*). Cf. Ph. Schaff, *History of the Christian Church,* VI, 1910, pp. 165–166.

18. The plan for this school was authorized by the Pope at Fray Luis' request; see *ibid.,* p. 20; "Cronica Fratris Ludovici de Valladolid," in *Analecta Sacri Ordinis Fratrum Praedicatorum,* XX (1932), 727–731; and R. Rius Serra, "Los rótulos de la universidad de Valladolid," in *Analecta Sacra Tarraconensia,* XVI (1943), pp. 95–97.

19. See Quétif-Echard, *op. cit.,* p. 837b, and P. Feret, *La faculté de Théologie de Paris et ses docteurs les plus célèbres,* IV, 1897, p. 336; see also H. Denifle-A. Chatelain, *Chartularium Universitatis Parisiensis,* IV (1897), p. 428.

20. Stockmann, *loc. cit.*, p. 17.

21. Claiming that sanctity and true religiosity were giving way to worldly interests in almost all parts of the Church hierarchy, he urged the adoption of special regulations that might help reverse or arrest these trends; yet he put greater emphasis on inner spiritual change than on administrative correctives. See K. Binder, "El Cardenal Juan de Torquemada y el movimiento de reforma eclesiástica en el siglo XV," in *Revista de Teología*, La Plata, III (1953), nu. 12, 42–65.

22. Thus following the adoption by the Council of the *Decretum irritans* denying the Pope's right to grant bishoprics and benefices (against which he spoke in June 1433; see J. Haller, *Concilium Basiliense*, 1897, vol. II, pp. 422–423; Mansi, xxx, 550–590), he opposed the *Avisamentum* by which the Council warned the Pope that he must follow the directives of that decree or else face deposition (*ibid., ibid.,* 56–61); he also rejected as invalid the Council's claim that, in his bull of December 15, 1433 *(Dudum sacrum)*, the Pope agreed to abide by all the decisions of the Council (Stockmann, *loc. cit.*, p. 20). These, however, were only his first steps in his protracted conciliar battle.

23. N. Valois, *Le Pape et le Concile (1418–1450)*, II, 1909, p. 112.

24. Stockmann, *op. cit.*, pp. 23–24; Candal, *op. cit.*, p. xxiv.

25. *Ibid.*, p. xxv. 21; *id.*, introd. to T.'s *Oratio Synodalis de Primatu*, 1954, p. xxxi.16. In his later discussions of the subject (especially in his commentary on Gratian's *Decretum* and his *Summa de Ecclesia*), Torquemada developed, but also limited this principle, so that ultimately he came to concede that, in matters of faith, the decisions of the Council may override decisions to the contrary of the Pope (see Vicente Proaño Gil, "Doctrina de Juan de Torquemada sobre el Concilio," in *Burgense*, I, pp. 89–94). For the differences between Torquemada and Guido Terreni, a 14th century proponent of papal infallibility, see Th. M. Izbicki, "Infallibility and the Erring Pope," in *Law, Church and Society*, ed. K. Pennington & R. Somerville, 1977, pp. 97–111. On the rise of the doctrine and its early phases of development, see B. Tierney, *The Origins of Papal Infallibility, 1150–1350*, 1972, pp. 842–864.

26. See Stockmann, *loc. cit.*, p. 27.

27. *Comment. in Decretum Gratiani Partes V,* 6 vols., Lyon, 1516.

28. *Summa de Ecclesia,* Cologne, 1480 (latest ed.: Venice, 1561).

29. Most of these papers, which were delivered in various Councils, were published by J. D. Mansi, *Sacrorum conciliorum nova et amplissima collectio,* Paris, 1901–1927, XXX, cols. 550–590; 590–606; 1072–1094;; XXXI A, 41–62, 63–127; XXXV, 43–56. For his *Oratio synodalis de Primatu*, see below, n. 34. His address to the Diet of Mainz was published by P. Massi, as appendix to his *Il Magistero Infallibile de Papa nella Teologia de Giovanni Torquemada*, 1957. T.'s *Flores sententiarum S. Thomae Aquinatis de auctoritate summi pontificis* appeared (according to Quétif-Echard, *op. cit.,* 840A) in Lyon, 1496, and Venice, 1562.

30. His *Tractatus de sacramento Eucharistiae* (written in 1436) was published in Lyon, 1578. The *Tractatus de veritate conceptionis Beatissimae Virginis* (written in 1437) was published in Rome, 1547. It was partly translated into English by E. B. Pusey and included in his work on the same theme: *First Letter to the Rev. J. H. Newman . . . in Regard to. . . . the Doctrine of the Immaculate Conception*, 1869. T's views on the position of Christianity toward forgiveness of sin are presented in his

Impugnationes of the propositions of Alfonso de Madrigal (see below, n. 31).

31. See his *Reprobationes XXXVIII articulorum Bohemorum* etc., written in 1442 (see Garrastachu, *loc. cit.*, pp. 196 and 301) and his *Symbolum pro informatione Manichaeorum* (written in 1461), ed. N. López Martínez and V. Proaño Gil, 1952. Notable are also (a) his refutation of some of the views of Agostino Favaroni which seemed to be akin to those of the Hussites (written in 1435); see Mansi XXX, cols. 979–1034; and cf. Izbicki, *Protector of the Faith*, p. 7; (b) his censures (written in 1442) of some of the "propositions" of the Spanish theologian Alfonso de Madrigal, better known as *el Tostado* (see Garrastachu, *loc. cit.*, p. 197); and (c) his *Defensiones* of the Revelations of St. Bridget of Sweden (written in 1434; Mansi, XXX, cols. 699–814).

32. See on this Joseph Gill, *The Council of Florence*, 1959, pp. 122–123, 274–275, 280, 283; Hefele-Leclercq, *Histoire des Conciles*, VII–I, 1916, p. 968; E. Candal, his introduction to T.'s *Apparatus super Decretum Florentinum Unionis Graecorum*, pp. xviii–xxii. Another difficult point of disagreement between the Greeks and the Latins concerned the concept of the Trinity. An insight into the controversies on all these issues from the Greek-Orthodox point of view is given by Ivan N. Ostroumoff, *The History of the Council of Florence*, transl. from the Russian by Basil Pokoff, 1971.

33. See Stockmann, *loc. cit.*, pp. 20–21, against Quétif-Echard and Touron who placed this appointment in 1431.

34. This debate, which centered on the question of the Primacy, was staged by Eugene IV in September 1439; see Torquemada's *Oratio synodalis de Primatu*, ed. E. Candal, 1954.

35. The appointment was made while Torquemada was staying in Bourges

as member of the papal delegation to the French king (see Valois, *op. cit.*, II, p. 225, p. 2). The following year Eugene granted Torquemada the bishopric of Cádiz which, in 1442, was exchanged for that of Orense; see Beltrán de Heredia, "Colección de documentos," in *Archivum Fratrum Praedicatorum*, VII, p. 218; and see *ibid.*, p. 229.

36. See Touron, *op. cit.*, p. 427; Stockmann, *op. cit.*, p. 29.

37. See *ibid.*, pp. 32–33. Prior to this nomination Pius II appointed Torquemada to the see of León, but the appointment was not confirmed by King Enrique IV; see Beltrán de Heredia, "Colección . . . ," *loc. cit.*, VII, pp. 227; *id.*, "Noticias . . . ," *ibid.*, xxx, pp. 137–140.

38. Stockmann, *op. cit.*, p. 33.

39. L. Pastor, *The History of the Popes*, II³, 1906, p. 9.

40. Georg Voigt, *Enea Silvio de' Piccolomini*, I, 1856, p. 208.

41. See, for instance, J.J.I. Döllinger, *Fables Respecting the Popes in the Middle Ages*, 1872, p. 247, n. 1, where he rates Torquemada's *Summa* as the "most important work of the Middle Ages on the question of the extent of papal power"; see also Joseph Schwane, *Dogmengeschichte der mittleren Zeit*, 1887, III, p. 102, 520–521, 565–575; IV, 292–293; and Aug. Langhorst, in *Stimmen aus Maria-Laach*, XVII (1879), Freiburg im Breisgau, p. 447: "That Torquemada is . . . one of the chief representatives of the orthodox Roman Church's teaching is not disputed by any one."

42. "Those who will read the accounts of the sessions of the Council of Basle . . . ," said Castillo, "will greatly esteem the faith, the constancy, the doctrine, the sanctity, the religiosity, and the Catholic heart of Juan de Torquemada." Castillo made that evaluation with reference to Torquemada's

defense of the Papacy. See his *Historia General de Santo Domingo y su Orden*, I, p. 488a.

43. See N. Antonio, *Bibliotheca Hispana Vetus*, p. 286a.

44. See Garrastachu, *loc. cit.*, pp. 191–217, 291–322; Quétif-Echard, *op. cit.*, 839–842; Antonio, *op. cit.*, pp. 288–292.

45. This title, bestowed on Torquemada by Eugene IV in 1439 (see above, p. 424), was reconferred on him by Pius II in 1458 (see L. Pastor, *Geschichte der Päpste*, II, p. 7).

46. For the reforms adopted by the Council of Constance see Creighton, *op. cit.*, II, pp. 96–99; Hefele-Leclerqc, VII (I), pp. 443–476, 484–504.

47. See E. Candal's introduction to Torquemada's *Apparatus super decretum Florentinum unionis Graecorum*, pp. xv–xvii, xix–xxv, xxix–xxxiii.

48. The influence of Torquemada's teaching on Catholic thinking, which was still strongly felt during the fifth Lateran Council (1516), was later carried forward by men like Bellarmine and rose to great heights during the 19th century, when the Vatican Council (1869–1870) elevated the doctrine of papal infallibility to the status of a dogma. For the controversy that evolved around this issue (since 1867), and often around T.'s specific views, see especially the works of J. J. Döllinger *et al* (Janus, *The Pope and the Council*, 1869), who opposed the doctrine, and J. Hergenröther (*Anti-Janus*, 1870), who defended it. See also K. Binder, *Konzilsgedanken bei Kardinal Juan de Torquemada*, pp. 212–240.

49. See Torquemada's *Tractatus contra Madianitas et Ismaelitas* (cited below as *Tractatus*), p. 42: Vidimus ante nos et legimus processum quemdam Toleti factum per quosdam impios homines ... qui capita fationum et iniquitatum Tolleti comisarum fuere, quemadmodum scilicet domino nostro

Nicholao Pape quinto per quemdam eorum collegam cum certis litteris ad curiam romanam demandarunt.

50. *Ibid.*, p. 45; ... prout tam ex regie magestatis litteris quam ex aliorum fide dignorum relationibus intelligere potuimus.

51. See above, pp. 331–332.

52. See *Tractatus*, pp. 42–43.

53. *Claros Varones de Castilla*, ed. J. Domínguez Bordona, 1954, p. 108.

54. Juan de la Cruz, *Coronica de la Orden de Predicadores*, Lisbon, I, 1567, 188ᵛ.

55. See Antonius Senensis, *Bibliotheca ordinis Fratrum Praedicatorum*, Paris, 1585, p. 148.

56. *Historia General de Santo Domingo y de su orden de predicadores*, Primera Parte, Valencia, 1587, lib. iii, cap. 32, p. 488b.

57. *Ibid., ibid.*; and cf. above, n. 9.

58. *Ibid., ibid.*

59. *Ibid., ibid.*

60. Balthazar Porreño, *Elogios de los Papas y Cardenales que ha tenido la Nación Española*, Ms. in Cod. Biblioth. Vaticanae Barber. lat. 3571, saec. xvii, fol. 85ʳ–87ᵛ.

He writes: "Hernando del Pulgar en el libro de los illustros varones dice que era Iudio en venganca de cierta pesadumbre que tuvo con un pariente del dicho Cardenal, pero mintio." It is likely that by the "Cardinal's relative" Porreño meant Tomás de Torquemada, the chief Inquisitor. He adds: "The cardinal is defended against Pulgar's assertion by Hernando del Castillo, Antonius Possevinus in his *Apparatus Sacer*, II, by the Sienese [Antonius Senensis] and others."

Pulgar's statement on Torquemada's Jewish origin has led certain scholars (among them Henry C. Lea, *History of the Inquisition of Spain*, I, p. 120) to conclude that his nephew, Tomás de Torquemada, the Inquisitor General, was likewise a New Christian. This, however, remains unproven. Tomás' father was doubtless Juan de Torquemada's brother and, like Juan, the son of Alvar Fernández, but not necessarily of the same mother. Zurita, in any case, was sure that Tomás de Torquemada was "de limpio y noble linaje" (see *Anales de la Corona de Aragón*, lib. XX, cap. 49). Tomás' exclusion from the convent he had founded in Avila of "anyone descended, directly or indirectly, from Jews" (see Lea, *op. cit.*, II, p. 286), reflecting a racism unnatural for conversos, likewise suggests an Old Christian origin.

61. See "El Memorial contra los Conversos," in *Sefarad*, XVII, p. 325.

62. See López Martínez, *Los Judaizantes Castellanos*, pp. 389–390.

63. *Ibid.*, p. 389.

64. *Ibid., ibid.*

65. Torquemada, *Tractatus*, p. 39. The full title given at the opening of the work in ms. Vat. lat. 2580 is: *Tractatus contra Madianitas et Hysmaelitas adversarios et detractores filiorum que de populo Israelitico originem traxerunt*. On the original title and the change it may have undergone, see below, n. 81.

66. See below, Appendix F.

67. *Ibid.*, p. 41. The translation is according to the Vulgate which Torquemada used as his biblical source.

68. *Ibid., ibid.*

69. *Ibid., ibid.*

70. See Psalms 83.7.

71. *Tractatus*, p. 41.

72. *Ibid., ibid.*

73. *Ibid.*, p. 42; Psalms 76.2.

74. According to Torquemada, a *fidelis Christi* is signified especially by two beliefs: (a) in God and (b) in the mystery of the incarnation. See Torquemada's *Summa de Ecclesia*, lib. I, cap. 19, f. 1.

75. *Ibid.*, p. 42. The printed text has here by mistake *conversatio* instead of *conversio*.

76. *Ibid., ibid.* A similar thought is ex-

pressed in the opening of Nicholas V's bull *Humani generis*. See Benito Ruano, *Toledo, etc.*, p. 198.

77. *Tractatus*, p. 42.

78. *Ibid., ibid.*

79. *Ibid., ibid.*

80. *Ibid., ibid.*

81. *Ibid.*, p. 43. From this point on to the end of the treatise the term *Idumaei* used before (pp. 41, 42) is replaced by *Madianitae*. It is obvious that Torquemada preferred to relate his denigrating epithets to the Midianites (who were also known enemies of the Israelites) rather than to the Idumeans, whom the Jews identified with Rome and Christianity. We may assume, however, that the original title of the work was: *Tractatus contra Idumaeos et Ismaelitas*.

82. *Ibid.*, pp. 45–46.

83. This is according to the Vulgate (Deut. 1.13): *Date ex vobis viros sapientes et gnaros, et quorum conversatio sit probata in tribubus vestris*.

84. *Ibid.*, p. 46: nec quid sit fides canonica, nec quando quis hereticus veniat iudicandus, adhuc plene noverunt.

85. *Ibid.*, p. 47: *celeritas sit inimica iudicii*. See Cicero, *Pro domo sua ad pontifices*, in *Ouvres completes*, ed. Nisard, II, 1852, p. 727.

86. According to the Vulgate: *causam quam nesciebam, diligentissime investigabam*.

87. Gregory, *Moralium libri XXXV*, lib. 19, c. 25, 46 (*Morals on the Book of Job*, Library of Fathers, v. 27, p. 434).

88. *Tractatus*, p. 47; Pope Eusebius, Ep. II ad episcopos Thusciae, ML 7, 1110.

89. *Tractatus*, p. 48.

90. Augustine, Sermon 351, 10; ML 39, 1546; C. I. Ca., I, *Decretum*, C. II, q. 1, c. 1; Constantinus, *ibid.*, C. II, q. 1, c. 2.

91. *Tractatus*, p. 48.

92. *Ibid.*, p. 50; cf. Augustine, *De Trinitate*, c. 3, n. 5–6; ML 42, 823.

93. *Tractatus*, p. 50; cum nullus illorum convictus fuerit, aut sponte confessus, aut pertinax in aliquo errore repertus,

non poterant dicere cum vertitate quod essent heretici. And cf. above, n. 89.

94. *Ibid.*, p. 48.

95. *Ibid.*, *ibid.*

96. See above, pp. 355, 375.

97. *Tractatus*, p. 48.

98. Psalms 5.10; Jeremiah 9.2, 7.

99. Psalms 5.11: *Judica illos, Deus.*

100. *Tractatus*, p. 48: nullus convictus de heresi aut quocumque errore.

101. *Ibid.*, p. 45.

102. *Ibid.*, p. 51: impietatis et malignitatis consilio.

103. Psalms 83.4.

104. *Tractatus*, p. 51.

105. Psalms 83.4.

106. *Tractatus*, p. 51.

107. *Ibid.*, p. 52.

108. *Ibid.*, *ibid.* Cf. Esther 13.15 (according to the broadened version of Esther in the Vulgate). Torquemada spells out more clearly what was indicated by the Relator in designating Marcos García as Haman (cf. below, p. 613). His judgment is fully confirmed by García's own words in the "Memorial," see below, pp. 501–504.

109. *Ibid.*, p. 53: "qui malus est, vel de generatione mala vel dampnata, semper presumitur quod sit malus et dampnatus de illa specie mali super que fuit pronunciatus sive dampnatus malus, *quousque transeat quarta generatio*."

110. *Ibid.*, pp. 53–54.

111. *Ibid.*, p. 53.

112. See *Decretalium* VI, lib. V, tit. xii: *De regulis iuris*, reg. viii.

113. *Tractatus*, p. 53. The reference is to the Gloss of Joannes Andreae, see *ibid.*, n. 64.

114. *Ibid.*, *ibid.*

115. *Ibid.*, pp. 53–54.

116. Wisdom of Solomon, 12.10.

117. *Tractatus*, p. 54.

118. The reference is to Wladislaw II, formerly Jagiello, Grand Duke of Lithuania, who became King of Poland in 1386, and on that occasion was converted to Christianity. His son was Casimir IV who ascended the throne in 1447.

119. The Bosnian King Stephanus Thomas was converted to Catholicism in 1445. Years later (in 1460) Torquemada wrote a tract against Bosnian Bogomilism. See his *Symbolum pro imformatione Manichaeorum*. ed. N. López Martínez and V. Proaño Gil, 1958, p. 23, n. 68.

120. *Tractatus*, pp. 54–55.

121. Ezekiel, 18.20.

122. Cf. the Relator's "Instrucción," *loc. cit.*, p. 351; and see above, p. 414.

123. *Ibid.*, p. 55. Augustine, *On the Good of Marriage*, in Library of Fathers, vol. 22, p. 293.

124. *Tractatus*, p. 56. Chrysostom, *The Homilies on the Gospel of St. Matthew*, homily III, 5 (Nicene and Post Nicene Fathers, v. X, 1888, p. 17).

125. *Ibid.*, p. 16.

126. Chrysostom, *In Mattheam homilia III*, C. 3, MG 57, 34 and 36; and see *Tractatus*, pp. 55–56.

127. *Ibid.*, p. 56.

128. *Ibid.*, pp. 56–57.

129. *Ibid.*, p. 56.

130. Actually, Pseudo-Ambrosius, *Lib. de sacramentis*, c. 4, n. 12 (ML 16, 421); see *Tractatus*, p. 58.

131. The words quoted are likewise from Pseudo-Ambrosius, *loc. cit.* above, n. 128.

132. Ezekiel 36.25; *Tractatus*, p. 58.

133. *Ibid.*, *ibid.*

134. *Ibid.*, *ibid.*

135. *Ibid.*, *ibid.*

136. *Decret. Gregorii IX*, lib. III, t. 42, c. 3.

137. Jerome, *Epistle* 130.9 (*Letters and Select Works*, transl. by W. H. Fremantle, 1892, p. 266a).

138. Which read: "But if the wicked turn from all his sins . . . and keep all my statutes . . . he shall surely live . . . None of his transgressions . . . shall be remembered against him."

139. *Tractatus*, p. 59.
140. *Ibid., p. 75.*
141. Four chapters are devoted to the first proposition (3–6), five to the second (7–11), while another chapter (12) summarizes the conclusions arrived at in all the nine chapters mentioned.
142. *Tractatus*, p. 61.
143. *Ibid.*, pp. 61–62; cf. Augustine, *Enarrationes in Psalmis*, 78.2 (ML 36, 1010); cf. *Expositions on the Book of Psalms*, IV, Library of Fathers, vol. 32, 1850, p. 84.
144. *Expositions on Psalms*, 79.2; *Tractatus*, p. 62.
145. Psalms 94.14.
146. Augustine, *Expositions on Psalms*, 79.2.
147. *Tractatus*, pp. 62–63.
148. *Expositions on Psalms*, 79.2.
149. *Ibid., ibid.*
150. *Ibid., ibid: Ista igitur electio, istae reliquiae, ista plebs Dei quam non repulit Deus, hereditas eius dicitur.*
151. *Expositions on Psalms*, 94.7. Torquemada passes in complete silence over this passage of Augustine, too. It is possible, moreover, that it was because of this passage, containing so disparaging an assessment of the Jews, that Torquemada, while trying to lean on Augustine, preferred the Saint's comment on Psalms 78.2 to that on Psalms 94.7. Both comments, however, follow the same line of argument and demonstration.
152. See below, appendix D (1).
153. *Tractatus*, p. 73.
154. See de Lyra on Micah 4.6–7 (on *Colligam* etc.); and see Jerome, *Commentariorum in Michaeam lib. I*, cap. IV, 478 (ML 25, 1188–1189).
155. *Tractatus*, p. 73.
156. De Lyra on Micah 4.6, second interpretation on *Congregabo* and his first comment on *et eam quam eieceram* and also on *Et ponam*.
157. *Tractatus*, p. 73.
158. See above, pp. 463, 466.
159. See above, pp. 465, 467.

160. See *Tractatus*, pp. 79, 83. 85, 87.
161. *Ibid.*, p. 89.
162. *Ibid., ibid.*
163. *Ibid.*, p. 90.
164. *Ibid., ibid.;* Ordinary Gloss and Nicholas de Lyra on Titus I.10.
165. *Tractatus*, pp. 90–91.
166. *Ibid.*, p. 91.
167. *Ibid., ibid;* Hebrews XI.32.
168. *Tractatus*, p. 91.
169. *Ibid.*, p. 92.
170. *Ibid., ibid.*
171. *Ibid.*, p. 93.
172. *Ibid., ibid.*
173. *Ibid.*, pp. 93–94.
174. *Ibid.*, pp. 67–69.
175. *Ibid.*, p. 68.
176. *Ibid., ibid.*
177. *Ibid.*, p. 69.
178. *Ibid.*, p. 67.
179. *Ibid.*
180. Luke 2.25–32, 36–38; *Tractatus*, p. 76.
181. *Ibid.*, pp. 75–78; p. 75: omnes de genere iudeorum elegit.
182. *Ibid.*, p. 78.
183. *Ibid.*, pp. 99–129.
184. *Ibid.*, p. 99.
185. *Ibid.*, p. 100; de Lyra on Romans XI.5.
186. Thomas Aquinas, *Expositio in Omnes Sancti Pauli Epistulas*, Rom. XI, lectio I, ed. Vives, 1889, p. 535.
187. Glossa Ordinaria on Romans XI.6.
188. Referring perhaps to the destruction of the Second Temple; but Thomas' text, in Vives' edition, has here *illo* (that) instead of *alio* (the other), and thus we may have here, in either case, a printer's or a copyist's error.
189. Here Torquemada's printed text has,) instead of *gratuitatem* (as in the Vives' ed. of Aquinas), *gratuitam*, which seems to have been the correct version.
190. See Thomas Aquinas, *op. cit.*, above, n. 186, p. 535.
191. *Tractatus*, p. 100, according to de Lyra on Romans XI.3 (on *et ego relictus sum solus*): quia prophetyae Spiritus non semper tangit corda prophetarum etc.

The word *prophetyae* was added by Torquemada.

192. *Tractatus*, p. 101. Glossa Interlinearis on Romans XI.11–12: *diminutio eorum*—pauci eorum qui conversis fuerunt, scilicet apostoli, divitie sunt gentium.

193. Romans, XI.12.

194. *Tractatus*, p. 101.

195. Romans, XI.15.

196. *Tractatus*, p. 102; de Lyra on Romans XI. 15.

197. Thomas Aquinas, *Commentarii in Epistolam ad Romanos*, c. 11, lectio 2, ed. Vives, pp. 538a and 539a; gentiles sunt fideles qui tepescent.

198. *Ibid., ibid.*

199. *Tractatus*, p. 102.

200. *Ibid., ibid.*

201. *Ibid.*, p. 103.

202. *Ibid., ibid.*; Glossa Ordinaria and Nicholas de Lyra on Romans XI. 16.

203. *Tractatus*, p. 103; Glossa Ordinaria on Romans XI. 16.

204. *Tractatus*, p. 103.

205. *Ibid., ibid.*

206. *Ibid., ibid.*

207. *Ibid., ibid.*

208. *Tractatus*, p. 104.

209. *Ibid.*, p. 105.

210. See Marcos García's "Memorial," *loc. cit.*, p. 334.

211. These explanatory words were added by Torquemada, see *Tractatus*, p. 106.

212. Romans XI. 25–26; see the Interlinear and Ordinary Glosses on Isaiah 59.20.

213. *Tractatus*, p. 106.

214. *Ibid., ibid.*

The "Memorial"

1. Some half a dozen manuscripts of the "Memorial" are extant in various Spanish archives and one in the Bibliothèque Nationale in Paris dating from 1567, which is probably the oldest. It was published by Eloy Benito Ruano in *Sefarad*, XVII (1957), pp. 314–351 (with a brief introduction and a few notes), and republished in his collection of articles on the conversos, entitled *Los Origines del Problema Converso*, 1976, pp. 103–132. For the passage missing in the printed text, see my article, "Did the Toledans in 1449 Rely on a Real Royal Privilege?" (*Proceedings of the American Academy for Jewish Research*, XLIV [1977], pp. 102–105). And see also below, n. 13, for what seems to be sufficient indication that the Memorial was written, at least partly, in response to the Relator's Instruction to Barrientos.

2. That the *Sentencia* was examined by the city's *letrados* (experts in ecclesiastic and civil law) is stated explicitly in its preface. See Martín Gamero, *Historia de Toledo*, p. 1037; and cf. my article, mentioned above, n. 1 (*loc. cit.*, p. 107, n. 26).

3. On the differences between the *Petition* and the *Sentencia* in the severity of their attacks upon the conversos, see above, p. 383. On the more reserved stand taken by the *Sentencia* as compared with that of the "Memorial," see my above-mentioned study in *PAAJR*, XLIV (1977), pp. 115–116.

4. As suggested by E. Benito Ruano, "El Memorial contra los conversos del bachiller Marcos García de Mora," in *Sefarad*, XVII (1957), p. 318.

5. See, for instance, above, pp. 1215, n. 41; 281–282.

6. Even though the Instruction of the Relator and the Pope's bulls, in the original and in translation, were received by Barrientos at the same time (see on this above, p. 393), we must assume that it took several weeks before all these papers were prepared by the Relator and their contents became known to the rebels. This does not make it very likely that the writing of the "Memorial" began before November, or was completed before the end of that month. And see on this above, *ibid.*

7. See "Memorial," *loc. cit.*, pp. 340–343.

8. See *ibid.*, p. 321.

9. *Ibid.*, *ibid.*

10. *Ibid.*, *ibid.:* the "cruelties and inhumanities" committed by Alvaro de Luna were, says García, "causadas, promovidas e incitadas" by the conversos.

11. *Ibid.*, pp. 322, 323, 326, 335, 339, 346, and elsewhere. Regarding the name *Hamomo* see above, p. 1240, n. 4.

12. *Ibid.*, p. 322. In all probability, the sharp denunciation of the Relator in this and other places of the "Memorial" (see especially *ibid.*, pp. 346, 349) came in reply to the biting criticisms which the Relator uttered against García in his Instruction (see *loc. cit.*, pp. 344, 348, 354, 355). Also García's attempt to present himself as a nobleman and "son of an honored man and a civic hidalgo" ("Memorial," *loc. cit.*, p. 346) was made in reaction to the Relator's description of García as a man who belonged to the rustic class (of "villano linage de la Aldea de Maçarambros, donde es su naturaleza" ("Instrucción," *loc. cit.*, p. 354). Attesting this is García's own statement ("Memorial," *loc. cit.*, p. 344): porque el dicho Mose Hamomo se trabajo de me deshonrrar e de menguar mi fama e honrra (because the said Mose Hamomo made an effort to dishonor me and besmirch my reputation and honor), he, García, had no choice but to speak of his own merits. For this purpose he went into a discussion of the three existent kinds of nobility, concluding that he owned at least two of them, while the Relator possessed none (*ibid.*, pp. 345–347).

13. *Ibid.*, p. 321.

14. *Ibid.*, *ibid.*

15. *Ibid.*, p. 322. The correct version should have been "treinta años," and thus we find it in the Petition (*Halconero*, p. 521): ". . . como a treinta años y mas tiempo" (and cf. *Crónica de Juan II*, p. 664b).

Similarly corrupt is the preceding statement in the "Memorial," *loc. cit.*, p. 321: "de quatro años de esta parte." The copyist of ms. 9-5849 of the Academia de la Historia, Madrid, tried to correct this error by replacing "quatro" with "sesenta" (f. 250ᵛ), no doubt bearing in mind the year 1391, in which he saw the beginning of converso influence in Spain, but considering the period of Alvaro's rule, the change is obviously unacceptable. The Salamanca ms. 455 has in both places: *quarenta años*, and this is probably what García wrote in the heat of his exaggerative censures. This phrasing, like other indications, shows that the manuscript was not checked and never made ready for formal use.

16. *Ibid.*, pp. 322–323.

17. *Ibid.*, p. 323.

18. *Ibid.*, *ibid.*

19. *Ibid.*, p. 320.

20. *Ibid.*, p. 331.

21. *Ibid.*, p. 336. The phrase appears not in Psalms, but in Deut. 32–20, and its correct translation is probably: *an unruly generation*. García, however, followed the translation of the Vulgate, which says here: *generatio perversa est*. To this formulation García added: *adulteros;* and this is not a mistranslation of *infideles filii*, Deut. 32.10), for García included among the derogatory titles also *fixos infieles* (p. 336).

22. *Ibid.*, p. 335: *'am to'ēy lēvav* (a people of an errant heart) is rendered by the Vulgate: *semper hi errant corde.* García translated it: *siempre me erraron en su corazón*, which means: they have always missed God in their thinking, or: could never attain the true knowledge of God, or the understanding of His will.

23. *Ibid.*, pp. 333–334. The confusion of Titus, Paul's disciple, with Titus the Emperor and conqueror of Jerusalem is only one of several indications of

García's poor historical knowledge and ignorance of Christian biblical exegesis (cf. above, n. 21, and below, notes 37 and 95a). But this is rather incidental. Of significance is his reference to Titus as the "avenger of Christ's blood," for it not only reflects the traditional Christian view of the Deicide as the cause of Jerusalem's destruction, but also the view that the true followers of Christ should *keep* avenging the "injuries" done Him. This is a recurring theme in the Memorial (see *ibid.,* pp. 322 and 341), and it shows that the same religious agitation launched against Jews in times of pogroms was now directed against the Marranos as if they were not Christians at all. Thus, while charges of quite a *new* kind were henceforth employed against the conversos, they combined with, but did not replace the old ones. It was no doubt the blend of all these arguments that gave the campaign against the New Christians its special effectiveness and force. And see further on this below, p. 983.

24. "Memorial," *loc. cit.,* pp. 333–334.

25. Such are the attributes "vindictive," "adulterous," "arrogant," "vainglorious," and "trained in all evil arts" (*ibid.,* p. 334); and cf. Titus 1. 5–16.

26. The strictly moral censures found in Paul's invectives (Titus 1.12), are directed not against the Jews of Crete, but against the Cretan *gentiles,* including their converts to Christianity, and the "prophet" he cites there as witness for those censures was the Greek poet Epimenides, as indicated by both Augustine (see *Glossa Ordinaria* on Titus 1.12) and Jerome (see his *Commentaria in Epistolam ad Titum,* ML 26, pp. 571–573).

27. Juan de Torquemada, as we have seen, bluntly labels that "addition" (which was doubtless found also in the summary of the *pesquisa*) one of the

gross falsifications of the Toledans, designed to crown their racial theory with the authority of the Apostle. See above, p. 472.

28. "Memorial," *loc. cit.,* p. 320. García's designation of the synagogue as a "congregation of beasts" echoes Chrysostom's reference to the Synagogue as "a lodging for wild beasts" (see his *Discourses against Judaizing Christians,* Discourse I, cap. 3, transl. P. W. Harkins, pp. 10–11).

29. "Memorial," *loc. cit.,* pp. 320–321.

30. *Ibid.,* p. 321.

31. *Ibid.*

32. See *ibid.,* 95, 9–10.

33. Augustine, *Enarrationes in Psalmis,* 94.10. The expression "forty years" in verse 10 is taken by Augustine as a mystical allusion to the "totality of time" *(iste numerus indicat integritatem saeculorum),* equaling in meaning the word "always," which appears in the Vulgate's translation of the phrase: "a people of an errant heart" (*semper* isti errant corde, *ibid.,* 94.10). What it indicates, according to Augustine, is that this people has *always* exacerbated God *(ibid., ibid.).*

34. *Ibid.,* on Psalms 94.11.

35. *Ibid., ibid.*

36. See Cassiodorus, *Expositio in Psalterium,* who follows closely in Augustine's footsteps and explains the Jews' failure to enter "His rest" as the "eternal death" that awaits those who *non meruerunt ad satisfactionis ejus munera pervenire* (*ibid.,* on Psalms 94.11; ML 70, p. 675).

37. It is questionable, of course, whether the influence referred to was a direct one. So close at this point is García's view to Augustine's that it is difficult to see why, in presenting it, García failed to mention the Saint's name, or cite from his words such statements about the Jews as *genus tale hominum quod me semper exacerbat usque in finem saeculi* (*ibid.,* 94.10), which could have

greatly bolstered his case. We are inclined, therefore, to believe that he drew his theory of condemnation not directly from its original authors, but from others (perhaps contemporary preachers) who summarized it in their own manner. His inadequate knowledge of biblical literature, evidenced by his other references to the Bible (which are usually erroneous or inaccurate; cf. above, n. 21 and below, n. 88), likewise supports this conclusion.

38. Augustine, *Enarrationes*, 94, verse 11.

39. Augustine, *Sermones*, 7.2 (ML 38, 63) and especially *Sermo* 122.5 (ML 38, 683).

40. See his *Postillae* on Psalms 94, where christological and literal interpretations go hand in hand. Thus de Lyra explained the term "My rest" as the "Land of Promise," i.e., the Land of Israel (see his comments on verses 8 and 11), but added that David (i.e., the author of the Psalm) also signified by that term the "land of the living, which is the peace of the blessed" (see his comment at the conclusion of the chapter).

41. "Memorial," *loc. cit.*, p. 336; and cf. the Relator's Instruction, *loc. cit.*, pp. 343–344.

42. "Memorial," *loc. cit.*, p. 336.

43. Instruction, *loc. cit.*, pp. 349–350.

44. "Memorial," *loc. cit.*, pp. 336–337.

45. *Ibid.*, p. 336.

46. See above, pp. 361–362.

47. See on all this below, p. 1140.

48. "Memorial," *loc. cit.*, p. 337.

49. *Ibid., ibid.:* ". . . acoceáronlos y truxéronlos y tráenlos debaxo de los pies como a enemigos de la ley y verdadera fée de Jusuchristo y como enemigos de los dichos Reynos, espeçial de esta ciudad." "Y tráenlos" (in the opening part of the sentence) is no doubt a relic from the original formulation which the scribe changed from the present to the past tense; ms. Salamanca 455, f. 23° reads here: *Y acoceanlos y traenlos por los pies.*

50. "Memorial," *loc. cit.*, p. 321. By this statement he no doubt intended to explain the appearance of the Apostles who came from the Jews and a few other "exceptions."

51. *Ibid.*, p. 334.

52. *Ibid.*, p. 331: e fueron fallados judaiçar e guardar todas las ceremonias judaicas.

53. See above, p. 317.

54. "Memorial," *loc. cit.*, p. 330.

55. *Ibid.*, pp. 330–331.

56. See *ibid.*, pp. 330 and 332: a los que dellos fincaron vibos sin ser *asaetados* e *enforcados*. Also according to the *Cronicón de Valladolid* for the year 1449 (see *CODOIN*, XIII, pp. 18–19), Juan de la Cibdad was hanged after he had died from an arrow shot (despues de meurto de una saeta). And cf. the *Crónica de Don Alvaro de Luna*, ed. Carriazo, p. 244, which likewise says that the said Juan was hanged after he had died.

57. "Memorial," *loc. cit.*, p. 331.

58. *Ibid.*, the reference is to Hostiensis; see below, n. 70.

59. See on this whole development in E. Vacandard, *The Inquisition*, 1918 (transl. by B. L. Conway), pp. 75–83.

60. *Ibid.*, pp. 76, 79: "In as much as repentent heretics were imprisoned for life [by the Church authorities themselves], it seems certain that the severer penalty served for obstinate heretics [who were delivered to the secular arm] must have been the death penalty at the stake."

61. We refer here to the edicts issued by Emperor Frederick II, the foremost lay ruler in Christendom, from 1220 to 1239; to the laws and practices of the City of Rome (the seat of the Popes) since 1231, and those followed by other towns and cities in Italy (such as Milan, 1233) and France. See on this H. Ch. Lea, *A History of the Inquisition of the Middle Ages*, I, 1958, pp. 321–326, and Vacandard, *op. cit.*, 78–83.

62. See *ibid.*, especially pp. 77–81.

63. *Summa Theologica*, II, ii, Q. 11, art. 4.

64. Hostiensis on *Ad abolendam* (De Haereticis), see his *In Quintum Decretalium librum Commentaria*, tit. 7, c. 9 (ed. Venice, 1581, p. 36b).

65. See the comments of Ioannes Andreae on the decretal *Ad abolendam* (on *Debitam*), quoted from his *Novella* in Eymeric's *Directorium inquisitorum*, II, Rome, 1585, p. 182a; and cf. Vacandard, *op. cit.*, p. 128.

66. See Hostiensis, *op. cit.*, p. 36b.

67. See "Memorial," *loc. cit.*, p. 331.

68. *Ibid., ibid.*

69. *Ibid.*, pp. 331–332.

70. *Ibid.*, p. 332. The authority mentioned here in the printed text is "Pedro Enrique", and Benito Ruano, in his introduction to the Memorial (*ibid.*, p. 318), and also in his second edition of this document (in *Los Origines del Problema Converso*, 1976, p. 98), included this "Pedro Enrique," together with Baldus and Bartolus, among the "authorities of the first rank" (primera fila de autoridades) used by García. There was, however, no expert on canon law by the name of Pedro Enrique. As the contents indicates, the reference was to Henricus de Segusio (Hostiensis), and "*Pedro* Enrique" was a scribal error for "*por el* Enrique," a phrase García used also in other places (see *loc. cit.*, pp. 327, 331, and 333).

71. See *Decretales Gregorii IX*, lib. V, tit. vii, cap. 15. And cf. H. Ch. Lea, *A History of the Inquisition of the Middle Ages*, I, ed. 1958, p. 484, who differentiates between the first part of the law, urging the death penalty for "persistent heretics," and the second part which deals with the less stubborn deviators, who "*redire voluerint*" (and not *noluerint*, as spelled erroneously in the given text), even though their desire to "return" to the faith was prompted by fear of death. For heretics of the latter kind the law ordered a punishment less severe than

death (namely, perpetual imprisonment).

72. See Hostiensis, *In Quintum Decretalium Librum Commentaria*, 1581, p. 40b.

73. "Memorial," *loc. cit.*, p. 332.

74. *Ibid., ibid.*: "no ouo en ello otro error saluo de tolerar a los que dellos fincaron vibos sin ser asaetados e enforcados," as was done to Juan de Cibdad.

75. *Ibid., ibid.*

76. *Ibid., ibid.*

77. *Ibid., ibid.*

78. *Ibid., ibid.* Relying on "L. Arriani, in De hereticis et mathematicis" (should be: L. Ariani, in De haereticis et Manichaeis), which appears in Justinian's Code (lib. I, tit. 5, lex 5), García handles the text all too freely. The law refers only to the Manichaeans "who may, by means of witchcraft, even put the elements in turmoil." García, as we have seen, broadened the reference to embrace all heretics, while omitting the mention of magic as a heretical *modus operandi*. Instead of "by means of witchcraft" he here used the word "naturally." The change is significant. Since the middle of the 13th century "heresy" was often associated with "magic," and the employment of sorcery was also attributed to the Jews as the "sons" or "servants" of the devil. Before long this association was also to be claimed in Spain. In the middle of the 15th century, however, such an attribution to the conversos would obviously appear preposterous, and García preferred to suppress the reference to magic in the Roman law and ascribe the disastrous effect of heresy to the "natural" impact of the "religious" deviation.

79. *Ibid., ibid.*

80. *Ibid.*, p. 333.

81. *Ibid., ibid.*

82. *Ibid.*, p. 333.

83. *Ibid., ibid.*

84. See above, pp. 501–502.
85. See "Memorial," *loc. cit.,* p. 333: Siguese pues que no puede ser imputado a crimen lo echo cerca de la toma de los dichos bienes, saluo lo no echo, para lo qual ay remedio, que los acauemos de perseguir y entonçes nuestros actos y mouimientos seran gratos e apaçibiles *ante conspectum Domini* y ante las gentes.
86. *Ibid.,* p. 333.
87. See above notes 24–25; Titus I. 1–12.
88. The "ordinance" he refers to, says García, is "indicated and written" in the third book of the Law (see "Memorial," *loc. cit.,* p. 334). Actually, however, it is found in the fifth (Deuteronomy 23. 3–9).
89. "Memorial," *loc. cit.,* p. 334.
90. That García's argument hit home, however, is evidenced by the fact that even some conversos came to regard it as true. See Hernando del Pulgar, *Letras,* ed. J. Domínguez Bordona, 1949, p. 138; and cf. my study, "Americo Castro and his View of the Origins of the Pureza de Sangre," in *PAAJR,* XLVI–XLVII (1979–1980). pp. 401–402.
91. See Juan de Torquemada, *Tractatus,* p. 95.
92. Deut. 23. 4, 8. Nicholas de Lyra (who at this point follows Saadia Gaon) rather bypasses the reasons offered in the Law for the total rejection of the Ammonites and Moabites (see Deut. 23. 5–7), and sees their main crime in their brazen attempt to seduce Israel to idolatry (see Glossa Ordinaria and Nicholas' *Postillae* on Deut. 23.4).
93. *Ibid.,* p. 335.
94. See González-Tejada, II, p. 245, c. 14: . . . praecepit, ut judaeis non liceat christianas habere uxores . . . nulla officia publica eos opus est agere etc.
95. See *ibid.,* I, p. 398f. (canon 34).
96. *Ibid.,* II, pp. 305–306.
97. See *ibid.,* II, p. 308, (c. 65).
98. See above, p. 403. Some Christian

commentators denied the assumption that the law referred to converts from Jewish origin (see above, p. 401, and below, p. 570), and the very formulation of this law, it seems, gave legitimate grounds for such interpretations. Yet whatever the law-maker had in mind when he used the phrase "those who are of the Jews," his avoidance to employ the term "converts" in this instance betrays his realization that such an enactment would go counter to the historic policy of the Church.

99. *Ibid.,* p. 335.
100. *Forum Judicum,* lib. xii, tit. II, 1. 10 (cf. above, *Sentencia-Estatuto,* notes 11–12).
101. *Ibid., ibid.*
102. "Memorial," *loc. cit.,* p. 335; see above, pp. 399–400.
103. For this assertion of García, which is missing in the Memorial as published in *Sefarad,* XVII (1957), see my study in *PAAJR,* XLIV (1977) indicated above, n. 1.
104. See above, pp. 401–402.
105. "Memorial," *loc. cit.,* p. 335.
106. *Ibid.,* p. 336.
107. *Ibid., ibid.*

The Privilege

1. The "Privilege" was published several times—first, by Antonio Paz y Mélia, in his collection *Sales españolas, o agudezas del ingenio nacional,* part I, Madrid, 1890 (Colección de escritores castellanos, t. LXXX, pp. 51–62); second, by H. Pflaum (later: Peri), in *REJ,* vol. 86 (1928), pp. 144–150, preceded by an introductory study of this document, pp. 131–143; thirdly, and finally, by N. López Martínez, as appendix II to his *Los Judaizantes Castellanos,* pp. 383–387.

Two manuscripts of the "Privilege" were preserved in the Biblioteca Nacional, Madrid: 13043 and 9175. Ms.

9175 is from the 16th century, ms. 13043 seems to have originated in the 18th century (see Pflaum, *loc. cit.*, p. 133). Pflaum published the version of ms. 9175, Paz and López that of ms. 13043, unaccompanied by comparisons and remarks. The only critical edition is that of Pflaum, and it is this edition that we shall cite in the following. Brief discussions of the "Privilege" are found in Baer's *History*, II, pp. 280–281, and Kenneth R. Scholberg's *Sátira e invectiva en la España Medieval*, 1971, pp. 349–352.

2. This is also suggested by the scribe of ms. 9175 who indicated (at the top of the manuscript's first page) that the "Letter of Privilege" was written by "some Old Christian *hijo dalgo* who did not prosper" (see Pflaum, *loc. cit.*, p. 144, n. 2).

3. See his *Judaizantes Castellanos*, p. 383.

4. See his study, "Une ancienne satire espagnole contre les Marranes," in *REJ*, 86 (1928), pp. 131–143; remarks on the date: pp. 142–143.

5. Privilege, *loc. cit.*, pp. 144–145.

6. *Ibid.*, p. 146.

7. *Ibid., ibid.*

8. *Ibid.*, p. 145.

9. *Ibid., ibid.*

10. *Ibid.*, pp. 145, 147.

11. *Ibid.*, pp. 146–147.

12. *Ibid.*, p. 148.

13. *Ibid.*, p. 147.

14. *Ibid., ibid.*

15. *Ibid.*

16. *Ibid.*, p. 146.

Alonso de Cartagena

1. See M. Martínez Añíbarro y Rives, *Intento de un Diccionario Biográfico de Autores de la Provincia de Burgos,* Madrid, 1889, pp. 88–115; Nicolás Antonio, *Bibliotheca Hispana Vetus,* II, Madrid, 1788, pp. 261–279; J. Amador de los Ríos, *Historia crítica de la literatura Española,* VI, Madrid, 1865, pp. 26–29, 67–73, 200,

316–320, 331; *id., Estudios sobre los Judíos de España,* Madrid, 1848, pp. 384–405; Luciano Serrano, *Los conversos Don Pablo de Santa María y Don Alfonso de Cartagena,* Madrid, 1942, pp. 119–260; Francisco Cantera Burgos, *Alvar García de Santa María y su familia de conversos,* Madrid, 1952, pp. 416–464, 490–495; Manuel Alonso, introd. to Alonso de Cartagena's *Defensorium Unitatis Christianae,* Madrid, 1943, pp. 17–57; E. García de Quevedo, *De bibliografía burgense,* 1941; Hernando del Pulgar, *Claros Varones de Castilla,* ed. J. Domínguez Bordona, Madrid, 1954, pp. 125–128; Menéndez y Pelayo, *Bibliografía Hispano-Latina Clásica,* I, 1902, pp. 571–585, 823–824; *id., Biblioteca de Traductores Españoles,* ed. E. Sánchez Reyes, I, 1952, pp. 289–310; Enrique Flórez, *España Sagrada,* v. 26 (1771), pp. 388–400.

2. See his coplas on Don Alonso in R. Foulché-Delbosc, *Cancionero Castellano del Siglo XV,* I, 1912, p. 676 (also with slight differences, in *España Sagrada,* v. 26, pp. 400–402). Cartagena's poetry, however, has not survived. B. J. Gallardo (*Ensayo de una biblioteca española* etc., 1966, II, 253–254) and J. Amador de los Ríos (*Estudios,* 392–405, and *Historia crítica de la Literatura Española,* VI, 67–73) believed that Alonso de Cartagena was the author of the love poems grouped in the *Cancionero general* of the 15th century under the name of "Cartagena;" but M. Jiménez de la Espada (in his "Notes and Illustrations" on *Las Andanças é Viajes de Pero Tafur,* etc., 1874, pp. 378–398), Menéndez y Pelayo (*Antología de Poetas líricos Castellanos,* 1944, III, 130–138), and recently F. Cantera (*Alvar García,* pp. 571–582, and "El Poeta Cartagena, etc." in *Sefarad,* 28 [1968], pp. 3–39) have shown that none of these poems were penned by Don Alonso.

3. See his coplas cited above, n. 2 (first copla).

4. See Amador de los Ríos, *Obras de Don Iñigo López de Mendoza*, introd., p. cxxiii, n. 22.

5. See Juan de Lucena, *De vita felici*, ed. A. Paz y Mélia, 1893, pp. 112–113.

6. See Foulché-Delbosc, *op. cit.*, II, p. 75; and see also his *Estrenas* to Cartagena, *ibid.*, p. 109.

7. Pulgar says that he was "so revered and commanded so great an authority that in his presence . . . no one dared say or do anything improper." See *Claros Varones*, p. 126.

8. Judging by the epitaph on his tomb which states that he was 71 years old when he died on July, 1456; see Cantera, *op. cit.*, p. 416. L. Serrano (*op. cit.*, pp. 119–120), however, maintained that he was born either in 1385 or 1386, since he was 70 years old when he died, according to his first anonymous biographer who was a contemporary of Don Alonso; see *De actibus . . . Alfonsi de Cartagena*, Biblioteca Nacional, Madrid, ms. 7432, f. 89.

9. On the date of his conversion, which was doubtless identical with that of his father, see my *Marranos of Spain*, 1973, p. 224. Paul was interested in spreading the notion that he and his sons were converted in 1390—that is, prior to the riots of 1391, and not in the year of those riots, which might place them in the category of forced converts. The real date of their conversion, however, was most probably July or August 1391. In the Prologue to his *Additiones* to the *Postilla* of Nicholas de Lyra, Paul of Burgos says that Alonso was converted to Christianity when he did not yet know to call the letters by their names *(prius literas nominare nouisses)*. Paul may have been interested in showing that Alonso did not manage to inherit any knowledge from his Jewish education. In any case, contrary to what was said by Amador, *Estudios*, p. 390, n. 3, it is difficult to find in his style signs of Hebrew influences

(cf. Cantera, *op. cit.*, p. 492, n. 62).

10. See Serrano, *op. cit.*, pp. 122.

11. *Ibid.*, p. 123.

12. *Ibid.*, p. 124.

13. *Ibid.*, p. 129.

14. Such as translations into Castilian of Cicero's *De officiis* and *De senectute* (1422). In the same year he wrote in Latin *Memoriale virtutum*, which was translated into Castilian in 1474. See Cantera, *op. cit.*, pp. 455–456, 459, 464; and Serrano, *op. cit.*, pp. 241–242, 246–247, 249.

These and other works of Cartagena (including his translations from Seneca) place him among the main contributors to the rise of humanism in Spanish literature. See on this Ottavio di Camillo, *El humanismo castellano del siglo XV* (transl. Manuel Lloris), 1976, pp. 113–193, 203–226.

15. See above, pp. 205–206.

16. See Alvar García, *Crónica*, año 1420, c. 30 (*CODOIN*, 99, p. 132); cf. Cantera, *op. cit.*, p. 417.

17. *Crónica de Juan II*, año 1421, cap. 2.

18. *Ibid., ibid.*, cap. 3; Alvar García, *op. cit.*, *CODOIN*, 99, p. 199.

19. *Crónica de Juan II*, año 1421, cap. x.

20. *Ibid., ibid.*, caps. xi–xii.

21. *Ibid., ibid.*, cap. xxxiv; and cf. Serrano, *op. cit.*, p. 126, n. 26.

22. *Crónica de Juan II*, año 1423, cap. 2.

23. Alvar García, *op. cit.*, in *CODOIN*, 99, p. 344; cf. Serrano, *op. cit.*, p. 127.

24. Perhaps it was in those days that Alonso de Cartagena joined the circle of Alvaro's allies who swore to "defend, protect and aid him, and guard his person, estate and honor against all the persons in the world" (see *Crónica de Don Alvaro de Luna*, ed. Carriazo, p. 396).

25. Cantera, *op. cit.*, pp. 423–424.

26. Serrano, *op. cit.*, p. 106; and see above, p. 206.

27. *Ibid.*, pp. 140–143. Don Alonso's speech on this subject, in Castilian translation,

appeared in *La Ciudad de Dios,* XXXV
(1894), pp. 122ff. The original Latin text
is found in Biblioteca Nacional,
Madrid, ms. 2347, f. 409.

28. Serrano, *op. cit.,* 146–148 (on the basis of
De actibus . . . Alfonsi de Cartagena,
Biblioteca Nacional, Madrid, Ms. nu.
7432).

29. Serrano, *op. cit.,* pp. 150–151.

30. Hefele, *Conciliengeschichte,* VII, 1874, p.
64b.

31. I. e., the debate which began in mid
April, 1439 and ended with the Pope's
deposition by the Council on June 15
of that year. See on this Creighton, *op.
cit.,* III, pp. 10–18.

32. In the meeting of April 1439; see on it
ibid., ibid., pp. 10–14.

33. See Aeneas Sylvius Piccolominus, *De
gestis Concilii Basiliensis* etc. (ed. D.
Hay and W. K. Smith), 1967, lib. I, p. 10.

34. *Ibid.,* p. 20.

35. *Ibid.,* p. 96.

36. *Ibid.,* pp. 29, 31.

37. For the position of the Castilian
government in Basle, see *Historia de
España,* XV, pp. 136–139, 140–143.

38. Serrano, *op. cit.,* p. 153.

39. *Ibid.,* p. 154.

40. Concerning the decision in Basle see
above, pp. 276–278; concerning the
cedula, see above, pp. 292–294.

41. See *Defensorium,* p. 64.

42. *Ibid.,* p. 66. While he actually cites
Bede (without mentioning his name),
Don Alfonso attributes the passage to
Augustine; and indeed the idea was
Augustinian. See *City of God,* XII, 22–23
(transl. by Ph. Levine in Loeb
Classical Library: *City of God,* vol. IV,
pp. 108–113); and see Bede's *Hexameron,*
lib. I, ML 91, 30. See also Bede in
Glossa Ordinaria, Gen. 2.21–22; cf. ML
91, 30.

43. See *Defensorium,* p. 66.

44. While rightly attributing the idea to
Augustine, Cartagena presents two
citations in support of this claim, one
(not verbatim) from Augustine, *City of*

God, XII, c. 22 and 28 (Loeb ed. cited
above, pp. 109–110 and 129), and the
other from Bede (*Hexameron,* lib. I,
ML. 91, 30), which he also attributes to
Augustine. See *Defensorium,* p. 66.

45. *Ibid.,* p. 67; Gen. 11.6.

46. *Ibid.,* p. 67: Omnes virtute aut vicio
personarum, non ex differentia
carnalis originis, distinguendos.

47. *Ibid.:* Omnes tamen gentiles et nulli
legi scripte alligati tunc erant.

48. *Defensorium,* p. 66: Allii quidem lumine
naturalis rationis utentes, honestatem
vivendi viam, aliquali cognitioni dei
coniunctam, tenuerunt.

49. Augustine, *City of God,* XV.1.

50. *Ibid.,* XV.8; XVI. 11–12.

51. See on this Maguire, *op. cit.,* pp. 43–57.

52. *Defensorium,* pp. 66–68.

53. *Hominum genus,* see above, p. 529.

54. *Defensorium,* pp. 72–73.

55. Gen. 12.1–3; *Defensorium,* p. 68.

56. *Ibid.,* p. 72.

57. *Ibid.,* p. 74.

58. *Ibid.,* p. 70.

59. Malachi, 1.2.

60. *Defensorium,* p. 70.

61. See Augustine, *Epistolae,* 186.15, 194.39
(ML 33, 821, 888).

62. *Defensorium,* p. 71: nec voluntas dei
iniusta esse non potest, venit enim de
occultissimis meritis (see Augustine,
De diversis quaestionibus, LXXXIII, lib.
I., q. 68 (ML. 40, 72).

63. *Defensorium,* p. 71; Peter Lombard,
Sententiae, lib. I, dist. 41, 2–3 (ML 192,
633–634).

64. *Defensorium,* p. 71: "We cannot assume
that that singularity of love proceeded
without a cause."

65. Job. 5.6. This is according to the
Vulgate, which differs greatly from
the Hebrew meaning. Says Cartagena:
"The reason for the special favor
conceded to that people with respect
to the flesh of Christ, which was to be
taken from it, does not stem from the
people's merit." And following St.
Thomas, without mentioning his

name, he adds: "But if someone will again ask, why He chose this people above all others that Christ might be born thereof, let him hear what Augustine says: "Seek not to judge, if you wish not to err" (see *Summa Theologica*, II^a, II^ae, q, 98, art. 4; and cf. *In Ioannis Evangelium Tractatus*, trac. xxvi⁴ (ML, 35, 1608). For these divine secrets cannot be known to men, nor should they be inquired into" (*Defensorium*, p. 75).

66. Augustine, *De bono coniugali*, c. 15 (*On the Good of Marriage*, in Library of Fathers, v. 22, p. 293).

67. *Defensorium*, pp. 74–75; for Augustine, see above, nn. 61, 64; for Thomas, see *Summa Theologica*, I^a, II^ae, q. 98, art. 4.

68. *Defensorium*, p. 73.

69. *Summa Theologica*, I^a, II^ae, q. 98, art. 5.

70. Nor was it limited to that people, for there were worshippers of God outside it, too. See *City of God*, XVIII, cap. 47 (ed. Loeb, vol. VI, pp. 54–55).

71. *City of God*, XVI, 12 (Loeb ed., vol. V, p. 71).

72. St. Thomas, *Summa Theologica*, I^a, II^ae, q. 98, art. 6 (reply obj. 2: A law should not be given save to a people, since it is a general precept).

73. *Summa Theologica*, I^a, II^ae, q. 98, articles 4 (reply obj. 1) and 5 (answer).

74. According to Thomas, "Abraham was the first to receive the promise of the future birth of Christ"; he was "the first to cut himself off from the society of the unbelievers;" and he was the first in whom the sign of circumcision was instituted as a "sign of faith."

75. *Summa Theologica*, I^a, II^ae, q. 98, art. 5.

76. Augustine, *City of God*, XVIII, cap. 28 (ed. Loeb, vol. V, pp. 462–465, and other places.

77. *Defensorium*, p. 72.

78. *Defensorium*, p. 76; follows Jerome, Epistle to Damasus, (ML 22, 382, *Epistulae*, XXI.4).

79. *Defensorium*, p. 79.

80. *Ibid.*, pp. 76–77; without mentioning

Thomas, Cartagena here, too, follows *Summa Theologica*, I^a, II^ae, Q. 107, art. 1 (vol. viii, p. 293) and art. 3, answer and replies to objections 1 and 2 (vol. viii, p. 300).

81. *Defensorium*, p. 85.

82. *Ibid., ibid.*

83. Including Jesus' doctrine of "love those who hate you and pray for those who persecute you," in accordance with Origen, *Homiliae in Numeros*, ix.3, on Numbers 16. 44–45 (MG 12, 627–628), who deduced it from the Pentateuch's account about Moses' and Aaron's prayer for their enemies; see *Defensorium*, pp. 77–78.

84. *Ibid., ibid.*, p. 85.

85. *Ibid., ibid.*

86. Isaiah 60.1; *Defensorium*, p. 81.

87. *Ibid., ibid.*

88. *Ibid., ibid.*

89. *Ibid., ibid.:* "gentes autem non sic quasi ad suum sed tanquam ad alienum lumen, ut suum sua fidelitate faciant, invitantur."

90. *Ibid.*, p. 80.

91. *Ibid.*, p. 88: Nec enim Iherusalem ad gentes conversa est, sed gentilis populus ad Iherusalem convertitur.

92. *Ibid., ibid.:* Neque enim Israel deos gentium recepit, sed gentes deum Israel receperunt.

93. Galatians 3. 38.

94. *Defensorium*, p. 90.

95. *Ibid.*, pp. 89–90.

96. *Ibid.*, p. 95.

97. *Ibid.*, p. 94.

98. *Ibid.*, pp. 98–99.

99. *Ibid.*, p. 99.

100. Deut. 18.15; *Defensorium*, p. 95.

101. *Ibid., ibid.* That Jeremiah referred in this statement to Jesus is obvious, according to Cartagena, from the following: When he addressed himself to the "hope of Israel," the prophet asked: "Why will you be as a stranger in the land and as a wayfarer who turns aside to tarry for the night?" And "who was the other

savior of Israel who was to walk like a stranger on the road and like a wayfarer who was seeking shelter for the night except Him who said of Himself: 'The foxes have holes, the birds have their nests, but the son of man does not have a place to lay his head.' " *Ibid.*, p. 96.

102. *Ibid.*, p. 95.

103. *Ibid.*, p. 96. Cf. Jerome, *Commentaria in Isaiam Prophetam*, lib. XIII, cap. 45, vers. 14–17 (ML 24, 446–447).

104. *Defensorium*, p. 96.

105. *Ibid., ibid.*

106. *Ibid.*

107. *Ibid.*, p. 97.

108. *Ibid.*; cf. the different interpretations in the Glossa Interlinearis on Acts 2.39: *omnibus etiam gentibus qui loco vel a noticia dei longe sunt*, and the Glossa Ordinaria on the same verse: *quod ad gentium vocationem pertinet especialiter.*

109. *Defensorium*, pp. 101–102.

110. *Ibid.*, p. 102.

111. See Glossa Interlinearis on Hosea 3.4 (on *Quia dies multos*) and 3.5 (on *Et post haec*); see de Lyra on Hosea 3.5 (on *in novissimo dierum*. For the view of Jerome, see his *Commentarium in Osee*, lib. I, cap. 3, vers. 4–5 (ML 25, pp. 844–845).

112. See Glossa Interlinearis and de Lyra's interpretation of Hosea 3.5 (on *in novissimo dierum*).

113. *Defensorium*, 102; quod utique apertis occulis videmus.

114. *Ibid.*, p. 97.

115. *Ibid.*, pp. 124–125.

116. *Ibid.*, p. 126; Romans 11. 25–26.

117. *Ibid.*, p. 126.

118. *Ibid.*, p. 125.

119. *Ibid.*, p. 126.

120. *Ibid.*, p. 127.

121. See, for instance, Hiernoymus de Sancta Fide, *Contra Iudaeos* (written in 1412), 1552, pp. 4v–5n; Petrus de la Cavalleria, *Zelus Christi*, Venice, 1592, pp. 23v ff., 51vff.; Paulus de Sancta

Maria, *Scrutinium Scripturarum*, Burgos, 1591, pars II, dist. vi, caps. 2, 3, pp. 501a, 504–505.

122. Matthew 27.25.

123. Also in the course of the persecution of the Conversos following the outbreak of the Toledan revolt, the call to avenge the blood of Christ was doubtless raised many times. The duty to take that vengeance is a recurring theme in García's agitation (see his "Memorial," *loc. cit.*, pp. 333, 337, 341).

124. *Defensorium*, pp. 166–167.

125. See *Summa Theologica*, III, Q. 47, art. 4.

126. *Defensorium*, p. 143.

127. *Ibid., ibid.*

128. *Ibid., ibid.*

129. According to common Christian interpretation, the Apostle referred here by "Princes" to the demons or the experts in the knowledge of the Law. See Glossa Ordinaria and Interlinearis. Nicholas de Lyra, however, presents as an alternative interpretation: "principes hic dicuntur sacerdotes et scribe iudeorum." Cartagena accepts only this interpretation which specifically refers to the Jews; see *Defensorium*, p. 143.

130. I Corinthians 1.8; *Defensorium*, p. 143.

131. *Ibid., ibid.*

132. Luke, 23.34.

133. *Defensorium*, p. 143; Bede, *In Lucae Evangelium Expositio*, lib. 6, on Luke 23. 13–14, 21, 34 (ML 92, 616).

134. *Defensorium*, p. 143.

135. *Ibid.*, p. 144.

136. Bede on Luke 23. 34 (see his *In Lucae Evangelium Expositio* (ML 92, 616).

137. This is why in quoting Bede Cartagena cites the *second* part of his statement—i.e., that those who were ignorant were to be forgiven, but omits the first part that speaks of those who *knew,* and preferred to crucify rather than confess.

Cartagena's new treatment of the

theme of the Passion was expressed especially in his attempt to limit the direct responsibility for Jesus' crucifixion to a tiny fraction of the Jewish people. In dealing with the question of the divine forgiveness promised to the culprits on account of their ignorance, Cartagena veers his way between Augustine and Thomas, with a clear leaning toward the former (see Augustine on John 5.18, 15.23; Thomas Aquinas, *Summa Theologica*, III. 47.5: 54.68–71). He completely disagrees with those Christian theologians who since the 13th century stressed more and more the element of intention, rather than of ignorance, that motivated, in their opinion, the Jews' share in the Passion. For the evolution of this attitude in Christendom, see Jeremy Cohen, "The Jews as the Killers of Christ in the Latin Tradition, from Augustine to the Friars," in *Traditio*, 39 (1983), pp. 1–27.

138. *Defensorium*, p. 144.
139. *Ibid.*, p. 149.
140. *Ibid*, p. 146.
141. *Ibid.* Augustine, *Contra Julianum*, lib. VI, c. 14.43 (ML 44, 847).
142. Isidore, *De summo bono*, I, xxii, 5 (ML 83, 589).
143. *Defensorium*, p. 148.
144. *Ibid., ibid.*
145. *Ibid., ibid.*
146. *Ibid.*, pp. 214–215.
147. This is according to the concept of Bartolus (see below, n. 160).
148. *Defensorium*, pp. 150–151 (end of the third theorem, cap. 6).
149. Plato, *The Republic*, book II (*The Dialogues of Plato*, transl. by B. Jowett, 1924, p. 49ff).
150. *Defensorium*, p. 173; and see Aristotle, *Politics*, lib. I, c. 2.
151. *Defensorium*, p. 173. cf. Corpus Iuris Civilis, *Digest*, L. xvii. 32 (De diversis regulis iuris antiqui): Quod attinet ff.

152. *Ibid.*, p. 148.
153. *Ibid., ibid.* Cartagena evidently differentiated between *individual* qualitites, which are part of man's nature, and *collective* characteristics, which are produced by circumstances and may disappear in a changed situation. Thus he says: "Although the gentiles are superior to the Israelites in potency and other temporal qualities, once the two groups are united under the amplitude of the faith, they become indivisible and indistinguishable" like the rivers that enter the sea (*ibid.*, p. 149). In contrast, he believed that individual qualities, such as those that form "natural" nobility, are so deep-rooted as to be almost in-eradicable. The past history of the Jews and their present condition bear testimony to this, he averred.
154. This is the main thrust of the fourth theorem, pp. 153–317.
155. *Defensorium*, pp. 154–155.
156. *Ibid.*, pp. 155–156; cf. Torquemada, *Tractatus*, p. 54.
157. *Defensorium*, p. 156.
158. *Ibid.*, pp. 156–157. The word *azilim* in Hebrew, which is taken to mean noblemen, is found in the Old Testament only once (Exod. 24.11).
159. *Defensorium*, p. 162.
160. Cf. Bartolus, *Code*, lib. xii, De dig-nitatibus, law 1; and see "Memorial," *loc. cit.*, 345ff.
161. *Defensorium*, p. 161.
162. *Ibid.*, p. 162; according to the Vulgate translation of Numbers 1.15.
163. *Ibid.*, 165; i.e., Petrus Comestor—author of *Historia Scholastica*, ML 198, 1055–1722.
164. *Defensorium*, p. 165.
165. *Ibid., ibid.*
166. *Ibid.*, pp. 163–164.
167. *Ibid.*, p. 160; *ubi culmen regni est, summam nobilitatem inesse.*
168. *Ibid.*, p. 161.
169. *Ibid.*, p. 162–163.

170. *Ibid.,* pp. 170, following Aristotle, *Politics,* lib. I, cap. 2.

171. *Ibid.,* pp. 172–173.

172. *Ibid.,* p. 173.

173. John 8.34.

174. *Defensorium,* p. 175.

175. *Ibid.,* p. 174.

176. *Ibid., ibid.* This is according to Corpus Iuris Civilis, Digest, V.I *(De Iudiciis),* 4: *Lis nulla* ff.

177. *Ibid.,* pp. 174–175.

178. *Ibid.,* p. 206.

179. *Ibid.,* p. 210.

180. *Ibid., ibid.*

181. *Ibid., ibid.*

182. *Ibid., ibid.*

183. *Ibid.,* pp. 210–211. It should be noted, however, that the priestly families, although they were denied the theological nobility, might prove, according to Cartagena, rich veins of nobility in other respects. Following de Lyra, Cartagena asserts that the leaders of the people from the tribe of Levi (the sacerdotal tribe) were intermarried with the royal tribe of Judah, so that the priestly tribe has a basis for a claim to secular nobility and eminence (see *Defensorium,* pp. 159–160; cf. de Lyra on Genesis 19.10.

184. *Defensorium,* p. 213.

185. *Ibid.,* p. 215.

186. *Ibid.,* p. 216.

187. *Ibid., ibid.*

188. *Ibid.,* pp. 217–218.

189. *Ibid.,* p. 219.

190. *Ibid.,* p. 220.

191. *Ibid.,* p. 222.

192. *Ibid.,* pp. 221–222.

193. *Ibid.,* p. 222; see Corpus Iuris Civilis, Codex, IX. LI (De sententiam passis), 1: Cum salutatus ff.

194. *Ibid.,* p. 223.

195. Timothy, 2.6.

196. Decretum, I, Distinctio 48, cap. 1.

197. Jerome, Epistle 69 (ad Oceanum), 9, ML 22, 663 (for English ed. see Jerome, *The Principal Works,*

transl. by W.H. Fremantle, 1893, p. 148a.)

198. Decretum, I, Dist. 48, c. 2 I (ed. Friedberg, p. 174); *Defensorium,* p. 246 (cap. 29).

199. *Ibid., ibid.*

200. See above, p. 553.

201. *Defensorium,* p. 256.

202. *Ibid.,* p. 257.

203. *Ibid.,* pp. 250–251.

204. Job, 1.11; the word "a little" (paululum) is according to the Vulgate.

205. *Defensorium,* 252.

206. *Ibid., ibid.*

207. Job, 2.4; *Defensorium,* p. 253.

208. John XXIII Extrava. Comm. Lib. V, tit. 2, cap. 2 *(Dignum arbitrantes),* ed. Friedberg, II, p. 1290.

209. *Defensorium,* pp. 266–267.

210. *Ibid.,* p. 273.

211. *Ibid., ibid.;* "For in dogmatizing even the slightest schism one tries to tear apart the only Church and fights the whole Church which is indivisible."

212. *Ibid., ibid.*

213. *Ibid.,* p. 289.

214. *Ibid.,* pp. 289, 293.

215. *Ibid.,* p. 293.

216. *Ibid.,* p. 296.

217. *Ibid.,* p. 301.

218. *Ibid., ibid.*

219. *Ibid.,* p. 302.

220. *Ibid.,* p. 315.

221. *Ibid.,* pp. 316–317.

222. *Ibid.,* p. 319.

223. *Ibid., ibid.*

Diego de Valera

1. See José Simón Díaz, "La familia Chirino en Cuenca," in *Guía* (Revista semanal de enseñanza y oposiciones), Madrid, I, 1944 (April 20), no. 171, pp. 3–6, based on data revealed by an inquisitional investigation, in 1631, about the family's purity of blood. See also *id.,* "El helenismo de Quevedo y var-

ias questiones más," in *Revista de Bibliografía Nacional,* Madrid, VI (1945), pp. 87–118 (see especially p. 98).

2. See *Epístolas de Mosen Diego de Valera,* published by the *Sociedad de Bibliófilos Españoles* (and edited by José Antonio de Balenchana, 1878, pp. 169–229. Balenchana believed that the treatise was written in 1441, because Valera says in his prologue to the work that he was *detached from civil or active life*—a description that suited his condition at the time, when he lived in Cuenca separated from the Court (*ibid.,* p. xxii, and p. 169, n. 1). Valera, however, deals in this work with themes related to the racial attack on the conversos, and his discussion echoes in many places arguments made by Cartagena and Torquemada. It would be easier to see him as a follower in the footsteps of the abovementioned great converso thinkers than a pathbreaker for their ideas on the issues involved. As for Balenchana's reason for his assumption: in 1451, when Valera served as tutor to the grandson of Pedro Destúñiga (the Count of Plasencia), he could see himself, no less than in 1441, "detached from civil or active life." In that condition, we may add, he could find ample time for both the contemplation and research he needed for the writing of his treatise. We believe therefore that his *Espejo* was composed c. 1451, after the appearance of Cartagena's *Defensorium* with which the *Espejo* has much in common.

3. For detailed accounts of Valera's life and works, see J. de M. Carriazo's introductions to Valera's *Crónica de los Reyes Católicos,* 1927, and *Memorial de Diversas Hazañas,* 1941; Lucas de Torre, *Mosen Diego de Valera,* 1914; H. Sancho de Sporanis, "Sobre Mosen Diego de Valera," in *Hispania,* Madrid, vol. VII (1947), pp. 531–553; Pascual de Gayangos, "Mossen Diego de Valera" in *Revista Española de Ambos Mundos,* III

(1855), pp. 294–312. On Valera's essays see J. A. de Balenchana's introduction to *Epístolas y otros varios tratados de Mosen Diego de Valera,* 1878; Carriazo, introd. to Valera's *Crónica de los Reyes Católicos,* pp. lxxix–lxxxix and xc–xcix; Gino de Solemni, in *Romanic Review,* XVI (1962), pp. 87–88. On his poetry, see Menéndez y Pelayo, *Historia de la Poesía castellana en la Edad Media,* II, 1914, pp. 225–242; Puymaigre, *La cour litteraire de Don Juan II,* 1973, I, p. 208; II, pp. 198–204. On his historical works, see (in addition to Carriazo) Julio Puyol, "Los Cronistas de Enrique IV," in *Boletín* de la Acad. de la Historia, Madrid, 1921 (79), pp. 118–126; G. Cirot, *Les histoires générales d'Espagne entre Alphonse X et Philippe II,* 1904, pp. 40–44; *id.,* "Les decades d'Alfonso de Palencia, etc.," in *Bulletin Hispanique,* xi (1909), pp. 425–442; Antonio Paz y Mélia, *El cronista Alonso de Palencia,* 1914, xxxix–xliv, lxxi–lxxxi, 428–469; *idem, Series de los más importantes documentos del archivo y biblioteca del . . . Duque de Medinaceli,* 1915, pp. 44, 72–74, 78, 82. N. Antonio, *Bibliotheca Hispana Vetus,* II, lib. X, cap. 13, §§ 708 ff; B. J. Gallardo, *Ensayo de una Biblioteca Española,* IV, 1889, pp. 870–875.

4. See *ibid.,* p. 173, 176; and see Bartolus, De dignitatibus, in his *Commentaria Codicis,* lib. XII, tit. 1, §§ 24–29; cf. Cartagena, above., pp. 562–563.

5. *Epístolas,* p. 219.

6. *Ibid.,* p. 185; see Innocent III, *De contemptu mundi,* lib. 1, cap. 17 (PL, 217, 709): *Natura liberos genuit, sed fortuna servos constituit.*

7. *Epístolas,* p. 185.

8. *Ibid.,* pp. 179, 183.

9. *Ibid.,* pp. 180, 194.

10. *Ibid.,* pp. 213–214; Valera, however, indicates the different customs that prevail in this respect in central and western Europe (see *ibid.,* p. 214).

11. *Ibid.,* pp. 212–213.

12. *Ibid.,* p. 211.

13. *Ibid.,* p. 208.
14. *Ibid.,* pp. 211–212.
15. *Ibid.,* pp. 209–210.
16. *Ibid.,* p. 208.
17. His reference at this point to Jesus' lineage as "the noblest" (nuestro Redenptor. . . . este linaje escogió para sy por el más noble) must be related to his basic concept that "nobler," when applied to a national entity, simply means "better" in the religious sense (see *ibid.,* p. 208).
18. The same argument, somewhat modified and amplified, was used by Valera also seven years later (in 1458), in response to a sermon delivered in Cuenca by a certain friar and master of theology (Serrano), who disputed the right of the New Christians to join the Spanish nobility. In rebutting the friar's racial assertions which caused the conversos much "injury and opprobrium," Valera pointed out, among other things, that the "kings of the Goths, who sprang from the tribe of Dan," were the forebears of the "illustrious kings" of Spain, and that the English delegation at the Council of Basle demanded to be seated before the Castilian on the ground that England's Kings drew their origin from Joseph of Arimathaea. "It would certainly take me a long time," said Valera, "to offer an account of all the princes and lords who descended from the Jewish stock" (see ms. of the Library of the University of Salamanca, no. 455, f. 68ʳ).
19. *Epístolas,* p. 209.
20. *Ibid., ibid.* In further explanation of this regeneration, Valera compares the converts who regain their capacities for nobility to "those who come out from captivity and recover the liberty which they had lost" *(ibid.).* It is almost certain that we have here a summary of Cartagena's elaborate discussion of this point (see above, p. 568), although Valera does not employ Cartagena's

proofs, including the example of the Roman law of *postliminium* (see *Defensorium,* pp. 219–220).
21. *Epístolas,* p. 210.
22. *Ibid.,* pp. 210–211.

The Political Views of the Toledan Rebels

1. See above, p. 321.
2. See his *Les Controverses des statuts de pureté de sang en Espagne du xvᵉ au xviiᵉ siècle,* 1960, p. 36.
3. Benito Ruano, *Toledo en el siglo xv,* p. 155.
4. See his article "La rebelión toledana de 1449", in *Archivum* (Oviedo), XVI (1966), p. 405.
5. *Ibid.,* p. 411.
6. *Ibid.,* pp. 413–414.
7. *Ibid.,* p. 414.
8. See above, p. 311.
9. *Crónica del Halconero,* cap. 375, p. 510; *Crónica de Juan II,* año 1449, cap. 5, p. 663b; and other places.
10. *Ibid., ibid.,* p. 664a.
11. See my article, "Did the Toledans in 1449 Rely on a Real Royal Privilege?", in *PAAJR,* XLIV (1977), especially, pp. 106–110.
12. See "El Memorial contra los conversos del bachiller Marcos García de Mora," in *Sefarad,* XVII, p. 320.
13. *Ibid., ibid.:* a quien, según Dios, Ley, raçón e derecho pertenesçe la administraçión de los Reynos e Señoríos de Castilla e de León.
14. The words we added in brackets suggest García's implied thought, especially as indicated in the words we italicized in the following sentence.
15. "Memorial," *loc. cit.,* p. 339.
16. This was essentially also the position of the mutinous nobles as expressed in their statements of 1425 and 1440 (cited above, pp. 239, 251), and it lay at the basis of their justification of their various conspiracies and uprisings against the King. If such statements

indicate anti-monarchism, those nobles, too, should have been opposed
to kingly rule as a form of
government. And this is palpably
absurd. Among the utterers of the
above criticisms against Juan II of
Castile were Alfonso V King of
Naples and Juan I King of Navarre.

17. *Sefarad,* xvii, p. 322.

18. This is stressed by Marcos García in
his "Memorial" as it is in the rebels'
Petition. See *Halconero,* pp. 524–526,
and "Memorial," *loc. cit.,* p. 341: "vos
señor diste[i]s la corona que Jesu-
christo vos dió por vuestra nobleça e
virtudes al dicho malo tirano." And
see, *ibid.,* p. 338: ". . . ca por esta causa
saldrá el dicho Rey de la seruidumbre
en que a estado y está . . . por el tirano
poderío del dicho don Aluaro de
Luna."

19. *Ibid.,* p. 341.

20. *Ibid.,* p. 338; cf. also 328.

21. *Ibid.,* p. 341: en otra manera, necessario
es usar de todos los remedios
defensorios.

22. For the origin of this view in the
writings of the Church Fathers (from
the 4th century on) and its reemergence in the medieval West (in
the 9th century), see A. J. Carlyle, *A
History of Mediaeval Political Theory in
the West,* I, pp. 149ff., 215–216; II, pp.
61–63; III, pp. 47–48. See also Bracton,
De legibus et consuetudinibus Angliae, I,
1.2; III, 9.3. For expressions of the same
conception in Spain, see *Espéculo,* I, 1.3;
Partidas, II, 1.5, 1.7.

23. See Bracton, *op. cit.,* I, 8.5; and cf. A. J.
Carlyle, *op. cit.,* I, pp. 230–239; III, p. 38.

24. *Partidas,* I, 1.19; *Espéculo,* introduction
(see *Opúsculos Legales,* published by
the Academia de la Historia, Madrid,
1836, p. 2).

25. Carlyle, *op. cit.,* III, pp. 56–58.

26. *Partidas,* II, tit. I, law 5.

27. *Ibid., ibid.,* tit. I, law 7.

28. *Ibid., ibid.*

29. *Espéculo,* I, 1.3.

30. *Ibid.,* I, 1.13.

31. *Partidas,* II, tit. II, laws 2, 4; tit. V, law 8.

32. *Espéculo,* I, 1.9; *Partidas,* I, tit. i, law 16.

33. *Ibid.,* I. tit. i, laws 17, 19.

34. *Córtes de los antiguous reinos de León y de
Castilla,* I, 1861, p. 542 (cap. 64); III, 1866,
p. 491.

35. Carlyle, *op. cit.,* VI, p. 5; *Cortes de León
y de Castilla.* II, xxviii, pp. 371–372,
Tercero Tractado, § 9.

36. *Ibid.,* III, 9. 19 (p. 111).

37. *Ibid.,* III, 15. 14 (p. 391).

38. *Ibid.,* III, 16.11 (pp. 406–407).

39. *Ibid., ibid.*

40. See above, p. 294.

41. *Cortes de León y de Castilla,* III, XVIII,
p. 458.

42. The ordenamiento given in reply to
this petition was issued by Fernán
Díaz de Toledo (see *Cortes de León y de
Castilla,* III, p. 494) and bears the
marks of his peculiar style.

43. *Ibid.,* III, p. 483.

44. *Ibid.,* III, p. 492.

45. Carlyle, *op. cit.,* VI, p. 188.

46. This is evident from the 63 petitions
submitted by the Cortes of Valladolid
(1447), of which more than half spoke
bluntly and obtrusively against the
failures and abuses of the royal
administration. See *Cortes de León y de
Castilla,* III, pp. 495–575; and cf.
Manuel Colmeiro's Introduction to
the above proceedings, I, 1883, pp.
505–515.

47. "Memorial," *loc. cit.,* pp. 323, 327, 338,
339, 343, 344, 345, 346, 347, 349.

48. See "Memorial," *loc. cit.,* p. 327, 338.

49. *Ibid.,* p. 339.

50. *Ibid., ibid.* (dañada y reprouada).

51. *Ibid., ibid.* p. 339.

52. Thomas Aquinas, *Summa Theologica,*
2.2, q. 42, art. 2.

53. Aristotle, *Politics,* III, 5. 4–5; IV. 8–3;
Ethics, VIII, 10.

54. Isidore of Seville, *Etymologies,* IX. 3.

55. John of Salisbury, *Policraticus,* IV. 1–4;
VIII, 17.

56. Bracton, *De legibus Angliae,* 5. 8. 5.

57. Bartolus, *De Tyrannia*, in *Humanism and Tyranny*, ed. Emerton, 1925, p. 132; and see also *ibid.*, pp. 130, 131.

58. Memorial, *loc. cit.*, p. 338.

59. *Ibid., ibid.*

60. *Las Siete Partidas*, II, tit. v. law 14.

61. See Aristotle, *Ethics*, viii, 10; cf. Thomas Aquinas, *De regimine principum*, lib. iv, cap. 1.

62. *Halconero*, pp. 257–258 (in the letter addressed to the King by the admiral of Castile Fadrique Enriquez and his brother Pero Manrique, *adelantado mayor* of León, on Feb. 20, 1439.

63. See *Cortes de León y de Castilla*, III, pp. 458–460, 481–485, 491–493.

64. "Memorial," *loc. cit.*, p. 339.

65. *Ibid.*, p. 338.

66. *Ibid., ibid.*

67. *Ibid.*, p. 339.

68. *Ibid.*, p. 341.

69. *Ibid.*, p. 342.

70. See John of Salisbury, *Policraticus*, IV, caps. 1, 3. and other places.

71. "Memorial," *loc. cit.*, pp. 340 and 325.

72. *Ibid., ibid.;* and see also p. 348.

73. *Ibid.*, p. 325.

74. *Ibid., ibid.*

75. *Ibid., ibid.*

76. *Ibid.*, p. 341.

77. *Ibid., ibid.;* and see also pp. 350–351 where he speaks of the possible need of the city to resort to "remedios defensorios" against the Pope as well as the King of Castile.

78. *Ibid.*, p. 350. The appeal to a "future Council" of the Church will be made if the Pope "will refuse to inform himself duly" of the Toledan case. Also earlier he points to the need of a Council when he says that the Pope could gain "full knowledge" of the case after hearing the opinion of the "venerado Concilio" (p. 341).

79. See Aeneas Sylvius' letter to Pope Nicholas V of Nov. 25, 1448, in L. Pastor, *Geschichte der Päpste*, I, 1901, p. 42.

80. On the position of Castile toward the Papacy during the Council of Basle, see L. Suárez Fernández, *Castilla, el Cisma y la crisis Conciliar (1378–1440)*, 1960, pp. 115–141. On Aragon's position in the conflict, see V. Balaguer, *Historia de Cataluña*, III, 1862, pp. 513–514, 519, 523, 526.

81. J. N. Figgis, *Studies of Political Thought from Gerson to Grotius*, 1907, pp. 53–60.

82. See *ibid.*, p. 35, where Figgis offers a terse summary of his view: "Eugenius IV is the forerunner of Louis XIV"; and see *id., The Divine Right of Kings*, 1922, pp. 39–65. It must be noted, however, that Figgis tends to overrate the impact of the papal claims to *plenitudo potestatis* (especially since the days of Boniface VIII) on the development of the principle of the Divine Right of Kings. As we see it, that principle owed its rise and growth to inward political needs of the monarchy no less than to outside papal pressures. It served as answer to the encroaching baronial forces as it did to those of the Church, and the factors responsible for its evolution, therefore, must be looked for in the growth of feudal power, which paralleled the rising ambitions of the Church.

83. "Memorial," *loc. cit.*, p. 325.

84. *Ibid.*, p. 341.

85. While it is true that Second Adventists, like Militz, often referred to the Holy Spirit, it is also true that ardent conciliarists referred to it just as often (see J.A.W. Neander, *General History of the Christian Religion and Church*, V, Boston, 1854, transl. by Joseph Torrey, pp. 95, 115, 117, 119, 132, 177–179, and many other places). So common indeed was the mention of the Holy Spirit by the followers of the Conciliar theories, that Traversarius, a supporter of the Pope, describing in a letter to Emperor Sigismund how decisions were adopted in the Council

of Basle, said that, in that Council, "the voice of the cook, so to say, has as much value as that of a bishop or archbishop" and "whatsoever this raging mob decrees is ascribed to the Holy Spirit" (see Ambrosius Traversarius, *Latinae Epistulae,* ed. L. Mehus, II, 1759, col. 238).

Old Christian Apologies for the Conversos

1. See his *Generaciones y Semblanzas,* ed. J. Domínguez Bordona, 1954, pp. 89–95.
2. See above, p. 517.
3. In 1450 or 1455; see Domínguez Bordona's introduction, *ibid.,* p. xx, n. 1.
4. *Ibid.,* p. 94: condenar a todos e non acusar a ninguno.
5. *Ibid.,* pp. 90–91.
6. *Ibid.,* p. 91.
7. *Ibid., ibid.*
8. *Ibid.,* p. 92.
9. *Ibid.,* pp. 92–93.
10. *Ibid.,* p. 93.
11. *Ibid., ibid.*
12. *Ibid., ibid.*
13. *Ibid.,* p. 94.
14. *Ibid.,* p. 91.
15. *Ibid.,* p. 94.
16. See on him T. Muñoz y Soliva, *Noticias de los Obispos de Cuenca,* 1860, pp. 146–159; *id., Historia de la ciudad de Cuenca,* II, 1867, pp. 314–326; J. Amador de los Ríos, *Historia crítica de la literatura Española,* VI, 1865, pp. 254, 285; N. Antonio, *Bibliotheca Hispana Vetus,* lib. x, cap. II, 570–579; Quétif-Echard, *Scriptores Ordinis Praedicatorum,* I, part 2, pp. 813ᵇ–815ᵃ. A. Touron, *Histoire des hommes illustres de l'ordre de Saint Dominique,* 1746, pp. 441 ff.; J. de Mata Carriazo, in his introd. to the *Refundición de la Crónica del Halconero,* 1946, p. cxxxiii–cl; Luis G. A. Getino, *Vida y obras de Fr. Lope de Barrientos,* 1927, pp. v–xcvi.
17. See Getino, *op. cit.,* pp. lxxxiii–lxxxiv.
18. *Ibid.,* pp. 202–203.
19. *Ibid.,* p. 203: como el arness con el fornido jubon.
20. *Ibid., ibid.*
21. *Ibid.,* p. 191.
22. And see on this Nicholas G. Round, "Politics, Style and Group Attitudes in the *Instrucción del Relator,*" in *Bulletin of Hispanic Studies,* vol. XLVI, no. 4 (1969), p. 294, n. 1.
23. *Sefarad,* XVII (1957), p. 342.
24. *Ibid.,* pp. 342–343.
25. On Cartagena's early intervention with the King against the rebels, see the prologue to his *Defensorium,* pp. 61–62.
26. Getino, *op. cit.,* p. 191.
27. "Contra algunos zizañadores de la nación de los conuertidos del pueblo de Israel," *ibid.,* pp. 181–204.
28. See his "Instrucción," *loc. cit.,* p. 356.
29. See below, pp. 649–650.
30. *Crónica de Juan II,* año 1450, cap. I (BAE, vol. 68, pp. 670–671).
31. "Instrucción," *loc. cit.,* p. 343.
32. Getino, *op. cit.,* p. 182. Barrientos uses here the term *Hebreos* (instead of *Judíos*) to indicate the community of ethnic origin (not of religion) between the conversos and the Jews in Haman's time.
33. *Ibid., ibid.*
34. *Ibid.*
35. "Instrucción," *loc. cit.,* p. 344.
36. Getino, *op. cit.,* pp. 183–184.
37. *Ibid.,* p. 201.
38. "Instrucción," *loc. cit.,* p. 389.
39. Getino, *op. cit.,* p. 193.
40. *Ibid.*
41. *Ibid.;* "Instrucción," *loc. cit.,* p. 348; see above, p. 410.
42. "Instrucción," *loc. cit.,* p. 344.
43. See above, pp. 570–571.
44. Getino, *op. cit.,* p. 185: en la fe primera nacieron.
45. *Ibid.,* pp. 183–184.—That the number of Judaizers among the conversos was, in Barrientos' opinion, small appears also from the special treatise he composed

on the 65th decree of the 4th Toledan Council. There he writes: "But if someone should say: *many are found among the converts, or among the descendants of the Jews,* who *follow the faith of the Jews,* we shall answer: It is possible that there are *some.*" (Ms. of the Biblioteca Nacional, Madrid, nu. 1181, f. 28). This is, however, how he formulated his opinion according to the Spanish translation of the treatise, while according to the printed Latin original, his answer to the above question was: "It is possible" (*possibile est;* see appendix I to Alonso de Cartagena's *Defensorium,* p. 336). Nothing definite or final may be said regarding the accuracy of any of these formulations, except to indicate that the printed Latin text is notable for its many omissions, which seems to offer greater reliability to the version of the translation. Also, in view of the opinions expressed by Barrientos on this subject in his edition of the Relator's *Instrucción,* it is more likely that his answer was in accord with the Spanish presentation. The question may of course be conclusively settled only by comparing the Spanish translation to other Latin manuscripts (if such become available). But whatever adjective he used in referring to the Judaizers ("many" or "some"), it is clear that he admitted only the *possibility* of their existence, not its *actuality* or even *probability.*

46. Getino, *op. cit.,* p. 194.

47. *Ibid., ibid.*

48. *Ibid.,* pp. 194–195; the same idea was later expressed by Pulgar, in his *Letras,* ed. Domínguez Bordona, 1949, pp. 64–65, and *Crónica de los Reyes Católicos,* ed. Carriazo, I, 1943, pp. 348–349, in the speech he attributed to Gómez Manrique (in 1478).

49. Getino, *op. cit.,* p. 195.

50. *Ibid., ibid.*

51. *Ibid.*

52. *Ibid.,* p. 188.

53. *Ibid.,* p. 184.

54. *Ibid.,* p. 186.

55. *Ibid.,* p. 201.

56. See Fermín Caballero, *Doctor Montalvo,* 1873, p. 19; see on him also N. Antonio, *Bibliotheca Hispana Vetus,* lib. x, §811–816.

57. Caballero, *op. cit.,* p. 23.

58. *Ibid.,* pp. 21, 23.

59. *Ibid.,* pp. 49, 114.

60. See Montalvo's preface to his annotated edition of the *Fuero Real,* reprinted with a Spanish translation by Caballero, *op. cit.,* p. 98.

61. Caballero, *op. cit.,* pp. 38, 39–40.

62. See *Memorias de Enrique IV,* II (Colección Diplomática), 1835–1913, pp. 74–75. Formally, the invitation for Montalvo to participate in that meeting was issued by the King (*ibid.,* p. 74a.).

63. Caballero, *op. cit.,* p. 50.

64. *Ibid.,* pp. 56–57.

65. *Ibid.,* p. 60.

66. See *Fuero Real de España,* lib. iv, tit. 3, 1. 2 (ed. 1781, with Montalvo's glosses, II, pp. 339–353).

67. Caballero, *op. cit.,* p. 66.

68. *Ibid.,* p. 25.

69. See *Fuero Real de España,* II, 1781, p. 339b (lib. iv, tit. 3): . . . ad quod facit tractatus quidam levis, quem de mandato Illustrissimi Domini nostri Regis Joan. II super factis Toleti contingentibus invalide compilavi.

70. See above, pp. 331 and 1230–1231, n. 12.

71. In 1548 Cardinal Siliceo, in a writ defending his *limpieza* statute, criticized Montalvo for his interpretation of Paul's words about the "unruly" converts from Judaism in his letter to Titus I. 1–10 (see *Fuero Real,* II, 1781, p. 349a). Siliceo defined these comments of Montalvo as assuredly "heretical" and "opposed to the understanding of the holy doctors" (BNM, ms. 13038, f. 21rv), but did not indicate that their author was a converso. Judging by Siliceo's habit of

denigrating his converso critics and opponents, one can hardly assume that he would have failed to mention Montalvo's Jewish ancestry, if the latter had been a New Christian.

72. See the convincing analysis of his character by Caballero (*op. cit.,* pp. 50–55 and 209–212).

73. See *Partidas,* I, tit. 7, l.1 (7th ed., 1528, with Montalvo's glosses).

74. Although the printing of the large work was completed in 1500 (see Caballero, *op. cit.,* p. 96), it was, in all likelihood, submitted to the press before Montalvo's death (in 1499).

75. *De la Unidad de los Fieles,* see *ibid.,* pp. 48, 115. According to Nicolás Antonio, however, Montalvo's treatise appeared under the heading "That the Jews converted to the faith are entitled to the public offices and ecclesiastic honors" (see *Bibliotheca Hispana Vetus,* lib. X, cap. iv, § 813).

76. *Fuero Real,* ed. 1781, II, p. 339b.

77. *Ibid.*

78. *Ibid.,* p. 340a.

79. *Ibid.,* p. 340ab. The argument betrays the influence of Torquemada's views, which may have been communicated to him by his converso counsellors, or perhaps by a draft of Torquemada's abridged presentation that may have been at their disposal.

80. *Ibid.,* p. 340b.

81. *Ibid., ibid.* Cf. Cartagena's comments on this subject in his *Defensorium,* pp. 142–144; and see above, p. 550.

82. *Fuero Real,* II, p. 340b.

83. *Ibid.,* p. 342ab.

84. *Ibid.,* p. 343b.

85. *Ibid., ibid.*

86. *Ibid.,* 343b–344a.

87. *Ibid.,* p. 347b–348, 349a.

88. *Ibid.,* p. 343ab; cf. *Córtes de León y de Castilla,* I, 1861, p. 533 (cap. 57).

89. *Fuero Real,* p. 343b.

90. *Ibid.,* pp. 342b–343a, 345b–346a; cf. Jerome's letter against Rufinus, *Decretum,* CICa, I, Dist. 56, c. 5.

91. *Fuero Real,* II, p. 343a.

92. *Ibid.,* p. 342a.

93. *Ibid.,* pp. 346b–347a.

94. *Ibid.,* p. 347a.

95. *Ibid.,* p. 349a.

96. *Ibid.,* p. 349ab.

97. Gonzalez-Tejada, II, p. 308.

98. *Fuero Real,* II, p. 349b.

99. *Ibid.,* p. 352a.

100. *Ibid.,* p. 345a.

101. *Ibid.,* p. 352b.

102. *Ibid., ibid.*

103. *Ibid.,* p. 353a.

The Historiographic Evidence

1. See on him as chronicler, F. Cantera, *Alvar García de Santa María,* 1952, pp. 99–127; J. Amador de los Ríos, *Historia Crítica de la Literatura Española,* VI, 1865, pp. 216–223; and B. Sánchez Alonso, *Historia de la Historiografía Española,* I, pp. 302–304.

2. On the various revisions of the Halconero, see Carriazo's detailed discussion in his introduction to the *Refundición de la Crónica del Halconero,* 1946, pp. ix–xv.

3. See on this above, p. 290.

4. *Halconero,* p. 520.

5. *Ibid.,* p. 523; this after alluding to them as "infidels" and "heretics" (pp. 521–522).

6. See above, pp. 354–364.

7. *Halconero,* p. 531.

8. *Ibid., ibid.*

9. *Ibid.*

10. Preserved in the Biblioteca Universitaria de Santa Cruz de Valladolid, no. 434.

11. *Ibid.,* f. 282a: *Luego el común con el fauor que les dio Pero Sarmiento apoderaronse en las puertas e puentes e torres.*

12. *Ibid.: non se mostraua claramente;* cf. *Halconero,* p. 518.

13. Ms. 434 of the Biblioteca de Santa Cruz, f. 282a.

14. *Ibid.,* f. 285a.

15. *Ibid.: personas q' a el plazia.*

16. See *Halconero*, p. 523 (passage cited above and its continuation).

17. See ms. 434 of the Santa Cruz Library, f. 288a; cf. *Halconero*, p. 525. We may also assume that the words *malos homes* in the concluding section of the Petition—a section missing in the *Halconero* and found only in the *Abreviación*—replaced titles such as *ereges* or *infideles*. Cf. Carriazo's introduction to the *Refundición del Halconero*, pp. cxciii–cxciv.

18. See ms. 434 of the Santa Cruz Library, f. 62a.

19. San Andrés, outside of Valladolid; see *Crónica de Alvaro de Luna*, p. 435.

20. Actually, after approximately two months; see *ibid., ibid.*

21. See ms. 434 of the Santa Cruz Library, ff. 304–305^A; cf. Carriazo, introduction to *Refundición*, p. ccii.

22. *Ibid.*, p. lxxxii; Elias Tormo, RAH, *Boletín*, 90 (1927), pp. 272–273.

23. *Refundición*, introduction, pp. clxxxi.

24. See ms. 434 of the Santa Cruz Library, f. 282a; cf. *Halconero*, pp. 518–519.

25. Ms. 434 of the Santa Cruz Library, ff. 283–3a. This interpolation has no connection with what preceded and followed it, and its explanation of the rebellion's cause differs from the Abbreviator's earlier account, which imputes the insurrection to the citizens' outrage over Alvaro's mistreatment of their privileges (*ibid.*, f. 279–279a). In that account the Abbreviator followed his source (*Halconero*, p. 511), but he obviously disagreed with the above imputation and looked for an opportunity to refute it. His description of the collection of the loan and its consequences, which followed his report of Sarmiento's claim that he wished to help the city defend its *privileges*, was to serve as proof that all talk about the privileges was humbug and that the real cause of the rebellion was quite different.

26. On the *Crónica* of Juan II, see Galíndez de Carvajal, introd. to the *Crónica de Juan II*, BAE, 68, pp. 273–275; Prologue to the edition of Guzmán's *Crónica* by Monfort, Valencia, 1779, pp. VII–XVIII; J. Amador de los Ríos, *Historia Crítica*, VI, pp. 212–216; R. Foulché-Delbosc, "Étude Critique sur Fernán Pérez de Guzmán," *Revue Hispanique*, XVI (1907), pp. 26–55.

27. Rarely does the *Crónica* abbreviate sharply; in one case it omits a whole chapter (the one describing the greatness of Alvaro de Luna), and on several occasions it replaces documents with a summary of their contents. Only a few chapters and passages found in the *Crónica de Juan II* are not included in the *Refundición*.

28. That some chapters of the *Crónica* of Guzmán follow closely in the footsteps of the *Halconero* may be accounted for by the fact that the *Refundición* used those chapters in virtually their original form.

29. According to Carriazo, from page 420 on (approximately from the middle of 1441) the *Halconero* contains the version of the *Refundición*, which was incorporated into it by some compiler. However, if Carriazo was right in this conclusion, while we, on the other hand, were correct in assuming that the *Crónica* of Guzmán followed the *Refundición* (as is evident from its procedure from 1435 to 1439), we should have noticed a renewal of the parallelism between Guzmán's *Crónica* and the *Halconero* from the middle of 1441. But a careful comparison of this part of the *Halconero* with Guzmán's *Crónica de Juan II* shows that the unlikes are more numerous than the likes, just as they are in the other parts.

30. *Crónica de Juan II*, cap. 5, p. 663b.

31. *Ibid., ibid.*, p. 664a.

32. *Ibid.*

33. *Ibid.*

34. *Ibid.*, p. 663b.
35. *Ibid.*, p. 664a.
36. *Ibid.*, *ibid.*
37. *Ibid.*
38. Thus the term "cruel punishment" (*cruel justicia, ibid.*) was occasionally used by him to indicate death by fire—a punishment often meted out to heretics.
39. See *Halconero*, p. 522.
40. See *Crónica de Juan II*, cap. 5, p. 664b.
41. See *Halconero*, p. 523.
42. *Crónica de Juan II*, p. 664b.
43. See *Halconero*, p. 521; *Crónica de Juan II*, p. 664b.
44. *Ibid.;* cf. *Halconero*, p. 524.
45. *Ibid.*, pp. 521–522.
46. *Crónica de Juan II*, p. 664b: *personas infieles é malas*, instead of *ynfieles e herejes* in the Petition (see *Halconero*, p. 523). The word *infieles* (infidels) could be taken as a synonym for Jews.
47. See *Crónica de Juan II*, p. 667b: *ninguno ni algunos de los que habia desterrado y echado fuera de la dicha cibdad*.
48. *Ibid.*, *ibid.*
49. *Abreviation*, f. 299.
50. *Crónica de Juan II*, p. 670a.
51. *Ibid.*, p. 670ab.
52. *Ibid.*, p. 670b.
53. *Ibid.:* á otros levantábades cosas que nunca pensaron; and cf. *ibid.*, 664a; *Abreviación*, ms. 434, and above, p. 630.

That Sarmiento, using torture, exacted from conversos fictitious confessions not only of religious but also *political* crimes is attested by the author of *Succesos en la ciudad de Toledo contra los conversos* (from 1449 to 1467), who must have had at his disposal fuller versions of the *Halconero*, and possibly other sources as well (see BNM, ms. 2041, f. 42ʳ; "*encarcelados y artormentados vigorosamente* les hizo decir . . . achacandoles que eran *traidores a Dios* y a la ciudad, y porque el maestre toleraba sus maldades y *sacrilegios* querian entregar la ciudad al Rey").

54. *Crónica de Juan II*, p. 670b.
55. *Ibid.*
56. *Ibid.*
57. *Ibid.*, p. 671a.
58. *Ibid.*
59. This summarizes the contents of CIC, *Codex Iustinianus*, I, 14, 4–5 (ed. Kriegel, 1895, p. 68a).
60. *Crónica*, 671a.
61. *Ibid.*, *ibid.*
62. *Ibid.*, p. 671b. See the original text of the chapter in Gratian's *Decretum*, CICa, I, pp. 293–294.
63. It is not at all impossible to assume that one of the Relator's aides was collaborating with Guzmán in editing the *Crónica de Juan II* and that this person was entrusted by Guzmán with the editorial supervision of the passages in question.
64. On the *Cuarta Crónica General* and the problem of its authorship see R. Menéndez Pidal, *Crónicas Generales de España*, 1898, pp. 93–97; G. Cirot, *Les Histoires générales d'Espagne*, 1904, p. 8; B. Sánchez Alonso, "Las Versiones en Romance de las Crónicas del Toledano," in *Homenaje ofrecido a Menéndez Pidal*, 1925, I, pp. 347–350; id., *Historia de la Historiografía Española*, 1941, pp. 319–321.
65. See Fita, in RAH, *Boletín*, XXXIII (1898), pp. 248–249.
66. Cartagena also wrote a brief *vita* of Juan II in the *Crónica de Juan II* edited by Guzmán (see BAE, vol. 68, pp. 693a–695b). In this account Cartagena refrained from touching on any of the crucial events of the reign, save the downfall of Alvaro de Luna. Concerning this Cartagena says that the "incredible love" of the King for Alvaro, which lasted for about thirty eight years, turned, due to "change of fortune," into "hate and ill will," which led to Alvaro's arrest and execution (*ibid.*, 693b). Thus, in the *Crónica de Juan II* Cartagena clearly sought to ascribe Alvaro's fall to the

King's altered attitude; but the author of the *Defensorium* and the leader of the struggle on behalf of converso rights must have felt a desire to disclose to posterity at least some of Alvaro's faults and misdeeds that accounted for the rift between him and the conversos. The disclosures of the *Crónica* under review could well fit the provenance of Alfonso de Cartagena.

67. *CODOIN*, 105–106 (1893). The chapter on Juan II in the other version—ms. 9563 of the Biblioteca Nacional, Madrid—deals with the period of Fernando de Antequera.

68. *CODOIN*, 106, pp. 138–140.

69. *Ibid.* p. 138.

70. *Ibid.*, pp. 138–139.

71. *Ibid.*, p. 139.

72. *Ibid.*: e echó de fuera della á mano armada a los alcaldes e caualleros vecinos de la dicha cibdad e á los conversos, e robóles cuantas faciendas tenian.

73. *Ibid.*

74. *Ibid.*

75. *Ibid.*

76. *Ibid.*

77. *Ibid.*, p. 140.

78. *Ibid.*

79. *Ibid.*, pp. 137–138.

80. It is notable that the chapter on Juan II in this *Crónica* ends with the severe accusation against Alvaro that, during Castile's war against Granada in 1431, he received from Granada's King a huge bribe which moved him to interrupt the campaign (*ibid.*, pp. 140–141). The same charge is presented in Valera's *Crónica Abreviada de España* (see his *Memorial de Diversas Hazañas*, ed. Carriazo, 1941, p. 307) as an unproven allegation. In the *Cuarta*, however, it appears more like an established fact. Obviously, if Alvaro was guilty of treason, he fully deserved the punishment that ended his life.

81. See below, pp. 724–725.

The Aftermath of the Rebellion

1. See *Crónica*, año 1450, cap. 1, p. 671a. According to Higüera, Cardinal Torquemada expressed the same view of the commitments which the Prince gave the Toledans under oath, saying that "such oaths should not be made; [if made, they are invalid] and being invalid, they should not be observed" (see Higuera's *Historia Eclesiástica*, lib. 28, cap. 7; ms. 1290 of Bibl. Nacional, Madrid, f. 232^r); and see below, p. 659, and n. 59.

2. That is, prior to his entrance into Toledo and prior to Sarmiento's departure from the city. See above, pp. 324, 349.

3. See above, pp. 336–338.

4. See *Colección Diplomática*, in *Memorias de D. Enrique IV de Castilla*, II, 1835–1913, pp. 28a–37a. Fernando de Luxán was chosen to be executor of the bull out of the seven Church dignitaries nominated by the Pope for that task; the choice was made by the royal administration (see *ibid.*, pp. 30a and 32a).

5. *Ibid.*, pp. 26a–28a and 37a–38b.

6. *Ibid.*, p. 32a.

7. *Ibid.*, p. 32b: nin alguno presuma de participar con el dicho Pero Sarmiento, nin con sus familiares e complices e satelites e ayudadores e allegados e consintientes e culpados en los dichos maleficios, nin fablando, non estando, nin seyendo, nin andando, nin saludando, nin dando posada a el, nin a los otros sobredichos, nin a alguno dellos, nin comiendo, nin bebiendo, nin moliendo, nin cosiendo manjar, nin potage para ellos, nin les dando agua, nin fuego, nin les ministrando otra qualquier cosa, nin algund solas de piedad, nin participando con ellos salvo solamente en los casos otorgados por el derecho.

8. See *ibid.*, pp. 30a and 32a.

9. Opposed to this massive retaliation was Alonso de Cartagena, whose advice in

this matter was evidently not heeded. See his *Defensorium Unitatis Christianae*, 1943, p. 316; and see below, pp. 575–576.

10. See Benito, *Toledo*, doc. 19, p. 202, and see *Colección Diplomática*, pp. 30ab.

11. *Ibid.*, pp. 37b–38a.

12. The Sentence, including the bull, appears in Alonso de Oropesa, *Lumen ad Revelationem Gentium*, cap. 43, ms. Ambrosiana, ff. 302r–311v, and in the Spanish translation of Oropesa's work by Luis A. Díaz y Díaz: *Luz para conocimiento de los Gentiles*, pp. 536–549. And cf. preceding chapter, n. 40.

13. See *ibid.*, p. 543: hemos sido requeridos con insistencia justificada por el procurador fiscal y promotor del mismo poderosisimo señor Rey. Of the six executors nominated by the Pope according to Oropesa's work (f. 305ᵛ), only one (i.e., the Bishop of Seville) is mentioned in the bull as published by Benito Ruano (p. 200). The Bishop of Palencia, therefore, was among those who replaced the original nominees.

14. Oropesa, *op. cit.*, p. 545; and the same on pp. 543–544.

15. *Ibid.*, p. 544: y que no los deshonréis ni de palabra ni de obra ni permitáis que los deshonren.

16. *Ibid.*, p. 545.

17. *Ibid.*, p. 544: ni tengáis la osadia, ni alguno la tenga, de dogmatizar en adelante lo contrario de lo que se ha dicho.

18. *Ibid.*, p. 546.

19. *Colección Diplomática*, p. 38b.

20. *Crónica*, año 1451, cap. 1, p. 672ab. According to this account, the executions mentioned (in Valladolid, Seville and Burgos) took place in 1451. But the dates and events indicated in the *Crónica* from 1450 on are not infrequently mixed up. In all probability, the punishments referred to in chapter one of the year 1451 took place in 1450, not long after

the publication of the bull *Si ad reprimandas*.

21. See the bull *Regis Pacifici* in Benito, *op. cit.*, doc. 22, p. 215; published also by Beltrán de Heredia, in *Sefarad*, XXI (1961), p. 44.

22. *Ibid.*, *ibid.*

23. *Crónica*, año 1451, cap. 3 (p. 673ab).

24. *Ibid.*, *ibid.*, p. 673b.

25. *Ibid.*, *ibid.*

26. Benito Ruano, *op. cit.*, doc. 23, p. 216.

27. *Ibid.*, *ibid.*, pp. 216–217.

28. *Ibid.*, p. 217.

29. *Ibid.*, p. 218.

30. *Ibid.*, p. 219.

31. *Ibid.*, *ibid.*

32. See below, p. 724.

33. See Benito Ruano, *op. cit.*, doc. 23, p. 220.

34. See *Crónica*, año 1481, cap. 7, p. 675b, and *Crónica de Alvaro de Luna*, p. 267. For the date of March 30th see Benito, *op. cit.*, p. 74, n. 17 (on the basis of Ms. 19703/12 of BNM).

35. *Crónica de D. Alvaro de Luna*, p. 267.

36. *Ibid.*, p. 268.

37. See Benito Ruano, *op. cit.*, p. 74, n. 17 (on the basis of ms. 19703/12 of BNM).

38. In his letter of March 21 to the city, the King made it clear that his decision to pardon the city and its inhabitants was influenced in large measure by the "supplications and requests" of his son Prince Enrique (see *ibid.*, doc. 23, p. 217). The Prince's actions, however, were largely determined by Pacheco. And see above, p. 673.

39. See Higuera, *op. cit.*, lib. 28, cap. 14; Ms. 1290, f. 250ʳ: La ciudad escrivio por este tiempo al Rey suplicandole tubiese por bien esta firme en la gracia que avia hecho que, *mudando la voluntad que tenia de favorecer a los conversos,* no diesse licencia para que entrassen en Toledo ni tubiessen officios publicos.

40. Benito, *op. cit.*, doc. 26, pp. 222–223.

41. See above, p. 667.

42. Benito, *op. cit.*, p. 76.

43. *Ibid.*, docs. 27–28, pp. 223–227.

44. Raynaldus, *Annales Ecclesiastici,* ann. 1451, *nu.* 6, p. 380.

45. *Ibid., ibid.*

46. See CICa, ed. Friedberg, II, Sextus, lib. V, tit. iii, cap. 16; cf. Lea, *History,* II, p. 41.

47. See Benito Ruano, *op. cit.*, pp. 74–75, and *ibid.*, p. 75, n. 18

48. See Raynaldus, *op. cit.*, ann. 1451, no. 5, p. 379ab; the bull is also included in Higuera, *op. cit.*, lib. 28, cap. 14; ms. 1290, ff. 250ᵛ–251ᵛ.

49. In the letter the King sent to the cities of his kingdoms following Alvaro's execution, he stated that Alvaro had solicited bulls from the Pope without the King's knowledge and against his wish (see *Crónica*, año 1452, cap. 3, p. 686b). Also Fernán Pérez de Guzmán, speaking of Alvaro, said that "the Pope has not denied any petition of his" (*Generaciones y Semblanzas*, ed. J. Domínguez Bordona, 1954, p. 134).

End of Alvaro de Luna

1. See *Crónica de Don Alvaro de Luna*, ed. J. de Mata Carriazo, 1940, pp. 295–320 (caps. 100–107).

2. For the occurrences leading to the execution, as well as for the execution itself, see *ibid.*, cap. 128, pp. 429–434; *Crónica*, año 1453, cap. 2, pp. 682b–683b; for the date of the execution see Rizzo, *op. cit.*, appendix B, especially pp. 353–355.

3. See *Crónica de Juan II*, p. 67; *Cuarta Crónica General, CODOIN,* 106, p. 135; *Palencia, Crónica,* I, pp. 109–110.

4. See, for instance, C. Silió, *Don Alvaro de Luna*, 1915, pp. 23–24; A. Ballesteros y Beretta, *Historia de España,* III, 1922, p. 105; L. Suárez Fernández, in *Historia de España,* XV, p. 206.

5. See Manuel José Quintana, *Don Alvaro de Luna*, 1885, pp. 193–194; also Rizzo, *op. cit.*, pp. 164–16, 170–171, who sees the Queen's influence as a major factor in the King's decision to rid himself of Alvaro, begins his narrative of the plot against Alvaro with Alonso de Vivero, to whom he attributes the foremost share in its birth and progress.

6. Amador de los Ríos, *Historia,* III, 1876, pp. 51–54, 58–59.

7. *Ibid., ibid.*, pp. 56–57.

8. *Ibid., ibid.*, pp. 43–45.

9. *Ibid., ibid.*, p. 47.

10. *Ibid., ibid.*, p. 50.

11. *Ibid., ibid.*, pp. 62–63.

12. *Ibid., ibid.*, 47, and n. 1.

13. See above, p. 206.

14. See above, pp. 238–239.

15. See above, pp. 292–294.

16. See above, p. 520.

17. See above, p. 1209, n. 31.

18. See Alvar García de Santa María, *Crónica del Rey Don Juan II*, published in *CODOIN*, 100 (1891), año 1431, cap. 24, pp. 302–311.

19. See above, p. 388.

20. That this was, in fact, Alvaro's attitude is conclusively proven by the bull *Humani generis*, and especially by the "Sentence" of its executor, both of which could not have been issued without Alvaro's cooperation. See above, pp. 666–667.

21. Graetz, *Geschichte*, VIII, 1890³, p. 148.

22. *Ibid., ibid.*, pp. 190–191, n. 2.

23. *Ibid., ibid.*, pp. 153–154. Admitting that the conversos had a grudge against Alvaro, Nicholas Round did not see in their relations with him sufficient cause to seek his destruction (see *The Greatest Man Uncrowned*, pp. 63–64). Despite his great mastery of the sources and numerous insightful observations, Round's major conclusion concerning Alvaro's fall does not square, in our judgment, with historical reality. His thorough work, however, must be carefully consulted in any study of the subject.

24. See Lea, *History,* I, 1905, p. 147.

25. *Ibid., ibid.*

26. *Ibid., ibid.*, p. 148.

27. *Ibid., ibid.,* p. 147.
28. *Ibid., ibid.*
29. *Ibid., ibid.,* pp. 147–148.
30. V. Beltrán de Heredia, "Las Bulas de Nicolás V acerca de los Conversos," in *Sefarad*, XXI (1961), pp. 29–30; see above, p. 667.
31. *Ibid., ibid.,* p. 34.
32. *Ibid., ibid.,* pp. 25, 35.
33. *Ibid.,* p. 35.
34. *Ibid.,* p. 34.
35. For some of these developments in modern scholarship, see my article, "¿Motivos o Pretextos? La Razón de la Inquisición," in Ángel Alcalá, ed. *Inquisición Española y mentalidad inquisitorial*, 1984, pp. 26–36.
36. Heredia, *loc. cit.,* p. 39: "De no ser así, el pontífice no se hubiere prestado a la maniobra."
37. *Ibid., ibid.,* p. 32.
38. See above, pp. 497, 600.
39. Heredia, *loc. cit.,* p. 34.
40. Luciano Serrano, *Los Conversos D. Pablo de Santa María y D. Alonso de Cartagena*, 1942, p. 180.
41. Amador de los Ríos, *Historia*, III, p. 58.
42. See Cantera, *Alvar García*, p. 427.
43. *Ibid.,* p. 428.
44. *Ibid.,* p. 79.
45. *Ibid.,* pp. 78–79, 244, 427–428.
46. *Crónica de Don Alvaro de Luna*, ed. cit., p. 381.
47. Cantera, *op. cit.,* p. 244.
48. *Crónica de D. Alvaro de Luna*, ed. cit., p. 332.
49. See *ibid.,* p. 301, where he refers to Alvaro's *muy sentido y avisado juicio;* p. 320: *El Maestre . . . conosçió con su discreçión;* p. 328: *pensó como caballero muy sentido;* and other places.
50. Thus he did not seem to have suspected Ruiz de Mendoza, Perafán de Rivera, and others who were involved in the conspiracy. See *ibid.,* pp. 404–406, 416 and many other places.
51. *Crónica de Don Alvaro de Luna*, p. 391;

Cartagena is also mentioned as the first of these emissaries in the *Crónica de Juan II*, año 1452, cap. i, p. 680, and in Valera's *Crónica Abreviada de España*, cap. xiv, published by J. de Mata Carriazo as an addendum to Valera's *Memorial de diversas Hazañas*, 1941, p. 332.
52. *Ibid.,* p. 392.
53. *Ibid., ibid.*
54. *Ibid., ibid.*
55. *Ibid., ibid.*
56. From the *Crónica de Juan II*, año 1452, cap. i, p. 680[a], one may conclude that Alfonso de Cartagena, along with other emissaries of the King, went to see Alvaro several times for the same aforesaid purpose. This, however, could hardly happen after the Bishop's encounter with Alvaro as described in the foregoing. Both Cartagena's self-respect and awareness of his lack of influence on Alvaro would prevent him from repeating the attempt.
57. *Ibid.,* p. 404.
58. *Ibid.,* p. 393.
59. *Ibid.,* p. 409.
60. *Crónica de Juan II*, año 1452, cap. I, p. 680b.
61. *Ibid., ibid.*
62. *Crónica de D. Alvaro*, p. 406.
63. Cantera, *op. cit.,* p. 77.
64. *Ibid.,* p. 427.
65. Alonso de Palencia, *Crónica de Enrique IV*, transl. by A. Paz y Mélia, I, 1904, p. iii.
66. *Ibid.,* pp. iii–112.
67. See *Memorias de D. Enrique IV de Castilla*, II, pp. 124–125.
68. *Ibid., ibid.*
69. Although it in no way affects our thesis, we should however note that some doubt persisted regarding the identity of this Relator. Miguel de Portilla y Esquivel, in his *Historia de la Ciudad de Compluto*, Alacalá, 1725, I, 447, cites an epitaph on the tomb of Doña María, mother of the Relator Fernán Díaz de Toledo, in which Luis

Díaz de Toledo is mentioned as the *second Relator*. The epitaph, however, is not entirely to be relied on. As Rodrigo Amador de los Ríos stated, "because of the bad state of the inscription, which was produced long after the death of Doña María (at least, in the 16th century), Portilla did not succeed in reading it clearly and thus gave room to many doubts and confusions" (see his article "La Parroquia de Santa María la Mayor de Alcalá de Henares y su abandonada capilla del Relator," in *Boletín de la Real Academia de Bellas Artes de San Fernando*, XVIII [1898], p. 250, n. 11). And, indeed, in one place Portilla says that the epitaph "calls *Diego Díaz* the Second Relator, and because of the effaced part of the inscription, "it is impossible to establish whether he was the husband or the son of that Señora, although the fact that he is called the second Relator indicates that he was the younger brother of Don Fernando" (see *op. cit.*, I, pp. 232, 236–239, 446, 447, 586, 587). It is clear that Portilla was not even sure of the name of the "second Relator"—i.e., whether it was Luis or Diego, though he seems to have finally decided on the former (judging by the text of the inscription he produced), and it is also clear that he could gather nothing definite about his relationship to Doña María (he could be her husband or her son, wrote Portilla; but it did not occur to him that he could be her grandson). Apart from this, the author of the epitaph mentioned was not well informed of the first Relator, since his inscription contains a number of gross errors, such as those relating to the dates of the demise of Fernán Díaz de Toledo and his mother-in-law (see Portilla, *op. cit.*, I, pp. 446, 447).

Rodrigo Amador de los Ríos wrote (*loc cit.*, p. 251, end of note 1) that *in no place* "do we find a notice about either

D. Diego or D. Luis whom Portilla entitles as the second Relator according to the epitaph." As we have seen, however, Luis Díaz de Toledo is described as Relator in the document we have cited from the *Memorias de Enrique IV* (see above, n. 67), and there can be hardly any doubt that the reference there is to the Relator's son. If Fernán Díaz de Toledo had a brother called Luis (like his son, mentioned above), the probabilities are that in 1467 that brother had already reached old age, and why should the rebels appoint an old man, unknown for any previous achievement, to the arduous tasks entrusted to D. Luis, according to the above cited document? Thus among the errors and erasures of the epitaph cited by Portilla in his aforementioned work, at least one true fact stands out—namely, that Luis Díaz de Toledo was the *second Relator*.

70. *Crónica de Don Alvaro de Luna*, p. 350, and other places.

71. *Memorias de Enrique IV*, II (*Colección Diplomática*) p. 74.

72. *Ibid.*, p. 75.

73. *Ibid.*, p. 76.

74. *Ibid.*, p. 76b.

75. *Ibid., ibid.*

76. *Ibid.*

77. *Crónica de Juan II*, año 1452, cap. 2, p. 682b.

78. *Ibid.* The division of opinion that developed on that occasion is also reflected in the contradictory views on the legitimacy of the King's Council expressed by Diaz de Montalvo, one of the jurists who attended the first and second meeting (*ibid.*, p. 75a). In his comments on the *Fuero Real*, lib. I, tit. 4 *(De los que no obedecen el mandamiento del Rey)*, he justifies the King's position and the procedure followed in reaching the verdict against the Constable, while in his gloss on the *Partidas* (Partida I, tit. 7, ley 1) he

denies the judicial grounds of the sentence and sees it as procedurally null and void. See on all this, F. Caballero, *Doctor Montalvo* (vol. III of his *Conquenses Ilustres*), 1873, pp. 50–53, 105–107, 209–210.

79. *Crónica*, año 1452, cap. 2, p. 682b.

80. See Amador, *Historia*, III, p. 62, n. 1.

81. That a murmuring campaign against Alvaro was the cause of the King's dissatisfaction with Alvaro is also indicated by the *Crónica* of Alvaro de Luna, except that the author, faithful to his policy of avoiding explicit reference to the converso leaders, ascribes this agitation to Vivero only.

82. The mutual dislike and constant irritation that marked the relations between Alvaro and the Queen may well be reflected in the testimonies adduced in a legal examination of Alvaro's sentence around the beginning of the 16th century. See León de Corral, *Don Alvaro de Luna* (segun testimonios inéditos de la época), 1915, pp. 47–49, 66–69.

83. See Valera, *Crónica Abreviada*, ed. cit., p. 214.

84. None of the 15th century sources offers us evidence to the effect that the Queen was the mainspring of the conspiracy against Alvaro. According to the *Crónica de Juan II* (año 1447, cap. 3, p. 654ab, and año 1452, cap. 1, p. 678a), the author of the idea was the King; he informed the Queen of his wish to dispose of Alvaro and asked for her cooperation, which was readily given. Similarly, the historian Alonso de Palencia ascribes the decision to destroy Alvaro to the King who, unable to endure any longer his "servitude" to the Constable, was determined to free himself from "that humiliating yoke" (*Crónica de Enrique IV*, I, 1904, pp. 108, 112). Likewise the *Crónica de D. Alvaro de Luna* does not see the Queen, but Alonso

Pérez de Vivero as the prime mover of the conspiracy (*ibid.*, p. 295ff.) and attributes the Queen's involvement in the plot to Vivero's persuasions (*ibid.*, p. 296, 307).

Moreover, judging by Diego de Valera, it was not the Queen, but Alvaro himself, who undermined the King's affection for him. According to Valera, the breach in their relations started with their differences over the King's second marriage. Alvaro learned of the King's intent to send Valera secretly to France to negotiate his marriage with the French King's daughter, while he, Alvaro, was secretly negotiating the King's marriage with Isabel of Portugal. When Alvaro confronted the King with his discovery, Valera tells us, "such things passed between them [i.e., the King and Alvaro] that the Constable remained very offended and the King no less annoyed. And from then on he [i.e., the King] always disliked him, although he disguised and concealed it with great sagacity" (*Crónica Abreviada*, ed. cit., pp. 314–315). It follows that the Queen did not have to use her influence to alienate the King from Alvaro. The disaffection had occurred before he met her.

This reference to the hidden hostility that Juan II felt for Alvaro de Luna may help us understand Valera's other statement that, by arranging for the marriage of Isabel to the King, the Constable "drew the knife which cut off his head" (see *ibid.*, p. 314). Most probably, he referred to the Queen's decisive share in obtaining the collaboration of the Count of Estúñiga which was considered essential for Alvaro's surrender (a view especially favored by Valera who was the Count's agent and a major actor in the events that resulted from that collaboration). Accordingly, the Queen was seen by him as "instrument," not as instigator of the conspiracy. And the same view may have been shared by Santillana when he praised her as the *quarta liberadora*, in line with Judith, Esther and Mary, the "spouse and mother of God" (see his "Coplas a la Reyna," in *Cancionero Castellano del Siglo XV*, ed. by R. Foulché-Delbosc, I, 1912, p. 501).

85. This was clearly discerned by Palencia (see *op. cit.*, I, p. 108).

86. See *Historia de España*, XV, pp. 204–207.

87. See above, pp. 594–595.

88. A clear reflection of this view can be seen in the King's letter to his kingdoms in which he sought to justify his sentence against Alvaro. In issuing that sentence, the King explained, he only exercised his right to do justice which was "entrusted to me by God," so that "all recognize . . . *the place he holds on earth by God's authority*" (*Crónica de Juan II*, año 1452, cap. 3, p. 690ab).

89. On his Jewish origin see above, p. 1265, n. 1.

90. It is difficult to dismiss as historically worthless Pedro Jerónimo de Aponte's claim (in his additions to the *Tizón de España*, BNM, ms. 6043, f. 1627ᵛ) that Vivero was of converso origin, as does N. Round, *op. cit.*, p. 64. The statement of the historian Lope García de Salazar, a contemporary of Alonso Pérez, that his father was a "good man of Vivero" and "an hidalgo" (see his *Libro de buenas andanzas e fortunas*, ed. A. Rodríguez Herrero, 1955, p. 60) does

not necessarily conflict with the assertions of the *Crónica de Alvaro de Luna* (p. 295) that he was a man of a low station and of "little value." We know, after all, nothing of the fortunes of Alonso's family or of his mother who may have been a New Christian. In any case, the indication of his base social condition may allude to his converso descent as may his profession (accountancy) and his repeated designation as *Judas* or his *"heir"* (*ibid.*, p. 300) who delivered his lord to the "power of the Jews" (p. 324)—i.e., the conversos.

Nor is it easy to explain Juan II's withdrawal from his intent to charge Alvaro with Vivero's murder (*Memorias*, pp. 43–44, 46) unless we assume that Vivero was a converso. If he was, the Relator may have come to fear that if Alvaro were to be sentenced for that murder, the sentence might stir the dangerous accusation that he was martyred by the conversos for the "just punishment" he imposed on one of their "despicable traitors." As a result, Vivero's name was not even mentioned in either the trial or the related royal document (see *Crónica de Juan II*, pp. 684–691).

Closing the Circle

1. See *Crónica de Juan II*, p. 629a.
2. See document published by Benito Ruano, *op. cit.*, pp. 262–265.
3. See RAH, *Memorias*, p. 121ab.
4. See above, p. 317.

BOOK THREE
Enrique IV and the Catholic Kings

Enrique IV: His Aims and Tactics

1. See above, p. 649.
2. See above, p. 673.
3. See the title accompanying his signature on the marriage contract (of

Feb. 1455) between Enrique IV and the Infanta Juana of Portugal, in *Memorias*, p. 140b; see also Diego de Valera, *Memorial de Diversas Hazañas*, ed. Carriazo, 1941, p. 20. In later royal documents (of May 28, 1455 and June 12, 1455), however, he is entitled as the King's secretary, *referendario,* major notary of his *privilegios rodados* and member of his Council, but not as his Relator (see *Col. Dipl.,* p. 143b, and F. Fita, in RAH, *Boletín,* XII [1888], p. 76).

4. Colmenares, *Historia de Segovia,* ed. 1970, cap. 29, n. 20.

5. See Valera, *op. cit.,* p. 15, and Palencia, *Crónica de Enrique IV,* I, p. 167. Enrique chose him as one of his ambassadors to Portugal to negotiate his proposed marriage with Juana, Alfonso V's sister. Palencia speaks of him in most disparaging terms.

6. For Diego Arias de Avila see *Colección Diplomática,* p. 139a, in a document from February 1455. Dávila is described there not only as *contador mayor,* but also as the King's secretary, *escribano mayor* (for his privileges) and public notary of the Court and "todos los sus regnos e señorios." In his *Crónica de Enrique IV* (cap. 20; BAE, vol. 70, p. 111a), Diego Enríquez del Castillo refers to him (in 1457) as the King's *Contador mayor e Tesorero* (see also Palencia, *op. cit.,* I, pp. 93–94, 160–161). For Alvar Gómez de Cibdad Real, see *Colección Diplomática,* p. 147b (cedula from August 2, 1455). He first appears as the King's secretary (together with Alvar García de Villa Real) in the King's matrimonial agreement of February 1455 (*ibid.,* p. 139a); and see Palencia, *op. cit.,* I, p. 235.

7. See Castillo, *op. cit.,* p. 141a (cap. 68).

8. See *ibid.,* p. 101ab, in Castillo's first chapter which is devoted to a description of Enrique's physiognomy and habits. The attractive picture of the King drawn by Castillo need not be taken as a fictitious sketch of an adulating court chronicler. It should be noted that Castillo's *Crónica,* which was written during Enrique's lifetime, is replete with criticisms of the King's conduct, while his summary evaluation

of Enrique's traits and efforts, penned after the King's death, reflects sincere admiration (see his *Crónica,* p. 222ab).

Another contemporary portrayal of Enrique, not very different from that of Castillo, is found in a fifteenth century manuscript preserved in the Escorial and published in its entirety by A. Rodríguez Villa, *Bosquejo biográfico de Don Beltrán de la Cueva,* 1881, pp. 5–6. Enrique was seen in a positive light also by Pedro de Escavias, who held various offices in Enrique's administration and was a member of his Council. The chapter on Enrique in his *Repertorio de Principes de España* (ms. in the Escorial, still unpublished) was printed by J. B. Sitges in his *Enrique IV y la excelente Señora,* 1912, appendix A, pp. 381–408 (see especially pp. 407–408).

Not free of some critical remarks, but on the whole commending the King, is also Pulgar's description of Enrique (*Claros Varones de Castilla,* ed. J. J. Domínguez Bordona, 1954, pp. 9–20). The main negative feature of this description is provided by Pulgar's claim that Enrique was demonstrably impotent—a claim which he attempted, but failed, to prove, and must be further questioned in light of the fact that Pulgar was chronicler of Queen Isabella, the legitimacy of whose rule rested entirely on Enrique's assumed impotence.

Another functionary of the Catholic Kings, Diego de Valera, spoke of Enrique in both laudatory and derogatory terms. His averments that the King knew Latin like a scholar, was an avid reader and a masterly writer *(in toda letra)* add important features to Enrique's image (see Valera, *op. cit.,* p. 259).

9. See Castillo, *op. cit.,* p. 104b (cap. 8): for the Moors "persecute our religion" and "usurp our lands."

10. However suggestive of his desire to add Catalonia to his dominions (see

below, p. 749), the War of Aragon was, in all likelihood, also seen by Enrique as a national necessity—as a means of dealing a crippling blow to his most dangerous foe, Juan II of Aragon, who kept meddling in Castile's affairs. Only a short time before the Catalonians had asked Enrique to become their King, a conspiracy of Castilian nobles, aimed at toppling Enrique's rule, had been organized with Juan's aid. According to Valera (*op. cit.*, pp. 42–43), that conspiracy caused Enrique a great deal of fear and anxiety (*"De lo qual . . . el rey rescibiese gran turbación;" "Él temía mucho este ayuntamiento de los grandes"*).

11. *Colección Diplomática*, p. 354b (§2); cf. Palencia, *op. cit.*, I, p. 259. Reflecting Enrique's attitude toward Christianity is Escavias' statement: "Fue muy devoto a iglesias y monesterios" (Sitges, *op. cit.*, p. 407), which is repeated by Pulgar (*op. cit.*, pp. 14–15), Valera (*op. cit.*, p. 294) and others.

12. Palencia was undoubtedly the most extreme—and most biased—critic of Enrique. According to Palencia, Enrique had no virtues, only vices; he was devious, corrupt, and tyrannical; he did not care for the people's welfare, but only to satisfy his perverted lusts; he was not in any sense devoted to religion, but openly and flagrantly anti-Christian ("A true scourge of God was Don Enrique, an enemy of the faith as much as a friend of the Moors"; Palencia, *op. cit.*, I, p. 466).

13. P. Aguado Bleye, *Manual de Historia de España*, I, 1967, p. 798a.

14. See Juan de Mariana, *Historia General de España*, lib. 22, cap. 20. Mariana assumed that the claim about Enrique's impotence was a "fable," largely "forged to please the Kings Don Fernando and Doña Isabel." The assumption is true to the extent that it relates to the evolution of the charge in Spain's public opinion. The "fable,"

however, had appeared a considerable time before Ferdinand and Isabella ascended the throne or even became political factors (see below, pp. 751–752).

15. Sitges, *op. cit.*, pp. 57–58.

16. Orestes Ferrara, *Un Pleito Sucesorio*, [1945], pp. 23–29.

17. Tarsicio de Azcona, *Isabel la Católica*, 1964, pp. 34–43.

18. J. N. Hillgarth, *The Spanish Kingdoms*, II, 1978, pp. 318–322.

19. M. Lafuente, *Historia General de España*, lib. 3, cap. 30.

20. A. Ballesteros y Beretta, *Historia de España*, III, 1922, p. 110.

21. See, for instance, Valera, *op. cit.*, pp. 22, 35, where Enrique is chided by the nobles of his entourage for taking unnecessary risks during the war against the Moors. Perhaps more than on other occasions ·he displayed exemplary courage when, in October 1467, he went, without any military force, to Segovia, to negotiate with rebels who on many occasions proved to have been his mortal foes (see Castillo, *op. cit.*, cap. 104).

22. Valera, *op. cit.*, p. 295.

23. That Enrique held this exalted view of kingship is indicated by his own pronouncements on the subject which were, however, phrased with some restraint. See below, notes 24, 25, 26, 27 and 190.

24. See Castillo, *op. cit.*, pp. 101b–102a (cap. 2).

25. *Ibid.*, p. 111a (cap. 20).

26. *Ibid.*, p. 150ab (cap. 82).

27. *Ibid.*, p. 148b (cap. 79).

28. Ibid., p. 177b (cap. 113).

29. Note his treatment of the Toledan rebels Marcos García amd Fernando de Avila who were "arrastrados e justiciados muy cruelmente" (*Crónica de Juan II*, año 1449, cap. ix, p. 668a; see also *Abreviación del Halconero*, ms. 434 de la Biblioteca de Santa Cruz (Universidad de Valladolid), cap. 172, f. 296). That this punishment was

executed at Enrique's orders is explicitly stated in the *Cuarta Crónica General, CODOIN*, 106 (1893), p. 140.

30. See the titular description of Escavias' *Repertorio* (in Sitges, *op. cit.*, 381). This description, if it was not written by Escavias, was framed by a contemporary of Enrique IV (whom he calls *nuestro señor*).

31. See on this above, pp. 385ff.; 421ff.; 517ff.; 610ff.; 619ff.; 1230, n. 12.

32. See below, pp. 631, 636, 645, 655, 656.

33. Lea, *History*, I, p. 148.

34. The above date is suggested on the basis of P. Thureau-Dangin's *Bernardino of Siena* (transl. by G. von Hügel, 1906, pp. 27–28), according to which Bernardino's first meeting with Ferrer took place at Alexandria, Piedmont, between 1402 and 1409.

35. A major element in his campaign against the Jews was his fierce opposition to the taking of usury (as all lending of money at interest was then called). For some of the views that shaped his attitude toward money lending, see I. Origo, *The World of San Bernardino*, 1962, pp. 92–97. A more systematic analysis of his economic concepts is offered by Raymond de Roover, *San B. of Siena and Sant'Antonio of Florence*, 1967, pp. 16–38.

36. On Capistrano see Wadding, *Annales Minorum*, 1734, vols. IX to XIII (indices); Graetz, *Geschichte*, VIII (1890), pp. 192–199; C. Roth, *History of the Jews of Italy*, (1946, pp. 158–159, 249–250, 274–275), and J. Hofer, *St. John Capistran*, transl. by P. Cummins, 1943, pp. 66–68, 268–281. Hofer, who believed that "individual Jews" were actually guilty of sacrilegious crimes such as host desecration (*ibid.*, p. 276), tried to minimize Capistrano's share in the Breslau executions of 1453. His contentions, however, are roundly denied by Wadding, *Annales Minorum*, XII, 1735, p. 142 (§26) and *Acta*

Sanctorum, October, X (1861), §§234–235, pp. 342b–343a, where he is described as a leading force in the anti-Jewish persecution.

37. See on him C. Roth, *op. cit.*, pp. 170–176; A. Milano, *Storia degli ebrei in Italia*, 1963, pp. 198–200; Graetz, *Geschichte*, VIII (1890), pp. 255–261.

38. See Baer, *Die Juden*, II, pp. 305–312 (§§292–293) and p. 322. This situation remained fundamentally unchanged also in Enrique IV's time (see *ibid.*, pp. 323–325). Noteworthy are the special grants (partial or full exemption from taxes) given by Enrique IV to the Jews of Soria and Alfaro for their military and other services (*ibid.*, pp. 331–334, §§319–320).

39. *Fortalitium Fidei*, lib. 3. consider. 11, art. 8; ed. Lyon, 1511, f. 232v.

40. *Ibid., ibid.*

41. *Ibid.*

42. *Ibid.*

43. *Ibid.*, Prologue, f. 3a.

44. See the King's order, dated May 28, 1455, published by F. Fita in RAH, *Boletín*, XII (1888), pp. 72–76; republished by Baer, II, pp. 327–328.

45. *Ibid.*

46. Colmenares, *Historia de Segovia*, 1640, caps. 33 (§2), pp. 399–400ab, 35 (§§7,13); Zacuto, *Yuḥasin*, ed. Filipowski, 1857, p. 226b; according to Colmenares, fifteen Jews were condemned, according to Zacuto only eight: two were garroted, two burned, four hanged.

47. José de Sigüenza, *Historia de la Orden de San Gerónimo*, I, 1907, pp. 363b–364b (lib. III, cap. 27).

48. *Ibid.*, 364b.

49. *Ibid.*, p. 366a (lib. III, cap. xviii).

50. *Ibid.*, p. 366b. This is against Sigüenza, *ibid.*, p. 366b, who claims that the bishops' reaction was positive and that "this was the first general inquisition made by the bishops in the kingdom of Castile." Sigüenza admits that he got no confirmation of this allegation beyond what he found in his

Order's archives. What he found, however, were probably courteous expressions of consent by some bishops to Oropesa's proposal which were not accompanied by any personal commitments.

51. *Ibid.*, p. 367a–368a.

52. *Ibid.*, p. 368a: . . . y dexo assentada y quieta aquella ciudad.

53. *Ibid.*, p. 368b; see L. A. Díaz y Díaz, in *Studia Hieronymiana*, I, 1973, p. 257.

54. See V. Beltrán de Heredia, "Las bulas de Nicolás V acerca de los conversos de Castilla," *Sefarad*, xxi (1961), pp. 35, 44–45.

55. *Ibid.*, p. 35.

56. See on this also below, pp. 892–893.

57. See Sigüenza, *op. cit.*, I, p. 368a.

58. See Espina, *op. cit.*, lib. 3, consideratio xii, quintus punctus, f. 236a.

59. Palencia, *op. cit.*, I, p. 364 (Década primera, lib. vi, cap. 6).

60. *Ibid.*, pp. 364–365.

61. Castillo, *op. cit.*, cap. 53 (p. 130ab); cf. Sigüenza, *op. cit.*, I, pp. 366b–367a.

62. Castillo, *op. cit.*, p. 130b.

63. Sigüenza, *op. cit.*, I, p. 367a.

64. *Ibid., ibid.*

65. See Juan Torres-Fontes, *El Itinerario de Enrique IV de Castilla*, 1953, p. 149.

66. Sigüenza, who assumed that this incident had occurred prior to Oropesa's work as inquisitor in Toledo (*ibid.*), was obviously mistaken. Castillo seems to have described the events in proper chronological order.

67. See Isaac Abravanel, *Wells of Salvation* (*Ma'aynei ha-Yeshu'ah*), XII, ii, 6 (Comm. on Minor Prophets and Hagiographa, Tel-Aviv, 1960, p. 412b); cf. Baer, *History*, II, p. 291.

68. Castillo, *op. cit.*, p. 150a (cap. 81).

69. Palencia, *op. cit.*, I, p, 362; III, p, 264.

70. Pulgar, *Claros Varones*, pp. 56–57.

71. *Crónica del Halconero*, cap. 384, pp. 539–540.

72. Castillo, *op. cit.*, cap. vii; BAE, vol. 70, p. 104b.

73. Palencia, *op. cit.*, I, p. 147.

74. This seems to be the conclusion one should draw from Enrique's desire to have his government run by opponents of Pacheco (which would prevent him from dismissing Barrientos) and from the help Don Lope offered him to attain this aim; see below, p. 748.

75. See Escavias, in Sitges, *op. cit.*, pp. 387–388.

76. *Ibid.*, p. 388.

77. Castillo, *op. cit.*, cap. xvi, p. 114b.

78. See *ibid.*, cap. XLIII (pp. 122b–123b) and cap. XLIV (p. 124ab); see above, pp. 718 and 1282, n. 10.

79. *Ibid.*, pp. 129–130.

80. *Ibid.*, p. 128a; *Colección Diplomática*, no. 87, pp. 290–291.

81. Castillo, *op. cit.*, pp. 134a–135b (caps. 60, 62).

82. *Colección Diplomática*, no. 92, p. 302a.

83. *Ibid., ibid.*

84. *Ibid.*, p. 302b.

85. *Ibid.*, p. 302a.

86. Castillo, *op. cit.*, pp. 136a–137a (cap. 63).

87. Sitges, *op. cit.*, p. 134.

88. Castillo, *op. cit.*, p. 136a (cap. 63).

89. *Ibid.*, p. 137ab (cap. 64).

90. *Ibid.*, p. 139a (cap. 65); *ibid.* (cap. 66).

91. *Ibid., ibid.*

92. *Colección Diplomática*, p. 326.

93. *Ibid.*, p. 327.

94. *Ibid.*, pp. 328b–329a.

95. *Ibid.*, p. 329b.

96. *Ibid.*, p. 330b.

97. *Ibid.*, p. 329a.

98. *Ibid.*, pp. 331b–332b.

99. See Galíndez de Carvajal, *Crónica de Enrique IV*, in Torres Fontes' *Estudio* about this *Crónica*, 1944, p. 220.

100. Castillo, *op. cit.*, pp. 138b–139a (cap. 65).

101. *Ibid.*, cap. 66, p. 139ab; *Colección Diplomática*, pp. 340a–345b.

102. Castillo, *op. cit.*, p. 140a (cap. 67); Palencia, *op. cit.*, I, pp. 422–423.

103. *Colección Diplomática*, pp. 366a–367b (nos. IV–VI).

104. *Ibid.*, p. 365.

105. *Colección Diplomática*, p. 329a, 330a.

106. *Ibid.*, 366b (no. iv).

107. *Ibid.*, p. 366a (no. iv).

108. *Ibid.*, p. 366b. That the assertion concerning the *many* "bad Christians" (which no doubt irked Oropesa) was included in the document may be explained by its ascription to the nobles who had advised the King about the heresy's dimensions. It could not, after all, be denied that the nobles *had* made that claim. On Oropesa's view of the converso problem, see in detail below, pp. 889–896.

109. See below, pp. 871–873.

110. Castillo, *op. cit.*, pp. 140b–141a (cap. 68).

111. *Ibid.*, p. 141ab (cap. 69).

112. *Ibid.*, p. 141a (cap. 69).

113. *Ibid.*, p. 141a (cap. 68).

114. See on this above, pp. 737–738, 741.

115. See below, pp. 786, 788, 809.

116. Castillo, *op. cit.*, p. 144b (cap. 74); Palencia, *op. cit.*, I, pp. 457–458 (Década I, lib. 7, cap. 8).

117. Pulgar, *op. cit.*, pp. 132–133; and see on him above, p. 1230, n. 12.

118. Palencia, *op. cit.*, I, pp. 532–533 (Década I, lib. 8, cap. 8).

119. *Ibid.*, p. 534.

120. *Ibid.*, p. 533.

121. *Ibid.*, p. 534. One of the authors mentioned by Palencia as opposed to Don Francisco's views was the bishop of Ampurias, Antonio de Alcalá, who died in 1459—i.e., six years before Enrique's dethronement (see Paz y Mélia's note, *ibid.*, p. 534). Did the Alfonsine party make use of a work written prior to the outbreak of the civil war?

122. According to Gil González Dávila, *Teatro Eclesiástico*, II, 1647, p. 451, King Enrique later sent Don Francisco to Rome as his ambassador to the papal court. This embassy no doubt provided the basis for Don Francisco's rise in the ecclesiastical hierarchy. Before long Sixtus IV appointed him his datary, bishop of Coria and (in

1476) his legate to Genoa, where he concluded an alliance between the Genoese republic, King Fernando of Sicily and the Pope. According to Pulgar (*Claros Varones de Castilla*, ed. Domínguez Bordona, p. 132), Don Francisco was about to be created Cardinal when death overtook him at the age of 55.

123. See *Colección Diplomática*, pp. 124–125. According to his own testimony upon signing (on May 28, 1467) a copy of the Testament of Juan II, Luis Díaz de Toledo, besides serving as Relator, was then "oidor, referendario, secretary, Major Notary of the Rounded Privileges and member of the Council of our Lord, the King Don Alfonso of Castile and León."

124. Palencia, *op. cit.*, II, pp. 48–51 (Década I, lib. 9, cap. 6).

125. Published by Martín Gamero, *Historia de Toledo*, pp. 1040–1045.

126. Ms. N-44 of Colección Salazar of the Real Academia de la Historia, Madrid, ff. 199^r–201^r, and ms. 2041 of the Biblioteca Nacional, Madrid, ff. 36^r–40^r.

127. Palencia, *op. cit.*, II, p. 48.

128. RAH, ms. N-44 of Colección Salazar, f. 199r.

129. Palencia, *op. cit.*, II, p. 48.

130. *Ibid., ibid.*

131. See ms. 2041 of BNM, 36^v; and see what I wrote concerning this in my *Marranos of Spain*, 1973, pp. 263–264.

132. Palencia, *op. cit.*, p. 49.

133. *Ibid.*

134. Martín Gamero, *op. cit.*, pp. 1041–1042; ms. N-44 of Colección Salazar, ff. 199^r, 200^r.

135. Palencia, *op. cit.*, II, p. 49.

136. *Ibid.*, pp. 49–50.

137. *Ibid.*, p. 50.

138. *Ibid.*, p. 49.

139. *Ibid.*, p. 50; cf. Martín Gamero, *op. cit.*, p. 1044

140. Colección Salazar, ms. N-44, f. 199^r.

141. Martín Gamero, *op. cit.*, p. 1040.

142. *Ibid.*, pp. 1040–1041.

143. Both Pero López and Alvar Gómez bore the titles of Major Judges; López' authority, however, extended to both criminal and civil cases, while that of Gómez was limited to civil cases only. See Colección Salazar, ms. 44, f. 199ʳ.

144. Martín Gamero, *op. cit.*, p. 1040.

145. *Ibid.*, p. 1041.

146. *Ibid.;* Colección Salazar, ms. N-44, f. 199ʳ.

147. Palencia, *op. cit.*, II, p. 50.

148. Martín Gamero, *op. cit.*, p. 1041.

149. See above, p. 779.

150. Martín Gamero, *op. cit.*, p. 1041; Colección Salazar, ms. N-44, f. 199ʳ.

151. Martín Gamero, *op. cit.*, pp. 1041, 1045.

152. Palencia, *op. cit.*, II, p. 51.

153. *Ibid., ibid.*

154. Colección Salazar, ms. N-44, f. 199ᵛ.

155. Martín Gamero, *op. cit.*, p. 1042.

156. *Ibid.*, p. 1042.

157. *Ibid.*, pp. 1042–1043; Colección Salazar, ms. N-44, f. 199ᵛ. The monastery of San Bernardo (on the other side of the Tagus) belonged to the Order of San Cistel. From there the Duke proceeded to Ocaña, where Pacheco stayed at the time (*ibid.*, f. 200ʳ).

158. *Ibid., ibid.*

159. *Ibid.*

160. *Ibid.*

161. Martín Gamero, *op. cit.*, p. 1043.

162. *Ibid.;* Colección Salazar, ms. N-44, f. 199ᵛ; see also Palencia, *op. cit.*, II, p. 51.

163. Colección Salazar, ms. N-44, f. 200ʳᵛ.

164. Martín Gamero, *op. cit.*, p. 1043.

165. *Ibid.*

166. *Ibid.*, pp. 1043–1044.

167. *Ibid.*

168. According to Palencia, "*all* [Toledan] conversos, covered with opprobrium, went into exile without their possessions [which had been confiscated] (*op. cit.*, II, p. 51). The sequential events of Toledo's history, however, deny this extreme assertion.

169. Judging by Pedro de Mesa (in Martín Gamero, *op. cit.*, pp. 1044–1045), the qualification of the conversos for office was to be determined by an Inquisition.

170. *Ibid.*, p. 1044.

171. Colección Salazar, ms. N-44, f. 200ᵛ.

172. Palencia, *op. cit.*, II, pp. 114–115.

173. *Ibid., ibid.*, p. 115.

174. *Ibid.*

175. *Ibid.*, pp. 113–114.

176. *Colección Diplomática*, p. 125a, and see above, n. 123.

177. Benito Ruano, *Toledo en el siglo XV*, pp. 241–242 (doc. 41).

178. Castillo, *op. cit.*, pp. 158ᵃᵇ–159ᵃ (caps. 89–90).

179. *Ibid.*, cap. 101, pp. 167b–168a.

180. *Ibid.*, 168ab; Palencia, *op. cit.*, II, pp. 83–93 (Década I, lib. x, cap. 1).

181. Castillo, *op. cit.*, cap. 103, p. 169a.

182. Palencia, *op. cit.*, II, pp. 100–101; Década I, lib. X, cap. 3.

183. Castillo, *op. cit.*, p. 170a (cap. 104).

184. *Ibid., ibid.*

185. *Ibid.*, cap. 110 (p. 173ff).

186. Benito Ruano, *op. cit.*, p. 106, and pp. 244–246 (doc. no. 44).

187. Castillo, *op. cit.*, p. 175b (cap. 112).

188. See Benito Ruano, *op. cit.*, pp. 249–251 (doc. 48).

189. *Ibid.*, pp. 262–265 (doc. 59).

190. Castillo, *op. cit.*, cap. 115 (p. 178ab).

191. *Ibid.*, p. 179ab (cap. 118); Palencia, *op. cit.*, II, pp. 177–189 (Década II, lib. 1, cap. 4); *Colección Diplomática*, p. 564a; for the full text of the agreement, see *ibid.*, pp. 561–566.

192. *Ibid.*, p. 564a.

193. Castillo, *op. cit.*, cap. 116 (p. 178b). Also Galíndez de Carvajal, following Castillo, accepted "fatigue" as the sole explanation of the King's conduct. See his *Crónica de Enrique IV*, published by J. Torres Fontes, together with his *Estudio* of this *crónica*, p. 333 (cap. 101).

194. According to Christian traditions, Judas either regretted his crime and

committed suicide (Matt. 27.3–5) or died an unnatural death (Acts, 1.16–18).

195. Castillo, *op. cit.*, cap. 113 (p. 177b).
196. Palencia, *op. cit.*, II, pp. 171–175 (Decada II, lib. I, cap. 3).
197. Hillgarth, *op. cit.*, II, p. 338.
198. Palencia, *op. cit.*, III, 107–116 (Década II, lib. 7, cap. 9).
199. *Ibid.*, p. 108.
200. *Ibid., ibid.*
201. *Ibid.*, pp. 108–109.
202. *Ibid.*, p. 109.
203. *Ibid., ibid.*
204. *Ibid.*, p. 108.
205. *Ibid., ibid.*
206. *Ibid.*, pp. 109–110; This is the date given by Palencia, *op. cit.*, III, p. 113 (Década II, lib. vii, cap. 9). Castillo (*op. cit.*, cap. 160, p. 214a) offers no date for the outbreak, while according to Valera (*op. cit.*, p. 242) it occurred on April 17, 1474. The *Crónica Castellana* (BNM, ms. 1780, f. 131b, col. 2) states that the riots broke out on April 17, 1474, thus combining, in a way, the indications of Palencia and Valera. Other authors, too (among them Galíndez, *op. cit.*, pp. 448–449), dated the riots in 1474; but Juan Gómez Bravo in his *Catálogo de los Obispos de Córdoba*, I, 1778, p. 356b, has shown, on the basis of the Actos Capitulares of the Cathedral, that the disturbances had occurred before April 1, 1473, which excludes all the dates found in the manuscripts save that of Palencia.
207. Palencia, *op. cit.*, III, p. 110. The historians of Cordova, relying no doubt on credible sources, give the name of the blacksmith as Alonso Rodrigues (see Francisco Pabón, "La Cruz del Rastro," in *Tradiciones Cordobeses*, Córdoba, 1863, I, p. 49, and R. Arellano y Ramírez, *Historia de Córdoba*, IV, p. 263), and they also assert that the Archdeacon of Pedrucha (a small town near Cordova) and other canons and "respectable individuals took a major part" in founding that fraternity (see Pabón, *loc. cit.*, p. 46).

208. Palencia, *op. cit.*, III, p. 110.
209. *Ibid.*
210. *Ibid.*, p. 111.
211. *Ibid.*, pp. 111–112.
212. *Ibid.*, pp. 112–113.
213. *Ibid.*, p. 111.
214. *Ibid.*, pp. 112–113.
215. *Ibid.*, p. 114.
216. *Ibid.*
217. *Ibid.*, p. 115.
218. *Ibid., ibid.*
219. *Ibid.*, p. 114.
220. *Ibid.*, p. 118.
221. Pulgar, *Crónica de los Reyes Católicos*, ed. Carriazo, 1943, I, p. 53.
222. Palencia, *op. cit.*, III, p. 119 (Década 2, lib. 7, cap. 10).
223. *Ibid., ibid.*
224. Valera, *op. cit.*, p. 245.
225. Palencia, *op. cit.*, p. 133.
226. *Ibid.*
227. *Ibid.*, pp. 131–132, 232–234.
228. *Ibid.*, p. 134.
229. *Ibid.*; cf. my remarks on the size of this militia in my *Marranos of Spain*, 1973, pp. 261–265.
230. Palencia, *op. cit.*, III, p. 134.
231. *Ibid., ibid.*, p. 231 (Década II, lib. IX, cap. 8).
232. *Ibid.*
233. *Ibid.*
234. *Ibid.*
235. *Ibid.*
236. *Ibid.*
237. *Ibid.*, p. 232.
238. *Ibid.*
239. *Ibid.*, III, pp. 107, 123, 231.
240. *Ibid.*, p. 123, n. 1.
241. Castillo, *op. cit.*, p. 214b (cap. 161).
242. *Ibid.*
243. *Colección Diplomática*, p. 693 (no. 199).
244. Castillo, *op. cit.*, p. 215a (cap. 161); Palencia, *op. cit.*, III, pp. 123–127.
245. Castillo, *op. cit.*, p. 214b.
246. *Ibid.*, p. 215a.
247. *Ibid.*

248. *Ibid.*, p. 214b (cap. 160).

249. See Castillo, *op. cit.*, p. 221b (cap. 168); Sitges, *op. cit.*, p. 247.

250. See appendix H.

Alonso de Espina

1. Numerous short biographies of Espina are included in histories of the Franciscan order, theological dictionaries and general Encyclopedias. Some of these will be listed here: L. Wadding, *Annales Minorum*, XII, 1735 (2nd ed.), p. 144, ann. 1452, no. xxxi; Christophorus Wolf, *Bibliotheca Hebraea*, II, 1721, pp. 1115–1123; Guilielmus Cave, *Scriptorum ecclesiasticorum Historia Literaria*, 1687, Appendix, pp. 143–145; Francesco de Gonzaga, *De Origine Seraphicae Religionis Franciscanae eiusque progressibus*, 1587, f. 863; Jo. H. Sbaralea, *Supplementum . . . ad Scriptores trium ordinum S. Francisci a Waddingo aliisve descriptos*, editio nova, I, 1908, pp. 29–30; J. Bartolocci, *Bibliotheca Magna Rabbinica*, IV, 1693, p. 408; Th. Crenius, *Animadversiones philologicae et historicae*, *III*, 1705, pp. 86–87; Joseph Rodríguez de Castro, *Biblioteca Española*, I, 1781, pp. 354–355; Juan de San Antonio, *Bibliotheca Universa Franciscana*, I, 1732, pp. 51–52; Nicolás Antonio, *Bibliotheca Hispana Vetus*, II, 1788, lib. x. cap. ix, §§480–489, pp. 279–280; Quétif-Echard, *Scriptores Ordinis Praedicatorum*, 1721, Pars I, vol. II, pp. 61–62 (on Guilielmus Totani).

2. See Wadding, *op. cit.*, p. 144.

3. For Palencia's date of birth (July 21, 1423), see his biography by Tomás Rodríguez, "El Cronista Alonso de Palencia," in *La Ciudad de Dios*, 2.ª época, XV (1888), p. 19. That the town of Palencia was his birthplace was proven by the same biographer, *ibid.*, *ibid.*, pp. 17–22.

4. See Atanasio López, "Descripción de los manuscritos existenes en la Biblioteca Provincial de Toledo," in *Archivo Ibero-Americano*, año xiii (num. 75), 1926, p. 355.

5. Gonzaga, *op. cit.*, f. 863.

6. *Crónica de Juan II*, año 1452, cap. 2, p. 683a; *Crónica de D. Alvaro de Luna*, ed. Carriazo, 1940, pp. 429–430; according to this *Crónica*, it was Alonso de Espina who first informed Alvaro that he was about to be executed (the men who guarded the Constable were to tell him nothing "except that the king ordered him to pass to Valladolid"), *ibid.*, p. 429.

7. *Crónica de D. Alvaro de Luna*, ed. Carriazo, pp. 429–432; *Crónica de Juan II*, año 1452, cap. 2 (BAE, 68, p. 683); *Fortalitium Fidei*, lib. IV, consideratio nona (155th battle between the Christians and the Moslems), ed. Nuremberg, 1494, f. 263ᵛa. All the following references to the *Fortalitium*, unless otherwise indicated, are according to the Lyon edition of 1511.

8. Diego de Valera, *Memorial de Diversas Hazañas*, ed. Carriazo, 1941, p. 10; Diego de Colmenares, *Historia de Segovia*, 1640, cap. xxxi, 3, pp. 365–366.

9. *Ibid.*, *ibid.*; and see Valera, *op. cit.*, p. 10.

10. *Fortalitium Fidei*, ed. Lyon, 1511, f. 190ʳa, lib. 3, undecima crudelitas. According to Nicolás Antonio, *Bibl. Hispana Vetus*, lib. x, cap. 9, §486, their number was 24.

11. No manuscript was preserved of these sermons, although they were widely distributed. According to N. Antonio, *ibid.* (who relies in this on Daza), they were "recited" by the whole of Spain.

12. For the dates of the beginning and completion of the work, see my article: "Alonso de Espina: Was he a New Christian?", in *PAAJR*, XLIII (1976), p. 109, n. 4 (cited below as "Alonso de Espina").

13. Espina, *op. cit.*, lib. 2, prima heresis, f. 75ʳa; secunda heresis, ff. 80ᵛb–82ᵛb. These sermons, too, are not extant. According to Antonio, *Bibl. Hisp. Vetus*,

lib. X, cap. 9, §487, a work of Espina by the name of *De Fortuna* was still extant in Antonio's time in the library of the Escorial. Since it was dedicated to King Juan II (d. 1454), it may have been Espina's first literary production.

14. See José de Sigüenza, *Historia de la Orden de San Jerónimo*, I, 1907 (2nd ed.), pp. 364b–365a.

15. *Ibid.*, pp. 363–364. The approach was made through a letter of the Franciscans, among them Espina (who is designated confessor to the king), to the General of the Hieronymites, Fray Alonso de Oropesa. The letter is dated August 10, 1459 (see Sigüenza, *op. cit.*, I, p. 364b.

16. See above, pp. 735–736.

17. *Crónica de Enrique IV*, cap. 53, BAE, vol. 70, p. 130ab; and see above, p. 742.

18. Menéndez y Pelayo, *Historia de los Heterodoxos Españoles*, ed. E. Sánchez Reyes, 1946, II, pp. 383, 473. In the index to his *History of the Inquisition in Spain*, IV, p. 569, Lea does not include Alonso de Espina, Inquisitor for Barcelona, under the title of Espina, the author of the *Fortalitium*.

19. See Carreras y Candi, "L'Inquisició barcelonina substituida per l'Inquisició castellana, 1446–1487," in *Anuari de l'Institut d'estudis catalans*, 1909–1910, pp. 144–145.

20. See F. Cantera, "Fernando de Pulgar y los conversos," in *Sefarad*, IV (1944), p. 319; and see my "Alonso de Espina," *loc. cit.*, pp. 107–108.

21. See Sbaralea, *op. cit.*, p. 29a.

22. Gonzaga, *op. cit.*, f. 863; Wadding, *op. cit.*, ann. 1246, no. 39.

23. The *Fortalitium Fidei* appeared anonymously, and the question of its provenance caused a great deal of confusion, especially in the West. The unknown author of the *Memorial Histórico de Segovia*, written in 1522 (see RAH, *Boletín*, XIV [1889], pp. 214–261) was perhaps the first Spanish scholar in the 16th century to identify Espina's

authorship of the *Fortalitium* (*ibid.*, p. 220). That *Memorial*, however, remained unpublished until 1889: and the first published work in which that identification was made was probably Garibay's *Compendio historial de las chronicas y universal historia . . . de España*, lib. 16, cap. 46 (ed. Antwerp, 1571, p. 1151). For later designations of Espina as the author of the *Fortalitium*, see my "Alonso de Espina," *loc. cit.*, pp. 112–114.

Of the various proofs offered of Espina's authorship, the most decisive was supplied by Espina himself. In the fourth book of the *Fortalitium* (consideratio nona, 155th battle, ed. Nuremberg, 1494, f. 263ᵛa), he refers to his having received the confession of Alvaro de Luna before the latter's execution (and see on this above, pp. 814 and 1289, n. 6).

On the editions of the *Fortalitium*, see Atanasio López, *loc. cit.*, pp. 375–379. Already in the 15th century, the *Fortalitium* was translated into French (see *ibid.*, p. 381).

24. There is no question, in my judgment, that many lines of communication lead from Espina to Eisenmenger (1700) and from there to Rohling (1882) and later German antisemitism. The various ramifications of this important subject call for special investigation.

25. *Epistolae obscurorum Virorum*, 1689, p. 83.

26. See Mariana, *Historia de España*, lib. 22, cap. 13 (BAE, vol. 31, p. 139a); Wolf, *op. cit.*, II, p. 1123. Both these scholars, however, limited their positive evaluation of Espina to the vast scope of his theological learning. Mariana considered the title of Espina's book "magnificent," but "not elegant," perhaps alluding by this to Espina's effective but violent language in which he discussed many of his subjects.

27. See, for instance, N. López Martínez, *Los Judaizantes Castellanos*, 1954, pp. 78–79, 84–85, and M. de la Pinta

Llorente, *La Inquisición Española*, 1948, pp. 19–20.

28. See my article, "Alonso de Espina," *loc. cit.*, pp. 114–118.

29. Wolf, *op. cit.*, I, p. 193; II, p. 1122.

30. See my article "Alonso de Espina," *loc. cit.*, p. 116.

31. Rodríguez de Castro, *op. cit.*, p. 354.

32. *Boletín* de la Real Acad. de la Historia, VII (1885), p. 179.

33. Amador, *Historia*, III, pp. 136, 145; *idem, Estudios*, pp. 344–345; *idem, Hist. crítica de la literatura Española*, VI (1865), p. 309.

34. *Historia de los Heterodoxos Españoles*, ed. Sánchez Reyes, 1963, II, p. 471.

35. Lafuente, *Historia General de España*, V, 1869 (2nd ed.), p. 133.

36. C. Sánchez Albornoz, *España, un Enigma Histórico*, 1962, II, p. 255; and cf. pp. 253, 288.

37. Américo Castro, *The Structure of Spanish History*, 1954, pp. 539–540. Only isolated Spanish scholars expressed doubt about Espina's Jewishness. See R. García Villoslada and B. Llorca, *Historia de la Iglesia Católica*, III², 1967, p. 529, n. 25.

38. See N. Antonio, *op. cit.*, lib. 4, cap. 9, 48, and my article on Espina, *loc. cit.*, p. 116.

39. See *Archivo Ibero-Americano*, XIII (1926), pp. 348–359. I am grateful to Prof. F. Márquez Villanueva who, remarking on my study of Espina, called my attention to this most interesting work in a letter dated January 26, 1977.

40. *Ibid.*, pp. 349–351.

41. Atanasio López, *loc. cit.*, p. 371.

42. *Ibid.*, p. 370; according to López, Espina shows in his work "vastissima erudición y da pruebas de conocer a fondo los idiomas hebreo y arabe, por lo cual recurre frecuentamente a los libros talmúdicos."

43. *Ibid., ibid.*, p. 371.

44. See above, no. 11.

45. *Ibid.*, pp. 154–155.

46. *Ibid.*, pp. 121–147, 156–165.

47. *Ibid.*, pp. 151–154.

48. *Fortalitium*, lib. III, sexta consideratio (opening), f. 163ᵛ: "For just as the devil has a thousand ways of causing harm, so has the Jew, his son."

49. See my "Alonso de Espina," *loc. cit.*, pp. 143–144, and other places.

50. *Fortalitium*, lib. III, consid. 7, tertius punctus, f. 185ᵛa: perpetui servi diversis in mundi partibus.

51. *Ibid., ibid.*

52. H. L. Strack, *The Jew and Human Sacrifice*, 1909, pp. 253–258.

53. *Speculum historiale*, lib. 30, cap. 25.

54. *Ibid.*, p. 277.

55. See *Bonum Universale de Apibus*, II, 29, 23, ed. 1627, pp. 304ff. Cf. Strack, *op. cit.*, pp. 174–175.

56. *Fortalitium*, lib. iii, septima consideratio, quinta crudelitas, f. 187ʳb; *De apibus*, cap. 20, p. 303; Strack, *op. cit.*, pp. 182–183.

57. Concerning the toponym given by Espina (the "territory of Luis de Almanza"), see P. Leon Tello, *'Emeq ha-Bakha de Yosef ha-Kohen*, 1964, pp. 406–407, 360; and cf. *Fortalitium*, lib. III, septima consideratio, decima et undecima crudelitates, ff. 189ᵛa, 190ʳa.

58. *Ibid.*, sept. cons., undecima crudelitas, f. 190ʳ.

59. *Ibid., ibid.*, f. 190ʳb–190ᵛa.

60. Strack, *op. cit.*, p. 239.

61. *Fortalitium*, lib. 3, sept. cons., octava crudelitas, f. 188.

62. *Ibid.*, nona crudelitas, ff. 188ᵛb–189ᵛa.

63. *Ibid.* f. 189ʳb.

64. *Ibid.*, decimatertia crudelitas, f. 191ʳb: si unum curant quinquaginta occident.

65. *Ibid.*, sexta crud., f. 187ʳb.

66. *Ibid., ibid.* According to Espina, this happened in the days of Pope Clement VI, 1345.

67. *Ibid.*, quarta crudelitas, ff. 186ʳa–187ʳa.

68. *Ibid.*

69. As proof Espina cites Leviticus 20:17.

70. *Fortalitium*, consideratio ii, ff. 108ᵛb–109ᵛa. See on all this my article on Espina, *loc. cit.*, pp. 152–154.

71. See *Speculum historiale*, lib. 30, cap. 25; *Fortalitium*, sept. cons. secunda crud., ff. 185ᵛa–186ʳb. For the statement cited, see *ibid.*, f. 186ʳa.

72. *Ibid., ibid.:* zelo dei flammatus.

73. *Ibid.*, f. 186ʳb.

74. See my *Don Isaac Abravanel*, 1982⁴, pp. 54–55.

75. *Fortalitium*, lib. III, nona consideratio, secunda expulsio, ff. 216ʳ–218ʳ.

76. *Ibid., ibid.*, secunda expulsio, f. 218ʳa.

77. Espina's story resembles in many details Chaucer's *Prioress's Tale* about the martyrdom of a Christian child named Hugh of Lincoln (see his *Canterbury Tales*, ed. W. W. Skeat, 1900², pp. 181–188), the historical kernel of both narratives being the blood libel perpetrated at Lincoln in 1255 (it was recorded by the monk Matthew Paris [d. 1259] in his *Historia Major*, ed. Luard [Rolls Series], V, pp. 516–518, and in the contemporary annals of the Abbey of Burton-on-Trent: *Annales monastici*, ed. Luard [Rolls Series], I, p. 340 (see on all this Joseph Jacobs, "Little St. Hugh of Lincoln," in *Transactions of the Jewish Historical Society of England*, I [1893–94], pp. 89–135). The accounts of this blood libel, however, are devoid of any miracle, while the motif of the miracles performed to a boy who sang antiphons in praise of the Virgin and because of this was killed by Jews, is found in many Marian tales circulated, most probably from the 12th century on, in the Netherlands, France and Germany (see Charleton F. Brown, "Chaucer's *Prioress's Tale* and its Analogues," in *Publications of the Modern Language Association of America*, XXI, 2 [1906], pp. 486–518). It was following the blood libel of Lincoln that the legend of the martyred anthem-singing boy was combined with the case of Hugh of Lincoln. Brown believed that the source of both Chaucer and Espina must have been a Latin version of the legend which was produced in England in the 13th or 14th century and did not come down to us (see *ibid.*, pp. 510–517; and see also Brown's article, "The Prioress's Tale," in *Sources and Analogues of Chaucer's Canterbury Tales*, ed. Bryan and Dempster, 1958, pp. 461–464).

78. *Fortalitium Fidei*, lib. 3, tertia expulsio, ff. 218ʳa–219ᵛb. It is worth noting that most other versions of the legend which refer to the fate of the Jews tell of their voluntary conversion to Christianity under the influence of the miracles performed by the Virgin (see Brown's article, "Chaucer's Prioress's Tale and its Analogues," *loc. cit.*, pp. 488, 491, 492, 497). One version speaks of the execution of the Jew who killed the Christian boy and the *expulsion* of the other Jews from the *town* in which the crime was committed (see *ibid.*, p. 488). Another speaks of the *burning* of the Jews of the *city* in which the outrage occurred (*ibid.*, pp. 496–497). None mentions, as Espina does, a royal order to *kill all the Jews of the country* where the crime was perpetrated, with the exception of a few who were expelled after having been divested of their properties. These data may have been contributed by Espina together with the name *Alfonso* of Lincoln which he substituted for *Hugh*.

79. See below, n. 80.

80. *Fortalitium*, lib. 3, tertia expulsio, f. 219ᵛb.

81. *Ibid., ibid.*, 219ʳb–219ᵛa. For the source of this legend, see below appendix G.

82. See above, p. 837.

83. *Fortalitium*, lib. ii, sexta consideratio, octava heresis, f. 87ʳ.

84. *Ibid.*, ff. 75–77; Martín Gamero, *Historia de Toledo*, p. 1037.

85. On the connection between the beliefs in magic and demons in medieval Christian Europe, see Lynn Thorn-

dike, *A History of Magic and Experimental Science*, II, pp. 466, 551–552, 603–604; III, 428; IV, 310, 491, and many other places; and see what I wrote concerning this in my paper, "La razón de la Inquisición," in *Inquisición Española y mentalidad inquisitorial*, ed. A. Alcalá, 1984, p. 35.

86. Moreover, even respecting this single case, the *Pesquisa* cannot tell us that its inquirers really knew what was done with the Hosts. See *Fortalitium*, f. 77ʳb: sacerdos quidam eiusdem gentis consecravit die quadam quinque hostias, quarum unam sumpsit & alias tradidit fratribus suis, et nescitur quid factum est de illis.

87. See above, p. 372.

88. See my *Marranos of Spain*, 1973², pp. 44, 49 and other places.

89. *Fortalitium*, lib. II, sexta consideratio, prima heresis, f. 73ʳff.

90. *Ibid.*, 74ᵛab.

91. *Ibid.*, f. 74ᵛ.

92. *Ibid.*, f. 75ʳ.

93. *Ibid.*, secunda heresis, f. 82ʳab.

94. *Ibid.*, ibid.

95. *Ibid.*, ibid., prima heresis, f. 75ʳa.

96. See my *Marranos of Spain*, pp. 57–58.

97. *Fortalitium*, lib. II, prima heresis, 75ᵛ.

98. *Ibid.*, ibid.

99. *Ibid.*, f. 78ᵛa.

100. *Ibid.*, ibid.

101. *Ibid.*, ibid.

102. *Ibid.*, f. 74ᵛa.

103. Of the other claims of the *Pesquisa*, we shall first mention here the charge that the conversos take their children to the synagogues and there instruct them in Jewish lore. This charge, too, is flatly denied by both Jewish and converso sources that describe the generation of 1450 as Christianized and totally ignorant of Judaism. We have noted that the reason given for that ignorance was the *absence* of any Jewish training, because it was deliberately denied the children by their parents, who wanted them to grow up as Christians (see my *Marranos of Spain*, pp. 45–46, and above, p. 410).

There remain only three more Jewish customs which the *Pesquisa* imputes to the Marranos, and which are mainly concerned with the dying or the dead. The *Pesquisa* (or Espina) tells us nothing of their scope, their frequency, their following, or their evidential basis. On the whole, we should remark, such customs die hard, and they may have persisted also among non-Judaizers. The progress of Marrano Christianization, however, must have limited the adherents of these customs, too, to a dwindling minority. Yet Espina, in agreement with his method and habit, attributed them to the *whole* Marrano group.

104. *Ibid.*, f. 75ʳ.

105. *Ibid.*, f. 76.

106. *Ibid.*, f. 79ᵛb.

107. *Ibid.*, undecima consideratio, f. 102ᵛb.

108. *Ibid.*, f. 103ʳa.

109. *Ibid.*

110. A good example of this is Espina's story about the Host desecration by the Jews of Segovia and the death of King Enrique III of Castile through poison administered to him by his physician Don Meir Alguadez (*Fortalitium*, lib. III, decima consideratio, undecimum mirabile, ff. 223ʳᵛ). The persecutions related to the "discovery" of these "facts" (i.e., the background of Espina's account) did, most probably, occur as reported, while the "facts" themselves (the core of the story) may be safely considered fictitious. Nevertheless, Espina's tale was accepted in its entirety as true by various scholars, not only during the reign of the Inquisition (see, for instance, Garibay, *Compendio*, lib. 15, cap. 58), but also in the middle of the 19th century (see Rafael Floranes, "Vida literaria del Canciller Mayor de Castilla D. Pedro López de Ayala," in *CODOIN*, xix [1851], p. 262).

The Alboraique

1. Short sections of the *Alboraique,* together with a brief résumé of the satire, were first published by Isidore Loeb in his article "Le livre Alboraïque," in *REJ,* xviii (1889), pp. 238–242, which was reprinted by Fidel Fita in the *Boletín* of the Academia de la Historia, Madrid, vol. XXIII (1893), pp. 378–383. The sections cited by Loeb were taken from ms. 356, fonds espagnol, of the Bibliothèque Nationale, Paris, ff. 60ʳ–70ᵛ, which contains a curtailed text of the work. The full text was published by López Martínez, *op. cit.,* pp. 391–404, on the basis of ms. 17891 of the Biblioteca Nacional, Madrid. K. R. Scholberg used this version for his account of the *Alboraique* (*op. cit.,* pp. 352–353). See also Baer's remarks in his *History,* II, pp. 394–397, 501–502 (n. 73).

2. See Loeb, *loc. cit.,* p. 238; Fita, *Boletín,* XXIII (1893), p. 410; López Martínez, *op. cit.,* p. 54, n. 15.

3. *Id., op. cit.,* p. 391; the Paris ms., f. 60ʳ reads here: "60 years," which is no doubt an error.

4. That he referred to the conversions of 1391 is evident also from his remark that the Christians who attacked the Jews "baptized most survivors [of the pogroms] by *force*" (los quedaron vivos . . . por la mayor parte los bautizaron por fuerza"), *ibid.*

5. *Ibid.,* p. 393.

6. *Ibid.,* p. 403. The Paris ms., f. 70ᵛ, reads here "viuido" (lived?) instead of "venido" (came) and "1488" instead of "1400" years. Following the Paris version, Loeb, Fita and López assumed that the *Alboraique* was written in 1488 (see above, n. 16); but the assumption is untenable. Apart from leaning on a sentence which hardly makes sense, it disregards the contents of the passage in question. It seems unlikely for the author of the *Alboraique* to have said that the various Jewish sects, of whom he speaks in that passage (such as the Sadducees and Pharisees), *lived 1488 years ago,* as if they ceased to exist after the arrival of Jesus. In addition, the above assertion is followed by the statement: *hay mas cativos ciegos entre los xrianos y moros* ("there are more blind captives among the Christians and the Moors"). There is obviously no connection between this and the preceding sentence if the latter is read according to the Paris manuscript. Both sentences, however, appear sensible and well connected if we follow the version of the Madrid ms., which speaks of the conversos' "infidel fathers," who "came [to Spain] 1400 years [ago]"—that is, immediately after the destruction of the Second Temple. The author refers to them also in the earlier part of the passage and calls them the "captives" of Vespasian (*ibid.,* p. 402). Accordingly, he states at the conclusion of the same passage that "there are more blind captives among the Christians and the Moors," meaning thereby the Jews who were carried captive by the Romans to other Christian countries (besides Spain) and to North Africa, the land of the Moors (cf. *Josippon,* ed. Flusser, 1980, I, pp. 432–433). As we see it, "1488 marked the year in which the ms. was *copied.* The scribe, who read "viuido" instead of "venido," considered Jesus' year of birth more suitable than "1400" to indicate the time in which the aforesaid sects "lived" (or, as he may have understood: flourished) in Palestine.

7. *Ibid.,* p. 394.

8. See Baer, *History,* II, pp. 292–295; *Die Juden,* II, pp. 437–444.

9. See Alboraique, *loc. cit.,* p. 394: . . . . *los que yban al turco y quemaron en Valencia de Aragon este año, y los que huyeron y los que se desterraron de esta gente yvan ayudar al turco por derramar sangre de los xrianos* (". . . those who went to the Turk and whom they burned in

Valencia of Aragon this year, and those of them who fled [the Valencian Inquisition] and exiled themselves went to help the Turk to spill the blood of Christians").

That the Inquisition of Aragon in 1467 burned Judaizers who sought to leave Spain must of course be considered questionable. A Castilian scribe who copied the manuscript after 1481 may have substituted, we assume, the word "burned" for a term such as "punished" in the original; he may have taken it for granted that conversos pronounced guilty of a design to aid the Turks got no lesser punishment than burning.

10. The Paris ms., f. 62ʳ: *ansy los que quemaron como los que se rrestrataron [desterraron?] en Valencia de Aragon fueron mill y quatrocientos y sesenta y siete.* The scribe here abridged the original version (see above, n. 22) by combining two sentences into one.

11. *Ibid.*, p. 391. See the Qoran, 17.1. Actually the Alboraique (*al-boraq* in Arabic)—an animal with a woman's face, a mule's body and a peacock's tail—is said to have carried Mohammed from Mecca to the Temple Mount in Jerusalem, from which he was taken to heaven.

12. *Ibid.*, pp. 391–392.

13. Decree 34; see González-Tejada, I, 1849, p. 398.

14. Cf. Proverbs, 26.11

15. Alboraique, *loc. cit.*, p. 394.

16. *Ibid.*, p. 393.

17. *Ibid.*; see below, p. 850, and above, p. 372.

18. Alboraique, *loc. cit.*, p. 401.

19. *Ibid., ibid.*

20. López Martínez, *op. cit.*, p. 394: "Synagoga de diablos" (instead "of Satan" as in Revelation, II. 9).

21. *Ibid.*, p. 395.

22. *Ibid.*, p. 394.

23. Actually, Moses; see Deut. 32.24.

24. Alboraique, *loc. cit.*, pp. 395–396.

25. *Ibid.*, p. 396.

26. Palencia, *Crónica*, III, pp. 230.

27. See my *Marranos of Spain*, p. 252.

28. See *ibid.*, pp. 216–220.

29. Alboraique, *loc. cit.*, pp. 396, 397.

30. *Ibid.*, p. 397; the *Alboraique* cites here the verse of the Vulgate: *rapere pauperem dum atrahit eum.*

31. *Ibid.*, p. 396 (see also p. 393: *maldita generacion*).

32. *Ibid.*, pp. 402–403. Cf. *Fortalitium*, lib. III, consid. 3, f. 109.

33. The author does not forget to add that the conversos *(malos cristianos)* were sodomites, a habit in which they followed the Jews, who originated that practice and transmitted it to the Moors (Alboraique, *loc. cit.*, p. 401).

34. *Ibid.*, p. 403.

35. *Ibid., ibid.*

36. *Ibid., ibid.*

37. *Ibid.*, p. 402. The mention of Valladolid among the cities which were free of Judaizers is another indication that the manuscript was written before 1488. Although the first arrests of the Inquisition in Valladolid took place on September 28, 1488 (see *Cronicón de Valladolid*, in *CODOIN*, XIII [1848], p. 176) its activity in that city no doubt began earlier; and it must have been preceded by some public discussion, for a tribunal was assigned to Valladolid already in 1485 (see Lea, *History*, I, p. 554). It is hard to assume that the author of the *Alboraique* was unaware of all this if, indeed, he wrote the work in 1488. To be sure, the Paris ms. (f. 69ᵛ) reads here, instead of Valladolid, *Valls*, which Loeb (*loc. cit.*, p. 241, n. 1) took as a corruption of *Valderas*; but the author mentions on this occasion the largest and most famous towns of Old Castile, and there was no reason for him to list among them the small town of Valderas.

38. See his remarks in RAH, *Boletín*, XXIII (1893), pp. 410, 424.

39. López Martínez, *Los Judaizantes*, p. 402.
40. See his "La Inquisición de Torquemada," RAH, *Boletín*, XXIII (1893), p. 424.

Alonso de Oropesa

1. See above, pp. 735–736, 742–743, 760–761.
2. Except that its pedigree went far back, and as such it was probably of noble origin. See below, p. 896.
3. In 1449, Oropesa tells us, he was "officio y joven converso en nuestra casa de Guadalupe;" see his *Luz para conocimiento de los gentiles* (cited below as *Luz*), transl. from the Latin by Luis A. Díaz y Díaz, 1979, p. 62.
4. L. A. Díaz y Díaz, "Alonso de Oropesa y su obra," *Studia Hieronymiana*, 1973, I, p. 255.
5. José de Sigüenza, *Historia de la Orden de San Jerónimo*, 1907, I, p. 361b. Sigüenza does not know the date of this appointment, but Díaz believes that it occurred between 1451 and 1452 (see his article mentioned above, note 4, *loc. cit.*, p. 255). However, considering the large amount of writing he did in Guadalupe (from the middle of 1450), it does not seem likely that his transfer to Talavera occurred before 1453.
6. Sigüenza (*op. cit.*, I, p. 361b) says that it was in Talavera that he began to preach, but according to Oropesa's own account (see below, n. 8), he started his sermonizing in Guadalupe.
7. Sigüenza, *op. cit.*, I, p. 361b.
8. See his *Luz*, pp. 62–64.
9. *Ibid., ibid.* The work has been preserved in three manuscripts, the best of which is that of the Biblioteca Ambrosiana in Milan (the other two are found in the Biblioteca Pública Provincial of Guadalajara and the Biblioteca Universitaria of Salamanca). For a detailed description of the three manuscripts, see Díaz y Díaz, *ibid.*, pp. 48–57. I have used a reproduction of the Ambrosiana ms., as well as a typed transcription of it which Prof. Albert A. Sicroff was kind enough to lend me.
10. *Ibid.*, pp. 65, 85, 97 and many other places. Sigüenza, (*op. cit.*, I, p. 372a) says that although Oropesa must have had the intention of writing a second part, "he neither did nor could do so; nor was it necessary since he accomplished his purpose" in the so-called first part. Sigüenza, however, is here in error, as Díaz has correctly pointed out (see his introd. to *Luz*, pp. 31–35). Oropesa not only refers throughout his work to his plan to write a second part, but also indicates many of the themes he intended to discuss in it.
11. *Ibid.*, p. 66.
12. See Sigüenza, *op. cit.*, I, p. 363a; and see above, pp. 734–735.
13. *Luz*, p. 761. That Oropesa had intended to write that introduction before he concluded his book is evident from his reference to Carrillo in the last chapter (p. 759) as "the *most reverend father* and *most illustrious señor*" without mentioning the archbishop's name. He assumed of course that the introduction, which he was planning to add, would make it clear whom he meant by those titles. Since the contents and spirit of that introduction are identical with those of his last chapters, it stands to reason that it was written shortly after he had completed the book.
14. That he was considered neutral is indicated by the fact that when Don Antonio de Veneris, the legate of Pope Paul II, tried to initiate peace negotiations between Enrique IV and the rebel party, he was advised by leading men of both sides that the most suitable man for such negotiations was Alonso de Oropesa "whom all loved and respected" (Sigüenza, *op. cit.*, I, p. 383a); cf. Castillo, *Crónica de Don Enrique IV,* cap. 100, ed. BAE, vol. 70, pp. 166b–167a.
15. *Luz*, pp. 62, 75.

16. Sigüenza, *op. cit.*, I, p. 388a.

17. Cited above, n. 4. Prior to this study of Díaz, Oropesa's work was briefly discussed, on the basis of Sigüenza's summary (see above, n. 5), by A. A. Sicroff, *Les controverses*, 1960, pp. 71–74. B. Sevisenti's article, "Un documento de la lucha anti-Judáica," in *Boletín de la Academia Argentina de letras*, VII (nos. 25–26), 1939, pp. 137–150, includes only a few remarks on the manuscripts of the *Lumen*, as well as its Latin table of contents. Short notes on Oropesa and his *Lumen* are also found in Nicolás Antonio, *Bibliotheca Vetus Hispana*, lib. x, cap. 10, nos. 565–566; Menéndez y Pelayo, *Historia de los Heterodoxos Españoles*, II 1963, pp. 471–472; M. Andrés Martín, *Historia de la Teología in España (1490–1570)*, I, 1962, pp. 195–196, and Américo Castro, *Aspectos del vivir hispánico*, 1947, pp. 108–111.

18. See above, no. 3.

19. See his introduction to Oropesa's *Luz*, p. 24, n. 15.

20. See Díaz y Díaz' article, "Alonso de Oropesa," *loc. cit.*, p. 307.

21. See *Defensorium*, p. 320.

22. In the second chapter of his book (p. 90), Oropesa speaks of the bloody riots that took place "less than a year ago in various cities, town and places." If we take the date of the disturbances in Ciudad Real (July, 1449) as an indication of the time therein referred to, we may assume that he started writing the *Lumen* c. July, 1450.

23. The title of Cartagena's book, *Defensorium unitatis christianae*, is actually embedded in the subtitle of Oropesa's work: *De unitate fidei et de concordi et pacifica aequalitate fidelium*.

24. See his introd. to Oropesa's *Luz*, p. 24, n. 15.

25. *Ibid., ibid.*

26. *Luz*, p. 112.

27. *Ibid.*, p. 108.

28. Cf. Isaiah 5. 1–7.

29. *Luz.*, pp. 118–119.

30. See *Defensorium unitatis christianae*, I, caps. 1–4; II, theorem I, cap. 5, p. 106: This is why all faithful *israelite dicantur et semen abrahe.*

31. *Luz*, p. 124.

32. Augustine, *City of God*, XVI, xii (Loeb ed. vol. V, p. 71). According to Augustine, Abraham opened the third of the five ages of the history of mankind before the appearance of Christ (see *Ibid.*, XXII, xxx (Loeb ed. vol. VII, p. 383).

33. *Luz*, pp. 124, 130.

34. *Ibid.*, pp. 124–125.

35. *Ibid.*, pp. 123–124.

36. *Ibid.*, pp. 129–130; 142–143, 150. The influence of the written law extended beyond the sphere of Israel, Oropesa points out: "There were many faithful among the gentiles in that period" who "admired the People of God and its holy law, its ceremonies and its worship" even though they remained under the Natural law" (*ibid.*, p. 143, following Augustine, *City of God*, lib. xviii, cap. 47; ed. Loeb, vol. VI, pp. 52–55).

37. *Ibid.*, pp. 230–232.

38. *Ibid.*, pp. 156–181, 193–203.

39. *Ibid.*, pp. 183–191. This is, of course, according to the *City of God*, lib. X, cap. xiv (ed. Loeb, III, pp. 312–314); cf. Thomas Aquinas, *Summa Theologica*, I^a, II^{ae}, Q. 98, art. 2; Q. 99, art. 6; De Lyra, on Exod. 32.4.

40. *Luz*, p. 218.

41. *Ibid.*, pp. 376.

42. *Defensorium*, I, cap. 6, p. 80, following I Cor. 2.6.

43. *Defensorium*, cap. 5, p. 75.

44. *Ibid.*, cap. 6, pp. 78–79.

45. *Ibid.*, p. 79; see Augustine, *Contra Faustum*, lib. 18.4 and 19.9, and cf. *id.*, Epistles, 145 (to Anastasius, 3).

46. *Defensorium*, pp. 76–77.

47. *Ibid., ibid.*

48. Colossians, 3.14.

49. *Defensorium*, I, cap. 6, p. 77.

50. Origen, *Homiliae in Numeros*, IX, 4; MG 12, 68.

51. Psalms, 119.105; *Defensorium*, I, cap. 9, p. 85.

52. Deut. 9. 6–8, 13; Isaiah, 48.

53. For the attitude toward the Election in Jewish thought and the literature on the subject, see my "Américo Castro and His View of the Origins of the *Pureza de Sangre*," in *PAAJR*, vols. XLVI–XLVII (1979–1980), pp. 399–400. On the Christian view of the Election see W. A. Copinger, *Treatise on Predestination, Election, and Grace*, 1889.

54. See Gen. 17.1–8, 15.1, 5–6; Exod. 6. 3–4, 7; and other places.

55. Oropesa, *op. cit.*, cap. 13, p. 151; Deut. 9.5–6.

56. Thomas Aquinas, *Summa Theologica*, I^a, II^ae, Q. 98, art. 4.

57. *Luz*, pp. 154–155; cf. Augustine, *Homilies on the Gospel according to John*, 26.4.

58. *Luz*, p. 155.

59. Deut. 7.6, 7.7, 10.15.

60. Cicero, *De Republica*, 2.42.

61. Augustine, *City of God*, XIX, 21 (ed. Loeb, VI, p. 207); and cf. *ibid.*, lib. II.21.

62. *Luz*, p. 134.

63. *Defensorium*, p. 71. For Augustine's words on the hidden merits, see his *De diversionibus quaestionibus*, LXXXIII, q. 68.4 (ML 40, 72).

64. Peter Lombard, *Sententiae*, lib., I, dist. 41.2–3 (ML 192, 633–634).

65. *Defensorium*, p. 71.

66. Job 5.6, according to the Vulgate: *Nihil in terra sine causa fit* (in the sense: without a cause). The Hebrew original, however, should be translated (approximately) thus: "For trouble does not grow out of dust." And, see *Defensorium*, pp. 71–72.

67. *Luz*, pp. 128–155.

68. *Ibid.*, p. 135.

69. *Ibid.*, pp. 134–135.

70. *Ibid.*, pp. 135–136.

71. *Ibid.*, p. 136.

72. *Ibid.*, p. 153.

73. *Ibid.*, p. 151, 150.

74. *Ibid.*, p. 296.

75. *Ibid.*, p. 289.

76. *Ibid.*, p. 272.

77. It may perhaps be argued that the positive achievements Oropesa ascribed to the Jewish people related to the brief epochs in its history (i.e., the intervals between its long sinful periods) in which it followed the will of God. But Oropesa nowhere says this. What is more likely, in our opinion, is that the two opposed assessments presented in his work reflect two conflicting influences which he could not reconcile—that of the converso apologists, especially of Torquemada, and that of the Church Fathers, especially of Chrysostom. Ultimately, the latter influence prevailed.

78. *Defensorium*, p. 81.

79. *Ibid.*, p. 100.

80. *Ibid.*, pp. 99–100.

81. See on this Jeremy Cohen, "The Jews as the Killers of Christ," in *Traditio*, 39 (1983), pp. 1–27; and see above, pp. 550–551, n. 137.

82. Acts 3.13; *Luz*, pp. 253, 261.

83. I Thessalonians 2.14–15.

84. Luke 23.34.

85. *Luz*, pp. 251–253 and other places.

86. I Thess. 2.16; *Luz*, p. 263.

87. *Ibid.*, pp. 268, 273.

88. *Ibid.*, p. 262.

89. *Ibid.*, p. 326.

90. *Ibid.*, p. 283.

91. *Ibid.*, p. 273.

92. *Ibid.*, p. 271.

93. *Ibid.*, p. 314.

94. *Ibid.*, p. 249.

95. Augustine, *City of God*, lib. XVIII, cap. 46 (ed. Loeb, VI, pp. 46–51); see also *id., Sermones*, 201.3 (ML 38, 1032–1033).

96. *Luz*, p. 250.

97. *Ibid.*, p. 249.

98. *Ibid.*, pp. 268, 278–280, 307, 312–313.

99. *Ibid.*, pp. 249, 264, 275, 266, 289; see also pp. 251, 273.

100. *Defensorium*, p. 174.
101. *Luz*, p. 320.
102. *Ibid.*, 624.
103. *Luz*, p. 322.
104. *Ibid.*, pp. 271–272.
105. *Ibid.*, p. 272.
106. *Ibid.*, pp. 269, 271.
107. *Luz*, p. 495.
108. *Ibid.*, p. 496; see also pp. 674–675.
109. *Ibid.*, p. 320.
110. *Ibid.*, p. 316.
111. *Ibid.*, p. 384.
112. *Ibid.*, p. 408, citing a comment of the *Glossa Ordinaria* on Colossians 3.11.
113. *Luz*, p. 228; cf. Jerome, *Cartas de San Jerónimo*, bilingual edition by D. Ruiz Bueno, 1962, II, p. 840 (epist. 148.21).
114. *Luz*, p. 408.
115. Apocalypse 5. 9–10.
116. I Peter 2.9.
117. Matthew 8. 11–12; *Luz*, p. 562.
118. As indicated above, p. 870.
119. *Luz*, p. 605.
120. *Ibid.*, p. 606: "Even if he had committed a million crimes before he was baptized, they will not be counted against him."
121. Acts 4.27–28.
122. Matt. 26.78.
124. Psalms 2.2; *Luz*, pp. 454–455.
125. *Luz*, p. 609.
126. Acts 18.24–25.
127. *Luz*, p. 623.
128. *Ibid.*, p. 262.
129. *Ibid.*, pp. 252–253.
130. Deut. 23.4–10.
131. *Luz*, p. 563.
132. *Ibid.*, *ibid.*
133. *Ibid.*
134. See "Memorial," *loc. cit.*, p. 334; and cf. above, p. 505. Garcia may indeed have been the first to have employed those laws in support of his position. The Relator, whose "Instruction" to Lope de Barrientos was written a few months before the "Memorial," does not mention this argument in a word, perhaps because it was not yet

current at the time, or because he found it disconcerting to tackle it. Instead he points to the Mosaic Law as the champion of full and unreserved equality between the Jews and the converts to their faith (see above, p. 404).

135. Pulgar, *Letras*, ed. J. Domínguez Bordona, 1949, p. 138; and see my article "Américo Castro and His View of the Origins of the *Pureza de Sangre*," in *PAAJR*, XLVI-XLVII (1979–1980), pp. 401–402.
136. *Luz*, pp. 629–630.
137. *Ibid.*, p. 649.
138. Deut. 18.18–19.
139. Acts 3.22–23.
140. *Luz*, pp. 564–565.
141. *Ibid.*, pp. 653–654.
142. I Tim. 3.6.
143. *Luz*, pp. 565–566, 658.
144. *Ibid.*, pp. 565–566.
145. *Ibid.*, pp. 680–682.
146. *Ibid.*
147. See above, p. 420.
148. See his "Instruction," in Cartagena's *Defensorium*, pp. 348–349.
149. *Luz*, pp. 663–665.
150. *Ibid.*, pp. 684–686; *Defensorium*, p. 246.
151. *Luz*, p. 225.
152. *Ibid.*, Oropesa says here that he intends to elaborate on this matter in the second part of his work (which was not written).
153. *Ibid.*, p. 82.
154. *Ibid.*
155. *Ibid.*, pp. 495–496.
156. *Ibid.*, p. 496.
157. See, for instance, *ibid.*, p. 746.
158. *Ibid.*, p. 675.
159. *Ibid.*, p. 728.
160. *Ibid.*, pp. 713–714, 716–717, 737–738, 743.
161. *Ibid.*, p. 306.
162. *Ibid.*, p. 89.
163. *Ibid.*, p. 91.
164. *Ibid.*, p. 92.
165. *Ibid.*, p. 89.
166. *Ibid.*, p. 761.
167. *Ibid.*, pp. 699–700.

168. *Ibid.*, p. 62.
169. *Ibid.*, p. 707.
170. *Ibid.*, p. 82.
171. *Ibid.*, p. 707.
172. *Ibid.*, p. 705.
173. *Ibid.*, p. 706.
174. Sigüenza, *op. cit.*, I, p. 368a.
175. Related to this is Díaz y Díaz' remark (*Luz*, p. 17) that Oropesa's "entire work" indicates that the Judaizers were a minority (*los menos*).
176. Menéndez y Pelayo, *Historia de los Heterodoxos*, II, p. 472.
177. *Luz*, p. 77.
178. *Ibid.*, p. 585.
179. Sigüenza, *op. cit.*, I, p. 368a.
180. *Luz*, 101. Américo Castro, who, as he admits, had not read Oropesa's work, inferred correctly from Sigüenza's remarks that Oropesa did not censure but defended the conversos (see his *Aspectos del vivir Hispánico*, p. 109). From this, however, he wrongly concluded that Oropesa was "surely a converso" (*ibid.*, p. 110).
181. *Ibid.*, p. 75.

The Chroniclers of Enrique IV

1. See above, pp. 636, 645, 657ff.
2. Regarding Sánchez de Arévalo, see his four chapters on Enrique from his *Compendiosa Historia Hispánica*, included as appendix in Castillo's *Crónica del Rey Enrique el quarto*, ed. J. M. de Flores, 1787², pp. 123–130. For Castillo's references to the conversos, see above, pp. 742 and 897. Escavias' discussion of the riots in Andalusia is included in the chapter from his *Repertorio de Príncipes de España*, made public by Sitges, *op. cit.*, pp. 405–406.
3. See his *Memorial de diversas Hazañas*, ed. Carriazo, 1941, pp. 134–135.
4. *Ibid.*, p. 240.
5. *Ibid.*, p. 245; *Crónica Castellana*, BNM, ms. 1780, f. 131a.
6. See his *Crónica de los Reyes Católicos*, ed. Carriazo, I, 1927, p. 127.
7. *Ibid.*; *ibid.*

8. *Ibid.*
9. *Ibid.*; note.
10. Pulgar's father was a Toledan escribano who must have served—and befriended—one or more of the great nobles for his son to become the King's page (see Pulgar's *Crónica de los Reyes Católicos*, ed. Carriazo, 1943, introd., p. XVII). That Pulgar was a New Christian is apparent, as F. Cantera has pointed out ("Fernando de Pulgar y los Conversos," *Sefarad*, IV [1944], pp. 296–299), from his letter to Cardinal Mendoza, in which he identified himself with the conversos, against whom the people of Guipúzcoa enacted a statute forbidding them to marry their sons and daughters and live in their territory (see Pulgar's *Letras*, ed. J. Domínguez Bordona, 1949, pp. 137–138).
11. *Ibid.*, pp. 63–69.
12. *Ibid.*, pp. 63–64.
13. *Ibid.*, p. 64; and cf. above, pp. 617, 1271 n. 48.
14. *Ibid.*, p. 65–66.
15. *Ibid.*, *ibid.*
16. *Ibid.*, p. 67.
17. *Crónica de los Reyes Católicos*, I, pp. 343–351. Amador's suggestion that Manrique, who was an "eloquent orator," may have been the author of the speech (*Historia Crítica*, VII, p. 338) cannot be upheld. Evidence that Pulgar wrote this address comes from his "Letter to a Friend in Toledo," which contains the same ideas in the identical language (see above, notes 11–16). This, however, was not an imagined oration of the kind produced by Livy and other classical historians to explain some situation in a remote past. It was a speech attributed to a *contemporary* of Pulgar and no doubt heard by a large audience. We must conclude therefore that Pulgar composed that speech for Manrique, who followed the chronicler's line of thought if not his particular phrasing.
18. *Ibid.*; *ibid.*, p. 347.

19. *Ibid.*, p. 350.
20. *Ibid.*, p. 345.
21. *Letras*, p. 68.
22. See his introd. to Pulgar's *Crónica*, p. L. The entire letter was first published by Carriazo in the above introd., pp. XLIX–LI. For emendations of the text and further analysis, see Cantera, "Pulgar y los conversos," *loc. cit.,* pp. 295–310. Carriazo believed that he was the first to have read this letter, which apparently was also the view of Cantera (*ibid.,* p. 302; and cf. Carriazo's introd. to Pulgar's *Crónica,* pp. LI–LII). Both were obviously unaware that the letter had been published in English translation by Adolfo de Castro in his *History of Religious Intolerance in Spain,* transl. by A. Parker, 1853, pp. 17–20.

The authenticity of the letter cannot be questioned not only because of its style (which is Pulgar's), but also because of its contents. It stands to reason that Pulgar exaggerated the number of Judaizers both to show the inquisitors that he respected their claim regarding the scope of the Judaic heresy, and to use this claim as basis for his argument that while cruel punishment could be considered for few, it could not be applied to many—an argument which was countered by his pro-inquisitional critic (see Cantera's article mentioned above, *loc. cit.,* p. 317). However, since the letter was obviously tampered with, one may question the authenticity of the words *diez mil niñas* which appear in the middle of his statement: "there are young maidens between the ages of ten and twenty in Andalusia, ten thousand *niñas,* who have not left their homes since their birth and never heard or knew any other doctrine save the one they saw enacted by their parents" (see Carriazo, *ibid.,* p. L). The words *diez mil niñas* disrupt the flow and structure of the sentence; the *precise* round number of "ten thousand" (without *más* or

hasta) does not agree with Pulgar's style; nor does the word *niñas* fit mature young women of eighteen, nineteen or twenty years of age. And why the second description of the girls as *niñas* after he had described them as "young maidens"? These words therefore seem to be interpolated. Pulgar's original sentence may have read: There are numerous young maidens in Andalusia etc.

23. Pulgar, *Crónica,* I, pp. 334–337.
24. *Ibid.; ibid.,* pp. 438–440.
25. *Ibid.,* p. 439.
26. *Ibid.,* II, pp. 210–211.
27. *Ibid.,* pp. 353–354.
28. *History of Religious Intolerance in Spain,* p. 17.
29. Transl. A. Paz y Mélia, 1904–1908.
30. For Valera's view of the King see his *Memorial,* pp. 294–295; for Pulgar's see his *Claros Varones de Castilla,* ed. J. Domínguez Bordona, 1954, pp. 9–20. Escavias' description of the King was published by Sitges, see above, p. 1282, n. 8. Resembling these portrayals of Enrique is Sánchez de Arévalo's "image" of the King (see above n. 2, *loc. cit.,* cap. 39) which, though highly adulatory, is not valueless.
31. *Historia de Don Enrique IV de Castilla,* 1776, BNM, ms. 1350, f. 328ᵛ (cited by J. Torres-Fontes, *Estudio sobre la "Crónica de Enrique IV" del Dr. Galíndez de Carvajal,* 1946, p. 29).
32. *Un Pleito sucesorio* [1945], p. 171.
33. See Galíndez de Carvajal, in BAE, 70, p. 537b; see also L. Pfandl, "Über Alonso de Palencia," in *ZfRP,* LV (1935), p. 350.
34. Zúñiga, *Annales,* p. 349f.
35. *El Cronista Alonso de Palencia,* 1914, p. xxxviii.
36. Amador, *Historia Crítica,* VII, pp. 160–161.
37. R. Ballester, *Fuentes Narrativas de la Historia de España,* 1908, p. 175.
38. Menéndez y Pelayo, *Antología de los poetas líricos Españoles,* ed. E. Sánchez Reyes, II, 1944, p. 287.; see also what he wrote on Palencia, *ibid.,* II, p. 294.

39. Paz y Mélia, *op. cit.*, p. xiii, n. 1.

40. See his *Estudio*, p. 28.

41. See Castro's *La Realidad histórica de España*, 1966, p. xxii, and his last major work, *The Spaniards*, 1971, p. 74.

42. RAH, *Boletín*, vols. 78 and 79.

43. *Ibid.*, vol. 79 (1921), pp. 11–12.

44. See Amador, *Historia Crítica*, VII, p. 141 ff.; Antonio M. Fabié, *Discursos leidos ante la Real Academia de la Historia*, 1875, pp. 5–104; Menéndez y Pelayo, *Biblioteca de Traductores Españoles*, ed. E. Sánchez Reyes, 1953, IV, pp. 14–27; Tomás Rodríguez, "El cronista Alfonso de Palencia," in *La Ciudad de Dios*, XV (1888).

45. Nicolás Antonio, *Biblioteca Hispana Vetus*, II, 1788, ff. 331–334, 796–810; J. A. Pellicer y Saforcada, *Ensayo de una biblioteca de Traductores Españoles*, 1778, pp. 7–23; B. J. Gallardo, *Ensayo de una Biblioteca española etc.*, II, 1866, cols. 1004–1010; D. I. Dormer, in his revised work of F. Andrés de Uztarroz, *Progressos de la Historia en el reyno de Aragon*, 1680, pp. 254–255; Diego Clemencín, *Eloqio de la reina Católica doña Isabel*, 1821, p. 67, n. 3.

46. "Los cronistas de Enrique IV," in RAH, *Boletín*, 79 (1921), p. 18.

47. *Ibid.*, p. 19.

48. Lev. 19.31; Deut. 18.11.

49. Jer. 10.2.

50. *History of Magic and Experimental Science*, IV, 1953, pp. 413–484.

51. "Los Cronistas," *loc. cit.*, p. 18. Similarly, Sitges charged Palencia with an "eagerness to speak evil of everybody" (*Enrique IV y la Excelente Señora*, 1912, p. 18). The number of persons Palencia censured, however, was markedly smaller than that of those he praised; and these were overwhelmingly Old Christian.

52. *Ibid., ibid.*; cf. Palencia, *Crónica*, II, p. 431.

53. *Ibid.*, p. 435; *Los Cronistas, loc. cit.*, pp. 18–19.

54. *Ibid.*, p. 19.

55. *Ibid.*, cf. Palencia, *Crónica*, III, p. 272.

56. "Los Cronistas," *loc. cit.*, p. 18.

57. Palencia, *Crónica*, II, p. 49.

58. *Ibid.*, p. 51.

59. *Ibid.; ibid.*

60. See above, pp. 779–780.

61. Palencia, *Crónica*, II, p. 50.

62. *Ibid.*, III, p. 108.

63. *Ibid.*, p. 109.

64. *Ibid.*, p. 108.

65. *Ibid.*, p. 111.

66. *Ibid.*, p. 108.

67. *Ibid., ibid.*

68. See above, p. 741.

69. Paz y Mélia (*op. cit.*, p. xxxix) believes that Palencia began to write his *Crónica* in 1478—i.e., shortly after he had left the Court. It is unlikely, however, that a creative author such as Palencia could have avoided all writing throughout his period of service for the Kings, especially after the threat to their rule had vanished with the defeat of the Portuguese at Toro in 1476.

70. Palencia, *La Guerra de Granada*, transl. Paz y Mélia, 1909, p. 24.

71. *Ibid., Crónica*, III, p. 125.

The Catholic Kings

1. See above, p. 805 and Appendix E.

2. *Ibid.*, p. 1126.

3. Palencia, *op. cit.*, IV, p. 269.

4. See V. Balaguer, *Los Reyes Católicos*, I, 1892, pp. 381–382.

5. On the divided attitude of these classes, see below, pp. 1072–1073.

6. Bernáldez, *Memorias del reinado de los Reyes Católicos*, 1962, pp. 95–96, 99: *el que mas procuró en Sevilla esta Inquisición;* F. X. García Rodrigo, *Historia Verdadera de la Inquisición*, 1877, pp. 66–71.

7. Pulgar, *Crónica de los Reyes Católicos*, (ed. Carriazo), I, p. 342.

8. For Manrique's speech, see *ibid.*, pp. 343–350; for the main ideas of the speech, see Pulgar's *Letras*, ed. J.

Domínguez Bordona, 1949, pp. 63–69), and Lope de Barrientos, in his *Obras,* ed. Getino, *op. cit.,* pp. 194–195; cf. above, p. 617.

9. See the text of the Synod's resolution

on this issue, in J. Caro Baroja, *Los Judíos en la España Moderna y Contemporánea,* III, 1961, appendix II, p. 280.

10. Cortes of Toledo, 1480, 76 (CLC, IV, p. 149).

BOOK FOUR
The Origins of the Inquisition

The Lesson of the Sources

1. M. Menéndez Pelayo, *La Ciencia española,* I, 1947, p. 237.
2. *The Marranos of Spain,* 1973².
3. *Ibid.,* pp. 60–61.
4. *Ibid.,* pp. 10–11; see especially notes 24, 26, 27. *Sefer Hamada,* Hilkhot teshuvah, I, 1, 3; II, 2, 4, 5.
5. See my *Marranos of Spain,* pp. 69–72.
6. *Ibid.,* pp. 66–67 and other places.
7. *Ibid.,* pp. 72–76, 211–215.
8. Isaac Abravanel on Ezekiel 20.32; (Com. on Later Prophets, Jerusalem, 1956, 520a); and see my *Marranos of Spain,* p. 184.
9. See above, n. 8, cited text; Comm. on Ezek. 20, 32–37 (ed. 1956, p. 520b); Comm. on Isaiah 43.6 (ed. 1956, p. 206b).
10. See my *Marranos of Spain,* p. 184.
11. *Ibid.,* pp. 184–185.
12. Arama, *'Aqēdat Yizḥaq,* V. pp. 149a–150b; and see my *Marranos of Spain,* p. 154.
13. *Ibid.,* p. 155, 141–142; and cf. *'Aqēdat Yizḥaq,* V. 163a.
14. See my *Marranos of Spain,* p. 175.
15. *Ibid.,* p. 174.
16. *Ibid.,* p. 201.
17. *Ibid., ibid.*
18. Lea, *History,* I, p. 120.
19. Baer, *Die Juden,* II, pp. 303, 328, 574a (and see index of Old Christian names).
20. See Baer's *History* (Hebrew), p. 537, n. 23.
21. I refer to the works of Fernán Díaz, Cartagena, Torquemada and Valera which are discussed in the present

study. A fifth Marrano apology from the mid 15th century, authored by Bachiller Palma, is preserved in manuscript in the Biblioteca Capitular of Toledo, of whose date, author and other relevant characteristics we have a fair description by Ramón González Ruiz (in *Toledo Judáico:* Symposio, Toledo, April 1972, II, pp. 31–48). Despite my repeated requests to allow me the examination of this manuscript, I was denied this privilege on the grounds that Señor González was engaged in the study of the work and its preparation for publication.

22. See my *Marranos of Spain,* pp. 19–22 and other places.
23. See above, p. 420.
24. On Pedro Regalado see the chapter on him by Antonio Daza in his *Excellencias de la Ciudad de Valladolid,* 1627.
25. See L. G. A. Getino, *Vida y obras de Fray Lope de Barrientos,* 1927, p. 197.
26. *Ibid.,* p. 201.
27. *The Marranos of Spain,* pp. 96–121.
28. See *ibid.,* p. 198, n. 139; Pulgar, *Crónica,* II, p. 210.
29. See above, p. 733.
30. See Lea, *Chapters from the Religious History of Spain,* 1890, p. 453.
31. See on these coplas K. R. Scholberg, *op. cit.,* pp. 331–338.

The Social-Economic Reasons

1. See above, pp. 411, 572–573.
2. See Pulgar's "Letter to a Toledan Friend," where he repeatedly attributed

the hatred for the Marranos to the "greed" *(cobdicia)* of the lower classes and their "ambition" to rise socially (*Letras,* ed. Domínguez Bordona, pp. 63–69). More elaborately and emphatically were the same thoughts expressed in Pulgar's report of the speech which Gómez Manrique, governor of Toledo, addressed to the anti-Marranos in the city. The speech, which bears the stamp of Pulgar's ideas, was either written or inspired by the chronicler, and then rephrased by Pulgar for his *Crónica* (see Pulgar, *Crónica,* ed. Carriazo, I, pp. 343–350); and see above, pp. 901, 1300, n. 17.

The 1473 outbreak against the Marranos in Cordova was related by Valera to the Old Christians' "great jealousy" of the "very rich" New Christians and the former's resentment of the conversos' haughty conduct in the public offices they had acquired with their wealth (see Valera, *Memorial,* ed. Carriazo, p. 240). Also when speaking of the pogrom in Jaén, he stressed the desire for robbery as its cause and exonerated the Marranos of any blame (*ibid.,* pp. 244–245).

3. Palencia, see above, p. 741.

4. See above, pp. 617, 892.

5. See above, pp. 664–679.

6. See Delgado Merchán, *op. cit.,* p. 419; and see above, pp. 330, 803.

7. *Córtes de León y de Castilla,* III, p. 803.

8. *Halconero,* p. 522.

9. Gamero, *op. cit.,* p. 1038.

10. *Ibid., ibid.*

11. See Zaccuto, *Sefer Juchassin,* 1857, 224b; and cf. Baer, II, p. 226.

12. In his account for the first year of Enrique III's reign, Ayala refers to the bitter quarrel that broke out between the Duke of Benavente and the Archbishop of Santiago over the Duke's proposal to appoint Juan Sánchez de Sevilla as the King's Contador Mayor. The Archbishop opposed the proposal on the ground that Juan Sánchez was engaged in tax-farming, and as tax-farmer his activity should be supervised by the Contador Mayor (*Crónica de Enrique III,* año primero, 1391, cap. 7; *BAE,* vol. 68, p. 168a). Despite the archbishop's reasonable objection, Juan Sánchez assumed the disputed office, although we do not know precisely at what time. In any case, in 1397 he is officially mentioned as "Contador Mayor" of the King and Treasurer of the Queen (Baer, I, 246).

13. *Crónica de Juan II,* año 1419, cap. 1 (*BAE,* v, 68, p. 377a).

14. See the Relator's "Instrucción," *loc. cit.,* p. 352.

15. *Ibid.*

16. See *Crónica de Juan II,* año 1416, cap. x (*BAE,* 68, p. 372a).

17. *Crónica del Halconero,* p. 71 (cap. 58).

18. *Ibid.,* año 1429, cap. xxii (p. 43); *CODOIN,* 106 (1893), p. 119.

19. See above, p. 1281, n. 90.

20. Martín Gamero, *op. cit.,* p. 1037.

21. F. Cantera, *La Familia Judeo-conversa de los Cota de Toledo,* 1969, pp. 16–17.

22. See Francisco Márquez Villanueva, "Conversos y Cargos Concejiles en el siglo xv," in *RABM,* lxiii, 2 (1957), p. 508, n. 27.

23. *Ibid.,* p. 507, n.17.

24. See above, p. 776.

25. Bernáldez, *op. cit.,* p. 100 (cap. 44). See Fita (above).

26. Márquez Villanueva, *loc. cit.,* p. 509, n. 30 (on the basis of L. Serrano y Sans, *Noticias biográficas de Fernando de Rojas,* pp. 252, 266); Márquez, *loc, cit.,* p. 507, n. 20.

27. Delgado Merchán, *Historia documentada de Ciudad Real,* 1907. pp. 424–425; Márquez Villanueva, *loc. cit.,* pp. 508, 513, n. 44, 517, n. 67.

28. See on him José Gómez-Menor, *Cristianos Nuevos y Mercaderes de Toledo,* 1970, p. xxxiv.

29. Márquez Villanueva, *loc. cit.,* p. 505, n.

11 (on the basis of Benito Fernández Alonso, *Los Judíos de Orense*, 1904, p. 35).

30. See *Crónica de Juan II*, año 1421, cap. 19 (p. 405b).
31. "Instrucción," *loc. cit.*, p. 352.
32. Delgado Merchán, *op. cit.*, pp. 246–249.
33. See above, p. 783.
34. See Márquez Villanueva, *loc. cit.*, p. 533, n. 123.
35. *Ibid.*, p. 509, n. 32.
36. Cantera, *La Familia de los Cota*, 1969, p. 14.
37. Márquez, *loc. cit.*, p. 507, n. 20.
38. *Ibid.*; and see F. Pinel y Monroy, *Retrato del buen Vasallo*, 1677, p. 116.
39. J. de M. Carriazo' introduction to Valera's *Crónica de los Reyes Católicos*, 1927, pp. XLV–LXII.
40. Baer, II, p. 142.
41. Cf. Amador, *Historia*, III, pp. 62–63 (n. 1).
42. Baer, I, p. 614.
43. See Manuel Serrano y Sanz, *op. cit.*, pp. lxxix, clxiii, and other loci.
44. See on him M. Kayserling, *Christopher Columbus*, 1894, p. 26.
45. See above, pp. 515–516, 828–829.
46. See above, p. 239.
47. See above, p. 346.
48. For the large number of escribanos among the habilitated Judaizers in Toledo in 1495 and 1497, see F. Cantera and P. Leon Tello, *Judaizantes del arzobispado de Toledo*, 1969, p. xviii.
49. Cantera and Tello, *op. cit.*, p. xix, denoted this industry as "very typical" of the Jews.
50. See J. Vicens Vives, *An Economic History of Spain*, p. 249.
51. *Cortes of Burgos*, §11 (CLC, II, p. 151).
52. Cortes of Ocaña, 1469, §21 (CLC, III, p. 803).
53. See J. de Mata Carriazo, "La Inquicisión y las rentas de Sevilla," in *Homenaje a Don Ramón Carande*, 1963, 22 tax-farmers (pp. 104–105) and the two

mayordomos of the city were likewise conversos (pp. 97–99).
54. See above, p. 311.

The Rise of Racism

1. L. Ranke, *Fürsten und Völker von Süd-Europa im sechsgehenten und siebzehenten Jahrhundert*, I, 1837[2], p. 246. In characterizing the Spanish people, it should be noted, Ranke precedes the term "Germanic" to "Romanic," perhaps to allude at the dominant influence of the Germanic element in the attitude of the Spaniards toward the Jewish "progeny." He seems to have believed in the basic commonship of the two Spanish races (soon to be called by many "Aryan") as against that of the alien racial elements—i.e., of "Jewish" and "Moorish" descent (the Spanish "Moors" were considered half-Arabic—i.e., racially kindred of Jews). The first edition of Ranke's book appeared in 1827.
2. See José M. Sánchez de Muniain, *Antología General de Menéndez Pelayo*, I, 1956, p. 62 (letter to Juan Valera of Oct. 17, 1887).
3. Américo Castro, *The Spaniards*, 1971, p. 67; and earlier, in his *Structure of Spanish History*, 1954, and other works.
4. *Castro, The Structure*, p. 531.
5. See my "Américo Castro and his View of the Origins of the *Pureza de Sangre*," *loc. cit.*, pp. 397–457.
6. See above, pp. 562–563, 581; see also p. 1110.
7. See the quotations from the *Dialogi* of Petrus Alphonsi in my study "Alonso de Espina: Was he a New Christian?," in *PAAJR*, XLIII (1976), pp. 125–126, and some of Baer's remarks on Avner of Burgos in his *History of the Jews in Christian Spain* (Hebrew edition), 1959, pp. 206–208, 515–516.
8. See his *Scrutinium*, p. 512; and Matt. 23.33.
9. See the long list of offensive descriptions of the Jewish race assembled

from Petrus de la Cavalleria's *Tractatus Zelus Christi Contra Iudaeos, Sarracenos et Gentiles* by Amador de los Ríos, *History*, III, pp. 108–109.

10. Hieronymus de Sancta Fide, *Contra Iudaeos*, 1412, pp. 130–195.

11. See his letter to his son Alfonso preceding his *Additiones* to the *Postilla* of Nicholas de Lyra, in *Biblia*, Nuremberg, 1487, and Sanctotis' introductory *Vita* to Paul's *Scrutinium Scripturarum*, 1591, p. 10.

12. See above, pp. 279–282.

13. See Pulgar, *Letras*, 1949, p. 64 (todos somos nascidos de una masa e houimos un principio noble), and especially p. 67.

14. *Las Siete Partidas*, VII, tit. XXIV, 3.

15. See above, p. 582.

16. See Juan de Lucena, *Libro de Vita Beata*, in *Opusculos Literarios de los siglos XIV a XVI*, ed. A. Paz y Mélia, 1892, p. 152.

17. J. Parkes, *The Conflict of the Church and the Synagogue*, 1961, p. 158.

18. See, for instance, above, pp. 513–516, 849–852.

19. Replying to the critics of his racial statute, Siliceo says that it is right to castigate the nobles who, out of their greed for money and estates *(hacienda)*, pollute their blood by marrying persons of Jewish descent; see ms. 13038 of Bibl. Nacional, Madrid, f. 81ᵛ.

20. These were the classes of the urban population that the Relator no doubt had in mind when he referred to *ciudadanos* (see below, n. 21). Lower classes were usually indicated as *labradores*.

21. See his "Instrucción," republished as appendix II to Alonso de Cartagena's *Defensorium*, 1943, p. 354: "hay muchos Linages en Castilla, fijos, e Nietos e Vis-nietos de el linage de Israel, ansi legos, como Clerigos, ansi de el linage de Nobles, como de caballeros, e Ciudadanos." He points out that a

similar situation exists in Aragon and in "todas las Españas;" see *ibid.*, pp. 354–355.

22. "Instrucción," *loc. cit.*, pp. 343, 347 (twice).

23. See Carriazo's introduction to his edition of Pulgar's *Crónica de los Reyes Católicos*, 1943, p. LI; F. Cantera, "Fernando de Pulgar y los conversos," in *Sefarad*, IV (1944), p. 309.

24. *Ibid.*, p. 319; and cf. Carriazo, *op. cit.* above, n. 23, p. LV.

25. F. Pérez de Guzmán, *Generaciones y Semblanzas*, ed. J. Domínguez Bordona, 1954, p. 90.

26. *Ibid.*, p. 93.

27. Palencia, *Crónica de Enrique IV*, III, p. 124: como *nación aparte;* and thus also in the Latin original: *tamquam segregata natio;* see Academia de la Historia, Madrid, ms. 9–6482, f. 355.

28. Barrientos identifies that "nation" with the New Christians; see Getino, *op. cit.*, p. 199.

29. Diego de Valera, *Epístolas*, 1878, p. 207.

30. *Ibid.*, p. 208.

31. "Instrucción," *loc. cit.*, p. 343.

32. Valera, *op. cit.*, p. 208.

33. J. de Torquemada, *Tractatus Contra Madianitas et Ismaelitas*, p. 45, and many other places.

34. "Instrucción," *loc. cit.*, p. 243.

35. See my work on Alonso de Espina, *loc. cit.*, p. 150 (n. 103).

36. See his "Memorial," in *Sefarad*, xvii (1975), p. 321: *xénero judáico;* p. 325.

37. Enríquez del Castillo, *Crónica del Rey Enrique IV* (BAE, vol. 70), pp. 144b–145a (cap. 74).

38. Palencia, *op. cit.*, III, p. 124.

39. See Louis R. Loomis, "Nationality at the Council of Constance," in *American Historical Review*, XLIV (1939), pp. 524–525.

40. *Ibid.*, p. 526.

41. *Ibid.*

42. *La Ciudad de Dios*, XXXV (1894), p. 350.

43. Américo Castro, "Las Castas y lo

Castizo," in *La Torre,* Puerto Rico, no. 35–36, 1961, p. 78.

44. *Ibid.,* p. 67.

45. *The Spaniards in their History,* transl. by W. Starkie, 1950, p. 190.

46. José Ortega y Gasset, *Invertebrate Spain,* transl. by M. Adams, 1937, p. 22.

47. *Ibid.*

48. With the second conquest of Murcia by Jaime I of Aragon who delivered the city to Castile which had first gained it from the Moslems in 1243.

49. See his articles, "The Development of a National Theme in Medieval Castilian Literature," *Hispanic Review,* III (April, 1935), pp. 149–161; "The Incipient Sentiment of Nationality in Medieval Castile," in *Speculum,* xii (1937), pp. 351–358; and "National Sentiment in the Poems of Fernán González, etc." in *Hispanic Review,* xvi (1948), pp. 61–68.

50. See María Rosa Lida de Malkiel, *Juan de Mena,* 1950, pp. 539–545.

51. *Ibid.,* pp. 542–543, n. 7.

52. See *Cancionero Castellano del Siglo XV,* ed. R. Foulché-Delbosc, I, 1912, p. 524 (no. 202). I cannot see how *España* may be understood here in terms of "political geography," as suggested by Lida (*op. cit.,* p. 543, no. 7).

53. See *Cancionero Catellano* (cited above, no. 49), p. 720 (nos. 126–127); and cf. *ibid.,* p. 721 (no. 136), 725 (no. 169), and 743 (no. 331). To Guzmán, the various political units in the peninsula were kingdoms, principalities or provinces of one "nation"—Spain. Occasionally, he applies the term "nation" also to Castile (as in no. 169), which attests his inclination to identify the two concepts.

54. García's "Memorial," *loc. cit.,* p. 341; cf. p. 342: *y oyr nuestros pueblos e los naturales dellos.*

55. See above, n. 36.

56. The contradictory terms *xenero christiano* and *xenero judaico,* which likewise appear in García's "Memorial" (pp. 323, 325), seem to indicate his belief that all the Christian peoples of Spain were being amalgamated in a common ethnic entity *(genero)* which will never intermingle with the Jews.

Ferdinand of Aragon

1. Thus we do not hear it proposed by García, though he justified the burning of alleged Judaizers in Toledo, during the rebellion (see his "Memorial," *loc. cit.,* pp. 331–332); or by any of his followers whose opinions are echoed in the satires we have discussed (see above, pp. 512–516, 849–854).

2. See above, pp. 676–679.

3. First published by Fidel Fita in RAH, *Boletín,* xv (1889), p. 448–453., and later by B. Llorca, in *Bulario Pontificio de la Inquisición Española,* 1949, pp. 49–55.

4. *Ibid.,* pp. 51–54.

5. *Ibid.,* p. 49. According to the Kings' letter, the papal bull said: *algunos malos christianos* (some bad Christians). The Pope, however, was obviously informed by the Kings that there were *many (quamplurimi)* deviators among the converts (see *ibid.,* p. 51).

6. *Ibid.,* pp. 49–50.

7. *Ibid.,* pp. 54–55.

8. *Ibid.,* p. 55.

9. Raynaldus, *Annales,* t. xxi, 1727, ann. 1451, §6, p. 380b.

10. Reg. Vat. 518, f. 206ᵛ.

11. See his bull of August 1, 1475, published by Lea in *American Historical Review,* I (1896), p. 49.

12. RAH, *Memorias de Enrique IV de Castilla,* p. 366a.

13. See Fidel Fita, "Lá Inquisición anormal, ó anticanónica, planteada en Sevilla," in RAH, *Boletín,* XV (1889), pp. 448, 450.

14. The word *premio* stands here no doubt for *premia* or *apremio*; cf. *Partidas,* VII, tit. 24, 1. vi; "Fuerça nin premia deuen

façer a ningund judio porque se torne christiano."

15. CICa, ed. Friedberg, II, Sextus, lib. V, tit. ii, cap. 13; and see *Boletín*, xv, p. 450.

16. See Ortiz' "Tratado contra la carta del protonotario de Lucena," in *Los Tratados del doctor Alonso Ortiz*, 1493, ff. LI^v–C^v.

17. Tarsicio de Azcona, *Isabel la Católica*, 1964, p. 400.

18. Isidore's view is expressed in the 57th decree of the 4th Toledan Council (633) and see above, p. 1187, n. 27.

19. For the position of Pope Gregory the Great, see above, p. 1187, n. 30. For the view of Thomas Aquinas, see *Summa Theologica*, II^a, 2^a, qu. 10, articles 8, 10. Duns Scotus, who in principle considered forced conversion permissible, regarded it as valid only when carried out by a sovereign (*Opera omnia*, VIII, 1639, p. 275; Sent. IV, hist. 4, qu. 9). In 1391, however, the Kings of both Castile and Aragon were opposed to Martinez' campaign; hence even according to Duns Scotus, the forced conversions that occurred in that year lacked legal force.

20. See Fita, *loc. cit.*, p. 455.

21. Pulgar, *Cronica* (ed. Carriazo), I, 1943, pp. 439–440, and Pope Sixtus IV's bull of April 18, 1482, in Llorca, *op. cit.*, pp. 67–72.

22. See Coulton, *The Inquisition*, 1929, p. 65.

23. Machiavelli, *The Prince*, xxi.

24. Guicciardini, *Storia d'Italia*, vi, 12.

25. Segni, *Storie Fiorentine*, 1725, p. 335 (Segni completed this history c. 1557).

26. See Llorente, *Histoire critique de l'Inquisition d'Espagne*, I, pp. 142–143.

27. J. del Castillo y Mayone, *El Tribunal de la Inquisición*, 1835, p. 1.

28. Adolfo de Castro, *History of the Jews in Spain*, transl. E. D. G. M. Kirwan, 1847, pp. 122, 150.

29. *Los Judeoconversos en España y America*, 1978, pp. 36–37.

30. *Ibid.*, p. 33; cf. Pulgar, *op. cit.*, I, p. 337.

31. Lea, *History*, II, p. 317.

32. Authors like G. A. Bergenroth (*Calendar of State Papers*, I, pp. 37, 45–46) and U. R. Burke (*A History of Spain*, II, p. 307) denied her financial disinterestedness in the Inquisition. Their condemnatory statements about Isabella, however, were inferred from her conduct *after* the establishment of the Holy Office.

33. This is similar to the financial considerations that accompanied his decision on the Expulsion. See my *Don Isaac Abravanel*, 1982^4, pp. 51, 281 (n. 67).

34. Domínguez Ortiz, *op. cit.*, p. 37.

35. *Ibid.*, *ibid.*

36. Tarsicio de Azcona, *op. cit.*, pp. 415–422.

37. Llorente, *Histoire*, I, p. 399.

38. Lea, *History*, II, p. 367.

39. Tarsicio de Azcona, *op. cit.*, pp. 417–418.

40. See Ranke, *op. cit.*, pp. 243–244.

41. *Ibid.*, pp. 244–245.

42. K. J. von Hefele, *The Life and Times of Cardinal Ximenes*, transl. J. Dalton, 1885, p. 314.

43. F. Guizot, *The History of Civilization* (transl. by W. Hazlitt), I, 1911, p. 201.

44. See V. Balaguer, *Los Reyes Católicos*, I, 1892, pp. 366–373.

45. *Bulario de la Orden de Santiago*, lib. 1, f. 36.

46. See above, p. 733.

47. See his *Católica Impugnación*, 1961, with an introductory study by F. Márquez [Villanueva], pp. 4–53.

48. Lea, *History*, IV, pp. 248–249.

49. Perhaps the most summarized view of this group was expressed by Pius Bonifacius Gams who said: "The Spanish Inquisition was introduced by the State, was governed and directed by the State, was a tool in the hands of the State, was abolished by the State" (*Die Kirchengeschichte von Spanien*, 1956, III/2, p. 93).

For the changing attitudes of Catholic scholars toward the Spanish Inquisition, see E. Schäfer, "Die Katholische Geschichtschreibung und die Inquisition," in *Der Alte Glaube,* Leipzig, IX, issues of Dec. 6 and Dec. 13, 1907.

50. Lea, *History,* IV, pp. 248–249.
51. Gams noted that out of the 44 Inquisitors-General of the Spanish Holy Office, the State dismissed 12, the Popes only one (*op. cit.,* p. 93, n. 1).
52. Lea, *History,* II, p. 317.
53. *Ibid.,* I, p. 21.
54. *Ibid., ibid.,* p. 189.
55. *Ibid., ibid.*
56. *Ibid., ibid.*
57. *Ibid.*
58. *Ibid.,* I, p. 22; II, pp. 378–379.
59. *Ibid., ibid.*
60. See Sandoval's *Historia de la vida y hechos del Emperador Carlos V,* I, 1955, lib 1, año 1516, c. 59, p. 61a. According to Adolfo de Castro (*op. cit.,* pp. 116–117), Sandoval said: "This King had long since thrown his confessor overboard, as a troublesome merchant, telling the latter that he was more influenced by motives of personal interest than regard for his conscience." However inaccurate as a quotation, the sentence correctly describes Ferdinand, provided we agree that his "personal interests" and his political interests were virtually identical.
61. Lea, *History,* I, pp. 189–190.
62. Adolfo de Castro, *op. cit.,* p. 173.
63. *Ibid.,* pp. 173–174.
64. *Ibid.* p. 175.
65. Lea, *History,* I, pp. 189–190.
66. Lea, *Chapters from the Religious History of Spain,* 1890, pp. 469–487.
67. See on this below, p. 1090.
68. Pulgar, *Crónica,* I, pp. 439–440.
69. B. Llorca, *Bulario Pontificio,* pp. 67–72.
70. See Llorente, *Historia Crítica de la Inquisición en España,* 1980, I, p. 296; *Histoire,* I, 1817, p. 398.
71. Lea, *History,* I, p. 194. This is Lea's

translation of a passage from a letter by Gonzalo de Ayora, dated July 16, 1507, to Miguel Pérez de Almazán, King Ferdinand's secretary (published by Cesáreo Fernández Duro, in RAH, *Boletín,* XVII (1890), pp. 446–452). See also the recorded charges raised against Lucero by Ayora as procurador of Cordova before King Ferdinand, which were published by F. Márquez Villanueva in his *Investigaciones sobre Juan Álvarez Gato,* 1960, pp. 405–409, 410–413. And see concerning this Márquez, *ibid.,* pp. 147–152.

72. *Ibid.,* and see Lea, *History,* I, p. 195.
73. *Ibid.,* p. 211.
74. *Ibid.,* p. 195.
75. *Ibid.,* p. 211.
76. *Ibid.,* p. 193.
77. See Ferdinand's letter published by Armando Cotarelo y Valledor, *Fray Diego de Deza,* 1905, pp. 350–351.
78. Lea, *History,* I, p. 196.
79. *Ibid.,* p. 197.
80. Modesto Lafuente, *Historia General de España,* VII, 1922, p. 250.

The Racial Substitute

1. Andrés Bernáldez, *Memorias del reinado de los Reyes Católicos,* ed. Manuel Gómez-Moreno y Juan de M. Carriazo, 1962, pp. 102–103 (cap. 44).
2. *Ibid.,* p. 102.

The Parallel Drive

1. See above, p. 920.
2. See L. à Páramo, *De Origine et progressu Oficii Sanctae Inquisitionis,* 1598, pp. 138–139; G. de Talavera, *Historia de nuestra Señora de Guadalupe,* Toledo, 1597, ff. 90ᵛ–91ᵛ; José de Sigüenza, *op. cit.,* II, pp. 29–41; F. Fita, "La Inquisición en Guadalupe," in RAH, *Boletín,* XXIII (1893), pp. 283–288. For the literature on the subject, see Lea, *History,* I, 171; II, pp. 286, 367; III, 88, 115–116; Baer, *History,* II,

pp. 337–338, 353–354; Domínguez Ortiz, *op. cit.*, 67; A. Sicroff, *op. cit.*, 76–87; T. de Azcona, "Dictamen en defensa de los judíos conversos de la Orden de San Jerónimo a principios del siglo xvi," in *Studia Hieronymiana*, II (1973), 347–380; H. Beinart, "The Judaizing movement in the Order of San Jerónimo," in *Scripta Hierosolymitana*, VII (1961), pp. 168–192 (deals with the trials of five Hieronymite friars by the Inquisition of the Order).

3. Beinart says (*loc. cit.*, p. 168) that from Oropesa's *Lumen* "we learn that even in those days apostasy had been discovered in the monastery of the order at Guadalupe." No intimations of such "discoveries," however, are found in Oropesa's work, and naturally they cannot provide a "clue," as Beinart claims, to the "condition of the Order in general" (*ibid.*, p. 169).

4. Sigüenza, *op. cit.*, II, p. 30b.

5. See on him *ibid.*, p. 29b. Sigüenza, who praises his "sanctity and prudence," indicates that Orense aspired to the "quietude of his cell," and was "afflicted" by the thought of the burden imposed on him by his election as General.

6. See Fita, *loc. cit.*, p. 284.

7. *Ibid.*

8. We gather this from the decision of the Order in 1486 which states that "se hallaron en el [the Convent of Guadalupe] algunos frayles, corrompidos con estos errores y fueron condenados por hereges, quemados publicamente" (Sigüenza, *op. cit.*, II, p. 33a). Of course, "algunos" may mean here more than several, but probably no more than a small number.

9. *Ibid.*, p. 32a. Talavera, who was himself prior of Guadalupe and no doubt had all the records of the monastery at his disposal, stated unreservedly (*op. cit.*, pp. 90–91) that Marchena was burned together with the Judaizers of Guadalupe in 1485. Beinart, however, asserted that he was burned "apparently in 1488," since "before his death he managed to appear for the prosecution in the trial of Diego de Zamora" (a friar of the convent of San Bartolomé de Lupiana) which began in 1489 (*loc. cit.*, pp. 169, 184, n. 94). But the record of the Inquisition, on which Beinart relied, does not say that Marchena testified in Zamora's trial, but that he confessed (perhaps in his own trial) that he had expressed "doubts about the faith" to Diego de Zamora, of which the latter failed to inform the Inquisition. The aforesaid communication to Zamora, the record adds, took place "eight or nine months before Marchena was burned" (see Archivo Histórico Nacional, Inquisición, leg. 188, no. 13 moderno, f. 10^r).

10. See Lea, *History*, II, 286.

11. See Sigüenza, *op. cit.*, II, p. 32a.

12. *Ibid.*, p. 32b.

13. *Ibid.*, p. 33a.

14. *Ibid.*, p. 34ab.

15. *Ibid.*, p. 34b.

16. *Ibid.*, *ibid.*

17. *Ibid.*

18. *Ibid.*, pp. 34b–35a.

19. *Ibid.*, p. 35a.

20. *Ibid.*

21. *Ibid.*

22. *Ibid.*, pp. 35ab.

23. *Ibid.*, pp. 35b–37b.

24. *Ibid.*, p. 37b.

25. *Ibid.*, p. 38a. There is no apparent ground for Beinart's assertion that "every possible effort was made [by the Order] to conceal the existence of the Judaizing movement among the monks" (*loc. cit.*, p. 170). On the contrary: the issuance of the limpieza statute by the Order and the great struggle against its revocation served in themselves as forceful announcements that the Order saw itself endangered by Judaizers. Above all, the inquisitional actions in

Guadalupe, in which a number of friars were publicly burned (among them the above mentioned Marchena), and the establishment of an independant Inquisition by the Order, which condemned many members of the Order to harsh punishments, were meant to be publicized rather than hidden. As Sigüenza, (*op. cit.,* II, p. 39a) put it: "Hicieronse *castigos públicos y exemplares,* hasta llegar con algunos a la hoguera, y otros en carceles perpetuas reclusos, otros privados de exercisio de las ordenes" (italics are mine, B. N.). In fact, what the Order strove for was not to purge itself clandestinely from its alleged sinners, but to serve as a *model* to all other organizations, religious and secular, in the country as to how to deal with the conversos in their midst.

26. Sigüenza defines him as "hombre seuero y riguroso con los otros, y consigo mas . . . a quien nunca se rendia" (p. 35b).

27. *Ibid.,* p. 39a.

28. *Ibid., ibid.*

29. *Ibid.,* p. 40a. According to Tarsicio de Azcona, "Dictamen en defensa de los Judíos conversos de la Orden de San Jerónimo a principios del siglo XVI," in *Studia Hieronymiana,* II (1973), p. 358, n. 28, two friars had already been sent to Rome in 1489 to attain papal support of the statute.

30. Sigüenza, *op. cit.,* 60b–61a. Pleased as they were with the papal decree, Gonzalo and his friends agreed to permit the Order's converso vicars and confessors to continue in their positions. Sigüenza explains this surprising decision by their desire not to "inflame the ulcer" and avoid expected "inconveniences." Motivating their decision, however, was no doubt the realization that their achievement had aroused King Ferdinand's anger, which they sought to allay or, at least, reduce.

31. See S. Simonsohn, "La 'Limpieza de Sangre' y la Iglesia," in *Actas del II Congreso Internacional: Encuentro de las tres Culturas,* Toledo, 3–6 Octubre 1983, p. 309.

32. The only exception seems to have been the bull of 1511 authorizing a *limpieza* statute for the Cathedral Church of Badajoz. See A. Domínguez Ortiz, *Los conversos de origen Judío despues de la expulsión,* 1955, p. 62.

33. José de Rújula, *Indice de los colegiales* etc., 1946, p. xxxi.

34. H. C. Lea, *History,* II, p. 287.

The Unchanged Goal

1. See BNM, ms. 13038, ff.

2. See the two versions of this letter published by Adolfo de Castro in his *History of the Jews of Spain,* translated by E. D. G. M. Kirwan, Cadiz, 1847, pp. 160–161. The version published by Isidro de las Cagigas in his edition of *Libro Verde de Aragón,* Madrid, 1929, p. 107, was obviously not the one submitted by Siliceo to the Pope (see below, p. 1066) as it could not serve as basis for the reply allegedly given by the Jews of Constantinople. Siliceo's final version must have therefore been closer to, or identical with one of the drafts published by Castro.

3. See the two formulations of the reply in Castro, *op. cit.* pp. 161–163; see also *Libro Verde De Aragón,* pp. 107–108.

4. *Ibid.,* p. 107.

5. *Ibid.,* p. 108.

6. Cf. BNM, ms. 13038, ff. 23ʳ–28ʳ, and other places.

7. This was indeed the view of Adolfo de Castro, *op. cit.,* pp. 163–164.

8. See Siliceo's assertion in the aforecited ms. 13038, f. 79ʳᵛ.

9. On the vacillation of Charles V and his conflicting decisions concerning the *Limpieza,* see Lea, *op. cit.,* II, pp. 289–290.

10. See ms. 13038, f. 24ᵛ.

11. See *ibid.,* ff. 48ʳ, 33ᵛ, 30ʳ, 22ᵛ, 26ʳ, 28ʳ.

12. See *ibid.,* f. 81ʳ–82ᵛ.

13. *Ibid.*, f. 23^v–24^r.
14. *Ibid.*, f. 24^v.
15. Lea, *op. cit.*, II, p. 293.
16. Note his description of the conversos as "bulliciosos" (BNM, ms. 13038, f. 27^r.)
17. Lea, *op. cit.*, II, p. 293.
18. Cf. ms. 13038, f. 89^v.
19. *Ibid.*, ff. 24^v–25^r.
20. Lea, *op. cit.*, II, p. 292.
21. *Ibid.*, *ibid.*

Struggling Assimilation

1. Ms. p. 13038 of BNM, f. 25v.
2. See above, pp. 416–417.
3. López Villalobos, *Cartas Castellanas*, no. 45, published by the Sociedad de Bibliófilos Españoles; republished by Domínguez Ortiz, *op. cit.*, Appendix VI (p. 249).
4. Cardinal Mendoza y Bobadilla, *Tizón de la Nobleza española*, Barcelona, 1880.
5. See above, p. 988.
6. See José Gómez-Menor, *Cristianos Nuevos y Mercaderes de Toledo*, 1970, especially pp. xv–xvii, 59–76, and the documents, p. 15ff.
7. Accordingly, Siliceo claimed that converso women wielded a strong influence on their Christian husbands, presumably on behalf of Jewish interests; see aforecited ms. 13038, f. 82^v.
8. Spinoza, *Works*, I (*Theologico-Political Treatise*), transl. by R.H.M. Elwes, I, 1951, p. 56.
9. The trend toward the phenomenon noticed by Spinoza was already indicated toward the end of the 16th century in Bautista Perez's report to the Suprema (see Lea, *History*, III, p. 236).

The Insidious Pretext

1. E. Vacandard, "Inquisition," in *Hastings Encyclopaedia*, VII, pp. 335–336.
2. Lord Acton, *Letters to Mary Gladstone*, ed. H. Paul, 1913, p. 147; Selections from the *Correspondence of Lord Acton*, ed. Figgis and Laurence, 1917, pp. 55, 217.

The Destructive Urge

1. Of the considerable literature on the Moriscos, mention must be made of Pascual Boronat y Barrachina, *Los Moriscos españoles y su Expulsión*, 1901 (2 vols.); Lea, *The Moriscos of Spain*, 1901; *id.*, *History*, III, pp. 317–410; and L. Marmol Carvajal, *Rebelión y castigo de los Moriscos de Granada* (BAE, vol. XXI).
2. See my remarks on this subject in my article, "La Razón de la Inquisición," in *Inquisición Española y mentalidad inquisitorial*, ed. Angel Alcalá, 1984, p. 28.
3. W.E.M. Lecky, *History of the Rise of Rationalism in Europe*, 1865, p. 387.
4. See above, p. 1063.
5. Lea, *History*, III, p. 492.
6. *Ibid.*, *ibid.*, p. 489.
7. John L. Motley, *The Rise of the Dutch Republic*, II, 1903, pp. 169–170; and see the decree of the Inquisition of Madrid dated Feb. 16, 1568, which confirms the judgment of the Inquisition of Netherland, according to which all the people of that country were defined not only as rebels to their King but also as heretics or fautors of heresies who deserved capital punishment (published in Dutch translation by Pieter Bor Christiaensz in his *Oorsprongk, Begin, en Vervolgh der Nederlandsche Oorlogen*, I, 1679, p. 226).

According to T. M. Lindsay, *A History of the Reformation*, II, 1516, pp. 255–256, the order threatening mass-annihilation was issued by the Council of Tumults against acts of *treason*, and not of *heresy*. But rebellious acts such as opposing the Inquisition were considered both treacherous and heretical, and the spirit that imbued the tribunal's activity was indicated by the statement of one of its leaders, Juan de Vargas, who said of the people of the northern provinces: "The heretics have broken open the Churches, the orthodox have done nothing to hinder them; therefore they ought all of them to be hanged together." Lindsay concedes that by this indictment he "brought the whole population of the Netherlands within the grip of the public executioner." In any case, the Council of Tumults was a vehicle of Philip II, who was both inspired and guided by the Inquisition.

8. *Ibid., ibid.*
9. Lea, *History,* III, pp. 334–340, 388–390.
10. Jeremiah, 17.9.
11. W. N. Rule, *History of the Inquisition,* 1868, p. 222.

Expulsion

1. On the manipulative and arbitrary attachment of crimes such as blasphemy, bigamy and witchcraft to the sphere of the Inquisition's jurisdiction, see Lea, *History,* IV, 206, 316ff, 328ff.
2. See above, pp. 833–839.
3. See below, n. 5.
4. See Baer, II, pp. 348–349 (§337); 357–359 (§344). Documents published by F. Fita, "La Inquisición de Jerez de la Frontera," in RAH, *Boletín,* XV (1889), 323–325, 327–328, show that the expulsion from that town was delayed until July 7, 1484.
5. Baer, *History* (Hebrew), 1959, p. 411 (emphasis added). If we are right in assuming, as Baer did, that the royal decision to expel the Jews from Andalusia resulted from the advocacy of the Inquisition, we must also assume that the Kings found it necessary formally to accept at least the main reasons the Inquisition offered for its

proposition. An echo of these reasons we hear in Ferdinand's letter to the inquisitors of Aragon (dated May 12, 1486), which begins with the words: "Devotos padres. Porque por experiencia parece, que *todo el danyo, que en los cristianos se ha fallado del delito de la heregia,* ha procedido de la conversacion e pratica, que con los jodios han tenido las personas de su linage . . ." (Baer, I, p. 913). As we see it, the King attributes his decision to the alleged lesson of "experience," of which he had no doubt been repeatedly informed by those who had constantly dealt with the problem—namely, the Inquisitors. By way of presenting his allegedly own thinking, he tells the Inquisitors that he accepted their argument and resolved to act accordingly.

6. Baer, I, pp. 912–913 (§563).
7. Lea, *History,* I (Documents, I), p. 569.
8. *Ibid.,* p. 569.
9. On the trial of the Santo Niño de La Guardia, see F. Fita, "El Proceso y Quema de Jucé Franco," in RAH, *Boletín,* XI (1887), pp. 13–115; Lea, *Chapters from the Religious History of Spain,* 1890, pp. 437–468; *id., History,* I, pp. 133–134.
10. The text of the edict was published by Amador, *Historia,* III, pp. 603–607 and (a more accurate version) by F. Fita, in *Boletín,* XI (1887), pp. 512–520.
11. Lea, *Chapters from the Religious History of Spain,* p. 457.
12. F. Fita, in RAH, *Boletín,* XI (1887), p. 14.

APPENDICES

The Number of the Marranos in Spain

1. Y. Baer, *A History of the Jews in Christian Spain,* II, 1966, p. 246.
2. A. Domínguez Ortiz, *Los Judeoconversos en España y América,* 1978, p. 192.
3. *The Marranos of Spain,* pp. 238–248.
4. *Ibid.,* pp. 240–241, 246–247.
5. *Ibid.,* pp. 255–270; Baron, *A Social and Religious History of the Jews,* XIII, 1969, p. 337, n. 4.
6. *Schevet Jehuda,* ed. Wiener, 1855, Hebrew section, p. 128.

7. *The Spanish Kingdoms,* II, 1978, p. 149, n. 2.

8. *REJ,* XIV, p. 171.

9. *Guerra de Granada,* transl. by A. Paz y Mélia, V, 1909, p. 25.

10. See *The Marranos of Spain,* pp. 266–267.

11. See Fernando de Pulgar, *Crónica de los Reyes Católicos,* ed. Carriazo, I, 1943, p. 337.

12. On the total number of Seville's population at the time, see what I wrote in *The Marranos of Spain,* pp. 264–265, n. 2.

13. Loeb, in *REJ,* XIV, p. 171; Baer, *Untersuchungen über Quellen und Komposition des Schebet Jehuda,* 1936, p. 29; *id., History,* II, p. 471, n. 15.

14. *The Marranos of Spain,* pp. 258–259; see also *ibid.,* pp. 239–241.

15. *Ibid.,* p. 241, n. 4.

16. *Ibid.,* pp. 241–242.

17. *History,* X, p. 375, n. 2.

18. See Arévalo's account in A. Neubauer, *Medieval Jewish Chronicles,* I, 1887, p. 98; Zacuto, *Sefer Yuhasin,* ed. Filipowski, 1857, p. 225b.

19. *Geschichte,* VIII³, p. 113.

20. See Amador, *Historia,* II, pp. 531–552; L. Suárez Fernández, *Documentos acerca de la Expulsión de los Judíos,* 1964, pp. 65–72.

21. See Isaac Abravanel, *Ma'aynei ha-Yeshu'ah,* Ferrara, 1551, 8b; and cf. my *Don Isaac Abravanel,* 1982⁴; pp. 55, 280, n. 60.

22. Graetz, VIII, 1890³, n. 10, pp. 462–463.

23. Ibn Verga, *Shevet Yehuda,* 46th persecution (ed. Baer-Shohat, 1947, p. 118)—16,000; Usque, *Consolation,* ed. Martin A. Cohen, 1964, p. 194 (dialogue 3, chapter 21)—15,000 (Usque confuses the persecutions of 1391 and 1412 and is evidently misinformed); Bzovius, *Annales Eccles.* ad annum 1412—over 20,000; a contemporary Catalonian source cited by R. Chabas, in *RABM,* VI [1902], p. 3)—25,000; Mariana, *Hist. General de España,* lib. XIX, cap. 12; BAE, vol. 31, p. 486—35,000 Jews (as against 8,000 Moors).

24. See above, p. 202.

25. Alami, *Iggeret Musar,* ed. Jellinek, 1872, p. 10b.

26. Zacuto, *op. cit.,* p. 225b.

27. Ms. G-15 of Academia de la Historia, Madrid, f. 169 (Colección Salazar, vol. 12-3-4, of the 16th century). Alvar García de Santa María, a converso, said that the petition for retrieving the expulsion decree submitted by Seville's Jews to Fernando of Antequera was based on the argument that if they were thrown out of their homes in mid winter they *would die of cold in the fields.* Alvar García considered the argument false. Fernando, the Regent, however, must have thought differently; and, as we know from Alami (see above, n. 25), his judgment was correct.

28. Alami, *op. cit.,* p. 10b.

29. *Ibid., ibid.*

30. See above, p. 193.

31. See Graetz, VIII, 1890³, p. 111, n. 2.

32. *Ibid., ibid.*

33. No doubt, Valencia de Don Juan, south of Leon.

34. South of Valencia de Don Juan.

35. *Ibid.,* pp. 110–111.

36. *Sefer Yuhasin,* p. 225b. That the conversion of "1412" continued beyond that year in both Castile and Aragon also following the periods of Ferrer's intensive agitation is evident from such facts as the conversion of 120 Jews in Guadalajara in March 1414 following a sermon preached by a Franciscan friar (see King Fernando I's letter to Ferrer, in Baer, II, p. 277, doc. 282, and F. Vendrell's remarks in *Sefarad,* XIII [1953], p. 92) and the conversion of the remainder of the community of Fraga (in Catalonia) in 1418 (see notification of Pope Martin V, of May 13, 1418, in J. Goñi Gaztambide's article, "Conversión de la Alajama de Fraga," in *Hispania Sacra,* XIII [1960], p. 2).

37. Baer, *Die Juden,* I, pp. 159–160, and II, p. 292f.

38. See on this *The Marranos of Spain*, pp. 244–245.

39. According to Bernáldez, that increase must have been high. Referring to the conversos, he says: "Todo su hecho era crecer e multiplicar" (*Historia de los Reyes Católicos*, cap. 43, BAE, vol. 70, p. 600a).

40. See Eugenio Alberi, *Relazioni degli Ambasciatori Veneti al Senato*, Serie Iᵃ, vol. Iº, Florence, 1859, p. 29.

41. See J. Liske, ed., *Viajes de Extranjeros por España y Portugal*, 1878. pp. 55–56, 67. Popielovo (Nicolaus von Popplau) visited Spain in 1484–1485.

42. See A. Hershman, *R. Yiẓḥaq ben Sheshet*, 1955–1956, pp. 194–195.

Diego de Anaya and His Advocacy of Limpieza

1. F. Ruiz de Vergara y Alava, *Vida del Illustrissimo Señor Don Diego de Anaya Maldonado*, 1661, pp. 47–49.

2. Joseph de Roxas y Contreras, *Historia del Colegio Viejo de S. Bartholomé*, I, 1766, pp. 56–58.

3. See Antonio Domínguez Ortiz, *Los Conversos de origen Judío despues de la Expulsión*, 1955, p. 57.

4. See Ruiz de Vergara, *op. cit.*, p. 47.

5. That of Benedict XIII's bull is found in Arch. Segre. Vaticano, Reg. Aven. 344, f. 736ʳ⁻ᵛ; that of the bull of Martin V is found in Arch. Vat. Reg. Lateran, 195, f. 127ᵛ.

6. See his *Les Controverses des Statuts de Pureté de Sang en Espagne de XVᵉ au XVIIᵉ Siecle*, 1960, p. 89, n. 101.

7. "Memorial," *loc. cit.*, p. 347.

8. The Old Christians of the anti-Marrano party designated themselves as *lindos* also in 1467 (see A. Martín Gamero, *Historia de Toledo*, 1862, p. 1040).

9. See Sicroff, *op. cit.*, p. 89, n. 101.

10. *Ibid., ibid.*

11. See José de Rújula y de Ochotorena, *Indice de los Colegiales del Mayor de San Ildefonso y menores de Alcalá*, 1946, p.

VIII. In fact, this policy was pursued by most colleges throughout the 15th century and beyond; see *ibid.*, pp. xiv (concerning the College of San Bartolomé, see pp. xvi, xvii, xxiv, xxv).

12. See Sicroff, *op. cit.*, pp. 89–90, n. 101.

13. See, for instance, Moses Arragel's letter to Luis de Guzmán, Master of Calatrava, where he employs the term *lympia sangre* (or *pura sangre*) in the sense of noble origin (*Biblia. Antiguo Testamento*, published by the Duke of Berwick and Alba, 1918–1921, I, p. 4). Diego Enríquez del Castillo, the chronicler of Enrique IV, describes Gonzalo de Saavedra as being of *limpia sangre* (in the sense of *noble* origin; see *Crónica del Rey Don Enrique IV*, BAE, vol. 68, p. 141a) and cites the constable Miguel Lucas de Iranzo's reference to King Enrique as *noble e de limpia sangre* (*ibid.*, p. 183b). In a similar manner, and late in the century, Pulgar says of Alfonso Carrillo, Archbishop of Toledo, that he was "de los fidalgos e de limpia sangre del reino de Portogal" (*Claros Varones de Castilla*, ed. J. Domínguez Bordona, p. 116).

14. Such terms, indeed, were used by the Colegio de Santa María del Monte Olivete in Salamanca when, in its statutes of 1517, it included a stipulation that the students must be offspring of legitimate marriages (see L. Sala Balust, *Constituciones, Estatutos y Ceremonias de los antiguos Colegios seculares de la Universidad de Salamanca*, I, 1962, p. 145, §6), and by the Colegio de Santa María Magdalena in 1516 (see *ibid.*, II, p. 23, §12, lines 615–616). Similar enactments we have also from the beginning of the 17th century in the Constituciones Latinas of the Colegio de Santa Catalina, 1603, § 4 (see *ibid.*, II, p. 390) and the constitutions of the College of San Ciriaco y Santa Paula of 1612 (see José de Rújula, *op. cit.*, p. xxxv). For later regulations of Spanish

Colleges taking the same stand on the subject of illegitimacy, see *ibid.*, pp. xxxvi–xxxvii, xl.

The enactments of statutes to this effect, however, might be attributed—at least, to some extent—to the growing influence of the *limpieza* policy: illegitimate children could well be descendants of Jews, Moors, or heretics.

15. See L. Sala Balust, *op. cit.*, III, 1964, p. 10, n. 5.
16. See J. Goñi Gaztambide, "Recompensas de Martín V a sus electores españoles," in *Hispania Sacra*, V (1958), pp. 259–397.

When Did Sarmiento leave Toledo?

1. See *Crónica*, año 1450, cap. 1, p. 670a.
2. *Ibid., ibid.*
3. *Ibid.*, p. 671a.
4. *Halconero*, cap. 383, p. 538.
5. *Crónica*, año 1450, cap. 1, pp. 670a–671a.
6. See *Refundición*, Carriazo's introd., pp. xv–xvi, cxxx–cxxxix, and other places.
7. *Abreviación*, cap. 175, f.299.
8. Benito Ruano, *Toledo en el Siglo XV*, p. 57.
9. *Ibid.*, p. 58.
10. *Halconero*, cap. 383, p. 539.
11. See above, n. 6.
12. *Crónica*, año 1450, cap. 1, p. 671a.
13. *Halconero*, cap. 383, p. 538.
14. *Ibid., ibid.*, p. 539.
15. *Colección Diplomática*, nu. xvi, p. 26
16. Benito Ruano, *op. cit.*, p. 71.
17. See above, pp. 349–350.
18. Benito Ruano, op. cit. p. 62.
19. *Ibid., ibid.*
20. *Crónica*, año. 1450, cap. 1, p. 671b (como estaba dubdoso de su vida).

Juan de Torquemada
I. Race and the Jewish People

1. Torquemada, *Tractatus*, p. 67.
2. *Ibid.*, p. 105.

3. *Ibid.*, p. 103.
4. *Ibid.*, p. 102.
5. *Ibid.*, p. 67.
6. *Ibid.*, p. 68.
7. *Ibid., ibid.*; Deut. 26.18–19.

II. More on the Judaizers

1. *Tractatus*, p. 96.
2. *Ibid.*
3. *Ibid.*
4. *Ibid.*
5. *Ibid.*, p. 182.
6. *Ibid.*, p. 183.
7. *Ibid.*, p. 186.
8. *Ibid., ibid.*
9. *Ibid.*, p. 187.
10. *Ibid.*, p. 188.

III. On the Reliability of Torquemada's Testimony

1. See his introduction to Torquemada's *Tractatus contra Madianitas et Ismaelitas*, 1957, p. 30.
2. See my *Marranos of Spain*, pp. 44–49.
3. See his introduction to Torquemada's *Tractatus*, p. 30.
4. *Ibid., ibid.*
5. *Ibid.*, p. 7

The Gibraltar Project

1. Palencia, *Crónica de Enrique IV*, transl. Paz y Mélia, III (1905), p. 233 (Década II, lib. ix, cap. 8).
2. *Ibid., ibid.*, p. 130 (lib. viii, cap. 2).
3. *Ibid.*, pp. 132–133.
4. *Ibid.*, pp. 232–233.
5. *Ibid.*, pp. 228–229.
6. *Ibid.*, p. 230.
7. *Ibid.*, p. 229.
8. *Ibid.*, pp. 233.
9. *Ibid.*, pp. 233–234.
10. *Ibid.*, p. 234.
11. *Ibid.*, IV (1908), p. 268 (Década III, lib. xxvii, cap. 5).
12. *Ibid.*, page 269.
13. *Ibid.*, pp. 267–268.

14. *Ibid.*, p. 268.
15. *Ibid.*, p. 269; and see what I wrote concerning the conversos' settlement in Gibraltar in my *Marranos of Spain*, 1973², pp. 251–254.
16. Palencia, *op. cit.*, IV, p. 269.

The Death of Enrique IV

1. Palencia, *Crónica de Enrique IV*, III, p. 299 (Década II, lib. X, cap. ix); according to Palencia, the last attack began with a "sudden and abundant flow of blood." In the anonymous portrayal of Enrique published by Rodríguez Villa, *Boquejo Biográfico de D. Betrán de la Cueva*, p. 6, the king's eating is described as *"destemplado"* (irregular); it also indicates that occasionally he suffered in the loins. Valera's description of the king's sickness ("pains in the loin, loose bowels, and blood in the urine") seems to combine intestinal and kidney trouble. In his last two days, he adds, Enrique became "so deformed that his sight aroused astonishment" (see his *Memorial de diversas Hazañas*, ed. Carriazo, 1941, p. 292).
2. Castillo, *Crónica*, cap. 166, p. 220a; cap. 164, p. 220a *(desque infermó en Segovia)*.
3. *Ibid.*, cap. 168, p. 221b. Based on the clinical symptoms indicated in the sources, G. Marañon arrived at the conclusion that Enrique IV died of poison. See his *Ensayo biológico sobre Enrique IV de Castilla y su tiempo*, 1930, p. 60.
4. Castillo, *Crónica*, cap. 164, p. 218b.
5. *Ibid., ibid.*
6. *Ibid.*
7. See his *Histoire de la revalité de la France et de l'Espagne*, III, 1801, p. 286.
8. Palencia, *op. cit.*, III, p. 252 (Década II, lib. X, cap. 1).
9. *Ibid.*, II, p. 9 (Década I, lib. ix, cap. 1).
10. *Ibid., ibid.*
11. J. B. Sitges, *Enrique IV y la Excelente Señora*, 1912, pp. 160–161, on the basis of

Rades y Andrada, *Crónica de Calatrava*, p. 77.
12. Palencia, *op. cit.* II, pp. 153–154 (Decada I, lib. X, cap. x).
13. V. Balaguer, *Los Reyes Católicos*, I, 1892, p. 75.

Espina's Source for the "Tale of the Two Tents"

1. See his *Josef Haccohen et les croniquères juives*, 1888, p. 102.
2. See Samuel Usque, *Consolations for the Tribulations of Israel*, transl. by M. A. Cohen, 1965, pp. 283–284.
3. *Ibid.*, pp. 285–286.
4. See his introduction to his commentary on Kings (at the end of the section dealing with the Kings of Judah) and his *Wells of Salvation (Ma'aynei ha-Yeshu'ah)*, Well II, palm *(tamar)* 3, toward the end of the opening section; and see my *Don Isaac Abravanel*, 1982⁴, pp. 65–66, 75.
5. Since Usque contains no chapter on the expulsion of the Jews from Spain, it stands to reason that Abravanel did not finish his *Yemot 'Olam*, which could have served Usque as a source for such a chapter. If the unfinished manuscript came into Usque's hands, it may not have carried the name of the author, and consequently Usque, unsure of its provenance, indicated it simply as *libro ebraico*.

This interpretation of the initials in question appears to me correct because in the majority of the cases (eleven out of nineteen) these initials appear as *L. Eb., l. Eb.*, or *li. Eb.*, which may well stand for *libro ebraico*, and one of the indications in capital letters *(LI. EB.)* may likewise stand for the same designation *(LIBRO EBRAICO)*. The remaining seven markings in capital letters *(L.I.E.B.)* are probably distortions of *LI. EB* or *Li. eb.* by some proof-reader who misunderstood their meaning.

Yemot Olam was not published, and

no ms. of it is extant, perhaps because it remained unfinished. Another work by Abravanel, *Eternal Justice,* met the same fate, probably for the same reason (see my *Don Isaac Abravanel,* pp. 85 and 289, n. 12).

6. See above, chapter on Espina, note 70.

The Abuse of the Conversos as "Judaizers"

1. See above, p. 256.
2. See above, p. 259.
3. See above, p. 1208, n. 11.
4. See González-Tejada, III, p. 736ff.
5. See above, pp. 355 and 1235, n. 28.

Bernáldez on the Conversos' Occupations

1. *Historia de los Reyes Católicos Don Fernando y Doña Isabel,* caps. 43 and 44; BAE, vol. 70, pp. 598b–602a; cf. the new edition of his work: *Memorias del Reinado de los Reyes Católicos,* ed. M. Gómez Moreno y J. de M. Carriazo, 1962, pp. 94–103.
2. See the introduction of the editors of the aforementioned *Memorias,* p. xxi.
3. See above, pp. 1053–1054.
4. *Historia,* p. 610a.
5. *Ibid., ibid.*
6. *Ibid.* (italicization is mine, B.N.).
7. *Ibid.,* p. 599a: "e ovo su impinacion é lozanía de muy gran riqueza y vanagloria de muchos sabios e doctos, e obispos etc."
8. See Abravanel, Commentary on Deuteronomy 4.15; cf. my *Don Isaac Abravanel,* 1982⁴, p. 119.
9. *Judeoconversos en España y America,* 1978, p. 21.
10. He may have been influenced in this by Espina, who expressed a similar thought. See above, p. 731.
11. See above, p. 780.

Racism in Germany and Spain

1. See *Seminar,* an annual extraordinary number of *The Jurist,* I, (1943), pp. 48, 73, published by the Washington School of Canon Law, The Catholic University of America.
2. *Ibid.,* p. 71.
3. *Ibid., ibid.*
4. *Ibid.,* p. 70.
5. See Martín Gamero, *Historia de Toledo,* p. 1038.
6. *Ibid.,* p. 1039.
7. See his study "Nationalism and Race in Medieval Law," *loc. cit.,* p. 71.
8. See his article "Marranos and Racial Antisemitism," in *Jewish Social Studies,* II (1940), pp. 239–248.
9. *Ibid.,* pp. 242–243.
10. *Ibid., ibid.*
11. Cited by Jacob Katz in his Hebrew article on the Hep-Hep riots in Germany in 1819, *Zion* (Jerusalem), XXXVIII (1973), p. 106; cf. L. Börne, *Gesammelte Schriften,* Leipzig, I, p. 217 (from his article "Für die Juden").
12. See Eleonore O. Sterling, *Judenhass,* 1969, pp. 125–129.
13. *Ibid.,* p. 170.
14. Sterling also says that in the first half of the nineteenth century the "idea of extermination" was mostly presented in the form of a demand to annihilate Judaism, and that National Socialism "developed" this demand into a plan to annihilate the Jews (*ibid.,* pp. 169–170). Nazism, however, could also build on more concrete plans to eliminate the Jews which German antisemitism had put forth in the first half of the 19th century. Especially did the racist agitation of the forties repeatedly project the expulsion of the Jews as a solution of the Jewish problem (see *ibid.,* p. 129), and Nazism harped for some time on this idea as an alternative to extermination. For a fuller account of this development, see A. Bein, *Die Judenfrage,* 1980, I, pp. 215ff; II, pp. 158ff.
15. See Roth, *loc. cit.,* p. 243.
16. See my article, "Antisemitism," in *Encyclopaedia Hebraica,* IV (1950), cols. 493a–513a.

The Converso Conspiracies Against the Inquisition

1. The enmity of the Inquisitors toward the conversos was repeatedly stressed by the New Christians, while Pope Sixtus IV denounced the excesses they committed out of avarice and disregard of justice. See Pulgar, *Crónica de los Reyes Católicos*, ed. Carriazo, I, 1943, p. 337; II, p. 340; and see the Pope's bulls of January 29, February 2, and April 18, 1482, in B. Llorca, *Bulario Pontificio de la Inquisición Española*, 1949, pp. 59ff., 63ff., and 67ff. The latter bull, which censures the Inquisitors of Aragon, may likewise be taken as reflecting primarily the Inquisition in Castile.

2. See his *Historia*, III, p. 247, n. 2.

3. First in RAH, *Boletín*, XVI (1890), pp. 450–456, and later in his *España Hebrea*, I (1889), pp. 185–190.

4. *Ibid.*, p. 85.

5. *Ibid.*, p. 191. The cited description of Núñez was made by a 17th century author on whom Fita relied; and see below, n. 6.

6. *Ibid.*, pp. 195–196.

7. *Ibid.*, pp. 193–195.

8. *Ibid.*, p. 194.

9. *Ibid.*, pp. 187–188.

10. See above, pp. 806, 1122; Palencia, *Crónica*, III, p. 133. See on this, my *Marranos of Spain*, 1973², pp. 251–254.

11. By 1480, all the great nobles in Andalusia were bound to the Kings' obedience. See Balaguer, *Los Reyes Católicos*, I, pp. 371–372, 382.

12. Fita, *op. cit.*, p. 193.

13. *Ibid, ibid.*

14. Bernáldez, *Memorias del Reinado de los Reyes Católicos*, ed. Gómez-Moreno and Carriazo, 1962, cap. xliv, pp. 99–100.

15. See Amador, *Historia*, III, p. 243; Lea, *History*, I, 1905, pp. 162–163; Graetz, *Geschichte*, VIII, 1889³, pp. 289–290.

16. Fita, *op. cit.*, I, p. 186.

17. *Ibid.*, p. 192.

18. This is also the view of Fita, *ibid.*, p. 193.

19. See F. Fita, "La Inquisición Toledana," in RAH, *Boletín*, XI (1887), pp. 290–294.

20. *Ibid.*, p. 291.

21. *Ibid.*, pp. 292–293.

22. *Ibid.*, p. 293.

23. *Ibid., ibid.*

24. See above, pp. 782–783.

25. See on this Lea, *op. cit.*, I, p. 246.

26. Palencia, *Crónica de Enrique IV*, vol. IV, p. 117.

27. Fita, *op. cit.*, p. 293.

28. *Ibid., ibid.*

29. See Ms. 13038 of the Biblioteca Nacional, Madrid, f. 17ʳ.

30. *Ibid.*, ff. 17ᵛ–18ʳ.

31. Lea, *History*, I, p. 274.

32. *Ibid.*, p. 255.

33. *Ibid.*, p. 250.

34. Baer, *History*, II, p. 368.

35. *Ibid.*, p. 369.

36. *Ibid., ibid.*

37. *Ibid.*, p. 370.

38. *Ibid.*, p. 369.

39. *Ibid.*, p. 370. Apart from charging him with heretical notions and performance of Jewish "ceremonies," the Inquisition accused him of having "taught, at his home, the benedictions of these ceremonies to a certain Jew" (see the Inquisitional document published by Lea, *History*, I, appendix xii, p. 601). Baer, who was not struck by the strangeness of the claim that a converso taught a Jew (!) Jewish benedictions, not only failed to question the accusation, but also broadened it by saying that Francisco de Santafe "did much to propagate the Jewish religion" (*History*, II, p. 371), or, as he put it in the original of the above work: he "spread the Jewish religion among *many*" (*Toledot*, ed. 1959, p. 434). How much farther can one go in accepting or underscoring the findings of the Holy Office? The Inquisition "discovered" that Francisco taught Jewish benedictions to *one Jew only*,

but Baer takes this as evidence of a campaign!

Baer draws further proof of Francisco's Judaism from the Inquisition's report that he was circumcised (see *ibid., ibid.;* and cf. Lea, *op. cit.,* I, p. 601). We are not surprised that the Inquisition mentioned this fact, or that it passed in silence over the other related fact—namely, that in 1485, when Arbués was assassinated, Francisco was at least 75 years old; and thus his being circumcised proved nothing. Francisco must have been born a short time before Lorki's conversion c. 1410 (see *Libro Verde de Aragon,* p. 45; and see above, pp. 202–203), and there is every reason to assume that, from early childhood, he was indoctrinated in Christianity by his father, the ardent convert. Baer, however, decided, against the evidence we possess (*Libro Verde,* p. 45), that Francisco was not Lorki's son but his *grandson.* He gave us no reason for this unreserved decision, and we cannot think of any. As we see it, old age did not necessarily exclude one from serving as the Governor's assessor, and Montesa, who was deputy chief justice of Saragossa, was also, we are told, an old man. Of course, as grandson, Francisco de Santafe *might* have been raised by a Judaizing father, and this could offer support to the claim of the Inquisition, as well as to Baer's view of his Jewishness.

40. *Los Orígenes de la Inquisición en Aragón: S. Pedro Arbués, Mártir de la Autonomía Aragonesa,* 1984, p. 64.

41. Lea, *op. cit.,* I, p. 250.

42. Alcalá, *op. cit.,* p. 60.

43. *Ibid.,* p. 33.

44. See his *Orígenes de la Dominación Española en America,* I, 1913, pp. cliii–clxx, dix–dxx.

45. *Ibid.,* p. clxix.

46. *Ibid.,* p. clxv.

47. *Ibid.,* p. dxvia.

48. *Ibid.,* p. dixa–dxva.

49. *Ibid.,* p. clxix.

50. *Ibid., ibid.*

51. This is also the view of Serrano, *ibid.*: *Todo hace presumir que Montesa y Paternoy no se habían puesto en acuerdo para lanzar tal acusación contra el Tesorero de Fernando el Católico.*

52. *Ibid.,* p. clxxi.

53. Despite the great notoriety of the case, both Bernáldez and Palencia, as well as Valera, pass in complete silence over the murder of Arbués and the massive punishment that followed. Indubitably, they disqualified or at least questioned the veracity of the pertinent official reports. The only contemporary historian who discussed the murder of Arbués was Pulgar. As the official chronicler, who was well aware of Ferdinand's stand on the matter, Pulgar's refusal to follow the official line might have cost him his office. The pragmatic converso decided to yield, though probably not without much hesitation and before becoming subject to royal pressure. He reported the murder only in 1488, that is, three years after its occurrence, and without mentioning Arbués' name. Pulgar, evidently, tried to play down the event. According to him, the murder resulted not from a conspiracy against the Holy Office, but from a plot of "some" conversos against a certain "judge who, they believed, solicited the Inquisition out of his enmity [for the New Christians] rather than out of zeal for the faith" (Pulgar, *op. cit.,* II, p. 340).

BIBLIOGRAPHY

The bibliography consists, with a few exceptions, of works mentioned in the notes.

Abreviación del Halconero, ms. 434, Bibl. de Santa Cruz, University of Valladolid.

Academia de la Historia, Madrid, *Colección de Fueros y Cartas Pueblas de España,* 1852.

————*Córtes de León y de Castilla,* I–V.

————*Memorias de Don Enrique IV de Castilla,* II, 1835–1913.

————*Opúsculos Legales,* 1836.

————*Memorial Histórico Español,* I, 1851.

————*Colección de documentos inéditos para la historia de España.*

Acta Sanctorum, ed. J. Bollandus et al., 1643–1867.

Acton, J.E.E.D., *Letters to Mary Gladstone,* ed. H. Paul, 1913.

————*General Correspondence,* ed. Figgis and Laurence, 1917.

————*History of Freedom and Other Essays,* 1907.

Aeneas Sylvius Piccolominus, *De gestis Concilii Basiliensis Commentariorum libri II,* ed. Denys Hay and W. K. Smith, 1967.

Alami, Solomon, *Iggeret Musar,* ed. Jellinek, 1872; ed. Habermann, 1946.

Albertus Aquensis, *Historia hierosolymitana,* in *Recueil des historiens des croisades: Historiens occidentaux,* IV, 1879.

Alcalá, Angel, ed. *Inquisición Española y Mentalidad Inquisitorial,* 1984.

————*Los orígenes de la Inquisición en Aragon: S. Pedro Arbués, Martir de la Autonomía Aragonesa, 1984.*

Altamira, R., *Historia de España*, 1900.

———"Spain under the Visigoths," in *Cambridge Medieval History*, II, 1980.

Amador de los Ríos, José, *Historia de los Judíos en España y Portugal*, I–III, 1875–1876.

———*Estudios históricos, políticos y literarios sobre los Judíos de España*, 1848.

———*Historia crítica de la Literatura Española*, V–VII, 1865.

———"La poesía política en el siglo XV, la privanza y el suplicio del condestable don Alvaro de Luna," in *Revista de España*, XXIII (1871) and XXIV (1872).

———ed., *Obras* de Iñigo López de Mendoza (Marqués de Santillana), 1852.

Amador de los Ríos, Rodrigo, "La parroquia de Santa María la Mayor de Alcalá de Henares," in *Boletín de la Real Academia de Bellas Artes de San Fernando*, Madrid, XVIII (1898).

Andreae, Joannes, *In quinque decretalium libros novella commentaria*, with an introd. by S. Kuttner, 1964; *In sextum decretalium librum novella commentaria*, 1581.

Anglería, Pedro Mártir de, *Epistolario*, transl. J. López de Toro, II, 1955.

Annales Monastici of the Abbey of Burton-on-Trent, ed. Luard, Rolls Series, I.

Antist, V. J., *Vida de San Vicente Ferrer*, 1575; reprinted in *Biografía y Escritos de San Vicente Ferrer*, ed. M. J. de Garganta and V. Forcada, 1956.

Antonio, Nicolás, *Biblioteca Hispana Vetus*, I, 1788.

Antonio González, Francisco, and Tejada y Ramiro, Juan, *Colección de Cánones de la Iglesia Española* (a bilingual edition, Latin-Spanish), II, 1850.

Applebaum, S., "A Note on the Work of Hadrian in Cyrene," in *Journal of Roman Studies*, XL (1950).

Aptowitzer, A., ed., *Sefer R.E.B.Y.H.* (Rabiah), 1964–1965.

Arama, Isaac, *Aqedat Yizhaq*, ed. Ch. J. Polak, 1882

Archivum Fratrum Praedicatorum, VII (1937); XXX (1960).

Aristeas, Letter of, transl. M. Hadas, 1951.

Aristotle, *Works*, ed. W. B. Ross, 1921–1931.

Arragel, Moses, *Biblia, Antiguo Testamento*, published by Duke of Berwick and Alba, 1918–1921.

Ashtor, E., *The Jews of Moslem Spain*, I–II, 1973–1984.

———"Quelques observations . . . sur la thèse de Pirenne," in *JESHO*, XIII (1970).

Augustine, *Obras*, bilingual edition, Latin-Spanish, in 22 vols., ed. BAC.

Avi-Yonah, M., *The Jews Under Roman and Byzantine Rule*, 1976.

Ayala, Pero López de, *Poesías,* 1920.

———Crónicas de Pedro I, Enrique II, Juan I y Enrique III de Castilla, ed. C. Rosell (BAE, vols. 66, 68).

Azcona, Trasicio de, *Isabel la Católica,* 1964.

———"Dictamen en defensa de los Judíos conversos de la orden de San Jerónimo a principios del siglo xvi," in *Studia Hieromyniana,* II (1973).

Bachrach, B. S., "A Reassessment of Visigothic Jewish Policy," in *AHR,* LXXVIII (1973).

———*Early Medieval Jewish Policy in Western Europe,* 1977.

Baer, Y. F., *A History of the Jews in Christian Spain,* I–II, 1961.

———*Studien zur Geschichte der Juden im Königreich Aragonien etc.,* 1913.

———*Untersuchungen über Quellen und Komposition des Schebet Jehuda,* 1936.

———*Die Juden im christlichen Spanien,* I–II, 1929–1936.

———On the Disputations of R. Yehiel of Paris and Nahmanides (Hebrew), in *Tarbitz,* II (1931).

Balaguer, V., *Los Reyes Católicos,* I, 1892.

———*Historia de Cataluña,* III, 1862.

Ballester y Castell, Rafael, *Las Fuentes narrativas de la historia de España durante la edad media, 417–1474,* 1927².

Ballesteros y Beretta, A., *Historia de España,* III, 1922.

———*Alfonso X el Sabio,* 1963.

———"Don Yuçaf de Écija," in *Sefarad,* VI (1946).

Baron, S. W., *Social and Religious History of the Jews,* I–XVIII.

———"The Jewish Factor in Medieval Civilization," in *AAJR, Proceedings,* XII (1942).

Bartolocci, J., *Bibliotheca magna rabbinica,* 1683.

Bartolus de Saxoferrato, *In tres libros codicis lucidissima commentaria,* 1543.

———"De Tyrannia," in *Humanism and Tyranny,* ed. Emerton, 1925.

Baur, F. Ch., *History of Christianity in the First Three Centuries,* I, 1878.

Beinart, H., "The Judaizing Movement in the Order of San Jerónimo," in *Scripta Hierosolymitana,* VII (1961).

Bell, I., *Jews and Christians in Egypt,* 1924.

Beltrán de Heredia, V., "Colección de documentos inéditos para ilustrar la vida del Cardenal Juan de Torquemada," in *Archivum Fratrum Praedicatorum,* VII (1937).

———"Las bulas de Nicolás V acerca de los conversos de Castilla," in *Sefarad,* XXI (1961).

Benavides, Antonio, ed., *Memorias de D. Fernando IV de Castilla*, II, 1860.

Benito Ruano, E., *Toledo en el siglo XV*, 1961.

———"Don Pedro Sarmiento," in *Hispania*, XVII (1957).

———"El Memorial contra los conversos del bachiller Marcos García de Mora," in *Sefarad*, XVII (1957).

———"La Sentencia-Estatuto," *Revista de la Universidad de Madrid*, VI (1952).

———"El Origen del condado de Salinas," in *Hidalguía*, V (1957).

Bergenroth, G. A., *Calendar of Letters, Dispatches and State Papers*, I, 1862.

Bernáldez, Andrés, *Memorias del reinado de los Reyes Católicos*, ed. Carriazo, 1962.

———*Historia de los Reyes Católicos*, ed. C. Rosell, BAE, 70.

Bernstein, S., ed., Lament on Jewish Martyrs (Hebrew), in *Sinai*, 29 (1951).

Binder, K., *Wesen und Eigenschaften der Kirche bei Kardinal Juan de Torquemada*, 1955.

———*Konzilsgedanken bei Kardinal Juan de Torquemada*, 1976.

———"El Cardenal Juan de Torquemada y el movimiento de reforma eclesiastiástica en el siglo XV," in *Revista de Teología*, La Plata, III (1953).

Blumenkranz, B., *Juifs et chrétiens dans le monde occidental, 430–1096*, 1960.

Bofarull y Sans, F., *Los Judíos en el Territorio de Barcelona*, 1910.

Börne, L., *Gesammelte Schriften*, I, 1880.

Boronat y Barrachina, P., *Los Moriscos españoles y su Expulsión*, 1901.

Bracton, Henry de, *De legibus et consuetudinibus Angliae*, 1640.

Brown, Charlton F., "Chaucer's Prioress's Tale and its Analogues," in *Publications of the Modern Language Association of America*, XXI, 2 (1926).

———"The Prioress's Tale," in *Sources and Analogues of Chaucer's "Canterbury Tales*," ed. Bryan and Dempster, 1958.

Budinszky, Alexander, *Die Universität Paris und die Fremden an derselben im Mittelalter*, 1876.

Bulario de la Orden de Santiago.

Burke, U. R., *A History of Spain*, II, 1895.

Burriel, A. M., *Informe de la Imperial ciudad de Toledo*, 1780.

Caballero, Fermín, *Doctor Montalvo*, 1873.

Cabello y Lapiedra, Luis Mª., *La capilla del Relator ó del Oidor*, etc., 1905.

Cagigas, Isidro de, *Libro Verde de Aragon*, 1929.

Cahen, C., "Y a-t-il eu de Rahdanites?," in *REJ*, 123 (1964).

Camillo, Ottavio di, *El humanismo castellano del siglo XV*, transl. Manuel Lloris, 1976.

Cantera Burgos, F., *Alvar García de Santa María y su familia de conversos*, 1952.

———"La Conversión del célebre talmudista Salomón Lewi," *Boletín de la Biblioteca Menéndez Pelayo*, XV (1933).

———*La familia judeoconversa de los Cota de Toledo*, 1969.

———*Sinagogas de Toledo, Segovia y Córdoba*, 1973.

———"Fernando de Pulgar y los Conversos," in *Sefarad*, IV (1944).

———"El Cancionero del Baena" etc., in *Sefarad*, XXVII (1967).

———"El Poeta Cartagena etc.," in *Sefarad*, 28 (1968).

———*Christian Spain*, in WHJP, *The Dark Ages*, ed. C. Roth, 1966.

———*La usura judía en Castilla*, 1932.

Cantera Burgos, F., and León Tello, P., *Judaizantes del arzobispado de Toledo*, 1969.

Cappa, R., *La Inquisición Española*, 1888.

Carlyle, R. W. and A. J., *A History of Medieval Political Theory in the West*, I–VI, 1927–1936.

Caro Baroja, J., *Los Judíos en la España Moderna y Contemporánea*, I–III, 1961.

Carreras y Candi, "L'Inquisició barcelonina substituida per l'Inquisició Castelana, 1446–1487," in *Anuari de l'Institut d'estudis catalans*, 1909–1910.

Carrete Parrondo, Carlos, *Fontes Iudaeorum Regni Castellae*, I–IV, 1985–1992.

———Introduction to Anton de Montoro, *Cancionero*, 1984.

Carriazo, J. de Mata, "La Inquisición y las rentas de Sevilla," *Homenjae a Don Ramón Carande*, 1963.

Carrillo de Huete, Pero, *Crónica del Halconero de Juan II*, ed. Carriazo, 1946.

Cartagena, Alonso de, *Defensorium unitatis Christianae*, ed. Manuel Alonso, 1943.

———"Discurso pronunciado . . . en el Concilio de Basilea acerca del derecho de precedencia del Rey de Castilla sobre el Rey de Inglaterra," *La Ciudad de Dios*, XXXV (1894).

Castillo, Hernando de, *Primera Parte de la Historia General de Santo Domingo y de su Orden*, 1587.

Castillo y Mayone, Joaquín del, *El Tribunal de la Inquisición*, 1835.

Castro, Américo, *España en su Historia*, 1948.

———*The Structure of Spanish History*, 1954.

———*De la Edad Conflictiva*, 1961.

———*The Spaniards*, 1971.

————"Las Castas y lo Castizo," *La Torre*, Puerto Rico, no. 35–36, 1961.

————*Los Españoles: como llegaron a ser lo*, 1959.

————*Aspectos del vivir hispánico*, 1949.

Castro y Rossi, Adolfo de, *History of the Jews of Spain*, transl. E.D.G.M. Kirwan, 1847.

————*Sobre el Centón Epistolario* etc., 1875.

————*History of Religious Intolerance in Spain*, transl. T. Parker, 1853.

Catalina García, Juan, *Castilla y León durante los reinados de Pedro I, Enrique II, Juan I y Enrique III*, I, 1891.

Cave, Guilielmus, *Scriptorum ecclesiasticorum historia literaria*, 1687.

Chabás, R., on Vicente Ferrer, in *RABM*, VIII (1903).

Chabot, J.-B., "Trois episodes concernant les Juifs," in *REJ*, XXVIII (1894).

Charles, R. H., *Apocrypha and Pseudepigrapha of the Old Testament*, 1913.

Chaucer, G., *Canterbury Tales*, ed. W. W. Skeat, 1900.

Chazan, R., *European Jewry and the First Crusade*, 1987.

Chía, Julian de, *Bandos y Bandoleros in Gerona*, I, 1888.

Christiaensz, P. B., *Oorsprongk, Begin, en Vervolgh der Nederlandsche Oorlogen*, I, 1679.

Chronica Fratris Ludovici de Valladolid, in *Analecta Sacri Ordinis Fratrum Praedicatorum*, XX (1932).

Chrysostom, J., *Discourses Against Judaizing Christians*, transl. P. W. Harkins, c. 1979.

————*The Homilies on the Gospel of St. Matthew*, ed. Nicene and Post Nicene Fathers, X, 1888.

Cicero, Marcus Tullius, *Works*, LCL.

————*Ouvres complètes*, ed. Nisard, II, 1852.

Cirot, G., *Les histoires générales d'Espagne entre Alphonse X et Philippe II*, 1904.

————"Les décades d'Alfonso de Palencia," in *Bulletin Hispanique*, XI (1909).

Codera, F., "Narbona, Gerona, y Barcelona bajo la dominación Musulmana," in IEC, *Anuari*, III (1909–1910).

Cohen, Jeremy, *The Friars and the Jews*, 1981.

————"The Jews as the Killers of Christ," in *Traditio*, 39 (1983).

Cohen, Martin A., "Reflections on the Text and Context of the Disputation of Barcelona," in *HUCA*, XXXV (1964).

Colmeiro, Manuel, *Córtes de León y de Castilla*, I, 1883.

————*Historia de la Economía política de España*, I–II, 1965.

Colmenares, Diego de, *Historia de Segovia*, 1640.

Comestor, Petrus, *Historia Scholastica*, Migne, PL, 198.

Copinger, W. A., *Treatise on Predestination, Election, and Grace*, 1889.

Corpus Iuris Canonici, ed. Ae. Friedberg, I–II, 1879–1881.

Corral, León de, *Don Alvaro de Luna*, 1925.

Cotarelo, E., "Algunas noticias nuevas acerca de Rodrigo Cota," RAH, *Boletín*, XIII (1926).

Cotarelo y Valledor, A., *Fray Diego de Deza*, 1905.

Coulton, G. G., *The Inquisition*, 1929.

Cowley, A. E., *Aramaic Papyri of the 5th Century B.C.*, 1923.

Creighton, M., *History of the Papacy*, 1882–1894.

Crenius, T., *Animadversiones philologicae et historicae*, 1705.

Crescas, H., "Letter to Jews of Avignon," in Wiener's ed. of *Shebet Jehuda*, 1855.

Crónica Castellana de Enrique IV, ms. 1780 of BNM.

Crónica de Alvaro de Luna, ed. Josef Miguel de Flores, 1784; ed. Cariazzo, 1940.

Crónica del Rey Don Alfonso el onceno, ed. Rosell, BAE, 66.

Cronicón de Valladolid, ed. P. Sainz de Baranda, *CODOIN*, XIII (1848).

D'Abadal i de Vinyals, Ramón (on the Black Death in Spain), Prologue to *Historia de España*, XIV.

Dahn, F., *Urgeschichte der romanischen und germanischen Völker*, I, 1881.

———*Die Könige der Germanen*, VI, 1885.

Daiches, S., *The Jews in Babylonia in the time of Ezra and Nehemia According to the Babylonian Inscriptions*, 1910.

Danvila, F., "El robo de la Judería en Valencia en 1391," RAH, *Boletín*, 8 (1886).

Davis, Gifford, "The Development of National Themes in Medieval Castilian Literature," *Hispanic Review*, III (1935).

———"The Incipient Sentiment of Nationality in Medieval Castile," *Speculum*, XII (1937).

———"National Sentiment in the Poems of Fernán González etc.," *Hispanic Review*, XVI (1948).

Daza, Antonio, *Excelencias de la Ciudad de Valladolid*, 1527.

De Actibus . . . Alfonsi de Cartegena, ms. 7432, BNM.

De Clerq, V. C., *Ossius of Cordova*, 1954.

Delgado Merchán, L., *Historia documentada de Ciudad Real*, 1907².

Denifle, H., in *Historisches Jahrbuch*, Munich, VIII (1887).

Denifle, H. S., and Chatelain, A., *Chartularium Universitatis Parisiensis*, IV, 1873.

Díaz de Montalvo, Alonso, ed., *El Fuero Real de España*, 1781.

——ed., *Las Siete Partidas*, 1807.

Díaz de Toledo, Fernán, "Instrucción," published by F. Caballero in his *Doctor Montalvo*, 1873, and M. Alonso, as appendix to his edition of Cartegena's *Defensorium*, 1943.

Díaz Martín, L. V., *Itinerario de Pedro I de Castilla*, 1975.

Díaz y Díaz, L. A., "Alonso de Oropesa y su obra," *Studia Hieronymiana*, I, 1973.

Dill, S., *Roman Society in Gaul in the Merovingian Age*, 1926.

Dinur, B., *A Documentary History of the Jewish People* (Hebrew), 8 vols., 1958–1969.

Dio Cassius, *Roman History*, LCL.

Döllinger, J.J.I. [pseud. Janus], *The Pope and the Council*, 1869.

——*Fables Respecting the Popes in the Middle Ages*, 1872.

Domínguez Ortiz, A., *La clase social de los conversos Judíos de Castilla en la edad moderna*, 1955.

——*Los Judeoconversos en España y America*, 1978.

Dormer, Diego Iosef, ed., Francisco Andrés de Uztarroz, *Progressos de la Historia en el reyno de Aragon*, 1680.

Dozy, R., *Recherches sur l'histoire et la littérature de l'Espagne pendant le moyen âge*, I–II, 1965³.

——*Spanish Islam*, 1913.

Duran, Profiat, "Kelimat ha-Goyim," in *Hazofe mᵉ-erez Hagar*, III, 1914.

——*Al tehi ka-avotekha*, in *Qovez Vikuḥim*, Breslau, and P. M. Heilpern, *Even Boḥan*, II, 1946; ms. 8° 757 of the National University Library, Jerusalem, ed. A. Poznanski.

Duns Scotus, Joannes, *Opera Omnia*, VIII, 1639.

Elliott, J. A., *Imperial Spain*, 1469–1716, 1964².

Enelow, H. G., ed., *Menorat ha-Maor*, 1930.

Enríquez del Castillo, Diego, *Crónica del Rey D. Enrique IV*, 1953 (BAE, 70).

Epistolae Obscurorum Virorum, 1689.

Escavias, Pedro de, *Repertorio de Principes de España*, ms. in the Escorial, X-ii-1; chapter on Enrique IV in J. B. Sitges, *Enrique IV* etc., 1912, as appendix 1.

Escolano, Caspar, *Década Primera de la Historia de Valencia*, I, 1610.

Espina, Alonso de, *Fortalitium Fidei*, Lyon, 1511.

Esteve Barba, Francisco, *Alfonso Carillo de Acuña, Autor de la unidad de España*, 1945.

Eusebius of Caesarea, *Historia Eccesiastica*, PG, 20.

————*Chronicorum libri duo, PG,* 19.

————*Chronica,* Hieronymite version, *PL,* 27.

Eymeric, Nicolaus, *Directorium inquisitorum,* II, 1585.

Fabié, Antonio María, *Discursos leidos ante la Real Academia de la Historia,* 1875 (on Alonso de Palencia).

Fabricius, J. A., *Bibliotheca Latina mediae et infimae aetatis,* ed. Mansi, 6 vols., 1858–1859.

Fages, H., *Histoire de Saint Vincent Ferrier,* 1892–1894.

Feret, Pierre, *La faculté de Théologie de Paris et ses docteurs les plus célèbres,* 8 vols., 1894–1904.

Fernández Duro, Cesáreo, "Noticias de la vida y obras de Gonzalo de Ayora," in RAH, *Boletín,* XVII (1890).

Fernando Alonso, B., *Los Judíos de Orense,* 1904.

Ferrara, Orestes, *Un Pleito Sucesorio,* 1945.

Figgis, J., *Studies of Political Thought from Gerson to Grotius,* 1907.

Fita, Fidel, *La España Hebrea,* I–II, 1889–1898.

————"La Inquisición Toledana," in RAH, *Boletín,* XI (1887).

————"La Judería de Madrid en 1391," in RAH, *Boletín,* VIII (1886).

————"La Judería de Segovia [en 1391]," in RAH, *Boletín,* IX (1886).

————"Edicto de los Reyes Católicos (31 Marzo, 1492) desterrando de sus estados a todos los judíos," in RAH, *Boletín,* XI (1887).

————"Los conjurados de Sevilla contra la Inquisición en 1480," in RAH, *Boletín,* XVI (1890).

————"El Papa Honorio primero y San Braulio de Zaragoza," in *La Ciudad de Dios,* IV, V (1871), and VI (1871).

————"Placitum de los judíos en tiempo de Chintila," in *Suplementos al Concilio nacional Toledano,* V, 1881.

————"El proceso y Quema de Jucé Franco," in RAH, *Boletín,* XI (1887).

Flannery, E. H., *The Anguish of the Jew,* 1964.

Floranes, Rafael, "Vida literaria del Canciller Mayor de Castilla D. Pedro López de Ayala," in *CODOIN,* XIX (1851).

Flórez, Enrique, *España Sagrada,* 26 (1771).

Foulché-Delbosc, R., *Cancionero Castellano del siglo XV,* I, 1912.

Fraker, Ch. F., *Studies on the Cancionero de Baena,* 1966.

Freedy and Redford, in *JAOS,* 90 (1970).

Friedberg, Aemilius, *Corpus Iuris Canonici,* I–II, 1879–1881.

Fuks, A., "The Jewish Revolt in Egypt," in *Aegyptus,* 33 (1953).

Gaillard, G.-H., *Histoire de la rivalité de la France et de l'Espagne*, III, 1801.

Galíndez de Carvajal, Lorenzo, Introd. to *Crónica de Juan II*, ed. Rosell, BAE, 68.

———*Crónica de Enrique IV*, published by J. Torres-Fontes together with an *Estudio* of this *Crónica*, 1944.

Gallardo, B. J., *Ensayo de una Biblioteca Española de libras raros y curiosos*, II, 1966.

Gams, P. B., *Die Kirchengeschitę Spaniens*, II (i), 1956.

———*Series Espiscoporum Ecclesiae Catholicae*, 1857.

García de Santa María, Alvar, *Crónica de Juan II de Castilla*, CODOIN, 99–100.

García Rodrigo, F. X., *Historia Verdadera de la Inquisición*, 1876.

García-Gallo, A., "Los fueros de Toledo," in *AHDE*, XLV (1975).

García de Quevedo, E., *De Bibliografía burgense*, 1941.

García Villoslada, R., and Llorca, B., *Historia de la Iglesia Católica*, III, 1967.

Garganta, J. M. de, and Forcada, V., editors *Biografía y Escritos de San Vicente Ferrer*, 1956.

Garibay, Estevan de, *Compendio Historial de las Chronicas y universal Historia de todos los Reynos de España*, 1628.

Garrastachu, J. Mª., "Los manuscritos del Cardenal Torquemada en la Biblioteca Vaticana," *La Ciencia Tomista*, XXII (1930).

Gayangos, Pascual de, "Mosen Diego de Valera," *Revista Española de Ambos Mundos*, III (1885).

Getino, L.G.A., *Vida y obras de Fr. Lope de Barrientos*, 1927.

Gill, Joseph, *The Council of Florence*, 1959.

Giménez, J., and Martínez de Carvajal, "San Raimond de Peñafort y las Partidas de Alfonso X el Sabio," in *Anthologica Annua*, Rome, III (1955).

Ginzberg, L., *Genizah Studies*, II, 1929.

Girbal, E. C., *Los Judíos de Gerona*, 1870.

Gómez Bravo, Juan, *Catálogo de los obispos de Córdoba*, I, 1778.

Gómez de Cibdareal, Fernán, *Centón Epistolario*, 1775.

Gómez de la Serna, Pedro, *Los Códigos Españoles*, II, 1872.

Gómez-Menor, José, *Cristianos Nuevos y Mercaderes de Toledo*, 1970.

Goñi Gaztambide, J., "Recompensas de Martín V a sus electores Españoles," in *Hispania Sacra*, XI (1958).

———"El Concilio de Basilea," in *Historia de la Iglesia en España*, III (1), ed. J. Luis González Navalín, 1980.

Gonzaga, Francesco de, *De Origine Seraphicae Religionis Franciscanae eiusque progressibus*, 1587.

González, J., *El reino de Castilla en la época de Alfonso VIII*, I, 1950.

González Dávila, Gil, *Teatro eclesiástico de las iglesias metropolitanas y catedrales de los reinos de las dos Castillas*, II, 1647.

González Palencia, A., *Los Mozárabes de Toledo en los siglos XII y XIII*, IV (1930).

Goodenough, E. R., *Introduction to Philo Judaeus*, 1962.

Görres, F., "Character und Religiospolitik des vorletzten spanischen Westgotenkönigs Witiza," in *ZfWT*, 48 (1905).

———"Das Judentum im westgotischen Spanien von König Sisebut bis Roderich (612–711)," *ZfWT*, 48 (1905).

Graetz, H., *Geschichte der Juden*, I–VIII.

———"Die westgothische Gesetzgebung in Betreff der Juden," in *Jahresbericht des jüdisch-theologischen Seminars*, Breslau, 1958.

———"Der historische Hintergrund ... des Buches Esther, etc.," in *MGWJ*, XXXV (1886).

Grayzel, S., *The Church and the Jews in the 13th Century*, 1966.

Gregory of Tours, *The History of the Franks*, II, transl. O. M. Dalton, 1927.

———*Historiae Francorum libri decem*, PL, 71.

Gregory the Great, *Morals on the Book of Job*, Library of Fathers, v. 27

Guicciardini, Francesco, *Della historia d'Italia*, 1775–1776; *The Histoire of Guicciardin*, transl. by G. Fenton, 1618³.

Guichot, J., *Historia de la Ciudad de Sevilla*, III, 1898.

Guido de Baysio, *Rosarium Decretorum*, 1481.

Guillén, Claudio, "Un padrón de conversos Sevillanos," in *Bulletin Hispanique*, 1963.

Guizot, F., *The History of Civilization*, transl. W. Hazlitt, I, 1911.

Gutman, Y., *The Beginnings of Jewish Hellenistic Literature*, (Hebrew), I, 1974.

———"The Wars of the Jews in the Days of Trajan," in *Sefer Asaf* (Hebrew), 1953.

Guttmann, Jacob, *Das Verhältniss des Thomas von Aquino zum Judenthum und zur jüdischen Literatur*, 1891.

———*Die Scholastik des dreizehnten Jahrhunderts in ihren Beziehungen zum Judenthum und zur jüdischen Literatur*, 1902.

Haller, J., *Concilium Basiliensis*, 1897.

Hardouin, J., *Acta Conciliorum et Epistolae decretales*, 1714–1715.

Harnack, A., *The Expansion of Christianity in the First Three Centuries*, transl. J. Moffatt, I–II, 1904–1905.

Hefele, K. J. von, *The Life and Times of Cardinal Ximenes,* transl. J. Dalton, 1885.

Henricus de Segusio (Hostiensis), *In Quintum Decretalium librum Commentaria,* 1581.

Hergenröther, J., *Anti-Janus,* transl. J. B. Robertson, 1870.

Herodotus, *Works,* LCL.

Hieronymus, *Epistulae,* PL, 22.

————*Commentaria in Isaiam Prophetam,* PL, 24.

————*Commentaria in Osee,* PL, 25.

————*Commentaria in Epistolam ad Romanos,* PL, 30.

————*Commentariorum in Michaeam lib. I,* PL, 25.

————*Commentaria in Epistolam ad Titum,* PL, 26. And see Jerome; Jerónimo.

Higuera, Román de la, *Historia eclesiástica de la imperial ciudad de Toledo y su tierra,* BNM, ms. 1290, vols. VI–VII.

Hillgarth, J. N., *The Spanish Kingdoms,* I–II, 1978.

————"La conversión de los Visigodos," in *AST,* XXXIV (1961).

Hinojosa, Gonzalo de la, *Continuacio de la Crónica de España de Jiménez de Rada, CODOIN,* 106.

Hispania Judaica (I: History), ed. J. M. Solà-Solé, S. G. Armistead, J. H. Silverman, 1980.

Historia General de Santo Domingo y de su orden de predicadores, Primera parte, Valencia, 1587.

Hofer, J., *St. John Capistran,* transl. P. Cummins, 1943.

Hoschander, J., *The Book of Esther in the Light of History,* 1923.

Huici Miranda, A., *Las Grandes Batallas de la Reconquista durante las invasiones Africanas,* 1956.

Innocent III, *De contemptu mundi,* PL, 217.

Isaac ben Moses, *Or Zaru'a,* I, 1862.

Isidore of Seville, *Historia Gothorum,* MGH.

————*De summo bono,* PL, 83.

————*Etymologiarum sive Originum libri XX,* ed. W. W. Lindsay, I–II, 1911.

Izbicki, T. M., *Protector of the Faith,* 1981.

————"Infallibility and the Erring Pope," in *Law, Church and Society,* ed. K. Pennington and R. Somerville, 1977.

Jacobs, J., *Jewish Contribution to Civilization,* 1919.

————"Little St. Hugh of Lincoln," in *Transactions of the Jewish Historical Society in England,* I, 1893–94.

Jerome, *The Principal Works,* transl. W. H. Fremantle, 1893.

Jerónimo, San, *Cartas*, bilingual edition (Latin-Spanish), ed. D. Ruiz Bueno, I–II, 1962 (BAC).

Jiménez de la Espada, M., Notes and Illustrations on *Andanças y Viajes de Pero Tafur (1435–1439)*, 1874.

Jiménez de Rada, Rodrigo, *Rerum in Hispania gestarum chronicon*, 1545.

John of Salisbury, *Policraticus* (without the first three books), transl. J. Dickinson, 1927; the first three books, transl. J. B. Pike, in *Frivolities of Courtiers and Footprints of Philosophers*, 1938.

Joseph ha-Kohen, *Emeq ha-Bakha*, 1852.

Josephus, *Works*, 9 vols., transl. Thackeray, Marcus and Feldman, LCL, 1961–1965.

Juan de la Cruz, *Crónica de la Orden de Predicadores*, Lisbon, I, 1567.

Juan de Lucena, *De Vida Felici*, ed. A. Paz y Mélia, 1893.

Julian de Toledo, *Historia Vambae Regis*, MGH, *Scriptores rerum Merovingicarum*, V.

Juster, J., *Les Juifs dans l'Empire Romain*, II, 1914.

———"The Legal Condition of the Jews Under the Visigothic Kings," ed. A. M. Rabello, in *Israel Law Review*, XI (1976).

Kamen, H., *The Spanish Inquisition*, 1965.

Katz, Jacob, "The Hep-Hep Pogroms of 1819 in Germany," in *Zion* (Jerusalem), XXXVIII (1973).

Katz, S., *The Jews in the Visigothic and Frankish Kingdoms of Spain and Gaul*, 1937.

Kaufmann, E., *History of Israel's Religion*, IV-1 (Hebrew), 1967.

Khurdadbe, Ibn, *Routes and Kingdoms*, transl. into English by A. Sprenger, *Journal of the Asiatic Society of Bengal*, 1844, and published in French translation by C. Barbier de Meynard in *Journal Asiatique*, sixth series, V, 1865.

Kisch, Guido, "Nationalism and Race in Medieval Law," in *Seminar*, an annual extraordinary number of *The Jurist*, I, 1943.

Klamroth, E., *Die jüdische Exulanten in Babylonien*, 1912.

Klausner, J., *History of the Second Temple*, I–V (Hebrew), 1949–1951.

———*Jesus of Nazareth*, 1929.

Kobak, J., ed. *Jeschurun*, I–IV (Hebrew), 1856–1878.

Kraeling, H., *The Jewish Community at Antioch*, 1932.

Krauss, S., *Studien zur byzantinisch-jüdischen Geschichte*, 1914.

Krush, B., ed., *Scriptores rerum Merovingicarum*, II, 1888 (MGH).

Kümmel, W. G., *Introduction to the New Testament*, transl. H. C. Kee, 1975.

Ladero Quesada, M. Ángel, *La Ciudad Medieval (1248–1491)*, 1976.

Lafuente, M., *Historia General de España*, 1857.

Landau, L., *Das apologetische Schreiben des Josua Lorki an den Abtrünnigen Don Salomon ha-Lewi*, 1906.

Langhorst, A., "Der Cardinal Turrecremata und das Vaticanum über die Jurisdictions-gewalt der Bischöfe," in *Stimmen aus Maria-Laach*, XVII (1879).

Layna Serrano, F., *Historia de Guadalajara y de los Mendozas*, 1942.

Lea, H. C., *A History of the Inquisition of Spain*, I–IV, 1905.

——*A History of the Inquisition of the Middle Ages*, I–III, 1888.

——*Chapters From the Religious History of Spain*, 1890.

——*The Moriscos of Spain*, 1901.

——"The First Castilian Inquisitor," in *AHR*, I (1895).

——"Ferrand Martínez and the Massacre of 1391," in *AHR*, I (1896).

Lecky, W.E.M., *History of the Rise of Rationalism in Europe*, 1865.

Lederer, S., *Der Spanische Cardinal Johann von Torquemada*, 1879.

Leon Tello, P., *Los Judíos de Toledo*, I–II, 1979.

——*Emeq ha-Bakha de Yosef ha-Kohen*, 1964.

Lévi-Provençal, E., *España Musulmana (711–1031)*, in *Historia de España* (ed. R. Menéndez Pidal), IV, 1950.

——"Alphonse VI et la prise de Tolede (1085)," in *Hesperis*, XII (1931).

Lewin, M. B., *Otzar ha-Geonim*, IX *(Quiddushin)*, 1940.

Lewis, Archibald R., *Naval Power and Trade in the Mediterranean*, 1954.

Lindo, E. H., *The History of the Jews of Spain and Portugal*, 1848.

Liske, Javier, ed., *Viajes de Extranjeros por España y Portugal*, 1878.

Llaguno Amirola, Eugenio de, *Sumario de los reyes de España*, 1781.

Llorca, B., "San Vicente y su labor en la conversión de los Judíos," in *Razón y Fe*, CLII (1955).

——*Bulario Pontificio de la Inquisición española en su periodo constitucional (1478–1525)*, 1949.

Llorente, J. A., *Historia Crítica de la Inquisición en España*, 1980.

——*Noticias históricas de las tres provincias Vascongadas*, IV, 1808.

Loeb, Isidore, *Joseph Haccohen et les croniqueures juives*, 1888.

——"La controverse de 1263 à Barcelone," in *REJ*, XV (1887).

——"Le Livre d'Alboraïque," in *REJ*, XVIII (1889), pp. 238–42.

——"La correspondance des Juifs d'Espagne avec ceux de Constantinople avec une lettre adressée en 1550 par les Juifs de Provence," 1888.

Lombard, M., "La route de la Meuse etc., in *L'Art Mosan*, 1953.

Lombard, Petrus, *Sententiae*, PL. 192.

Loomis, Louis L., "Nationality at the Council of Constance," in *American Historical Review*, XLIV (1939).

Lopes, Fernão, *Chronica de D. Pedro*, ed. G. Macchi, 1966.

López, Atanasio, "Descripción de los manuscritos existentes en la Biblioteca Provincial de Toledo," in *Archivo Ibero-Americano*, XIII (1926).

López de Mendoza, Iñigo, *Obras*, ed. J. Amador de los Ríos, 1852.

López de Meneses, A., "Una consecuencia de la peste negra en Cataluña: el pogrom de 1348," in *Sefarad*, 19 (1959).

López Martínez, Nicolás, *Los Judaizantes Castellanos*, 1954.

López Mata, Teófilo, "Morería y Judería," in RAH, *Boletín*, 129 (1951).

Lucas de Túy, *Historia Galliae, PL*, 96.

———*Crónica de España*, transl. Julio Puyol, 1926.

Lucas de Torre, *Mosen Diego de Valera*, 1914.

Lucena, Juan de, *Libro de Vita Beata*, ed. A Paz y Mélia, 1892.

Lynch, C. H., *Saint Braulio, Bishop of Saragossa*, 1938.

Lynch, C. H., and Galindo, P., *San Braulio*, 1950.

MacCay, Angus, "Popular Movements and Pogroms in 15th-Century Castile," in *Past and Present*, 55 (1972).

Macdonald, I. I., *Don Fernando de Antequera*, 1946.

Machiavelli, N., *Chief Works and Others*, transl. A. Gilbert, 1965.

Maguire, W. E., *John of Torquemada: The Antiquity of the Church*, 1957.

Mahaffy, J. P., *A History of Egypt Under the Ptolemaic Dynasty*, 1914.

Mansi, J. D., *Sacrorum conciliorum nova et amplissima collectio*, 1901–1927.

Mantuano, Pedro, ed., *Seguro de Tordesillas* (by D. Pedro Fernández de Velasco, Conde de Haro), 1784².

Marañón, G., *Ensayo biológico sobre Enrique IV de Castilla y su Tiempo*, 1930.

María Quadrado, J., "La judería de la ciudad de Mallorca en 1391," in RAH, *Boletín*, IX (1886).

Mariana, Juan de, *Historia General de España*, BAE, vols. 30–31.

Mariéjol, Jean, *The Spain of Ferdinand and Isabella*, transl. B. Keen, 1961.

Marmol Carvajal, L., *Rebelión y Castigo de los Moriscos de Granada*, BAE, 21.

Márquez [Villanueva], F., *Investigaciones sobre Juan Alvarez Gato*, 1960.

———"Conversos y Cargos concejiles en el siglo XV," in *RABM*, LXIII (1957).

———Introd. to Hernando de Talavera's *Católica impugnación*, 1961.

Martín, Andrés, *Historia de la Teología en España (1490–1570)*, I, 1962.

Martínez Alcubilla, Marcelo, ed., *Códigos antiguos de España*, I, 1885.

Martínez Añíbarro y Rives, Manuel, *Intento de un Diccionario Biográfico y Bibliográfico de Autores de la Provincia de Burgos*, 1889.

Martínez Ferrando, J. Ernesto, *San Vicente Ferrer y la Casa real de Aragon*, 1955.

Martín Gamero, A., *Historia de la ciudad de Toledo*, 1862.

Maspero, G., *The Passing of the Empires*, transl. M. L. McClure, 1900.

Massi, P., *Magistero Infallibile del Papa nella teologia di Giovanni da Tourquemada*, 1957 (includes Torquemada's address at the Diet at Mainz).

McKenna, S., *Paganism and Pagan Survivals in Spain up to the Fall of the Visigothic Kingdom*, 1938.

Memorial Histórico de Segovia, in RAH, *Boletín*, XIV (1889).

Memorias de Don Enrique IV de Castilla, ed. RAH, II, 1835–1913.

Memorias de Don Fernando II, ed. Miguel de Manuel Rodríguez, 1800.

Menaḥem ben Zeraḥ, *Zĕda la-Derekh*, 1567.

Mendoza y Bobadilla, Francisco de, *Tizón de la Nobleza*, 1880.

Menéndez y Pelayo, M., *Historia de los Heterodoxos Españoles*, ed. E. Sánchez Reyes, I, 1963.

———*Biografía Hispano-Latino Clásica*, I, 1902.

———*Biblioteca de Traductores Españoles*, ed. E. Sánchez Reyes, I, 1952.

———*Antología de Poetas líricos Castellanos*, ed. E. Sánchez Reyes, 1944.

———*Historia de la Poesía Castellana en la Edad edia*, 1914.

———*La Ciencia Española*, I, 1947.

Menéndez Pidal, R., *La España del Cid.*, I, 1947.

———*The Spaniards in their History*, transl. by W. Starkie, 1950.

———*Crónicas Generales de España*, 1898.

———ed., *Primera Crónica General de España*, II, 1955.

———"El compromiso de Caspe," in *Historia de España*, XV.

———ed., *Historia de España*, vols. IV, V, XIV, XV.

Mercadel, García, *Viajes de extranjeros por España y Portugal*, 1932.

Meyer, E., *Der Papyrusfund von Elephantine*, 1912.

———*Die Entstehung des Judenthums*, 1896.

Milano, A., *Storia degli ebrei in Italia*, 1963.

Millas, J. M., "San Vicente Ferrer y el antisemitismo," in *Sefarad*, X (1950).

Milne, J. Grafton, *Egypt Under Roman Rule*, 1898.

Minguella y Arnedo, T., *Historia de la Diócesis de Sigüenza*, II, 1912.

Mommsen, T., *Römische Geschichte*, V, 1909.

Moses ha-Kohen de Tordesillas, *'Ezer ha-Emuna*, ed. Y. Shamir, I–II, c. 1972.

Motley, J. L., *The Rise of the Dutch Republic*, 1903.

Muñoz y Romero, T., *Colección de Fueros Municipales*, I, 1847.

Muñoz y Soliva, T., *Noticias de los Obispos de Cuenca*, 1860.

———*Historia de la Ciudad de Cuenca*, 1867.

Nahmanides, *Kitvei R. Moshe ben Naḥman*, ed., Ch. Chavel, 1971.

Neander, A., *General History of the Christian Religion and Church*, transl. J. Torrey, 1854.

Netanyahu, B., *Don Isaac Abravanel*, 1982⁴.

———*The Marranos of Spain*, 1973².

———"Alonso de Espina: Was He a New Christian?," in *PAAJR*, XLIII (1976).

———"Did the Toledans in 1449 Rely on a Real Royal Privilege?", in *PAAJR*, XLIV (1977).

———"On the Composition Date of *Haqanah* and *Hapeliah*," in *Jubilee Volume in honor of S. W. Baron*, 1975.

———"Américo Castro and his View of the Origins of the *pureza de sangre*," in *PAAJR*, XLVI–XLVII (1979–1980).

———"La Razón de la Inquisición," in *Inquisición Española y mentalidad Inquisitorial*, ed. A. Alcalá Galve, 1984.

———"Antisemitism," *Encyclopaedia Hebraica* (1950), IV, cols. 493–513.

Neubauer, A., *Medieval Jewish Chronicles*, I, 1887.

———Paul's Letter to Meir Alguades, in *Israelitische Letterbode*, X (1884–1885); published also by I. Abrahams in *JQR*, XII (1900).

Nicolaus de Lyra, *Postilla*, in *Biblia*, Nuremberg, 1487.

Oesterley, W.O.E., *The Jewish Background of the Christian Liturgy*, 1925.

Olmstead, A. T., *History of the Persian Empire*, 1948.

Origen, *Homiliae in Numeros*, PG, 12.

Origo, I., *The World of San Bernardino*, 1962.

Orlandis, José, *La España visigotica*, 1977.

Oropesa, Alonso de, *Lumen ad Revelationem Gentium*, ms. A3INF Ambrosiana, Milan; *Luz para conocimiento de los gentiles*, transl. L. A. Díaz y Díaz, 1979.

Orosius, Paulus, *Historiarum adversum Paganos libri vii*, ed. C. Zangemeister, 1882.

Ortega y Gasset, J., *Invertebrate Spain*, transl. M. Adams, 1937.

Orti y Lara, M., *La Inquisición*, 1932.

Ortiz, Alonso, *Los Tratados*, 1493.

Ortiz de Zúñiga, Diego, *Annales ecclesiásticos y seculares de . . . Sevilla*, 1677.

Ostroumoff, N., *The History of the Council of Florence*, transl. Basil Pokoff, 1971.

Otto, H., "Alexander IV und der deutsche Thronstreit," in MIOG, XIX (1898).

Pabón, F., "La cruz del Rastro," *Tradiciones Cordobeses*, 1863.

Pacios López, A., *La Disputa de Tortosa*, I–II, 1957.

Palacky, F., *Literarische Reise nach Italien im Jahre 1837*, c. 1838.

Palencia, Alfonso de, *Crónica de Enrique IV*, transl. A. Paz y Mélia, vols. I–IV, 1904–1908.

———*Guerra de Granada*, transl. A. Paz y Mélia, 1909.

Paramo, Ludovicus à, *De Origine et progressu Officii Sanctae Inquisitionis*, 1598.

Paris, Matthew, *Historia Major*, ed. Luard, Rolls Series, V.

Parkes, James, *The Conflict of the Church and the Synagogue*, 1961.

———*The Jew in the Medieval Community*, 1938.

———*The Jew and His Neighbor*, 1930.

———*Antisemitism*, 1963.

Pastor, L., *Geschichte der Päpste*, I, 1901; *The History of the Popes*, II, 1906[3].

Paulus Burgensis, *Scrutinium Scripturatum*, 1591.

———*Additiones* to the *Postilla* of Nicolas de Lyra, in *Biblia*, Nuremberg, 1487.

———*Edades Trovadas* or *Siete Edades del Mundo*, in Foulché-Delbosc, *Cancionero Castellano del Siglo XV*, II, 1915, pp. 155–88.

Paz, Julian, *Archivo General de Simancas, Catálogo I: Diversos de Castilla*, 1904.

Paz y Mélia, A., *El cronista Alfonso de Palencia*, 1914.

———*Series de los mas importantes documentos del archivo y biblioteca del . . . Duque de Medinaceli*, 1915.

———*Sales Españolas o agudezas del ingenio nacional*, I, 1890.

Pellicer y Saforcada, J. A., *Ensayo de una biblioteca de Traductores Españoles*, 1778.

Pérez de Guzmán, Fernán, ed., *Crónica de Juan II*, BAE, 68.

———*Generaciones y Semblanzas*, ed. J. Domínguez Bordona, 1954.

Pérez Villanueva, Joaquín, and Escandell Bonet, Bartolomé, eds., *Historia de la Inquisición en España y America*, I, 1984.

Peters, Edward, *The Magician, the Witch and the Law*, 1978.

Petrie, W. M. Flinders, *A History of Egypt: XIXth to XXXth Dynasties*, 1905.

Pflaum, H., "Une ancienne satire espagnole contre les Marranes," in REJ, 86 (1928).

Pinel y Monroy, F., *Retrato de Un buen vasallo*, 1677.

Pinta Llorente, M. de la, *La Inquisición Española*, 1948.

Pirenne, H., *Mohammed and Charlemagne*, 1937.

Plato, *The Dialogues*, transl. by B. Jowett, 1924.

Porreño, Balthazar, *Elogios de los Papas y Cardenales que ha tenido la nación Española*, Ms. in Cod. Biblioth. Vaticanae Barber, lat. 3571.

Porten, B., *Archives from Elephantine*, 1968.

Portilla y Esquivel, Miguel de, *Historia de la Ciudad de Compluto*, 1725.

————"La Parroquia de Santa María la Mayor de Alcalá de Henares y su abandonada capilla del Relator," in *Boletín de la Real Academia de Bellas Artes de San Fernando*, XVIII (1898).

Proaño Gil, V., "Doctrina de Juan de Torquemada sobre el Concilio," in *Burgense*, I (1960).

Pseudo-Ambrosius, *De Sacramentis libri sex*, PL, 16.

Puig y Puig, Sebastián, *Pedro de Luna*, 1920.

Pulgar, Fernando de, *Crónica de los Reyes Católicos*, ed. Carriazo, 1943.

————*Claros Varones de Castilla*, ed. J. Domínguez Bordona, 1954.

————*Letras*, ed., J. Domínguez Bordona, 1949.

Pusey, E. B., *First Letter to the Reverend J. Newman . . . in regard to . . . the doctrine of the Immaculate Conception*, 1869.

Puymaigre, T. J. B., *La cour littéraire de Don Juan II, roi de Castille*, 1873.

Puyol, Julio, "Los cronistas de Enrique IV," in RAH, *Boletín*, 78–79 (1921).

Quétif-Echard, *Scriptores ordinis Praedicatorum*, I, 1719.

Quintana, M. J., *Vidas de los Españoles Celebres*, III, 1833.

Rabello, A. M., *The Jews in Visigothic Spain in the Light of the Legislation* (Hebrew), 1983.

Rades y Andrada, Francisco de, *Crónicas de las tres órdenes y cavallerías de Santiago, Calatrava y Alcántara*, 1572.

Ramírez, Eusebio, "Perdón a Cuenca por haber seguido a Doña Blanca de Borbón," in *RABM*, XXVII (1924).

Ramírez de Arellano, Rafael, "Matanza de Judíos en Córdoba. 1391," RAH, *Boletín*, 38 (1901).

————and Díaz de Morales, *Historia de Córdoba*, I, 1919.

Ranke, L., *Fürsten und Völker von Süd-Europa im sechsgehenten und siebzehnten Jahrhundert*, I, 1837.

Rawlinson, G., *History of Ancient Egypt*, II, 1882.

Raymond de Roover, *San Bernardino of Siena and Sant'Antoni of Florence*, 1967.

Raynaldus, Odericus, *Annales Ecclesiastici*, 1738–1746.

Refundición de la Crónica del Halconero, ed. Carriazo, 1946.

Régné, J., "Étude sur la condition des Juifs de Narbonne de Vᵉ au XIVᵉ siècle," in *REJ*, 55 (1908).

Reinach, T., *Textes d'auteurs grecs et romaines relatifs au Judaïsme*, 1895.

Reinaud, J., *Invasions de Sarrazins en France, et de France en Savoie, en Piemont et en Suisse*, 1836.

Relación de todo lo que pasó al hacer el Estatuto de Limpieza que tiene la Santa Iglesia de Toledo . . . el qual se hizo siendo Arzobispo Don Juan Martínez Siliceo. Año de 1547. BNM, ms. no. 13038.

Renan, E., *Averroès et Averroïsme*, 1861.

Rius Serra, R., "Los rótulos de la universidad de Valladolid," in *AST*, XVI (1943).

Rizzo y Ramírez, J., *Juicio Crítico y significación política de Don Alvaro de Luna*, 1963.

Roberts, C. H., *An Unpublished Fragment of the Fourth Gospel*, 1935.

Rodríguez, Tomás, "El Cronista Alfonso de Palencia," *La Ciudad de Dios*, 1888.

Rodríguez de Castro, J., *Biblioteca Española*, I, 1781.

Rodríguez Villa, A., *Bosquejo biográfico de Don Beltrán de la Cueva*, 1881.

Rojas y Contreras, Joseph de (Marqués de Alventos), *Historia del Colegio Viejo de San Bartolomé*, III, 1770.

Rosa Lida, María, *Estudios de literatura española y comparada*, 1966.

Roscher, W., "The Status of the Jews in the Middle Ages Considered from the Standpoint of Commercial Policy," in *Historia Judaica*, VI (1944).

Rosell, Cayetano, ed., *Crónicas de los Reyes de España*, BAE, 66, 68, 70.

Rostovtzeff, M., *The Social and Economic History of the Hellenistic World*, II, 1967.

Roth, Cecil, *A History of the Marranos*, 1932.

———*History of the Jews of Italy*, 1946.

———*The Spanish Inquisition*, 1937.

———ed. *The Dark Ages*, WHJP, 1966.

———"The Disputation of Barcelona, 1263," in *Harvard Theological Review*, XLIII (1950).

———"Marranos and Racial Antisemitism," in *Jewish Social Studies*, II (1940).

———ed., a dirge on Toledan Jewry, 1391, in *JQR*, 39 (1948).

Roth, Norman, "The Jews and the Moslem Conquest of Spain," in JST, 37 (1976).

Round, Nicholas G., *The Greatest Man Uncrowned*, 1986.

————"Politics, Style and Group Attitudes in the 'Instrucción del Relator,' " in *Bulletin of Hispanic Studies*, XLVI (1969).

Ruiz de Vergara y Alava, F., *Vida de don Diego de Anaya Maldonado*, 1661.

Rújula y Ochotorena, José de, *Índice de los Colegiales del Mayor de San Ildefonso y menores de Alcalá*, 1946.

Rule, N. W., *History of the Inquisition*, 1868.

Russell, P. E., *The English Intervention in Spain and Portugal in the Time of Edward III and Richard II*, 1955.

Saavedra, E., *Estudio sobre la invasión de los Arabes en España*, 1892.

Sáez, Emilio, *El libro del Juramento del Ayuntamiento de Toledo*, AHDE, XVI (1945).

————*Ordenamiento dado a Toledo por el infante don Fernando de Antequera . . . en 1411*, in *AHDE*, XV (1944).

Sala Balust, L., *Constituciones, estatutos y ceremonias de los antiguos colegios seculares de la Universidad de Salamanca*, III, 1964.

Salazar y Mendoza, Pedro de, *Crónica de el Gran Cardenal de España*, 1625.

Salva, Anselmo, *Las Cortes de 1392 en Burgos*, 1891.

San Antonio, Juan de, *Bibliotheca Universa Franciscana*, I, 1732.

Sánchez-Albornoz, C., *España, Un enigma Histórico*, 1962.

————*España Musulmana*, I, 1960.

Sánchez Alonso, B., *Historia de la Historiografía española*, 5 vols., 1941–1952.

————"Las versiones en Romance de las Crónicas del Toledano," *Homenaje ofrecido a Menéndez Pidal*, I, 1925.

Sánchez de Arévalo, Rodrigo, four chapters on Enrique IV from his *Compendiosa Historia Hispanica*, published as appendix to Enríquez del Castillo's *Crónica de Enrique IV*, ed. Flores, 1779.

Sánchez Belda, L., ed., *Cronica Adefonsi imperatoris*, 1950.

Sánchez de Muniain, José M., ed., *Antología General de Menéndez Pelayo*, I, 1956.

Sancho de Sporanis, H., "Sobre Mosen Diego de Valera," in *Hispania*, Madrid, VII (1947).

Sanctotis, Ch., *Vita Pauli*, biographical introd. to Paul of Burgos' *Scrutinium Scripturarum*, 1591.

Sandoval, Prudencio, *Historia de la vida y hechos del Emperador Carlos V*, I, 1955 (BAE, 80).

Sauneron, S., and Yoyotte, J., "Sur la politique Palestinienne des rois Saïtes," in *VT*, II, 1952.

————"La campagne nubienne de Psametique II," *BIFAO*, 50 (1952).

Sbaralea, J. H., *Supplementum . . . ad Scriptores trium ordinum S. Francisci a Waddingo aliisve descriptos*, I, 1908.

Schäfer, E. H. J., *Beiträge zur Geschichte des spanischen Protestantismus und der Inquisition im 16. Jahrhundert*, I–III, 1902 (1969²).

——"Die katholische Geschichtschreibung und die Inquisition," in *Der alte Glaube*, Liepzig, Dec. 6 and 13, 1907.

Schaff, Philip, *History of the Christian Church*, VI, 1910.

Schirmann, J., ed., a dirge, *Kobez al Jad*, N.S. III (1), 1939.

Scholberg, K. R., *Sátira e invectiva en la España Medieval*, 1971.

Scholem, G., *Elements of the Kabbalah and its Symbolism* (Hebrew), 1976.

——*Major Trends in Jewish Mysticism*, 1941.

Schöne, A., *Die Weltchronik des Eusebius in ihrer Bearbeitung durch Hieronymus*, 1900.

Schwane, Joseph, *Dogmengeschichte der mittleren Zeit*, 1882.

Scott, S. P., *The Visigothic Code*, 1910.

Schottus, Andraeas, *Hispaniae illustratae*, I, IV, 1608.

Senensis, Antonius, *Bibliotheca Ordinis Fratrum Praedicatorum*, 1585.

Sengi, B., *Storie Fiorentine*, 1725.

Sergeant, L., *The Franks*, 1898.

Serrano, Luciano, *Los Conversos D. Pablo de Santa María y D. Alfonso de Cartagena*, 1942.

——*Los Reyes Católicos y la Ciudad de Burgos*, 1943.

Serrano y Sanz, Manuel, *Orígenes de la dominación Española en America*, 1913.

Sevisenti, B., "Un documento de la lucha anti-Judáica," in *Boletín de la Academia Argentina de Letras*, VII (nos. 25–26), 1939.

Shaw, R. Dykes, "The Fall of the Visigothic Power in Spain," in *The English Historical Review*, LXXXII, April 1906.

Sicart, R., article on Anaya y Maldonado in *Dictionaire d'histoire et de geographie ecclesiastiques*, II.

Sicroff, A. A., *Les Controverses des Statuts de Pureté de Sang en Espagne de XVᵉ au XVIᵉ siècle*, 1960.

Sigüenza, José de, *Historia de la Orden de San Jerónimo*, I–II, 1907–1909.

Silió, César, *Alvaro de Luna y su Tiempo*, 1935.

Simón Díaz, José, "La familia Chirino en Cuenca," in *Guía*, Madrid, 1944.

——"El Helenismo de Quevedo" etc., in *Revista de Bibliografía Nacional*, VI (1945).

Simonsohn, S., "La Limpieza de Sangre y la Iglesia," *Actas del II Congreso Internacional: Encuentro de las tres culturas*, Toledo, 1983.

Sitges, J. B., *Enrique IV y la excelente Señora*, 1912.

———*Las Mujeres del Rey Don Pedro I de Castilla*, 1910.

Sobrequés Callicó, J., "La peste negra en la península Ibérica," in *Anuario de Estudios Medievales*, 7 (1970–1971).

Solenni, Gino V. M. de, "On the Date of Composition of Mosen Diego de Valera's *El doctrinal de principes*, in *The Romanic Review*, XXVI (ed. J. L. Gerig).

Spinoza, B., *Works*, I, transl. R.H.M. Elwes, 1951.

Stähelin, F., *Der Antisemitismus des Altertums*, 1905.

Starr, J., *The Jews in the Byzantine Empire, 691–1204*, 1939.

———"Byzantine Jewry on the Eve of the Arab Conquest," *JPOS*, XV (1935).

Sterling, E. D., *Judenhass*, 1969.

Stern, M., *Greek and Latin Authors on Jews and Judaism*, I–II, 1974–1980.

Strack, H. L., *The Jew and Human Sacrifice*, 1909.

Suárez Fernández, L., *Nobleza y Monarquía*, 1959.

———*Documentos acerca de la expulsión de los Judíos*, 1964.

———on Pedro I de Castilla, in *Historia de España*, ed. R. Menéndez Pidal, vol. XIV.

———on Juan II de Castilla and Alvaro de Luna, in *Historia de España*, v. XV.

———*Castilla, el Cisma y la crisis conciliar (1378–1440)*, 1960.

Succesos en la ciudad de Toledo contra los combersos, etc., ms. 2041, BNM.

Tadmor, H., ed., WHJP, *The Restoration: The Persian Period*, 1983.

Talavera, Gabriel de, *Historia de Nuestra Señora de Guadalupe*, 1597.

Tcherikover, A., *The Jews in Egypt in the Hellenistic-Roman Age in the Light of the Papyri* (Hebrew), 1945

———*Jews and Greeks in the Hellenistic Period* (Hebrew), 1930.

———and Fuks, A., *Corpus Papyrorum Judaicarum*, I–II, 1960.

Thomas Aquinas, *Summa Theologica* and *Summa contra gentiles* (transl. by the Dominican Fathers).

———*On the Governance of Rulers*, transl. of *De Regimine principum*, by G. B. Phelan, 1938.

———*Exposition in Omnes Sancti Pauli Epistulas*, ed. Vives, 1889.

Thomas de Cantimpré, *Bonum universale de Apibus*, 1627.

Thompson, E. A., *The Goths in Spain*, 1969.

———"The Conversion of the Visigoths to Catholicism," in *Nottingham Medieval Studies*, IV (1960).

Thorndike, Lynn, *A History of Magic and Experimental Science,* III–VI, 1934–1941.

Thureau-Dangin, P., *Bernardine de Siena,* transl. G. von Hügel, 1906.

Ticknor, George, *History of Spanish Literature,* 1965[6].

Tierney, B., *The Origins of Papal Infallibility, 1150–1350,* 1972.

Toni, Teodoro, "Rodrigo Sánchez de Arevalo," *AHDE,* XII (1935).

Torquemada, Juan de, *Summa de Ecclesia,* 1561.

——*Comentaria in Decretum Gratiani Partes V,* 6 vols., 1516.

——*Oratio Synodalis de Primatu,* ed. E. Candal, 1954.

——*Apparatus super decretum Florentinum unionis Graecorum,* ed. E. Candal, 1942.

——*De corpore Christi mystico,* ed. J. F. Stockmann, 1951.

——*Tractatus de Sacramento Eucharistiae,* 1578.

——*Tractatus de veritate conceptionis Beatissmae Virginis,* 1547 (partly translated into English by E. B. Pusey and included in his work on the same theme).

——*Tractatus contra Madianitas et Ismaelitas,* ed. N. López Martínez and V. Proaño Gil, 1957.

——*Flores Sententiarum S. Thomae Aquinatis de auctoritate summi Pontificis,* 1496 and 1562.

——*Symbolum pro informatione Manichaeorum,* ed. N. López Martínez and V. Proaño Gil, 1958.

Torre, Fernando de la, *Cancionero y obras en prosa,* ed. A. Paz y Mélia, 1907.

Torre y Franco-Romero, Lucas de, *Mosén Diego de Valera,* 1914.

Torrejoncillo, F., *Centinnela contra Judíos,* 1693.

Torres-Fontes, J., *El Itinerario de Enrique IV de Castilla,* 1953.

Torrey, H. C., "The Date of the Crucifixion according to the Fourth Gospel," in *Journal of Biblical Literature,* L (1931).

Touron, A., *Histoire des hommes illustrés,* III, 1746.

Traversarius, Ambrosius, *Latinae Epistulae,* ed. L. Mehus, I–II, 1759.

Trials of Hieronymite friars by the Inquisition, manuscripts of Archivo Histórico Nacional, Madrid, leg. 188 and others.

Usque, S., *Consolaçam as Tribulaçoens de Israel,* 1806; transl. and ed. Martin Cohen, *Consolation for the Tribulations of Israel,* 1965.

Vacandard, E., *The Inquisition,* transl. B. L. Conway, 1918.

——"Inquisition," *Hastings Encyclopaedia,* VII.

Valdeavellano, L. G. de, *Historia de España,* I (2), 1955.

————*Sobre los Burgos y los Burgueses de la España Medieval,* 1960.

Valdeón Baruque, Julio, *Enrique II de Castilla: La Guerra Civil y la consolidación del Régimen (1361–1366),* 1976.

————*Los Judíos de Castilla y la revolución Trastámara,* 1968.

————"La Judería Toledana en la guerra civil de Pedro I y Enrique II," in *Simposio, Toledo Judáico,* I, 1972.

Valera, Diego de, *Epistolas,* ed. Antonio de Balenchana, 1878.

————*Crónica de los Reyes Católicos,* ed. Cariazzo, 1927.

————*Memorial de Diversas Hazañas,* ed. Cariazzo, 1941 (includes Valera's *Crónica Abreviada de España*).

Valls Taberner, F., *San Ramón de Peñafort,* 1936.

Valois, N., *Le Pape et le Concile (1418–1450),* II, 1909.

Vendrell, F., *La actividad proselitista de San Vicente Ferrer durante el reinado de Fernando I de Aragon,* in *Sefarad,* XIII (1953).

Vera y Figueroa, J. Antonio de, *El Rei Don Pedro Defendido,* 1648.

Verga, Solomon ibn, *Shevet Yehuda,* ed. Baer-Shohat, 1947; *Schevet Jehuda,* ed. Wiener, I, 1855.

Vicens Vives, J., *An Economic History of Spain,* transl. F. M. López-Morillas, 1969.

————*Fernando el Católico, 1458–1478,* 1952.

————*Juan II de Aragon,* 1955.

Vignau, V., *Índice . . . de Sahagún,* 1874.

Villanueva, J. L., *Viaje literarrio a las Iglesias de España,* vols. 18, 22.

Vincent de Beauvais, *Speculum Historiale,* 1494.

Voigt, Georg, *Enea Silvio de' Piccolomini,* I–III, 1856–1862.

Wadding, L., *Annales Minorum,* 1734–1735.

Weiss, M., *Vor der Reformation* (drei Aufsätze in den *Historisch-politische Blättern,* LXXIX), 1877.

Wilcken, U., "Zum alexandrinischen Antisemitismus des Altertums," *APHK,* XVII (1909).

Willrich, H., "Caligula," in *KLIO,* III (1903).

Winckler, Hugo, *Alttestamentliche Untersuchungen,* 1892.

Wolf, Christophorus, *Bibliotheca Hebraea,* II, 1721.

Wolfson, H. A., *Philo,* I–II, 1948.

Yehuda ha-Levi, *Diwan,* ed. Brody, II, 1909.

Yoyotte, J., "Sur la voyage Asiatique de Psametique II," in *VT,* I (1951).

Zacuto, A., *Sefer Yuhasin,* ed. Filipowski, 1857.

Zarco Cuevas, Eusebio Julián, *Catálogo de los manuscritos castellanos de la Real Biblioteca de El Escorial*, 1929.

Zarza, Samuel, appendix to *Shebet Jehuda*, ed. Wiener, 1859.

Zeumer, K., ed., *Leges Visgothorum*, 1902, (MGH, *Legum*, sectio I, v. I).

Ziegler, A. K., *Church and State in Visigothic Spain*, 1930.

Zosimus, *Historia Nova*, ed. Mendelssohn, 1887.

Zurita, Jerónimo de, *Anales de la Corona de Aragon*, III, 1862.

ACKNOWLEDGMENTS

In the long years during which this work was written, I enjoyed the cooperation of many scholars and librarians in Spain, Britain, France, Italy, Israel, and the United States, who offered me their help with a love of learning and a warmth of feeling that always evoked my deepest appreciation. Their large number, however, compels me to limit the following acknowledgments only to the few whose assistance extended across many years or covered the entire manuscript.

Of these I must mention first Professor C. Moron Arroyo, my colleague at Cornell University, to whom I am profoundly indebted for his unfailing readiness to assist me in obtaining manuscripts and rare books in Spain and the United States even when this assistance involved much effort and placed heavy demands on his time. I am similarly grateful to my friend the late Professor Joseph B. Sermoneta of the Hebrew University, who repeatedly secured for me important documents from the library of the Vatican.

To Mrs. Ruth Rigby I owe special thanks for carefully checking the style of the manuscript and for offering many graceful suggestions with due consideration for the flow of my language. I am also grateful to Veronica Windholz, my copy editor, for her painstaking attention to detail.

It was fortunate for this work that Jason Epstein, editorial director at Random House, was its final reviewer. Careful as he was not to affect my line of thought, he raised a number of important questions that led me to add a short chapter and elaborate on several points. His meticulous perusal of the manuscript resulted in many stylistic refinements, and the artistry of his editorial work left its traces in more than a few places. My gratitude to him is abiding.

Finally, I wish to acknowledge the enduring and constant help of my wife, Cela. She was my first research assistant, my first reader, and my first critic, whose astute judgment I always valued. She also deciphered and retyped my revised drafts, copied many texts in the libraries we worked in, and cataloged and filed the huge quantities of materials gathered in the course of my researches. Judging by the sheer volume of her work, it took a good part of her life; and who can find words adequate enough to express due gratitude for such an effort? Nor can I duly acknowledge her support in times of travail and tragedy. Yet here are my thanks, inexpressible as they are.

INDEX

ABOUT THE AUTHOR

B. NETANYAHU is internationally known as historian of the Jews and Marranos in Spain and as author of works on the Jewish question in both medieval and modern times. Best known among his works on medieval themes are his study of Alonso de Espina, propagator of the establishment of the Inquisition in Castile (1975), and his books *Don Isaac Abravanel* and *The Marranos of Spain*, whose conclusions concerning Marrano Christianization provoked widespread scholarly debate.

Professor Netanyahu was editor in chief of the *Encyclopedia Hebraica*, general editor of the *World History of the Jewish People*, and co-editor of the *Jewish Quarterly Review*. He is a fellow of the American Academy for Jewish Research, member of the Real Academia de Bellas Artes y Ciencias Históricas de Toledo, and professor emeritus at Cornell University.

ABOUT THE TYPE

The text of this book was set in Janson, a misnamed typeface designed about 1690 by Nicholas Kis, a Hungarian in Amsterdam. In 1919 the matrices became the property of the Stempel Foundry in Frankfurt. It is an old-style book face of excellent clarity and sharpness. Janson serifs are concave and splayed; the contrast between thick and thin strokes is marked.